A RHETORICAL HISTORY OF THE UNITED STATES VOLUME VI

Significant Moments in American Public Discourse

A Rhetorical History of the United States
Significant Moments in American
Public Discourse
Volumes I–X

Under the General Supervisory Editorship of
Martin J. Medhurst
Texas A & M University

Editors:

Rhetoric and Reform in the Progressive Era

Edited by
J. MICHAEL HOGAN

A RHETORICAL HISTORY OF THE UNITED STATES
Significant Moments in American Public Discourse

VOLUME VI

Michigan State University Press
East Lansing

Copyright © 2003 by Michigan State University Press

♾ The paper used in this publication meets the minimum requirements of ANSI/NISO
Z39.48–1992 (R 1997) (Permanence of Paper).

Michigan State University Press
East Lansing, Michigan 48823–5202

Printed and bound in the United States of America.

09 08 07 06 05 04 03   1 2 3 4 5 6 7 8 9 10

LIBRARY OF CONGRESS CATALOGING-IN-PUBLICATION DATA

Rhetoric and reform in the Progressive Era / edited by J. Michael Hogan.
    p. cm. —(A rhetorical history of the United States; v. 6)

    ISBN 0-87013-637-2 (alk. paper)

    1. United States—Politics and government—1901-1953. 2. Progressivism (United States politics)
3. Rhetoric—Political aspects—United States—History—20th century. 4. Social reformers—United
States—History—20th century. 5. Social movements—United States—History—20th century.
6. United States—Social policy. I. Hogan, J. Michael, 1953–   . II. Series.

E743.R47 2003
973.91—dc21   2002008953

Book design by Sans Serif Inc.

Visit Michigan State University Press on the World Wide Web at:
www.msupress.msu.edu

In memory of Douglas Birkhead

The following individuals, department, colleges, and universities provided subvention funds to help offset the initial publication costs of this ten volume series. Michigan State University Press expresses its sincere thanks to each.

A. CRAIG BAIRD DISTINGUISHED PROFESSORSHIP
University of Iowa

COLLEGE OF ARTS AND SCIENCES
Indiana University

COLLEGE OF LIBERAL ARTS
Texas A&M University

DEPARTMENT OF COMMUNICATION
Texas A&M University

DEPARTMENT OF COMMUNICATION ARTS & SCIENCES
The Pennsylvania State University

DEPARTMENT OF COMMUNICATION AND CULTURE
Indiana University

DEPARTMENT OF COMMUNICATION STUDIES
Northwestern University

SCHOOL OF SPEECH
Northwestern University

CONTENTS

INTRODUCTION
Rhetoric and Reform in the Progressive Era

J. Michael Hogan

The Progressive Era is, in a sense, a historical fiction. Defined neither by an epoch-making event, nor by a dominant personality, nor by a particular policy or program, the era lacks the specific historical referents of, say, the Jacksonian era or the New Deal. In the conventional view, the Progressive Era took its name from a nationwide movement for social and political reform, but as Peter Levine has suggested, a "movement that attracted Upton Sinclair and J. Edgar Hoover, W. E. B. Du Bois and Robert Taft, Herbert Hoover and the young Franklin D. Roosevelt can hardly be called a movement at all." Since the label "Progressive" sounded "unequivocally positive" at the time, "practically everybody embraced it," from the founders of the NAACP to the "white supremacists who perfected racial apartheid in the South." With "racists and liberals, elitists and populists, technocrats and democrats" all calling themselves Progressives, "the term often meant nothing more specific than an enthusiasm for change."[1]

Even the *Encyclopedia Britannica* hedges when defining progressivism. "Generally speaking," the *Britannica* states, "progressivism was the response of various groups to problems raised by the rapid industrialization and urbanization that followed the Civil War." Yet the *Britannica* concedes that the origins and the nature of progressivism are "complex" and "difficult to describe," and that "there was not, either in the 1890s or later, any single Progressive movement. The numerous movements for reform on the local, state, and national levels were too diverse, and sometimes too mutually antagonistic, ever to coalesce into a national crusade."[2]

Perhaps "progressivism" describes only a mood or an attitude, like the Cold War or the Era of Good Feelings. Perhaps Progressives shared little more than gut-level emotions, feelings of fear and uncertainty, or an "enthusiasm for change." Most Progressives did share certain "common assumptions and goals," as the

Britannica suggests: the "repudiation of individualism and laissez-faire, concern for the underprivileged and downtrodden, the control of government by the rank and file, and the enlargement of governmental power in order to bring industry and finance under a measure of popular control."[3] Yet other Progressives preached "rugged individualism" or feared popular government, and even those who did share basic assumptions disagreed over specific measures. In general, Progressives spoke a rhetoric of reform, morality, and the "public interest," but they advocated a wide variety of specific initiatives, and their conceptions of morality and the "public interest" often differed radically.

In retrospect, we recognize that many progressive reforms were neither forward looking nor liberal minded, most notably those dealing with the "Negro question" and the "uplift" of foreign peoples. In addition, we now understand that Progressives "lost at least as many battles as they won," and that "conservative opponents of change remained powerful in many places" as the Progressive Era drew to a close.[4] So why do textbooks continue to refer to the period between the turn of the century and World War I as the "Progressive Era"? Perhaps, as Steven J. Diner suggests, it is simply because "historians routinely use this label and readers recognize it more readily than any other."[5] Yet this volume suggests that there may be something more that distinguishes the Progressive Era: a *rhetorical renaissance* that changed how Americans *talked* about politics and society.

The discourse of progressivism clearly broke from the rhetoric of Reconstruction, the Gilded Age, and even the Populist Era. It represented a new common language of political and social analysis that was reform oriented, moralistic, and optimistic about the possibilities for human "progress." Progressives disagreed over many specifics, but all sensed the need for fundamental reforms in response to rapid social change and unprecedented political challenges. Progressives looked for answers in new sciences, new professions, new organizations, and new political structures. But above all else, they looked for answers in a revitalized public sphere. Progressives had faith that a democratic public, properly educated and deliberating freely, provided the best hope for the future of the American democracy.

As Levine has noted, Americans in the Progressive Era confronted "powerful forces that transformed almost everyone's life and that seemed beyond the capacity of government to shape or control." The challenges seemed overwhelming: "The frontier was closed; cities had grown to unprecedented size. There were terrible slums and factories that perpetually darkened the sky. Corporations had accumulated astounding wealth but seemed insensible to the needs of workers and consumers. Social classes had become more distinct, self-conscious, and mutually hostile than ever before in American history."[6] Convinced that existing political and social institutions were incapable of solving such problems, Progressives set out to reinvent those institutions, to revive the citizenry's sense of civic responsibility, and to rejuvenate deliberative democracy. Those efforts, according to many political and social commentators, remain instructive today. Faced with a democratic crisis with many parallels to our own loss of political faith, the Progressives pointed the way toward a revitalized public sphere.

Problematizing "Progressivism"

History textbooks generally date the Progressive Era from the turn of the century to the start of World War I, and most have little difficulty identifying its major causes, ideas, and leaders. Thus, for example, Billington and Ridge's *American History after 1865*, a textbook that evolved through nine editions over four decades, confidently dates the "Progressive Period" from 1900 and 1917 and offers the following assessment of its causes and character: "The triumph of conservatism and imperialism in the 1890s forced middle-class Americans to ask an important question. Should the results of industrialization be farm peasantry, worker poverty, and the exploitation of colonial peoples? And how could these evils be remedied? The answer, they believed, was two-fold: they must: 1) restore the government to the hands of the people, and 2) use that popularly controlled government to regulate industry, finance, transportation, agriculture, and foreign policy in the interest of the many rather than the few. As they carried out that program in the early twentieth century, the United States entered on that phase of its history known as the Progressive Period."[7] According to Billington and Ridge, journalistic "muckrakers" pointed the way during this period of democratization and reform, and the era "reached a climax" under Woodrow Wilson.[8]

Historical scholarship has long cast doubt on such tidy textbook generalizations. As early as the mid-1950s, one of the classic studies, Richard Hofstadter's Pulitzer prize-winning *Age of Reform*, described progressivism as "a rather vague and not altogether cohesive or consistent movement" that aimed at "some not very clearly specified self-reformation." Hofstadter also was among the first to sense "much that was retrograde and delusive" in progressivism—even "a little that was vicious." Setting "impossible standards" and driven by "moral absolutism," Progressives encouraged a certain "ruthlessness in political life" by turning unrealistic ambitions into holy crusades. As Hofstadter concluded: "It is hardly an accident that the generation that wanted to bring about direct popular rule, break up the political machines, and circumvent representative government was the same generation that imposed Prohibition on the country and proposed to make the world safe for democracy."[9]

New Left revisionists have even more aggressively challenged the textbook wisdom. In *The Triumph of Conservatism*, for example, Gabriel Kolko argued that "the period from approximately 1900 until the United States' intervention in the war"—the period "labeled the 'progressive' era by virtually all historians"—was, in fact, "really an era of conservatism." In Kolko's view, it was no coincidence that "the results of progressivism were precisely what many major business interests desired." According to Kolko, big business "defined the limits of political intervention, and specified its major form and thrust." Kolko sensed no "conspiracy" behind all this, but instead attributed it to "a basic consensus among political and business leaders as to what was the public good." Nevertheless, the effect was to divert radical challenges posed by agrarian discontent, labor unrest, and socialism into cosmetic reforms. Political capitalism "redirected the radical potential of mass grievances and aspirations—of genuine progressivism"—by channeling them into reform efforts that were "frequently designed by businessmen to serve the ends of business."[10]

Recent scholarship has raised still more challenges to the conventional wisdom. Reflecting an emerging consensus that the label itself is impossible to define or even "meaningless,"[11] historian Peter Filene wrote an "obituary for the Progressive Era" in 1970. This supposed new epoch, he concluded, in fact had no unifying theme, no common purpose or program.[12] A survey of the historical scholarship would seem to support such a conclusion. As a national phenomenon—as an "era" or as a "movement"—progressivism has been interpreted as everything from a genuine grassroots movement that democratized American politics and forged a new social consciousness, to an elitist, authoritarian, and bureaucratic effort to impose order, efficiency, and discipline on an unruly society. Because of the diversity of the reformers and the mixed bag of initiatives they promoted, historians simply cannot agree on the causes, character, or effects of progressivism.

One manifestation of this difficulty is the regional or even local focus of much of the literature on the Progressive Era. We now have studies of "Yankee,"[13] Southern[14] and Midwestern[15] progressivism, urban[16] and rural[17] progressivism, and progressivism in dozens of specific states. Not surprisingly, many have studied Wisconsin progressivism,[18] but scholars also have studied progressivism in Vermont,[19] California,[20] Ohio,[21] Illinois,[22] Minnesota,[23] and Oklahoma.[24] As a group, these studies reinforce the sense that there was not just one but many Progressive movements. By illuminating the differing agendas and styles of Progressives across the nation, they reflect the "heterogeneity" that, according to Ellen Fitzpatrick, "has discouraged historians who have sought to define a singular Progressive movement."[25]

Still more doubts about the textbook portrait have emerged out of social histories of African Americans, women, workers, immigrants, and other marginalized groups in the Progressive Era. Clearly, many Progressives did *not* champion what we today would consider enlightened or "progressive" racial ideals. As C. Vann Woodward and others have demonstrated, it was during the so-called Progressive Era that Jim Crow laws spread throughout the South and "the doctrine of racism" gained acceptance, even within "respectable scholarly and intellectual circles."[26] Even the reform-minded "muckraking" journals, as Karlyn Campbell has noted, "ridiculed, derided, and stereotyped" African Americans, "consistently reinforcing ideas of white supremacy" and even blaming the victims for the problem of lynchings.[27] As Raymond Hall has concluded, "the Progressive Era may have meant advancement and progress for the nation as a whole, but it was . . . the nadir for black people."[28] This seeming paradox—the fact that the "first great liberal movement of the twentieth century" was "unmistakably caught up in a powerful tide of racism"—is what inspired historian David W. Southern to dub race relations the "malignant heritage" of the Progressive Era.[29]

Women fared somewhat better than African Americans during the Progressive Era. As Ellen Fitzpatrick has noted, women of this generation enjoyed "unparalleled opportunities in American higher education," and university-trained women "exercised leadership in early-twentieth-century reform circles, not only by actively participating in public life, but by writing extensively about social problems."[30] Middle-class women in general, as Nancy Dye has written, became heavily involved in politics and social reform, as they "came to the realization that in modern industrial society, the doctrine of separate spheres no longer held: the home and the community were inextricably bound together, and those concerns once defined as the private responsibility of the individual housewives and mothers were in actuality public and political."[31] Yet the middle-class reformers often failed to "overcome the barriers of race and class in their attempts to restructure the relationship between the home and the community at large,"[32] and minority and working-class women remained largely untouched by progressive reform. Meanwhile, the suffrage movement stalled throughout much of the period, with no new states won between 1896 and 1910 and the Susan B. Anthony federal suffrage amendment seemingly "moribund."[33] All in all, then, the Progressive Era was a time of great progress for some women, but for others little changed. By the end of the era, women remained, for the most part, second-class citizens.

Finally, the great paradox of the Progressive Era remains the apparent contradiction between liberal reform and the aggressive, even belligerent foreign policies of the period. As Billington and Ridge expressed the textbook view, the "liberal domestic program" of the progressive presidents "contrasted sharply" with their foreign policies, as throughout the period the United States "warred ruthlessly on subject peoples, dominated weaker neighbors, and exerted its power over much of the world."[34] In trying to account for this paradox, Robert Wiebe, in another of the classic studies of the era, wrote of "certain predilections" or "habits of mind" that led Americans at the time to separate the whole world into just two camps—the "civilized powers" and the "barbarians"—and to draw a "clear moral differential" between them. Framed in these terms, American projections of power abroad could be perceived, not as reactionary or imperialistic, but as noble and beneficial to the "natives." Claiming to uplift "backward" peoples and to advance "civilization," many Americans viewed overseas interventionism *as* progressive reform in "a misty extension of ideas that informed progressivism at home."[35]

Thus, the Progressive Era remains a historical enigma. Not only did self-proclaimed Progressives often have little in common, but also not "everything that happened in the period, or for that matter everything done under the banner of reform," represented "progressive" change—at least by "any modern definition" of that term.[36] Especially in race relations and foreign affairs, the contradictions seem obvious. At home, blacks suffered through the worst period in race relations since the Civil War (including an epidemic of lynchings), while abroad America warred against supposedly "barbarian" peoples—all in the name of "civilization" and "progress." It is little wonder, then, that historians have come to question the "progressive" label. In some ways, the period between the turn of the century and World War I was among the most reactionary in American history.

Yet by focusing only on the diversity and paradoxes of progressivism, we overlook important commonalities that, *at the time*, shaped the essential spirit of the age. Most notably, "practically all self-described progressives" believed in a "national interest" or "public good" superior to "special interests and market outcomes."[37] And however else they may have differed, most Progressives agreed that this "national" or "public" good was ultimately revealed, not through philosophical reflection or scientific investigation, but by the nation's leaders and citizens deliberating among themselves. Like most recent scholarship, this volume acknowledges the diversity, tensions, and inconsistencies of the Progressive Era. Yet it also highlights what Progressives had in common: a commitment to robust democratic speech and public deliberation. Focusing on the *discourse* of the era, it reveals the essence of progressivism for those who lived it: an implicit faith in the power of words to change the world for the better.

Progressive Discourse and Deliberative Community

For many Progressives, the essential problem of the era was not corruption in government, nor the "Negro question," nor poverty in the urban tenements, nor even the trusts. On these questions, Progressives disagreed. But virtually all Progressives shared an abiding concern with public opinion and its role in the democratic process. For Progressives, the essential problem of the era was what John Dewey would later call "the problem of the public": the need for improvements in "the methods and conditions of debate, discussion, and persuasion."[38] As a group, Progressives feared that, in an increasingly complex world, powerful special interests had supplanted the "voice of the people," and whatever their other differences, they all agreed on the need to reinvent and revitalize the public sphere. This concern with public deliberation was at the core of Robert La Follette's progressivism, for example. As Levine has noted, La Follette believed that the "surest way for voters to form wise judgments . . . was for them to *deliberate* together about public affairs," and so he proposed a number of "practical measures to increase the quantity, quality, and inclusiveness of public deliberation." For La Follette, it was important that government be "open and fair," but citizens also had a "corresponding responsibility to act cooperatively and wisely."[39]

Theodore Roosevelt may have sniffed at La Follette and others he considered overzealous, but he sounded many of the same themes. Even in the speech that some consider his repudiation of the reform spirit, "The Man with the Muckrake," TR actually celebrated "every writer or speaker" who exposed evil practices and proclaimed the rhetoric of exposure "indispensable to the well-being of society." Like La Follette, however, Roosevelt believed that the right of free speech carried with it certain responsibilities—above all, the responsibility to be "absolutely truthful." He objected to those who made "financial or political profit out of the destruction of character," and he worried about the corruption of the public dialogue by "sensational, lurid, and untruthful" exposés. Such exposés, he insisted, often did "more damage to the public mind" than the alleged abuses themselves, because they fostered "a morbid and vicious public sentiment," a "moral color-blindness," and a "general attitude either of cynical belief in . . . public corruption or else of a distrustful inability to discriminate between the good and the bad." In TR's view, irresponsible public advocacy only impeded reform. As TR himself summarized the essential point of the speech: "Hysterical sensationalism is the very poorest weapon wherewith to fight for lasting righteousness."[40]

Neither admitted it at the time, but the muckrakers actually "shared an uneasy partnership with Theodore Roosevelt."[41] Not only did they help build public support for TR's regulatory efforts, but more important, they shared his faith in the power of rhetoric and informed public opinion. Trusting in the essential rationality, wisdom, and morality of the American people, the muckrakers believed that with "information and guidance, the people would be capable of selecting proper principles and leaders."[42] Unfortunately, as Kevin Mattson has argued, the muckrakers overlooked a key prerequisite to democratic participation: forums for public deliberation. They assumed that simply informing the public would bring about reform, but without "the means of deliberating about effective democratic action," the public remained "passive" in the face of the corruption exposed by the muckrakers.[43]

For later progressive activists and intellectuals, the creation of regular forums of public debate and decision making—forums where an active, enlightened, and freely deliberating "democratic public" might emerge—thus became "a goal in and of itself."[44] Many progressive initiatives, from a "social centers" movement that opened public school buildings to evening town meetings and public debates,[45] to the founding of many of the civic and voluntary associations that still exist today,[46] reflected this ambition. In their efforts to educate the public, to cultivate public deliberation, and to give more organized and efficient expression to public opinion, Progressives turned settlement houses into community forums, and they revived the Chautauqua movement—a national program of educational meetings and discussions "organized for—and by—farmers."[47] In small Midwestern cities they appointed "civic secretaries" to organize public meetings and debates, and they invented school newspapers and student governments to teach young people about civic engagement. Meanwhile, debate and forensics clubs flourished in colleges and universities, and the University of Wisconsin even formed a Department of Debating and Public Discussion, which encouraged off-campus public debates by distributing background papers on such issues as the income tax and woman suffrage.[48] The Progressive Era also gave birth to the "university extension," which brought academic knowledge to the common folk in hopes of promoting more informed public discussion.[49] Even the movement to build municipal parks and playgrounds during the Progressive Era grew out of this concern with democratic community, as such facilities were seen as investments in "neighborliness" and good citizenship.[50]

All across America, ordinary citizens of the Progressive Era gathered in schools, in churches, and even in tents to listen to speakers, to debate among themselves, and to render their judgments on the issues of the day. These exchanges between citizens, as Mattson has suggested, were for the most part "serious, passionate, and normally quite civil," and "many citizens took action based upon what they had learned from one another within these deliberative sessions."[51] Women's clubs and mothers' clubs, for instance, typically began as literary discussion groups but eventually played a significant role in the major reforms of the day, including food safety, housing, services to the poor and disabled, and child labor.[52] Even disenfranchised black women, organized in colored women's clubs, assumed a "public" role as they pushed for better resources in segregated schools and other community needs.[53] By participating in community deliberations or in educational and lobbying groups, Americans of the Progressive Era "learned the necessary skills of a democratic public: how to listen, how to argue, and how to deliberate."[54] If the Progressive Era may be distinguished by nothing else, it marked a remarkable renaissance of public discussion and deliberation. The Progressive Era was, in short, a most "rhetorical" of times.

Progressive efforts to rebuild deliberative communities reflected the belief, later given expression by John Dewey, that "the public" did not exist at all in the absence of "effective and organized inquiry." An "organized, articulate Public" came "into being," according to Dewey, only when people associated with others and communicated *in* public *about* public affairs.[55] Through their various initiatives to bring the public "into being," Progressives aspired to nothing short of a "perfectly deliberative democracy"—a democracy, as Levine has written, that would "function much like an idealized jury but enlarged to include the whole public."[56] In their utopian ideal, Progressives envisioned the public deliberating much like a sequestered jury, free of extraneous forces and influenced only by the persuasiveness of the arguments put before them. Making the comparison explicit and suggesting the faith that Progressives had in the moral wisdom that emerged out of collective deliberation, muckraker Lincoln Steffens described public opinion as a "jury that can not be fixed."[57]

Yet many of the key terms of progressive ideology—organization, efficiency, rationality, expertise, and science—also contained the seeds of a very different view of democracy and public opinion. This view, expressed only occasionally during the Progressive Era but clearly manifested during World War I and throughout the 1920s, held that the "public good *could not* emerge from a democratic process that included everyone, because too many people lacked sufficient virtue and knowledge."[58] Advocates of this view pushed for a paternalistic central government, guided by experts rather than the collective will, and some advocated tougher voter registration rules and even literacy tests in the name of "good government"—that is, as "progressive" reforms. According to these advocates, it fell upon government, experts, and other elites to organize, direct, and articulate public opinion. In this view, public opinion was not seen as rising up out of collective deliberation, but rather as manufactured and manipulated "from above."[59]

This view of democracy and public opinion did not emerge out of a reactionary backlash against progressivism. To the contrary, it was implicit in the writings of some of the leading Progressives, including Herbert Croly and the young Walter Lippmann. In one of the most influential political treatises of the era, *The Promise of American Life*, Croly endorsed the "superior political wisdom" of Alexander Hamilton and concluded that the "national public interest" must be determined by experts and affirmed by a strong, charismatic national leader through "positive and aggressive action."[60] In his 1914 book, *Drift and Mastery*, Lippmann proclaimed the "scientific spirit" the "discipline of democracy" and likewise argued for a strong central government guided by experts rather than public opinion.[61] Lippmann's antidemocratic skepticism did not reach full flower until after the Great War, of course, when he published *Public Opinion*[62]—"the most damaging critique of public opinion and democracy yet written."[63] Yet the foundations of Lippmann's doubts were laid nearly a decade earlier by what Danbom has called "scientific progressivism." Instead of the Christian principles that "fueled the initial thrust" of the Progressive movement, the scientific Progressives placed their "faith in the expert rather than the goodness of the average citizen" and "yearned for an organized and efficient America rather than a morally regenerate one."[64]

In one sense, Woodrow Wilson's election signaled the triumph of scientific progressivism. An expert himself on government and politics, Wilson embodied his own academic theory of presidential leadership. As president, he cast himself not merely as a public persuader or educator of the masses, but as "the chief interpreter" of those "broad, enduring principles" that constituted what he called the "true majority sentiment."[65] For Wilson, the presidency was not merely a "bully pulpit," but was actually a forum for articulating the public consensus *on behalf* of "the people." As Levine has argued, Wilson advocated "calm, national discussion aimed at consensus," but he did more to promote political conformity than genuine dialogue. Levine concludes: "Wilson's fault was to declare himself the sole arbiter of the public interest and to demand acquiescence rather than real consensus. . . . In general, Wilson assumed that his own beliefs and values epitomized the national interest."[66]

Wilson's wartime propaganda agency, the Committee on Public Information (CPI), epitomized the antidemocratic tendencies of scientific progressivism. In the most aggressive attempt ever to manufacture public opinion "from above," the CPI thoroughly saturated the popular media with pro-war rhetoric and severely restricted the expression of dissent. Although staffed largely by Progressives,[67] the CPI pioneered many of the manipulative techniques of modern mass persuasion, in the process giving rise to the negative connotations associated with the term "propaganda" itself. By the end of the war, a very different view of public opinion prevailed. No longer was the public viewed as an "active deliberating body," but rather as "a passive object to be manipulated by mass propaganda."[68]

After the war, many Progressives carried what they had learned in the CPI into the newly emerging industries of advertising and public relations. Edward Bernays, for example, would later recall that his work with the CPI had given him his "first real understanding of the power of ideas as weapons and words as bullets." From his work with the CPI, Bernays learned "one basic lesson": "that efforts comparable to those applied by the CPI to affect the attitudes of the enemy, of neutrals, and people of this country could be applied with equal facility to peacetime pursuits. In other words, what could be done for a nation at war could be done for organizations and people in a nation at peace."[69] Inspired by that insight, Bernays went on to found one of the first public relations firms in the nation and to write two of the landmark works on the manipulation of public opinion, *Crystallizing Public Opinion* (1923) and *Propaganda* (1928).

This, then, is the ironic legacy of the Progressive Era: that a movement that aspired to empower the democratic polity instead magnified the power of central government, bureaucratic agencies, and experts in propaganda. As wartime propaganda experts turned their talents to peacetime pursuits, the progressive dream of an informed and engaged democratic public gave way to the modern, "scientific" view of mass communication and "opinion management." As Mattson has concluded: "A radical change occurred during World War I and into the 1920s: the concept of a democratic public, which was widespread during the Progressive Era, no longer constituted a key element in the American political imagination."[70] Instead of leaving a revitalized public sphere, the Progressive Era—that most "rhetorical" of times—instead gave way to the modern age of public relations and propaganda.

A Rhetorical History of the Progressive Era

This volume provides further evidence of the remarkable diversity of those who called themselves Progressives. Examining the rhetoric of politicians, social reformers, and advocates for a variety of causes, it reveals how some of the leading public advocates of the Progressive Era arrived at very different conclusions about the best paths to reform. At the same time, however, it also demonstrates their shared commitment to public deliberation and "serious speech"—speech "in search of truth," speech intended to aid citizens in their "common search for understanding."[71] The Progressives spoke and wrote prolifically, and they believed in the power of words—especially *their* words—to effect positive change. Whether running for political office, writing political treatises, or speaking in the diverse and vibrant public forums of the day, all contributed to a rhetorical renaissance that distinguishes the Progressive Era from both the Gilded Age and the later era of mass communication and opinion management. All contributed to a rebirth of democratic deliberation and a revitalized public sphere.

Robert Kraig begins our rhetorical history of the Progressive Era with a wide-ranging reflection on what he calls the "second oratorical renaissance." Neglected in most historical accounts of the period, this "renaissance" represented more than just a renewed interest in the teaching and practice of oratorical skills. Grounded in broader theories of enlightened leadership and republican governance, the second oratorical renaissance harkened back to the classical rhetorical tradition of Cicero and Quintillian—a tradition passed down to America's founders and, in the public memory of the Progressive Era, most perfectly realized in the antebellum golden age of American oratory. "When great oratorical statesmen returned to the national stage during the Progressive Era," Kraig observes, "they symbolized for their followers a return to the political virtues of the past." They recalled a time when the political system was "more perfectly democratic, when power was wielded not by irresponsible political machines and mammoth corporations, but by platform giants whose only real hold was their capacity to convince their fellow citizens to lay aside selfish and parochial interests." In telling the story of this second oratorical renaissance, Kraig demonstrates how, *rhetorically*, this era of innovation and experimentation was in fact something of a throwback. In pursuing the overarching objective of progressive reform—the revitalization of the democratic public sphere—Progressives longed for a *return* of the well-educated, disinterested oratorical statesmen. "The yearning for the glories of a past age was part of a general nostalgia for lost virtues during the first two decades of the twentieth century," Kraig concludes, "a time when social thought was at once nostalgic and forward looking."

In chapter 2, Leroy Dorsey tackles the great historical enigma of the Progressive Era: Theodore Roosevelt. Dismissed as something of a phony Progressive, both by Progressives in his own day—most notably, Robert La Follette in his *Autobiography*[72]—and by later historians,[73] Roosevelt still puzzles those who cannot reconcile his progressive domestic agenda with his attacks on the muckrakers, his celebration of the "strenuous life," and his glorification of war. Yet, as Dorsey shows, the fundamental principles undergirding all of Roosevelt's rhetoric were, in the context of the times, thoroughly progressive, and those principles remained consistent throughout his career—from his earliest writings as a historian and social commentator in the 1880s and 1890s through his Bull Moose and preparedness campaigns near the end of the Progressive Era. Convinced that genuine and lasting social reform rested upon the moral and physical strength of individual Americans, Roosevelt's "rhetorical progressivism" may be jarring to modern sensibilities, but it reflected the progressive emphasis on moral character and the responsibilities of democratic citizenship.

In chapter 3, Christine Oravec shows how progressive conceptions of "the people" and the "public spirit" were manifested in the early conservation movement. As Oravec shows, the conservation policies of the Roosevelt administration may have arisen out of scientific and technological premises, but they were popularized "by rhetorically constituting a nationwide conservationist public—a public that continues to warrant political action today." Seizing upon "conservation" itself as a term that encompassed both preservationist and developmentalist impulses, Gifford Pinchot, W J McGee, and Roosevelt himself transcended controversies over policy with a "constitutive" rhetoric that created a conservationist "public" and rendered the wise management of natural resources a moral, spiritual, and even patriotic duty. As the unifying principle for a new social movement, "conservation" not only popularized a "reformist, well-managed, middle-of-the-road" approach to natural resources, but also left a legacy that sustains the conservation movement to this day: a "rhetorical culture" that grounds conservation in "the spirit of the people."

In chapter 4, Douglas Birkhead addresses a key topic in any history of the Progressive Era: the changing business of journalism. In most accounts of progressivism, of course, the muckrakers play a role; their exposés are described as the engine of progressive reform, and their ethos defines a central image of the era: that of the "socially responsible reporter-reformer."[74] As Birkhead suggests, however, journalism evolved through the same sort of identity crisis—and attracted many of the same criticisms—as many other professions, businesses, and institutions of the Progressive Era. The press "entered the twentieth century on the verge of corporate oligopoly," Birkhead writes, "maligned as much as any other industry in the country." In this context, the rise of muckraking, as well as the larger movement to professionalize journalism, may be seen as *rhetorical* efforts "to counter criticisms that journalism had devolved from an exalted 'Fourth Estate' into a base commercial enterprise." Unlike efforts to professionalize other occupations, the drive to professionalize journalism had little to do with "empowering journalists as an occupational group." It aimed, instead, to legitimize the press as "a socially responsible corporate institution." The "economic exploitation of technology" radically changed journalism during the Progressive Era, but Birkhead shows how the professionalization of journalism was not so much a "revolution" as a "rhetorical frame for understanding that change."

In chapter 5, James Aune offers a close reading of the speeches and judicial opinions of Oliver Wendall Holmes Jr., the man who, perhaps more than any other, "helped define the peculiar place of legal rhetoric in our public life." Holmes, Aune argues, is also the one figure who perhaps "best captures the tensions and contradictions in American progressive thought." He was, on the one hand, "the first American to argue for an empirical and behavioral view of the law, one that purged it of traditional moral associations." He also was a "hero" to labor leaders and progressive politicians, including Theodore Roosevelt. On the other hand, he was a controversial figure, criticized for his "pragmatic view" of the law and, in later years, reviled for his Darwinism, atheism, and philosophical skepticism. In studying Holmes and the continuing contest over his reputation and legacy, Aune argues that "Holmes's career helps us understand . . . the sweeping transitions in the American language of public life that occurred between the Civil War and the New Deal." The "ambiguities and contradictions" in Holmes's "romantic realism" remain "part of American liberalism" even today, as evident in the "various reflections" and "projections of social anxiety on to the figure of Holmes by several generations of legal scholars."

Malcom Sillar's subject in chapter 6, William Jennings Bryan, also illustrates the ambiguities and contradictions of progressive thought. Contrasting sharply with Holmes, Bryan elevated religion over science, ordinary citizens over experts, and the rights of the individual over those of the community. Identified more with the populism of the 1890s than with the Progressive Era, Bryan in fact carried his passion for social reform into the twentieth century—and thus was no less a Progressive than Holmes or Theodore Roosevelt. Yet, as Sillars shows, Bryan's progressivism had a distinctively Jeffersonian flavor in an era that more often celebrated Hamilton. Breaking from the crowd, Bryan exposed the contradiction inherent in progressive imperialism, and he demonstrated (to the satisfaction of his many supporters, at least) the *anti*progressive implications of evolutionary theory. Like most Progressives, Bryan remained strangely silent about "progress" for African Americans. And like most early Progressives, he had a strong faith in reason, the power of persuasion, and the wisdom of the ordinary citizen. According to Sillars, Bryan was neither the wild-eyed radical nor the fundamentalist reactionary that his critics caricatured throughout his career. Rather, he was among the earliest proponents of a "modern liberalism" that emphasized *both* active government and individual rights—a liberalism that "redefined" the Democratic Party and drew new lines of distinction between Democrats and Republicans.

In chapter 7, James Darsey recovers one of the genuinely radical voices of the Progressive Era: Eugene Victor Debs. In "Eugene Debs and American Class," Darsey illuminates how Debs "expressed the drama of class struggle" in the "American vernacular" and put working-class issues "so firmly onto the main stage of American politics that mainstream political parties were forced. . . . to respond." Elaborating on Debs's adaptations of Marxist theory, his unabashed sentimentalism, and his embrace of many of the prevailing assumptions and issues of the Progressive Era, Darsey shows how Debs promoted a uniquely American notion of "class" with an equally distinctive "working-class eloquence." Dismissed for many years as a champion of lost causes and a dangerous radical, it comes as little surprise that Debs was excluded from the first official attempt to forge a canon of great American orators: Brigance's *History and Criticism of American Public Address.*[75] Nearly sixty years later, however, the standards of eloquence that excluded Debs themselves seem "rigid, quaint, and alien," and we recognize in Debs "a prototypical version of our own more direct, less studied public discourse." For "good or ill," Darsey concludes, Debs "helped to break the stranglehold of an essentially republican eloquence and to displace it with a rough-and-tumble, democratic, extemporaneous, middle-class public speech, colored by American pragmatism and its plutonian cousin, American anti-intellectualism." As such, Debs "forces us to confront in profound ways the ideological tests to which we put candidates for canonization, our assumptions about an ideal discourse, even the desirability of that ideal, and the changing style of what we used to call 'oratory.'"

In chapter 8, Robert Terrill and Eric King Watts investigate W. E. B. Du Bois's disputes with both Booker T. Washington and Marcus Garvey as they flesh out his concept of "double-consciousness." Examining how double-consciousness informed Du Bois's rivalries with both Washington and Garvey, they extend our understanding of the concept and show how it was "refigured in Du Bois's thought as Pan-Africanism." As the authors point out, "double-consciousness" was the product of Du Bois's academic training and the racial politics of the Progressive Era, and they acknowledge that it provided "a useful lens for revealing and exploring the complexities of the African-American experience." Yet it did not prove so effective as a rhetorical stance "around which to assemble political action or through which to attempt social change." For Du Bois, "double-consciousness" meant *retaining* the complex and problematic dual identity of African Americans—as Africans *and* Americans—in a productive tension. Yet "to get work done in the world," Terrill and Watts conclude, "sometimes you must come down firmly somewhere," and Du Bois's "commitment to multivocality and against monolithic leadership" may have "precluded his own rise as the undisputed leader of a movement or institution."

In chapter 9, Brian McGee continues our exploration of race relations with an investigation into "the ways in which race fit into the rhetoric of progressivism." Rather than an era of "progress" for African Americans, as McGee notes, the Progressive Era "marked the worst period for race relations since the Civil War." McGee uncovers at least part of the explanation in the two prevailing "rhetorics of race" at the time: the subjugationist and the developmentalist. If there was a "commonplace" among whites in the Progressive Era, McGee argues, it was belief in the inferiority of African Americans as a group. For white Americans, including most Progressives, the race issue revolved around what, if anything, to do about to the presence of an "inferior race" in America. For subjugationists, there was little chance that African Americans would ever progress sufficiently to qualify for full democratic citizenship. They viewed the permanent exclusion of blacks from the body politic as a progressive reform necessary to safeguard democracy. Developmentalists, on the other hand, held out hope for the intellectual and moral improvement of African Americans, and they viewed white assistance in that process as a progressive imperative. While they envisioned African Americans *someday* achieving the qualifications necessary for democratic citizenship, however, they emphasized that this process might take a generation or more. Thus, in the short term, developmentalists reached essentially the same conclusion as the subjugationists: "that progress could be made only by excluding African Americans from the mainstream of public life." Illustrating the subjugationist and developmentalist perspectives with the rhetoric of novelist Thomas Dixon Jr. and Theodore Roosevelt, respectively, McGee shows how both promoted black disenfranchisement at home and imperialism abroad as progressive reforms. Given this consensus, McGee concludes, the resurgence of the Ku Klux Klan in the 1920s can be seen as an ironic rhetorical legacy of the Progressive Era.

In chapter 10, Jennifer Borda examines efforts to push forward the campaign for woman suffrage during the Progressive Era. Far from the "doldrums" of the suffrage crusade, the period between the mid-1890s and the end of the Progressive Era was, in fact, a period of significant activity led by three different and rhetorically intriguing leaders: Carrie Chapman Catt, Alice Paul, and Harriot Stanton Blatch, the daughter of Elizabeth Cady Stanton. As Borda demonstrates, each of these suffrage leaders brought a different strategic philosophy and rhetorical style to the cause, yet all bore the rhetorical imprints of the Progressive Era. Exploring how different elements of progressive ideology shaped the leadership of each of these three leaders, Borda shows how the woman suffrage movement made the "crucial transition into the new century" as a "distinctively progressive movement"—one that, "like progressivism itself," remained "a diverse and ever-changing movement throughout the period."

In chapter 11, Carl Burgchardt investigates another prominent woman of the Progressive Era, Jane Addams. Focusing on Addams's anti-war rhetoric, Burghchardt illuminates a dimension of her public persona rarely featured in historical and biographical accounts: her reputation as an outspoken opponent of imperialism and war. Enjoying widespread celebrity for her work at Hull House, Addams served as an important voice for a wide variety of reforms throughout the Progressive Era and became known, as Wiebe has observed, for redefining social work, not as "a personal concern for an individual's spiritual and mental elevation," but rather as "the scientific analysis of a life in process."[76] Generally, Americans accepted her pacifist and anti-war views as a natural extension of her efforts to improve the lives of workers, women, and children. When she spoke out against World War I, however, Addams became embroiled in controversy, with critics questioning her motives, her intelligence, and even her loyalty. In the face of such reactions, Addams was forced to abandon her characteristically confident, detached, and scholarly rhetorical style for more emotional defenses of her own motives and character. With her progressive faith in the power of reasoned discourse to uplift humanity shaken by the irrationality of war, one of the most outspoken and popular public advocates of the Progressive Era retreated into a "cautious, defensive rhetorical posture."

In chapter 12, historian Judith Allen investigates "the most important feminist theorist of the Progressive Era," Charlotte Perkins Gilman. Focusing on Gilman's nonfiction rather than her more frequently studied literary works, Allen reveals in great detail how Gilman supported herself as a public lecturer and illuminates her distinctively feminist take on such "quintessential Progressive Era preoccupations" as prostitution, birth control, and immigration. As Allen suggests, some of Gilman's views seem "uncongenial and even ludicrous to late-twentieth-century readers." Gilman criticized libertarian sexual mores and birth control, for example, and she sounded nativist and racist themes in her discourse on immigration. In the context of that very different age, however, Gilman's views were, at once, both in the mainstream of progressive discourse and original and critical extensions of that discourse from a feminist perspective. "Not only was Gilman a significant exemplar of progressivism," Allen concludes, but her work also "placed feminism firmly within the progressivist agenda." She might not sound like a "progressive feminist" or a "feminist Progressive" to modern ears, but at the time Gilman "was what progressivism was, what feminism was, warts and all."

In the voices of the Progressive Era, we hear both echoes of the past and harbingers of the future. As Danbom has emphasized, Progressives often "looked backward rather than forward."[77] In this volume Robert Kraig illustrates how that was true in a *rhetorical* sense: many Progressives longed, not for a *new* rhetoric for the modern age, but for a "renaissance" of an oratorical golden age. At the same time, we hear in the voices of the Progressive Era many of the themes and stylistic tokens of today's political discourse, including some of the more troubling tendencies in modern electioneering. As Roderick Hart has noted, the first presidential campaign of the Progressive Era—the campaign of 1900—not only had some of the same sloganeering and "smarminess" of today's presidential campaigns, but even some of the issues sound familiar.[78] Hart quotes one historical summary of that campaign that, as he notes, has "a particularly contemporary ring": "Bryan preached—Roosevelt shouted. The Nebraskan quoted scripture—the Rough Rider waved the flag. The great Democratic leader was an artist with words—his Republican rival was a better tub-thumper."[79]

The legacies of the Progressive Era include not only image making in political campaigns, but also the "rhetorical presidency" and the rhetoric of special-interest politics. The conflict between preservation and "wise use" in the rhetoric of environmentalism dates back to the Progressive Era, as do tensions in the rhetoric of law between collective needs and individual rights. Religion and science are perhaps no more reconciled today than they were in the Progressive Era, and we continue to debate the causes of poverty, crime, and social deviance—all hot topics for the budding social scientists of the Progressive Era. We remember the Progressive Era—and we quote such figures as W. E. B. Du Bois and Charlotte Perkins Gilman—as we reflect on what it means to be black or female in America, and echoes of Debs and Addams can still be heard in pleas for workers' rights and "social justice." The more we hear the voices of the Progressive Era, the more we understand Nancy Dye's claim that "the Progressive Era marks the beginning of contemporary America."[80] Not only have we yet to settle many of the central controversies of that day, but we still look to the Progressive Era for guidance in solving many of today's social and political challenges.

In the conclusion to this book, we will reflect at greater length on the legacies and lessons of the Progressive Era. We will examine how memories of the Progressive Era have once again become prominent in our public discourse as we address—at the start of the twenty-first century—many of the same problems the historical Progressives faced: rapid technological and social change, economic and racial inequalities, fragmented communities, and civic decay. Before reflecting on those legacies, however, we should first listen closely to the voices of the original Progressives. Before asking what they might have to teach us today, we must first understand what they had to say in their own—and, in many ways, unique—historical context.

Notes

1. Peter Levine, *The New Progressive Era: Toward a Fair and Deliberative Democracy* (Lanham, Md.: Rowman and Littlefield, 2000), xi.
2. Encyclopedia Britannica Online, s.v. "United States, History of," <http://search.eb.com/bol/topic?eu=121263&sctn=5> (accessed 13 January 2001).
3. Ibid.
4. Steven J. Diner, *A Very Different Age: Americans of the Progressive Era* (New York: Hill and Wang, 1998), 202.
5. Ibid., 13.
6. Levine, *New Progressive Era*, ix.
7. Ray A. Billington and Martin Ridge, *American History after 1865*, 9th ed. (Totowa, N.J.: Littlefield, Adams, 1981), 113.
8. Ibid., 131.
9. Richard Hofstadter, *The Age of Reform: From Bryan to F.D.R.* (New York: Vintage Books, 1955), 5, 12, 16, 18.
10. Gabriel Kolko, *The Triumph of Conservatism: A Reinterpretation of American History, 1900–1916* (1963; reprint, New York: Free Press, 1977), 2, 280, 282, 285–86.
11. Robert M. Crunden, "Progressivism," in *The Reader's Companion to American History*, ed. Eric Foner and John A. Garraty (Boston: Houghton Mifflin, 1995), 869.
12. Peter Filene, "An Obituary for the 'Progressive Movement,'" *American Quarterly* 22 (1970): 20–34.
13. David W. Southern, *The Malignant Heritage: Yankee Progressives and the Negro Question, 1901–1914* (Chicago: Loyola University Press, 1968).
14. Dewey W. Grantham, *Southern Progressivism: The Reconciliation of Progress and Tradition* (Knoxville: University of Tennessee Press, 1983); Paul D. Casdorph, *Republicans, Negroes, and Progressives in the South, 1912–1916* (University: University of Alabama Press, 1981); William A. Link, *The Paradox of Southern Progressivism, 1880–1930* (Chapel Hill: University of North Carolina Press, 1992).
15. Russel B. Nye, *Midwestern Progressive Politics: A Historical Study of Its Origins and Development, 1870–1958* (East Lansing: Michigan State University Press, 1959).
16. John D. Buenker, *Urban Liberalism and Progressive Reform* (New York: Scribner, 1973); Roy Lubove, *The Progressives and the Slums: Tenement House Reform in New York City, 1890–1917* (1962; reprint, Pittsburgh: University of Pittsburgh Press, 1963); James J. Connolly, *The Triumph of Ethnic Progressivism: Urban Political Culture in Boston, 1900–1925* (Cambridge: Harvard University Press, 1998).
17. Robert W. Cherny, *Populism, Progressivism, and the Transformation of Nebraska Politics, 1885–1915* (Lincoln: University of Nebraska Press, 1981).
18. David P. Thelen, *The New Citizenship: Origins of Progressivism in Wisconsin, 1885–1900* (Columbia: University of Missouri Press, 1972); Robert S. Maxwell, *La Follette and the Rise of the Progressives in Wisconsin* (1956; reprint, New York: Russell and Russell, 1973); Herbert F. Margulies, *The Decline of the Progressive Movement in Wisconsin, 1890–1920* (Madison: State Historical Society of Wisconsin, 1968); Roger T. Johnson, *Robert M. La Follette, Jr. and the Decline of the Progressive Party in Wisconsin* (Madison: State Historical Society of Wisconsin, 1964).
19. Winston A. Flint, *The Progressive Movement in Vermont* (Washington, D.C.: American Council on Public Affairs, 1941).
20. George E. Mowry, *The California Progressives* (Chicago: Quadrangle Books, 1963).
21. Hoyt L. Warner, *Progressivism in Ohio, 1897–1917* (Columbus: Ohio State University Press, 1964).
22. Thomas R. Pegram, *Partisans and Progressives: Private Interest and Public Policy in Illinois, 1870–1922* (Urbana: University of Illinois Press, 1992).
23. See Carl H. Chrislock, *The Progressive Era in Minnesota, 1899–1918* (St. Paul: Minnesota Historical Society Press, 1971).
24. Danney Goble, *Progressive Oklahoma: The Making of a New Kind of State* (Norman: University of Oklahoma Press, 1980).
25. Ellen Fitzpatrick, *Endless Crusade: Women Social Scientists and Progressive Reform* (New York: Oxford University Press, 1990), xii.

26. C. Vann Woodward, *The Strange Career of Jim Crow,* 3d ed. (New York: Oxford University Press, 1974), 74.

27. Karlyn Kohrs Campbell, "The Power of Hegemony: Capitalism and Racism in the 'Nadir of Negro History,'" in *Rhetoric and Community: Studies in Unity and Fragmentation,* ed. J. Michael Hogan (Columbia, S.C.: University of South Carolina Press, 1998), 38.

28. Raymond Hall, *Black Separatism in the United States* (Hanover, N.H.: University Press of New England, 1978), 53.

29. Southern, *Malignant Heritage,* 1.

30. Fitzpatrick, *Endless Crusade,* xii–xiii.

31. Nancy S. Dye, introduction to *Gender, Class, Race, and Reform in the Progressive Era,* ed. Noralee Frankel and Nancy S. Dye (Lexington: University Press of Kentucky, 1991), 3.

32. Ibid., 5.

33. Eleanor Flexner, *Century of Struggle: The Woman's Rights Movement in the United States,* rev. ed. (Cambridge: Harvard University Press, 1975), 256.

34. Billington and Ridge, *American History after 1865,* 131.

35. Robert H. Wiebe, *The Search for Order, 1877–1920* (New York: Hill and Wang, 1967), 237.

36. Diner, *A Very Different Age,* 13.

37. Levine, *New Progressive Era,* 18.

38. John Dewey, *The Public and Its Problems* (1927; reprint, Athens, Ohio: Swallow Press, 1991), 208.

39. Levine, *New Progressive Era,* xiii.

40. Theodore Roosevelt, "The Man with the Muckrake," in *American Rhetorical Discourse,* 2d ed., ed. Ronald F. Reid (Prospect Heights, Ill.: Waveland, 1995), 676–78.

41. David Mark Chalmers, *The Muckrake Years* (Huntington, N.Y.: Robert E. Krieger, 1980), 68.

42. Ibid., 66.

43. Kevin Mattson, *Creating a Democratic Public: The Struggle for Urban Participatory Democracy during the Progressive Era* (University Park: Pennsylvania State University Press, 1998), 15.

44. Ibid., 8.

45. Ibid., 48–67.

46. See Robert D. Putnam, *Bowling Alone: The Collapse and Revival of American Community* (New York: Simon and Schuster, 2000), 383–88.

47. Levine, *New Progressive Era,* 16.

48. Ibid., 16.

49. See Mattson, *Creating a Democratic Public,* 25–29.

50. Michael J. Sandel, *Democracy's Discontent: America in Search of a Public Philosophy* (Cambridge: Harvard University Press, 1996), 209–10.

51. Mattson, *Creating a Democratic Public,* 1.

52. Diner, *A Very Different Age,* 20–21.

53. See Jacqueline A. Rouse, "Atlanta's African-American Women's Attack on Segregation, 1900–1920," in *Gender, Class, Race, and Reform,* 10–23.

54. Mattson, *Creating a Democratic Public,* 45.

55. Dewey, *The Public and Its Problems,* 177, 184.

56. Levine, *New Progressive Era,* 12.

57. Quoted in ibid., 12.

58. Ibid., 18–19.

59. Mattson, *Creating a Democratic Public,* 12.

60. Herbert Croly, *The Promise of American Life* (1909; reprint, Boston: Northeastern University Press, 1989), 190.

61. Walter Lippmann, *Drift and Mastery* (1914; reprint, Englewood Cliffs, N.J.: Prentice-Hall, 1961), 151.

62. Walter Lippmann, *Public Opinion* (1922; reprint, New York: Free Press Paperbacks, 1997).

63. Mattson, *Creating a Democratic Public,* 118.

64. David B. Danbom, *"The World of Hope": Progressives and the Struggle for an Ethical Public Life* (Philadelphia: Temple University Press, 1987), 113.

65. J. Michael Hogan and James R. Andrews, "Woodrow Wilson (1856–1924)," in *U.S. Presidents as Orators: A Bio-critical Sourcebook*, ed. Halford Ryan (Westport, Conn.: Greenwood, 1995), 115.

66. Levine, *New Progressive Era*, 20.

67. As Diner has observed, the CPI "attracted all sorts of progressives," including the "prototypical reformer" who headed it, George Creel. Progressives initially viewed the CPI as an agent of social reform. As Stephen Vaughn has noted, many Progressives within the agency "believed the war had evoked a new spirit of self-sacrifice and cooperation. They were drawn to the committee in hope that they might fight society's evils and make a better world." As it turned out, of course, those hopes were dashed. As Diner notes, Progressives soon realized that the "war had brought out the worst in human nature, had failed to instill a larger common purpose, and had encouraged a 'cult of irrationality' which contradicted progressives' faith in the reasonableness of an intelligent citizenry." Instead of ushering in a new era of social reform and progress, "postwar politics turned decisively against progressive social engineering" (Diner, *A Very Different Age*, 261–63); Stephen Vaughn, *Holding Fast the Inner Lines: Democracy, Nationalism, and the Committee on Public Information* (Chapel Hill: University of North Carolina Press, 1980), 23–24.

68. Mattson, *Creating a Democratic Public*, 115.

69. Quoted in Scott M. Cutlip, *The Unseen Power: Public Relations. A History* (Hillsdale, N.J.: Lawrence Erlbaum Associates, 1994), 165, 168.

70. Mattson, *Creating a Democratic Public*, 115.

71. E. J. Dionne Jr., *They Only Look Dead: Why Progressives Will Dominate the Next Political Era* (New York: Touchstone Books, 1997), 261.

72. Robert M. La Follette, *La Follette's Autobiography: A Personal Narrative of Political Experiences* (Madison, Wis.: La Follette, 1913), esp. 387–89, 478–85.

73. See Richard Hofstadter, *The American Political Tradition and the Men Who Made It* (New York: Vintage Books, 1948), 206–37. As Collin has noted, Hofstadter later seemed to change his attitude toward Roosevelt. In such later works as *The Age of Reform* (1954) and *Anti-intellectualism in American Life* (1963) he credited TR with moderate yet significant reforms that served to calm the nation's fears of extremism and prevent class conflict. See Richard H. Collin, *Theodore Roosevelt and Reform Politics* (Lexington, Mass.: D. C. Heath and Co., 1972), xiii.

74. Hofstadter, *Age of Reform*, 186.

75. William Norwood Brigance, ed., *A History and Criticism of American Public Address*, 2 vols. (New York: McGraw-Hill, 1943).

76. Wiebe, *Search for Order*, 150.

77. Danbom, "The World of Hope," vii.

78. Roderick P. Hart, *Campaign Talk: Why Elections Are Good for Us* (Princeton: Princeton University Press, 2000), xv.

79. Ibid. Hart is quoting from E. H. Roseboom and A. E. Eckes, *A History of Presidential Elections: From George Washington to Jimmy Carter* (New York: Macmillan, 1970), 126–27.

80. Dye, introduction to *Gender, Class, Race, and Reform in the Progressive Era*, 9.

The Second Oratorical Renaissance

Robert Alexander Kraig

I wish there were some great orator who could go about and make men drunk with this spirit of self-sacrifice. I wish there were some man whose tongue might every day carry abroad the gold accents of that creative age in which we were born a nation; accents which would ring like tones of reassurance around the whole circle of the globe.

WOODROW WILSON, "An Address on Robert E. Lee"

During the Progressive Era, there was an outpouring of nostalgia for the bygone age when oratory seemed to dominate American life. Publishing houses produced a rash of multivolume oratorical anthologies, in which the formative events of history could be experienced as a sequence of great speeches by fabled orators. Dozens of magazine articles and newspaper editorials lamented the decline of American oratory from its heroic heights before the Civil War. Although this view had been conventional since at least the 1870s, the intensity and frequency of these regrets intensified. There was a running debate about whether it was possible in a modern industrial society for oratory to recover its former influence. Some maintained that even if the contemporary equivalents of Patrick Henry and Daniel Webster were to appear in the political arena, their burning eloquence would make little impression on impatient and distracted modern audiences.

Curiously, at the same time that so many were mourning the decline of the art, oratory was becoming more influential in American politics than it had been since antebellum times. In national and state election campaigns, on the hugely popular Chautauqua circuit, and in the rise of a new breed of reform politician, oratory was again playing a determining role. There were again great debates in Congress, and, in a development that would have significant repercussions for the rest of the century, the presidency was being transformed into a mighty platform for oratorical leadership. Another constellation of great orators at least the equal of any other in U.S. history was on the rise, and yet most commentators remained profoundly dissatisfied. The second great oratorical renaissance in America was dogged by the remembrance of the first.

1

This tension between contemporary discourse and the idealized memory of past practice could be so strongly felt because Progressive Era America was still a self-consciously oratorical culture. The generation that produced Woodrow Wilson, Robert M. La Follette, and William Jennings Bryan—all of whom were born shortly before the Civil War—was the last in American history in which a significant number of young people grew up believing that to become influential leaders they had to submit themselves to years of intensive oratorical training. For this generation, and indeed for all previous generations in American history, the great orators of the past were models for imitation, and the figure of the orator had a romance and a social importance that is hard to imagine today. In the Gilded Age there had been a profusion of public speaking, and despite persistent doubts about its quality, it still meant something to be an accomplished orator. Because oratory retained a commanding place in the literary canon, the educated had been exposed to the landmarks of British and American public address. Those who had gone to college had spent long hours in Latin and Greek recitations, declaiming Demosthenes and Cicero. Aspiring orators had studied Pitt, Burke, Bright, Brougham, Everett, Sumner, Chase, and the other luminaries of English and American oratory. Even those with the most rudimentary of educations had declaimed Webster's second reply to Hayne. The ritual of reading great speeches and attempting to imbibe their wisdom and spirit gave oratorical culture a distinctive texture.[1]

For the generation of Wilson, La Follette, and Bryan, the term "orator" still denoted something more profound than mere fluency of speech. It was a signifier in a civic language that is now lost, and it was part of a broader worldview about the kinds of leaders that ought to govern in a well-structured republic. Part and parcel of the shared generational experience of reading and admiring the canon of oratorical classics was the exaltation of the iconic orators who produced them. As in the classical model of the ideal orator in Cicero and Quintilian, these figures had reputations not for elocution only, but also as educated and disinterested statesmen who applied their generous talents for the benefit of the commonweal. This mythic conception of oratorical power was a complex referent that could have varying meanings. Indeed, discussions of oratory often reflected unresolved social tensions that centered on the relationship between leadership and democracy. When great oratorical statesmen returned to the national stage during the Progressive Era, they symbolized for their followers a return to the political virtues of the past. For many, the golden age of American oratory before the Civil War was associated with a political system that was remembered as more perfectly democratic, when power was wielded not by irresponsible political machines and mammoth corporations, but by platform giants whose only real hold was their capacity to convince their fellow citizens to lay aside selfish and parochial interests. Oratory in the early twentieth century still carried the resonance of this idealized past because the heroism of great orators was still an integral part of the collective memory of history between the Revolution and the Civil War. For many conservatives who feared the increasingly mass cast of the political system, the iconic Whig orators of the pre–Civil War period symbolized rule by the "best men"—that is, by an educated and disinterested elite. They saw men such as Bryan and La Follette not as the heirs to Webster and Clay, but as dangerous demagogues who could not be trusted with the power of popular eloquence.

The various meanings imputed to the art of oratory during the Progressive Era were not merely the fanciful creations of a romantically inclined generation. On the contrary, they were modernized variants of themes that stretch back to the early days of the republic. The role of oratory in a democratic political system had been contested ground throughout the entire pre–Civil War era. Although they were applied to vastly different circumstances, concerns about the use of oratorical power in the Progressive Era were recognizably similar to those that had vexed the Federalists and the American Whigs. It is a testament to the continuity of the oratorical tradition that something of these old debates was transposed into contemporary political controversies. The fading of this oratorical culture marks a major break in the history of American public address. There would continue to be highly influential public speaking after the second oratorical renaissance, but it would not have the same range of connotations for speakers or their audiences.

In the historiography of the late nineteenth and early twentieth century, historians and political scientists have tended to pass lightly over the immense social and cultural significance of oratory. Arthur Link, for instance, writes that in the Progressive Era "the American people admired oratory above all other political skills," and Robert Ferrell reports that it was "an era still reverent of the golden age of oratory that opened with Webster and Hayne, Calhoun and Clay." Yet neither Link nor Ferrell, nor most other historians, follow up such observations with sustained analysis of what difference this esteem of oratory might have made in the political culture of the time.[2] One of the cardinal features of oratorical culture was a distinct historical consciousness that connected speakers and their audiences to the orators of the past. To appreciate the meaning of American oratory's second renaissance for its participants, and to understand its place in the rhetorical history of America, we need to come to terms with the antebellum culture that exalted the great orator above all other figures. Thus, before turning to the postbellum social environment that produced the greatest speakers of the Progressive Era, and the oratorical revival of the late nineteenth and early twentieth century that catapulted them into the limelight, this chapter will first trace the development of the oratorical culture that emerged during the early days of the republic and flowered in the golden age of American oratory during the decades before the Civil War.

The Rhetorical World of the Founders

Eloquence was viewed with a mixture of awe and trepidation by the eighteenth-century statesmen who framed the federal Constitution. For them, it was a mighty force for good, an essential power in a republic. They lived, as Gordon Wood has said, in a "rhetorical world" in which statesmen were expected to be orators. Yet ancient and modern history furnished abundant proof to them that eloquence had the potential not only to build commonwealths but to rip them asunder. Thus eighteenth-century leaders both respected and feared the potential of rhetoric. This combined adoration and anxiety would inform the founding generation's conception of a well-formed republic and of the kind of leaders it required.[3] For them, the immense potential of oratory for good or ill made it essential that its power be wielded by enlightened statesmen who could be trusted to use it in the most responsible manner. It also required oratory to be institutionally contained within assemblies made up of responsible guardians of the commonwealth. This relationship between the nature of eloquence and prescriptions for statesmanship in the eighteenth-century mind was critical to the formation of a complex of ideas that would remain remarkably influential from the early national period through the Progressive Era.

The late-eighteenth-century view of rhetoric in the Anglo-American world had its roots in two distinct yet overlapping traditions: the classical and Renaissance humanist vision of eloquence as the foundation of civilization, and Enlightenment verbal skepticism, with its great concern for the dangers of linguistic deceit and corruption. Renaissance humanists had rehabilitated the classical rhetorical tradition, epitomized by the writings of Cicero and Quintilian, which linked eloquence to wisdom and power and held the eloquent leader to be a great civilizing and nation-building force. As Thomas Gustafson writes, in the Renaissance, eloquence "became what it had been for Cicero and what it would be for American revolutionaries: the instrument for advancing civil liberty."[4] For Enlightenment thinkers, however, rhetoric was more often than not an instrument of deception and tyranny. The most influential broadside against eloquence came from John Locke, who believed that the deceit of rhetorical language was the primary cause of such disorders as the English Civil War and constituted the primary barrier to the unity of politics and reason. His proposed solution, following Francis Bacon, was a transparent and neutral discourse "to free language from the confoundments of rhetoric."[5] In England and America, Locke's highly influential views were leavened somewhat by English republican thinkers who were unwilling to forsake the power of eloquence as an instrument for social reform. The two orientations existed side by side because the link between republicanism and eloquence proved hard to break, even during the apogee of enlightened rationalism.[6]

Owing to this mixed intellectual inheritance, late-eighteenth-century Americans were of two minds on rhetoric.[7] On the one hand, they placed profound importance on it. "To the revolutionary generation," explains Gordon Wood, "rhetoric lay at the heart of an 18th-century liberal education and was regarded as a necessary mark of a gentleman and an indispensable skill for a statesman, especially for a statesman in a republic." Rhetorical education blossomed in the United States after 1750, and this education emphasized the civic uses of eloquence. At Princeton during the last third of the century, John Witherspoon taught rhetoric to a generation of future leaders, among them James Madison, in order that they might become more effective statesmen. "The grace of elocution and the power of action," Witherspoon taught, "might not only acquire a man fame in speaking, but keep up his influence in public assemblies." The emphasis on rhetorical attainment was epitomized by ambitious men such as the young John Adams, who dreamed of becoming an American Cicero.[8] This view of eloquence reached its zenith in the afterglow of independence from Great Britain, when faith in the virtue and incorruptibility of the people was at its highest. In the words of Kenneth Cmiel, "eloquent language, almost all agreed, was critical to the new regime. Republicanism was governed by discussion as opposed to force of fiat." Adams believed that the new republic would become a rhetorical meritocracy, because "The constitutions of all the States in the Union are so democratical that eloquence will become the instrument for recommending men to their fellow-citizens, and the principle means of advancing through the various ranks and offices of society."[9]

The experience of governance under the Articles of Confederation swung the pendulum decidedly in the opposite direction. Although it escaped sustained attention for many years, in the last two decades a number of scholars have pointed to the pronounced antioratorical character of *The Federalist Papers*.[10] Alexander Hamilton, for example, in his argument against large assemblies, expressed great anxiety about the effects of popular oratory upon uneducated audiences. Hamilton assumed that when oratory operated on people of "limited information" and "weak capacities," it became a power that turned passion against reason and led to the ascendancy of demagogues rather than genuine statesmen. As Fisher Ames put it, "In democracies, it is no matter who is chosen to rule. Demagogues, though not chosen, will rule." The most famous statement of this view among major Enlightenment thinkers came from Thomas Hobbes, who derisively defined popular democracy as "no more than an aristocracy of orators, interrupted sometimes with the temporary monarchy of one orator." In this view, it was presumed that leadership based on popular oratory would, in Hamilton's words, make "Ignorance . . . the dupe of cunning, and passion the slave of sophistry and declamation."[11]

The reaction against popular oratory by the Federalists reflected the complex relationship they saw between rhetoric and leadership. Oratory was essential in a republic, but if it fell into the wrong hands, it would destroy the conditions required for virtuous leadership. The Federalists' antioratorical pronouncements are best understood as an aspect of their reaction against the increasingly egalitarian democracy of the 1780s. The men who framed the Constitution and argued for its ratification in the state conventions were appalled by what they saw in the state legislatures under the Articles of Confederation—a factious scramble of interests conducted by ill-educated, narrow-minded, and self-interested new men.[12] The poor construction of republican institutions and the resulting low quality of representatives, they believed, meant that there was no buffer between popular agitations and public policy. The result was rule by unscrupulous demagogues who fed off the passions of the people. Yet the Federalists' anxieties about democracy and demagoguery should not be misunderstood as a blanket repudiation of the deeply embedded association between rhetoric and republicanism that characterized late-eighteenth-century thought. Within the context of their rhetorical culture, the men who wrote using the pseudonym "Publius" were not objecting so much to rhetoric itself as to bad rhetoric from the wrong mouths to inappropriate audiences.

The Federalists believed, as most national leaders would until the 1820s, that a republic could not operate in the general interest unless it was governed by the best men. According to Gordon Wood, "the most enlightened of that enlightened age believed that the secret of good government and the protection of popular liberty lay in ensuring that good men—men of character and disinterestedness—wielded power." Although the architects of the Constitution would come to differ on how these leaders were to be induced to come forward, there was no disagreement that they must be found. As James Madison put it in *The Federalist Papers*, "the aim of every political constitution is, or ought to be, first to obtain for rulers men who possess most wisdom to discern, and most virtue to pursue, the common good of the society."[13]

The complete orator had the same qualities as the ideal statesman: a deep liberal education and a disinterested regard for the common good.[14] The connection was so close between the orator and the statesman that writers often used the terms together, sometimes interchangeably. At one level, it was thought that wisdom and virtue were prerequisites for true eloquence. The most influential advocate of this view was Bolingbroke.[15] On a second level, it was thought that the power of eloquence was only safe in the hands of leaders with the attributes of genuine statesmen. The first two American treatises on rhetoric both embraced this neoclassical ideal. John Witherspoon and John Quincy Adams defended oratory against its detractors by arguing that because it could be used for good or ill, it was imperative that the civically virtuous master its power. The ideals of the orator and the statesman thus formed a mutually reinforcing complex of beliefs about the kind of person who should wield the power of eloquence in a stable republic.[16]

One of the animating impulses behind the federal Constitution of 1787 was the empowerment of leaders who possessed the capacities and virtues of the ideal statesman and the complete orator. For the statesmen who met at Philadelphia, rhetorical success with popular audiences was not associated with the possession of such attributes. If leadership fell to those who could best appeal to mass meetings, or for that matter to ill-educated state legislators, then the new republic would not be ruled by virtuous statesmen, and all the well-known horrors of ancient democracy would be relived on a much wider scale. For deliberative rhetoric to contribute to the stability and sagacity of government, its scope had somehow to be constricted. Federalist political rhetoric itself reflected this doctrine. That the Federalists wrote and spoke primarily for the educated is evidenced by the character of their discourse, which made few, if any, allowances for those who lacked a broad liberal education. This restricted conception of audience was also promoted by the increasingly popular Scottish rhetoric textbooks—especially those of George Campbell and Hugh Blair—which were intended to teach gentlemen how to speak and write to each other and almost completely ignored popular eloquence.[17] Reflecting these assumptions, discussions of political oratory in eighteenth-century America focused on rhetoric within legislatures made up of educated statesmen and had little to say about rhetoric out-of-doors, directed to the people at large.[18]

Within the context of postrevolutionary leveling, Hamilton and his Federalist allies feared that the awesome power of eloquence had breached the containments of rank and merit. The Constitution was, in part, an attempt to contain this problem by devising a mixed government that could not be easily controlled by any one faction or overwhelmed by any single popular agitation, and in which the more enlightened part of the community might lead. In a House of Representatives with large electoral districts and a Senate that was not popularly elected, there would be institutional space for free deliberation by disinterested statesmen.[19] Eloquence within this sphere would be safer both because it would emanate from and be directed at men of character and because of the many checks against precipitous action built into the Constitution. Delay was thought crucial to wise action for, as Fisher Ames said in his famous speech on the Jay Treaty, "the movements of passion are quicker than those of understanding." The Federalists did not seek to banish political oratory but to institutionally restrict it in such a way that its benefits would be maximized and its dangers controlled. Public discourse would have a powerful effect on the sifting and winnowing of national opinion, but it would be a restrained discourse by and for gentlemen, rather than for the public at large.[20]

Although not usually in the foreground, the parallel to ancient history lurked in the background of the discussions of oratorical statesmanship in the new republic. Those who framed the Constitution, and their intellectual heirs during the first four decades of the nation's existence, were acutely aware of the difference between the kind of republican government they sought to construct and the direct democracies of antiquity. "We know from history," wrote Fisher Ames, "that every democracy . . . is delivered bound hand and foot into the keeping of ambitious demagogues." In the difference between ancient democracy and modern republicanism lay the gap between neoclassical and classical oratory. One of the best-developed statements of this was offered by Edward Tyrrell Channing in 1819, in his inaugural address as the Boylston professor of rhetoric and oratory at Harvard. According to Channing, the founders departed from the classical conception of popular oratorical leadership, where a single orator could hold the destiny of the state in his hands, while embracing a more limited vision of refined rhetorical leadership within stable republican institutions.[21] However, the ideal of the oratorical statesman, despite the protestations of men such as Channing, could not help but become more popular in the increasingly egalitarian democracy of the next century. In this changed context, the founders' confinement of deliberative oratory to the chambers of the House and Senate would prove impossible to maintain. Ironically, their own classicism would form the basis for a more expansive view of the orator's mission. The linkage between rhetoric and republicanism, drawn from the classical tradition, would justify a much broader use of political oratory in the new century.[22] In the evolving environment of antebellum America, the intellectual heirs to the Federalists would come to believe that the virtuous oratorical statesman needed to address a mass audience. How he would do this would be a point of considerable contention, but by the 1830s the orator's scope would be truly national.

The Antebellum Oratorical Republic

In antebellum America, oratory quickly became both an essential medium of communication and a dominant social ideal. Oratorical standards and training were no longer the exclusive province of gentlemen, and it seemed that anyone who wished to advance needed to become an orator. The great orator became a cultural icon whose exploits were chronicled in epic terms and upon whom young men patterned themselves. Yet even in the increasingly egalitarian democracy of the nineteenth century, the neoclassical concept of the oratorical statesman—a man of broad learning and deep civic virtue who wielded his eloquence responsibly—continued to have effect. For an influential segment of society, the rise of mass democracy was viewed with great trepidation, and the spread of popular eloquence was seen as a menace to American civilization. Not unlike the Federalists, these critics believed that only genuine statesmen should rule and that demagoguery threatened to tear the commonwealth asunder as it had in ancient times. Ironically, this strand of thought informed the outlooks of the most renowned speakers of the so-called golden age of American oratory. The Jacksonian opposition that ultimately coalesced in the American Whig Party became the home of the traditional view of statesmanship and, not coincidentally, of the nation's most celebrated orators. Within this new social and political environment, however, the doctrine of oratorical statesmanship would undergo important changes. Despite the Federalist undertones of their project, the bearers of the old neoclassical conception of leadership would pursue a most un-Federalist solution to the perceived decadence of modern party politics. They came to believe that the only way to create the political conditions in which enlightened and disinterested statesmen would rule was to eloquently address a mass audience. It was within this ideological framework of defending traditional ideals against the encroachments of a new political style that mass oratory and disinterested statesmanship became most firmly linked.

Beginning in the early national period, commentaries repeatedly proclaimed that the new republic was inundated with spoken eloquence.[23] "It may perhaps be afforded," wrote Richard Rush in 1804, "that since the days of Athens, there have been no people among whom oratory has flourished as it has among the people of the American states." Rush was only one of a parade of contemporary commentators who paid homage to the American obsession with oratory. The United States, they believed, had a greater volume of public speaking than any nation on record. As Alexander Everett put it in 1809, "There never was a country where eloquence had a better field for its display than the United States: from the town-meeting to the national congress, every mode of transacting business affords a theater for the orator." By the 1830s this assertion was so commonplace that even the most careful observers conceded it. As Joseph Story wrote in 1834, "it is probably true (as has been often asserted) that no people exceed the Americans in facility and exuberance of speech; and no people use this facility and exuberance upon more public occasions, from the stump orator, at home, to the representative in the national legislature." A writer for the *New-England Magazine* observed that "in no other nation, either ancient or modern, have the opportunities for the elevation of eloquence, especially the eloquence of public debate, been so numerous and favourable, or the inducements to aim at excellence in it so strong and inspiring as in the United States. . . . Who can deny that the Americans are the most 'talking and speech-making' race, that the world has produced!"[24]

So important was oratorical accomplishment in the early national period that proficiency in eloquence was often said to be the distinguishing quality of the new nation. Favorable comparisons to ancient Greece and Rome, as well as to contemporary Britain, were commonplace. It became a great national cliché that a young man ought to cultivate eloquence if he wished a career at the bar, in public service, or in the ministry. Over the first fifty years of national existence oratory penetrated every level of American society. Literature and poetry were dominated by oratorical standards, and learning was diffused by itinerant speakers on the lyceum circuit. In addition to its role in government, law, and religion, oratory was the mode of public ritual, the medium of the nation's literature, and a major source of popular entertainment. Much more than a practical medium of communication, it became an art that was cultivated for its own sake.[25]

In its political capacity, the antebellum "cult of oratory," as Lawrence Buell has termed it, reflected the transformation of the older elite rhetorical creed of the eighteenth century into a general cultural style for a more upwardly mobile and egalitarian polity. The Revolution had sparked an unprecedented expansion of the public sphere in which many, more than ever before, could aspire to active involvement. Rhetoric, in part because it had been the mark of the gentleman, now became the object of study for newly empowered segments of society. John Quincy Adams asked his students at Harvard, "Is there among you a youth, whose bosom burns with the first of honorable ambition; who aspires to immortalize his name by the extent and importance of his services to his country?" If so, "let him catch from the relics of ancient oratory those unrested powers, which mould the mind of man to the will of the speaker, and yield the guidance of a nation to the dominion of the voice."[26]

Many American boys who could not attend Harvard headed this call. The general belief that they should do so was reflected by the strong emphasis on rhetorical education in the early national period.[27] In higher education, rhetoric was at the center of the curriculum and was typically taught by college presidents. Its aim was to produce liberally educated and rhetorically effective civic leaders to guide the new republic. As Samuel Knapp reported in his *Lectures on American Literature*, "no country on earth has ever laboured harder to make orators than our own. In addition to the fifty-three colleges, where classical education are given, there are hundreds of minor institutions in which every rule of rhetorick is committed to memory; and every student can give you all the maxims, from Blair, Campbell, and others, necessary to make an orator." This attitude was manifest not only in formal college curricula, but also in the popularity of practical public speaking texts. The major elocution manuals, which focused on delivery and gesture, went through dozens of editions.[28] Rhetoric texts were so widely distributed that one would even reach a young Maryland slave named Frederick Douglass.[29] The importance with which rhetorical education was treated in antebellum culture was also reflected in repeated statements of dissatisfaction with its quality and method. Revealing the persistence of classical models in the rising oratorical culture, many believed that training could not suffice if it was any less thoroughgoing than it had been in ancient Greece and Rome, where young men had received their educations in schools of rhetoric.[30]

Interest in the cultivation of the rhetorical arts was paralleled by an expansion of the potential audience for political oratory. Legislative proceedings in the new nation became ever more public, and great debates such as deliberations over the War of 1812, the Missouri Compromise, and Daniel Webster's clashes with Robert Y. Hayne and John C. Calhoun over the meaning of the Constitution would captivate national attention.[31] Increasingly, even commonplace performances were recorded to be read by contemporary audiences and, the ambitious orator dared to hope, by posterity as well. By the 1830s legislative oratory was aimed at dual audiences: a small primary audience within the sound of the speaker's voice and a much larger secondary reading audience. Although next-day newspaper reports of congressional speeches did not become the norm until the telegraph came into wide use in the early 1850s, the explosion of oratorical literature reached critical mass during the 1830s, by which time it was often complained that most congressional speeches were aimed not at advancing deliberation but at each legislator's constituents back home, who expected their representative to gain credit for his region by making great utterances in a national forum.[32]

Such loquaciousness, even among backbenchers, was inspired by the heroic stature accorded the orator in the antebellum imagination. The orator as hero was an ideal type that was held up to encourage tireless exertions in the pursuit of rhetorical excellence. "Let not a view of the extensive qualifications that combine in the orator, deter any from attempting their acquisition," Richard Rush implored in the first decade of the new century. "The character when reached is of that high kind, which seems to determinate the endeavors of enterprise, and satisfy the expectations of generous ambition." Eloquence, pronounced another writer, opens to the orator "the widest avenue to distinction. Compared to it, the influence of the other attributes, which elevate to rank and confer authority, is feeble and insignificant." Expressing the classicism that was apparent in most commentaries on oratory, John Quincy Adams told his Harvard students that "in the flourishing periods of Athens and Rome, eloquence was POWER. . . . The talent of public speaking was the key to the highest dignities; the passport to the supreme domination of the state." Ralph Waldo Emerson thought the status of the orator in antiquity had been achieved in America by the 1830s: "Who can wonder at the attractiveness of Parliament, or of Congress, or the bar, for our ambitious young men, when the highest bribes of society are at the feet of the successful orator? He has his audience at his devotion. All other fames hush before his. He is the true potentate."[33]

While eighteenth-century leaders had been timid about popular exploitation of the power of eloquence, antebellum Americans exalted it—to the point that Hobbes's famous nightmare vision of an "aristocracy of orators" was sometimes miscast in a positive light. Many unreservedly embraced the older classical vision of the orator dominating his audience and even the entire society. Descriptions of the suasive force of these orators were extravagant by modern standards. As a Southerner explained, "The orator is complete master of his audience. He is, so to speak, their dictator; for what greater despotism can there be than that over the reason, the passion and the feelings. His is the rod of Moses—with it he sways back the sea of humanity and returns it at his pleasure."[34] Such characterizations of the commanding power of the orator pervaded the antebellum periodical literature. So too did paeans to the great orators of antiquity, particularly Demosthenes and Cicero. In fact, it seemed impossible for antebellum writers to discuss eloquence or to rate contemporary speakers without reference to those two great classical masters.[35] When Americans were not gazing backward at orators through the mists of time, they were looking across the Atlantic. The two great British oratorical models, sometimes referred to as the Demosthenes and the Cicero of their country, were Pitt and Burke.[36] Although these two luminaries had a dominant place in the American oratorical imagination, British speakers such as Henry Brougham, Richard Sheridan, the younger William Pitt, and George Canning also enjoyed considerable celebrity.[37] If anything, antebellum Americans were more enamored of British oratorical exploits than were the British themselves. British observers thought Americans were peculiarly obsessed with oratory.[38]

Despite the outpouring of literature exalting the orator, the old fears of degenerate eloquence by no means disappeared. These fears were an integral part of the complex of ideas that inspired the iconic Whig orators of the golden age. Moreover, those who most exalted these great oratorical statesman were often the very people who worried most about demagoguery. As in the 1780s, concerns about popular rhetoric were closely related to a perceived crisis in the quality of republican leadership. Throughout the antebellum period, and particularly after the rise of modern party politics, there were repeated calls for the restoration of independent statesmanship in the face of what was seen as the corruption of public life by ill-educated, partisan, self-interested mediocrities.[39] Although those who lamented the absence of statesmen in antebellum America had many differences, they shared a vision of enlightened leadership in which the ideal statesman was a genius of almost universal knowledge, disinterested beyond reproach, independent of economic dependencies and party attachments, and commandingly eloquent.[40]

The worry that the republic was no longer being led by genuine statesmen was augmented by the parallel concern that the power of oratory was falling into dangerous hands. Despite, and perhaps because of, society's obsession with oratory, concerns about the subversive potential of speech did not dissipate even at the height of the first American oratorical renaissance. Indeed, even the defenders of eloquence believed that because the orator operated on the passions, he played with fire. The power of eloquence was described as "awful," "fearful," and "terrible" by its warmest proponents.[41] The orator, noted one writer, works with "the smouldering and smothering volcanoes of feeling that cannot be approached without hazard, and, when roused, burst into fury and desolation. These are to be managed and controlled, and not let loose, but under the decree of terrible necessity." This linkage between the power of speech and combustible human passions explains why many antebellum writers were so concerned that eloquence not be misused. "For its proper use the possessor must give an account in the courts above," one writer declared. Channing, although he was to teach rhetoric and oratory at Harvard for thirty-two years, held that "Our institutions and privileges are too costly, to be the prey or theme, of stormy and troubled eloquence, such as kindled the old republicks to madness, and led them to deal with the state and its glory as playthings for their passions." Another writer warned that oratory was "even in its best form dangerous from the uncertainty of the hands . . . into which so potent an instrument of authority over the people may fall."[42]

It was the increasing uncertainty of these "hands" that most troubled antebellum critics. Even before the Jacksonian ascension there was a palpable sense of anxiety about the thoroughness with which young speakers were being educated. The admonition that the aspiring orator must get the statesman's broad liberal education to use the art safely was a constant refrain as Jeffersonians and Federalists, National Republicans, Whigs, and Southerners of all parties paid homage to the neoclassical ideal of the liberally educated, civically virtuous orator passed down from Cicero and Quintilian. The strand of eighteenth-century thought which held that in a well-functioning republic the orator was a statesman and the statesman an orator thus continued to be passionately defended throughout the antebellum period.[43] The unease about the misuse of speech that was an undercurrent throughout the first fifty years of the nation's existence became much more urgent with the rise of Jackson.[44] Before then, many believed that the unrestrained eloquence that did so much damage in the ancient world had been checked by the wise construction of American institutions. An essayist observed during the Monroe administration that while in ancient "popular assemblies" eloquence was "called out in all its fervor and force," in modern America "deliberative bodies" were "select and small." As a result, "warm tumultuous feelings, which so often rent and agitated the assemblies of the people, are now banished and unfelt. In a word impassioned oratory has in some degree *departed* with the *crowd*."[45] However, the emergence of Jackson and modern party politics convinced a highly influential group of American elites that the "crowd," far from departing, had taken control of affairs. The year of Jackson's election to the White House would be remembered by generations of adherents to the traditional standards of statesmanship—leading Progressive Era orators such as Henry Cabot Lodge, Woodrow Wilson, and Theodore Roosevelt among them—as the fateful year when the civic virtues of the old republic came crashing down.

The implementation of the spoils system and the other accouterments of modern party politics challenged the fundamental assumptions of neoclassical leadership. Now capacity and character, it seemed, would have nothing to do with the holding of office. The party hacks who insolently grasped the reins of government appealed directly to the people in impassioned colloquial language rather than in the controlled and refined idiom that elite leaders had used to avoid the undue excitement of popular feeling. This "rude license of pen and tongue," this "Jacobinism of the press and the rostrum," the Whigs believed, imperiled the "tranquillity of the republic" by threatening to drive the public mind into "delirium."[46] The most searing condemnations came when President Jackson appealed over the head of the Senate to the people, most notoriously in his bank veto message of 1832. Webster, Clay, and their associates believed that such rhetoric would subvert all the carefully contrived checks against rule by popular passion built into the Constitution. Visions of disorder and conflict stemming from direct popular rule by the agency of passionate rhetoric frequently recurred in Whig condemnations of Jackson. Webster arraigned him for using "the most reprehensible means for influencing public opinion" and thus dividing rather than unifying the country. Jackson's veto message, Webster thundered, appealed "to every prejudice which may betray men into a mistaken view of their own interests, and to every passion which may lead them to disobey the impulses of understanding. . . . It is a state paper that finds no topic to eliciting to use, no passion too flammable for its address and solicitation." In the judgment of Alexander Everett, "It was obvious, that those to whom the administration of the government was intrusted, were seeking to maintain their power by a most dangerous appeal to those very passions which government was established to control."[47]

This division between Whigs and Democrats over political speech reflected a clash of rhetorical cultures. As Christine Oravec has observed, the Democrats "favored discourse addressed primarily to the public, rather than deliberative assemblies. . . . Theirs was a rhetoric of mass communication in a politically pluralistic society, as distinguished from a specialized rhetoric addressing a ruling elite." The Whigs' most frequent charge was that the Jacksonian mode of address presaged destruction of the realm of independent deliberation in which statesmen settled policy separate from the popular demands of the moment.[48] This reaction against Jacksonian rhetoric was not merely an isolated response by those who had lost a single, bitterly contested election. Neo-Federalist conceptions of rhetoric and statesmanship persisted in elite circles well after Jackson departed the scene.[49] A particularly clear example was James Russell Lowell's condemnation of Andrew Johnson's 1865 speaking tour. Lowell argued that Johnson was open "to very grave reprehension if he appeal[s] to the body of the people against those who are more immediately its representatives than himself." According to Lowell, such appeals tended to "deride us from a republic . . . to a mass meeting, where momentary interests, panic, or persuasive sophistry . . . may decide by a shout what years of afterthought may find it hard, or even impossible, to undo."[50]

Although the Whigs' diagnosis of the dangers of popular oratory had Federalist overtones, their solution was very different. The Whigs and their predecessors developed, to paraphrase Madison's language in the *The Federalist*, Number 10, an oratorical remedy to the diseases most incident to oratorical culture. They embraced the maxim of the classical rhetorical tradition that the best redress for bad speech was good speech.[51] If demagogues were addressing the mass public, then wise and just speakers had to do so as well. In this vein, the Whigs developed a species of refined yet popularly directed oratory that aimed to instill in the general public an appreciation of the central tenets of American history and character as the Whigs understood them. The founding generation had not anticipated this use of mass-directed oratory to constitute a virtuous citizenry. Whig oratory sought less to settle definite policy through oratory than to create a basis for governing by imparting a body of shared knowledge and beliefs upon which stable constitutional government depended. It was within this intellectual context that the cultural ideals of the statesman and the orator were most firmly joined. To propagate the appropriate social values, the Whig orator, like the Ciceronian orator, needed to be a man of deep learning, sterling civic character, and enlightened popular appeal. Like the orators of antiquity, the Whig orator had to address more than an elite audience.

A style of oratory suited to this purpose evolved gradually. It had its roots in the rapid expansion of the genre of patriotic occasional address during the early national period.[52] At the same time a more publicly oriented brand of legislative rhetoric also emerged. As debates in Congress became more public, the Jeffersonian idea that the republican statesman ought to educate his constituents became one of the objects of legislative oratory. Over time, this didactic function changed the nature of deliberative rhetoric. Debates in the colonial assemblies—where gentleman addressed each other with little public scrutiny—had been sharp and vituperative. By the late 1820s, proto-Whigs such as Daniel Webster had developed a more polite style of deliberative oratory that was better gauged to meeting the dual ends of persuading fellow legislators and imparting public virtues to a large secondary audience without unduly exciting popular passions.[53]

The Whigs made a sharp distinction between such statesmanly oratory and nonstatesmanly discourse. A Whig writer explained this distinction in hypothetical terms in 1848. "The same multitude were addressed by two orators," the writer imagined. "The first of these orators considered in his mind that the people he addressed were to be controlled by several passions." This, of course, was a Democratic orator. "But now a second orator arises, a Chatham, a Webster, a Pericles, a Clay; his generous spirit expands itself through the vast auditory, and he believes he is addressing a company of high-spirited men, citizens. . . . at once, from a tumultuous herd, they are converted into men . . . their thoughts and feelings arise to an heroic height, beyond common men or common times." This second orator "addressed the better part of man's nature, supposing it to be in him—and it *was* in him." In this vision, oratory became a force for the inculcation of republican values and institutions, as a "tumultuous herd" is transformed by the voice of the good person speaking well into a body of citizens interested in the greater good of their country. Just as ancient authorities and Renaissance humanists had believed that speech created civilization, so the Whigs believed they could create a virtuous republic by using oratory to draw out from the body of the people the virtue that was buried within them. This was the raison d'être of the Whig way of speaking: the promotion of national consensus through the preservation and extension of shared civic values. As Webster told an audience during the 1840 presidential campaign: "It is our duty to spare no pains to circulate information, and to spread the truth far and wide. Let us persuade those who differ from us, if we can, to hear both sides. Let us remind them that we are embarked together, with a common interest and a common fate. And let us, without rebuke or unkindness, beseech them to consider what the good of the whole requires, what is best for them and for us."[54]

This was the grand ideal, but the reality of rhetorical practice was more perplexing for the Whigs. Once they began seeking to persuade public opinion, they found it difficult to resist adopting more and more popular forms of address. Frustrated by the electoral dominance of the Democrats, the Whigs in 1840 put on the most popular presidential campaign to date. The Log Cabin Campaign was characterized by songs, slogans, festivals, and stump speaking by all of the major Whig leaders, including their presidential nominee, William Henry Harrison. Webster privately agonized over the style of the campaign but ultimately agreed to participate.[55] John Quincy Adams also fretted over the 1840 campaign. "This practice of itinerant speech-making has suddenly broken forth in this country to a fearful extent," he complained. "Immense assemblages of the people are held—of twenty, thirty, and fifty thousand souls—where the first orators of the nation address the multitude, not one in ten of whom can hear them, on the most exciting topics of the day." Instead of attending to their official duties, party leaders seemed to think it their function to "rave, recite, and madden round the land."[56]

Adams's fear that violence and civil unrest might result from such popular passion was an expression of the older neoclassical creed of circumscribed oratorical statesmanship. Yet, as W. G. Howard pointed out at the time, the Log Cabin Campaign was actually a step toward the classical oratorical practice of direct interaction between statesmen and populace: "Our country seems fast approaching to the peculiar state which called forth the unrivaled efforts of Grecian oratory. We seem destined to *enact* Greece, if I may say so, on a gigantic scale." The repeated contact between popular audiences and its greatest oratorical statesmen, Howard imagined, would raise American oratorical standards to new heights and "Eloquence will probably exercise a greater influence hereafter than it has hitherto done."[57] Even during the 1840 campaign, however, Whig orators continued to exalt the ideal of independent deliberation, in which genuine statesmen transacted the nation's business through the medium of eloquent debate and determined the common good free from the interference of party and popular passion. As Webster told his audience in a speech entitled "Whig Principles and Purposes," he and his colleagues were beseeching "all good men to unite with [them] in an attempt to bring back the deliberative age of the government, to restore to the collected bodies of the people's representatives that self-respect, decorum, and dignity, without which the business of legislation can make no regular progress, and is always in danger either of accomplishing nothing, or of reaching its ends by unjustifiable and violent means"[58]

This dream of restoring an older order of statesmanship motivated many of the most illustrious orators of the antebellum era.[59] It also partially accounts for the enormous symbolic significance they had for their contemporaries. Although the 1830s and 1840s were seen as a golden age of oratory, its greatest glories were inextricably linked to fears of decadence and decline. There was a negative quality, a sense of resistance against a new and threatening order of popular democracy, reflected by both the contemporary and the historical image of the iconic orators of the antebellum period. The outsized reputations of the leading statesmen of the era were larger-than-life amplifications of traditional leadership virtues. Faith in men such as Webster, Clay, and Calhoun meant so much to their adherents because they personified cherished ideals that seemed to be under siege in Jacksonian America. Reading the speeches of a Webster or an Everett, one feels in the presence of immensely superior individuals, scrupulously versed in all relevant history and philosophy, viewing the entire political and social landscape with a piercing insight that could not be matched by ordinary persons. That such peerless leaders should rule implied that others should not.[60]

The Gilded Age Interregnum and the Education of the Progressive Orators

The reputations and rhetoric of the Whig orators produced important generational echoes. Even when the great Whig orators still strode the Senate, and especially once they had departed, they symbolized an ideal of heroic leadership that was perceived as lost—a bygone age of statesmanship and oratory in which the best men led through the brilliance of their imperishable words. The Whigs, for their part, had hoped to restore the world of the founders, but through their own style of leadership they actually helped redefine the ideals of statesmanship. In the posthumous reputations of the most famous oratorical statesmen, and in the printed texts of the great speeches they left behind, something of the tension and anxiety about who should lead was passed down to subsequent generations. The leading politicos of Gilded Age America never fully escaped the shadow cast by the great orator-statesmen of the antebellum era. For some, the story of their gallant leadership would become as mystical and full of romance as the tales of medieval chivalry. In this romantic myth there was a uniquely powerful association between commanding oratory and exalted statesmanship, and an enduring resonance of what that association implied. The ideal would never again have the central place in the cultural imagination that it occupied during the 1830s and 1840s, but it would still be powerful enough to help shape the ideals, values, and public careers of many emerging American leaders. The ideal survived despite the perceived decay of oratory after the Civil War and had a renewed influence during the Progressive Era, when great rhetorical exigents created new opportunities for orators.

In terms of raw volume, there was more public speech than ever before in the postbellum era, yet few doubted that the state of oratory was in decline. Dorsey Gardner articulated the conventional view when he stated in 1872 that "as a motive-power in government, reliance upon oratory itself has imperceptibly passed away." Many explanations were advanced for this, including the increased reach of the press and the detachment of speaking from decision making.[61] The complaint that Congress no longer made its decisions through public debate was one of the chief grievances of the liberal reformers of the 1870s and 1880s.[62] What leading postbellum orators seemed to lack most was compelling questions of the kind that animated antebellum oratory. Moreover, the old vision of the great speaker addressing the most challenging issues of the day was out of step with the propensity of the Gilded Age ruling class to eschew weighty and potentially unsettling issue-based rhetoric in favor of distracting oratorical entertainment. E. L. Godkin, the influential editor of the *Nation*, observed that the paradigmatic rhetorical genre of the period was no longer deliberative oratory but after-dinner speaking. "The essentials of an after-dinner speech," Godkin reported, were "that it should be humorous or lively; that it should touch every topic lightly, and should make no heavy or prolonged draughts on any one's sober-mindedness; that it should not attempt to edify or instruct." As a result of the popularity of this genre, Godkin observed, "the style acquired for success in after-dinner oratory is accordingly carried into all oratory."[63] This tendency was evident in the deterioration of the postbellum lyceum. Gilded Age audiences, as Joseph Gould explains, "wanted to laugh with the humorists or thrill to the pyrotechnics of a fundamentally empty display of oratory."[64]

Another sign of decay was the condition of rhetorical education in colleges, where the civic content so central to the teachings of men such as John Witherspoon, John Quincy Adams, and Edward Tyrrell Channing had been gradually melting away since the 1840s. Divorced from its public mission and bereft of any specific purpose aside from utilitarian skill development, rhetorical instruction became increasingly dry and mechanical. By the late nineteenth century, Kenneth Cmiel observes, "the old tradition was gone. Composition, unlike rhetoric, taught skills; it was not part of the larger formation of character." Contemporary critics of rhetorical education were well aware of this trend. The young Woodrow Wilson, for example, wrote about it in Princeton's college newspaper in the late 1870s. "We have witnessed here," he wrote, "a divorcement of oratory from debate . . . brought about by false, undiscriminating criticism which exalts correctness to supremacy— an undisputed throne—which does not of right belong to it." Without proficiency in a more substantive brand of oratory, Wilson warned his classmates, "we must be ciphers in the world's struggles for the settlement of principles and the advancement of causes."[65]

As the ground of Wilson's arraignment of undergraduate rhetoric instruction suggests, the old values were still available to young people who were inclined in that direction. Significantly, despite the declining quality of rhetoric courses, other parts of the college curriculum continued to encourage interest in oratory. Membership in debate societies remained one of the rites of passage for many undergraduates into the 1890s, and rhetorical exercises continued to be staples of the college experience. Perhaps most important, the classics curriculum, one of the chief sources of oratorical culture, remained entrenched in American colleges for the rest of the century.[66] Even as rhetoric was gradually being squeezed out of the college curriculum by the modern organization of academic departments, many aspiring politicians during the late nineteenth century cut their teeth on Burke and Webster and grew up believing that the great statesman was a great orator. The ambitious young William Borah, A. E. Whitehead writes, "read the speeches of Cicero, Demosthenes, Sheridan, Fox, Pitt, Burke, Lincoln, Douglas, and Phillips." The twenty-year-old Jonathan Dolliver immersed himself in oratorical classics and constantly practiced his elocution because, as he wrote his brother, he wished to make himself "a fluent and attractive orator." Oratory, he declared, "is the best hold a man can get in the world. It is the sure forerunner of influence among men." Robert M. La Follette, Albert Beveridge, William Jennings Bryan, and countless others who would rise to prominence during Progressive Era drenched themselves in the old oratorical tradition.[67]

A paradigm case of how the oratorical tradition was conveyed to the generation of speakers who would rise to prominence during the Progressive Era was that of Woodrow Wilson.[68] The singular influence on Wilson's early mental life was his father, the Reverend Joseph Ruggles Wilson, who was a man fully imbued with antebellum oratorical culture. The elder Wilson had received a first-class rhetorical education in college and, through the study of great speeches and incessant elocutionary drill, had made himself into one of the leading pulpit orators in the Southern Presbyterian Church. The Reverend Wilson also taught rhetoric at Jefferson College and "sacred oratory" at Columbia Theological Seminary. For him, the cultivation of oratorical ability was the centerpiece of a young man's education, and the accomplished orator, be he a statesman or a preacher, had to strive not only to appear but actually to be Quintilian's good man skilled in speaking. He was also nostalgic for the bygone era when oratory had a more central place in American society. Throughout his life he never tired of telling how he had seen the great Webster speak in person, nor of bemoaning the fallen state of contemporary public discourse.[69]

It is understandable that the son of such a man would absorb at least some of the fathers' interest in oratory. In the case of the younger Wilson the inherited enthusiasm was unadulterated. In his early years, his father frequently drilled him to build his verbal abilities. One of their more interesting joint projects was a series of failed attempts to improve the speeches of Webster.[70] By late adolescence, Woodrow was practicing his elocution by reading great speeches aloud in his fathers' empty church. He continued this drill in college at Princeton—then the College of New Jersey—where his classmates often found him in the woods reciting Burke and Bright, Everett and Webster, and in law school at the University of Virginia. As he wrote to a school friend, "I think an orator *is* made, in great part, and if there be in me any stuff worth the working, I intend to make as much of an orator out of myself as indefatigable labor can bring out of the materials at hand." Chafing at what he saw as the weakness of Princeton's rhetoric instruction, Wilson wrote a series of editorials in the college newspaper on the subject. "Only as the constant companions of Demosthenes, Cicero, Burke, Canning, and Webster," he advised his classmates, "can we hope to become orators."[71] Taking his own advice to heart, he supplemented his own rhetorical education by reading great speeches, by devouring the biographies of great statesmen, by carefully studying Maurice Bautain's *Art of Extempore Speaking*, along with several other shorter works on eloquence, and by founding a debate society that was devoted to extemporaneous debate. His dream was to make himself into an oratorical statesman of the first rank—an American Gladstone.[72]

Wilson's obsession with making himself an orator was paralleled by the importance he placed on oratorical leadership in his embryonic political writings. "It is natural," he wrote on several occasions, "that orators should be the leaders of a self-governing people." Notably Whiggish in outlook, especially during his student years, Wilson believed that oratory was essential to creating a virtuous citizenry committed to a common national interest. His early political speculations culminated in his well-known argument that the establishment of English-style cabinet government in the U.S. Congress would transform American government, creating a system in which decisions were made in open debate by leaders who were both orators and statesmen.[73]

Despite his burning desire to fill this role himself, the young Wilson ultimately concluded that there was no hope for such a career in the barnyard of Gilded Age politics. His perception of the political scene paralleled the conventional wisdom of the era that there was no longer any place in politics for the educated and disinterested. Some notes Wilson wrote around the time he made this decision reveal the decisive influence of the assumption that the age of great orators and statesmen had passed. The notes began with the question: "Why have we no great *statesmen?*" Wilson answered: "Because there is no opportunity for personal leadership and predominant influence." He asked further: "Why have we no great political *orators*? Because there is no inspiration—there are no *themes* to inspire—no *causes* to incite. Before the war there were *constitutional* themes of the greatest magnitude—hence the orators of whom Webster was the greatest. Same applies to the statesmen-giants of the preceding generation. *Now* what call for giants?"[74] Wilson could have no way of knowing, when he made his anguished decision to abandon his plans to become a statesman in the early 1880s, that the "call for giants" would come again in his own lifetime and that he would at length achieve his fondest ambitions.

While Wilson's story offers an example of how oratorical culture was transmitted to the leaders of his generation, his path to power was atypical. Although an unusual number of young men who would in all likelihood have entered politics in previous generations chose not to do so in the late nineteenth century, there were contemporary stimuli that prompted many with aspirations similar to Wilson's to take the plunge into active politics.

One very important and yet overlooked influence on the young Americans who would rise to leadership during the Progressive Era was the transformation of popular British political oratory during the last two decades of the century. Americans who came to maturity in the last quarter of the nineteenth century had the examples of liberal orator-statesmen such as John Bright and William Gladstone, who used platform oratory to achieve almost mythic status among the British masses. Traditionally, popular oratory in England had been more harshly stigmatized than it ever had been in the United States.[75] However, after Gladstone's Midlothean Campaigns in 1879 and 1880, it became general practice for the chiefs of the major parties to advance the leading issues before Parliament through spectacular speaking tours. Because successful tours were taken as evidence of public sentiment, they often had a large influence on the course of legislation. These tours came to dominate public attention, reaching not only huge in-person audiences, but also the entire reading public by means of sophisticated newspaper transcription syndicates. As a result of this system, newspaper readers were able to follow the speaking tours of their leaders with the daily intensity of modern sports fans. According to one English commentator, this system made it possible for "the orator of modern times" to "exert an influence of which his ancestors never dreamed." It was well understood at the time that this rhetorical innovation had revolutionized political communication, and there was general agreement that platform oratory had displaced parliamentary debate and political pamphlets as the primary means of opinion formation.[76] Even more significantly, in an age when Americans were very attentive to English affairs, the prominence of British platform oratory reinforced the traditional republican linkage between eloquence and principled national statesmanship.[77] Gladstone in particular, whose active political career extended into the 1890s, achieved a oratorical reputation in his own lifetime that is unequaled in the annals of British and American statesmanship.[78]

Although the oratorical events across the Atlantic were more exciting, there was no shortage of contemporary domestic inspirations during the postbellum era. It is important to understand that the perception of a decline in oratory during the late nineteenth century reflected the previous stature of oratory as much as an absolute decline. By the standards of our own time, postbellum America too was an oratorical culture, and the older romantic view of oratory continued to have powerful resonance. E. L. Godkin proclaimed that America at the centennial was the most oratorical nation in world history: "The faculty of fluent speech in public was never in so flourishing a condition as it is at this moment in the United States. . . . The number of persons capable of making a respectable off-hand speech on the stump or after dinner, was never so great, in proportion to population, as it is now." English professor William Mathews thought the volume of speech was oppressive: "In this country . . . every third man is an orator. . . . Not only in the court-houses and representative halls, but everywhere, we are literally deluged with words,—words,—words. Everybody seems born to make long speeches, as the sparks fly upwards."[79]

Pulpit oratory, public lectures, and speeches in support of social reforms, such as temperance and women's suffrage, and economic reforms, such as the organization of labor unions and relief for impoverished farmers in the South and Midwest, flourished during the 1870s and 1880s. One of the most notable late-nineteenth-century oratorical campaigns was orchestrated by the Farmers' Alliance, which at its peak claimed to have forty thousand orators crisscrossing the South and Southwest. Every fourth year, presidential campaigns employed thousands of surrogate orators to convey their messages to a mass audience. These mass campaigns proved an especially fertile training ground for young orators. For example, four of the leading speakers of the early twentieth century—Theodore Roosevelt, Albert Beveridge, Jonathan Dolliver, and William Jennings Bryan—got their starts as surrogate orators in the 1884 contest between James G. Blaine and Grover Cleveland.[80] Congressmen and senators continued to take their speaking very seriously and to distribute their printed orations throughout the land. Critics charged that their speeches were mere window dressing or obfuscation, while actual decisions were made in secret, but no one accused the nation's representatives of silence.

Despite this profusion of public speech, there continued to be a profound sense that something essential was lacking. With the exception of orators such as Robert Ingersoll, who was considered a first-tier orator by his contemporaries and inspired an inordinate number of future orators, few of these speakers seemed to measure up to the standards of the past. Chauncey Depew, the acknowledged master of after-dinner speaking, was much more representative of Gilded Age oratory than the eccentric Colonel Ingersoll.[81] But this persistent sensation of loss could also be an inspiration. Men of middle age or older could and did impart something of the old luster of oratory to the rising generation. In 1875, Charles Francis

Adams proclaimed that college men could be of greatest service to their country if they followed the example of the statesmen of the past and cultivated "every element that can contribute to the formation of a noble style and exalted oratory. . . . Oratory is not a trick. It is a great force in the state." In as pure a statement of the neoclassical vision of oratorical statesmanship as can be found anywhere in the antebellum era, Adams declared that the "single voice" of the oratorically trained and deeply educated statesman "may not only elevate the character of his own generation, but spread a healthy influence over that of many yet to come. . . . There is not a youth in the hearing of my voice at this moment who, if he possess the requisite qualifications, may not contribute more to the happy destiny of America, then did all the noblest orators upon that of either Greece or Rome." In a speech at Hamilton College in 1872, Charles Dudley Warner, co-author with Mark Twain of *The Gilded Age*, expressed the romantic attachment to oratory many of his generation still felt:

> Twenty-one years ago in this house I heard a voice calling me to ascend the platform, and there to stand and deliver. The voice was the voice of President North; the language was an excellent imitation of that used by Cicero and Julius Caesar. I remember the flattering invitation. . . . To be proclaimed an orator, and an ascending orator, in such a sonorous tongue, in the face of a world waiting for orators, stirred ones' blood like the herald's trumpet when the lists are thrown open.[82]

In addition to such flesh-and-blood reminiscences, history continually reminded the new generation of the past glories of oratory. To those looking backward, the history of pre–Civil War America seemed, in Daniel Boorstin's words, like "a series of events connecting famous orations." Postwar Americans were "inclined to see . . . great orations as the dominant creative 'events' in the making of the nation" and "to think of the national history between the Revolution and the Civil War as . . . having been largely enacted in great speeches." Reading history in this way gave particular prominence to the Whig orators because they had supported the concept of Union that was vindicated in the Civil War and because they had produced, more than any other group, lasting oratorical literature. Webster's postwar reputation was especially renowned: his posthumous celebrity easily overshadowed Lincoln's and rivaled that of the leading founding fathers.[83]

In this way, the afterglow of American oratory's golden age was bright enough to inspire many who came to maturity during the post–Civil War decades. Members of yet another generation of young men, aspiring to a substantial role in the affairs of state, grew up believing that to be great leaders they needed to make themselves orators, just as Demosthenes, Cicero, Pitt, Burke, Webster, and all the great orator-statesmen had done.

The Progressive Era Oratorical Revival

In 1872 novelist Charles Dudley Warner wistfully recalled the early 1850s as "a world waiting for orators." During the Progressive Era, these expectations were revived and the orator was again accorded Emerson's "highest bribes of society." As La Follette declared in 1905, the orator "holds the balance of power. It is the orator, more than ever before, who influences the course of legislation and directs the destinies of states." Oratory's second renaissance spanned roughly the interval between William Jennings Bryan's "Cross of Gold" speech at the 1896 Democratic National Convention and Wilson's great "swing around the circle" on behalf of the

League of Nations in late 1919. The intellectual context within which this revival took place was no less complex than that which informed the golden age of American oratory before the Civil War.[84]

Although the idea that oratory was in decline had been common currency in the 1870s and 1880s, such lamentations markedly intensified in the 1890s. Even as oratory reemerged as a potent political force, discussion of its decline continued in the popular press and in more intellectual journals. This irony did not go unnoticed at the time. "Much is said in these days to the effect that oratory is no longer effective or useful," Chauncey Depew observed in 1902. "But it is the experience of political leaders of all denominations that the orator never had a larger field or could exercise more influence than to-day." Curtis Guild agreed. "Among a certain highly educated but imperfectly informed class," he remarked, "it is generally accepted as an axiom that political speeches no longer convert nor even influence public opinion." Yet "men who study political events at first hand are aware that the influence of oral personal appeal is not decreasing but increasing."[85]

The cultural significance of political oratory in the Progressive Era can only be fully understood with reference to its perceived decline. The conception of true oratorical statesmanship, influenced by the legendary reputations of the great Whig orators, was an exalted standard of eloquence and intellectual mastery that overshadowed the renewal of oratory as an active influence in public affairs. Nor was this romanticism unique to discussions of oratory. The yearning for the glories of a past age was part of a general nostalgia for lost virtues during the first two decades of the twentieth century, a time when social thought was at once nostalgic and forward looking. Reflecting this duality, conceptions of oratory were being modernized to meet the requirements of modern mass communication in the advanced print age.

In the first decade of the new century, the enlarged political importance of oratory was most apparent in the increasingly spectacular conduct of presidential campaigns, the emergence of the Chautauqua circuit as a major agency of political reform, and the techniques used by insurgent leaders to defeat political machines in a number of states. In the venue of presidential campaigns, Bryan's stunning oratorical victory at the 1896 Democratic National Convention, followed by his whirlwind campaign speaking tour, shocked many of those who had confidently announced the demise of oratory as a force in history. Bryan's unlikely nomination in Chicago, wrote one contemporary observer, "led to an immense amount of discussion as to the present condition and the future possibilities of eloquence. For quite a number of years it had been taken for granted that the age of oratory has gone by forever; that the time when a brilliant speaker could dominate the minds of a great assemblage will never return; and that the remarkable masters of eloquence whose forensic efforts are as familiar as their names have left behind them no successors whatsoever." In his campaign tour of 1896, Bryan traveled eighteen hundred miles and addressed an estimated five million people.[86] In the 1900 campaign Bryan gave more speeches than all previous candidates for president combined, excluding his own efforts four years earlier, and Theodore Roosevelt, nominated in part because of his popular-speaking capacities, gave more speeches than all preceding vice presidential candidates combined. According to a contemporaneous estimate, Roosevelt gave six hundred seventy-three speeches in forty-three states within an eight-week span; not to be outdone, Bryan spoke at such a frenetic pace that he managed to deliver thirty speeches in a single day. Herculean oratorical journeys such as Roosevelt's and Bryan's were repeated throughout the era. Hiram Johnson, the Progressive Party's vice presidential nominee in 1912, gave five hundred campaign speeches in twenty-two states. Eugene Debs, the perennial standard bearer of the Socialists, drew unprecedented visibility and support for his party through his incessant speaking tours. In the 1908 campaign, for example, he gave twenty speeches a day for seven weeks. Oratorical ability now became one of the criteria to be considered in making up national tickets.[87]

These oratorical spectaculars were not limited to the candidates themselves. Each party dispatched thousands of orators to scour the countryside and stir excitement with short statements of issues and emotionally charged harangues. Although presidential campaigns had relied increasingly on legions of barnstorming orators in the 1870s and 1880s, contemporaries believed there was an explosion of such oratory after 1896. So ubiquitous was this phenomenon that a new term—"spellbinder"—was coined for these campaign orators. Although there are many stories concerning the origin of the term "spellbinder," and it may go as far back as the election of 1884 between Cleveland and Blaine, the spellbinder system reached its apotheosis in the first decade of the twentieth century. A spellbinder was any speaker who took to the stump during a presidential campaign, even if he were a more dignified orator in normal times. Hence men such as Chauncey Depew, Henry Cabot Lodge, Thomas B. Reed, and former President Benjamin Harrison were counted among the ranks of spellbinders. These speakers drew large and enthusiastic audiences, making it possible to disseminate the message of each campaign more widely than ever before. Not only were spellbinders an integral part of the presidential canvass, they were the single most costly item in campaign budgets. Each major party had a speakers' bureau that carefully tracked the distribution of its orators throughout the country, making sure they were deployed to maximum effect as the campaign progressed. Cleveland Bacon was one of the many who saw the mass of spellbinders that fanned out every fourth year as a new birth for oratory. "A new phase of political oratory has developed," he wrote, and "however one may regard its desirability, not since the days of the antislavery excitement have meetings attracted interest so widespread and audiences so vast. Far from the voice having lost its power as an instrument of instruction, one may well question if a new career for the orator has not just begun."[88]

The most compelling presidential canvass in this era of spectacular campaigns was the epic contest in 1912, where two of the most profound orators in all American history dueled over the future of the American experiment in the modern industrial age.[89] With Republican incumbent William Howard Taft relegating himself to the sidelines, Wilson, the Democratic standard bearer, and Roosevelt, the nominee of the newly formed Progressive Party, crisscrossed the country on behalf of their sharply contrasting visions of domestic reform. Roosevelt, who knew that his chances of winning were remote, undertook (according the estimate of journalists at the time) the longest presidential campaign tour in American history to that point—a grueling coast-to-coast excursion in which he gave one hundred fifty major speeches in thirty-two states—in the hope that he could build long-term support for his new party.[90] The campaign was notable not only for the volume of its oratory, but also for the depth and far-reaching significance of its themes. Wilson gave arguably the most eloquent series of speeches in the history of American presidential campaigns, in which he painted a beautiful picture of small-scale entrepreneurial capitalism and town-meeting democracy that he maintained was being ruined by the trusts. Roosevelt offered a blunt and piercing critique of modern industrial society in which he argued that only an energetic federal government could check the destructive power of large corporations. As historian John Milton Cooper Jr., has observed, the 1912 election was "the greatest debate ever witnessed in an American presidential campaign," pitting "the most colorful politician since the Civil War" against "the most articulate politician since the early days of the Republic." The only campaign in American history on a comparable philosophical plain was the election of 1800 between John Adams and Thomas Jefferson.[91]

The expansion of the Chautauqua circuit in the first decade of the new century afforded another forum for the political orator. By the 1880s, the condition of the postbellum lyceum paralleled the decline of political oratory generally, as entertainment increasingly displaced the consideration of issues and causes.[92] In the Progressive Era, however, the exciting reform issues of the day helped renew the taste for serious oratory at the same time the circuit was becoming a much larger-scale enterprise. Community-based Chautauquas had proliferated during the last two decades of the nineteenth century, especially in the Midwest and the West, but the perfection of the circuit system and the innovation of the big-tent Chautauqua in 1904 led to exponential expansion. By the time Wilson was inaugurated as president, the circuit Chautauqua had grown well beyond its regional base and was becoming a national institution. At its height, it passed through ten thousand communities and reached forty million people each year. Nor was the influence of the lecture circuit limited to the commercial Chautauquas. The Socialists, for instance, had their own far-flung lyceum circuit. The commercial Chautauquas, however, provided a venue for a surprisingly wide spectrum of opinion. Chautauqua, to be sure, offered an outlet for the oratory of mainline politicians such as House Speaker Joe Cannon and Senator Warren G. Harding, as well as for many inspirational and educational speakers, but by far the most popular were the reform orators, the more outspoken the better.[93] Indeed, up until American entrance into the First World War, reform speakers were a bigger draw than entertainers and musicians. As the operator of the largest circuit, Harry P. Harrison, later recalled: "There were gifted orators by the dozens and Chautauqua grabbed them, and the orators grabbed Chautauqua, to air all colors of opinion." The reform oratory that captivated Chautauqua audiences was characterized by its vehemence. To hold an audience in a hot tent for hours required both sensationalism and showmanship. According to a contemporary account of one of the most popular speakers, Robert La Follette, he "denounced graft with resistless power . . . and carried the people on the stream of his burning eloquence. . . . He seldom speaks for less than three hours . . . [and] not withstanding the heat and weather and the hard seats, the people remain to hear his burning words." The way headliners such as La Follette, Dolliver, Beveridge, and Debs used the Chautauqua to propagate reform ideas reminded some of the power of antebellum oratory. As one commentator observed in 1912, "The progressive movement that now is sweeping the country owes its strength very largely to the chautauqua, just as the abolition movement gained its momentum chiefly from the free platform of the lyceum." William Allen White agreed, arguing that "the Progressive Party was born from a dozen Chautauqua speeches."[94]

In general during the Progressive Era, oratory that advanced issues and ideas became a more important part of the political landscape than it had been for a generation. Theodore Roosevelt turned the presidency into a "bully pulpit," and Wilson would go still further in his exploitation of the presidential platform. Oratory again became one of the surest tickets to political preferment.[95] It was one of the chief methods by which a slew of educated, reform-minded leaders of serious oratorical capacity rose to prominence during the era. Bryan and Roosevelt were joined in the field by such men as Dolliver, La Follette, Beveridge, Borah, Albert Cummins, Newton Baker, Clarence Darrow, and Hiram Johnson. The spectacular nature of their oratorical performances often drew both regional and national attention to their causes. In his 1900 Wisconsin gubernatorial campaign, for example, La Follette traveled sixty-five hundred miles and gave two hundred sixteen speeches in sixty-one Wisconsin counties. In 1910, Hiram Johnson stumped California for eight consecutive months in his successful campaign for governor. Governor Woodrow Wilson of New Jersey gained a national reputation as a reformer, which he parlayed into the Democratic presidential nomination in 1912, largely through his highly publicized state speaking tours and a national speaking tour in 1911. It was not uncommon for leading insurgent orators to tour on behalf of one another, and state and national political campaigns joined the Chautauqua circuit as great training grounds for the rising orators of the era. La Follette, who became a model for reformers across the country, is a paradigm case of this phenomenon of oratorical publicity. His spectacular reform campaigns, in which he toured the state in both election and nonelection years, and his Chautauqua swings each summer brought him a tremendous amount of newspaper publicity. Another notable insurgent politician whose career exemplified the value of oratorical talent in the Progressive Era was Senator Jonathan Dolliver of Iowa. Before his premature death, Dolliver's mesmerizing oratory in the Senate and on the stump marked him a rising star in the GOP. Most important, La Follette, Johnson, Dolliver, and the other "new men in public life"—as the *Nation* called the group of reform-minded politicians that were coming into prominence at the turn of the century—saw oratory not as a form of entertainment with which to aid digestion of public dinners, but as a force for purifying American politics.[96]

Yet despite all the evidence of political oratory's renewed vitality, the revival was dogged by continued talk of decline and degradation. In 1913, the year after the greatest oratorical campaign in the history of presidential elections, Samuel Eliot Morison wrote that "Down to the last half-century oratory was one of the most potent forces in moulding public opinion and in arousing popular enthusiasm in America. Since then our susceptibility to the power of human speech has gradually declined and with this loss has come a deterioration in the quality of our oratory." Remarks such as Morison's were common currency, so common in fact that the decline of oratory can be considered one of the great clichés of the era. Why, when oratory was more politically consequential than it had been since the Civil War, was there such persistent talk of its demise? The answer suggests much about the meaning of oratory in the realm of ideas. When commentators spoke of the decline of oratory, they referred not merely to the aggregate flow of oral discourse, but to a broader complex of political values that left many unimpressed by the oratorical extravaganzas enacted during campaign years or each summer on the Chautauqua circuit. In fact, the mass cast of discourse in the era was precisely what concerned many of those who believed oratory was in decline. Under the conditions of the new mass oratory, worried *Nation* editor Rollo Ogden, oratory risked becoming merely a source of popular entertainment. "As the crowd pays less and less attention to what" orators actually say, Ogden predicted, "it will flock denser than ever to the spectacle and excitement which their very manner of saying it offers."[97]

Although it did not reach a similar level of intensity, the critique of popular eloquence in the Progressive Era paralleled the reaction against Jacksonian rhetoric. For many of the prophets of decline, a true orator was not merely a glib talker but a well-educated and disinterested statesman who spoke eloquently on behalf of carefully wrought principles. It is evident that there was still an inexorable connection in many minds between the highest attributes of leadership and dignified oratory. "If we are to have a new period of oratory in public life," William Everett argued in 1898, "it must be through a higher class of men going to the legislatures and to Congress." Although this idea had never really disappeared during the Gilded Age, there was a renewed commitment to it in the 1890s. The image of the ideal oratorical statesman, as it had been earlier in the century, was of a man of broad learning and selfless devotion to the commonweal who used the power of eloquence to instruct the people and to aid the forces of social and political progress. The true orator, wrote one commentator, "drawing from his well-filled storehouse of knowledge and experience, utilizing his careful study of the conditions of human society, the teachings of history, science, and philosophy discusses grave questions of science, of statesmanship, of morals, in words so weighty, in sentences so replete with meaning, in a style so polished and forceful, that his oration becomes a monument of great attainment to be studied by future generations for its lessons of wisdom." Oratory as mass entertainment was assailed for not fulfilling this essential republican function. With the triumph of oratorical spectacle, Ogden complained, "political oratory is certain to decline—to decline, that is, as a means of influencing the progress of ideas or leading men to undertake serious political action." The great orator, another writer proclaimed, "raises men above themselves, instead of entertaining them on the every day plane of revelry and anecdote."[98]

Behind all of this was remembrance of the old oratorical tradition, with its pantheon of mythic statesman-orators. The vitality of this cultural memory was evinced by the outpouring of oratorical nostalgia that took place around the turn of the century. At the same time that many magazines and newspapers were lamenting the decline or predicting the possible revival of oratory, publishing houses were issuing a rash of large, multivolume collections of classic orations, many edited by famous men such as Bryan, Depew, Reed, and Supreme Court Justice David Brewer. These gilded editions, often containing ten to fifteen volumes that could be purchased on a subscription basis, claimed to contain the best oratory of all time, from Demosthenes to that most classical of Gilded Age orators, Ingersoll. These were the kind of coffeetable books that people used to display in their homes to advertise their family's commitment to polite learning. Regardless of the extent to which these books were actually read, their popularity betokened the continuing cultural significance of the oratorical tradition during the Progressive Era.[99]

Whether in the press or in anthologies, discussions of oratory were but one aspect of the general appeal of lost values for Progressives and conservatives alike.[100] When the men and women of the Progressive Era thought back to the supposedly purer antebellum years—before the growth of large corporations and the rise of modern politics—they thought of statesmen who were also orators. After dwelling on some of the most famous orators in English and American history, for example, George F. Hoar wrote: "Gladstone was the last of a school of oratory, and the last of our time—I hope not for all time—of a school of statesmen. When he entered upon a discussion in Parliament, or on the hustings, he elevated it to the highest possible plane. The discussion became alike one of the highest moral principles and the profoundest political philosophy. He seemed to be speaking as our statesmen of the Revolutionary time, and the time of the framing of the Constitution. He used to speak to all generations alike." This recollection of oratory past was a staple of the age. "In the overflow of public speaking of the present day," wrote Henry L. Dawes, "no one looks for, or would think of finding, anything which would remind him of Fisher Ames or Daniel Webster." Another commentator similarly remarked, "We have in Congress no longer any Websters, Clays, Bentons, and Calhouns. And not only is that true, but the best speakers there do not fulfill even in a lesser degree the ends to which the Senators and Representatives of old addressed themselves." The perceived gap between contemporary orators and the iconic orators of old explains how one writer could declare in 1910 that "No art is so neglected in these days as that of oratory. . . . The world has always rewarded its great orators generously, and unless human nature has undergone a fundamental change, it is even now holding precious laurels in store for those who shall charm its ears with golden speech. Why is it that there are so few who think these laurels worth winning?"[101]

The appeal of the spellbinders and Chautauqua orators, as well as the reaction against them, reflected the persistence of traditional conceptions of oratory. Popular orators were often heralded as modern-day representatives of the Websterian tradition. An example was the Barnumesque hyperbole one Chautauqua bureau chose to advertise its headline speaker, Congressman Champ Clark of Missouri: "He is magnificent mentally, and with his wonderful knowledge of history, of law, and of men, he holds a record of oratory and debate that few have equaled and none surpassed. He is magnificent morally, with a courage of his convictions that is clean cut and unshaded. . . . His speech against Tammany has achieved a fame that surpasses that of Daniel Webster."[102] There were, however, distinct regional and class dimensions to the reputations of insurgent orators. While the plain people of the Midwest might take men such as Clark, Bryan, and La Follette to be worthy successors to Webster and Lincoln, detractors, especially in the Northeast, labeled them and other reform politicians "boy orators," which implied that they lacked the wisdom of orators of the highest type. "What the country needs to-day," wrote one critic, silently invoking Quintilian, "is not boy oratory, but virile oratory, the oratory of its wisest, ablest, most thoughtful citizens—'good men who understand speaking.'" The insurgent orators suffered in comparison to this mythic ideal. As Thomas Reed declared, "Men who stir the surface of thought for the moment may be inferior and command little permanent respect, but the great orators have left too many handsome landmarks behind them to be confounded with rhetoricians and men of the moment."[103]

The basis of Woodrow Wilson's appeal to conservatives, before he entered the political arena and showed himself to be a Progressive, reflected this yearning for a return to a nobler brand of leadership. In the first decade of the new century, many of the more respectable periodicals had taken up the old mugwump call for a return to enlightened intellectual leadership. George Harvey, the influential publisher of *Harper's Weekly* and the owner of the venerable *North American Review,* promoted Wilson as the personification of this ideal. Harvey, who would be instrumental in securing for Wilson the New Jersey Democratic nomination for governor in 1910, was initially inspired by Wilson's oratorical capacities. After hearing his inaugural address at the occasion of his elevation to the presidency of Princeton University in 1902, Harvey remarked to his assistant: "That man could win the people; I want to know about him." After reading some of Wilson's writings, Harvey came to the conclusion that Wilson reflected in his person the best American traditions of statesmanship. Harvey stated in a widely commented-upon speech at the New York Lotus Club in 1906: "For nearly a century before Woodrow Wilson was born the atmosphere of the Old Dominion was surcharged with true statesmanship. The fates directed his steps along other paths, but the effect of growth among the traditions of the fathers remained." Wilson, Harvey believed, was "by instinct a statesman," whose "grasp of fundamentals, the seemingly unconscious application of primary truth to changing conditions, the breadth in thought and reason" all manifested "a sagacity worthy of the best and noblest Virginia traditions." In commending Wilson to his ideological cohorts, Harvey thus drew on the most sanctified American tradition of enlightened and disinterested leadership. Because Wilson possessed the wisdom of a genuine statesman and was "truly eloquent," Harvey argued that he was the perfect leader to make necessary changes while fending off the dogmas and schemes of radical reformers and demagogues.[104]

Many of the rising insurgents politicians, in contrast to Harvey's idealized image of Wilson, shocked respectable sensibilities with the tone and the venues of their speech. La Follette, noted a writer who witnessed his standard Chautauqua speech, "was inflammatory, and even incendiary to a painful degree. . . . He may for the moment secure the cheers of irresponsible hearers, but he will assuredly lose the confidence of thoughtful supporters." Another critic said of La Follette: "This is not oratory, it is passion. It is fanaticism. It is demagoguery. It is not force, it is frenzy." Not only were the insurgents not genuine statesman to their detractors, they also specialized in less-than-respectable genres of public speech. The carnivalesque spectacle surrounding stump harangues and Chautauqua speaking was not reminiscent of the dignified congressional oratory of the antebellum giants. Bryan, for example, when he insisted on continuing on the Chautauqua circuit after he became Wilson's secretary of state, was excoriated by the eastern press for sullying the decorum of the office. He was "billed in circus style to appear between Swiss yodelers, bell-ringers, and sleight-of-hand performers," Oswald Garrison Villard sniffed in the *Nation*. "We are deeply outraged by the spectacle. . . . We can most sincerely assure Mr. Bryan that in this part of the country our feeling is shared by all those who reverence our institutions and believe in their being dignified by those entrusted with the duty of governing." Wilson's famous stumping tours as governor of New Jersey were not the same, Villard continued, because "no jugglers or xylophone artists were included in the programme." Even Dolliver, who was regarded as a more "respectable" orator than Bryan, was assailed by his opponents for his frequent appearances on the Chautauqua circuit.[105]

This gulf between the oratory of old and the more popular brand of speaking that characterized the Progressive Era was one reason so many could continue to proclaim the demise of the art even as it became more politically consequential. It was repeatedly pointed out that congressional speaking, the venue of most of the idols in the history of American oratory, continued to have little discernable influence on public opinion. According to House Speaker Reed, it had "lost its old proportion, and now struggles in vain for an audience as wide as yore. No metropolitan papers published a synopsis of the debates, and a member acquainted with its business cannot tell what is going on after three days absence." As Herold Truslow Ross observes, Albert Beveridge, who as a young man embraced the oratorical tradition with enthusiasm, was surprised when he entered the U.S. Senate in 1899 to find that it no longer was "carrying on the traditions of the Websterian period, wherein the great questions of the day were brought upon the floor for discussion and where those who wished to condemn or defend the policies rose to speak in a lofty and dignified fashion." This cherished vision of exalted legislative oratory was reflected by the palpable longing that it be restored to its old station. A political ally advised Dolliver that if he championed railroad regulation, "he had a chance as a parliamentary debater . . . such as no American Senator had since the fight over slavery and emancipation." When a debate in the House or Senate did draw national attention—such as the contest between Beveridge and Hoar on Philippines policy in 1900 or the clash between Senate standpatters and Republican insurgents led by Dolliver, La Follette, and Beveridge over the Payne-Aldrich Tariff in 1909—there were frequent expressions of hope that congressional oratory was on the upswing. One commentator gushed in 1911 that "Never in recent times has debating in the United States Senate been on a higher plane of ability than in the session now ending." In 1912 the House chamber, which liberal reformers had scorned as a barrier to debate throughout the postbellum era, was remodeled. When it opened in 1913, there were great expectations that the new chamber would lead to the revival of legislative oratory. This hope persisted at least through the end of Wilson's presidency. When the debate over ratification of the Treaty of Versailles began in 1919, commentators again predicted that a debate on the level of the great antebellum contests was in the offing.[106]

This attachment to the ideal of a more deliberative politics in which oratory was the determining influence on national policy was more than mere nostalgia. The ideal of oratorical statesmanship overlapped with broader currents of political thought shared by reformers and conservatives alike during the Progressive Era. Indeed, the significance of oratory in this era was consonant with broader ideological currents of the age, which placed renewed emphasis on disinterested moral leadership by educated men. Like their mugwump predecessors, many Progressives believed that only such leaders could run government in the true public interest.[107] The complexity of modern problems, the growing belief in the necessity of governmental solutions, and the general fear of social and economic disorder fueled a deep desire for leadership that was educated and yet also popular. As Herbert Croly wrote in *The Promise of American Life,* the most important political treatise of the era, "The process of educating men of moral and intellectual stature sufficient for the performance of important constructive work cannot be disentangled from the process of national fulfillment by means of intelligent collective action. American nationality will never be fulfilled except under the leadership of such men." The challenge in a republic, according to Croly, was to find a way to link intellectual qualifications and the ability to move mass opinion. "The gulf between individual excellence and effective popular influence still remains to be bridged; and until it is bridged, an essential stage is lacking."[108]

Because the image of exalted leadership was intertwined with that of the great orator, one of the best ways to stake a claim to the mantle of leadership during the progressive years was through oratory. Oratory was also closely associated with another mantra of progressivism—democracy. Traditionally oratory was seen, in Santayana's words, as a consummately "republican art," an agency both for reaching the public and for making the public's demands manifest. A staple of progressive thought was that there was a common will underlying public opinion, a will that could purify public policy if it were only permitted to express itself.[109] An orator, unlike a politician who operated in the secrecy of caucuses and committees, did his work in public and was utterly dependent for his authority on the favor of the people. In fact, in the absence of modern opinion polling, a rousing speaking tour was usually taken to be proof of the popularity of a speaker's positions. As we have seen, the concept of the ideal orator was also celebrated by conservatives who wished for leaders who could instill calm, restraint, and respect for traditional principles against the demands of insurgent orators and muckraking journalists.[110]

Progressive social thought, as has often been observed by historians, was a curious combination of yearning for a past golden age of greater economic and political freedom and great hope for the potential rewards of modernity. The partial revival of oratory, although reflecting a commitment to traditional political values, also reflected the modernist strand of progressivism. The massive oratorical crusades unleashed by each major party during presidential campaigns were an innovative attempt to extend the reach of mass communication beyond the reading public. The techniques of surrogate oratory would reach their apex during the First World War, in the efforts of Wilson's propaganda agency, the Committee on Public Information, and during the League of Nations controversy, in the dueling publicity campaigns of the League to Enforce Peace and the Liberty League. The publicity techniques insurgent orators used to reach the public were also dependent on mass communication. Their barnstorming tours were sensational stories that were covered by the newspapers, which greatly magnified their influence beyond immediate audiences. Sometimes such tours drew national attention, and most successful insurgent orators exhibited a high level of media savvy. For instance, La Follette's decision to become the first governor in Wisconsin history to address the state legislature in person was informed by the expectation that the resulting press coverage would generate public pressure on behalf of his agenda. Although some argued that modern developments such as the expansion of the domain of print had supplanted the orator, more astute observers saw newspaper coverage as one key to the oratorical revival.[111] As Bryan declared, "The age of oratory has not passed; nor will it pass. The press, instead of displacing the orator, has given him a larger audience and enabled him to do a more extended work." In light of this recognition, orators were often counseled to pay greater attention to the much larger secondary reading audience than to their immediate hearers. As Brander Matthews remarked: "as it happens often, the very best way to arouse the reverberation of the press is to say what you have to say in a speech which the newspapers must report." Similarly, the Chautauqua circuit relied on innovations of marketing and organization that allowed the orator to reach a much larger in-person audience in a shorter amount of time than ever before. The circuit was planned so that the orator could shuttle from site to site, addressing a full house each night. This made it possible for La Follette, for instance, to speak in twenty-five states during the summer of 1905. Similar techniques were used by campaign speakers' bureaus.[112]

The short and direct speaking style pioneered by spellbinders was also a modernization of old oratorical standards to meet the demands of contemporary political persuasion. Spread-eagle oratory did not disappear all at once, but it was increasingly scorned.[113] As Rollo Ogden advised, "Give us the heads of your discourse . . . and let your elaborations go." Traditionalists, who believed that oratory depended for its force on powerful emotional appeals built up in the course of elaborate speeches, were countered by rhetorical modernists, who held that the unadorned simplicity of modern public speaking did not rob oratory of its former power. As Brander Matthews wrote, "Although the wings of the orator have been clipped, and he is no longer encouraged to soar into the blue empyrean, but must keep his footing on the earth, never were more occasions offered to him for the exercise of the art." Ogden agreed, holding that despite the revolution in speaking style, "there is no real ground for thinking that pungent and informed public speaking has lost its power."[114]

This view was vindicated, at least in the short term, by the political career of Woodrow Wilson, who embodied the era's conflicting oratorical standards better than any other leader. The other major orator who might have done so was Dolliver, but he died unexpectedly in 1910.[115] As a respected man of letters, Wilson, unlike Bryan and La Follette, could not be accused of "boy oratory." His style was dignified, and his prose, while certainly not ornate, was elegantly chiseled. Wilson's major rival, Theodore Roosevelt, had the impeccable social and educational credentials of the traditional statesman, but he also had a notorious proclivity to indulge in vituperative harangues and was too much the spellbinder even for some of his strongest supporters.[116] Wilson, on the other hand, could not be accused of being undignified or overly popular in his speech. In addition, his rhetoric elevated issues and events to a philosophical plane. Like the orators of old, he always seemed to treat fundamental questions. The simplicity of his language, on the other hand, made him more accessible to mass audiences than orators such as Beveridge, who spoke in the grandiloquent style of the nineteenth century. Roosevelt's friend Henry Cabot Lodge, a man of the old school of statesmanship, would claim that because Wilson did not use classical allusions in his speeches or lace them with literary references, he was not truly educated. But Lodge's view was a throwback. By this time, orators no longer had to use such devices to be considered intellectual.[117] Wilson's style was a near perfect synthesis of old and new. His prose was simple, direct, and conversational. His speeches were shorter than had been the norm for political addresses. He spoke extemporaneously most of the time, which meant that he spoke with his immediate audience in view. Yet his speeches also read remarkably well. His discourse was reasoned, even when on the campaign trail, and yet carried emotional intensity. Wilson somehow managed, not unlike Lincoln before him, to seem both modern and classical. His oratory helped him embody both the restoration of old values of leadership and progress toward the promise of a modern democracy. By combining the élan of the old oratory with the necessities of modern mass communication, he would prove to be the apotheosis of the second oratorical renaissance.

The Rise of The Oratorical Presidency

The wish for a return of great congressional debates, so frequently expressed since the end of the Civil War, was answered in 1919 in the Senate contest over the League of Nations. "In the annals of senatorial eloquence," John Milton Cooper Jr., has recently written, "these debates did not match the olympian heights attained in the previous century by such immortals as Daniel Webster, John C. Calhoun, and Charles Sumner." But they "did set a standard that would not be matched again in the twentieth century except at a few times during the civil rights debates of the 1950s and '60s."[118] Fittingly, perhaps, this outstanding debate was overshadowed by President Wilson's dramatic speaking tour in September of 1919.

The most lasting legacy of Progressive Era rhetoric has been the shift in emphasis from congressional debate to presidential rhetoric. Even during the golden age of American oratory, presidents spoke infrequently and by custom almost never used written or oral public discourse as a means of influencing the legislative process. During the oratorical revival of the Progressive Era, however, the inhibitions against popular presidential rhetoric began to loosen. William McKinley went on tour to build support for his Philippines policy, Roosevelt pioneered use of speaking tours as a weapon against Congress, and even the stolid Taft took to the platform on behalf of arbitration treaties with Great Britain and France. However, Wilson was responsible, above all, for extending the rhetorical reach of the presidency. In *Constitutional Government* (1908), his last major scholarly work, he provided the theoretical justification for a president who used popular rhetoric to insert himself into the legislative process. Once he was inaugurated as president in 1913, Wilson would put his academic theory into practice, setting an example that would be followed by the other leading presidents of the twentieth century.[119]

Wilson's innovation had two major precedents, one foreign and the other domestic. The first of these, which has escaped the attention of American presidential scholars, was the shift in British official oratory from forensic exchanges in the House of Commons to extraparliamentary speaking tours. In this Gladstonian system, which became dominant after the Midlothean Campaigns of 1879–80, the prime minister and the leaders of the opposition party promoted their legislative programs in Parliament by appealing to the public directly from the stump. This change in the character of British political rhetoric received substantial attention on both sides of the Atlantic and was seen by many as a necessary innovation in a modern mass democracy. As one English writer explained, in terms that foreshadowed Wilson's rationale for an oratorical presidency in the United States, "a democracy would be merely a congeries of atoms unless its thoughts and wishes could find articulate expression; and it is round a popular leader that the ideas, vague and indeterminate, of a people may be said to crystallize themselves. Hence the need for the platform as a vehicle of expression. Still more is there need of a channel through which the statesman may reach the public mind."[120] It is certain that Wilson, who even more than most educated Americans of his generation took a keen interest in English affairs, was aware of the dominance of extraparliamentary oratory in British politics when he wrote *Constitutional Government*.[121]

The immediate domestic precedent for Wilson's innovation was the presidency of Theodore Roosevelt. As a vice presidential candidate in 1900, Roosevelt had already shown a zest for spellbinding. Once president, he conceived of his office as a "bully pulpit," thereby bucking a century-long precedent of relative presidential silence. "As President," J. Michael Hogan recounts, "[Roosevelt] continued to popularize his ideas with public speaking tours of exhausting dimensions. During one tour in 1903 he covered fourteen thousand miles by rail and several hundred miles by stagecoach or carriage. During sixty-five days on the road, he made 265 speeches.

Virtually everywhere he went the audiences were large and enthusiastic. The energetic new president proved a 'dream come true' for American reporters and the reading public."[122] Roosevelt's speech making took two distinct forms. First, he addressed the moral duties of citizenship in general terms. Concerned that the radicalism of labor on the one side and the reactionary inclinations of capital on the other might ultimately destroy the republic, he consciously sought to promote in the populace a republican commitment to a common national interest. His sermonizing was so notorious that one journal dubbed him "Our Preacher President."[123] Second, Roosevelt became the first president to barnstorm as a means of focusing pressure on Congress to pass specific legislation. His best-known effort came as part of his campaign to promote the Hepburn Bill on railroad regulation, during which he spoke to nearly any organization that would tender an invitation.[124] Although Roosevelt avoided speaking when Congress was discussing railroad regulation and tried to limit his focus to general principles so as not to interfere with the legislative process, his departure from precedent was striking and could not help having a great impression on Wilson, who, in a series of lectures at Columbia University, first unveiled his new theory of popular presidential leadership in 1907—a year after the successful conclusion of Roosevelt's campaign for the Hepburn Bill.[125]

Although these precedents were important, Wilson's new doctrine of presidential leadership was above all the culmination of his thirty-year intellectual search for a way to place oratorical statesmen at the head of American government. The nation was adrift, he had believed since his earliest political writings, because it lacked the kind of leadership that could make the connection between public opinion and constructive statesmanship. In his approach, Wilson reflected a synthesis of the republican and democratic strands of the oratorical tradition. His ideal orator expressed the popular will while refining it and directing it toward the broader common interest. For most of his academic career, Wilson had assumed that such integrative leadership could only come from Congress, from modernized equivalents of the leading American Whig orators and the leading debaters of the mid-nineteenth-century British Parliament. Although he had for many years advocated cabinet-style government as the institutional arrangement most likely to produce such leaders, in the 1890s he had begun to explore ways to make the American executive into the locus of constructive national leadership. Inspired by Grover Cleveland's example, he had proposed in the late 1890s that the president might use his annual message to rally public opinion and force Congress to consider his agenda, but he still thought Congress could ultimately ignore the president in the absence of more formal executive powers. The Spanish-American War furnished still more inspiration. As he wrote in 1900, "Much the most important change to be noticed is the result of the war with Spain upon the lodgment and exercise of power within our federal system: the greatly increased power and opportunity for constructive statesmanship given the President, by the plunge into international politics. . . . The President of the United States is now, as of course, at the front of affairs, as no president, except Lincoln, has been since the first quarter of the nineteenth-century." Wilson also noticed that presidential rhetoric was drawing more attention than it had since the Civil War: "There is no trouble now about getting the President's speeches printed and read, every word."[126] By 1907, Wilson had crossed an intellectual Rubicon and was prepared to argue that skillfully deployed rhetoric could make the American president the forceful leader of a unified national government.

The decisive step in this intellectual journey was Wilson's realization that the president had a built-in ethos unmatched by anyone else in the country. His early rhetorical training had emphasized the importance of ethos in persuasion. The way the people looked to McKinley for guidance during the Spanish-American War, followed by Roosevelt's charismatic leadership, convinced him that the president's cultural authority was growing. "There can be no mistaking the fact," he said, "that we have grown more and more inclined from generation to generation to look to the President as the unifying force in our complex system, the leader both of his party and of the nation."[127] This rhetorical insight was the pivot of Wilson's argument for an oratorical presidency in *Constitutional Government*. If the president could command an attentive national audience that took his utterances seriously as expressions of national sentiment, then he could rally public opinion behind specific policy proposals. In a modern republic, Wilson maintained, the part of the government with "the most direct access to opinion has the best chance of leadership and mastery; and at present that part is the President." Wilson argued that this development had been hastened by the marginalization of oratory in Congress, where discussion came more in closed committees and party caucuses than in debate on the floor.[128] With Congress ceding the field of public opinion formation, immediate access to an attentive national audience gave the president a unique rhetorical opportunity. The president, Wilson said, "is the only national voice in affairs." As such, "When he speaks in his true character, he speaks for no special interest. If he rightly interpret the national thought and boldly insist upon it, he is irresistible." The nation's "instinct is for unified action, and it craves a single leader."[129] Because Wilson assumed that there was a connection between oratorical talent and the other characteristics of high statesmanship, he believed that such a president would likely use this power to promote a great constructive agenda. Unlike members of Congress, who saw issues from state and local perspectives, the president was free to develop a commanding vision of national affairs.[130]

Wilson's reconstruction of the presidency was an intellectual outgrowth of the oratorical culture that he had embraced in his youth. Wilson had believed throughout his life that the first-rate orator was a great constructive and unifying force in a republic. As we have seen, one of the dominant preoccupations of Progressive Era political thought was the question of how democratic leadership could be reconciled with leadership in the genuine public interest. Wilson squared the circle by drawing on the figure of the neoclassical orator. Belief in this ideal made it possible for Wilson to assume, without extended argument, that a system which made oratorical ability a qualification for high office would also tend to elevate educated and principled leaders.[131] The dominant paradigm of interpretation in presidential studies, however, neglects the influence of the oratorical tradition on Wilson's theory of the presidency.

In recent years, Wilson's innovation has received a great deal of attention from political scientists writing about the emergence of what they call the "rhetorical presidency."[132] "The modern doctrine of presidential leadership," Jeffrey Tulis, James Ceaser, and others argue, "was consciously formulated and put into practice by Woodrow Wilson." In the historical narrative offered by these scholars, the framers of the Constitution had so feared demagoguery that they deliberately stigmatized popular presidential rhetoric. By reversing this tradition and tying presidential power to the transient winds of public sentiment, they contend, Wilson degraded the balanced constitutional system and ruined the possibility of independent statesmanship. By laying the theoretical and institutional groundwork for a "rhetorical presidency," they claim, Wilson successfully overturned the Aristotelian political science of the founders, with its emphasis on institutional space where leaders could discuss issues of national importance absent the immediate pressure of public opinion, and inaugurated a new sophistic age in which genuine deliberation has been replaced by empty political sloganeering masquerading as public knowledge.[133]

Laying aside the appraisal of modern presidential rhetoric advanced by Tulis and other critics, and their implicit assumption that the nineteenth-century political system produced more genuine deliberation than is present today, it is clear that by limiting their analysis to the institution of the presidency, these political scientists have oversimplified American rhetorical history, asserting far too great a continuity between the founders' conception of rhetoric and oratorical practice from 1787 to 1913. In addition, the antirhetorical emphasis of *The Federalist Papers*—practically the exclusive source for their analysis of the founders' position on rhetoric—was a reaction against the excesses of the state legislatures under the Articles of Confederation. Taken in full, the founders had a nuanced understanding of rhetoric, seeing it both as a dangerous and a necessary power in a republic. While their concern about the misuses of rhetoric, which had been heightened by recent political events, prompted them to devise institutions they hoped would keep it in the hands of disinterested statesmen, their simultaneous belief that eloquence was a vital republican capacity helped spark the subsequent explosion of popular oratory during the early national period. By the Jacksonian period, it was widely conceded that the public would of necessity be addressed directly by political leaders, although there were profound disagreements about who was qualified to address a mass audience and over the proper form and substance of this speech. The Whig ideal of the oratorical statesman, who addressed the public in an ennobling and uplifting manner, was in part a response to anxieties about the abuses of popular speech. While theorists of the rhetorical presidency recount the continued tradition of presidential reticence in the last two-thirds of the nineteenth century—an era, it should be noted, in which the balance of power tilted decidedly toward Congress—they ignore this broader evolution of oratorical culture. They seem strangely insensible to the prominent place of oratory and orators in the cultural imagination, and the central role popular rhetoric actually played in nineteenth- and early-twentieth-century politics. They also seem entirely unaware of the influence of British extraparliamentary oratory.

Most significantly, the assumption of the rhetorical presidency theorists that a system which gives popular rhetoric a prominent role must necessarily lead to the degradation of statesmanship and serious deliberation manifests an undiluted verbal skepticism that, although it may be common among social scientists living in the second half of the twentieth century, was not shared in the main by Wilson and his contemporaries. It is telling that these scholars offer no evidence that Wilson's *Constitutional Government* was considered radical by his contemporaries. To the contrary, Wilson remained the darling of conservative Democrats, a group that acutely feared popular oratory and admired traditional statesmanship, long after the publication of his book. Even after he entered politics and revealed himself as an ideological Progressive, there were surprisingly few attacks on his dramatic rhetorical innovations as a governor and as president. This was likely because Wilson embodied the cultural ideal of the educated and principled orator who could be trusted as a steward of the public interest. A Bryan or La Follette presidency, on the other hand, might well have prompted an antioratorical backlash.

Within the oratorical tradition, Wilson's viewpoint did tilt toward those who believed that the character of eloquent speakers was a strong safeguard against the misuses of rhetoric. Since his earliest writings, Wilson had taken the Aristotelian view that the good person speaking well would tend to win out over base speakers, provided the system gave such orators equitable access to the public mind. In the intellectual history of American oratory, Wilson's reformation of presidential rhetoric is comparable to what the American Whigs attempted to do for legislative oratory in the 1830s and 1840s. Like the Whigs, Wilson's innovation was intended to adapt traditional political values to a rapidly changing environment. Like the Whigs, Wilson was searching for a means of creating a more unified polity that could act on pressing national problems. Like the Whigs, Wilson saw a necessary connection between oratory and genuine leadership and recognized popular eloquence as a potential means of empowering independent and disinterested statesmen. For both

Wilson and the Whigs, the character of true orators assured that they would not be dragged down to the level of transient public opinion.

There is direct evidence that Wilson himself saw the connection between his theory of the presidency and the Whig ideal. Immediately preceding his analysis of the presidency in *Constitutional Government,* he invoked the most celebrated oratorical contest of the antebellum golden age:

> There is one debate to which every student turns with the feeling that in it lay the fire of the central dramatic force of all our history. In the debate between Mr. Hayne and Mr. Webster the whole feeling and consciousness of America was changed. Mr. Hayne had uttered, with singular eloquence and ringing force, the voice of a day that was passing away; Mr. Webster the voice of a day that had come and whose forces were to supersede all others. There is a sense in which it may almost be said that Mr. Webster that day called a nation into being. What he said has the immortal quality of words which almost create the thoughts they speak. The nation lay as it were unconscious of its unity and purpose, and he called it into full consciousness. It could never again be anything less than what he had said it was. It is at such moments and in the mouths of such interpreters that nations spring from age to age in their development.

Wilson went on to say that the nation faced in the modern industrial age, as it had in 1831, a moment when great orators were needed to give voice to underlying changes that had not yet gained conscious recognition. Only after establishing this association between Webster's rhetorical triumph over Hayne and present exigencies did Wilson go on to unveil his theory that the American president might become the supreme spokesman for national progress.[134]

Soon after he entered office in 1913, Wilson demonstrated the practicality of his claim that rhetoric could augment the influence of the president. Wilson used speaking tours to great effect as governor of New Jersey and as president during the preparedness controversy of 1916. However, despite repeated threats to take to the stump during legislative impasses, his most frequent rhetorical tact as president was not the speaking tour but the address to Congress. No president had spoken in Congress since Thomas Jefferson abandoned the practice of giving the State of the Union message in person in 1801. To great fanfare, Wilson returned to the Federalist practice on 8 April 1913, in a speech launching the first of his New Freedom reforms. Ultimately, Wilson addressed Congress twenty-five times—substantially more often than any president before or since. These addresses helped Wilson to pass the most ambitious domestic reform agenda ever enacted to that point in American history and to lead the nation along the torturous path from neutrality to active participation in World War I. Once the war had been entered, he defined the nation's war aims and his vision of a revised world order in a series of eloquent addresses before the Senate. The last great political act of his career was his momentous three-week speaking tour on behalf of the League of Nations in September of 1919. As is well known, this epic tour was cut short by Wilson's physical breakdown following his speech in Pueblo, Colorado, on 25 September.

While future presidents—especially Roosevelt, Kennedy, Johnson, Reagan, and Clinton—would also rely heavily on public address, Wilson's self-conscious identification with the oratorical tradition separates him from these later-day rhetorical presidents. The oratorical tradition Wilson so admired was more than a cultural style. It was at base an ethical tradition that required its adherents to live up to an exalted code of conduct. In an age dominated by the standards and practices of public relations and advertising, this connection between eloquence and character has atrophied. Wilson's model of the presidency has been disembodied in the sense that the modern rhetorical presidency does not operate within the intellectual tradition that informed its creation. There was a rich intellectual universe that animated oratorical culture from Fisher Ames to Woodrow Wilson that has now all but vanished. Wilson himself recognized this passing from his sickbed during his lonely and bitter final year as president. As the White House doctor recorded, "The President this afternoon spoke to me for quite a while on the lack of oratory these days." Wilson recited a favorite passage from Webster and "was almost moved to tears as he repeated the quotation." Webster would not be an icon for future generations, nor would it mean so much to be an orator.[135]

What is also missing now is the spiritual sense that the eloquence of a single eminent orator can remake the world. Wilson was much more of a realist than his historical reputation suggests, yet his close identification with the pantheon of famous orators did encourage him to believe that there were great moments in history when society could be induced, through the agency of eloquence, to make great leaps forward. When he was planning his political strategy for the ratification of the Treaty of Versailles, Wilson thought back to Webster's famous triumph over Hayne in 1831. According to Wilson, Webster had not reinvented the nation out of whole cloth, but he had, in a single brilliant speech, made the northern public realize that they had gradually come to see themselves not merely as the residents of individual states, but as the citizens of a great and perpetual union. Wilson saw the controversy over the League of Nations in similar terms. When he reached the West Coast during his momentous speaking tour in September of 1919, where the immense, enthusiastic crowds made many believe that the tour was succeeding, he saw himself as consummating a mission that had been begun by the long line of orators who preceded him. As he reached the apex of his tour, Wilson self-consciously identified his errand with the prophethood of all the great orators of the American past. "After saturating myself most of my life in the history and traditions of America," Wilson declared, "I seem suddenly to see a culmination of American hope and history—all the orators seeing their dreams realized, if their spirits are looking on; all the men who spoke the noblest sentiments for America heartened with the sight of a great nation responding to and acting upon those dreams."[136]

Notes

1. On the traditional components of oratorical training see Robert Hariman, "Relocating the Art of Public Address," in *Rhetoric and Political Culture in Nineteenth-Century America*, ed. Thomas W. Benson (East Lansing: Michigan State University Press, 1997), 173–74.

2. Arthur S. Link, "Woodrow Wilson: The Philosophy, Methods, and Impact of Leadership," in *Woodrow Wilson in the World Today*, ed. Arthur P. Dudden (Philadelphia: University of Pennsylvania Press, 1957), 10; Robert H. Ferrell, *Woodrow Wilson and World War I* (New York: Harper and Row, 1985), 2. Also see, for example, Sean Dennis Cashman, *America in the Age of Titans: The Progressive Era and World War I* (New York: New York University Press, 1988), 124.

3. Gordon S. Wood, "The Democratization of the American Mind," in *Leadership in the American Revolution* (Washington, D.C.: Library of Congress, 1974), 72. For an example of the late-eighteenth- and early-nineteenth-century view of eloquence see Dugald Stewart, *Elements of the Philosophy of the Human Mind: Volume III*, in *The Collected Works of Dugald Stewart*, ed. William Hamilton (Edinburgh: Thomas Constable and Co., 1854), 4:157–61.

4. Thomas Gustafson, *Representative Words: Politics, Literature, and the American Language, 1776–1865* (Cambridge: Cambridge University Press, 1992), 122, 118–25. Also see Jerrold E. Seigel, *Rhetoric and Philosophy in Renaissance Humanism: The Union of Eloquence and Wisdom, Petrach to Valla* (Princeton: Princeton University Press, 1968); and

S. Michael Halloran, "Tradition and Theory in Rhetoric," *Quarterly Journal of Speech* 62 (1976): 236–37.

5. The strongest assault on eloquence came in Locke's tremendously influential *Essay on Human Understanding,* in the chapter "On Words," which John Bender and David E. Wellbery call "one of the most virulent antirhetorical tirades on record." John Bender and David E. Wellbery, "Rhetoricality: On the Modernist Return to Rhetoric," in *The End of Rhetoric,* ed. Bender and Wellbery (Stanford, Calif.: Stanford University Press, 1990), 8–14. Also see Gustafson, *Representative Words,* 130–68.

6. Highly influential republican thinkers such as Bolingbroke and Hume were among the defenders of eloquence. See Henry St. John, Viscount Bolingbroke, "Letters or Essays Addressed to Alexander Pope, Esq.: Essay the First Concerning the Nature, Extent, and Reality of Human Knowledge," in *The Works of Bolingbroke: With a Life* (1754; reprint, Philadelphia: Carey and Hart, 1841), 3:129–30; David Hume, "Of Eloquence," in *The Philosophical Works of David Hume* (1742; reprint, Edinburgh: Adam Black and William Tait, 1826), 3:119.

7. See Gustafson, *Representative Words,* 6, 118–20.

8. Wood, "Democratization of the American Mind," in *Leadership in the American Revolution,* 70; John Witherspoon, "Lectures on Eloquence," 1768, in *The Selected Writings of John Witherspoon,* ed. Thomas Miller (Carbondale: Southern Illinois University Press, 1990), 256. Also see Sandra Marie Gustafson, "Performing the Word: American Oratory, 1630–1860" (Ph.D. diss., University of California, Berkeley, 1993), 2–3. On eighteenth-century rhetorical education see Gordon E. Bigelow, *Rhetoric and American Poetry of the Early National Period* (Gainesville: University of Florida Press, 1960), 24–25; S. Michael Halloran, "Rhetoric in American College Curriculum: The Decline of Public Discourse," *Pre/Text* 3 (1982): 250–54; Gregory Clark and S. Michael Halloran, "Introduction: Transformations for Public Discourse in Nineteenth-Century America," in *Oratorical Culture in Nineteenth-Century America: Transformations in the Theory and Practice of Rhetoric* (Carbondale: Southern Illinois University Press, 1993), 2–3, 7. On John Adams's romance with oratory see James Michael Farrell Jr., "John Adams and the Ciceronian Paradigm" (Ph.D. diss., University of Wisconsin, Madison, 1988); Gustafson, *Representative Words,* 147, 234–36; and Bernard Bailyn, *Ideological Origins of the American Revolution* (Cambridge: Harvard University Press, 1967), 26.

9. Kenneth Cmiel, *Democratic Eloquence: The Fight over Popular Speech in Nineteenth-Century America* (New York: Morrow, 1990), 40, 46–47; John Adams, "To the President of Congress," 5 September 1780, in *The Works of John Adams, Second President of the United States: With a Life of the Author,* ed. Charles Francis Adams (Boston: Little, Brown and Co., 1852), 7:250, 249.

10. Gustafson, *Representative Words,* 287–91. The attacks on popular eloquence in *The Federalist Papers* are the launching-off point for the group of political scientists who have written on the modern rhetorical presidency. See James Ceaser, Glen E. Thurow, Jeffrey Tulis, and Joseph M. Bessette, "The Rise of the Rhetorical Presidency," *Presidential Studies Quarterly* 11 (1981): 158–71; Jeffrey Tulis, "The Decay of Presidential Rhetoric," in *Rhetoric and American Statesmanship,* ed. Glen E. Thurow and Jeffrey D. Wallin (Durham, N.C.: Carolina Academic Press, 1984), 101–4; Jeffrey K. Tulis, *The Rhetorical Presidency* (Princeton: Princeton University Press, 1987), 26–56; Joseph M. Bessette, *The Mild Voice of Reason: Deliberative Democracy and American National Government* (Chicago: University of Chicago Press, 1994), 237; and James W. Ceaser, *Presidential Selection: Theory and Development* (Princeton: Princeton University Press, 1979), 321–27.

11. "No. 58: Hamilton," in Alexander Hamilton, James Madison, and John Jay, *The Federalist Papers,* ed. Clinton Rossiter (1787; reprint, New York: Penguin, Mentor Books, 1961), 360; Fisher Ames, "Phocion IV," 1 May 1801, in *Works of Fisher Ames,* ed. W. B. Allen (Indianapolis: Liberty Classics, 1983), 1:284; Thomas Hobbes, *De Corpore Politico, or The Elements of Law, Moral and Politick,* in *The English Works of Thomas Hobbes,* ed. William Molesworth (London: John Bohn, 1966), 4:141. This same critique would later be leveled against the Jeffersonians by the Federalists. See Fisher Ames, "Falklands II," 6 February 1801, in *Works of Fisher Ames,* 1:311–17.

12. On the relationship between Federalist leadership doctrines and their reaction against the state of political affairs under the Articles of Confederation, see Gordon S. Wood, "Interests and Disinterestedness in the Making of the Constitution," in *Beyond Confederation: Origins of the Constitution and American National Identity*, ed. Richard Beeman, Stephen Botein, and Edward C. Carter II (Chapel Hill: University of North Carolina Press, 1987), 71–77; Gustafson, *Representative Words*, 291–92; and Elaine K. Swift, *The Making of an American Senate: Reconstitutive Change in Congress, 1787–1841* (Ann Arbor: University of Michigan Press, 1996), 14–23.

13. Gordon S. Wood, *The Radicalism of the American Revolution* (New York: Alfred A. Knopf, 1992), 109; "Federalist No. 57: Madison," in *Federalist Papers*, 350. Also see Wood, "Making of the Constitution," in *Beyond Confederation*, 69–109; Ralph Ketcham, *Presidents above Party: The First American Presidency, 1789–1829* (Chapel Hill: University of North Carolina Press, 1984), 62–68; Meyer Reinhold, "The Classics and the Quest for Virtue in Eighteenth Century America," in *The Usefulness of Classical Learning in Eighteenth Century America*, ed. Susan Ford Wiltshire (University Park, Pa.: American Philological Association, 1977), 6–26; Thomas G. West, "The Classical Spirit of the Founding," in *The American Founding: Essays in the Formation of the Constitution*, ed. J. Jackson Barlow, Leonard W. Levy, and Ken Masugi (New York: Greenwood, 1988), 11–21; Charles S. Sydnor, *American Revolutionaries in the Making: Political Practices in Washington's Virginia* (New York: Free Press, 1965), 13–18, 112; and Gerald Stourzh, *Alexander Hamilton and the Idea of Republican Government* (Stanford, Calif.: Stanford University Press, 1970), 65–70.

14. For Cicero's classic statements on the qualifications of the orator and Quintilian's reiteration of the Ciceronian ideal, see Cicero, *De Oratore*, in *Cicero on Oratory and Orators*, trans. J. S. Watson (Carbondale: Southern Illinois University Press, 1970), 37, 42–45; and *Quintilian on the Early Education of the Citizen-Orator*, ed. James J. Murphy, trans. J. S. Watson (Indianapolis: Bobbs-Merrill, Library of Liberal Arts, 1965), 71–72. For overviews of the neoclassical ideal of the orator, see Halloran, "Tradition and Theory in Rhetoric," 235–36; Halloran, "Rhetoric in American College Curriculum," 246; Cmiel, *Democratic Eloquence*, 25; and Gustafson, *Representative Words*, 126–27. For the antebellum view of Cicero's orator see, for example, "Characteristics of the Statesman," *Southern Quarterly Review* 6 (July 1844): 107; and "Political Education—Statesmanship," *American Review* 3 (April 1846): 355.

15. Bolingbroke, "A Letter on the Spirit of Patriotism," in *Works of Lord Bolingbroke*, 2:366, 367–68. Bolingbroke's remarks upon eloquence were cited in eighteenth- and nineteenth-century American essays on oratory. See, for example, "On Eloquence," *Columbian Magazine* 1 (September 1787): 622; and [Francis Walker Gilmer], *Sketches of American Orators* (Baltimore: Fielding, Lucas, Jr., 1816), 47.

16. Witherspoon, "Lectures on Eloquence," in *The Selected Writings of John Witherspoon*, 231, 305; John Quincy Adams, *Lectures on Rhetoric and Oratory* (Cambridge, Mass.: Hilliard and Metcalf, 1810), 1:63–65, 20. Also see Stewart, *Elements of the Philosophy of the Human Mind*, 4:157–61.

17. George Campbell, *The Philosophy of Rhetoric*, ed. Lloyd F. Bitzer (Carbondale: Southern Illinois University Press, 1988); Hugh Blair, *Lectures on Rhetoric and Belles Lettres*, 6th ed. (1783; reprint, London: A. Strahan, T. Cadell, and W. Creetch, 1796). On this point also see Wood, "Democratization of the American Mind," in *Leadership in the American Revolution*, 67–69; Andrew W. Robertson, *The Language of Democracy: Political Rhetoric in the United States and Britain, 1790–1900* (Ithaca, N.Y.: Cornell University Press, 1995), 2–3, 22n. 6; and Cmiel, *Democratic Eloquence*, 35–36.

18. Witherspoon, "Lectures on Eloquence," in *The Selected Writings of John Witherspoon*, 258, 305; Adams, *Lectures on Rhetoric and Oratory*, 1:257–59. On the lofty ideals of statesmanship that the Federalists inherited from the English country party and radical republican thinkers, see Wood, *Radicalism of the American Revolution*, 104–5; Wood, "Making of the Constitution," in *Beyond Confederation*, 83–89; Ketcham, *Presidents above Party*, 70; and Swift, *Making of an American Senate*, 15. Fisher Ames articulated all of the major premises of neoclassical statesmanship in his essay on Hamilton. Ames, "A Sketch of the Character of Alexander Hamilton," July 1804, in *Works of Fisher Ames*, 1:510–19.

19. "No. 10: Madison," in *Federalist Papers*, 82–83; "No. 63: Probably Madison," in *Federalist Papers*, 384. Also see Bessette, *Mild Voice of Reason*, 237; Wayne Fields, *Union of Words: A History of Presidential Eloquence* (New York: Free Press, 1996), 10–11; and Swift, *Making of an American Senate*, 19–23.

20. Fisher Ames, "Speech on the Jay Treaty," 28 April 1796, in *Works of Fisher Ames*, 2:1157. For one of the more influential proposals on how to develop a new leadership class that would live up to these ideals, see Thomas Jefferson, *Notes on Virginia*, in *The Works of Thomas Jefferson*, Federal ed., ed. Paul Leicester Ford (New York: G. P. Putnam's Sons, Knickerbocker Press, 1904), 4:60–65.

21. Fisher Ames, "The Mire of Democracy," 1805, in *Works of Fisher Ames*, 1:4–5, 6; Edward Tyrrell Channing, "The Orator and His Times," 8 December 1819, in *Lectures Read to the Seniors in Harvard College* (Boston: Ticknor and Fields, 1856), 3, 4, 8, 15–16. Also see [Edward Tyrrell Channing], review of *Philosophical Essays*, by James Oglivie, *North American Review and Miscellaneous Journal* 4 (March 1817): 380; and Fisher Ames, "Speeches in the Convention of Massachusetts," 15 January 1788, in *Works of Fisher Ames*, 1:543.

22. See especially Caleb Bingham, "Extracts from an Oration on Eloquence, Pronounced at Harvard University, on Commencement Day, 1794," in *The Columbian Orator: Containing a Variety of Original and Selected Pieces; Together with Rules Calculated to Improve Youth and Others in the Ornamental and Useful Art of Eloquence* (Boston: Manning and Loring, 1797), 32–33.

23. For general discussion of America's golden age of oratory see Richard Beale Davis, *Intellectual Life in Jefferson's Virginia, 1790–1830* (Chapel Hill: University of North Carolina Press, 1964), 363–65, 371–85; Daniel J. Boorstin, *The Americans: The National Experience* (1965; reprint, London: Sphere Books, Cardinal, 1988), 308–15; Daniel Walker Howe, *Political Culture of the American Whigs* (Chicago: University of Chicago Press, 1979), 25–26; Lawrence Buell, "New England Oratory from Everett to Emerson," in *New England Literary Culture: From Revolution through Renaissance* (Cambridge: Cambridge University Press, 1986), 139–42, 153; James Perrin Warren, *Culture of Eloquence: Oratory and Reform in Antebellum America* (University Park: Pennsylvania State University Press, 1999); Lewis Pearson Simpson, "The Era of Joseph Stevens Buckminster: Life and Letters in the Boston-Cambridge Community, 1800–1815" (Ph.D. diss., University of Texas, 1948), 400–6; Barnet Baskerville, *The People's Voice: The Orator in American Society* (Lexington: University Press of Kentucky, 1979), 32–87; and Gustafson, *Representative Words*, 373–74. The veneration of the successful orator was especially profuse in the South. See W. Stuart Towns, *Oratory and Rhetoric in the Nineteenth-Century South: A Rhetoric of Defense* (Westport, Conn.: Praeger, 1998), 1; Kenneth S. Greenberg, *Masters and Statesmen: The Political Culture of American Slavery* (Baltimore: Johns Hopkins University Press, 1985), 12–16; Wilbur J. Cash, *The Mind of the South* (New York: Alfred A. Knopf, 1951), 51, 130; Davis, *Intellectual Life in Jefferson's Virginia*, 365–85; Edward K. Graham, "The History of Southern Oratory during the Federal Period, 1788–1861," in *The South in the Building of the Nation*, vol. 9 of *History of Southern Oratory*, ed. Thomas E. Watson (Richmond, Va.: Southern Historical Publications Society, 1909), 31–37; William R. Taylor, *Cavalier and Yankee: The Old South and American National Character* (New York: George Brazilliar, 1961), 82–83; Francis Pendleton Gaines, *Southern Oratory: A Study in Idealism* (Tuscaloosa: University of Alabama Press, 1946); and William Martin Reynolds, "Deliberative Speaking in Ante-Bellum South Carolina: The Idiom of a Culture" (Ph.D. diss., University of Florida, 1960).

24. [Richard Rush], "The American Lounger No. LXXVIX," *Port Folio* 4 (28 January 1804): 1; [Alexander Hill Everett], "Silva No. 52: Eloquence," *Monthly Anthology and Boston Review* 6 (June 1809): 382–83; [Joseph Story], "Statesmen—Their Rareness and Importance: Daniel Webster," *New-England Magazine* 7 (August 1834): 90; "Remarks on Eloquence of Debate," *New-England Magazine* 7 (August 1834): 107. Also see [William Powell Mason and William Jones Spooner], "Modern Oratory," *North American Review and Miscellaneous Journal* 7 (July 1818): 215; Samuel L. Knapp, *Lectures on American Literature, with Remarks on Some Passages of American History* (New York: Elam Bliss, 1829), 213–18; "Intelligence," *Monthly Anthology and Boston Review* 3 (September

1806): 502–3; [John Blair Linn], *Miscellaneous Works, Prose and Poetical, by a Young Gentlemen of New-York* (New York: Thomas Greenleaf, 1795), 27–28; "Inchiquin the Jesuit Letters," *Port Folio* 5 (May 1811): 392–93; [Samuel Cooper Thatcher], review of *Lectures on Rhetoric and Oratory,* by John Quincy Adams, *Monthly Anthology and Boston Review* 8 (April 1810): 249–50; [Edward Everett], "Webster's Speeches," *North American Review* 41 (July 1835): 231–39; Adams, *Lectures on Rhetoric and Oratory,* 68–72, 257–59; review of *Life and Eloquence of Rev. Sylvestor Larned,* by R. R. Gurley, *American Review* 1 (January 1845): 111; and [W. G. Howard], "Ancient and Modern Eloquence," *Southern Literary Messenger* 8 (March 1842): 169.

25. On American oratorical exceptionalism see, for example, "Remarks on Eloquence of Debate," 107; "The Schools of Modern Eloquence," *Knickerbocker or New-York Monthly Magazine* 1 (May 1833): 270–71; "Intelligence," 503; "Inchiquin, The Jesuit Letters," 392; [Rush], "The American Lounger," 1. There was a self-conscious discussion in the antebellum years of the relations between modern and ancient eloquence, and how American oratory measured up to the Greek and Roman exemplars. See, for example, [Howard], "Ancient and Modern Eloquence," 170–81; [Mason and Spooner], "Modern Oratory," 212; "Intelligence," 503; Bingham, "Extract from an Oration on Eloquence," in *Columbian Orator,* 32; "Modern Oratory," *Southern Literary Messenger* 18 (June 1852): 370–75; [Thatcher], review of *Lectures on Rhetoric and Oratory,* 249; "Oratory," *Western Journal and Civilian* 9 (October 1852): 60–62; Knapp, *Lectures on American Literature,* 227; A. M. Judson, "Eloquence," *Southern Literary Messenger* 20 (September 1854): 539; "Inchiquin: The Jesuit Letters," 392; [Rush], "The American Lounger," 1; and "Remarks on Eloquence of Debate," 107. On the prominence of the lecture circuit see, for example, Edward Everett Hale, "Lectures and Lecturers," in *Modern Eloquence,* ed. Thomas B. Reed (Philadelphia: John D. Morris and Co., 1900), 4:xv–xxvii. For discussion of the dominance of oratory over other arts see Bigelow, *Rhetoric and American Poetry,* 29–32; Simpson, "The Era of Joseph Stevens Buckminster," 401–3; and Baskerville, *People's Voice,* 82–83.

26. Buell, "New England Oratory," in *New England Literary Culture,* 153; Adams, *Lectures on Rhetoric and Oratory,* 30. Also see [Howard], "Ancient and Modern Eloquence," 169; "Remarks on Eloquence of Debate," 106; [Rush], "The American Lounger," 1; and [Mason and Spooner], "Modern Oratory," 213.

27. By far the most influential text on rhetoric in antebellum rhetoric was Blair's *Lectures on Rhetoric and Belles Lettres.* See Warren E. Guthrie, "The Development of Rhetorical Theory in America, 1635–1850" (Ph.D. diss., Northwestern University, 1940), 83–85; Albert Kitzhaber, *Rhetoric in American Colleges, 1850–1900* (Dallas: Southern Methodist University Press, 1990), 49–52; Cmiel, *Democratic Eloquence,* 40; Davis, *Intellectual Life in Jefferson's Virginia,* 366–67; and Bigelow, *Rhetoric and American Poetry,* 33.

28. Knapp, *Lectures on American Literature,* 218. Also see Rush, "The American Lounger," 1; and "Intelligence," 502–3. On the diffusion of rhetorical texts see Marie Hochmuth and Richard Murphy, "Rhetorical and Elocutionary Training in Nineteenth Century Colleges," in *History of Speech Education in America,* ed. Karl R. Wallace (New York: Appleton-Century-Crofts, 1954), 161–63; and Thomas M. Conley, *Rhetoric in the European Tradition* (New York: Longman, 1990), 248. On college rhetorical education see Halloran, "Rhetoric in American College Curriculum," 250–54; Howe, *Political Culture of the Whigs,* 25; Warren, *Culture of Eloquence,* 10–11; Clark and Halloran, "Transformations in Public Discourse," in *Oratorical Culture in Nineteenth-Century America,* 2–3; Ronald F. Reid, "Edward Everett and Neoclassical Oratory in Genteel America," in *Oratorical Culture in Nineteenth-Century America,* 38; S. Michael Halloran, "From Rhetoric to Composition: The Teaching of Writing in America to 1900," in *A Short History of Writing Instruction from Ancient Greece to Twentieth-Century America,* ed. James J. Murphy (Davis, Calif.: Hermagoras Press, 1990), 177; S. Michael Halloran, "Rhetoric and the English Department," *Rhetoric Society Quarterly* 17 (winter 1987): 8; and John P. Hosher, "American Contributions to Rhetorical Theory and Homiletics," in *History of Speech Education in America,* 131.

29. The text that inspired Douglass was Caleb Bingham's *Columbian Orator.* See Gregory P. Lampe, *Frederick Douglass: Freedom's Voice, 1818–1845* (East Lansing: Michigan State University Press, 1998), 12, 9–13.

30. See, for example, [Edward Everett], "Speeches of Henry Clay," *North American Review* 25 (October 1827): 448; [Channing], review of *Philosophical Essays*, 380; "Oratory," 61; "Political Education—Statesmanship," 362; [William Wirt], *The Old Bachelor* (Richmond, Va.: Enquirer Press, 1814), 196–99; "Eloquence and Eloquent Men," *New-England Magazine* 2 (February 1832): 99–100; and Judson, "Eloquence," 539.

31. [Everett], "Speeches of Henry Clay," 427–29, 430–33; Wood, "Democratization of the American Mind," in *Leadership in the American Revolution*, 73ff; Cmiel, *Democratic Eloquence*, 15.

32. On the development of print-directed oratory see [Everett], "Speeches of Henry Clay," 425, 430–33; [George Stillman Hillard], review of *Speeches on Various Occasions*, by Edward Everett, *North American Review* 44 (July 1837): 138; and Alexis de Tocqueville, *Democracy in America*, trans. Henry Reeve (1838; reprint, New York: Alfred A. Knopf, 1945), 90–93. On the instantaneous reporting of congressional debates in the 1850s, see Robertson, *Language of Democracy*, 15, 83. On the public influence of great debates in the antebellum United States, also see my "The Narration of Essence: Salmon P. Chase's Senate Oration Against the Kansas-Nebraska Act" *Communication Studies* 48 (fall 1997): 234–53.

33. [Rush], "The American Lounger," 1; "Intelligence," 503; Adams, *Lectures on Rhetoric and Oratory*, 1:19; Ralph Waldo Emerson, "Eloquence," in *The Complete Works of Ralph Waldo Emerson*, Concord edition (Boston: Houghton Mifflin, 1912), 7:63.

34. "Popular Eloquence," *Southern and Western Literary Messenger and Review* 13 (December 1847): 741. Also see John Williamson Crary Sr., *Reminiscences of the Old South from 1834 to 1866* (Pensacola, Fla.: Perdido Bay Press, 1984), 47–48; Emerson, "Eloquence," in *Complete Works*, 7:65; "Remarks on the Eloquence of Debate," *New-England Magazine and Review* 13 (December 1847): 106; Judson, "Eloquence," 539; "Eloquence," *American Quarterly Review* 21 (June 1837): 296; "Eloquence," *Southern Literary Messenger*, 165–66; and "Forensic Eloquence," *Knickerbocker or New-York Monthly Magazine* 21 (June 1843): 532–33.

35. See, for example, "The Schools of Modern Eloquence," 259; "Eloquence," *Southern Literary Messenger*, 164–65; "Popular Eloquence," 740–41; [Howard], "Ancient and Modern Eloquence," 180–81; William Wirt, *Sketches of the Life and Character of Patrick Henry* (Philadelphia: James Webster, 1817), 36, 47, 49, 106–7; "How Shall Life by Made the Most of?" *American Review*, 416; [Linn], *Miscellaneous Works*, 28; Adams, *Lectures on Rhetoric and Oratory*, 1:72; Bingham, "Extract from an Oration on Eloquence," in *Columbian Orator*, 31–32; "Inchiquin: The Jesuit Letters," 392–93; "Remarks on Eloquence of Debate," 107.

36. See, for example, "Inchiquin: The Jesuit Letters," 392; and "Remarks on Eloquence of Debate," 108–12. On Chatham see, for example, T. Romeyn Beck, "The Earl Chatham," *Knickerbocker or New-York Monthly Magazine* 36 (July 1850): 39–48; "Characteristics of the Statesman," 127; and "Popular Eloquence," 741. On Burke see, for example, "Eloquence," *American Quarterly Review*, 316–20; "The Schools of Modern Eloquence," 264; and "Rhetoric," *Port Folio* 5 (February 1811): 118.

37. [Gilmer], *Sketches of American Orators*, 45; [Howard], "Ancient and Modern Eloquence," 180, 182. On the profound shaping influence of British oratory on the American character see, for instance, Alexander Hamilton Bullock, *Intellectual Leadership in American History: An Address Delivered before the Society of Phi Beta Kappa, at Brown University, Providence, June 18, 1875* (Worcester, Mass.: Charles Hamilton Printer, 1875), 27–28.

38. [Everett], "Speeches of Henry Clay," 429; "American Eloquence," *United States Review* 34 (July 1854): 40; Harriet Martineau, *Retrospect of Western Travel* (London: Saunders and Otley, 1838), 2:47; [Abraham Hayward], "American Orators and Statesmen," *Quarterly Review* 67 (1841): 20, 51; Alexander Mackay, *The Western World, or Travels in the United States in 1846-7* (London: Richard Bentley, 1849), 1:293. Also see "American Oratory," *Once a Week*, 3d ser., 2 (29 January 1869): 576; and Tocqueville, *Democracy in America*, 90–93.

39. See especially [Story], "Statesmen—Their Rareness and Importance," 89; and "How Shall Life Be Made the Most of?" 419–20. Also see Knapp, *Lectures on American Literature*, 217–18; James Dunwoodie Brownson DeBow, "Characteristics of the Statesman,"

DeBow's Review 20 (January 1855): 37–39, 47, 49–54; and John Quincy Adams, *Memoirs of John Quincy Adams, Comprising Portions of His Diary from 1795–1848* (Freeport, N.Y.: Books for Libraries Press, 1969), 9:311–12, 361. On the Whig view of statesmanship, see Thomas Brown, *Politics and Statesmanship: Essays on the American Whig Party* (New York: Columbia University Press, 1985), 8–12, 20–21, 172, 189; and Marshall, "The Strange Stillbirth of the Whig Party," 462–63. On Southern views see Greenberg, *Masters and Statesmen*, 4–7, 12; Brown, *Politics and Statesmanship*, 159–69; and William Barney, *The Road to Secession: A New Perspective on the Old South* (New York: Praeger, 1972), 137–39. For the contrasting Jacksonian view, which did not rely on the leadership of great men, see Lawrence Frederick Kohl, *The Politics of Individualism: Parties and the American Character in the Jacksonian Era* (New York: Oxford University Press, 1989), 125–33.

40. See, for instance, "Political Education—Statesmanship," 355; "Characteristics of the Statesman," 107–8, 114, 128; "Eloquence," *Southern Literary Messenger* 1 (December 1834): 165; "Character of a Perfect Statesman," *New-England Magazine* 1 (August 1831): 142–44; "American Oratory," *Southern Quarterly Review* 5 (April 1841): 362–65, 372; [Alexander Hill Everett], "Life of Henry Clay," *North American Review* 33 (October 1831): 395; [Story], "Statesmen—Their Rareness and Importance," 93; "Mr. Clay—The Texas Question," *American Review* 1 (January 1845): 77; and [Salmon P. Chase], "Life and Character of Henry Brougham," *North American Review* 33 (July 1831): 257.

41. See, for example, the depiction of Calhoun in "American Oratory," *Southern Quarterly Review*, 366. Also see "Popular Eloquence," 739.

42. Henry Coleman, "On Eloquence," *New-England Magazine* 2 (May 1832): 378; "Modern Oratory," 370; "Eloquence," *American Quarterly Review*, 300; [Edward Tyrrell Channing], "The Abuses of Political Discussion," *North American Review and Miscellaneous Journal* 4 (January 1817): 197; [George Frederick Holmes], "The Athenian Orators," *Southern Quarterly Review* 20 (October 1851): 374–75, 377. See also "Thoughts on the Times," *Port Folio* 3 (30 April 1803): 1; "Characteristics of the Statesman," 118, 128–29; Adams, *Lectures on Rhetoric and Oratory*, 1:65; review of *Education in South Carolina*, by Thomas Cooper, *North American Review* 14 (April 1822): 317; [Channing], review of *Philosophical Essays*, 380; and [Mason and Spooner], "Modern Oratory," 214.

43. See review of *Education in South Carolina*, by Thomas Cooper, 312; "Political Education—Statesmanship," 360; Judson, "Eloquence," 537. Also see Knapp, *Lectures on American Literature*, 213, 220; Adams, *Lectures on Rhetoric and Oratory*, 1:65; and Charles H. Lyon, "Oratory," *Knickerbocker or New-York Monthly Magazine* 17 (February 1841): 139–40. For modern discussions of this ideal in antebellum America see Cmiel, *Democratic Eloquence*, 14, 24–26; Howe, *Political Culture of the Whigs*, 215; Davis, *Intellectual Life in Jefferson's Virginia*, 366–67; and Gustafson, *Representative Words*, 118–21. There were attempts to modernize the classical statesman, most notably by William Wirt. See Wirt, *Patrick Henry*, 43–67; and [Wirt], *The Old Bachelor*, 196–99. For discussion of Wirt's project see Davis, *Intellectual Life in Jefferson's Virginia*, 376ff; Taylor, *Cavalier and Yankee*, 83–89; Gustafson, *Representative Words*, 188–91, 232–33; and Theodore R. Marmor, *The Career of John C. Calhoun: Politician, Social Critic, Political Philosopher* (New York: Garland Publications, 1988), 22.

44. This undercurrent of unease about degenerate oratory was also apparent in fiction, especially in the works of Hawthorne and Melville. See David Warren Shawn, "The Transformation of Oratory in Antebellum America: Democrats, Demagogues, and the Quest for Citizenship" (Ph.D. diss., Boston University, 1998), 207–8, 218–22, 276–84. This was also a major theme for Thoreau. Warren, *Culture of Eloquence*, 15–16.

45. "American Eloquence," *Western Review and Miscellaneous Magazine* 2 (March 1820): 108. See especially [Mason and Spooner], "Modern Oratory," 212; and [Franklin Dexter], "Fine Arts," *North American Review* 26 (January 1828): 219.

46. "Political Symptoms and Popular Rights," *American Quarterly Review* 19 (June 1836): 367–68. On the reaction against colloquial and passionate language see Cmiel, *Democratic Eloquence*, 55–56, 61, 72–72; and Robertson, *Language of Democracy*, 73–74. There was an older disagreement between Jeffersonians and Federalists over the use of passionate language in public discourse. See Marmor, *Calhoun*, 20–24. On antiparty thought in the Anglo-American political culture of the eighteenth and early nineteenth century, see Ketcham, *Presidents above Party*, vii–xi, 4, 157–58; 201, 204–5, 224, 228.

47. Daniel Webster, "Whig Principles and Purposes," in *The Works of Daniel Webster*, 7th ed. (Boston: Little, Brown, and Co., 1853), 2:51; Daniel Webster, "Veto of the Bank Bill," 1:502–39, in *The Papers of Daniel Webster, Series Four: Speeches and Formal Writings*, ed. Charles M. Wiltse (Hanover, N.H.: Dartmouth College/University Press of New England, 1986), 1:528, 529; [Alexander Hill Everett], "General View of the Course of Administration," in *The American Annual Register for the Year 1832–33*, vol. 8 (New York: William Jackson, 1835), 12. Also see "Remarks on Eloquence of Debate," 116; "The Administration: The Party," *American Whig Review* 15 (April 1852): 293; William Henry Harrison, "Inaugural Address," 4 March 1841, in *A Compilation of the Messages and Papers of the Presidents* (Washington, D.C.: Bureau of National Literature, 1897), 5:1872–73; and Cmiel, *Democratic Eloquence*, 63–64.

48. Christine Oravec, "The Democratic Critics: An Alternative American Rhetorical Tradition of the Nineteenth Century," *Rhetorica* 4 (1986): 405. For Whig critiques of Jacksonian rhetoric see "Political Symptoms and Popular Rights," 369; and [Everett], "General View of the Course," 293. On Jacksonian rhetoric also see Thomas M. Lessl, "Andrew Jackson," in *U.S. Presidents as Orators*, ed. Halford Ryan (Westport, Conn.: Greenwood, 1995), 65–76. On the Whig reaction against Jacksonian rhetoric and the Whig view of deliberation see Marshall, "The Strange Stillbirth of the Whig Party," 447; and Brown, *Politics and Statesmanship*, 49.

49. Fears that party politics would destroy genuine deliberation did not begin with Jackson. "Whether the age of oratory will ever return I know not," John Adams declared in 1806. "At present its seems to be of little use, for every man in our public assemblies will vote with his party, and his vote is counted before he takes his seat" (John Adams to Benjamin Rush, 23 July 1806, in *The Spur of Fame*, 59). Also see John Adams to Benjamin Rush, 19 September 1806, *The Spur of Fame*, 64. The ideal of independent legislative deliberation, where public decisions were adjusted and public policy decisions actually made in the course of debate, was expressed repeatedly in the antebellum period. For especially lucid statements of the ideal see Adams, *Lectures on Rhetoric and Oratory*, 1:23, 266; Thomas Cooper, *Two Essays: 1. On the Foundation of Civil Government, 2. On the Constitution of the United States* (Columbia, S.C.: D. and J. M. Faust, 1826), 34; Witherspoon, "Lectures on Eloquence," in *The Selected Writings of John Witherspoon*, 305; "Eloquence," *American Quarterly Review*, 319; "Modern Oratory," 371; [Howard], "Ancient and Modern Eloquence," 170; and [John Gorham Palfrey], "Congressional Eloquence," *North American Review* 52 (January 1841): 143–44.

50. [James Russell Lowell], "The President on the Stump," *North American Review* 102 (April 1866): 538. Also see [Howard], "Ancient and Modern Eloquence," 171; and Daniel Webster, "The Rhode Island Government," January 1848, in *Works of Daniel Webster*, 6:225, 227.

51. For statements of this view, see Adams, *Lectures on Rhetoric and Oratory*, 1:65; and "Modern Oratory," 371.

52. William Tudor, "A Discourse to Have Been Delivered before the Society of Phi Beta Kappa on the Anniversary of the Day after Commencement at Cambridge, August 30, 1810," *Monthly Anthology and Boston Review* 9 (September 1810): 155; [Everett], "Webster's Speeches," 244–45. On the early development of the most characteristic variant of the genre, the Fourth of July oration, see "The Festival of Independence in Connecticut," *Monthly Magazine and American Review* 1 (July 1799): 241–44; Peter Thatcher, "An Address to the Members of the Massachusetts Fire Society, May 31, 1805," *Monthly Anthology and Boston Review* 2 (June 1805): 319–21; and John Adams to H. Niles, 13 February 1818, *Works of John Adams*, 10:284. On the general development of commemorative speaking in antebellum America see Baskerville, *People's Voice*, 37–39, 40–44.

53. Marmor, *Calhoun*, 28–29; Wood, "Democratization of the American Mind," in *Leadership in the American Revolution*, 80; Howe, *Political Culture of the Whigs*, 220–22.

54. "Calhoun's Speech against the Conquest of Mexico," *American Whig Review* 7 (April 1848): 225; Daniel Webster, "Mass Meeting at Saratoga," 22 August 1840, in *Works of Daniel Webster*, 2:34. The idea that social unity could be created through rhetoric distinguished the Whigs from the Democrats. See also Howe, *Political Culture of the Whigs*, 27; and Warren, *Culture of Eloquence*, 4–5, 15–16, 27, 143.

55. By all accounts, Webster's popularized style was extremely effective. Sydney Nathans, *Daniel Webster and Jacksonian Democracy* (Baltimore: Johns Hopkins University Press, 1973), 131; Cmiel, *Democratic Eloquence*, 61. For an account of the campaign see Robert Gray Gunderson, *The Log-Cabin Campaign* (Lexington: University of Kentucky Press, 1957).

56. Adams, *Memoirs of John Quincy Adams*, 10:352–53, 355–56.

57. [Howard], "Ancient and Modern Eloquence," 169.

58. Daniel Webster, "Whig Principles and Purposes," in *Works of Daniel Webster*, 2:47.

59. Howe, *Political Culture of the Whigs*, 216; Brown, *Politics and Statesmanship*, 217; Robert A. Ferguson, *Law and Letters in American Culture* (Cambridge: Harvard University Press, 1984), 211, 237; Nathans, *Daniel Webster and Jacksonian Democracy*, 7. See also Kohl, *Politics of Individualism*, 133–35; and Ketcham, *Presidents above Party*, 174–75.

60. Edwin Black has provocatively argued that in linguistic universe of Whig rhetoric, sovereignty of self was given over to the great orator. Edwin Black, "The Sentimental Style as Escapism, or The Devil with Daniel Webster," in *Form and Genre: Shaping Rhetorical Action*, ed. Karlyn Kohrs Campbell and Kathleen Hall Jamieson (Falls Church, Va.: Speech Communication Association, 1978), 78.

61. Dorsey Gardner, "Oratory and Journalism," *North American Review* 114 (January 1872): 86–87; Nathanial Hawthorne, "The French and Italian Notebooks," 8 July 1858, in *The Centenary Edition of the Works of Nathanial Hawthorne*, ed. William Charaut et al. (Columbus: Ohio State University Press, 1962–88), 14:367; William Mathews, *Oratory and Orators* (Chicago: S. C. Griggs and Co., 1878), 54; Howe, *Political Culture of the Whigs*, 303.

62. For commentary on the increasing irrelevance of congressional oratory see "The Gift of Gab," *Nation* 3 (26 July 1866): 75; [E. L. Godkin], "Rhetorical Training," *Nation* 20 (4 May 1875): 145; "Oratory and Debating," *Saturday Review* 61 (29 May 1886): 741; Gamaliel Bradford, "The Progress of Civil Service Reform," *International Review* 13 (September 1882): 268; "Culture and Politics: The Way to Avoid Becoming a Political Pessimist," *Boston Herald*, 4 June 1882, 9; [Jacob D. Cox], "The House of Representatives," *Nation* 26 (4 April 1878): 227; [Arthur George Sedgwick], "The Disappearance of 'Great Men' from Public Life," *Nation* 32 (3 February 1881): 71; and [E. L. Godkin], "The Way Congress Does Business," *Nation* 16 (27 February 1873): 146. For secondary accounts of the postwar decline of congressional oratory also see Stephen E. Lucas, "Debate and Oratory," in *The Encyclopedia of the United States Congress*, ed. Donald G. Bacon, Roger H. Davidson, and Morton Keller (New York: Simon and Schuster, 1995), 2:612; Baskerville, *People's Voice*, 93; Kenneth G. Hance, Homer O. Henderson, and Edwin W. Schoenberger, "The Later National Period, 1860–1930," in *A History of Criticism of American Public Address, Volumes 1–2*, ed. William Norwood Brigance (New York: McGraw Hill, 1943), 1:136–44; and Robert Weibe, *The Search for Order, 1877–1920* (New York: Hill and Wang, 1967), 33–34.

63. [E. L. Godkin], "Great Speeches," *Nation* 44 (14 April 1887): 311. Also see Arthur Reed Kimball, "The Passing Art of Oratory," *Outlook* 58 (29 January 1898): 280; Ralph Curtis Ringwald, *Modern American Oratory: Seven Representative Orations* (New York: Henry Holt and Co., 1898), 40–43; and "After-Dinner Oratory," *Scribner's Magazine* 21 (February 1897): 254–55.

64. Joseph E. Gould, *The Chautauqua Movement: An Episode in the Continuing American Revolution* (New York: State University of New York, 1961), 75. Also see Frederick J. Antczak, *Thought and Character: The Rhetoric of Democratic Education* (Ames: Iowa State University Press, 1985), 74.

65. Cmiel, *Democratic Eloquence*, 240; [Woodrow Wilson], editorial, *Princetonian*, 27 February 1879, in *Papers of Woodrow Wilson*, ed. Arthur S. Link et al. (Princeton: Princeton University Press, 1966–94), 1:461. Also see Charles Francis Adams, *An Address Delivered at Amherst before Members of the Social Union, 7 July, 1875* (Cambridge, Mass.: Riverside Press, 1875); Kitzhaber, *Rhetoric in American Colleges*, 31, 141, 175, 204; Halloran, "From Rhetoric to Composition," 175–76; Halloran, "Rhetoric in American College Curriculum," 250–54; Halloran, "Rhetoric and the English Department," 5, 8; Harold Monroe Jordan, "Rhetorical Education in American Colleges and Universities, 1850–1915" (Ph.D. diss., Northwestern University, 1952), 41, 64–65; Donald C. Stuart,

"The Nineteenth Century," in *The Present State of Scholarship in Historical and Contemporary Rhetoric*, ed. Winifred Bryan Horner (Columbia: University of Missouri Press, 1983), 137–38; Giles Wilkeson Gray, "Some Teachers in the Transition to Twentieth-Century Speech Education," in *History of Speech Education in America*, ed. Karl R. Wallace (New York: Appleton-Century-Crofts, 1954), 424; and Conley, *Rhetoric in the European Tradition*, 248.

66. On the history of debate societies in general see David Potter, "The Literary Society," in *History of Speech Education in America*, 238–58. Also see Jordan, "Rhetorical Education in American Colleges and Universities," 353; Thomas Jefferson Wertenbaker, *Princeton, 1746–1896* (Princeton: Princeton University Press, 1946), 203, 329; and Jacob N. Beam, *The American Whig Society of Princeton University* (Princeton: American Whig Society, 1933).

67. A. E. Whitehead, "William E. Borah," in *A History and Criticism of Public Address, Volume 3*, ed. Marie Hochmuth (New York: Longmans, Green and Co., 1955), 367; as quoted in Thomas Richard Ross, *Jonathan Prentiss Dolliver: A Study in Political Integrity and Independence* (Iowa City: State Historical Society of Iowa, 1958), 31, 37–38. On the rhetorical educations of these orators see, for instance, Albert Beveridge, *The Art of Public Speaking* (Boston: Houghton Mifflin, 1924), 4–15; Herold Truslow Ross, "Albert J. Beveridge," in *History and Criticism of Public Address*, 2:919–22; Carol Lahman, "Robert M. La Follette, in *History and Criticism of Public Address*, 2:948–51, 952–64; and Myron G. Phillips, "William Jennings Bryan," in *History and Criticism of Public Address*, 2:894–97, 900–4.

68. For a much more comprehensive account of Wilson, see my "Woodrow Wilson and the Lost World of the Oratorical Statesman" (Ph.D. diss., University of Wisconsin, Madison, 1999).

69. Stockton Axson, *"Brother Woodrow": A Memoir of Woodrow Wilson*, ed. Arthur S. Link (Princeton: Princeton University Press, 1993); Joel L. Swabb Jr., "The Rhetorical Theory of Rev. Joseph Ruggles Wilson, D.D." (Ph.D. diss., Ohio State University, 1971).

70. "Diary of Dr. Cary T. Grayson," 27 May 1919, in *Papers of Woodrow Wilson*, 59:528; "A Memorandum by Cary Travers Grayson," 30 March 1920, in *Papers of Woodrow Wilson*, 65:145; Axson, *"Brother Woodrow,"* 20.

71. Woodrow Wilson to Robert Bridges, 1 January 1881, in *Papers of Woodrow Wilson*, 2:10; [Woodrow Wilson], editorial, *Princetonian*, 7 June 1877, in *Papers of Woodrow Wilson*, 1:274–75. For first-hand accounts of Wilson's training see Robert H. McCarter, interview by Henry Wilkinson Bragdon, 15 July 1940, Henry Wilkinson Bragdon Collection, Mudd Library, Princeton University, box 63, folder 12; Fletcher Durell, "Recollections of Woodrow Wilson by a College Classmate," Bragdon Collection, Princeton University, box 62, folder 3; Edward P. Davis, "Memorandum Concerning Woodrow Wilson," 1925, Ray Stannard Baker Papers, Library of Congress, container 104; Woodrow Wilson, "Shorthand Diary," 21 July 1876, in *Papers of Woodrow Wilson*, 1:157; Woodrow Wilson to Robert Bridges, 10 August 1878, in *Papers of Woodrow Wilson*, 1:395; and Woodrow Wilson to Robert Bridges, 24 May 1881, in *Papers of Woodrow Wilson*, 2:70.

72. Maurice Eugine Marie Bautain, *The Art of Extempore Speaking: Hints for the Pulpit, the Senate, and the Bar* (1857; reprint, New York: Charles Scribner, 1859); [Woodrow Wilson], "Constitution for the Liberal Debating Club," in *Papers of Woodrow Wilson*, 1:245–49; [Woodrow Wilson], "Social Debating Clubs," *Princetonian*, 6 February 1879, in *Papers of Woodrow Wilson*, 1:455; Jessie Bones Brower to Ray Stannard Baker, 11 October 1925, Baker Papers, Library of Congress, container 101. On Bautain's rhetoric see Kathleen Kerwin Pendergast, "The Origin and Organogenesis of the Rhetorical Theory of the Abbé Bautain" (Ph.D. diss., Syracuse University, 1974).

73. Woodrow Wilson, "Cabinet Government in the United States," *International Review* 6 (August 1879), in *Papers of Woodrow Wilson*, 1:493–510; Woodrow Wilson, "Congressional Government," 1 October 1879, in *Papers of Woodrow Wilson*, 1:548–74.

74. Wilson notebook, Woodrow Wilson Papers, Manuscript Division, Library of Congress, Washington, D.C., ser. 1, reel 1.

75. Stephen H. Browne, "Contesting Political Oratory in Nineteenth-Century England," *Communication Studies* 43 (1992): 191–202.

76. C. B. Roylance Kent, "The Platform as a Political Institution," *Living Age* 237 (25 April 1903): 243–44, 247. On the dominance of extraparliamentary oratory in Britain also see Henry Jephson, *The Platform: Its Rise and Progress* (London: Macmillan, 1892), 2:606–7, 508–23, 564–67, 603–4; [James Bryce], "Political Influence of the Press in England," *Nation* 37 (29 November 1883): 444–45; and Earl Curzon of Kedleston, *Modern Parliamentary Eloquence: The Rede Lecture, University of Cambridge, November 6, 1913* (London: Macmillan and Co., 1914), 15–16. For an account of the operation of the oratorical agencies that transcribed and sold extraparliamentary speeches to the press, see Alfred Kinnear, "The Trade in Great Men's Speeches," *Contemporary Review* 75 (March 1899): 439–44. The best contemporary scholarship on the rise of the platform system in late-nineteenth-century Britain has been done by Matthew. See H. C. G. Matthew, "Rhetoric and Politics in Great Britain, 1860–1950," in *Politics and Social Change in Modern Britain*, ed. P. J. Waller (Sussex: Harvest Press Limited, 1987), 34–58; and H. C. G. Matthew, *Gladstone, 1875–1898* (Oxford: Clarendon Press, 1995), 41–51, 93–97. Also see Robert Kelley, *The Transatlantic Persuasion: The Liberal-Democratic Mind in the Age of Gladstone* (New York: Alfred A. Knopf, 1969), 202–3, 221–23, 231–34.

77. On the fixation of educated Americans on English models during the Gilded Age see John Tomsich, *A Genteel Endeavor: American Culture and Politics in the Gilded Age* (Stanford, Calif.: Stanford University Press, 1971), 75–76; and Morton Keller, *Affairs of State: Public Life in Late Nineteenth Century America* (Cambridge: Harvard University Press, 1979), 292.

78. On the cultural importance of Gladstone's oratorical success in late-Victorian Britain see Patrick Joyce, *Visions of the People: Industrial England and the Question of Class, 1848–1919* (Cambridge: Cambridge University Press, 1991), 38–55; James Vernon, *Politics and the People: A Study of English Political Culture, c. 1815–1867* (Cambridge: Cambridge University Press, 1993), 117–25, 146–51, 251–53; Eugenio F. Biagini, *Liberty, Retrenchment, and Reform: Popular Liberalism in the Age of Gladstone, 1860–1880* (Cambridge: Cambridge University Press, 1992), 370–425; Patrick Joyce, *Democratic Subjects: The Self and the Social in Nineteenth-Century England* (Cambridge: Cambridge University Press, 1994), 88–104, 213–24; and John Belchem and James Epstein, "The Nineteenth-Century Gentleman Leader Revisited," *Social Policy* 22 (1997): 174–93.

79. [E. L. Godkin], "Rhetorical Training," 75; William Mathews, *Words: Their Use and Abuse* (Chicago: S. C. Griggs and Company, 1876), 154. Also see "American Oratory," *Once a Week*, 577; David Swing, *Club Essays* (Chicago: Jansen, McClurg and Co., 1881), 163; James H. McBath, "The Platform and Public Thought," in *The Rhetoric of Protest and Reform, 1878–1898*, ed. Paul Boase (Athens: Ohio University Press, 1980), 320–41; Buell, "New England Oratory," in *New England Literary Culture*, 162–65; Keller, *Affairs of State*, 240, 246; and Weibe, *Search for Order*, 33–34. For later recollections of the importance of oratory in small towns see Beveridge, *Art of Public Speaking*, 4–9; and Clarence Darrow, *Farmington* (Chicago: A. C. McClurg and Co., 1904), 203–6.

80. Lois Scoggins Self, "Agrarian Chautauqua: The Lecture System of the Southern Farmers' Alliance Movement" (Ph.D., diss., University of Wisconsin, Madison, 1981), 64; Donald H. Ecroyd, "The Populist Spellbinders," in *Rhetoric of Protest and Reform*, 132–52; Ross, "Albert J. Beveridge," in *History and Criticism of Public Address*, 919.

81. On Ingersoll's influence see, for example, Beveridge, *Art of Public Speaking*, 10–13; and Carl R. Burgchardt, "The Will, the People, and the Law: A Rhetorical Biography of Robert M. La Follette, Sr." (Ph.D. diss., University of Wisconsin, Madison, 1982), 7–8. On Depew's career see Baskerville, *People's Voice*, 108–10; and Robert T. Oliver, *A History of Public Speaking in America* (Boston: Allyn and Bacon, 1965), 356–57.

82. Charles Francis Adams, *An Address Delivered at Amherst before Members of the Social Union*, 11, 13, 25, 30; Charles Dudley Warner, "What Is Your Culture to Me?" *Scribner's Monthly* 4 (August 1872): 471–72. Also see, for example, Henry Ward Beecher's Whiggish book on oratory, which went through numerous reprints throughout the late nineteenth and early twentieth century. Henry Ward Beecher, *Oratory* (1876; reprint, Philadelphia: Penn Publishing, 1897).

83. Boorstin, *The National Experience*, 310; Irving Bartlett, "Daniel Webster as a Symbolic Hero," *New England Quarterly* 45 (1972): 484–507.

84. Warner, "What Is Your Culture to Me?" 470; Emerson, "Eloquence," in *Complete Works*, 63; La Follette, quoted in Burgchardt, "Rhetorical Biography of Robert M. La Follette," v. For general surveys of oratory in the Progressive Era, see Baskerville, *People's Voice*, 115–39; Oliver, *History of Public Speaking in America*, 473–517; Cmiel, *Democratic Eloquence*, 248–52; Daniel J. Boorstin, *The Americans: The Democratic Experience* (New York: Random House, 1973), 462–74; and Hance, Henderson, and Schoenberger, "The Later National Period," in *History of Criticism of American Public Address*, 111–52.

85. Chauncey M. Depew, foreword to *The Library of Oratory: Ancient and Modern* (New York: E. R. Du Mont, 1902), 1:iii; Curtis Guild Jr., "The Spellbinder," *Scribner's Magazine* 32 (November 1902): 565. For contemporaneous discussion of the decline literature see Kimball, "The Passing Art of Oratory," 280; Harry Thurston Peck, "Some Notes on Political Oratory," *Bookman* 4 (November 1896): 208–18; Henry L. Dawes, "Has Oratory Declined?" *Forum* 18 (October 1894): 146; E. Jay Edwards, "Is Oratory a Lost Art?" *Chautauquan* 14 (January 1892): 445; [Rollo Ogden], "Effective Public Speaking," *Nation* 76 (15 January 1903): 44–45; Brander Matthews, "The Four Ways of Delivering an Address," *Cosmopolitan* 25 (July 1898): 331–32; Edward Everett Hale, "Memories of a Hundred Years: The Orators-Modern American Oratory," *Outlook* 71 (7 June 1902): 405; "Oratorical Traditions," *Current Literature* 30 (June 1901): 642–43; Guild, "The Spellbinder," 561; William O. Stoddard, "Orators," *Outlook* 48 (30 December 1893): 1233; Joel Benton, "Reminiscences of Eminent Lecturers," *Harper's New Monthly Magazine* 96 (March 1898): 603; "Women to the Rescue," *Munsey's Magazine* 25 (May 1901): 293; Lorenzo Sears, *The History of Oratory from the Age of Pericles to the Present Time* (Chicago: S. C. Griggs and Co., 1896), 415; Francis Rogers, "The Neglected Art of Oratory," *Scribner's Magazine* 47 (March 1910): 374, 376; "Oratory and Eloquence," editorial, *New York Times*, 3 September 1919, 12; and Champ Clark, *My Quarter Century of American Politics* (New York: Harper and Brothers, 1920), 2:346.

86. Peck, "Some Notes on Political Oratory," 208. The statistics on the extent of Bryan's 1896 tour come from Phillips, "William Jennings Bryan," in *History and Criticism of Public Address*, 904.

87. Luther B. Little, "Campaign Orators," *Munsey's Magazine* 24 (November 1900): 281; William Dudley Foulke, "The Spellbinders," *Forum* 30 (February 1901): 658–72; Guild, "The Spellbinder," 561, 565; Michael A. Weatherson and Hal W. Bochin, *Hiram Johnson: Political Revivalist* (Lanham, Md.: University Press of America, 1995), 60; Francis L. Broderick, *Progressivism at Risk: Electing a President in 1912* (New York: Greenwood, 1989), 114–21, 172–80. For the development of the presidential campaign tour in the late nineteenth century, see Michael McGerr, *The Decline of Popular Politics: The American North, 1865 to 1928* (New York: Oxford University Press, 1986), 143–44.

88. Cleveland Frederick Bacon, "Itinerant Speechmaking in the Last Campaign," *Arena* 25 (April 1901): 418. Also see Thomas Brackett Reed, "Oratory Past and Present," in *Modern Eloquence*, ed. Reed (Philadelphia: John D. Morris and Co., 1900), 4:vi.

89. On the historical importance of the 1912 campaign, also see my "The 1912 Election and the Rhetorical Foundations of the Liberal State," *Rhetoric and Public Affairs* 3 (fall 2000): 363–95.

90. "Roosevelt Party Find Wilson In Lead," *New York Times*, 23 September 1912, 2; Theodore Roosevelt to William Dudley Foulke, 1 July 1912, *The Letters of Theodore Roosevelt*, ed. Elting Morison, John M. Blum, and Alfred D. Chandler Jr. (Cambridge: Harvard University Press, 1951–54), 7:568; Theodore Roosevelt to Horace Plunkett, 3 August 1912, *Letters of Theodore Roosevelt*, 7:591, 593, 594; Theodore Roosevelt to Arthur Hamilton Lee, 14 August 1912, *Letters of Theodore Roosevelt*, 7:598.

91. John Milton Cooper Jr., *The Warrior and the Priest: Theodore Roosevelt and Woodrow Wilson* (Cambridge: Harvard University Press, 1983), 140.

92. Gould, *Chautauqua Movement*, 75; Antczak, *Thought and Character*, 74.

93. Gould, *Chautauqua Movement*, 81–82, 95–96; John E. Tapia, *Circuit Chautauqua: From Rural Education to Popular Entertainment in Early Twentieth Century America* (Jefferson, N.C.: McFarland and Co., 1997), 53–57, 76–77, 78–80; Antczak, *Thought and Character*, 80–85; Mary Ann D. Hartman, "The Chautauqua Speaking of Robert La Follette" (Ph.D. diss., Bowling Green State University, 1969), 15, 43–44, 47; R. B. Tozier, "A Short Life-History of the Chautauqua," *American Journal of Sociology* 40 (July 1934): 71;

John E. Tapia, "Circuit Chautauqua Program Broachers: A Study in Social and Intellectual History," *Quarterly Journal of Speech* 67 (1981): 167.

94. Harry P. Harrison (as told to Karl Detzer), *Culture under the Canvass: The Story of Tent Chautauqua* (New York: Hastings House, 1958), 117; Robert Stuart Mac Arthur, "Chautauqua Assemblies and Political Ambitions," *World To-Day* 9 (October 1905): 1075–76; French Strother, "The Great American Forum," *World's Work* 24 (September 1912): 553; William Allen White, quoted in Tapia, *Circuit Chautauqua*, 55. Also see David P. Thelen, *Robert M. La Follette and the Insurgent Spirit* (Madison, Wis.: University of Wisconsin Press, 1985), 41; Paul M. Pearson, "The Chautauqua Movement," *Annals of the American Academy of Political and Social Science* 40 (March 1912): 211–16; J. Anthony Lukas, *Big Trouble* (New York: Simon and Schuster, 1997), 432; and Broderick, *Progressivism at Risk*, 174, 177.

95. "Campaign Orators," *Century* 60 (August 1900): 634; Reed, "Oratory Past and Present," in *Modern Eloquence*, 4:vi.

96. Burgchardt, "Rhetorical Biography of Robert M. La Follette," 129, 112–15, 142–45, 154–62, 171–75, 190–91; Weatherson and Bochin, *Hiram Johnson*, 26–34; Robert E. Burke, "The Political Oratory of Hiram Johnson," *Journal of the West* 27 (1988): 20–27; Ross, *Dolliver*, 38–39, 43–76, 158–62, 231–35, 284–85; Frank Parker Stockbridge, "How Woodrow Wilson Won His Nomination," *Current History* 20 (July 1924): 561; Frank Parker Stockbridge, "With Governor Wilson in the West," *World's Work* 22 (August 1911): 14713–16; James Kerney, *The Political Education of Woodrow Wilson* (New York: Century Co., 1926), 132–33; [Rollo Ogden], "New Men in Public Life," *Nation* 70 (March 1900): 216–17. On the rise of a new crop of leaders based on oratorical ability around the turn of the century see John Milton Cooper Jr., *Pivotal Decades: The United States, 1900–1920* (New York: W. W. Norton and Co., 1990), 28–29, 122–23; and William Bayard Hale, "'Friends and Fellow Citizens': Our Political Orators of All Parties, and the Ways They Use to Win Us," *World's Work* 23 (April 1912): 673–83.

97. Samuel Eliot Morison, *The Life and Letters of Harrison Gray Otis, Federalist* (Boston: Houghton Mifflin, 1913), 1:248; [Rollo Ogden], "Political Verbomaniacs," *Nation* 95 (29 August 1912): 184. Also see "Campaign Orators," 633; Kimball, "The Passing Art of Oratory," 280–81; Ralph Curtis Ringwalt, *Modern American Oratory: Seven Representative Orations* (Henry Holt and Co., 1898), 40–41; and "Oratory and Eloquence," editorial, *New York Times*, 3 September 1919, 12.

98. [William Everett], review of *History of Oratory and Orators*, by Henry Hadwicke, *Nation* 63 (5 November 1896): 351; T. J. Morgan, "Boy Oratory," *The Independent* 48(10 September 1896): 1231; [Ogden], "Political Verbomaniacs," 184. Also see "Campaign Orators," 634; and [Rollo Ogden], "Long Speeches," *Nation* 64 (27 May 1897): 391. On the difference between base and refined oratory, and the qualifications of the true orator, see especially Beveridge, *Art of Public Speaking*, 4–13, 25–28, 32; Hugh Price Hughes, "The Secret of Success in Oratory," *Review of Reviews* 5 (January 1892): 62; and Chauncey Depew, ed., foreword to The *Library of Oratory: Ancient and Modern*, 15 vols. (New York: E. R. Du Mont, 1902), 1:i–ii.

99. Oratorical anthologies published around the turn of the century include William Jennings Bryan, ed., *The World's Famous Orations*, 10 vols. (New York: Funk and Wagnalls, 1906); Ringwalt, *Modern American Oratory* (1898); David Brewer, ed., *The World's Best Orations*, 10 vols. (Saint Louis: Fred P. Kaiser, 1899); Reed, ed., *Modern Eloquence*, 15 vols. (1900); Depew, ed., *The Library of Oratory*, 15 vols. (1902); Guy Carleton Lee, ed., *The World's Orators*, 10 vols. (New York: G. P. Putnam Sons, 1900); Mayo W. Hazeltine, ed., *Orators from Homer to William McKinley*, 24 vols. (New York: P. F. Collier and Sons, 1902); Edwin Du Bois Shurter, *Masterpieces of Modern Oratory* (Boston: Ginn and Co., 1906); Rossiter Johnson, *Masterpieces of Eloquence: A Library of Ancient and Modern Oratory with Critical Studies of the World's Greatest Orators* (New York: T. Nelson, 1906); Alexander K. McClure, ed., *Famous American Statesmen and Orators*, 6 vols. (New York: F. F. Lovell, 1902); Sherwin Cody, ed., *A Selection from the World's Great Orations* (Chicago: A. C. McClurg and Co., 1904); Elbert Hubbard, *Little Journeys to the Homes of Eminent Orators* (East Aurora, N.Y.: Roycrofters, 1903); and Mayo W. Hazeltine et al., eds., *Masterpieces of Eloquence: Famous Orations and Great World Leaders from Early Greece to Present Time*, 25 vols. (New York: P. F. Collier and Sons, 1905). A number of

histories of oratory also appeared around the same time as the anthologies. See, for example, Lorenzo Sears, *The History of Oratory* (1896); Henry Hardwicke, *The History of Oratory and Orators* (New York: G. P. Putnam's Sons, 1896); and Thomas Wentworth Higginson, *American Orators and Oratory* (Cleveland: Imperial Press, 1901). Another example of revived interest was the large number of editions of Henry Ward Beecher's defense of oratory went through between 1892 and World War I. Henry Ward Beecher, *Oratory* (1876).

100. On the nostalgic strand of thought in the era see, for example, David B. Danbom, *"The World of Hope": Progressives and the Struggle for an Ethical Public Life* (Philadelphia: Temple University Press, 1987), 240; Carl N. Degler, *Out of Our Past: The Forces That Shaped Modern America*, rev. ed. (New York: Harper and Row, 1970), 368–77; Samuel P. Hays, *The Response to Industrialism, 1885–1914* (Chicago: University of Chicago Press, 1957), 92; Richard Hofstadter, *The Age of Reform: From Bryan to F. D. R.* (New York: Vintage Books, 1955), 257; and Robert Crunden, *Ministers of Reform: The Progressives' Achievement in American Civilization* (Urbana: University of Illinois Press, 1984), x.

101. George F. Hoar, "Some Famous Orators I Have Heard," *Scribner's Magazine* 30 (July 1901): 63; Dawes, "Has Oratory Declined?" 146; Benton, "Reminiscences of Eminent Lecturers," 603; Rogers, "The Neglected Art of Oratory," 374, 376. Also see Stoddard, "Orators," 1233–35; Hale, "Memoirs of a Hundred Years," 405–6; Bryan, introduction to *World's Famous Orations*, xxi; Charles Cotesworth Pinckney, "The Great Debate of 1833," *Lippincott's Magazine* 63 (January 1899): 107–16; Clark, *My Quarter Century of American Politics*, 1:7–9, 2:347; Ainsworth Rand Spofford, "The Eloquence of Congress: Historical Notes," *Records of the Columbia Historical Society* 9 (1906): 177–97; Ringwalt, *Modern American Oratory*, 10–11; and Peck, "Some Notes on Political Oratory," 209–10.

102. Quoted in Tapia, *Circuit Chautauqua*, 54.

103. Morgan, "Boy Oratory," 1231; Reed, "Oratory Past and Present," in *Modern Eloquence*, 3:xiv.

104. George Harvey quoted in William Inglis, "Helping to Make a President," *Collier's* 58 (7 October 1916): 15; George Harvey, "Colonel Harvey's Speech Proposing Wilson for the Presidency," 3 February 1906, in *Papers of Woodrow Wilson*, 16:299–301. Also see Kerney, *Political Education of Woodrow Wilson*, 14; and Axson, *"Brother Woodrow,"* 151, 275–76.

105. Mac Arthur, "Chautauqua Assemblies and Political Ambitions," 1076; Burgchardt, "Rhetorical Biography of Robert M. La Follette," 157; [Oswald Garrison Villard], "The Bryan Scandal," *Nation* 97 (18 September 1913): 256–57; Ross, *Dolliver*, 185–86. For discussion of Bryan's flogging in the metropolitan press see, for example, "Chautauqua Stars," *Everybody's* 33 (September 1915): 323–34; and George Harvey, "Mr. Bryan Rides behind," *North American Review* 199 (March 1914): 321–34.

106. Reed, "Oratory Past and Present," in *Modern Eloquence*, 4:viii; Ross, "Albert J. Beveridge," in *History and Criticism of Public Address*, 933; Ross, *Dolliver*, 197, 244–64; "Great Debating in the Senate," *American Review of Reviews* 43 (March 1911): 271–72. Also see Champ Clark, "Is Congressional Oratory a Lost Art?" *Century* 81 (December 1910): 307–10; [Ogden], "Interest in Parliamentary Oratory," *Nation* 72 (9 May 1901): 369–70; Ringwalt, *Modern American Oratory*, 12. For examples of the hope that good debates in Congress raised see, for example, [Rollo Ogden], "Congress Again Debating," *Nation* 75 (24 April 1902): 320–21; and "Senators' League Debate Will Rank with Famous Parliamentary Bouts," *New York Evening Post*, 29 July 1919, 9. On the new House chamber see "Clearing the Decks for Debate," editorial, *Chicago Record-Herald*, 8 April 1913, 4; editorial, *New York Evening Post*, 9 April 1913, 6; and [Francis Ellington Leupp], "Oratory and the New House," *Nation* 96 (19 June 1913): 612–13. On the prospects for a revival of legislative oratory also see "Campaign Orators," 634; Sears, *History of Oratory*, 416; and [Rollo Ogden], "Changes in Public Oratory," *Nation* 68 (30 March 1899): 236; and [Rollo Ogden], "Interest in Parliamentary Oratory," 369–70.

107. Leon Fink, *Progressive Intellectuals and the Dilemmas of Democratic Commitment* (Cambridge: Harvard University Press, 1997), 210–12; Danbom, *"The World of Hope,"* 102, 174–75; George E. Mowry, *The Era of Theodore Roosevelt and the Birth of Modern America* (New York: Harper and Row, 1958), 88–90; Wiebe, *Search for Order*, 161–63; Robert H. Wiebe, *Businessmen and Reform: A Study of the Progressive Movement* (1962; reprint, Chicago: Ivan R. Dee, 1989), 9, 206–7.

108. Herbert Croly, *The Promise of American Life* (New York: Macmillan, 1909), 428, 442.

109. George Santayana, *Character of Opinion in the United States*, in *The Works of George Santayana*, Triton ed. (New York: Charles Scribner's Sons, 1937), 8:7. Also see John P. Altgeld, *Oratory: Its Requirements and Rewards* (Chicago: Charles H. Kerr, 1901), 54–57; James A. Morone, *The Democratic Wish: Popular Participation and the Limits of American Government* (New York: Basic Books, 1990), 113; Danbom, "The World of Hope," 176; and Wiebe, *Businessmen and Reform*, 102.

110. On the conservative desire for sound leadership that could resist the onslaught of reform see Mowry, *Era of Theodore Roosevelt*, 40–43.

111. Robert M. La Follette, *La Follette's Autobiography* (1911; reprint, Madison, Wis.: University of Wisconsin Press, 1960), 105; Lahman, "Robert M. La Follette," in *History and Criticism of Public Address*, 949. On surrogate speaking as an agency of propaganda during World War I see Stephen L. Vaughn, "Public Speaking and the CPI," chapter 7 in *Holding Fast the Inner Lines: Democracy, Nationalism, and the Committee on Public Information* (Chapel Hill: University of North Carolina Press, 1980), 116–40. On the publicity campaigns of the League to Enforce Peace and the Liberty League, see John Milton Cooper Jr., *Breaking the Heart of the World: Woodrow Wilson and the Fight for the League of Nations* (Cambridge: Cambridge University Press, 2001), chaps. 3–4.

112. Bryan, introduction to *World's Famous Orations*, x; Burgchardt, "Rhetorical Biography of Robert M. La Follette," 190–91; Matthews, "The Four Ways of Delivering an Address," 331. On the effect of the reading audience on oratory also see Altgeld, *Oratory*, 53–54, 27–29; [Everett], review of *History of Oratory and Orators*, 351; [Ogden], "Congress Again Debating," 320; and Matthews, "The Four Ways of Delivering an Address," 332.

113. "An Orator under Control," *New York Tribune*, 2 February 1916, 8; "The Lure of the Platform," *New York Evening Post*, 4 September 1919, 8; "Senator's League Debate Will Rank with Famous Parliamentary Bouts," *New York Evening Post*, 29 July 1919, 9; "Deflation," *New Republic* 9 (18 November 1916): 64–65; [Rollo Ogden], "The New Style of Oratory," *Nation* 85 (21 November 1907): 463. On the style of the spellbinders see Guild, "The Spellbinder," 574–75; and Bacon, "Itinerant Speechmaking in the Last Campaign," 414.

114. [Ogden], "Changes in Public Oratory," 236; Matthews, "The Four Ways of Delivering an Address," 332–33; [Ogden], "Effective Public Speaking," 44–45. For the argument that oratory could not be as powerful as it once was in modern society see Clark, "Is Congressional Oratory a Lost Art?" 308; Morison, *Life and Letters of Harrison Gray Otis*, 1:248; Peck, "Some Notes on Political Oratory," 209, 210; "Oratorical Traditions," 642–43; Ringwalt, *Modern American Oratory*, 12; [Ogden], "Interest in Parliamentary Oratory," 370; James Bryce, *The American Commonwealth* (New York: Macmillan and Co., 1888), 2:613–14; [Everett], review of *History of Oratory and Orators*, 351; Kimball, "The Passing Art of Oratory," 278–80; [Leupp], "Oratory and the New House," 612–13; and "The Excess of Oratory," *Spectator* 85 (4 August 1900): 138.

115. Albert Beveridge called Dolliver "beyond all possible doubt the greatest orator in the contemporaneous English-speaking world." Beveridge, quoted in Ross, *Dolliver*, 241–42. Also see Hale, "'Friends and Fellow Citizens,'" 683; and Frank Luther Mott, "Master of Oratory," *Palimpsest* 5 (February 1924): 60–77.

116. On Roosevelt see, for example, [Rollo Ogden], "The President Stumping," *Nation* 87 (1 October 1908): 304–5. On Roosevelt's popular brand of oratory also see Cmiel, *Democratic Eloquence*, 248–50; and Cooper, *Pivotal Decades*, 29–30.

117. Lodge also charged that the one classical allusion he ever read in a Wilson speech was wrong. Henry Cabot Lodge, *The Senate and the League of Nations* (New York: Charles Scribner's Sons, 1925), 220–21.

118. Cooper, *Breaking the Heart of the World*, 124. For a much less favorable contemporary assessment of the debate, see Newton D. Baker to Hugh C. Wallace, 27 September 1919, Newton D. Baker Papers, Library of Congress, box 11.

119. Woodrow Wilson, *Constitutional Government in the United States* (1908; reprint, New York: Columbia University Press, 1961).

120. Kent, "The Platform as a Political Institution," 247.

121. "News Report On Governor's Conference at Spring Lake, New Jersey," 13 September 1911, in *Papers of Woodrow Wilson*, 23:321–22; "A Memorandum by Stockton Axson,"

August 1919, in *Papers of Woodrow Wilson*, 67:605; Woodrow Wilson, "Notes on States-manship," 5 June–15 September 1899, in *Papers of Woodrow Wilson*, 11:126. In 1892 Wilson reviewed Henry Jephson's influential book on the rise of the English platform. Woodrow Wilson, review of *The Platform: Its Rise and Progress*, by Henry Jephson, in *Papers of Woodrow Wilson*, 8:31–33. Wilson would have also been reminded of Glad-stone's famous platform exploits in 1904, when he read John Morley's monumental biography of the great English orator. See "From Wilson's Diary for 1904," 2 January 1904 and 3 January 1904, in *Papers of Woodrow Wilson*, 15:116, 117. Wilson might have read about the rise of British platform oratory as early as 1883, in an article by his friend James Bryce in his favorite periodical, the *Nation*. Bryce, "Political Influence of the Press in England," 444–45.

122. J. Michael Hogan, *The Panama Canal in American Politics* (Carbondale: Southern Illi-nois University Press, 1986), 31–32. Also see Leroy G. Dorsey, "Reconstituting the American Spirit: Theodore Roosevelt's Rhetorical Presidency" (Ph.D. diss., Indiana University, 1993), 13–15, 210–12, 217–18.

123. "Our Preacher President," *Independent* 61 (13 December 1906): 1431–32. Also see Leroy G. Dorsey, "Theodore Roosevelt and Corporate America, 1901–1909: A Reexam-ination," *Presidential Studies Quarterly* 25 (1995): 725–39.

124. Tulis, *Rhetorical Presidency*, 97–98, 106, 108; Carol Geldman, *All The President's Words: The Bully Pulpit and the Creation of the Virtual Presidency* (New York: Walker and Com-pany, 1997), 1–2, 4.

125. On the influence of Roosevelt's presidency on Wilson see Edward S. Corwin, "Depart-mental Colleague," in *Woodrow Wilson: Some Princeton Memoirs*, ed. William Starr Myers (Princeton: Princeton University Press, 1946), 28; Arthur S. Link, *Wilson: The New Free-dom* (Princeton: Princeton University Press, 1956), 146–47; Link, "Wilson: Philosophy, Methods, and Impact," in *Woodrow Wilson in the World Today*, 5–6; Daniel D. Stid, "Woodrow Wilson and the Rise of the Rhetorical Presidency," in *Leadership, Rhetoric and the American Presidency: Brigance Forum, April 19, 1995* (Crawfordsville, Ind.: Wabash College, 1995), 6; and Daniel D. Stid, *The President as Statesman: Woodrow Wilson and the Constitution* (Lawrence: University Press of Kansas, 1998), 44, 48.

126. Woodrow Wilson, "Leaderless Government," 5 August 1897, in *Papers of Woodrow Wil-son*, 10:304; Woodrow Wilson, "The Preface to the Fifteenth Edition of *Congressional Government*," 15 August 1900, in *Papers of Woodrow Wilson*, 11:570.

127. Wilson, *Constitutional Government*, 60, see also p.68.

128. Ibid., 110–11. On the marginalization of Congressional oratory, see pp. 109–11.

129. Ibid., 68.

130. Ibid., 70, 116–17.

131. Although he did not do so in *Constitutional Government*, Wilson had argued this thesis in great detail in a series of essays and books in the 1870s and 1880s.

132. Tulis, "The Decay of Presidential Rhetoric," in *Rhetoric and American Statesmanship*, 107. See also Ceaser, Thurow, Tulis, and Bessette, "The Rise of the Rhetorical Presi-dency," 158–71; Tulis, *Rhetorical Presidency*, 16–22, 130–36; and Bessette, *Mild Voice of Reason*, 191–92.

133. Ceaser, Thurow, Tulis, and Bessette, "The Rise of the Rhetorical Presidency," 158–71; Ceaser, *Presidential Selection*, 321, 325–26; Tulis, "The Decay of Presidential Rhetoric," in *Rhetoric and American Statesmanship*, 107; Tulis, *Rhetorical Presidency*, 179.

134. Wilson, *Constitutional Government*, 48–49. Also see Wilson's earlier interpretations of Webster's reply to Hayne in Woodrow Wilson, *Division and Reunion, 1829–1889* (New York: Longmans, Green, and Co., 1893), 44–48 and Woodrow Wilson, *A History of the American People*, 5 vols. (New York: Harper and Broths, 1902), 4:27–28.

135. "A Memorandum by Cary Travers Grayson," 30 March 1920, in *Papers of Woodrow Wil-son*, 65:145. On the gap between the old oratorical tradition and modern political cul-ture see, for example, Hariman, "Relocating the Art of Public Address," in *Rhetoric and Political Culture*, 163.

136. Diary of Edith Benham, 14 January 1919, in *Papers of Woodrow Wilson*, 54:62–63; Woodrow Wilson, "A Luncheon Address in Portland," 15 September 1919, in *Papers of Woodrow Wilson*, 63:283.

Preaching Morality in Modern America: Theodore Roosevelt's Rhetorical Progressivism

Leroy G. Dorsey

2

Richard Watson Jr. observed that at the turn of the twentieth century, "there was a sense of dissatisfaction with things as they were."[1] Many in the urban middle class believed that America faced an overwhelming number of economic, political, and social problems. Economically, corporations began wresting control over whole industries from small business owners and frequently abused the public trust by fixing prices and selling unsafe products. Richard Hofstadter noted that some within the middle class also took offense for more selfish reasons: once they invested their savings in corporate securities, they found that the "power to make the vital economic decisions of society" had passed from them into the "hands of the masters of corporations."[2] Politically, George Mowry observed, corrupt practices "ran from the bottom of the American political structure upward into state and national government."[3] Ward bosses, legislators, and other public servants regularly took bribes from criminals and captains of industry to safeguard their respective activities. As a result, middle- and lower-class people found their taxes raised and the services provided inadequate.[4] Socially, modern cities appeared to act as breeding grounds for the worst in human character. Reformers believed that virtuous country folk, exposed to the brothels, gambling dens, and bars in the city, were transformed into immoral brutes. "Such unfortunates," Mowry concluded, "became the flotsam of the slums, making the saloon their church and the dive their home."[5]

Progressivism was the response to this seeming deterioration of American culture. According to Watson, Progressives "assumed they could remove the causes for dissatisfaction and assure human progress." More specifically, they believed that stronger local and national government could alleviate many of society's ills.[6] Comprised of people from all walks of life with many different agendas, Progressives succeeded in bringing about lasting reforms in areas such as workers' rights, political propriety, and social justice. Mowry summarized the accomplishments of the Progressive movement: "Undoubtedly it altered the standards of political honesty and public morals. It inquired into the national structure of production and tried to redistribute wealth more equitably among all the nation's people. . . . And . . . it demonstrated that the federal government . . . was the master of even the largest industrial combinations."[7]

One of the most recognized yet least understood figures of the Progressive Era is Theodore Roosevelt. According to many scholars, Roosevelt did not deserve the label of reformer. According to Richard Hofstadter, for example, Roosevelt was a conservative masquerading as a Progressive: "It is hard to understand how Roosevelt managed to keep his reputation as a strenuous reformer," since he had "no passionate interest in the humane goals of reform." As proof, Hofstadter offered Roosevelt's unwillingness to "bust" the corporate trusts despite the president's public declarations to the contrary.[8] Henry Pringle noted that the president was not reform minded until his affiliation with the Bull Moose Party in 1912; until then, "he stood close to the center and bared his teeth at the . . . liberals of the extreme left."[9] Even Mowry, one of Roosevelt's most sympathetic biographers, noted Roosevelt's hostility toward the early Progressives. Mowry observed that the "progressive movement owed much to Theodore Roosevelt as he left office"; however, "detractors of Roosevelt have claimed that he had little part in the origins of the progressive movement, that he simply reaped where other men had sown, and that he then usually proceeded to vilify his benefactors. . . . [This is] unquestionably true."[10]

Roosevelt has not fared much better in more recent biographies. Lewis Gould discussed the various regulatory policies that Roosevelt supported as president but did not treat those initiatives as part of the larger progressive impulses of the day.[11] Both Nathan Miller's work and the most recent account of Roosevelt's life by H. W. Brands remind us of Roosevelt's hostility toward progressive reformers prior to his presidency. Like Pringle, they consider Roosevelt a reformer only after his affiliation with the Progressive Party in 1912. Even then, their accounts focus more on the private, political machinations of the man and his party than on his principles of reform.[12]

The reluctance of historians to treat Roosevelt as a genuine Progressive—especially before 1912—is in part attributable to a problematic distinction between Roosevelt's rhetoric and the "reality" of his achievements. Mowry disapproved when critics attacked President Roosevelt for "talking reform loudly and accomplishing little or nothing at all," but even Mowry perpetuated the distinction by apologetically observing that Roosevelt "secured what he could" from Congress.[13] Hofstadter, of course, condemned Roosevelt most harshly for his failure to follow up on his progressive rhetoric. Suggesting that Roosevelt's rhetoric was disingenuous and ultimately meaningless, Hofstadter concluded, "Nothing was farther from [Roosevelt's] mind than to translate his moral judgments into social realities; and for the best of reasons: the fundamentally conservative nationalist goals of his politics were at cross-purposes with the things he found it expedient to say, and as long as his activity was limited to the verbal sphere the inconsistency was less apparent."[14]

Clearly, Roosevelt has not been counted among the great Progressives of his day. As Mowry suggested, Progressives often had a "missionary desire to create a heaven on earth," yet Roosevelt was a practical politician who often clashed with more idealistic reformers.[15] It also may be true, as Hofstadter suggested, that Roosevelt's mind "did not usually cut very deep" on the great issues of the day.[16] Yet not all Progressives fit the same mold; there was not one but many Progressive movements, each with its own agenda.[17] While some stressed the role of professionalism or scientific management in solving social problems,[18] others—

including Roosevelt—emphasized the moral foundations of reform. Finally, Roosevelt's often aggressive views on foreign policy have marked him, in the minds of some biographers and historians, as a reactionary rather than a Progressive. With most accounts of the Progressive Era focusing on domestic reform,[19] and with many Progressives opposing foreign involvements as a drain on the nation's resources, Roosevelt's passion for international affairs and his advocacy of the martial spirit and expansionism seem anything *but* "progressive."[20]

To gain a more substantial and coherent understanding of Roosevelt's place in the Progressive Era, his discourse as public official, chief executive, and private citizen must be reassessed. A close analysis of his public discourse reveals not only a consistency in his commitment to reform, but also a commitment to *moral* principles that, for him, represented the essential guidelines for genuine progress both at home and abroad. Stated another way, this analysis contests the conventional wisdom that Roosevelt's rhetoric was meaningless and that he did not qualify as a "Progressive" until, at best, late in his career. It demonstrates how, in a rhetorical sense, Roosevelt was the consummate Progressive: a reformer with a strong faith in the power of rhetoric to shape public opinion and in the power of public opinion, in turn, to bring about meaningful social reform.

The principles underlying Roosevelt's "rhetorical progressivism" were largely those articulated in what Arthur Link called the "most significant formulation of progressive political theory" of the era: Herbert Croly's *The Promise of American Life.*[21] Published in 1909, Croly elaborated a progressive philosophy in perfect harmony with Roosevelt's words and actions. Roosevelt's "influence is written large across the book," Arthur M. Schlesinger Jr. wrote, and "Croly's broad argument is in essence a justification and generalization of Roosevelt's political position."[22] Croly himself wrote that Roosevelt "was the first to realize" that a person "could no longer really represent the national interest without becoming a reformer."[23] Croly's work articulated many of the distinctive strains of Roosevelt's progressivism: the belief that moral concerns were the essence of reform, and that for "civilized democracy" to survive, the "common citizen" needed to be "something of a saint"; the call for a "technical" efficiency to bring about the practical rather than the ideal; the necessity of foreign interventions where indigenous people were incapable of efficiently governing themselves; the use of history to rediscover the "principles" that would lead to "American national fulfillment"; and the emphasis not merely on charity but on individual and collective responsibility.[24]

These principles of reform were central to Roosevelt's rhetoric throughout his life and informed both his domestic and foreign policies. They constituted a distinctive brand of progressivism—a "rhetorical progressivism"—that placed more emphasis on attitudinal than structural reform. Roosevelt's brand of progressivism did not trust to mere legislation to bring about lasting reform; for him, laws were secondary to improvements in human *character*. Like a minister, Roosevelt preached to America about character, hoping to build a *moral* foundation for political, economic, and social progress, both at home and abroad.

The essay explores Roosevelt's "rhetorical progressivism" in two major sections. First, I discuss the manifestations of Roosevelt's reform principles in domestic affairs. Before he became president, Roosevelt campaigned to reinvigorate the nation's moral conscience, condemning the sins of greed and pride in the rich corporate officers and public officials who abused the public trust. For Roosevelt, a new emphasis on moral principle and personal character was necessary to guide the practical reform of business and government. As president, he became the nation's secular preacher, using the "bully pulpit" to preach against the greed of the big corporations, particularly the railroad trusts. At the same time, he warned against the sin of envy, which he charged was behind many unwarranted attacks on the trusts. As the nation's voice of morality, Roosevelt offered his audience a chance at practical salvation: support the national government's administrative regulation of corporations. After leaving the presidency, Roosevelt continued to promote reform in essentially moral terms in two well-known but generally miscast addresses: "The New Nationalism" and "A Confession of Faith." In both speeches, he continued his decades-old public campaign to uplift the character of the nation by applying his transcendent principles of righteousness to human welfare, equality of opportunity, and the regulation of corporations.

The essay's second major section examines Roosevelt's rhetorical progressivism in foreign affairs. Prior to his presidency, Roosevelt repeatedly called for America to prepare for its international role by strengthening its military. To that end, he wrote several book-length histories designed to inspire twentieth-century Americans to embrace the moral and martial virtues of America's pioneers. As president, Roosevelt continued to call upon the nation to recognize its responsibilities in the world. To that end, he took a number of initiatives that, by today's standards, might not seem "progressive," yet which were completely consistent with the progressive principles he articulated in domestic affairs. For Roosevelt, expansion and the exercise of military power by morally advanced societies were, by definition, "progressive" acts, for they advanced the "progress" of civilization. Later, Roosevelt also cast America's participation in World War I as something of a "progressive" imperative, for at stake was the continued "progress" of "civilized" society.

Ultimately, judgments of Roosevelt's credentials as a Progressive should not rest upon interpretations of his personal sentiments or on his presumably selfish political aspirations. Nor should legislative victories be the sole measure of his progressive achievements. As a historian Roosevelt took a longer view of the evolution of culture, and as a political leader he aspired to build the moral and spiritual foundations for such long-term "progress." For Roosevelt, progressivism meant something more than a platform of legislative goals or programmatic reforms. For him, progressivism meant moral leadership and the transformation of the public character through rhetorical advocacy and inspiration.

Rhetorical Progressivism and Domestic Affairs

THE EARLY YEARS

Born into an upper-middle-class New York City family in 1858, Theodore Roosevelt's notion of private responsibility and public service came largely from his father. Theodore Sr. taught his son that in order to serve a higher good, he must be strong, both morally and physically. "No one had a greater influence upon his namesake," Miller wrote of the elder Roosevelt, who imbued his son "with a strong sense of moral values." By example, young Roosevelt watched his father's "disciplined sense of obligation as a Christian" spur him to become an "early supporter of almost every humanitarian endeavor in the city." The senior Roosevelt believed that with good fortune came an obligation to perform service for those less fortunate.[25]

Following his graduation from Harvard in 1880, Roosevelt enrolled in Columbia Law School. He soon realized, however, that the practice of law did not fulfill his desire for public service. Miller noted that when Roosevelt discovered that the "heroes of the bar were the attorneys for big corporations," his enthusiasm waned.[26] The teaching of the law, Roosevelt wrote in his *Autobiography*, "seemed to be against justice. . . . It did not seem to me that the law was framed to discourage as it should sharp practice, and all other kinds of bargains except those which are fair and of benefit to both sides." Since he deemed that the law did not promote "social fair dealing," he looked for other forums in which to express his vision of social justice.[27]

To better serve the public, Roosevelt decided upon a career in government, enjoying political prosperity with a succession of important positions. From 1882 through 1884, he served in the New York State Assembly. According to Carleton Putnam, Roosevelt gained a reputation as a champion who would do what was necessary to "stop great wealth from holding itself above the law."[28] To that end, he sponsored a number of pro-labor initiatives. During his term, he called for legislation that would limit the hours that women and children could work, that provided for greater safety measures to protect factory workers, and that established a bureau of labor statistics.[29] While the young assemblyman "refused to associate actively with labor men," many of whom he believed were demagogues, Howard Hurwitz wrote that "Roosevelt's shibboleth . . . was reform."[30]

After a self-imposed exile as a Dakota rancher following the death of his wife and mother in 1884, and a failed campaign for mayor of New York City in 1886, Roosevelt accepted an appointment as a member of the federal Civil Service Commission in 1889. During his six-year tenure as commissioner, Roosevelt called for an end to political patronage, criticizing even his own party for rewarding wealthy contributors with civil service positions.[31]

Eventually tiring of his civil service work, Roosevelt accepted the presidency of the New York City Police Board in 1895. In that post he attended to reform at a personal as well as a managerial level. Jay Berman noted that the new president himself "embarked on a series of nightly inspection tours," hoping to catch an officer "off his beat, drunk, sleeping, abusive or otherwise delinquent."[32] On a larger scale, Roosevelt declared war on all types of vice and corruption.[33]

In his final two posts before the presidency—governor of New York from 1899 to 1900 and vice president in 1901—Roosevelt continued to etch his vision of reform in the public consciousness. Early in his administration as governor, he worked both to improve housing conditions in the tenements and to decrease the dangerous conditions in sweatshops.[34] Roosevelt's stint as vice president began inauspiciously. According to William Harbaugh, Roosevelt had little to do: after presiding over the Senate for four days, Congress adjourned for its recess, leaving the new vice president with no administrative duties. During this time, he made several public appearances to speak about philanthropy.[35]

Roosevelt's practical accomplishments, while impressive, only begin to reflect his commitment to social progress. Throughout the last decades of the nineteenth century, he used his talents as a writer and a speaker to influence public opinion, to fire the imagination of individuals regarding their responsibility to themselves and to the culture. To that end, Roosevelt tapped into one of the dominant strains of progressivism at the time—a strain inspired by evangelical Protestantism.[36] According to Arthur Link and Richard McCormick, the Protestant revivals of the early 1800s spurred a "reform mentality" in progressive advocates that became "an all-consuming urge to purge the world of sin." Many Progressives believed that the use of "moralistic appeals" would make "people feel the awful weight of wrong in the world" and compel "them to accept personal responsibility for its eradication."[37] Robert Crunden noted that by the 1890s, "America remained dominated by patterns of religious thought"; such thought had given rise to the Social Gospel movement, which called on the churches to help more directly with alleviating poor living and working conditions.[38]

Roosevelt, however, extended the rhetoric of the Social Gospel beyond the church. For him, moral responsibility rested with individuals, not institutions, and he railed against people in positions of power who abused the public's trust. As Croly observed, Roosevelt was akin to "Thor wielding . . . a sledge-hammer in the cause of national righteousness," hoping that the "sympathetic observer" who was not "stunned by the noise of the hammer" would be "rewarded by . . . gleams of insight."[39] In popular periodicals and in speeches, he became the nation's secular preacher, identifying the sinners in the community and calling upon them to repent. "The doctrine that I preach," Governor Roosevelt declared to the members of a New York social club in 1899, "is a doctrine that was old when the children of Israel came out of Egypt . . . the doctrine that teaches us that men shall prosper as long as they do their duty to themselves and their neighbors alike" by upholding those "rules of conduct which were set down in the Sermon on the Mount."[40]

Roosevelt's rhetoric of reform was more sermonic than deliberative, exhorting individuals to embrace what he considered to be progressive ethical ideals. For him, the character of individuals was the key to national greatness. He did not propose programs so much as he preached against "sinful" behaviors.

With industrialization and the rise of the business class, Roosevelt preached mostly about the "sin" of greed. He did not criticize the wealthy per se. To the contrary, he applauded those "men who use their wealth aright . . . for good in the community."[41] Rather than vilify the moneyed class, he assured readers of the *Review of Reviews* that even the "poor man . . . is better off in the long run because other men are well off."[42] Yet with wealth came responsibilities; men of means shouldered a "heavy moral obligation" to the nation.[43] In no uncertain terms, Roosevelt rebuked those who were concerned not with the public interest but only with getting richer. He especially disdained those who got rich off other people's money or who earned money through illegal means.

As sociologist Stanford Lyman has observed, greed is a religious sin when "man finds a deity in things."[44] When the desire for material things is elevated to a sacred level, not only is the Supreme Being displaced, but also the fraud, treachery, and indifference associated with greed may "engender severe social conflicts and personal misfortunes."[45] Roosevelt's rhetoric reflected this view of greed. He railed against the "short-sighted selfishness" of merchants who regarded "everything merely from the standpoint of 'Does it Pay?'" Such men refused to "take any part in politics" because they were "short-sighted enough to think that it will pay . . . better to attend purely to making money, and too selfish to be willing to undergo any trouble for the sake of abstract duty."[46] Such men were dangerous, Roosevelt wrote in *The Forum*, because they measure "everything by the shop-till" and are "unable to appreciate any quality that is not a mercantile commodity."[47] For Roosevelt, the "mere materialist" did not understand what constituted real progress. For genuine progress to occur, he believed that "appeals for civic and national betterment" had to be based "on nobler ground than those of mere business expediency."[48]

Roosevelt especially disliked those greedy businessmen whose very success led to civic disengagement. A successful merchant, Roosevelt wrote in 1886, "pompous, self-important . . . and accustomed because of his very success to be treated with deferential regard, as one who stands above the common run of humanity, naturally finds it very unpleasant to go to a caucus or primary where he has to stand on an equal footing with his groom and day-laborers."[49] Too many of them, Roosevelt told the Liberal Club in New York several years later, "plume themselves upon being good citizens if they even vote." To Roosevelt, this sort of civic aloofness was "unpardonable." To "find men of high business . . . saying that they really have not got time to go to ward meetings . . . [or] to take a personal share in all the important details of practical politics," he declared, was nothing less than "contemptuous."[50]

Above all, Roosevelt condemned the wealthy businessman who achieved that status by illegal means. To him, crooked rich men were worse than common criminals. There were not great numbers of them, he assured his readers in 1895, but they were "curses to the country"[51] because of the example they set: "The conscienceless stock speculator who acquires wealth by swindling his fellows, by debauching judges and corrupting legislatures, and who ends his days with the reputation of being among the richest men in America, exerts over the minds of the rising generation an influence worse than that of the average murderer or bandit, because his career is even more dazzling in its success, and even more dangerous in its effects upon the community."[52] Those who became successful through "deceit," "chicanery," and "unscrupulous cunning," Roosevelt wrote five years later, represented one of the most dangerous influences in American culture. Their success, attained "by the sacrifice of the fundamental principles of morality," threatened to poison the moral climate of the entire nation.[53]

In addition to sinful businessmen, Roosevelt lashed out against public officials who lacked the proper moral fiber. "Government employees, as a whole," Civil Service Commissioner Roosevelt wrote in the *Atlantic Monthly* in 1892, were "hard-working, not overpaid men, with families to support."[54] Many honest legislators worked from "eight to fourteen hours a day" and were "obliged to incur the bitterest hostility" from their critics, he noted in *The Century*.[55] Yet enough public officials had become corrupt to constitute an "aristocracy of the bad." Speaking before the New York Assembly early in 1884, he declared that those who "fatten in the public offices upon the plunder wrung from the working man" with "the support of all that is vile and bad" represented a "standing danger to the community."[56] As New York City Police Commissioner, Roosevelt vowed to end the "wholesale corruption of the Police Department" by enforcing the Sunday Closing Law and rooting out those officers who "blackmailed and bullied" small liquor-sellers into closing but allowed the wealthy and politically connected liquor-sellers to remain open.[57] Again, Roosevelt seemed as concerned with the moral example set by such actions as with the violations themselves: "If public officers are to execute the laws at their caprice, at the caprice of a section of their constituents, then we not only expect to see corruption flourish in our great cities, to see the growth of a black-mailed and lawbreaking body of liquor-sellers, and the growth of venality among public officials and of indifference to law among citizens, but we may expect to see in other communities the white-capper and the lyncher flourish, and crimes of every kind go unpunished unless punished by the exercise of the right of private vengeance."[58]

In Roosevelt's view, public officials needed to point the way toward the "higher life."[59] Pointedly casting governmental abuses in religious terms, he applied the eighth commandment to politics: the politician, he wrote as governor in 1900, "shalt not steal." "We can afford to differ on the currency, the tariff, and foreign policy," he argued, "but we cannot afford to differ on the question of honesty if we expect our republic permanently to endure." As usual, Roosevelt minimized the prevalence of such governmental corruption by declaring that the "number of public servants who actually take bribes is not very numerous." Yet for even a few public officials to "give certain corporations special legislative and executive privileges because they have contributed heavily to campaign funds" threatened the moral foundations of the entire political system. Such actions came "dangerously near the border-line of the commandment."[60]

In criticizing corrupt businessmen and politicians, Roosevelt echoed other reformers of his day. Yet Roosevelt also directed some of his "sermons" at the reformers themselves, particularly those "preachers of vague discontent" who "denounce the present conditions of society . . . for shortcomings which they themselves have been instrumental in causing."[61] In Roosevelt's view, some preached reform only to bring credit to themselves. These "men of morbid vanity," he wrote, often quenched their "thirst for notoriety" by "denouncing those who are really forces for good." The socialist who raved against the existing order or the man who demanded "the immediately impossible in temperance," he observed, only strengthened the forces of evil.[62] These were "head-in-the-air social reformers."[63] They were epitomized by the "maudlin sentimentalist" who did not understand that a "man can occasionally be helped when he stumbles" but that it was "useless to try to carry him when he will not or cannot walk; and worse than useless to try to bring down the work and reward of the thrifty and intelligent to the level of the capacity of the weak, the shiftless, and the idle."[64] Offering the "Negro problem" as an example, Roosevelt maintained that while legislation had set Negroes free, some starry-eyed reformers believed that legislation could also bring immediate equality to the ex-slaves. These "parlor socialists" did not understand that "great advances in general social well-being" could not come through "some far-reaching scheme" or by supporting the "pauper-producing, maudlin philanthropy of the free soup-kitchen and tramp lodging-house."[65] True reform, in short, was an evolutionary rather than a revolutionary process. Addressing a New York audience in 1893, he reminded them that a "man who goes into politics should not expect to reform everything right off."[66]

Instead of the "Quack remedies" and "wild schemes" of the impatient reformer, Roosevelt called on the public to embrace "practical reform." That meant having realistic expectations about what changes could be made and how quickly. He noted that in New York, it took at least two years of sustained work to bring about meaningful changes, but patience had paid off: "we have broken the power of the ward boss and the saloon-keeper to work injustice; we have destroyed the most hideous of the tenement houses in which poor people are huddled like swine in a sty; we have made parks and playgrounds for the children in the crowded quarters."[67] Instead of striking out at the evils of modern life "in a spirit of ignorant revenge," Governor Roosevelt observed in his 1900 "Annual Message" that the alleviation of social problems could only come through "careful study of conditions, and by action which while taken boldly and without hesitation is neither heedless nor reckless."[68]

Above all, Roosevelt believed that practical reform required a foundation in moral ideals. Reform must be cultivated slowly, he cautioned City Club members in 1899, since he believed that "Evil can't be done away with through one spasm of virtue."[69] Writing for *The Century* in the summer of 1900, he hoped to illuminate the differences between the false prophets of change and the morally upright, practical reformers who represented the true agents of progressive reform. Those "head-in-the-air" reformers only alienated "from the cause of decency keen and honest men . . . who grow to regard all movements for reform with contemptuous dislike because of the folly and vanity of the men who in the name of righteousness preach unwisdom and practise uncharitableness." True and lasting reform required an "unending struggle for righteousness." It required practical men who would "take the time and trouble," who were "far-sighted and resolute," and who combined "sincerity with sanity." It required an "atmosphere of enthusiasm and practical endeavor." Like Abraham Lincoln, who worked "through practical methods to realize [the] ideal" of slavery's abolition and the restoration of the Union, modern Americans needed to avoid a "compromise with dishonesty [and] with sin" and persist in the quest for reforms consistent with the "laws of righteousness, of decency, [and] of morality."[70]

Ultimately, then, true reform was moral, practical, and evolutionary. It also required "manly" strength. In "The Manly Virtues and Practical Politics," Roosevelt called upon men of "honesty and unselfish desire" to heed the call to political battle with "men of far lower ideals than [their] own." While political action resulted from the "joint action of many men" and compromise was sometimes necessary, Roosevelt insisted that the reformer "must not lose his own high ideal . . . [and] stand firmly for what he believes." Moreover, he needed to be strong, like the soldier in a holy battle for righteousness. A "man desirous of doing good political work," Roosevelt declared, needed to exhibit the "rougher, manlier virtues, and above all the virtue of personal courage, physical as well as moral." Such a man, "vigorous in mind and body," must be able to hold his own "in rough conflict with [others], able to suffer punishment without flinching, and, at need, to repay it in kind with full interest." For Roosevelt, the reformer who served the nation well usually possessed "some of the hardy virtues which we admire in the soldier who serves his country well in the field."[71]

Just as Croly warned that "no amount of moral energy" could alone lead to genuine reform, Roosevelt thus added courage and strength—the willingness to fight—to his list of requirements for true reform.[72] Writing in *The Outlook* in 1895, he praised the reformer who was willing to step down "into the hurly-burly," who was "not frightened by the sweat and the blood[,] . . . who 'haunts not the fringed edges of the fight, but the pell-mell of men.'"[73] This emphasis on the "manlier" virtues, perhaps more than anything else, distinguished Roosevelt's "rhetorical progressivism" from both the reformers of his own day and later Progressives. And it would remain an essential element of his progressive philosophy throughout his tenure as president.

THE PRESIDENTIAL YEARS

By dint of an assassin's bullet, Vice President Roosevelt found himself propelled into the presidency on 14 September 1901. Upon entering the office, Roosevelt noted in his *Autobiography* that one of the most important questions he faced "was the attitude of the Nation toward the great corporations."[74] This issue, perhaps more than any other, produced the historical controversy surrounding his commitment to reform.

As the twentieth century opened, the new industrial combines held unprecedented power. As Mowry has written, "The larger combines had placed the small producers of their raw materials into a state of semibondage," often extending their control "from the wholesaler to the retailers of their products" and engaging in practices that allowed them to "either swallow or ruin effective competitors."[75] Now, according to Sean Cashman, "many important industries were dominated by a few large corporations" that created a "veritable plutocracy," seemingly more powerful than local and state governments.[76] As Watson has observed, Roosevelt wanted to determine "whether big business could be controlled."[77] In his view, antitrust legislation had failed to prevent the consolidation of these entities or to inhibit their power, and government agencies designated to expose corporate abuses, such as the Bureau of Corporations, met with mixed results. Publicity alone had thus far failed to change the trusts' behaviors.[78]

Roosevelt took particular interest in the railroad industry. One of his first acts as president was to order his attorney general to file suit under the Sherman Antitrust Act against the Northern Securities Corporation, a railroad trust controlled by J. P. Morgan and John D. Rockefeller that threatened to control the entire Northwest and beyond. The Supreme Court eventually ruled that Northern Securities did in fact constrain trade and ordered its dissolution.[79] The president, however, was not finished with the railroad trusts. During his last term, Roosevelt pushed for passage of the Hepburn Act. This act not only gave the Interstate Commerce Commission the power to regulate railway rates, but also to examine the financial records of interstate utilities. According to Mowry, the Hepburn Act represented a "landmark in the evolution of federal control of private industry."[80]

By the end of his presidency, Roosevelt had overcome obstacles of partisan politics, institutional inertia, and public apathy to win several legislative victories against corporate America. Yet some scholars still judge Roosevelt a failure in his crusade against the trusts. Roosevelt "blasted dishonesty in business" with "some of the showiest language that had ever been used in the White House," according to Hofstadter, yet he never was really "keen to find wrongdoing among the trusts."

He engaged "in a few cleverly chosen prosecutions which gave substance to his talk about improving the moral code of the corporations," yet according to Hofstadter, the most "intense and rapid growth of trusts in American business history took place during Roosevelt's administration."[81]

Such judgments overlook how Roosevelt's campaign against the trusts had the sort of higher moral purpose that, in essence, defines the modern "rhetorical presidency." Prior to Roosevelt's presidency, as Tulis has noted, "attempts to move the nation by moral suasion" were "almost unknown."[82] Roosevelt not only changed that, but also aimed to enlist public opinion as a tool of social reform. In calling upon the public to hold corporations to higher moral standards, he not only hoped to change the behavior of the corporations, but also to transform the public itself. "Skillful presidents not only adapt to their audiences," Karlyn Campbell and Kathleen Jamieson have observed, but they also "engage in a process of transforming those who hear them into the audiences they desire."[83] Toward that end, as Ceasar and others suggest, the discourse of modern, "rhetorical" presidents often soars "above the realm of calm and deliberate discussion of reasons of state or appeals to enlightened self-interest" to call the public to a "common purpose and a spirit of idealism."[84] This is precisely what Roosevelt did as he exploited what Fairbanks has called "the ministerial aspects of presidential leadership" to draw out the larger moral lesson of the controversy over the trusts.[85] "What as a nation we need," Roosevelt declared in summarizing that lesson, "is to stand by the eternal, immutable principles of right and decency, the principle of fair dealing as between man and man, the principles that teach us to regard virtue with respect and vice with abhorrence."[86]

As the object lessons in Roosevelt's secular sermons, the trusts represented "real and great evils" that stood out even more "in all their ugly baldness in times of prosperity," as the president put it in remarks to a Rhode Island audience in the summer of 1902. The "wicked who prosper," he conceded, "are never a pleasant sight."[87] Yet Roosevelt's concerns transcended the abuses of the trusts; he was more concerned with the larger lessons about human character taught by corporate abuses: "The man who gives himself up to the service of his appetites, the man who the more goods he has the more he wants, has surrendered himself to destruction. . . . Material prosperity without the moral lift toward righteousness means a diminished capacity for happiness."[88] As in his prepresidential rhetoric, Roosevelt condemned some industrialists for succumbing to "wolfish greed and vulpine cunning"; those businessmen had earned the "seared soul" of the damned.[89] In the final analysis, however, Roosevelt worried not so much about specific corporate abuses as about the moral example that set for the rest of the nation: "If we make it the only ideal before this Nation, if we permit the people of this Republic to get before their minds the view that material well-being carried to an ever higher degree is the one and only thing to be striven for, we are laying up for ourselves not merely trouble but ruin."[90]

The railroad corporations were simply the best illustration of what happened when business was not guided by moral principle. Of all the industrial combines, these stood as the most powerful and the most destructive, and some believed that the railroad magnates stood on the verge of controlling not only the transportation industry but the country itself.[91] As proof of their insatiable greed, Roosevelt detailed their "unjust practices," including driving smaller shippers "out of business, until practically one buyer of grain . . . had been able by his illegal advantages to secure a monopoly on the line."[92] Such practices, he repeated two years later, put a "premium upon unscrupulous and ruthless cunning in railroad management."[93]

During his presidency, Roosevelt continued to balance his criticisms of corporate businessmen with denunciations of those writers—"muckrakers," he called them—who exaggerated corporate abuses in numerous newspapers, magazine articles, and books. Pringle noted that "even the muckrakers, who had brought into the light so many of the evils on which Roosevelt acted, were to learn, in pained surprise, that he endorsed them with distinct reservations." For Pringle, this illustrated Roosevelt's "energetic efforts to appease the right wing" and, ultimately, called into question Roosevelt's commitment to reform.[94] To Roosevelt's mind, however, the muckrakers' incessant and sensational exaggerations of corporate offenses also violated basic ethical standards. Moreover, they did not serve the public good; they demoralized rather than educated, inflamed rather than energized. As a steward of the public welfare, Roosevelt could not let that stand unchallenged. Any writer who divided rich from poor, who aimed to damage all businessmen, or who engaged in "ignorant agitation" was, to Roosevelt's mind, an "enemy of the Republic."[95]

Roosevelt's criticism of those who recklessly attacked the trusts climaxed, of course, in his "Man with the Muck-Rake" speech in April of 1906. While targeted at journalists, the speech aimed especially at those whose revelations of government and big business abuses Roosevelt considered exaggerated or particularly lurid. "It was inevitable," Link noted, "that the muckraking technique would be adopted by publishers and writers of dubious integrity and exploited merely for financial gain."[96] Roosevelt clearly had these publishers and writers in mind as he spoke to an audience assembled for the laying of a cornerstone for a government building in Washington, D.C.

As president, Roosevelt often capitalized on public ceremonies to deliver his sermonic speeches, realizing that not only would he have a crowd in attendance, but that he would also attract national media coverage. In his muckrakers speech, the president used just such an occasion to transform a literary figure into a national political icon: the "man with the muck-rake," whose "vision is fixed on carnal instead of spiritual things." After working for so long in cleaning filth off the floor, constantly looking down into that which was vile, such a person could no longer see good and, as a result, became "one of the potent forces for evil." In Roosevelt's view, the "reckless assaults" by some journalists on the character of government and business officials had created just such an evil—a "morbid and vicious public sentiment." For him, the "wild preachers of unrest and discontent, the wild agitators against the entire existing order . . . the men who preach destruction" had become the "most dangerous opponents of real reform." Instead of righting wrongs, they committed sins of their own. "No good whatever will come from that warped and mock morality which denounces the misdeed of men of wealth and forgets the misdeeds practiced at their expense," he concluded, or which "foams with rage if a corporation secures favors by improper methods, and merely leers with hideous mirth if the corporation is itself wronged."[97]

Roosevelt conceded that most journalists were not muckrakers, and he applauded those who exposed real corruption or illegal practices. But, he concluded, those demagogic journalists who had created an "epidemic of indiscriminate assault upon character" had gone too far and caused a kind of "moral color-blindness": over time people would no longer "believe in the truth of the attack, nor in the honesty of the man who is attacked . . . it becomes well-nigh hopeless to stir them either to wrath against wrong-doing or to enthusiasm for what is right."[98]

Roosevelt extended his critique of public morality well beyond the corporate officers and the muckrakers. For him, every American had an obligation to promote righteousness and the national good, and he lamented that the public itself sometimes seemed to succumb to the sin of envy. Delivering a speech in front of the Alamo in 1905, the president warned his listeners that the "money-making" from modern industrialism had created "in the minds of the poor people an attitude of sullen envy toward men of wealth, which is infinitely more damaging to the people who hold it than any action of the man of wealth could be." For him, an attitude of "rancorous envy" stimulated the tendency for men to engage in "mob violence" and "mob rule."[99] Speaking before the National Education Association meeting in 1905, he further reminded his audience that if they did not "attach an exaggerated importance to the rich man who is distinguished only by his riches, this rich man would have a most insignificant influence." In other words, every citizen bore some of the moral responsibility for whatever evils resulted from the accumulation of great wealth: "It is generally our own fault if [the wealthy man] does damage to us, for he damages us chiefly by arousing our envy or by rendering us sour and discontented. . . . [It] is wicked folly to let ourselves be drawn into any attack upon the man of wealth. . . . Moreover, such an attack is in itself an exceptionally crooked and ugly tribute to wealth, and therefore the proof of an exceptionally ugly and crooked state of mind in the man making the attack."[100] Several months later, Roosevelt returned to the theme that envy led to immorality and hypocrisy. "We often see the very man who in public is most intemperate in his denunciation of wealth," he declared before an Atlanta audience, but "in his private life most eager to obtain wealth, in no matter what fashion, and at no matter what moral cost."[101]

Throughout his presidency, Roosevelt continued to speak out against the "apostles of discontent" who, out of envy, sought to "teach you that our social and industrial conditions are all wrong" and must be changed through revolution.[102] The true path to national greatness, he suggested, lay not in bringing down the rich but in the hard work and moral virtue of each and every American. "The principles of righteousness," he declared, "underlie all real national greatness."[103] While speaking at a banquet late in 1902, he declared that, "armed with the old homely virtues," America could defeat all of its "present evils."[104] As he told a group of miners during the summer of 1905, the "hand of the Lord" sometimes seemed "heavy upon the just," and it was not always possible to "ward off disaster." But the "chance for leading a happy and prosperous life" could be "immensely improved" if only one strove to be "decent [and] industrious."[105]

These were the base principles of Roosevelt's distinctive brand of "rhetorical progressivism": the principles of righteousness and selflessness. The federal government could not instill such principles in men, he suggested, but it did have an obligation to protect the public against corporations run by men who lacked such principles. As Roosevelt stated in August of 1902, a "trust is an artificial creature not wholly responsible to any legislation, either by state or nation."[106] Yet to his mind, the federal government did have the authority and the power to at least mitigate the damages done by big corporations. At a Union League Club meeting early in 1905, Roosevelt warned that the public would not long stand for the "use of the vast power conferred by . . . wealth in its corporate form, without lodging somewhere in the Government the still higher power of seeing that this power" is used "for and not against the interest of the people as a whole." According to Roosevelt, the right of the national government to deal with corporate businesses had been ordained since the beginning of the republic: "All great business concerns are engaged in interstate commerce, and it was beyond question the intention of the founders of our Government that interstate commerce in all its branches and aspects should be under national and not State control."[107]

Roosevelt's "rhetorical progressivism" in some measure tapped into the new fascination with administrative science in the early 1900s. According to David Danbom, the turn of the century saw many Progressives "put their faith in professional expertise" as the key to social progress. They believed that "public-spirited experts" and "scientific administration and management" could "move society in a desirable direction."[108] In this view, agencies run by experts trained in their field would "preside over a narrowly delineated functional area—railroad rates, food and drugs, banking, public health, commerce—so that specialized expertise might be brought to bear on public problems."[109] Roosevelt, to a degree, conceptualized the national government as this sort of dispassionate organization working systematically for the public good.

Yet for Roosevelt, the core issues in controversies over the trusts were always moral rather than administrative or practical. His charge to the Interstate Commerce Commission (ICC), for example, was to do the "square thing" for all involved in regulating the railroads: "If the railroad wants more than it is entitled to have, then [the ICC] must decide against it; if the public ignorantly demands that the railroad shall do more than it can with propriety do, then just as fearlessly [the ICC] must antagonize public sentiment, even if the public sentiment is unanimous."[110]

Roosevelt thus viewed the national government as something of an impartial arbitrator. At a banquet in Dallas in 1905, he again declared that the purpose of governmental regulation was not to enforce a particular solution but rather to assure a "square deal" for all: "[It was not possible] to give every man the best hand. If the cards do not come to any man, or if they do come, and he has not got the power to play them, that is his affair. All I mean is that there shall not be any crookedness in the dealing. . . . All any of us can pretend to do is to come as near our imperfect abilities will allow to securing through governmental agencies an equal opportunity for each man to show the stuff that is in him; and . . . with the intention of safeguarding each man, rich or poor . . . in his rights, and giving him as nearly as may be a fair chance to do what his powers permit him to do; always provided he does not wrong his neighbor."[111]

Unlike the scientific Progressives, who "did not believe that a thoroughgoing regeneration of character . . . was necessary" for social progress, Roosevelt continually returned to the theme that practical progress rested upon a moral base in the individual.[112] Croly summarized this synthesis between technical efficiency, ethics, and the "individual workman": the "excellent performance" of work, Croly argued, demanded that "thoroughly competent performers" be "morally and intellectually, as well as scientifically and manually" prepared, and be held to moral standards "applied as incorruptibly as those born of specific technical practices."[113] Like Croly, Roosevelt articulated a rhetoric of technically efficient government, but his fundamental expression of progressive reform involved the reconstitution of virtue in all Americans. "Let us never forget," he declared during a 1907 Memorial Day address, "that [regulating corporate activity] is not merely a matter of business but also a matter of morals." What everyone needed to understand was that even with increased legislative power, government administration could only do so much; corporate rate fixing, bribery, and blackmail, which did "irreparable moral harm" to the entire nation, could not be completely stopped through lawmaking.[114]

Ultimately, the solutions to social problems rested on individual morality and responsibility. The president observed that what we have to "demand in ourselves . . . is honesty—honesty to all men. . . . Demand honesty—absolute, unflinching honesty—together with courage and common sense, in public servant and in business man alike."[115] The federal government could do its part to "scourge sin" and "bid sinners fear," he wrote in a 1908 message to Congress, but it was the individual expression of "honesty . . . in all walks of life, in big things and in little things" that would "bring nearer the day when greed and trickery and cunning shall be trampled under foot by those who fight for the righteousness that exalteth a nation."[116] Just as Croly had maintained that the "Promise of American life" was to be fulfilled by "subordinating the satisfaction of individual desires to the fulfillment of a national purpose," Roosevelt gave voice to the idea that only through the morally inspired work of the individual would all Americans collectively achieve greatness.[117] Some historians have recognized that Roosevelt's principles of corporate responsibility were "progressive." However, it was ultimately his call to the broader public to embrace and to enforce righteousness that distinguished his progressivism from those who believed that only the coercive powers of government could rein in the giant corporations. His public messages reflected a faith in transcendent truths, in the power of rhetoric to help the public embrace those truths, and in the power of public opinion, in turn, to control the corporations. That is what distinguished Roosevelt from many other Progressives during his presidency, and he continued to preach this distinctive brand of "rhetorical progressivism" after he left office.

THE FINAL YEARS

While Roosevelt decided in 1904 not to run for a third term, he still planned to exert his influence over the presidency by naming his successor. He picked his vice president, William Howard Taft, as his heir apparent in the 1908 election. In Roosevelt's mind, Taft's victory over William Jennings Bryan in the that election, bringing with it Republican control of both the House and the Senate, would perpetuate Roosevelt's own legacy.[118] Taft, however, would soon disappoint his predecessor.

As Taft settled into the White House, Roosevelt kept himself isolated from the political news by going on safari in Africa.[119] When he returned to America in June 1910, Harbaugh observed, he discovered that his successor "had been proving a political failure." Taft appeared the antithesis of Roosevelt: he submitted rather than fought, and he seemed unwilling to explore problems in any depth. In addition, Taft angered Progressives with several decisions. First, he supported a contingent of progressive insurgents in Congress who wanted a lower tariff to expose American corporations to more foreign competition (only to later go along with a conservative bill that actually raised the tariff). Second, he replaced Roosevelt's secretary of the interior with Richard Ballinger, a man sympathetic to opening natural resources to development. Inevitably, Ballinger clashed with Gifford Pinchot, Roosevelt's chief of forestry, who publicly accused the new interior secretary of scheming to give valuable Alaskan coal lands to a private company. Taft backed Ballinger and fired Pinchot, further riling Progressives. Finally, Taft joined Republican conservatives in a campaign to defeat progressive Republicans in several Midwestern primary elections.[120]

Taft's actions led many progressive Republicans to look to Roosevelt for leadership.[121] Roosevelt was not yet ready to leave the party, but in the summer of 1910 he began a three-week speaking tour of the West. During that tour, he articulated the "New Nationalism," his progressive platform including such reforms as worker compensation laws, a graduated income tax, and children's and women's labor laws. Many people applauded his philosophy; Taft and the Republican old guard were appalled.[122]

While generally acknowledging Roosevelt's progressivism after his presidency, historians have characterized him as something of an extremist during this period. They point to his 31 August 1910 speech at Ossawatomie, Kansas, as evidence of a revolutionary change in his attitudes toward progressive reform. Amos Pinchot noted that in the "New Nationalism" speech, Roosevelt "took by far the most radical stand of his life," a stand that surprised many of his followers.[123] Harbaugh similarly labeled the speech "radical," likening Roosevelt's ideas about capital and labor to "words that could have been uttered by Marx."[124] Even Brands, who acknowledged that most of the ideas in that speech had been uttered during Roosevelt's presidency, concluded that the colonel's "striking statement" placed "the mark of the zealot on Roosevelt's forehead."[125]

These assessments fail to appreciate that the "New Nationalism" rested upon the same principles of righteousness and responsibility that had informed Roosevelt's brand of progressivism throughout his career. The speech represented the culmination of Roosevelt's decades-long crusade for moral reform. Now, however, he gave those themes their most striking expression. "Never were selfishness, hedonism and materialism so universally denigrated," Danbom wrote, and "never were selflessness, sacrifice, service . . . and devotion to the public interest more widely celebrated."[126]

Roosevelt spoke on a number of specific topics at Ossawatomie, including conservation, the tariff, corporate influence in the political process, a graduated income tax, the regulation of women and children labor, a direct primary, and workmen's compensation laws. But linking all of the various issues was an old refrain: virtuous character must undergird practical reform. To substantiate this idea, Roosevelt likened the struggle for progressive reform to another struggle faced decades earlier by many in his audience. Before an audience of Civil War veterans, Roosevelt reflected on the past, for the "great deeds of the past," in his view, acted as "spurs to drive us onward in the present."[127]

According to Roosevelt, the Civil War was itself a struggle to destroy special privilege. He called on his audience to forget the "bitterness" of that struggle and to contemplate instead all the good that ultimately resulted. "The essence of any struggle for healthy liberty," Roosevelt declared, "has always been . . . to take from some one man . . . the right to enjoy power, or wealth, or position . . . which has not been earned by service to his . . . fellows. That is what you fought for in the Civil War." As a result of that "long struggle for the rights of man—the long struggle for the uplift of humanity," America had achieved equality of opportunity and become the "mightiest nation upon which the sun shines." The colonel acknowledged those in charge—the military leaders—for their contributions, but, as always, he recognized that success came only through the determination and sacrifice of each individual soldier. "It would all have been worthless," he reminded his listeners, "if the average soldier had not had the right stuff in him. . . . In the last analysis . . . vitally necessary though it was to have the right kind of organization . . . it was even more vitally necessary that the average soldier should have the . . . right character."[128] The lessons from the Civil War—the elimination of special privilege and the moral uplift of the nation—reflected the essence of Roosevelt's "rhetorical progressivism."

Roosevelt's "New Nationalism" thus became a continuation of the same fight. Just as "the special interests of cotton and slavery threatened our political integrity," he declared, "so now the great special business interests too often control and corrupt the men and methods of government for their own profit." Just as the Grand Army rendered "life worth living for our generation," he continued, the "New Nationalism" would put "the national need before sectional or personal advantage" and would demand "that the representative body shall represent all the people rather than any one class or section of the people." For him, everyone was entitled to justice, the special interest as well as the common individual: "Every man will have a fair chance to make of himself all that in him lies," and, as a result, this "equality of opportunity means that the commonwealth will get from every citizen the highest service of which he is capable." The ultimate goal of reform was to remove those obstacles that kept "countless men from being good citizens by the conditions of life with which we surround them."[129]

While changing the laws was necessary, it was not enough; only individual initiative could lead to lasting reform. As Croly stated the spirit behind Roosevelt's progressivism: "It is none the less true that any success in the achievement of the national purpose will contribute positively to the liberation of the individual, both by diminishing his temptations . . . and by enveloping him in an invigorating rather than an enervating moral . . . atmosphere."[130] Roosevelt, as always, tied social reform to personal virtue. The government might "help any man who stumbles," but ultimate responsibility rested with each individual: "if he lies down, it is a poor job to try to carry him; but if he is a worthy man, try your best to see that he gets a chance to show the worth that is in him." In sum, Roosevelt's "New Nationalism" envisioned a moral revival. "We must have . . . a genuine and permanent moral awakening," he announced, "without which no wisdom of legislation or administration really means anything." His "New Nationalism" may have envisioned "radical" legislation, but at bottom it echoed what he had advocated for decades: a moral rebirth. New legislation had become necessary only because some men had corrupted public ethics in pursuit of selfish gain: "We are face to face with new conceptions of the relations of property to human welfare, chiefly because certain advocates of the rights of property as against the rights of men have been pushing their claims too far. The man who wrongly holds that every human right is secondary to his profit must now give way to the advocate of human welfare, who rightly maintains that every man hold his property subject to the general right of the community to regulate its use to whatever degree the public welfare may require it."[131]

Although Roosevelt won praise for his speech and helped progressive Republicans capture their nominations in some states, the Democrats gained control of the House and of governorships in twenty-six states as a result of the 1910 election, including the home states of both Roosevelt and Taft. Progressive congressmen then clamored for the next year and a half for the former president to challenge his successor for the 1912 nomination, agitating a divisive spirit in the Republican ranks.[132]

Still blaming himself for the political troubles of the Republicans since he left the presidency, Roosevelt announced his candidacy for the Republican nomination in the spring of 1912 and campaigned vigorously against Taft. While not totally unexpected, Brands wrote, it "hit the Republican Party like a thunderclap," since many Republicans liked Roosevelt but "weren't eager to help him split the party."[133] The voting public, however, clearly preferred Roosevelt. In one presidential primary after another, Roosevelt won the delegates, even in Taft's home state. Still, Roosevelt failed to win the nomination at the Republican National Convention in June 1912. To win the nomination, Roosevelt needed 70 of the 254 delegates in dispute; the Republican National Committee, comprised of Taft loyalists, gave Taft 235 and Roosevelt only 19.[134]

Stung by the defeat, Roosevelt bolted from the party and became the candidate of the Progressive or "Bull Moose" Party. Convening in August 1912, Harbaugh noted, the Progressive Party convention represented a "triumph of ideals" but a "failure of politics." Roosevelt's acceptance speech, "A Confession of Faith," called for the reform of America's political and social landscape, repeatedly bringing his listeners to their feet in cheers. Yet few of the insurgent Republicans who had courted him prior to the convention ultimately supported Roosevelt, and some Progressives condemned him for spurning African-American supporters who, in turn, left the convention to join with Taft.[135] Despite the hopelessness of his campaign, Roosevelt campaigned vigorously for the "permanent moral awakening" he had called for at Ossawatomie.

The Bull Moose convention illustrated vividly the moral impulse in Roosevelt's rhetoric. Joseph Gardner described it as less a "political convention" than an "old-time camp meeting of religious revivalists," complete with the singing of "Onward, Christian Soldiers."[136] According to Brands, Roosevelt brought the "Lord smack into politics" at the convention, and the crowd responded like new converts at a tent revival.[137] For fifty-five minutes after he appeared, the crowd cheered steadily for Roosevelt, and it interrupted his address more than one hundred times with thunderous applause.[138] Nothing could have been more appropriate in such a setting than an acceptance address entitled "A Confession of Faith." Roosevelt's "sermon" merged the practical with the pious, arguing that both were necessary for social progress and lasting reform.

"We promise nothing which will jeopardize honest business," Roosevelt promised in the address. "We promise adequate control of all big business and the stern suppression of the evils connected with big business." To that end, he called for Americans to support legislation in a wide array of areas: to protect industrial workers from harm and to give them a minimum wage; to thwart the judicial system in serving the corporate interests; to establish presidential primaries as well as the election of senators by popular vote; to support women's suffrage; to conserve the nation's resources more vigorously; to supervise and to regulate corporate entities with more powerful agencies in the national government; and to strengthen the country's military forces.[139]

Yet, as always, Roosevelt sought ultimately to energize the sense of moral responsibility in all Americans. His complaint against the major parties, he suggested, focused more on their moral indifference than on their political platforms. "The old parties are husks," he declared, "with no real soul within either." They were "boss-ridden and privilege-controlled . . . neither daring to speak out wisely and fearlessly what should be said on the vital issues of the day."[140] Both upheld a legalism that "subordinates equity to technicalities," and both allowed uncaring corporate owners to subject their workers to "unnecessary hazards." Above all, however, both made their "bread and butter by thwarting the wishes of the people." They had allowed government to be "misrepresentative instead of representative."[141] When he had been president, by contrast, Roosevelt understood that all else rested on the support of "the people." "When on any point I did not have that backing," he said, "when on any point I differed from the people, it mattered not whether I was right or whether I was wrong, my power vanished."[142]

Roosevelt clearly cast his Bull Moose campaign as a crusade for moral principle rather than a quest for political power. "It matters little what befalls any of us who for the time being stands in the forefront of the battle," he said. "I hope we shall win. . . . But, win or lose, we shall not falter." By casting the coming election as a struggle for the soul of the nation, as a war to protect the "eternal principle of righteousness," Roosevelt expressed the moral, democratic, and nationalistic threads that lay at the heart of his progressive "crusade": "Now to you . . . who, in your turn, have come together to spend and be spent in the endless crusade against wrong, to you who face the future resolute and confident, to you who strive in a spirit of brotherhood for the betterment of our nation, to you who gird yourselves for this great new fight in the never-ending warfare for the good of humankind, I say in closing. . . . We stand at Armageddon, and we battle for the Lord."[143]

Roosevelt campaigned determinedly against Taft and Woodrow Wilson, but to no avail. Wilson won a landslide victory, and with the Republicans divided, Democrats gained control of the Senate and retained control of the House as well.[144] Yet if we take Roosevelt at his word, his Bull Moose campaign had a higher purpose: to articulate a different *kind* of progressivism in the 1912 campaign, a more genuine and fundamental progressivism rooted in the principles of righteousness and decency. If his goals had been merely legislative, Roosevelt may well have been satisfied with the outcome of the election; Wilson's legislative agenda was not all that different from his own. For Roosevelt, however, the Bull Moose campaign was about more than policies and programs. It was a crusade for confirmation of the moral principles he had championed throughout his career.

Rhetorical Progressivism and Foreign Affairs

THE EARLY YEARS

Roosevelt's celebration of the martial spirit began in childhood. Indirectly, Theodore Sr. acted as the catalyst for Theodore Jr.'s passionate interest in the military. At an early age, the young Roosevelt was haunted by his father's refusal to fight in the Civil War—even though that refusal came at the behest of his Southern-born wife. According to Brands, Theodore Jr.'s sister, Corinne, assigned her "brother's obsession with war to a desire to compensate for their father's deficiency in this regard."[145]

Roosevelt's "obsession" with war was clear in his writings in the 1880s. Roosevelt focused on war in his most respected scholarly work, *The Naval War of 1812*.[146] His best-selling popular history, *The Winning of the West*, also revealed Roosevelt's fascination with war. According to one review of that work, Roosevelt showed a "keen appreciation of what the frontier experience meant to the people who underwent it and to the rest of the nation."[147] What it "meant" for the settlers, of course, was almost constant war, not only against the Native Americans but against nature itself.

When he became assistant secretary of the navy in 1897, Roosevelt became a vocal advocate of building up the fleet.[148] To cap his one-year appointment and to illustrate the importance of a strong navy, Roosevelt disobeyed the secretary of the navy's warning not to issue any orders regarding America's response to the destruction of the *Maine* and dispatched Dewey's fleet to Hong Kong. This paved the way for the destruction of the Spanish fleet during the Spanish-American War and American control of the region.[149]

America's war with Spain also gave Roosevelt the opportunity to demonstrate his own martial skills. Resigning from his post as assistant secretary, he organized a cavalry regiment of volunteers whose deeds have since entered into American folklore. Chronicling those exploits a year later in *The Rough Riders*, he recalled how he sensed that the Spanish-American War "would be as righteous as it would be advantageous to the honor and the interests of the nation."[150] Roosevelt's glorification of his own military exploits seemed to confirm his "obsession" with war.

"Progressivism" generally calls to mind a philosophy of domestic social reform. Progressives sought mainly to ameliorate social injustice, political corruption, and corporate abuses at home, not to change the world.[151] Progressives generally said little about war and imperialism, according to Robert Johnson, simply because they "devoted little attention to foreign policy matters."[152] Watson also observed that Progressives lacked any unified and coherent philosophy of international relations. "There is no clear-cut relationship," he wrote, "between progressivism in general and any particular position on foreign policy." According to Watson, progressive advocates "moved in and out of every divergent position" on foreign policy.[153]

Nevertheless, the tendency among modern scholars has been to suggest that Roosevelt's emphasis on international affairs and his "obsession" with war prove that his progressivism was not genuine. In Hofstadter's view, for example, Progressives—by definition—opposed militarism, for war is the "Nemesis of the liberal tradition."[154] More recently, Johnson has written of the progressive "suspicion" of "traditional power politics," as manifested in the imperialism of Roosevelt's day. Some Progressives, as Johnson notes, "did not question American cultural imperialism" and supported American economic expansion.[155] Similarly, Watson has noted that Progressives endorsed a "vigorous policy of foreign trade and overseas investment" as a means to promote "order and stability at home."[156] Yet Progressives, according to most later scholars, generally opposed the use of military force to advance American interests overseas.

In terms of Theodore Roosevelt's own principles, however, the meaning of a "progressive" foreign policy was quite different. Not only did international engagement and even war build righteous character, in Roosevelt's view, but America also had a moral obligation to advance "civilization" around the world—by force, if necessary. Just as Croly would later defend the "vigorous assertion of a valid foreign policy" and the "righteous use of superior force" as progressive principles,[157] Roosevelt spent considerable energy prior to his presidency articulating a "progressive" rationale for an aggressive foreign policy.

Roosevelt's "rhetorical progressivism" revolved around a simple and consistent idea that he applied both at home and abroad: "No nation can achieve real greatness," he wrote in 1896, "if its people are not both essentially moral and essentially manly."[158] Early in his career, he repeated this age-old theme in a number of forums, often as a "lesson of the past" in his historical works. In his *Winning of the West*, for example, Roosevelt demonstrated the necessity of expansion and the subjugation of backward peoples to the "progress" of civilization. As he portrayed the westward spread of America's pioneers, it became the story of how they tamed "brutal and lazy" people "incapable of self-motivated productive labor."[159] In Roosevelt's view, the Americans had every right—indeed, they had a duty—to displace the nomadic tribes, for "the man who puts the soil to use must of right dispossess the man who does not, or the world will come to a standstill."[160] Roosevelt criticized the false sentimentality of those who questioned the morality of warring against such people. To him, it was a "warped, perverse, and silly morality which would forbid a course of conquest that has turned whole continents into the seats of mighty and flourishing civilized nations." The displaced people were but "scattered savage tribes, whose life was but a few degrees less meaningless, squalid, and ferocious than that of the wild beasts with whom they held joint ownership."[161]

The parallels to the foreign policy debates of his own day were obvious. It infuriated Roosevelt when people rationalized international passivity by claiming that the United States had no right to expand into the Philippines or other inhabited areas. Where "savages" unfit for self-government held sway, America had both a right and a duty to expand. It was "criminal folly" to advocate a principle in foreign policy that "would have made the entire North American continent . . . the happy hunting ground of savages," he told an audience in New York in 1899.[162] Similarly, he suggested in a speech in Detroit in 1900 that if America had no right to expand overseas, then it had no right to conquer the American West: "The men who are making speeches on the unrighteousness of our expanding in the Philippines might with as much justification incite the Sioux and the Apache tribes to outbreak against us, on the ground that we have no right to retain South Dakota or Arizona."[163] Thus Roosevelt suggested that critics of expansion were not true "Progressives," for they opposed the advancement of civilization and the spread of Christian and democratic virtues.

The chief tool of Roosevelt's "progressive" internationalism was, of course, a battleship navy, and Roosevelt spoke and wrote prolifically on that subject early in his career. He believed that a powerful fleet would not only provide the means to assure the "progress" of "civilization" abroad, but also be a source of inspiration and honor at home. In *The Naval War of 1812*, he revealed the two "most practical lessons" that history could teach: the need for "efficient ships" and the need for "efficient men" to sail them. Roosevelt pointed time and again to the need for a navy "unsurpassed" by that of all other nations. He illustrated his point with reference to Great Britain's world leadership. "In every sea," he wrote, ships of all sizes could be found flying England's colors: "from the stately ship-of-the-line, with her tiers of heavy cannon and her many hundreds of men, down to the little cutter carrying but a score of souls and a couple of light guns." According to Roosevelt, England's offensive, sea-going navy played the key role in advancing "civilization" during the nineteenth century. For him, the historical lesson was clear: if the United States aspired to world leadership and the "progress" of civilization, it would need a first-class navy, manned with crews trained to "fight with pluck."[164]

As assistant secretary of the Navy, Roosevelt expanded upon that historical lesson in a famous speech to the Naval War College in 1897, "Washington's Forgotten Maxim." Starting from the premise that preparedness was the best assurance of peace, Roosevelt argued that the construction of a "first-class fleet of first-class battleships" would do more to assure peace than "any arbitration treaty which the wit of man can devise." Common sense dictated that the country follows this path, since "never once in the course of its history" had the United States "suffered harm because of preparation for war, or because of entering into war." To the contrary, history illustrated that "incalculable harm" resulted from a "foolish failure to prepare for war or from reluctance to fight when to fight was proper." Preparation for war, Roosevelt suggested, was ultimately a "progressive" measure—a means of promoting civilization and protecting the weak. "Better a thousand times err on the side of over-readiness to fight," he concluded, "than to err on the side of tame submission to injury, or cold-blooded indifference to the misery of the oppressed.[165]

Roosevelt's rhetoric of preparedness reflected more than a simple "obsession" with war. It reflected his deep-rooted belief that the progress of civilization rested upon the willingness of both individuals and the nation to embrace great challenges, not just in war, but in all aspects of life. That, of course, was the theme of Roosevelt's most famous prepresidential address, "The Strenuous Life." Delivered before the Chicago Hamilton Club in April of 1899, "The Strenuous Life" explored the implications for both individuals and nations of the most fundamental principles of Roosevelt's "rhetorical progressivism."

Among Roosevelt's more philosophical addresses, "The Strenuous Life" criticized that "base spirit of gain and greed" that led both people and nations to a "life of slothful ease." When "men fear work or fear righteous war," Roosevelt proclaimed, civilization was doomed, and nations likewise survived only by taking on great challenges. "We cannot sit huddled within our own borders," he declared, "and avow ourselves merely an assemblage of well-to-do hucksters who care nothing for what happens beyond." Such a course would lead the nation to "rot by inches" and "go down before other nations which have not lost the manly and adventurous qualities." For civilization to progress, Americans needed to embrace the "life of toil and effort, of labor and strife." Genuine progress depended on "the man who does not shrink from danger, from hardship . . . and who out of these wins the splendid ultimate triumph." Invoking Lincoln and Grant, Roosevelt called upon his audience to apply this lesson to the nation as a whole. Just as the "wisdom of Lincoln" and the "armies of Grant" ended slavery, restored the Union, and placed America "once more as a helmeted queen among nations," modern Americans, to be "really great people," would have to insist that their nation "strive in good faith to play a great part in the world." Roosevelt concluded on a sermonic note: "I preach to you . . . that our country calls not for the life of ease but for the life of strenuous endeavor. . . . If we stand idly by, if we seek merely swollen, slothful ease and ignoble peace, if we shrink from the hard contests where men must win a hazard of their lives . . . then the bolder and stronger peoples will pass us by. . . . Let us therefore boldly face the life of strife, resolute to do our duty well and manfully; resolute to uphold righteousness by deed and word; resolute to be both honest and brave, to serve high ideals, yet to use practical methods."[166]

Well before assuming the presidency, Roosevelt thus articulated what he believed was the essence of a truly "progressive" foreign policy: righteousness backed by martial strength. Specifically, modern Americans needed to recapture the spirit of their pioneer ancestors. They needed to be willing to defend their honor, as well as to enforce justice. To later historians, such views may seem the antithesis of "progressivism"; Roosevelt displayed what seems today nothing more than a crude "obsession" with war and an even cruder hostility toward "backward" peoples. In the final analysis, however, Roosevelt was simply championing the same basic principles that guided his domestic reform agenda: the principles of righteousness among the privileged and justice for the oppressed.

THE PRESIDENTIAL YEARS

According to Harbaugh, no aspect of the presidency "more fascinated Roosevelt than the conduct of foreign affairs."[167] Despite the nation's strong isolationist tradition, President Roosevelt embarked on a number of provocative foreign policy initiatives. During his tenure, Roosevelt intervened in a number of regions to safeguard America's interests, including Venezuela, the Dominican Republic, Cuba, the Philippines, and Panama.[168] Meanwhile, he continued to call for the upgrading of the navy to a fleet of sea-going battleships. Roosevelt pressed his executive power to the limit as he pursued his foreign policy agenda, and he continuously urged the nation to embrace what he believed were its international responsibilities.

While scholars generally have conceded that Roosevelt accomplished much in foreign affairs, many sense a contradiction between his progressive domestic agenda and what Gould has called his "bravado" in foreign affairs.[169] According to Mowry, for example, the supposedly progressive Roosevelt was "often ruthless in his power against" America's "weaker foreign neighbors."[170]

Roosevelt would no doubt have been puzzled by such criticism. To his mind, American intervention in such places as Cuba and the Philippines had always been to the benefit of the native people, not to the benefit of Americans. When American forces ended their four-year occupation of Cuba after the Spanish-American War, for example, Roosevelt insisted that they had left that island nation "in a better condition than it ever has been in all the centuries of Spanish rule."[171] Four months later he elaborated on the benefits of American intervention in Cuba by declaring that America had "administered it on a plane higher than it had ever reached," improved its education, health care, and government, and established the "deep and broad foundations upon which civil liberty and national independence must rest."[172] Similarly, Roosevelt insisted that when America intervened in the Philippines, it "acted in the interest of the [natives] themselves."[173] In both cases, he portrayed American intervention as something of a "progressive" imperative. Speaking specifically of Cuba in his "Second Annual Message," he argued that it would have been "unworthy of a mighty and generous nation . . . to refuse to stretch out a helping hand to a young and weak sister republic just entering upon its career of independence."[174] Speaking at a Founders' Day banquet in late 1902, he again cast American intervention as consistent with the "spirit of great humanity" and part of the burden of a great and forward-looking nation: "No nation as great as ours can expect to escape the penalty of greatness, for greatness does not come without trouble and labor. . . . Scant is our patience with those who preach the gospel of craven weakness. . . . We know that the future is ours if we have in us the manhood to grasp it, and we enter the new century girding our loins for the contest before us, rejoicing in the struggle."[175]

Roosevelt offered similar defenses of his interventions in Venezuela and the Dominican Republic. With both cases involving conflicts with European nations, Roosevelt creatively reinterpreted the Monroe Doctrine as a mandate for the United States to "police" the Western Hemisphere. This so-called Roosevelt Corollary to the Monroe Doctrine, announced in his "Fourth Annual Message," had a strongly moral and progressive tone with its emphasis on efficiency, decency, and the interests of "civilized" society. As Roosevelt summarized the doctrine: "If a nation shows that it knows how to act with reasonable efficiency and decency in social and political matters, if it keeps order and pays its obligations, it need fear no interference from the United States. Chronic wrong-doing, or an impotence which results in a general loosening of the ties of civilized society, may . . . require intervention by some civilized nation, and in the western hemisphere the adherence of the United States to the Monroe Doctrine may force the United States . . . to the exercise of an international police power."[176]

Roosevelt stretched the limits of his "progressive" foreign policy in what Gould has called the "most disputed and controversial act" of his presidency: securing the rights to build the Panama Canal.[177] According to Pringle, Roosevelt deluded himself "when he praised the ethics" of his actions in Panama.[178] Most later biographers and historians agree: by first negotiating a treaty with Columbia for the right to build a canal across its isthmus of Panama, and then using military force to support a revolution by locals unhappy with the Columbian senate's rejection of that treaty, Roosevelt acted in a manner both reprehensible and illegal. His deployment of American warships to protect the revolution and the one-sided treaty that the administration quickly secured from the new Panamanian government—the Hay-Buneau-Varilla treaty—epitomize, in conventional wisdom, Roosevelt's heavy-handed approach to foreign affairs.[179] Even at the time, the president's opponents charged that Roosevelt had usurped the war-making powers of Congress and disregarded a congressional mandate to build the canal in Nicaragua if a treaty could not be successfully negotiated with Columbia within a "reasonable time."[180] While Roosevelt responded to these charges when the Senate debated the new treaty, for the most part he ignored the specific allegations in his public rhetoric both during and after the ratification debate. In Roosevelt's view, the contributions of the canal to the progress of "civilization" far outweighed any concerns over his means in obtaining the canal rights.

Defending his actions in Panama in numerous venues, Roosevelt emphasized that the benefits of the canal would be "by no means limited merely to its material effects upon our business prosperity."[181] For Roosevelt, the building of the canal would demonstrate the nation's embrace of its duties and obligations to the entire civilized world. It would signal America's arrival as a great world power. In his "Third Annual Message," he did respond to specific concerns about his treatment of Columbia. That nation had shown itself to be "utterly incapable of keeping order on the Isthmus," he noted, and only America's "active interference" had enabled Columbia to preserve any "semblance of sovereignty."[182] More commonly, however, Roosevelt did not answer the charges so much as he celebrated the canal project as a symbol of "progress." A canal between the oceans, he announced to a Connecticut audience in 1902, would be one of the "greatest, probably the greatest, engineering feats of the twentieth century."[183] It would reflect and promote America's emergence as a great world power, he wrote in his "Special Message" to Congress in 1906, and all Americans could take the "highest pride" in the "gigantic" undertaking.[184]

Roosevelt apparently convinced Congress with such arguments, but controversy over the canal would continue for many years. During construction of the canal, journalistic muckrakers wrote about jobbery, disease, exploitation of workers, and administrative incompetence on the isthmus, thereby threatening Roosevelt's vision of the canal as a great symbol of American achievement. In response, Roosevelt launched a major campaign to focus attention on the positive achievements of the canal workers. Traveling to the isthmus and later publicly distributing a "Special Message" to Congress on the project, Roosevelt silenced the critics and began a national celebration of the canal. In the "Special Message," dated 17 December 1906, Roosevelt used words and pictures to celebrate every aspect of the project, from the actual digging to the provisions made for the workers. He especially boasted of the achievements in health and sanitation. The isthmus, he noted, "had been a byword for deadly unhealthfulness," but under the leadership of Dr. William Gorgas, the chief health officer on the isthmus, American sanitation workers had made the canal zone "healthy and attractive." These Americans had labored unceasingly to cut back vegetation from housing, dig drainage ditches, pave streets, and establish the "most modern hygienic" sewer and water services in an effort to eliminate the mosquitoes that transmitted yellow fever. Only a "single mosquito" had been seen during his visit, Roosevelt reported, and that one was "not of the dangerous species." According to the president, Dr. Gorgas's "army" of health workers had reduced sickness and the death rates on the isthmus to the point where they compared favorably with those within the United States.[185]

The imagery of war pervaded Roosevelt's rhetoric on the canal. While visiting the isthmus, Roosevelt spoke to the workers as if they were soldiers in a great war. "You here who do your work well in bringing to completion this great enterprise," he told them, "stand exactly as the soldiers of a few . . . of the most famous armies" in history. Time and again he compared the American canal workers to a "mighty army . . . a brigade," even referring to excavating machinery on occasion as their "howitzers." He encouraged them to develop a "healthy spirit of emulation" between the "different shovel and locomotive crews," just as the "different gun crews" on a battleship competed "in matters of marksmanship." And just as American warriors in the past had triumphed over impossible odds, Roosevelt promised the workers that they too would relish the "feeling of triumph" once they completed their "mighty work" of "conquest" down on the isthmus. In the end, he assured them, they would earn the "same credit" that was given to "the picked men of a victorious army."[186]

Roosevelt ultimately celebrated not just the "soldiers" of the canal zone but the progressive spirit of all Americans who took pride in the project. The whole "American Nation," he said, took "especial pride" in assuming its "world duty." Only a "big nation" could undertake such a "work for all mankind." The "American People" had demonstrated "not only faith, but resolution," he said before a Florida audience in 1905, and had refused to be "swept one way or the other by mere sensationalism." As a result, the "stupendous work" on the isthmus had brought "honor" and a "thrill of pride" to all Americans.[187] In the end, it testified to the progressive spirit of every American.

Finally, Roosevelt emphasized one last requirement of what he portrayed as a "progressive" foreign policy during his presidency: a battleship navy. According to naval historians Harold and Margaret Sprout, never before had a president exhibited such a "fanatical desire for a big navy," and, not surprisingly, his efforts met with considerable resistance.[188] "No argument for naval expansion," historian George Davis has observed, "escaped the most heated opposition."[189] With America at peace and isolationist sentiment still strong in Congress, few shared Roosevelt's urgency about the need for a big navy. According to congressional critics of Roosevelt's naval build up, a bigger and more formidable navy would only benefit the munitions makers and invite war by signaling America's aggressive intentions.[190]

For Roosevelt, however, the navy was more than a tool of war. Like the Panama Canal, the navy was also to serve as a symbol of American "progress"—a practical instrument for managing the nation's international responsibilities, to be sure, but also a testament to the nation's "coming-of-age" as an agent of moral force in the world. Roosevelt reminded the public in 1905 that, with the completion of the canal, the Caribbean would become a "highway for the nations of mankind."[191] No longer would America be able to rest secure in its geographical isolation. American needed a strong navy to keep the peace in the whole region. A strong navy, Roosevelt wrote to Congress in 1901, represented the "very lightest premium for insuring peace which this nation can possibly pay." The "insurance" provided by a strong navy represented the "best guarantee of peace."[192]

As he often did in his writings before becoming president, Roosevelt looked to history for proof that a strong navy was of "literally incalculable worth." During all the great crises in America's history, he reminded a Massachusetts audience in 1902, the navy played a pivotal role. A strong navy, he contended, prevented America's national "disgrace" during the Spanish-American War.[193] By contrast, he argued before a Maryland audience in 1906, "our parsimony in not preparing an adequate navy" prior to the War of 1812 "cost in the end literally thousands of dollars for every one dollar we thus foolishly saved."[194] History thus taught a clear lesson: Americans needed the "insurance" of a strong navy—the "most potent guarantee of peace."[195]

In the twentieth century, Roosevelt thus suggested, a strong navy was needed to maintain peace and to safeguard America's interests around the world. In addition, it would help preserve progressive yet manly virtues, which he articulated at Carnegie Hall in 1903: "[I]f we are to advance in broad humanity, in kindliness, in the spirit of brotherhood . . . it must be by developing strength in virtue and virtue in strength, by breeding and training men who shall be both good and strong . . . and who at the same time have both the courage and the strength to strive mightily for the right."[196] Two years later, Roosevelt even invoked the wisdom of George Washington, the isolationists' hero, to argue that a strong navy was necessary to, in Washington's words, "observe good faith and justice toward all nations." Speaking at the University of Pennsylvania, Roosevelt concluded: "It is neither the conscientious man who is craven at heart, nor yet the bold and strong man without the moral sense, who is of real use to the community; it is the man who to strength and courage adds a realizing sense of the moral obligation resting upon him. . . . So, in the world at large, the nation which is of use in the progress of mankind is that nation which combines strength of character, force of character, and insistence upon its own rights, with a full acknowledgment of its own duties toward others. Just at present the best way in which we can show . . . our loyalty to the teachings of Washington . . . is to see to it that the work of building up our navy goes steadily on."[197]

Roosevelt dramatically demonstrated the symbolic power of a strong navy in 1907 when he sent America's new battleship fleet on a world cruise. Ignoring criticisms that the cruise might provoke a war, Roosevelt ordered the fleet to assemble at Hampton Roads, Virginia, on 1 December 1907. Two weeks later, sixteen gleaming white battleships departed the port with, as Gould has written, an "ample complement of reporters to record what took place."[198] The cruise had the desired effect: it captured the attention of the public both at home and abroad. Hundreds of articles appeared in the American press, not only telling the story of the cruise but also endorsing Roosevelt's naval philosophy and celebrating the progress of naval technology.[199] Never before had Americans witnessed such a concentration of naval might, and thousands turned out to welcome the fleet at each of its North American stops. "In every corner of the nation," James Reckner has written, the "pageantry and splendor" of the cruise promoted "public knowledge of, interest in, and sympathy" for the navy. At foreign ports, the reception was equally impressive. Foreign newspapers also marveled at the "greatest naval experiment ever undertaken," and wherever the fleet anchored it inspired large celebrations. Whether in Latin American, Australia, or the Far East, hundreds of thousands of spectators welcomed the fleet with parades, athletic competitions, and fireworks displays. As Reckner has concluded, "no earlier episode in American history had so . . . convincingly identified the United States as a major actor on the world stage."[200]

The cruise of the great white fleet proved a fitting capstone to Roosevelt's foreign policy initiatives. Symbolizing as nothing else his conception of a "progressive" foreign policy, the cruise announced to the world America's acceptance of the challenges of world leadership. It symbolized in many ways the seeming contradiction of Roosevelt's "rhetorical progressivism": the simultaneous celebration of militarism and peace. For some historians, this apparent contradiction reveals the hypocrisy of Roosevelt's foreign policy rhetoric. In the final analysis, however, it was consistent with what he had said all along: that virtue without strength meant nothing.

THE FINAL YEARS

Attempting to leave politics behind following his loss in the 1912 presidential election, Roosevelt led a disastrous expedition down an uncharted river in South America.[201] Despite being physically weakened and infected with malaria as a result of the ordeal, Roosevelt felt compelled to enter what would be his last full-fledged political battle when he returned to the United States in the summer of 1914. Harbaugh concluded that when Germany invaded Belgium late that summer, Roosevelt "had thrown himself into the mightiest struggle of his career—the campaign to persuade the American people to enter World War I and to prosecute it with vigor after they had entered it."[202] Publishing in popular forums, including the *Outlook*, the *New York Times*, and the *Kansas City Star*, and compiling articles in such books as *America and the World War* and *Fear God and Take Your Own Part*, he repeatedly attacked President Wilson's policies. He sharply criticized Wilson's decision to remain neutral and to try to end the European conflict through mediation. By 1916, Roosevelt had become the chief voice for military preparedness and universal military service.[203]

When America declared war in the spring of 1917, Roosevelt felt vindicated. He also relished the opportunity to participate personally in the Great War. He hoped to raise a volunteer division to fight in Europe, and he wrote several letters to the secretary of war asking for permission. He even called upon his bitter foe, Wilson, to endorse the "Roosevelt Division." Despite widespread public support for the venture, Wilson refused. Over the next year and a half until his death in January 1919, Roosevelt wrote over one hundred editorials blasting the Wilson administration's war policies and the anti-war attitudes of many of his fellow citizens.[204]

Roosevelt's passionate call for America to enter the European war ran counter to prevailing sentiments prior to 1915. Peace Progressives in the Senate, Johnson wrote, were "suspicious of American involvement in power politics" and argued that America should not get involved in the European conflict.[205] Many other Progressives opposed American participation because they feared that the war would interfere with domestic reform.[206] Link and McCormick observed that as "late as the eve of American entry into the war, Wilson himself had given strong expression to the conviction that war and progressivism were antithetical."[207] After America's entry into the war, however, many Progressives came to accept or even embrace it as something of a progressive crusade. Lending their expertise, organizational skills, and rhetorical energies to the war effort, Progressives eventually joined enthusiastically in the war effort. According to Danbom, many Progressives came to think that the war actually might help the nation to "achieve unity and brotherhood and efficiency."[208] For many, the war became a vehicle for the cultural and social development of the nation. "No wartime task was carried out in a more progressive manner," Link and McCormick concluded, "than that of raising and training an American army. . . . Kept from alcohol, warned against prostitutes, inspected for disease, tested for intelligence, and ministered to . . . by army chaplains, the army was rendered as morally and scientifically 'fit to fight' as the wisest and most religious progressives of the day could make it."[209]

Nevertheless, scholars have tended to cast Roosevelt's pro-war campaign as a betrayal of progressivism. Mowry noted that the Progressive Party did not support Roosevelt's early pro-preparedness position, citing that "some of the most militant opposition" to American involvement in Europe "was voiced by Progressives."[210] Pringle and Brands both have suggested that Roosevelt abandoned his progressive ideals only because of his personal animosity toward Wilson.[211] Again, however, Roosevelt's four-year pro-war campaign not only foreshadowed the attitudes of many other Progressives, but was perfectly consistent with the progressive principles he had articulated throughout his career. Rather than celebrate war per se, Roosevelt advocated American participation because he viewed the European conflict as an affront to progressive principles. In Roosevelt's view, the German war machine threatened the continued progress of "civilization" itself.

From the beginning of the European conflict, Roosevelt demonized and dehumanized the Germans. In an article that appeared less than two months after the invasion of Belgium, he lamented how Europeans were unprepared as "hell yawned under [their] feet . . . and woe smote them as it smote the peoples we read of in the Old Testament." He compared the German military machine to the forces of nature: destructive, chaotic, and an impediment to human progress. According to Roosevelt, the enemy erupted as "volcanic fires" tearing through the "smiling surface of civilization." He even likened the invasion of Belgium to the best-known disaster of his day: "What occurred in Europe," he wrote, "is on a giant scale like the disaster to the *Titanic*. . . . Suddenly, in one awful and shattering moment, death smote the floating host. . . . At one stroke they were hurled from a life of effortless ease back into elemental disaster; to disaster in which baseness showed naked."[212]

Even after the United States declared war against Germany in 1917, Roosevelt continued a steady drumbeat of attacks on the Germans' character and motives. Writing numerous articles for the *Kansas City Star*, he created a vivid portrait of how a military force—without moral purpose—not only produced barbarous behavior but also threatened all the progress that "civilization" had thus far achieved. The German social system, he alleged, was a system based on "brutal insolence to the weak." It had produced a "conscienceless" society.[213] Unlike President Wilson, who absolved the German people of blame by insisting in his "War Message" that it was not "upon their impulse that their government acted in entering this war," Roosevelt condemned all things German.[214] "Our war is as much with the German people as with their Government," he wrote in "German Hatred of America," "and we should regard with loathing all Americans who any way attempt to justify or defend Germany's actions." After all, he maintained, the German people had rallied behind their government's "systematic infliction of hideous brutality . . . obscene cruelty . . . wholesale slaughter . . . [and] foul treachery and bestiality."[215] Roosevelt cataloged long lists of atrocities perpetrated by the German military and sanctioned by its people: slaughtering children, destroying churches and hospitals, torturing prisoners, crucifying soldiers, and raping women. For him, a culture that waged war in this fashion was right out of the "Dark Ages."[216]

Roosevelt extended his condemnation of the German people to German Americans who remained loyal to the fatherland. In an essay published in the *Kansas City Star*, for example, he criticized the "Shadow Huns" who "stir dissensions among our own people and weaken us in the prosecution of the war."[217] In another essay in the *Star*, entitled "Pillar-of-Salt Citizenship," Roosevelt retold the biblical story of Lot's wife who had been turned into a pillar of salt because "she could not resist looking back to the land she had left." German Americans, he suggested, deserved the same fate if they could not let go of their loyalty to the homeland.[218]

Even worse, to Roosevelt's mind, were those Americans who decried the use of military force as inherently immoral, the peace-at-any-cost pacifists who opposed America's entry into the war because they opposed war itself. In a 1914 newspaper article entitled "Summing Up," Roosevelt accused the "peace-at-any-price men" of a "crime against morality" for failing to "uphold righteousness as the all-important end toward which we should strive." These "professional peace-prattlers," he suggested, reflected a dangerous spiritual softness in the American national character.[219] Employing religious imagery, he depicted the pacifists as false prophets who fostered an evil indifference in the guise of upholding righteousness. In 1915, he wrote that "professional pacifists preach the utter flabbiness and feebleness, moral and physical, which inevitably breeds cowardice."[220] In 1916, he added that those who "preach the doctrine of milk-and-water . . . have in them a softness of fibre."[221] In 1917, he even seemed to blame the war itself on the pacifists: "We followed the foolish prophets of pacifism when with quavering voices they told us that if we were only harmless enough nobody would hurt us, and that preparedness brought on war. We tried the experiment. We did not prepare. And we have the war."[222]

Roosevelt reserved perhaps his harshest criticisms for those who refused to fight for religious reasons. In a speech in Minneapolis in 1917, he dismissed the possibility that some conscientious objectors might be sincere in their beliefs. The "bulk" of them were actually "traitorous pro-Germans," or just plain "slackers"— lazy men who desired "to avoid any duty that interferes with their ease and enjoyment." Regardless of their motive, this "sissy type of pacifist" represented a clear sign of the "rotting out of the virile virtues" in the American character. The pacifists typified "the unlovely senile side of civilization." However sincere their motivations, those who put "peace above righteousness" worked to "serve the devil against the Lord," according to Roosevelt, and as such they posed perhaps an even greater threat to "civilization" than the war itself.[223]

Roosevelt's glorification of war thus was limited to wars that served righteous causes and advanced "civilization." "Among the noblest deeds of mankind," he wrote in the *New York Times* in 1914, were the "great wars for liberty"; he found glory not in all wars but only "in wars for the relief of oppressed peoples, [and] in wars for putting an end to wrong-doing in the dark places of the globe." He called upon Americans to "pray for the peace of righteousness," yet also to cultivate the "strength and the loftiness of spirit which will back righteousness with deeds and not mere words." "Mere words," such as those of peace treaties or arbitration agreements, were worth "absolutely nothing" during times of crisis "with no sanction of force behind them."[224] In one of Roosevelt's best-known essays, "Fear God and Take Your Own Part," he summarized his attitude toward war in the sermonic tones common to his presidential rhetoric: "Peace is not the end. Righteousness is the end. When the Saviour saw the money-changers in the Temple he broke the peace by driving them out. At that moment peace could have been obtained readily enough by the simple process of keeping quiet in the presence of wrong. But instead of preserving peace at the expense of righteousness, the Savior armed himself . . . and drove the money-changers from the Temple. Righteousness is the end, and peace a means to the end, and sometimes it is not peace, but war which is the proper means to achieve the end."[225]

In Roosevelt's view, then, war was not an end in itself, nor was war a personal "obsession." Nor did he sense any contradiction between his campaign urging America's participation in World War I and the progressive ideals he had expressed throughout his career. To the contrary, he viewed that war as the ultimate challenge to the continued progress of "civilization." For Roosevelt, World War I was a quintessentially progressive crusade, a war for righteousness and justice against the forces of barbarism and evil.

Conclusion

For some historians and biographers, Theodore Roosevelt is a study in conflicting images and philosophical contradictions. In the conventional view, he was both a conservative and a Progressive, a scholar and a cowboy, a hunter and a conservationist, a war monger and a peace maker, a man of principle and a political opportunist. In attempting to account for these conflicting images, some have suggested that he changed over the course of his life. Others distinguish his "progressive" views on some issues from his "reactionary" attitudes on others. This chapter has suggested a different way of understanding the supposed contradictions of Roosevelt's career: they were not contradictions at all but elements of Roosevelt's distinctive yet coherent brand of "rhetorical progressivism."

In some respects, Roosevelt embraced traditional progressive principles: a belief in the necessity of a strong national government to effect social and political reform, a faith in science and administrative expertise, and an emphasis on moral improvement. Yet Roosevelt's "rhetorical progressivism" was distinguished, at bottom, by his emphasis on the *character* of individuals. He believed in the power of words to shape individual and public morality. To that end, he constantly "preached" about the "sins" of both individuals and nations. In rhetoric often sermonic in tone, Roosevelt promoted long-term attitudinal changes over short-term legislative reforms. For him, the foreign and domestic problems of the early twentieth century would be solved only when individuals of high character—people guided by the principles of righteousness and justice—developed the will and the strength to *enforce* what was right. For Roosevelt, legislative reform was never enough; there had to be "progress" in human character if America was to meet its domestic and international responsibilities in the modern age.

Domestically, Roosevelt's "rhetorical progressivism" exposed the evils corrupting civilization. He condemned the greedy who elevated material gain above all else and the reformers who, out of envy, overzealously condemned the rich. He wrote and spoke prolifically on the need for every American to embrace both virtue and the "strenuous life" necessary to uphold it. In foreign affairs, he likewise reduced great controversies and even wars to simple questions of character. Whether restoring order in the Dominican Republic, building the Panama Canal, or participating in the Great War, America needed to stand for the same principles that defined the virtuous individual. According to Roosevelt, a truly progressive foreign policy consisted of the principles of righteousness backed by the courage and strength to enforce them—even through war, if necessary.

From the vantage point of our own day, as Danbom has suggested, some of the efforts of reformers such as Roosevelt may appear "silly." It may seem fruitless to "concentrate on human character" in promoting social change, and the concept of "moral progress" may seem like a "joke."[226] As Morone observed, today's notions of reform range "from technical fiddles," such as "currency adjustments, [and] incentives to boost national savings," to "far-reaching improbables." What is missing from such efforts, he concludes, are efforts to renew "the public sphere" and infuse it with "workable forms of popular participation" in our democratic institutions.[227]

Ironically, Roosevelt would have agreed. His "rhetorical progressivism" rested on the assumption that rhetoric made a difference and that public opinion could be uplifted and energized into a powerful force for moral progress. Not only exploiting the "bully pulpit" but also constantly "preaching" to the public both before and after his presidency, Roosevelt tried to build a foundation in public opinion for lasting and righteous reform. That his views did not always fit the progressive "mold" in his day or ours should not detract from our appreciation of Roosevelt's impact on the progressive tradition. His was a distinctive progressivism—a "rhetorical progressivism" emphasizing character over legislation—but it was no less sincere or consistent than the many other strains of progressive thought in the first two decades of the twentieth century.

Notes

1. Richard L. Watson Jr., *The Development of National Power: The United States, 1900–1919* (Boston: Houghton Mifflin, 1976), 59.
2. Richard Hofstadter, *The Age of Reform: From Bryan to F. D. R.* (New York: Vintage Books, 1955), 220.
3. George E. Mowry, *Theodore Roosevelt and the Progressive Movement* (New York: Hill and Wang, 1946), 9.
4. George E. Mowry, *The Era of Theodore Roosevelt and the Birth of Modern America, 1900–1912* (New York: Harper and Row, 1958), 59.
5. Ibid., 91.
6. Watson, *Development of National Power*, 59.
7. Mowry, *Theodore Roosevelt and the Progressive Movement*, 10.
8. Richard Hofstadter, *The American Political Tradition and the Men Who Made It* (New York: Vintage Books, 1954), 225–27.
9. Henry F. Pringle, *Theodore Roosevelt: A Biography* (New York: Harcourt, Brace and Co., 1931), 208.
10. Mowry, *Theodore Roosevelt and the Progressive Movement*, 33.
11. See Lewis Gould, *The Presidency of Theodore Roosevelt* (Lawrence: University Press of Kansas, 1991).
12. See Nathan Miller, *Theodore Roosevelt: A Life* (New York: William Morrow and Co., 1992); H. W. Brands, *T. R.: The Last Romantic* (New York: Basic Books, 1997).
13. Mowry, *Theodore Roosevelt and the Progressive Movement*, 34.
14. Hofstadter, *American Political Tradition*, 229–30.
15. Mowry, *Era of Theodore Roosevelt*, 114.
16. Hofstadter, *Age of Reform*, 207; Hofstadter, *American Political Tradition*, 230.
17. Blaine A. Brownell, "Interpretations of Twentieth-Century Urban Progressive Reform," in *Reform and Reformers in the Progressive Era*, ed. David R. Colburn and George E. Pozzetta (Westport, Conn.: Greenwood Press, 1983), 14; Watson, *Development of National Power*, 84.
18. See Arthur S. Link, *American Epoch: A History of the United States since the 1890s*, 2d ed. (New York: Alfred A. Knopf, 1966), 68–69.
19. On domestic reform, see ibid., 70–72; Watson, *Development of National Power*, 61–85; Hofstadter, *Age of Reform*, 174–214; Richard L. McCormick, *The Party Period and Public Policy: American Politics from the Age of Jackson to the Progressive Era* (New York: Oxford University Press, 1986), 263–88; James A. Morone, *The Democratic Wish: Popular Participation and the Limits of American Government* (New York: Basic Books, 1990), 97–128.
20. On Roosevelt's passion for foreign adventurism, see William H. Harbaugh, *The Life and Times of Theodore Roosevelt* (New York: Collier Books, 1963), 180. For criticisms of Roosevelt's foreign policies as reactionary, see Pringle, *Theodore Roosevelt: A Biography*, 166–67; Mowry, *Era of Theodore Roosevelt*, 163–64.
21. Link, *American Epoch*, 79.
22. Arthur M. Schlesinger Jr., introduction to *The Promise of American Life* by Herbert Croly, ed. Arthur M. Schlesinger Jr. (1909; reprint, Cambridge: Harvard University Press, 1965), xiii.
23. Croly, *Promise of American Life*, 168.
24. See ibid., 28 (history), 174–75 (emphasis), 289–314 (foreign), 438–39 (technical), 454 (moral).
25. Miller, *Theodore Roosevelt: A Life*, 31–32.
26. Ibid., 106.

27. Theodore Roosevelt, *Theodore Roosevelt: An Autobiography* (New York: Charles Scribner's Sons, 1929), 54.

28. Carleton Putnam, *Theodore Roosevelt: The Formative Years, 1858–1886* (New York: Charles Scribner's Sons, 1958), 1:272.

29. Howard L. Hurwitz, *Theodore Roosevelt and Labor in New York State, 1880–1900* (New York: Columbia University Press, 1943), 106–7.

30. Ibid., 104.

31. Pringle, *Theodore Roosevelt: A Biography*, 52, 92, 122, 126, 129.

32. Jay Berman, *Police Administration and Progressive Reform: Theodore Roosevelt as Police Commissioner of New York* (New York: Greenwood Press, 1987), 56–57.

33. Ibid., 94.

34. Hurwitz, *Theodore Roosevelt and Labor*, 191–98.

35. Harbaugh, *Life and Times*, 142–43.

36. David B. Danbom notes that the 1890s and the first few years of the 1900s were dominated by this religious rhetoric of reform. See *"The World of Hope": Progressives and the Struggle for an Ethical Public Life* (Philadelphia: Temple University Press, 1987), 80.

37. Arthur S. Link and Richard L. McCormick, *Progressivism* (Arlington Heights, Ill.: Harlan Davidson, 1983), 23.

38. Robert M. Crunden, *Ministers of Reform: The Progressives' Achievement in American Civilization, 1889–1920* (New York: Basic Books, 1982), 40–41.

39. Croly, *Promise of American Life*, 174.

40. Theodore Roosevelt, "Property and the State, May 15, 1899," in *Campaigns and Controversies*, vol. 14 of *The Works of Theodore Roosevelt*, National ed. (New York: Charles Scribner's Sons, 1926), 328, 40–41.

41. Theodore Roosevelt, "Character and Success, March 31, 1900," in *American Ideals/The Strenuous Life/Realizable Ideals*, vol. 13 of *Works*, 383.

42. Theodore Roosevelt, "How Not to Help Our Poorer Brother, January, 1897," in *Works*, 13:161.

43. Theodore Roosevelt, "The College Graduate and Public Life, August, 1890," in *Works*, 13:36.

44. Stanford M. Lyman, *The Seven Deadly Sins: Society and Evil* (New York: St. Martin's Press, 1978), 234.

45. Ibid., 235.

46. Theodore Roosevelt, "Machine Politics in New York City, November, 1886," in *Works*, 13:81–82.

47. Theodore Roosevelt, "American Ideals, February, 1895," in *Works*, 13:10.

48. Ibid., 13:11.

49. Roosevelt, "Machine Politics," in *Works*, 13:81.

50. Theodore Roosevelt, "The Duties of American Citizenship, January 26, 1893," in *Works*, 13:282–83.

51. Roosevelt, "American Ideals," in *Works*, 13:6, 9.

52. Ibid., 13:6.

53. Theodore Roosevelt, "Latitude and Longitude among Reformers, June, 1900," in *Works*, 13:342.

54. Theodore Roosevelt, "Political Assessments, July, 1892," in *Works*, 14:138.

55. Theodore Roosevelt, "Phases of State Legislation, January, 1885," in *Works*, 13:60.

56. Theodore Roosevelt, "The Mayor's Power of Removal, March 12, 1884," in *Works*, 14:34.

57. Theodore Roosevelt, "The Enforcement of Law, September, 1895," in *Works*, 14:187.

58. Theodore Roosevelt, "The Higher Life of American Cities, Dec. 21, 1895," in *Works*, 13:305.

59. Roosevelt, "Higher Life," in *Works*, 13:297.

60. Theodore Roosevelt, "The Eighth and Ninth Commandments in Politics, May 12, 1900," in *Works*, 13:387–88.

61. Roosevelt, "How Not to Help," in *Works*, 13:164–65.

62. Roosevelt, "Latitude and Longitude," in *Works*, 13:347.

63. Roosevelt, "How Not to Help," in *Works*, 13:162.

64. Ibid., 13:165.

65. Ibid., 13:162–63.

66. Roosevelt, "Duties of American Citizenship," in *Works*, 13:285.

67. Roosevelt, "How Not to Help," in *Works*, 13:162.

68. Theodore Roosevelt, "Annual Message, January 3, 1900," in *State Papers as Governor and President*, vol. 15 of *Works*, 41–42.

69. Theodore Roosevelt, "A Word to Reformers, May 9, 1899," in *Works*, 14:320.

70. Roosevelt, "Latitude and Longitude," in *Works*, 13:342, 351, 353–54.

71. Theodore Roosevelt, "The Manly Virtues and Practical Politics," in *Works*, 13:27–28, 32–33.

72. Croly, *Promise of American Life*, 149.

73. Roosevelt, "Higher Life," in *Works*, 13:298, 300.

74. Roosevelt, *Theodore Roosevelt: An Autobiography*, 423.

75. Mowry, *Era of Theodore Roosevelt*, 10.

76. Sean Dennis Cashman, *America in the Age of the Titans: The Progressive Era and World War I* (New York: New York University Press, 1988), 38, 40.

77. Watson, *Development of National Power*, 108.

78. Ibid., 107.

79. Mowry, *Era of Theodore Roosevelt*, 131.

80. Ibid., 205.

81. Hofstadter, *American Political Traditions*, 224–25.

82. Jeffrey Tulis, *The Rhetorical Presidency* (Princeton: Princeton University Press, 1987), 5–6.

83. Karlyn K. Campbell and Kathleen H. Jamieson, *Deeds Done in Words: Presidential Rhetoric and the Genres of Governance* (Chicago: University of Chicago Press, 1990), 5.

84. James W. Ceasar, Glen E. Thurow, Jeffrey Tulis, and Joseph M. Bessette, "Rise of the Rhetorical Presidency," *Presidential Studies Quarterly* 11 (1981): 163.

85. James D. Fairbanks, "The Priestly Functions of the Presidency: A Discussion of the Literature on Civil Religion and Its Implications for the Study of Presidential Leadership," *Presidential Studies Quarterly* 11 (1981): 224.

86. Theodore Roosevelt, "The Spirit of Class Antagonism, October 25, 1905," in *The Roosevelt Policy: Speeches, Letters and State Papers, Relating to Corporate Wealth and Closely Allied Topics*, ed. William Griffith (1919; reprint, New York: Kraus Reprint Co., 1971), 1:317.

87. Theodore Roosevelt, "Necessity of Establishing Federal Sovereignty over Trusts, August 23, 1902," in *Roosevelt Policy*, 1:32.

88. Theodore Roosevelt, "At Bangor, Maine, August 27, 1902," in *Addresses and Presidential Messages of Theodore Roosevelt, 1902–1904* (New York: G. P. Putnam's Sons, 1904), 36–37.

89. Theodore Roosevelt, "Industrial Peace, November 11, 1902," in *Roosevelt Policy*, 1:102.

90. Theodore Roosevelt, "Material Welfare and the Spiritual Life, March 12, 1905," in *Roosevelt Policy*, 1:250.

91. Watson, *Development of National Power*, 108.

92. Theodore Roosevelt, "Progress Made toward Federal Control of Corporations, April 3, 1903," in *Roosevelt Policy*, 1:114–15.

93. Theodore Roosevelt, "Administrative Control of Railways, October 19, 1905," in *Roosevelt Policy*, 1:304.

94. Pringle, *Theodore Roosevelt: A Biography*, 427.

95. Theodore Roosevelt, "Wise and Unwise Methods of Remedying Trust Evils, September 2, 1902," in *Roosevelt Policy*, 1:52.

96. Link, *American Epoch*, 77.

97. Theodore Roosevelt, "Muck-Rakers, April 14, 1906," in *Roosevelt Policy*, 2:368–70, 376–77.

98. Ibid., 2:369, 371.

99. Theodore Roosevelt, "Federal Supervision of Railways as an Executive Not a Judicial Function, June 22, 1905," in *Roosevelt Policy*, 1:276.

100. Theodore Roosevelt, "False Standards Resulting from Swollen Fortunes, July 7, 1905," in *Roosevelt Policy*, 1:284–85.

101. Theodore Roosevelt, "Corporate Activity and 'Law Honesty,' October 20, 1905," in *Roosevelt Policy*, 1:311.

102. Theodore Roosevelt, "Individual Citizenship the Basis of National Success, October 4, 1906," in *Roosevelt Policy,* 2:423.

103. Roosevelt, "Necessity of Establishing," in *Roosevelt Policy,* 1:38–39.

104. Roosevelt, "Industrial Peace," in *Roosevelt Policy,* 1:101.

105. Theodore Roosevelt, "Temperance and the Wage Earner, August 10, 1905," in *Roosevelt Policy,* 1:290–91.

106. Roosevelt, "Necessity of Establishing," in *Roosevelt Policy,* 1:37.

107. Theodore Roosevelt, "Federal Regulation of the Interstate Railways, January 30, 1905," in *Roosevelt Policy,* 1:241–42.

108. Danbom, *"The World of Hope,"* 114–15.

109. Morone, *Democratic Wish,* 116–17.

110. Theodore Roosevelt, "The Square Deal, April 5, 1905," in *Roosevelt Policy,* 1:254.

111. Ibid., 1:253.

112. Danbom, *"The World of Hope,"* 119.

113. Croly, *Promise of American Life,* 436.

114. Theodore Roosevelt, "Regulating the Railways by Law, May 30, 1907," in *Roosevelt Policy,* 2:515–16.

115. Roosevelt, "Regulating the Railway," in *Roosevelt Policy,* 2:516–17.

116. Theodore Roosevelt, "'The Campaign against Privilege,' January 31, 1908," in *Roosevelt Policy,* 2:722, 736–37.

117. Croly, *Promise of American Life,* 22.

118. See Joseph L. Gardner, *Departing Glory: Theodore Roosevelt as Ex-president* (New York: Charles Scribner's Sons, 1973), 97.

119. Harbaugh, *Life and Times,* 347. For Roosevelt's account of his trip, see *African Game Trails,* vol. 4 of *Works.*

120. Harbaugh, *Life and Times,* 358.

121. Cashman, *American in the Age,* 99–103.

122. Harbaugh, *Life and Times,* 366–69.

123. Amos R. E. Pinchot, *History of the Progressive Party, 1912–1916,* ed. Helene M. Hooker (Washington Square, N.Y.: New York University Press, 1958), 115.

124. Harbaugh, *Life and Times,* 367.

125. Brands, *T. R.,* 675–76.

126. Danbom, *"The World of Hope,"* 150.

127. Theodore Roosevelt, "The New Nationalism, August 31, 1910," in *Social Justice and Popular Rule—Essays, Addresses, and Public Statements Relating to the Progressive Movement (1910–1916),* vol. 17 of *Works,* 6.

128. Ibid., 17:5–6, 7, 9.

129. Ibid., 17:5, 7, 10–11, 19–20, 22.

130. Croly, *Promise of American Life,* 409.

131. Roosevelt, "The New Nationalism," in *Works,* 17:17, 21.

132. John A. Gable, *The Bull Moose Years: Theodore Roosevelt and the Progressive Party* (Port Washington, N.Y.: Kennikat Press, 1978), 11; Cashman, *American in the Age,* 104.

133. Brands, *T. R.,* 706.

134. Cashman, *American in the Age,* 111; Brands, *T. R.,* 713.

135. Harbaugh, *Life and Times,* 410, 417–18.

136. Gardner, *Departing Glory,* 261.

137. Brands, *T. R.,* 716.

138. Gardner, *Departing Glory,* 261.

139. Theodore Roosevelt, "A Confession of Faith, August 6, 1912," in *Works,* 17:254, 258–81.

140. Ibid., 17:262, 268.

141. Ibid., 17:260.

142. Ibid., 17:297–98.

143. Ibid., 17:298–99.

144. Cashman, *American in the Age,* 119–20.

145. Brands, *T. R.,* 19.

146. Miller, *Theodore Roosevelt: A Life,* 116–17.

147. John M. Cooper Jr., "Theodore Roosevelt: On Clio's Active Service," *Virginia Quarterly Review* 62 (1986): 26.
148. Miller, *Theodore Roosevelt: A Life*, 252–53.
149. Harbaugh, *Life and Times*, 98.
150. Theodore Roosevelt, *The Rough Riders* (1899; reprint, New York: Signet, 1961), 13.
151. See Mowry, *Era of Theodore Roosevelt*, 85–105; Cashman, *America in the Age*, 45; Hofstadter, *Age of Reform*, 174–214; Lewis L. Gould, "The Progressive Era," in *The Progressive Era*, ed. Lewis L. Gould (Syracuse, N.Y.: Syracuse University Press, 1974), 1–10; Link and McCormick, *Progressivism*, 11–25.
152. Robert D. Johnson, *The Peace Progressives and American Foreign Relations* (Cambridge: Harvard University Press, 1995), 3.
153. Watson, *Development of National Power*, 60.
154. Hofstadter, *Age of Reform*, 272–73.
155. Johnson, *Peace Progressives*, 31.
156. Watson, *Development of National Power*, 60.
157. Croly, *Promise of American Life*, 310, 312.
158. Theodore Roosevelt, "The Monroe Doctrine, March, 1896," in *Works*, 13:177.
159. Theodore Roosevelt, *The Works of Theodore Roosevelt: The Winning of the West—An Account of the Exploration and Settlement of Our Country from the Alleghanies to the Pacific*, Elkhorn edition (New York: Charles Scribner's Sons, 1906), 11:52.
160. Ibid., 8:107.
161. Ibid., 11:51–52, 8:107.
162. Roosevelt, "America's Part of the World's Work, February 13, 1899," in *Works*, 14:316.
163. Roosevelt, "The Prophecies of Mr. Bryan, September 7, 1900," in *Works*, 14:385.
164. Theodore Roosevelt, *The Naval War of 1812, or The History of the United States Navy during the Last War with Great Britain* (1882; reprint, New York: Haskell House Publishers, 1968), 23–31, 65, 135, 218–19, 421, 445–47.
165. Theodore Roosevelt, "Washington's Forgotten Maxim, June, 1897," in *Works*, 13:183, 185, 187.
166. Theodore Roosevelt, "The Strenuous Life, April 10, 1899," in *Works*, 13:321–23, 331.
167. Harbaugh, *Life and Times*, 180.
168. Miller, *Theodore Roosevelt: A Life*, 383–409, 449–51.
169. Gould, *Presidency of Theodore Roosevelt*, 73.
170. Mowry, *Era of Theodore Roosevelt*, 163.
171. Theodore Roosevelt, "Charleston Exposition, April 9, 1902," in *Addresses and Presidential Messages*, 6–7.
172. Theodore Roosevelt, "The Administration of the Island Possessions, August 22, 1902," in *American Problems*, vol. 16 of *Works*, 272–73.
173. Ibid., 16:278.
174. Theodore Roosevelt, "Second Annual Message, December 2, 1902," in *Works*, 15:150.
175. Theodore Roosevelt, "At the Founders' Day Banquet of the Union League, Philadelphia, November 22, 1902," in *Addresses and Presidential Messages*, 93, 97, 99.
176. Theodore Roosevelt, "Fourth Annual Message, December 6, 1904," in *Works*, 15:254, 257.
177. Gould, *Presidency of Theodore Roosevelt*, 91.
178. Pringle, *Theodore Roosevelt: A Biography*, 301.
179. See Richard H. Collin, *Theodore Roosevelt's Caribbean: The Panama Canal, the Monroe Doctrine, and the Latin American Context* (Baton Rouge, La.: Louisiana State University Press, 1990).
180. See J. Michael Hogan, *The Panama Canal in American Politics: Domestic Advocacy and the Evolution of Policy* (Carbondale: Southern Illinois University Press, 1986), 34–35.
181. Theodore Roosevelt, "At the Capitol Building, Montgomery, Ala., October 24, 1905," in *Presidential Addresses and State Papers*, 4:528–29.
182. Roosevelt, "Third Annual Message," in *Works*, 15:209.
183. Roosevelt, "Administration of the Island Possessions," in *Works*, 16:273.
184. Theodore Roosevelt, "From a Special Message to Congress on the Panama Canal, January 8, 1906," in *Addresses and Papers of Theodore Roosevelt*, ed. Willis F. Johnson (New York: Unit Book Publishing Co., 1909), 299–300.

185. Theodore Roosevelt, "Special Message, Delivered December 17, 1906, to the Senate and House of Representatives," in *A Compilation of the Messages and Papers of the Presidents*, (New York: Bureau of National Literature, 1923), 15:7309–10, 7312.

186. Theodore Roosevelt, "Special Message, December 17, 1906" in *A Compilation of the Messages*, ed. James D. Richardson (Washington, D.C.: GPO, 1914), 10:7697, 7699, 7708; Theodore Roosevelt, "Special Message of the President of the United States Concerning the Panama Canal, Communicated to the Two Houses of Congress on December 17, 1906," in *Senate Documents*, 59th Cong., 2d sess., 1907, 10:10, 24, 30–33.

187. Theodore Roosevelt, "Special Message, December 8, 1908," in *Compilation of the Messages*, 10:7611; Theodore Roosevelt, "Special Message, February, 17, 1909," in *Compilation of the Messages*, 10:7649; Roosevelt, "Special Message, December 17, 1906," in *Compilation of the Messages*, 10:7697, 7708; Theodore Roosevelt, "To the Long Island Medical Society at Oyster Bay, New York, July 12, 1905," in *Presidential Addresses and State Papers*, 4:431; Theodore Roosevelt, "At Jacksonville, Florida, October 21, 1905," in *Presidential Addresses and State Papers*, 4:506–7.

188. Harold Sprout and Margaret Sprout, *The Rise of American Naval Power, 1776–1918* (Princeton: Princeton University Press, 1946), 263.

189. George T. Davis, *A Navy Second to None: The Development of Modern American Naval Policy* (New York: Harcourt, Brace and Co., 1940), 141–42, 150, 152.

190. John J. Fitzgerald speaking in regard to the Naval Appropriation Bill, 58th Cong., 2d sess., *Congressional Record* (12 February 1904), 38, 2079; and Jack Beall speaking in regard to the Naval Appropriation Bill, 58th Cong., 3d sess., *Congressional Record* (15 February 1905), 39, 2667.

191. Theodore Roosevelt, "At Williams College, Williamstown, Mass., June 22, 1905," in *Presidential Addresses and State Papers*, 4:404.

192. Theodore Roosevelt, "Message Communicated to the Two Houses of Congress at the Beginning of the First Session of the Fifty-Seventh Congress, December 3, 1901," in *Addresses and Presidential Messages*, 323.

193. Theodore Roosevelt, "At Haverhill, Massachusetts, August 26, 1902," in *Addresses and Presidential Messages*, 28.

194. Theodore Roosevelt, "Heroism and Preparation—The Navy's Two Requirements, Address on the Reinterment of the Remains of John Paul Jones, April 24, 1906," in *Works*, 16:247.

195. Theodore Roosevelt, "Letter Accepting the Republican Nomination for President of the United States, September 12, 1904," in *Presidential Addresses and State Papers*, 3:54.

196. Theodore Roosevelt, "At Carnegie Hall, New York, N.Y., February 26, 1903, upon the Occasion of the Bicentennial Celebration of the Birth of John Wesley," in *Addresses and Presidential Messages*, 113–14.

197. Theodore Roosevelt, "The Ideals of Washington, Feb. 22, 1905," in *Works*, 13:501–2.

198. Gould, *Presidency of Theodore Roosevelt*, 263.

199. On media coverage of the naval cruise, see Leroy G. Dorsey, "Sailing into the 'Wondrous Now': The Myth of the American Navy's World Cruise," *Quarterly Journal of Speech* 83 (1997): 447–65.

200. James R. Reckner, *Teddy Roosevelt's Great White Fleet* (Annapolis: Naval Institute Press, 1988), x, 24–25, 43–107, 123–26, 159.

201. Harbaugh, *Life and Times*, 435–36. This trip culminated in a minor adventure classic written by Roosevelt: see *Through the Brazilian Wilderness*, vol. 5 of *Works*. .

202. Harbaugh, *Life and Times*, 439.

203. Ibid., 444–54.

204. Ibid., 470–75.

205. Johnson, *Peace Progressives*, 45.

206. Watson, *Development of National Power*, 219.

207. Link and McCormick, *Progressivism*, 106.

208. Danbom, *"World of Hope,"* 192, 203.

209. Link and McCormick, *Progressivism*, 107. Danbom, *"World of Hope,"* 192, 203.

210. Mowry, *Theodore Roosevelt and the Progressive Movement*, 320.

211. Pringle, *Theodore Roosevelt: A Biography*, 584; Brands, *T. R.*, 766–68; Harbaugh, *Life and Times*, 455–56.

212. Theodore Roosevelt, "The Duty of Self-Defense and of Good Conduct toward Others, September 27, 1914," in *America and the World War/Fear God and Take Your Own Part,* vol. 18 of *Works,* 3–4.

213. Theodore Roosevelt, "The Ghost Dance of the Shadow Huns, October 1, 1917," in *Roosevelt in the Kansas City Star: War-Time Editorials by Theodore Roosevelt* (Boston: Houghton Mifflin, 1921), 7; Theodore Roosevelt, "Pillar-of-Salt Citizenship, October 12, 1917," in *Roosevelt in the Kansas City Star,* 17.

214. Woodrow Wilson, "Wilson's Address to Congress Advising That Germany's Course Be Declared War against the United States, April 2, 1917," in *The Messages and Papers of Woodrow Wilson* (New York: Review of Reviews, 1924), 1:378.

215. Theodore Roosevelt, "German Hatred of America, November 13, 1917," in *Roosevelt in the Kansas City Star,* 50.

216. Theodore Roosevelt, "Thank Heaven, April 2, 1918," in *Roosevelt in the Kansas City Star,* 128; Theodore Roosevelt, "The German Horror, May 2, 1918," in *Roosevelt in the Kansas City Star,* 145–46; Roosevelt, "German Hatred of America," in *Roosevelt in the Kansas City Star,* 50.

217. Roosevelt, "The Ghost Dance of the Shadow Huns," in *Roosevelt in the Kansas City Star,* 7.

218. Roosevelt, "Pillar-of-Salt Citizenship," in *Roosevelt in the Kansas City Star,* 16.

219. Theodore Roosevelt, "Summing Up, November 29, 1914," in *Works,* 18:164.

220. Theodore Roosevelt, "Peace Insurance by Preparedness against War, August, 1915," in *Works,* 18:311.

221. Theodore Roosevelt, "America First—A Phrase or a Fact? January, 1916," in *Works,* 18:261.

222. Theodore Roosevelt, *National Strength and International Duty* (Princeton: Princeton University Press, 1917), 77.

223. Theodore Roosevelt, "The 'Conscientious Objector,' September 28, 1917," in *The Foes of Our Own Household/The Great Adventure/Letters to His Children,* vol. 19 of *Works,* 173.

224. Theodore Roosevelt, "The Peace of Righteousness," in *Works,* 18:69.

225. Theodore Roosevelt, "Fear God and Take Your Own Part, 1916," in *Works,* 18:206, 225.

226. Danbom, *"World of Hope,"* 241.

227. Morone, *Democratic Wish,* 336.

Science, Public Policy, and the "Spirit of the People": The Rhetoric of Progressive Conservation

Christine Oravec

3

In 1890, the U.S. Census Bureau called an end to a century of unlimited development by announcing the closing of the frontier.[1] Eighteen years later, a speaker at the White House Conference of Governors on the conservation of natural resources associated the end of the frontier with the potential shortage of arable land: "We now turn to the only remaining resource of man upon this earth, which is the soil itself. How are we caring for that, and what possibilities does it hold out to the People of future support? We are only beginning to feel the pressure upon the land. The whole interior of this continent, aggregating more than 500,000,000 acres, has been occupied by settlers within the last 50 years. What is there left for the next 50 years? How long will the remainder last? No longer can we say that 'Uncle Sam has land enough to give us all a farm.'"[2] Other speakers warned of the impending depletion of such important resources as oil, timber, clean air, metals, and water.[3] By the turn of the century it had become apparent that the United States could no longer exploit its wilderness territories to provide for the material needs of the nation.

The speeches delivered at the Governors' Conference expressed a growing concern over the dwindling reserves of raw materials necessary for the nation's economic welfare. But more than reflecting generalized concern, the speakers argued for public action in the form of policies that might be designated progressive in nature. The majority of those attending supported constraints at the level of national government on the overconsumption of natural resources. Further, their presence at such a prestigious venue signaled a general willingness to engage in collective action to effect those constraints.[4] One of the most effective techniques for managing waste and abuse, they proposed, was the creation of a social movement that would shape and give expression to a public conservation ethic. As with other progressive campaigns, conservation required broad public involvement as well as governmental intervention.

The Progressive Era thus may be considered the seedbed of what scholars today call the movement for conservation. One indicator of this relationship is that the standard dates of the early conservation movement (roughly from the 1890s to 1917) coincide with the conventionally accepted period of progressivism.[5] In addition, issues in the history of progressivism parallel comparable issues in the history of conservation. Specifically, the nature and composition of the conservation movement has been closely tied to the characterization of progressivism as a social phenomenon.

One of the most important issues in the scholarly literature concerns what kind of social activity might be labeled "conservationist" or "progressivist." Controversy still exists over whether progressivism was sufficiently homogenous and organized to be termed a "social movement."[6] The types of social phenomena considered under the term "progressivism," so diverse as to include even the segregation of blacks and whites and the passage of Jim Crow laws, have varied widely over time.[7] Similarly, many groups with divergent interests have claimed to have originated conservationism, from professional foresters of the late 1880s to mountaineering clubs of the early 1920s. Even today, the term "conservation movement" either refers to any collective activity concerning the managed use of natural resources or identifies one of several campaigns for the development of an environmental consciousness.[8]

Another more particular issue involves the socioeconomic makeup of both progressivism and the conservationist movement. The social origin of progressive leaders has been hotly disputed since the beginning of scholarship on the subject. They have been characterized as advocates of the people against the dominant powers; middle-class, conservative "Mugwumps"; public intellectuals; immigrants, minorities and women; and even the upper ranks of big business.[9] These variations have in turn influenced the way scholars characterize the constituency of the conservation movement.

For example, Samuel P. Hays, one of the most important historians of the early twentieth century, uses the conservation movement to provide key evidence for his thesis on the Progressives' social constitution. His book, *Conservation and the Gospel of Efficiency: The Progressive Conservation Movement, 1890–1920*, identifies the core leadership of conservation as a small group of scientists, technicians, bureaucrats, and forward-looking politicians who embraced the increasing industrialization of the new twentieth century. Furthermore, he demotes citizens' groups and activists to the role of camp followers manipulated into supporting the specialists' campaigns for modernization and the professionalization of power. Efficiency, rationality, and social control: these premises, according to Hays, are the lynchpins of progressivism as well as the true foundations of conservationism.[10]

Whether Hays is correct, the two issues of the nature and makeup of the conservationist constituency remain central to the discussion of progressivism in the movement. This chapter discusses these two issues and advances an alternative pair of theses: first, the conservation movement may be seen not only as an objective social phenomenon, but also as a construction constituted by its own rhetoric; and second, as a result of this construction, conservationism depended upon a claim to public opinion and support to legitimize its very existence.[11]

Although superficially similar, these theses differ from Hays's in two important ways. First, Hays suggests that the scientific and bureaucratic "gospel of efficiency" was an ideological device used by specialists to adjust the public to increasing technological and industrial complexity. Instead, this chapter argues that conservationist language may also be seen as actively constitutive discourse that helped bring about the widespread cultural phenomenon termed the conservation movement.

And, rather than determining that only one group was central to the movement's goals, as does Hays, this argument suggests that conservationist discourse created a conception of a "people" or a "public" that engaged the collective participation of both scientific bureaucrats and citizen activists alike. In other words, I argue that conservation, in addition to reflecting a particular social configuration, was also a product of the language, culture, and public communication of its age. As Richard L. McCormick states, "Progressivism . . . [and here one could include conservationism as well] was the first reform movement to be experienced by the whole American nation."[12]

This chapter explicates the process by which the progressive conservationists developed bureaucratic policy out of scientific and technological premises, and then popularized this policy by rhetorically constituting a nationwide conservationist public—a public that continues to warrant political action today. I first shall discuss some of the pressures and problems that provided a context for the conservationist cause. Next, I shall examine in detail how such speakers and writers as W J McGee and Gifford Pinchot formulated specific language, first to originate conservation as a social movement, and then to advocate a public policy based upon the "spirit of the people." In the course of this examination, I hope to show how rhetorical discourse both constructed a social movement grounded in progressivism and also positioned the people of the United States as constituents of a progressivist public culture.

Organization and Opposition in Early Conservation

By the beginning of the twentieth century, a growing number of Americans had become sensitive to the need for conserving natural resources but did not yet conceive of the necessity for a unified national policy. The extent of the awareness may be gauged by the appearance between 1865 and 1890 of a large number of agencies, clubs, and associations concerned about the rapid consumption of resources. For example, the National Association for the Advancement of Science sent memorials to Washington in 1873 and 1889 calling for a governmental policy of forest management; the congressional supporters of the Yellowstone Park Bill in 1872 sought to protect the area as a natural curiosity;[13] the U.S. Geological Survey under Clarence King and John Wesley Powell mapped the West, particularly its water supplies, with a view toward regulating future development;[14] the Audubon Society, organized in 1886 by magazine editor George Bird Grinnell, advocated the protection of wild birds;[15] the Boone and Crockett Club, started by Theodore Roosevelt in 1888, moved to preserve big game for the purposes of sport;[16] and the Sierra Club supported the preservation of wilderness soon after the campaign to create Yosemite National Park.[17]

If the policies of these groups seemed confusingly at odds, the legislative policy of government must have seemed no less confused.[18] Some of the earliest federal conservation measures—the Timber Culture Act of 1873, the Desert Land Act of 1877, the Timber and Stone Act of 1878, and the Mineral Land Act of 1866— were passed by Congress to regulate private development of resources, but each of these acts were criticized for being vague and unenforceable.[19] The internal policy of government itself was decentralized and poorly organized. Gifford Pinchot noted that before the movement took hold, there existed three separate federal bureaus concerned with minerals, four or five with streams, six with forests, and a dozen with wildlife, soils, and other miscellaneous resources. Only after seven years of serious administrative, congressional, and local opposition did the Forest Service assume sole control over forest reserves.[20]

Criticism of the federal government's ill-organized attempts at conservation came from at least two opposing yet equally unorganized groups: the business interests and the preservationists. The first group, comprised chiefly of farmers, ranchers, and industrialists, often promoted the development of the new states and territories to serve their own interests. They united in protest most effectively when governmental actions alienated the greatest number of these interests. The mass complaints against the Cleveland forest reservations of 1897 and the protests during the Denver Public Lands Convention of 1907 are examples of such unification.[21]

The arguments of the business interests against conservation centered upon the needs and desires of local rather than national populations. Residents claimed that the centralization of conservation efforts violated state and local rights, and that forest reservation in particular retarded the development of the newest states in the Union. In light of these arguments, conservationists were pressed to demonstrate the benefit and appeal of their programs to the general citizenry.[22]

The other group of opponents consisted of dedicated preservationists, such as John Muir and much of the Sierra Club, who challenged the government's plans to allow limited use of forest reserves and right-of-ways in the nation's parks. To answer the preservationists, the conservationists needed to establish a legitimate and respectable history of respect for the public welfare in the face of accusations that they represented political and business interests. The debate between preservationists and conservationists pitted the scenic and spiritual uses of the land against the most publicly beneficial and productive use, with the preservationists claiming historical precedence and a record of nationwide support.[23]

The requirements of justifying their cause thus forced conservationists to choose a tenuous middle path between those who would have resources available for general use and those who would have them preserved from any practical use. The conservationists needed to demonstrate nothing less than the support, or at least the understanding, of a major part of the public, including both businessmen and "nature lovers." In addition, conservationists needed to create a movement broad enough in its appeal to be identified neither as the fabrication of scientific specialists, nor as the promotion of a political administration.

Their efforts culminated in the Conference of Governors of 1908, almost universally recognized then and now as the key event in the early history of conservation. It was the first of a series of well-publicized meetings and commissions which confirmed that a movement was in the making.[24] In the wake of the conference, speakers for the movement claimed with some justification that nearly every individual in the United States had somehow been exposed to the terms and principles of conservation.[25] Furthermore, the doctrine of the movement pervaded such major magazines as the *Century,* the *Outlook, The World's Work,* and *McClure's.*[26] By the end of the first decade of the twentieth century the movement appeared to have received, if not support, then at least recognition from a significant portion of the American public.

For many during the Progressive Era, the conservation movement spoke for the "public interest" of America regarding its natural resources. Thus the language used by speakers and writers for the movement was carefully chosen and shaped to represent the public welfare. In particular, leaders of the movement transformed the term "conservation" from a word within the scientific lexicon to an expression connoting the moral and spiritual resources of a people. In the course of this transformation, "conservation" became a term that justified and legitimized its own use.

"Conservation" as a Self-Identifying Term

The number and diversity of individual organizations concerned with the difficulty of managing natural resources resulted, in part, from the complexity of the problem itself. The lack of a major identifying principle shared among each of these organizations also caused confusion. Between 1902 and 1908, however, representatives of the movement quite consciously decided that "conservation" best served the purpose of self-identification.[27] Narrowly construed, conservation stood for such practical goals as preventing the waste of natural resources, using resources wisely, and distributing national wealth among the whole population.[28] Even so, the connotations of the term were also broad enough to include moral and ethical justifications for collective action. Examination of the scientific, political, moral, and even religious connotations of "conservation" illustrates the transformation of an ostensibly neutral term into powerfully evocative discourse.

The primary technical function of the term conservation was to encompass two differing standards for managing natural resources under one overarching principle. The first standard was the temporary withdrawal of natural resources from immediate use, to allow for long-range planning and the minimizing of waste; and the second standard involved the cultivation of plans for the gradual use and development of the resources in the interest of the general public. Gifford Pinchot, in his book of essays *The Fight for Conservation*, articulated the two standards: "The first great fact about conservation is that it stands for development. There has been a fundamental misconception that conservation means nothing but the husbanding of resources for future generations. There could be no more serious mistake. Conservation does mean provision for the future, but it means also and first of all the right of the present generation to the fullest necessary use of all the resources with which this country is so abundantly blessed."[29] Though the emphasis still remained upon consumption, the term conservation represented an effort to fulfill demands both by preservationists for saving portions of wilderness and by developers for using resources.

The efficacy of subsuming two standards of management under one term may be measured by the response of the opposing groups. Earlier, when vast tracts of forest lands were preserved under executive order, preservationists had little cause for complaint while developers protested the "locking up" of valuable lands. Then, as plans were implemented for developing the lands, such as those under the Forest Management Act of 1897, preservationists objected and developers found it to their advantage to comply.[30] To the degree that conservation became an identifying principle under which at least one opposing interest perceived some advantages, the movement was able to mediate between the two demands. Moreover, it became possible for both individuals and groups on either extreme to confess an interest in preserving nature and developing resources simultaneously.

Another function of the term was to coordinate differing policies for managing the several natural resources, such as minerals, water, and forests. Scientists discovered that conservation fulfilled this function admirably, for the same principles could be applied to the selective cutting of forests, the impoundment of waters, and the moderate development of minerals, soils, and grazing lands. The first college textbook on conservation claimed: "Conservation is not a simple subject which can be treated with reference to a single resource, independently of the others; it is an interlocking one. The conservation of one resource is related to that of another. Thus the conservation of coal is to be accomplished in a large measure by the substitution of water as a source of power. The conservation of the metals is to be largely accomplished by the substitution of cement and stone and brick and other products."[31] To the scientists and technicians involved in the new movement, the power of conservation lay not so much in the originality of its techniques as in its broad comprehension of many independent problems. Conservation designated a paradigm of scientific thought that approximated the certainty of a natural law.

Yet for conservation to function as a unifying principle for a social movement, conservationists needed not only a scientific paradigm but also a fundamental ethical or moral truth. According to Gifford Pinchot, conservation implied an ethical attitude toward the use of natural resources: "I was riding my old horse Jim in Rock Creek Park one day—I think it was February 1907—when suddenly the idea . . . occurred to me . . . that all these natural resources which we had been dealing with as though they were in watertight compartments actually constituted one united problem. That problem was the use of the earth for the permanent good of man. . . . The idea was so new that it did not even have a name. Finally Overton Price suggested that we should call it 'conservation' and the President said 'O.K.' So we called it the conservation movement."[32] With its emphasis on the "permanent good of man," conservation promoted the responsibility of the individual to the group, an altruistic imperative that soon became a patriotic and spiritual one.[33] Further, association of conservation with the established bureaucracy in Washington lent a political legitimacy to the concept that complemented its scientific and social legitimacy.

Theodore Roosevelt's address to the Conference of Governors made explicit the connection between effective management of resources and governmental efficiency. In a phrase later quoted frequently in the literature of the movement, Roosevelt exhorted his listeners to "remember that the conservation of natural resources, though the gravest problem of today, is yet but part of another and greater problem to which this Nation is not yet awake, but to which it will awake in time, and with which it must hereafter grapple if it is to live—the problem of national efficiency, the patriotic duty of insuring the safety and continuance of the Nation."[34]

In a similar vein, Pinchot related that his work, with "more bureaus than any other man in Washington," made it the most "natural thing in the world that the relations of forests lands, and minerals, each to each should be brought to my mind."[35] Governmental organization, particularly the Rooseveltian view of government centralized in the federal bureaucracy, reflected and stimulated a view of nature itself as an organized whole.[36]

Sometimes speakers for the movement emphasized the analogy between nationalism and the need to manage natural resources across state and local boundaries. Progressive ideologist W J McGee, for example, proclaimed a "new Union among the States" based upon the interrelationship of natural resources: "The fundamental principle of equity and law that each shall so use his own as not to injure others is felt to apply not only between man and man within each State, but between State and State throughout the entire Union; and it is felt as never before that each State owes a sacred duty to each other commonwealth in connection with each resource, indeed with each unit measure of that resource."[37] C. H. Forbes-Lindsay, travel writer and historian of the Panama Canal, made explicit the comparison between the unity of nature and that of the federal organization of states: "In the foregoing summary of the relation of the forests to the river and the soil, we have a good illustration of the interdependence of our natural resources. This close connection and coordination pervades the entire question of conservation and development. In it we find the basis of the principle that each element of the problem must be considered as an integral part of a whole inseparably related to the other parts. In it, too we find the logic of the proposition that independent action by the several States would not be feasible and Federal regulation must control."[38]

John L. Mathews, an avid student of Mississippi waterway development, also recognized that cooperation among the states was necessary to promote conservation. He perceived the Rooseveltian plan of encouraging parallel legislation in each of the states as an administrative innovation designed to bridge the "twilight zone" between national and state jurisdictions: "These means appear before trial to offer a happy means of bringing about co-legislation without infringing upon the dignity of any member of the Union." Significantly, Mathews argued that governmental organization on such a scale could be brought about, not by executive fiat, but by "the organization of public sentiment."[39]

In making such arguments McGee and Mathews drew from contemporary progressive political theory, which sought to strike a balance between federal and local interests. Ideally, according to progressive thinking, neither individualism nor social homogeneity should dominate national policy; instead, progress was assisted through "specialization, organization, and group participation" of individual units in the collective.[40] Like Spencerian organisms, progression from simple to complex forms of organization occurred in government as well, with centralized government superior to any intermediate form. As John Morton Blum, quoting Theodore Roosevelt, wrote: "A simple and poor society can exist as a democracy on a basis of sheer individualism. But a rich and complex industrial society cannot so exist; for some individuals, and especially those artificial individuals called corporations, become so very big that the ordinary individual . . . cannot deal with them on terms of equality. It therefore becomes necessary for these ordinary individuals to combine in their turn . . . in order to act in their collective capacity through that biggest of all combinations called the government."[41] Taken to its extreme, this position allowed for little intermediate private or group organization, a policy criticized as "social atomism."[42] In its most sanguine aspect, however, the members of the public, much like the states themselves, were to relate to the central government as individual units in an organized and efficient configuration.

The belief in "federation and combination" of individual units into a collective whole may have provided a compromise between the positions of federal and state government and certainly contributed to the symbolic importance of the Governors' Conference and other interstate meetings. Cooperation among the states and between the central government and the states had political advantages as well. Roosevelt needed support from Republican constituencies in the West, and he often traded concessions to individual states for general adherence to national policies.[43] Occasionally, the call for cooperation between the state and the nation was interpreted as reinforcing states' rights as well as federalism.[44]

But in addition to the political utility that supported Roosevelt's emphasis upon cooperation between constituent units of government, the principle of conservation also depended upon a concept of the nation as a whole. Herbert Croly, a leading progressive theorist, encouraged individuals to direct their interests toward the nation and its "historic mission" of progressive democratization.[45] Likewise, the principle of conservation appeared to elicit a sincere patriotic response. The writing of such scholars as Charles R. Van Hise became infused with the patriotic grandeur of conservation: "'The part of wisdom is to cooperate' . . . The new movement can no more be stilled than can the tides, which depend upon the movements of the planets, because it rests upon as fundamental a cause—a severe limitation of the natural resources of the nation. . . . Those who play their part in this great revolution in ideals, the most fundamental and the most necessary that has ever confronted the nation, will receive the blessing of posterity."[46] For Van Hise, the new patriotism was to be distinguished from the false expansiveness of what traveler and Western chronicler Rudolf Cronau called "our boasting

SCIENCE, PUBLIC POLICY, AND THE "SPIRIT OF THE PEOPLE"

91

spread-eagle orators."[47] Rather, conservationism projected a more modest and practical voice: the progressive "patriotism of making things better."[48]

Eventually, conservation so effectively united the scientific, moral, and political goals of the movement that some began to think of it as the "true moral welfare" that was the ultimate goal of humankind—in other words, as a kind of secular religion. For W J McGee, the ethical doctrine of conservation—the greatest good for the greatest number—"was better expressed in an utterance of two millenniums past—'A new commandment give I unto thee, that ye love one another.' . . . Whatever its material manifestations, every revolution is first and foremost a revelation in thought and spirit."[49] It was often assumed that true understanding of the principles of conservation came about through spiritual revelation, much like Gifford Pinchot's experience in Rock Creek Park.

The religious imagery of conversion served the conservationists' goals precisely because of its strong implications for social activity, particularly the conversion of the unbeliever. Indeed, Gifford Pinchot appealed directly to the missionary spirit in his book *The Fight for Conservation*: "Among the first duties of every man is to help in bringing the Kingdom of God on earth. The greatest human power for good, the most efficient earthly tool for the future uplifting of the nations is without question the United States."[50] The leaders of the movement encouraged each individual to promote the conservation gospel, "second only . . . to the great fundamental questions of morality," by applying Christian virtue to the common good.[51] The patriotic and religious tenors in the writings of progressive conservationists became inseparably entwined.

This powerful combination of faith and politics also infused the elaborate rituals and ceremonies of the movement. The Governors' Conference, for example, was referred to in terms reminiscent of religious services. "The Conference took on from time to time the aspect of a confessional," wrote the editor of the *Century*, "The serious and devoted spirit—as of men administering a solemn trust—was inspiring, and at times electric in its manifestation. Dr. Edward Everett Hale struck the keynote in the passage which preceded his invocation, and the fervor with which the whole assembly joined him in the Lord's Prayer was most impressive. The *patriotism of making things better* was the bugle-call that aroused every one to enthusiasm."[52]

Similarly, *The World's Work* described the conference reports as constituting an "experience meeting," with each governor giving personal testimony of his state's efforts at conservation.[53] *Outlook* magazine, in describing Roosevelt's entrance at the conference, emphasized the personally enlightening quality of the experience when it stated that "suddenly the assemblage seem[ed] electrified by a new nervous force!"[54] Finally, McGee brought out both secular and religious overtones when he compared the conference to one of the two sacred documents of American history, the Declaration of Independence (the first meeting of the National Conservation Commission being the Constitution).[55]

Judging from the reviewers' responses to the Governors' Conference, readers fully associated the patriotic with the religious auspices of these public events. According to the "social gospel," religion was associated directly with economic and political progress, and the test of religion appeared to be humanity's continued moral and social improvement.[56] The emphasis upon mutual spiritual and social progress required spiritual superiority even from the nation's leadership. Herbert Croly asked for "some democratic evangelist—some imitator of Jesus" to lead America toward national democracy, and his readers no doubt recognized an implicit comparison between Croly's evangelist and Roosevelt himself.[57]

Conservation as an identifying term was particularly useful in transforming what could have been a bureaucratic reorganization or a scientific concept into a movement that engaged the moral, patriotic, and even spiritual responsibility of the individual to the general public. As Samuel P. Hays wrote, the response of the general public to the concept "tinged the conservation movement with the emotion of a religious crusade."[58] Nevertheless, conservationists proceeded further to justify the principles of conservation by designating its constituency as the American "people." In doing so, they placed the movement firmly within a temporal context and conferred upon it a continuous and respectable claim to public authority.

W J McGee and "the People"

The concept of conservation served well to unify and identify the scientific, ethical, and political themes of the movement. However, conservationists needed to justify further the philosophy of managing natural resources when opponents questioned conservation as a regulatory principle guiding public policy. Even after 1908, preservationists still rejected the policy of conservation for use, while developers attacked what seemed to be the intent to preserve resources for indefinite periods of time.[59] In response to such opposition, the conservationists developed a public policy that was grounded first in the principles of neo-Lamarckian science, and second in progressive political theory. The result was the construction of a concept of "the people," whose interests the conservation movement claimed to represent.

The scientific theory supporting the conservationists' ideas was labeled "neo-Lamarckianism" after Charles Darwin's famous predecessor, Jean Baptiste Lamarck. Lamarck postulated that various environmental influences, such as severity of climate or lack of food supply, directly influenced the physical characteristics of members of a species—hence his famous analogy of a giraffe developing a long neck from stretching to reach leaves on the highest trees. Further, Lamarck had claimed that such variations would be passed on to descendents. Thus giraffes born to parents living among tall trees would be well adapted to their surroundings from birth, and this adaptation would secure the continued existence of the species. Although Lamarck's theory was later proven to be misguided, it was taken quite seriously at the time. Scientists did not yet understand that mutations in the gene cells, not direct environmental influences, produced variations in the characteristics of species. For example, Darwin himself toward the end of his life pronounced that environmental factors were major causes of species variation.

Nevertheless, the social and political version of Lamarck's theory, termed neo-Lamarckianism, was widely accepted outside of the scientific community and extended Lamarck's credibility among Americans well into the early twentieth century. The neo-Lamarckians argued that humans were obligated to use their unique characteristics of self-awareness and ingenuity to continually improve the environment, and hence the species. Progressive reform did not harm humankind by allowing less well-adapted individuals to survive, as the social Darwinists claimed. Instead, neo-Lamarckians believed that rational management of the environment was the only natural mechanism of human advancement. Judging from their popularity, neo-Lamarckian principles successfully reflected American cultural beliefs in pragmatism, self-determination, and the influence of the frontier experience upon the national character.[60]

By founding their social policy upon neo-Lamarckian principles, speakers for conservation consequently placed the movement within a temporal framework encompassing the evolutionary history of humankind, as well as the history of the nation. Note, for example, this excerpt from Roosevelt's introductory speech at the Governors' Conference:

"The steadily increasing drain on these natural resources has promoted to an extraordinary degree the complexity of our industrial and social life. Moreover, this unexampled development has had a determining effect upon the character and opinions of our people. The demand for efficiency in the great task has given us vigor, effectiveness, decision, and power, and a capacity for achievement which in its own lines has never yet been matched. . . . [I]t is safe to say that the prosperity of our people depends directly on the energy and intelligence with which our natural resources are used. It is equally clear that these resources are the final basis of national power and perpetuity. Finally, it is ominously evident that these sources are in the course of rapid exhaustion."[61] From the conservationists' evolutionary viewpoint, natural resources not only existed as an organized system, but they also exerted a force inevitably modifying the characteristics of future generations and guaranteeing the progress of humanity.

To lend immediacy to the growing perception of limits on the available resources, advocates of conservation further constructed a history of wasteful consumption that, conveniently enough, paralleled the history of progress. This history of waste continued from the ancient past through the present and made every conservation measure a necessary and urgent action. The following paragraph from the president's speech underscores that urgency: "This Nation began with the belief that its landed possessions were illimitable and capable of supporting all the people who might care to make our country their home; but already the limit of unsettled land is in sight, and indeed but little land fitted for agriculture now remains unoccupied save what can be reclaimed by irrigation and drainage. . . . We began with an unapproached heritage of forests; more than half of the timber is gone. We began with coal fields more extensive than those of any other nation . . . and many experts now declare that the end of both iron and coal is in sight."[62] Thus influenced by neo-Lamarckian principles, conservationists associated evolutionary human development with the immediate need to direct and regulate that development in order to justify their own policies and programs.

The language that most effectively communicated both the temporal inevitability of conservation and the contemporary urgency of its tasks permeated the writing of the ethnologist, geologist, and popularizer of science W J McGee (1853–1912). As the acknowledged intellectual leader of the movement (Pinchot labeled him the "scientific brains" of conservation and attributed to him the creation of the "greatest good" formula), McGee himself remained comparatively unknown to the public. His personal influence was exerted primarily from within the bureaucracy—as vice president and secretary of the Inland Waterways Commission, editor of the *Proceedings* of the Conference of Governors, leader of the Bureau of Ethnology, and president of the National Geographic Society.[63] Though he did publish some of his ideas in such widespread outlets as *The World's Work, American Review of Reviews,* and *Conservation* magazine, his more scholarly publications were unavailable to the majority of Americans.[64]

Despite his obscurity, McGee's influence pervaded the conservationists' public literature. According to historian Whitney Cross and Gifford Pinchot's own testimony, McGee collaborated with Pinchot in anonymously composing many of the official published statements of the conservation movement, including several of Theodore Roosevelt's addresses. In these official statements, as well as in his more popular public works, McGee framed the conservation movement as the culminating episode of a great evolutionary pageant rooted in the principles of neo-Lamarckian evolution and progressive social theory. Further, by infusing the language of important public discourses with his distinctive style, McGee placed a unique rhetorical stamp upon the social policy of conservation.

The foundation of McGee's complex evolutionary theory was a sophisticated blend of Darwinian and neo-Lamarckian concepts. Consistent with the Darwinism of his time, McGee accepted that competition and natural selection determined variations among species. In Whitney Cross's paraphrase of McGee's views, "gradually the competitive pressures for existence among the species of live organisms had developed variation among them heightening the nervous sensitivity of certain groups."[65] Beginning in 1894, however, McGee's papers before the Smithsonian Institution raised controversy by insisting that "the characters of organisms are determined through interaction with environment."[66] McGee claimed that extreme environmental forces produced similar characteristics, even among different species: "The potency of environment in shaping organisms is still more clearly shown in desert lands. . . . Here all plants interact with the in-organic external in such manner that even unrelated species assume likeness in form and feature."[67] The overarching influence of the environment was highly significant for McGee. Although certain species dominated through competition and natural selection, environmental causes powerfully affected all living species, including humanity.

According to McGee's evolutionary theory, humanity as a species was noteworthy on two counts: first, the effect of environmental influences on humans was primarily spiritual rather than physical; second, humanity exhibited the particular distinguishing trait of adaptability, the ability to escape the immediate confines of environmental influence:

> The failure of the law [of physical variation], when extended to mankind, is apparent only. The desert nomads retain common physical characteristics, but develop arts of obtaining water and food, and these acts are adjusted to the local environment; dwellers alongshore do not suffer modification in bodily form, but their arts are modified and they become fishermen and sailors; the mountaineers do not acquire the physical characters of the subhuman animals of the mountains, but learn to use weapons and to protect themselves from bodily injury by artificial devices. . . . Thus development, differentiation, transformation, are no less characteristic of the human genus than of lower organisms—indeed, it is in this noblest of organisms that plasticity or adjustability to diverse conditions culminates—but the differentiation is intellectual rather than physical, cerebral rather than corporeal.[68]

McGee's references to adaptability and spirituality are typical of efforts to accommodate the theory of natural selection to neo-Lamarckian claims for environmental influence.

An additional factor, besides spirituality and adaptability, ultimately differentiated mankind from animals and distinguished McGee's variety of evolutionary thought. Instead of viewing the individuality of humans as their most important trait, producing virility, independence, and the ability to compete, McGee emphasized the adaptability of the *cooperative* or *social* tendencies. "The essential unit is the organization rather than the organism," McGee stated, and society was the chief means of adapting to, or conquering, the natural environment.[69] He even claimed that the rough-and-ready mountaineering character, exemplified by the independent Swiss, did not create competition among individuals, but produced a "regard for neighbor," "altruistic government," and "nationhood," through "ceaseless strife against rocks and ice."[70] McGee's interest in the social implications of evolution transformed the figure of Turner's frontier explorer into a representative of the public spirit.

Consequently, societal organization played an unusually important role in McGee's theory of natural evolution. Rather than wreaking destruction, society interacted with nature, much like the interaction of advanced and primitive species, to produce a collective benefit: "Thus the growth of cooperation begins with independent association and ends with interdependent association or organization—a hierarchic association or organisms in which each has its special function and all have individual and collective profit, while all are dominated by the big brained organism for the good of his world, be it small or large."[71] Even if cooperation required consumption, as when an Indian ingested a plant for food, the merger naturally led to a kind of spiritual exaltation on a universal scale: "Thus the cooperation beginning in simple tolerance sometimes ends in bodily union—a union so complete that the component organisms are transformed unto each other and transfigured into an exalted unity far transcending individual or specific quality."[72] For McGee, the primary virtues ultimately resulted from societal development and institutionalization. "Justice, truth, mercy, and probity" derived not from individual experience, but from socially productive organization.[73]

Applying the general values of social organization to questions of environmental responsibility, McGee turned to an examination of the relationship between the American people and the land. As mentioned previously, his view of the relationship sprang from two discordant sources. On one hand, the Darwinian precepts of natural selection and survival of the fittest pictured humanity as dominant over nature. Recounting the history of humanity's conquest of fire, the wheel, and wild beasts, McGee noted, "Many minor advances too, have come out of our West: [but] they all marked Conquest over Nature; and they grew up and were given freely by virtue of the strenuous life arising in a region of stressful extremes."[74] Insofar as Darwin (and Teddy Roosevelt!) were correct, conservationists had a moral obligation to exploit natural resources as a means of waging battle with the forces of nature: "On its face the Conservation Movement is material—ultra-material. At first blush the moral and the social in which cults arise and from which doctrines draw inspiration may not appear. Yet in truth there has never been in all human history a popular movement more firmly grounded in ethics. . . . No forests, no streams; no iron, no ships; no coal, no power; no farms, no food—for these verifies are but seed of thought and feeling."[75] Through statements such as these, McGee appeared committed to the conquest of nature, however respectfully, to insure the survival and dominance of humankind.

Yet McGee's recognition of the human impulse to conquer nature seemed contradictory to the neo-Lamarckian aspects of the conservation creed: the avoidance of waste, the reservation of resources until needed, and the obligation to future generations. Without natural resources to develop, the American people would lose its character as a nation: "When the lotus-eaters forgot the travail of the nation's birth and condemned their own posterity to perdition unknown, national spirit oozed out of their fingertips. They wasted what Nature saved through the ages, scattered that which their sires garnished, ceased to consider the fate or even the fact of posterity. . . . Thus unity grew lax, and patriotism weakened; standards of morality sank below normal instead of rising steadily as is their wont; and the budding notion of national efficiency was chilled back."[76] Because their distinctive character depended upon the influence of their natural environment, Americans would do well not to destroy it.

The fundamental incompatibility between Darwinian science and the ethics of neo-Lamarckianism required a transcending notion reconciling both positions and simultaneously providing a basis for justifying the conservation movement to its diversified and critical audience. McGee provided such a notion in his concept of "the People." Within the progressive tradition, the idea of designating the social collective as a people went back as far as Turner's description of the American population created and shaped by the forces of its Western environment.[77] In addition, reformist economist Henry George and many populist leaders used the term "the people" to describe the productive working classes, as did at least one progressive historian, J. Allen Smith.[78] Most Progressives, however, implied that "the people" included all the social and economic classes of the nation.[79]

McGee's particular contribution to the progressive idea of "the people" was to integrate his intricate neo-Lamarckian evolutionary theory with the social policy of a widely popular movement. As a continuing society with its roots in primal history and its future manifest in the American destiny, for McGee "the People" was a *sociobiological* entity, the most efficient possible unit of human organization and development. America as a nation was neither a biological species nor a social collective; it was both. The earlier evolution of "the People" was grounded in its more primitive biological origins, but its future survival required conscious, rational management of the social organism and its surrounding environment.

Given these biological origins, then, the urge to conquer nature was itself neither good nor evil; it was a temporary stage in the evolutionary development of "the People."[80] As society developed throughout successive stages, its very existence depended upon a blend of primitive and progressive forces—a "balance between impulse and responsibility"—that resulted only if "the People" overcame their impulse to conquer Nature and turned their energies toward cooperation.[81] Society also depended upon an intelligent and reflective awareness of humankind's place in the natural flow of history, a perspective that McGee provided throughout his historical review. "All our national extravagances are shocking to sensibilities once awakened," McGee stated, and he hoped that the civilized response of society would embarrass individuals into curbing their lust for material gain.[82]

Finally, through his concept of "the People," McGee prepared the way for viewing the future of the American people as a patriotic and even spiritual consummation of the gospel of conservation. As always, the source of patriotic pride remained the environment. But in the grand evolutionary pageant of conservation, the various elements of the environment were elevated to characters of epic proportions that acted out their parts on the stage of human history. As a result, the new environmental consciousness became part of a civic ritual: "Just as the Land for which the Fathers fought was at once the tangible basis and the inspiration for patriotism in an earlier day, so in this day the birthright Land, the soil-making Forests, the native Minerals, and the life-giving Waters inspire Patriotism anew. Each is well worthy of story and song and shrine; and each inspiration is warmer and the whole are knit in closer union by reason of each other."[83] Significantly, the consummation of the ritual evoked an "exaltation" much like that of the ceremonies surrounding the Governors' Conference: "A new Patriotism has appeared. . . . Its object is the conservation of national resources; its end the perpetuation of People and States and the exaltation of Humanity. The keynote of its cry unto the spirits of men is *The Greatest Good for the Greatest Number for the Longest Time*."[84] The exaltation was a social rather than an individual experience, resembling the kind of aroused popular opinion that Gifford Pinchot called "public spirit."

The arousing of an "exaltation" or "public spirit" among the movement's constituency was a primary goal of the major conservationists. To effect this result, they built a requirement for a successful rhetorical appeal into the very fabric of their discourse. Conservationists repeatedly evoked the idea of the American people to lend credibility to their claims. By doing so, they reinforced the perception of their movement, not as a special interest group or a bureaucratic creation, but as a natural evolutionary trend representing all of the American public.

To perceive the weaving together of McGee's ideology with the discourse of the movement, two official documents, the *Preliminary Report* of the Inland Waterways Commission and the *Proceedings* of the Governors' Conference, bear close examination. The Inland Waterways Commission (of which McGee was the commissioner) was the organization responsible for the proposal of a nationwide governors' conference. In response to "numerous commercial organizations of the Mississippi Valley," the president authorized a report on the feasibility of a nationwide waterways development program.[85] The language referring to the group of private business interests making the request, however, was phrased in McGee's unique idiom. "The Commission is fully aware that its creation was due to a demand of the people," stated the preliminary report.[86] The president's own message to Congress transmitting the report was also heavily interspersed with references to "the widespread interest and demand from the people" and the "increased commerce growth, and prosperity of our people" to result from water management.[87] The claim for a popular mandate was strong enough to bring about intense prospective media interest in the subsequent Governors' Conference and in the concerns of conservation.[88]

As might be expected (McGee was the editor and author of many of the speeches), the *Proceedings* of the Governors' Conference also was liberally infused with language attesting to the interest of the people. The need for a strong popular appeal was great enough, in fact, to alter the character of the proceedings from a meeting of scientific specialists to a gathering of state representatives and other public figures: "In the course of discussion the further idea was brought out more clearly than before that the State Governor is of necessity the chief sponsor for the welfare of his commonwealth. Soon as suggested, this idea modified the plan for the meeting, and led to the decision that it should be primarily a Conference of Governors and only secondarily a meeting of experts able authoritatively to convey information both to the Governors and the Commission."[89] Apparently after the Denver meeting of 1907 and other gatherings of the opposition, it was important to emphasize the presence of representatives from all the states to establish the public mandate of the conference.[90]

Throughout the conference public discourse placed impressive emphasis upon "the People" as a political and environmental force. Two examples serve to underscore this emphasis. First, the reprinting of the letter from the Inland Waterways Commission to the president recommending a governors' conference showed the direct influence of McGee's idiosyncratic style. When the letter was printed in the Preliminary Report, references to "the people" remained in lowercase. However, in the Conference of Governors' report, "the People" acquired a remarkable precedence: "We are of the opinion that the time has come for considering the policy of conserving these material resources on which the permanent prosperity of our country and the equal opportunity of all our People must depend; we are also of the opinion that the policy of conservation is so marked an advance on that policy adopted at the outset of our National career as to demand the consideration of both Federal and State sponsors for the welfare of the People."[91] Interestingly, in a later article for *Popular Science Monthly*, McGee claimed that administrative agencies ranked in status with other branches of government (such as the executive or judiciary) as a result of their constitution by "the People." For McGee, even Roosevelt's progressive conception of administrative bureaucracy was a product of the evolution of the human species.[92]

The second indication of the increased importance attached to the concept of "the People" at the Governors' Conference is found in Roosevelt's opening address. After tracing the evolution of environmental consciousness from primitive times, Roosevelt talked of "the People's" spiritual and patriotic responsibility to fulfill their historical destiny: "When the People of the United States consciously undertake to raise themselves as citizens, and the Nation and the States in their several spheres, to the highest pitch of excellence in private, State, and national life, and to do this because it is the first of all the duties of true patriotism, then and not till then the future of this Nation, in quality and in time, will be assured [great applause]."[93] A more neo-Lamarckian statement could not have been composed for this address. In Roosevelt's view, conscious awareness and political action would bring about the evolutionary success of the American public. As befitted the "big-brained species," "the People's" own intelligence and adaptability would insure their survival.

Through the idioms of such intellectual leaders as W J McGee, the conservationists succeeded in providing the public with an effective account of the relationship between nature and society. They identified the movement with contemporary scientific and social thought, while providing the relatively new institution with a long and distinguished history. The movement's final task, then, was to support its claims to represent the people by communicating its basic principles to the vast numbers of the public and receiving their active support.

"Public Spirit" and the Response to Conservation

To earn the designation of a social movement, the conservationist impulse required more than intellectual self-justification and moral self-control; it also required wide recognition from the American public. Certainly a social movement of considerable force would legitimate the actions already taken by the government and provide a counterforce to the thoughtless consumption and monopolistic greed that threatened the remaining resources.[94] But more important, the conservation movement required popular as well as institutionalized support because it based its very concept of truth upon the role of a people in control of their own destiny. The form of the movement—as an organization with a popular base—was therefore made to correspond to its basic ideological premises through the effect of public discourse.[95]

The creation of a movement that claimed public support depended upon the expressed beliefs of its leadership in the efficacy of public opinion—in Pinchot's phrase, "public spirit." Despite Samuel P. Hays's claim that conservationists distrusted the enthusiastic response that followed the Governors' Conference, chief forester and presidential confidant Gifford Pinchot considered popular support essential, if not key, to the movement's success.[96] As early as 1903, Pinchot indicated his views in a letter to correspondent R. C. Melward: "Nothing permanent can be accomplished in this country unless it is backed by a sound public sentiment. The greater part of our work, therefore, has consisted in arousing a general interest in practical forestry throughout the country and in gradually changing public sentiment toward a more conservative treatment of forest lands."[97] As the years went on, Pinchot intensified his belief. By 1908 enough congressional opposition to conservation emerged for Pinchot to value above all other accomplishments the creation of a favorable public opinion: "The essential thing to be achieved, if our natural resources are to be preserved, is far less the taking of specific and individual measures than the creation of a mental attitude on the part of our people, the creation of an habitual and effective public sentiment which will look ahead."[98] Furthermore, Pinchot attributed previous mishandling of the public lands to "an unhealthy public sentiment," and he had no reason to change his opinion throughout the life of the movement.[99]

For Pinchot, the antidote to unhealthy public opinion was the cultivation of a healthy public spirit. "Our whole future is at stake in the education of our young men in politics and public spirit," Pinchot wrote, and he defined the phrase in the terms of patriotism and spirituality: "Among the first duties of every man is to help in bringing the Kingdom of God on earth. . . . Public spirit is the means by which every man can help toward this great end. Public spirit is patriotism in action; it is the application of Christianity to the commonwealth; it is effective loyalty to our country, to the brotherhood of man, and to the future."[100] Yet Pinchot displayed considerable pragmatic understanding of the mechanism of public opinion. He presumed that public opinion produced public welfare by virtue of the legitimacy of its origins; he recognized the need to take action at the peak of public enthusiasm; and he noted the responsiveness of representatives of government to their constituents' desires.[101]

Pinchot's interest in the mechanism of popular support led to the conservation movement becoming the "most conspicuous cause on the American scene" for its time, and conservation itself "the most-talked-about subject in America." To achieve these results, Pinchot turned to a typical device of public communication—the publicity campaign.[102] Using media as varied as pamphlets, tracts, letters, speeches, and pictures in educational and journalistic settings, Pinchot promoted the Forest Service into one of the most important bureaus of the Roosevelt administration.[103] He extended the range of the audience to include farmers and business people, Easterners and Westerners, and the educated and the uneducated as well, through the public schools. To accommodate such a wide audience, Pinchot and his associates distributed generally useful and informative materials, adopted a popular instead of a technical style, and actively encouraged communication between the central organization of the movement and the general public.

An example of Pinchot's effective use of informative materials was a series of Forest Service circulars and bulletins dealing with the history, development, and principles of the movement. Editions concerning conservation were issued with increasing frequency from 1905 through 1912, appearing in the same series with instructional pamphlets demonstrating principles of forest management and timber cultivation.[104] Some bulletins were particularly important, notably Pinchot's own *Primer of Forestry* (Division of Forestry bulletin no. 24), which was published in sequence from 1899 through 1905 and attained a circulation of a million copies.[105] The circulars sometimes contained reprints of speeches that would not ordinarily have reached a wide audience, such as Roosevelt's address before the Society of American Foresters in 1903, or excerpts from the proceedings of the American Forest Congress of 1905.[106] Yet the major purpose of the bulletins was to provide those working on the land with ways to understand and implement the principles of conservation.

Though their purpose required a direct instructional approach, occasional bulletins imitated the epic themes and styles suited to recounting the history of the people. Treadwell Cleveland Jr., in the "widely distributed" *Primer of Conservation*, finished his description of humanity's early struggle with the elements by proclaiming, "It is difficult for us to realize that we, standing at the height of western civilization, are in fact vastly more dependent upon tabulary nature than is the savage of the South Seas."[107] An excerpt on the roots of American conservation from Roosevelt's Conference of Governors speech then followed Cleveland's description, completing a short natural history of conservation from ancient to modern times.

The embellishment of a direct, informational message with the epic language of the conservation story was a conscious strategy of Pinchot's publicity campaign. Conservationists needed the spiritual support of farmers, cattle ranchers, and business people, even though these groups and their representatives in Congress found the scientific rationale for supporting conservation difficult to accept.[108] At least one business owner, George L. Knapp, reminded conservationists of the need to transform technical information into an attractive public style: "A forest officer defended to me the proposed inclusion of 94,000 acres of treeless land in the Gunnison reserve on the ground that the 'abuse of land contiguous to the national forests has a detrimental effect on the forests themselves.' Both the English and the logic are typical."[109]

To increase their efficiency in transmitting scientific, ideological, and social truths, conservationists developed a unique theory of style. Training in this form of rhetoric began with internal instruction to Forest Service employees and extended to educational materials and political publications. "Above all things a perfunctory, cut-and-dried report should be avoided," advised the Forest Service's *Use Book*; "Supervisor's reports must be concise as possible, but must have full information."[110] Likewise, the express goal of the Forest Service publications was "to convert scientific information into common knowledge" through "brief pamphlets, cheaply gotten up and written in a nontechnical style."[111]

The need to communicate scientific truth to the general public in an effective style extended to the areas of education and political activism. As stated by educator L. A. Mann in one of the first forestry textbooks, "The highest type of scientific writing is that which sets forth scientific facts in language which is interesting and easily understood by the millions who read."[112] In the field of political activity, the National Conservation Association promised bulletins "deal[ing] simply and without reservation with conservation measures pending or proposed. If a bill promotes conservation the Association will tell the truth about it, no matter who its authors may be or what interests are behind it."[113] By emphasizing simplicity and attractiveness in their use of language, the conservationists believed they served a widespread constituency while accurately reporting scientific truths.

Gifford Pinchot's own discussion of the social and moral implications of communication illuminates the conservationists' conception of style. According to Pinchot, efficiency and clarity of language was a moral imperative. Quoting from the Forest Service's *Use Book*, which was distributed to every service employee, Pinchot wrote: "'Use direct clear-cut language. Avoid unwieldy words where shorter, simpler ones will express the idea equally well. Be concise. . . .' The first object of a letter that does its job is to establish or continue living, moving, productive relations between two persons who are or ought to be interested, and so to get things done. But that is only the beginning. It has also to create or maintain good working confidence and cooperation between two individuals or two organizations. . . . To quote St. Paul again: 'Except ye utter words that are easy to understand, how shall it be known what is spoken?'"[114] Evidently, the conservationists' infusion of scientifically accurate information with spiritual and moral implications extended even to their theory of communication.

Yet when the morality of style was applied to mass-produced literature, it resulted in a strangely mixed pattern. Although attempting to be clear and precise, at times the conservationists were hortatory and expansive in a way similar to the nineteenth-century "spread-eagle orators" reviled by Rudolph Cronau. Conservationists often employed such elaborate techniques as epic narrative, allusion, and analogy to encourage the growth of public spirit. This curious blend of scientific accuracy and rhetorical effusion could be found throughout the speeches and writings of the major conservationists.

At one extreme, W J McGee infused scientific exposition with the expansive cadences and figures of biblical prose. His speech before the National Geographic Society in 1895 compared the struggle for survival with Christ's parable of the sower: "Commonly the trees bear multitudes of seeds, that the species may survive even though many seeds fall on stony ground and many young shoots may choke among brambles."[115] Moreover, through references to such biblical characters as Moses and Joshua, McGee imposed an epic manner upon the conservation story, "In good time came Theodore Roosevelt—in whom East and West met in ceaseless struggle for supremacy making him the typical American of his generation—and as President he . . . pushed on toward the reclamation of the rivers for navigation and other uses, an effort in which his hands were held up by many—notably James Rudolph Garfield, first as Commissioner of Corporations and later as Secretary of the Interior."[116] As noted, McGee's epic style also influenced the writing of more popular works, such as Forest Service bulletins and presidential addresses. By blending the style of exaltation with scientific reportage, McGee aimed to inspire as well as to educate.

At the other extreme, Gifford Pinchot demonstrated an alternative to rhetorical expansiveness with simple, almost humble storytelling and illustration. Pinchot's more homey analogies and anecdotes frequently combined a scientific truth with a moral point: "Suppose a man adrift at sea in an open boat with a little water, enough to last him with ordinary use for five days, an infinitesimal chance of being picked up, and the certainty that he could not make land in less than twenty days. What would any of us say to him if, under these circumstances, he not only drank all the water he wanted, but used the rest of it to wash his hands with and then threw it over the side? Yet we are not only using all the coal we want, but we are throwing a lot of it away."[117] Pinchot's style of speaking impressed its listeners not only with its simplicity of style and language, but with its memorable analogies and metaphors.[118] His simple comparisons were often directed to the interests of the particular audience addressed. Thus, in a speech to businessmen at the Aldine Club in New York City, Pinchot said:

> The country has accepted our idea—the application of common sense to common problems for the common good. Why should we not think ahead for the country as a family or businessman does?
> The National Conservation Commission. . . . [has] found that every year there are three and a half times as many trees cut as our forests can grow. . . .
> Our water powers run away every year in sufficient power to turn every wheel and to drive every car we have.[119]

To a civic interest group in New Rochelle, New York, Pinchot elaborated on several familiar comparisons:

> Another, and usually plausible, form of attack, is to demand that all land not now bearing trees shall be thrown out of the national forests. For centuries forest fires have burned through the Western mountains, and much land thus deforested is scattered throughout the national forests awaiting reforestation. This land is not valuable for agriculture, and will contribute more to the general welfare under forest than in any other way. To exclude it from the national forests would be no more reasonable than it would be in a city to remove from taxation and municipal control every building lot not now covered by a house.
> It would be no more reasonable than to condemn and take away from our farmers every acre of land that did not bear a crop last year, or to confiscate a man's winter overcoat because he was not wearing it in July.[120]

And he exercised his talent for the telling aphorism at the St. Paul Roosevelt Club:

> The brand of politics served out to us by the professional politician has long been composed largely of hot meals for the interests and hot air for the people. . . .
> To try to divert the march of an aroused public conscience from this righteous inevitable conflict by means of obsolete political catch-words is like trying to dam the Mississippi with dead leaves.[121]

Whether through elaborate discourse or simple analogies, the rhetorical style of the conservationists simultaneously elicited the understanding and evoked the emotions of the public audience.

In addition to the accessibility gained by an engaging style, popular support derived from the sense of direct involvement evoked by the rhetoric of the movement. Pinchot initiated the directive for writers to engage readers in active dialogue. In several early Forest Service circulars he posted the following note:

To the Public

The Forest Service exists to promote forestry throughout the whole country for every practical purpose and for the benefit of all. Its knowledge, advice, and co-operation are at the disposal of all forest users. . . . Inquiries relating to forests, forest trees, forest products, and the industries depending upon them are solicited and welcomed. Information and counsel upon forest legislation may be sought. All communications should be addressed to:

The Forester
United States Department of Agriculture
Washington, D.C.[122]

The readership did respond, to the extent that letter writing became an important part of Pinchot's campaign for forestry.[123]

Later in the movement Pinchot's major lobbying organization, the National Conservation Association, encouraged participation by increasingly explicit and lengthy appeals. Several bulletins in the Forest Service publication series expressing the policy of the association toward current legislation addressed the readers directly:

Your officers have seen with the keenest satisfaction the vigorous and effective support and cooperation which the members of the Association have given and are giving in its work. . . . Had it not been for your letters, your telegrams, and your help in many ways, there would be a far less satisfactory story to tell about the fight of the Association against bad legislation.

I want very specially to urge every member of the Association to get behind these bills for the conservation of great natural resources in the interest of the people. Letters from all members to their Senators and Congressmen . . . will be of great assistance.[124]

Through such appeals, conservationism's large number of passive members could identify their private efforts at influencing governmental policy with the aims of the movement and the "interest of the people" in conserving natural resources.

Of the many efforts to acquire public support, including the creation of a theory of public communication, the emphasis upon communicability of style, and the making of direct appeals to the public, the best indicator of the strength of the movement for conservation lay in its claim to represent a significant number of Americans. Conservationists both exposed multitudes of people to the movement and argued for the representative nature of their constituency. The size of the conservationists' immediate audience may be estimated from reported circulation statistics. Pinchot stated publicly that the movement reached nine million newspaper readers in the last months of 1907. Privately he estimated that Forest Service news releases appeared in thirty to fifty million copies of newspapers each month.[125] By 1909 the Forest Service's mailing list alone included seven hundred eighty-one thousand names and did not diminish significantly in number by 1910.[126]

The flood of information often produced secondary effects helpful in organizing the movement and in winning supporters. Historian Elmo Richardson, for example, has noted that Forest Service employees in the West created local publicity campaigns based on conservationist literature that reached cattle ranchers, foresters, and newspaper editors.[127] Additional audiences for conservation were created through intensive efforts in public schools and colleges, where practical forestry was taught to illustrate evolutionary theory and to facilitate vocational training.[128] Because of the very pervasiveness of their influence, in part, the conservationists had difficulty identifying the precise makeup of their following. At least

AND THE "SPIRIT OF
THE PEOPLE"

103

they could claim to represent the various social and vocational classes more widely than any of the special interests or competing preservationist groups.

Given the available evidence, conservationists' claims to represent the public certainly seemed justified. The mailing lists of the Forest Service and Pinchot's active campaigning brought the message of conservation to cattle ranchers, timber harvesters, farmers, journalists, educators, owners of businesses, and members of the social and cultural elite.[129] Organizations representing technical professions and economic interests, including the American Societies of Civil Engineers and Mechanical Engineers, the American Institutes of Electrical Engineers and Mining Engineers, the National Electric Light Association, the National Farmer's Congress, the National Fire Protection Association, the American National Livestock Association, the Lakes-to-the-Gulf Deep Waterways Association, the National Council of Commerce, the National Board of Trade, the AFL, and the United Mine Workers, officially endorsed conservation.[130] The National Lumber Manufacturer's Association, the Weyerhauser Lumber Company, and the superintendent of the Homestake Mining Company nominally supported conservation, which raised some controversy, given the conservationists' professed antipathy toward big business and monopolies.[131] Yet the attraction of conservation to scientists, business people, and agriculturalists was understandable, for the movement offered fresh and effective ideas for enhancing the productivity of the land, supported by the recent scientific thought and consistent with national policy.[132]

The attraction of conservation to other major segments of the population was more difficult to explain in terms of direct economic benefit. Yet the same population that enjoyed periodical essays on natural history or travel in national parks— the educated and politically aware urban middle class—enthusiastically endorsed conservation, just as it had endorsed other progressive causes.[133] Such groups as the General Federation of Women's Clubs, the Daughters of the American Revolution, and the American Civic Association directly supported progressive conservation.[134] Moreover, a variety of well-known individuals, including William Jennings Bryan, Andrew Carnegie, James J. Hill, Jane Addams, Carrie Chapman Catt, Samuel Gompers, and Mark Hanna, suggested a certain broadness of representation even within the leadership of society.[135] Prepared by the themes of scientific observation and appreciation of nature in the writings of John Muir and others, and stimulated by the wave of political and social progressivism, the influential upper middle and middle class joined scientists, engineers, farmers, and even organized labor in support of conservation.[136]

By meeting the requirements of a scientific and technological age and the constraints of public effectiveness, the conservationists created a body of discourse through which Americans could find a place within a vast popular movement. Whether the movement actually reached the nine million newspaper readers in the last months of 1907, as Pinchot claimed, the very word "conservation" evoked a strong response from many social and vocational groups throughout the country. Interestingly, that positive and inclusive public response has remained strong throughout the twentieth century. In concluding, I shall attempt to characterize the nature of early conservation as a movement and suggest that the popularity of its message lay in its appropriation of the public interest in its language and ideology, an appropriation that continues today.

Conservation in a Progressive Culture

In the context of this scholarly overview, the movement for conservation might be seen as a positive, forward-looking, and even revolutionary development in public attitudes, in much the way early historians characterized progressivism itself. Conservation from this perspective diverged sharply from the exploitative and rapacious use of natural resources by business and private interests characteristic of the nineteenth century in America. With evangelistic zeal, adherents of the movement claimed that a new stage in the evolutionary history of the American people as a species had been reached through self-consciousness, spiritualism, and Rooseveltian bureaucracy. The Forest Service in particular, and government conservationists in general, became the new century's standard for efficiency in government and in the management of natural resources. Compared to the attitudes and events of the previous century, the conservationism of the early twentieth was a veritable revolution in human, and natural, affairs.

Unlike preservationism, for example, conservationism may be identified as a particularly progressive movement. First, its discourse demonstrated a greater interest in social change, however that change may be perceived; and second, its version of social change coincided with contemporary ideas of social progress. Between the two positions on the relationship of society and nature, only conservation developed a language suited to the creation of a widely popular social movement. The term "conservation" admirably served to identify the predominant scientific, political, and moral principles of the movement, and "the people" provided a legitimate rationale for action. The choice of such language suggested particular beliefs in the social progress of humanity and, by implication, of its public audience. By privileging the human side of the nature-humanity dialectic, the conservationists consciously and systematically cultivated a movement justified by the very concept of the public and its material needs.

Conservation, however, may not have been as revolutionary as its leaders claimed or as progressive historians have implied. The conservationist rhetoric of social policy drew from ideas of progress that had already penetrated American culture by the first decade of the twentieth century. Those ideas, based in neo-Lamarckian evolution, flourishing American nationalism, developing social consciousness, and barely secularized spiritualism, were combined by scientists and bureaucrats to generate a forceful and pragmatic program for public action. But the founding principles of this form of public action were already embedded in the immediate intellectual, social, and cultural context—indeed, in progressivist thinking itself.

Members of the constituency of conservation may also be seen as less than revolutionary in their attitudes. The ideas that spawned conservationism proved irresistible to the educated, rising middle class, who was invested in the inevitability of social progress and enticed by the possibility of effecting significant change. The many social service organizations endorsing conservation during the Progressive Era attested to the "do-good" attitude of their members. Conservation in this view can be seen as possessing a reformist, well-managed, middle-of-the-road orientation toward public action, a view typical of many recent historians' characterizations of the Progressive movement itself.

The argument over whether the conservation movement was either strikingly revolutionary or moderately reformist will continue as long as scholars of progressivism base their arguments upon social and economic grounds. Yet one might adopt a third, alternative view. Seen through the lens of language and culture, the widespread acceptance of the conservation movement in the first decade of the twentieth century did signal a profound, if not revolutionary, change in the relationship between humankind and nature. This change was as much a product of the constitutive power of rhetorical discourse as it was a result of the social or political forces of the early twentieth century.

In this view, the thematically precise construction of "the people" generated by conservationists determined to a considerable degree both the constitution of the movement and the enthusiastic response from its audience. Conservationist rhetoric persuaded the American public that progress was a "natural" process, scientifically verified and spiritually endorsed. Therefore, according to the concept of "the people," change could be brought about by the people *themselves*, if they only possessed sufficient public spirit. Thus the phenomenon of a social movement was brought about by its own constitutive language.

The profound change generated by this rhetorical construction, moreover, lay in an altered conception of the relationship between society and nature. Conservationists and their public constituency reevaluated the idea that the individual's personal encounter with nature was necessary or even desirable to effect change. Nature was now government's responsibility; efficiency (today termed technical rationality) was the preferred means of dealing with nature, and the public, particularly the mass public, became the intermediary between the self and the natural experience. Conservationism (later as environmentalism) paradoxically became the most institutionalized, bureaucratized, and regulatory popular movement of the twentieth century—not only because of its technocratic leadership and middle-class support, but also because of its scientific and political discursive rationale.

In many ways, the conservationism of today has not substantially changed from that of 1908. The language of controlled perpetuation and use of natural resources (now phrased in terms of "sustainable development") and the genetic, organic growth of administrative resources (today rationalized in the form of "sociobiology" or, more recently, "evolutionary ecology") haunts the discourse of contemporary environmentalism. When presidents and vice presidents claim to be conservationists, they echo the progressive, neo-Lamarckian, quasispiritualized, bureaucratic language of nearly a century ago.

The legacy of the conservation movement, then, is not so much the efficiency of its reforms or its potential for change, but its creation of a rhetorical culture. Theodore Roosevelt, Gifford Pinchot, and W J McGee have succeeded indeed; according to every existing attitude poll and survey, they have constituted a conservationist public. By apprehending their bureaucratic discourse, we have voluntarily stepped into positions they have created for us. In other words, we *are* "the people." We have an identity, a history, and a location in environmental affairs. We even call ourselves conservationists. The legacy of conservation is the creation of a "people" who justify their interactions with nature, for better or worse, in utilitarian, enlightened, and progressive terms.

Notes

1. Roderick Nash, *Wilderness and the American Mind*, 3d ed. (New Haven: Yale University Press, 1982), 143. The definitive statement on the closing of the frontier was Frederick Jackson Turner's reference to the census bulletin of 1890 at the 1893 meeting of the American Historical Association: "'Up to and including 1880 the country had a frontier of settlement, but at present the unsettled area has been so broken into by isolated bodies of settlement that there can hardly be said to be a frontier line. . . . ' This brief official statement marks the closing of a great historic movement." Turner's further claim that "the existence of an area of free land, its continuous recession, and the advance of American settlement westward, explain American development" underscored the urgency of retaining areas of underdeveloped land to preserve the particular character of American life. "The Significance of the Frontier in American History," in *The Frontier in American History* (New York: Henry Holt and Co., 1948), 1.

2. Conference of Governors, *Proceedings*, 13–15 May 1908, ed. W J McGee (Washington, D.C.: GPO, 1909), 67; for similar sentiments, see also 7 and 74. (Hereafter cited as *Governors' Conference.*) The White House Conference of Governors on the conservation

of natural resources was the first of a series of prestigious national conferences of governors that have continued from 1908 to today.

3. Ibid., 32, 40, 148, 179–80.

4. Daniel O. Buehler, "Permanence and Change in Theodore Roosevelt's Conservation Jeremiad," *Western Journal of Communication* 62 (1998): 440–41.

5. Arthur S. Link and Richard L. McCormick, *Progressivism* (Arlington Heights, Ill.: Harlan Davidson, 1983), 1; Roderick Frasier Nash, *American Environmentalism: Readings in Conservation History,* 3d ed. (New York: McGraw-Hill, 1990), 69–71.

6. Peter G. Filene, "An Obituary for 'The Progressive Movement,'" *American Quarterly* 22 (1970): 20–34; Richard L. McCormick, *The Party Period and Public Policy: American Politics from the Age of Jackson to the Progressive Era* (New York: Oxford University Press, 1986), 268–69.

7. C. Vann Woodward, "Progressivism: For Whites Only," chap. 14 in *Origins of the New South, 1877–1913:* A History of the South, ed. Wendell Holmes Stephenson and E. Merton Coulter (Baton Rouge: Louisiana State University Press and the Littlefield Fund for Southern History of the University of Texas, 1951), 9:369–95.

8. Samuel P. Hays, *Beauty, Health, and Permanence: Environmental Politics in the United States, 1955–1985* (Cambridge: Cambridge University Press, 1987), 13–15.

9. Benjamin Parke De Witt, *The Progressive Movement: A Non-partisan, Comprehensive Discussion of Current Tendencies in American Politics* (Seattle: University of Washington Press, 1915), 113–14; 142–43; 191–92; Richard Hofstadter, *The Age of Reform: From Bryan to F. D. R.* (New York: Random House, Vintage Press, 1955), 137–48; Leon Fink, *Progressive Intellectuals and the Dilemmas of Democratic Commitment* (Cambridge: Harvard University Press, 1997), 13–51; Steven J. Diner, *A Very Different Age: Americans of the Progressive Era* (New York: Hill and Wang, 1998), 3–13; Robert H. Wiebe, *Businessmen and Reform: A Study of the Progressive Movement* (Cambridge: Harvard University Press, 1962), 206–24.

10. Samuel P. Hays, *Conservation and the Gospel of Efficiency: The Progressive Conservation Movement, 1890–1920* (New York: Atheneum, 1974), 1–4; for a comparable emphasis upon the scientific and bureaucratic foundations of Roosevelt's concept of government, see Alan Trachtenberg, *The Incorporation of America: Culture and Society in the Gilded Age* (New York: Hill and Wang, 1982).

11. I derive the idea of the constitutive function of the rhetoric of the people from Maurice Charland, "Constitutive Rhetoric: The Case of the *Peuple québécois,*" *Quarterly Journal of Speech* 73 (1987): 133–50. See also Trachtenberg, *The Incorporation of America,* 180–81.

12. McCormick, *Party Period,* 272; Link and McCormick, *Progressivism,* 9.

13. Frank Graham, *Man's Dominion: The Story of Conservation in America* (New York: M. Evans, 1971), 78; Hans Huth, *Nature and the American: Three Centuries of Changing Attitudes* (Berkeley and Los Angeles: University of California Press, 1957), 154–55; Frank E. Smith, *The Politics of Conservation* (New York: Random House, Pantheon Books, 1966), 151; Nash, *Wilderness,* 108.

14. John R. Ross, in "Man over Nature: Origins of the Conservation Movement," *American Studies* 16 (spring 1975): 49–62, discusses the relationship between the U.S. Geological Survey and the early conservationists. See also Hays, *Conservation,* 6, for a review of the survey's work.

15. Nash, *Wilderness,* 152–53. John F. Reiger, particularly in chapters 5 and 6 in *American Sportsmen and the Origins of Conservation* (New York: Winchester Press, 1975), argues that conservation began with hunters and hunting societies, and magazines such as Grinnell's *Forest and Stream.* Also, Mark Neuzil and William Kovarik, in chapter 1 of *Mass Media and Environmental Conflict: America's Green Crusades* (Thousand Oaks, Calif.: Sage, 1996), discuss the contributions of hunting and fishing magazines to the movement.

16. Graham, *Man's Dominion,* 41.

17. Christine Oravec, "Conservationism vs. Preservationism: The 'Public Interest' in the Hetch Hetchy Controversy," *Quarterly Journal of Speech* 70 (1984): 445.

18. Roy M. Robbins, *Our Landed Heritage: The Public Domain, 1776–1936* (1942; reprint, New York: Peter Smith, 1950), 325.

19. John Ise, *The United States Forest Policy* (New Haven: Yale University Press, 1920), 43–45, 48–40, 55–60; Graham, *Man's Dominion*, 70–71.

20. Gifford Pinchot, *Breaking New Ground* (New York: Harcourt, Brace and Co., 1947), 319–21; Smith, *The Politics of Conservation*, 98–99; Hays, *Conservation*, 139.

21. E. Louise Peffer, *The Closing of the Public Domain, 1900–1950* (1951; reprint, New York: Arno Press, 1972), 17; Hays, *Conservation*, 256–57; Robbins, *Our Landed Heritage*, 315–21.

22. Elmo R. Richardson, *The Politics of Conservation: Crusades and Controversies, 1897–1913*, University of California Publications in History, vol. 70 (Berkeley and Los Angeles: University of California Press, 1962), 30.

23. Robert Underwood Johnson, *Remembered Yesterdays* (Boston: Little, Brown, and Co., 1923), 300–4.

24. Robert Gottlieb, *Forcing the Spring: The Transformation of the American Environmental Movement* (Washington, D.C.: Island Press, 1993), 24; Stephen Fox, *John Muir and His Legacy: The American Conservation Movement* (Boston: Little, Brown, and Co., 1981), 130; Charles R. Van Hise, *The Conservation of Natural Resources in the United States* (New York: Macmillan, 1926), 67; Gifford Pinchot, *The Fight for Conservation* (New York: Doubleday, Page, 1910), 1; U.S. Department of the Interior, *Forest Service Circular: A Primer of Conservation*, by Treadwell Cleveland Jr., no. 157 (1908); J. Leonard Bates, "Fulfilling American Democracy: The Conservation Movement, 1907 to 1921," *Mississippi Valley Historical Review* 44 (1957): 32; Samuel Eliot Morison and Henry Steele Commager, *The Growth of the American Republic*, 4th ed. (New York: Oxford University Press, 1950), 2:399–401. Frank E. Smith, in *The Politics of Conservation*, states only that "a much publicized Governor's Conference on Conservation was held at the White House . . . but it changed few votes in Congress" (108).

25. Pinchot, *Fight for Conservation*, 41.

26. Robbins *Our Landed Heritage*, 311–12, and Johnson, *Remembered Yesterdays*, 278–313, discuss the influential work of the *Century* editorialists during the early years of the forest reserves. Popular interest shifted from "genteel" magazines to more topical, reform-oriented magazines after 1890, and conservationists followed suit; they wrote for *McClure's* and *Collier's* as well as the *Century*. Roosevelt himself was on the staff of the *Outlook* for a short period, and Pinchot used *The World's Work* as an outlet for his more popular writings. See Frank Luther Mott, *A History of American Magazines, 1865-1885* (1938; reprint, Cambridge: Harvard University Press, 1957), 3:1–14, 430–31; and *A History of American Magazines, 1885-1905* (Cambridge: Harvard University Press, 1957), 4:779.

27. "The word 'conservation' in its present sense did not come into official use until the Theodore Roosevelt administration," claimed writer and editor Paul Brooks, as quoted in Paul Russell Cutright, *Theodore Roosevelt: The Making of a Conservationist* (Urbana, Ill.: University of Illinois Press, 1985), 238.

28. Pinchot, *Fight for Conservation*, 42–47.

29. Ibid., 42.

30. Hays, *Conservation*, 36–48.

31. Van Hise, *The Conservation of Natural Resources*, 362.

32. Gifford Pinchot, "How Conservation Began in the United States," *Agricultural History* 11 (1937): 262–63. The importance of this event in the history of conservation is underscored by Pinchot in *Breaking New Ground*, 322–26.

33. Bates, "Fulfilling American Democracy," 31; Hays, *Conservation*, 72.

34. *Governors' Conference*, 12. See also *National Conservation Association: What It Is* (n.p., n.d.), 1, and Trachtenberg, *The Incorporation of America*, 194.

35. Pinchot, *Breaking New Ground*, 322.

36. Ross, "Man over Nature," 52; Hays, *Conservation*, 72.

37. W J McGee, "The New Union among the States," *American Review of Reviews*, March 1909, 320. McGee requested that no periods be placed after the first two initials of his name to conserve ink.

38. C. H. Forbes-Lindsay, "Taking Stock of Our National Assets: The Far-Reaching Significance of the White House Conference," *Craftsman*, July 1908, 377. For similar

thoughts, see "The White House Conference," *Outlook*, 23 May 1908, 148; a skeptical view is expressed in "The Governors at Washington," *Nation* 86, no. 2238 (1908):460.

39. John L. Mathews, "The Conservation of Our National Resources," *Atlantic* 101, no. 5 (1908): 695.

40. Thomas L. Hartshorne, *The Distorted Image: Changing Conceptions of the American Character since Turner* (Cleveland: Case Western University Press, 1968), 31; Charles Forcey, *The Crossroads of Liberalism: Croly, Weyl, Lippmann, and the Progressive Era, 1900–1925* (New York: Oxford University Press, 1961), 21–46, discusses progressive journalist Herbert Croly's organic concept of federalism and governmental organizations.

41. John Morton Blum, *The Republican Roosevelt*, 2d ed. (Cambridge: Harvard University Press, 1977), 109–10.

42. Hays, *Conservation*, 269–70.

43. Richardson, *The Politics of Conservation*, 25, 40–46.

44. "The Conference of Governors," *Independent*, 21 May 1908, 1151.

45. George E. Mowry, *The Era of Theodore Roosevelt, 1900–1912* (New York: Harper and Row, 1958), 97.

46. Charles R. Van Hise, "Patriotism and Waste," *Collier's*, 18 September 1909, 41.

47. Rudolf Cronau, "A Continent Despoiled," *McClure's Magazine*, April 1909, 640.

48. "Patriotism That Counts," in "Topics of the Time," *Century*, July 1908, 475.

49. W J McGee, "The Conservation of Natural Resources," in *Mississippi Valley Historical Association Proceedings, 1909–1910* (Cedar Rapids, Iowa, 1911), 378.

50. Pinchot, *Fight for Conservation*, 95.

51. *Governors' Conference*, 3.

52. "Patriotism That Counts," 475 (Hale's emphasis). On the subject of patriotism in conservation see also Gifford Pinchot, "A New Patriotism," *The World's Work*, May 1908, 10235–37.

53. "The Governors' Conference and a New Patriotic Impulse," *The World's Work*, July 1908, 10420.

54. "The White House Conference," *Outlook*, 146.

55. McGee, "A New Union," 317; see also Graham Taylor, "National Movement to Conserve Natural Resources," *Charities and the Commons*, 3 October 1908, 8, for mention of the Declaration and the Constitution; and "The *Governor's Conference* and a New Patriotic Impulse," *The World's Work*, 10420, for mention of the Revolution and the Civil War.

56. Henry F. May, *The End of American Innocence: A Study of the First Years of Our Own Time, 1912–1917* (New York: Knopf, 1969), 12–14; Hofstadter, *The Age of Reform*, 149–52.

57. Forcey, *Crossroads of Liberalism*, 46.

58. Hays, *Conservation*, 145.

59. J. Horace McFarland, "Shall We Have Ugly Conservation?" *Outlook*, 13 March 1909, 594; J. R. McKee, "The Public and the Conservation Policy," *North American Review*, October 1910, 499.

60. Increasingly scholars have recognized the neo-Lamarckian flavor of evolutionary theory in the U.S. in the later part of the nineteenth century. See for example, the work of Peter J. Bowler, *Darwinism* (New York: Twayne Publishers, 1993), and Cynthia Eagle Russett, *Darwin in America: The Intellectual Response, 1865–1912* (San Francisco: W. H. Freeman, 1976). One index of the influence of neo-Lamarckian thought upon the nontechnical literature of conservation is reference to noted authorities in the field. For example, neo-Lamarckian Nathaniel Shaler is mentioned by Pinchot in *Fight for Conservation*, 9; by James J. Hill in his *Governors' Conference* speech, 64; in "Patriotism That Counts," 475, and by Forbes-Lindsay, "Taking Stock," 377.

61. *Governors' Conference*, 7.

62. Ibid.

63. Pinchot, *Breaking New Ground*, 325–26; Smith, *The Politics of Conservation*, 101; and Gottlieb, *Forcing the Spring*, 25. The only biography I have been able to locate was written by his sister, Emma R. McGee, *The Life of W J McGee; Distinguished Geologist, Ethnologist, Anthropologist, Hydrologist, etc. in Service of United States Government with Extracts from Addresses and Writings* (Farley, Iowa: Torch Press, 1915). This small volume of reminiscences contains a useful bibliography of his scientific publications.

64. In addition to McGee's conservationist writings, which are cited throughout, there was a short series in the magazine *Science* reporting on the official conferences and policies of the movement (see, for example, "Recent Steps in the Conservation Movement," *Science*, 2 April 1908, 539–40; "Current Progress in Conservation Work," *Science*, 26 March 1909, 490–96; "Water as a Resource," in the conservation issue of the *Annals of the American Academy of Political and Social Science* (Philadelphia, 1909), 521–50; and such articles as "Our Great River," *The World's Work*, February 1907, 8575–84; and "How One Billion of Us Can Be Fed," *The World's Work*, February 1912, 443–51.

65. Whitney Cross, "W J McGee and the Idea of Conservation," *Historian* 40 (spring 1953): 158.

66. W J McGee, "The Relation of Institutions to the Environment," in *Annual Report of the Board of Regents of the Smithsonian Institution, 1895* (Washington, D.C.: GPO, 1896), pt. 1, 704; Cross, "W J McGee and the Idea of Conservation," 152; Ross, "Man over Nature," 52.

67. McGee, "Relation of Institutions," in *Annual Report*, 701–2, 706.

68. Ibid., 704–5.

69. Ibid., 705.

70. W J McGee, "National Growth and National Character," *National Geographic Magazine*, June 1899, 195. McGee was a hydrographer and a geologist, so it is not surprising for him to attribute the highest levels of human development to migratory wandering and intermingling between coastal and highland desert peoples, as he does in the 1895 Smithsonian address. The American public, however, had identified with mountaineers for more than sixty years; this may have led McGee to make an obligatory comparison between the Swiss and the American characters in the *National Geographic* article.

71. McGee, "Relation of Institutions," in *Annual Report*, 707–8.

72. Ibid., 707.

73. Ibid., 711.

74. McGee, "Conservation of Natural Resources," in *Historical Association Proceedings*, 367.

75. Ibid., 376.

76. W J McGee, "The Cult of Conservation," *Conservation*, September 1908, 472.

77. David W. Noble, *Historians against History: The Frontier Thesis and the National Covenant in American Historical Writing since 1830* (Minneapolis: University of Minnesota Press, 1965), 41–49, is an interesting analysis of Turner's use of the term "people" to designate Americans in his historical writings.

78. Bates, "Fulfilling American Democracy," 30–40, discusses the possibly substantial but indirect influence of socialist thinking upon conservationists of the period; Eric F. Goldman, *Rendezvous with Destiny: A History of Modern American Reform* (New York: Knopf, 1953), 48–49, discusses the Populists' use of the word "people."

79. Grant McConnell, *Private Power and American Democracy* (New York: Random House, Vintage Press, 1966), 37; Goldman, *Rendezvous with Destiny*, 147, 83.

80. McGee, "The Conservation of Natural Resources," in *Historical Association Proceedings*, 367.

81. Ibid., 366.

82. Ibid., 374. In the campaign for national organization and efficiency and against waste, Rooseveltian conservationists paradoxically found themselves attacking individualism under the leadership of a president noted for that very trait. See the attacks on individualism in Pinchot, "Foundations of National Prosperity," 748; Van Hise, "Patriotism and Waste," 41; and George L. Knapp, "The Other Side of Conservation," *North American Review*, April 1910, 465–81, reprinted in *Selected Articles on the Conservation of Natural Resources*, Debater's Handbook Series, comp. C. E. Fanning (Minneapolis: H. W. Wilson, 1913), 23.

83. McGee, "The Cult of Conservation," 472.

84. Ibid., 469 (McGee's emphasis).

85. Inland Waterways Commission, *Preliminary Report*, 60th Cong. 1st sess., 1908, S. Doc. 325 (Washington, D.C.: GPO, 1908; reprint, Arno Press, 1972), 15.

86. Ibid., 18.

87. Ibid., iii, vii.

88. Grant McConnell, "The Conservation Movement—Past and Present," *Western Political Quarterly* 7 (1954): 463–78, in *Readings in Resource Management and Conservation*, ed. Ian Burton and Robert W. Kates (Chicago: University of Chicago Press, 1960), 191. All indications point to the success of the various conservation conferences in effecting a strong and enthusiastic response. "The Conference [of Governors] was already upon a level of thought and of emotion that can be accurately described as the mood of high and practical patriotism," effused one writer. "It is not too much to say, then, that President Roosevelt and Mr. Gifford Pinchot have changed the attitude of the American people toward the earth that they live on and given a new direction to the national thought." "The Governor's Conference and a New Patriotic Impulse," *The World's Work*, 10420, 10419.

89. *Governors' Conference*, vii.

90. The legitimacy of the conference was also an issue for Caspar Whitney, in "The View-Point: Governor's Conference at the White House," *Outing*, July 1908, 490; for him, the conference was "more truly representative of the American people than Joe Cannon's time-serving House of Representatives."

91. *Governors' Conference*, viii.

92. W J McGee, "The Five-Fold Functions of Government," *Popular Science Monthly*, September 1910, 274–85, reprinted in part in Emma McGee, *The Life of W J McGee*, 198–99.

93. *Governors' Conference*, viii.

94. Smith, *The Politics of Conservation*, 108.

95. Van Hise, *Conservation of Natural Resources*, 394; Bates, "Fulfilling American Democracy," 39; McConnell, "The Conservation Movement," 191, 197.

96. See, for example, Hays's own dismissive description of the work of women's groups in forestry (*Conservation*, 142–44) compared to Pinchot's appeal for support and acknowledgment of their contributions in *Fight for Conservation*, 106. Hays's statement that the conservationists "viewed with distrust" the enthusiasm of the public (*Conservation and the Gospel of Efficiency*, 145) is not supported in their published discourse.

97. Gifford Pinchot, as quoted in Harold R. Pinkett, *Gifford Pinchot: Private and Public Forester* (Urbana, Ill.: University of Illinois Press 1970), 53.

98. Pinchot, "Foundations of National Prosperity," 742; see also M. Nelson McGeary, *Gifford Pinchot: Forester-Politician* (Princeton: Princeton University Press, 1960), 90.

99. Gifford Pinchot, "The Conservation of Natural Resources, *Outlook*, 12 October 1907, 293; also see the reprint of this article in *Fight for Conservation*, 12.

100. Pinchot, *Fight for Conservation*, 95–96.

101. Ibid., 98, 91, 97–98.

102. McConnell, "The Conservation Movement," 189; McGeary, *Gifford Pinchot*, 98.

103. Pinkett, *Gifford Pinchot* 81; McGeary, *Gifford Pinchot*, 50. For a detailed account of the growth and scope of Pinchot's publicity bureau activities, see Stephen Ponder, "Federal News Management in the Progressive Era: Gifford Pinchot and the Conservation Crusade," *Journalism History* 12, no. 2 (1986): 42–48; and "Government Publicity and Conservation: Gifford Pinchot and the Frontier Press," *Mass Communication Review* 22, nos. 1 and 2 (1995): 64–74.

104. See the U.S. Department of Agriculture, *Forest Service Circulars: A Primer of Conservation; The Future Use of Land in the United States*, no. 159 (1908); *The Status of Forestry*, no. 167 (1909); and *The Forests: Their Use*, by Overton Price, no. 171 (1909). Forestry circulars had been long used for public education; the conservationists simply appropriated the publications for their own needs. See, for example, *Division of Forestry Circulars: Request to Educators for Cooperation*, no. 1 (1886); *A Circular for Educational Men*, no. 2 (1887); *Forest Service Circulars: Addresses at the American Forest Congress*, no. 35 (1905); and *The Forest Service: What It Is and How It Deals with Forest Problems*, no. 36 (1905).

105. Pinkett, *Gifford Pinchot*, 53.

106. Forest Service Circular, *Forestry and the Lumber Supply*, no. 25 (1903), and *Circular*, no. 35.

107. *Circular*, no. 157, 4.

108. Hays, *Conservation*, 133–34; Richardson, *The Politics of Conservation*, 18.
109. Knapp, "The Other Side of Conservation," 22.
110. U.S. Department of Agriculture, Forest Service, *The Use Book: Regulations and Instructions for the Use of the National Forests* (Washington, D.C.: GPO, 1907), 151–53, 155.
111. *Congressional Record*, 30 March 1908, 4137.
112. L. A. Mann, as quoted in Richard Boerker, *Our National Forests* (New York: Macmillan, 1919).
113. *National Conservation Association, What It Is.*
114. Pinchot, *Breaking New Ground*, 289; U.S.D.A. Forest Service, *Use Book*, 160.
115. McGee, "Relation of Institutions," in *Annual Report*, 701.
116. McGee, "Conservation of Natural Resources," in *Historical Association Proceedings*, 371.
117. Pinchot, "Foundations of National Prosperity," 744.
118. McGeary, *Gifford Pinchot*, 399; Pinkett, *Gifford Pinchot*, 85.
119. *New York Times*, 10 January 1909, sec. 2, p. 20.
120. *Minneapolis Journal*, 27 December 1909, p. 3, col. 2–3.
121. *New York Times*, 12 June 1910, p. 11, col. 1, 3.
122. *Circular*, no. 36, 2.
123. Pinchot, *Breaking New Ground*, 289–90. Pinchot was emphatic about his standards for letter writing: "The form of a letter is far more important than many people think. Few things show the character and purpose of an organization better than its mail, both incoming and outgoing. The outgoing mail carries the message and the quality of its source. The incoming mail brings the proof of failure or success" (189).
124. *National Conservation Association Bulletin*, 21 December 1912, 1; 3 January 1912.
125. McGeary, *Gifford Pinchot*, 88; *Cong. Rec.*, 30 March 1908, 4138; Ponder, "Federal News Management," 44.
126. Pinkett, *Gifford Pinchot*, 82; McGeary, *Gifford Pinchot*, 88; Ponder, "Federal News Management," 44.
127. Richardson, *The Politics of Conservation*, 27.
128. Pinkett, *Gifford Pinchot*, 87–88.
129. McGeary, *Gifford Pinchot*, 88; also, *New York Times*, 7 March 1910, p. 5, col. 3.
130. *Governors' Conference*, xxv–xxviii; Taylor, "National Movement to Conserve Natural Resources," 9.
131. Hays, *Conservation*, 29; Edith Jane Hadley, "John Muir's Views of Nature and Their Consequences" (Ph.D. diss. University of Wisconsin, 1956), 607.
132. Hays, *Conservation*, 29, 39, 64, 123, 139; Jackson Lears, *No Place of Grace: Antimodernism and the Transformation of American Culture, 1880–1920* (New York: Pantheon, 1981).
133. Hofstadter, *Age of Reform*, 131–32.
134. Ibid., 143–46.
135. Bates, "Fulfilling American Democracy," 36; *Governors' Conference*, xxv, and xxx–xxxi; Blum, *The Republican Roosevelt*, 39.
136. Smith, *The Politics of Conservation*, 115; McGeary, *Gifford Pinchot*, 235, 267, 283. According to his biographer, Pinchot in later life was sensitive to the labor vote "far more than most politicians of his day."

The Progressive Reform of Journalism: The Rise of Professionalism in the Press

Douglas Birkhead

4

A familiar historical generalization is that journalism served as the voice of the Progressives during the early years of the twentieth century. The influence of journalism on public discourse was felt in two principal ways. First, the classic power of oratory to move crowds was transformed by an emerging mass press into a formidable force for shaping public moods and perceptions. The effect was unprecedented. The coverage of rhetorical events as news stories instigated and sustained the defining social and political movements of the day. Second, the press went far beyond being a common carrier of public communication. It also contributed to the national forum with its own formidable rhetoric of exposure. Richard Hofstadter, in *The Age of Reform*, drew upon the image of the muckraking journalist to describe the typical progressive attitude as that of the socially responsible reporter-reformer.[1] The identity of the Progressive Era owes much of its coherence to the heralding work of journalism.

And yet the press entered the twentieth century on the verge of corporate oligopoly, maligned as much as any other industry in the country.[2] Competition for newspaper circulation spawned the sensationalistic "yellow journalism" of the 1890s, evoking virulent public criticism. Muckraking itself was very much a commercial venture, boosting the readership of newly founded national magazines and disappearing after a decade as reader interest waned. Progressive legislation regulating business practices was directed at the press itself in 1912, prohibiting hidden ownership, disguised advertising, and falsified circulation claims.[3]

As Arthur Mann suggests, a central reality of the Progressive Era was its contradictions.[4] Henry George presaged the incertitude with his *Progress and Poverty* in 1879, which characterized the maldistribution of the nation's growing wealth as "the great enigma of our times."[5] Unalterably reconfigured as an industrial society, the country remained responsive to pastoral myths. The more the nation urbanized, the less attractive the city was perceived to be as a living environment. The clamor against political corruption did not deter calls for more government management and control. Policies of imperialistic expansion competed with sentiments of isolationism. The equivocal signposts of the period have perplexed historians. Was progressivism a status revolt? Of which class? Were issues of reform the essential driving force, or was it the impulse for organization and order? How did the era relate to its immediate past? How did it portend the future?

This state of affairs both in history and in historiography should invigorate historians of rhetoric. If conventional rhetorical scholarship involves the chronology, analysis, and contextualization of exemplary texts, the Progressive Era, with its interpretive ambiguities, calls for more innovative approaches. The standard anthology of great rhetorical texts glosses over the gritty task of communication in seeking communal meaning in bewildering or threatening circumstances and the role of public discourse in organizing social resources to confront them. The nation broke forth into the modern world as if emerging from a chrysalis, with all its memories and many of its habits of a prior life intact. The significance of discourse during the period went beyond exhortation for action. It involved what had to be addressed in facing problems of reorientation, new modes of social coordination, fresh strategies for survival, and the reconciliation of palpable loss and beckoning opportunity.

The challenge to explore the deeper dynamics of communication in the Progressive Era extends to its journalism. The most easily collectible texts from the turn of the century are the muckraking exposés. An impressive canon could be gleaned from the roughly two thousand articles in the genre. A representative volume might include the likes of Ida Tarbell excoriating Standard Oil, Lincoln Steffens uncovering the corruption of municipal government, David Graham Phillips condemning the Senate, and Thomas Lawson laying bare the manipulations of Wall Street. Muckraking journalists and others also wrote books and novels depicting the social and political ills of the times. Their writing did embody a kind of collective voice of great importance in shaping the progressive experience and in achieving whatever ends historians might identify as the progressive legacy.

But muckraking itself was not a revolution in journalism, a conclusion Hofstadter drew in celebrating the "business of exposure" as the fundamental critical accomplishment of progressivism. Hofstadter knew that the American press has a long history of access for reformers and crusaders, not to mention firebrand publishers, eccentric editorial gadflies, and even seditious founding fathers. Rather, he rested his claim of the uniqueness of muckraking on the distinction that its practitioners had gained entry to a new mass press not previously available. Market penetration was indeed a revolutionary transformation in journalism by the end of the nineteenth century. But the opportunity to convey messages, shape perceptions, arouse emotions, and direct actions on a large scale was not limited to reformers. It was a commodity for sale, a coveted source of profit and power. Hofstadter underestimated the scope of the runaway communications revolution. The mass press was as much a danger to progressive ideals as it was their vocal outlet. The development of the press in the decades after the Civil War followed a typical pattern of commercial and industrial growth in America. A period of "New Journalism," in which contemporary approaches to reporting were crafted, represented a stage in product development when news was reformulated for mass appeal. New printing plants were as technologically advanced as any other factory system in the country. Publishers such as Joseph Pulitzer, William Randolph Hearst, and Frank A. Munsey became famous business barons. Competition led to sensationalistic excesses. Fear and loathing of the press were simmering critical sentiments at the conception of progressive alarm over political, social, and economic conditions.

Hofstadter's portrait of the progressive mind drawn in the image of the "socially responsible reporter-reformer" is partially an anachronism. A full theory of social responsibility characterizing the role of the American press in society was not developed until after World War II.[6] But the image is not so much slightly askew in time as is Hofstadter's unqualified reference to it. A knowledgeable press observer from the period would have recognized the notion of a socially responsible journalist as a rhetorical construct. A socially responsible, or professional, reporter was precisely the representative persona being promoted by the press to counter criticism that journalism had devolved from an exalted "Fourth Estate" into a base commercial enterprise. What Hofstadter took as the model for the typical Progressive was being rhetorically crafted by the press itself during the historical period he was describing.

This chapter is an account of the rhetorical struggle to rehabilitate the identity of the press through professionalization. The principal contention of the analysis is that the professionalism movement in journalism, while similar in voice and appearance to other organizational efforts among occupations at the time, had very little to do with empowering journalists as an occupational group. The rise of corporate journalism did not generate an occupational crisis to which professionalism was the solution. The drive to have journalists recognized as professionals was only peripherally a movement of occupational self-interest. What occurred in the name of professionalism primarily involved legitimating the press as a socially responsible corporate institution.

The sustained acceleration of development after the Civil War contributed to a pervasive social awareness of a profound transformation in the press. Two general themes of interpretation emerged in the literature of press commentary and analysis. One theme was a critical evaluation of the change in economic terms. The second was a more optimistic, largely progressive assessment of the transformation in terms of technological progress. Professionalism was a concept used to extend and establish the technological assessment as the appropriate version of the new social reality. The effort was reflected in the writing and activities of publishers, editors, reformers, and ultimately educators as they attempted to fashion a new professional sanction for the press. The ideology of the press shifted from a political emphasis to a focus on social surveillance as a public service. The professional imperative called for objectivity and standardization, a new discipline in the newsroom that coincided with production efficiency and market strategies. Professionalization of the press actually reduced the autonomy of the individual practitioner. The analytical and narrative focus of this study is how journalism dealt with the problem of defining its own modernity.[7]

Professionalism in Journalism: A Historical Overview

The ideological thrust of American journalism for much of its history has been to resist the role of the state as an intruder into its forum-marketplace. Perceived since its inception as a political instrument, the press nevertheless operated and developed on combined principles of politics and proprietorship. Removal of authoritarian government controls under the First Amendment meant the press as a commercial enterprise achieved deregulation. The new freedom was a political concession to libertarian sentiment following the American Revolution. It involved a liberal interpretation of press freedom as an extension of the natural right of individual free speech.

The economic base of the press shifted from political patronage to a market of readers in the first half of the nineteenth century. The press as a democratic political instrument still remained a central public perception. This image of the press was boosted by the elaboration of the concept of public opinion in democratic theory by the 1830s.[8] The press's identification with the process of public opinion formation advanced the notion of newspaper consumption as a form of political participation. Alexis de Tocqueville attributed the relatively large circulation of American newspapers to the impulse of Americans to involve themselves in self-government. He described the readership of newspapers as an important form of political association through which common sentiment formed as a prelude to political action.[9]

After 1840 newspapers were considered second only to elections as a reflection of the popular will. Lord Bryce, observing a more industrialized press in the last quarter of the nineteenth century, still found the significance of journalism to be its contribution to the political system, determining that a periodic press was in many ways superior to elections as an expression of public opinion in America. He explained the mass-market orientation of a growing number of newspapers as essentially an extension of a classless democratic tradition.[10]

The perception of the press as a democratic institution in keeping with free speech, political participation, and the mechanics of public opinion formation held through the early stages of journalism's commercialization. Based largely on the notion that the central figure of journalism was the editor-publisher, and that the authoritative function of journalism was editorial expression, the image of the press as a political institution was finally challenged at the end of the century. Substantial commentary appeared, focusing on a perceived revolutionary shift in the nature of journalism. Most of these observations were evoked by the impact of changed news practices. The most historically visible illustration of the New Journalism was the raucous press of New York, particularly the legendary circulation war between Pulitzer and Hearst. But in more general terms, the commentary corresponded with the coalescence of new technological, managerial, and marketing techniques into the imposing presence of corporate journalism. Powerful and competing new images of the press emerged. On the one hand, newspapers were described in the metaphor of their technological transformation: "I am persuaded that the ideal newspaper is an emotionless machine; that the function of this machine is solely to give the news; that it attains its maximum usefulness when every wheel in the gigantic machine runs smoothly, grinding out its daily grist without emotion, dispassionate, unswerving, relentless."[11] In a darker version of the change, journalism was depicted as not just a neutral machine but as industrialized big business, engaged in the production of an unregulated commodity of unquestionable political and social value. "Journalism to-day is a business. To write of it as such is to write of it as it is," Lincoln Steffens wrote in describing the "inside view" of modern journalism in 1897.[12] "The fundamental principle of metropolitan journalism today," wrote another critic, "is to buy white paper at three cents a pound and sell it at ten cents a pound."[13] An ideological crisis in the identity of the press was at hand.

In response, a new institutional presentation was negotiated, a progressive posture for journalism adapted to the realities of the press's new corporate structure. That posture was an interpretation that largely accepted modern journalism in its technical and organizational complexity, and in its range of production. The case for acceptance was argued on the merits of mass communication as a vital social service to industrial society. The key ideological resource in the rhetorical reconstruction of the press was the concept of professionalism. The professionalization of journalism became the project by which the traditional political sanction of journalism was extended into a professional one.

It is important to distinguish this historical experience of professionalization from the typical process for other occupations. Emerging professional groups usually saw in themselves the characteristics of occupations that had historical social prominence even in traditional society, such as medicine and law. Modern professionalism developed as a concept in the image of such classic professions, evolving into a set of ideas and theories concerning the proper application of knowledge in society and the handling of critical occupational functions. For most aspiring professions, the process of professionalization was a concerted effort of practitioners to organize themselves. The rewards of a professional identity included authority and prestige, material gain, and the autonomy of practitioners, or at least their relative independence in organizational settings of practice.[14]

Arising as a status ideal in the latter half of the nineteenth century, professionalism had so influenced the public sense of modern social order by the turn of the century that it has been described as a unified movement of middle-class aspirations.[15] Progressives typically were identified as the personification of the professionally minded. Burton Bledstein proposes that a professional culture may be seen emerging everywhere, "in popular culture, the academy, indeed in the ordinary habits of middle-class life as an individual learned the hygienic way to bathe, eat, work, relax, and even to have sexual intercourse."[16] As a general cultural value, professionalism was associated with the proper application of expertise and the appropriate management of activity, and became the gauge of performance in both public and private life. Professionalism was an ideological resource to be exploited by the press.

Professionalization of journalism began as an "order of discourse" consistent with the "new social space" of the corporate press, organized along bureaucratic management lines.[17] News handling on large urban newspapers had evolved into a number of occupational specialties. The role of the reporter was central, but it was integrated into a hierarchy of editorial control through which the reporter's relationship with the reader was mediated. The work of the reporter was tempered if not dominated by production schedules, circulation and advertising pressures, and the ideological leanings of the publisher-owner. A conventional path of professionalization for journalism logically would have been the amelioration of this intrusion, involving more autonomy of practice for the reporter. Instead, professionalism became a rhetorical means for defining the organizational management of news as the focus of social responsibility. The press claimed professional status on the basis of controlling the quality of its product. The process in effect celebrated the standardization of the role of the journalist as a production component in the mass media industry.[18]

The use of professionalism to sanction the efficiency of business was an anomaly, but it was not unique to journalism. Professionalism became associated with a "science of management" during the Progressive Era. Louis D. Brandeis told a 1912 commencement audience at Brown University that the trades of finance, manufacturing, merchandising, and transportation were becoming professionalized through their enlightened management of labor and resources.[19] The trappings of professionalism were worked into the business ethic as scores of trade associations came into existence, each with their codes and creeds covering standards of performance. In making its professional claim for the entire media industry, the press competed with the similar assertion of such diverse enterprises as bottling and brick manufacturing, stock breeding, and producing plumbing supplies.[20]

The Power in the Image

"If one begins a study of American journalism," muckraker Will Irwin wrote for *Collier's* in 1911, "he finds himself perplexed by a multiplicity of squirrel tracks and a scarcity of main roads."[21] To look for any authoritative formulation of the larger principles of journalism in relation to its time is to find none. Modern journalism "has burst into the world with a flair of trumpets, but it has not even crept into the slow consciousness of the philosophers."[22]

Journalism had become a great contradiction. Everywhere there was the sense that it had fundamentally changed, but nowhere was there a clear grasp of its new parameters or purpose. It was at once praised and condemned, feared for its influence and chastised for its loss of leadership and power. Its decline was eulogized and its ascension heralded; it was dismissed as a lost profession and defended for its new professional ideals. Journalism and the press, Irwin recognized, were in the throes of a conceptual crisis.

Providing a vivid perceptual field to the disorder in interpretation was the physical reality of change. If population growth and its shift to urban centers were important factors in the transformation of society and its worldview, the press grew even faster during the period and thrived in the environment of the city. Emery notes that from 1870 until the end of the century, when the population of the country doubled and the degree of urban concentration tripled, the number of daily newspapers in America quadrupled and their combined circulation increased sixfold.[23] After 1870, the ratio of newspapers to urban centers increased until the turn of the century, and after 1880 newspaper circulation expanded at a more rapid rate than the urban population.[24] By 1900, the circulation figure for dailies, more than fifteen million, nearly equaled the number of American households. In 1910, the circulation of dailies exceeded the number of families in the nation.[25] Journalism had become a mass phenomenon. Penny papers had eliminated the appeal of journals in public houses and reading rooms by midcentury, but it was the industrial press of the century's end that achieved the capacity to bring the newspaper into every home.

Moreover, circulation was an aspect of journalism reported, promoted, and celebrated by the press. Newspapers competed for distribution not only for profits but for prestige. Behind the impulse for mass circulation was more than the value and authority of popular support derived from democratic tradition. Circulation as a standard of success reflected what Wiebe has described as a new quantitative ethic, an abdication of traditional values.[26] In the cultural flux of the times, Americans grasped for virtue in the fundamental fact that life now seemed to exist on a larger scale: "For lack of anything that made better sense of their world, people everywhere weighed, counted, or measured it."[27]

Evident in the altered proportions of life was the technological foundation that permitted, or forced, the new scale. The significant difference between late-nineteenth-century technology and the industrial mechanisms and techniques introduced earlier in the century can be attributed to the underlying empirical shift from revolutionary practical invention to the even more far-reaching application of scientific knowledge. The gradual extension of mechanization and inanimate power was radically boosted by the development of new materials and new means of power. The result, as Geoffrey Barraclough notes, was a "second industrial revolution," extending so deeply into the materiality, patterns, and outlook of everyday life as to mark the beginning of contemporary society.[28]

The advancing technology of journalism, obliterating traditional limitations of time, space, and production, was as striking to the mind as any other manifestation of the age. In journalism, it seemed, was finally realized the potential of the telegraph and cable. Newspapers used wood paper and multiple presses, the linotype and photography, typewriters and the telephone. Inventiveness had gathered into the electro-mechanical factory of the newspaper and its web and tendrils of communication. The press was an interconnected machine, each newspaper a terminal of production.

The awe in mass circulation was in the speed, scope, and intricacy of the technical accomplishment. From ephemeral spark to temporarily forged metal, from metal plate to paper, the journey of news and commentary to the reader was a chain of complex conversions. Output was achieved and maintained in a daily routine of multiple editions, a rhythmic flood of cheap, personal copies. Production rose for leading dailies from a maximum of eighty-five thousand copies a day in 1870 to three hundred thousand in 1890. By 1900, the capacity of the largest printing mechanisms exceeded one million copies a run.[29]

Newspapers also grew in bulk. Eight-page issues were a common measure of size in 1870. The potential number of pages in the metropolitan dailies increased by a continuous factor of two until "double octuple" presses had the capacity to run 128-page issues by the turn of the century. Each doubling in size presented the technical drawback of halving production, a reducing factor more than compensated for by larger, faster, and more efficient machines.[30]

The presence of the newspaper as a physical structure and force in the city gained a prominence during the period never felt or witnessed before. The expansion in equipment and organization cramped backroom print shops and conventional storefront quarters, giving rise to original plant design and journalism's own architecture. The newspaper building in many cities became a monument to the new industrial and financial power of the press, as well as a reflection of its occupational specialty to publicize.

The most remarkable examples were to be found in New York. The press helped to inaugurate the era of the modern office building, one observer noted among its achievements in an assessment written in 1903, having "turned Park Row with its single line of straggling structures into a series of the most imposing edifices in the world."[31] Historian W. A. Swanberg writes that the commanding landmark of 1875 was the 260-foot *Tribune* campanile. But the structural domination of the district was effected appropriately enough in 1890 upon completion of the Pulitzer Building, home and tribute to the *World* newspaper.[32] The tallest building in New York at the time was built for the city's largest mass-circulation daily. The 309-foot structure ascended from basement pressrooms, housing steam and electrical power plants and ten quadruple presses, to a gilded dome of executive editorial suites. Pulitzer's "20-story shout of triumph" rose above the *Sun, Times, Herald,* and *Tribune* with calculated arrogance.[33] The building "fitly crowned and attested" to the publisher's success, wrote *Harper's Weekly.*[34] The *World* itself devoted a special edition to its significance and dimensions as well as to the circulation, advertising, press capacity, and paper poundage of the journal as a marvel of production.[35] Also published in the *World* was a document that certified that the $2 million "People's Palace" had been constructed without debt or mortgage. The building was presented as a symbol of financial independence for a newspaper of extraordinary business aggressiveness and motivation.

The prestige of occupying the city's tallest building gravitated to the *Times* when that newspaper was moved to new quarters in 1905, but the most intriguing architectural response to Pulitzer's play for the skyline of New York was engineered by James Gordon Bennett of the *Herald* in 1893. Bennett not only rejected the challenge to reign over "Printing-house Square" with the tallest office, he abandoned Park Row altogether. He chose his ground at Broadway and Sixth Avenue and built an Italian palace of arcades, polished columns, and a red-tile roof. The low but spacious two-story structure was Bennett's reply "to the newspaper proprietors who have erected giant office buildings, in which the editorial forces occupy garrets and the pressmen are crowded into dark cellars," wrote an advocate of the project in *Harper's Weekly.*[36] The edifice, reminiscent of the Renaissance despite its distracting location near an elevated railway, was designed as "a rebuke to the utilitarianism of the American metropolis, an appeal to something better than sky-scraping ugliness."[37] If Pulitzer's building was meant to symbolize business success yet financial independence, Bennett's was intended as an expression of noncommercial journalism. "The *Herald* is rich beyond the dreams of avarice," extolled the *Harper's* article, a public institution envisioned by its proprietor to succeed him as a kind of "journalistic republic."[38] The statement of its architecture, however, was less an invocation to humanism than a paean to the blend of science and the arts. Through the arcades, the inner walls of terra-cotta and pyrolyth were penetrated by arched, plate-glass windows to expose the workshop: "The fascinating rush and whir of men and machinery late at night, when the place is ablaze with electric lights and the entire mechanical force is straining to get the paper printed in time for the early trains, will be one of the most notable sights of New York."[39]

Residents of the city had read about the wondrous production process occurring in the industrial grotto of the *World*. At the *Herald* it was exposed to the passerby:

> The whole course of the white paper is in full view from the street, as it spins from its damp rolls in continuous webs, flashes between the whirling cylinders, turns, reverses, enters the marvelous folding apparatus and finally appears pasted, folded, counted, and ready for delivery.
>
> The stereotype metal is melted in sight of the public in two huge pots, over which hangs a metal hood to carry off the hot air, by means of an electric fan in the exhaust duct. Five casting-boxes are arranged in a semicircle in front of the melting pot, so that the whole process of casting the shining plates from which the paper actually takes its impressions can be seen in all its detail by outsiders.[40]

Augmenting the glory of the building was its power plant:

> This wonderful system of machinery is interchangably operated by steam or electricity. Two huge black-marble switchboards, glittering with brass levers, control the electrical force. When steam-power is undesirable, the huge dynamos are brought into play, and when everything else fails, a turn of the wrist connects the operating mechanism with the electric-lighting mains in the street. In this way there can be no failure in the presswork or lighting apparatus. No matter what breakdown occurs, the *Herald* will be printed on time.[41]

Along the low Roman roof line of the structure like a row of sentinels were twenty mechanical owls, winking electric eyes at regular intervals. In the double-rose window of the pediment was a clock regulating the flashing of the eyes and a wavering dial measuring the wind.

To many, however, Bennett's palace only presented a double facade. Behind the marble was a factory and behind the factory a business, despite the disclaimers and the distraction of the exposed inner mechanics. Not much different was Pulitzer's display of his debt-free independence beneath a gilded dome. As imposing on the senses as the technological basis for journalism's new scale was evidence that the change was economic as well as technical, involving a movement toward financial empire as much as an extension of scientific progress.

If there was a preponderant critical theme of the times, it was that wealth and capital were laying a pattern of control over society, a subjugation more subtle yet as onerous as political despotism. At the turn of the century, the largest corporations dwarfed state governments, and the capital of some trusts exceeded the expenditures of the federal government.[42] The Spencerian analogy between the laws of nature and the regulating principles of the economic environment was philosophically flawed but metaphorically persuasive: business flourished and multiplied to excess in the favorable climate for expansion, then consolidated into fewer select enterprises during the periodic cooling periods in the economy. The edges for survival were size and the capacity to control the terms of transaction and competition. The overall result was both expansion in the nation's wealth and its concentration in large, complex, and commanding units of finance and production.

The economic development of the country transcended the superlatives that might have been used to describe the period of growth immediately following the Civil War. The disorientation that came later was not from the pace, but from the sustained acceleration. From 1865 to 1880, the assets of the nation doubled. At the start of Reconstruction, manufacturing investment stood at about $500 million, rising to nearly $3 billion in 1878. By 1900, the nation's assets had doubled again, and total manufacturing capital exceeded $8 billion. The value of American production was more industrial than agricultural by 1890; ten years later the cities outproduced the farmlands two to one. During the decade of the 1890s the country became the richest industrial producer in the world.[43]

The multiplication in wealth through industrial bounty was accompanied by an equally compelling statistical curve of combination and centralization. By 1890, the year of the Sherman Antitrust Act, approximately one hundred combinations existed in industries as diverse as petroleum, leather, wire nails, and bicycles. The era of consolidation had barely dawned before it was comprehended as a national threat. After the economic chill of 1893, the drive to combine began in earnest. The concentration of manufacturing followed the lead of railroads, where hundreds of independent lines had merged into six principal networks by 1904. The same year more than three hundred corporations existed in industry that were capitalized at $10 million, up from a dozen before 1900. The struggle in steel brought the $1.5 billion United States Steel Corporation into existence in 1901.[44]

The rise of finance capitalism took American business beyond the realm of common mercantile understanding. "A great industrial nation is controlled by its system of credit," Governor Woodrow Wilson declared in 1911.[45] The dimensions of "Morganization," the penetration of bankers and financiers into the ownership and directorate structure, were genuinely imperial. A congressional committee reported in 1912 that the allied financial interests of the ultimate figure in acquisitive banking, J. P. Morgan, included control of 341 directorships in 112 corporations, with combined assets of more than $22 billion.[46] On the one hand, the enterprise of America had created technological wonders that were vaulting the country into a dynamic and material future; on the other, it was laying the basis for a challenge of the authority of democratic stewardship of national affairs.

The economic transition of journalism was not on the billion-dollar scale of the railroads, petroleum, or steel, nor did combination characterize the immediate end of capitalization. The book value of all of American printing and publishing in 1879 stood at $80 million; in 1889 it was $234 million. By 1904 it had reached $450 million. The concentration of the industry at the turn of the century was not significant on the national level. The four largest enterprises produced no more than 1 percent of the value brought to the market by publishing concerns. In chemical manufacturing the degree of concentration by this measure was 24 percent, in petroleum, 47 percent, and in rubber, 100 percent.[47] Contraction had already begun in some markets, however, and the decline in the number of newspapers was a trend after 1914. Chains as an indication of concentrated ownership were a familiar phenomenon even before 1900. The monopolistic behavior of the wire services not only became a legal controversy before the close of the century, but also contributed significantly to a perception of news as a commodity of exchange. Newsprint, the physical raw material of the press, was controlled by a virtual paper trust going into the twentieth century, a market condition fought by publishers at the level of international trade.

The penetrating image of the press in economic terms, however, was shaped by the emergence of the corporate entity of the newspaper organization. The term "corporate" is not meant in the purely technical sense of stock ownership, although such corporations indeed accounted for more than 70 percent of the revenues of newspapers by 1909. Commercial journalism characterized the enterprise of cheap dailies since the 1830s; the business stature of the press after the 1880s requires a referent that denotes not only its economic orientation, but also suggests something of its scope, complexity, and spirit as a financial and industrial institution. The conventional representation of the press as such an institution is "big business"; Mott's expressive description is the newspaper as Leviathan.[48] The newspaper as a corporation, collectively comprising a corporate press, perhaps defines in a figurative and almost literal sense what journalism became as an enterprise during the period.[49]

The metropolitan daily at midcentury was a financial investment dear enough to engender mercantile respectability, and the frontier beckoned the itinerant printer. The sum of $100,000 was considered a reasonable stake for starting a newspaper in a large city, although H. J. Raymond managed to launch the *New York Daily News* in 1851 for $69,000.[50] By the 1870s there were reports of million-dollar papers, and nineteenth-century historian Frederic Hudson boasted that in 1869 the Bennetts had refused an offer to buy the *Herald* for more than $2 million.[51] Papers in difficulty could be had for nominal sums: Pulitzer's winning bid for the bankrupt *Saint Louis Dispatch* was $2,500 in 1878; Adolph S. Ochs paid one-tenth that amount to acquire the *Chattanooga Times* the same year.[52]

The inevitable pressure of development, however, raised the stakes of ownership beyond even the daring entrepreneur. The lockstep relationship of technical progress with expanding cost and investment had begun with exploitation of the telegraph. The cost of wire dispatches was not just in the considerable toll expenses, but was, more important, in the nurturing of a public appetite for perishable news, of an expensive and resource-demanding hunger for instant inventory in the fashion of the moment. The result was a necessary expansion in all news-gathering operations. The multiplying capacity of the improved presses was matched by the rise in the cost of their purchase and maintenance. The complexity and specialization in the technology of mass production was mirrored in the human support system of the process. The financial potential of marketing to every household was conditioned on laying all elements of the capital base to scale.

Pulitzer bought the *World* from a financier, Jay Gould, who had acquired the property as an ante in a railroad deal. The purchase price of $346,000 bought little more than a wire-service franchise. Pulitzer's capital came from the subsequent success of the newspaper, the spectacular exception that established the rule of success for the modern newspaper. In a little more than a decade after Pulitzer assumed control of the *World* in 1883, the morning and evening editions of the paper were reaching a million readers; the enterprise was expending $2 million a year on production costs and salaries for thirteen hundred employees; the value of the journal was estimated at $10 million; and Pulitzer was believed to be making $1 million a year.[53] When Hearst came to New York to do battle in 1895, he girded for combat by liquidating the family holdings in copper mining for $7.5 million in ready cash. Again, the confrontation was exceptional in American journalism, but its influence on the perception of the press, and ultimately on its structure and practice, cannot easily be overestimated.

If the observer of the press at the end of the century was for some reason insensitive to its new proportions, either in terms of production or finance, technology or capital, it is unlikely he or she as a regular reader could have failed to notice that the newspaper itself had changed as a tangible, sensate object of communication. Irwin had argued that the power of the newspaper had shifted to its news columns; virtually everyone already recognized that the appeal of journalism was not in the expression of opinion, but in the depiction of the drama and detail of contemporary life. Newspapers told "true" stories; they also provided information considered essential to make one's way in a complex world. Both functions served to portray realities and had wide appeal, although preference for news that entertained or for news as accurate and objective intelligence tended to be class related.[54] The American says to his journalists, surmised a writer in *North American Review,* "Give me the news and I will comment on it myself. Only don't forget I have to do fourteen hours' work to-day and that I want to be amused."[55] As expressed in a *Scribner's* article, the ideal journal of the 1890s provided for a different kind of coping: "What the man wants who newly finds himself with incalculably increased material opportunities before him is not, at first, thoughts that will strengthen his hold upon the eternal verities. No. It is information that will put him in direct touch with the actualities of the passing hour; information that will teach him all about his environment, and what he is to do there, and how he is to conduct himself in order to keep the place that he has got, and to extend it, to push himself further on."[56] In either taste, one exhibiting a desire to consume life as sensation, the other exuding the aspiration of an ascending social class to profit from a mastery of experience, there was a relative indifference to the pulpit or the political platform of the editorial page. In both was a mutual appreciation for the concrete and specific content of the news item.

The appeal and visibility of news was enhanced by innovations in presentation: the breakaway in typography and layout, and the introduction of better graphics, color, and photography. The market for news was tested by experiments in departmentalization, variety of coverage, sensationalism, and objectivity. Advertising moved off the front page to dominate the newspaper from the inside. Ads grew to full pages and cataloged a retail cornucopia. Advertising surpassed the sale of newspapers as a source of revenue by 1900; publishers thereafter sold the attention of readers as their primary transaction of business. "The newspaper whose subscribers paid for it died with the birth of news," wrote Irwin.[57] More accurately, the subsidy of the press was assumed by a higher bidder than the traditional political patron.

The perception of change in the nature of the press was forced by the raw stimuli of growth, mechanization and electrification, incorporation, financial and expressive redirection, promotion, and novelty. Lost in the momentum and display of the physical transformation was a comfortable familiarity with the press as a vital adjunct to the political process, a manifestation of freedom, an institution of democracy. "For whether or not politics is boiling, the newspaper goes on day by day with its function of bringing the world to our doors," observed Irwin.[58] Not since the appearance of the Penny Press was journalism so exposed to fundamental reevaluation. As Irwin set the extremes in judgment: "The condemners say that the metropolitan newspaper has grown venal, that advertisers and great financial interests control it; that its sensationalism has vitiated the public taste; that it has lost all power of leadership in good causes. The defenders answer that it is more free and independent than ever before; that it gives its readers better mental pabulum than they want; that it leads our civilization; that it has more influence than ever the written word exercised before."[59] The press was embarked on a fresh current; at issue was the moral comprehension of the new reality.

Journalism Lost

Prominent among the themes of commentary on journalism at the turn of the century was a sense of decline, a felt perception of lost heritage and fallen prestige. This sense that journalism had lost a golden past was typical of the reactions of many Americans to the eclipse of community values in the wake of urbanization and industrialization. Wiebe writes of this general mood: "In a manner which eludes precise explanation, countless citizens in towns and cities across the land sensed that something fundamental was happening to their lives, something they had not willed and did not want, and they responded by striking out at whatever enemies their view of the world allowed them to see. They fought, in other words, to preserve the society that had given their lives meaning. But it had already slipped beyond their grasp."[60]

The new journalism was clearly a phenomenon spreading from the cities, alien to village concepts of communication. On the values of the self-contained community, however, rested the stature of the newspaper as a public forum, pulpit, and the "printed diary of the hometown."[61] For the press, which depended upon the continuity of tradition for official sanction, a disconnection with the past and historical principles represented a serious challenge of mission and purpose, and ultimately of its libertarian brand of freedom. Many citizens were inclined to make the press account for a breach of faith.

The culmination of legitimacy for the press was the evolution of its "Fourth Estate" ideology, a presentation of purpose evident in profile by the time the press was formally exalted by the Bill of Rights, but not fully developed until newspapers were seen as catalytic to the formation of public opinion. This variation in democratic theory was not elaborated until the early decades of the nineteenth century.[62] As historian George Boyce observes for the English press (an analysis easily extended to American journalism), the basic arguments for a libertarian press as a vital link between public opinion and governing institutions were devised during the transition of journalism from political patronage to commercialism: "inevitably, increased sales could only be achieved if a newspaper could claim in some way to be independent, to represent public opinion, and to be able to give the public an authentic and reliable news service: in short, a newspaper had to be worth buying."[63] The strategic proclamation of the Penny Press was political independence, a new freedom guaranteed by the attachment of journalism to the marketplace. In order to appeal to "the great masses of the community—the merchant, mechanic, working people," James Gordon Bennett set his intentions in the first number of the *New York Herald:* "In debuts of this kind many talk of principle—political principle—party principle, as a sort of steeltrap to catch the public. We mean to be perfectly understood on this point, and therefore openly disclaim all steeltraps, all principle, as it is called—all party—all politics."[64] A Boston journal editorialized: "The time has come when the respectable portion of the community no longer looks to the big sixpenny, lying oracles of politics for just notions of government. . . . The low price of the penny papers endows their publishers with a philanthropical spirit of disinterestedness, and a regard to the purity of public morals not dependent upon pecuniary considerations."[65]

Even the system of distribution, a dependence on street sales to anonymous readers, promoted political autonomy, Bennett claimed.[66] Frederic Hudson, writing in 1872, expressed a common assessment of the development by describing the rise of an independent press as the culmination of journalistic history, advancing the prevalent political emphasis in interpreting journalism's shift in economic fortunes.[67]

The press did not become apolitical upon finding a wider market, however, although there was a new penetration and variety in news coverage and a general discouragement of direct political sponsorship. Partisanship continued as a wide editorial practice. Indeed, the commercialized press actually assumed a broader political function than the party press. It not only reserved the right of political commentary, but also insisted that newspapers spoke for the popular will. The purchase of a journal was considered a form of suffrage, and circulation a kind of mandate. In the economics of the press was seen a pure democracy, the reins of control held by a buying public.

Although the cheap, market-exploiting newspaper was a product of the city, it gave rise to the image of the independent editor as the driving force of journalism, a personification of the craft that was compatible with community values. Some editors became public figures in national life, but through a manner of recognition that was not very much different from the style of status that was bestowed upon regional and local editors who rose to prominence in community-oriented culture. The distinction between metropolitan and rural life was not yet abrupt, and notable journalists everywhere drew their social identity from the same basic allegiance to, and participation in, a civic culture that embraced both city and village.[68] The prestige of journalism, as embodied in the practice of the independent editor, approached that of the traditional professions, which in turn derived their stature from the reputations of practitioners in a community context. Historian Robert Sobel writes: "As the penny press came to dominate the newspaper scene, and the independent newspapers became near-universal, the editor took his place alongside the clergyman and doctor as a leading citizen and respected figure. After the Civil War, many professional men lost much of their power to a rising business class, but not so the publisher-editor of the influential newspapers, who made the adjustment to the new dispensation with a minimum of difficulty."[69] At least the appearance of independence gave journalism the basis for a professional claim as a calling in the traditional sense, one that celebrated the individual practitioner pursuing an occupational mission as a public service. Recognition and acceptance were anchored in a local social hierarchy, and the mercantile aspects of the occupation actually strengthened its professional prospects.

In these terms, journalism was developing a professional consciousness and identity by the 1850s, focused primarily on the role of the editor and involving a perceived province in the formation and voicing of public opinion. Looking back on developments in 1875, press commentator Charles Wingate wrote, "During the past twenty years, journalism has become prominent, if not pre-eminent, as a profession. The press is to-day the most potent agency for good or evil; and editors, far more than statesmen, are the guides of current opinion.[70]

The grist of public opinion was "authentic news," as well as the commentary of editors; reputations were founded on news policy in addition to editorial insight and direction. News, however, was not yet divorced from editorials, even though it was being distinguished as a separate category of newspaper content. News, especially political reporting, reflected the critical and moral aims of the journal that published it. The power of the press was still in the explication of issues with sentiment: "When the people feel that in their newspaper they have a watch set on their politicians whose fidelity to their principles can not be suspected, they give to the paper thus situated, vast confidence and power," wrote Henry Watterson, editor of the *Louisville Courier-Journal*.[71] "It is just here that is the test of a true journalist—the capacity to see quickly and to express correctly the tendencies of public opinion," observed Samuel Bowles of the *Springfield Republican*.[72] On his business side the journalist was a "merchant of news," where enterprise and industry gained him the success and honor of the mercantilist. News, however, was more than a commodity. It was intelligence "to be diffused among the masses," and the journalist drew his position from professing to a higher calling than commerce and trade: "That the journalist has it in trust and stewardship to be the organ and mould of public opinion, to express and guide it, and to seek, through all conflicting private interests, solely the public general good. Herein his work is allied to the statesman's, the politician's, and takes rank as it takes tribute of letters, science and the law."[73]

Entering the last quarter of the nineteenth century with a professional profile defined in terms of traditional values and precepts, journalism experienced what many observers considered a conversion downward during the subsequent process of industrialization and incorporation. Journalists of the new cast were perceived, "not as blundering men, but as fallen angels."[74] The changing nature of the press was viewed as a degradation, a violation of an almost sacred trust. New York editorial writer Frank Colby observed at the turn of the century, "The press, it seems, is a tutelary institution of superhuman origin, having no other office than to safeguard our liberties and uplift our souls, and when it is perverted to a baser use it is as if an imp were to blow some ribald tune through Gabriel's trumpet."[75] In the flux of meaning and interpretation, professionalism became a double-edged sword by which critics symbolized a journalism lost as advocates of the press heralded its professional development. The status symbol itself was being redefined, and journalism would emerge in the twentieth century with fresh professional trappings, paradoxically more secure as a semiprofession than during its brief ideological experience as a consummate "noble profession."

The falling away of the "Fourth Estate" image of the press and its professional corollary was marked by the displacement of the independent editor as the personality of the newspaper. The passing of an early generation of prominent New York editors—Raymond, Bennett, Greeley, Bryant—before 1880, and the loss of an almost rearguard echelon of personal editors—Dana, Godkin, Horace White of Chicago and New York, Grady of Atlanta—during the careers of the iconoclastic Pulitzer and Hearst presented a powerful metaphor for the downturn and demise of an era. The modern newspaper "has swallowed up the editor," declared *Bookman* magazine in 1903.[76] The evolution of the corporate press had pushed aside character in journalism for two common denominators: principle for profit and prestige for production. Looking back in 1909, a writer for *Arena* observed that the press of the past had been represented by "real men, editors whose personalities dominated their papers and gave the Fourth Estate in America its moral as well as political power; but to-day that race is well-nigh extinct."[77] The journalist of journalism was no longer the editor and could not, in good faith, be identified as the publisher in his counting room, notwithstanding his new power and prominence. "The great editor—the leader of public thought—has been pushed from his throne, and in his place sits a nameless thing, opinionless and usually money mad, a sightless, soulless corporation—a *publishing company*."[78] Journalism as a profession had grown faceless, and the press was being assessed as if it had suffered a fall from grace. Worse was the judgment for journalism because it "had hitherto pretended to be a profession," and neither business prestige nor commercial success could atone for the betrayal of a higher cause.[79]

Journalism had emerged from a nebulous profession of letters to become, in the person of the independent editor, a kind of literary profession of public affairs and public opinion. Modern journalism brought the "news store," a complex organizational form of social surveillance and reportorial commentary on life that left the occupation without a professional frame in any traditional sense. For those who sought to interpret the change from a traditional perspective, journalism was now morally formless and bereft of direction. As Tiffany Blake of the Chicago *Tribune* wrote in 1911: "Journalism is without any code of ethics or system of self-restraint or respect. It has no sense of standards of either work or duty. Its intellectual landscapes are anonymous, its moral distinction confused. The country doctor, the village lawyer knows his place and keeps to it, having the consciousness of superiority. The journalist has few, if any, mental perspectives to fix his horizon; neither chart of precedent nor map of discovery upon which his sailing lines and travel lines have been marked."[80] The inevitable logic of such plaintive emotion was a felt need to impose order and control; either journalism would find and save its own soul or have ethical regulation and purpose imposed upon it.

The press might have seemed a cultural juggernaut in its influence on the daily discourses and diversions, the habits of mind, and even the passions of the people. In terms of political persuasion, enlightenment, and the reflection of the popular will in public decision making, however, the newspaper was seen as a waning force in society. In this contradiction was a crisis of class and of democracy, an uncertainty over the venerable notion of the common man as a responsible citizen in a society of urban, labor, immigrant, and anonymous masses.

Prominent among those who grappled with this dilemma was E. L. Godkin, perhaps the last of the legendary editors, who lent his character and personality to the *Nation* and to the *New York Evening Post* in a long career that ended in 1900. By the 1890s, he noted, a generation of readers had already grown accustomed to turning to the press for amusement; that it should "exert its old influence on opinion, is scarcely to be expected, and this old influence will not soon or easily be regained."[81] If politics were the measure, "the role of the press has so greatly diminished that, in some localities, the newspapers have ceased to have any part in it at all."[82] Yet Godkin could also write of newspapers, "It is not too much to say that they are, and have been for the last half-century, exerting more influence on the popular mind and the popular morals than either the pulpit or the book press has exerted in five hundred years. They are now shaping the social and political world of the twentieth century."[83] Newspapers had once focused the mind; "Now, nothing can be more damaging to the habit of continuous attention than newspaper-reading."[84] The press was a force of color in a "chromo" civilization.

Journalist and author Francis Leupp, writing for *Atlantic Monthly* in 1910, observed that the traditional power of the press had been drawn from the relationship of the newspaper with the common citizen of fair intelligence and education: "It is he who has been weaned from his faith in the organ of opinion which satisfied his father, till he habitually sneers at 'mere newspaper talk'; it is he who has descended from reading to simply skimming the news, and who consciously suffers from the errors which adulterate, and the vulgarity which taints, the product."[85] For such a reader, the modern newspaper indeed had lost its effectiveness as an organ of persuasion and was unrepresentative as a mirror of thought. However, Leupp also warned: "But there is another element in the community which has not his well-sharpened instinct for discrimination; which can afford to buy only the cheapest, and is drawn to the lowest, daily prints; which, during the noon hour and at night, finds time to devour all the tenement tragedies, all the palace scandals, and all the incendiary appeals designed to make the poor man think that thrift is robbery. Over that element we find the vicious newspaper still exercising an enormous sway; and, admitting that so large a proportion of the outwardly reputable press has lost its hold on the better class of readers, what must we look for as the resultant of two such unbalanced forces?"[86] There was a fear that the press was, in effect, filling its own power vacuum. As the newspaper grew politically impotent as an organ of conscious deliberation, its influence as a coarse stimulus of the masses was increasing.

Giving credence to the apprehension was a perspective of commentary drawing upon the new social sciences. A social body and a public mind had been discovered to be analogous to the human organism, susceptible to similar disorders and amenable to parallel diagnoses. Journalism could be "pathological," its reading matter an environment in which "the community mentally dwells, the malaria of which it is constantly inhaling."[87] The function of news became the role of "bringing men to social consciousness," with useless news being "worse than useless, because it detracts one's attention from his work to no purpose."[88] As observed by Godkin and Leupp as perceptive laymen, the reading of newspapers was seen by science as a potential disease, not only a possible drain of mental energy but also a dissolvent of the social fabric. "The function of the newspaper," one could read in the *Annals of the American Academy*, "is to control the state through the authority of facts, not drive nations and social classes headlong into war through the power of passion and prejudice."[89] If newspapers "should neglect or fail to mend their ways," spoke the oracular *American Journal of Sociology*, "the penalty—unavoidable in the long run—which threatens them is moral decline, contempt, and a place among the forces of disorder and evil."[90]

Scientific critics of the press assumed that journalism was a public function, involving a public responsibility. The tradition of a free press could be looked upon with utilitarian detachment as a social artifact that did not necessarily endow the public good in contemporary society. The vital question, from the social standpoint, could be the question of control.[91] The options of control were anticommercial and bureaucratic, including the alternative of self-regulation in the form of a more socially responsible professional commitment. Social scientific thinking helped to define the press as a new force in society and contributed to the ground rules that would ultimately frame its social acceptance.

To reevaluate the press in terms of force and influence was to devise a center for its ideological reinterpretation. Irwin's analysis of journalism, more than any other consideration, was a discourse on the paradox of its effect on society, the "contradiction in the very cant phrase that we hear most commonly concerning newspapers—'the power of the press.'"[92] It was in resolution of this contradiction that Irwin offered his primary thesis: "The 'power of the press' is greater than ever before. They who deny this are looking back to the old age when all party lines were definite, when men first swallowed a formula and then bent their intellectual powers to prove it. That was the golden age of the editorial; and those pangyrists of older times assume that the editorial page still swings all the power of the press. The world runs differently now since Darwin. The power of the press has shifted; it is less tangible than it was in the days of Greeley, Dana, MacCullough, and Medill, but it is just as great. Indeed, line for line, it is greater, if for no other reason than that in the last generation not everyone was a newspaper reader, while now the audience of the daily press includes all human beings with two eyes and an elementary education."[93] If the editor had been pushed from his throne, a new personification of journalism had emerged; "This has come to be the age of the reporter."[94] Gone was the intellectual sway of the editorial: "In even its simplest form, news is the nerves of the modern world."[95]

Finding a new source of power for the press in news, however, only began any deliberation of the legitimacy of such a power in a corporate press. On this issue, Irwin perhaps made a more incisive contribution than his elaboration of the nature of news. He set the ideological question in appropriate terms for a new theory of press responsibility: "Again: is journalism a business or a profession? In other words, should we consider a newspaper publisher as a commercialist, aiming only to make money, bound only to pay his debts and obey the formal law of the land, or must we consider him a professional man, seeking other rewards before money, and holding a tacit franchise from the public for which he pays by observance of an ethical code? No other perplexity of journalism is so involved as this."[96] The question cut to the core of concern and criticism of the press at the turn of the century and framed an alternative reminiscent of traditional values, yet one that Irwin and others would reshape to suit the modern condition and configuration of journalism.

Invasion of the Inner Sanctum

The incongruous spectacle of the Fourth Estate as an image in society, as Boyce suggests, was that of an institutional being whose head was in politics and whose feet were in commerce.[97] The equilibrium of such a figure required a rather large head; nevertheless, the dualism of politics and business was not an uneasy collaboration of functions in the press, even as late as the 1880s. The commercialism of the press, as already noted, could be defended on political grounds as engaging newspapers in the democracy of the marketplace, advancing their independence from political party or faction. As long as editors held to the purpose of serving public opinion as their ultimate calling, the dualism was symbolically symbiotic. The office study of the editor was an inviolate inner sanctum beyond the counting room; the business of journalism was a bodily function of an essentially intellectual existence.

In the last quarter of the nineteenth century the stasis was disrupted. One focus of the perception of change in the press was the apparent corruption of journalism's ends by its once perfunctory commercial means. The new journalism "put the cart before the horse"; its élan had become a "mercenary spirit."[98] Boyce writes of this experience as it occurred at a somewhat later period for the English press: "The newspaper world appeared more and more to be a mirror of the worst aspects of the capitalist world, with its transformation into a major enterprise, and the consequent emergence of the great commercial corporation. Concentration of ownership became the order of the day, and the celebrated nineteenth century figure, the editor, declined in power and prestige as the business managers came into their own. The press lost the mystique of being regarded as an estate: it was now described in down-to-earth terms as an industry."[99] In America, this theme of criticism reflected a whole current of misgiving about the American condition gathering since the 1870s, "a pattern of complaint and concern about the results and dislocations of the new age of industrialism."[100] The capitalist domination of the press was a corollary to what became the progressive diagnosis of the American dilemma going into the twentieth century. It was a view of journalism prevalent enough among observers of the press to represent a principal thesis of interpretation on the significance and direction of change. It was, in rudimentary form, a paradigm of meaning for a perceived revolution in communication, one that pushed to describe a new and dark reality.

In 1875, the business posture of journalism was not yet a significant source of embarrassment. The function of journalism to sell a commodity brought no particular opprobrium; indeed, the proprietor of a newspaper could make a supplementary claim of distinction on his merits as a merchant as well as a guardian of public opinion. "Probity has the same reward in public confidence," wrote Manton Marble of the *New York World*.[101] "Shrewd and farsighted combinations bring to the merchant of news—or of flour, or of pork—profit and credit."[102] The province of journalism is to inform, to teach, and "to render unto Caesar the things that are Caesar's," offered a Missouri editor.[103]

"The recognition of the fact that the newspaper is a private and purely business enterprise will help to define the mutual relations of the editor and the public," Charles Dudley Warner of the *Hartford Courant* told a meeting of the Social Science Association in 1881.[104] Newspapers could be honorably sold as articles of value according to the principles of market demand: "If the buyer does not like a cloth half shoddy, or coffee half chicory, he will go elsewhere. If the subscriber does not like one newspaper, he takes another, or none."[105]

The talk about newspapermen as if they were brokers in an exchange shocked the sensibilities of listeners as the industrialization of the press accelerated. In the 1890s Lincoln Steffens would write of such conversations in exposé fashion; in

1911 Irwin reported as an unexpected admission that "more than one editor of a newspaper without fear and without reproach has declared to me that it is nothing but a business."[106] A critical mood developed in a relatively short period of time that transformed an open discourse on economic function into a startling disclosure of hidden truth.

The focus of attention in press commentary may be seen passing like a lamp through a house, from the sanctum of the editor to the counting room, and ultimately to the professional newsroom. By the turn of the century the financial quarter of journalism was fully exposed to criticism. That journalism had a troublesome economic dimension was virtually a cliché of analysis. "Ingenuous reformers of the press seem to think the whole question turns on the raw, obvious influence of money," observed the *Atlantic Monthly*.[107] An economic argument not only was the culmination of direct attacks on advertising as a source of influence, but consisted of conclusions that sensationalism was a marketing ploy, that publishers by nature were a capitalist breed, and that a broad alliance of business interests including the press was a potential threat to a free society. Indeed, virtually every evil and shortcoming attributed to journalism could be traced in some manner to its economic structure and behavior, from the "black eruption" of its typeface to the selectivity or invasiveness of its news coverage. Economics had turned a political regency into a "commercial thraldom," a study into a workshop, a profession into a trade.

The contours of press criticism during the period may be sketched from rudimentary statistical evidence. In a content analysis of popular periodical literature from 1890 to 1914, George Howard Phillips has revealed a lively and even debate, but one in which the contention that journalism was dangerously under the sway of advertising, wealth, and profits went relatively unchallenged by press defenders.[108] The prevailing focus of criticism of the press was less personal and individual than it was institutional. Critics tended to reprehend the press as corporate entity and societal force, writing negatively about the press and newspapers in general, and owners, publishers, and the business office as anonymous components. Discussed more favorably were named journalists and newspapers or subordinate occupational abstractions, such as journalists, artists, cartoonists, and photographers. The content of newspapers generally was viewed with disfavor, as was the performance of the press in terms of gathering, editing, and displaying the news. Accuracy and truth were frequently questioned. Nevertheless, the journalist as an individual practitioner and journalism as a specific calling and career went relatively unscathed.[109]

The press was not being condemned principally in occupational terms, but for corporate irresponsibility and perceived misbehavior as a societal establishment. The fundamental tenets of the press's functions and structure were being examined. While observers outside journalism tended to be more frequently critical, much of the commentary, both favorable and unfavorable, was generated from within the press itself. More than half of the commentators who published views on the press during the period had journalistic credentials.[110] The critical current of the times was not so much intellectual as journalistic, and the press as the object of critique brought a mainstream response. Some critical observers viewed the condition of the press with a paralyzing nostalgia; a very few saw the situation in terms of a proletarian struggle. The central channel of critical interpretation, however, if not in volume at least in the force and influence of the analysis after 1900, was essentially progressive.[111]

The progressive discontent was with the amoral management and display of economic power, and the progressive impulse was for self-control and rational discipline within the institutions of society, in part to counterbalance a moral weakness and indifference perceived in the American public itself.[112] From the

Progressives came a counterargument to their own critical assessment of changes in the press. In their formula for reform they conceded the principal contention of press advocates and defenders: that modern journalism signaled the rise of an essential agency for integrating a complex society. As much as the industrialization of the press could be seen in troubling economic terms, the more compelling image in the new century was the development of journalism in terms of its mechanics. This perspective came to define the "revolution" in communication, and to identify the rise of the press as a modern institution for serving society's surveillance and information dissemination needs. Its professionalization was a process to legitimize, in management terms, this new role.

"Society's New Set of Nerves"

The fact that economic criticism of the press did not ultimately frame the prevailing interpretation of journalism's transformation was consistent with the meaning of change that was emerging in the whole of American culture. The tension in the basic dualism in the image of industrialization—social displacement and human degradation versus material fulfillment and the exploitation of invention and energy—was being eased by an almost spiritual attraction developing in American society toward technology. In the chaos of change and reorganization, the linear development of technology stood out as an alluring standard of progress. The contrast between the boiler and the dynamo seemed to offer a qualitative difference. The belching smokestack would not be the symbol of Western civilization, Charles and Mary Beard would write looking back on the turn of the century, for the revolution in industry was followed by still more revolution. The steam engine, heavy and static, was associated with a "fixed kind of social apparatus, gloomy and depressing," but electricity and internal combustion represented a radical departure in mechanics "fraught with social destiny."[113] Technology had evolved a kind of democratic dimension with the introduction of small machines and appliances that made the engine itself a common consumer product. The disruptions and inequalities resulting from industrial expansion might be the temporary effects of social adaptation to a central historical force of technological improvements. The tantalizing solution to the problem of industrialization was perhaps a deeper commitment to the machine. The meaning of modern journalism would emerge in the context of this vision of an industrial Second Coming.

As Lewis Mumford discerned in American literature, the industrial process by the 1890s had replaced the frontier as a compelling source of imagination and experience.[114] Writing in 1926, Mumford noted the change in the curious cultural lag of children's stories, which at the turn of the century featured the exploits of the frontier when the West was fading as a popular mythical theme. Even the child's mind would eventually be directed to technological exploits, the adventures of invention, science, aviation, and the motor car. The literature of technology had its precursors as well: the utopian models of nineteenth-century idealists moved from the pastoral community to the technological city by the 1880s.[115] Indeed, the machine had long intruded into the vision of man's appropriate destiny with nature, before the future was dreamed of in terms of cities, nation, and empire.[116] By the late nineteenth century the utopian novel had become a distinct genre, embodying "happy technological fantasies, where everyone enjoyed a life of abundance and ease supported by efficient machines and a sense of duty easily discharged in a few hours a day."[117]

Such currents of fancy set ironic parameters on defining the age. Even those who wrote of the brutalities of industrialization could not easily conceive of reforms that did not extend a technological civilization. As Mumford lamented over the proposals of Upton Sinclair, "What was weak in Mr. Sinclair's program was the assumption that modern industrial society possessed all the materials essential to a good social order. On this assumption, all that was necessary was a change in power and control: the Social Commonwealth would simply diffuse and extend the existing values."[118] The critical temperament of the progressive observer was characterized by moral indignation over economic irregularities in industrial society, but that fervor was moderated and bound by constructive precepts: confidence in the adaptability of democracy, a new intellectual faith in a "logic of possibility" to intervene in the social environment, and optimism over the potential of the machine to improve the human condition.[119] This technological assumption could be seen in the tendency of critics to draw an ethical distinction between a system of distribution and one of production. It was reflected in arguments that displayed a critical bias toward treating consumers rather than laborers as the victims of the economic order, a society best served by higher standards of production. It was evident in the pervasive imperative of Progressives for efficiency, in their admiration of scientific management of the workplace, in their ambivalent attitude toward the corporation as a model of organization, and even in their stance regarding the concentration of power in the monopolies and trusts. The great crime was "stealing the means of production," in Irwin's phrase. The great struggle was not against industrial organization, but for a release of its benevolent promise.

Sinclair, more radical than most in his critique of contemporary society, nevertheless dreamed of an "Industrial Republic," where "a man will be able to buy anything he wishes, from a flying machine to a seven-legged spider made of diamonds," and where electronic music might be as free as the air.[120] Inspired by the technological fiction of Edward Bellemy, whose influence ran through the work of many muckrakers, Sinclair proclaimed that history had worked its progress in two waves, the roll of political revolutions and the final industrial tide that could shortly sweep away the last inequities of society. Industrial competition had done its work: it had forged the discipline of workers and administrators, and "built us up a machine for satisfying all the material needs of civilization," if only it could be properly run.[121] Herbert Croly saw industrialism as a similar historical force, one that was working toward a historic compromise between Jeffersonian and Hamiltonian democratic ideals.[122] To muckraker David Graham Phillips, industry's physical sources of power were "efficient agents of democracy, the strong and inevitable unshacklers of the bodies and minds of mankind."[123] Howard Mumford Jones has read the literature and journalism of the period and found them crackling with the rhetoric of an Age of Energy.[124] To Phillips, the machine itself had a voice and spoke as a prophet: "I, the machine, will make your burden into a blessing, your toil into labor, the noble, the dignified, the producer of civilization and self-respect. I will widen your horizon until you see that all men are brothers, brothers in the business of, by business enterprise, increasing and creating wants, and of, by business enterprise, satisfying them. I will give you ideals that are true and just—not loyalty to idle thieving prince, not slavery to irrational superstition, not bondage to bloody soldier-tyrant, but intelligent loyalty to truth and justice and progress. I will make you masters of nature and of yourself, servant of the true religion and the true morality."[125] Even when the progressive critic focused on his principal theme of corruption in politics and capitalism, he could not help noting, as John Moody and George K. Turner observed in writing on monopolies in railroads, steel, and oil, that corporate concentration made a "splendid machine" of logic and efficiency.[126]

What the Progressives felt about technology they must have felt with special keenness about the technical structure of journalism. The movement itself, as Hofstadter suggests, was sustained by its journalism.[127] Muckraking was the spectacular exploitation of a new national medium, the wide-circulation magazine. The press was perhaps a model of an industry in technological transformation moving toward a new social role. Muckraking was the technique of exposure, the revelation of facts upon which to build an illuminated, if not enlightened, reality. More broadly, progressivism called for decision-making information and, at the subjective level, uniform expressions of value to nurture an integrated culture. The means of modern journalism were well suited to the motives of the reformers who undertook to establish the morality of the new century.[128] In the mind of most Progressives, the press had surpassed the educational system as the institution of mass indoctrination and challenged the pulpit as society's most influential instrument of exhortation. In 1903 S. S. McClure, in the seminal issue of his magazine that reported the trendsetting disclosures of Lincoln Steffens, Ida Tarbell, and Ray Stannard Baker, described the failure of legal, religious, and educational institutions to stem the corruption of law. "There is no one left; none but all of us," he wrote as if gathering a national congregation, one that journalism would presume to address by institutional default. Here, as Hofstadter noted, was the essence of the progressive spirit.[129]

Practitioners and defenders of the press had long been committed to the view that journalism was transformed as an institution as it underwent technological development. Journalism historian Calder Pickett found the technological interpretation of progress in journalism common among the attitudes of many of the prominent figures of the New York press throughout much of the nineteenth century.[130] William Cullen Bryant had viewed technology, especially the coming of the telegraph, with transcendental sublimity; Benjamin Day marveled at the revolutionary impact of both the telegraph and Richard Hoe's press. James Gordon Bennett was a skeptic on the railroad but an admirer of the steamship, and a visionary on the coming of instantaneous communication. Greeley praised all mechanization and treated invention as news, while Raymond of the *Times* thought the mechanics of printing alone exceeded the contribution to society of all the speculating philosophers of the ancient world. Pulitzer used the dimensions of technology to describe the scope of his own success.[131]

Advocates and critics of the press alike came to comprehend the new journalism as the culmination of a series of inventions. "Newspapers, prior to the discovery of the telegraph and the railroads, were insignificant and unimportant," wrote a Philadelphia publisher.[132] "With the invention of modern machinery and the typewriter, the use of electricity, the use of the telegraph and the telephone, a new era set in," observed press analyst James Edward Rogers in 1909.[133] To participants such as *Tribune* editor Whitelaw Reid, the process of development had been inevitable, even beyond the control of the men who engaged in it, "and nothing could then wholly avert the moral changes which soon began to accompany an unexampled facility of production."[134] The progressive observer did not substantially disagree and even largely accepted the capitalist corollary: production conforms in content to public taste. The modern press had made every citizen a reader, a physical achievement sustained only by providing what society would buy to read. Reform had to raise the moral consciousness of consumers themselves. The ethical diffuseness of this argument, and the fact that it represented for Progressives a central economic reality, tended to erode and compromise their critique of the press. The "mighty engine" of the press they essentially respected; its bending to a business point of view they could almost accept as inherent in its structural design.

For the most part, critics were content to reprimand the stewardship of business without divorcing the impressive capacity of the press from its economic orientation. Its commercialization, to draw from an editorial in the *Nation*, could be seen as "an incident of our passing from the day of small things to the time of large undertakings."[135] Arthur Reed Kimball, a muckraker sensitive to the "journalization" of culture (the influence of the press on patterns of thought, speech, and literature), did not extend his unsettling analysis to question the "claims of capital": "The blunt fact, offered not in apology, but in recognition of a condition as opposed to a theory is, of course, that capital does, and must, control the policy of the newspaper, to maintain which a large investment is necessary."[136] Steffens reminded reformers of their own stake in the newspaper of wide dissemination: "A business it is, and a business it must always be. All this talk we hear of a subsidized newspaper is essentially wrong. The idealists, even more than the moneymakers, should insist that the good newspaper be so made that it will pay; since it is not the paper but the readers they are after and the profits are the proof of the reading."[137]

In his economic analysis of the American newspaper and study of its psychological effect on the reader, Rogers describes a somber reality of class control and base advertising influence but is able to conclude little more than a tautology: "The American is sensational and so is his paper, the American is democratic and so is his paper. The successful, up-to-date editor does little more than adapt his newspaper to the demands and temperament of the public."[138] Hamilton Holt, the progressive managing editor of the *Independent,* called for occupational resistance to the influence of the advertiser and was a leading proponent of the endowed journal, but did not discount mass circulation as a protective dimension of the press and believed public disclosure of problems was itself a significant factor in gathering moral force in society.[139]

Giving precise expression to the progressive attitude toward the press and ideologically justifying its critical compromises was the contribution of Irwin with his long, definitive series in *Collier's* in 1911. From his original intent of exposing the shame of the press in muckraking fashion, Irwin shifted to the task of revealing the underlying principles of modern journalism. Production factors, instantaneous communication, and the emergence of an information culture had led to the functional realignment of journalism as a service industry. What defamed journalism as a commercial enterprise—its corporate processes and structure—could be given benign relevance through the presentation of the press as an indispensable public utility with a redefined constitutional franchise.

Irwin's thesis on the power of the press was based on a view that journalism had evolved in a manner consistent with the development of a technological society. The origins of the press had been a functional response to contemporary society in embryo: "With the increasing complexity of modern life arose a need for some method of communication better and more general than word of mouth or palace proclamation; so was born the newspaper."[140] At an inevitable moment news was "invented" following the manifestation of a news function in society and concurrent with the development of the mechanical means to address it: the railroad, the telegraph, the transatlantic cable, and the cylinder press. The discovery was not unlike the release of a new form of energy: "Blindly, as progress goes, our editors had stumbled upon a private want, a public need, hitherto unsatisfied; a new factor in democracy. They held the triggers of a force whose full power they failed to understand. Our Constitution and State codes, formed for an eighteenth century civilization and warped awkwardly sometimes to fit the needs of a new industrial era, failed in nothing as it failed in providing curbs for this new force— the power of news. . . . This force surprised civilization; it was born without the law; its power kept it above the law."[141] Ultimately from the crucible of the chemist came the secret to wood-based web paper, surmounting the last barrier to mass journalism.[142]

The influence of traditional journals had been focused and intentional; the effect of contemporary journalism was not conditional on either the motives or the determination of its practitioners, but on the potential of its machines. The power of news was a factor of its production: its wide circulation "without limitation from the mechanical plant," its "long-distance effect upon the public mind," the sum of its "constant iteration."[143]

In the new social order the importance of news was organic, and a vital fix to the modern psyche: "we need it, we crave it; this nerve of the modern world transmits thought and impulse from the brain of humanity to its muscles; the complex organism of modern society could no more move without it than a man could move without filaments and ganglia."[144] The priority of news set the press between the citizen and his social environment and rivaled the authority of other institutions: "On the commercial and practical side, the man of even small affairs must read news in the newspapers every day to keep informed on the thousand and one activities in the social structure which affect his business. On the intellectual and spiritual side, it is—save for the Church alone—our principal outlook on the higher intelligence. The thought of legislature, university, study, and pulpit comes to the common man first—and usually last—in the form of news. The tedious business of teaching reading in public schools has become chiefly a training to consume newspapers."[145] The ethical dilemma of the press, and conversely of society in relation to its journalism, was the problem of harnessing this new medium of energy and penetration.

Irwin did not ignore the familiar alarms of the period. The economic system included the reality of advertising influence, of proprietors who shared the values of a corporate class, and of the web of interlocking ownership between newspapers and other industries.[146] Indeed, Irwin gathered the themes that have occupied press criticism to the present. The draining concession of his critical argument, a perspective that has also largely carried forth, was to subsume the economic transformation of the press in a more forceful process of modernization. Businessmen themselves were caught up in this great revolution: "In the complex organization of modern society grow large and rooted injustices, often the fault of no one man, at worst the fault of only a few. The agents of these systems may be above the ordinary in private virtue. They are but operatives, each tending, oiling, and repairing one little wheel in a great machine."[147] The economic structure of the press could be exonerated with less difficulty than most of the nation's other industrial systems: "No Rockefeller or Gould, Quay or Coker, built it up; on the contrary, it grew from the editorial and business policy not only of the ruthless Bennett and Hearst, but of the conscientious Greeley and Medill. It arose with the growth of the times."[148]

The business of the press was in an "involved and disorganized condition" following expansion, but Irwin saw the system moving on its own momentum toward a higher ethical plane: yellow journalism was in decline, truth had been demonstrated to be a practical and valuable commodity in the marketplace, and good will was proving to be an asset. He discounted the need for legislative intervention, the feasibility of an endowed press, and the practicality of an adless paper.[149] The transformation of the press had brought a complex new institution into being. Its scope and efficiency could not be separated from its free enterprise orientation, its corporate organization, or the capital investment of its technological base. But its power and intrinsic importance to modern life gave it prerogatives that extended beyond the boundary of property rights. It held a "tacit franchise" that required leadership beyond the business attitude.[150] Irwin argued that a rationale counter to commercialism already was a factor in contemporary journalism. It could be found in the existing structure of the press, regulating but not changing basic managerial relationships, modifying but not upsetting journalism's market orientation. It was evident at all levels of responsibility: in the "noble dissatisfaction" of journalists coming to realize the importance of their work, in principles guiding the honest editor through the quandary of making news decisions, and in ethics marking the conscientious publisher as a "professional man."[151] A vision of responsibility could distinguish a profession even in an industry. The appropriate reform of journalism was to leave its successes intact.

The Professional Attitude

Irwin's appeal to a professional ideal for the press to counteract what he concluded were the troublesome economic side effects of its technical achievement was ironic. Journalism had already experienced the rise and fall of a professional identity in the figure of the nineteenth-century editor, whose status as the prominent personality of the newspaper had faded with the appearance of the large news organization. This loss of stature had been widely described as the decline of journalism as a profession. Irwin, however, was not reaching back for a traditional value of occupation in community. He was reaching out for a new meaning of professionalism in society, a renegotiated concept that was emerging in a professionalism movement affecting many occupations, including the "reprofessionalization" of traditional professions.

Indeed, the history of professionalism in America follows a contour of emphasis and deemphasis, the loss of prestige and its recovery, as the organizing concept is made to conform to new values. The rise of modern professionalism in the late nineteenth century, significant and pervasive enough to be a major theme of middle-class culture, depended upon the breakdown in the monopoly of authority held by a small number of traditional professions to allow other claims to be recognized. However, the credibility of modern professionalism required that most of the traditional professions also recover—ideologically and bureaucratically revamped—to carry on the important appearance of tradition. Journalism's tenure as a "noble profession" after 1850 had been brief and tenuous, but the choice of professionalism as an organizing ideal again at the turn of the century was wholly consistent with the times.

The professional trend in American industrial society from 1880 onward involved both a restructuring of the marketplace and the collective quest for status by career-oriented specialists proliferating in the division of labor. In a deeper effect, the trend changed patterns of everyday habits, responses to problems, and attitudes toward self-reliance. The movement was class related, the spread of a set of essentially middle-class values through much of society and culture. Although the professionalization of journalism was an event of this process, it was not a typical occurrence of the movement. The central vehicle of professional activity was the occupational group, assisted in most cases by like-minded allies in government and higher education. Typically occupational specialists, particularly in service fields, came to recognize a basic similarity in their relation to consumers or clients and the highly ritualized relationships of the traditional professions. After a period of identifying itself as a distinct collectivity, the occupational group with a professional vision began to emulate the established professions in detail, especially with the aim of acquiring government sanction through government licensing and of benefiting from the exclusivity and prestige of college training.

The professionalization of journalism was only marginally activated by an occupational motivation. The principal impetus for journalism to professionalize was the need to resolve a public crisis of confidence in an industrial institution. Irwin's "tacit franchise" in effect was a professionalization of the First Amendment, calling for institutional responsibility to control a force "born without the law" whose power "kept it above the law."[152] Irwin's ideas were influential but hardly original. Similar notions on the appropriate means of controlling the press had been voiced before. "Like a railway, a great metropolitan newspaper is a quasi-public institution," observed an article in *Era* in 1903. "It is as dependent on popular suffrage and as responsible to the people for the right use—which means the best use—of its powers and privileges as if these were matters of legal franchise."[153] A decade earlier in *Contemporary Review*, Henri de Blowitz, a correspondent for the *London Times*, had described himself as "haunted" and "besieged" because the press had no formal training for its practitioners to learn professional rules, "yet journalism governs the world, and this state within the State thrives continually more and more; striking, punishing, recompensing, immortalizing, or plunging into oblivion, all that exists, all which, because of its intrinsic interest, pushes to the light in the immense assemblage of human institutions which make up the social order."[154]

The journalist had become "his own temple, god and prophet," Blowitz lamented.[155] "Can a body of journalists be created whose professional education, established training, and certified attitudes will reassure the public conscience?"[156] Similar sentiments appeared in *Forum*: "That journalism is, that it must be, a profession appears to me so clear that I do not see how the statement can be questioned. That it is often degraded to the level of a business enterprise, that it falls into the hands of persons who ignore its relations to the public welfare, means simply that it fails to recognize the responsibilities inherent in its very nature. But from those responsibilities there is no honorable way for the journalist to escape, any more than there is for the physician and the clergyman to escape from the responsibilities of their respective callings."[157] In 1904 the case was offered in the *Harvard Graduate*: "the press indeed has become a mighty engine, but its rapid development has brought with it great abuses. Its chief fault is that, reveling in the freedom it enjoys, it has shown in much too slight a degree a sense of public responsibility for the use it makes of its freedom. The time has come when journalism, in its own and the public interest, should become a genuine profession, when it should become subject to self-imposed ethics, such as governs the other professions, and when it should not exercise unregulated powers."[158] Pulitzer himself in 1904 gave voice to the essential danger at hand: "Once let the public come to regard the press exclusively a commercial business, and there is an end of its moral power. Its influence cannot exist without public confidence."[159]

Pulitzer's response was to endow a professional school of journalism at Columbia for $2 million. For one of the nation's leading business figures, the press had become a public service institution fighting off its own baser instincts: "Nothing less than the highest ideals, the most scrupulous anxiety to do right, the most accurate knowledge of the problems it has to meet, and a sincere sense of its moral responsibility will save journalism from subservience to business interests seeking selfish ends, antagonistic to the public welfare."[160] Consistent with his view that higher education should work hand in hand with the journalism industry to advance professionalism as a symbol of the press, Pulitzer set the condition that business was not to be taught in the journalism curriculum: "I am sure that, if my wishes are to be considered, business instruction of any sort should not, would not, must not form any part of the work of the college of journalism. . . . nothing, in fact, is more inconsistent and incompatible with my intentions or repugnant to my feelings than to include any of the business or commercial elements of a newspaper in what is to be taught in this department at Columbia College."[161] The press was the technological equal of any institution, consistent with the "March of Progress" that had revolutionized transportation, manufacturing, agriculture, and education. But the press was not maintaining the pace: "All professions, all occupations but one, are keeping step with that majestic march. Its inspiration has fired all ranks of the marching army, or must we except the standard bearers? The self-constituted leaders of the people—what are they doing? Standing still, lost in self-admiration, while the hosts march by?"[162] Without professional recognition, without official sanction of its institutional authority, the press could not renew its vital social mission: "It is not too much to say that the press is the only organized force which is actively and as a body upholding the standard of civic righteousness. There are many political reformers among the clergy, but the pulpit as an institution is concerned with the Kingdom of Heaven, not with the Republic of America. There are many public-spirited lawyers, but the bar as a profession works for its retainers, and no law-defying trust ever came to grief from a dearth of legal talent to serve it. Physicians work for their patients and architects for their patrons. The press alone makes the public interest its own."[163]

Symbolically, Pulitzer's endowment of the Columbia school was to higher education what his $2 million Pulitzer building, the "People's Palace," had been to the city. Both in their fashion were monuments to the modern institutionalization of the press, the publicity of responsible power through the prestige of architecture on one hand, and the university on the other. Both were unlikely triumphs in their day, a skyscraper for a factory and a professional school for a commercial enterprise. To match the gilded dome on the horizon of the city, journalism was presented in the university as the practice of a moral corporate trust. Pulitzer's vision of the press was neither corrupt nor venal. It was an expression of belief offered in the material and ideological coin of the emerging industrial culture. Pulitzer's petition for professionalism was quintessentially progressive in character. A process of deception is not implied: the contradictions and paradoxes in Pulitzer's presentation of the press was not an ambiguity suppressed, but a conflict in meaning forcefully debated to resolution. Pulitzer's interpretation emerged as essentially the prevailing perception of the contemporary press. Any frame of understanding would have involved in some sense an intellectual captivity, participants not fully aware of their own motivations. Pulitzer's persuasive edge in making his professionalism argument was the genius of his metaphorical investments in the tangible symbols of his cause.

The fit of an occupational ideal of individual autonomy to an industrial bureaucracy would not be perfect: journalism would be destined to a perennial state of semiprofessionalism, to a continuous dynamic of emerging professionalism, to a faith in a "spirit of professionalism" rather than in the exact example of the established professions. The case for distinguishing the working journalist, the salaried employee of the newspaper, as the focus of the profession was problematic. Overriding the difficulty was the perception of the press as a whole having a professional mission: "The collection, publication, and distribution of news has become a business of dignity and importance."[164] Pledge the press to a professional mandate, and the status of professionalism would accrue to the existing press system. As important as the need for reform of the press was, the greater necessity was to clear away the dangerously ambivalent public attitude toward the powerful new medium. The drive to professionalize journalism had to convince both press and public alike. The project was essentially ideological: deeply affected were neither the structure nor the procedures of modern journalism, but the manner in which they were interpreted. Journalism was changed by the economic exploitation of technology; professionalism was the rhetorical frame for understanding that change.

Notes

This chapter expands and revises, from a rhetorical perspective, an earlier article on journalism history, "The Power in the Image: Professionalism and the Communications Revolution," *American Journalism* 1 (winter 1984): 1–14.

1. Richard Hofstadter, *The Age of Reform: From Bryan to F. D. R.* (New York: Vintage Books, 1955), 186.

2. An analysis of the press in terms of the concept of oligopoly can be found in Joseph P. McKerns, "The Emergence of Modern Media, 1900–1945," in *The Media in America: A History*, 2d ed., ed. William David Sloan, James G. Stoval, and James D. Startt (Scottsdale, Ariz.: Publishing Horizons, 1993), 301–4.

3. Linda Lawson, *Truth in Publishing: Federal Regulation of the Press's Business Practices, 1880–1920* (Carbondale: Southern Illinois Press, 1993).

4. See the introduction, p. 2, and "Partial Success," 205, in *The Progressive Era: Major Issues of Interpretation*, ed. Arthur Mann (Hindsdale, Ill.: Dryden Press, 1975).

5. Henry George, as quoted in *Major Problems in the Gilded Age and the Progressive Era*, ed. Leon Fink (Lexington, Mass.: D. C. Heath, 1993), 6.

6. For a discussion of the development of social responsibility theory, see Fred S. Siebert, Theodore Peterson, and Wilbur Shramm, *Four Theories of the Press* (Urbana: University of Illinois Press, 1956).

7. This study constructs and interprets the discourse on the American press as it appeared in popular periodicals and other commentary at the turn of the century.

8. Paul Palmer, "The Concept of Public Opinion in Political Theory," in *Essays in History and Political Theory in Honor of Charles Howard McIlwain* (Cambridge: Harvard University Press, 1936), 242.

9. Alexis de Tocqueville, *Democracy in America* (New York: Alfred Knopf, 1945), 2:113.

10. James Bryce, *The American Commonwealth* (New York: Macmillan, 1921), 2:840.

11. Remarks quoted in "The Ideal Newspaper," *Current Literature* 48 (March 1910): 335.

12. Lincoln Steffens, "The Business of a Newspaper," *Scribner's* 22 (October 1897): 447.

13. J. W. Keller, "Journalism as a Career," *Forum* 15 (August 1893): 691.

14. See Philip Elliott, *The Sociology of Professions* (New York: Herder and Herder, 1972); Terence J. Johnson, *Professions and Power* (London: Macmillan Press, 1972); Magali Sarfatti Larson, *The Rise of Professionalism: A Sociological Analysis* (Berkeley and Los Angeles: University of California Press, 1977).

15. Burton Bledstein, *The Culture of Professionalism: The Middle Class and the Development of Higher Education in America* (New York: W. W. Norton and Co., 1976).

16. Ibid., 80.

17. The terms are Michel Foucault's. See his *The Birth of the Clinic: An Archaeology of Medical Perception* (New York: Pantheon, 1979).

18. For recent accounts of journalism history from a labor perspective, see Hanno Hardt and Bonnie Brennen, eds., *News Workers: Toward a History of the Rank and File* (Minneapolis: University of Minnesota Press, 1995); and William S. Solomon and Robert W. McChesney, eds., *Ruthless Criticism: News Perspectives in U.S. Communication History* (Minneapolis: University of Minnesota Press, 1993).

19. Louis D. Brandeis, *Business—A Profession* (Boston: Small, Maynard and Co., 1914), 1–12.

20. See Max Radin, *Manners and Morals in Business* (Indianapolis: Bobbs-Merrill, 1934); J. Whitney Bunting, ed., *Ethics for Modern Business Practice* (New York: Prentice-Hall, 1953); Edgar L. Heermance, *Codes of Ethics: A Handbook* (Burlington, Vt.: Free Press, 1924); and Alfred D. Chandler Jr., *The Visible Hand: The Managerial Revolution in American Business* (Cambridge: Harvard University Press, 1977). See also Gabriel Kolko, *The Triumph of Conservatism: A Reinterpretation of American History, 1900–1916* (Glencoe, Ill: Free Press, 1963).

21. Will Irwin, "The American Newspaper—I: the Power of the Press," *Collier's* 46 (21 January 1911): 15.

22. Ibid.

23. Edwin Emery, *The Press and America: An Interpretative History of the Mass Media*, 3d ed. (Englewood Cliffs, N.J.: Prentice-Hall, 1972), 285. For a close examination of the pivotal decade of the 1870s, see Jeffrey B. Rutenbeck, "Newspaper Trends in the 1870s: Proliferation, Popularization, and Political Independence," *Journalism and Mass Communication Quarterly* 72 (summer 1995): 361–75.

24. Alfred McClung Lee, *The Daily Newspaper in America: The Evolution of a Social Instrument* (New York: Macmillan, 1937), 65, 70.

25. Melvin L. DeFleur and Sandra Ball-Rokeach, *Theories of Mass Communication* (New York: David McKay, 1966), 29–31.

26. Robert H. Wiebe, *The Search for Order, 1877–1920* (New York: Hill and Wang, 1967), 40.

27. Ibid., 43.

28. Geoffrey Barraclough, *An Introduction to Contemporary History* (Baltimore: Penguin Books, 1967), 43–64.

29. Lee, *Daily Newspaper in America*, 119.

30. Ibid., 120–22.

31. Day Allen Willey, "The Development of the Modern Newspaper," *Era* 11 (May 1903): 417.

32. W. A. Swanberg, *Pulitzer* (New York: Charles Scribner's Sons, 1967), 162–63.

33. Ibid., 163.

34. "New York World," *Harper's Weekly* 34 (18 January 1890): 47.

35. Calder M. Pickett, "Technology and the New York Press in the Nineteenth Century," *Journalism Quarterly* 37 (summer 1960): 407.

36. James Creelman, "The New York Herald and Its New Home," *Harper's Weekly* 37 (2 September 1893): 842.

37. Ibid.

38. Ibid., 843.

39. Ibid.

40. Ibid.

41. Ibid.

42. Hofstadter, *Age of Reform*, 229–32.

43. The discussion of America's economic growth draws upon Emery, *Press and America*; Allan Nevins, *The Emergence of Modern America, 1865–1878* (New York: Macmillan, 1927); William Miller, *A New History of the United States* (New York: Dell Publishing, 1969); Francis G. Walett, *Economic History of the United States* (New York: Barnes and Noble, 1963); Matthew Josephson, *The Robber Barons* (New York: Harcourt, Brace and World, 1962); and U.S. Department of Commerce, *Historical Statistics of the United States: Colonial Times to 1970* (Washington, D.C.: Bureau of the Census, 1970).

44. The most enduring theme of criticism of the press is consolidation of ownership.

45. Woodrow Wilson, as quoted in Louis Brandeis, *Other People's Money and How the Bankers Use It* (New York: Frederick A. Stokes, 1932), 1.

46. Hofstadter, *Age of Reform*, 232.

47. U.S. Department of Commerce, *Historical Statistics of the United States*, 687.

48. Frank Luther Mott, *American Journalism: A History, 1690–1960*, 3d ed. (New York: Macmillan, 1962), chap. 32.

49. For a general discussion of the emergence of a corporate identity for American business, see Martin J. Sklar, *The Corporate Reconstruction of American Capitalism, 1890–1916* (New York: Cambridge University Press, 1988).

50. Lee, *Daily Newspaper in America*, 166; Thomas C. Cochran, "Media as Business: A Brief History," *Journal of Communication* 25 (autumn 1975): 156.

51. Lee, *Daily Newspaper in America*, 166.

52. Swanson, *Pulitzer*, 44; Henry Steele Commager, *The American Mind: An Interpretation of American Thought and Character since the 1880's* (New Haven: Yale University Press, 1950), 70.

53. Emery, *Press and America*, 325.

54. See Michael Schudson, *Discovering the News: A Social History of American Newspapers* (New York: Basic Books, 1978), chap. 3.

55. Max P. O'Rell, "Lively Journalism," *North American Review* 150 (March 1890): 368.

56. Aline Gorren, "The Ethics of Modern Journalism," *Scribner's* 19 (April 1896): 509.

57. Will Irwin, "The American Newspaper—IX: The Advertising Influence," *Collier's* 47 (27 May 1911): 15.

58. Irwin, "American Newspaper—I," 15.

59. Ibid.

60. Wiebe, *Search for Order*, 44.

61. See James Melvin Lee, *History of American Journalism* (Boston: Houghton Mifflin, 1923), 406.

62. The first analysis of public opinion in political terms was conducted late in the eighteenth century. This analysis was tied to the concept of majority opinion and inferred the sense of many in agreement in judgment through individual reflection. It was a fashionable concept regarding the will of the French Revolution, and by the first quarter of the nineteenth century had become a central consideration of democratic theory. By that time the press was recognized as a chief instrument in its formation and expression. (See Palmer, "Concept of Public Opinion," in *Essays in History and Political Theory*, 240–42.) The concept of public opinion was closely tied to the development of representative democracy as a rationalization of its legitimacy and authority. That governments heed the opinion of the public became an ethical imperative, as V. O. Key suggests, in the democratic push to overturn exploitive autocratic regimes (V. O. Key Jr., *Public Opinion and American Democracy* [New York: Alfred A. Knopf, 1967], 4). Its enthronement in place of kings, however, was that of a virtual stranger. The rise of the public represented the emergence of influential elements in society to challenge authoritarian governments. As frightening as their apparent numbers was their anonymity: they did not bear titles or live on estates, yet their power was evident in commerce and in an agitating common interest that seemed to manifest itself in the environment of the city, despite the city's lack of tight social organization. To authoritarian rulers, the public was the "crowds," and they attempted the earliest evaluation of public opinion by sending agents into public gathering places. Even to the radicals of democratic sentiment, however, the public was an amorphous phenomenon, an abstraction for a mythical assembly of a whole agitating social class. Public opinion became the ideological concept for the deliberation of this class. Newspapers came to be recognized as primary channels of its expression, the authoritative counters to official government institutions. See also Brendan Dooley, "From Literary Criticism to Systems Theory in Early Modern Journalism History," *Journal of the History of Ideas* 51 (July–September 1990): 461–86.

63. George Boyce, "The Fourth Estate: The Reappraisal of a Concept," in *Newspaper History: From the Seventeenth Century to the Present Day*, ed. Boyce, James Curran, and Pauline Wingate (London: Constable, 1978), 20.

64. *New York Morning Herald*, 6 May 1835.

65. Quoted from Lee, *American Journalism*, 191, attributed to the *Boston Herald*.

66. *New York Morning Herald*, 21 November 1837.

67. Frederic Hudson, *Journalism in the United States from 1690 to 1872* (New York: Harper and Bros., 1873).

68. For a description of the prevailing civic culture as the framework of intellectual life of the times, see Thomas Bender, "The Culture of Intellectual Life: The City and the Professions," in *New Directions in American Intellectual Life*, ed. John Hipham and Paul K. Conklin (Baltimore: Johns Hopkins University Press, 1979).

69. Robert Sobel, *The Manipulators: America in the Media Age* (Garden City, N.Y.: Anchor Press/Doubleday, 1976), 12.

70. Charles Wingate, ed., Introduction to *Views and Interviews on Journalism* (New York: F. B. Patterson, 1875), 7.

71. "Henry Watterson," in ibid., 21–22.

72. "Samuel Bowles," in ibid., 45.

73. "Manton Marble," (editor of the *New York World*) in ibid., 216.

74. Frank M. Colby, "Attacking the Newspapers," *Bookman* 15 (August 1902): 534.

75. Ibid.

76. Henry Thurston Peck, "Henry Watterson," *Bookman* 18 (October 1903): 635.

77. Richard A. Haste, "The Evolution of the Fourth Estate," *Arena* 41 (March 1909): 349.

78. Ibid.

79. Brooke Fisher, "The Newspaper Industry," *Atlantic* 89 (June 1902): 746.

80. Tiffany Blake, "The Editorial, Past, Present and Future," *Collier's* 48 (23 September 1911): 35.

81. E. L. Godkin, "The Influence of the Press," *Nation* 65 (25 November 1897): 411.

82. Ibid.

83. E. L. Godkin, "Newspapers Here and Abroad," *North American Review* 150 (February 1890): 202.

84. Ibid.

85. Francis Leupp, "The Waning of the Press," *Atlantic* 105 (February 1910): 155.

86. Ibid., 155–56.

87. See Deolos F. Wilcox, "The American Newspaper: A Study in Social Psychology," *Annals of the American Academy* 16 (July 1900): 76; Henry Wood, "The Psychology of Crime," *Arena* 8 (October 1893): 530.

88. Wilcox, "American Newspaper," 57, 87.

89. Ibid., 87.

90. "Is an Honest and Sane Newspaper Press Possible?" *American Journal of Sociology* 15 (November 1909): 334.

91. See Wilcox, "American Newspaper," 89.

92. Irwin, "American Newspaper—I," 15.

93. Ibid.

94. Ibid.

95. Ibid.

96. Ibid.

97. Boyce, "Fourth Estate," in *Newspaper History,* 27.

98. See Fisher, "The Newspaper Industry," 746; Rollo Ogden, "Journalism in New York," *Nation* 57 (3 August 1893): 78–79.

99. Boyce, "Fourth Estate," in *Newspaper History,* 36.

100. Louis G. Geiger, "Muckrakers—Then and Now," *Journalism Quarterly* 62 (autumn 1966): 469.

101. "Manton Marble," in *Views and Interviews,* 216.

102. Ibid.

103. William Hyde, editor of the *Missouri Republican,* in *Views and Interviews,* 197.

104. Charles Dudley Warner, as quoted in Lee, *American Journalism,* 354.

105. Ibid.

106. See Lincoln Steffens, "The Business of a Newspaper," *Scribner's* 22 (October 1897); Irwin, "American Newspaper—I," 15.

107. "The Simplicity That Never Was," *Atlantic* 105 (January 1910): 139.

108. George Howard Phillips, "An Analysis of 835 Articles in the Leading American Periodicals for the Period 1890–1914 to Determine What Was Said about American Daily Newspapers" (Ph.D. diss., University of Iowa, 1962). See the excellent bibliography, invaluable for the present study.

109. Ibid., chap. 5.

110. Ibid., chap. 6.

111. Two other useful historical studies of commentary on the press are Marion Tuttle Marzolf, *Civilizing Voices: American Press Criticism, 1880–1950* (New York: Longman, 1991); and Hazel Dicken-Garcia, *Journalistic Standards in Nineteenth Century America* (Madison: University of Wisconsin Press, 1989).

112. See David B. Danbom, *"The World of Hope": Progressives and the Struggle for an Ethical Public Life* (Philadelphia: Temple University Press, 1987).

113. Charles Beard and Mary R. Beard, *The Rise of American Civilization* (New York: Macmillan, 1928), 714.

114. Lewis Mumford, *The Golden Day* (New York: W. W. Norton, 1926), 23. A variation of Mumford's thesis on the replacement of the frontier in the public imagination is offered in David W. Noble, *The Progressive Mind, 1908–1917* (Chicago: Rand McNally, 1970). In Noble's analysis, what the Progressives sought to describe was a new frontier force in industrialism and technology, one that allowed for economic expansion and social mobility. Pointing the American identity toward the future were historians such as Charles Beard, and speaking of harmony through technological order were Frederick Taylor, Henry Ford, and Thorstein Veblen. Noble writes of the progressive conceptual effort as an Americanization of Marx, placing the Marxist theory of progress into a middle-class frame.

115. Robert H. Walker, ed., *The Reform Spirit in America* (New York: G. P. Putnam's Sons, 1976), 558.

116. See Leo Marx, *The Machine in the Garden* (New York: Oxford University Press, 1964). See also Alan Trachenberg, *The Incorporation of America: Culture and Society in the Gilded Age* (New York: Hill and Wang, 1982).

117. Walker, *Reform Spirit in America*, 558.

118. Mumford, *The Golden Day*, 243.

119. See Jay Martin, "The Literature of Argument and the Arguments of Literature: The Aesthetics of Muckraking," in *Muckraking: Past, Present and Future*, ed. John M. Harrison and Harry H. Stein (University Park: Pennsylvania State University Press, 1973), 101–2.

120. Upton Sinclair, *The Industrial Republic* (New York: Doubleday, Page and Co., 1907), 239.

121. Ibid., 61. See Edward Bellamy, *Looking Backward* (Boston: Houghton, Mifflin, 1888).

122. See Herbert Croly, *The Promise of American Life* (New York: Macmillan, 1909). On Croley see Charles Forcey, *The Crossroads of Liberalism: Croly, Weyl, Lippmann, and the Progressive Era, 1900–1925* (New York: Oxford University Press, 1961); David W. Noble, *The Paradox of Progressive Thought* (Minneapolis: University of Minnesota Press, 1958); and Howard Mumford Jones, *The Age of Energy* (New York: Viking Press, 1970), 425–29.

123. David Graham Phillips, *The Reign of Gilt* (New York: James Pott and Co., 1905), 163.

124. Jones, *Age of Energy*.

125. Phillips, *Reign of Gilt*, 177–78.

126. John Moody and George K. Turner, "Masters of Capital in America: The Seven Men," *McClure's* 37 (August 1911): 427–28, one of a series of muckraking articles.

127. Hofstadter, *Age of Reform*, 185.

128. Ibid.

129. S. S. McClure, editorial, *McClure's* 20 (January 1903): 336. See Hofstadter, *Age of Reform*, 202–3.

130. Pickett, "Technology and the New York Press."

131. Ibid., 398–407.

132. George W. Ochs, "Journalism," *Annals of the American Academy* 28 (July 1906): 38.

133. James Edward Rogers, *The American Newspaper* (Chicago: University of Chicago Press, 1909), 14–15.

134. Whitelaw Reid, as quoted in Arthur Reed Kimball, "The Profession of Publicist," *Atlantic* 92 (December 1903): 807.

135. Editorial, *Nation* 74 (12 June 1902): 459.

136. Kimball, "The Profession of Publicist," 807.

137. Lincoln Steffens, "The New School of Journalism," *Bookman* 18 (October 1903): 173–74.

138. Rogers, *American Newspaper*, 185.

139. See Hamilton Holt, *Commercialism and Journalism* (Boston: Riverside Press, 1909); and the biography by Warren F. Kuehl, *Hamilton Holt* (Gainesville: University of Florida Press, 1960).

140. Will Irwin, "The American Newspaper—II: The Dim Beginnings," *Collier's* 45 (4 February 1911): 14.

141. Ibid., 16.

142. Ibid., 17.

143. Ibid.

144. Will Irwin, "The American Newspaper—V: What Is News?" *Collier's* 46 (18 March 1911): 16.

145. Ibid.

146. At least four of Irwin's articles in the series could be considered primarily economic interpretations of the press.

147. Irwin, "The American Newspaper—IX," 15.

148. Ibid., 14.

149. See Will Irwin, "The American Newspaper—IV: The Spread and Decline of Yellow Journalism," *Collier's* 46 (4 March 1911): 18–20, 36; "The American Newspaper—XIII: The New Era," *Collier's* 47 (8 July 1911): 15–16, 25; "The American Newspaper—XV: The Voice of a Generation," *Collier's* 47 (29 July 1911): 15–16, 23, 25.

150. Will Irwin, "The American Newspaper—VI: The Editor and the News," *Collier's* 47 (1 April 1911): 18.
151. Irwin, "American Newspaper—I," 15; Irwin, "American Newspaper—XV," 23.
152. Irwin, "The American Newspaper—VI," 18; Irwin, "The American Newspaper—II," 16.
153. Paul Tyner, "The Ideal Newspaper," *Era* 11 (May 1903): 474.
154. Henri de Blowitz, "Journalism as a Profession," *Contemporary Review* 63 (23 January 1893): 38.
155. Ibid., 39.
156. Ibid., 41.
157. William Morton Payne, "What a Daily Newspaper Might Be Made," *Forum* 16 (November 1893): 364.
158. Samuel W. McCall, "The Newspaper Press," *Harvard Graduate* 13 (September 1904): 43.
159. Joseph Pulitzer, "The College of Journalism," *North American Review* 178 (May 1904): 659.
160. Ibid., 658.
161. Quoted from Albert Alton Sutton, *Education for Journalism in the United States from Its Beginning to 1940* (Evanston, Ill.: Northwestern University, 1945), 13.
162. Pulitzer, "College of Journalism," 662.
163. Ibid., 679–80.
164. Albert Shaw, "Making a Choice of a Profession," *Cosmopolitan* 35 (June 1903): 156.

Justice Holmes's Rhetoric and the Progressive Path of the Law

James Arnt Aune

5

The term "Progressive" implies a linear notion of history, one that evolutionary Darwinism spread to all fields of knowledge in the United States by the late nineteenth and early twentieth century. As Edward A. Purcell Jr. points out, the modern disciplines of political science, sociology, economics, and psychology were created under the inspiration of the new evolutionary naturalism. The new philosophy of pragmatism examined "'mind' as an adaptive physiological function of the body rather than as a separate spiritual entity." Political science pointed to "group conflict as the central reality of politics." The social sciences generally came to be based on the assumptions of objectivism (elimination of the "personal factor"), particularism (the nominalistic reduction of observed phenomena to individual units), and functionalism (the doctrine that knowledge was based on and confined to practical operations).[1]

The cultural difficulty that progressive naturalism faced was the problem of "value" in a world without God. As Wayne Booth and other rhetorical critics of scientific naturalism have argued, the "modern dogmas" of skepticism, positivism, relativism, and emotivism seemed to undercut the very possibility of reasoned communication.[2] Later critics of both the intellectual and political sides of the Progressive movement criticized them for their distrust of popular democracy and their uncritical celebration of the planning and organizing capabilities of the centralized state—a celebration that seemed to culminate at best in a government of unresponsive bureaucracy and at worst in totalitarianism.[3]

The figure who best captures the tensions and contradictions in American progressive thought is Justice Oliver Wendell Holmes Jr. He was the first American to argue for an empirical and behavioral view of the law, one that purged it of traditional moral associations. He emerged early as a hero to labor leaders and progressive politicians such as Theodore Roosevelt. He mentored future leaders in law and politics, including Felix Frankfurter, Harold Laski, and even Alger Hiss. Yet Holmes's Darwinism, atheism, and philosophical skepticism eventually made him a controversial figure, especially when Communist and Nazi totalitarianism seemed to require a strong moral response from the Western democracies

The outline of Oliver Wendell Holmes Jr.'s life can be summarized briefly.[4] He was born 8 March 1841 in Boston, Massachusetts, son of Oliver Wendell Holmes, the physician and author. The Puritan emphasis on duty and calling remained a strong part of his cultural milieu, even if Puritan religious belief did not. He attended Harvard College from 1857 to 1861, where he received the standard, if uninspiring, education of a young American aristocrat of his day. Holmes's greatest interest during his college years was in art history, spurred by a reading of John Ruskin. He displayed some enthusiasm for the abolitionist cause, but his faith in abstract political principles was soon shattered by his three years of service in the Union army. He was wounded three times.[5]

After the war he studied at Harvard Law School, read law in two Boston law offices, and was admitted to the bar in 1867. He had an active law practice in Boston from 1867 to 1882. During that time he edited the twelfth edition of Kent's *Commentaries on American Law* (1873) and gave an influential series of lectures, collected in *The Common Law*, at Lowell Institute in Boston (1880–81).[6] His growing reputation as a legal scholar led to his appointment as professor of law at Harvard Law School, from which he resigned abruptly to accept an appointment as a member of the Supreme Judicial Court of Massachusetts from 1882 to 1902. He was chief justice of the court from 1899 to 1902.[7]

During his years as a state supreme court justice he developed a reputation as an eloquent ceremonial speaker. His "Memorial Day Address" (1883) and "The Soldier's Faith" (1895) were widely reprinted. The latter speech made a particular impression on Theodore Roosevelt, who, according to Holmes, seems to have mistaken it for a "jingo document."[8] An address to the Boston University School of Law in 1897, "The Path of the Law," remains the single most cited piece of legal writing in the United States.[9]

Holmes's argument for a pragmatic view of the law, against the natural rights, formalist jurisprudence of the time, made him a controversial figure.[10] His dissents in a few labor cases that came before the Massachusetts court made him suspect as a closet "socialist" in the eyes of the business elite.[11] President Roosevelt appointed him to the Supreme Court in 1902, hoping that he would support Roosevelt's efforts at progressive reform, although the president was disappointed in Holmes's opinions in some cases, notably *Northern Securities Company v. United States* (1904). Holmes's dissents in cases such as *Lochner v. New York* (in which a majority of the Court struck down a New York law limiting the number of hours worked by bakers) gave him a growing reputation as principled antagonist to the Court's use of the doctrine of "substantive due process" to strike down legislation that would interfere with "freedom of contract."

After World War I, Holmes began to attain popularity among liberals and the Left, partially because of his seemingly strong defense of free speech, and partially because of a public relations campaign by Felix Frankfurter and other young progressive thinkers.[12] By 1932, when he retired from the Court, his eloquence and learning (as well as his formidable mustache) had made him the American ideal of the Supreme Court justice.[13] His courageous Civil War service and longevity—not many Americans could say that they had fought in the Civil War *and* knew Alger Hiss (one of his last law clerks)—made him the stuff of popular legend. Catherine Drinker Bowen wrote a best-selling, semifictionalized biography, *Yankee from Olympus*, that was later made into a successful stage play and film, *Magnificent Yankee*.[14]

Soon after Holmes's death, however, a reaction set in. A group of Jesuit law professors began a campaign against Holmes in the 1940s, arguing that his atheism and skepticism made him closer to Nazism than to American ideals.[15] The publication of his letters to the English legal scholar Sir Frederick Pollock seemed to confirm the growing image of Holmes as "savage, harsh, and cruel, a bitter and lifelong pessimist who saw in the course of human life nothing but a continuing struggle in which the rich and powerful impose their will on the poor and weak."[16] The controversy over Holmes as a person and as a legal theorist continues to the present day. Was he a pragmatist or a utilitarian? Did he anticipate the insights of legal realism and law-and-economics, or was he merely a muddled thinker more interested in writing pithy aphorisms than in developing a coherent system of thought? Holmes simultaneously wrote too much (over two thousand legal opinions, a book of speeches, two books of legal theory, and several posthumously published collections of his letters) and too little (he gave his audiences his conclusions in stark, often shocking form, leaving out an explanation of the reasoning process that led him to those conclusions). The enormous quantity of his writings and his enigmatic style have meant that there is plenty of evidence for all the competing interpretations of Holmes.[17]

The purpose of the present essay is not to settle once and for all the debates over Holmes's character and philosophy. It is not even to examine his career as a legal theorist and practitioner. Holmes is of interest to the student of American rhetoric and public affairs both as an eloquent orator and writer of judicial opinions. Perhaps more than any other legal rhetor, he has helped define the peculiar place of legal rhetoric in our public life. There has been very little analysis of Holmes as a rhetor, despite the fact that his speeches, and especially his aphorisms, are still quoted today: "the marketplace of ideas," "the life of the law is not logic but experience," "law as the magic mirror of American civilization," "certainty generally is illusion and repose is not the destiny of man," "shouting fire in a crowded theater," "the whole purpose of man is to form general propositions, only adding that no general proposition is worth a damn." In this essay I propose to examine Holmes's epideictic oratory, notably the "Memorial Day Address" and "A Soldier's Faith"; his speech "The Path of the Law," his only explicit statement of his legal philosophy; and his most often cited legal opinions: the dissent in *Lochner v. New York*, his free speech dissents, and his notorious support of sterilization of the mentally retarded in *Buck v. Bell.* I make three arguments about Holmes. First, his jurisprudence cannot be understood without careful analysis of his epideictic oratory. Viewed by themselves, his opinions and his private letters explaining them justify a view of Holmes as a cynic. But his speeches reveal a more complex figure, seeking to find a way to continue the ideals of American republicanism in a world without religious faith. Holmes's materialist mysticism, which he shared with his favorite philosopher, George Santayana, remains a unique contribution to American philosophy, one that only appears in his occasional addresses. Second, Holmes's effort to solve the "problem of value" in a time of scientific naturalism, as Edward A. Purcell Jr. puts it, occurred through rhetorical performances that constituted a new audience, who would find in professionalism an antidote for despair and anxiety.[18] His writings are part of an American conversation on the relationships among politics, law, and morality that continues to the present day. Holmes constitutes a particular legal language: a way of seeing (and not seeing) the role of the legal professional in American society through the lens of what William Lewis has called the "romantic realism" of the law.[19] Third, Holmes's career helps us understand, as perhaps no other American orator does, the sweeping transitions in the American language of public life that occurred between the Civil War and the New Deal. The ambiguities and contradictions in Holmes's romantic realism remain part of American liberalism today, and they can be seen in the various reflections and projections of social anxiety onto the figure of Holmes by several generations of legal scholars.

Three Views of Holmes's Rhetoric

The public character of the American lawyer and judge is largely crafted through strategic, rhetorical documents. Some of the most eloquent prose in the American rhetorical tradition has been crafted by appellate and Supreme Court judges. Despite such legal eloquence and despite the centrality of law in American politics, there has been much less attention paid to legal argument in American rhetorical studies than to, say, presidential rhetoric or the rhetoric of social movements.

By the 1980s, however, the controversies over constitutional interpretation that had been ignited by the Warren court and, especially, *Roe v. Wade* seemed to inspire interest in legal rhetoric. The development of literary theory into a general theory of the "text" inevitably revived interest in classical rhetoric. The continuing assault on positivism by American pragmatists and their counterparts among French poststructuralists cleared a space for use of rhetorical categories for explicating the reality-creating functions of legal discourse. Narrative theory was a particularly congenial territory where legal and literary scholars could meet, since legal arguments almost always take the form of a story, "the facts of the case." The discovery of the cognitive functions of metaphor inspired several discussions of root metaphors in the law.[20] Several scholars began to write rhetorical criticism of judicial opinions and also began tracing the relationships between rhetorical education and legal education in Western culture.[21] The interest in rhetoric as practical reasoning that had been revived by Chaim Perelman and Stephen Toulmin in the 1950s seemed to some scholars to provide something of a corrective to excessively "literary" ways of looking at legal language.[22]

In one of his widely quoted aperçus Holmes referred to the law as "a magic mirror," in which "we see reflected, not only our own lives, but the lives of all men that have been!"[23] In "The Path of the Law," law is described as "the witness and external deposit of our moral life."[24] Although Holmes has been criticized for promoting a specialist's vision of the law and for radically separating morality and justice from the study of the law, he also can be credited with helping to introduce the historical study of the law in the United States. The life of the law was to be found in the experience of a people, not in the rarified legal axioms of Holmes's formalist predecessors. Indeed, the popularity of Holmes both inside and outside the legal community in the United States highlights the peculiar status of law in the American political tradition. As Alexis de Tocqueville wrote, political questions in America have a way of turning into legal questions, making prominent attorneys and judges much more "public" figures than in the other Western democracies.[25]

Despite the sheer volume of Holmes's speeches and judicial opinions, there have been only five extended discussions of Holmes's rhetoric: Dorothy Anderson's neo-Aristotelian, biographical study in 1962; Joan Schwarz's enthymematic analysis of "The Path of the Law"; Marouf Hasian Jr.'s 1992 study from the perspective of critical rhetoric; Richard Posner's 1988 study in his *Law and Literature: A Misunderstood Relation*, which treats Holmes's rhetoric from a purely literary standpoint; and Robert Ferguson's "Holmes and the Judicial Figure." I will discuss Schwarz's and Hasian's analyses when I examine "The Path of the Law" and the free speech opinions. Anderson's essay demonstrates how Holmes crafted a distinctive judicial and political philosophy through his speeches, judicial opinions, and letters—his logos. Ferguson discusses Holmes's creation of himself as a "judicial figure," the ethos of the ideal judge in the Progressive Era. Posner examines Holmes's distinctive style and use of pathos.

Together, Anderson, Ferguson, and Posner help us see how Holmes approximated the classical ideal of the orator, who, in S. M. Halloran's words: "became a kind of living embodiment of the cultural heritage. The ideal orator was conceived as the person of such broad knowledge and general competency that he could apply the accumulated wisdom of the culture to any particular case in a sufficiently logical fashion to move his hearer's minds (*logos*), and with enough emotional force to engage their passions (*pathos*). The name given to the third of the traditional modes of rhetorical appeal, *ethos*, underlines the importance of the orator's mastery of the cultural heritage; through the power of his logical and emotional appeals, he became a voice of such apparent authority that the word spoken by this person was the word of communal wisdom, a word to be trusted for the weight of the person who spoke it and of the tradition he spoke for."[26]

Anderson's "The Public Speeches of Justice Oliver Wendell Holmes" is one of the better examples of traditional public address studies.[27] She limits her focus to Holmes's occasional addresses but contends that these speeches reveal "his major premises about the infinite and universal, about life and living, that he sometimes hesitated to include in his judicial opinions."[28] Holmes called the speeches "chance utterances of faith and doubt," a phrase that Anderson characterizes as an "important clue" to his beliefs: "The philosophy expressed in his speeches is precisely a combination of faith and doubt—doubt enough to motivate thinking, faith enough to motivate action."[29]

Holmes's consistent rhetorical method was to state conclusions vividly, but without revealing all the steps in his thought process. The greatest contribution of the speaker, like that of the philosopher, was, in Holmes's words, to create "a lot of penetrating *aperçus* that are quite independent of all his spider work."[30] Anderson writes that each "of the occasional addresses includes one or another, and sometimes the whole set, of his *aperçus* about (1) the nature of the cosmos, (2) the search for truth, (3) the nature of life, and (4) the source of his value."[31]

For Holmes the "cosmos" is an "unimaginable whole," the meaning of life consists of refusing to set oneself against the universe "as a rival god," and "the key to happiness is to accept a like faith in one's heart, and to be not merely a necessary but a willing instrument in working out the inscrutable end."[32]

With this basic act of faith Holmes sets about a search for "bettable premises." These are his premises about fact and value, as he explained to Laski: "When I say that a thing is true I only mean that I can't help believing it—but I have no grounds for assuming that my can't helps are cosmic can't helps—and some reasons for thinking otherwise. I therefore define truth as the system of my intellectual limitations—there being a tacit reference to what I bet is or will be the prevailing can't help of the majority of that part of the world I count. The ultimate—even humanly speaking—is a mystery. . . . Absolute truth is a mirage."[33] Anderson summarizes the consequences of Holmes's "bettabilitarianism" very well: "Because he thought that curiosity felt in the face of the mystery of the universe was man's most human appetite and the satisfaction of it was as truly an end in itself as self-preservation, he encouraged his listeners to seek bettable premises through intellectual struggle, through a constant effort to see one's work in relation to the whole of things."[34] Once one finds one's bettable premises, one sets about squaring those beliefs with the "can't helps" of others, or at least of the majority. Holmes's view of truth and of morality was essentially social in character, only representing "the preference of a given body in a given time and place."[35] Anderson points out that Holmes did not clarify how a social view of the truth necessarily leads to the notion "that truth can be determined by majority vote or a show of power."[36]

Holmes's skepticism led not to passivity but to an emphasis on action. One must act to the full extent of one's powers. Holmes always emphasized his "Puritan ferment"—the will to act—in his occasional speeches: "Holmes seemed loath to leave a speech without saying that the end of life was life itself—to vent and realize the inner force."[37]

In a more whimsical vein, Holmes described his plan for creating a society of "jobbists," arguing that doing one's job to the best of one's ability is often more altruistic than setting about with the specific goal of changing the world.[38] Holmes was especially critical of the view that happiness could be "won simply by being counsel for great corporations and having an income of fifty thousand dollars."[39]

Anderson notes that William James criticized Holmes for being "unable to make any other than one set speech which comes out on every occasion." But she defends the clarity and consistency of the vision Holmes set before his audiences: "His constant effort was to make clear to his hearers that as parts of an unimaginable whole they must reconcile themselves to the fact that truth was not absolute, that in spite of this they must expend every intellectual effort to discover premises on which they were willing to act, and that having discovered these premises their joy would come from acting as hard as they could."[40]

Anderson also discusses "the development and arrangement" of Holmes's ideas. She asserts rather than proves that "the training in rhetoric which Holmes had at Harvard would be important, not because it gave him bits and pieces of technique, but because it stimulated his interest in rhetorical principles."[41] We know that Holmes studied rhetoric under Francis James Child, the holder of the Boylston Chair, and under James Jennison, instructor in elocution, but these years were the beginning of the end for classical rhetorical education at Harvard, and Holmes never discusses rhetoric in his many letters, other than in terms of style. He does refer to George Willis's *Philosophy of Speech* several times, but the book is really about pronunciation and grammar rather than public speaking.[42] Harold Laski asked Holmes three times in his letters if Holmes has read Aristotle's *Rhetoric*, about which Laski had become quite enthusiastic, but Holmes did not respond.[43] Holmes read Greek and Latin well, but he read classical philosophy and literature, not oratory or rhetorical theory. His well-known antipathy to Roman law may explain the absence of any interest in Cicero.[44] The one rhetorical theorist whom he did read was Alexander Bain, who is often credited with influencing Pierce and James in the development of pragmatism. Holmes read Bain's *Emotions and the Will.*[45]

Anderson makes some perceptive analyses of Holmes's rhetorical strategies. She describes his ethos this way: "He talked more like a man more keenly interested in telling you how he felt about things than in trying to convince or persuade."[46] She identifies the form of Holmes's reasoning as inductive, except when he made swift deductions at the beginning of a speech. His reasoning and his organizational pattern were never explicit. "His ideas are, indeed 'imparted by contagion' rather than by deliberate argument or persuasion. He makes us realize that true rhetoric is art."[47] Finally, the main characteristics of Holmes's style are rich metaphorical expressions, "pungent brevity," spontaneity, and a good ear for the sound of the words.[48]

Anderson's analysis has all the strength and weaknesses of traditional neo-Aristotelian analysis. She takes for granted that the occasional speeches fall within the purview of rhetorical studies but not the judicial opinions. Her interest in the social and political climate of the time is limited to influences on Holmes's ideas (she notes as influences only the pragmatist philosophers Morris R. Cohen and John Dewey, but not Darwin or Malthus). Perhaps most oddly, she never mentions his free speech jurisprudence.

Like Anderson, Richard Posner discusses Holmes's other contributions to American intellectual and cultural history, but with a greater focus on his legal writings. Holmes's contributions to jurisprudence, primarily in *The Common Law* and "The Path of the Law," supplied the "leading ideas for the legal-realist movement (more accurately, the legal-pragmatist movement)": (1) the idea that there is no such thing as a duty to perform a contract; rather, the law communicates clearly the consequences of breaking a contract, allowing the promisor to choose to perform *or* to pay damages; (2) the radical separation of law and morality—with his "bad man" theory of the law, which was connected to (3) the prediction theory of the law—law is what judges will do with a given case, "a fruit of his pragmatic preference for analyzing law in terms of consequences rather than of morally charged abstractions such as 'right' and 'duty'"; (4) the conviction that law is concerned with behavior rather than internal states, as manifested in his "reasonable person" theory of negligence, which remains the foundation of modern tort law.[49] Posner thus disagrees with G. Edward White and other recent writers who find little of enduring value in Holmes's jurisprudence.

According to Posner, Holmes's contributions as a Supreme Court justice were (1) the opposition to the use of the due process clause of the Fourteenth Amendment to prevent social and economic experimentation by the states; (2) his evolutionary notion of the Constitution—"it should not be allowed to kill the living polity in obeisance to the dead hand of the past";[50] (3) his crafting of the modern notion of free speech; (4) his challenge to the idea that the Supreme Court was free to disregard common law decisions of state courts in "diversity of citizenship" cases, a position that was confirmed in the *Erie* decision shortly after his death; (5) his role in establishing the principle that state prisoners convicted in violation of the Constitution could obtain a remedy via federal habeas corpus (in his dissent in *Frank v. Mangum* and in his majority opinion in *Moore v. Dempsey*).

Posner's most provocative comment about Holmes's place in American cultural and intellectual history points to his contributions as a distinctly *modern* thinker, like Nietzsche, Heidegger, Kafka, Gide, Sartre, the later Wittgenstein, and Richard Rorty, all of whom were "concerned with the personal and social implications of taking seriously the definite possibility that man is the puny product of an unplanned series of natural shocks having no tincture of the divine, and they have been suspicious of efforts to smuggle in God by the back door (perhaps by renaming him Progress, or Science, or Technology, or History, or the Class Struggle) in order to recreate the certitude and the sense of direction that Christianity had provided."[51] In perhaps his most controversial comment about Holmes, Posner contends that "solemn moralizers will never appreciate Holmes." His judicial opinions, particularly *Lochner v. New York* and *Buck v. Bell*, are masterpieces of rhetorical skill, and that was Holmes's offense, "[T]o those whose bent is strongly ethical—a common American tendency, puritanism and philistinism being salient features of our culture—the aesthetic conception of rhetoric is not only unworthy but insidious, a seductive art at the disposal equally of good and evil."[52] Posner adds a valuable insight into Holmes's rhetorical practice and rhetorical philosophy through his "bad man's theory of rhetoric" that parallels Holmes's "bad man theory of the law," centering on explaining and predicting the effects of rhetorical strategies rather than engaging in moral evaluation. I will discuss Posner's provocatively "amoral" rhetorical criticism of *Lochner v. New York* and *Buck v. Bell* later in this essay.

The heavy criticism of Holmes by recent legal scholars, especially Grant Gilmore and G. Edward White, reflects a one-sided focus on his judicial opinions and legal treatises to the neglect of his epideictic oratory. Posner rightly directs our attention to Holmes's creativity as a kind of materialist mystic searching for a way to live a full life after the death of God. One neglected figure in American intellectual history who may help clarify Holmes's distinctive philosophical stance is George Santayana, the Spanish-American philosopher who taught for many years at Harvard. Santayana, like Holmes, attempted to develop a theory of knowledge, ethics, and aesthetics on an atheistic and materialistic basis. Holmes refers to Santayana's works quite frequently in his letters to Pollock and Laski. We know that he was reading Santayana's *Life of Reason* at the time of the *Lochner* case, that he wrote Santayana a fan letter after the publication of *Winds of Doctrine,* and that he considered Santayana's philosophy as closest to his own.[53] Santayana shared with Holmes an antipathy to logic: "No syllogism is needed to persuade us to eat, no prophecy of happiness to teach us to love. . . . Reason is significant in action only because it has begun by taking, so to speak, the body's side."[54] He articulated an essentially aesthetic view of reasoning and ethics: morality as a "desired harmony between human beings and the natural conditions of their lives";[55] belief as a product of "animal faith," the "can't help's" that enable one to act in the midst of uncertainty;[56] a materialist mysticism centered on the eternal essences created by religion, art, and science as cultural forms;[57] and, finally, a strong sense of the importance of patriotism ("The object of patriotism is in truth something ideal, a moral entity definable only by the ties which a man's imagination and reason can at any moment recognise. If he has insight and depth of feeling he will perceive that what deserves his loyalty is the entire civilisation to which he owes his spiritual life and into which that life will presently flow back, with whatever new elements he may have added").[58] It is particularly Holmes's patriotism, as expressed in his ceremonial orations, that is foreign to the value system of recent scholars.

Holmes's identification with American values raises the issue of his ethos. Robert Ferguson helps us make sense of Holmes's crafting of his ethos in his judicial opinions. Ferguson was severely critical of Holmes in *Law and Letters in American Culture,* where he criticized Holmes for creating a narrowly specialized view of the law, a view "that no early American lawyer could have understood. . . . The antebellum lawyer addressed the people and used much the same language at the bar, from the bench, and behind the podium."[59] Holmes, however, wrote for what he once welcomed as "the little army of specialists." Holmes's influence on modern law would be "a deliberate rejection of comprehensive ideas and a corresponding loss in communicative power. Legal knowledge in the twentieth century would reach only the few; it would have less and less to do with America's general search for self-expression."[60]

In "Holmes and the Judicial Figure," however, Ferguson emphasizes the rhetorical nature of American judging. Judges, "alone in American officialdom, explain every action with a distinct and individual writing, which then becomes the measure of their performance. They are, in consequence, practicing literary craftsmen in ways that executive leaders and legislators are not. . . . The judicial opinion, like every other written text, thrives on the integration of ideas within a volatile series of choices about persona, point of view, description, narration, style, tone, symbol, and so on."[61]

Ferguson analyzes three of Holmes's opinions, concluding that Holmes is a master of the seeming incongruity between judicial review and democracy: "Judicial discourse is a tribal rite that reaffirms when properly rendered and perceived. The warrior-magician knows this and more. An always distinct clarity in action turns Justice Holmes into the perfect cultural totem—a venerated object that serves among a people as the emblem of ancestral connection and continuing cohesion." Holmes, for all his emphasis on specialization, "is committed to the belief that ruler and ruled must meet in a crucial moment of intellectual comprehension. . . . He reaches for the largest audience, and he insists upon a connection between professional knowledge and general explanation."[62] Holmes crafted an image of the ideal judge, perhaps best captured in the Charles Hopkinson portrait of Holmes, but also found in Catherine Drinker Bowen's semifictionalized biography, in the film *Magnificent Yankee,* and in the children's book *Mr. Justice Holmes* by Clara Ingram Judson. There are two statements in Judson's book that summarize well Holmes's public image among New Deal liberals:

> His outstanding contribution was in showing that law is not a dull, static thing, but experimental, fluid, realistic. His courage and faith and human understanding and the splendid language of his opinions still remain an inspiration on the bench of the highest court of the United States, where he served with honor for thirty years.[63]
>
> He brought to his work a keen intelligence, a shrewdness, a wide range of knowledge, a lively wit, a lofty vision—and a kind and honest heart. With the passing of years, the fame of Mr. Justice Holmes has steadily grown. His genius with the written word has attracted countless readers of his letters and speeches and opinions, and has helped to place him high among the nation's heroes. He is honored as a wise philosopher, an honest judge, and a great man.[64]

To summarize, Anderson, Posner, and Ferguson together create a well-rounded view of Holmes's rhetorical stance: his logos as a materialist mystic; his pathos as a master of rhetorical strategy and the patriotic appeal; and his ethos as the ideal American judge. His rhetorical stance parallels important developments in the political and legal culture of progressivism: the search for value in a time of secularization, the effort to redefine the American nation after the crises of Civil War and Reconstruction, and the rapidly developing importance of law as tool of social reform. I now turn to specific case studies of Holmes's rhetorical mastery, beginning with his epideictic oratory.

Holmes's Epideictic Orations

The noted literary critic Edmund Wilson has praised Holmes for being part of the "chastening of American prose style" that occurred after the Civil War.[65] Holmes thought highly of his own speeches. He sent a copy of the first collection of his speeches to Walt Whitman, who answered him: "When I came from the country yesterday, dear Judge Holmes, there greeted me that white little book with contents like the Puritan which it describes, . . . full of a high & mystical beauty."[66]

The oratorical form most foreign to current tastes is the nineteenth-century epideictic oration. Even rhetorical critics such as Edwin Black (who should know better) tend to confine it to the margins of the oratorical canon.[67] Robert Hariman writes that a "canyon of incomprehension divides the mentalities of the late twentieth century and the 'Golden Age' of American oratory."[68] And yet through a careful examination of "how the speech addresses a complex situation and organizes conflicting social goods through the artful interplay of conventional assurance, unspoken assertion, and distinctive restatement, one can discern how the language of the social text actually operates as a means for managing contingency and negotiating conflict."[69] It is at first a bit surprising that Holmes, the master of the ironic aperçu and the cynical puncturer of legal myths, should be so accomplished an epideictic orator, but his remarkable command of language and emotion was as evident in his speeches as in his judicial opinions.

Epideictic oratory at its best fuses the resources of language, a range of "fitting" emotions, and the ideals and virtues of the audience. In its original Greek meaning (*epideixis*), it is a "display" of the resources of language and imagery, often more "visual" than other oratorical forms, culminating in a series of tableaux. It makes fully public what may at first be a set of private emotions: hopes, fears, regrets, longings. It is also a display of a speaker's claim to *represent* a particular culture, time, and place. The epideictic orator's ambition is to become what Emerson called a "Representative Man."[70]

The rhetorical action in an epideictic oration is accomplished through a fitting movement of images and emotions, which evoke a natural rhythm. This rhythm may include negative emotions, but it culminates in a kind of purgation of them, usually in a set of sublime or transcendent images. In his analyses of the Romantic crisis poem, the literary critic Harold Bloom has demonstrated how particular tropes, poetic images, and psychological mechanisms of defense are united in a distinctive poetic "crossing."[71] Much successful epideictic oratory can be read in terms of this tripartite unity of trope, image, and emotional defense. In an earlier essay on Lincoln's second inaugural address, I found that the speech moved from flat irony to a height of religious and political transcendence, the "American Sublime."[72] Holmes's speeches typically follow a pattern similar to the Lincoln speech, although with a more ironic or reductive twist. A typical Holmesian "movement" of images and ideas is as follows:

1. Irony or reversal of fortune; a "swerve" away from what might be an anticipated beginning for the topic
2. A metonymic reduction: an acknowledgment of the insignificance of the topic in the larger scheme of things or (as in "The Path of the Law") a startling diminishment of the heroic claims of the subject matter
3. Another reversal: limiting the reduction by casting the audience's perceptions (sometimes auditory, sometimes visual) to a sublime moment: "an echo of the infinite," the glimpse of an "unfathomable process," " a hint of the universal law" ("The Path of the Law," 1895); "to be not merely a necessary but a willing instrument in working out the inscrutable end [of the universe]" (speech at Brown University, 1897); "But then I remembered the faith that I partly have expressed, faith in a universe not measured by our fears, a universe that has thought and more than thought inside of it, and as I gazed, after the sunset and above the electric lights there shone the stars" ("Law and the Court," speech to Harvard Law School Association of New York, 1913) [73] The conclusions always express what Dorothy Anderson calls the theme of the "unimaginable whole." Holmes's sublime images of height and depth counter the reductive cynicism that is the perennial temptation of the skilled professional. They also were particularly fitting responses to the widespread loss of religious faith among the educated classes in the Progressive Era.

"MEMORIAL DAY"

"Memorial Day" was delivered on 30 May 1884, at Keene, New Hampshire, before John Sedgwick Post No. 4, Grand Army of the Republic. This was Holmes's first important public address outside the law; he had the speech printed and sent copies to the Boston newspapers.[74] As George Frederickson writes in his remarkable study *The Inner Civil War*, a distinct shift in the cultural meaning of the Civil War took place in the 1880s among both Northerners and Southerners. There was increased observance of Memorial Day during this time, but it was essentially nonideological. Holmes had come out of the Civil War with a deep skepticism about political ideas. He had "substituted a stoical acceptance of nature and the universe for a belief in Divine Providence."[75] His relativism led to an endorsement of all beliefs that led to "the heroic fighting qualities" of "strenuousness and courage."[76] This praise of the military virtues as distinct from the political ideologies that drove the conflict was very appealing to this new mood among the public.

The introduction of "Memorial Day" begins in irony.[77] Holmes says that the speech is an answer to the question, Why do we still keep Memorial Day? He promises an answer "which should command the assent of those who do not share our memories" (4).

His metonymic, or reductive, move occupies the next few paragraphs. He declines to celebrate military victory or the political ideals that led to the conflict. Instead, he says that the experience of battle "taught its lesson even to those who came into the field" bitterly disposed against the other side: "You could not stand up day after day in those indecisive contests where overwhelming victory was impossible because neither side would run as they ought when beaten, without getting at last something of the same brotherhood for the enemy that the north pole of a magnet has for the south—each working in an opposite sense to the other, but each unable to get along without the other" (5). Even now, the "soldiers of the war need no explanations; they can join in commemorating a soldier's death with feelings not different in kind, whether he fell toward them or by their side" (5). For those who do not share "our" memories, the occasion may be like the Fourth of July: "It celebrates and solemnly reaffirms from year to year a national act of enthusiasm and faith. It embodies in the most impressive form our belief that to act with enthusiasm and faith is the condition of acting greatly"(6). Both sides felt deeply that "a man ought to take part in the war." This was not "simply the requirement of a local majority that their neighbors should agree with them." The feeling was right on both sides. "I think that, as life is action and passion, it is required of a man that he should share the passion and action of his time at peril of being judged not to have lived" (6–7).

The "use of this day is obvious." Holmes says that he cannot argue a man into a desire, although desire can be imparted "by contagion. Feeling begets feeling, and great feeling begets great feeling. We can hardly share the emotions that make this day to us the most sacred day of the year, and embody them in ceremonial pomp, without in some degree imparting them to those who come after us. I believe from the bottom of my heart that our memorial halls and statues and tablets, the tattered flags of our regiments gathered in the State-houses, and this day with its funeral march and decorated graves, are worth more to our young men by way of chastening and inspiration than the monuments of another hundred years of peaceful life could be" (7).

But, even if the day is forgotten, "it is enough for us that to us this day is dear and sacred. Accidents may call up the events of the war. You see a battery of guns go by at a trot, and for a moment you are back at White Oak Swamp, or Antietam, or on the Jerusalem Road. You hear a few shots fired in the distance, and for an instant your heart stops as you say to yourself, The skirmishers are at it, and listen for the long roll of fire from the main line" (8).

This heightening of the emotional excitement is immediately followed by a descent into the somber recollection of the presence of the dead. "For one hour, twice a year at least . . . the dead come back and live with us." He describes them: a "fair-haired lad, a lieutenant," dead at the battle of Ball's Bluff, of whom he heard the doctor say, "He was a beautiful boy." He caught the eye of another youthful lieutenant as the advance at Glendale began. They saluted each other, and when Holmes glanced his way again, he was gone. Also, Holmes added: "I see the brother of the last—the flame of genius and daring in his face—as he rode before us into the wood of Antietam, out of which came only dead and deadly wounded men" (9). He compares the men of his memory to Vandyke's portraits of those who fell in the civil wars of England: "High breeding, romantic chivalry—we who have seen these men can never believe that the power of money or the enervation of pleasure has put an end to them. We know that life may still be lifted into poetry and lit with spiritual charm" (9–10). The men were "the Puritans of our day. For the Puritan still lives in New England, thank God!" (10).

One person [Henry Abbott] is "always present to my mind." "I observed him in every kind of duty, and never in all the time that I knew him did I see him fail to choose that alternative of conduct which was most disagreeable to himself. He was indeed a Puritan in all his virtues, without the Puritan austerity; for, when duty was at an end, he who had been the master and leader became the chosen companion in every pleasure that a man might honestly enjoy" (11). Holmes depicts "the awful spectacle of his advance alone with his company in the streets of Fredericksburg." When Abbott died, "his death seemed to end a portion of our life also" (12).

G. Edward White, with his penchant for psychoanalyzing Holmes, notes that his depiction of the advance of his friend Henry Abbott to the head of his company in the streets of Fredericksburg is misleading, since Holmes was sick in the hospital with dysentery at the time. The speech is thus a kind of self-reproach for having missed "the battle that produced Abbott's legendary bravery."[78] White's conclusion seems a bit much; what is interesting to the rhetorician is Holmes's skill at portraiture here, an essential component of the commemorative oration.

Part of the cultural expectation of the time included a reinforcing of standard gender roles: We do not think only of the dead but also "those still living whose sex forbade them to offer their lives, but who gave instead their happiness" (13). One was a benefactress to the poor, another taught her children well. "The story of these and of their sisters we must pass in reverent silence" (13). He then recites a poem by one "of their own sex."

Solemnity yields to joy in the recognition that we can still meet our companions who survived. But we do not deceive ourselves: "We attribute no special merit to a man for having served when all were serving. We know that, if the armies of our war did anything worth remembering, the credit belongs not mainly to the individuals who did it, but to average human nature" (14). And we cannot live in the past: "we admit that, if we would be worthy of the past, we must find new fields for action or thought, and make for ourselves new careers" (15). Still, this generation that fought has been set apart: "Through our great good fortune, in our youth our hearts were touched with fire. It was given to us to learn at the outset that life is a profound and passionate thing. . . . But, above all, we have learned that whether a man accepts from Fortune her spade, and will look downward and dig, or from Aspiration her axe and cord, and will scale the ice, the one and only success which it is his to command is to bring to his work a mighty heart" (15).

He concludes on a note of mystic reverie: "Such hearts—ah me, how many!—were stilled twenty years ago; and to us who remain behind is left this day of memories. . . . Year after year lovers wandering under the apple boughs and through the clover and deep grass are surprised with sudden tears as they see black veiled figures stealing through the morning to a soldier's grave" (15).

While tempted to remain in this mood of sadness, Holmes continues, "But grief is not the end of all. I seem to hear the funeral march become a paean. I see beyond the forest the moving banners of a hidden column. Our dead brothers still live for us, and bid us think of life, not death—of life to which in their youth they lent the passion and glory of the spring. As I listen, the great chorus of life and joy begins again, and amid the awful orchestra of seen and unseen powers and destinies of good and evil our trumpets sound once more a note of daring, hope, and will" (16).

The control over the movement of ideas and emotions is flawless. The metaphors are striking: "awful orchestra," "hearts touched with fire." The emotions of grief, gratitude, and mystical yearning are juggled carefully. Only the reference to women seems jarring to present-day ears. The "portraits" represent a powerful strategy for enabling an audience not present to identify with the dead. He unites "everyone"—Northerner and Southerner, soldier and civilian, man and woman—in a single community. Conspicuous by absence, of course, is the black slave, who was to come to pay the price for national reunion during this time of cultural redefinition of the Civil War. Holmes's indifference to African-American civil rights would remain a virtual constant in his judicial career, with one or two rare exceptions.[79] When Holmes revisited the theme of "Memorial Day" twelve years later he continued to refine his almost Nietzschean—or, better perhaps, almost Roman—adulation of the military virtues.[80]

"THE SOLDIER'S FAITH"

"The Soldier's Faith" was delivered on Memorial Day, 30 May 1895, at a meeting sponsored by the graduating class of Harvard University.[81] It was published, evidently against Holmes's wishes, by the *Harvard Graduates Magazine* in December 1895 and was widely discussed in the press. Holmes complained to Sir Frederick Pollock that his views were misrepresented in these accounts as imperialistic and warmongering: "Fancy my speech of last Memorial Day being treated as a jingo document! Greatly to my disgust it was put over in the Harvard Magazine and only came out a few days ago. I quarreled with the editors about it in the summer, but now it seems to some of the godly as if I were preaching a doctrine of blood!"[82] Theodore Roosevelt loved the speech, which may have laid the groundwork for Roosevelt's later appointment of Holmes to the Supreme Court. He wrote to Henry Cabot Lodge, "By Jove, that speech of Holmes's was fine."[83]

"The Soldier's Faith" unites the Holmesian themes of the unknowable Whole, the need to act despite uncertainty, the inevitability of struggle, and the importance of patriotism. As White writes, "When one considers 'The Soldier's Faith' in terms of Holmesian metaphysics, the address becomes more than a jingoistic tract. Holmes was not glorifying conquest and brutality and slaughter, but rather juxtaposing them against the 'heroism' of stoic exposure to death in pursuit of 'gentlemanly' ideals."[84]

The speech begins with an ironic portrait: "Any day in Washington Street, when the throng is greatest and busiest, you may see a blind man playing a flute. I suppose that someone hears him. Perhaps also my pipe may reach the heart of some passer in the crowd." The crowd passing by no longer thinks much of occasions such as Memorial Day: "war is out of fashion, and the man who commands the attention of his fellows is the man of wealth. Commerce is the great power. . . . Moralists and philosophers . . . declare that war is wicked, foolish, and soon to disappear" (73).

Yet the combined efforts of "philanthropists, labor reformers, and men of fashion" result in a society "in which they may be comfortable and may shine without much trouble or danger." Holmes thus reframes the bloody contest between labor and capital in the Gilded Age as but part of a larger valorization of individualism and comfort, "by a rootless self-seeking search for a place where the most enjoyment can be had at the least cost." Scientists, socialists, and antivivisectionists are alike in their rejection of suffering and pain, and advanced writers point out "in story and in verse how hard it is to be wounded in the battle of life, how terrible, how unjust it is that any one should fail."[85] For Holmes, however, "the struggle for life is the order of the world, at which it is vain to repine." Despite the fact that all creeds have collapsed and the meaning of the universe is unknowable, "there is one thing I do not doubt, that no man who lives in the same world with most of us can doubt, and that is that the faith is true and adorable which leads a soldier to throw away his life in obedience to a blindly accepted duty, in a cause which he little understands, in a plan of campaign of which he has no notion, under tactics of which he does not see the use" (76).

In a remarkable passage using the figure of anaphora (Martin Luther King Jr. uses a similar pattern in the center of "Letter from Birmingham Jail"), Holmes captures the pain and repetitiveness of the soldier's life:

> If you have been in line, suppose on Tremont Street Mall, ordered to wait and to do nothing, and have watched the enemy bring their guns to bear upon you down a gentle slope like that from Beacon Street, have seen the puff of the firing, have felt the burst of the spherical case-shot as it came toward you, have heard and seen the shrieking fragments go tearing through your company, and have known that the next or the next shot carries your fate; if you have advanced in line and have seen ahead of you the spot which you must pass where the rifle bullets are striking; if you have ridden by night at a walk toward the blue line of fire at the dead angle of Spottsylvania, where for twenty-four hours the soldiers were fighting on the two sides of an earthwork, and in the morning the dead and dying lay piled in a row six deep, and as you rode have heard the bullets splashing in the mud and earth about you; if you have been on the picketline at night in a black and unknown wood, have heard the spat of the bullets upon the trees, and as you moved have felt your foot slip upon a dead man's body; if you have had a blind fierce gallop against the enemy, with your blood up and a pace that left no time for fear— if, in short, as some, I hope many, who hear me have known, you have known the vicissitudes of terror and of triumph in war, you know that there is such a thing as the faith I spoke of. (77)

Holmes then hearkens back to the dark visions of the "children of North," as memorialized in the works of the Beowulf poet, Milton, Dürer, Rembrandt, Schopenhauer, Turner, and Tennyson—the vision of the warrior gaining honor in death. He says, "War, when you are at it, is horrible and dull. It is only when time has passed that you see that its message was divine." And this message is something we need in "this snug, over-safe corner of the world." "We need it in this time of individualist negations, with its literature of French and American humor, revolting at discipline, loving fleshpots, and denying that anything is worthy of reverence,—in order that we may remember all that buffoons forget." He sees a similar message in the dueling of students at Heidelberg, and even in polo players: "If once in a while in our rough riding a neck is broken, I regard it, not as a waste, but as a price well paid for the breeding of race fit for headship and command" (80–81).[86]

Holmes concludes with the usual gesture of muted mysticism, reciting a "little song sung by a warlike people on the Danube," "a song of oblivion and peace" (83). If the speech was not, ultimately, as White writes, a "jingoistic" document, it does represent part of a continuing reflection on the nature of public virtue in the Gilded Age, a search for a resolution to what writers in the late twentieth century would come to call a "crisis of masculinity." Despite the fact that the law appeared to many as yet another "snug, over-safe corner of the world," as White writes, Holmes was to invest legal professionalism with the same intensity that he brought to the commemoration of the Civil War dead.

"THE PATH OF THE LAW"

Oliver Wendell Holmes delivered "The Path of the Law" at the dedication of a new building at the Boston University School of Law on 8 January 1897. The speech was published in the *Harvard Law Review* in March 1897.[87] He did not include the speech in his *Occasional Speeches*, his "chance utterances of faith and doubt," as he called them.[88] He did, however, include it in the 1920 edition of his *Collected Legal Papers*. Holmes had tried to write systematic legal theory in *The Common Law*, but he had concluded that such system building was a waste of time. Nonetheless, the speech has continued to attract scholarly interest. A conference on the speech was held at the University of Iowa in 1997. In March 1997 *Harvard Law Review* reprinted the speech with commentary by the most important legal scholars of the present day, joining an already impressive bibliography of scholarly articles on the subject. This is an unusual amount of attention to be paid to a ceremonial speech.

The primary interest of legal scholars has been in the conceptual unity of Holmes's philosophy of law. Holmes advances three controversial theses in the speech: first, to know the law means to be able to *predict* what courts will do; second, to know the law requires a radical separation between law and morality, treating the law as a "bad man" does, enabling a rational calculation of whether punishment will occur for certain actions; finally, there is no logic of the law, no universal system of axioms from which legal truth can be derived; judges legislate, and we will have better law when they recognize that fact and learn cognate disciplines such as economics that will make for better decisions. Scholars continue to debate whether Holmes was a utilitarian or a pragmatist, whether he anticipated the field of law-and-economics, or whether he was simply an incoherent thinker, more interested in promoting his public image through his witty aperçus than in articulating a philosophy of law.

My argument, however, is that the speech is interesting precisely for its rhetorical purposes: the constitution of a particular kind of community for its audience. "The Path of the Law" is a remarkable specimen of epideictic oratory, one that transcends the usual "sentimental style" of nineteenth-century speech making. It is an essential moment in the rhetorical redefinition of the law during the Progressive period. "The Path of the Law" begins by proclaiming that the study of law is not a "mystery," but it concludes, as Holmes's speeches always do, by drawing the audience's attention "higher," to a glimpse of truths that cannot be grasped by mere mortals. Luban calls this a "weird" conclusion in light of the dismissal of "mystery" in the introduction, but this sort of paradoxical play on words is essential to Holmes's purpose.[89] Much like Stanley Fish's characterization of Plato's *Phaedrus* as a "self-consuming artifact," Holmes's "The Path of the Law" hopes to constitute an audience able to sustain a sense of vocation in the midst of paradox and uncertainty.[90]

For purposes of analysis I will first summarize the arguments of the speech, drawing on Thomas C. Grey's useful labels for the main divisions.[91] As we shall see, the overall movement of the images and conceptual figures in the speech follows the irony-metonymy-sublime movement I identified earlier.

Introduction

Holmes frames the study of law in terms of an ironic opposition between mystery and science, concretion and abstraction, past and future.

The study of law is not a mystery, but a well-known profession. The object of our study is prediction, "the prediction of the incidence of the public force through the instrumentality of the courts" (391). The means of our study are the "sibylline leaves" of the legal reports, treatises, and statutes of the United States and England, "extending back for six hundred years." The effort of legal thought is to generalize these "oracles" into a system. Such a system retains only the "final analyses and abstract universals": "The reason why a lawyer does not mention that his client wore a white hat when he made a contract, while Mrs. Quickly would be sure to dwell upon it along with the parcel gilt goblet and the sea-coal fire, is that he foresees that the public force will act the same way whatever his client had upon his head." Holmes immediately draws an analogy between irrelevant concrete details and "the evil effects of the confusion between legal and moral ideas." The lawyer should not think of "the right or the duty as something existing apart from the breach, to which certain sanctions are added afterward" (391).

He previews the purpose and structure of the speech: "I wish, if I can, to lay down some first principles for the study of this body of dogma or systematized prediction which we call the law, for men who want to use it as the instrument of their business to enable them to prophesy in their turn, and, as bearing upon the study, I wish to point out an ideal which as yet our law has not attained" (392).

Part 1: "The Limits of the Law"

Holmes's strategy is to change the typical "container" of legal studies—a metonymic reduction accomplished by the dissociation of law and ethics.[92]

Holmes wants a "businesslike" understanding of the law. In order to attain such an understanding, one must dispel the confusion between "morality and law." He anticipates the objection that he is speaking the "language of cynicism." On the contrary, for Holmes, "[t]he law is the witness and external deposit of our moral life. Its history is the history of the moral development of the race. The practice of it, in spite of popular jests, tends to make good citizens and good men." Holmes's emphasis on the difference between law and morals is made for one end only: "learning and understanding the law." He summarizes part 1 with the notorious image of "the bad man theory" of the law: "If you want to know the law and nothing else, you must look at it as a bad man, who cares only for the material consequences which such knowledge enables him to predict, not as a good one, who finds his reasons for conduct, whether inside the law or outside of it, in the vaguer sanctions of conscience." The limits to law are not coextensive with any system of morals; sometimes it may simply have to do with the "habits of a particular people at a certain time" (393).

Part 2: "Not Logic but Experience"

Holmes continues to dissociate law and morality and introduces a second dissociation: logic and experience as different forms of rationality. Experience, Holmes's preferred form of rationality, in turn exists in the realm of the external, of observable behavior. The "inside" is the irrelevant realm of logic, ethics, and the search for motives.

The "bad man theory" entails a theory of law as prediction of what courts will do. The law is not a system of reason, a deduction from "principles of ethics or admitted axioms." Our "friend the bad man does not care two straws for the axioms and deductions," but does want to know what the courts are likely to do: "The prophecies of what the courts will do in fact, and nothing more pretentious, are what I mean by the law."

It is counterproductive to analyze such predictions in terms of morality. There really is no difference "between being fined and being taxed a certain sum for doing a certain thing." It doesn't matter from the standpoint of the law if the act is described in terms of praise or blame. "You see how the vague circumference of the notion of duty shrinks when we wash it with cynical acid and expel everything except the object of our study, the operations of the law." Holmes then analyzes the confusion between law and morality in the common law of contracts and torts. For example, "The duty to keep a contract at common law means a prediction that you must pay damages if you do not keep it—and nothing else" (394).

Part 3: "The Ideal of Instrumental Reason"

Holmes criticizes the use of history and continuity with precedent as the normative and rational basis of the law. He articulates a "Progressive," forward-looking view of the law. He thus rejects the law/politics dissociation emphasized by the legal formalists.

In addition to the confusion between law and morality, a second fallacy about law is "that the only force at work in the development of the law is logic." It is true that everything in the universe is part of a logic of cause and effect, but we should not let that fact lead us to "the notion that a given system, ours, for instance, can be worked out like mathematics from some general axioms of conduct" (396).

Legal training is certainly a training in logic, and part of the appeal of logic is that it flatters "that longing for certainty and for repose which is in every human mind. But certainty generally is illusion, and repose is not the destiny of man." Beneath logical form is always a judgment about "the relative worth and importance of competing legislative grounds." All a decision can do is "embody the preference of a given body in a given time and place" (397).

The problem with judges at the present time is that they have "failed adequately to recognize their duty of weighing considerations of social advantage." They are not at all conscious of the fact that they are imposing economic doctrines on the public that prevailed "about fifty years ago." When the "comfortable classes" of the community began to be afraid of socialism, they began to look to the courts for protection, since they could control the courts easier than the legislatures. The courts are deluded about their objectivity. If lawyers were instead trained "to consider more definitely and explicitly the social advantage on which the rule they lay down must be justified, they sometimes would hesitate where now they are confident, and see that really they were taking sides upon debatable and often burning questions" (398).

In addition to the consideration of social advantage, a useful addition to legal analysis is historical research. If we want to understand a rule, we can trace it back to England and even to the "German forests." But the main purpose of studying history is to encourage "an enlightened scepticism." History eventually will need to yield to more rigorous, social-scientific legal analysis: "For the rational study of the law the black-letter man may be the man of the present, but the man of the future is the man of statistics and master of economics. It is revolting to have no better reason for a rule of law than that so it was laid down in the time of Henry IV" (399).

Holmes summarizes this section by encouraging his audience "to follow the existing body of dogma into its highest generalization by the help of jurisprudence; next, to discover from history how it has come to be what it is; and, finally, so far as you can, to consider the ends which the several rules seek to accomplish, the reasons why those ends are desired, what is given up to gain them, and whether they are worth the price" (404).

Conclusion

Holmes compensates for the irony and reductiveness by constructing a mystical image of the ethos of the legal professional.

The most important thing, finally, is imagination, the command of ideas. He encourages his audience to read Kant and Descartes, to understand how philosophers often have more practical force on the lives of men than statesmen or generals. "We cannot all be Descartes or Kant, but we all want happiness. And happiness, I am sure from having known many successful men, cannot be won simply by being counsel for great corporations and having an income of fifty thousand dollars. An intellect great enough to win the prize needs other food beside success. The remoter and more general aspects of the law are those which give it universal interest. It is through them that you not only become a great master in your calling, but connect your subject with the universe and catch an echo of the infinite, a glimpse of its unfathomable process, a hint of the universal law" (406).

There are apparent contradictions in the speech, as numerous commentators have argued. The positivism of the "bad man" theory meshes poorly with the claim that the law is the "witness and external deposit" of our moral life. The rejection of mystery in the introduction hardly prepares the audience for the mystic notes of the conclusion, something that Grey says seems "tacked on, too little too late."[93] The connection between the life of the mind and the life of action seems to be, as David Luban puts it, "a mess."[94] It is not clear if the "bad man" is a typical corporation client (assuming that the discussion of "happiness" in the conclusion is carefully linked to the earlier discussion), or if he is simply an ironic figure for "homo economicus," rationally calculating costs and benefits. It is also not clear if judges are to be followers of the "bad man" and "prediction" theory; if so, how are their duties distinct from an attorney's?

Other commentators have attempted to explain the speech's seeming contradictions. In the only analysis of the speech by a rhetorician, Joan I. Schwarz identifies the key enthymemes in the speech and argues that the speech suffers from an incoherent shift from an exhortative strategy (in Edwin Black's terms: the law IS this way) to an argumentative synthesis or transcendence strategy identifying the ideal of the law, thus glossing over inconsistencies between his "positivist" and "policy science" views of the law.[95] William W. Fisher III argues that the speech offers three conflicting perspectives on American law: law as an instrument of business, law as an instrument of rational legislation, and law as a repository of wisdom.[96] Richard D. Parker contrasts three different personas crafted by Holmes: the "cynic," the "idealist," and the "romantic."[97]

Richard Posner characterizes the speech as "prophecy" about American law that is coming to be true: the growth of economics in the law, the unmasking of legal pretensions by the legal realists, and the deprofessionalization of the law into something more like business.[98] Robert W. Gordon, however, sees a unified purpose. He characterizes the "bad man" image as a "deliberate provocation," a device designed to shake Holmes's audience out of its complacency. Holmes's "disillusioned, de-moralized view leads on not to cynicism but to glory," the glory of the "tough-minded scientific naturalist" able, like a Stoic hero, to look the brute facts of reality in the face. "He discards the traditional roles for lawyers as seekers of justice, social mediators, and curators of the legal framework," substituting the role of "consequentialist policy analyst," doing little more than "temper[ing] the ambitions of reform movements." Like Posner, although less enthusiastically, Gordon sees Holmes as setting forth a path for a new conception of professional identity, one that would move progressive thinkers, New Deal liberals, and, most recently, practitioners of law-and-economics.[99]

We can read "The Path of the Law" as an epideictic speech in the classical sense: it identifies and commends a community's sense of virtue, it employs a grand style with startling metaphors and "sublime" moments, and it prepares the community constituted by the speech for future moral and political deliberation. Yet Holmes's peculiar loneliness in these years before his appointment comes out clearly as well, for it is not clear that the immediate audience is ready for the message he is presenting, and perhaps the best he could do is "keep them awake," as he wrote to Pollock, and jar them out of their dogmatic slumbers.

The ideal figure constituted by this speech was to come later, in Felix Frankfurter, Harold Laski, Walter Lippmann, and others, all of whom shared Holmes's antiutopianism, his advocacy of legislative supremacy and use of state force to change society, and his cynical distrust of the masses, "who usually like to hear loose-fibred and coarse-grained men drool."[100] Progressives, New Deal liberals, and Cold War realists shared Holmes's stance toward the world, if not the social Darwinist, even Nietzschean principles that he expressed privately.[101] "The Path of the Law" articulates better than any other document in American rhetorical history the dominant ideology of the law in the twentieth century: what William Lewis calls "romantic realism." In Lewis's view, "Legal decisions position the law as an heroic character capable of moderating, regulating and directing social action." Romantic realism paradoxically combines a high-romantic view of the lawyer's vocation with an essential cynical distrust of popular decision making and of the rationality of rhetoric and language.[102] Perhaps the best illustration of Lewis's theory is the conclusion to Holmes's speech "The Law," delivered at the Suffolk Bar Association dinner, 5 February 1885: "When I think . . . of the law, I see a princess mightier than she who once wrought at Bayeux, eternally weaving into her web dim figures of the ever-lengthening past—figures too dim to be noticed by the idle, too symbolic to be interpreted except by her pupils, but to the discerning eye disclosing every painful step and every world-shaking contest by which mankind has worked and fought its way from savage isolation to organic social life. . . . But when for the first time I was called to speak on an occasion as this, the only thought that could come into my mind, the only feeling that could fill my heart, the only words that could spring to my lips, were a hymn to her in whose name we are met here to-night—to our mistress, the Law."[103]

If there is a critical judgment to be made of Holmes's ideology in "The Path of the Law," it may lie in discerning the contours of what Philip Wander calls "The Third Persona," or the audience ignored or marginalized by the rhetoric.[104] Holmes's ethos is established in the speech through his wit, vivid language, and technical mastery of the law. The second persona, or the ideal auditor called into being by the speech, is very much like the progressive or New Deal lawyers mentioned earlier. The third persona, however, is the democratic public itself, who does not figure in the speech at all, except perhaps in the figure of the "bad man" or "good man" client who comes to the lawyer's office. The tension between the technical expertise of the legal liberal and the "irrational" populist impulses of the American public would come to be a defining characteristic of American liberalism in the next century. But it was Holmes's legal rhetoric in his judicial opinions that was to gain the greatest attention from his future audience.

Elements of Holmes's Judicial Strategy

While Holmes's epideictic speeches are neglected today, his judicial opinions remain the touchstone of eloquence for many jurists. Justice Anthony Kennedy, for example, recently pleaded for a law clerk who could make him sound like Oliver Wendell Holmes.[105] Edmund Wilson writes that Holmes "gave to these short pieces a crystalline form . . . hard and bright. . . . It is Holmes's special distinction— which perhaps makes him unique among judges—that he never dissociates himself from the great world of thought and art, and that all his decisions are written with awareness of both their wider implications and the importance of their literary form. He was not merely a cultivated judge who enjoyed dipping into belles lettres or amusing himself with speculation: he was a real concentrator of thought who had specialized in the law but who was trying to determine man's place, to define his satisfactions and duties, to try to understand what humanity is."[106]

Three rhetorical generalizations can be made about Holmes's opinions. First, he recognized, following his argument in "The Path of the Law," that there is inevitably a policy dimension to judging. Yet he combined this recognition with a conviction of the need to repress his own private ideological positions. Some of the intuitive leaps and supposed failures of legal "craft" in his opinions may serve as defenses against the contradictory position Holmes's philosophy of judging put him in.

Second, the opinions display astonishing brevity, especially in the dissents, with an emphasis on aperçus rather than carefully developed reasoning. Novick puts it this way: "Holmes's opinions had always been easy to read but difficult to understand. They flowed on in a conversational way, but distinct points were difficult to isolate and questions were presented in a kind of mosaic that one took in as a whole. It was an art form peculiar to Holmes." He also notes that Fuller had begun to ask Holmes privately to give more extended explanations in his opinions.[107] G. Edward White makes an interesting point about the brevity: "I think he was attempting to show that in a truly 'hard' case, if you force an extended explanation, that explanation will crumble to pieces on reflection. . . . One's job as a judge becomes to decide—that is what people count on one to do; that is what judges have the power to do where ordinary people do not—and not to agonize about why. Cryptic explanations, then, are intended to cut off thinking about issues that are sufficiently complicated and difficult to benumb the mind. At some point one has to stop thinking and choose."[108]

Third, the brevity helped contribute to what Dudziak calls his "rhetoric of assertion," the implication that it is inconceivable to hold an alternative point of view: "Through the invocation of danger, the identification of a community of believers, and the presentation of opinion as fact, Holmes rhetorically demanded his readers to believe he was right."[109]

Finally, despite Holmes's elitism, he consistently displayed a tendency to reject "lawyerly" language in favor of a fairly direct style. Holmes comments frequently in his letters about his colleagues' efforts to make him adopt a more traditional style—usually employing castration imagery. The tendency to allow clerks to draft opinions has largely done away with the communicative function of the judicial opinion in the United States, as Richard Posner and others have complained.[110]

There is need for a thorough study of the language and strategies in all of Holmes's opinions, a task that may be aided by recent advances in the computerized analysis of style, but such a thorough analysis needs to begin with a careful reading of his most influential opinions.[111]

LOCHNER V. NEW YORK AND THE "LIBERTY OF CONTRACT"

The *Lochner* case has become notorious as a symbol of "judicial activism," largely because of the force of Holmes's dissent. It was widely cited by labor activists and Progressives as an instance where the Court majority invented a mythical "liberty of contract" in order to preserve existing domination of labor by capital. Theodore Roosevelt referred to the decision in his "New Nationalism" speech of 1912 and used it as a justification for the progressive proposal that Congress be allowed to override Supreme Court decisions. Opponents of *Roe v. Wade* have, with some justification, drawn an analogy between the "substantive due process" notion of "right to privacy" advanced by Justice Blackmun with the "liberty of contract" in *Lochner*. Recent scholars have emphasized that the decision "did not introduce a reign of terror for social legislation."[112]

At issue in the case was a New York statute limiting the number of hours a baker could work to sixty per week or ten per day. While it was true that bakers suffered from serious work-related illnesses such as white lung or baker's leg (a swelling caused by standing all day), the case also reflected a conflict between master and journeymen bakers over the control of the workplace. Eileen Scallen has done a rhetorical analysis of Justice Peckham's majority opinion that struck down the statute, describing how he orchestrated the "presence" of the competing interests he was balancing through the use of repetitive structure, dominating metaphor clusters (especially the state as arbitrary parent), and slippery slope arguments resting on parallelism, anaphora, and alliteration for their force.[113] Judge Richard Posner, the chief judge of the Seventh Circuit Court of Appeals, has analyzed the opinion in his *Law and Literature*. Posner's analysis foregrounds some interesting issues in the rhetoric of law, as well as in the implications of Holmes's rhetoric for later constitutional law. I include the full text of Justice Holmes's dissent in order to compare Posner's reading of the opinion with my own.

> I regret sincerely that I am unable to agree with the judgment in this case, and that I think it my duty to express my dissent.
>
> This case is decided upon an economic theory which a large part of the country does not entertain. If it were a question whether I agreed with that theory, I should desire to study it further and long before making up my mind. But I do not conceive that to be my duty, because I strongly believe that my agreement or disagreement has nothing to do with the right of a majority to embody their opinions in law. It is settled by various decisions of this court that state constitutions and state laws may regulate life in many ways which we as legislators might think as injudicious or if you like as tyrannical as this, and which equally with this interfere with the liberty to contract. Sunday laws and usury laws are ancient examples. A more modern one is the prohibition of lotteries. The liberty of the citizen to do as he likes so long as he does not interfere with the liberty of others to do the same, which has been a shibboleth for some well-known writers, is interfered with by school laws, by the Post Office, by every state or municipal institution which takes his money for purposes thought desirable, whether he likes it or not. The Fourteenth Amendment does not enact Mr. Herbert Spencer's Social Statics. The other day we sustained the Massachusetts vaccination law.[114] United States and state statutes and decisions cutting down the liberty contract by way of combination are familiar to this court. Two years ago we upheld the prohibition of sales of stock on margins or for future delivery in the constitution of California.[115] The decision sustaining an eight hour law for miners is still recent.[116] Some of these laws embody convictions or prejudices which judges are likely to share. Some may not. But a constitution is not intended to embody a particular economic theory, whether of paternalism and the organic relation of the citizen to the State or of *laissez faire*. It is made for people of fundamentally differing views, and the accident of our finding certain opinions natural and familiar or novel and even shocking ought not to conclude our judgment upon the question whether statutes embodying them conflict with the Constitution of the United States.
>
> General propositions do not decide concrete cases. The decision will depend on a judgment or intuition more subtle than any articulate major premise. But I think that the proposition just stated, if it is accepted, will carry us far toward the end. Every opinion tends to become a law. I think that the word liberty in the Fourteenth Amendment is perverted when it is held to prevent the natural outcome of a dominant opinion, unless it can be said that the statute proposed would infringe fundamental principles as they have been understood by the traditions of our people and our law. It does not need research to show that no such sweeping condemnation can be passed upon the statute before us. A reasonable man might think it a proper measure on the score of health. Men whom I certainly could not pronounce unreasonable would uphold it as a first installment of a general regulation of the hours of work.

Whether in the latter aspect it would be open to the charge of inequality I think it unnecessary to discuss.[117]

Posner makes five arguments about Holmes's strategies intended to support his overall contention that the opinion is bad law but great rhetoric: "Would the dissent in *Lochner* have received a high grade in a law school examination in 1905? I think not. It is not logically organized, does not join issue sharply with the majority, is not scrupulous in its treatment of the majority opinion or of precedent, is not thoroughly researched, does not exploit the factual record, and is highly unfair to poor old Herbert Spencer. It is not, in short, a good judicial opinion. It is merely the greatest judicial opinion of the last hundred years. To judge it by 'scientific' standards is to miss the point. It is a rhetorical masterpiece, and evidently rhetoric counts in law; otherwise the dissent in *Lochner* would be forgotten."[118]

First, Posner identifies the ethical appeal of Justice Holmes that is established by a "serious and deferential tone" in the first sentence, a rapid change of subject, and a bold statement about the role of economic theory in the majority opinion. Posner writes that the force of this appeal "lies in the assurance with which it is made. It puts the reader on the defensive; dare he question a statement made with a conviction so confident and serene?"[119]

Second, this ethical appeal works because of the high information costs of the audience: "Holmes's method is more effective because in areas where our own knowledge is shaky we tend to take people at their own apparent self-evaluation and thus to give more credence to the confident than to the defensive."[120]

Third, Posner argues that Holmes is being disingenuous by adopting a "simple man" ethical appeal, since he was known to have been quite conversant with laissez-faire economic theory and was sympathetic to it himself.[121]

Fourth, the choice of "Mr Herbert Spencer's Social Statics" as a metonymy for laissez-faire is very concrete and effective.

Finally, Posner notes that when Justice Holmes "finally" introduces evidence he employs it badly. Posner chooses the one bad precedent, the vaccination case, to discuss in the text, arguing that vaccination conveyed an external benefit to those who may catch the disease, while the New York hours law did not. He does say (in a footnote) that the other examples do work.

In short, Holmes's dissent is not a good judicial opinion because of its lack of logical order, its lack of clear opposition to the majority, its sparse research, and its failure to use the factual record effectively in making the argument. In calling it a great judicial opinion, Posner points to its longevity, as well as to its "enchanting rhetoric" with all its "tricks," which have blinded us to the fact that the Supreme Court majority, by striking down laws such as the New York law, probably "made the United States marginally more prosperous than it would otherwise have been."[122]

Now, what is wrong with Posner's reading of the opinion? An examination of Justice Peckham's opinion, as well as Justice Harlan's dissent, reveals that much of Justice Holmes's strategy can be understood only in response to his colleagues as well as in its direction to a larger audience.

First, Posner directs our attention to the simultaneously arrogant yet "plain man" ethos of the introduction. Holmes's strategy reads to me more like an echo of Justice Peckham's own opening move, when he writes, "this is not question of substituting the judgment of the court for that of the legislature," and yet goes on to say, "we do not believe in the soundness of the views which uphold this law."[123] Sir Frederick Pollock commented on Justice Peckham's tone here as not giving credit "to the state legislature for knowing its own business," and as treating it "like an inferior court which has to give proof of its competence."[124]

Second, Holmes's "lack of evidence" for his argument that the majority is using a particular economic theory makes more sense when read against Justice Peckham's attribution of ulterior motives to the New York legislature, where he argues that this is not a public health but rather a labor law.[125] Holmes's seemingly ill-mannered tone toward his brethren must be compared to Justice Peckham's treatment of the New York legislature.

Third, Posner's own structuring of his argument is deeply rhetorical, in his own limited sense. He heightens the weakest part of Holmes's legal reasoning, the supposed weakness of the vaccination analogy, and deals with the strongest part only in a footnote.

Fourth, Posner misidentifies the "simple man" ethical appeal and the rapid, overly authoritative style of the opinion as being appropriate for audiences whose "own knowledge is shaky." The audience for this opinion, however, was not a potted plant. There were multiple audiences addressed by the dissent—some were present, some future, some anticipated, some unanticipated. One audience was the majority, the other, the rest of the minority. Posner never discusses Justice Harlan's dissent, which was much more lawyerly and perhaps freed Holmes to take a different rhetorical path. Harlan's opinion was also the original majority opinion, until one of the justices changed his vote. Thus, the timing of Holmes's dissent is of some interest both to the rhetorician and the legal historian. Another audience consisted of younger legal scholars for whom the *Lochner* decision came to be considered the opening move in the development of legal realism. Surely Justice Holmes knew, however limited his own optimism for social reform, that his words would have some effect on the larger progressive legal and political community. Interestingly, the labor movement itself—an audience for whom the information cost even of reading Justice Holmes's dissent was high, at least by Posner's standards—used the *Lochner* decision for intensifying strike action to gain the eight-hour day.[126]

Holmes's opinions and his close relationship with young Progressives such as Felix Frankfurter led to his increasing adulation by the *New Republic* crowd and by those who would come in time to be called "New Deal liberals." Holmes's constitutive rhetoric created and addressed a community of legal and political professionals who were willing to allow legislative experiments for the common good, who shared Holmes's skepticism about natural law and other moral and epistemological absolutes, and who sought a greater role for the new social sciences in the direction of public policy. It was the free speech opinions that led above all to Holmes's canonization as the "character" of ideal judge.

Holmes's aperçus in the free speech opinions have entered both into the lexicon of First Amendment law and into the public consciousness: "clear and present danger," "the free marketplace of ideas," "no right falsely to shout fire in a crowded theater," "every idea is an incitement," "life is an experiment," "fighting faiths." Scholars continue to argue about the genesis and significance of Holmes's ideas about free speech. What accounts for the seeming shift in his position between *Debs* and *Abrams?* Did Learned Hand, Harold Laski, and others persuade Holmes of the significance of free speech? Did Holmes possess a coherent First Amendment doctrine? Did his "economic" metaphor for free speech construct an inadequate grounding for the role of the First Amendment in a democratic society? My argument in this section is that Holmes's judicial rhetoric was shaped by the audience he had helped call into being, and that his free speech doctrine was and is a workable way of talking about the First Amendment. Holmes's opinions reached out to the widest possible consensus on the nature of free speech as a public good, and they exhibited his recurring willingness to live in the tension between his egalitarian Darwinism and his legal mysticism. In fact, free speech became the preferred site for mediating the claims of the democratic public and the aristocratic field of the law. Despite the Progressives' distrust of judicial review, Holmes carved out a distinctive place for the judicial protection of minority rights, one that was to reach its zenith on the Warren court.

SCHENCK V. UNITED STATES

In June 1917 Congress enacted an espionage and sedition statute, and then followed it in May 1918 with a more restrictive law against communications that displayed disloyalty or sedition.[127] The primary focus of the cases that reached the federal courts under the sedition statutes was on efforts to obstruct the draft. The Supreme Court ultimately upheld six convictions under the act, the first of which was *Schenck v. United States* (1919).[128] Holmes wrote the unanimous opinion of the Court.

Charles Schenck was general secretary of the Socialist Party in Pennsylvania. He was in charge of the party headquarters, which had sent out several thousand leaflets in August 1917 urging resistance to the draft. The leaflet argued that the draft violated the Thirteenth Amendment proscription of involuntary servitude and called for Americans to assert their rights. The leaflets were mailed to men in Philadelphia of draft age. Several recipients complained to the post office. Federal agents raided the Socialist Party offices and seized information related to the case. Schenck was convicted in the U.S. District Court for eastern Pennsylvania on 20 December 1917. He appealed to the Supreme Court, which heard oral arguments on 9–10 January 1919 and issued its decision on 3 March of the same year. The decision was nine to zero against Schenck.[129]

Even though the case was not sufficiently protective of free speech by later standards, it represented a pivotal point in the evolution of the concept of free speech. The law governing sedition up to that point had largely been governed by the "bad tendency" doctrine. Speech or printed matter that had a tendency to appeal to dangerous tendencies in the community could be restricted by the government.[130] In any case, "free speech" in the classic sense was viewed merely as freedom from "previous restraint." Speech could be punished for seditious libel after utterance or publication. As we saw in the *Lochner* case, the preferred notion of "liberty" in legal circles had been "liberty of contract." Part of the missing history of American liberalism has been the fact that the progressive reaction against "liberty of contract" was joined with a generalized reaction against individual rights of any kind. David Rabban argues that John Dewey, Herbert Croly, and other progressive social thinkers were largely indifferent to the rights of dissenters before and during World War I. He writes, "Some of them became active civil libertarians following the war and recognized government as a constant threat to civil liberties. In dramatic contrast to their prewar attacks on constitutional rights as barriers to social reform, they emphasized the centrality of constitutional free speech to the democratic themes they had elaborated before the war."[131] The story of Holmes and the World War I free speech cases is part of a complex process by which progressive thinkers began to shift from "utility talk" to "rights talk."[132]

The first sign of a rethinking of the progressive position came in the opinion of Learned Hand, then a federal district judge in New York, in the case of *Masses Publishing Company v. Patten* (1917). Hand had argued that the "bad tendency" doctrine needed to be replaced by an "objective standard" that takes into account the words uttered and the specific intent to incite crime. Hand, however, was overruled by the Circuit Court of Appeals. Holmes took an intermediate position in his opinion: (1) What is the context?: "the character of every acts depends upon the circumstances in which it is done. . . . The most stringent protection of free speech would not protect a man in falsely shouting fire in a theater and causing a panic"

(52). (2) Is there a "clear and present danger" that the words will bring about a substantive evil? (3) Is the evil one that Congress has a right to prevent?

The *Schenck* decision, other than the phrases "clear and present danger" and "falsely shouting fire in a theater," is not written in the characteristic Holmes style. As Max Lerner notes, Holmes tended to depersonalize his style when writing for the Court as a whole.[133] Holmes begins with a description of the indictment: (1) conspiracy to violate the Espionage Act of 15 June 1917, by attempting to cause insubordination in the armed services; (2) conspiracy "to use the mails for transmission of matter declared to be non-mailable by Title XII, section 2, of the Act of June 15, 1917"; (3) "an unlawful use of the mails for the transmission of the same matter." He then summarizes the arguments of the defendants: "They set up the First Amendment to the Constitution forbidding Congress to make any law abridging the freedom of speech, or of the press, and bringing the case here on that ground have argued some other points of which we must dispose" (49) The tone here is extremely detached. There is no sense of "tragedy" in the decision; that is, Holmes expresses no concern for the particular constitutional right being threatened.

The next paragraph deals with the argument by Schenck and Baer that the evidence was insufficient to prove that they were involved in sending the documents. Holmes refers to the facts that Schenck was in charge of the headquarters from which the documents were sent, and that a record of the minutes of the Executive Committee of the Socialist Party detailed the role of Schenck in arranging for the printing and distribution of the documents. Baer was a member of the Executive Committee as well, and there was evidence that she had taken the minutes of the meeting. Holmes concludes, "The argument as to the sufficiency of the evidence that the defendants conspired to send the documents only impairs the seriousness of the real defense" (50).

The third paragraph addresses the argument that the use of the evidence violated the Fifth Amendment. Holmes cites four precedents on this issue, more than in any other part of the opinion.

The fourth paragraph is a careful, even neutral description of the content of the pamphlet, concluding with a sentence that places the defendants in something of a dilemma: "Of course the document would not have been sent unless it had been intended to have some effect, and we do not see what effect it could be expected to have upon persons subject to the draft except to influence them to obstruct the carrying of it out" (51). Unlike later free speech cases, notably the Smith Act cases dealing with the Communist Party in the 1950s, this opinion makes no effort to depict the defendants as a serious threat to the nation.

The fifth paragraph lays out the constitutional issues, including the points about "falsely shouting fire" and "clear and present danger." Holmes emphasizes the role of context in determining meaning, contending that the sentiments expressed in the leaflet would have been legal in "many places and in ordinary times." The core argument is phrased thusly: "The question in every case is whether the words used are used in such circumstances and are of such a nature as to create a clear and present danger that they will bring about the substantive evils that Congress has a right to prevent. It is a question of proximity and degree. When a nation is at war many things that might be said in time of peace are such a hindrance to its effort that their utterance will not be endured so long as men fight and that no court could regard them as protected by an constitutional right." Since the statute punishes conspiracy as well as actual obstruction, "we perceive no ground for saying that success alone warrants making the act a crime." It is especially interesting that Holmes makes no attempt to justify Congress's decision to punish words as well as actions. He concludes the paragraph by saying that he has chosen to "add a few words" on free speech, since the controlling precedent, *Goldman v. United States,* does not refer to free speech "specially" (52).

The final paragraph deals with definition of "conspiracy to obstruct." The defendants had argued that the words of the Act of 1917 referred only to "the recruiting or enlistment service," not the draft itself. Holmes concludes, "But recruiting is gaining fresh supplies for the forces, as well by draft as otherwise. It is put as an alternative to enlistment or voluntary enrollment in this Act. The fact that the Act of 1917 was enlarged by the amending Act of 16 May 1918, c. 75, 40 Stat. 553, of course, does not affect the present indictment and would not, even if the former Act had been repealed. Rev St. par. 13" (53). Even if Holmes was usually more formal in his language in decisions written for the Court, this conclusion is quite different from his other majority opinions in its abruptness and flatness of affect. The strategic choice is oddly contradictory. The reader concludes that these defendants are really not worth much serious attention or concern, but if that is so, why are they being prosecuted by the federal government? In his characteristic metonymic strategy, Holmes reduces the case to a matter of a literal reading of a federal statute. Free speech, like liberty of contract, must yield to the force of the majority, even if the majority wishes to "go to hell." Holmes nonetheless refuses to provide any emotional support to the fears that led to the statute in the first place.

Several scholars have noted that Holmes treats speech in this decision as analogous to the notion of "attempt" in the criminal law. The question of criminality deals with "proximity" to the harm and the "degree" of the harm. White writes, "Spoken words urging resistance to the war were treated the same as an unsuccessful effort to poison an acquaintance . . . or to burn down a building."[134] David Rabban contends that Holmes relies on the "bad tendency" doctrine in *Schenck*. These readings, though, neglect the seemingly strategic ambivalence of the decision, an ambivalence that may prefigure the seeming shift in Holmes's position in *Abrams*. As H. L. Pohlman writes, the puzzle about *Schenck* is why Holmes wrote the decision he did. The jury had evidence to warrant the conviction; the law in question referred to "conspiracy," not "speech." Holmes could have dealt with the case solely on the conspiracy issue without dragging in the clear and present danger doctrine.[135]

Pohlman's contention is that Holmes conceptualized the limits of free speech by analyzing speech in terms of a general theory of legal liability. Free speech for Holmes was a "residue," what was leftover when speech did not satisfy the criteria of legal liability. Pohlman uses the concept of liability to read all the free speech decisions and contends that Holmes's position remains consistent throughout them. My argument is that Pohlman is correct about the oddity of the opinion, but his reduction of Holmes's position to a common-law notion of legal liability misses the significance of Holmes's relationship to Laski and Frankfurter. "Clear and present danger" remained a perfectly coherent doctrine in the eyes of later civil libertarian justices. Hugo Black criticized the Court's decisions in the Smith Act cases as ignoring the "clear and present danger" doctrine.[136] Efforts to "trash" Holmes's free speech opinions reflect the tendency of later scholars to project their own ambivalence toward the role of law and judicial review in a democracy onto Holmes.

ABRAMS V. UNITED STATES

The *Abrams* dissent is perhaps Holmes's single most widely quoted opinion.[137] If the *Lochner* dissent established Holmes as the friend of legislative experiment with social legislation, the *Abrams* dissent established him as the father of civil libertarianism in America. We know more about the circumstances of the writing of the dissent, as well as the experience of the defendants in the case, than most of the other cases that Holmes heard. Richard Polenberg's *Fighting Faiths* is an account of the case from the point of view of the defendants but draws its title from Holmes's opinion.[138] Holmes's letters to Laski, Pollock, and Frankfurter are particularly illuminating about his motivations. But in many ways the opinion speaks for itself. Holmes's gifts for metaphor, for economy of style and argument, and for his signature metonymy-to-mysticism rhetorical rhythm combine to make it a masterpiece.[139]

On 23 August 1918, a group of Russian immigrant anarchists, led by Jacob Abrams, were arrested in New York City for writing, printing, and distributing (actually, throwing them off a roof in the garment district) two leaflets—one in Yiddish, the other in English—condemning Woodrow Wilson for sending troops to Russia. The Yiddish leaflet called for a general strike. They were charged with violating the Sedition Act, were convicted in October 1918, and were sentenced to fifteen-to-twenty-year prison terms. Their first trial was noteworthy because of the prejudicial remarks of the judge, Henry DeLamar Clinton. The defense argued that the United States was not at war with Germany, and thus the Sedition Act did not apply. There was, however, a widespread perception at the time that the Bolsheviks were German spies.

The oral arguments before the Supreme Court were heard on 21 October 1919. The case was decided on 10 November 1919, on a seven-to-two vote. Justice Clarke wrote the majority opinion, which carefully followed Holmes's reasoning in *Schenck*. The leaflets created a clear and present danger, because they had been distributed "at the supreme crisis of the war" and were "an attempt to defeat the war plans of the Government."[140] Even if the defendants had urged that no arms be produced for war with Russia, a necessary result of their incitement would be to hinder the war effort against Germany.

And yet Holmes did not join the majority. Why? He had changed his mind, based on arguments from Learned Hand, Zechariah Chaffee, and Harold Laski, as well as on his growing irritation with the treatment of his young friends at Harvard.[141] Holmes wrote the dissenting opinion, joined by Justice Brandeis. It is longer (twelve paragraphs) than most of Holmes's other dissents. Paragraph one describes the indictment. His first sentence already diminishes the significance of the conspiracy: "This indictment is founded wholly upon the publication of two leaflets" (624). Paragraphs two and three are careful descriptions of the two leaflets, with numerous direct quotations.

Paragraph four begins by agreeing that counts one and two of the indictment are justified. The leaflets clearly are "abusive language about the form of government of the United States" and are written in "language intended to bring the form of the government into contempt." The fourth indictment—"conspiracy to incite curtailment of production of things necessary to the prosecution of the war"—is where the government has failed to prove its case. "[T]o make the conduct criminal that statute requires that it should be 'with intent by such curtailment to cripple or hinder the United States in the prosecution of the war.' It seems to me that no such intent is proved" (626).

Paragraph five discusses the statute in terms of the general doctrine of civil and criminal liability: "A man may have to pay damages, may be sent to prison, at common law might be hanged, if at the time of his act he knew facts from which common experience showed that the consequences would follow, whether he individually could foresee them or not. But, when words are used exactly, a deed is not done with intent to produce a consequence unless that consequence is the aim of deed. . . . . he does not do the act with intent to produce it unless the aim to produce it is the proximate motive of the specific act, although there may be some deeper motive behind" (627).

Paragraph six constructs an analogy: "A patriot might think that we were wasting money on aeroplanes, or making more cannon of a certain kind than we needed, and might advocate curtailment with success, yet even if it turned out that the curtailment hindered and was thought by other minds to have been obviously likely to hinder the United States in the prosecution of the war, no one would hold such conduct a crime." Holmes admits that the analogy may not deal with all the issues in the case, but it provides a transition to the core argument of the opinion. The last sentence is striking: "[M]y illustration . . . is enough to show what I think and to let me pass to a more important aspect of the case. I refer to the First Amendment to the Constitution that Congress shall make no law abridging the freedom of speech" (627).

Paragraph seven states that *Schenck, Frohwerk,* and *Debs* were rightly decided under the "clear and present danger" principle.

Paragraphs eight and nine contend that "Congress cannot forbid all effort to change the mind of the country," and that an "intent to prevent interference with the revolution in Russia might have been satisfied without any hindrance to carrying on the war in which we were engaged" (628).

Paragraph ten deals with the third count of the indictment, "intent to provoke resistance to the United States in its war with Germany." Holmes writes that "no such intent was proved or existed in fact. I also think that there is no hint at resistance to the United States as I construe the phrase" (628).

Paragraph eleven is a masterpiece of Holmesian irony, culminating in the remarkably complex sentence: "Even if I am technically wrong and enough can be squeezed from these poor and puny anonymities to turn the color of legal litmus paper—I will add, even if what I think the necessary intent were shown—the most nominal punishment seems to me all that possibly could be inflicted, unless the defendants are to be made to suffer not for what the indictment alleges but for the creed that they avow—a creed that I believe to be the creed of ignorance and immaturity when honestly held, as I see no reason to doubt that it was held here, but which, although made the subject of examination at the trial, no one has a right even to consider in dealing with the charges before the Court" (679). This sentence is an example of what I have called the metonymic moment in Holmesian rhetoric. It reduces the case to triviality, a triviality in which both defendants and the Court majority are implicated.

But then the rhythm of the opinion shifts, after the long-held note of the transitional paragraph, to a mystical and metaphorical reflection on the philosophy of free speech in a democracy. The first sentence of the last paragraph remains in the ironic mode: "Persecution for the expression of opinions seems to me perfectly logical. If you have no doubt of your premises or your power and want a certain result with all your heart you naturally express your wishes in law and sweep away all opposition." Holmes then reaches the heart of his justification for an expansive notion of free speech: "[W]hen men have realized that time has upset many fighting faiths, they may come to believe even more than they believe the very foundations of their own conduct that the ultimate good desired is better reached by free trade in ideas—that the best test of truth is the power of the thought to get itself accepted in the competition of the market, and that truth is the only ground upon which their wishes safely can be carried out. That, at any rate, is the theory of our Constitution." Holmes rejects the idea that the First Amendment left the common law of seditious libel in force: "I had conceived that the United States through many years had shown its repentance for the Sedition Act of 1798 by repaying fines that it imposed. Only the emergency that makes it immediately dangerous to leave the correction of evil counsels to time warrants making any exception to the sweeping command, 'Congress shall make no law . . . abridging the freedom of speech.'" Holmes's final sentence denies the rhetoricity of his own opinion: "I regret that I cannot put into more impressive words my belief that in their conviction upon this indictment the defendants were deprived of their rights under the Constitution of the United States" (630–31).

As usual with Holmes, skepticism and mysticism merge in this last paragraph. The connection is expressed clearly in a letter to Frankfurter in 1915: "every wise man is a mystic at bottom—not in the sense of unalterable communications from behind every phenomena—but in that of realizing that all ends in mystery if you only put it in the right place."[142] Holmes frequently referred to his "first great act of faith" in which he decided that he was "not God."[143] Humility and skepticism fit well with the pragmatic, consensus view of the truth expressed in his summary of the Constitution's defense of free speech: "It is an experiment, as all life is an experiment."

The language of skepticism and experimentalism fit well within the attitudes of young Progressives such as Frankfurter and Laski. Later generations questioned the doctrine of free speech in the *Abrams* dissent on a number of grounds. The most enduring has been the claim, put most forthrightly by the critical rhetorician Marouf Hasian Jr., that the "free marketplace of ideas" metaphor ignores the ways in which capitalism undermines equality of opportunity to speak.[144] Pnina Lahav argues that Holmes's defense of free speech was "libertarian," while Brandeis's was "republican." Holmes's social Darwinism, writes Lahav, "made him doubt the idea that the political process nurtured by the 'free trade' would yield progress. Social Darwinism predicted the survival of the socially powerful or those who could adapt and become powerful. . . . Thus, if the crowd so desires, the neutrality of the state toward the free trade of ideas, combined with social Darwinism, might well result in an illiberal, anti-progressivist value system." Brandeis, in contrast, defended free speech in the language of "republicanism," contending that it is an essential prerequisite for the practice of "civic virtue."[145]

The problem with these arguments is that they overrate the role of the "market" metaphor in the dissent. Note that Holmes does not use the phrase "free marketplace of ideas." What he actually writes is, "the best test of truth is the power of thought to get itself accepted in the competition of the market, and that truth is the only ground upon which their wishes safely can be carried out." Hasian and Lahav are simply prejudiced against any use of the concept "market," even though neither Marx nor most contemporary socialists after the fall of Communism ever expected that markets would be eliminated. The real difference between Holmes and Brandeis is that Brandeis appealed to the highest motives of his audience in defending free speech. Holmes built on the low yet solid ground of practicality and self-interest. Together, they crafted a notion of free speech that has been one of the political triumphs of American politics in the twentieth century.

A final criticism of Holmes's dissent is that it is incoherent. White writes that Holmes has four contradictory concepts of free speech: "(1) speech as 'another act we don't like,' personified by the 'criminal attempts' analogy; (2) speech as the 'search for truth,' personified by the reconfigured 'clear and present danger' test; (3) speech as the vehicle by which the 'dominant forces of the community' exercise their power; and (4) speech as the principle of freedom for the thought we hate." These formulas are "cumulatively inadequate."[146] It is unclear how these concepts are prima facie contradictory. In any case, to demand of Holmes that he construct an inflexible major premise from which later decisions could be formally deduced is hardly reasonable. Still, if any part of constitutional law has exhibited essential continuity in the twentieth century (with the possible exception of the Smith Act cases of the 1950s, which were nonetheless argued in terms of the "clear and present danger" topos), it is Holmes's formulation of the meaning of the First Amendment. It was only in 1969 that the Court revised the "clear and present" danger test in *Brandenburg v. Ohio*, and it seems pretty clear that the revision would have been congenial to Holmes. Finally, it is significant that White—like Lahav and Hasian—

does not cite the letter to Laski of 26 October 1919 in which Holmes proclaims his willingness to die for the principle of freedom of speech: "I fear we have less freedom of speech here than they have in England. Little as I believe in it as a theory I hope I would die for it and I go as far as anyone whom I regard as competent to form an opinion, in favor of it. Of course when I say I don't believe in it as a theory I don't mean that I do believe in the opposite as a theory."[147] In other words, Holmes's private opinion is consistent with what he wrote in *Abrams:* men are not gods, general theories aren't worth a damn, and yet free speech is one of those "can't helps" that are a foundation of a mystical, patriotic faith that Holmes hopes that he and others would die for. It is Holmes's patriotism, finally, that saves his concept of free speech from relativism or social Darwinism. Since patriotism has disappeared as a virtue in American academic rhetoric, it is no wonder that White and others can make no sense of Holmes's view of free speech.

BUCK V. BELL

Holmes's majority opinion in *Buck v. Bell* (1927) is one of the most disturbing judicial opinions in American history.[148] It was seized upon by Roman Catholic opponents of Holmes in the 1940s as a sign of his proto-Nazi leanings, and several later legal scholars have carefully demonstrated the terrible injustice done to Carrie Buck in this case. The Virginia law upheld by Justice Holmes was the actual model for the Hereditary Health Law in Nazi Germany, which led to the sterilization of thousands of the "genetically unfit." During the Nuremberg trials, an attorney for the Nazis referred to Holmes's opinion in *Buck v. Bell* in defense of their sterilization practices.[149] The purpose of this section of the essay, however, is not to rehearse the now-standard objections to Holmes's opinion. *Buck v. Bell* is interesting from the standpoint of rhetorical history for two reasons: it foregrounds the tension between eloquence and morality that has been at the heart of the rhetorical tradition since its inception, and it represents the precise topical point of strain in progressivism: its inability to develop a coherent set of political principles and rhetorical justifications for individual rights.

By the 1920s several states had passed laws requiring the sterilization of the retarded and the insane. By today's standards some surprising supporters of eugenics included Margaret Sanger, Emma Goldman, Norman Thomas, and the American Association of University Women. Some state courts had struck down sterilization statutes because of a lack of procedural safeguards. The model law devised by the biologist Harry Laughlin was adopted by Virginia in 1924, and it appeared to contain several procedural safeguards. The law provided standards for sterilization of "inmates of institutions supported by the State who shall be found to be afflicted with a hereditary form of insanity or imbecility." Aubrey Ellis Strode, the main sponsor of the Virginia law, was known for his then-liberal views on women's rights and fairer treatment for blacks, and he "thought of eugenics as altogether consistent with his progressive outlook."[150]

The unfortunate Carrie Buck had been committed to the Lynchburg State Colony for Epileptics and Feeble-Minded after giving birth to an illegitimate child. The superintendent asked a three-member board that she be sterilized because she was a "moral delinquent . . . of the moron class." He attempted to prove that Carrie's daughter, Vivian, was retarded as well, but in fact she made the honor roll a few years later at a Charlottesville public school. The law required that a guardian be appointed for Carrie, and in what appeared to be a "friendly suit," the guardian brought the case to the Virginia Supreme Court of Appeals and then to the Supreme Court. Carrie was duly sterilized and lived out her difficult life, finally dying, as Leuchtenberg writes, in "a hovel on a dirt road near Charlottesville with her second husband, a crippled alcoholic lost in fantasy—just the sort of ending that Justice Holmes and the eugenists would have predicted for someone with her genes."[151] The Supreme Court never reversed *Buck v. Bell*, and compulsory sterilization laws still remain on the books.[152]

Holmes's primary strategies in the opinion are to foreground the due process issues, to develop an analogy between forced sterilization and military service: "We have seen more than once that the public welfare may call upon the best citizens for their lives. It would be strange if it could not call upon those who already sap the strength of the state for these lesser sacrifices, often not felt to be such by those concerned, in order to prevent our being swamped with incompetence" (207).

Perhaps if Holmes had stopped with the military analogy the opinion would not have become so notorious. But he capped it off with the sentence, "Three generations of imbeciles are enough." Richard Posner, in an analysis that follows the *Lochner* discussion cited earlier, contends that this is "beautiful prose—vivid, passionate, topped off by a brilliant aphorism—but it is dubious legal reasoning." It is based on the unproven assumption that mental retardation begets crime, and he even breaks his own rule, articulated in *Lochner*, to avoid bringing his personal approval or disapproval of a statute into his legal analysis. Yet Posner, true to his conception of rhetoric, contends that it is a first-class piece of rhetoric and argues that "Scholarly analysis of the 'rhetoric' of judicial opinions would be more fruitful and certainly clearer, if scholars stopped trying to equate good rhetoric with goodness."[153]

A more interesting take on the opinion might be to view it, in Kenneth Burke's sense, as an example of a vocabulary—in this case of utilitarian moral reasoning—taken "to the end of the line," fulfilling its entelechy. The enthusiasm of the progressive social thinkers and jurisprudes for Holmes's judicial restraint, moral relativism, and emphasis on social experimentation would eventually need to be tempered with a new respect for "rights," entities whose existence Holmes scoffed at, yet whose importance in an age of totalitarianism would lead to the transformation of progressivism into post–New Deal liberalism, with its emphasis on strict scrutiny of laws that appeared to violate the rights of "discrete and insular minorities."[154]

Holmes's Afterlife: The Magic Mirror of Twentieth-Century Liberalism

In this essay I have emphasized both a close reading of Holmes's rhetorical strategies in his speeches and judicial opinions as well as a larger analysis of his place in the evolution of American legal and moral argument. Holmes was part of the modernist rethinking of the human place in a godless universe, as well as part of a kind of "masculine protest" against the lack of civic virtue in the Gilded Age. His solution to the crisis of faith following the Civil War and the rise of Darwinism was to emphasize the martial virtues and the satisfactions to be obtained by public service and professionalism. His Darwinism and his emphasis on social experimentation inspired a generation of progressive thinkers who, in turn, were to discover the limitations of a political language based on utility rather than on rights.

It remains to say a few words about the vicissitudes of Holmes's reputation, which I have alluded to throughout this essay. G. Edward White has described Holmes's "image" and reputation as falling into six distinct time segments.

1. *1881–1902: Holmes as Scientist.* Holmes's *The Common Law* and "The Path of the Law," as well as his work on an external theory of tort liability, has

helped create a modern, more scientific and pragmatic view of the law in place of the reigning legal formalism.

2. *1903–31: Holmes as Progressive.* Progressives wanted to experiment, as a way of *attaining* progress. They believed in government by experts and wanted to expand the executive branch of government, especially with administrative regulatory agencies. And they were incensed at judges who substituted logical axioms for empirical analysis. His supporters relied on two symbols in their praise of Holmes: the image of the socially conscious Puritan and the aristocrat as democrat.

3. *1932–40: Holmes as Myth.* These years represent the "apotheosis" of Holmes. The first full-length biography was published by Silas Bent in 1932. Karl Llewellyn paid tribute to him as a legal realist. Felix Frankfurter represented him as a "liberal" in the 1938 book *Mr. Justice Holmes and the Supreme Court.* The young lawyers whom Frankfurter sent to serve in the Roosevelt administration were inspired by the image of Holmes's pragmatism and his hatred of laissez-faire judges.

4. *1941–49: Demythologizing Holmes.* After the publication of the letters to Pollock, with their endorsement of Darwinism and contempt for the common man, Jesuit law professors, joined by Lon Fuller and Daniel Boorstin, sought to demythologize Holmes.

5. *1950–59: Holmes in Historical Context.* The major works about Holmes during this period, Commager's *The American Mind* and Howe's biography of Holmes, began to emphasize how distant Holmes's outlook was from the present day and began the process of situating him more clearly in his cultural context.

6. *1960–now: Holmes and Libertarianism-Egalitarianism.* The "rights revolution" of the 1960s inevitably led to the assault on Holmes's intellectual and moral character, beginning with Yosal Rogat's "The Judge as Spectator" and continuing with the White biography and the remarkable savaging of Holmes in the introduction to the three-volume edition of his public papers by Sheldon Novick.

The final chapter in the reception of Holmes lies in the more careful attempts at situating him in the history of the common law, notably by Neil Rosenberg and Richard Posner. The renewed attempt at canonization of Holmes by Richard Posner reflects the return to a utilitarian view of law after the seeming exhaustion of "rights talk."[155]

It may well be that the changing images of Holmes reflect the continuing need of otherwise rational students of the law for a figure onto whom they project their own ambivalence about their "Mistress, the Law."[156] That by the 1990s Holmes was no longer available to the general public as "The Magnificent Yankee" said as much about the changed fortunes and prestige of law in American democracy as it said about Holmes himself. The efforts of the legal process school in the 1950s to carve out a distinctive "craft" of the law, as opposed to the conflation of law and politics by legal realism, seemed to have failed. Conservatives such as Robert Bork and Antonin Scalia proclaimed a new originalism or textualism in constitutional interpretation, yet wielded judicial authority as politically as anyone on the Warren court. Critical legal studies scholars assaulted liberal legalism's romantic faith in the "rule of law" as mere "ideology."[157] The "rise and fall" of Justice Holmes in the American popular mind may finally have been completely parallel to the rise and fall of faith in law itself.

Yet the fall of Holmes's reputation in legal studies should not deter scholars of rhetoric from examining the role of legal rhetoric in American political culture. His philosophy of law shaped and reflected the larger public dialogue of the Progressive and New Deal Eras. Holmes contributed to the celebration of science and expertise by Progressives and to the liberal devaluation of popular democracy—

especially as practiced at state and local levels of government. His effort to define a secular faith influenced the growing divide between the "cultural elite" and the religious American public. Holmes's strictures about separating morality and law probably helped reinforce the "fact-value" split, targeted by contemporary rhetorical theorists such as Booth and Perelman as the source of the decay of public discourse. Further attention to Holmes's reputation may clarify some of the sources of the post–World War II rhetorical revival, since much of the quest for a "logic of value judgments," as Perelman called it, parallels the Jesuit critique of Holmes.[158]

On the other hand, the rhetorical scholar, like the legal scholar, must beware of projecting contemporary anxieties onto Holmes's rich body of epideictic and legal discourse. Holmes's commitment to "bettable premises" and his "soldier's faith" remain intriguing options in an age of continuing doubt that the universe has some sort of ultimate meaning. His epideictic oratory deserves a much wider audience, both among public address scholars and the general public.

Finally, if he did nothing else, Holmes's forthright defense of free speech at a time of its lowest popularity remains his distinctive contribution to the proper role of the law in a democratic polity. He taught an entire generation of progressive thinkers that free speech is one right that trumps social utility. Despite his elitism, he was one of the few Supreme Court justices in the twentieth century to write judicial opinions accessible to the general public. He remains *the* central figure in the American conversation about politics, law, and ethics. His progressive path of the law remains the one on which, for better or for worse, we still tread.

Notes

1. Edward A. Purcell Jr., *The Crisis of Democratic Theory: Scientific Naturalism and the Problem of Value* (Lexington: University Press of Kentucky, 1973), 5–6, 17, 21–42.
2. See Wayne Booth, *Modern Dogma and the Rhetoric of Assent* (Notre Dame, Ind.: University of Notre Dame Press, 1974).
3. See Purcell, *The Crisis of Democratic Theory,* on the attack by Robert Hutchins, Mortimer Adler, and Jesuit leaders on scientific naturalism; on the criticism of progressivism, see Christopher Lasch, *The True and Only Heaven: Progress and Its Critics* (New York: W. W. Norton and Co., 1991).
4. The biographical material on Holmes is huge. Catherine Drinker Bowen's *Yankee from Olympus: Justice Holmes and His Family* (Boston: Little, Brown, and Co.,1944) is semifictionalized and uncritical of Holmes but is still well worth reading. Felix Frankfurter was the original authorized biographer but gave the Holmes papers to his protégée, Mark DeWolfe Howe, whose two-volume biography was only one-third completed before his untimely death: *Justice Oliver Wendell Holmes: The Shaping Years, 1841–1870* (Cambridge: Harvard University Press, 1957); *Justice Oliver Wendell Holmes, II: The Proving Years, 1870–1882* (Cambridge: Harvard University Press, 1963). Grant Gilmore was then designated the authorized biographer, and he worked on it for fifteen years but evidently grew disgusted with Holmes, as his account in *The Ages of American Law* attests ([New Haven: Yale University Press, 1977], 49). New revelations about Holmes's romantic relationship with the Irish aristocrat Lady Castletown appeared in the 1980s; Morton Horwitz makes much of these revelations in his "The Place of Justice Holmes in American Legal Thought," in *The Legacy of Justice Oliver Wendell Holmes, Jr.,* ed. Robert W. Gordon, (Stanford, Calif.: Stanford University Press, 1992), 31–71. Liva Baker, *Justice from Beacon Hill: The Life of Oliver Wendell Holmes, Jr.* (New York: HarperCollins, 1991), is the most sympathetic of the recent biographers. Sheldon Novick, *Honorable Justice: The Life of Oliver Wendell Holmes* (Boston: Little, Brown, and Co., 1989), is thorough but neglects Holmes's legal theory. G. Edward White's *Justice Oliver Wendell Holmes: Law and the Inner Self* (New York: Oxford University Press, 1993) is an intellectual biography of Holmes but is marred by his endless psychoanalyzing of

Holmes, for whom he displays considerable personal distaste; for an effective criticism of White's book, see Adam J. Hirsch, review of *Justice Oliver Wendell Holmes: Law and the Inner Self*, by G. Edward White, *Virginia Law Review* 82 (1996): 385–411.

5. See Mark DeWolfe Howe, ed., *Touched with Fire: Civil War Letters and Diary of Oliver Wendell Holmes, Jr.* (Cambridge: Harvard University Press, 1947). Two works that discuss Holmes's relation to the Civil War and the later American struggle to define its cultural meaning are Edmund Wilson, *Patriotic Gore* (New York: Oxford University Press, 1962), 743–96; and George Frederickson, *The Inner Civil War: Northern Intellectuals and the Crisis of the Union* (New York: Harper and Row, 1965).

6. Oliver Wendell Holmes Jr., *The Common Law*, ed. Mark DeWolfe Howe (Cambridge: Harvard University Press, 1963); Frederic Rogers Kellogg, ed., *The Formative Essays of Justice Holmes: The Making of an American Legal Philosophy* (Westport, Conn.: Greenwood, 1984), includes his early scholarly essays, with a useful introduction. The meaning of Holmes's early legal scholarship, like his judicial opinions, remains controversial, especially his theory of torts. See especially David Rosenberg, *The Hidden Holmes: His Theory of Torts in History* (Cambridge: Harvard University Press, 1995).

7. See Mark Tushnet, "The Logic of Experience: Oliver Wendell Holmes on the Supreme Judicial Court," *Virginia Law Review* 63 (1977): 975–1052, for a thorough analysis of Holmes's opinions on the Massachusetts court.

8. Holmes to Pollock, 27 December 1895, *Holmes-Pollock Letters: The Correspondence of Mr. Justice Holmes and Sir Frederick Pollock, 1874–1932*, ed. Mark DeWolfe Howe, 2d ed. (Cambridge: Harvard University Press, 1961), 440.

9. Mary Ann Glendon, *Rights Talk* (New York: Free Press, 1991), 86.

10. The extent of Holmes's "pragmatism" remains unclear; for the most comprehensive attempt to locate Holmes within pragmatic philosophy, see Thomas C. Grey, "Holmes and Legal Pragmatism," *Stanford Law Review* 41 (1989): 787–870. As I will argue below, the most puzzling omission in all the accounts of Holmes's philosophical stance is his often-expressed admiration for the work of George Santayana. Still, a good working definition of "pragmatism" in Holmes and in jurisprudence generally is Richard Posner's: "I shall argue in short for a functional, policy-saturated, nonlegalistic, naturalistic, and skeptical, but decidedly not cynical, conception of the legal process; in a word (although I fear an inadequate word), for a pragmatic jurisprudence" (*The Problems of Jurisprudence* [Cambridge: Harvard University Press, 1990], 26). What Posner misses is Holmes's fundamental "mysticism." A thorough survey of various approaches to Holmes and intellectual history is Gordon, ed., *The Legacy of Oliver Wendell Holmes, Jr.*

11. *Commonwealth v. Perry*, 155 Mass. 117, 123 (1891) (arguing that a law passed by legislature to protect weavers was within the scope of legislative action); *Vegelahn v. Guntner*, 1676 Mass. 92, 104 (1896) (arguing that combinations of labor, i.e. unions, in this case for peaceful picketing, must be allowed just as combinations of business, i.e. trade associations, are).

12. For a recent account, see I. Scott Messinger, "Legitimating Liberalism: The New Deal Image-Makers and Oliver Wendell Holmes, Jr.," *Journal of Supreme Court History* (1995): 57–72. An essential element of Holmes's prestige among progressive lawyers such as Frankfurter was his freedom from anti-Semitism, an unusual quality in a Boston Brahmin of his day; on Holmes and his relation to Jewish intellectuals, see David A. Hollinger, "The 'Tough-Minded' Justice Holmes, Jewish Intellectuals, and the Making of an American Icon," in *The Legacy of Oliver Wendell Holmes, Jr.*, 216–28.

13. See Robert A. Ferguson, "Holmes and the Judicial Figure," in *The Legacy of Oliver Wendell Holmes, Jr.*, 155–85.

14. Bowen, *Yankee from Olympus*.

15. See especially Francis E. Lucey, "Jurisprudence and the Future Social Order," *Social Science* 16 (July 1941): 211–17. For discussions of the attack on Holmes, see Francis Biddle, *Justice Holmes, Natural Law, and the Supreme Court* (New York: Macmillan, 1961); and, especially, David H. Burton, "Justice Holmes and the Jesuits," *American Journal of Jurisprudence* 27 (1982): 32–45.

16. Gilmore, *The Ages of American Law*, 49.

17. A word about primary sources: the Holmes papers are available in microfilm from University Press of America; fortunately, they have been thoroughly examined by recent biographers. As John Pollock writes in his introduction to the Holmes-Pollock letters, "At the first blush you would take Holmes's script for a fine piece of calligraphy: it had a certain beauty of its own. But in the same second you became aware that something was surely amiss with your eyesight. What had seemed from their general shape and spacing to be words dissolved into hieroglyphics. The longer they were studied the more obscure they became, until you wondered whether any message at all lay hid therein. It was as if a demented fly had followed the writer's pen across the page" (*Holmes-Pollock Letters*, xxvii). Three volumes of the collected works have been published: Oliver Wendell Holmes Jr., *The Collected Works of Justice Holmes: Complete Public Writings and Selected Judicial Opinions of Oliver Wendell Holmes*, ed. Sheldon Novick, 3 vols. (Chicago: University of Chicago Press, 1995). In this essay, I use Oliver Wendell Holmes Jr., *The Occasional Speeches of Justice Oliver Wendell Holmes*, ed. Mark DeWolfe Howe (Cambridge: Harvard University Press, 1962), for the ceremonial speeches; for "The Path of the Law" and other extrajudicial legal writing I use Oliver Wendell Holmes Jr., *Collected Works*, ed. Novick; for the judicial opinions I cite the original publication in *United States Reports*. For the general reader, Max Lerner, *The Mind and Faith of Justice Holmes: His Speeches, Essays, Letters and Judicial Opinions* (New York: Modern Library, 1943), remains useful, although it has been superseded by Richard Posner, ed., *The Essential Holmes: Selections from the Letters, Speeches, Judicial Opinions, and Other Writings of Oliver Wendell Holmes, Jr.* (Chicago: University of Chicago Press, 1992). Posner's preface is an exceptionally perceptive and sympathetic account of Holmes's work.
18. Purcell, *The Crisis of Democratic Theory*.
19. William Lewis, "Of Innocence, Exclusion, and the Burning of Flags: The Romantic Realism of the Law," *Southern Communication Journal* 60 (1994): 4–21.
20. See especially Milner Ball, *Lying down Together: Law, Metaphor, and Theology* (Madison: University of Wisconsin Press, 1985).
21. See, for example, Peter Brooks and Paul Gewirtz, eds., *Law's Stories: Narrative and Rhetoric in the Law* (New Haven: Yale University Press, 1996); Marouf Hasian Jr., Celeste Michelle Condit, and John Louis Lucaites, "The Rhetorical Boundaries of 'the Law': A Consideration of the Rhetorical Culture of Legal Practice and the Case of the 'Separate but Equal' Doctrine," *Quarterly Journal of Speech* 82 (1996): 323–42; and John W. Cairns, "Rhetoric, Language, and Roman Law: Legal Education and Improvement in Eighteenth Century Scotland," *Law and History Review* 9, no. 1 (1991): 31–58.
22. See Richard Gaskins, *Burdens of Proof in Modern Discourse* (New Haven: Yale University Press, 1995).
23. Holmes, "The Law," in *Collected Works*, 3:469. Kermit L. Hall uses the term for the title of *The Magic Mirror: Law in American History* (New York: Oxford University Press, 1989).
24. Holmes, "The Path of the Law," in *Collected Works*, 3:392, 170.
25. Alexis de Tocqueville, *Democracy in America*, ed. Phillips Bradley (New York: Alfred A. Knopf, 1945), 1:290.
26. S. M. Halloran, "Tradition and Theory in Rhetoric," *Quarterly Journal of Speech* 62 (1976): 235–36.
27. Dorothy I. Anderson, "The Public Speeches of Justice Oliver Wendell Holmes," in *American Public Address: Studies in Honor of A. Craig Baird*, ed. Loren Reid (Columbia: University of Missouri Press, 1962), 5–25.
28. Ibid., 5.
29. Ibid., 6.
30. Holmes, cited in ibid., 7. Holmes's use of the term "aperçu" recurs through many of his letters.
31. Ibid.
32. Holmes, "Speech at Brown University, 1897," in *Collected Legal Papers*, 166, cited in Anderson, "Public Speeches," in *American Public Address*, 8.

33. Holmes to Laski, 11 January 1929, *Holmes-Laski Letters: The Correspondence of Mr. Justice Holmes and Harold J. Laski, 1916–1935*, ed. Mark DeWolfe Howe (Cambridge: Harvard University Press, 1953), 2:1125.

34. Anderson, "Public Speeches," in *American Public Address*, 9.

35. Ibid., 10.

36. Ibid.

37. Ibid., 12.

38. See Holmes letter to Lady Ellen Askwith, 3 March 1915, cited in Howe, *Justice Oliver Wendell Holmes*, 1:227 n.

39. Holmes, "The Path of the Law," in *Collected Works,*, 3:406.

40. Anderson, "Public Speeches," in *American Public Address*, 13.

41. Ibid.

42. George Willis, *The Philosophy of Speech* (London: Allen and Unwin, 1919).

43. Laski to Holmes, 26 January 1920, 14 August 1921, 27 January 1924, *Holmes-Laski Letters*, 2:236, 361, 585.

44. See Holmes, "The Path of the Law," in *Collected Legal Papers*, 403–4.

45. On Bain and pragmatism, see Grey, "Holmes and Legal Pragmatism," 803 n. 64.

46. Anderson, "Public Speeches," in *American Public Address*, 14.

47. Ibid., 19

48. Ibid., 21–22.

49. Posner, Introduction to *The Essential Holmes*, ix–xi.

50. Ibid., xii.

51. Ibid., xviii.

52. Ibid., xvii.

53. See Holmes to Pollock, 23 November 1905: "I am just turning to Santayana's last two volumes of *The Life of Reason* which I like better than any philosophy I have read—or nearly so" (*Holmes-Pollock Letters*, 1:122); 23 June 1906: "At all events his book was one which seemed to me to express the world as I should express it, more nearly than often befalls" (*Holmes-Pollock Letters*, 1:126–27); 6 April 1924: referring to *Scepticism and Animal Faith*, "Au fond, unless I mistake, he takes much the same view that I have taken en passant in one or two of my things. His philosophy is much nearer to my way of thinking than James's or Royce's" (*Holmes-Pollock Letters*, 2:132).

54. George Santayana, *The Life of Reason* (New York: Charles Scribner's Sons, 1953), 15.

55. John McCormick, *George Santayana: A Biography* (New York: Alfred A. Knopf, 1987), 17.

56. George Santayana, *Scepticism and Animal Faith* (New York: Dover Books, 1955), 186: "It might seem ignominious to believe something on compulsion, because I can't help believing it; when reason awakes in a man it asks for reasons for everything. Yet this demand is unreasonable: there cannot be a reason for everything."

57. See George Santayana, *Realms of Being* (New York: Charles Scribner's Sons, 1942).

58. Santayana, *The Life of Reason*, 162–63.

59. Robert Ferguson, *Law and Letters in American Culture* (Cambridge: Harvard University Press, 1984), 290.

60. Ibid.

61. Ferguson, "Holmes and the Judicial Figure," 155–56.

62. Ibid., 163, 184–85.

63. Clara Ingram Judson, *Mr. Justice Holmes* (Chicago: Follett, 1956), 6.

64. Ibid., 192. Mark DeWolfe Howe makes an interesting observation about the popular image of Holmes: "When he died in 1935 a cluster of popular myths surrounded his reputation. They had made him into a strangely unreal figure—gay dog, ardent soldier, impassioned liberal, puritan Yankee. When the process of reappraisal began, new fancies displaced old fables. He became the disciple of Hobbes and Austin, who had strayed perilously near to the pit of totalitarianism. He had banished moral values from the province of law and made might into right. The American response to these startling accusations against the nation's erstwhile hero was made through the favorite media of communication. It was felt that if movie and television spoke of Holmes, something of his dignity could be restored to him. The language of sentimentality might revive the legend if it could not revive the truth" (introduction to *Holmes-Pollock Letters*, 1:iv).

65. Wilson, *Patriotic Gore*, 637–38.

66. Holmes papers, B38 F38; cited in Novick, *Honorable Justice*, 196.

67. Edwin Black, "The Sentimental Style as Escapism," in *Rhetorical Questions* (Chicago: University of Chicago Press, 1993), 99ff.

68. Robert Hariman, "Afterword: Relocating the Art of Public Address," in *Rhetoric and Political Culture in Nineteenth-Century America*, ed. Thomas W. Benson (East Lansing: Michigan State University Press, 1997), 164.

69. Ibid.

70. See Ralph Waldo Emerson, "Representative Men: Seven Lectures," in *Essays and Lectures* (New York: Library of America, 1983), 613–761. Another fruitful subject for rhetorical criticism would be a comparison of Holmes to Emerson; Emerson, of course, was a friend of Holmes's family, and Holmes sent his first published essay to Emerson for comments. See Howe, *Justice Oliver Wendell Holmes: The Shaping Years*, 1:203, where Holmes praises Emerson for starting "the philosophical ferment in my mind."

71. See Harold Bloom, *A Map of Misreading* (New York: Oxford University Press, 1975); and Harold Bloom, *Wallace Stevens: The Poems of Our Climate* (Ithaca, N.Y.: Cornell University Press, 1977).

72. James Arnt Aune, "Lincoln and the American Sublime," *Communication Reports* 1 (winter 1988): 14–19.

73. "The Path of the Law," in Holmes, *Collected Works*, 3:391–406; "Address at Brown University Commencement 1897," *Collected Works*, 3:518; "Law and the Court," *Collected Works*, 3:508.

74. Novick, *Honorable Justice*, 176.

75. Frederickson, *The Inner Civil War*, 219.

76. Ibid., 220.

77. I am using the text of Holmes, "Memorial Day," in *Occasional Speeches*, 4–16; page numbers are hereafter noted parenthetically in the text.

78. White, *Justice Oliver Wendell Holmes*, 79.

79. See especially Yosal Rogat, "Mr. Justice Holmes: A Dissenting Opinion," *Stanford Law Review* 15, no. 3 (1962): 254–308, for a discussion of the Holmes judicial opinions cases dealing with black civil rights, although it is wise to remember Jan Vetter's observation about Rogat's influential assault on Holmes. Rogat only proved that Holmes was not fit to sit on the Warren Court of 1964; See Jan Vetter, "The Evolution of Holmes: Holmes and Evolution," *California Law Review* 72, no. 3 (1984): 343–68.

80. It has become characteristic to refer to Holmes as a "liberal," as opposed to a "republican," after the "republican revival in legal history in the 1980s" (see Pnina Lahav, "Holmes and Brandeis: Libertarian and Republican Justifications for Free Speech," *Journal of Law and Politics* 4, no. 3 [1988]: 451–82). A better understanding of Roman republicanism might lead one to call Holmes the "last republican." His philosophical skepticism, belief in free speech, glorification of the martial virtues, and intense patriotism (he left his estate to the United States of America, which did not quite know what do with it) mark him more as Roman republican than classical liberal in his sensibilities.

81. I use the text of Holmes, "The Soldier's Faith," in *Occasional Speeches*, 73–83. Subsequent references to the speech are included parenthetically in the text.

82. Holmes to Pollock, 27 December 1895, *Holmes-Pollock Letters*; Holmes is referring to "Sentimental Jingoism," an anonymous editorial published in the *New York Evening Post*, 16 December 1895, 6 (evidently written by his classmate Wendell P. Garrison), and to "Force as a Moral Influence," *New York Evening Post*, 17 December 1895, 6, written by E. L. Godkin and reprinted in *Nation* 61 (19 December 1895): 440.

83. Theodore Roosevelt to Henry Cabot Lodge, 5 June 1895, *Selections from the Correspondence of Theodore Roosevelt and Henry Cabot Lodge* (New York: Charles Scribner's Sons, 1925), 1:146.

84. White, *Justice Oliver Wendell Holmes*, 83.

85. Holmes expressed this hatred of sentimentality more colorfully in a letter to Dean Wigmore of Northwestern University in 1915: "Doesn't this squashy sentimentality of a big minority of people make you puke? . . . people who think that something particular has happened and that the universe is no longer predatory. Oh bring in a basin"

(cited in Richard Polenberg, *Fighting Faiths: The Abrams Case, the Supreme Court, and Free Speech* [New York: Viking Press, 1987], 211).

86. I do not know if this "rough riding" image was borrowed by Theodore Roosevelt during the Spanish-American War, but the theme is clearly one that rang true with Roosevelt. Santayana, too, in *The Life of Reason*, praises sport as way of preserving the martial virtues (128–29).

87. Oliver Wendell Holmes Jr., "The Path of the Law," *Collected Works*, 3:391:406 (originally published in *Harvard Law Review* 10 [1897]: 457–78); also *Harvard Law Review* 110, 5 (1997): 991–1009. Two anthologies of Holmes's work, Lerner's *The Mind of Faith and Justice Holmes* and Posner's *The Essential Holmes*, omit portions of the speech, although that fact is not clearly noted by either editor. Subsequent page references refer to the *Collected Works* version.

88. Holmes, "The Path of the Law," in *Occasional Speeches*, ix n. 4.

89. David Luban, "The Bad Man and the Good Lawyer: A Centennial Essay on Holmes's 'The Path of the Law,'" *New York University Law Review* 72 (December 1997): 1550.

90. Stanley Fish, *Self-Consuming Artifacts* (Berkeley and Los Angeles: University of California Press, 1972).

91. Thomas C. Grey, "Plotting 'The Path of the Law,'" *Brooklyn Law Review* 63 (1997): 19–58.

92. On dissociation, see Chaim Perelman and Lucie Olbrechts-Tyteca, *The New Rhetoric*, trans. John Wilkinson (Notre Dame, Ind.: University of Notre Dame Press, 1969), chap. 4, 413ff.

93. Grey, "Plotting 'The Path of the Law,'" 48.

94. Luban, "The Bad Man and the Good Lawyer," 1559.

95. Joan I. Schwarz, "Oliver Wendell Holmes's 'The Path of the Law': Conflicting Views of the Legal World," *American Journal of Legal History* 29 (1985): 235–50.

96. William W. Fisher III, "Interpreting Holmes," *Harvard Law Review* 110, no. 5 (1997): 1010–12.

97. Richard D. Parker, "The Mind of Darkness," *Harvard Law Review* 110, no. 5 (1997): 1033–38.

98. Robert W. Gordon, "The Path of the Lawyer," *Harvard Law Review* 110, no. 5 (1997): 1013–18.

99. Richard A. Posner, "The Path away from the Law," *Harvard Law Review* 110, no. 5 (1997): 1039–43.

100. Holmes to Laski, *Holmes-Laski Letters*, 1:430, 14 June 1922.

101. I confess here that I just do not buy the emphasis on the "cruel" Holmes described by Grant Gilmore; anyone who has spent time with professional men (and I do believe it is a male quality)—lawyers, professors, doctors—can attest to the occasional brutal cynicism in which courts, students, or patients are described, but this does not prevent these professionals, any more than it did Holmes, from fulfilling their professional duties competently and even with compassion. Even in the Holmes-Pollock letters, used by everyone from the Jesuit attack dogs of the 1940s to G. Edward White as evidence of Holmes's cruelty and cynicism, reveal different sorts of beliefs: he criticizes Beard and Parrington for their cynical interpretation of the founding fathers, suggesting that it is a bad habit to get into; his statement to Brandeis that he is more interested in reading fiction during his vacation than learning about mistreatment of women and children in factories is belied by the later letter (never cited by Holmes's critics) that he did in fact read the materials Brandeis suggested.

102. Lewis, "Of Innocence, Exclusion, and the Burning of Flags."

103. Holmes, "The Law," in *Occasional Speeches*, 22–23.

104. Philip Wander, "The Third Persona: An Ideological Turn in Rhetorical Theory," *Central States Speech Journal* 35 (1984): 209.

105. Edward Lazarus, *Closed Chambers* (New York: Times Books, 1998).

106. Wilson, *Patriotic Gore*, 781.

107. Novick, *Honorable Justice*, 256.

108. G. Edward White, "The Integrity of Holmes's Jurisprudence," *Intervention and Detachment: Essays in Legal History and Jurisprudence* (New York: Oxford University Press, 1994), 99; originally published in *Hofstra Law Review* 10 (1982). Frederic Rogers

Kellogg makes an additional observation about Holmes's brevity: "His writings are full of aphorisms as fascinating as they are unfashionable—and unfathomable—today. There is the feeling that Holmes was the messenger of glimpses of an understanding greater than he was given to explain" (introduction to *The Formative Essays of Justice Holmes,* ix).

109. Mary Dudziak, "Oliver Wendell Holmes as a Eugenic Reformer: Rhetoric in the Writing of Constitutional Law," *Iowa Law Review* 71 (March 1986): 859.

110. See Posner, *Problems of Jurisprudence,* 190; for a particularly chilling discussion of the role of clerks in the formation of constitutional law, see Edward Lazarus's controversial account of the Supreme Court during his service as clerk for Justice Blackmun in *Closed Chambers.*

111. A possible starting point would be to trace Holmes's use of topical reasoning, as suggested in Jack M. Balkin, "A Night in the Topics: The Reason of Legal Rhetoric and the Rhetoric of Legal Reason," in *Law's Stories,* 211–24.

112. The definitive history of the Court's decisions during this period is in David P. Currie, *The Constitution in the Supreme Court: The Second Century, 1888–1986* (Chicago: University of Chicago Press, 1990); see p. 50 for the "reign of terror" comment.

113. Eileen Scallen, "Presence and Absence in Lochner: Making Rights Real," *Hastings Constitutional Law Quarterly* 23, no. 3 (1996): 623–25.

114. *Jacobson v. Massachusetts,* 197 U.S. 11 (1905).

115. *Otis v. Parker,* 187 U.S. 606 (1905).

116. *Holden v. Hardy,* 169 U.S. 366 (1905).

117. *Lochner v. New York,* 198 U.S. 45, 74–76 (Holmes, dissenting [1905]).

118. Richard A. Posner, *Law and Literature: A Misunderstood Relation* (Cambridge: Harvard University Press, 1988), 285–86.

119. Ibid., 283–84.

120. Ibid., 283

121. Ibid.

122. Ibid., 286.

123. *Lochner v. New York,* 198 U.S. 45, 56, 61 (1905).

124. Frederick Pollock, *Law Quarterly Review* 3 (1905): 211.

125. *Lochner v. New York,* 198 U.S. 57.

126. David R. Roediger and Philip S. Foner, *Our Own Time: A History of American Labor and the Working Day* (London: Verso, 1989), 157–58.

127. For a thorough history of the Espionage Act, see David Rabban, *Free Speech in Its Forgotten Years* (Cambridge: Cambridge University Press, 1997), 248–98.

128. *Schenck v. United States,* 249 U.S. 47 (1919).

129. Ibid.

130. Holmes himself relied on the "bad tendency" doctrine in his opinion for the Court in *Patterson v. Colorado,* 205 U.S. 454 (1907). See Rabban, *Free Speech in Its Forgotten Years,* 132–46, for a discussion of Holmes's pre-*Schenck* free speech opinions.

131. Rabban, *Free Speech in Its Forgotten Years,* 217; see all of chapter 5, "Free Speech in Progressive Social Thought," 211–47, for a thorough discussion of Dewey and Croly on free speech.

132. See Vetter, "The Evolution of Holmes," 343–68. See also Glendon, *Rights Talk,* for the original criticism of the dominance of a discourse of individual rights in the United States since the 1960s. The last chapter of Rabban's *Free Speech in Forgotten Years* shows the similarities between the current criticism of rights talk and free speech from the Left and the prewar progressive position on free speech. He criticizes Cass Sunstein, Owen Fiss, and other left-wing opponents of free speech for neglecting the lesson that Progressives learned from the federal government's behavior during World War I (381–93). See Cass Sunstein, *Democracy and the Problem of Free Speech* (New York: Oxford University Press, 1993); Owen M. Fiss, *The Irony of Free Speech* (Cambridge: Harvard University Press, 1996).

133. Lerner, *The Mind and Faith of Justice Holmes,* 294.

134. White, *Justice Oliver Wendell Holmes,* 418.

135. H. L. Pohlman, *Justice Oliver Wendell Holmes: Free Speech and the Living Constitution* (New York: New York University Press, 1991), 66.

136. See Hugo Black's dissent in *Dennis v. United States*, 341 U.S. 494 (1951).

137. *Abrams v. United States*, 250 U.S. 616, 624 (1919).

138. Polenberg, *Fighting Faiths*.

139. Max Lerner, *Mind and Faith*, called it "the greatest utterance on intellectual freedom by an American, ranking in the English tongue with Milton and Mill" (306). Frankfurter wrote that it would "live as long as English prose retains its power to move." Frankfurter to Holmes, 12 November 1919, *Holmes and Frankfurter: Their Correspondence, 1912–1934*, ed. Robert M. Mennel and Christine L. Compston (Hanover, N.H.: University Press of New England, 1996), 55. G. Edward White, predictably, dismissed it and the later dissents as a "rhetorical spree" that masked the incoherence of Holmes's doctrine of free speech, White, *Justice Oliver Wendell Homes*, 413, 453.

140. *Abrams v. United States*, 250 U.S. 616 at 613.

141. See Rabban, *Free Speech in Its Forgotten Years*, 316–35, on Chafee and his influence on Holmes's *Abrams* dissent. As Polenberg discovered, Holmes read a number of books on free speech and related topics during the summer of 1919; Polenberg, *Fighting Faiths*, 221–28.

142. Holmes to Frankfurter, 12 October 1915, *Holmes and Frankfurter,*, ed. Mennel and Compston, 36.

143. Holmes to Laski, 22 October 1916, *Holmes-Laski Letters*, 1:29.

144. Marouf Hasian Jr., "The Rhetorical Turn in First Amendment Scholarship: A Case Study of Holmes and the 'Marketplace of Ideas,'" *Free Speech Yearbook* 31 (1993): 42–65.

145. Lahav, "Holmes and Brandeis," 458, 461.

146. White, *Justice Oliver Wendell Holmes*, 453.

147. Holmes to Laski, 26 October 1919, *Holmes-Laski Letters*, 1:217.

148. *Buck v. Bell*, 274 U.S. 207.

149. William E. Leuchtenberg, *The Supreme Court Reborn* (New York: Oxford University Press, 1995), 16–17.

150. Ibid., 9.

151. Ibid., 24.

152. Ibid.

153. Posner, *Law and Literature*, 288–89.

154. Justice Harlan Stone's phrase in the famous "Footnote Four" of *United States v. Carolene Products*, 323 U.S. 152–53 (1938); see John Hart Ely, *Democracy and Distrust: A Theory of Judicial Review* (Cambridge: Harvard University Press, 1980), for a thorough discussion.

155. Glendon, *Rights Talk*.

156. Holmes, "The Law," *Collected Works*, 3:470.

157. The best account of American jurisprudence in the twentieth century, up to critical legal studies, is Neil Duxbury, *Patterns of American Jurisprudence* (Oxford: Oxford University Press, 1995); more opinionated, but equally helpful, is Richard A. Posner, *Problems of Jurisprudence* (Cambridge: Harvard University Press, 1990).

158. Chaim Perelman, *The Realm of Rhetoric*, trans. William Kluback (Notre Dame, Ind.: University of Notre Dame Press, 1982), 26–28.

William Jennings Bryan: The Jeffersonian Liberal as Progressive

Malcolm O. Sillars

6

William Jennings Bryan was born in 1860 at Salem, in the Egyptian triangle of southern Illinois. He attended Illinois College in Jacksonville, near Springfield, where he was an avid debater, orator, and valedictorian of a class of eleven in 1881. He studied law in Chicago at Union School of Law, worked as a clerk for Lyman Trumbull, former U.S. senator and one-time political associate of Abraham Lincoln. His first practice was in Jacksonville, Illinois, but in 1888 he moved to Lincoln, Nebraska. A lifelong Democrat from a Democratic family, he was elected to Congress in 1890 and 1892 and was an unsuccessful senatorial candidate in 1894. In 1896, at thirty-six years of age, he was the youngest presidential candidate in U.S. history. He ran again and lost in 1900. He drafted the Democratic platform that conservative Alton B. Parker refused to run on in 1904. He was a losing presidential candidate again in 1908. He helped nominate and campaigned for Woodrow Wilson in 1912, and served as his secretary of state from 1912 to 1915. He campaigned for Wilson in 1916. He was active in the prohibition campaign and the antievolution campaigns after that. He died in 1925, shortly after the close of the Scopes trial, where he had his famous confrontation with Clarence Darrow.

Bryan was a consummate politician. But most of all, he was an orator. From "Character," his valedictorian address at Illinois College, to his last speech at Winchester, Tennessee, the political stump to Chautauqua, his was a life of speaking. One summary has it that he spent one-third of his nights in his bed at home, one-third in hotel rooms, and one-third in railroad cars on the road. From 1900 to 1916 he published the *Commoner*, a newspaper of his speeches and kindred articles. He also published numerous compilations of his speeches in book form beginning with the history of the 1896 presidential campaign, *First Battle*. And the final word on William Jennings Bryan may have been written in the scathing treatment he received for his role in economic reform and particularly for his role in the Scopes trial. Perhaps his intellect may be summed up in the observation that "The Boy Orator of the Platte" was like the Platte River, "six inches deep and six miles wide at the mouth."[1]

There is a good deal in popular lore that makes William Jennings Bryan easy to understand. Here is the usual scenario. He grew up in a staunchly Democratic and religious home. He championed the oppressed farmers of the West and South against the plutocracy. He supported free silver, income tax, direct election of senators, control of trusts and railroads, woman's vote, and a host of other reform proposals. He opposed imperialism. When he was unsuccessful in politics he turned to religion and supported those who would restrict freedom: prohibitionists and antievolutionists. He was destroyed on the witness stand at the Scopes trial in Dayton, Tennessee, by Clarence Darrow and in the newspapers of America by H. L. Mencken, among others. He talked so much that he did not have time to read and learn. So, the well from which he drank became less and less productive as time went on. It was only his magnificent voice that held his supporters and admirers to him—that, and the fact that he spoke their own banal thoughts.

A more careful examination of William Jennings Bryan and his rhetoric makes Bryan a more complex player in the Progressive Era. On many issues he anticipated the Progressives. They came to accept his positions after rejecting them when he first advanced them. He began as a Jeffersonian liberal who argued for individual liberty but came to see that "life, liberty, and the pursuit of happiness" could, in an industrial age, only be protected by government action. He separated from some Progressives with his objection to imperialism. But in this and in virtually every other issue he addressed, from free coinage of silver to antievolution laws, he provided a consistent image of a progressivism rooted in the freedom of the individual and in the protection of that freedom through democratic action.

Bryan and the Progressive Era

Historian Robert W. Cherny has described the town of Salem, Illinois, of 1870, when Bryan was ten years old:

In 1870, the town of Salem counted 342 people with identifiable occupations other than farmer or farm laborer. About a hundred worked as artisans: carpenters, saddle and harness makers, shoemakers, butchers, bakers, blacksmiths, milliners. Most artisans worked in their own shops, usually without assistance except from family members. Another seventy provided personal services, half as domestic servants, most of the others as launderers, saloonkeepers, hotel keepers, and barbers. The town counted nearly equal numbers of professionals—teachers, physicians, and lawyers—and of merchants, bankers, brokers, or agents. As county seat, Salem claimed nearly two dozen government officials, most of them serving the town and county. Manufacturing was limited and small in scale; members of the community purchased the flour and lumber produced by Salem's three mills. They also bought most of the plows, wagons, and carriages made in Salem's one manufacturing shop. The mills each employed four to six workers; the shop occasionally hired as many as eleven. Only one adult Salemite in five worked for wages, most of them as domestic servants, day laborers, teachers, or store clerks. Agriculture controlled the economic destiny of the entire population. If crops were good and prices steady, the merchants, artisans, proprietors, and professionals of Salem prospered along with the farmers. In his most famous speech, Bryan was to proclaim, "destroy our farms and the grass will grow in the streets of every city in the country." His dictum unquestionably held true for Salem and thousands of other towns like it.[2]

This was the America that Bryan knew, the America of farms and small towns, and it was to and for this America that he first spoke. Like Thomas Jefferson, his idol, Bryan viewed agrarian America as the ideal America. But the image of America as Salem, Illinois, was at that moment being reworked. The "myth of the garden," as Henry Nash Smith has called it, had a defined limit in John Wesley Powell's observation in 1874 that "All of the regions of the country west of the 100th or 99th meridian except a little in California, Oregon and Washington territory, is arid, and no part of that country can be . . . redeemed for agriculture, except by irrigation."[3] The concept of the yeoman farmer and the small towns that supported the family farm was on the way to ending as the dominant image of American life.

Bryan's America was giving way to a new industrial America. Jefferson, in his "First Inaugural Address," had argued for "the encouragement of agriculture, and of commerce as its handmaid."[4] But the late nineteenth and early twentieth centuries would see a revolution of a non-Jeffersonian variety—an America defined neither by agriculture nor by commerce, but by industry.

Iron and steel produced on an average day at blast furnaces "increased from no more than forty-five tons before the Civil War to more than four hundred tons in the early twentieth century."[5] By 1900, America produced double the amount of steel produced in England and was now the world's greatest producer of iron, steel, and coal.[6] Oil production, unheard of before 1860, would become a major industry. A national transportation system developed to move industrial production. "By 1915, when the railroads boasted some 250,000 miles of track, hardly an important community in the country lay outside this extensive system."[7] The railroads brought raw materials to the major cities and dispersed the manufactured products to be sold across the nation and the globe. They were also a major consumer of iron and steel.

In this period, the major cities were created—not only the large industrial centers such as Boston, New York, Cleveland, Chicago, and Minneapolis, but also the smaller industrial centers such as Fall River, Massachusetts; Patterson, New Jersey; and Rochester, New York. Identified with them were "bedroom communities" such as Lake Forest, Greenwich, and Brookline. The nature of the economy changed and the social system changed with it. To populate these large urban centers there was a gradual but steady movement of population from rural to urban centers. Twenty-eight percent of the population lived in places of twenty-five hundred or more inhabitants in 1850, almost 40 percent in 1900, and well over 50 percent by 1920.[8]

Between 1820 and 1930 America also experienced what Samuel P. Hayes has called "one of the largest and most significant migrations in world history" as over thirty-seven million people immigrated. The third move, between 1900 and 1930, was not like the previous wave of immigrants, who were primarily from Britain and northern Europe, but instead consisted of people from southern and eastern Europe: Italians, Poles, Greeks, and Russians; they were mostly Catholic, Greek Orthodox, or Jewish, spoke a foreign tongue, and numbered almost nineteen million.[9] This migration brought laborers to the cities who had never heard of Thomas Jefferson or seen Western democracy at work.

But the Progressive Era is defined by more than massive changes to an industrial economy. It is marked by the organization of all facets of the society and the rise of the expert. Producers, laborers, and farmers all organized in order to better control the economic conditions under which they worked. "Industrialism," Samuel Hayes notes, "had shifted the context of economic decisions from personal relationships among individuals to competition among well organized groups."[10]

Not only was this organization society characterized by the rise of groups such as the National Association of Manufacturers, the American Federation of Labor, and the Farmer's Cooperatives, it permeated all parts of American life. The National Association for the Advancement of Colored People, the Federal Council of Churches of Christ in America, the National Consumer's League, and the National Conference of Catholic Charities are only a few of the organizations founded to influence national society and policy in these years. The Progressive Era was the beginning of a modern era, when only the organized would influence society.

This reorganization around special interests occurred even in higher education. The German system of higher education was brought to the United States, and many scholars went to Germany to study. That system emphasized research for the public benefit, the Ph.D., and the structure of the university around disciplines. The restructuring of the old gentleman's English educational system began with Johns Hopkins and Cornell Universities and rapidly expanded into the land-grant state universities in the West and the older, private institutions of the East. Along with university expansion and reorganization came the founding of professional associations and journals: "Beginning with the founding of the American Economic Association in 1885 and the American Academy of Political and Social Science in 1890 a host of discipline-defined organizations and journals developed."[11] This was the period when the forerunners of the National Communication Association (1914), the Association for Education in Journalism and Mass Communication (1910), and the Society of Professional Journalists (1909) were formed.

The general move toward professionalism and expertise, both in the industrial economy and in academe, established the intellectual base of progressivism. Eldon J. Eisenach identifies nineteen persons as "the authors of progressive public doctrine," thirteen of whom were academics, including Jane Addams, John Dewey, Charlotte Perkins Gilman, and Edward Alsworth Ross. Ross is mentioned here not because he is as well-known today as the others, but because this professor of economics and sociology at Stanford University, the University of Nebraska, and the University of Wisconsin was not only "the most prominent American social theorist of his day," but also a personal friend of William Jennings Bryan.[12]

This intellectual core of progressivism was reflected in the public arena by a host of individuals, including Theodore Roosevelt, Albert Jeremiah Beveridge, Robert La Follette, Woodrow Wilson, and Bryan. In varying degrees and on varying issues they advocated that government be used to organize the society for the moral benefit of the people. A complex society, such as the United States, could not be run on pure principles of individual freedom. The Puritan notion of community had to be developed to control the seemingly moral vacuum of selfish individualism that seemed to Progressives to threaten America at the turn of the century.[13]

With the concentration of wealth and population came urban social problems of housing, sanitation, social stability, and political corruption. So it seemed to many that something was wrong and something had to be done. Farmers, particularly in the plains states and in the South, rebelled against low prices, expensive credit, excessive railroad rates, and a federal government they saw as indifferent to their plight or actively engaged as agents of a plutocracy. Bryan's career spans what is now known as the Progressive Era, and he may justifiably be considered a Progressive because of many of the reforms that he advocated. While primarily oriented to the agrarian problems, he discovered the problems of industrial workers early in his life. As a law student in Chicago, he wrote to his fiancée, Mary Baird, about his unhappiness with the conditions of laborers in the city and of their domination by big business. He visited the shops of George Pullman and commented that the workers were prepared to rebel against low pay and poor working conditions, which they did a few years later.[14]

Bryan's active political career spans the Progressive Era, and he spoke out on virtually every issue of that era. What has to be obvious is that there was not one face to progressivism but several faces. Bryan's rhetoric defines one of those faces. It can be delineated by following Bryan's career through a series of issues. His definition of progressivism influenced the nature of the Democratic Party and the nature of reform down to today. It covered many facets but was always grounded in agrarian liberalism.

Bryan as Jeffersonian Liberal

The agrarian myth was the first element of liberalism on which Bryan's rhetoric turned. His definition of a "business man" in his 1896 Democratic Convention speech popularly known as the "Cross of Gold," illustrates it beautifully. In that speech, Bryan's agrarian bias is evident not only in the contrasting images of the plutocrat and the yeoman, but also in the sheer weight of words he uses to describe the two parts of society who work directly with nature: the farmer and the miner.

> We say to you that you have made the definition of a business man too limited in its application. The man who is employed for wages is as much a business man as his employer, the attorney in a country town is as much a business man as the corporation counsel in a great metropolis; the merchant at the cross-roads store is as much a business man as the merchant of New York; the farmer who goes forth in the morning and toils all day—who begins in the spring and toils all summer—and who by the application of brain and muscle to the natural resources of the country creates wealth, is as much a business man as the man who goes upon the board of trade and bets upon the price of grain; the miners who go down a thousand feet into to earth, or climb two thousand feet upon the cliffs, and bring forth the precious metals to be poured into the channels of trade are as much business men as the few financial magnates who, in a back room, corner the money of the world. We come to speak for this broader class of business men.[15]

Bryan would later support conservation as a national responsibility to preserve the watershed and clean drinking water. But even in 1911 he confessed, "I am one who has been blind, during part of my life, to the needs that are now so clearly recognized." Even then he felt the problem was more a state than a federal problem, and he spent most of his speech at the National Conservation Congress speaking of farmers and their closeness to the soil. Conservation, for Bryan, was clearly linked to the agrarian myth.[16]

Bryan's reform motives are not only rooted in agrarianism. He was also totally committed to the Jeffersonian ideas of individual freedom, inalienable rights, covenants, and limited government. On some questions he sounded more like Andrew Jackson, both activist and Populist.[17] But there is no doubt that Thomas Jefferson was his chief idol. Over and over again, on virtually every issue, as this analysis will show, he cited Jefferson, particularly the Declaration of Independence: "We hold these truths to be self-evident, that all men are created equal; that they are endowed by their Creator with certain unalienable Rights; that among these are Life, Liberty, and the Pursuit of Happiness."

Bryan never wavered from what he saw as Jeffersonian principles. "A Jeffersonian democrat," he wrote in 1912, "is one who believes with Jefferson in his conception of government. Jefferson trusted the people and believed that they were the source of power and authority. Anything that brings the government nearer to the people and makes it more responsive to the will of the people is Jeffersonian. I regard the election of senators by the people, the initiative and referendum, etc., as in line with Jeffersonian principles. In legislation the application of Jeffersonian principles leads us to consider the interests of the whole people rather than the demands of a class. Jefferson's motto of equal rights to all and special privileges to none is the fundamental law that governs legislation and the administration of government."[18]

Bryan's reforms all focused on protecting the rights of, and making the system work for, the individual. The direct election of senators, woman's suffrage, initiative referendum and recall, tariff reduction, and many other issues he linked to individual freedom. But he also argued for government action that would limit individual action. Certainly the income tax, controls on trusts, free silver, banking regulation, railroad regulation, the Pure Food and Drug Act, and a host of other reforms involved the essential contradiction that he shared with most Progressives between supporting individual freedom and advocating a more activist federal government. For instance, he argued early for a plan of government-guaranteed bank deposits, although it would not be until the New Deal that Americans would adopt it. He settled for an amended Reserve System with regional offices and government, not banker control, but what he wanted were guaranteed deposits to protect the individual. Here is Bryan's speech in Topeka, Kansas, on 28 August 1908:

> Why not make the depositor secure? The United States Government requires the deposit of specific security when it entrusts money to a national bank, altho[ugh] it can examine the bank at any time; the State requires security when it deposits money in a bank; the county requires security and the city requires security; even the banks require security from the officials who handle money. Why should the depositor be left to take his chances?
>
> Not only is the depositor without protection, but the security given to nation, state, county and city lessens his security. They are preferred creditors; they have a mortgage on the gilt-edged assets and the depositor must get along as best he can with what remains. Why are the interests of depositors thus neglected?[19]

Still, Bryan's earliest political positions clearly remained in the tradition of Jeffersonian liberalism. His first major speech as a congressman from Nebraska was delivered on 16 March 1892 and supported a report of the Ways and Means Committee (of which he was a member) to reduce the tariff on manufactured goods. His argument was that the "wool tariff is the keystone of the protective arch" and must end because it does not benefit the wool growers and because its cost is passed on to the consumer. His argument was simple and direct, expressing fundamental concern for the ordinary person:

> The reason why I believe in putting raw material upon the free list is because any tax imposed upon raw material must at last be taken from the consumer of the manufactured article. You can impose no tax for the benefit of the producer of raw material which does not find its way through the various forms of manufactured products and at last press with accumulated weight upon the person who uses the finished product.[20]

Removing the tariff was not "class legislation," as some of his opponents had claimed: "It is sufficient evidence, Mr. Chairman, that this bill does not advance class legislation that the Republican party is solidly opposing it. If it were class legislation we could reasonably expect their united support." This not-so-subtle identification of the Republican Party as the true exponent of class legislation was followed by his characterization of the tariff opponents as "saying simply what every honest man says, 'Let me alone to enjoy the results of my toil.'"[21] Clearly, his position on the tariff was in the long-standing Democratic tradition of greater individual freedom and less governmental interference.

Tariff reform had been Bryan's main issue as he campaigned for a house seat from Nebraska's First Congressional District in 1890 and 1892. The income tax was his second most important issue as he went on the stump in the fall of 1891. In January 1894 he debated with New York Democrat Bourke Cockran over Bryan's plan to add an income tax to replace the revenue lost because of tariff reduction. Bryan "favored a graduated income tax that began with the incomes of $2500 and would affect only between 50,000 and 80,000 people, but the [Ways and Means] committee directed him to provide for a straight 2 percent tax on personal and net corporate incomes of over $4000." Cockran argued that the tax was a socialistic measure that would cause a collapse in democratic government if all persons did not share equally.[22] Bryan argued that the exemptions were typical in tax laws, citing New York and Connecticut: "The gentlemen who are so fearful of socialism when the poor are exempted from an income tax view with indifference those methods of taxation which give the rich a substantial exemption. They weep more because fifteen millions are to be collected from the incomes of the rich than they do at the collection of three hundred millions upon the goods which the poor consume. And when an attempt is made to equalize these burdens, not fully, but partially only, the people of the South and West are called anarchists."[23] He found the income tax no more invasive of privacy than other taxes.[24] He defended "the people of the South and West," and by implication himself, as "the staunchest supporters of government, . . . the best friends of law and order," and "willing to protect the rights of property, even while they demand that property shall bear its share of taxation."[25] While others found the income tax a dangerously radical proposal, for Bryan it was a simple extension of Jeffersonian liberalism.

The Campaign of 1896

Bryan is best remembered for his advocacy of currency reform and, more specifically, for the free coinage of silver at sixteen to one. His congressional campaign platform in 1890 called for free coinage and, after extensive study, he settled by the end of July 1891 on the ratio of silver to gold at sixteen to one.[26] By the Democratic Convention of 1896 he was a leader in the cause, and after his most famous speech on the subject, "Cross of Gold," he won the nomination at age thirty-six, becoming the youngest presidential candidate ever.

That nomination and the subsequent campaign split the Democratic Party and, to a lesser extent, the Republican Party. Free silver and other issues had already led to the formation of the People's Party, which joined with Bryan by giving him its nomination. Bryan campaigned extensively, while the Republican candidate, William McKinley, carried on a front-porch campaign, with carefully selected groups brought to his home in Marion, Ohio. Mark Hanna, McKinley's campaign manager, raised and spent $16 million to the Democrats' $600,000, almost double sixteen to one. Hanna's campaign was replete with voter fraud, vote purchasing, and political blackmail of the unsubtle variety, such as notices to workers that "Bryan men need not return to work if Bryan were elected."[27] Republicans used the argument that McKinley's election would bring "the full dinner pail," and that Bryan's would mean economic disaster. Immediately after the election, Republican newspapers such as the *New York Weekly Tribune* ran stories of new plant openings and expansions attributable to the election: "McKinley Starts Great Plant," "He Lights the Fires in the Furnace of the Niagara Iron and Steel Works," "Southern Iron Industry Already Feels the Effect of McKinley's Election," "Brighter Days for Labor," and "Thousands of Unemployed Hands Securing Work." These are just a few of the headlines in one issue of the *Tribune* proclaiming that McKinley's election had ended the recession.[28]

Bryan's espousal of free silver and his association with the People's Party, Tom Watson, John Peter Altgeld, Eugene Debs, and others made him a fine target for some of the worst personal abuse ever in a political campaign. *Harper's Weekly* published a cartoon on its cover with Bryan's face and the words "free silver" on a coin, which was held up as a mask before a dark and sinister Altgeld, carrying the torch of anarchy, with the caption "Leader Altgeld and his mask."[29] In this cartoon and others, Bryan was portrayed as a naïve dupe of more sinister forces, but, more frequently, the criticism was not so kind. When Bryan was nominated by the People's Party at the Saint Louis Convention in July 1896, the *New York Times* said of that association:

> It is inconceivable that the sober-thinking, self-respecting, clean, and orderly people of any section should be carried away by the hysterical, senseless, vituperative yawplings of orators drawn from Coxey's Army of Commonwealers, or that anybody who has learned anything about the pranks of the freaky delegates to the St. Louis Convention should contemplate for a moment the casting of a vote that would give an irresponsible, unregulated, ignorant, prejudiced, pathetically honest and enthusiastic crank complete or partial control of the Government.[30]

Harper's Weekly saw McKinley's election as a "Defeat of Socialism," which had been unknowingly advanced by the ignorant:

> If Mr Bryan and his party have not adopted the full programme of the cult which in Europe is struggling for the realization of the dreams and fantasies of Karl Marx, it is because, in their ignorance, the candidate and most of his political associates do not yet understand the logic of their attitude.[31]

The *New York Weekly Tribune* (the paper founded by Horace Greeley) was considerably stronger in its views than even the title of its editorial, "Good Riddance," would indicate:

> The people have dismissed it [the Bryan candidacy] with no uncertain tones. Hereafter let there be whatever controversies men may please about the tariff, about the currency, about the Monroe Doctrine, and all the rest. But let there never again be a proposition to repeal the Moral Law, to garble the Constitution, and to replace the Stars and Stripes with the red rag of Anarchy. On those other topics, honest men may honestly differ, in full loyalty to the Republic. On these latter there is no room for two opinions, save in the minds of traitors, knaves and fools.
>
> The thing was conceived in iniquity and was brought forth in sin. It had its origin in a malicious conspiracy against the honor and integrity of the nation. It gained such monstrous growth as it enjoyed from assiduous culture of the basest passions of the least worthy members of the community. It has been defeated and destroyed because right is right and God is God.
>
> Its nominal head was worthy of the cause. Nominal, because the wretched, rattle-pated boy, posing in vapid vanity and mouthing resounding rottenness, was not the real leader of that league of hell. He was only a puppet in the blood-imbued hands of Altgeld, the anarchist, and Debs, the revolutionist, and other desperadoes of that stripe. But he was a willing puppet, Bryan was, willing and eager. Not one of the masters was more apt than he at lies and forgeries and blasphemies and all the nameless iniquities of that campaign against the Ten Commandments. He goes down with the cause, and must abide with it in the history of infamy. He had less provocation than Benedict Arnold, less intellectual force than Aaron Burr, less manliness and courage than Jefferson

Davis. He was the rival of them all in deliberate wickedness and treason to the Republic. His name belongs with theirs, neither the most brilliant nor the most hateful in the list.

Good riddance to it all, to conspiracy and conspirators, and to the foul menace of repudiation and anarchy against the honor and life of the republic.[32]

Bryan, however, remained amazingly calm and refused to respond in kind to such vicious attacks on his integrity and his intelligence. He made his case, and even in defeat he was not bitter. He set about preparing for the next campaign by editing a collection of his speeches. Its title indicated that there would be other campaigns. This had been only the *First Battle*.

Why was Bryan so vilified? Because he was seen as a populist, a socialist, or an anarchist. Yet the Democratic platform that Bryan helped construct and on which he ran in 1896 was strikingly different from the People's Party platform. For instance, it did not include government ownership of railroads and telegraphs, opting only for greater regulation of railroads to control the formation of trusts.[33] Bryan indicated after his nomination by the People's Party that its "platform is, on many questions, substantially identical with the Chicago [Democratic] platform; it goes beyond the Chicago platform, however, and endorses some policies of which I do not approve."[34] It is quite clear that he was referring to government ownership of railroads. Only once, and only briefly in 1906, did he espouse such a proposal.[35]

Bryan's support for initiative referendum and recall, direct election of senators, an end to lifetime appointments, one term for the president and the vice president, and similar proposals inspired some of the attacks on him. He also offended some with his support for trust busting and regulation and for the income tax. He identified these and other positions as an attack on the "plutocrats." However, the greatest source of opposition to Bryan seems to have been on the "money question."

In some ways, bimetallism appears to be an insignificant question. The Republican platform called for the institution of free silver by international agreement.[36] That had been the ingenious suggestion of William McKinley, soon to be their nominee. It was a compromise between the silver Republicans of the West and the gold Republicans of the East. On the surface, at least, it was a rather minor issue of whether to have free coinage immediately and unilaterally or to wait for international agreement. But it still left the impression that the Republicans were for "sound money" and that the Democrats were not.

The underlying struggle was between creditor and debtor. After the Civil War, when money was plentiful, it was borrowed from financial institutions. That was a period of inflation. Subsequently, a series of laws were enacted to shrink the money supply. Money was less plentiful and more expensive, so debtors were obligated to pay back loans with money more valuable than the money they had borrowed. Republicans and gold Democrats argued for "sound money." Bryan and his supporters argued for an "honest dollar." In his Madison Square Garden acceptance speech, 12 August 1886, he made the question quite simple: "What is the test of honesty in money? It must certainly be found in the purchasing power of the dollar. An undoubtedly honest dollar would not vary in its general purchasing power; it would be absolutely stable when measured by average prices. A dollar which increases in purchasing power is just as dishonest as a dollar which decreases in purchasing power. . . . It cannot be successfully claimed that monometallism or bimetallism, or any other system, gives an absolutely just standard of value. . . . Bimetallism is better that monometallism, not because it gives us a perfect dollar— that is a dollar absolutely unvarying in its general purchasing power—but because it makes a nearer approach, to stability, to honesty, to justice, than a gold standard possibly can."[37]

The gold standard, he claimed, "depresses prices, and transfers to the pockets of the creditor class an unearned increment. . . . [T]he crusade against silver must inevitably raise the purchasing power of money and lower the money value of all other forms of property."[38]

Free coinage of silver may have been, as many have argued, too complex an issue to explain. The understanding that one was out of a job, or was unable to purchase enough goods and services, or was losing the farm was difficult to link to a proposal for free coinage of silver at a sixteen-to-one ratio. Added to that, some of the problems of depression were alleviated as the campaign continued. According to Coletta, by August the price for farm products had begun to increase. Wheat, for instance, went from "47 cents a bushel in 1894 to 53 cents in August of 1896, and to a three-year high of 84 cents in December." By the campaign of 1900, silver was a minor issue because increased gold production in Alaska, South Africa, and Australia and general prosperity had eliminated the problem.[39]

Still, Bryan had moved into what for some was radical territory—the manipulation of the money supply by the government—and he had drawn what seemed like a class line. He would address the currency question again when he advised President Woodrow Wilson on provisions of the Federal Reserve Act. But it was free coinage of silver that brought charges that he was a crackpot, a radical, a socialist, or an anarchist. His metaphor at the Chicago Convention polarized in religious terms those who worked from those who controlled the money: "You shall not press down upon the brow of labor this crown of thorns, you shall not crucify mankind upon a cross of gold."[40]

In fact, Bryan's arguments were not rooted in class distinctions but in the democratic tradition of majority rule and Jeffersonian liberalism. The money question itself was, for Bryan, a matter of establishing stability so all could compete equally and freely, not a declaration of war by one class against another.

Before the proposal for free coinage of silver there had been many government efforts to control the money supply, such as the printing of Civil War greenbacks and various post–Civil War restrictions and silver purchase acts. Free coinage of silver was seen by its supporters as a natural way of adjusting the money supply. There is lots of silver, they thought, so it should be coined, almost like a free enterprise act. But it was a powerful step toward legitimizing the government's responsibility for the welfare of the people. In that way it was a step toward progressive reform, particularly when linked to other proposals for government regulation of industry.

Labor Policy

The Democratic campaign of 1896 has often been portrayed as a failure because Bryan emphasized the single issue of free silver which, as I have noted, was difficult for working people to understand. He did not appeal to a natural constituency, the working people of the East and Midwest. He did not follow Jacob Coxey's proposals, as stated in the People's Party platform, for the employment of the unemployed on public works projects.

His strongest pro-labor argument was, as a matter of fact, aimed in exactly the opposite direction, away from federal governmental action. He opposed the use of the injunction by the federal government in labor disputes, arguing that such disputes were more properly the responsibility of local and state governments. The Democratic Party platform stated this point of view clearly: "We denounce arbitrary interference by Federal authorities in local affairs as a violation of the Constitution of the United States and a crime against free institutions, and we especially object to government by injunction and a new and highly dangerous form of oppression by which Federal Judges, in contempt of the laws of the states and rights of citizens, become at once legislators, judges [and] executioners; . . . [we approve of] trials by jury in certain cases of contempt."[41]

In his letter accepting the nomination for president, Bryan acknowledged "the absolute necessity for the prompt and vigorous enforcement of laws and the preservation of the public peace." He grounded that view on the constitutional separation of powers: "It will be noticed that, while the United States guarantees to every state a republican form of government and is empowered to protect each state against invasion, it is not authorized to interfere in the domestic affairs of any State except upon application of the Legislature of the state or upon the application of the executive when the Legislature cannot be convened."[42]

The *New York Times* was quick to see that this general reference was intended to mean something more specific and sinister in Bryan's statement. "He wilfully ignores the fact that transportation of inter-State commerce and the United States mails are not the 'domestic affairs' of any State and cannot be left to the protection of any faithless Governor with whom a state for the time being may be afflicted. In other words, Mr. Bryan stands by the Anarchist Altgeld sheltering himself by a mischievous perversion of the doctrine of states rights."[43] Englishman Sidney Brooks, writing about Bryan four years later in the *Contemporary Review,* found that "In England, where property is much less sacred, individual rights more respected and legislation far more socialistic than in the States, so violent an innovation on the ordinary principles of jurisprudence [injunction] would be unthinkable. . . . Englishmen may get an envious idea of the American respect for property when an attack on such a system [judicial injunction] can be described as, and really believed to be, 'a crime against society.'"[44]

In addition to the states' rights argument, Bryan argued in his 1896 acceptance letter for passage of the Senate bill providing for trial by jury in "certain contempt cases" that "have grown out of the injunction proceedings." This was a position that he was to hold throughout his life.[45] In his 1908 Labor Day address in Chicago he argued that "an industrial dispute shall not, in itself, be regarded as a sufficient cause for injunction. If an injunction [is] issue[d] in an industrial dispute, it must be based on acts which would justify an injunction if there were no industrial dispute involved." Unlike the Republicans, he found no ambiguity in these words. He would have restricted the use of injunctions to situations in which laws had been violated; he opposed the use of injunctions for the benefit of the employers' side in a labor dispute. And if a dispute was subject to injunction, he said the case should be decided by a jury trial.[46]

Bryan then formed the issue between himself and his 1908 opponent William Howard Taft. "Mr. Taft takes issue with us. He is thoroughly aroused by what he regards as a menace to the courts." But, Bryan argued, the jury is better able to judge the merits of the case, particularly since the judge who hears the case is the same person who issued the injunction. He also questioned the fact that in "eighteen years of anti-trust legislation, only one man has been given a penal sentence for violating the federal [antitrust] law, . . . and that man was a member of a labor organization rather than a trust magnate."[47] Again, Bryan's position was not especially radical; it had to do with the separation of powers between state and federal government and his preference for legal decisions made by juries.

By 1908 Republicans were agreeing with Bryan on many points. Both parties supported an eight-hour workday and an employer's liability act. Both supported, as Bryan had in 1900 and 1904, the establishment of a Department of Labor: "The first step toward the elevation of labor to its proper position in the nation's deliberations is to be found in the establishment of a Department of Labor," Bryan argued, "with a cabinet officer at its head. The wage earners deserve this recognition, and the President is entitled to the assistance which such an official could render him."[48]

Bryan continued to argue for the arbitration of labor disputes, and in his 1908 Chicago Labor Day address he indicated that he saw the government as a major force for good. The Declaration of Independence, he argued in true Jeffersonian fashion, says that governments are instituted to protect life, liberty, and the pursuit of happiness. The second and third of these "are really parts of the first, for life means nothing to the individual if it is confined to mere animal existence. . . . Liberty is necessary for the realization of man's possibilities." And for Bryan, the "pursuit of happiness" meant equal opportunity ensured by the government:

> And what constitutes the pursuit of happiness? He must have house and friends—family and society. He must have food or he will starve. He must have clothing and shelter. He must have books, he must have instruments with which to work. . . . One of the great problems of today is to secure an equitable distribution of the proceeds of toil. . . . The Democratic party proclaims that each individual should receive from society a reward for his toil commensurate with his contribution to the welfare of society. . . . A good government is the best legacy that a parent can leave to his child. Riches may take the wings of the morning and fly away, but government is permanent, and we cannot serve posterity better than by contributing to the perfection of the government. That each child born into the world may feel that it has here an opportunity for the most complete development, and a chance to win through service, the largest possible happiness and honor.[49]

In a question-and-answer session at Cooper Union on 21 April 1908, Bryan was asked: "If you were elected to office what would you do regarding the unemployed?" "In the short term," he answered, "I believe it is the duty of the government to provide that no one shall suffer without his fault. . . . No humane government, no humane people will ever let a man or woman die from want. We must meet an immediate need immediately, furnishing labor if labor can be furnished, giving work if the government can supply it, and giving aid if work cannot be supplied." As for a "permanent cure," Bryan proposed that some laws be repealed and other laws passed to provide "a more equitable distribution of the proceeds of human toil." Bryan denied that this meant socialism. He said, "I believe that individualism is better than Socialism if you will remove the abuses that have grown up about individualism."[50] Thus, as he prepared for his third presidential campaign, he still emphasized the rights of the individual, but he had become even more progressive. He was willing to support the government welfare and work programs that he had shied away from in 1896. Government had become the necessary, permanent instrument for assuring life, liberty, and the pursuit of happiness.

Gender and Race

Clearly, the emphasis on individual rights was central to Bryan's progressivism. Throughout his political life he argued for such proposals as the popular election of senators, initiative referendum and recall, disclosure of campaign contributions, and even, in 1896, for a one-term limitation for the presidency.[51] Similarly, Bryan supported woman's suffrage in his first congressional platform in 1890. He spoke most openly for it in the 1914 Nebraska canvass on the issue, and subsequently he advocated a national suffrage amendment. He took a public position, in the words of Mary Baird Bryan, "when woman suffrage became a real issue before the American people."[52] It was probably at her urging that he did so. She was a member of the Congressional Committee of the National American Woman's Suffrage Association.[53]

His arguments for woman suffrage were quite traditional. At Alliance, Nebraska, he said: "Are women qualified to vote? The voter needs intelligence and morals—is not woman man's equal in both? Go to the Nebraska penitentiary and you will find three hundred and fifty inmates—only five are women—less than two percent. Go to the churches and you will find that the women outnumber the men there. Now, if the women have the good sense to keep out of the penitentiary and are moral enough to go to church are they not fit to go to the polls?"[54]

For Bryan, as for many who argued for suffrage, women were not only the equal of men but their moral superiors. He claimed that "the strongest argument in favor of woman suffrage is the mother argument." Women loved their children more than men, he argued, "and as long as the ballot is given to those who conspire to rob the home of a child it is not fair—no one can believe it fair—to tie a mother's hands while she is trying to protect her home and save her child."[55]

Bryan probably did not endorse woman's suffrage when he ran for president because the base of his national support was in the South and the Southern Democrats were mostly opposed to extending the suffrage. Even after he involved himself in the debate over woman's suffrage, he at first supported state action in deference to Southern wishes. Like President Wilson, Bryan possibly changed to favoring a constitutional amendment, according to Coletta, because "the adoption [of] the prohibition amendment made it difficult to take the states' rights position seriously."[56]

While Bryan eventually abandoned the states' rights position on woman's suffrage, he always maintained the states' authority on the civil rights of African Americans. In this period of Jim Crow laws and the separate-but-equal doctrine, Bryan bought the Southern position. Perhaps he was naïve, but more likely he was political. The South was a solid base of his political power, and African Americans were mostly Republicans. On several occasions he was called upon to explain the contradiction between his firm support of life, liberty, and pursuit of happiness and his acceptance of Southern restrictions on African Americans. At Cooper Union in 1908 he was asked, "Is the policy of disfranchising the Negro, advocated by Democrats of the South, in accord with the spirit of brotherhood?" At first, Bryan tried to answer by suggesting that educational qualifications on voting affected both "white" and "colored." He "called attention to the fact, that the colored man in the South who is disfranchised by an educational qualification has a chance to bring himself within the qualifications. . . . And in every state in the South where they have an educational qualification there are colored men who do vote." Then he changed the subject, pointing out that "[T]he Republican of the North, who objects to that, has fastened up the Filipino a colonial system under which no man, however intelligent, can hope to share in the destiny of this nation." The "colored man of the south" lived under a law that applied to everyone, he argued, while the Filipino lived under laws that applied only to them: "If a black man objects to the law in the south, I ask him why he helps to foster upon a brown man in the Orient a more odious qualification than is fostered upon the black man of the south."[57]

Bryan admitted that such an argument was only a way of saying that a "Republican cannot in justice" ask such a question. He then answered "more frankly," exposing the social fears behind his position. "The white man in the south puts on that qualification as a matter of self-protection," he argued, and there was not "a Republican community in the North that would not add it on when necessary." It was done by Republicans in Washington, D.C., he pointed out, where they "disfranchised white men in order to disfranchise black men, and they would do it anywhere else, if necessary, to prevent what occurred in the South under carpet-bag government."[58]

His answer was even more specific in 1923. No longer a candidate for office, the racial basis of his view is clear. One race was more advanced than the other and should rule, he claimed, but that did not mean that blacks would be denied legal equality:

> The problem which the whites of the south had to solve did not involve the question of equality before the law; . . . no one denied that the blacks are entitled to equal-protection in their rights. The question is: which race shall control the government and make the laws under which both shall live? The more advanced race will always control, as a matter of self-preservation, not only for the benefit of the advanced race but for the benefit of the backward race also. . . .
>
> It is no reflection upon the black race to say that they could not formulate laws and administer government as well as the whites. It is only a few centuries since the ancestors of the colored people of the south were brought from Africa as slaves. They have made wonderful progress and they have made it because they have been associated with and helped by white people. Slavery among the whites was an improvement over independence in Africa.[59]

Bryan expressed a rather different view on 8 August 1900, when he launched his second presidential campaign primarily on the issue of imperialism in the Philippines. Then he said, "It was God himself who placed in every human heart the love of liberty. He never made a race of people so low in the scale of civilization or intelligence that it would welcome a foreign master."[60] As usual, he answered charges of inconsistency in his position with a charge of a more serious inconsistency in his political opponents. Such an argumentative evasion was only a diversion from the more basic question of racial equality. On that, though he claimed "equality before the law," he accepted white supremacy. For Bryan, unlike such Republican Progressives as Albert Jeremiah Beveridge, racial differences were not inherent but were a matter of environment.

In 1901 he found it "unfortunate" that President Roosevelt had invited Booker T. Washington to dinner at the White House: "It will give depth and acrimony to a race feeling already strained to the utmost." There were four phases to "the Negro question," he said, legal, educational, political, and social. Negroes should have the same legal and educational rights as whites. The educational qualifications in Southern states did not deny the Declaration of Independence or that all men were created equal, "but upon the theory that when races of different degrees of civilization . . . must live together under the same government . . . then the more advanced race has always exercised the right to impose conditions upon those less advanced. . . . [W]hile every race is capable of self government, a race may not be capable of sharing upon equal terms in the control of a government whose blessings are enjoyed by, and whose burdens are imposed upon, several races differing in advancement." In the social phase he quoted Abraham Lincoln against social equality in 1858. He argued that social equality would only bring on greater antagonism between the races.[61]

In 1901 and 1903 Bryan spoke out about lynching, particularly in the case of a "Negro school teacher" who was clubbed, burned, and lynched because he shot a county superintendent in Bellville, Illinois, who had refused to renew his teaching certificate. The teacher was no rapist, said Bryan, but a man who had educated himself and did what, under similar circumstances, a white man might have done. What was the cause of this increase in racial prejudice? Bryan speculated, "Is it unreasonable to suppose that the efforts on the part of some Republican leaders to force the appointment of colored men upon protesting white people had something to do with it? These appointments have embittered the whites and the protests made by the whites have embittered the Negroes, and the two races are more hostile than at any time since the war."[62]

In the same year Bryan published President Roosevelt's letter defending the appointment of a "colored man" in Charleston, South Carolina. "If, as you hold," Roosevelt said, "the great bulk of the colored people are not yet fit in point of character and influence to hold such positions, it seems to me that it is worthwhile putting a premium upon the effort among them to achieve character and standing which will fit them." Bryan objected to Roosevelt's publication of this response as an "extreme statement," arguing that "No party advocates the exclusion of the colored man from all political positions. Mr. Cleveland appointed Negroes to office and these appointments were confirmed by a democratic senate." But "why does the President refuse to apply the same rule in the north that he does in the south? He respects the prejudice of white republicans in the north, but he takes occasion to lecture white democrats in the south. . . . As the president is a candidate for re-election and may need the votes of colored delegates, his letter will not be viewed as a disinterested statement of his views."[63]

It is not possible that Bryan was unaware of the discriminatory laws of the south or how unequal "separate but equal" was. He first responded that there was no discrimination on the basis of race but soon abandoned that for the argument that the more advanced race had to lead the way in governing. Finally, he attempted to shift the burden by claiming that the Republicans were as bad or worse in their policies.

It is difficult to understand today how a "Progressive" could not be concerned about equal rights for all, especially one who quoted so often from the Declaration of Independence. But the entire Progressive movement was strangely silent on racial matters. President Theodore Roosevelt invited Booker T. Washington to dinner, once, and he appointed black officeholders in areas of significant black population.[64] But that was all, and in this repressive era of "separate-but-equal" doctrine, Jim Crow laws, race riots, and lynchings, most Progressives were, at best, silent. Even the intellectual theorists of progressivism did not treat racial discrimination as an issue. Edward Alsworth Ross, Bryan's friend and a leading theorist of progressive reform, sounded a great deal like Bryan when he argued in his 1901 book, *Social Control*, for "the uplifting of the American Negro" by the combined influences of church, school, contact with whites, and industry. These would develop in the Negro "new and higher wants," coupled with the training to new skills, which were "the best lever for raising the idle, quarreling, sensual Afro-American."[65] And Herbert Croly, in his 1910 book *The Promise of American Life*, condemned slavery as evil but made no mention of the status of African Americans in the Progressive Era.[66]

On another racial front, Bryan was opposed to weakening the Chinese Exclusion Act because the Chinese, unlike the Europeans, did not want our institutions, our civilization, or our ideals. To the Chinese, he wrote in the *Commoner*, "The United States is a field to be exploited and nothing more." There was no indication that Bryan considered the Chinese inherently inferior, and he seemed to find inter-marriage acceptable. For Bryan, Chinese exclusion was a matter of economics and protection of democracy: "At present we have no racial disfunction between employer and employee (except that presented by the Negro problem), and one race problem is enough."[67] One of Bryan's first responsibilities as secretary of state under Wilson's administration was to deal with controversy over a California law that prohibited Japanese from owning property. He went to California in a vain attempt to convince the California legislature and progressive Republican Governor Hiram Johnson to repeal the law.[68]

There also is no evidence to support the popular view that Bryan was anti-Semitic. He was accused of anti-Semitism in the 1896 campaign because he attacked the Rothchild bankers. In attacking the Rothschilds, he said, he and his supporters were "not attacking a race; we are attacking greed and avarice which knows no race or religion."[69] His strong identification with Christian fundamentalism, particularly in his later years, and his objection to denouncing the Klan in 1924 undoubtedly caused some to assume that he was anti-Semitic, but even then there was no other evidence of such a bias.[70]

There is considerable evidence to the contrary, including his objection to Henry Ford as a presidential candidate because Ford accepted the *Protocols of Zion*, the anonymous work that charged that the Jews were planning world domination. There is additional evidence of his friendship with prominent Jews and his belief that Jews were part of the universal brotherhood.[71]

The issue of race forced William Jennings Bryan into argumentative distortions of the reality of the conditions in the Southern states. His responses were primarily political, parrying charges of inconsistency with charges of inconsistency. He never acknowledged this challenge to his belief in equality, brotherhood, and the Declaration of Independence. He may not have even recognized the inconsistency of his position. Bryan's view of racial equality was clearly developmental, however. Some races were more advanced than others by virtue of civilization, education, and democracy. But others could learn. They were not forever rooted in inferior status. This view was clearest when he argued against imperialism.

Imperialism and Foreign Policy

Anti-imperialism became a central argument when Bryan ran for president for the second time, in 1900. The focal point of the argument was the Philippines. The United States had liberated them from the Spaniards but the United States, unlike in Cuba, chose to hold control of the islands. This led to a battle with its former allies, the Philippine insurgents led by Emilio Aquinaldo. The imperialists had their most eloquent advocate in Albert Jeremiah Beveridge of Indiana. Elected to the Senate in 1899, he toured the Philippines, taking extensive notes, and returned to argue "the Philippine question" in the Senate on 9 January 1900. Beveridge advocated that the United States retain the Philippines for its economic wealth as the gateway to China, and because it was the destiny of the Anglo-Saxon race to govern: "We will not renounce our part in the mission of our race, trustee, under God, of the civilization of the world. And we will move forward to our work, not howling out regrets like slaves whipped to their burdens, but with gratitude for a task worthy of our strength, and thanksgiving to Almighty God that He has marked us as his chosen people henceforth to lead in the regeneration of the world."[72]

For Beveridge and other Progressives, imperialism and progressivism were linked. He cast his imperialism as progressive by arguing that our stewardship over the Philippines was an obligation of which "every other progressive nation stands ready to relieve us."[73] Bryan's rejection of imperialism put him clearly at odds with the mainstream of Progressives. Yet in his own way he was thoroughly progressive. He rejected dollar diplomacy and the acquisition of territory but he was no isolationist. America, for Bryan, had an obligation to lead the world to peace and democracy.

Bryan began arguing against imperialism in the winter of 1898–99, probably with his speech "Naboth's Vineyard" in Denver, Colorado. That speech, as the title indicates, was about violation of biblical commandments: "'Thou shalt not covet!' 'Thou shalt not bear false witness' 'Thou shalt not kill'—three commandments broken, and still a fourth, 'Thou shalt not steal' to be broken in order to get a little piece of ground!"[74] On 22 February 1899, he delivered "America's Mission" in Washington, D.C., where the question of race was the climax of the speech: "Much has been said of late about Anglo-Saxon civilization. Far be it from me to detract from the service rendered to the world by the sturdy race whose language we speak. . . . But the process of race evolution was not complete when the Anglo and the Saxon met. . . . Great has been the Greek, the Latin, the Slav, the Celt, the Teuton and the Anglo-Saxon, but greater than any of these is the American, in whom are blended the virtues of them all. . . . Anglo-Saxon civilization has taught the individual to protect his own rights, American civilization will teach him to respect the rights of others. . . . Anglo-Saxon civilization has carried its flag to every clime and defended it with forts and garrisons. American civilization will imprint its flag upon the heart of all who long for freedom."[75]

It came as no surprise, then, when Bryan made the campaign of 1900 a referendum on imperialism. His acceptance address at Indianapolis on 8 August began as a continuation of the campaign of 1896. The 1900 "contest," he said, is between "Democracy" and "plutocracy." "The Republican Party is dominated by those influences which constantly tend to substitute the worship of mammon for the protection of the rights of man."[76] He directed this characterization so that most of the speech was a refutation of the arguments for imperialism and the annexation of the Philippines. The Declaration of Independence served as Bryan's basis for rejecting a colonial empire: "But, if it were possible to obliterate every word written or spoken [by Patrick Henry, Thomas Jefferson, George Washington, Abraham Lincoln, and Henry Clay] in defense of the principles set forth in the Declaration of Independence, a way of conquest would still leave its legacy of perpetual hatred, for it was God himself who placed in every human heart the love of liberty. He never made a race so low in the scale of civilization or intelligence that it would welcome a foreign master."[77]

To "the four principal arguments" in "defense of imperialism," Bryan answered in order. First, imperialism was not necessary to make us a "world power": "[F]or more than a century this nation has been a world power. For ten decades it has been the most potent influence in the world. . . . Because our Declaration of Independence was promulgated others have been promulgated. Because our patriots of 1776 fought for liberty others have fought for it. Because our Constitution was adopted other constitutions have been adopted. . . . I would not exchange the glory of this Republic for the glory of all the empires that have risen and fallen since time began."[78]

Second, Bryan disputed "that our commercial interests in the Philippine Islands and in the Orient make it necessary for us to hold the islands permanently," citing Benjamin Franklin's reply to Lord House's assertion that British control over the American colonies was necessary to keep American trade out of the hands of foreigners: "Neither the obtaining or retaining of any trade, howsoever valuable, is an object for which men may justly spill each other's blood."[79] A "war of conquest," he concluded, was "as unwise as it is unrighteous." The expenses were greater than the profits, he said, and the profits all go to a few. Moreover, the costs were borne by the farmers and laborers through taxes, immigration, and capital, leaving "our shores to employ oriental labor in the Philippines."[80]

Third, Bryan labeled the argument that annexation would facilitate the spread of the Christian religion the "gun powder gospel." In the Philippines, he said, it was "a sufficient answer to say that a majority of the Filipinos are now members of one branch of the Christian Church; but the principle involved is one of much wider application and challenges serious consideration." Bryan concluded, "Imperialism finds no warrant in the Bible. The command 'Go ye into all the world and preach the gospel to every creature,' has no Gatling gun attachment."[81]

Finally, Bryan refuted the argument that "there is no honorable retreat from the position which the nation has taken." He answered by noting that we had shed American blood in Cuba, "yet the President has promised the Cubans independence." "The flag still floats over our dead [in Mexico City], but when the treaty with Mexico was signed, American authority withdrew to the Rio Grande and I venture the opinion that during the last fifty years the people of Mexico have made more progress under the stimulus of independence and self-government than they would have made under a carpet-bag government held in place by bayonets."[82]

These four arguments tell a lot about Bryan. They point to the centrality of the Declaration of Independence in his thinking and to his belief that the American civilization was the highest. They reveal his belief that non–Anglo-Saxons could improve and could govern themselves. The Anglo-Saxon was more advanced, in Bryan's view, but not inherently superior. Bryan's anti-imperialist arguments also assumed that the Christian religion was a superior faith to be propagated around the world—but not by force. Furthermore, the American laborers and farmers (the people) had to be protected against those who would use policy to strengthen the rich and powerful.

Finally, Bryan argued against manifest destiny, which he saw as "the subterfuge of the invertebrate," as "It obliterates the distinction between right and wrong and makes individuals and nations the helpless victims of circumstance."[83] Human beings were capable of protecting the weak through government action. Any people could choose democracy and righteousness. In this argument against destiny, he was stating a principle that, although overlooked by most critics, would anchor his case against evolution in the 1920s.

Instead of destiny, duty, or profits, Bryan emphasized brotherhood: permitting others to choose their own course and turning to love, not force, as a basis for international relations. In July of 1906, he explained the five blessings that American civilization would "carry to the rest of the world": "education, knowledge of the science of government, arbitration as a substitute for war, appreciation of the dignity of labor, and a high conception of life."[84] While not an imperialist in his thinking, he was an interventionist.

His statements against imperialism, force, and war caused many of his critics to see Bryan as a pacifist.[85] But Bryan was no pacifist and he was no isolationist. He held the rank of colonel in the First Nebraska Volunteers, although he never saw action in the war with Spain. As secretary of state under Woodrow Wilson, he supported sending American forces to Vera Cruz to intercept munitions shipments to the Huerta forces during the Mexican revolution. He agreed to send arms to the Constitutionalists there, threatened action in San Domingo, and used the Marines in Haiti. Nor was he a pacifist when he volunteered for service in World War I and, at Wilson's suggestion, served instead as a speaker in liberty bond drives and similar war-related activities.[86]

It is true that Bryan sought every opportunity to avoid war. He resigned as secretary of state when Wilson's commitment to preparedness and his treatment of Germany tilted the president away from a policy of strict neutrality, and he opposed dollar diplomacy. Even at the age of thirteen, he looked forward to the day when "it will not be necessary to shoot at a man to convince him that you are right and to blot out a nation to prove to them that their principles are false," but he was not a pacifist.[87]

Bryan's strongest and most consistent position in international affairs was his advocacy of arbitration to settle disputes. Not surprisingly, Bryan's plan grew out of his earlier proposals for the mediation of labor disputes. In 1905 he suggested that international disputes be submitted "to a permanent tribunal" made up of five persons, "one by each country from among its own citizens, one by each country from another country, and a fifth by agreement between them." There would be no hostilities for a year while the tribunal investigated and reported.[88] As noted earlier, Bryan considered arbitration as a substitute for war, one of the "blessings which the Christian nations are . . . duty bound to carry to the rest of the world." On 26 July 1906 he spoke to the Interparlimentary Union in London on the occasion of their endorsement of a plan similar to his.[89] He subsequently, in his own words, "lost no opportunity to lay the plan before Peace Advocates wherever they assembled [and] . . . explained the plan to President Taft and he incorporated a part of it into his treaties with Great Britain and France." After Bryan became secretary of state he pressed for arbitration treaties and secured the ratification of thirty of them. The idea of arbitration also was included in the covenant of the League of Nations.[90]

Even so, there was some concern that Bryan would oppose the League of Nations. However, in March 1919, as President Wilson was in Paris, he wrote a widely distributed statement in support of the League. He proclaimed the League of Nations "the greatest step toward peace in a thousand years." One of the main reasons for his support was that the League provided for his idea of investigation of the disputes before hostilities began. He disagreed with the League on several points but chose to support it as "the best thing we can get."[91] His most important reservation he had raised in a written debate with former President Taft in 1917 over the proposed "League to Enforce Peace." Bryan, debating the negative, made his first argument an objection to the use of force: "What new hope does the proposed employment of great force hold out? Over and over again, this hope has been found empty and vain. Force as a means of promoting peace has been 'weighed in the balance and found wanting.' Reliance upon it gives to diplomacy a threatening tone, breeds conspiracies and intrigues and inspires hatred instead of friendship."[92]

His own plan for the investigation of disputes during a cooling-off period without the threat of force made more sense to him than forced arbitration:[93] "When the President [Woodrow Wilson] declares that a peace to be lasting 'must be a peace without victory,'" said Bryan, "he sets forth an essential condition, however unpleasant that philosophy may be to those who, accustomed to think in terms of force, have not considered the greater power of love. . . . The saying 'Speak softly but carry a big stick' may be witty; but it is not statesmanship. The man who speaks softly does not need a big stick; and, if he yields to temptation and equips himself with one, the tone of his voice is very likely to change."

This was not the first or the last time Bryan would argue that love and brotherhood should guide national and international policy. In July of 1906 he spoke at the Interparliamentary Union at the House of Lords in London. Pointing to the fresco by Maclise of the death of Lord Nelson in battle, he paid tribute to those who gave their lives for their country. But, he said, "a life devoted to the public, and ever flowing, like a spring, with good, exerts an influence upon the human race and upon the destiny of the world as great as any death in war." He hoped that the world could come to the day when "we will begin to understand that the whole human race is but a larger family. . . . All movements in the interest of peace have back of them the idea of brotherhood. If peace is to come in this world, it will come because people more and more clearly recognize the indissoluble tie that binds each human being to every other. If we are to build permanent peace it must be on the foundation of the brotherhood of men."[94]

One political scientist, writing in 1961, found Bryan to be the least realistic of all the secretaries of state. From a "realist" perspective, according to Richard Challener, Bryan clearly failed in that office: "The realists look almost in vain for Secretaries of State who understand the operations of the balance of power, thought in terms of the national interest, or recognized the necessity of balancing commitments with a willingness to utilize the instruments of coercion if need arose. Bryan, it is scarcely necessary to say, abjectly fails to meet the realist criteria. With his rejection of power politics, his penchant for moralizing, his addiction to platitudinous speeches, and his reliance on the tenants of Christian pacifism, Bryan seems to be the symbol of virtually every error that is condemned by contemporary critics of the American diplomatic tradition."[95] Granted, Bryan was no realist; he was an idealist. He was supremely optimistic about people and their ability to choose the right course if given all the facts. Foreign policy was, for him, an extension of a domestic policy rooted in Christian love and in the realization of principles of equality and unalienable rights. Such "unrealistic" views cost him the support of many Progressives. Herbert Croly, writing in 1910 before Bryan's third presidential campaign and his term as secretary of state, saw in Bryan's objection to power politics a basis for disqualifying him as a leader of Progressives: "In seeking to prevent his countrymen from asserting their national interest beyond their own continent, he was also opposing in effect the resolute assertion of the national interest in domestic affairs. He stamped himself as an anti-nationalist, and his anti-nationalism has disqualified him for effective leadership of the party of reform [progressivism]."[96]

It is probably no surprise that Croly found Theodore Roosevelt the ideal Progressive because he "represented both the national idea and the spirit of reform. . . . The whole tendency of his programme is to give a democratic meaning and purpose to the Hamiltonian tradition and method. He proposes to use the power and the resources of the Federal government for the purpose of making his countrymen a more complete democracy in organization and practice; but he does not make these proposals as Mr. Bryan does, gingerly and with bad conscience. He makes them with a frank and full confidence in an efficient national organization as the necessary agent of the national interest and purpose." Many Progressives shared Croly's conviction that there was a natural connection between progressivism and an aggressive foreign policy.[97]

David Danbom, while acknowledging the connection, makes a distinction within progressivism that is useful in understanding Bryan. He says that progressivism had two sources, a Christian one and a scientific one. People such as Croly and Roosevelt represented the scientific wing of the movement, while Wilson and Bryan leaned more toward the Christian emphasis.[98] That did not mean that Bryan rejected the idea of direct action in the national interest. As I pointed out earlier, the arbitration treaties, the involvement in Latin America, and his argument for the "white man's burden" all pointed to an active nation. It does mean, however, that Bryan viewed America more as the Puritans' "city on the hill"—a nation that might change others by example rather than by force. In this sense, Bryan fashioned a nonimperialistic progressivism; Bryan's America would take no territory to exploit, but it would seek to change other nations to make them more like the image Bryan had of American democracy.[99]

There is ample evidence that Bryan's views on foreign policy were an outgrowth of his views on domestic policy. His cooling-off treaties, for instance, had their origin in his advocacy of "a similar plan for the settlement of labor disputes."[100] The examples already provided demonstrate rather clearly that he conceived of all the nations of the world as having at least the potential for being like the United States. They, like the United States, were moving toward an ideal state, the fulfillment of the Jeffersonian dream. Just as he accepted his presidential defeats without questioning the essential good judgment of the people, he believed that a liberated people abroad could also exercise democracy with wisdom. Such a view was probably unrealistic, but it represented, again, his faith in the ability of humans to change and enjoy the benefits of democracy.

Like his domestic policy, Bryan's foreign policy was activist. He wanted America to take the lead in improving other nations by making them more like the United States. Also, like his domestic policy, it was rooted in Jeffersonian liberalism, a combination of his agrarian and individualist biases. In those ways there was no difference in principle between his domestic and foreign policies. They both represented a commitment to government action as a way to bring about the Jeffersonian ideal.

Prohibition and Evolution

Bryan's dedication to the Jeffersonian ideal in the Christian progressive tradition would have been the way he was remembered had it not been for the last years of his life, when he turned to campaigning for prohibition and against the teaching of evolution. For in both these campaigns he has been judged as using the government not to liberate, but to restrict individual liberty. Bryan continued to campaign for the League of Nations, for the outlawing of child labor, and for other progressive reforms, but, until recently, historians have focused on his inconsistencies in the later years. Stephen Jay Gould has expressed the common view as a question: "How could this man have then joined forces with the cult of biblical literalism in an effort to purge religion of all liberality, and to stifle the same free thought that he had advocated in so many other contexts?[101]

But as Gould and others have conceded, Bryan did not believe that he had been inconsistent.[102] A careful examination of his antievolution crusade through the Scopes trial until his death five days later shows how he was able to make his "last crusade" a continuation of his earlier life's work.

Bryan's position on prohibition might be explained from his lifelong commitment as a teetotaler and the realization that prohibition had a long-standing connection to the liberal reform movements dating back to the early nineteenth century. At that time, temperance, antislavery, woman's rights, Indian rights, child labor, and a host of other reform issues were joined together. Bryan's delay in espousing prohibition may have been a product of the political realities he faced. His election to Congress in Nebraska's First District was made possible in 1890 and 1892 only because he could hold the Irish and German Democratic wards in Omaha, and there was no room for talk of prohibition there if he wanted to be elected. It is also quite possible that Bryan regarded abstinence from alcohol to be an individual decision. He came reluctantly to support a constitutional amendment for prohibition after his career as an active candidate for national office was over.

He was first active in promoting abstinence. In 1909, for instance, he wrote the article "Why Sign the Pledge?" for the *Christian Endeavor World*. At that time, at least, he seemed ambiguous about legal restrictions on alcohol but clear in his advocacy of abstinence: "Whatever differences of opinion may exist as to the success of regulation from without, no one can question the success of that method of regulation which locks the door from within. The strongest advocate of personal liberty must admit man's right to use that personal liberty to refuse to touch, taste, or handle; the most rabid opponent of regulation will confess that a man not only may, but can, so regulate his own life as to reduce the demand for liquor to the extent of one man's consumption; no matter how bitterly opposed a man may be to prohibition, in theory or in practice, he cannot deny but that a man can absolutely prohibit the use of liquor so far as he himself is concerned."[103]

At the 1912 Nebraska State Democratic Convention, he fully espoused the "righteous cause" of prohibition, but he favored state action. He did not want it to be a national issue that might hurt the Democratic Party in the election of 1912. After he resigned as secretary of state in 1915, he toured Ohio by train between 25 and 30 October in his first significant campaign for national prohibition. When the Eighteenth Amendment to the Constitution was passed on 29 January 1919, Bryan called it "the greatest moral reform of the generation" and said that the United

States should take the lead among the "civilized nations in the banishment of intoxicating liquor from the globe."[104]

Bryan's arguments rested on the proposition that alcohol is a poison that "weakens the body, impairs the strength of the mind and menaces the morals." If this is a false proposition, he argued, prohibition and any other attempt to regulate liquor would fail. "If this proposition is sound," on the other hand, he argued that it would be "difficult" to find a valid reason for permitting the manufacture and sale of alcoholic liquors as a beverage." Bryan anticipated the more modern view of alcohol abuse as a type of "disease": "Suppose a man applied for a license to spread hog cholera throughout the country; would you give him a license? No. . . . Why, then, will you license a man to spread disease among human beings—disease that destroys the body, robs the mind of its energy and underestimates the morals of men?"[105]

His arguments in the *Commoner* push for national prohibition focused on saloons. In 1911 he had argued in favor of maintaining an antisaloon ordinance in Lincoln, Nebraska, while permitting people to purchase liquor to consume at home. That possibility did not come up in his arguments for national prohibition, but his arguments remained aimed at the saloons, the brewers, and the distillers, whom he saw as representing an illegitimate private interest, much as he had seen the bankers, the trusts, and the imperialists of earlier eras.[106]

However, once he turned from abstinence to prohibition, he did not talk of personal liberty (except to note that the question had been answered).[107] Nor did he quote Jefferson or the Declaration of Independence, as he did so often in his arguments on other issues. In his willingness to use the government for the moral uplift of the nation, and in his vision of America leading the whole world to prohibition, he sounded much like the other Progressives of his day.

The same cannot be said, of course, about his position on evolution. In opposing the teaching of evolution, Bryan set himself apart from most Progressives and, according to legend, brought about his own demise under Clarence Darrow's questioning at the Scopes trial. Because the Scopes trial identified Bryan as a bigot to the intellectual community, and because he died shortly after, the trial stands with the free silver campaign as one of the defining moments of his life. It is seen as a complete contradiction to all of his earlier arguments for freedom of the individual. So, his role in the antievolution campaign deserves some serious attention. One historian's description of Bryan's demise at the end of the trial serves as the usual characterization and a point of departure: "The excitement quickly evaporated. Many spectators pushed up to Darrow to shake his hand, but Bryan was largely ignored. Several ministers offered their congratulations, but scores of Fundamentalists who previously had regarded him as their champion seemed to feel let down and turned away."[108] However, according to the same historian, four days after the trial ended and the day before his death, Bryan traveled around the countryside and spoke to more than fifty thousand people.[109] The Scopes trial may testify more to the anti-Bryan bias of the press than to Bryan's own failure. If Bryan was rejected by his followers, it was strictly to the extent that they read and believed the newspapers.

The trial format, particularly the questioning of Bryan by Darrow, does not provide a basis for understanding Bryan's objection to evolution. From a contemporary vantage point, Bryan was not the only person who should have been embarrassed. In the words of theologian Carlyle Marney:

> Neither Bryan, nor Darrow, nor any of the fundamentalists, nor their "liberal" tormenters understood the nature of language. Both were literalists of the same type. The only thing more disgraceful than Mr. Bryan's answers at Dayton was the set of Mr. Darrow's questions.

The quality of both question and answer reveals an ignorance of language, myth, and meaning as appalling as the whole set-up was sordidly unreal and shameful. Nothing could have been won there. Nothing was at stake. The questions had changed already.[110]

The opposition set up in the questioning of a literalist biblical interpretation against a positivist science was already out-of-date in the theological and scientific communities.

Darrow's questioning probably did prove that Bryan did not know very much about ancient civilizations or the science then popular. It also revealed what seems to surprise most people: that Bryan was not a complete literalist when he acknowledged that many statements in the Bible, such as "Ye are the salt of the earth," were "given illustratively." Bryan surprised Darrow with his statements that the writer of Joshua, who had the sun stand still, "may have used language that could be understood at that time," and that the six days of creation described in the Bible were "not six days of twenty-four hours."[111] Those views, however, should not have surprised anyone who really understood Bryan. But it did and still does. In 1981 fundamentalist Jerry Falwell edited a book in which he argued that "Bryan lost the respect of the fundamentalist when he subscribed to the idea of periods of time for creation rather than twenty-four hour days."[112] But a careful analysis of all his statements on evolution in the years before the trial clearly justifies the conclusion of Beverly Barnett: "Bryan made mistakes during the trial, the worst was probably his consenting to take the witness stand and be examined by Darrow. But his concessions on literalism were no mistake."[113]

Fundamentalism has two interpretative legs on which it stands. The stronger leg is inerrancy. Here Bryan was solid. The Bible is true! Bryan modified the second leg, literalism, but he was not alone among fundamentalists on that score.[114] Nonetheless, his concessions on the literal interpretation of the Bible separated him from some fundamentalists and from the popular view of fundamentalism.

However, the emphasis on literalism, and what to many was Bryan's dogmatism and ignorance, draws attention away from Bryan's more basic conflict with his fundamentalist supporters. Fundamentalism took form in the late nineteenth century to counter the influence of scientific evolution, higher criticism, and the social gospel.[115] While Bryan decried this modernism on the first two issues, he was clearly a believer in the social gospel. "The Prince of Peace," his most widely delivered speech in the United States and abroad, clearly supported this social element: "Again, Christ deserved to be called the Prince of Peace because He has given us a measure of greatness which promotes peace. . . . Service is the measure of greatness; it always has been true; it is true to-day, and it always will be true, that he is greatest who does the most of good. . . . The human measure of human life is its income; the divine measure of a life is its outgo, its overflow—its contribution to the welfare of all."[116] This social gospel constitutes a sharp break with fundamentalism's emphasis on individual salvation, aligns him with his progressive views examined earlier, and reveals a different light for William Jennings Bryan's antievolution campaign. A careful examination of his arguments on evolution reveals how he came to his antievolution position progressively and thoughtfully over about a twenty-three-year period.

In his earlier speeches, such as "The Prince of Peace," Bryan had taken a comparatively moderate position: "I do not carry the doctrine of evolution as far as some do; I am not yet convinced that man is a lineal descendant of the lower animals. I do not mean to find fault with you if you want to accept the theory; all I mean to say is that while you may trace your ancestry back to the monkey if you find pleasure or pride in doing so, you shall not connect me with your family tree without more evidence than has yet been produced."[117]

As time went on, however, he became firmly opposed to the theory of evolution and its teaching as a scientific fact. Restricting the teaching of evolution brought him up against the charge that he would restrict freedom of thought. Bryan clearly was troubled by the changes that his antievolutionary crusade threatened "freedom of conscience." In his last speech at Winchester, Tennessee, he noted that Christians voluntarily tied their own hands. Though in the majority, they agreed not to teach Christianity in the public schools. They built colleges and schools to teach their religion. But atheists and agnostics did not build schools. Bryan suggested that they build their own schools to teach their "religion." Private citizens would not be denied the right to think or say what they wanted, Bryan concluded, but teachers were employees of the state.[118]

This argument was not a new one for Bryan. It is clear from many other speeches and from his correspondence in the 1920s that he felt a need to address the free speech argument against his position. Mary Bryan, his wife, told of their "last conversation":

> We spoke of the narrow margin between this perfectly legitimate work as touching the public servant, and an encroachment on individual religious belief which is a sacred domain. We agreed that care must be taken at this point that no religious zeal should invade this sacred domain and become intolerance.
> Mr. Bryan said, "Well, Mamma, I have not made that mistake yet, have I?" And I replied, "You are all right so far, but will you be able to keep to this narrow path?" With a happy smile, he said, "I think I can." "But," said I, "can you control your followers?" and more gravely he said, "I think I can." And I knew, he was adding mentally, "by the help of God."[119]

Bryan was concerned that he and his followers not violate other's rights to free speech. However, he was also true to his long belief in majority rule. In the Winchester speech he proudly states: "I have the largest majority on the side with me I have ever had in any fight I have ever had." In his earlier "reform" efforts (popular election of senators, income tax, prohibition, and woman suffrage), he said he had begun with only minority support. In "this fight against the brute doctrine that robs the heart of love of God and belief in the Bible," he claimed to be "on the side of an immense majority."[120]

Confident that he was not violating individual freedom and strengthened in the belief that, despite his detractors, the majority supported him, Bryan developed his antievolution argumentative strategy to reflect not narrow biblical interpretations, but the social liberalism that marked his life. Bryan's argument against evolution was probably most carefully laid out in the trial summation speech that he finished writing after the trial and that was published after his death. None of the arguments or evidence was new, but they provide a good look at Bryan's case against evolution. That speech developed Bryan's position against evolution in five indictments:

1. "It [evolution] disputes the truth of the Bible account of man's creation and shakes faith in the Bible as the Word of God"[121]
2. "The evolutionary hypothesis, carried to its logical conclusion, disputes every vital truth of the Bible"[122]
3. "It [evolution] diverts attention from pressing problems of great importance to trifling speculation"[123]
4. "By paralyzing the hope for reform, it [the evolutionary hypothesis] discourages those who labor for the improvement of man's condition"[124]
5. "If taken seriously and made the basis of a philosophy of life, it [the evolutionary hypothesis] would eliminate love and carry man back to the struggle of tooth and claw"[125]

The argument on the first indictment took but three sentences, concluding: "It [evolution] not only contradicts the Mosaic record as to the beginning of human life, but it disputes the Bible doctrine of reproduction according to kind—the greatest scientific principle known."[126] The second indictment developed the bulk of his arguments. In length, his elaboration made up half the discussion of the five indictments. It covered more than the simple statement the indictment implies: "The evolutionary hypothesis carried to its logical conclusion disputes every vital truth of the Bible."[127] That argument illustrated that Bryan's "vital truth of the Bible" was not about literal interpretations.

Charles Darwin was Bryan's proof that evolution led "down and down and down to helpless and hopeless agnosticism."[128] He found the key to the "downward pathway" to the "brute level" in Darwin's statement: "Then arises the doubt, can the mind of man which has, as I fully believe, been developed from a mind as low as that possessed by the lowest animals, be trusted when it draws such grand conclusions?"[129] Bryan reinforced the Darwin quotation by introducing the testimony of George Romanes, "a distinguished biologist," about "the appalling contrast between the hallowed glory of that creed which once was mine, and the lonely mystery of existence as I now find it,—at such times I shall ever feel it impossible to avoid the sharpest pang of which my nature is susceptible."[130]

To Darwin and Romanes he added the survey research of Bryn Mawr psychology Professor James H. Leuba, which showed that scientists and students alike were losing their faith in God.[132] It is then that Bryan turned to his central indictment of evolution: that it disputed every "vital truth of the Bible."

Bryan's objection to evolution was not rooted in science, nor in a literalist reading of the Bible. It was rooted in the same liberalism that made him favor direct election of senators, free coinage of silver, woman suffrage, and antitrust legislation. For Bryan, social Darwinism threatened the realization of the ideal America.

This argument was probably best developed in his speech on the fifth day of the Scopes trial. He turned the tables on Darrow by noting that Darrow, in his defense of Richard Loeb and Nathan Leopold, had blamed their murder of Bobby Franks on their reading of Nietzche, "the only great author who tried to carry [survival of the fittest] to its logical conclusion." When Darrow denied it, Bryan read verbatim from Darrow's statements at the trial.[132] Darrow's statement set the basis for Bryan's position that evil followed the teaching of evolution:

I will guarantee that you can go down to the University of Chicago today, into its big library, and find over a thousand volumes of Nietzsche's, and I am sure I speak moderately. If this boy is to blame for this, where did he get it? Is there any blame attached because somebody took Nietzsche's philosophy seriously and fashioned his life on it? And there is no question in this case but what it is true. Then who is to blame? The university would be more to blame than he is. The scholars of the world would be more to blame than he is. The publishers of the world—and Nietzsche's books are published by one of the biggest publishers in the world—are more to blame than he. Your Honor, it is hardly fair to hang a 19-year-old boy for the philosophy that was taught him at the university.[133]

Bryan used Darrow's defense of Loeb to summarize this indictment. That argument made clear what he meant when he said that evolution "carried to is logical conclusion disputes every vital truth of the Bible":

Psychologists who build upon the evolutionary hypothesis teach that man is nothing but a bundle of characteristics inherited from brute ancestors. That is the philosophy which Mr. Darrow applied in this celebrated criminal case. "Some remote ancestor"—he does not know how remote—"sent down the seed that corrupted him." You cannot punish the ancestor—he is not only dead but, according to the evolutionists, he was a brute and may have lived a million years ago. And he says that all the biologists agree with him—no wonder so small a per cent of the biologists, according the Leuba, believe in a personal God.

This is the quintessence of evolution, distilled for us by one [Darrow] who follows that doctrine to its logical conclusion. Analyze this dogma of darkness and death. Evolutionists say that back in the twilight of life a beast, name and nature unknown, planted a murderous seed and that the impulse that originated in that seed throbs forever in the blood of the brute's descendants, inspiring the killings innumerable, for which the murderers are not responsible because coerced by a fate fixed by the laws of heredity! It is an insult to reason and shocks the heart. That doctrine is as deadly as leprosy; it may aid a lawyer in a criminal case, but it would, if generally adopted, destroy all sense of responsibility and menace the morals of the world. A brute, they say, can predestine a man to crime, and yet they deny that God incarnate in the flesh can release a human being from this bondage or save him from ancestral sins. No more repulsive doctrine was every proclaimed by man; if all the biologists of the world teach this doctrine—as Mr. Darrow says they do—then may heaven defend the youth of our land from their impious babblings.[134]

The third indictment, that evolution "diverts attention from pressing problems of great importance to trifling speculation," also reflected Bryan's central concern with social welfare. "The science of 'How to Live' is the most important of all science," he said, and that science, especially as taught to the gifted two percent of the population who are college graduates, must be "used for the benefit of society and not against the public welfare."[135]

The fourth indictment was also centered around the issues of social liberalism. The evolutionary hypothesis, "by paralyzing the hope for reform, . . . discourages those who labor for the improvement of man's condition." It essentially picked up where the second indictment left off regarding the effect of evolution on human actions:

Evolution chills their enthusiasm by substituting aeons for years. . . . It is represented as a heartless process, beginning with time and ending in eternity, and acting so slowly that the rocks cannot preserve a record of the imaginary changes through which it is credited with having carried an original germ of life that appeared sometime from somewhere. Its only program for man is scientific breeding, a system under which a few supposedly superior intellects, self-appointed, would direct the mating and the movements of the mass of mankind—an impossible system. . . . It is because Christians believe in individual regeneration and in the regeneration of society through the regeneration of individuals that they pray "Thy Kingdom come, Thy will be done in earth as it is in heaven." Evolution makes a mockery of the Lord's prayer![136]

For Bryan the ability of individuals to change, as Christ can change them, was the basis for social reform.

Then, in the fifth indictment, Bryan's argument went directly to the issue of the survival of the fittest—the central enemy of Bryan's vision. He drew his case against social Darwinism directly from *The Descent of Man*, where Darwin argued that civilized people protected the weak, who "propagate their kind," while the "savages" who survived "commonly exhibit a vigorous state of health."[137] Bryan's argument was most forceful at this point:

Darwin reveals the barbarous sentiment that runs through evolution and dwarfs the moral nature of those who become obsessed with it. Let us analyze the quotation just given. Darwin speaks with approval of the savage custom of eliminating the weak so that only the strong will survive and complains that "we civilized men do our utmost to check the process of elimination." How inhuman [is] such a doctrine as this! He thinks it injurious to "build asylums for the imbecile, the maimed, and the sick," or to care for the poor. Even the medical men come in for criticism because they "exert their utmost skill to save the life of everyone to the last moment." And note his hostility to vaccination because it has "preserved thousands who, from a weak constitution would, but for vaccination, have succumbed to smallpox"! All of the sympathetic activities of civilized society are condemned because they enable "the weak members to propagate their kind." Then he drags mankind down to the level of the brute and compares the freedom given to man unfavorably with the restraint that we put on barnyard beasts.

The second paragraph of the above quotation shows that his [Darwin's] kindly heart rebelled against the cruelty of his own doctrine. He says that we "feel impelled to give to the helpless," although he traces it to a sympathy which he thinks is developed by evolution; he even admits that we could not check this sympathy "even at the urging of hard reason, without deterioration of the noblest part of our nature." "We must therefore bear" what he regards as "the undoubtedly bad effects of the weak surviving and propagating their kind." Could any doctrine be more destructive of civilization? And what a commentary on evolution! He wants us to believe that evolution develops a human sympathy that finally becomes so tender that it repudiates the law that created it and thus invites a return to a level where the extinguishing of pity and sympathy will permit the brutal instincts to again do their progressive (?) work.[138]

Further, Bryan quoted from Benjamin Kidd's book, *Science of Power,* that it was Nietzsche who "denounced Christianity as the 'doctrine of the degenerate,' and democracy as 'the refuge of weaklings.'" In "due time" he noted, this "gave Germany the doctrine of the superman translated into the national policy of the superstate aiming at world power."[139]

Earlier, in his book *In His Image* (1922), Bryan had extended this indictment of Darwinism to the creation of class struggle: "To destroy the faith of Christians and lay the foundation for the bloodiest war in history would seem enough to condemn Darwinism, but there are still two other indictments to bring against it. First, that it is the basis of the gigantic class struggle that is now shaking society throughout the world. Both the capitalist and the labourer are increasingly class conscious. Why? Because the doctrine of the 'Individual efficient for himself'—the brute doctrine of the "survival of the fittest"—is driving men into a life-and-death struggle from which sympathy and the spirit of brotherhood are eliminated. It is transforming the industrial world into a slaughter-house."[140]

Bryan's five indictments, laid out so clearly in the final undelivered summation before the court, can be found in the Winchester speech and in all his other arguments against evolution. Clearly, only the first indictment ("It disputes the truth of the Bible accounts of man's creation and shakes faith in the Bible as the word of God") addressed the issue of Clarence Darrow's questioning, which has dominated the negative impression of Bryan through the years.[141] That indictment he disposed of in three sentences. His argument in the four other indictments built the case for rejecting evolution because it served as the intellectual basis for rejecting his social gospel. For Bryan, humans were a special creation of God who had the obligation to accept God and to help one another achieve moral regeneration and a society of love and mutual support.

It is not clear when Bryan took up the antievolution argument. He says in the Winchester speech that it was "about twenty-three years ago" (1901). He did not study it in college but began reading Darwin when he was "about the age of forty" because of what he learned about the effect of Darwin on "college boys."[142] It was

World War I that led him to make the connection between Darwin and the Niet-zsche: "When we went into the war I got an idea somehow—the impression grew upon me that Nietzsche had something to do with the war. I had never read any of his books consecutively. I had read extracts. But I had the impression that he had something to do with the war, so I got his books and read them. By that time I had something more to say about Darwinism, for I found that Nietzsche took Darwin-ism and carried it to its logical conclusion. I found that it was Darwinism that was at the basis of that damnable doctrine that might makes right that had spread over Germany."[143]

So it was, he said, that in January 1919 he delivered "Back to God," which led to "Brother or Brute" and then to "The Menace of Darwinism."[144] Almost immedi-ately, by public statement and private correspondence, Bryan was told that his un-derstanding of evolution was flawed. Lloyd C. Douglas wrote in *Christian Century* in November 1920:

> A considerable volume of water has passed under the bridge, in the realm of science, since Mr. Bryan first came out as a biologist. Practically the whole theory of evolution has been rephrased during that time. Perhaps the genial ex-secretary of state is unaware of that fact. Surely, he must be unaware of it, for his lectures still carry opportunities for the introduction of the same old sto-ries, the same old misquotations, and the same old attacks against "Darwin-ism." His references to evolution have not grown an inch or gained a pound for twenty years.
>
> Meanwhile, let it be repeated, science has been busy. Mr. Bryan may have wished to inform himself upon this subject, or he may not; but science has been assiduously devoting itself to a sincere and honest investigation of the known facts.
>
> One of the interesting features of modern scholarship in this field—which may come as a shock to Mr. Bryan, should he ever have this matter brought to his attention—is the fact that the present-day scientist has long since left off talking of evolution in terms of "Darwinism." Mr. Bryan rarely speaks of evo-lution: his designation for it is "Darwinism." Ah—how he does put Darwin on the grille! Cannot some friend inform him, for his own sake, that Charles Robert Darwin is related to evolution, in the thought of the scholar, exactly as Robert Fulton is related to steam navigation, and as Langley is related to aero-nautics, and as Dr. Harvey is related to present-day surgery?[145]

B. L. Miller of the Department of Geology at Lehigh University wrote Bryan on 10 May 1921, stating that he was "unfamiliar with the modern ideas of evolution" and suggesting that he read *Organic Evolution* by Richard S. Lull, *The Origin and Evo-lution of Life* by Henry Fairchild Osborn, and *Darwin and after Darwin* by George John Romanes. Henry Fairchild Osborn was among others who reported on Bryan's misunderstanding of evolution and of whose writings Bryan was aware.[146]

In 1905 sociologist Edward Alsworth Ross discussed Darwin's *Descent of Man* with Bryan. He claimed Bryan was prone to dismiss the evidence of which he was aware. Bryan, he said, "gave no sign of having considered what the evidence mar-shaled by Darwin points to; he regarded Darwin's hypothesis that man has evolved as a 'theory' set up to rival the Creation dogma, not a generalization emerging irre-sistibly from an immense number of significant facts. For him the classical author-ities and logic settled things—rather than 'facts.'"[147]

So Bryan knew, though not in detail, that the scientists studying evolution began questioning Charles Darwin's theories from the beginning. Natural selec-tion, a mechanical practice that Bryan attacked most strongly, was a concept that most scientists had already rejected.

Scientific thought questioned Darwinism in four broad categories: theistic evolution, Lamarckism, orthogenesis, and mutation theory. Theistic evolution emphasized an order to evolution, with humans at the head of the system created so by a controlling God. This view lost its power among scientists in the late nineteenth century, and even though some continued to argue for it, theistic evolution was difficult to prove, to say the least, in field or laboratory. Lamarckism argued that characteristics acquired during the life of an organism could be passed on to its offspring. Orthogenesis argued that evolution was directed by forces originally within the organism itself. The mutation theory explained the creation of new life forms but was "appropriated by Mendelian genetics to denote the spontaneous modification of a gene."[148]

It was this Mendelian adaptation that won out and had the most force by the time of the Scopes trial. As early as 1904 Hugo Devries gave a series of lectures published as *Species and Varieties: Their Origin by Mutation.* He said, "my work claims to be in full accordance with the principles laid down by Darwin."[149] However, he and other exponents of the gene mutation theory undermined social Darwinism because "the varieties between individual human beings were mere fluctuations with no evolutional significance, so there would be little point in allowing a free-for-all struggle to weed out the weakest.[150] Other followers of this theory believed that it was quite different from Darwin. Regardless of the position taken, it is easy to understand how Bryan's opponents, such as Lloyd C. Douglas, could decry Bryan's insistence on attacking Darwinism and natural selection. It showed, they argued, that he was out of touch with what was going on in evolutionary theory. It set the basis for William Berryman Scott of Princeton University to label Bryan an "ignoramus."[151]

There is evidence that Bryan understood that such changes had taken place, although he appeared unaware of the details or the significance of the changes. He acknowledged in the undelivered trial summation, published after his death, that "natural selection is being abandoned, and no new explanation is satisfactory even to scientists."[152] In his *New York Times* article of 26 February 1922, he said, "many evolutionists adhere to Darwin's conclusions while discarding his explanations [sexual and natural selection]."[153]

However, even as he acknowledged the changes, he explained that he attacked "Darwinism because it is a definite hypothesis." "Darwin's hypothesis or guess is the only application of evolution to man that has any considerable number of supporters," he said, and none of the alternatives denied the essential thread of Darwin's theory, that humans descended from animals.[154] Bryan argued that no species had ever yet been traced to another species.[155] He argued most strongly that the connection between humans and animals had not been proven, nor had evolution tried to explain the origin of life. He even said that he could accept evolution through the lower animals but the human race had to be by special creation.[156] He wrote to Dr. Howard A. Kelly, a Baltimore supporter, suggesting that his total rejection of evolution was an argumentative strategy:

> I agree with you that the days mentioned in Genesis mean periods of indefinite length of twenty-four hour days, and I would not be concerned about the truth or falsity of evolution below man but for the fact that a concession as to the truth of evolution up to man furnishes our opponents with an argument which they are quick to use, namely, if evolution accounts for all the species up to man, does it not raise a presumption in behalf of evolution to include man? I see no reason for conceding a change of species until they are able to trace some one species to another. If we concede evolution up to man, we have only the Bible to support us in the contention that evolution stops before it reaches man and that man was made by separate act as Moses describes; whereas our position is much stronger, I think, if we compel our

opponents to prove evolution step by step instead of giving them the benefit of a presumption based upon an unbroken line of change up to man. The Tennessee law does not deal with evolution below man but prohibits the teaching of the doctrine that man is a descendent of any lower form of life.[157]

Why not theistic evolution? After all, Bryan had agreed that the seven days of creation did not need to be seven literal days. From the same assumption, many argued that evolution was consistent with the biblical account; it was simply God's way of achieving what is shown in Genesis.[158] But Bryan was as firmly against theistic evolution as he was any other variety, as illustrated by 1923 letter to the *Presbyterian Advance*:

> The theistic evolutionist leads the Christian, blindfolded, back to the beginning of life, or to some more distant point, and then assumes the existence of God, by this time God is so far away that consciousness of his presence and a sense of responsibility to him are greatly impaired, if not lost. Theistic evolution is an anesthetic that deadens the patient's pain while atheism removes his religion.
>
> The church is not greatly menaced today by the atheist on the outside but it is menaced by theistic evolutionists on the inside. They progressively dilute the Word of God with scientific speculation until its authority is destroyed and it becomes but a man-made book, full of errors.[159]

In the trial summation he attacked theistic evolution (and, without naming it, higher criticism) as "using weasel-words like 'poetical,' 'symbolical' and 'allegorical' to suck the meaning out of the inspired record of man's creation."[160]

One of the most interesting exchanges in the Bryan Papers came after Bryan offered, through the Reverend C. N. Baylor of Morgantown, West Virginia, to give one hundred dollars to any professor in the University of West Virginia who could show that the teachings of the Bible and evolution were in harmony. A botanist, R. C. Spangler, believed that he could. Bryan asked Spangler to answer six questions. The last five questions Spangler answered "yes." They had to do with accepting miracles, supernatural events, virgin birth, resurrection, and Christ's appearance to his disciples. The first question was "Are you willing to put in writing and sign a statement declaring that you believe that you are a descendant of an ape?" Spangler answered "no," because contemporary biologists "except those ignorant of the facts of biology don't believe that."[161]

Bryan agreed that Spangler should get the money but pointed out "as the two are inconsistent, I feel sure that you will ultimately reject one or another and I am trusting that you will reject evolution instead of the Bible." Further, Bryan said: "So far as I know, no effort has been made to connect man with any other line of descent [than apes]. Therefore, it would be interesting to have a sketch of your family tree. If you are sure that you have brute blood in your veins you must attach yourself to some other beast if not the ape. There is considerable discussion just now as to whether one is permitted to select his brute ancestor or is compelled to accept any family tree that the pseudo-scientists may give him. One man recently told me that he would prefer to come from a Jersey cow if he had to come from any animal, while another, who is fond of hunting, preferred the setter dog as an ancestor. What is your choice? . . . Tell us, I pray, to what ape, or if not an ape, to what other animal, bird, reptile, or fish do you pay your respects on Father's Day?"[162]

Evolution made humans into brutes no matter what form it took, and this characteristic was, for Bryan, a central weakness that could not be overcome. Although he was under attack by other Christians, he insisted his was the majority view of both Protestants and Catholics.[163] Further, he claimed the question was more than a Christian issue; it was a broadly religious one. He encouraged the

prosecution in the Scopes trial to get the services of Samuel Untermeyer, the distinguished New York Jewish lawyer: "He has had large experience in big cases and is a
match for any of the men on the other side. Being a Jew he ought to be interested
in defending Moses from the attacks of the Darwinites."[164]

Though the central objective of antievolution legislation was that evolution
not be taught as a "fact," Bryan's real concern was that it not be allowed to impede
social reform. In this, Bryan was different from many fundamentalists, who rejected the social gospel and saw Christianity as concerned only with the salvation
of the individual soul. For Bryan, Christianity justified social reform. He was also
opposed to the doctrine of predestination that some Christians, such as Andrew
Carnegie and John D. Rockefeller, joined with evolution theory to justify social
Darwinism. It was at Salem's Cumberland Presbyterian Church that Bryan was converted at fourteen, and "the Cumberland Presbyterians rejected the doctrine that
only a select few were predestined to salvation."[165]

During the 1920s Bryan continued to campaign for economic and social reform. He opposed the repeal of the excess profits tax, and he favored the creation
of departments of health and education, a referendum on a declaration of war, veterans bonuses, voting by mail, a disarmament conference, and government ownership of telephone, telegraph, and the merchant marine.[166] He did not put these
aside as he turned to antievolution legislation. Why should he? In his scheme of
things, religion and politics were merged. His religion spoke to assumptions about
the nature of humans and their capacity to change and reform society. He had great
faith in the people. He worried that he might be seen as ignorant and that he might
be violating his own principles of freedom of speech. Beyond that, his antievolution campaign, in content and strategy, was an argumentative defense of his brand
of social liberalism. For Bryan, Christianity, Jeffersonian liberalism, and progressivism were intertwined.

Bryan's Argumentative Practice

Jeffersonian progressivism not only describes Bryan's beliefs, but it was also the
dominant influence on his argumentative practice. He was committed to majority
rule and the ultimate persuasion of truth, and his rhetorical practices were oriented
to communicating with reasonable human beings. As Bryan prepared for a trip to
South Africa in 1909, he wrote his son William Jennings Bryan Jr., for his "instruction in case accident should come to us":

> The most potent influence in human life is man's sense of responsibility to
> God. The most necessary thing for society is that each member shall learn
> Christ's measure of greatness, namely service, and apply it; the aim of govern-
> ment is justice and the best guaranty of justice is to be found in the maxim: the
> people have a right to have what they want.
> Corruption of government comes from the attempt to substitute the will
> of the minority for the will of the majority.[167]

As a maxim to guarantee justice, it is easy enough to see the problems of "the
people have a right to have what they want." But it is a stark statement of the ma-
joritarian principle (linked through service to a human's responsibility to God)
that was at the center of Bryan's public life.

To his Jeffersonian liberalism Bryan brought a consummate conviction about
the democratic process. He organized for every convention and controlled most of
the platform, even in 1904 and 1924, when conservatives were nominated. His

commitment to majority rule never weakened, even in defeat. It was a major argument against the teaching of evolution. Lawrence W. Levine summarizes Bryan's position as follows: "If the majority of the people who believe in Christianity did not demand that their views be taught at public expense, by what right did the minority who believe in atheism, agnosticism, and evolution demand this privilege? No one, he protested, was trying to abrogate the inherent rights of anyone else. All the fundamentalists wanted was that the rights of all in matters of conscience and religious belief be equally protected."[168]

One can search Bryan's statements, public and private, for evidence that he lost faith in persuasion and the rule of the majority but it will not be found. One will find evidence that Bryan believed there were dark forces of plutocracy, greed, or atheism aligned to warp the majority will, but one will not find evidence that he believed that the majority view would not someday, with the proper persuasion, be right. He decried, for instance, the dominance of the eastern conservative newspapers and argued between 1918 and 1920 for a federally funded national nonpartisan bulletin controlled by the Republican and Democratic parties to provide information on political issues with each party having equal space. Many of the intellectual Progressives saw the press as an important agent in producing a better society. John Dewey even attempted to found a newspaper, *Thought News,* to achieve that objective. Bryan's proposed journal would not have attempted to move the society one way or another. It would have maintained its objectivity by having bipartisan editing and presenting both sides of issues. Bryan's paper represented his attempt to clarify public argumentation. It was a correction—an idealized one at that—to an essentially sound system.[169]

His view was an idealized version of Aristotle's argument that "truth and justice are by nature more powerful than their opposites; so that, when decisions are not made as they should be, the speakers with the right on their side have only themselves to thank for the outcome."[170] For Bryan, truth, justice, responsibility to God, and majoritarianism were all wrapped up together. The communication of all points of view was essential to make such a system most effective, but there was no doubt about his commitment to persuasion as the basis for a moral democracy.

The nature of the persuasion he used, however, is not very well understood. Some said that they were charmed by his voice. Others claim that he uttered simple platitudes that appealed to simple-minded people. Most people know little more about Bryan than that he was humiliated by Darrow at the Scopes trial, and that the close of his speech on the silver plank at the Democratic Convention in 1896 is one of the most memorable perorations in American history. But, more commonly, Bryan's persuasion was argumentative. He typically searched for issues, took clear positions, argued them carefully, marshaled evidence, and refuted opposition arguments. In these ways, his rhetoric reflected the ideal of Progressives who wanted a careful analysis of social problems. He was no Theodore Roosevelt, arguing both sides of an issue to seize the middle ground. He was no Russell Conwell, stringing a series of stories together as one strings beads. Bryan argued.

This inclination can be seen in every speech. Frequently, the major points are summarized at the beginning and organized in the body of the speech with clear numerical signposting. In his 1920 speech "Brother or Brute," for instance, he argued that war is the ultimate outcome of seeing humans as brutes. Then he argued the steps to brotherhood: "first, a belief in God"; "second, man must believe in God in order to understand that he is made in the image of is maker"; "third, I present the moral code of Christ as the only moral philosophy that fits into every human need and furnishes a solution to every problem that can vex the heart of people or society"; "Fourth, Christ taught that service is the measure of greatness"; "Fifth, Christ taught the peaceful means of settling disputes; we are commanded to overcome evil with good."[171] Each of these steps was a point from which to advance to the next claim. Similar practices can be found in many of his speeches.[172] When such listings were not used, there was still a clear identification of the issues that dominated the structure of his speeches.

Bryan's most popularly noted "failure" was his 12 August 1896 acceptance address at Madison Square Garden, "enemy country." In order to be sure that the speech and his explanation of—and carefully reasoned argument for—the free coinage of silver was not garbled by the newspapers, he read it for an hour and forty minutes from manuscript in the sweltering heat. Bryan recalled the event as follows:

> Following the determination . . . [to have the newspapers get the speech in an accurate form] I read the speech, only laying the manuscript aside when near the conclusion. The delivery was a disappointment to those present, as I knew it would be. The *World*, speaking of it the next morning, said:
>
> > "To put it in blunt, sincere language, the great Bryan demonstration at the Madison Square Garden was a disappointment. Mr. Bryan read a speech tempered in tone, and beautifully phrased, but failed to fire the great multitude who came to see and hear him. When the young orator rose to speak the temperature in the building was 97 degrees Fahrenheit, but before he finished the thermometer showed a fall of two degrees."
>
> The *Journal*, though giving a more friendly account of the reception accorded the speech, said:
>
> > "It cannot be denied that the audience was disappointed in the circumstance that Mr. Bryan read his speech. Nevertheless, he was listened to with the deepest attention and the salient points of the speech were received with tumultuous applause."
>
> The reading of the speech was much discussed in both a serious and a comic vein by the opposition papers. The incident gave rise to a number of cuts and caricatures, one of the best of which represented me as a boy, reading a long roll of manuscript, while father Knickerbocker was returning to his house with a complacent look upon his face and a fire extinguisher under his arm. Beneath the picture were the significant words, "A false alarm."[173]

That speech is seen as a special case. A close observer would argue otherwise. It was special in that it was read from manuscript and was perhaps more dense, but in its emphasis on reason, on argument, it was typical of Bryan's speeches. Bryan's speeches typically established the background of the issue, built constructive arguments, and refuted opposing arguments. In the "Cross of Gold" speech, he set the historical scene in two pages, spent five pages in refutation of specific opposition arguments, used an additional two pages to analyze the Republican confusion on the coinage issue, and closed with a two-and-a-half page peroration beginning with Carlyle's struggle between "the idle holders of idle capital" and the "struggling masses, who produce the wealth and pay the taxes of the country." He ended, of course, with the cross of gold metaphor.[174]

Another element that illustrates Bryan's argumentative practice is the prevalent use of refutation. On every issue he was oriented not only to presenting his own view, but also to refuting opposition arguments. The "Cross of Gold" speech, the 1900 acceptance address, "Imperialism," and a host of others feature refutation. Perhaps refutation was more important to Bryan because he always seemed to be on the political "outside." He also was a reformer and, therefore, had to argue against the status quo. However, his refutation was more than a necessity; it was a consistent and essential part of his rhetoric.

Bryan was also more inclined to develop evidence than most assume. His first major speech in the House of Representatives, on the tariff, used extensive figures on the amount of wool produced per capita in the states, the dollar value of sheep in the nation, and the dollar value of the wool crop; quotations from Alexander Hamilton and Henry Clay; a report of the Bureau of Statistics; and a host of other sources.[175] This tendency has already been noted in other speeches, particularly his use of authoritative testimony from economists and especially from American heroes, including Jefferson, Jackson, Lincoln, and Henry. Even his speeches on prohibition and evolution show a greater emphasis on evidence than his opponents would have one believe. His evidence may not have been from reputable sources by opposition standards, but the importance of evidence in his speeches on every issue, and throughout his life, cannot be denied.

Part of Bryan's argumentative approach to speaking was an inclination to narrow the issues to a single question. In every campaign he centered on a paramount issue—free silver, imperialism, trusts, prohibition, or evolution. In several speeches he openly argued for this rhetorical strategy. In "The Price of a Soul" he noted how great orators, and even Christ, tended to reduce great controversies to a single question: "He [Christ] understood the value of the question in argument. If you will examine the great orations delivered at crises in the world's history, you will find that in nearly every case the speaker condensed the whole subject into a question, and in that question embodied what he regarded an unanswerable argument."[176]

Bryan has been criticized for this strategy. It probably hurt his chances with working class audiences in the east to reduce the whole populist crusade in 1896 to the issue of free coinage of silver. There were many other arguments that were closer to the interests of his audience. Some populists, such as Henry Demarest Lloyd, complained that the emphasis on free silver in 1896 pushed other reforms, such as direct election of public officials, public ownership of railroads and telegraphs, and public works projects for the unemployed, into the background and made silver the "great and pressing issue of the impending campaign." "Free silver," said Lloyd, "is the cow-bird of the Reform movement. It waited until the nest had been built by the sacrifices and labor of others, and then it laid its eggs in it, pushing out the others which lie smashed on the ground. It is now flying around while we are expected to do the incubating."[177] Free silver at sixteen to one was also too complicated for the average person to understand. Mark Hanna (William McKinley's campaign manager) said, "He's talking silver all the time and that's where we've got him."[178]

Paola E. Coletta, Bryan's most sympathetic and thorough biographer, says of the 1896 New York acceptance address: "Bryan could have been notified in Nebraska and lived up to his reputation as an orator with an extemporaneous speech in New York. Even better, he should have spoken on the income tax or on government by injunction, the two issues which appealed most to the working men of the East. Moreover, he had dwelt at greatest length on the money question, which most observers deemed the least important issue in the campaign, the most difficult to explain to ordinary men, and the one most misinterpreted because it was consonant with the selfish interest of the silver kings."[179]

Some have argued that Bryan's failure in 1908 was that he never found "a paramount issue, arguing that 'Shall the People Rule?' held neither the appeal of free silver in 1896 nor that of antiimperialism in 1900. One reporter who accompanied Bryan in 1908 thought Bryan spent the entire campaign testing 'issue after issue, trying to find a good paramounter,' only to dismiss them as 'duds.'"[180]

Finding the "paramounter" was indeed an important part of Bryan's argumentation. For Bryan, however, the paramount issue was more than just the most important issue: it was the basic cause. The gold standard, imperialism, the trusts, and evolution were the causes of other problems. That was Bryan's sense of argument. Go to the heart of the matter, find the underlying source of the problem, destroy or change that element, and the remainder of the system collapses. In this sense Bryan was a more intellectual speaker (perhaps I should say classical speaker) than most because he saw a reasoned pattern, identified the relationships, and recognized the nature of a chain of reasoning.

The argumentative practice of finding a root cause or a paramount issue is a powerful way of arguing, as long as the audience is homogenous. But the audience of the Progressive Era was becoming increasingly diverse, with more and stronger groups dedicated to particular points of view. The successful presidential candidates in the twentieth century have avoided the "paramount issue" practice and argued from broader questions of public policy rather than from specific issues, and never from a paramount issue. Perhaps Bryan's 1908 "Shall the People Rule?" was more like a successful twentieth-century theme than any of his paramounters.

Bryan's analytical approach should have appealed to Progressives, but did not because of his tendency to ignore new information and ideas that might have led him to modify his positions. Sociologist Edward Alsworth Ross, a personal friend of Bryan's, provided some insight into the tendency:

> Bryan's organ like voice was so pleasing that often while listening to him I lost the thread of his discourse in my enjoyment of his rich, musical tones. His was one of the most powerful intellects I have known; but absorbed in politics from his twenties on, he failed to keep up with the general progress of thought, so that in some sectors his outlook was antiquated.
>
> As I looked through Mr. Bryan's book-shelves I notices they showed many "crank" books presented by the authors; but the works of the great *contemporary* authorities in economics, money, etc. were not there. From our many conversations it became plain to me that Mr. Bryan regarded economic truth as reposing on the authority of great classical thinkers like Adam Smith, Mill, Cairnes and Walker and not as something continually developing out of the study of economic life. For instance, he felt that the qualifications economists were beginning to make in the quality theory of money were designed merely to prop the gold standard.
>
> When he was in California in 1899 I tried to impress him with the effect upon the public mind of the sensational gold-strikes in the Klondyke and South Africa, arguing that in the new circumstances the free-silver position might have to be given up. His reaction was that of the debater. He would not consider these new gold supplies as a serious factor in shaping monetary policy, but merely suggested how to parry arguments based upon them. He would say, "Tell them this," or "meet that point this way." I went away with the conviction that Mr. Bryan was no realist.[181]

So it was with evolution. Evolutionary theory might change, but that was of little significance because the theory of evolution still had humans descending from animals, driven by forces over which they had no control. That was not the real world for Bryan. In his world, humans had a God-given role above all other animals to improve themselves and to improve society. As the emphasis of his speeches showed, social Darwinism and Nietzsche's superman had to be defeated by cutting off their head—biological evolution.

Some, like Ross, have argued that Bryan held people by his delivery and style rather than by the substance of his speeches. John Scopes said of Bryan's speech at his trial that he found himself "not listening to what he was saying, but to how he was saying it, . . . letting his oratorical talent hypnotize [him]. The longer he talked, the more complete was the control he had over the crowd."[182] There is no doubt that Bryan had a magnificent voice, and stylistically he made effective use of analogies, antithesis, parallelism, and Ciceronian climax. Contrary to his image as a narrow, biased pontificator, he also was well regarded in his day for the sense of humor he displayed in his speeches.

But argument was the center of Bryan's rhetorical method. In many ways, he was perhaps the most rhetorical Progressive of a very rhetorical age. His almost constant travel to campaign for various causes, his Chautauqua speeches, his newspaper, the *Commoner*, his numerous articles in other newspapers and magazines, and his books (frequently collections of speeches) all mark him as tremendously prolific. He was probably so busy speaking, writing, and listening that he had little time to read the current theories of the time. He was less intellectual than Woodrow Wilson, with whom he shared many political ideas. He was probably not as well read as Theodore Roosevelt. Yet his was an argumentation based on finding issues, driving those issues back to a paramount issue or cause, and, with evidence and argument, seeking to persuade. That emphasis on reason revealed an incredible confidence in the ordinary citizen. He believed that "the common man" would understand, follow, and, eventually, support his side of a controversy. Such a faith is at the basis of the enlightened origins of the Democratic Party. If the people are to use the government to assure life, liberty, and the pursuit of happiness, they must be able to reason. In this, Bryan's argumentation represented Jeffersonianism in the modern age.

Conclusion

Massive changes took place in American society at the turn of the century. Great forces were at work changing America from an agricultural to an urban and industrial nation. National pressure groups of various political, social, religious, and even academic orientations were creating a new society of elites who jockeyed for position in the new age.

Bryan sought to use government to preserve the rural, agrarian, and individualistic impulses of Jeffersonian liberalism. He advocated such means as direct election of senators, initiative referendum, and recall. He sought to level the playing field for all in the economic world through currency reform, tariff reform, restrictions on injunctions, and a graduated income tax. He looked for direct intervention of the government, first on the local and state level, but eventually on the federal level, through labor and health departments, regulation of trusts and railroads, public ownership of utilities, guaranteed bank deposits, a federal reserve system, woman's suffrage, child labor laws, prohibition, and antievolution laws.

His progressivism was, like Woodrow Wilson's, an attempt to produce a "new freedom," but he came to it earlier than Wilson did. Many of the proposals for which Bryan earlier had been vilified became accepted progressive measures even to his vilifiers, including Theodore Roosevelt. He was willing to see the government, on behalf of the American people, spread an idealized version of American democracy throughout the world. He objected vigorously to imperialism but accepted a role for America as an activist "city on the hill."

Bryan, like most Progressives, was unconcerned about "separate but equal" doctrine and repression of civil liberties for African Americans. While he did not believe the Anglo-Saxon race was inherently better than other races, he did see some races as more educated to democracy and therefore more able to make and enforce the laws. This racism was reinforced by his commitment to the Democratic Party, with its base in the South, and by the fact that more African Americans were Republicans. Bryan was, nonetheless, supremely oriented to the ability of individuals to change. He believed in the power of persuasion and in the active participation of the government in defining the nature of individual freedom in an industrial society.

Under the leadership of William Jennings Bryan, the Democratic Party was re-defined. It became a much more progressive party than it had been before Bryan came on the political scene. Many of the divisions between Democrats and Republicans that have become obvious since Franklin Delano Roosevelt grew from the lines drawn by Bryan at the turn of the century. His progressivism argued that the traditional American liberal's desire for the freedom of the individual could only be attained by active government attempts to balance the powerful forces of the modern era. Furthermore, he defined modern liberalism not only as reasoned but as moral, and he saw no contradiction between his liberalism and his religion. Government, like the people, must be moral, he argued, and if it was not, then it, like the people, could change. Change came through persuasion. His faith in the individual, in reason, and in the ability of "the people" to govern themselves marked him as a distinctively Jeffersonian, yet modern Progressive.

Notes

1. Mark Sullivan attributes "the boy orator of the Platte" to Bryan's friends and the comments on the Platte River to Ohio Republican Joseph B. Foraker. Mark Sullivan, *Our Times: 1900–1925* (New York: Charles Scribner's Sons, 1936), 1:193.

2. Robert W. Cherny, *Righteous Cause: The Life of William Jennings Bryan* (Boston: Little, Brown, and Co., 1985), 3.

3. Henry Nash Smith, *Virgin Land: The American West as Symbol and Myth* (Cambridge: Harvard University Press, 1950), 196.

4. Thomas Jefferson, "First Inaugural Address," in *American Rhetorical Discourse*, ed. Ronald F. Reid (Prospect Heights, Ill.: Waveland Press, 1995), 228.

5. Samuel P. Hays, *The Response to Industrialism, 1885–1914* (Chicago: University of Chicago Press, 1957), 13.

6. Carl N. Degler, *The Age of the Economic Revolution, 1876–1900* (Glenview, Ill.: Scott Foresman Co., n.d.), 31.

7. Hays, *Response*, 8–9.

8. Degler, *Economic Revolution*, 50–51.

9. Hays, *Response*, 58–59.

10. Ibid., 70.

11. Eldon J. Eisenach, *The Lost Promise of Progressivism* (Lawrence: University of Kansas Press, 1994), 13.

12. Ibid., 31, 35; Edward Alsworth Ross, *Seventy Years of It* (New York: D. Appleton-Century Co., 1936), 87. There are some notable omissions to the Eisenach list (Charles Beard, Herbert Croly, and Walter Lippmann, for instance). Eisenach omitted them because they wrote later, after the Progressive movement was well underway. However, these omissions do indicate that intellectual progressivism is much more substantial than any simple list can encompass. The list does indicate, however, that intellectual progressivism was substantial.

13. There is no firm beginning or ending point to the Progressive Era. Hays, for instance, uses 1885–1914; Arthur Link uses 1880–1930. For many, progressivism lived on in the Franklin Roosevelt years and still lives today.

14. Paolo E. Coletta, *Political Evangelist, 1860–1908*, vol. 1 of *William Jennings Bryan* (Lincoln: University of Nebraska Press, 1964), 25.

15. William Jennings Bryan, "In the Chicago Convention," in *Speeches of William Jennings Bryan* (New York: Funk and Wagnalls Co., 1909), 1:240–41.

16. William Jennings Bryan, "Mr. Bryan's Speech at the Conservation Congress," *Commoner*, 20 October 1911, 5–6. "The Conservation Problem," *Commoner*, 9 June 1911, 11.

17. Herbert Croly, *The Promise of American Life* (New York: Macmillan, 1910), 156.

18. William Jennings Bryan to May K. Foy, 5 June 1912, Occidental College Library, Los Angeles, boxes 5–6.

19. Bryan, "Guaranteed Deposits," in *Speeches*, 2:143.

20. Bryan, "The Tariff," in *Speeches*, 1:5–7.

21. Ibid., 1:13.

22. Coletta, *Political Evangelist*, 56–58.

23. Bryan, "An Income Tax," in *Speeches*, 1:174.

24. Ibid., 1:169–73.

25. Ibid., 1:173–74.

26. Coletta, *Political Evangelist*, 42, 67.

27. Ibid., 201.

28. "McKinley Starts Great Plant," *New York Weekly Tribune*, 11 November 1896, 20.

29. "Leader Altgeld and his mask," cartoon, *Harper's Weekly*, 18 July 1896, cover. Altgeld was the governor of Illinois who pardoned three anarchists convicted of complicity in the Haymarket murders of 1896 and opposed as unconstitutional President Cleveland's use of regular army troops in the 1894 Pullman Strike.

30. "W. J. Bryan, Populist," *New York Times*, 26 July 1896, 1. "Coxey's Army of Commonwealers" refers to bands of unemployed who, under the leadership of Jacob Coxey and others, marched on Washington in the winter of 1893–94 to advocate a $500 million federal program for work relief on road construction and local improvements to relieve unemployment and increase the amount of money in circulation.

31. "The Defeat of Socialism," *Harper's Weekly*, 14 November 1896, 1114.

32. "Good Riddance," *New York Weekly Tribune*, 4 November 1896, 10.

33. William Jennings Bryan, *First Battle* (Chicago: W. B. Conkey Co., 1896), 271–76, 406–9. There are other differences in the platforms but they are relatively insignificant to my purposes here. The Democratic platform omits initiative, referendum, and recall, and the People's Party platform omits tariff for revenue only, for example, but such items were not inconsistent with Bryan's views.

34. Ibid., 297.

35. Coletta, *Political Evangelist*, 375–78.

36. Ibid., 119.

37. Bryan, "At Madison Square Garden," *First Battle*, 321.

38. Ibid., 322.

39. Coletta, *Political Evangelist*, 203. Louise W. Koenig, *Bryan: A Political Biography of William Jennings Bryan* (New York: G. P. Putnam's Sons, 1971), 252.

40. Bryan, "In the Chicago Convention," 249.

41. Bryan, "Democratic Platform," *First Battle*, 408.

42. Ibid, 410.

43. *New York Times*, 9 September 1896, 4.

44. Sidney Brooks, "Bryanism," *Contemporary Review* 78 (1890): 638–39.

45. Bryan, *First Battle*, 412. See also "To Central Labor Union," 17 July 1908, Nebraska State Historical Society, MS 5, box 2, folder F8; "Labor," 7 September 1908, Nebraska State Historical Society, MS 464, box 5, folder 10.

46. Bryan, "Labor."

47. Ibid.

48. Ibid.

49. Ibid.

50. William Jennings Bryan, "Answers at Cooper Union," 21 April 1908, Occidental College Library, Los Angeles, boxes 1–4.

51. Bryan, *First Battle*, 414.

52. William Jennings Bryan and Mary Baird Bryan, *Memoirs of William Jennings Bryan* (Chicago: John C. Winston and Co., 1925), 467. Paolo E. Coletta, *Political Puritan, 1915–1925*, vol. 3 of *William Jennings Bryan* (Lincoln: University of Nebraska Press, 1969).

53. Coletta, *Political Puritan*, 80. Coletta notes that four Western states (Wyoming, Colorado, Idaho, and Utah) gave women the vote in the 1890s. Between 1910 and 1914 Washington, California, Oregon, Kansas, Arizona, Illinois, Montana, and Nevada made it thirteen states where women had the vote. By 1917, New York, North Dakota, Nebraska, Rhode Island, and Arkansas gave enough congressmen with women constituents to secure a national amendment.

54. William Jennings Bryan to Charles Bryan, n.d., Occidental College Library, Los Angeles, boxes 3–4. (Speech at Alliance, Nebraska, was in the letter.)

55. Bryan and Bryan, *Memoirs*, 506.

56. Coletta, *Political Puritan*, 82.

57. Bryan, "Answers at Cooper Union."

58. Ibid.

59. Bryan, "White Supremacy," 7 March 1923, Occidental College Library, Los Angeles, box 1–4.

60. Bryan, "Imperialism," in *Speeches*, 2:24.

61. William Jennings Bryan, "The Negro Question," *Commoner*, 1 November 1901, 1–2. See also William Jennings Bryan, "The Race Problem," *Commoner*, 21 August 1903, 1–2.

62. William Jennings Bryan, "Another Negro Burned," *Commoner*, 26 June 1903, 2.

63. William Jennings Bryan, "White and Black," *Commoner*, 9 January 1903, 11.

64. Arthur A. Ekirch Jr., *Progressivism in America* (New York: New Viewpoints, 1974), 135–36.

65. Edward Alsworth Ross, *Social Control: A Survey of the Foundations of Order* (New York: Macmillan, 1901), 336.

66. Herbert Croly, *The Promise of American Life* (New York: Macmillan, 1910), 72–84.

67. William Jennings Bryan, "Mr. Bryan on Chinese Exclusion," *Commoner*, 30 March 1906, 3–4.

68. Coletta, *Political Evangelist*, 214–22.

69. Bryan, *First Battle*, 581. Coletta, *Political Evangelist*, 191.

70. Richard Hofstadter, *The Age of Reform: From Bryan to F.D.R.* (New York: Vintage Books, 1955), 77–81.

71. Willard H. Smith, *The Social and Religious Thought of William Jennings Bryan* (Lawrence, Kans.: Coronado Press, 1975), 42–45.

72. Albert Jeremiah Beveridge, "The Philippine Question," in *American Public Addresses, 1740–1952*, ed. A. Craig Baird (New York: McGraw-Hill, 1956), 202.

73. Ibid.

74. Bryan, "Naboth's Vineyard," in *Speeches*, 2:6–8.

75. Bryan, "American's Mission," in *Speeches*, 2:15–16.

76. Bryan, "Imperialism," in *Speeches*, 2:17.

77. Ibid., 2:24.

78. Ibid., 2:39–40.

79. Ibid., 2:41.

80. Ibid., 2:41, 43.

81. Ibid., 2:43–44.

82. Ibid., 2:37, 45.

83. Ibid., 2:47.

84. Bryan, "The White Man's Burden," in *Speeches*, 2:217

85. Richard Hofstadter, *The American Political Tradition and the Men Who Made It* (New York: Alfred A. Knopf, 1948), 196; Paxton Hibben, *The Peerless Leader: William Jennings Bryan* (New York: Farrar and Reinhart, 1929), 357.

86. Paolo E. Coletta, *Progressive Politician and Moral Statesman, 1909–1915*, vol. 2 of *William Jennings Bryan* (Lincoln: University of Nebraska Press, 1969), 165, 198, 204–5. Coletta, *Political Puritan*, 57–60. Koenig, *Bryan*, 520–21.

87. Bryan and Bryan, *Memoirs*, 383.

88. Ibid., 385.

89. Bryan, "The White Man's Burden," in *Speeches*, 2:217. Bryan, "At The Peace Conference," in *Speeches*, 2:226–31.

90. Bryan and Bryan, *Memoirs*, 385, 386–87.

91. Lawrence W. Levine, *Defender of the Faith, William Jennings Bryan: The Last Decade, 1915–1925* (New York: Oxford University Press, 1965), 136–47. Bryan supported Wilson until after the defeat of the League of Nations in the Senate. After that he supported a compromise with Henry Cabot Lodge and the Republicans who controlled the Senate.

92. William Jennings Bryan to C. W. Bryan, 13 March 1919, Occidental College Library, Los Angeles, box 31. William Howard Taft and William Jennings Bryan, *World Peace* (New York: George H. Doran, 1917), 29.

93. Taft and Bryan, *World Peace*, 37–38, 111.

94. Bryan, "At the Peace Conference," in *Speeches*, 2:230, 231.

95. Richard Challener, "William Jennings Bryan," in *An Uncertain Tradition: American Secretaries of State in the Twentieth Century*, ed. Norman A. Graebner (New York: McGraw-Hill, 1961), 80.

96. Croly, *Promise*, 157.

97. Ibid., 169. Ekirch, *Progressivism in America*, 275. Eisenach, *Lost Promise of Progressivism*, 48–70. David B. Danbom, *"The World of Hope": Progressives and the Struggle for an Ethical Public Life* (Philadelphia: Temple University Press, 1987), 151.

98. Danbom, *"World of Hope,"* 151.

99. Eisenach, *Lost Promise of Progressivism*, 48–70, contains an interesting discussion of the link between progressivism and the "New England narrative." One analyst has called Bryan a "Missionary Isolationist." The analysis is not significantly different from what I have presented here. It does, however, illustrate the dangers of using terms like "isolationist" to characterize a public figure like Bryan. Kendrick A. Clements, *William Jennings Bryan: Missionary Isolationist* (Knoxville: University of Tennessee Press, 1982).

100. Bryan and Bryan, *Memoirs*, 384.

101. Stephen Jay Gould, "William Jennings Bryan's Last Campaign," *Natural History* 96 (November 1997): 16.

102. See, for instance, Gould, "Last Campaign"; Levine, *Defender of the Faith*; Coletta, *Political Puritan*; and Smith, *Social and Religious Thought*.

103. William Jennings Bryan, "Why Sign the Pledge?" Occidental College Library, Los Angeles, boxes 3–4.

104. Coletta, *Political Puritan*, 60–66, 78.

105. William Jennings Bryan, "Prohibition," *Commoner*, January 1916, 13, 60–66, 78.

106. William Jennings Bryan, "The Liquor Question in Lincoln," *Commoner*, 7 April 1911, 1–4; Bryan, "Prohibition," 13–15; William Jennings Bryan, "Democracy's Deeds and Duties," *Commoner*, January 1917, 14–19.

107. Bryan, "Democracy's Deeds and Duties."

108. Koenig, *Bryan*, 651.

109. Ibid., 657.

110. Carlyle Marney, "Dayton's Long Hot Summer," in *D-Days at Dayton*, ed. Jerry R. Tompkins (Baton Rouge: Louisiana State University Press, 1965), 135.

111. *The World's Most Famous Court Trial* (Cincinnati: National Book Co., 1925), 285–86, 299.

112. Jerry Falwell, Ed Dobson, and Ed Hindson, *The Fundamentalist Phenomenon* (Garden City, N.Y.: Doubleday, 1981), 86. Although Dobson and Hindson are identified as the authors of this book and Falwell is identified as the "editor," it is clear that it represents Falwell's beliefs.

113. Beverly J. Barnett, "William Jennings Bryan's Theological and Hermeneutical Stance in the Scopes Trial: A Rhetorical Study" (Master's thesis, University of Utah, 1984), 182.

114. Ibid., 152–84. See also Ernest R. Sandeen, *The Roots of Fundamentalism* (Chicago: University of Chicago Press, 1970), 107–12; and Nancy T. Ammerman, "North American Protestant Fundamentalism," in *Fundamentalism Observed*, ed. Martin E. Marty and R. Scott Appleby (Chicago: University of Chicago Press, 1991), 1:5–7.

115. Sandeen, *Roots*, 267–68.

116. William Jennings Bryan, "The Prince of Peace," in *Speeches*, 2:285.

117. Ibid., 2:267.

118. Frank A. Pattie, "The Last Speech of William Jennings Bryan," *Tennessee Historical Quarterly* 6 (1947): 272–73.

119. Bryan and Bryan, *Memoirs*, 485–86.

120. Pattie, "Last Speech," 267, 270.

121. Bryan and Bryan, *Memoirs*, 537.

122. Ibid.

123. Ibid., 547.

124. Ibid., 548.

125. Ibid., 550.

126. Ibid., 537. What is revealed here is that Bryan's concept of science, like that of most fundamentalists, was Baconian. Science was for Bryan "classified knowledge." Facts were gathered from biblical texts and scientific data to discover inductively the laws of nature. Theories (what he called "guesses") were useful but could not be true science until observable evidence was available to establish them as true. Ammerman, "North American," in *Fundamentalism Observed*, 9. See, for instance, William Jennings Bryan, "The Menace of Darwinism," *Commoner*, April 1921, 5.

127. Bryan and Bryan, *Memoirs*, 537.

128. Ibid., 539.

129. Ibid.

130. Ibid., 541. It should be noted that J. N. Rodeheaver, in a 1922 letter to Bryan, criticized Bryan for omitting from his lecture "The Bible and Its Enemies" that Romanes returned to Christianity in his last years through higher criticism. J. N. Rodeheaver to Bryan, 18 November 1922, Bryan Papers, Library of Congress, box 36. Bryan responded by pointing out that while Romanes "was working his way back when he died," his statement is still there that "for a quarter of a century he was unable to pray because of an undue regard for reason as against the heart and will." Bryan to Rodeheaver, 29 November 1922, Bryan Papers, Library of Congress, box 36. What this shows is that Bryan's concentration was on the issues as he saw them. It also shows that he made few changes in his arguments or his evidence. Many of the statements in his later speeches are almost verbatim from earlier speeches.

131. Bryan and Bryan, *Memoirs*, 541–43.

132. *Most Famous Trial*, 178.

133. Ibid., 179–80. Bryan indicates that he bought the book containing Darrow's speech from the Leob Leopold case "here in town. I bought four copies the other day; cost me $2; anybody can get it for 50 cents apiece, but he cannot buy mine. They are valuable." To which Dudley Field Malone, an attorney for the defense and a former associate of Bryan's in the Department of State, responded, "I will pay $1.50 for yours. (Laughter)" So, one of his best arguments was in a fifty-cent book he found in Dayton (*Most Famous Trial*, 179). An interesting sidelight here is that Bryan also turns the tables on Darrow in his undelivered trial summation speech when he noted Darrow's argument that "Dicky Loeb, the younger boy, had read trashy novels, of the blood and thunder sort. He even went so far as to commend an Illinois statute which forbids minors reading stories of crime. Here is what Mr. Darrow said: 'We have a statute in this state, passed only last year, which forbids minors reading stories of crime. Why? There is only one reason; because the legislature in its wisdom thought it would have a tendency to produce these thoughts and this life in the boys who read them.' If Illinois can protect her boys, why cannot this state protect the boys of Tennessee" (Bryan and Bryan, *Memoirs*, 546).

134. Bryan and Bryan, *Memoirs*, 546–47.

135. Ibid., 548.

136. Ibid., 548, 549.

137. Ibid., 550.

138. Ibid., 550–51; Bryan quotes from Charles Darwin, *The Descent of Man, and Selections Related to Sex* (Princeton: Princeton University Press, 1981), 168–69. The question mark in parenthesis (?) is part of Bryan's published argument.

139. Bryan and Bryan, *Memoirs*, 553.

140. William Jennings Bryan, *In His Image* (New York: Fleming H. Revell, 1922), 125–26.

141. Bryan and Bryan, *Memoirs*, 537.

142. Pattie, "Last Speech," 271.

143. Ibid.

144. Ibid., 271–72.

145. Lloyd C. Douglas, "Mr. Bryan's New Crusade," *Christian Century*, 25 November 1920, 11–12. Douglas was a Lutheran minister, essayist, and wrote such novels as *Magnificent Obsession*, *The Robe*, and *The Big Fisherman*.

146. B. L. Miller to Bryan, 10 May 1921, Bryan Papers, Library of Congress, box 34. Levine, *Defender of the Faith*, 286–88.

147. Ross, *Seventy Years of It*, 88. Interesting as a sidelight is the fact that Ross's conception of sciences is the same as Bryan's (see note 126). Ross also supports the idea that social Darwinism was Bryan's principle objection to evolution. He says that Bryan "held that such a conception of man's origin [as found in the *Descent of Man*] would weaken the cause of democracy and strengthen class pride and the power of wealth."

148. Peter J. Bowler, *The Eclipse of Darwinism* (Baltimore: Johns Hopkins University Press, 1983), 7–8.

149. Ibid., 200.

150. Ibid., 202.

151. William Berryman Scott, as quoted in Pattie, "Last Speech," 276.

152. Bryan and Bryan, *Memoirs*, 533.

153. William Jennings Bryan, "God and Evolution," *New York Times*, 26 February 1922, sec. 7, p. 1. See also Bryan to Heber D. Curtis, 22 May 1923, Bryan Papers, Library of Congress, box 37; Bryan to Arthur W. Stalker, 31 January 1921, Bryan Papers, Library of Congress, box 33; Bryan to George McReady Price, 13 April 1922, Bryan Papers, Library of Congress, box 35.

154. Bryan, "God and Evolution," 1; Bryan to editor, *Madison* (Wisconsin) *Capital Time*, 15 April 1922, Bryan Papers, Library of Congress, box 35; Bryan to F. A. Paddock, 7 March 1923, Bryan Papers, Library of Congress, box 37.

155. Bryan and Bryan, *Memoirs*, 532–33; Bryan to J. B. Steere, 28 August 1922, Bryan Papers, Library of Congress, box 35.

156. Bryan and Bryan, *Memoirs*, 534; Bryan to F. M. Reed, n.d., Bryan Papers, Library of Congress.

157. Bryan to Howard A. Kelly, 22 June 1925, Bryan Papers, Library of Congress, box 47. See also Bryan, "God and Evolution," 1.

158. There are also many arguments against theistic evolution that are not central to this discussion; see Bowler, *Eclipse of Darwinism*, 54.

159. William Jennings Bryan, "Mr. Bryan Speaks for Himself," *Presbyterian Advance*, 6 December 1923, 18.

160. Bryan and Bryan, *Memoirs*, 537.

161. R. C. Spangler to Bryan, 29 April 1922, Bryan Papers, Library of Congress, box 35.

162. Bryan to R. C. Spangler, 26 May 1922, Bryan Papers, Library of Congress, box 35.

163. Bryan to editor, *Chicago Tribune*, 14 June 1923, box 37, Bryan Papers, Library of Congress, box 37; Bryan to C. H. Thurber, 22 December 1923, Bryan Papers, Library of Congress, box 38.

164. Bryan to S. K. Hicks, 10 June 1925, Bryan Papers, Library of Congress, box 47.

165. Cherny, *Righteous Cause*, 10.

166. Levine, *Defender of the Faith*, 188–94; William Jennings Bryan, "A Constructive Program," *Commoner*, January 1919, 5.

167. Bryan to William Jennings Bryan Jr., 20 December 1909, Occidental College Library, Los Angeles, boxes 21–22.

168. Levine, *Defender of the Faith*, 278.

169. Cherny, *Righteous Cause*, 160; Coletta, *Political Puritan*, 8; William Jennings Bryan, "Speech on the 1920 Convention Platform," Occidental College Library, Los Angeles, box 1; Bryan, "A Constructive Program"; John Durham Peters, "Satan and Savior: Mass Communication in Progressive Thought," *Critical Studies in Mass Communication* 6 (1989): 147–63.

170. Aristotle, *The Rhetoric of Aristotle*, trans. Lane Cooper (New York: D. Appleton-Century-Crofts, 1932), 5.

171. William Jennings Bryan, "Brother or Brute," *Commoner*, November 1920, 11.

172. See, for instance, "The Liquor Question in Lincoln," *Commoner*, 7 April 1911, 1–4; "The White Man's Burden," in *Speeches*, 2:212–25; "Imperialism," in *Speeches*, 2:17–49. Michael J. Hosteller has commented on the "rhetorically complex structure and arguments" in Bryan's undelivered Scopes trial final argument published after his death. Michael J. Hosteller, "William Jennings Bryan as Demosthenes: The Scopes Trial and

the Undelivered Oration, 'On Evolution,'" *Western Journal of Communication* 62 (1998): 165–80.

173. Bryan, *First Battle*, 314–15.
174. Bryan, "In the Chicago Convention," in *Speeches*, 1:238–49.
175. Bryan, "The Tariff," in *Speeches*, 1:3–11.
176. William Jennings Bryan, "The Price of a Soul," in *Speeches*, 2:337.
177. Koenig, *Bryan*, 217.
178. Mark Hanna, as quoted in Coletta, *Political Evangelist*, 164.
179. Ibid.
180. As quoted in Cherny, *Righteous Cause*, 115.
181. Ross, *Seventy Years of It*, 87–91.
182. John Scopes, as quoted in Cherny, *Righteous Cause*, 178.

Eugene Debs and American Class

James Darsey

> *Americans, while occasionally willing to be serfs, have always been obstinate about being peasantry.*

F. SCOTT FITZGERALD, *The Great Gatsby*

7

enry James, in his 1877 novel *The American*, gives to a Frenchman, M. de Bellegarde, the task of articulating the absence of rigid, hierarchical class structures in the United States: "Being an American, it was impossible you should remain what you were born, and being born poor—do I understand it?—it was therefore inevitable that you should become rich. You were in a position that makes one's mouth water; you looked round you and saw a world full of things you had only to step up to and take hold of."[1] Bellegarde's American witness, Christopher Newman, is happy to confirm Bellegarde's understanding. Newman, on whose confusion and frustration over the entailments of French hierarchy the novel turns, later affirms his American sense of egalitarianism in a discussion of nobility: "'A title? What do you mean by a title?' asked Newman. 'A count, a duke, a marquis? I don't know anything about that, I don't know who is and who is not. But I say I am noble. I don't exactly know what you mean by it, but it's a fine word and a fine idea; I put in a claim to it.'"[2] It is, for Newman, all a matter of "energy and ingenuity."[3]

James's characters express a conceit fondly held by Americans of the nineteenth century. Letters home from immigrants to the United States reflect the appeal of—and belief in—a classless society in their new country. "This is a free country and nobody has a great deal of authority over another," wrote a transplanted Swede in 1850. "There is no pride and nobody needs to hold his hat in his hand for anyone else. This is not Sweden, where the higher classes and employers have the law on their side so that they can treat subordinates as though they were not human beings." In 1890, Johann Schmitz used almost identical language, even to the metonymy of the doffed hat, in a letter to his brother back home: "And what is nicer yet is the fact that this is a free land. No one can give orders to anybody here, one is as good as another, no one takes off his hat to another as you have to do in Germany."[4]

Whether the United States was ever the egalitarian utopia it prides itself on being is a more complicated question than Christopher Newman or the letters of self-satisfied immigrants might suggest. The voluminous literature on class in America is fractious, given to inconsistent findings, and often divided along ideological lines.[5] The theory of American exceptionalism, which holds the United States to be unique in its relative lack of class structure, has, like the evil antagonist in so many slasher films, been repeatedly vanquished, especially by avowedly Marxist labor historians, only to arise miraculously from the grave to fight again. Much of the confusion arises from imprecise notions of class, the necessarily very local studies used to address the question of class division, and a failure to distinguish the material marks of class from class consciousness.

Beginning in the Gilded Age, language and material experience in the United States achieved a consonance that make invocations of "class consciousness" and "class interests" less controversial than they are for earlier historical periods. Leon Fink, who, like most contemporary labor historians, disputes the idea of American exceptionalism, nonetheless recognizes the power of the democratic idea of equality in the United States and its reality, relatively speaking, in much of American history. Fink focuses on the late 1870s as the provenance of serious class consciousness in the United States, identifying the Noble and Holy Order of the Knights of Labor as "the first mass organization of the North American working class." Marking the significance of this development in American politics, Fink continues: "the labor movement in the Gilded Age turned the plowshares of a consensual political past into a sword of class conflict."[6]

Fink's argument does not rest on the presence of labor organizations or on economic data. Identifying himself as part of a new school of labor historians practicing a "cultural approach" to their subject, Fink applauds "an explicit focus on consciousness [that] has emerged through the study of language and rhetoric," and he insists that "the sustained coordination of language and social action," such as emerges in the labor movement of the Gilded Age, "should be reason enough to credit a distinct set of thought and ideals, a group outlook, at least to the same extent that one would infer an outlook from the language and actions of other groups, such as the 'liberal middle class.'"[7] Fink finds just such "sustained coordination of language and social action in the labor movement in the United States at the turn of the last century," which, he notes, "not unlike its nineteenth-century British counterpart, spoke a 'language of class' that was 'as much political as economic.'"[8]

One of the preeminent spokespersons addressing the interests of the increasing population of industrial wage workers in fin de siècle America, Eugene Debs, founder of the American Railroad Union, reluctant leader of the Pullman strike in 1893, relentless foe of the elitist craft unionism represented by Samuel Gompers and the American Federation of Labor, untiring advocate of integrated industrial unionism, and five-time Socialist Party candidate for president, had an important role in reshaping the American political vocabulary so that it could give voice to lived experience and the emergence of class consciousness.[9]

The precipitousness of the change is indicated in Debs's reflection, in 1914, on the Homestead strike only forty-five years earlier. "There was no class-conscious labor movement or press, such as we have today, to interpret Homestead in the light of the class struggle," Debs opined.[10] Debs's sense of his own time is remarkably consistent with Leon Fink's assessment that the language of class struggle and class consciousness becomes liminal in the United States only in the 1870s. Even then, the myth of classlessness is so tenacious that Debs must often unmask its pretensions directly, as he does in a 1905 speech in Chicago: "President Roosevelt would have you believe that there are no classes in the United States," Debs chides. "He was made president by the votes of the working class." Debs continues:

> Did you ever know of his stopping over night in the home of a workingman? Is it by mere chance that he is always sheltered beneath the hospitable roof of some plutocrat? Not long ago he made a visit here and he gave a committee representing the working class about fifteen minutes of his precious time, just time enough to rebuke them with the intimation that organized labor consisted of a set of law-breakers, and then he gave fifteen hours to the plutocrats of Chicago, being wined and dined by them to prove that there are no classes in the United States, and that you, horny handed veteran, with your wage of $1.50 a day, with six children to support on that, are in the same class with John D. Rockefeller! Your misfortune is that you do not know you are in the same class. But on election day it dawns upon you and you prove it by voting the same ticket.[11]

In Debs's own case, though his essential causes and sympathies were remarkably consistent over his career, an explicit, self-conscious articulation of the class struggle as the central motive in history is not featured in his rhetoric until after his time in jail at Woodstock, Illinois, for his role in the Pullman strike of 1894—the time, according to the legend Debs himself helped to foster, of his conversion to socialism.[12] Speaking on behalf of the International Workers of the World (IWW) at Grand Central Palace in 1905, Debs offers an interpretation of a society clinging tenaciously to a democratic ideal while increasingly stratified economically: "In the evolution of capitalism, society has been divided mainly into two economic classes; a relatively small class of capitalists who own tools in the form of great machines they did not make and cannot use, and a great body of many millions of workers who did make these tools and who do use them, and whose very lives depend upon them, yet who do not own them."[13] "The Socialist Party," Debs avers in a 1908 article in the *Independent*, "is the political expression of what is known as 'the class struggle.' This struggle is an economic fact as old as history itself, but it is only within the past generation that it has become a thoroughly conscious and well organized political fact."[14] Others may have spoken in the patois of marginal immigrants or ideological groups already accustomed to thinking in class terms; Debs expressed the drama of class struggle and the coming cooperative commonwealth in the American vernacular and put working-class issues so firmly onto the main stage of American politics that mainstream political parties were forced, however incrementally and reluctantly, to respond.

Equality and Stratification in Fin de Siècle America

To those who lived through the Industrial Revolution in the United States, the accompanying sense of dislocation was both acute and intense. Historian Robert Wiebe writes: "As the network of relations affecting men's lives each year became more tangled and more distended, Americans in a basic sense no longer knew who or where they were. The setting had altered beyond their power to understand it, and within an alien context they had lost themselves. In a democratic society who was master and who was servant? In a land of opportunity what was success? In a Christian nation what were the rules and who kept them? The apparent leaders were as much adrift as their followers."[15] Nor are the anxieties we attribute to the period in retrospect merely the post hoc realization of historians. In 1914, looking back over the tumultuous changes of the previous forty years, Walter Lippmann, in his second book, *Drift and Mastery*, wrote, "We are unsettled to the very roots of our being. There isn't a human relation . . . that doesn't move in a strange situation. . . . There are no precedents to guide us, no wisdom that wasn't made for a simpler age. We have changed our environment more quickly that we know how to change ourselves."[16]

Americans in the decades following the Civil War moved from the farm into the city, where they mixed with masses of immigrants from Europe, exchanged agrarian for industrial work, and witnessed an astonishing production of new wealth and its concentration in a very small number of hands. There are countless recitations of increasing economic inequality in America during the final two decades of the nineteenth century and the first two decades of the twentieth. Walter Licht reports that "in 1890, the top 1 percent of wealth holders owned 51 percent of all property, the bottom 44 percent just 1.2 percent." Licht goes on to note that the top 1 percent included approximately 125,000 families, owning on average $264,000 of personal property, while the bottom 44 percent comprised 5.5 million families owning, on average, $150 of property.[17]

Figures such as these are not simply statistical abstractions through which one generation looks back at the material conditions of another; they were an important part of the substance with which social reformers at the turn of the last century attempted to create class consciousness. "We have but to study the figures in the report of the federal board of industrial relations which indicate unerringly the ugly fact that one third of the American wage-earners is in a poverty-stricken condition," Eugene Debs moaned in an editorial in the *National Rip-Saw*, "that two-thirds of the male workers are paid less than fifteen dollars per week, that half the wage-earning fathers receive less than fifty dollars per month, that half the women wage-workers receive less than a dollar a day, and that one out of every twelve persons who die in New York City, the great American metropolis, is buried as a pauper in the pottersfield."[18] On the dedication of Henry Frick's "four million dollar castle" on Fifth Avenue in New York City, Debs wrote, "The splendors of it are dazzling, the immensity of it overwhelming," signaling with both adjectives the great distance between Frick's material position and that of working-class men and women, in particular Frick's "old employees" at Homestead, "murdered by Pinkertons, because they wanted wages enough to live in decency and provide their children with bread."[19] Addressing the court just prior to his sentencing for violation of the Espionage Act, Debs called the court's attention "to the fact this morning that in this system five percent of our people own and control two-thirds of our wealth; sixty-five per cent of the people embracing the working class who produce all wealth, have but five per cent to show for it."[20]

In the face of enormous and undeniable inequalities of wealth and power, turn-of-the-century capitalists tried to reorder the fragmented social landscape by dividing the world into the disciplined and virtuous versus the undisciplined and degraded. Early theories of management espoused a theory of human nature, now referred to as "theory X," which assumed humankind to be lazy, irresponsible, and unmotivated. Andrew Carnegie took it to be a basic fact of human nature that "ability and energy" were the possession of the few.[21] William Graham Sumner reflected the same perspective when he called cupidity, selfishness, envy, malice, lust, and vindictiveness the "constant vices of human nature."[22] Sumner claimed that "the weak who constantly arouse the pity of humanitarian and philanth[r]opists are the shiftless, the imprudent, the negligent, the impractical, and the inefficient, or they are the idle, the intemperate, the extravagant, and the vicious."[23] Where discipline was naturally lacking in inferior men, superior men were duty bound to impose it, primarily through the application of the principles of scientific management, a movement that reached its zenith under the influence of Frederick W. Taylor in the second decade of the twentieth century.

The powerful attempted to give moral sanction to their dominance by co-opting the language of rectitude and merit and characterizing economic inequality in terms of traditional Puritan hierarchies, hierarchies that could be both hierarchical and democratic inasmuch as they were predicated on putatively corrigible elements of character. The guardians of privilege in turn-of-the-century America were particularly adept at exploiting the Janus-faced nature of America's ideals.[24] Against the claim that industrial capitalism was destructive of individualism, apologists for the new order made the bold assertion that strong individual character was the foundation for their success. With the benison of Herbert Spencer's exegesis of sacred history, stern, moralistic John D. Rockefeller presented himself as the embodiment of Puritan virtue; J. P. Morgan pronounced "character" the basis for all of his transactions;[25] Carnegie defended "individualism" as the only defensible basis for civilization;[26] and Russell Conwell defended the wealthy as, on the whole, honest men whose wealth was a result of their honesty, "the very best people in character as well as in enterprise."[27] Drawing on the tradition of Calvinism updated with social evolutionism, such views held wealth to be a sign of God's grace; poverty signaled moral failing.

The subrogation of moral value by "the great bitch goddess Success," despite its apparent meanness, was an attempt to provide some standard for a disordered world and reason to new hierarchies of wealth. The empirical threatened to overwhelm considerations of the ethical. As Robert Wiebe notes, "For lack of anything that made better sense of their world, people everywhere weighed, counted, and measured it."[28] John D. Rockefeller was indisputably rich, and he and others like him were objects of near-universal envy. If values could not find a common celebration, the achievements of production, profits, and growth could.

The values of the countinghouse, though, were a poor substitute for the sacred. They lacked in genuine transcendence and in disinterested expression, and they fostered competition rather than community. There was no escaping the worldliness of wealth, nor that the greatest exponents of the gospel of wealth were its beneficiaries. In the face of immense poverty, particularly during the periodic depressions of the last half of the nineteenth century, there was an irremediable suspicion that the tremendous aggregation of wealth in the hands of the few was not right. Writing on the Panic of 1873, one of Debs's compeers, A. M. Simons, editor of the *International Socialist Review*, wrote: "The capitalist henceforth becomes purely a parasitic owner, who may be an idiot, an infant, an insane person, a ward of the court but who, while the law protects his ownership of corporation shares, can still levy a tax upon every man working either with hand or with brain."[29] Simons's argument undermines the meritocratic warrant for hierarchy underlying both Calvinism and social evolutionism.

Eugene Debs and the Classification of America

Sean Wilentz identifies this period of radical economic stratification with the fourth stage in the formation of an American working class, the period "from the upheavals of the 1880s to the era of World War I," which included "the advent of national and international monopoly capital, a remaking of the American working class, bitter conflicts between employers and workers, and a fragmentation of the American labor movement."[30]

Just as their capitalist counterparts sought divisions by which they might give order to the great confusion that was industrial society, so too did turn-of-the-century social reformers. A class consciousness, new in the experience of American workers, arose from a growing awareness that workers were part of a distinct and relatively stable underclass, a class that, by virtue of its relative stability, began to define its interests in opposition to the interests of those who owned the means of production, whose wealth and status and power, it seemed increasingly apparent, wage workers could never hope to achieve. "Ownership of the means of life of one class by another class, such as we have in the United States and in every other capitalist nation on earth, means class rule and class war; class supremacy and class subjection," wrote Debs. "It means that the few who own shall grow extremely rich without producing anything while the great mass who produce all shall remain in poverty."[31]

Not surprisingly, what Debs and his fellow reformers concluded regarding the moral signification of great wealth stood in diametrical opposition to the conclusions of the Carnegies and the Conwells. In a 1914 editorial in the *National Rip-Saw,* Debs provided a particularly colorful statement of a favorite theme, that the great wealth of the capitalist class was, far from being a symbol of their superior moral character, in truth, indicative of their ruthlessness, rapaciousness, and mendacity: "There are no titled rulers on earth and no blood-sucking vampires any where who can beat American capitalists, banded together in corporations and trusts, when it comes to the brutal, heartless repression of their slaves who produce their wealth. Not even women or children are spared. Nothing is sacred to them. The rights of men are to them food for laughter and scorn. All the decencies, dignities and amenities of civilized life are trampled under their hoofs in their mad war to increase their profits and keep down their slaves."[32] Countering any pretension that turn-of-the-century life represented an evolutionary high-water mark, Debs, with his bestial images, suggests the degeneration of decency, dignity, and civilization. In a 1917 editorial defaming the prosecution of the leaders of various strikes around the country, Debs iterates the theme of the degraded character among capitalists: "Capitalism, corner-stoned in industrial robbery and buttressed by political corruption, is essentially craven and cowardly. It does not fight in the open. It fights as it robs, in the most sneaking and cowardly way."[33]

Debs turned capitalist, Spencerian theories of human nature and the practical realization of those theories in scientific management on their head, and he held the innate virtue, or manhood, of the working class against the degradation and depravity of the owning class.[34] He decried the view of human nature forwarded by the capitalists as "a low estimate of moral worth, which affirms that all men are corrupt and denies that any man has honor, which repudiates self-respect and scorns manhood."[35] "I would not be a capitalist:" Debs thundered to the applause of an IWW convention. "I would be a man; you cannot be both at the same time":

> The capitalist exists by exploitation, lives out of the labor, that is to say the life, of the working man; consumes him, and his code of morals and standard of ethics justify it and [sic] this proves that capitalism is cannibalism.
> A man, honest, just high-minded, would scorn to live out of the sweat and sorrow of his fellowman—by preying upon his weaker brother.
> We purpose [sic] to destroy the capitalist and save the man. We want a system in which the worker shall get what he produces and the capitalist shall produce what he gets. That is a square deal.[36]

That the ethos of wealth was ultimately unconvincing is suggested, not only in the equation of capitalism with cannibalism and bestiality, but also in Debs's swipe at President Theodore Roosevelt's "square deal," a slogan Roosevelt first used following the settlement of a mining strike in 1902. Roosevelt's "square deal" described an ideal of peaceful coexistence between big business and labor unions, an ideal that Debs and others thought purely phantasmagorical.[37] While Roosevelt and other exponents of the gospel of wealth preached rugged individualism against unionism and touted a doctrine of unlimited opportunity, achievement was undeniably the possession of a very few. The elitism bred of industrial capitalism was repugnant to the American ideals of egalitarianism and democracy.[38] The exercise of unjustified power for personal gain, as reformers saw it, was not individualism but usurpation, an attempt at tyranny. Debs placed ultimate responsibility for the condition of workers squarely on workers themselves, but he firmly rejected a "rank individualism" of the sort espoused by Theodore Roosevelt and others, an individualism that proscribed the right of workers to organize and to act collectively on their own behalf.[39]

Debs and Marx

Had Debs done no more than resurrect the hoary icons of the past against the false ethic of wealth, he could be easily dismissed as a simpleminded reactionary, a Don Quixote of American labor. But Debs was not a fallow imitator. He helped to introduce into the American political argot a vocabulary previously confined to the margins, spaces occupied by foreigners and anarchists, the vocabulary of Marxism. Although it is generally agreed that Debs was not a great Marxist theorist, and that he, in fact, left a great many contradictions unresolved in his casual assimilation of Marxism into native American thought, the influence of Marxism on Debs's thinking is undeniable.

Perhaps the most direct evidence of Debs's Marxist leanings is his adoption of a materialist conception of history and a dialectic of class struggle as the central motive in history. In a summary statement, Frederick Engels reveals the relationship of these ideas in Marxist theory:

> Then it was seen that all past history, with the exception of its primitive stages, was the history of class struggles; that these warring classes of society are always the products of the modes of production and of exchange—in a word, of the economic conditions of their time; that the economic structure of society always furnishes the real basis, starting from which we can alone work out the ultimate explanation of the whole superstructure of juridical and political institutions as well as of the religious, philosophical, and other ideas of a given historical period.[40]

Debs's analysis is a virtual echo of Engels:

> We are engaged today in a class war; and why? For the simple reason that in the evolution of the capitalist system in which we live, society has been mainly divided into two economic classes—a small class of capitalists who own the tools with which work is done and wealth is produced, and a great mass of workers who are compelled to use those tools. Between these two classes there is an irrepressible economic conflict.[41]
>
> Now it is a fact that politics is simply the reflex of economics. The material foundation of society determines the character of social institutions—political, educational, ethical and spiritual. In exact proportion as the economic foundation of society changes the character of all social institutions changes to correspond to that basis.[42]

Armed with this analysis, Debs exposed the false alternatives represented by the Republican and Democratic Parties, which he often referred to as the Republican-Democratic Party, "the double-headed political monstrosity of the capitalist class"[43]:

The capitalist class is represented by the Republican, Democratic, Populist and Prohibition parties, all of which stand for private ownership of the means of production, and the triumph of any one of which will mean continued wage-slavery to the working class. . . .

The Republican and Democratic parties, or, to be more exact, the Republican-Democratic Party, represent the capitalist class in the class struggle. They are the political wings of the capitalist system and such differences as arise between them relate to spoils and not to principles.[44]

"As a rule," Debs opines elsewhere, emphasizing what he holds to be the only true division in society, "large capitalists are Republicans and small capitalists are Democrats, but workingmen must remember that they are all capitalists."[45] Debs's rejection of the legitimacy of the major political parties is reminiscent of Garrisonian abolitionists, but his characterization of "a life and death struggle between two hostile economic classes"[46] and of "war upon the capitalist class, and upon the capitalist system"[47] was foreign to American thought and came directly from Marxist theory, as Debs acknowledged both overtly and by quotation. In this, he was distinguished even from such close political neighbors as the Christian Socialists, whose socialism tended to reflect sources other than Marx.[48]

The language of class division and class warfare is apparent in some of Debs's earliest writings, including a commentary on events at Andrew Carnegie's Homestead, Pennsylvania steelworks in 1892. In his essay in the *Locomotive Fireman's Magazine* for August 1892, Debs notes Carnegie's "aristocratic" inclinations and accuses Carnegie of being a combination of "plutocrat and pirate," who had "concluded that the time had arrived for him to array himself in purple," accompanied by "autocratic pomp and parade." Debs continues his harangue, making Carnegie simply an example of the "Christless capitalists" and "plutocratic pharisees" who rob labor of the capital that the "workingmen" have created and who use that capital to introduce new machinery that serves to ensure that the division between owner and laborer will be permanent and unbridgeable, and that "the pariahs were to remain pariahs forever."[49] That Debs chooses in essence to reprint the 1892 article in his analysis of the events at Ludlow is indicative of a considerable continuity in Debs's mind between his pre-Marx and post-Marx thinking.

Continuities notwithstanding, prior to his incarceration at Woodstock and his introduction to Marxist thinking, Debs lacked any abiding sense of the causes of or potential solutions to the great economic inequities he observed. Charles Lomas notes that "in a four year period at the end of the nineteenth century," Debs was "successively a leading Populist, a Bryanist, a utopian colonizer, and a founder of the Socialist Party."[50]

After Woodstock, Debs, with considerable consistency, features the evils of private ownership of the means of production as the centerpiece of his revolutionary program. Even more than the idea of class struggle, it is this focus on control of the means of production that most clearly marks the innovations in Debs's thinking as a result of his conversion to socialism. "Capitalism owns the tools and controls the jobs yet confesses that it cannot employ the workers, therefore the workers are bound to seize the tools, lay hold of the jobs, and employ themselves," exhorts Debs in a 1914 editorial in the *National Rip-Saw.*[51] "The Socialist party is the only party which stands for the taking over of the mines and other public utilities by the people and operating them for the benefit of the people, and this will put an end to the bloody misrule of capitalism forever," he declares in another editorial.[52]

Debs's understanding of Marx was not a profound one. Though he proudly notes his ownership of a copy of Marx's *Capital,* Debs nowhere claims to have read it,[53] and when he does quote Marx directly, it is generally from *The Communist Manifesto.*[54] When Debs undertakes economic analysis or engages aspects of

Marxist thought more technical than the quotation of such shibboleths as "Work-ingmen of all countries unite," Karl Kautsky's popular Marxist "catechism," *The Class Struggle,* is the likely source. James Cannon recognizes Kautsky as "the best popularizer of Marxism known in this country in the epoch before the First World War" and the source from which Debs learned the essentials.[55] Responding to sev-entieth birthday greetings from Kautsky, Debs fulsomely acknowledges this intel-lectual and theoretical debt: "It was from you, dear comrade, that I learned some of my earliest and most precious lessons in socialism, and I have always felt myself in debt, gratefully and with a deep sense of appreciation, to your gifted pen for having opened my eyes to the light which guided me into the socialist movement. I was in jail, one of the innumerable victims of capitalism, sitting in darkness as it were, when your pamphlets first came into my hands and your influence first made itself felt in my life, and I have since wondered often how any one, however feeble and benighted mentally, could read your crystal-clear Marxian expositions and interpre-tations without becoming and remaining a socialist."[56] Debs gushes in this letter, counting the birthday greeting from Kautsky "a great joy . . . and an honor I esteem beyond words, in which my beloved wife Katherine shares gladly, to receive from Karl and Luise Kautsky such a flattering testimonial of regard on the occasion of the anniversary of my natal day."[57] Debs's effusiveness betrays his own insecurity as a socialist and reveals the importance to Debs of the benison of such an acknowl-edged Marxian authority as Kautsky. Debs's analyses of surplus labor,[58] the com-modification of labor,[59] the periodic crises endemic to capitalist production,[60] the superfluity of the capitalist class,[61] and the evils of private ownership of the means of production[62] are all readily recognizable in Kautsky's handy catechism.

The first chapter of Kautsky's *The Class Struggle,* the beginnings of an elabora-tion of the first section of the program adopted by the German Social Democracy at Erfurt in 1891, is "The Passing of Small Production." In 1908, in a speech before the American Federation of Labor, Debs condensed Kautsky's evolutionary tale into the most recent fifty years: "No matter whether you have studied this economic question or not, you cannot have failed to observe that during the past half century society has been sharply divided into classes—into a capitalist class upon the one hand, into a working class upon the other hand. I shall not take the time to trace this evolution. I shall simply call your attention to the fact that half a century ago all a man needed was a trade and having this he could supply himself with the simple tools then used, produce what he needed and enjoy the fruit of his labor. But this has completely changed. The simple tool has disappeared and the great machine has taken its place. The little shop is gone and the great factory has come in its stead. The worker can no longer work by and for himself."[63] Debs's account is less historical than lamentation, an expression of sorrow and fear; it testifies to the felt nature of the dramatic changes in turn-of-the-century America. He mourns for the security of the "simple tool" and the "little shop," marks of an uncompli-cated and egalitarian way of life, which had succumbed to the complexity of the "great machine" and the social, political, and economic hierarchy created by the machine, a hierarchy in which workers no longer controlled their only real asset, their ability to labor. What makes class division relatively permanent is control of the means of production by the capitalist class.

It seems quite likely that Debs not only found Kautsky more accessible than Marx and Engels, but was also comfortable with what Robert Tucker has identified as Kautsky's "moderate" tone, "devoid of the spirit of radical alienation from ex-isting society that stamps so many of the writings of Marx."[64] Though he proudly counted himself a radical—as, for example, when he wrote to William Allen White of a speaking tour, "Our meetings down here are all crowded to the doors and the more radical the speech the greater the enthusiasm and the heartier the approval"[65]—and though he spent much of his career in the company of radicals and revolutionaries, Debs consistently disavowed anarchism and other extremist ideologies.[66] Debs and Kautsky both believed in the necessity of a revolution that would overthrow capitalism, but both also foreswore violence in favor of the exercise of power through parliamentary and electoral means.[67]

Kautsky also provides Debs with firm theoretical justification for Debs's advocacy of integrated, industrial organization over the craft union model for skilled workers represented by Samuel Gompers and the American Federation of Labor. "Today," wrote Kautsky, "the worst enemies of the working-class are not the stupid, reactionary statesmen who hope to keep down the labor movement through openly repressive measures. Its worst enemies are the pretended friends who encourage craft unions, and thus attempt to cut off the skilled trades from the rest of their class."[68] Compare Debs's plea to railroad workers: "You are not united now, but helplessly divided and the railroads and your own craft union officials mean to keep you so." Later in the same article, Debs writes "TODAY CRAFT ORGANIZATION SIMPLY MEANS INDUSTRIAL DISORGANIZATION."[69] A decade earlier, speaking in defense of the IWW's strategy of vertical organization of all workers within an industry, Debs declared, "Craft division is fatal to class unity. To organize along craft lines means to divide the working class and make it prey of the capitalist class."[70]

In some respects Debs reflected the intellectual currents of his day in reading Marxism as a science, a set of laws that operate of necessity in determining the course of history.[71] Jean-Paul Sartre once wrote: "in contradiction to revolutionary realism which asserts that the least little result is attained with difficulty and amidst the greatest uncertainties, the materialist myth leads certain minds to a profound reassurance as to the outcome of their efforts. It is impossible, they think, for them to fail. History is a science, its consequences are already inscribed, we have only to decipher them."[72] Debs's was one of those "certain minds" so led. Despite, in many respects, his marked atavism, Debs was very much attuned to trends in progressive, as well as Marxist, thinking that valorized scientific method, and he sought constantly to extend the scope of science to include even such venerable representatives of human studies as history.

Especially in letters concerning his health, Debs praises the demonstrable powers of "scientific treatment" and credits his "scientific osteopath" for getting him on his feet again.[73] Still on the subject of health, but addressing more the administration of health care than the substance of treatment, Debs wrote to Stephen Marion Reynolds: "I cannot see why a department of health would not be in order and why it should not be organized and maintained upon a sound and scientific basis and do good work."[74] The shift from the science of medicine to a science of medical administration is indicative of Debs's eagerness to extend scientific principles to the management of social issues and suggests his kinship with tendencies in progressivism that resulted in, for example, the city manager model for municipal governments and the rise of civil service bureaucracies based on expertise. Blurring the line between the science of medicine and scientifically based public policy, Debs contrasts the "scientific propaganda" of Margaret Sanger on birth control to the "idiotic" attitude of federal authorities toward her campaign.[75]

The confluence of modern history with science is explicitly celebrated by Debs when he notes approvingly that Harry Tichenor's *The Creed of Constantine* freely quotes "Gibbon, Froude, Comte, Darwin, Haeckel and other historians and scientists."[76] Science, even when not explicitly mentioned, is always the antithesis to "superstition," especially the oppressive superstitions traveling under the name of religion. Congratulating Upton Sinclair on Sinclair's pamphlet "Profits of Religion," Debs writes "Every wage slave in America ought to have one of these put into his hands, and if possible into his gray matter to dislodge the superstition placed there by priestcraft which keeps him in bestial subjection to his capitalist master and his mercenaries, the priests and professors and politicians and editorial hirelings."[77] The ascendancy of the scientific ethos over the priestly ethos is so complete in Debs's view that the domain of theological questions is abolished and its quondam problems are turned over to science. In a 1904 letter to Clara Spalding Ellis, Debs responds to the theological question of immortality by answering, in part, "The most scientific minds have thus far failed to demonstrate the immortality of human life."[78]

Science was subsumed under the broad rubric "reason," and in his celebration of reason, Debs was in complete accord with the thinking of the Progressive Era. Just as capitalists sought to bring reason and efficiency to industrial production, progressive reformers sought to bring reason to government, child rearing, and other arenas of human activity. At the same moment that business schools were created at leading universities to teach the new science of management, graduate schools inaugurated offerings in education, social work, and the emerging field of sociology. The uses to which science was rightly put were contested ground, but the authority of science itself was unquestionable. The evolutionary theories of Spencer and Darwin, for example, were enlisted on both sides of the debate. If capitalists found in evolutionary theory a sociobiological justification for their superior position, Debs found therein a guarantee of the ultimate triumph of socialism and the cooperative commonwealth. "Evolution is the order of nature, and society, like the units that compose it, is subject to its inexorable law," Debs proclaimed.[79] "I could not begin to tell you the story of social evolution this afternoon; of how these things are doing day by day, or how the world is being pushed into Socialism, and how it is bound to arrive, no matter whether you are for it or against it. It is the next inevitable phase of civilization."[80]

Debs's mechanistic and formal understanding of Marx is encouraged by Kautsky. "The capitalist social system has run it course," Kautsky affirms, "its dissolution is now only a question of time. Irresistible economic forces lead with the certainty of doom to the shipwreck of capitalist production. The substitution of a new social order for the existing one is no long simply desirable, it has become inevitable."[81] Kautsky's confidence is underwritten by scientific facts. "These are no utopian suggestions," Kautsky avers, "but scientific conclusions based on definite facts."[82] "All the ability and interests of the delegates [to the 1904 Socialist party convention] are absorbed in producing a scientific platform," Debs similarly assures his readers.[83]

It was a simplistic and naïve understanding of history and causation even in Debs's own day, for as Walter Licht has noted, "The labor upheavals of the era, in this regard, cannot simply be laid to the economy because there was nothing simple about the economy," but it was an understanding that allowed Debs to see with an unshakable certitude an underlying and progressive order in a history that was on its surface confused and unsettled.[84]

An interpretation that holds Marxian materialist history to be inexorable in its teleology must confront what James Aune has called "the central, unresolved problem in Marxism," "the relationship between structure and struggle."[85] As C. J. Arthur has put it, "any Marxian attempt to resolve the apparent antithesis between mechanical determination and self-conscious activity must include the point that *in the first instance* material circumstances condition us, however much we revolutionise those conditions later. We cannot create our being by some undetermined pure act."[86] Debs did not have the benefit of those thinkers whose efforts to reconcile this problem in Marxian theory are explored by Aune, thinkers such as Lenin, Lukács, Gramsci, Marcuse, Raymond Williams, and Habermas, nor is it likely that Debs would have availed himself of such insights had they been available to him.

Debs had an intuitive understanding of the necessity of what he often called propaganda,[87] and its function was demonstrative rather than persuasive: "The eyes of millions of wage-slaves await to be opened. Don't waste time splitting hairs, but make every bit of your time and every atom of your energy count in awakening the slumberers and arousing them to action."[88] Debs praised Francis Marshall Elliott for the use of "his brilliant pen to arouse the workers":[89] "The workers themselves must be made to see . . . and to understand that only they can organize and educate and fit themselves for industrial mastery and industrial freedom. And this supreme fact can only be made clear to the great mass of the workers by the more intelligent and class-conscious of themselves. It cannot be taught to them in the language of the professor or by the logic of the lawyer or in the abstruse terms of the economist, but must be made clear to them in the simple every-day, readily-understood vernacular of their own class."[90] Debs consistently uses the prophetic language of apodeictic to describe his efforts and the efforts of other advocates for the socialist cause.[91] Debs's conception of himself as the "tongue of working class," a conception readily affirmed by his followers,[92] did not include the sense of argument as oppositional interests entailed in the term "persuasion."[93] Though advocating a position that the majority of the working class did not hold, Debs did not believe his interests to be antagonistic to those of his audience. He believed himself to have a synecdochical relationship to the working class—he was one of "the more intelligent and class-conscious of themselves"—and he simply revealed to the working class, awakened it to, its own true advantage.[94]

Debs's preferred term for his work was "education." "Nothing is of more importance than the education, the true education of the working-class," he maintained.[95] "The campaign of the Socialist Party is and will be wholly educational," he counseled his readers in 1904.[96] Ten years later, Debs provided a statement of his own vision of the mission of the socialist labor paper the *National Rip-Saw:* "The Rip-Saw, realizing the vitally essential need of education, will use all its influence to spread the truth among the workers to the end that they may be organized in powerful industrial unions, as well as in their own revolutionary political party."[97] For Debs, the problem was ignorance, a defect of the audience really, and when that defect was corrected, enlightenment was inevitable. "Read and think and study," demanded Debs in a spirit entirely consistent with the self-improvement ethic of the time, "and the light will dawn and the night of slavery will end."[98] The relationship expressed between cause and effect is scientific inasmuch as the material act leads inexorably to the desired result without consideration of other factors; the change of mind (or heart) is, in Burkean terms, entirely scenic, comporting quite properly with Debs's extensive use of metaphors of vision and sightedness.[99]

Although religion is a term that is an anathema to Marxist theory, it is probably fair to suggest that Debs's conception of Marxism was essentially religious. Echoes of John 8:32, "You shall know the truth, and the truth shall set you free," occur throughout Debs's rhetoric, where the liberating truth is recognition of the class struggle and of the necessity of a proletarian revolution to establish a cooperative commonwealth, and there is a pronounced tendency in Debs's discourse to make Marxist materialism continuous with the Christian ethic.[100] The intentions of its creators notwithstanding, Marxism lends itself to such conceptions,[101] and Debs freely mixed the language of the Bible and the language of class conflict: "The hordes of hell are all against us, but the hosts of justice are on our side," he pronounces.[102] Congratulating John Reed on an article Reed had published in the *Liberator*, Debs exclaims "Success to the Liberator! It is a flaming evangel of the revolution."[103] Sounding like a latter-day Elijah, Debs declares, "Ah, but Socialism cannot be kept out [of] a Labor organization any more than the rays of the rising sun can be prevented from dispelling the lists of darkness. Hail to Socialism, in which the miner can lift his bowed form from the earth and stand erect, a new being throbbing with immortal life."[104] Explaining how he became a socialist, Debs said, "I was to be baptized in socialism in the roar of conflict and I thank the gods for reserving to this fitful occasion the fiat, 'Let there be light!'—the light that streams in steady radiance upon the broad way to the socialist republic."[105] "All that is essential in our material life and all that is vital and fundamental in religion are embraced in the emancipating program of the labor movement," Debs exulted in a 1916 front-page proclamation.[106] When Debs extols Harry Tichenor's call for a new religion, one that replaces "pious platitudes" with a "soulful plea for the emancipation of the oppressed and the crowning of emancipation with the brotherhood of the race," a religion "divine because it is rational and rational because it is divine," there can be little doubt that Debs is thinking of scientific socialism.[107]

Sentimental Sources of Debsian Socialism

Debs's identification of a working class in the United States and his sympathies with that class antedate his acquaintance with Marx in any form. At the time Debs was introduced to Marxist thought he was, after all, in jail for his role leading a workers' strike against the Pullman Car Company. Long before Debs read Marx or converted to socialism, he evinced a pathetic, visceral, sentimental connection to the unfortunate and downtrodden. "It makes a person's heart ache to go along some of the main sts [sic] in the city and see men women & children begging for something to eat," he wrote in a letter to his father and mother in the fall of 1874.[108]

The language of the heart is an important and consistent theme throughout Debs's rhetorical career. Though disparaging of "maudlin sentimentalism," Debs's socialist instincts are strongly sympathetic.[109] "It cuts me to the quick and makes my heart bleed for those comrades," Debs writes to Frank O'Hare about a canceled labor rally.[110] On wishing the readers of the Rip-Saw a "RIGHT HAPPY NEW YEAR," Debs apologizes that the greeting may be trite in its expression, but assures them that "there is nevertheless heart in it." He goes on to note the "peculiar attachment" that the Rip-Saw has for its readers,[111] and still later, he praises Harry Tichenor for pouring out "his great heart to his readers."[112] Writing in 1914 about Kelley's army of unemployed, Debs offers the following plaintive portrait: "Kelley's army and like bodies of homeless, workless, hopeless human beings present pictures tragic and heart-breaking enough to bring tears to the eyes of a stone image. Driven from pillar to post these victims of capitalism present an object lesson of the utter cheapness of human flesh and blood. There is nothing left of many of them but their exploited bones and these are scarce worth a place in the pottersfield. They are not wanted anywhere. They are worked out and worthless, and as mere human beings they are greater nuisances than vagabond dogs. That is the view taken of them by the beneficiaries of the system which wrecked them."[113] In the same issue of the Rip-Saw, Debs makes another appeal steeped in pathos on behalf of hop pickers, lamenting "the horrible outrages, involving hunger, rags, filth, torture indescribable, and living death to which the three thousand hop pickers were subjected under the domination of the plutocratic brutes who fattened upon their misery and degradation."[114]

There is scarcely an issue of the Rip-Saw during Debs's tenure as an editorial writer that does not feature the melodramatic opposition of heroic workers fighting against "inhuman monsters to keep starvation from their wives and children. . . . See them," Debs implores his readers, "shot down, hundreds of them, as if they were dogs."[115] His criticism of maudlin sentimentalism notwithstanding, Debs himself could be shamelessly bathetic in exploiting women and children as a rhetorical resource. He pictures children "in their early, tender years . . . seized in the iron clutch of capitalism . . . forced into industrial dungeons [where] they are riveted to the machines; they feed the insatiate monsters and become as living cogs in the revolving wheels. They are literally fed to industry to produce profits . . . millions of babes that fester in the sweat shops, are the slaves of the wheel, and cry out in agony, but are not heard in the din and roar of our industrial infernalism."[116] The sentimentalism in Debs's rhetoric is omnipresent and so unabashed that Debs himself was perceived by many of his followers as the heart as well as the reasoning brain of the labor movement. "Help, Gene!" wrote Carlo Tresca from a jail cell in Minnesota, signaling with the use of the abbreviated first name a kind of kinship felt by many,[117] "You are the heart, the brain of the worker in America."[118] David Karsner, Debs's authorized biographer, reports that on Karsner's first visit with Debs in the Atlanta Federal Penitentiary, Debs, "while he had not received a single paper or periodical since he came to Atlanta, June 14th, 1919," still "knew, felt, all the important happenings and did not need to be enlightened." "I can feel the vibrations of the warm, firm and tender hearts beating in unison for freedom and democracy all over the world," Debs is quoted as saying. "The swelling note of their song reverberates through these corridors, and I know they are active."[119]

If much of the passion in Debs's rhetoric seems today balanced precariously between the lurid and the merely trite, it was undoubtedly less so for Debs's own readers and auditors. Debs's nineteenth-century models, most notably Wendell Phillips and Robert Ingersoll, were schooled in the rhetorical theories of George Campbell, Richard Whately, and Adam Smith, theories with a pronounced pathetic influence.[120] Edwin Black finds in both Britain and the United States in the nineteenth century a rhetorical style he terms "sentimental," a style marked by "the detail with which it shapes one's responses" the way it seeks to regulate "every shade of the auditor's feelings as the speech unfolds."[121]

The sentimental style is intimately connected to the genre of melodrama, a genre that has its provenance in the French Revolution and which, as Black notes of the sentimental style, served to structure strictly audience responses in an effort to clarify a confusing moral landscape. As Peter Brooks has written, melodrama finds its genesis "in a world where the traditional imperatives of truth and ethics have been violently thrown into question, yet where the promulgation of truth and ethics, their instauration as a way of life, is of immediate, daily, political concern."[122] Such was the world Debs lived in and addressed, a world in which capitalists and laborers battled, sometimes figuratively, sometimes literally, over the meaning of the vastly transmogrified social landscape in fin de siècle America.

Marxism is not without sentiment. It is a doctrine rooted in empathy for the plight of the working class and dedicated to the liberation of that class, and the sentimental style is not absent from the writings of even the most sober Marxist theorists, including Karl Kautsky. In a Dickensian moment, Kautsky writes, "Extension of the hours of labor, abolition of holidays, introduction of night labor, damp and overheated factories filled with poisonous gases, such are the 'improvements' which the capitalist mode of production has introduced for the benefit of the working class."[123] Or consider this example: "Many a slave-holder has in former times torn husband from wife and parents from children, but the capitalists have improved upon the abominations of slavery; they tear the infant from the breast of its mother and compel her to entrust it to strangers' hands."[124]

The availability of Marxist models notwithstanding, the most direct and significant model for Debs's own melodramatic style was the man from whom Debs took his middle name, Victor Hugo. Bernard Brommel notes, "As an adult Eugene declared that *Les Misérables* impressed him more than any other book, and excerpts from this book and others appeared in his speeches and writings,"[125] and Nick Salvatore affirms that, even in his early years, Debs "frequently reread" *Les Misérables* in the original French.[126] In "Victor Hugo and the Socialists," Debs identifies *Les Misérables* as Hugo's "masterpiece," a book that "has been read and read again by millions and millions," an "immortal novel,"[127] and in "Fantine in Our Day," Debs holds Jean Valjean to be "the noblest of heroes" and Fantine, the "sublimest of martyrs."[128]

Hugo's prose can be extravagant, especially when he describes the plight of children or the poor. Compare this passage, just before Cosette is rescued from her oppressive foster family by Jean Valjean, to the passages from Debs quoted above: "She walked bent forward like an old woman, with the weight of the bucket dragging on her thin arms and the metal handle biting into her small chilled hands, pausing frequently to rest; and each time she put the bucket down a little of the water slopped on to her bare legs. And this was happening to a child of eight in the woods at night, in winter, far from any human gaze. Only God was there to see, and perhaps her mother, alas, for there are things that rouse the dead in their graves."[129] The specificity of the images and the piling on of cruel details combine, as the passage unfolds, to dictate to the reader every "degree of heat" and "drop of moisture."[130] In a novel that begins with the sentencing of the young Jean Valjean to hard labor for stealing a loaf of bread, his dependents, "Those unhappy beings, God's creatures, left without support, guidance, or shelter," are consequently "scattered no one knows where. Each presumably went its own way to become lost in that cold murk that envelops solitary destinies, the distressful shadows wherein disappear so many unfortunates in the sombre progress of mankind."[131] And over the course of twelve hundred pages, Hugo provides scenes depicting the fall of Fantine into prostitution and later her consumptive death, the degradation of Éponine, the squalid life of the urchins of Paris, the noble death of Gavroche, the life and hard times of a wheelwright and his washerwoman daughter—"It was hard on her too, bent over a washtub, soaked to the waist rain or shine and the wind cutting into you. Even if it's freezing you have to get the washing done. . . . The tubs leak and you're soaked through to your petticoats"—in short, the miseries of the canailles, *les misérables*.[132] The themes are commonplaces in late-nineteenth- and early-twentieth-century reform rhetoric, and if the treatment in Hugo reaches a higher state of artfulness than it does in most, the kinship and the marks of the melodramatic imagination are unmistakable.

Hugo's influence on Debs does not end with style. Almost every one of Debs's substantive themes can be found in *Les Misérables*. The language of the poor and the working class is Hugo's language. In *Les Misérables*, all of the sympathetic characters either come from poverty or voluntarily suffer it—Jean Valjean, Fantine, Cosette, Gavroche, Éponine, even Marius. Compare Hugo, speaking in his own voice directly to his reader, to Debs, in Deb's famous statement at his sentencing for violation of the Espionage Act. Debs declares, "Your Honor, years ago I recognized my kinship with all living being, and I made up my mind that I was not one bit better than the meanest on earth. I said then, and I say now, that while there is a lower class, I am in it, while there is a criminal element I am of it, and while there is a soul in prison, I am not free."[133] In a similar vein, Hugo admonishes his readers: "Let us have compassion for those under chastisement, Alas, who are we ourselves? Who am I and who are you? Whence do we come and is it quite certain that we did nothing before we were born? This earth is not without some resemblance to a gaol. Who knows but that man is a victim of divine justice? Look closely at life. It is so constituted that one senses punishment everywhere."[134]

In Hugo's world, the poor are poor and the criminal, criminal because a corrupt social system has made them that way. Early in *Les Misérables*, M. Myriel, newly appointed bishop of Digne, counsels his flock: "[Society] is responsible for the darkness it creates. The soul in darkness sins, but the real sinner is he who caused the darkness."[135] It is a theme sounded in the epigraph to *Les Misérables* and returned to throughout. In a section of the novel titled "The Lowest Level," Hugo brings together themes of fundamental human equality, of the need for education to combat ignorance, and of the systemic distortions of human nature created by modern society. "Humanity is our common lot. All men are made of the same clay. There is no difference, at least here on earth, in the fate assigned to us. We come of the same void, inhabit the same flesh, are dissolved in the same ashes. But ignorance infecting the human substance turns it black, and that incurable blackness, gaining possession of the soul, becomes Evil."[136] These themes are prominent in and inextricable from Debs's speaking and writing. Thus, when Debs refers to capitalism as "the system from which these crimes and cruelties flow in natural sequence,"[137] to the "tramp and the hobo" as "victims of capitalism,"[138] or to "the poverty produced by capitalism,"[139] when he declares "I belong in prison. . . . I belong where men are made to suffer for the wrongs committed against them by a brutalizing system,"[140] we should hear not only the voice of American scientific progressivism, but Hugo's sentimental socialism as well.

The issue of individual versus societal responsibility was a difficult one for Debs. In the era of "rugged individualism," "the strenuous life," and "the law of competition," the American ethic of personal accountability was strong and was eagerly reinforced by capitalists and their proponents. Debs was not immune to the power of this American tradition, and he struggled throughout his career with the conflict between a persistent individualism, most often expressed as a challenge to his audience's "manhood," and an emergent corporatism and class identity, to be fulfilled in the coming cooperative commonwealth.[141] Debs became a synecdoche for the great dilemma of American socialism.

Fortunately for Debs, faced with this dilemma, his mentor, Hugo, was no simple, soft-headed sentimentalist. Among the many lengthy digressions in *Les Misérables* is a bit of hard-edged economic analysis in which Hugo identifies "Problem One" as "the production of wealth," and "Problem Two" as "its distribution":

> Problem One embraces the question of labour and Problem Two that of wages, the first dealing with the use made of manpower and the second with the sharing of the amenities this manpower produces.
> A proper use of manpower creates a strong economy, and a proper distribution of amenities leads to the happiness of the individual. Proper distribution does not imply an *equal* share but an *equitable* share. Equity is the essence of equality.
> These two things combined—a strong economy and the happiness of the individual within it—lead to social prosperity, and social prosperity means a happy man, a free citizen, and a great nation.[142]

England, Hugo continues, suffers an imbalance in her solution to the two problems: "She is highly successful in creating wealth, but she distributes it badly," and as a result, she is brought "inevitably to the two extremes of monstrous wealth and monstrous poverty."[143] Hugo brings his analysis to a socialistic conclusion, "All the amenities are enjoyed by the few and all the privations are suffered by the many, that is to say, the common people: privilege, favour, monopoly, feudalism, all these are produced by their labour. It is a false and dangerous state of affairs whereby the public wealth depends on private poverty and the greatness of the State is rooted in the sufferings of the individual: an ill-assorted greatness composed wholly of materialism, into which no moral element enters."[144] The parallels between Hugo's England and the economic conditions in Debs's United States are obvious. Hugo's solution to this dangerous imbalance includes elements familiar from Debs's own program: "a fair and brotherly relationship between work and wages," the democratization of private property, "not by abolishing it, but by making it universal, so that every citizen without exception is an owner," and especially "compulsory free education," making knowledge "the criterion of manhood."[145] "Read and think and study," Debs exhorts his readers, repeating Hugo's prescription, "and the light will dawn and the night of slavery will end. It is better, far better to stand up than to crawl; to be a man than to be a slave."[146]

There are other parallels, other ways in which Debs is indebted to Hugo. Debs may have learned his uncompromising attitude and his commitment to principled victory from Hugo, who wrote, "But principles cannot be fragmented: truth is the whole, and it does not admit of compromises."[147] Debs's belief in the inexorability of progress, his idea of what that progress should bring, and his comfort with revolution as the sometimes necessary vehicle to progress may owe as much to Hugo as to Marx.[148] Debs might well have made his credo Hugo's celebration of "the glorious warriors of the future, the prophets of Utopia, whether they are successful or not," "Even when they fail they are deserving of reverence, and perhaps it is in failure that they appear most noble. Victory, if it is in accord with progress, deserves the applause of mankind; but an heroic defeat deserves one's heartfelt sympathy. The one is magnificent, the other sublime. For ourselves, we prefer martyrdom to success, John Brown is greater than Washington, Pisacane greater than Garibaldi," Debs declared.[149]

While Hugo was no more American than Marx, he was certainly more widely read in the U.S., and the melodramatic style he represented seemed as well suited to *Uncle Tom's Cabin* as to *Les Misérables*. In a centenary oration on Voltaire, Hugo expressed his faith in the power of the passions: "Jesus wept; Voltaire smiled. Of that divine tear and of that human smile the sweetness of present civilisation is composed."[150] So when Debs speaks of coal miners, "these slaves whose labor makes possible the firesides of the world, while their loved ones shiver in the cold," when he says, "I know something of the conditions under which they toil and despair and perish. I have taken time enough to descend to the depths of these pits, that Dante never saw, or he might have improved upon his masterpiece. I have stood over these slaves and I have heard the echo of their picks, which sounded to me like muffled drums throbbing funeral marches to the grave, and I have said to myself, in the capitalist system, these wretches are simply following their own hearses to the potter's field," he does not require his listeners to adopt a alien and abstract philosophy, he appeals instead to fundamental and universal sympathies.[151] Debs spoke a language that appealed to the concrete experiences of workers in the United States. Hyperbolic, filled with stark antitheses presenting a Manichaean division of the world into forces of darkness and forces of light, Debs's language rendered Marx and Hugo as idiomatic as a poem by Debs's friend James Whitcomb Riley.

Debs's Issues

Eugene Debs had a deep commitment to the idea of equality, a sympathy deeply rooted in the tradition of the Declaration of Independence, but also in the kindred legacy of the French Revolution, the latter sympathetically communicated to Debs largely through the work of Victor Hugo, especially *Les Misérables*, and he was deeply offended by the gross inequality he saw in industrializing America. Coupled with a class analysis sharpened by Marxist sources, Debs's passionate egalitarianism provided a powerful source of moral criticism in a society that had lost its way. Debs applied his peculiar brand of socialism to a wide range of issues facing Americans at the turn of the last century.

Racism, according to Debs, makes no sense except as it serves the ruling class "to have the 'white trash' and the 'niggers' making senseless war on one another in their common undoing."[152] Only in the Socialist Party, he declares, is there no color line. Though Debs had his own conflicts regarding race,[153] and though he, in a manner resembling Booker T. Washington, insisted that "economic freedom" not "social equality," was the real issue,[154] once he had found the motive of history in the class struggle, Debs never allowed race to obscure the clarity of his vision: "The class struggle is colorless," Debs reminded his readers, "The capitalists, white, black and other shades, are on one side and the workers, white, black and all other colors, on the other side."[155] Along with Ida B. Wells and others, Debs decried lynchings of blacks by white supremacists. Lynching, Debs declared, was "shocking and disgraceful, an impeachment of civilized government and the utter repudiation of law and order, . . . an atrocious and revolting crime."[156]

On the issue of prohibition, Debs departed from progressive thinking in decrying the Eighteenth Amendment and its attempt to outlaw the "manufacture, sale or transportation of intoxicating liquors," but he was doggedly consistent with progressive sociology in arguing that the answer to the abuse of alcoholic beverages lay in addressing the social circumstances that caused the abuse. In a letter to Charles R. Jones, head of the Prohibition Party, Debs, a man known to enjoy a drink on occasion, wrote, "I admit all you say about the liquor evil and we differ only in the way this evil shall be destroyed. Prohibition will never do it. Besides, there is but one way to get at the root of the evil and that is by abolishing the profit system of which intemperance, like prostitution, is the legitimate fruit." "The socialists," Debs continued, "are right in refusing to be led away from the main issue and to give attention to the thousand and more of ills that flow from capitalism, private ownership, profit and exploitation."[157] After prohibition had taken effect, bringing in its wake many of the troubles Debs had predicted it would bring, Debs sneered at the disingenuousness of its rationale. "Whiskey, wine and beer will be made as long as corn and wheat and grapes grow," Debs wrote to fellow socialist J. A. C. Meng, "and instead of foolishly and vainly trying to stamp it out with the iron heel of prohibition and suppression it is infinitely saner to educate and enlighten the people," iterating one of his favorite themes, "and to give attention to surrounding them with conditions that make for temperance, morality and sane and sweet human living."[158] The basic progressive belief in the causal power of social conditions eclipses the ethic of personal responsibility here as elsewhere, though in Debs's own mind there was a continual struggle between them.

Debs loosely connected prohibition to the exploitation of women in an exposé of a businessman's smoker in Oklahoma City. The activities at the smoker included not only drinking (six thousand bottles of beer, according to the account), but dancing by "a female from Chicago" clad in "'September Morn' raiment."[159] Prohibition and the exploitation of women had, with racism and other social ills, common provenance in the system of capitalist production. "MANY INSTANCES ARE GIVEN OF IMMORALITY FORCED UPON GIRLS BY THEIR EMPLOYERS OR THEIR SUPERIORS AT THEIR PLACES OF EMPLOYMENT, THE PENALTY OF REFUSAL BEING THE LOSS OF POSITION," Debs quotes from a report commissioned by the governor of Maryland. "Could there be a more terrific indictment of the capitalist system which forces helpless girls to yield up their chastity, suffer themselves to be debauched, and damn their very souls for the sake of earning a wretched living?" he queries, sounding a theme common in fin de siècle novels and speeches and echoing Fantine's fall in *Les Misérables*.[160] "The face of Fantine, in which we behold 'the horror of old age in the countenance of a child,' is the mirror which reflects society's own sin and shame," Debs charges.[161]

If not always completely consistent with his emphasis on 'manhood' and 'manliness,' Debs's embrace of women's issues, including suffrage, was consistent with his larger emphasis on the fundamental equality of all human beings. In a pamphlet titled "Woman—Comrade and Equal," Debs repudiates any apparent inconsistency: "I am glad to align myself with a party that declares for absolute equality between the sexes. Anything less than this is too narrow for twentieth-century civilization, and too small for a man who has a right conception of his manhood."[162] "The socialist movement knows no color line and no sex discrimination," he affirms in a 1915 editorial. "All workers regardless of race, nationality or sex are equally welcome and all are received and hold their membership upon absolutely equal terms."[163] Addressing the situation of women in particular, Debs assured readers of the *Rip-Saw*, "The man who is so wanting in sense of fairness and common justice as to deny to women the rights he claims for himself is a living certificate of the absolute necessity of releasing woman from his ignorant and brutal domination."[164] The appeal is vintage Debs: no abstruse theory, simply a heartfelt appeal to a fundamentally American common sense of equality and fair play. Reporting on relatively narrow defeats of the suffrage amendment in New Jersey, New York, Massachusetts, and Pennsylvania in November 1915, Debs emphasized the power of the capitalist cabal allied against the amendment, "Never was the old saying that 'politics make strange bed-fellows' better exemplified. Cardinal Manning, in the name of the holy church, was in political alliance with booze and boodle and with the blear-eyed deformities of capitalist misrule to prevent women from having a share in the control of government and in the administration of public affairs."[165]

The connection between women and children in Debs's rhetoric has already been alluded to. Children are an easy subject for *argumentum ad misericordium*, the commonness of the appeal in no way diminishing the horrific conditions under which many children in the United States labored before the institution of child labor laws, and "humanitarian progressivism," in the estimate of Robert Wiebe, made the child its "central theme."[166] Along with muckraking child labor reformers such as Jacob Riis and photographer Lewis Hine, Debs regularly drew attention to the plight of child laborers. "Child labor is child murder," Debs rails, exhibiting a mode of vilification typical in his rhetoric, "and capitalism is the guilty monster."[167] Juxtaposed to another of his characteristic editorial epigrams on the disenfranchisement and exploitation of women, Debs charges that "Child labor is the scarlet letter, the badge of shame of the capitalist system. Capitalism is the only system in all the world's history that deliberately devours its own offspring."[168] Drawing on some of the most powerful and resonant political vocabulary in American culture, Debs derides any pretense that the United States is an enlightened or humane society, "If there is a crime that should bring to the callous cheek of capitalist society the crimson of shame, it is the unspeakable crime of child slavery; the millions of babes that fester in the sweat shops, are the slaves of the wheel, and cry out in agony, but are not heard in the din and roar of our industrial infernalism."[169]

Remarkably, for all the pathetic potential in child labor, and notwithstanding Debs's own tendency to exploit the sentimental, Debs never significantly developed the child labor appeal. The relatively bloodless, abstract charges presented here provide a fair representation of Debs's rhetorical use of children. It is likely that Debs's experience with children, especially child laborers, was limited. Debs himself never had any children, and there is a patronizing distance in notes to friends when Debs, with typical effusiveness, refers to children in the household. "Dear Mrs. Sandburg and her sweet-souled mother and the three darling little gods of your heavenly household," Debs writes to Carl Sandburg in one such letter.[170] Without extending the argument too far into the realm of speculative psychology, Debs's rhetorical treatment of children suggests that he may not have been entirely comfortable with them and thus may not have had any real passion for them in their special status as children.

Debs was typical of progressive reformers in the faith he put in education and self-improvement, but the educational system was simply another battleground in the class war. A strong exponent of the "People's College," Debs saw the established university system in the United States as one more structure reinforcing capitalist domination.[171] In 1896, Debs charged that "as a general proposition, universities are aristocratic institutions." American universities are descended from European universities, "which, *nolens volens*, created a class of superior beings as separate and distinct from labor as if the lines defining their limits had been rivers of fire," he continued.[172] "The university," he wrote "to use a figure of speech, is itself a capitalist and has never had anything in common with labor and, therefore, is not doing its 'share,' whatever that may be, in solving any labor problem."[173] Almost twenty years later, in a scathing rebuke of Harvard's president for his testimony before a federal board on labor unrest, Debs sneered, "either his sycophancy and senility are betraying his true character or . . . the highest education in a capitalist college cannot save its victim from moral and spiritual degeneration."[174]

Influenced by Hugo no doubt, and by his own experiences and those of his friends and colleagues, crime and punishment under capitalism occupied a significant share of Debs's attention. Crime, Debs consistently maintained, was produced by capitalism.[175] The solution was not imprisonment of the putative criminal but overthrow of the system that produced the criminal. In his own chapter synopses for his most extended work on the subject, the book *Walls and Bars*, Debs forwards the following theses:

> XIV. Capitalism and Crime.
>
> Capitalism and crime almost synonymous terms.—Private ownership of the means of the common life at bottom of prison evil.—Capitalism must have prisons to protect itself from the criminals it has created.
>
> XV. Poverty and the Prison.
>
> Intimate relation between poor-house and prison.—Poverty the common lot of the great mass of mankind. . . .—Abolish the social system that makes the prison necessary and populates it with the victims of poverty.
>
> XVI. Socialism and the Prison.
>
> Socialism and prison antagonistic terms.—Socialism will abolish the prison as it is today by removing its cause.—Capitalism and crime have had their day and must go.[176]

Predictably, Debs also opposed capital punishment, "a relic of barbarism," on the grounds that "We are now sufficiently enlightened to understand that what is known as crime is in a large measure due to unfortunate environment; that crime is in fact a disease, an infirmity, and that every consideration of humanity demands that the unfortunate victim of society's weakness or maladjustment, shall be treated with the same degree of patience, and with all the skill that science has made available."[177] The topoi are all recognizable to the student of progressive thought: the causal relationship between environment and behavior, the faith in enlightenment, reason, and science, the basic sympathy for the downtrodden. "I know by close study of the question exactly how men become idle," Debs declaimed in a wide-ranging speech in 1908, "I don't repel them when I meet them. I have never yet seen the tramp I was not able to receive with open arms. He is a little less fortunate than I am. He is made the same as I am made. He is a child of the same Father. Had I been born in his environment, had I been subjected to the same things to which he was I would have been where he is."[178]

Consistent with his renunciation of capital punishment and his abjurement of violent protest, Debs also condemned war generally, and toward the end of his career, World War I consumed an increasing share of Debs's attention and energy. It was, after all, for his protest against the First World War, specifically his speech in

Canton, Ohio, on 16 June 1918, that Debs was sentenced to the federal penitentiary for violation of the Espionage Act of 1917. On the question of war, as on so many other issues, Debs follows Victor Hugo and Jesus Christ. Debs quotes Hugo extensively against war generally in an editorial titled "Victor Hugo on War" in the *National Rip-Saw* in 1917,[179] and there is plenty of material in *Les Misérables* that Debs might have chosen to support his argument.[180] In his address to the court during his trial for violation of the Espionage Act of 1917, Debs admonishes his audience: "the Prince of Peace" did not say "'Kill one another' but 'love one another.'"[181]

Debs's first editorials against World War I for the *National Rip-Saw* appeared in the September 1914 issue, and it was a rare issue of the *Rip-Saw* thereafter that did not find Debs fulminating against the war and the possibility of U.S. intervention. From the outset, Debs characterized the war as the murder of workers by workers at the behest of the master class.[182] "The monster of capitalism is aroused and his lust to kill cannot be appeased until he has had his fill of blood," Debs cried, "Certainly all this slaughter of the innocents is not to be in vain. Socialists who are and ever had been set against war will find it less difficult after this war is over to open the eyes of the people to the cause of war and to enlist them in the only war the civ[i]lized human beings should fight in, and that is the war against war and the system that breeds war."[183] In 1915 in an editorial for the *Appeal to Reason* titled "The Prospect for Peace," Debs argued that the only hope for a true peace lay in an international conference of working-class people against the war, for "capitalist nations have no honor and . . . the most solemn treaty is but a 'scrap of paper' in their mad rivalry for conquest and plunder."[184] Accepting the Socialist Party's nomination as its presidential candidate in April 1916, Debs described "The terrible war now raging in Europe which has transformed nation after nation boasting of their civilization and Christianity into hideous slaughterhouses, where millions of our brothers have turned brutes and been shot like dogs; where king and kaiser and czar rule and bureaucracy and aristocracy and plutocracy, all rotten to the core and buttressed by dead men's bones are supreme."[185] In all of Debs's protestations against the war, there is the insistent refrain that it was a capitalistic war, the product of a selfish, rapacious, immoral, and misguided economic system. "I have full faith that you will rise to the demand and declare to the world in clear and unmistakable terms the attitude of the party toward war and toward the ruling class system which has forced this frightful catastrophe upon mankind," Debs wrote in April 1917 to Adolph F. Germer, national executive secretary of the Socialist Party of America.[186] Contrasting plutocratic with proletarian preparedness, Debs notes, "the owning class want war but do not fight. The producing class fight but do not want war."[187] And in the same issue of the *Rip-Saw*, Debs elaborates the point: "Did you ever see a millionaire who had his legs shot off in war? I never have and do not expect to. Millionaires reap the golden harvests of war while poor fools die like hogs at slaughter on fields of battle."[188]

Again and again, Debs decried the false banner of nationalism as a justification for war, noting "the NATION is the CAPITALIST CLASS."[189] On 8 March 1917, the *New York Times* headlined a report on a Debs speech the previous night: "DEBS URGES STRIKE IF NATION FIGHTS, Exhorts Workers at Cooper Union Not to Bear Arms for 'Capitalist Government' . . . Wall Street, He Declares, Is behind the Agitation for War, and Labor is Victimized." In the body of the story Debs is quoted as saying, "you never had a country. When the working people own this country and other countries there will be no war. I tell you it is better to live for your country than to die for Rockefeller and Morgan."[190]

Consistent with his antinationalistic universalism, Debs—like the last man he supported for president before running himself, William Jennings Bryan—opposed imperialism. Where Bryan had been concerned primarily with the Philippines,

Debs, in addition to deploring the imperialist ambitions he saw behind the First World War, repeatedly condemned U.S. policy toward Mexico. In August 1914, Debs declared the absolute right of the Mexican people to "drive out the foreign robbers. American, British and German capitalists have gobbled up the choicest portions of the empire and it is not in the least strange that they are hated and despised by their despoiled and wretched victims."[191] The retaliatory measures taken after Francisco "Pancho" Villa's raid on New Mexico were characterized by Debs as "the prelude to the invasion of Mexico if Wall street [sic] is allowed to play out its hand."[192] And the following year, taking a swipe at both defenders of the war with Mexico and America Firsters, Debs queried, "If 'America for Americans' is a patriotic slogan what's the matter with 'Mexico for Mexicans.'"[193] Imperialism, as Debs saw it, was simply foreign policy driven by the profit motive, a policy that benefited capitalists to the detriment of the working class.

Though progressivism was too large and too diffuse a movement to be identified precisely with specific issues, Debs's positions largely accorded with the general tenor of progressive thinking in the early years of the twentieth century. Indeed, as socialist positions of the first two decades of the new century found their way into mainstream politics, it became increasingly difficult for Debs's successor, Norman Thomas, to differentiate radical socialism from simple reformism and later the New Deal.

Debs and the Americanization of Class

Debs's denigration of nationalism was consistent with his vision of a worldwide workers' utopia. "The narrow patriotism that turns into hate at the boundary line belongs to the jungle-age of the past," Debs exhorted in 1916, in part remarking on the war then in progress. "The wider and nobler patriotism which embraces the earth and whose appeal is to all races and all nations is finding lodgment in the souls of men and in due time will conquer the world."[194] Such appeals to what Debs called "international patriotism" emerge in Debs's rhetoric early in World War I,[195] which must be understood as the immediate exigence for this line of argument, but Debs also recognized that such universalism was a necessary part of Marxian socialist theory.[196]

For all its debts to Marx and other sources, however, and notwithstanding the charges of un-Americanism hurled at Debs, Debs's ideas of socialism, class, and class warfare were firmly rooted "in the American grain."[197] Documenting Debs's essential Americanism is a significant part of the burden of Nick Salvatore's argument in his acclaimed biography of Debs. Salvatore writes: "Quote as he might Marx, Engels, Lasalle, or Kautsky (with little acknowledgment of the differences among them), the roots of his own social thought remained deeply enmeshed in a different tradition."[198] Mark Pittenger concurs, characterizing Debsian socialism as having "a distinctly American flavor, a good-humored earthiness, and a midwestern twang," and Pittenger attributes at least some of these attributes to the influence of Laurence Gronlund.[199]

Rhetorical assessments of Debs have, over the years, come to similar conclusions. Offering no support for their opinion, Ernest Wrage and Barnet Baskerville declare that, "although Debs often spoke in a Marxist idiom, he had been influenced only superficially by Marx and other revolutionary importations. His was an indigenous radicalism, a native growth like that of Laurence Gronlund, Edward Bellamy, Henry Demarest Lloyd, and Upton Sinclair."[200] Ronald Lee and James Andrews, though they overstate the case in arguing that Debs "shunn[ed] the themes of Marxist doctrine," properly find "the *topoi* of traditional opposition politics in America" at the heart of Debs's discourse.[201]

Debs himself was acutely aware of the uniqueness of the American situation and of the need to adapt to it. "There has never been the kind of socialist movement there should be and would be if it were rooted in American traditions, American history and American conditions," Debs counseled Claude G. Bowers in a letter written near the end of Debs's life. "The fundamental principles are of course everywhere the same but there is a different psychology in every nation, different economic and political conditions, and these have not been wisely reckoned with by socialists or they would be much farther along with the American movement."[202]

Debs understood that notions of class were alien if not repugnant to Americans, and he credited, with "a feeling of profound obligation akin to reverence," immigrants "for their noble work in laying the foundations, deep and strong, under the most trying conditions, of the American [socialist] movement," for their efforts to "engraft the class-conscious doctrine upon their inhospitable 'freeborn' American fellow citizens."[203] The botanical metaphor in the last sentence reveals Debs's sensitivity to the fact that, even were it desirable, European socialism could not simply be transplanted onto American soil. "In the matter of tactics we cannot be guided by the precedents of other countries," he counsels readers in a preconvention issue of the *Socialist Review*. "We have to develop our own and they must be adapted to the American people and to American conditions."[204]

Adapting his case to American conditions, Debs uses a distinctly American vocabulary. "Aristocracy" is a prominent devil term in Debs's discourse. Largely unquestioned as a given in the greater part of European history, "aristocracy" was one of the great *bêtes noires* of the American Revolution, and Debs carries that antipathy forward deriding craft unions for evincing "some of the most vulgar and offensive aristocracy" he has known;[205] condemns universities as aristocratic institutions, which have "always served the purpose of creating an aristocracy of D.D.'s, LL.D.'s, etc., often as obnoxiously exclusive as a titled nobility created by kings";[206] reviles his sometime-opponent Victor Berger as an "aristocrat and {not} a socialist"[207] and Woodrow Wilson as "an aristocrat and autocrat";[208] and as the First World War escalated, sneers at "the aristocratic gentry who are howling for preparedness."[209]

Debs contrasted "the American aristocracy" with "the American democracy."[210] Consistent with this opposition and with the legacy of the American Revolution, he features "freedom" as a god term and "slavery" as a devil term throughout his public editorials and speeches. "Liberty and slavery are primal words, like good and evil, right and wrong; they are opposites and coexistent," proclaims Debs.[211] Having disabused his readers of the illusion that they have elected the president of the United States, "the actual president" being "located at 26 Wall street [*sic*]," Debs charges that John D. Rockefeller "holds his title as ruler by the divine right of being the owner of the means whereby the people live." Shaming his audience with the memory of the American Revolution against such notions as divine right and the slavery of monarchical rule, Debs continues: "As long as Rockefeller is allowed to own the nation's bread he will control the nation's life, and all our boasted freedom is silly mockery and false pretense. The freedom we have is the freedom to work on Rockefeller's terms and the freedom to be assassinated by his gunmen if we refuse."[212] Rockefeller was simply one of Debs's favorite synecdoches for the capitalist class. The slavery created by surplus labor was endemic to industrial capitalism:

> The capitalist for whom you work doesn't have to go out and look for you; you have to look for him and you belong to him just as completely as if he had a title to your body; as if you were his chattel slave.
>
> He doesn't own you under the law, but he does under the fact.[213]

Surplus labor created the conditions wherein "thousands of section men" must "slave away at their miserable jobs twelve hours a day at 11¢ or 12¢ an hour, or a total of $35.00 per month for 12 hours of daily slavery."[214]

In Debs's construction, there is a class hierarchy in the United States, but it is essentially illegitimate and contrary to American notions of equality. Debs operates in a mode that is fundamentally epideictic here, agreeing with and reinforcing American ideals while finding their realization deeply flawed. The capitalist class is, in truth, discredited royalty returned in the thin guise of meritocracy rather than divine right. Note the enthymematic construction as Debs defends the legitimacy of the Western Labor Union: "If it is held that the American Federation [of Labor] had prior jurisdiction, it may be answered that George the Third and Great Britain had prior jurisdiction over the colonies."[215] Debs could count on the fact that virtually no American in 1902 would assent to the proposition that George III legitimately ruled the colonies by virtue of chronological precedence.

Debs regularly capitalized on the premises of the American Revolution whereby subjugation to monarchy was synonymous with slavery. In an editorial titled "Lexington and Ludlow," he made a characteristic comparison between the struggle of labor versus capital and that of the colonists versus royal rule:

> April twentieth is a red letter date in American annals.
> It was on April twentieth, 1775 that the battle of Lexington was fought. . . .
> The battle of Lexington signaled the death of king rule and the overthrow of political despotism in the United States.
> One hundred and thirty-nine years later, on April 20th, 1914, the anniversary of Lexington was celebrated by Rockefeller and the ruling class in free America by the murder of working-class women and babies at Ludlow, Colorado. . . .
> Ludlow, where on April 20th, 1914, the gunmen of the ruling class murdered the mothers, wives and babes of the working class signaled the revolutionary struggle for the end of king rule in industry and the overthrow of industrial despotism in the United States.[216]

Debs rarely missed an opportunity to cast the efforts of unions and working-class organizations in the American tradition.[217] The abolition of class stratification in the United States would come about with the creation of a commonwealth in which the means of production are owned by the workers, a solution that, while it ran counter to American notions of property, restored the ideal of equality.

Goading the workers to action, Debs contrasted their present condition with the promise of the American Revolution, "the fundamental American rights of free speech, free press and free assemblage," and he regularly traded on the heroic status of the founding fathers and other American luminaries.[218] Patrick Henry and Robert Emmett are named by Debs as personal heroes: "They were the inspiration for my maiden speech before the Occidental Literary Club."[219] On more than one occasion, Debs alludes to Patrick Henry's "Liberty or Death" speech, once even mixing his allusion to Henry with one to Marx: "If they insist upon war let it come. We have nothing to lose but our chains."[220] Making his case against World War I, Debs invokes Thomas Paine,[221] and in defense against charges that he had violated the Espionage Act of 1917, he allies himself with "George Washington, who is now revered as the father of his country, [who] was denounced as a disloyalist; . . . Sam Adams, who is known to us as the father of the American Revolution, [who] was condemned as an incendiary, and Patrick Henry, who delivered that inspired and inspiring oration, that aroused the Colonists, [who] was condemned as a traitor."[222] In that same address, Debs quotes Benjamin Franklin "There never was a good war or a bad peace."[223] "Washington, Adams, Paine—these were the rebels of their day. At first they were opposed by the people and denounced by the press. You can remember that it was Franklin who said to his compeers, 'We have now to hang together or we'll hang separately by and by,'" Debs continues, implicitly identifying his own actions, now on trial, to the actions of those now in the national pantheon.[224] Writing to Robert M. La Follette in 1909 regarding the situation in Mexico, Debs declares the inconsistency in honoring "the memories of Jefferson, Paine, Sam Adams, Franklin, and other patriots of our own country" while not honoring "Magon and his compatriots who are fighting to deliver their own unhappy country from the Diaz despotism based upon force and plunder."[225]

Debs did not restrict himself to Revolutionary heroes when seeking to frame current causes in the context of an anointed American past. Prominent Americans from the nineteenth century, including Wendell Phillips, Ralph Waldo Emerson, and most especially Abraham Lincoln, figure prominently in Debs's arguments. Deriding a proposed program of forced marriages for military conscripts, Debs invokes Ralph Waldo Emerson—"Ye Gods! How the mighty have degenerated"—and alludes to Lincoln's "Gettysburg Address."[226] He also quotes Lincoln in the Canton, Ohio, speech itself, the speech for which Debs was prosecuted under the Espionage Act. In turn, Debs himself was compared by others to Lincoln and other American demigods,[227] and he had the temerity to compare himself to Jefferson and others.[228]

Debs and Working-Class Eloquence

Richard Weaver, in one of his classic essays, identifies the defining characteristic of "old rhetoric," the rhetoric of the nineteenth century, as the quality of "spaciousness," a quality manifested in a heavy dependence on "uncontested terms," bespeaking a fundamental unity and stability of ideology in a culture; "large resonant" phrases; a respectful distance, which served to obscure impertinent details; and a monumental, Olympian status for the orator, transcending the individual voice and speaking on behalf of all humankind.[229] Kenneth Cmiel traces the evolution of civic discourse in the United States from a two-tiered system in the eighteenth century; to a more democratic, rough and tumble, "middling" eloquence in the Jacksonian era; to a turn toward a Saxon Romanticism, "a middling style trying to transcend itself" in the mid-nineteenth century;[230] to an attempt, after the Civil War, by the "best men" to try to "reform the authoritative texts about the English language in the hopes of reasserting their authority [and 'gentle speech'] in America,"[231] an effort opposed by a Victorian emphasis on standards set by linguistic scholarship over taste, a move in the linguistic world parallel to the rise of science and expertise in other realms. As Cmiel tells the story, there is a century-long struggle over the proper place of slang, colloquial usage, neologisms, in short, nonaristocratic forms of speech in the public forum. Cmiel and Weaver are largely in agreement that the dominant modes of speech in the nineteenth century exhibited refinement, elevation, and taste, modes that were not, in Weaver's terms, "impertinent."

Debs, in contrast to this nineteenth-century ideal, could be decidedly impertinent in his public declamations. Though he claimed the great nineteenth-century exemplars Wendell Phillips and Robert Ingersoll as his oratorical models, what Debs took from them were those qualities that caused Phillips to be identified as a master of abuse and Ingersoll as a blasphemer and heretic, an early modernist.[232] Decrying "soft words," Debs declared, "Like Garrison we shall be harsh as truth and implacable as justice. Like Phillips we shall apply the lash of scorpions to the hypocrites in high places and denounce the oppressors of the poor though every friend desert us. Like Lowell we shall speak out, 'though all earth's systems crack.'"[233]

Examples of Debs's unsparing directness abound. There is his use of colloquial, working-class language and slang, reflecting his working-class ideology; there are uses bordering on the prurient; and there is his unrelenting sarcasm. The need of a preconvention board member conference Debs dismisses as "simply a piece of damphoolism."[234] He often refers to "the plute press,"[235] run by the likes of Harrison Grey Otis, "the notorious scab-in-chief of the rat-publication known as the Los Angeles Times [sic]." "Go to it," Debs urges strikers against the paper, "ye mutineers of Los Angeles against the barbarous scab-infested, stench-breeding domination of Harrison Grey Otis and his filthy organ, the allies and abettors of political corruption and industrial slavery and the arch enemies of freedom and justice."[236] John D. Rockefeller is "that pious degenerate,"[237] "henceforth the synonym of theft, arson, rapine and black-handed assassination. The blood of a thousand Christs would not cleanse his blackened heart and hell itself would spew out his canting, cannibalistic soul."[238] Judge A. G. Dayton is a "low and servile judicial functionary, [a] bootlicking lackey of Wall Street."[239] "Anthony Comstock, the relentless and bogus purist . . . died recently, though not nearly soon enough," Debs pronounces with unveiled contempt.[240] The Mine Owner's Association "and their Standard Oil backers and pals" are "gory-beaked vultures."[241] They are among "labor's age-long enemies, the blood-sucking vampires and their vast brood of mercenaries and microbes,"[242] with their "swaggering assassins in uniform,"[243] "greasy hirelings," and "degenerate courts."[244] Referring to the militias of Colorado and Michigan, Debs writes, "If there is anything human about the soldiers who have charged upon women and children, broken into houses and robbed them, swaggered through the streets like cowardly bullies, crazy drunk, assaulting helpless men and insulting and outraging their wives; if there is anything human about these filthy beasts it is sadly out of place in their vile and degenerate carcasses."[245] He shrilly casts "Mine owners and their official hirelings" as "the coldest-blooded murderers, woman-ravishers and baby-roasters that ever figured in the annals of crime."[246] Debs railed against hypocrisy and rarely missed an opportunity to expose the distance between noble profession and craven practice: "The owners of the present plants have some rights Uncle Sam is bound to respect and among these is the inalienable right to pluck, fleece, gouge, rob, burglarize and skin the American people as long as there is a pin-feather in sight."[247] The capitalist parties "gush with nauseating slobber,"[248] and Debs pictures Republican candidate for president Charles Evans Hughes "spewing his vomit."[249] Writing of the American Federation of Labor (AFL) convention of November 1914, Debs sneers, "For twenty years they have been 'boring from within' and their boring has penetrated about the length of a mosquito's nozzle in a ram's horn."[250] Through such uses, Debs helped to create a place in national politics for a "new rhetoric," direct, detailed, often damnatory, that gradually displaced the diffuse, unfocused "spaciousness" of old oratory. If the old rhetoric was dignified and aristocratic, Debs's was scrappy and democratic.

The democratic impetus in Debs's rhetoric is reflected in his favorite stylistic figure, alliteration. "In China," Debs jeers, "the *h*eathen *h*ordes, *f*anned into *f*renzy by the *s*ordid *s*pirit of modern *c*ommercial *c*onquest, are presenting to the world a *c*arnival of *c*rime almost equaling the 'refined' exhibitions of the world's 'civilized' nations."[251] Referring to "the proletariat of the rugged and sparsely settled Mountain states," the source of "class-conscious trades unionism in the West," Debs declares it impossible that they "*c*ould be long *c*ontent to *c*reep along in the *c*reaking *c*hariot of *c*onservatism, even though it still bear [sic] traces of the union label."[252] Outlining his platform as the Socialist Party nominee for president in 1916, he writes that the Socialist Party would work to "liberate the children from the slave-pens in which they are *d*warfed, *d*iseased and *d*eformed."[253] "The *p*romptest action should be taken by the *p*eople everywhere to checkmate this infernal scheme of the *p*lunderbund to *p*erpetuate its *p*ower by buttressing it with a militarism that derives its *p*ower from the *p*ollution and *p*erversion of the *p*lastic minds of little children under *p*retense of educating and fitting them for *p*atriotic service to their country."[254] "Oh, what a *s*pectacle," Debs mourns as the United States prepared to enter the First World War, "what a *s*hameless, *s*ordid, *s*oulless, ghastly *s*pectacle is here seen in all its naked horror and repulsiveness."[255] Not only does Debs extend his alliterations to improbable and virtuosic lengths, he mixes them in complex combinations as in the following excerpt: "If we are ever to be saved it must be by ourselves and not by our exploiters, and if we are ever to be saved from slaughter like sheep, cattle and swine, we have got to quit going into capitalist class wars and fighting capitalist class battles."[256] Debs begins with a repetition of the *v* and quickly introduces a repeated *s*: **e**ver, **s**aved, **s**elves; **s**aved, **s**laughter, **s**heep. Then **c**attle is connected to the *t* in slaugh**t**er, a return to the s in **s**wine, reprise of the t in go**t** and qui**t**; **g**ot prepares for **g**oing; the hard t resumes in in**t**o, capi**t**alis**t**, figh**t**ing, and ba**t**tles, which rhymes with ca**tt**le, and a hard c is introduced in **c**apitalist **c**lass. There is, in this sentence, an intricate weaving of sounds, each new sound introduced in the context of an established theme.

Stylistic figures based on repetition are among the most democratic of verbal turnings. Figures based on comparison or contrast—metaphor, simile, oxymoron, antithesis, hyperbole—require the listener or reader to know something, outside the text, about at least one of the terms or about general standards, part of the context in which the text occurs. Even so common a simile as "cold as ice," if the audience is to be enlightened regarding the quality of some unfamiliar object, requires that the audience know something about ice. And such an understatement as "A nuclear bomb could ruin your whole day," common enough to be seen on bumper stickers, requires, in fact, that a complicated rhetorical transaction be completed if the dark humor is to have its intended effect. A figure such as allusion requires that the auditor/reader possess specific historical or cultural knowledge, and such figures as enallage, metaplasmus, and hyperbaton require prior knowledge of the general rules of a language's spelling, grammar, and normal usage. Figures based on repetition, in contrast, are contained entirely within the text and require only that a pattern existing in the text be recognized by the audience. Alliteration and assonance are figures based on the repetition of sounds. They are entirely available to the auditor/reader within the text, and they are, in that way, thoroughly democratic rhetorical ornaments.

Like Thomas Paine in *Common Sense*, Debs said nothing that had not been said by others, sometimes using the same characteristic vocabulary. There is a marked consistency, a common use of caricature, metonyms, and favored epithets, among socialist writers and speakers of Debs's era. The synecdochical use of "hand" and "brain" to denote the reduction of human beings to the status of tools provides an example. Kautsky adumbrates this act of reduction when he writes of "establishments that once counted their *workmen* by hundreds" becoming "giant concerns [a certain irony in the use of the term here] that employ thousands of *hands*,"[257] and in A. M. Simons's *Class Struggles in America*, published in 1903 by Charles H. Kerr, the socialist publishing house in Chicago that also published some of Debs's writings, Simons writes of every man working "with hand or with brain."[258] Compare these uses to Debs's lamentation: "Why he's a factory hand—a hand, mind you, and he gets a dollar and a quarter a day when the factory is running. . . . Just a hand! A human factory hand! Think of a hand with a soul in it! . . . The working hand is what is needed for the capitalist's tool and so the human must be reduced to a hand. No head, no heart, no soul—simply a hand."[259] Among the most characteristic of these common stylistic tokens is the representation of capitalists as "parasites." A. M. Simons writes of the industrial capitalist in the process of becoming "purely a parasite,"[260] and Kautsky describes the capitalist class as a small group, which, "together with their parasites, appropriate all the tremendous advantages that have been wrung from nature" by science.[261]

What Debs did provide was an uncommon degree of embellishment in a form that had astonishing resonance with his working-class, largely uneducated audiences, many of them recent immigrants and non-native speakers. Coming out of the tradition of Victor Hugo and nineteenth-century oratory, Debs adapted those rhetorical conventions with remarkable effect to a putatively modern, rational, scientific discourse. It was a leveling move and it put a working-class discourse at the highest levels of politics in the United States. Debs, of course, was not the only spokesperson engaged in the democratization of public rhetoric at the turn of the last century, but he occupied a particularly prominent place, a place based entirely on his rhetorical power.

Assessing Debs's Achievement

For all his prominence and despite, perhaps in part because of, the passions he inspired in his day, Eugene Victor Debs was not included in the original effort by the Speech Association of America to provide a canonical overview of American public address. Samuel Gompers—founder of the AFL, a man thoroughly vilified by Debs as "fat witted,"[262] a man singularly responsible for the failure of the 1894 Pullman strike and the subsequent dissolution of Debs's American Railway Union,[263] a "miserable traitor and coward," and "a tool of the capitalist class"[264]—was the sole representative of the labor movement in the three-volume *A History and Criticism of American Public Address*.[265] Herold Truslow Ross, writing on Debs in an alternative volume put together by students of A. Craig Baird on the same model as the *History and Criticism* volumes, suggests some of the reasons for Debs's exclusion from the official effort. Ross realizes of Debs that many may dismiss him as "a champion of lost causes and a dangerous radical in times of national peril."[266]

Debs may have been the champion of lost causes in the short term, but the long view now available to us reveals that much of what he promoted is an established part of the American scene, most notably his vision of worker organization as realized in the Congress of Industrial Organizations (CIO). By the time the Congress of Industrial Organizations merged with the American Federation of Labor in 1955, the industrial model of CIO had long overwhelmed the craft model of the AFL.[267] Unions are racially and sexually integrated; prohibition has been repealed; women have gained the right to vote; child labor laws have been enacted; worker safety laws govern working conditions in most industries. The Socialist Party's 1908 platform included a proposal for "immediate government relief for the unemployed workers by building schools, by reforesting of cut-over and waste lands, by reclamation of arid tracts and the building of canals, and by extending all other useful public works," which sounds very much like the WPA of the New Deal.[268]

However Debs's programmatic achievements are measured, what is not open to question is that his rhetoric represents a marked departure from the style valorized in the nineteenth century, still the reigning model for oratory in the early, literary days of modern rhetorical criticism, the model that guided the *History and Criticism* project, especially the first two volumes edited by William Norwood Brigance. The bow to historical effect notwithstanding, all of the speakers included in those volumes conformed to certain expectations, the norms of nineteenth-century oratory.

Of particular significance to rhetorical and political history is Debs's influence on the ways that "class" and class analysis have entered the political vocabulary of the mainstream. Debs's contemporary, Henry James, may have, from his decidedly highbrow perspective in a decidedly highbrow medium, poked gentle fun at the idea of a classless America, but Eugene Debs, in his repeated campaigns for the presidency, in his editorials, and in his lecture tours where miners and railroad and factory workers came to hear the man from Terre Haute speak, took "America's forbidden thought" on the road.[269] According to Nick Salvatore, "Debs at his best brought an understanding of class into the center of American political discourse."[270]

From Debs's time forward, class has been a rhetorical resource available to mainstream politicians in the United States, especially Democrats needing a locus of conflict around which to structure their dramatic narratives. Franklin Delano Roosevelt, in his first inaugural address, spoke of driving the "money changers from the temple," and in one of the most audible speeches in contemporary political history, Mario Cuomo told "A Tale of Two Cities." Jesse Jackson has built his career as a Democratic gadfly, always trying to remind the party of its traditional obligations to the working class even as "New Democrats" have sought a "third way." None of this is intended to deny that Americans are still strikingly ambivalent about notions of class. In 1992, Michael Dukakis's effort to oppose Main Street to Wall Street failed to resonate with Americans, 94 percent of whom reportedly identified themselves as middle class.[271] But even the willingness to collapse class into the great undifferentiated middle confirms the passing of the republican ideal that guided the country from the colonial period through the nineteenth century. The democratization of American politics and its accompanying rhetoric, forwarded by Debs and others, is now so thorough that when Al Gore, in the 2000 presidential election, took up the cause of "working families" against big corporate interests, his opponent, George W. Bush, was able, with some credibility, to dismiss Gore's appeal as "misguided," an attempt to foment "class warfare." Bush's dismissal, however, did not, at least ostensibly, take the form of denying the legitimacy of middle- and working-class claims while reasserting the authority of a superior class. Rather, Bush denied any opposition of class interest in the United States, and for at least a time in the campaign, conceded that if there were an opposition of interests, Bush had his own "blueprint for the middle class."[272]

Nearly sixty years after the publication of the original two volumes of *A History and Criticism*, the standard of nineteenth-century eloquence so much in evidence there—an elite standard comfortable to the elite academy, a standard held to be the universal measure of public discourse—seems rigid, quaint, and alien, a discourse suitable for high, starched collars, while in the rhetorical style of Debs and other working-class rhetors we recognize a prototypical version of our own more direct, less studied public discourse. Debs's discourse, for good and ill, helped to break the stranglehold of an essentially republican eloquence and to displace it with a rough-and-tumble, democratic, extemporaneous, middle-class public speech, colored by American pragmatism and its plutonian cousin, American anti-intellectualism.

Even as he defended the choices that were made for *A History and Criticism of American Public Address*, editor William Norwood Brigance conceded the folly of attempting to fix for all time a roster of the most influential speakers in American history, thus codifying a set of historical values "in a world wherein values ought frequently to be reassessed."[273] Whether or not a period of nearly sixty years in any way passes for "frequently," Debs is exemplary of the need for such periodic reassessment. Specifically, Debs's case forces us to confront in profound ways the ideological tests to which we put candidates for canonization, our assumptions about an ideal discourse, even the desirability of that ideal, and the changing style of what we used to call "oratory."

Notes

1. Henry James, *The American*, Everyman Paperback ed. (1877; reprint, London: J. M. Dent, 1997), 103.
2. Ibid., 116.
3. Ibid., 125.
4. Both letters quoted in Carl Degler, *Out of Our Past*, Colophon ed. (New York: Harper and Row, 1970), 275–76.
5. See, for example, Sean Wilentz, "Against Exceptionalism: Class Consciousness and the American Labor Movement, 1790–1920," *International Labor and Working Class History* 26 (1984): 1–24; Nick Salvatore, "Response," *International Labor and Working Class History* 26 (1984): 25–30; Michael Hanagan, "Response," *International Labor and Working Class History* 26 (1984): 31–36; Steven Sapolsky, "Response," *International Labor and Working Class History* 27 (1985): 35–38; Sean Wilentz, "A Reply to Criticism," *International Labor and Working Class History* 28 (1985): 46–55. See also Joseph Rayback, *A History of American Labor* (New York: Macmillan, 1966); Walter Hugins, *Jacksonian Democracy and the Working Class: A Study of the New York Workingmen's Movement, 1829–1837* (Stanford, Calif.: Stanford University Press, 1960); Sean Wilentz, "The Rise of the American Working Class, 1776–1877: A Survey," in *Perspectives on American Labor History: The Problems of Synthesis*, ed. J. Carroll Moody and Alice Kessler-Harris (De Kalb: Northern Illinois University Press, 1989), 83–151; Walter Licht, *Industrializing America: The Nineteenth Century* (Baltimore: Johns Hopkins University Press, 1995); Ronald Story, "Social Class," in *Encyclopedia of American Social History*, ed. Mary Kupiec Cayton, Elliot J. Gorn, and Peter W. Williams (New York: Charles Scribner's Sons, 1993), 1:467–82.
6. Leon Fink, *In Search of the Working Class: Essays in American Labor History and Political Culture* (Urbana: University of Illinois Press, 1994), 16, 20. Nick Salvatore, in his award-winning biography of Debs, traces the emergence of class consciousness in the microcosm of Terre Haute, Indiana, as it parallels changes in Debs's thinking. Nick Salvatore, *Eugene V. Debs: Citizen and Socialist* (Urbana: University of Illinois Press, 1982).
7. Fink, *In Search of the Working Class*, 91, 92.
8. Ibid., 18.
9. For a review of assessments of Debs's significance, see James Darsey, "Prophetic *Ethos* as Radical Argument: The Legend of Eugene Debs," *Quarterly Journal of Speech* 74 (1988): 435, 447f.; James Darsey, *The Prophetic Tradition and Radical Rhetoric in America* (New York: New York University Press, 1997), 86.
10. Eugene Debs, "Homestead and Ludlow," in *Eugene V. Debs Speaks*, ed. Jean Tussey (New York: Pathfinder, 1972), 217.
11. Eugene Debs, "Revolutionary Unionism," in *Writings and Speeches of Eugene V. Debs*, ed. Arthur Schlesinger Jr. (New York: Heritage Press, 1948), 216.
12. Darsey, "Prophetic *Ethos*," 439–40.
13. Eugene Debs, "Industrial Unionism," in *Debs Speaks*, 123.
14. Eugene Debs, "The Socialist Party's Appeal [1908]," in *Debs Speaks*, 164.
15. Robert Wiebe, *The Search for Order, 1877–1920* (New York: Hill and Wang, 1967), 42–43, 40f.
16. Walter Lippmann, *The Essential Lippmann*, ed. Clinton Rossiter and James Lare (Cambridge: Harvard University Press, 1982), 32.
17. Licht, *Industrializing America*, 183.
18. Eugene Debs, "Patriotism and Pauperism," *National Rip-Saw*, December 1915, 3.
19. Eugene Debs, "Frick's Fifth Avenue Castle," *National Rip-Saw*, February 1915, 3.
20. Eugene Debs, as quoted in David Karsner, *Debs: His Authorized Life and Letters* (New York: Boni and Liveright, 1919), 49.
21. Andrew Carnegie, "Wealth," in *1864–1957*, vol. 2 of *Great Issues in American History*, ed. Richard Hofstadter (New York: Vintage Books, 1958), 80.
22. William Graham Sumner, "The Forgotten Man," in *American Forum: Speeches on Historic Issues, 1788–1900*, ed. Ernest J. Wrage and Barnet Baskerville (Seattle: University of Washington Press, 1960), 232.

23. Ibid., 236.
24. Robert Wiebe notes how easily social Darwinism could be made to "read like a cata-logue of mid-nineteenth-century values" (*Search for Order*, 136, 161).
25. Ibid., 134.
26. Carnegie, "Wealth," in *1864–1957*, 79–84.
27. Russell Conwell, "Acres of Diamonds," in *American Forum*, 271.
28. Wiebe, *Search for Order*, 43.
29. A. M. Simons, *Class Struggles in America* (Chicago: Charles H. Kerr, 1906), 101.
30. Wilentz, "Rise of the American Working Class," in *Perspectives on American Labor His-tory*, 84–85.
30. Eugene Debs, "Industrial Democracy," *National Rip-Saw*, August 1914, 3.
31. Eugene Debs, "Are They 'Un-American'?" *National Rip-Saw*, May 1914, 4.
32. Eugene Debs, "Cowardly Attacks upon Labor," *National Rip-Saw*, February 1917, 4.
33. On the gendered entailments of "virtue" in Debs's time, see Darsey, *The Prophetic Tra-dition*, 236 n. 25. Surrounded by such examples as Mother Jones and Kate Richards O'Hare, Debs did sometimes, rather self-consciously and explicitly, broaden his focus to acknowledge the role of women, but "manhood" is always the controlling and paramount term. Note in the following how "womanhood" is incorporated and then subsumed under the "manful" response: "They [the Socialists of Oklahoma] are ap-pealing to the sober sense, the honesty, the love of justice and fair play, the manhood and womanhood of the state. They realize that a crisis is upon them and they are man-fully battling to meet the issues squarely and to decided once for all [*sic*]" (Eugene Debs, "Disfranchising [*sic*] Labor in Oklahoma," *National Rip-Saw*, April 1916, 11).
34. Eugene Debs, "Our Presidential Candidates," *National Rip-Saw*, May 1916, 11.
35. Debs, "Industrial Unionism," in *Debs Speaks*, 133.
36. Throughout his career, Debs denied that the interests of workers and private corpora-tions could be "harmonious," "nor can there be such a thing as 'mutual confidence' between them" (Eugene Debs, "Mutual Confidence and Harmonious Relations," *Na-tional Rip-Saw*, April 1916, 4).
37. "[T]he social attitudes of most Americans of the period [the Gilded Age] were *not* sim-ply pecuniary," writes R. Jackson Wilson, "but combined a devotion to practicality with an intense moralism and idealism." R. Jackson Wilson, *In Quest of Community: Social Philosophy in the United States, 1860–1920* (London: Oxford University Press, 1970), 53.
38. Eugene Debs to Carl D. Thompson, 26 November 1910, *Gentle Rebel: Letters of Eugene V. Debs*, ed. J. Robert Constantine (Urbana and Chicago: University of Illinois Press, 1995), 68.
39. It is the bulk of Salvatore's argument to trace the evolution of Debs's thought, and in doing so, he illuminates the inconsistencies in Debs's thinking. Salvatore, *Eugene V. Debs.*
40. Frederick Engels, "Socialism: Utopian and Scientific," in *Marx and Engels: Basic Writ-ings on Politics and Philosophy*, ed. Lewis S. Feuer (Garden City, N.Y.: Anchor, 1959), 88–89. Given the complexities in the evolution of Marxist theory, it may be objected that a single quotation from Engels cannot be considered representative, but according to Robert K. Merton: "Whatever other changes may have occurred in the development of theirs during the half-century of their work, they [Marx and Engels] consistently held fast to the thesis that 'relations of production' constitute the 'real foundation' for the superstructure of ideas" ("Sociology of Knowledge," in *Twentieth Century Sociology*, ed. Georges Gurvitch and Wilbert E. Moore [New York: Philosophical Library, 1945], 373). Included in this superstructure of ideas is the political system.
41. Eugene Debs, "Revolutionary Unionism," in *Debs: His Life, Writings and Speeches* (Chicago: Charles H. Kerr, 1908), 427; see also Debs, "Industrial Unionism," in *Debs Speaks*, 446f.
42. Eugene Debs, "The Issue," in *Writings and Speeches*, 306.
43. Eugene Debs, "What's the Matter with Chicago?" in *Debs Speaks*, 75.
44. Eugene Debs, "The Socialist Party and the Working Class," in *Writings and Speeches*, 127; This theme becomes one of the recurrent themes in Debs's speaking and writing:

- Needless is it for me to say to the thinking workingman that he has no choice between these two capitalist parties, that they are both pledged to the same system and that whether the one or the other succeeds, he will still remain the wage-working slave he is today.
- The working class must get rid of the whole brood of masters and exploiters, and put themselves in possession and control of the means of production. . . . It is therefore a question not of "reform," the mask of fraud, but of revolution. The capitalist system must be overthrown, class rule abolished and wage slavery supplanted by cooperative industry (Eugene Debs, "The Outlook for Socialism in the United States," in *Debs Speaks*, 64–65).

See also Eugene Debs, "Reply to John Mitchell," in *Debs: His Life, Writings and Speeches*, 175.

45. Debs, "The Outlook for Socialism in the United States," in *Debs Speaks*, 65.
46. Debs, "The Socialist Party and the Working Class," in *Writings and Speeches*, 126.
47. Eugene Debs, "Class Unionism," in *Writings and Speeches*, 202.
48. Paul Boase, "Christian Socialism and the Social Gospel," in *The Rhetoric of Protest and Reform, 1870–1898*, ed. Paul H. Boase (Athens: Ohio University Press, 1980), 248.
49. Quoted extensively by Debs in his 1914 essay "Homestead and Ludlow," in *Debs Speaks*, 218, 219, 220, 221.
50. Charles Lomas, "Urban Mavericks and Radicals," in *Rhetoric of Protest and Reform*, 49.
51. Eugene Debs, "Capitalism Self-Condemned," *National Rip-Saw*, April 1914, 4.
52. Eugene Debs, "Private Ownership," *National Rip-Saw*, July 1914, 4.
53. Eugene Debs, "How I Became a Socialist," in *Debs Speaks*, 48. Bernard Brommel makes the claim that Debs read *Capital* during his stay at Woodstock in 1895. He may have support for this claim, but he does not produce it. Bernard J. Brommel, *Eugene V. Debs: Spokesman for Labor and Socialism* (Chicago: Charles H. Kerr, 1978), 208.
54. For example, Eugene Debs, "On Race Prejudice," in *Debs Speaks*, 93; Debs, "Industrial Unionism," in *Debs Speaks*, 136; Eugene Debs, "Sound Socialist Tactics," in *Debs Speaks*, 191. Scott Molloy asserts that Debs read *The Communist Manifesto* while in Woodstock Jail but does not claim that Debs read *Capital*. Scott Molloy, "Eugene V. Debs," in *Encyclopedia of the American Left*, ed. Mari Jo Buhle, Paul Buhle, and Dan Georgakas (Urbana: University of Illinois Press, 1992), 186.
55. James P. Cannon, introduction to *Debs Speaks*, 13. Salvatore concurs with Cannon, listing a number of authors over whom Debs "pored" while in Woodstock, ending the list with "especially Karl Kautsky, the German popularizer of Karl Marx" (Salvatore, *Eugene V. Debs*, 150).
56. Eugene Debs to Karl Kautsky, 4 December 1925, *Gentle Rebel*, 260.
57. Ibid., 261.
58. For example, Debs, "Industrial Unionism," in *Debs Speaks*, 123; Debs, "Capitalism Self-Condemned," 4.
59. For example, Debs, "Industrial Unionism," in *Debs Speaks*, 122; Eugene Debs, "Hughes and Labor as a Commodity," *National Rip-Saw*, August 1916, 3; Eugene Debs, "Labor Is Not a Commodity," *National Rip-Saw*, June 1916, 3.
60. For example, Debs, "Capitalism Self-Condemned," 4.
61. For example, Eugene Debs, "Unionism and Socialism," in *Writings and Speeches*, 118.
62. For example, Debs, "Private Ownership," 4.
63. Eugene Debs, "Unity and Victory," in *Debs: His Life, Writings and Speeches*, 8–9.
64. Robert Tucker, introduction to *The Class Struggle*, by Karl Kautsky, trans. William E. Bohn (New York: W. W. Norton and Co., 1971), 3.
65. Eugene Debs to William Allen White, 27 January 1911, *Gentle Rebel*, 71.
66. On Debs's moderation, see Brommel, *Eugene V. Debs*, 211ff.; see also Eugene Debs to Joseph A. Labadie, 5 May 1908, *Gentle Rebel*, 52–53; Eugene Debs to William English Walling, 5 March 1913, *Gentle Rebel*, 84; Eugene Debs, "The Crisis in Mexico," in *Debs Speaks*, 185, 187.
67. Tucker, introduction to *The Class Struggle*, 3; Debs, "Sound Socialist Tactics," in *Debs Speaks*, 190–94.
68. Kautsky, *The Class Struggle*, 182.
69. Eugene Debs, "To the Railroad Workers," *National Rip-Saw*, September 1915, 16.

70. Debs, "Industrial Unionism," in *Debs Speaks*, 115. Writing in the *International Socialist Review*, plotting the socialist course for the election of 1912, Debs described the craft unions of the American Federation of Labor as "labor-dividing and corruption breeding" (Eugene Debs, "Danger Ahead," in *Debs Speaks*, 180).

71. For some discussion of these issues, see Jürgen Habermas, *Theory and Practice* (Boston: Beacon Press, 1973), esp. 238; Jean-Paul Sartre, "Materialism and Revolution," in *Philosophy in the Twentieth Century*, vol. 3, ed. William Barrett and Henry D. Aiken (New York: Random House, 1962), esp. 401; George Lichtheim, *The Concept of Ideology* (New York: Vintage, 1967), 34 n.

72. Sartre, "Materialism and Revolution," 424; See also Herbert Marcuse, *Reason and Revolution: Hegel and the Rise of Social Theory*, Beacon Press edition (Boston: Beacon Press, 1960), 317. Marcuse tries to avoid the determinism trap, but his equivocation is not entirely convincing (see pp. 317–19). Certainly, there are readings of Marx and Engels that lend themselves to interpretations such as Sartre describes. Even on a superficial level, without considering the consistency of historical materialism as a theory, Marx and Engels refer to capitalism as "a passing historical phase" that will be "swept away by the complete development of modern productive forces" of the "inevitable breaking up" of the state, by the operation of "natural laws of capitalist production. It is a question of these laws themselves, of these tendencies working with iron necessity toward inevitable results." See Karl Marx, *Capital: A Critique of Political Economy*, selections reprinted in *Marx and Engels*, 139, 135, 146; Engels, "Socialism," in *Marx and Engels*, 107. See also Maurice Cornforth, *Materialism and the Dialectical Method*, 4th ed. (New York: International Publishers, 1971); George Novack, *An Introduction to the Logic of Marxism*, 5th ed. (New York: Pathfinder, 1971).

73. Eugene Debs to Theodore Debs, 18 May 1912, *Gentle Rebel*, 75; Eugene Debs to Theodore Debs, 12 August 1917, *Gentle Rebel*, 126.; Eugene Debs to Theodore Debs, 21 April 1912, *Gentle Rebel*, 74.

74. Eugene Debs, to S. M. Reynolds, 17 August 1916, *Gentle Rebel*, 112.

75. Eugene Debs, "Margaret Sanger and Birth Control," *National Rip-Saw*, May 1916, 4.

76. Eugene Debs, "Tichenor's *Creed of Constantine*," *National Rip-Saw*, January 1917, 5.

77. Eugene Debs to Upton Sinclair, 28 October 1918, *Gentle Rebel*, 145. Writing on the issue of Irish home rule, Debs prescribed the need to get rid of "priestcraft, superstition and ignorance" before any substantial would be possible. Eugene Debs, "The Home Rule That Ireland Needs," *National Rip-Saw*, May 1914, 5. Similarly, the "long suffering Mexican people" were instructed to "put a finish to the priestcraft and superstition which have for centuries kept them down in physical and mental slavery" (Eugene Debs, "Mexico for the Mexicans," *National Rip-Saw*, July 1914, 4).

78. Eugene Debs to Clara Spalding Ellis, 6 February 1904, *Gentle Rebel*, 36.

79. Eugene Debs, "Socialism," in *Writings and Speeches*, 119.

80. Debs, "The Issue," in *Writings and Speeches*, 305–6. See also in *Writings and Speeches* Eugene Debs, "Prison Labor," 32; Debs, "Unionism and Socialism," 118, 119; Eugene Debs, "Craft Unionism," 186; Debs, "Class Unionism," 205; Eugene Debs, "The Growth of Socialism," 261, 267; Eugene Debs, "Revolution," 292; Debs, "The Issue," 306; Eugene Debs, "Labor's Struggle for Supremacy," 341; Eugene Debs, "Speech of Acceptance," 363, 365. See also in *Debs Speaks*, Debs, "The Outlook for Socialism in the United States," 66; Eugene Debs, "The Socialist Party's Appeal [1904]," 110; Debs, "Industrial Unionism," 122, 136, 141, 142; Debs, "The Socialist Party's Appeal [1908]," 168. See also Eugene Debs, "Speech at the Founding Convention of the Industrial Workers of the World," 119; Debs, "Industrial Unionism," 122, 136, 141, 142; Debs, "The Socialist Party's Appeal [1908]," 168; Eugene Debs, "The Canton, Ohio, Speech," in *Debs Speaks*, 267. See also Eugene Debs, "Brotherhood and Peace," *National Rip-Saw*, April 1914, 4; Ray Ginger, *The Bending Cross: A Biography of Eugene Victor Debs* (New Brunswick, N.J.: Rutgers University Press, 1949), 443. See also on the scientism of fin de siècle radicals in America, Aileen S. Kraditor, *The Radical Persuasion, 1890–1917: Aspects of the Intellectual History and Historiography of Three American Radical Organizations* (Baton Rouge: Louisiana State University Press, 1981), esp. 220–36 and Mark Pittenger, *American Socialists and Evolutionary Thought, 1870–1920* (Madison: University of Wisconsin Press, 1993). Salvatore describes Debs's faith in science and in the

scientifically foreordained progress of society as "almost Comtean" (Salvatore, *Eugene V. Debs*, 65).

81. Kautsky, *The Class Struggle*, 117.
82. Ibid., 128.
83. Eugene Debs, "The Socialist Party's Appeal (1904)," in *Debs Speaks*, 107.
84. Licht, *Industrializing America*, 183.
85. James Arnt Aune, *Rhetoric and Marxism* (Boulder, Colo.: Westview Press, 1994), 13; see also Kenneth Burke's discussion of the problem of determinism in Marxist thought. Kenneth Burke, *A Grammar of Motives* (Berkeley and Los Angeles: University of California Press, 1969), 258–59.
86. C. J. Arthur, introduction to *The German Ideology*, by Karl Marx and Frederick Engels, part 1 with selections from parts 2 and 3 and supplementary texts, ed. C. J. Arthur (New York: International Publishers, 1970), 23.
87. For example, Debs, "Danger Ahead," in *Debs Speaks*, 179; Debs, "Sound Socialist Tactics," in *Debs Speaks*, 199; Eugene Debs, "The Vital Question of Today," *National Rip-Saw*, March 1914, 28.
88. Eugene Debs, "Editorials," *National Rip-Saw*, April 1916, 4.
89. Eugene Debs, "Francis Marshal Elliott: Love and Farewell," *National Rip-Saw*, March 1916, 22.
90. Eugene Debs, "The Workers Must Organize," *National Rip-Saw*, April 1915, 3.
91. On the apodeictic aspects of prophecy, see Darsey, *The Prophetic Tradition*, 19.
92. On Debs's use of this metonymy, see Darsey, "Prophetic *Ethos*," 445–46. Carl Tresca, an Italian immigrant arrested in conjunction with an IWW strike in Minnesota in 1916 and charged as an accessory in the murder of a sheriff's deputy, illustrates how Debs's followers shared in his own conception of himself: "your voice is the voice of labor" (Carl Tresca to Eugene Debs, ca. 18 September 1916, *Gentle Rebel*, 113).
93. Kenneth Burke calls scientific language "a preparation for action," while rhetorical language is "an inducement to action" (*Grammar of Motives*, 42).
94. Debs, "The Workers Must Organize," National Rip-Saw, April 1915, 3. Debs's followers also believed in him as a representative of working-class interests. Walter Hurt describes him as "a voice proclaiming the Message of the Masses . . . an articulate sentiment, a personalized principle." Walter Hurt, *Eugene V. Debs: An Introduction* (Williamsburg, Ohio: Progress Publishing Co., nd.), 17. Aileen Kraditor writes of Debs: "He seems to have been unable to consider any belief, feeling, or hope that he had to be just his own; it was always the awakened workers thinking, feeling, and hoping through him." Kraditor, *Radical Persuasion*, 151.
95. Eugene Debs, "Education of the Workers," *Social Revolution*, April 1917, 4.
96. Debs, "The Socialist Party's Appeal [1904]," in *Debs Speaks*, 106.
97. Eugene Debs, "To the Readers of the *Rip-Saw*, Greetings," *National Rip-Saw*, February 1914, 1. See also Debs, "The Crisis in Mexico," in *Debs Speaks*, 184.
98. Eugene Debs, "Editorials," *National Rip-Saw*, September 1916, 3; see also Eugene Debs to Claude G. Bowers, 28 March 1907, *Gentle Rebel*, 47. Debs was entirely in accord with the thinking of other radicals on this issue. For some years, the masthead of the *National Rip-Saw* included the motto "Blind as a Bat to Everything but Right." In 1917, with a change in the paper's name to *Social Revolution*, the masthead featured, pictorially, the contrasting states of "Enlightenment" and "Ignorance" on the left and right sides of the masthead, respectively.
99. Burke, *Grammar of Motives*, 131.
100. In his most famous speech, the speech at Canton, Ohio, for which Debs was convicted under the Espionage Act of 1917, Debs declared "The truth alone will make the people free." Debs, "The Canton, Ohio, Speech," in *Debs Speaks*, 263. See also, "the truth that makes men free," in Eugene Debs, "Soft Words," *National Rip-Saw*, April 1914, 3.
101. On Marxism as religion, see Joseph Schumpeter, "Marx the Prophet," in *Capitalism, Socialism, and Democracy* (New York: Harper and Brothers, 1947); Karl Jaspers, *Reason and Anti-reason in Our Time*, trans. Stanley Godman (1952; reprint, Hamden, Conn.: Archon Books, 1971), 7–17; Mircea Eliade, *The Sacred and the Profane: The Nature of Religion*, trans. Willard R. Trask (New York: Harcourt, Brace and World, 1959), 206f.;

Kenneth Burke, *Rhetoric of Motives* (Berkeley and Los Angeles: University of California Press, 1969), 194; Burke, *Grammar of Motives*, 209.

102. Eugene Debs, as quoted in Ginger, *Bending Cross*, 334f. On the alliance of these appeals, see Kraditor, *Radical Persuasion*, 205–47. Although I will argue that Debs's conception of socialism was more religious than scientific (if a distinction must be made between the two), Debs did sometimes refer to socialism as a science. For example, see Debs, "The Socialist Party's Appeal (1904)," in *Debs Speaks,* 107. It is worthy of note that this reference to the socialist platform as "scientific" is immediately followed by a reference to Moses.

103. Eugene Debs to John Reed, 21 September 1918, *Gentle Rebel,* 144.

104. Eugene Debs to Mary Harris [Mother] Jones, 28 January 1901, *Gentle Rebel,* 31.

105. Debs, "How I Became a Socialist," in *Debs Speaks,* 47.

106. Eugene Debs, "The Worker and His Future," *National Rip-Saw,* October 1916, 1.

107. Debs, "Tichenor's *Creed of Constantine,*" 5.

108. Eugene Debs to Jean Daniel Debs and Marguerite Bettrich Debs, 29 September 1874, *Gentle Rebel,* 4.

109. Eugene Debs, "Francis Marshal Elliott: Love and Farewell," *National Rip-Saw,* March 1916, 22; Eugene Debs, "On Immigration," in *Debs Speaks,* 171; Eugene Debs, "A Plea for Solidarity," in *Debs Speaks,* 206.

110. Eugene Debs to Frank P. O'Hare, 14 February 1915, *Gentle Rebel,* 97.

111. Eugene Debs, "The New Year and the *Rip-Saw,*" *National Rip-Saw,* January 1917, 3.

112. Debs, "Tichenor's *Creed of Constantine,*" 5.

113. Eugene Debs, "Capitalism's Ghastly Joke," *National Rip-Saw,* May 1914, 5.

114. Eugene Debs, "Uncle Sam's Hop Pickers," *National Rip-Saw,* May 1914, 3.

115. Eugene Debs, "Heroes and Outlaws," *National Rip-Saw,* June 1914, 3.

116. Debs, "Industrial Unionism," in *Debs Speaks,* 138–39.

117. See Darsey, "Prophetic *Ethos,*" 443, on the letter to Debs from the daughter of Mabel Curry, which begins "Dearest Gene—Mother says I am to call you this instead of the 'Mister.'"

118. Carlo Tresca to Eugene Debs, ca. 18 September 1916, *Gentle Rebel,* 113. Brommel quotes Norman Thomas, Debs's successor as head of the Socialist Party, to the effect that "Debs wasn't the intellect of the Party but he was emphatically the heart of the Party" (Brommel, *Eugene V. Debs,* 206). Debs himself never opposed heart and brain, but apparently conceived of them in essential harmony as, for example, when he declares "Freedom must have its beginning in the brain and heart of the working-class" (Debs, "Education of the Workers," 4).

119. Karsner, *Debs,* 2.

120. See Darsey, *The Prophetic Tradition,* 79, on Phillips's nineteenth-century rhetorical education.

121. Edwin Black, "The Sentimental Style as Escapism, or The Devil with Dan'l Webster," in *Form and Genre: Shaping Rhetorical Action,* ed. Karlyn Kohrs Campbell and Kathleen Hall Jamieson (Falls Church, Va.: Speech Communication Association, 1978), 78.

122. Peter Brooks, *The Melodramatic Imagination: Balzac, Henry James, Melodrama, and the Mode of Excess* (New Haven: Yale University Press, 1976), 15.

123. Kautsky, *The Class Struggle,* 21.

124. Ibid., 27.

125. Brommel, *Eugene V. Debs,* 15.

126. Salvatore, *Eugene V. Debs,* 12.

127. Eugene Debs, "Victor Hugo and the Socialists," *National Rip-Saw,* January 1916, 4.

128. Eugene Debs, "Fantine in Our Day," in *Writings and Speeches,* 392.

129. Victor Hugo, *Les Misérables,* trans. Norman Denny (New York: Penguin Books, 1982), 351.

130. Black, "Sentimental Style," in *Form and Genre,* 78.

131. Hugo, *Les Misérables,* 94.

132. Ibid., 250.

133. Eugene Debs, "Statement to the Court," in *Writings and Speeches,* 437.

134. Hugo, *Les Misérables,* 1218.

135. Ibid., 30.

136. Ibid., 622. For other direct statements of the theme, see 97, 501, 622, 640, 987.
137. Debs, "Soft Words," 3.
138. Debs, "Capitalism's Ghastly Joke," 5.
139. Eugene Debs, "Child Labor and the Politicians," *National Rip-Saw*, October 1916, 3.
140. Karsner, *Debs*, 88.
141. See Salvatore, *Eugene V. Debs*, 19, 68, 72, 81, 96f., 103, 113, 118, 123, 124, 137, 171, 215, 216, 228f., 269. See also Darsey, "Prophetic *Ethos*," 438; Eugene Debs, "Dare to Be a Man," *National Rip-Saw*, August 1915, 3; Debs, "Editorials," *National Rip-Saw*, April 1916, 3. On the cooperative commonwealth, see Eugene Debs, "What's the Matter with Chicago," in *Debs Speaks*, 73–74; Eugene Debs, "The Socialist Party's Appeal [1904]," in *Debs Speaks*, 110; Debs, "The Socialist Party's Appeal [1908]," in *Debs Speaks*, 167; Debs, "To the Readers of the *Rip-Saw*, Greetings," 1.
142. Hugo, *Les Misérables*, 722.
143. Ibid., 722–23.
144. Ibid., 723.
145. Ibid., 723f.
146. Debs, "Editorial," *National Rip-Saw*, September 1916, 3.
147. Hugo, *Les Misérables*, 951.
148. Ibid., 1230, 1232, 1229, 56, 921, 951, 1005, 1228.
149. Ibid., 1044. On Debs's martyrdom, see Darsey, "Prophetic *Ethos*."
150. www.geocities.com/Athens/Academy/6361 (3 May 2002).
151. Debs, "Industrial Unionism," in *Debs Speaks*, 139.
152. Eugene Debs, "The Color Line," *National Rip-Saw*, April 1916, 3.
153. Salvatore, *Eugene V. Debs*, 104–5.
154. Debs, "On Race Prejudice," in *Debs Speaks*, 93.
155. Ibid.
156. Eugene Debs, "The Crime of Lynching and 'White Supremacy,'" *National Rip-Saw*, January 1917, 3.
157. Eugene Debs to Charles R. Jones, 1 June 1912, *Gentle Rebel*, 78.
158. Eugene Debs to J. A. C. Meng, 12 March 1926, *Gentle Rebel*, 281.
159. Eugene Debs, "Prohibition, Stockings and Garters," *National Rip-Saw*, May 1914, 3.
160. Eugene Debs, "Rich and Respectable Rottenness," *National Rip-Saw*, March 1916, 3. For other examples of this theme of lost feminine virtue, see James Darsey, "Literature at the Moral Frontier: The Sexuality of Women as Synecdoche" (paper presented at the seventy-fifth annual convention of the Speech Communication Association, San Francisco, November 1989).
161. Debs, "Fantine in Our Day," in *Writings and Speeches*, 395.
162. Eugene Debs, "Woman—Comrade and Equal," in *Writings and Speeches*, 452.
163. Eugene Debs, "Editorial," *National Rip-Saw*, October 1915, 3.
164. Eugene Debs, "The Women and Their Fight," *National Rip-Saw*, October 1915, 3. See also "Debs Speaks for Suffrage," *New York Times*, 18 October 1915, 4; Eugene Debs, "Editorial," *Social Revolution*, December 1917, 5.
165. Eugene Debs, "Triumph for Equal Suffrage," *National Rip-Saw*, December 1915, 4.
166. Wiebe, *The Search for Order*, 169.
167. Eugene Debs, "Editorials," *National Rip-Saw*, January 1917, 3.
168. Eugene Debs, "Editorials," *National Rip-Saw*, March 1916, 3.
169. Debs, "Industrial Unionism," in *Debs Speaks*, 139.
170. Eugene Debs to Carl Sandburg, 9 December 1922, *Gentle Rebel*, 220.
171. Eugene Debs, "The People's College," *National Rip-Saw*, February 1915, 20; Eugene Debs, "The People's College," *National Rip-Saw*, March 1915, 4.
172. Eugene Debs, "The American University and the Labor Problem," in *Debs Speaks*, 54.
173. Ibid., 55.
174. Eugene Debs, "The Apologetic Dr. Eliot," *National Rip-Saw*, March 1915, 4.
175. Eugene Debs, "Penitentiary Prosperity," *National Rip-Saw*, March 1916, 4.
176. Eugene Debs, *Walls and Bars* (1927; reprint, Chicago: Charles H. Kerr, 1973), 8–9.
177. Eugene Debs to Robert B. Sims, 23 May 1913, *Gentle Rebel*, 85.
178. Eugene Debs, "Revolutionary Unionism," in *Writings and Speeches*, 118.
179. Eugene Debs, "Victor Hugo on War," *National Rip-Saw*, April 1917, 4.

180. Hugo, *Les Misérables*, 291, 333, 573, 950.

181. Eugene Debs, as quoted in Karsner, *Debs*, 28–29.

182. Eugene Debs, "The Furies Have Been Let Loose," *National Rip-Saw*, September 1914, 3, and Eugene Debs, "The War and the Workers," *National Rip-Saw*, September 1914, 3.

183. Eugene Debs, "The European Slaughter Continues," *National Rip-Saw*, January 1915, 4.

184. Eugene Debs, "The Prospect for Peace," in *Debs Speaks*, 233.

185. Eugene Debs, "Letter of Acceptance," in *Debs Speaks*, 236.

186. Eugene Debs to Adolph F. Germer, 11 April 1917, *Gentle Rebel*, 122.

187. Eugene Debs, "Plutocratic and Proletarian Preparedness," *National Rip-Saw*, May 1916, 3.

188. Eugene Debs, "Preparedness and the Working Class," *National Rip-Saw*, May 1916, 16.

189. Ibid.

190. "Debs Urges Strike if Nation Fights," *New York Times*, 8 March 1917, 3. For other examples of Debs's anti-war rhetoric, see Eugene Debs, "The War and the Workers," *National Rip-Saw*, September 1914, 3; Eugene Debs, "If Only They Knew," *National Rip-Saw*, October 1914, 3; Eugene Debs, "The Destroyers Unmasked," *National Rip-Saw*, November 1914, 3; Eugene Debs, "The National Campaign This Year," *National Rip-Saw*, June 1916, 14; Eugene Debs, "Patriotism on Parade," *National Rip-Saw*, October 1916, 4; Eugene Debs, "Karl Leibknecht: Germany's Conquering Hero," *National Rip-Saw*, January 1917, 25–27. The war was also an important topic in Debs's letters between 1914 and 1917; see *Gentle Rebel*, 100, 105, 106, 107, 124–25, 274. See also Brommel, *Eugene V. Debs*, 147ff.

191. Debs, "Mexico for the Mexicans," 6.

192. Eugene Debs, "The Chase after Villa," *National Rip-Saw*, June 1916, 4.

193. Eugene Debs, "Editorials," *National Rip-Saw*, July 1917, 4. For other examples of Debs's treatment of the situation in Mexico, see Eugene Debs, "The War in Mexico," *National Rip-Saw*, August 1914, 3; Eugene Debs, "The Threatened Mexican Invasion," *National Rip-Saw*, September 1915, 3; Eugene Debs, "President Wilson and the Mexican Muddle," *National Rip-Saw*, May 1916, 3; Eugene Debs, "The Situation in Mexico," *National Rip-Saw*, August 1916, 4. See also Brommel, *Eugene V. Debs*, 55, 56.

194. Eugene Debs, "The Expanding New Life," *National Rip-Saw*, April 1916, 3.

195. Eugene Debs, "International Patriotism," *National Rip-Saw*, November 1914, 4.

196. Eugene Debs, "Internationalism," *National Rip-Saw*, January 1916, 4.

197. Irving Howe, "In the American Grain," *New York Review of Books*, 10 November 1983, 18–22.

198. Salvatore, *Eugene V. Debs*, 171; see also 153, 186–94, 229, 230.

199. Pittenger, *American Socialists and Evolutionary Thought*, 62; see also Salvatore, *Eugene V. Debs*, 103, 150, on Gronlund's influence on Debs.

200. Ernest J. Wrage and Barnet Baskerville, eds., *Contemporary Forum: American Speeches on Contemporary Issues* (Seattle: University of Washington Press, 1969), 7.

201. Ronald Lee and James Andrews, "A Story of Rhetorical-Ideological Transformation: Eugene V. Debs as Liberal Hero," *Quarterly Journal of Speech* 77 (1991): 29.

202. Eugene Debs to Claude G. Bowers, 16 January 1926, *Gentle Rebel*, 271.

203. Debs, "The Outlook for Socialism in the United States," in *Debs Speaks*, 61.

204. Debs, "Sound Socialist Tactics," in *Debs Speaks*, 190.

205. Eugene Debs, "The Common Laborer," *National Rip-Saw*, April 1914, 1. See also Eugene Debs, "The Railroad Eight-Hour Movement," *National Rip-Saw*, March 1916, 20.

206. Eugene Debs, "The American University and the Labor Problem," in *Debs Speaks*, 54.

207. Eugene Debs to Carl D. Thompson, 26 November 1910, *Gentle Rebel*, 68.

208. Eugene Debs to Emanuel Haldeman-Julius, 4 January 1926, *Gentle Rebel*, 262.

209. Eugene Debs, "Piracy Masked as Patriotism," *National Rip-Saw*, May 1916, 1.

210. Debs, "The American University and the Labor Problem," in *Debs Speaks*, 58.

211. Eugene Debs, "Liberty," in *Writings and Speeches*, 8.

212. Eugene Debs, "Rockefeller's Republic," *National Rip-Saw*, June 1914, 3.

213. Debs, "Revolutionary Unionism," in *Writings and Speeches*, 216.

214. Debs, "The Railroad Eight-Hour Movement," 20. For other examples, see Eugene Debs, "Declaration of Revolt," *Appeal to Reason*, 7 January 1911, 1; Eugene Debs, "John

Brown: History's Greatest Hero," in *Writings and Speeches*, 281; Debs, "The Canton, Ohio, Speech," in *Debs Speaks*, 275.

215. Eugene Debs, "The Western Labor Movement," in *Debs Speaks*, 84.

216. Eugene Debs, "Lexington and Ludlow," *National Rip-Saw*, May 1915, 3.

217. For example, see Eugene Debs, "Garrison, Lovejoy, and Bigelow," *Social Revolution*, December 1917, 5.

218. Eugene Debs to Otto Branstetter, 22 November [1919–21], *Gentle Rebel*, 161.

219. Eugene Debs, "Interview with E. V. Debs," interview by Ruth Crawford, *Terre Haute Star*, 7 November 1926, quoted in Brommel, *Eugene V. Debs*, 21.

220. Eugene Debs to Tom Mooney in care of John Snyder, ed., *World*, 30 November 1918, *Gentle Rebel*, 146; see also Eugene Debs to E. B. Ault, 30 November 1918, *Gentle Rebel*, 150.

221. Eugene Debs, "Thomas Paine, Anti-Militarist," *National Rip-Saw*, August 1916, 4.

222. Eugene Debs, "Address to the Court," in Karsner, *Debs*, 27–28.

223. Ibid., 28.

224. Ibid., 30.

225. Eugene Debs to Robert M. La Follette, 7 March 1909, *Gentle Rebel*, 61.

226. Eugene Debs, "Enforced Military Marriages," *Social Revolution*, June 1917, 3.

227. Darsey, "Prophetic *Ethos*," 435.

228. In addition to the examples above, see Brommel, *Eugene V. Debs*, 62.

229. Richard Weaver, "The Spaciousness of Old Rhetoric," in *The Ethics of Rhetoric* (1953; reprint, Davis, Calif.: Hermagoras Press, 1985), 164–85.

230. Kenneth Cmiel, *Democratic Eloquence: The Fight over Popular Speech in Nineteenth-Century America* (New York: William Morrow, 1990), 95.

231. Ibid., 122.

232. Irving Bartlett is using the phrase of one of Phillips's contemporaries when he characterizes Phillips's discourse as "the eloquence of abuse," and E. L. Godkin, also contemporary with Phillips and one of the few who shared many of his radical views, nonetheless felt constrained, as editor of the *Nation* magazine, to criticize Phillips's excesses. Irving H. Bartlett, "The Persistence of Wendell Phillips," in *The Antislavery Vanguard*, ed. Martin Duberman (Princeton: Princeton University Press, 1965), 111; Irving H. Bartlett, "Wendell Phillips and the Eloquence of Abuse," *American Quarterly* 11 (1959): 516. The phrase is Robert C. Winthrop's. E. L. Godkin, "Wendell Phillips as a Whipper-In," *Nation*, 8 February 1866, 166, quoted in Winona L. Fletcher, "Knight-Errant or Screaming Eagle? E. L. Godkin's Criticism of Wendell Phillips," *Southern Speech Journal* 29 (1963): 217.

233. Debs, "Soft Words," 3.

234. Eugene Debs to Theodore Debs, 9 November 1900, *Gentle Rebel*, 29.

235. For example, Eugene Debs to David Karsner, 30 July 1922, *Gentle Rebel*, 210; Eugene Debs, "The Plutocratic Press and Its Prostitutes," *Social Revolution*, July 1917, 3.

236. Eugene Debs, "Otis Still at Large," *National Rip-Saw*, January 1916, 3.

237. Eugene Debs, "A Matter of Principle," *National Rip-Saw*, July 1914, 3.

238. Eugene Debs, "The Rockefellers," *National Rip-Saw*, November 1915, 3.

239. Eugene Debs, "Judge Dayton's Infamy," *National Rip-Saw*, July 1914, 3.

240. Eugene Debs, "Conviction of William Sanger," *National Rip-Saw*, November 1915, 3.

241. Eugene Debs, "Arouse, Ye Slaves," in *Debs Speaks*, 146.

242. Eugene Debs, "Labor the Giant," *National Rip-Saw*, May 1914, 3.

243. Eugene Debs, "Uniformed Brutes," *National Rip-Saw*, May 1914, 5.

244. Eugene Debs, "Pat Quinlan Still Lives," *National Rip-Saw*, October 1916, 4.

245. Debs, "Uniformed Brutes," 4–5.

246. Eugene Debs to William E. Sweet," 28 August 1915, *Gentle Rebel*, 104.

247. Eugene Debs, "The Armor Plate Robbers," *National Rip-Saw*, March 1916, 4.

248. Eugene Debs, "There's a Difference," *National Rip-Saw*, May 1914, 4.

249. Eugene Debs, "The National Campaign," *National Rip-Saw*, September 1916, 3.

250. Eugene Debs, "A.F. of L. Convention," *National Rip-Saw*, January 1915, 4.

251. Debs, "The Outlook for Socialism in the United States," in *Debs Speaks*, 60. The first six paragraphs of this speech are built on alliteration, most involving intricate combinations of sounds as illustrated in this example. In this example, and in the remaining

examples in this section (unless otherwise noted), certain letters and words have been italicized to highlight the stylistic devices employed by Debs.

252. Debs, "The Western Labor Movement," in *Debs Speaks*, 87.

253. Eugene Debs, "Letter of Acceptance," *National Rip-Saw*, May 1916, 19.

254. Eugene Debs, "Training Children in Murder," *Social Revolution*, April 1917, 4.

255. Eugene Debs, "Dare to Be a Coward," *Social Revolution*, March 1917, 6. For other particularly colorful examples of Debs's use of alliteration, see Debs, "Piracy Masked as Patriotism," 1; Debs, "President Wilson and the Mexican Muddle," 3; Debs, "Letter of Acceptance," *National Rip-Saw*, 19; Debs, "The Armor Plate Robbers," 4; Debs, "The Rockefellers," 3; Debs, "Uncle Sam's Hop Pickers," 3; Debs, "Capitalism Self-Condemned," 4; Debs, "The Outlook for Socialism in the United States," in *Debs Speaks*, 60; Debs, "Industrial Unionism," in *Debs Speaks*, 139; and Debs, "On Race Prejudice," in *Debs Speaks*, 99.

256. Eugene Debs, "The Majority Report Should Prevail," *Social Revolution*, June 1917, 1.

257. Kautsky, *The Class Struggle*, 63 (emphasis added).

258. Simons, *Class Struggles in America*, 101.

259. "Unionism and Socialism," in *Writings and Speeches*, 124. See also, "The Canton Speech," in *Debs Speaks*, 271. If the metonymy was characteristic of Debs, the idea was common in socialist thinking. For example, see Upton Sinclair, *The Jungle*, Signet ed. (New York: New American Library, 1960), 126, 137, 142, 338.

260. Simons, *Class Struggles*, 101.

261. Kautsky, *The Class Struggle*, 43.

262. Eugene Debs, "Gompers and His 'Successful' Leadership," *National Rip-Saw*, July 1916, 6.

263. See, for example, Eugene Debs to Peter Damm, 22 April 1905, *Gentle Rebel*, 40–42. In this letter, Debs goes on at some length on Gompers's role, concluding: "These gentlemen ['Mr. Gompers and his Executive Board'] did what they had made up their minds from the start to do. They decided against the strike and turned down the strikers and thus delivered one of the final blows that crushed the strike," (41).

264. Eugene Debs to Robert Hunter," 4 February 1910, *Gentle Rebel*, 63.

265. Walter B. Emery, "Samuel Gompers," in *A History and Criticism of American Public Address*, ed. William Norwood Brigance (1943; reprint, New York: Russell and Russell, 1960), 2:557–79. A third volume was published under the editorship of Marie Hochmuth [Nichols] in 1955, but no additional labor spokespersons were included.

266. Herold Truslow Ross, "Eugene Victor Debs: Spokesman for Socialism," in *American Public Address: Studies in Honor of Albert Craig Baird*, ed. Loren Reid (Columbia, Mo.: University of Missouri Press, 1961), 273. Though the original publication date of this volume is considerably later that the original publication of the Brigance volumes, according to the editor's foreword, it is their near contemporary in conception (Reid, foreword to *American Public Address*, vii). Ronald Lee and James Andrews, writing thirty years after Ross, recapitulate and amplify Ross's assessment, adding acknowledgment of history's increasingly complicated evaluation of Debs. Lee and Andrews maintain that the current view of Debs is the result of a rehabilitation effort by liberal historians. Lee and Andrews, "A Story of Rhetorical-Ideological Transformation," 20–37.

267. Joseph G. Rayback, *A History of American Labor* (New York: Macmillan, 1966), 350–427.

268. Debs, "The Socialist Party's Appeal (1908)," in *Debs Speaks*, 162.

269. Paul Blumberg, *Inequality in an Age of Decline* (New York: Oxford University Press, 1980), quoted in Paul Fussell, *Class: A Guide through the American Status System* (New York: Summit Books, 1983), 15.

270. Salvatore, *Eugene V. Debs*, 344.

271. Kenneth Pins, "Battleground 1992 Finds U.S. Voters in a Quandary," *Des Moines Register*, 16 January 1992.

272. These themes were the common currency of the 2000 election. For example, see: Ian Christopher McCaleb, "Gore Says Bush Waging 'Class Warfare'; Bush Looses Blistering Battleground TV Ad," www.cnn.com/2000/ALLPOLITICS/stories/10/31/campaign.wrap/index.html (5 May 2002); David Greenberg, "What Bush Means When He Accuses Populist Gore of 'Class Warfare,'" slate.msn.com/?id=88669 (5 May 2002); Ralph Z.

Hallow, "Bush Hits Speech for Divisiveness," *Washington Times* (19 August 2000), A1; "Blueprint for the Middle Class: Real Plans for Real People," www.issues 2002.org/2001/Blueprint.html (5 May 2002).

273. Brigance, Introduction to *A History and Criticism of American Public Address*, viii.

W. E. B. Du Bois, Double-Consciousness, and Pan-Africanism in the Progressive Era

Robert E. Terrill and Eric King Watts

8

Theodore Vincent has noted that "in Black American history there are two personal feuds which stand out beyond all others, W. E. B. Du Bois vs. Booker T. Washington and W. E. B. Du Bois vs. Marcus Garvey."[1] If these feuds were only personal, of course, then today they would be a mere historical curiosity, marginalized men in heated disagreement about matters important only to them. But these were public disputes, carried out through various forms of public address—speeches, essays, and articles. While the combatants did engage in a certain amount of ad hominem, they mostly were arguing about what sort of public action African Americans should undertake to improve their situation in the United States. The themes and proposals that emerged during these debates reverberate throughout twentieth-century American race relations.

A comprehensive review of the issues argued within these debates is impossible. Du Bois and Washington disagreed primarily about what sort of education was appropriate for African-American youth, but of course this topic touched upon nearly every other aspect of African-American cultural life. Du Bois argued with Garvey about the efficacy of attempting to leave America for Africa, but these arguments were tinctured with issues of class and authority. We take as our focus the ways in which these men constructed for their audiences particular perceptions of African-American identity.

We capitalize on Du Bois's participation in both of these debates to use "double-consciousness" as our organizing thematic. Du Bois introduced this concept in his 1903 collection of essays titled *The Souls of Black Folk*, where it was intended to be juxtaposed against what Du Bois saw as Washington's narrow single-mindedness. Almost from its inception, double-consciousness became a trope of African-American identity that resonated particularly strongly with intellectuals and critics.

Today, it inhabits literary theory and cultural criticism as a central, though contested, hermeneutic device. Though double-consciousness has been engaged by many writers as an analytic heuristic, its effectiveness as a trope of public address has not been investigated. Thomas C. Holt has argued that to understand Du Bois, "one must endeavor to read his eloquent texts against the gritty backdrop of the organizational confrontations that simultaneously engaged him."[2] Concepts such as double-consciousness were not developed by Du Bois in the vacuum of the ivory tower, but instead were fashioned in the heat of political battle. By examining double-consciousness in this way, as a rhetorical trope manifested in the public discourse of W. E. B. Du Bois during the Progressive Era, we illustrate both the possibilities and the limitations of double-consciousness with regard to its potential to define an audience and foment action.

Both the critical utility and the contested nature of double-consciousness are illustrated in a recent exchange between rhetorical critics Stephen Browne and James Darsey. Browne discerns in Du Bois's essay "Of the Wings of Atalanta," the fifth chapter of *Souls*, three narrative strands, which he calls "the New South," "the Gospel of Wealth," and "Utopian Atlanta." On Browne's reading, the last of these narratives proposes an answer to the problem posed by the other two: how to craft a viable racial identity within the alienation of the modern city. He suggests that Du Bois's essay both endorses and enacts a certain form of double-consciousness as a proper and fitting response to this alienation. In other words, the form and the content of this essay argue for a "doubled" understanding of the modern city, one that straddles both the narrative of "the New South" and the narrative of the "Gospel of Wealth" without fully endorsing or rejecting either. As Browne puts it, Du Bois's essay suggests that the "capacity to anticipate and act upon a world not of one's making . . . is most fully realized when engaging both worlds at once."[3]

Darsey, responding to Browne, provides a more complex understanding of double-consciousness, suggesting that it provides "the perspective of no one, of one whose identity is not fixed or certain."[4] Yet this double-consciousness "does not entail homelessness" so much as "it entails a community required to see itself, at least part of the time, as an outsider would see it."[5] Like Browne, Darsey identifies the place of this "outsider" as defined by and attainable through education; it is through education that one is able to rise above the "veil," the central metaphor for racial estrangement that informs much of *Souls*. "Here, then," Darsey writes, "at last we have found Du Bois's home, above the Veil . . . a home beyond the color line, indeed beyond any provinciality."[6] Darsey shows how double-consciousness can be redrawn as lying not only between white and black, and not merely between dominant and oppositional urban narratives, but rather between a sort of "universal" culture above the "veil" and "the world as it is" below. The university, wherein this universal culture can be obtained through a broad-reaching education, is the earthly representation of this utopia.[7] It could be added, of course, that Du Bois surely understood also that the university often makes promises to African Americans that other institutions and mores deny.

Browne's essay demonstrates the usefulness of the concept of double-consciousness as a tool of critical textual explication. Throughout his analysis, Browne illustrates the way that double-consciousness is both instantiated and advocated within an exemplar of Du Bois's discourse. He argues that double-consciousness "describes not only a condition of being but also a means to imagine, structure, and express a certain view of the world."[8] In other words, Browne's critique shows one way in which double-consciousness might function as a rhetorical trope of African-American identity. Darsey's essay draws more broadly upon *Souls* to show that double-consciousness can be seen as expressing a more radical rhetorical position, neither consigned "to the world as it is" nor divorced from a "sense of political obligation"—in other words, Darsey suggests that an identity defined by double-consciousness *vacillates* between the idealized and the political.

We do not suggest that either of these readings is somehow "incorrect." Indeed, this essay is similar to both Browne's and Darsey's in that we, too, read exemplars of Du Bois's discourse carefully as a way to reveal the complexities of double-consciousness. However, we intend to extend our understanding of this term in two ways. First, we provide a thorough review of some recent critical engagements with double-consciousness, specifically to show that this concept and Du Bois's appropriation of it cannot be divorced from his academic training or from the racial politics of the Progressive Era. In fact, part of the doubleness in Du Bois's discourse might be a reflection of his inability, as a rhetor, to reject completely the assumptions of his day; Du Bois is striving to redefine key concepts such as racial identity, but to be effective every bold move that breaks new ground must remain rooted in the expectations of his contemporary audience.

Second, we challenge these recent critiques. Adolph Reed, for example, notes that "the double-consciousness notion by and large disappeared from Du Bois's writing after 1903," and he goes on to argue that, therefore, the effort of many contemporary theorists and critics of African-American discourse to extrapolate from Du Bois's writings a general theory of the African-American experience is misguided and, perhaps, dangerous.[9] We believe that Reed is mistaken when he suggests that this invalidates double-consciousness as a discursive concept; as Browne and Darsey have illustrated, double-consciousness remains useful as an interpretive paradigm, whether or not Du Bois one day abandoned it. Furthermore, we argue that rather than disappearing, double-consciousness was refigured in Du Bois's thought as Pan-Africanism. Thus, we augment our understanding of double-consciousness by viewing Du Bois's developing interest in Pan-Africanism during the first two decades of the twentieth century as a concrete instantiation of this concept.

Because Du Bois's personal history is so integral to his development of double-consciousness, we begin with a brief biographical sketch, concentrating on his early childhood and his education. Then we turn our attention to the way that *The Souls of Black Folk,* and the concept of "double-consciousness" that it introduces, is a product of Du Bois's intellectual milieu and the Progressive Era. We divide manifestations of double-consciousness into "internal" and "external," the first being an inner reflection of the second. We use this division to explore the implications of Du Bois's "veil" metaphor as it relates to Pan-Africanist thought, especially as it entails a romantic racial essentialism. Having thus laid the theoretical groundwork, we turn our attention specifically to Du Bois's public feuds with Washington and Garvey. Throughout, we suggest that while double-consciousness does provide a useful critical lens for revealing and exploring the complexities of the African-American experience, it seems not so effective as a rhetorical stance around which to assemble political action or through which to attempt social change. It prizes an ability to remain affiliated with, but uncommitted to, various ideological frameworks, but rhetorical success of a material kind might require becoming firmly grounded somewhere.

Doubled Life: Du Bois until 1903

In the opening paragraphs of his first autobiography, Du Bois described modern society as an organism and depicted himself—and all of black America—as one of the "rejected parts" of the social body, whose function it was to inform the remainder of disease. For Du Bois, the moral charge to tell of the ills of society began early in Great Barrington, Massachusetts, rooted in a fundamental belief in liberal democracy.

Born of Mary and Alfred Du Bois in 1868, William Edward Burghardt was reared in western Massachusetts in a town populated by farmers and artisans. The two principal sites of socialization for the young Du Bois in Great Barrington were the high school and town hall, foreshadowing the two principal interests, education and political action, between which he would vacillate throughout his adult life. Du Bois's fervent participation in school and in town meetings constituted a synergism between his critical voice and his mind that made civil interchange a concrete and practical requirement. For example, while in high school Du Bois witnessed repeated assaults on the patience of town folk at town meetings by "a particularly dirty, ragged, fat old man" who emerged from the woods to deplore public education. "Yet the town heard him gravely . . . and when he was through, they calmly voted the usual funds for the high school. Gradually as I grew up, I began to see that this was the essence of democracy: listening to the other man's opinion and then voting your own, honestly and intelligently."[10]

It is difficult to ascertain when Du Bois first recognized that racism and discrimination virtually prohibited him from participating in this sort of rational and ethical practice in the American polity. In *The Souls of Black Folk*, Du Bois invented a childhood moment when the revelation of the color line came upon him "all in a day, as it were"; a little white girl refused his greeting card "peremptorily, with a glance."[11] However, in his later autobiographical projects, the incident in *Souls* became incidental to descriptions of "picnics and festivals" in which Du Bois "took part with no thought of discrimination on the part of my fellows."[12] The apparent inconsistency itself may be a symptom of Du Bois's larger unwillingness to decide firmly whether he was inside or outside of the dominant culture.

Du Bois's experiences in the South only provided further grist for this sort of wavering stance. After graduation from Great Barrington High and following some financial finagling, he secured a scholarship to attend Fisk University in Nashville, Tennessee. Before going to college in 1885, Du Bois considered the entire world from the vantage point of Great Barrington, with occasional wider vistas provided by his job as a local correspondent of the *Springfield Republican*. But as his train crossed the Mason-Dixon Line, this world changed forever. Du Bois's "spiritual isolation" and parochialism were shattered by the voices and faces of black students who were familiar to the New Englander, but also vastly different.[13] Du Bois was astonished by the rich variety of "extraordinary colors" of black men and by the opulence of black girls, "the never-to-be-forgotten marvel . . . of the most beautiful beings God ever revealed to the eyes of 17."[14] Perhaps more significant than the racial sights revealed to Du Bois upon arriving at Fisk were the sounds of blackness, which called for a reevaluation of cultural affiliation. The renowned Fisk Jubilee Singers not only demonstrated the commercial benefits of black folk culture by raising impressive funds for the university, but their sorrowful songs kindled in Du Bois "a new loyalty and allegiance [that] replaced my Americanism: henceforward I was a Negro."[15]

Du Bois excelled at Fisk, capturing the admiration of classmates and professors. His studies further contributed to the development of a doubled perspective, since Fisk's President Cravath and Dean Spence were thoroughly committed to developing "African American versions of New England ladies and gentlemen—Black Puritans or Afro-Saxons, as they were sometimes half mockingly called."[16] In a sense, then, Du Bois was contrasted against himself in Tennessee. His adoration of and faith in European culture was strengthened by Fisk's emphasis on the classics—Greek and Latin—even while his exposure to the lived experience of black folk in the post-Reconstruction, "Jim Crow" American South made him skeptical of classical philosophy's ability to rationalize human oppression. Du Bois internalized this schism, taking it back to Massachusetts when he ventured into Harvard Yard.

Du Bois enrolled as a junior in Harvard College in 1888 and graduated cum laude with a B.A. in philosophy in 1890. In his autobiographies, Du Bois's accounts of his Harvard days reveal a serious scholar who was not fazed by the social isolation imposed on him by his white classmates. "In general," Du Bois wrote later, "I asked nothing of Harvard but the tutelage of teachers and the freedom of the library. I was quite voluntarily and willingly outside its social life." He protested, perhaps too much, that "this cutting off of myself from the white fellows, or being cut off, did not mean unhappiness or resentment. . . . I was in Harvard," he concluded, "not of it."[17]

The special tutelage of George Santayana, who instructed Du Bois in German philosophy, and William James, his professor in psychology and pragmatics, left a profound imprint—one that can be perceived in his commencement address, "Jefferson Davis as a Representative of Civilization." In this important speech, Du Bois utilized a rhetorical strategy he would later perfect in his attacks on the proponents of Washingtonian policies and programs. By characterizing Jefferson Davis as an exemplar of Anglo-Saxon culture, Du Bois was able to coax an audience into questioning the criteria recommending such a brutish model of the "Strong Man." Moreover, Du Bois reconstituted the dignity of the "Submissive Man" in a racialized version of Hegel's master-slave dialectic. Authorized by Hegel's phenomenology, Du Bois's political history logically premised black folk culture as the means for revising the standards of civilized living.[18] Du Bois's "Jefferson Davis" was received enthusiastically and helped pave the way for the funding of his doctoral studies at Harvard.

The transition to graduate school also brokered a change in primary intellectual interest, one that again contributed to a doubling of perspectives. Perhaps Du Bois's mentoring relationships with James and Santayana should have primed him to become a philosophy major, but James diverted him: "'If you must study philosophy you will; but if you can turn aside into something else, do so. It is hard to earn a living with philosophy.'"[19] David Levering Lewis is skeptical of Du Bois's explanation, or of James's motives, believing instead that Du Bois's scholastic record showed a dull sort of promise in philosophy.[20] At any rate, Du Bois studied politics and, under the guidance of Albert Bushnell Hart, history. In 1891, Du Bois earned his master's degree and worked on his thesis, "The Suppression of the Slave Trade to America." Upon learning of the Slater Fund for the education of qualified blacks, Du Bois launched a letter-writing campaign to former President Rutherford B. Hayes until, in 1892, he was awarded funds to study abroad.

Du Bois spent two years at the University of Berlin, where Gustav von Schmoller and Adolf Wagner modified his views on the interdependence of economics and politics, and Heinrich von Treitschke idealized the historical process by positing that "history is made by the powerful wills of great men through a process in which the masses play no significant part."[21] Du Bois was greatly impressed with Europe and traveled extensively while in Germany. He also grew more convinced of his uniqueness as a black scholar destined to wield his mighty intellect against the currents of history.[22] This "great man" conception of historical change skirted the boundaries of theology, but Du Bois was a confirmed agnostic: "Du Bois had replaced the notion . . . of God in scholasticism, with the notion of a relativistic prime force whose existence was arrived at by an empirical process that avoided transcendental categories. His concept was man-centered without being egotistical, moral without relying on theism, and categorical without being monistic."[23] In short, signaling another of the points of integration that characterize Du Bois's persona, for him morality was rational.

The development of a rational basis for moral intervention into the historical process was intoxicating for Du Bois—though it was in direct conflict with the sensibilities of Albert Hart, his Harvard dissertation advisor. Hart was trained in a classical Germanic method and believed that the historicity of an event did not admit moral challenges by scholars. He stressed an "objective" approach to historical study: "If Du Bois felt that he had special insight into the question of slavery or of contemporary black life by virtue of his blackness, Hart would probably have assured him that he had none."[24] This assurance was uncomfortable and unrealistic for a black scholar of Du Bois's temperament writing in the Progressive Era. For example, in his doctoral dissertation, "The Suppression of the Slave Trade in the United States, 1638–1870," Du Bois argued that the ineffectiveness of the 1808 federal trade ban was not the result of poor legislation, nor God's designed retribution on the Americas, but represented a moral failure produced by a series of strategic compromises and illegal acts by Northern shipping officials and Southern planters. "The Suppression of the Slave Trade" did more than detail the failure to suppress the slave trade; it empirically documented a moral lack. Thus, epistemologically, it can be read as an attempt to breathe ethical life into the science of history and sociology.

An edict of social reform based on a rational morality strongly charted Du Bois's course as a professor at Wilberforce, at the University of Pennsylvania—where he wrote his groundbreaking study, *The Philadelphia Negro*—and finally at Atlanta University. Between the years 1897 and 1910, Du Bois established a longitudinal sociological study of the Southern Negro, became integral to the Pan-African Congresses, founded the Niagara Movement, edited two periodicals, authored several poems, reviews, and essays, and, of course, gave poignant birth to *The Souls of Black Folk*.

Double-Consciousness, Progressivism, and The Souls of Black Folk

A few pages into *The Souls of Black Folk*, Du Bois wrote what Adolph Reed suggests "is probably . . . the most widely known and most frequently cited statement of any in Du Bois's entire corpus."[25] Sandra Adell notes that the passage is "very famous," and Arnold Rampersad thinks that this is the place at which Du Bois articulates "the most important concept" of that book.[26] Like many before us, we quote these two paragraphs in full:

> After the Egyptian and Indian, the Greek and Roman, the Teuton and Mongolian, the Negro is a sort of seventh son, born with a veil, and gifted with second-sight in this American world,—a world which yields him no true self-consciousness, but only lets him see himself through the revelation of the other world. It is a peculiar sensation, this double-consciousness, this sense of always looking at one's self through the eyes of others, of measuring one's soul by the tape of a world that looks on in amused contempt and pity. One ever feels his two-ness,—an American, a Negro; two souls, two thoughts, two unreconciled strivings; two warring ideals in one dark body, whose dogged strength alone keeps it from being torn asunder.
>
> The history of the American Negro is the history of this strife—this longing to attain self-conscious manhood, to merge his double self into a better and truer self. In this merging he wishes neither of the older selves to be lost. He would not Africanize America, for America has too much to teach the world

and Africa. He would not bleach his Negro soul in a flood of white Americanism, for he knows that Negro blood has a message for the world. He simply wishes to make it possible for a man to be both a Negro and an American, without being cursed and spit upon by his fellows, without having the doors of Opportunity closed roughly in his face.[27]

These paragraphs reveal the polysemic meanings and central tension expressed by double-consciousness as Du Bois develops the concept in *Souls*. On the one hand, it seems almost a blessing, a gift of second sight; African Americans possess particular powers of perception not granted to those of whom society requires a singularly defined identity. But this is a peculiar gift, purchased at the cost of true "self-conscious manhood," because a black man in America is compelled to "see himself through the revelation of the other [white] world." "One ever feels his twoness," if one is African American, because that is the mode of self-consciousness imposed upon African Americans who desire a public voice.

And while this form of identity may be imposed from the outside, that does not mean that those upon whom it is imposed are relieved of the burden of its maintenance. The two ideals are at war within the "one dark body," and coherence is maintained only through "dogged strength." Indeed, this is a heavy price to pay for any "gift" that might have been bestowed, but in the second paragraph the situation is complicated further—the consciousness of African Americans is a paradox. Du Bois reemphasizes and generalizes the "strife" involved in attempting to "merge [this] double self into a better and truer self," but then immediately argues that this merging should not entail the loss of either of the "older selves." One should strive for coherence, but at the same time the split imposed by the dominant culture should be retained. African Americans—especially the relatively privileged class to which Du Bois would direct his appeals for most of his life—must retain both components of their character simultaneously.

If Du Bois is saying that double-consciousness is a gift to be cherished not only by African Americans but also by the dominant culture, then attempts to merge the two halves into a whole are misguided and perhaps futile. If it is a curse, a source of strife that denies to African Americans an authentic vision of themselves, then it should be transcended through a merging of the two halves into a productive whole. The two choices are not necessarily incompatible, but they also do not fit together neatly; each entails a different view of the African-American experience. And that may be Du Bois's point—African Americans are doomed and gifted, and must be provided with the opportunity to be at once "both a Negro and an American." As Ernest Allen Jr. puts it, "What he [Du Bois] wished to eliminate was not the two-fold character of African-American life, but rather its most alienating, imposed characteristics."[28]

Double-consciousness, then, is itself doubled. It entails a motive to preserve some sense of doubleness, while at the same time it decries the inability to achieve coherent identity. Part of the reason for the indeterminacy of double-consciousness as Du Bois developed it lies in its genesis in the cultural and intellectual milieu of the early twentieth century. Du Bois did not invent this concept in a vacuum. Rather, his choice of this terminology to describe the experience of people of African descent in America was a precipitate both of his education and of ideas that were common in the social and critical thought of the day. As Browne points out, it does not diminish "the force of Du Bois's conception to note that versions of it had been circulating for some time," but it does deepen our understanding of double-consciousness to see that Du Bois did not simply appropriate it but rather used it as an inventional resource to generate a racial heuristic.[29]

Preludes to the "Veil"

Dickson D. Bruce Jr. notes that "Du Bois drew on two main sources" for his terminology. "One of these was essentially figurative, a product of European Romanticism and American Transcendentalism"; the other "was initially medical, carried forward into Du Bois's time by the emerging field of psychology."[30]

For Ralph Waldo Emerson, the American transcendentalist, double-consciousness summarized the tension between "the downward pull of life in society . . . and the upward pull of communion with the divine."[31] This is a tension between the actual and the ideal, between the earthbound and the eternal, between world and spirit—also, between public and private. Reed suggests that Emerson eventually resolved this conundrum by advocating that "one 'must ride alternately on the horses of his private and public nature,'" employing first one and then the other of these two selves depending on the circumstances.[32] This is not so much a deliberate act of will as a resignation to accept the essential and inevitable double-consciousness that defines the human condition. Neither self can be fully denied, but, at the same time, neither should always govern one's actions. The moment of transcendence—wherein one becomes a "transparent eyeball" and "part or parcel of God"—is not a moment of Hegelian synthesis but instead an abdication of the self, a loss of identity precisely because this doubled consciousness cannot be resolved while the self is left intact.[33] Darsey notices the echo of this formation in Du Bois's intellectual utopia, where he might walk arm-in-arm with the immortals, and this can be recast as a loss of the public self into the transcendent individual.[34] Du Bois recoiled, however, from the requirement that self need be abdicated through transcendence; the central problem of the African-American experience, for Du Bois, was the formation of a viable public, political identity, and selfless transcendence was not a possibility.

As for the psychological roots of the idea of double-consciousness, these were revealed to Du Bois by his Harvard mentor and teacher, William James. As Bruce points out, "the idea, if not the term" appears in *The Principles of Psychology . . .* published in 1890 at the very time that Du Bois was at Harvard."[35] James argued that "'man has a dual nature, and is connected to two spheres of thought, a shallower and a profounder sphere, in either of which he may learn to live habitually.'"[36] "Healthy consciousness" was the maintenance of an equilibrium, which different individuals are able to maintain to different degrees and through different means—but perhaps most productively through religion.[37] As we have noted, Du Bois was never a religious man, and so he recoiled from Jamesian transcendence just as he did from the Emersonian variety. But the idea that a viable and functional self might be crafted by maintaining a delicate equilibrium recurred throughout Du Bois's writing around the turn of the century.[38]

Whereas Emerson and James articulate a universal component of human existence, presumably common to all folk, Du Bois is interested in articulating an experience that is specific to African Americans. Further, while Emerson and James perceive the essential doubleness of human nature to correspond to a rift in the spheres within which humans are required to operate—the shallower and the profounder, in James's words—Du Bois articulates this doubleness as within, and as essential to, each African-American identity, constructed as a response to cultural exigencies. Finally, and characteristically, Du Bois does not acknowledge any external or formalized system of beliefs that might help him to resolve his two-ness. Only his sheer will holds the two selves together and thus maintains the semblance of a coherent identity; in the face of adversity, only "dogged strength alone" keeps the "two warring ideals" from being "torn asunder."

The "veil" is Du Bois's central metaphor for defining a line drawn through the African-American soul across which these two ideals are at war. Actually, as Donald Gibson points out, in Du Bois's writings during the first decades of the twentieth century the veil has many meanings, and "it is not always entirely clear just exactly what the veil means or where Du Bois stands in relation to it."[39] We limit ourselves to exploring two senses of the veil metaphor, "internal" and "external," especially with regard to Du Bois's attempts to permeate the division named by the metaphor. Du Bois's interest in Pan-Africanism is one such attempt, but it is best understood within the context of his other attempts. In other words, double-consciousness is a relatively empty form that needs to be filled out with realized particulars before it can be most productively appreciated. We consider two such particular manifestations of an "internalized" veil before discussing the "externalized" veil to which they are related.

THE INTERNAL VEIL

First, let us consider the division in Du Bois between scholar and activist, what Rampersad refers to as Du Bois's "divided career." As Rampersad puts it "the tension between his [Du Bois's] academic role and the free expression of his political and cultural views provided the main drama of his intellectual life" during the years that are the focus of this essay.[40] Reed suggests that "Du Bois's career can be read from one vantage point as a series of oscillations between scholarly pursuit and social activism." Such a wedding between scholarship and activism was not uncommon in Du Bois's day; many intellectuals of the Progressive Era showed no "reluctance to intervene in practical affairs."[41]

Further, Du Bois's experience as an African-American intellectual seemed to militate against scholarly isolation. Social science at the turn of the century experienced an epistemological dilemma precipitated by philosophy's inability to account for the troublesome intersection of racism and industrialization, and Du Bois's scholarly training invited him to "attempt to investigate the relationship between the political crisis of race and understanding's failure of confidence."[42] The rationalization of society provided a strong exigence for Du Bois because the demands placed on labor in general placed peculiar stress on black workers, whose progeny were Atlanta University's student body. "There was little danger, then, of my teaching or of their thinking becoming purely theoretical," Du Bois explained in *Darkwater*. "Work and wage were thrilling realities to us all."[43] Though he had once thought that "knowledge based on scientific investigation" was sufficient to combat racism, he had come to realize that the "cure wasn't simply telling people the truth, it was inducing them to act on the truth."[44]

While he did not abandon his commitment to scholarship, Du Bois gradually became a political advocate. Du Bois was frustrated by the state of knowledge regarding black life and blamed, in part, the impersonality of science, arguing that one cannot apprehend the complexity of Negro culture "from a car window."[45] Du Bois "continued to cling" to the scholarly tradition of empirical social scientific research in which he was trained at Harvard and in Germany, but he also increasingly began to produce social critiques that departed from that style so as to escape "complete conformity with the thoughts and confusions of then current social trends."[46] Du Bois wanted to articulate "new questions rather than simply responding to the views of white scholars" about race.[47]

Rampersad suggests that during his formative years at Atlanta University Du Bois carried on "two careers: one as an academic sociologist teaching and editing the Atlanta University Publications, the other as a political and cultural commentator whose *Souls of Black Folk* would establish him as the most insightful interpreter of the black experience on the American scene."[48] Of these two careers, Rampersad points out, "the dimension represented by [Du Bois's] career as advocate and cultural interpreter, poet and visionary, has in many instances proved ultimately more important" than the other.[49] Shamoon Zamir argues that in *Souls*, "Du Bois the theorist of action and Du Bois the idealist philosopher of history begin to give way to Du Bois the poet who tries to contest and appropriate the new universe."[50]

Thus, Du Bois's scholarly writing was not devoid of advocacy, and his more partisan writing was not devoid of scholarship; as Reed notes, "within his writings scholarly detachment and a hortatory posture often coexist even in a single text."[51] In *Souls* and in much of Du Bois's work, his formidable control of the English language allows him to inhabit both the realm of activist engagement and that of scholarly detachment. Through his prose this dichotomy is not resolved, but rather the tension inherent in the division is utilized as a generative force; the "veil" is permeated as scholarship becomes advocacy and advocacy becomes scholarship.

A second, and related, manifestation of the internalized "veil" in Du Bois's writing and thought most directly involves Du Bois's emerging sense of the role of Africa in African-American liberation. Bruce argues that "by double-consciousness Du Bois referred most importantly to an internal conflict in the African-American individual between what was 'African' and what was 'American.'"[52] It is this manifestation of the veil that Rampersad calls "the most acute and therefore, for the artist, the most alluring of black dilemmas, the reconciliation of his troubled presence in white America with his nostalgia for the mythic home from which he was torn."[53] Africa, as Du Bois put it in the long passage we quoted earlier, "has a message for the world"—and specifically, its message is an antidote to what Du Bois perceived as the overly materialistic milieu of the early twentieth century.

To witness Du Bois's most pointed critique of this materialism we must revisit the essay upon which Browne and Darsey concentrate, the fifth chapter of *Souls*, "Of the Wings of Atalanta." "You know the tale," Du Bois declares, but then reminds his readers of it: "how swarthy Atalanta, tall and wild, would marry only him who out-raced her; and how the wily Hippomenes laid three apples of gold in the way. She fled like a shadow, paused, startled over the first apple, but even as he stretched his hand, fled again; hovered over the second, then, slipping from his hot grasp, flew over river, vale, and hill; but as she lingered over the third, his arms fell round her, and looking on each other, the blazing passion of their love profaned the sanctuary of Love, and they were cursed." "If Atlanta be not named for Atalanta," Du Bois closes, "she ought to have been" (64–65). Thus Atlanta becomes a sign for the materialism that Du Bois saw as usurping other, more spiritual goals. "Atlanta," he wrote, "must not lead the South to dream of material prosperity as the touchstone of all success"; but "already the fatal might of this idea is beginning to spread" (66). Indeed, this "lust for gold" already had penetrated beneath the "Veil of Race," and the "ideals" of the black world already had begun to be usurped (67). This was dangerous, in part because such overriding material concerns signified a thorough "Americanization" and a corresponding loss of the ideals that, for Du Bois, defined the African history of the race. It negated the unique "gift" that people of African heritage had brought and could still bring to America.[54]

The antidote to this "Mammonism of America" (68) was the spirituality of the African—the health of the American body politic depended upon the inclusion of African Americans. "For Du Bois," Bruce notes, "the essence of a distinctive African consciousness was its spirituality, a spirituality based in Africa but revealed among African-Americans in their folklore, their history of patient suffering, and their faith."[55] Neither Browne nor Darsey address explicitly the way that this theme is manifested in "Of the Wings of Atalanta," but the forms of double-consciousness that they reveal are parallel to and supportive of this theme. Du Bois had argued in 1897, in "The Conservation of Races"—a speech that we will soon investigate in greater detail—that African Americans are "that people whose subtle sense of song has given America its only American music, its only American fairy tales, its only touch of pathos and humor amid its mad money-getting plutocracy."[56] He wrote similarly in *Souls* a half-decade later that African Americans had brought "three gifts and mingled them with yours: a gift of story and song—soft, stirring melody in an ill-harmonized and unmelodious land; the gift of sweat and brawn to beat back the wilderness, conquer the soil, and lay the foundations of this vast economic empire two hundred years earlier than your weak hands could have done it; the third, a gift of the Spirit."[57]

Elsewhere in *Souls*, Du Bois remembers an African song that his "grandfather's grandmother," who was "seized by an evil Dutch trader two centuries ago," used to sing, and that had been passed down to him through his family. "This was primitive African music," he writes, one of the "songs peculiarly characteristic of the slave" (207–8). This spirit is the great gift that the "African" can contribute to the "American," and as such Du Bois warned in 1897—echoing language he would use in *Souls*—that "it is our duty to conserve our physical powers, our intellectual endowments, our spiritual ideals."[58] Simple or complete racial assimilation was not a goal, nor even an ideal.

As Thomas C. Holt points out, Du Bois's "major biographers . . . portray him lurching between the antithetical and contradictory goals of black nationalism and racial integration."[59] Such a portrayal is a misrepresentation of Du Bois's position as it is articulated in his discourse. As Browne puts it, Du Bois's was a struggle "not for total assimilation, à la Washington, nor for separatism, à la Garvey, but for a world irreducible to those terms."[60] Du Bois was unwilling to withdraw permanently his support for either response to American racism; rather than lurching between extremes, Du Bois was attempting to hold the two in a productive tension parallel to, and supportive of, the tension between his scholarly activity and political activism.

THE EXTERNAL VEIL

The double-consciousness that Du Bois appropriated and modified from Emerson and James divides the soul. It is the inner reflection of another sense of division, an external one dividing not African-American consciousness but the African-American experience. But it is the externalized veil that perhaps most interested Du Bois, the translucent, semipermeable membrane that divides the African American against the dominant culture.

This orientation of the veil metaphor was emphasized when Du Bois introduced the figure in the opening narrative anecdote of *Souls*, the passage describing the peremptory glance with which his young white classmate refused his greeting card: "Then it dawned upon me with a certain suddenness," Du Bois wrote, "that I was different from the others; or like, mayhap, in heart and life and longing, but shut out from their world by a vast veil" (4). This is African-American doubleness as alienation, an inability to participate in the dominant culture of one's own country. Du Bois, as a Harvard graduate, may have felt this sort of alienation particularly strongly; if it were not for the fact that he was black, he most certainly would have been accepted into the ranks of the eastern intellectual elite. Instead, he was forced to work at "Negro" colleges in the South and Midwest—a substantial comedown from the prestige and salary that his white classmates at Harvard could have hoped to command. As Lewis describes it, "With no money, Slater Fund debts, no positions available at any white college or university, and rural Tennessee authorities dismayed by a German-trained scholar's offer to teach public school, Du Bois was a perfect illustration of one of Booker T. Washington's jokes about the perils of runaway education."[61] Rampersad notes, similarly, that Du Bois's "anxious search among black colleges for a teaching position" was "a choice forced on him, in spite of his highly sophisticated education, by the racism of his time."[62] Certainly, Du Bois was humiliated at having to ride through the South in segregated railway cars. Indeed, "the issue of Jim Crow public facilities infuriated Du Bois; many decades later he wrote about it in the language not of cool social science but of flesh and blood victimization."[63] In *Souls*, Du Bois wrote of one experience in the Jim Crow car, that "the discomfort lies chiefly in the hearts of those four black men yonder—and in mine" (93).

This manifestation of the veil, then, falls between the races, dividing America into two worlds, one black and one white. In his "forethought" to *Souls*, Du Bois explained that part of the purpose of the book is to leave "the world of the white man" and to step "within the Veil, raising it that you may view faintly its deeper recesses" (1–2). Though Du Bois tells his readers that "I who speak here am bone of the bone and flesh of the flesh of them that live within the Veil" (2), he seems to be able to traverse this barrier between the two worlds, lifting the veil and dropping it again at will. It serves as a literary device, then—a way for Du Bois to accomplish through language what he could not accomplish, for example, on that childhood playground or in that Jim Crow railroad car.

But Du Bois's concept is complex—doubled—for the veil also demarcates a divide that Du Bois unambiguously described as a "problem" to be solved. African Americans certainly should be allowed access to all the privileges and rights that America bestows on its white citizens; on this point, Du Bois was unequivocal. This veil—the one that restrains African Americans from full participation in the dominant culture of the United States—should be erased, transcended perhaps, as both Emerson and James seem to suggest about doubled consciousness.

Du Bois and the Limits of Progressive Era Essentialism

In "The Conservation of Races," Du Bois's explicit linking of things "African" with things "primitive" and therefore "spiritual" thuds against the contemporary ear. Such assertions would be greeted today, by many, as reactionary at least and as racist perhaps. To argue that there is emancipatory potential in such essentialism is to argue against generations of liberal thought and legal decisions.[64] We marshal three considerations, however, to Du Bois's defense; the first two flow from reading Du Bois against the cultural and intellectual background, and the third from a careful reading of this speech text itself.

ESSENTIALISM IN CONTEXT

First, the boldness of Du Bois's argument should not be underestimated. As Allen points out, "Du Bois was the first of any generation of black intellectuals—traditionally assimilationist-minded—to acknowledge publicly that there was something of moral and aesthetic value to be found in African-American folk culture."[65] In an age when African-American folk culture was almost totally rejected as holding any possible intrinsic worth, not only by whites but also by most blacks with access to the public sphere, Du Bois based a substantial part of his challenge to the dominant culture upon folk culture. "It is in this black peasantry, totally disenfranchised, that Du Bois believes the *spirit* of (Afro) American culture resides," and it is the peculiar gift of this spirit that, for Du Bois, warranted the inclusion of African Americans in society.[66]

Interestingly, this element of Du Bois's essentialism supports the permeation of the internal veil that divides the scholar from the "folk" of her or his own race. Zamir suggests that Du Bois himself was going through a process of discovery at the time he wrote *The Souls of Black Folk*, so that "if *Souls* is a journey into the world behind the veil for the white reader, it is also presented as a journey into unknown or half-known aspects of black life for Du Bois himself."[67] Gibson, similarly, suggests that "though Du Bois tells his readers at the beginning of the book that he is going to lift the veil in order to reveal the 'souls of black folk,' it would perhaps be more accurate to recognize that he is also sharing with his readers his *own* discovery of the 'souls of black folk.'"[68] *Souls*, then, is the site of yet another sort of permeation of the veil that Du Bois accomplished through his prose.

The second defense of Du Bois's essentialism that can be culled from his milieu is the simple fact that this manifestation of double-consciousness, like the concept itself, was common among white liberals of Du Bois's day. Reed supplies a great deal of evidence to support his claim that a certain class of Victorian intellectuals were haunted during the Progressive Era with a sense of their own inauthenticity and liminality. He argues that they internalized a "disaffection with the process of social rationalization associated with a consolidating mass industrial society" and became increasingly skeptical regarding society's ability to live up to its claims of perpetual progress.[69] Their own culture was "overcivilized," missing spiritual elements that seemed to exist only in more "primitive" cultures. "Their perception of their own lives as unreal," Reed argues, "presumed a sentimentalized view of lower-status 'others' considered less complex or cultivated."[70] James believed that the "integrity of the instinctive reactions, this freedom from all moral sophistry and strain, gives a pathetic dignity to ancient pagan feeling," and Jane Addams "acknowledged a preference in her work for recent immigrants over second- or third-generation ethnics because the former were 'more natural and cast in a simpler mold.'"[71] "Du Bois," Reed argues, "was part of a cohort of university-trained, reform-oriented, typically eastern intellectuals who mainly came to maturity during the last years of the nineteenth century and the first years of the twentieth and who shared a loosely defined outlook and intellectual and political *problematique*."[72]

It is not surprising, then, that Du Bois's own work recreated the assumptions of this cohort; "Of the Wings of Atalanta" easily can be read as just this sort of recreation. It is perhaps even less surprising that many liberal whites of the Progressive Era responded positively to Du Bois's writing. As Zamir points out: "At a time when the vast majority of African-Americans were illiterate or barely literate, and when the majority of literate southern whites were hardly interested in a book like *Souls*, Du Bois's audience was made up largely of northern middle-class and probably liberal whites."[73] This was an audience afflicted with "a real hunger . . . for a revival of the spiritual," and with whom Du Bois would have a problematic relationship throughout much of his life.[74]

ESSENTIALISM ARTICULATED

The third consideration that can be brought to the defense of Du Bois's essentialism is the manner in which Du Bois actually articulated this essentialism in "The Conservation of Races," delivered as an address in 1897 and then published as the second of the "occasional papers" of the American Negro Academy. In it, Du Bois did argue for a sort of essentialism, but in the carefully balanced style that characterized so much of his writing during this period. Of particular interest is his effort to work out the relationship between the biological determinism prevalent in the scientific discourse of his day and a more radical, sociohistorical definition of race.[75] Thus, Du Bois here was unwilling—perhaps unable—to reject completely the essentialist assumptions of his day but tempered their biological basis with sociohistorical sensitivity.

Du Bois began "The Conservation of Races," characteristically, by noting a dilemma: "the American Negro has always felt an intense personal interest in discussions as to the origins and destinies of races," yet investigations of racial differences have generally been to the disadvantage of African Americans. As a result, African Americans have been "led to deprecate and minimize race distinctions." But, on the other hand, "in our calmer moments we must acknowledge that human beings are divided into races."[76] "The question," he concluded, "which we must seriously consider is this: what is the real meaning of race?" But underlying this dilemma is another one, "that in this country the two most extreme types of the world's races have met," and that "the resulting problem . . . forms an epoch in the history of mankind" (74–75). So there were two dilemmas—one concerning the definition of race, and the other concerning the place of African Americans in America. Du Bois's answer to the first question was patently equivocal: his definition of race entailed both biological and sociohistorical elements. His answer to the second question was highly provocative for its time: African Americans should identify themselves as both Africans *and* Americans.

Du Bois's quest for the "real meaning of race" began where, for most of his contemporaries, it would have ended—biology. Du Bois noted the various scientific criteria that have been established—of "color, hair, cranial measurements and language"—but found them unsatisfactory because, "unfortunately for scientists," they are "most exasperatingly intermingled" (74). The best that can be suggested by science is that "we have at least two, perhaps three, great families of human beings—the whites and the Negroes, possibly the yellow race," but Du Bois went on to suggest that such "purely physical characteristics . . . do not explain all the differences" among the races. The differences that do reliably divide the human race into races "perhaps transcend scientific definition" but, "nevertheless, are clearly defined to the eye of the historian and sociologist" (75).

Du Bois then defined "race" in a way that does not so much break with as question the norms of thought prevalent in his cultural and intellectual milieu, "What, then, is a race? It is a vast family of human beings, generally of common blood and language, always of common history, traditions and impulses, who are voluntarily and involuntarily striving together for the accomplishment of certain more or less vividly conceived ideals of life" (75–76). This definition deserves careful attention. Its dominant stylistic feature, like so many of Du Bois's key passages, is equivocation. To say that a race is "generally of common blood" suggests that there may be some validity in biological determinants of race, while to say that a race is bound by "common history, traditions and impulses" suggests the social and historical criteria he seemed to endorse as an alternative to biological science. Such a group might be striving both "voluntarily and involuntarily," which suggests that at least some aspects of racial definition might not be determined by the race itself; the race might be defined, in part, by the goals it is forced to pursue. And even those goals themselves might be "more or less vividly conceived."

Du Bois demonstrated the superior discerning powers of his definition of race by showing that it yields "eight distinctly differentiated races"—as compared to the three distinguished through merely scientific methods. But Du Bois's new sociohistorical definition did not seem able, by itself, to shoulder the whole burden of race definition. "Certainly," he stated, "we must all acknowledge that physical differences play a great part, and that, with wide exceptions and qualifications, these eight great races of today follow the cleavage of physical race distinctions" (77). But "no mere physical distinctions would really define or explain the deeper differences—the cohesiveness and continuity of these groups," which are "spiritual, psychical, . . . undoubtedly based on the physical, but infinitely transcending them" (77).

Du Bois's repeated use of the term "transcending" is interesting, because he did not actually transcend the biological basis of his argument at all. Rather, the biological and the sociohistorical were always held in tension, being neither resolved through transcendence nor collapsed one into the other. No clear hierarchical distinction was made between them; although the sociohistorical distinctions are "deeper" than the biological distinctions, at the same time they were "based" upon those same biological distinctions.[77]

The political implication of this was that "only Negroes bound and welded together" can "work out in its fullness the great message [they] have for humanity"; therefore, the destiny of African Americans—whom he called "the advance guard of the Negro people"—"is *not* absorption by the white Americans" (79). This argument ended where it began, with African Americans in a fundamental dilemma: "No Negro who has given earnest thought to the situation of his people in America has failed, at some time in his life, to find himself at these crossroads; has failed to ask himself at some time: what, after all, am I? Am I an American or am I a Negro? Can I be both? Or is it my duty to cease to be a Negro as soon as possible and be an American?" (79–80). "It is such incessant self-questioning and the hesitation that arises from it," Du Bois concluded, "that is making the present period a time of vacillation and contradiction for the American Negro" (80).

Du Bois's preferred response to this vacillation was that African Americans participate in the American ideal but at the same time mark off the limits of identification with the white dominant culture beyond which they should not go. "We are Americans," he writes, "not only by birth and by citizenship, but by our political ideas, our language, our religion. Farther than that, our Americanism does not go. At that point, we are Negroes" (80–81). African Americans are "the harbinger of that black tomorrow which is yet destined to soften the whiteness of the Teutonic today." As such, Du Bois continued, African Americans have a "duty to conserve our physical powers, our intellectual endowments, our spiritual ideals" (80). Fully the final one-third of the address consisted of an extended appeal for more and stronger race organizations, both to advance the race within the dominant culture and to defend it against the forces of simple assimilation.

In "The Conservation of Races," then, Du Bois accomplished two tasks: he developed a sociohistorical definition of race and he proposed a solution to the American racial dilemma. But each of these two accomplishments was tempered; his definition of race retained some biological inflection, and his solution to the race problem entailed a continuation of racial differentiation. His essentialism, then, is at least problematized—it is not, for Du Bois, a simple task either to define what general characteristics might be attributed to African Americans or to resolve the relationship between Africans and Americans. So, while placing Du Bois's arguments into the context of his intellectual and cultural milieu brings into relief the boldness of many of his claims, it is also important not to overstate the case. Du Bois's essentialism was balanced, almost tentative, and fraught with tensions never quite fully resolved. Such an inherently unstable stance will prove, as Du Bois's confrontation with Booker T. Washington shows, a problematic foundation upon which to build a rhetorical movement.

Booker T. Washington and Progressive America

Progressive whites can be said generally to have harbored two attitudes toward African Americans: neglect and paternalism. Thomas K. McCraw, for example, suggests that "whatever it may have achieved elsewhere, progressive reform exhibited what several historians have called a 'blind spot' toward the problems of race."[78] Dewey W. Grantham Jr. argues that "despite the comprehensive nature of their proposed reforms, American liberals of the Progressive era gave little attention to the status of the Negro, which all agreed represented one of the nation's social and political problems."[79] And Lewis Gould notes that progressive reformers "overlooked the plight of black citizens and excluded that festering problem from the roster of change."[80] Those reformers who did explicitly attempt to improve the lot of African Americans did so, not surprisingly, from within the dominant racial ideology of the age. Grantham argues that such Progressives as Charles B. Aycock, Edwin A. Alderman, Walter Hines Page, Edgar Gardner Murphy, and Julia Tutwiler may have been genuinely interested in the advancement of African Americans, but it was an interest that was "also paternalistic and philanthropic; their solution lay within the framework of white supremacy."[81] Alex Lichtenstein even suggests that "when it came to the South's 'criminal class'—synonymous, in the minds of reformers, with 'the negro'—the chain gang . . . could operate as a form of state-sponsored noblesse oblige," helping the inherently inferior African Americans learn the advantages of hard work.[82] Raymond Hall thinks that "the Progressive Era may have meant advancement and progress for the nation as a whole, but it was . . . the nadir for black people."[83] David W. Southern makes this point most strongly, arguing that "the progressive movement, the first great liberal movement of the twentieth century, was unmistakably caught up in a powerful tide of racism."[84]

While it is difficult to make sweeping statements regarding the ideological motivations of the Progressives, it seems relatively safe to say that progressive whites, in general, were not explicitly interested in the problems of African Americans and most assuredly not interested in empowering African Americans to define their own issues and plans of action.[85] Thus, while Du Bois's ideas of double-consciousness, and perhaps even his romanticized ideas about Africa, surely resonated with the ideas of many liberal and socially conscious whites throughout the Progressive Era, it is also true that his single-minded concern with resolving American racial problems had little in common with most of what Reed identifies as Du Bois's "cohort." Indeed, in his appropriation of some of the terms and concepts of white intellectuals, he was subverting the paternalistic inflection of much of that thought. It was Booker T. Washington whose ideas on race and racial amelioration fit most comfortably within progressive ideology.

Washington is one of the great enigmas in the African-American political tradition. As John White notes, "there is no scholarly consensus on Booker T. Washington's achievement (or limitations) as a black leader."[86] Louis Harlan, one of Washington's biographers, admits that "he was too complex and enigmatic for historians to know what to make of him."[87] S. Jay Walker perhaps puts it best, noting that "more than half a century after his death, the meaning of Booker T. Washington's career, the career itself and its aftermath, remain a mystery—an enigma only compounded by successive studies."[88] Unquestionably, Washington was an adroit politician, capable of assuaging disparate and potentially hostile audiences; as Lewis suggests, his public rhetoric was a simple and straightforward blend of the "politics of compromise and the mien of ingratiation."[89] But he achieved this effectiveness through a rhetoric of ambiguity and, perhaps, duplicity; his motives and actions were often much more complex than they appeared, and there is compelling evidence to suggest that the face he presented to most of the public most of the time was not the only one available.

For example, his famous declaration in his 1895 Atlanta Exposition Address, that "in all things that are purely social we can be as separate as the fingers, yet one as the hand in all things essential to mutual progress," might easily have been seen as a sell-out to white racists, conceding the issue of civil rights. Indeed, soon after he delivered that speech, he wrote to some concerned white women in Boston to assure them that "if anybody understood me as meaning that riding in the same railroad car or sitting in the same room at a railroad station is social intercourse, they certainly got a wrong idea of my position."[90] On the other hand, at Atlanta Washington might have been deceiving the racist institutions of the South into supporting a program of economic black separatism whose long-range goal was the subversion of those very institutions.[91] The issue is further complicated by the fact that "while Washington publicly seemed to accept a separate and unequal life for black people, behind the mask of acquiescence he was busy with many schemes for black strength, self-improvement, and mutual aid." Indeed, "Du Bois and Washington were secretly cooperating as late as December 1904 in an effort to test the Tennessee Jim Crow law."[92]

The ambiguity may have been strategic, but it was submerged beneath a philosophy to which powerful whites in both the North and the South responded positively. "Southern leaders embraced Washington's philosophy of accommodation with unrestrained glee," and Northern politicians "grabbed the chance to dump the whole race problem into Washington's lap."[93] On the one hand, Washington's message of self-help and economic separatism, which some sympathetic interpreters have suggested qualifies Washington for a place within the black nationalist tradition,[94] "found easy lodgement [sic]" in a progressive rationale that was grounded in the equalizing of opportunity rather than the toppling of a racial caste system. On the other hand, Washington's veneer of conservatism—however deeply ingrained it may have been—helped to make Washington and Tuskegee attractive to those white liberals hoping to support something for the betterment of African Americans without encouraging a cultural revolution. The progressive impulse, after all, was to break the monopolies and expose the corruption that made the playing field uneven—but not to change the boundaries of the field. As Richard Hofstadter explains, the Progressives believed that "if the laws are the right laws, and if they can be enforced by the right men, . . . everything would be better."[95] The movement was reformist, not revolutionary, and called primarily for an end to those practices that prevented the fulfillment of "God's plan for democracy in the New World."[96] In the first decades of the twentieth century, it was far from decided, even among the most liberal of whites, that God's plan included complete equality for African Americans. Washington's ambiguity was a decorous fit within this conflicted liberal milieu and allowed Washington to build what Du Bois called the "Tuskegee machine," largely through the donations of white industrialists.

W. E. B. Du Bois, however, found no such comfort within the limitations placed on African-American identity and self-expression by Washington's manufactured leadership. For Du Bois, Washington's public persona displaced and, thus, hid from white view the troublesome complexities of African-American experience. Because Du Bois believed that double-consciousness, at least in some manifestation, was a necessary and valuable component of African-American identity, he perceived a danger in denying this essential complexity. From Du Bois's point of view, Washington's ambiguous rhetoric denied both the unique identity of African Americans and their unique "gift" to American culture.[97] Du Bois believed that Washington's rhetoric was dangerous because it legitimated a "monolithic" black voice. In its accommodation to white power, it undermined Du Bois's own efforts to constitute an African-American intellectual leadership.

Du Bois initially praised Washington's Atlanta Address, but he almost imme-diately began an ideological drift away from Washington's position.[98] In 1903, the publication of *The Souls of Black Folk* provided the impetus for an increasingly vocal and influential opposition to Washington, which would eventually culmi-nate in the National Association for the Advancement of Colored People (NAACP). The third chapter of *Souls,* "Of Mr. Booker T. Washington and Others," was developed from Du Bois's review of Washington's *Up from Slavery,* which had appeared two years earlier in the *Dial,* but Du Bois had "honed" and "expanded" it to the point that, as Lewis has said, "it was virtually a new piece altogether."[99] Gibson calls this essay "the most arresting chapter of the book"; Rampersad agrees that it is "the most controversial essay and the spearhead of the work" and "the key to the book's political intent."[100] The chapter is an extended and eloquent cri-tique of Washingtonian accommodation, in which Du Bois juxtaposed against Washington's monolithic race leadership a more multivocal model grounded both in his elitist predisposition and in the double-consciousness that he believed char-acterized the African-American intellectual.

This essay is an example of one of those instances in which Du Bois lifts the veil between the scholar and the activist. Rampersad claims that this "is a rigidly unpoetic" essay, and compared to other chapters in *Souls* it does display a more tightly structured sequence of linear argument and narrative.[101] But in and through the elements of this relatively taut structure Du Bois blended the tonalities of aca-demic inquiry with the rhetoric of advocacy. The essay began with and sustained the "scholarly narrative posture or radical of presentation" that Robert B. Stepto finds typical of the book, but it developed into a pointed and controversial criti-cism of Washington's political program.[102] Du Bois's critique of America's materi-alism also surfaced, as did his conflation of Washington's rise to power with the manifestation of this rise of Mammonism. A brief analysis of this chapter is war-ranted, then, because it illustrates both the contours of Du Bois's opposition to Washington and the limitations of this opposition.[103]

DU BOIS READS WASHINGTON:
SCHOLARLY DETACHMENT AS CRITICAL DEVICE

Du Bois began "Of Mr. Booker T. Washington" by remarking that "the most strik-ing thing in the history of the American Negro since 1876 is the ascendancy of Mr. Booker T. Washington. . . . Mr. Washington came, with a single definite pro-gramme, at the psychological moment when the nation was a little ashamed of having bestowed so much sentiment on Negroes, and was concentrating its ener-gies on Dollars."[104] These sentences show Du Bois observing the coming of Wash-ington from a safely academic distance, insulated both from the historical moment and from Washington's influence. From this perspective, Du Bois perceived Wash-ington not as an agent—his emergence was not even an event but a "thing"—but as a by-product of America's shifting interest from Negroes to dollars. Further, this passage suggested that Washington's rise as a leader corresponded to a regression in the fate of his people. Also of note is Du Bois's characterization of Washington's program as "single" and "definite"—a narrow program against which Du Bois jux-taposed his own more multivocal opposition. These opening sentences anticipated a number of key themes that persisted through the essay: that Washington's pro-gram was a passive accommodation to external circumstances; that his leadership was sponsored by sources outside the African-American community; that it was ex-cessively narrow and single-minded; and that it had a decidedly regressive aspect.

As Du Bois next approached the task of explaining Washington's rise, he retained the voice of academic detachment that he established in the opening sentences—the reader is invited to approach the text as historical and sociological diagnosis rather than as partisan argument. Du Bois noted that the seemingly impossible task of winning the "sympathy and cooperation of the various elements comprising the white South" was accomplished by the essential ambiguity of Washington's speech, as it could be decoded by both Southern radicals and conservatives to their own satisfaction. Washington has become, Du Bois added with deadpan irony, "the most distinguished Southerner since Jefferson Davis" (31). Furthermore, not only has Washington "won the applause of the South," but he also has gained the "admiration of the North" because he "intuitively grasped the spirit of the age which was dominating the North" and learned its "speech and thought of triumphant commercialism and the ideals of material prosperity" (31).

But, in thus learning the language of the whites Washington had "silenced . . . the Negroes themselves." In the face of this synthesis of the forces outside the veil, the African-American community within it could only murmur for a moment in confusion and then be quiet. Because Washington's leadership allowed no other voices to be heard, and because his voice was in such perfect harmony with the white North and South, Washington became "the one recognized spokesman of his ten million fellows" (32). The tale of Washington's methods, then, reveals leadership that silences a community through accommodation to forces external to it.

Thus far in the essay Du Bois maintained a highly objective, disinterested prose style, and he yet retained that style while he discussed two more items before he adopted a more partisan tone. First, he outlined a general view of the role of criticism in a free society. Du Bois warned that the "hushing of the criticism of honest opponents is a dangerous thing," that "honest and earnest criticism from those whose interests are most nearly touched,—criticism of writers by readers, of government by those governed, of leaders by those who are led,—this is the soul and safeguard of modern society" (33). African-American interests are served best when African Americans choose their own leaders through an applied criticism, and in turn such a critical practice also best safeguards the larger modern society. Monolithic, unilateral leadership is good for no one, but perhaps especially not for African Americans. The white world, Du Bois implied, retains its power in part *because* it allows a multiplicity of voices; however they differ in other respects, white Southerners and white Northerners both are free to express critical judgments. On the other side of the veil there is only silent opposition.

Second, Du Bois placed Washington against a tradition of African-American protest rhetoric. The detached, scholarly voice was still in evidence as Du Bois described two attitudes of protest: "revolt and revenge" and "adjustment and assimilation" (34). Then he described a third course, a middle view, which he aligned with Frederick Douglass and called "a new period of self-assertion and self-development." This middle course, perhaps because it is most amenable to a doubled stance, embodies the tension between revolt and assimilation. This is the mode of protest with which Du Bois aligned himself, together with "the educated and thoughtful colored men in all parts of the land," who are experiencing "a feeling of deep regret, sorrow, and apprehension at the wide currency and ascendancy which some of Mr. Washington's theories have gained" (33).

DU BOIS READS WASHINGTON:
CRITICAL PRACTICE AS SOCIAL ACTIVISM

Du Bois had not yet presented an extended critique of Washington, but now he seemed ready to do so. His preparation touched upon several central themes that characterized his rhetoric during the Progressive Era. First, he has argued for the importance of the voice of scholarly critique, and specifically for a critical voice centered between unproductive extremes—one perhaps especially inviting a doubled perspective. Second, Du Bois has mined the resources of African-American history, positioning his own discourse as a continuation of what he sees as one of the three African-American rhetorical traditions. The potential power of his own critic-activist stance, and presumably that of other African-American intellectuals, flows from within the race; positioning his critique of Washington as a continuation of this rhetorical tradition is consistent with his numerous claims throughout this era that African-American history harbors a potent "gift." Finally, Du Bois has demonstrated his ability to maintain the distanced stance of the academic, coolly surveying the territory from the window of his ivory tower. In the second half of the essay, however, Du Bois at last donned a more activist, personal, and partisan critical voice. The academic gloves came off, and Du Bois presented himself and self-assertive protest as the key to resisting Washington's monolithic leadership.

Du Bois retained from his nonpartisan stance his stated preference for a balanced position between extremes. Recall that Du Bois placed Washington in the least acceptable of three rhetorical traditions, that of total race assimilation. Here, he noted that Washington's extreme position has been "the object of criticism by two classes of colored Americans" (38). The criticisms of those at the opposite extreme of "revolt and revenge" might be dismissed, because "they hate the South blindly and distrust the white race generally" and favor "emigration beyond the borders of the United States" rather than an attempt to resolve the American race issue. Any such strategy is anathema to Du Bois, as is evident in his later critique of Marcus Garvey. On the other hand, those critics of Washington who favor self-assertion—those who occupy the middle ground where Du Bois has placed himself—demand an audience.

Advocates of this middle position, Du Bois wrote, "do not ask that ignorant black men vote when ignorant whites are debarred," but only that black men vote; they agree that "the low social level of the mass of the race is responsible for much discrimination against it," but that the lack of civil equality is "more often a cause than a result of the Negro's degradation"; and "they advocate, with Mr. Washington, a broad system of Negro common schools" but insist that such schools must rest on "the well-equipped college and university" (38–39).

Du Bois has provided a voice of critique not before heard, that of the African-American intellectual. But Du Bois has rooted this critical stance in an African-American tradition of self-assertive protest, and thus has empowered himself from within a tradition that Washington has abandoned. The vitality is evident in the text. The men he speaks for, Du Bois insisted, "are absolutely certain that the way for a people to gain their reasonable rights is not by voluntarily throwing them away and insisting that they do not want them; that the way for a people to gain respect is not by continually belittling and ridiculing themselves; that, on the contrary, Negroes must insist continually, in season and out of season, that voting is necessary to modern manhood, that color discrimination is barbarism, and that black boys need education as well as white boys" (39). At the same time, it is also evident that Du Bois was maintaining a critical high ground, eschewing one-sided polemic in favor of a balanced, "broad," or perhaps doubled critical stance. It is through criticism of this sort that he opposed Washington from within a black perspective, but as the essay concludes it seems that this mode of criticism is an agency by which African Americans might, through self-determination, stride across the veil.

The mode of criticism Du Bois has described and engaged in is next advocated as a civic duty. "In failing thus to state plainly and unequivocally the legitimate demands of their people," Du Bois warned, "even at the cost of opposing an honored leader, the thinking classes of American Negroes would shirk a heavy responsibility," one that surmounts divisions of South and North and divisions of attitude within the black race; it is a responsibility men have "to themselves, . . . to the struggling masses, . . . to the darker races of men whose future depends so largely on this American experiment, but especially . . . to this nation,—this common Fatherland" (39). Washington's efforts to appease South and North are not merely irrelevant but also dangerous, for it is because Washington has collapsed into one his roles as national black leader and racial accommodator that African Americans are unable to engage in the self-assertion required of participants in an active democracy. The American public sphere is crippled as a result, denied the gifts that only African Americans can bring. Du Bois called upon African Americans, "by every consideration of patriotism and loyalty," to oppose "by all civilized methods" Washington's course toward "industrial slavery and civic death." "We have no right," Du Bois argued, "to sit silently by while the inevitable seeds are sown for a harvest of disaster to our children, black and white" (40).

The trajectory of Du Bois's "discriminating and broad-minded criticism," which continues the historical trajectory of self-assertive protest, is next able to propel Du Bois across the veil to a position from which the dominant white culture can, and must, be criticized. It is the first duty "of black men to judge the South discriminatingly"; they should praise what is good in the South and "use the same breath" to denounce what is evil. The South needs this sort of criticism "for the sake of her own white sons and daughters, and for the insurance of robust, healthy mental and moral development" (40). Of course, when Du Bois symbolically moved across the veil, he did not fully enter the white world and abandon the black; his was not an assimilationist program. Rather, Du Bois's doubled criticism was turned toward both Washington and the white world. As the essay came to a close, criticism of Washington and of the white South were both advocated by turns, almost in alternating passages. For Du Bois, "the black men of America have a duty to perform, a duty stern and delicate,—a forward movement to oppose a part of the work of their greatest leader" (42). Though Washington's leadership has resulted in some actual advance, and these elements of it should be supported, it has also resulted in some relative retrogression, and these elements of it must be criticized. Telling the difference is delicate, but the criticism must be stern.

End of an Era

Booker T. Washington died late in 1915, having staved off all challenges to his status as the "leader of the race"—at least to the extent that this title was conferred by whites. Manning Marable reports that "Within a decade [of his death], nearly all Washington's former supporters had accepted most of the NAACP's views, and the Du Bois-Washington controversy receded into history."[105]

Perhaps the most essential difference between these two men was in the orientation of their rhetoric. Du Bois was interested in making room for more discourse; it was through continued and increasingly multivocal critique that the race problem might be solved. Washington, however, held what might be termed a "materialist" conception of rhetoric; his discourse was intended to usher into existence things like colleges and carpenters.[106] Washington's public single-mindedness also provided both white and blacks with a focal point that Du Boisian doubleness could never do. Du Bois noted in *Souls* that "it is as though Nature must needs make men narrow in order to give them force," and Du Bois's rhetoric never attained the sort of forceful currency within American culture that Washington's enjoyed (38).

Washington's death created a power vacuum, however, which seemed to suck Du Bois not only further into the public limelight but also into opposition with another charismatic race leader with idealized notions of Africa and African-American history. As Elliot P. Skinner puts it, "The battle waged between W. E. B. Du Bois, a

Harvard- and Berlin-trained natural aristocrat, and Marcus Garvey, a charismatic Jamaican-born immigrant, for accession to the leadership mantle of Booker T. Washington was one of heroic proportions."[107] In the next section, we trace the effects that this heroic feud had upon Du Bois's developing philosophy of Pan-Africanism.

Du Bois before Garvey: Incipient Pan-African Thought

Du Bois's biting criticism of Booker T. Washington and the Tuskegee machine helped to inspire others, including Monroe Trotter and George Forbes, editors of the *Guardian* in Boston, to mount their own attacks on Washington. Trotter was arrested while heckling Washington at a Boston church, sparking a national protest meeting organized by Du Bois. He "asked a group of young Negro intellectuals to meet in Ontario, Canada, in 1905. Here, the delegates initiated a protest organization called the Niagara Movement which, four years later, became the germinal seed for the creation of the National Association for the Advancement of Colored People."[108] The twenty-nine men who met in Fort Erie, Canada, in July 1905—race prejudice forced them across the border from their originally intended meeting site of Buffalo, New York—were brought there by a "call," written and circulated by Du Bois, which echoed the words of *Souls* in its invitation to those who shared an opposition to the "present methods of strangling honest criticism."[109] The second meeting of the Niagara movement took place at Harper's Ferry, West Virginia, the site of John Brown's famous raid, on 15–18 August 1906. At this conference—much more widely attended than the first, though no more widely reported in the Washington-controlled press—a permanent standing committee on Pan-Africanism was established.[110] To provide an editorial voice untouched by the Tuskegee machine, Du Bois and a handful of others founded the *Moon Illustrated Weekly*, which made its debut on 2 December 1905 as the voice of the Niagara Movement. It had a very small circulation, lasted for less than a year, and only four copies are now known to exist—but, as Lewis notes, it "turned the heat up higher and higher on the Wizard [Washington]."[111]

Du Bois's next editorial effort debuted in January 1907. The *Horizon* was, in Lewis's terms, "Du Bois's dress rehearsal for a career in propaganda journalism."[112] It appeared monthly, for the most part, surviving with a short subscriber list and with the infusion of many hundreds of dollars from the personal resources of Du Bois and his two partners, L. M. Hershaw and F. H. M. Murray. Du Bois's editorial column was called the "Over-Look," and it was a digest of announcements, reviews, opinions, and reprints, each under a separate heading—much like the editorial columns Du Bois would later write for the *Crisis*. Periodically interspersed among book and magazine recommendations and local and national news items were, usually under the heading "Africa," bits of information about that continent and its people. Of importance is a progression in these editorial sections from an unspoken assumption that African Americans have a distinct relationship to Africa to an explicit call for a Pan-African self-consciousness. This progression mirrors the relationship between the two arguments of "The Conservation of Races" and the ways that these two arguments are related to double-consciousness: in these *Horizon* editorials, at first double-consciousness was an intrinsic (though tacit) element of the African-American experience, and then it was explicitly advocated as a potentially powerful political stance.

In the very first issue, for example, Du Bois wrote a story condemning America's growing participation in the exploitation of the Congo. This same issue also noted that "there is a land of dark men far across the sea which is of interest to us," the "land of India, the land, perhaps, from whence our fore-fathers came," which is an incipient Pan-Africanist statement of a rather radical tincture for 1907.[113] Du Bois did not make an explicit argument, in these pages, that African Americans should develop any particular relationship to Africa or to Africans; he seemed instead to assume that they already understood such a relationship. He simply delivered the news, mostly in the same sort of academically precise prose he used throughout the first half of "Of Mr. Booker T. Washington and Others."

This academic detachment is not merely an artifact of Du Bois's journalistic style. For many of the short items that he included in his "Over-Look" Du Bois completely abandoned that style, choosing a tone of academic detachment consistently only when writing about Africa. Again in that first issue, for example, Du Bois wrote that "if the truth must be told, Theodore Roosevelt does not like black folk."[114] The April 1907 issue contains other examples of Du Bois's polemical style, as he tells his readers to "buy books. Do not merely read them but buy them, own them, make them yours." He also urges avoidance of the Sunday paper, for "it is an imp of Hell and child of the Devil" (13). By way of contrast, also in the April issue is a much longer and less strident section under the heading "Africa," reporting the new Dutch "sympathetic attitude towards the natives" in the Transvaal, the "state of affairs in Natal," the burgeoning industrial revolution in Nigeria, and the observation that "the outlook for reform in Congo is gloomy." Du Bois closes this entry with a plea: "the American Board of Commissioners for Foreign Missions who have withdrawn all their colored missionaries from Africa are respectfully asked to send them to Belgium, England, Portugal and—Georgia" (13–14). None of this news from Africa contains any explicit argument. The only departure from the studied voice of journalistic detachment is that last word, which is sufficient to suggest an analogy between the European colonial powers and the racist segregation of the United States but still does not endorse any particular point of view or call to action. Regarding the need for African Americans to buy books, Du Bois makes an explicit argument; regarding the need for African Americans to develop a relationship to Africa, Du Bois assumes it.

This stance and tone remained largely constant throughout most of Du Bois's columns in the *Horizon;* when discussing Africa, Du Bois reported on, or reprinted from, other works without comment. In June 1907, Du Bois reprinted a long transcript apparently from an address at the "annual meeting of the Aborigines Protection Society of London," portraying the "situation in South Africa" (20–21). In October of that same year, Du Bois printed a long quotation from a book by Theophilus E. S. Scholes, *Glimpses of the Ages*, which argued persuasively for the "Negro origin of the Egyptians" (32–33). One of Du Bois's strongest statements in the *Horizon* concerning the importance of Africa—but one that retained his characteristic reserve—appeared in the February 1908 issue, in his review of *Fanti Customary Laws* by John Mansah Sarbah. After noting that Sarbah is "a man of pure African blood," Du Bois noted that "the gaze of scholars" has turned toward "the Asian plateaux" in their search for "the cradle of Roman law," but that "if African dialects found the place in European schools which is occupied by Oriental languages, there is no knowing what the result might bring forth" (45–46). Thus, Du Bois prefigured the central argument eventually made at length by Martin Bernal in *Black Athena*.[115]

When Du Bois did break the veil of journalistic objectivity, it was often to draw out instructive parallels rather than to urge that any particular sort of relationship between Africans and African Americans be formed. In March 1908, under the heading "Mulattoes [*sic*]," Du Bois reprinted an article detailing "the fusion of the white and black races" in Cape Colony, South Africa, which made it "quite impossible to draw a color line which would be legally enforceable." Du Bois then commented that "Negroes are going to be men, with every right accorded to modern men. . . . We may not live to see it, but Rome was not built in a day" (50–51). The relevance of South Africa to America is assumed; the parallel that Du Bois was drawing rests upon that assumption.

As Du Bois's tenure as editor of the *Horizon* came to a close, he made more explicit appeals for the support of Pan-African ideals. For example, in the combined November-December issue of 1908, Du Bois urged solidarity and organization among African Americans so that they might more effectively support Liberia. "We must have a second and greater Pan-African movement," he urged. "The cause of Liberia, the cause of Haiti, the cause of South Africa is our cause, and the sooner we realize this the better" (79). This more explicit and strident tone regarding topics pertaining to Africa was a reflection of a shift in Du Bois's tone generally during his last few years before becoming affiliated with the NAACP. For example, in February 1910, under the heading "J'accuse," Du Bois began an explicit and powerful critique of the American South that he revisited several times that year (96). But this shift in tone also indicated Du Bois's gradual movement away from the tacit assumptions of his *Horizon* days and toward the more explicit and radical Pan-African program that would emerge over the next decade. In May 1910, Du Bois announced plans for a "Universal Races Congress" to be held in July 1911 in London. The motivation for this congress, according to Du Bois, was that "the interchange of material and spiritual goods between the different races of mankind has of late years assumed such dimensions that the old attitude of distrust and aloofness is giving way to a general desire for closer acquaintanceship" (107).

The final issue of the *Horizon*, in July 1910, contained a call for its subscribers to "join our membership" in the NAACP (121). Over protests by Ida B. Wells Barnett and Trotter regarding the undue influence of white organizers, Du Bois had accepted the position of director of research and publications in the new organization.[116] For twenty-four years Du Bois served as editor of the *Crisis;* the editorial content of the periodical was dedicated to disseminating information regarding discrimination, legal battles, and black culture. Despite Du Bois's claims that the *Crisis* was a "newspaper," it was in fact and in spirit much more.[117] The journal regularly interpreted events and characters for the purpose of instructing and constituting a racial philosophy to "fight the wrong with every human weapon in every civilized way" (16). Over the years Du Bois's editorials demonstrated a passion and corrosive wit that tunneled into a collective American unconscious, where he understood racist irrationality to fester. The *Crisis* was iconic; it dramatized the salubrious and serious performance of African-American struggles.

If the *Crisis* was a healthy and critical site for Du Bois's intellectual energies, the NAACP was an organization that frustrated and at times threatened to demoralize him. "We had on our board of directors many incongruous elements as was to be expected," Du Bois explained in his *Autobiography.* "Philanthropists like Oswald Villard; social workers like Florence Kelley; liberal Christians like John Haynes Holms and liberal Jews like the Spingarns; spiritual descendants of the Abolitionists like Mary Ovington and radical Negroes. Clashes now and then were inevitable."[118] Friction between Du Bois and various members of the board occurred regularly and over such disparate issues as his membership in the Socialist Party, his domination of *Crisis* editorial content, perceived racism among board members, and perceived hypersensitivity on Du Bois's part.[1193] Not the least source of friction was Du Bois's increasing emphasis on Pan-Africanism; with its focus on the legal requirements of American civil rights, the NAACP had no real interest in the anticolonial efforts of Africa.[120]

The shift in the tone and explicitness of Du Bois's Pan-Africanist arguments represents more than a shift in tactics, and it had effects beyond the board of the NAACP. Du Bois was no longer content merely to point out double-consciousness as a necessary condition of African-American life. Rather, in inviting his readers to accept and indeed to celebrate African connections that he perceived as presently dormant, Du Bois was fostering a form of double-consciousness where it might not otherwise have existed. This shift in rhetorical strategy and tone propelled Du Bois toward the second great clash of his public career, that with Marcus Garvey.

Marcus Garvey

Marcus Moziah Garvey was born in St. Ann's Bay, Jamaica, on 17 August 1887, the youngest of eleven children.[121] He attended the local schools, and perhaps also Birkbeck College in London, but was largely self-educated. At seventeen he left St. Ann's Bay for Kingston, where he honed his oratorical skills by attending the churches of successful preachers and listening carefully to the open-air speakers common in Kingston. In his early twenties, as Garvey traveled, he edited several short-lived periodicals, including *Garvey's Watchman* and *Our Own*, and later, *La Nacionale* in Costa Rica and *La Prensa* in Colon—each a precursor to the enormously successful *Negro World*. In London in 1912, Garvey read Booker T. Washington's *Up from Slavery*; years later, he would testify that after reading that book "my doom—if I may so call it—of being a race leader dawned upon me."[122] Back in Jamaica in 1914, Garvey established the "Universal Negro Improvement and Conservation Association and African Communities League" by publishing a manifesto; this organization and its attendant publications, ceremonies, and business enterprises would occupy most of Garvey's time until his death.

Garvey at first was not particularly successful at recruiting members or gaining financial support for his new organization and concluded that he needed support from African Americans. In particular, Garvey became interested in establishing a Tuskegee-like trade school in Jamaica, and thus wrote to Booker T. Washington seeking support for this idea. Washington, who surely received many such requests, responded politely and promised that if Garvey visited America, then he and his staff would make Garvey's visit "as pleasant and as profitable as we can."[123] In March 1916, Garvey landed in New York City. Booker T. Washington had died late in 1915, leaving an African-American power vacuum; the Ku Klux Klan was in resurgence, wreaking havoc throughout the American South; the "great migration," fueled in part by this increase in race hatred, had transplanted many rural, Southern, and nearly illiterate African Americans to Northern cities. All these factors conspired to create for Garvey a rhetorical situation that he would exploit masterfully.

In January 1918, he established in Harlem the *Negro World*, which within a year was "the most widely read black newspaper in America," and by the middle of 1919 Garvey was claiming over two million members in the American chapter of his UNIA.[124] The Black Star shipping line, which was to be Garvey's most spectacular failure, was established in June 1919. It was intended to carry both freight and passengers to all parts of the world and was to become the cornerstone for black economic independence and nationalism; it was funded through the sale of stock at five dollars per share, and thus was supported almost entirely by blacks. Though the UNIA eventually did purchase three ships, the Black Star Line met with a series of misadventures and near disasters.

A fairly typical example will suffice. One of Garvey's ships, the *Yarmouth*, was commissioned to take a load of whiskey to Cuba just before the Volstead Act went into effect; but only eighty miles offshore, as E. David Cronon tells the tale, "the *Yarmouth*'s engineer opened the sea cocks and an SOS was sent out that the ship was sinking." The crew threw much of the whisky overboard, where it was "at once picked up by a swarm of small boats that for some unexplained reason had been following the *Yarmouth*." Some weeks later, an attempt was made again to complete the journey with what was left of the cargo, "but during the jolly voyage the *Yarmouth*'s undisciplined crew made considerable inroads on the unguarded cargo of whisky and only a fraction of the original shipment was ever unloaded."[125] The captain of the vessel for that second attempt, Hugh Mulzac, tells the story differently, but adds that on the return trip Garvey ordered the *Yarmouth* to visit so many ports as a symbolic gesture that the seven hundred tons of coconuts it was commissioned to deliver to New York rotted in the hold.[126] A few years later, the *Yarmouth*, which had been purchased for $165,000, was sold for $6,000, for scrap.

As Garvey's movement grew, and as it became clear that incidents such as those involving the *Yarmouth* were more the rule than the exception, the UNIA and the Black Star Line began to draw fire from other black leaders. In January 1922, Garvey was arrested on charges of using the mail to defraud—he was accused of misusing money from the sale of stock. A "Garvey Must Go!" movement was begun, led by A. Philip Randolph and Chandler Owen and supported by Du Bois. After Garvey's trial had been delayed for almost a year, a "Committee of Eight" wrote an open letter protesting the delays to Attorney General Harry M. Daugherty. Eventually, Garvey would be convicted, imprisoned in Tombs Prison, and finally deported—both his dreams and the life savings of hundreds of African Americans irrecoverably lost. In the meantime, however, W. E. B. Du Bois brought Garvey into his rhetorical crosshairs.

Du Bois and Garvey

Garvey was almost immediately seen as a rival to Du Bois, having taken up, to some degree, the mantle of Booker T. Washington. Garvey appealed to the masses in a way that the infamously imperial W. E. B. Du Bois never could, and so challenged his ideal of intellectual race leadership in a way similar to Washington. While Garvey never would exert wide control of the black presses as Washington did, he did control his own press, and his *Negro World* had a circulation that easily surpassed that of the *Crisis.* As Rampersad points out, "By 1919, when Du Bois organized his first Pan-African Congress in Paris with the support of the NAACP, there existed two irreconcilable approaches to the 'Negro problem,' each supported by an institutional force."[127] While none of this probably pleased Du Bois, what rankled most was that he found himself in the awkward position of having to respond to allegations that his program was essentially the same as Garvey's. As we have noted, Du Bois's editorial comments on Africa had been shifting over time to a more explicit call for African Americans to recognize themselves as partly African. His increasing emphasis on the important role that Africa should play in the lives of African Americans made it difficult for many, particularly whites, to tell the difference between Garvey and Du Bois.

There were, indeed, substantial similarities in Du Bois's and Garvey's public positions. Skinner notes that "given their differences, both in style and outlook, and their lack of communication except by invective in the pages of the *Crisis* and the *Negro World*, it is surprising how similar the views of Du Bois and Garvey often were regarding the steps necessary to ameliorate the condition of African peoples."[128] Rampersad summarizes the similarities: "Both men saw the world as comprising separate cultures, each reflecting a distinct heritage and demanding freedom of expression. By the early twenties both believed that there are not superior and inferior races in the twentieth century, only temporarily backward peoples. Both saw the speciousness of the Anglo-Saxon claim to superiority based on technological progress usually of a destructive sort."[129] Though Garvey and Du Bois shared many basic assumptions, particularly about the importance of African independence for the eventual liberation of African Americans, the differences between their two programs were vital.

Garvey, working largely from within a black separatist rhetorical tradition, believed that there was no hope for whites and blacks to peacefully and productively inhabit the same country. As Bernard Boxill describes it, the separatist tradition in African-American political thought, unlike the assimilationist tradition, denies that a color-blind society is possible.[130] James Golden and Richard Rieke note that this tradition is based on the assumption that "the prejudice directed at the black man is derived from the color difference," and that attempts to achieve racial equality are necessarily futile; "so long as men are black and white, states this reasoning, they will hate each other."[131] The only solution, therefore, is the separation of the races.[132] Du Bois, over the course of his life, moved in a generally separatist direction. However, during the time of his public disagreement with Marcus Garvey, Du Bois still insisted that it should be possible, as he put it in *The Souls of Black Folk*, for an African American "to be both a Negro and an American, without being cursed and spit upon by his fellows, without having the doors of Opportunity closed roughly in his face."[133] Du Bois was never a simple assimilationist, but he did believe that African Americans should receive equal treatment in the United States.

One primary source of confusion was that Du Bois and Garvey used similar language—sometimes, remarkably so—to describe their programs. For example, Garvey was fond of using the phrase "Africa for the Africans" to describe that part of his agenda which included freeing Africa from colonial rule. The UNIA advocated "the cause of Africa for the Africans—that is, that the Negro peoples of the world should concentrate upon the object of building up for themselves a great nation in Africa."[134] "If Europe is for the white man, if Asia is for brown and yellow men," Garvey explained, "then surely Africa is for the black man."[135] "To us," Garvey said, "the white race has a right to the peaceful possession and occupation of countries of its own and in like manner the yellow and black races have their rights."[136]

In a letter published in June 1921, in the *New York Age*, Du Bois responded to a Bishop C. S. Smith by noting that he "mingles the Pan-African Congress and the Garvey movement as practically one idea. This is a grave mistake. The Pan-African Congress has nothing to do with any 'Africa for the Africans' movement."[137] However, in the February 1919 issue of the *Crisis*, Du Bois had argued for the end of African colonization and used the phrase "Africa for the Africans" to describe this point of view. Later, in 1922, after Garvey had become well known, Du Bois attempted to clarify his point under the heading "Africa for the Africans": "Again the editor distinctly believes that Africa should be administered for the Africans and, as soon as may be, by the Africans. He does not mean by this that Africa should be administered by West Indians or American Negroes. They have no more right to administer Africa for the native Africans than native Africans have to administer America."[138] Later in 1922, Du Bois laid out a "program" for the liberation of Africa and concluded that "after this program has been carefully and devotedly and successfully followed, Africa will belong to the Africans and no man will dare gainsay them—and perhaps no one will want to."[139]

Both men also decried the capitalist exploitation of Africa by white American and European powers. Garvey noted in 1923 that "an open appeal is being made to the white capitalists of different countries to invest in the exploitation of the oil fields, diamond, gold and iron mines of the 'Old Homeland.'"[140] He went on to note that "the British Empire today owes its present financial existence to the wealth which has been recruited from Africa, the wealth that we Negroes could have controlled fifty years ago, when there was not so much interest in Africa."[141] Similarly, Du Bois wrote in the *Crisis* in February 1919 that "What Europe, and indeed only a small group in Europe, wants in Africa is not a field for the spread of European civilization, but a field for exploitation. . . . Greed,—naked, pitiless lust for wealth and power, lie back of all of Europe's interest in Africa and the white world knows it and is not ashamed."[142] Later, in an essay entitled "The Souls of White Folk" and published in his 1920 book, *Darkwater*, Du Bois wrote in words that Garvey almost could have been paraphrasing: "Why, then, is Europe great? Because of the foundations which the mighty past have furnished her to build upon: the iron trade of ancient, black Africa, the religion and empire-building of yellow Africa, the art and science of the 'dago' Mediterranean shore, east, south, and west, as well as north."[143]

Both men, then, evidently believed that African Americans had an interest in a free Africa and used similar terms to describe this interest—but there were two important differences. The first was a difference in motive. For Garvey, the existence of an "Africa for the Africans" was more than a right; it was a necessity. African Americans could never hope to achieve equality or respect in America, so there *had* to be a free and independent Africa as a place of refuge and as an international symbol of race pride. "You and I can live in the United States of America for 100 more years," Garvey argued in 1922, but "so long as there is a black and white population, when the majority is on the side of the white race, you and I will never get political justice or get political equality in this country."[144] The progress of African Americans in America, Garvey proclaimed in 1924, "has been built upon sand." The white man will never tolerate black equality, because "the laws of self-preservation force every human group to look after itself and protect its own interest."[145] Thus, in an essay in which he explicitly attacked Du Bois, Garvey pleaded: "Let the Negro have a country of his own. Help him to return to his original home, Africa, and there give him the opportunity to climb from the lowest to the highest positions in a state of his own."[146] Elsewhere, explaining the aims of the UNIA, he noted that "the Association is determined to bring Negroes together for the building up of a nation of their own. And why? Because we have been forced to it."[147] Garvey's motivational trajectory, then, was traced from the United States and toward Africa; it was because Africa was at a distance from the United States that it was worthwhile for African Americans to support its independence. It represented a destination, partly spiritual and partly physical; its ameliorative powers lay in the possibility of escape.[148]

For Du Bois, on the other hand, at least in the 1920s, Africa was not a destination. Rather, its independence was important because of the meritorious effect it might have on domestic race relations. In December 1918, in a dispatch from aboard a ship bound for Paris for the first Pan-African conference, Du Bois explained the purpose of the conference emphatically as "not a 'separatist' movement." "Once for all," he continued, "let us realize that we are Americans" and that "there is nothing so indigenous, so completely 'made in America' as we. Any ebullition of action and feeling that results in an amelioration of the lot of Africa tends to ameliorate the condition of colored peoples throughout the world." In May 1919, again in the *Crisis,* he explained in detail his motives for going to Paris and concluded that "the world-fight for black rights is on!"[149] He meant that the fight for black rights was global; African Americans were not to support African liberation only because Africa should be free, but also because a free Africa might make it more likely that blacks would be free in America. In 1920, Du Bois wrote that "there can be no permanent uplift of American or European labor as long as African laborers are slaves." In that same essay, Du Bois again made it clear that he is not endorsing a separatist movement, for "this building of a new African State does not mean the segregation in it of all the world's black folk." The motivational trajectory here is from Africa and toward America; the function of a free Africa is to empower African Americans. "The Negroes in the United States and the other

Americas have earned the right," Du Bois wrote, "to fight out their problems where they are."[150]

For Marcus Garvey, African Americans should be identified primarily as Africans because such identification holds the promise of freedom *in Africa*. For W. E. B. Du Bois, African Americans should be concerned with and interested in events in Africa because those events might increase the likelihood of freedom *in America*. African Americans should not resolve their identities and become exclusively Africans, for Du Bois, because their freedom is contingent upon the recognition of their unique doubled nature. The distinction is not subtle, but it probably seemed so to members of the white press who were not aware of the divergent rhetorical traditions from which Garvey and Du Bois drew. As a result, these two men, who perhaps could not have been more different, were often lumped together, forced to co-inhabit the narrow ideological space reserved by whites for African-American rhetors. They fought bitterly.

DU BOIS CRITIQUES GARVEY

The substance of their attacks on each other is important not only because of what it reveals about each man, but also because of what it reveals about the presumptions that undergird their respective agendas. Given that Garvey was so greatly influenced by Washington—Garvey himself stated that his program "includes the program of Booker T. Washington and has gone much further"—it is perhaps not surprising that Du Bois's critique of Garvey bears a striking resemblance to Du Bois's critique of Washington.[151]

Like Du Bois's opposition to Washington, his opposition to Garvey began slowly. When Du Bois visited Jamaica in the spring of 1915, Garvey greeted him in a receiving line and later left his calling card at the place where Du Bois was staying, and when Garvey arrived in New York, he asked that Du Bois chair his first public lecture; Du Bois declined.[152] Du Bois did, however, dutifully note Garvey's lecture dates in the pages of the *Crisis*. In December 1919, Du Bois noted that some African-American periodicals had been "disowning the new radicals" but that the *Crisis* would not do so. "The *Crisis* holds no brief for the *Messenger*, the *Negro World*, and other periodicals," Du Bois was careful to point out, "but they have a right to speak" (247). In September of the following year, under the heading "The Rise of the West Indian," Du Bois suggested that "this mass of peasants, uplifted by war and migration, . . . and their new cry of 'Africa for the Africans' strikes with a startling surprise upon America's darker millions." While "the movement is as yet inchoate and indefinite, . . . it is not beyond possibilities that this new Ethiopia of the Isles may yet stretch out hands of helpfulness to the 12 million black men of America" (273).

Later in 1920, Du Bois's assessment of Garvey and the UNIA became more severe, though he retained vestiges of balanced assessment. In articles that ran in December 1920 and January 1921, in a critique that echoes strongly "Of Mr. Booker T. Washington and Others," Du Bois argued that while Garvey's goals are feasible, and indeed in some ways praiseworthy, his program was too narrow to accomplish them. Du Bois commented on both Garvey's character and his business acumen. On the first score, Du Bois noted that Garvey "has with singular success capitalized and made vocal the great and long suffering grievances and spirit of protest among the West Indian peasantry." Although there were a number of things about Garvey that "militate against him and his reputation," he could not find "the slightest proof that his objects were not sincere or that he was consciously diverting money to his own uses." Though "his general objects are so shot through with bombast and exaggeration that it is difficult to pin them down for careful examination,"

Du Bois admitted that "Garvey is an extraordinary leader of men" (284–85). The flaws in Garvey's program—as was the case with the flaws in Booker T. Washington's program—did not flow from flaws of sincerity in Garvey's character.

But Du Bois began the January installment by noting that "when it comes to Mr. Garvey's industrial and commercial enterprises there is more ground for doubt and misgiving than in the matter of his character" (285). Most of this article consisted of a long and critical investigative report regarding the financial condition of the UNIA and the Black Star Line, leading to the conclusion that Garvey's methods (like Washington's) make the realization of his goals impossible. Garvey's business ventures, for example, "have brought in few returns, involved heavy expense and threatened him continually with disaster or legal complication." Du Bois did give Garvey credit for a bold vision, and for the "great, human service" of popularizing an idea that had long lain dormant among African Americans, and even agreed that a scheme to "redeem Africa as a fit and free home for black men" is perhaps justifiable (285). But, Du Bois warned, "when Garvey forges ahead and almost *singlehandedly* attempts to realize his dream in a few years, with large words and wild gestures, he grievously *minimizes* his task and endangers his cause" (288, emphasis added). Du Bois summed up, "Garvey is a sincere, hardworking idealist; he is also a stubborn, domineering leader of the mass; he has worthy industrial and commercial schemes but he is an inexperienced business man. His dreams of Negro industry, commerce and the ultimate freedom of Africa are feasible; but his methods are bombastic, wasteful, illogical and ineffective and almost illegal" (289). For Du Bois, Garvey was mostly Booker T. Washington. He was relying primarily upon an economic program, but at the same time crippling that program through a single-handed narrowness and a proclivity for self-promotion.

In 1923, while Garvey was in the Tombs prison, Du Bois published in the *Century Magazine* an article that made these charges more explicit. Du Bois noted, for example, that Garvey was not troubled by double-consciousness, that he sought "to oppose white supremacy and the white ideal by a crude and equally brutal black supremacy and black ideal." Such a program naturally would be anathema to the balanced approach and position that Du Bois advocated so strongly during this period in his life. Garvey's mistake, he wrote, "did not lie in the utter impossibility of this program, . . . but in its spiritual bankruptcy and futility; for what shall this poor world gain if it exchange one race supremacy for another?" Garvey did not trust any whites—nor, indeed, many light-skinned blacks—enough to work with them productively. "His African program," Du Bois continued, "was made impossible by his own pig-headedness." Because of his single-mindedness about what was to be done and the complete impermeability of the color line in his scheme of thought, he failed; like Washington before him, Garvey was caught in a hopeless double bind. It was impossible, Du Bois argued, "for Garvey to establish any headquarters in Africa unless it was done by the consent of the very nations whom he was threatening to drive out of Africa!"[153]

GARVEY CRITIQUES DU BOIS

Whereas Du Bois's critique of Garvey paralleled—and might have been predicted from—his critique of Washington, Garvey's critique of Du Bois paralleled our own. That is, Garvey critiqued Du Bois on the basis of his doubleness. First, Garvey, as a separatist, did not believe that the black and white races should work together, much less intermingle. He warned against "race assimilation," for example, as the work of "traitors of their own race." He believed, he said, "in a pure black race just as how all self-respecting whites believe in a pure white race, as far as that can be."[154] The NAACP, he warned, was one of those groups that believed "that the nearer we approach the white man in color the greater our social standing and privilege and that we should build up an 'aristocracy' based upon caste of color." He was repulsed by his discovery, upon visiting the offices of the NAACP and the *Crisis,* that "the whole staff was either white or very near white."[155] This was, for Garvey, hypocrisy; indeed, he stated that "between the Ku Klux Klan and the More-field Storey National Association for the Advancement of 'Colored' People group, give me the Klan for their honesty of purpose towards the Negro."[156] Untroubled by double-consciousness, for Garvey all descendants of Africans were African. "Everybody knows," he wrote, "that there is absolutely no difference between the native African and the American and West Indian Negroes, in that we are descendants from one common family stock."[157] "The Negroes of Africa and America are one in blood," he wrote elsewhere. "They have sprung from the same common stock."[158] African Americans should resolve their hyphenated identities and become exclusively Africans; for Garvey, any other choice made no sense.

This tendency in Garvey's thought to divide the world neatly into racially segregated halves was implicated in a Manichaean class consciousness. Garvey's was a movement of the masses and held no appeal either to or for the members of Du Bois's "Talented Tenth."[159] In his rhetoric, Garvey repeatedly linked race and class divisions. "There is a vast difference between the white and black races," he wrote. "The two are at extremes. One is dazzlingly prosperous and progressive; the other is abjectly poor and backward."[160] The race traitors who favored assimilation, he argued, were "generally to be found among the men highest placed in education and society." Garvey viewed the increasing resistance to the UNIA from the upper classes of African-American leadership as class warfare. "Others of my race oppose me," he was convinced, "because they fear my influence among the people, and they judge me from their own corrupt, selfish consciences."[161] Garvey referred to the "Committee of Eight," who had written that open letter to the attorney general, as "good old darkies," who believed that "only professional men are respectable." Turning neatly on its head Du Bois's critique of Washington's privileging of vocational education, Garvey warned that "were it not for the ignorant element of Negroes, these very fellows would have starved long ago, because all of them earn their living either by selling out the race under the guise of leadership or by exploiting the race in business."[162]

Given Garvey's distrust of African Americans who work closely with whites and of African Americans who did not identify closely with the lower classes, it is not surprising that W. E. B. Du Bois became his chief target. Had Du Bois been content to identify himself simply as "American" or to remain safely isolated in the "ivory tower" of academia, he would not have drawn Garvey's ire. But because Du Bois refused to resolve those inherent tensions in his identity, he became to Garvey a token of all that was wrong with African Americans who were confused about their identity.

"Du Bois," Garvey wrote in 1923 in the *Negro World,* "represents a group that hates the Negro blood in its veins." After Du Bois's extended critique of Garvey appeared in the *Century Magazine,* Garvey responded that the editor of "the official organ of the National Association for the Advancement of 'certain' Colored People . . . bewails every day the drop of Negro blood in his veins, being sorry that he is not Dutch or French." In fact, Garvey went on, being "a little Dutch, a little French, and a little Negro . . . the man is a monstrosity. As a hater of dark people, Du Bois can lead the race only toward "losing our black identity and becoming, as nearly as possible, the lowest whites by assimilation and miscegenation." Du Bois, Garvey continued, "has absolutely no respect and regard for independent Negro effort but that which is supported by white charity and philanthropy," because he owes both his education and his current salary to the "charity and philanthropy of white people." Further, "if Du Bois' education fits him for no better service than being a lackey for good white people, then it were better that Negroes were not educated."[163] "Dr. W. E. B. Du Bois," Garvey pointed out elsewhere, highlighting further his anti-intellectual bias, "has been educated by white charity, [and] is a brilliant scholar, but he is not a hard worker. He prefers to use his higher intellectual abilities to fight for a place among white men in society, industry and in politics rather than use that ability to work and create for his own race that which the race could be able to take credit for."[164] Thus, Garvey critiqued Du Bois on precisely his most vulnerable point; saturated in a rhetoric of double-consciousness, Du Bois could not accomplish material work in the world the way that Garvey could.

Within Garvey's worldview, there was no way to position oneself between extremes. One was either white or black, rich or poor, an academic or a race leader. Attempting to straddle these dichotomies resulted in a weakened capacity to work in either one. This rhetoric proved immensely successful, appealing perhaps to individuals caught in a culture that denied to them a viable political identity. Garvey gave them a singular vision of their history and place in the world and a plan for bringing this vision into concrete reality. Du Bois, on the other hand, was attempting to foment double-consciousness as a way for African Americans to know and to make known their political situation; that is, Du Bois was crafting critics. Through his own critique and his cooperation with other influential black leaders, Du Bois contributed to the silencing of Garvey; however, he could offer the African-American masses no concrete program to substitute for Garvey's, and thus never was able to hold their attention for long.

Du Bois after Garvey: Separation and Independence

The story of the last three decades of Du Bois's life is one of decreasing satisfaction with the possibilities afforded African Americans in America and an increasing commitment to Africa. Du Bois's participation in the Pan-African Congresses of 1919, 1921, and 1923 had increasingly splintered his support among the board of the NAACP. By the end of the decade of the Harlem Renaissance, Du Bois had more fully recognized that the singular pursuit of the ballot by the civil rights organization obscured the oppressive economic operations of globalization. Moreover, the onset of the Great Depression bound the NAACP to fewer financial sources and exacerbated communist fears within the organization. Taken together, these forces exacted a severe toll on Du Bois's editorial and intellectual authority.[165] In 1931, James Weldon Johnson, a longtime supporter of Du Bois's programs, was replaced as executive secretary by Walter White. Du Bois depicted White as an authoritarian who routinely "went underground" to unseat opposition, and White's ability to raise *Crisis* funds during the Depression warranted his encroachment onto editorial and research territories formerly controlled by Du Bois.[166] With Du Bois chafing under White's leadership, "advocating new, deliberate, and purposeful segregation for economic defense," and publicly criticizing White's "unsound explanation of the historical stand of the NAACP on segregation," in the spring of 1934 Du Bois's departure seemed inevitable.[167] The board of directors voted in May that salaried employees could not publicly voice dissension, effectively forcing Du Bois to either shut up or get out. Based on Du Bois's primal screams against the imposition of silence, there really was no choice at all.

At the invitation of longtime friend, Atlanta University President John Hope, Du Bois ventured south once again in search of himself and of his vocation. Installed as department chair of sociology, Du Bois taught a half-load in order to return to a research dream deferred—the execution of "a systematic study of the essential facts of the present condition of the Negro race and to establish a way of continuing and making more complete and effective such a study."[168] He remained at Atlanta until 1944, when he was ousted (perhaps because of the jealousy of his superiors, perhaps because of a politically delicate research agenda), and at the age of seventy-six he was invited to rejoin the NAACP as director of special research.[169]

White and Du Bois almost immediately renewed their shadowboxing, with Du Bois accusing White of Machiavellian tactics to reduce him to the status of an executive surrogate and "ghost writer." Thus, his realliance with the NAACP was short-lived, and he was fired on 31 December 1948. Also in 1948, Paul Robeson invited Du Bois to join the Council on African Affairs, the only organization in the United States that dedicated all its resources to information and programmatic efforts against colonialism in Africa. By the time Du Bois became chair of the African Aid Committee in 1949, the council had already been branded as "subversive."[170] Meanwhile, Du Bois's strident participation in the peace movement and his New York senatorial Labor Party candidacy in 1950 attracted public scorn colored bright red by McCarthyite fear. Finally, on 8 February 1951, the council and Du Bois were indicted "for not registering as an agent of a foreign power in the peace movement."[171] By all accounts, the trial in November of the same year was a mockery; the government could not link Du Bois's efforts to strategic foreign policy and the case was summarily dismissed. The incident, however, left indelible scars on Du Bois. "I have faced during my life many unpleasant experiences," he recounted later, "the growl of a mob; the personal threat of murder; the scowling distaste of an audience. But nothing has so cowed me as that day . . . when I took my seat in a Washington courtroom as an indicted criminal."[172]

Despite having won the legal battle, Du Bois was effectively blacklisted in the United States as a communist sympathizer. So severe were some informal sanctions on Du Bois's intellectual productivity that "colored children ceased to hear my name."[173] Du Bois continued to write; his *Black Flame* trilogy, widely panned as literary tripe in the United States, sold well in the Soviet Union in the late 1950s and early 1960s.[174] Du Bois traveled extensively to the Soviet Union and China and was commonly regarded as a communist, though he did not officially join the party until 1961. At the behest of Ghana's President Kwame Nkrumah, Du Bois moved to Africa and accepted the position of director of the *Encyclopaedia Africana* project sponsored by that nation. Two years later, thoroughly disgusted with American willingness to exploit labor and developing nations in the name of progress, Du Bois satisfied the requirements for Ghanaian citizenship. William Edward Burghardt Du Bois died shortly thereafter on 27 August 1963, the eve of Martin Luther King's famous speech at the March on Washington. He was given a state's funeral and interred in Accra, Ghana.

Conclusion

Du Bois did not invent double-consciousness in a vacuum; the concept was closely related to ideas of Emerson and James with which he was familiar. But Du Bois refashioned this doubleness, translating it from an inherent characteristic of human experience to describe the specialized experience of African Americans. This set in motion Du Bois's argument, wholly original, that double-consciousness holds within it a potential for authenticity and therefore respect. Though much of his thinking during these years about the importance of Africa and the "gift" that African Americans might offer to the world rested on a romantic essentialism at odds with contemporary sensibilities, it is important to contextualize Du Bois's comments so that both their boldness and their tentativeness are brought into focus. "The Conservation of Races," in particular, illustrated the extent to which Du Bois was willing to break with the dominant ideas of his time and the extent to which he was constrained by them.

Du Bois's rhetoric in his famous public battle with Booker T. Washington demonstrated the potential for social action within the ideals of double-consciousness. Washington's ambiguity masked what for Du Bois was the fundamental dilemma in African-American experience: how to participate fully in the American ideal while retaining a separate identity as a person of African descent. Du Bois believed that Washington had impaled himself upon the horns of this dilemma; his color-blind vocational work ethic effectively erased African Americans from the public sphere. Du Bois advocated a more multivocal leadership and a wider sense of the roles that African Americans might play in America. For Du Bois, participation in the dominant culture *required* that African Americans retain their problematic identity: participation in public deliberation required both an authentic black public voice and a critical engagement with the dominant culture, and to deny this fundamental complexity would be to deny the "gift" that African Americans could contribute.

In Du Bois's search for this doubled, authentic, black public voice, double-consciousness became instantiated in Pan-Africanist thought; if African Americans were to identify themselves as both African and American, then they must cultivate a relationship with Africa. Du Bois's increasingly explicit attention to the place of Africa in the lives of his readers eventually drew him into conflict with Marcus Garvey. Garvey, as a separatist, did not believe that whites and blacks could coexist; African Americans should identify exclusively as Africans and revel in their separation from the corrupt, white, American mainstream. He attacked Du Bois bitterly as a man at least confused and likely malevolent. Garvey cast Du Bois as a hater of dark people because, for Garvey, the balanced double-conscious that characterizes Du Bois's rhetoric represented a man unwilling to commit to a definite social agenda.

Du Boisian double-consciousness has long enjoyed a productive resonance with critics and theorists of the African-American experience. It introduces a radical flexibility that can be emancipatory and models a balanced relationship between detachment and engagement that academic critics find useful. But both Washington and Garvey point out the central limitations of Du Bois's stance: to get work done in the world, sometimes you must come down firmly somewhere. Washington built Tuskegee as the concrete manifestation of his educational ideals; Garvey, similarly, built his UNIA and *Negro World*. Du Bois's critiques of both Washington and Garvey were devastatingly insightful, even as the stance he articulated might today inspire critics toward further insight, but his own commitment to multivocality and against monolithic leadership perhaps precluded his own rise as the undisputed leader of a movement or institution. Du Bois will always stand as a— perhaps *the*—towering intellectual of his time, but as a political actor Du Bois's appeal was limited to a rather select group. Du Bois's was not a rhetoric of simplification, and he sought to explore rather than cloak the complexities of being black in America. There is a potential emancipation in such discourse, for the understanding of multiple perspectives often is a prerequisite of empowerment. But also, as Washington and Garvey illustrate, there is a certain material force in a rhetoric that simplifies.

Notes

1. Theodore Vincent, as quoted in Manning Marable, *W. E. B. Du Bois: Black Radical Democrat* (Boston: Twayne, 1986), 113.
2. Thomas C. Holt, "The Political Uses of Alienation: W. E. B. Du Bois on Politics, Race, and Culture, 1903–1940," *American Quarterly* 42 (1990): 307.
3. Stephen H. Browne, "Du Bois, Double-Consciousness, and the Modern City," in *Rhetoric and Community: Studies in Unity and Fragmentation*, ed. J. Michael Hogan (Columbia, S.C.: University of South Carolina Press, 1998), 88.
4. James Darsey, "'The Voice of Exile': W. E. B. Du Bois and the Quest for Culture," in *Rhetoric and Community*, 96.
5. Ibid., 97.
6. Ibid., 102.
7. Ibid., 103, 106.
8. Browne, " Du Bois, Double-Consciousness," in *Rhetoric and Community*, 76.
9. Adolph Reed, *W. E. B. Du Bois and American Political Thought: Fabianism and the Color Line* (New York: Oxford University Press, 1997), 124.
10. W. E. B. Du Bois, *The Autobiography of W. E. B. Du Bois: A Soliloquy on Viewing My Life from the Last Decade of Its First Century* (New York: International Publishers, 1968), 92.
11. W. E. B. Du Bois, *The Souls of Black Folk* (New York: Penguin Books, 1989), 7.
12. W. E. B. Du Bois, *Dusk of Dawn: An Essay toward an Autobiography of a Race Concept* (New York: Harcourt, Brace and Co., 1940), 14.
13. Ibid., 23.
14. Du Bois, *Autobiography*, 107.
15. Ibid., 108.
16. David L. Lewis, *W. E. B. Du Bois: Biography of a Race, 1868–1919* (New York: Henry Holt, 1993), 60.
17. Du Bois, *Dusk of Dawn*, 34; Du Bois, *Autobiography*, 136.
18. David L. Lewis, *W. E. B. Du Bois: A Reader* (New York: Henry Holt, 1995), 17–19.
19. William James, as quoted in Du Bois, *Dusk of Dawn*, 39.
20. Lewis, *Biography*, 102.
21. Arnold Rampersad, *The Art and Imagination of W. E. B. Du Bois* (Cambridge: Harvard University Press, 1976), 44.
22. Keith E. Byerman, *Seizing the Word: History, Art, and Self in the Work of W. E. B. Du Bois* (Athens: University of Georgia Press, 1994).
23. Rampersad, *Art and Imagination*, 26.
24. Ibid., 33.
25. Reed, *American Political Thought*, 91; see also Holt, "Political Uses of Alienation," 301.
26. Sandra Adell, *Double-Consciousness/Double Bind: Theoretical Issues in Twentieth-Century Black Literature* (Urbana: University of Illinois Press, 1994), 13; Rampersad, *Art and Imagination*, 74.
27. Du Bois, *Souls*, 5. Subsequent references to *Souls* will be by parenthetical page number only, except where the context does not make the reference clear.
28. Ernest Allen Jr., "Ever Feeling One's Twoness: 'Double Ideals' and 'Double Consciousness' in *The Souls of Black Folk*," *Critique of Anthropology* 12 (1992): 261–72.
29. Browne, "Du Bois, Double-Consciousness," in *Rhetoric and Community*, 83.
30. Dickson D. Bruce Jr., "W. E. B. Du Bois and the Idea of Double Consciousness," *American Literature* 64 (1992): 299–300.
31. Ibid., 300.
32. Reed, *American Political Thought*, 100.
33. Shamoon Zamir, *Dark Voices: W. E. B. Du Bois and American Thought, 1888–1903* (Chicago: University of Chicago Press, 1995), 163–64.
34. Darsey, "'Voice of Exile,'" in *Rhetoric and Community*, 101.
35. Bruce, "Idea of Double-Consciousness," 303. Bruce also provides an account of the medical history of the "double-consciousness," dating its usage to 1817, and suggests that Du Bois may have been familiar with at least some of the history of the medical use of the term (303–5).
36. Reed, *American Political Thought*, 102.

37. Adell points out that James eventually abandoned "consciousness" entirely as a philosophical proposition, unconvinced that it could exist as an entity. "Fortunately," she continues, "by the time James got around to trying to persuade his students that consciousness did not exist, Du Bois had moved on. Had he been among a later group of students, Du Bois might have hesitated to use what had become, at least for James, a contentious concept" (*Double-Consciousness*, 14).

38. The "problematic question of how one achieves mature self-consciousness and an integrity or wholeness of self in an alienating environment" would become "the dominant focus—political and cultural—of Du Bois's life and work" (Holt, "Political Uses of Alienation," 304).

39. Donald Gibson, introduction to *The Souls of Black Folk*, xii.

40. Rampersad, *Art and Imagination*, 49.

41. Reed, *American Political Thought*, 43.

42. Zamir, *Dark Voices*, 1.

43. W. E. B. Du Bois, *Darkwater: Voices from within the Veil* (New York: Kraus-Thomson, 1921), 82.

44. Lewis, *Biography*, 213, 225.

45. Du Bois as quoted in M. Aldrich, "Progressive Economists and Scientific Racism: Walter Willcox and Black Americans," 1895–1910 *Phylon* 40 (1979): 8–9.

46. *W. E. B. Du Bois Speaks: Speeches and Addresses, 1890–1919*, ed. Philip S. Foner (New York: Pathfinder Press, 1970), 48; Du Bois, *Dusk of Dawn*, 25–26.

47. J. D. Smith, "Du Bois and Phillips: Symbolic Antagonists of the Progressive Era," *The Centennial Review* 24 (1980): 89.

48. Rampersad, *Art and Imagination*, 54–55. This duality was manifested in another way during the years 1904 to 1906, when Du Bois was editing the *Horizon*. Some of his best poetry was written in response to racist violence, Jim Crowism, and the Atlanta riots.

49. Ibid., 59.

50. Zamir, *Dark Voices*, 6.

51. Reed, *American Political Thought*, 43.

52. Bruce, "Idea of Double-Consciousness," 301.

53. Rampersad, *Art and Imagination*, 89.

54. As Browne points out, Du Bois's critique of Atlanta's greed itself seems doubled. It is clear that Du Bois feared the rise of Mammonism, "but, for all the intensity of that fear, Du Bois could still see and appreciate Atlanta's temptations" ("Du Bois, Double-Consciousness," in *Rhetoric and Community*, 87).

55. Bruce, "Idea of Double-Consciousness," 301.

56. W. E. B. Du Bois, "The Conservation of Races," in *W. E. B. Du Bois Speaks*, 81.

57. Du Bois, *Souls*, 214. These three "gifts" are expanded upon in much greater detail in Du Bois's *The Gift of Black Folk: The Negroes in the Making of America* (Millwood, N.Y.: Kraus-Thomson Organization, 1975).

58. Du Bois, "Conservation," in *W. E. B. Du Bois Speaks*, 81.

59. Holt, "Political Uses of Alienation," 305.

60. Browne, "Du Bois, Double-Consciousness," in *Rhetoric and Community*, 83.

61. Lewis, *Biography*, 150. In fact, Washington easily could have been describing Du Bois just as he appears in pictures taken soon after his return from Europe: "The white people who questioned the wisdom of starting this new school [Tuskegee] had in their minds pictures of what was called an educated Negro, with a high hat, imitation gold eye-glasses, a showy walking-stick, kid gloves, fancy boots, and what not—in a word, a man who was determined to live by his wits" (*Three Negro Classics* [New York: Avon Books, 1965], 92).

62. Rampersad, *Art and Imagination*, 48.

63. Lewis, *Biography*, 243.

64. However, as Reed points out, strains of this thought emerge into the contemporary public sphere in Afrocentrism (*American Political Thought*, 139). Much of the rhetoric of Malcolm X, particularly while he was a minister of Elijah Muhammad's Nation of Islam, also builds an emancipatory case on essentialist notions. Indeed, much of the rhetoric that might be termed "black nationalism" rests on at least some essentialist

principles, and the emergence of this thought into the discourse of the black intelligentsia can be traced, in large part, back to Du Bois. See Manning Marable, *Through the Prism of Race and Class: Modern Black Nationalism in the U.S.* (Dayton, Ohio: Black Research Associates, 1980); and Marable, *Black Radical Democrat*.

65. Allen, "Ever Feeling One's Twoness," 274.

66. Adell, *Double-Consciousness,* 22.

67. Zamir, *Dark Voices,* 139.

68. Gibson, introduction to *Souls,* xxiv.

69. Reed, *American Political Thought,* 108. But David P. Thelen argues persuasively that such psychological or "social tension" hypotheses concerning the origin of the Progressive movement are at least open to question ("Social Tensions and the Origins of Progressivism," *Journal of Southern History* 56 [1969]: 323–41). The thesis that guides Reed's investigation is that Du Bois's conception of double-consciousness has little to do with its later appropriation by contemporary theorists and critics; this may be so, but this does not diminish the potential theoretical utility of Du Boisian double-consciousness. We take up this matter later in this essay.

70. Reed, *American Political Thought,* 111.

71. Ibid., 112, 111.

72. Ibid., 107. Pan-Africanism had a counterpart in the thought of white Progressives, in their interest in a sort of pan-Europeanism. As Stanley Caine notes, "obligations to Europe pervaded the reform movement." Intellectuals, in particular, helped to "bring to light relevant parts of the European experience that would aid Americans in achieving a better society. As America's problems, revolving around urbanization and industrialization, came to resemble those with which Europeans were already dealing, many who had earlier viewed Europe with skepticism now sought to learn from its successes and failures" (Caine, "The Origins of Progressivism," in *The Progressive Era,* ed. Lewis Gould [Syracuse, N.Y.: Syracuse University Press, 1974], 17).

73. Zamir, *Dark Voices,* 137.

74. Bruce, "Idea of Double-Consciousness," 302.

75. See Reed, *American Political Thought,* 43–51.

76. Du Bois, "Conservation," in *W. E. B. Du Bois Speaks,* 73. Subsequent references to the text will be to this version by page number only. The speech can also be found in its originally printed form ("The Conservation of Races" [Washington, D.C.: American Negro Academy, 1897]).

77. Anthony Appiah believes that Du Bois's movement toward a sociohistorical definition of race is "uncompleted" in this early speech. We disagree, suggesting instead that what Appiah has uncovered in the text is not an arrested or uncompleted argument but rather an attempt by Du Bois to hold two competing and contradictory definitions of race in solution (Appiah, "The Uncompleted Argument: Du Bois and the Illusion of Race," *Critical Inquiry* 12 [1985]: 21–37).

78. Thomas K. McCraw, "The Progressive Legacy," in *The Progressive Era,* 192.

79. Dewey W. Grantham Jr., "The Progressive Movement and the Negro," *South Atlantic Quarterly* 54 (1955): 461.

80. Lewis Gould, introduction to *The Progressive Era,* 10.

81. Grantham, "Progressive Movement," 465.

82. Alex Lichtenstein, "Good Roads and Chain Gangs in the Progressive South: The Negro Convict is a Slave,'" *Journal of Southern History* 59 (1993): 91.

83. Raymond Hall, *Black Separatism in the United States* (Hanover, N.H.: University Press of New England, 1978), 53.

84. David W. Southern, *The Malignant Heritage: Yankee Progressives and the Negro Question, 1901–1914* (Chicago: Loyola University Press, 1968), 1.

85. Gould notes that "the period itself is . . . full of contradictions and paradoxes" (introduction to *The Progressive Era,* 8–9), and Caine suggests, vaguely, that "Progressivism began with the breaking of chains of intellectual and religious thought that bound Americans in the late nineteenth century to precepts and assumptions that militated against reform" ("Origins," in *The Progressive Era,* 11). Robert Crunden takes as his thesis that "progressivism was a climate of creativity within which writers, artists, politicians, and thinkers functioned" and goes on to argue that "Progressives shared no

platform, nor were they members of a single movement" (*Ministers of Reform: The Progressives' Achievement in American Civilization, 1889–1920* [New York: Basic Books, 1982], ix).

86. John White, *Black Leadership in America: From Booker T. Washington to Jesse Jackson*, 2d ed. (New York: Longman, 1990), 44.

87. Louis Harlan, *Booker T. Washington: The Making of a Black Leader, 1856–1901* (New York: Oxford University Press, 1972), vii.

88. S. Jay Walker, "Booker T. Washington: 'Separatist' in Golden Chains," in *Black Separatism and Social Reality: Rhetoric and Reason*, ed. Raymond L. Hall (New York: Pergamon Press, 1977), 56.

89. Lewis, *Biography*, 238.

90. Booker T. Washington, as quoted in Wilson J. Moses, *The Wings of Ethiopia: Studies in African-American Life and Letters* (Ames: Iowa State University Press, 1990), 99.

91. See J. P. Flynn, "Booker T. Washington: Uncle Tom or Wooden Horse," *Journal of Negro History* 54 (1969): 262–74.

92. Louis Harlan, *Booker T. Washington in Perspective* (Jackson: University Press of Mississippi, 1988), 111, 115.

93. Southern, *Malignant Heritage*, 13–14.

94. For Washington and black nationalism, see Moses, *Wings of Ethiopia*, 95–105. On Washington's fit within Progressive Era politics, see Grantham, "Progressive Movement," 475.

95. Richard Hofstadter, *The Age of Reform: From Bryan to F. D. R.* (1955; reprint, New York: Alfred A. Knopf, 1959), 202–3.

96. Crunden, *Ministers of Reform*, ix.

97. See, for example, Du Bois's *The Gift of Black Folk* for his exploration of the various contributions made by African Americans to American culture. Though much of this book focuses on the material contributions made by African Americans—through labor and in the armed services, for example—Du Bois also notes that "a Negro American literature has arisen of deep significance, and Negro folk lore and music are among the choicest heritages of this land" (Du Bois, *The Gift of Black Folk*, iii).

98. Houston A. Baker Jr., "The Black Man of Culture: W. E. B. Du Bois and *The Souls of Black Folk*," in *Critical Essays on W. E. B. Du Bois*, ed. William L. Andrews (Boston: G. K. Hall and Co, 1985), 131–32.

99. Lewis, *Biography*, 287. Du Bois's original review of *Up from Slavery* is "The Evolution of Negro Leadership," *Dial*, 16 July 1901, 53–55.

100. Gibson, introduction to *Souls*, xix; Rampersad, *Art and Imagination*, 69, 81.

101. Rampersad, *Art and Imagination*, 69.

102. Robert B. Stepto, "The Quest of the Weary Traveler: W. E. B. Du Bois's *The Souls of Black Folk*," in *Critical Essays on W. E. B. Du Bois*, 149.

103. Much of the following analysis relies on Robert E. Terrill and Michael C. Leff, "The Polemicist as Artist: Du Bois's Response to Booker T. Washington," in *Argumentation and Values: Proceedings of the Ninth SCA/AFA Conference on Argumentation*, ed. Sally Jackson (Annandale, Va.: Speech Communication Association, 1995), 230–36. See also James Andrews, Michael C. Leff, and Robert E. Terrill, *Reading Rhetorical Texts: An Introduction to Criticism* (Boston: Houghton Mifflin, 1998), 116–33.

104. Du Bois, *Souls*, 30.

105. Marable, *Black Radical Democrat*, 83.

106. See Michael Calvin McGee, "A Materialist's Conception of Rhetoric," in *Explorations in Rhetoric: Studies in Honor of Douglas Ehninger*, ed. R. E. McKerrow (Glenview, Ill.: Scott Foresman Co., 1982).

107. Elliot P. Skinner, *African Americans and U.S. Policy toward Africa, 1850–1924: In Defense of Black Nationality* (Washington, D.C.: Howard University Press, 1992), 521.

108. John L. Golden and Richard D. Rieke, *The Rhetoric of Black Americans* (Columbus, Ohio: C. E. Merrill, 1971), 235.

109. Lewis, *Biography*, 316.

110. Marable, *Black Radical Democrat*, 92.

111. Lewis, *Biography*, 327.

112. Ibid., 338.

113. W. E. B. Du Bois, *Writings in Periodicals Edited by W. E. B. Du Bois: Selections from the "Horizon"* (White Plains, N.Y.: Kraus-Thomson Organization, 1985), 3.

114. Du Bois, *Selections from the "Horizon,"* 3. In the interests of textual economy, further references to Du Bois's writings in the *Horizon* will be to this volume by parenthetical page number unless the reference is not clear from the context.

115. Martin Bernal, *Black Athena: The Afroasiatic Roots of Classical Civilization* (New Brunswick, N.J.: Rutgers University Press, 1987). Bernal's central argument is that features of Greek philosophy and religion can be traced to northern Africa.

116. Du Bois, *Autobiography,* 255.

117. W. E. B. Du Bois, *Writings in Periodicals Edited by W. E. B. Du Bois: Selections from the "Crisis"* (Millwood, N.Y.: Kraus-Thomson Organization, 1983), 1:153. All future references to Du Bois's works in the *Crisis* will be to this volume, by parenthetical page number, unless the reference is not clear from the context.

118. Du Bois, *Autobiography,* 256.

119. See W. E. B. Du Bois, *Selections, 1877–1934,* vol. 1 of *The Correspondence of W. E. B. Du Bois,* ed. Herbert Aptheker (Amherst: University of Massachusetts Press, 1973), 180, 191, 207.

120. Du Bois, *Autobiography,* 293.

121. The brief biographical sketch that follows is based primarily on E. David Cronon, *Black Moses: The Story of Marcus Garvey and the Universal Negro Improvement Association* (Madison: University of Wisconsin Press, 1955). Hal W. Bochin also provides an excellent brief biographical sketch of Garvey ("Marcus Moziah Garvey," in *African-American Orators: A Bio-critical Sourcebook,* ed. Richard W. Leeman [Westport, Conn.: Greenwood, 1996]), 151–62. And Du Bois provides his own "brief . . . history of the Garvey movement" (*Selections from the "Crisis,"* 283–84).

122. Marcus M. Garvey, *Philosophy and Opinions of Marcus Garvey* (New York: Atheneum, 1967), 2:126. Most of Garvey's important speeches and statements have been collected by his widow, Amy Jacques Garvey, in the two volumes of *Philosophy and Opinions.* The first volume was published in 1923, and the second followed in 1925, but most often today these two volumes are found together as a single volume, though retaining the original pagination. Most of the speeches and statements contained in these volumes are culled from Garvey's editorials in the *Negro World,* but many are undated and lack other references to their original place of publication.

123. Booker T. Washington, as quoted in Cronon, *Black Moses,* 19.

124. Hall, *Black Separatism,* 60; Cronon suggests a direct causal connection between "Garvey's amazing success in the rapid organization of the Negro masses" and "his establishment in January, 1918, of the Negro World, the U.N.I.A.'s New York newspaper" (*Black Moses,* 45). The *Negro World* was published weekly until 1933.

125. Ibid., 83.

126. Hugh Mulzac, "Memoirs of a Captain of the Black Star Line," in *Marcus Garvey and the Vision of Africa,* ed. J. H. Clarke and A. J. Garvey (New York: Random House, 1974), 127–28.

127. Rampersad, *Art and Imagination,* 148.

128. Skinner, *U.S. Policy toward Africa,* 523.

129. Rampersad, *Art and Imagination,* 149.

130. Bernard Boxill, "Two Traditions in African American Political Philosophy," in *African-American Perspectives and Philosophical Traditions,* ed. John P. Pittman (New York: Routledge, 1997).

131. Golden and Rieke, *Rhetoric of Black Americans,* 43.

132. Du Bois, near the end of his life, also commented in detail on these two dominant traditions in African-American political thought. "Historically, beginning with their thought in the eighteenth century and coming down to the twentieth," he wrote, "Negroes have tended to . . . emphasize two lines of action." The first is the assimilationist tradition, based upon "the assumption on one hand that most race prejudice is a matter of ignorance to be cured by information; and on the other hand that much discrimination is a matter of deliberate deviltry and unwillingness to be just." "The second group effort to which Negroes have turned," Du Bois continues, "is more extreme and decisive." This is the effort exemplified by the recurrent "back to Africa"

movements that Du Bois insisted appeal not only to the "inexperienced and to demagogues," but also "to the black man who is tired of begging for justice and recognition from folk who seem to him to have no intention of being just and do not propose to recognize Negroes as men" (*Dusk of Dawn*, 192–95).

133. Du Bois, *Souls*, 5.
134. Garvey, *Philosophy and Opinions*, 1:50.
135. Ibid., 1:25.
136. Ibid., 2:37.
137. W. E. B. Du Bois, *Writings by W. E. B. Du Bois in Periodicals Edited by Others* (Millwood, N.Y.: Kraus-Thomson Organization, 1982), 2:147.
138. Du Bois, *Selections from the "Crisis,"* 331.
139. Ibid., 331–32. On the next page of this issue of the *Crisis*, Du Bois issued a warning to "expect the Demagog [*sic*] among Negroes more and more." Du Bois does not mention Garvey by name, but it is clear that he must be referring to him.
140. Garvey, *Philosophies and Opinions*, 2:64.
141. Ibid., 2:66.
142. Du Bois, *Selections from the "Crisis,"* 168.
143. W. E. B. Du Bois, *Writings*, ed. Nathan Huggins (New York: Library of America, 1986), 930. An essay with the same title, and some of the same phrases, appeared in 1910 in the *Independent* (Du Bois, *Edited by Others*, 25–29).
144. Garvey, *Philosophy and Opinions*, 2:97–98.
145. Ibid., 2:103.
146. Ibid., 2:39.
147. Ibid., 2:96.
148. Care should be taken not to oversimplify Garvey's program. As Cronon points out, "It was never Garvey's intention that all Negroes in the New World would return to Africa and in this sense it is misleading to call his scheme a Back to Africa movement. Rather he believed like many Zionists that once a strong African nation was established Negroes everywhere would automatically gain needed prestige and strength and could look to it for protection if necessary" (*Black Moses*, 184–85). In another remarkable correlation between Du Bois's thought and Garvey's, Du Bois, in an unpublished letter written in 1897, lays out in some detail a plan for a line of ships to carry people and material to Africa. Like Garvey, Du Bois insists in this letter that not all African Americans should go to Africa; only the strongest and most intelligent would be worth the expenditure ("On Migration to Africa," in *Against Racism: Unpublished Essays, Papers, Addresses, 1887–1961*, ed. Herbert Aptheker [Amherst: University of Massachusetts Press, 1985], 43–49).
149. Du Bois, *Selections from the "Crisis,"* 167–68, 188.
150. Du Bois, *Writings*, 948.
151. Garvey, *Philosophy and Opinions*, 1:41.
152. Lewis, *Biography*, 456, 505.
153. Du Bois, *Edited by Others*, 176, 178.
154. Garvey, *Philosophy and Opinions*, 1:29.
155. Ibid., 2:56–57.
156. Ibid., 2:71.
157. Ibid., 1:52.
158. Ibid., 2:40.
159. As Edwin S. Redkey points out, because of the northern migration of African Americans in the decades just prior to Garvey's arrival, "Garvey's followers . . . were the same Southern black marginal farmers who had responded to the emigration appeals of Bishop Turner and his followers a generation earlier" (*Black Exodus: Black Nationalist and Back-to-Africa Movements, 1890–1910* [New Haven: Yale University Press, 1969], 177).
160. Garvey, *Philosophy and Opinions*, 2:7.
161. Ibid., 1:21, 23, 76.
162. Ibid., 2:303–4.
163. Ibid., 2:57, 310–11, 313, 318.
164. Ibid., 2:43.

165. Du Bois, *Dusk of Dawn*, 300–3.
166. Du Bois, *Autobiography*, 294.
167. Ibid., 297–98.
168. Ibid., 310.
169. John Hope had died in 1936, leaving the nearly seventy-year-old scholar without an strong administrative ally. Du Bois developed a strongly Afrocentric plan to link black scholars at land-grant universities in a "program of cooperative social studies" that could have rankled any number of potential enemies; Du Bois himself believed that his "sudden retirement then savored of a deliberate plot, although this cannot be proven" (ibid., 319–22).
170. Paul Robeson, *Here I Stand* (Boston: Beacon Press, 1958), 119.
171. Du Bois, *Autobiography*, 347.
172. Ibid., 379.
173. Ibid., 395.
174. L. W. Phillips, "W. E. B. Du Bois and Soviet Communism: *The Black Flame* as Socialist Realism," in *Socialist Realism without Shores* (Durham, N.C.: Duke University Press, 1995).

Rhetoric and Race in the Progressive Era: Imperialism, Reform, and the Ku Klux Klan

Brian R. McGee

What is democracy? What does democracy include? Does democracy really include Negroes as well as white men? Does it include Russian Jews, Italians, Japanese? Does it include Rockefeller and the Slavonian street-sweeper? And Tillman and the Negro farmhand?

RAY STANNARD BAKER, *Following the Color Line* (1908)

9

Criticism of the treatment of African Americans is part of the historical narrative of the Progressive Era, with Baker's *Following the Color Line* among the classics of the period. We should not be surprised to find an interest in the plight of African Americans in the muckraking publications of the period. If reform advocates were to crusade against poverty and social injustice, then a progressive critique of what was then called race prejudice or race hatred would seem inevitable.[1] With progressive social workers calling for "a new American society," one might assume that African Americans would have benefited from the political and economic reforms initiated by the emerging white middle class.[2]

Yet the Progressive Era is not known for any great improvements in black-white race relations. White Southern Progressives frequently claimed that they were promoting the best interests of African Americans in the Old South. As C. Vann Woodward has documented, however, the push to codify Jim Crow policies in law throughout the former Confederacy took place during the reign of progressivism, especially in the twenty years following the Supreme Court's 1896 decision in *Plessy v. Ferguson*.[3] Woodward concluded that, during the Progressive Era, "the doctrine of racism reacted a crest of acceptability and popularity among respectable scholarly and intellectual circles."[4]

For African Americans, this hostility was not difficult to discern. Howard University Professor Kelly Miller described the era in 1908 as one in which "[c]ivil privileges have been restricted, education opportunities, in some States at least, have been curtailed; the industrial situation . . . has become more ominous and uncertain, while the feeling between the races is constantly growing more acute and threatening."[5] W. E. B. Du Bois made essentially the same observation two years earlier, noting that step-by-step "the defenders of the rights of American citizens have retreated. The work of stealing the black man's ballot has progressed. . . . Discrimination in travel and public accommodation has so spread that some of our weaker brethren are actually afraid to thunder against color discrimination as such and are simply whispering for ordinary decencies."[6]

Far from being a time of progress for African Americans, the Progressive Era marked the worst period for race relations since the Civil War. As we understand the term today, little "progress" was made on racial justice during the Progressive Era. James Weldon Johnson's protagonist explained in *Autobiography of an Ex-coloured Man* (1912) that both blacks and whites in the South were suffering through a period of racial conflict "as lamentable" as it was "violent."[7]

Given the curious coexistence of the most famous national reform movement in United States history with the grim state of race relations at the century's turn, I wish to explore the ways in which race fit into the rhetoric of progressivism. By acknowledging the inferiority of African Americans and denying that this inferiority could be quickly overcome (if it could be overcome at all), white folk, including those whom we could describe as progressive, consigned African Americans to the margins of public life and denied their claim to the rights and responsibilities of citizenship. During the Progressive Era the expansion of African-American rights became at most a concern only of the far-off future. Further, I will argue that the twentieth-century Ku Klux Klan co-opted progressive rhetorics dealing with race. In this sense the Ku Klux Klan of the 1920s was a rhetorical legacy of the Progressive movement.

Race and the Progressive Agenda

Traditional historiography characterizes the Progressive Era as a time of great reforms that reduced political corruption and expanded democracy. It was, according to David H. Bennett, "an age of optimistic activism, an age of belief in the ability of an alert and rational citizenry to make a better tomorrow by reshaping institutions."[8] This movement composed of heterogeneous groups protested the unhappy by-products of U.S. industrialization and urbanization, and Progressives allegedly expressed "a new and intelligent concern for the poor and the underprivileged, for women and children, for the victims and the derelicts of society, for the immigrant, the Indian, and the negro[sic]."[9] In their 1942 summary of the Progressive movement, Samuel Eliot Morison and Henry Steele Commager pointed to the founding of the National Association for the Advancement of Colored People in 1909 as evidence of the progressive spirit.[10]

Curiously, in this climate of reform a leading Southern Progressive, Hoke Smith, could make the following claim in 1905: "This is a white man's country. . . . No matter how secure we may feel at present from negro domination, if . . . there is danger to the state at large . . . from this curse, it will be folly for us to neglect any means within our power to remove the danger."[11] How could a self-proclaimed Progressive utter such sentiments?

I maintain that two rhetorics, a rhetoric of *subjugation* and a rhetoric of *development*, were complicit in the Progressive movement's construction of African Americans as a problem requiring reform. Hoke Smith's words were consistent, strangely enough, with both of these rhetorics.

THE UNDEVELOPED AFRICAN AMERICAN

If one commonplace existed for all those who perceived themselves as white at the beginning of the twentieth century, it was the inferiority of African Americans as a group. That African Americans were members of a "backward" race and that white folk were the "forward" race was almost never seriously questioned in the white population. However, the moral and practical implications of this commonplace were not particularly obvious, and debates about what, if anything, should be the response to the presence of this inferior race in white America were common at this time.

In this debate, "development" and related terms such as "growth" and "progress" were central to the ongoing discussion. For one group, which employed what I will describe as a subjugationist rhetoric, African Americans were and always would be inferior to white folks. African Americans would always lag behind whites in their development, and the ability of African Americans to develop at all was sometimes questioned. As a result of these limitations, African Americans should be totally subjugated to white authority, or white civilization would be threatened by the social and political influence of an inferior race.

For another group, which used what I will call a developmental rhetoric, development of African Americans was perceived as possible, and providing an education for African Americans was perceived as an obligation of the white citizenry. Like the subjugationists, developmentalists noted that African Americans belonged to the inferior race. Unlike the subjugationists, developmentalists maintained that African Americans could become competent citizens one day, if and only if they received appropriate instruction from their more advanced white teachers.

The Subjugationists

While almost all whites agreed about the racial inferiority of African Americans, subjugationist rhetoric placed this assumption of inferiority in a context that made inferiority seem permanent. This inferiority was a fact of history and science, as Robert Bennett Bean's 1906 essay in *Century Magazine* illustrates. Where history was concerned, the tendency was to describe African Americans as members of an ancient race that had never shown any evidence of intellectual or cultural potential. According to Bean, African Americans "have been in contact continually with the highest civilizations of antiquity, but have never risen to the eminence of other nations, having retained their primitive condition, even as is now apparent in the Southern States."[12] The scientific research of the early twentieth century was also used by Bean, a professor of anatomy. Because the "negro brain [has] fewer nerve cells and nerve fibers . . . the possibilities of developing the negro are therefore limited, except by crossing with other races."[13] Given this evidence from history and science, Bean concluded that the "Caucasian and the negro are fundamentally opposite extremes in evolution."[14] Based on such reasoning, one can understand a congressman's assertion at the time "that the white race will demand and take the superior position is beyond controversy. Six thousand years of history proclaim his right to it."[15] From this perspective, white racial supremacy meant that white rule of inferior races was and always would be inevitable.

As further evidence of ineluctable African-American inferiority, the subjugationist position emphasized that African Americans would not do useful work without white supervision. For example, Hubert Howe Bancroft observed in 1912 that the "Americanized negro . . . depends upon the white man to do his mental work, his thinking and management for him, preferring himself only to serve. He is by nature and habit a servant . . . because of his mental inferiority."[16] The strongest version of this position suggested that the optimal answer to the problem posed by African Americans in the United States was their deportation to Africa, or, at least, regret that deportation had not already been chosen as the best solution: "Were it not better frankly to admit that the freed African in America is a failure, and that when made free he should have been sent away? He is a failure here, for effective work is not be obtained from him except under compulsion. As an American citizen he is a monstrosity."[17] Because African Americans were not motivated or effective workers, their contributions to U.S. civilization would always be minimal. As suggested below, the rhetoric of subjugation was consistent with the "permanent exclusion of the black body from the (white) body politic" as a progressive reform.[18]

While those employing a developmentalist rhetoric would hold out the hope that education would help African Americans to develop their moral sensibilities and cognitive abilities, subjugationist rhetoric noted that education for African Americans was of limited value at best and was harmful at worst. Initially, because education could not overcome inherited racial characteristics, there were inherent obstacles that African Americans could not overcome. As Howard W. Odum maintained in 1910, "back of the child, and affecting him [or her] both directly and indirectly, are the characteristics of the race. . . . The Negro has few ideals and perhaps no lasting adherence to an aspiration toward real worth. . . . The Negro shirks details and difficult tasks; he is incapable of turning his mind toward any other subject when once morbid curiosity holds his attention."[19]

Education from this perspective could not overcome fundamental racial attributes. Changing the child's environment might improve matters to some degree, but such a change would never compensate for the child's racial heritage. For example, William Benjamin Smith concluded in 1905 that "there is no hope whatever of any organic improvement, of any race betterment of the Negro, from any or from all extra-organic agencies of education or religion or civilization." Smith did not object to education for African Americans that would make them "more useful and productive," but nothing more could be expected of such education.[20] If education for African Americans had any value, it was industrial education. Higher forms of education were a waste of time for members of a race not suited to ambitious endeavors and having only limited intellectual capacities.

Further, because education encouraged unrealistic expectations among African Americans who were ultimately best suited for personal service or manual labor, education often rendered African Americans unwilling to accept the work that was available to them. Under the educational system of the South in the early twentieth century, Odum complained that the "young educated negroes are not a force for good in the community but for evil. . . . They feel that manual labor is beneath their dignity; they are fitted to do no other. They sneer at the idea of work, and they thus spread dissatisfaction among the members of their race."[21] Odum's conclusion was that new elementary school textbooks should be developed for the use of African-American children. Such textbooks would be better suited to developing the limited abilities of such children without encouraging envy of the white race.

For others employing a subjugationist rhetoric, the dangers of African-American education were not limited to African-American dissatisfaction and decreased productivity. One member of Congress, on the basis of incomplete data and with little consideration of alternative interpretations, concluded that education for African Americans was the cause of higher crime rates, as African-American illiteracy rates were declining at the same time that African-American prison populations were growing. For Thomas W. Hardwick, the "conclusion is irresistible that the more you educate the negro the more criminal he becomes."[22] James K. Vardaman, the former governor of Mississippi, independently reached a similar conclusion in 1906, noting that Mississippi census data showed that literate African Americans were "more criminal than the illiterate, which is true of no other element of our population."[23]

The existence of African-American intellectuals intuitively would challenge the subjugationist position, as observers during this period conceded that there were "hundreds, if not thousands, of black men in this country who in capacity are to be ranked with the superior persons of the dominant [white] race."[24] However, exceptional accomplishments by educated African Americans were accounted for with a biological explanation, as such African Americans were typically mulattoes whose white racial heritage explained their intellectual abilities. As noted above, Bean described African-American brains as smaller and less complex than the brains of whites. However, Bean also cited data supporting his claim that "the brain of the American negro weights more than the native African, which is no doubt because of the greater amount of white blood in the American negro."[25] For subjugationists, any African-American achievement was attributed to her or his white ancestry.

In summary, the rhetoric of subjugation maintained that racial differences were permanent and could not be overcome by any amount of education or time. After all, if "God Almighty had intended these two races to be equal, He would have so created them."[26] Given these unavoidable racial differences, any ill-conceived effort to expand the rights or opportunities of African Americans beyond their rightful limits would be vigorously resisted. As Florida congressman Frank Clark concluded, the United States "will always be a white man's country. If the black man and the yellow man each desire to remain with us, occupying the sphere in life for which God Almighty intended each, let them do so. If not content with that, then let them go elsewhere."[27] The "successfully developed black man," as Odum described him, would never consider "race agitation" or dispute the "uncontrovertible [sic]" fact of African-American inferiority.[28] However, Odum's was not the typical use of the term "developed."

The Developmentalists

While the rhetoric of subjugation rejected the possibility of moral or intellectual improvement for African Americans, the rhetoric of development was much more optimistic. Developmentalists conceded the backwardness and *current* inferiority of African Americans, but they held out the possibility that African Americans could *one day* grow morally and intellectually to the point of full participation in American public life. Further, developmentalists saw attempts to guide and direct the development of African Americans as a moral obligation of white folk that was consistent with the progressive spirit of reform.

The tenor of developmental rhetoric can be observed in several magazine articles on Southern prohibition published in the first decade of the century. These articles repeatedly described prohibition as a reform movement and pointed to the African-American presence in the South as a major cause of prohibition advocacy. For example, according to John E. White the saloon was the "ravager of the negro people," which "fed their animalism" and was "a debauching agent let loose by law upon them." Because the "Liquor Traffic only tended to complicate" the "sociological problem" posed by African Americans in the South, prohibition was warranted. African Americans constituted "a child-people element in our population," and the great majority of them were "ignorant and weak." Therefore, a legislative solution to the problem of alcohol consumption by African Americans was warranted. Just as disfranchisement of African Americans was a "movement in consideration of the true welfare of the negro race . . . [because] through such limitation only could the discipline of citizenship become possible," prohibition was a step taken by white folk in the interests of an as-yet undeveloped race.[29]

The well-known Southern prohibitionist A. J. McKelway also emphasized that prohibition protected members of the "weaker race," which was "demoralized by drink" and for which alcohol was "the chief source of his crime." Because African Americans lacked the Anglo-Saxon "inheritance of liberty," alcohol consumption led "the liberty bestowed upon the African" to "degenerate into license."[30] While many white Southerners were initially reluctant to give up alcohol themselves, the "moderate drinker in the South" was "willing to forego his privileges in order to protect the Negro from the unlimited sale of liquor."[31]

Frank Foxcroft described the Southern experience with prohibition in 1908 by comparing it with British imperialism: "What is the cause of this drift toward prohibition in the South? The obvious cause . . . is the presence of the negro. It is said that the vote for prohibition in the South represents exactly the same reasoning which excludes liquor . . . from great areas in Africa under the British flag; and that, wherever there is an undeveloped race, the reasons for restrictions upon the liquor traffic become convincing."[32] Again, the rationale for prohibition laws was the presence of an undeveloped race, or what A. J. McKelway called, "this child-race among us."[33] Unlike the subjugationists, however, this rhetoric did not maintain that African Americans could not or would not develop over time. White and Foxcroft in particular emphasized that alcohol and the saloons damaged both African Americans and working-class whites, though the harm done to African Americans was seen as more severe. Whether black or white, development was hampered by the presence of alcohol among inferior peoples.

A more complete example of the rhetoric of development is found in John Carlisle Kilgo's 1903 essay in the *South Atlantic Quarterly*. For Kilgo, African Americans, no less than their white counterparts, were evolving from a lower to a higher evolutionary stage. Rather than being unique, African Americans, like members of other races, "only manifest themselves in those forms peculiar to a race" at a particular "stage of moral and intellectual development."[34] African Americans were capable of evolution, and it was the duty of the African American "to lift himself from a lower plane of life to a higher one, to fit himself to fill the mission of a negro man in the world's progress, to render the very best service which he, as a member of a distinct race, can render."[35]

In response to the subjugationists, whom he explicitly criticized, Kilgo insisted that African Americans deserved every opportunity to develop: "There is a class of men who assert that the negro is extremely limited in his capacities. Some of these are extreme enough to assert that it is a waste of means and effort to attempt the development of the negro. There is an extremer [*sic*] class who boldly assert that the negro was ordained to a life of ignorance and degradation. Such men do not represent the world's best faith. . . . For a superior race to hold down a inferior one simply that the superior race may have the services of the inferior, was the social doctrine of mediaevalism."[36] Against the charges made by subjugationists that African Americans had little or no capacity for development, Kilgo insisted that African Americans "can grow" and had proven as much since coming involuntarily to the United States.[37] By helping African Americans to develop and by recognizing their ability to develop, whites were attending to a "grave responsibility" that also was a "rich opportunity" to see African Americans become useful and productive citizens to the mutual advantage of both races.[38]

In making his argument, Kilgo described African Americans as "a race just emerging from savagery" and whites as members of "a superior race." Further, he insisted that African-American problems involved "personal growth, not . . . social equality," as no one can be forced to see another person as his or her social equal.[39] With this understanding, however, Kilgo endorsed not only the industrial education represented by Booker T. Washington's Tuskegee Institute but also the right of African Americans to seek a university education. In contrast to the impoverished curriculum for African Americans suggested by many subjugationists, Kilgo, a college president, insisted that African Americans deserved the "strongest and highest influences" represented by Shakespeare and Raphael.[40]

That the rhetoric of development was more generous than the rhetoric of sub-jugation in describing the potential of African Americans is not in question. How-ever, references to the passage of *time* in the rhetoric of development are crucial in explaining the intersection of developmental and subjugationist rhetorics. For Kilgo and for other developmentalists, the development of African Americans would be a slow and deliberate process, requiring that both African Americans and their white teachers cultivate patience: "In passing from a lower to a higher plane of life and manhood, the negro must travel the ordinary way of progress along which all other races have come. He must be given time to grow. The evolution of racial character is slow and tedious, and no improved formula has been found by which a race can rise in a century to the highest duties and offices of an advanced civilization. The negro himself must learn this, and in learning it learn to be pa-tient, and like Abraham, follow a promise which was fulfilled centuries after he had passed away. . . . An effort to override the laws of the evolution of life will bring sure destruction, and the negro will find his worst enemy in that man who wishes to rush his progress by some process of false growth."[41]

Kilgo suggested here that a century might not be sufficient for African Ameri-cans to attain full citizenship. Indeed, African Americans might have to wait cen-turies, as had Abraham. Attempts to speed this process would only yield false results, especially as Kilgo emphasized elsewhere in the same essay that African Americans were "behind all other races" in their development and that the "Anglo-Saxon has two thousand years the start of the negro."[42] Other developmental rhetorics also emphasized the slow character of future African-American growth and development. For example, Edgar Gardner Murphy insisted that where African Americans were concerned, the "most imperative external element in the whole ed-ucational process is not equipment or wealth or peace, but *time,*—and, until time be accorded, the other opportunities for learning and for efficiency can have only a halting power."[43]

The emphasis on education and development as a slow, deliberate process al-lowed developmentalists to assert a moral imperative to educate African Americans while avoiding any meaningful challenge to the prevailing social order. As devel-opmentalists conceded that African Americans were members of an inferior race that was not yet ready to participate in politics, the rhetoric of development posed no challenge to then-current efforts to disenfranchise African Americans and to separate them from members of the more advanced race. Whether the time that must pass before sufficient African-American development took place was specified or not, politicians and social observers in the early twentieth century could rest as-sured that the obligation to take African Americans seriously as citizens was not coming anytime soon. African Americans "will win equality at some time," as one editorial noted, but the day and hour were not imminent.[44]

If subjugationists believed that they were making a permanent division be-tween the superior race and the inferior race for the sake of their descendants, the rhetorical logic of development was consistent with "temporary" disfranchisement and laws mandating racial segregation, where such temporary measures might be required to last for a generation or more. From both the subjugationist and devel-opmental perspectives, Jim Crow was good for the well-being of both races and was ultimately a kind of beneficial social and political reform.

To further illustrate how both the subjugationist and developmental rhetorics led to the progressive conclusion that African Americans could and should be ex-cluded from the white public sphere, I now turn to the discourse of the novelist Thomas Dixon Jr. and of Theodore Roosevelt. The former was a subjugationist, the latter a developmentalist. Yet both reached essentially the same conclusion: that progress could be made only by excluding African Americans from the mainstream of public life.

DIXON AND SUBJUGATIONIST RHETORIC

As Jack Temple Kirby notes, if "the turn-of-the-century marked a distinctive era for whites, it was certainly a definable epoch for blacks: it was the nadir of their post-emancipation existence in America."[45] One reason for the unhappy experience of African Americans in the early twentieth century was the ascendancy of subjugationist rhetoric among white Southern politicians, including many politicians who would be described as progressive. This subjugationist rhetoric could also be found in much public commentary and entertainment media. Rather than countering the rhetoric of subjugation, progressivism in some ways encouraged it.

A review of the life and discourse of novelist Thomas Dixon Jr. illustrates the vector of this rhetoric. While Dixon is barely remembered today, several of his novels enjoyed spectacular sales in the early years of the century. For over a decade Dixon's standing as a popular novelist and playwright almost guaranteed the commercial success of anything he wrote.[46] Famous for inspiring the pro–Ku Klux Klan film *The Birth of a Nation* (1915), Dixon, as historian Joel Williamson has noted, "probably did more to shape the lives of modern Americans than have some Presidents. Yet, his work and Dixon himself have been all but lost to historians."[47] Dixon's influence could be found in the huge audience reached by his books and plays and the movies inspired by his works. While Dixon appropriated the "same basic tropes as those used by" other white Southern novelists during his day, such as Page and Harris, his work was unique for its ability to inspire "rioting" and "frothing expressions of racial hate among whites."[48]

In his well-known work, Thomas Dixon's commitment to both progressive ideals and the exclusion of African Americans from public life illustrates the rhetoric employed in a subjugationist version of progressivism. As a successful minister in the late nineteenth century, Dixon's writing reveals the paternalistic attitude toward African Americans often associated with the educated white Southern elite (or "Bourbon" Democrats) in the years immediately following Reconstruction, a paternalism not unlike the developmental position described above. For example, in an essay published by the *Christian Union* in 1887, Dixon noted that racism was inevitable in both North and South and argued against suffrage for uneducated former slaves. However, he also contended that the "negro is made of the same material that the white man is made of. He has the same passions, the same heart, the same nature."[49] The younger Dixon's solution to the so-called Negro problem was thus to educate African Americans. He explicitly rejected the colonization of African Americans in Liberia. As late as 1896, Dixon insisted in a critique of chattel slavery that "democracy is the destiny of the race, because all men are bound together in the bonds of fraternal equality with one common love," a position far more in line with a developmental rather than a subjugationist rhetoric.[50]

By the time he published his first novel, *The Leopard's Spots* (1902), Dixon's description of African Americans had changed. Throughout *The Leopard's Spots* and his later novels, Dixon repeatedly and consistently described African Americans as predatory animals incapable of change and unable to improve their position in the natural order of things. In *The Leopard's Spots*, the African-American threat posed to Anglo-Saxons was indicated by Dixon's description of the "freed Negro" as "a possible Beast to be feared and guarded."[51] Indeed, Dixon was not content in depicting the "possible Beast" merely to compare African Americans to cats, leopards, and apes. In a passage that Dixon credits to the Yankee son of a Radical Republican in *The Clansman* (1905), Dixon portrayed African Americans as inferior even to some animals: "He [an African-American Union soldier] had the short, heavy-set neck of the lower order of animals. His skin was coal black, his lips so thick they curled both ways up and down with crooked blood-marks across them. His nose was flat, and its enormous nostrils seemed in perpetual dilation. The sinister bead eyes, with brown splotches in their whites, were set wide apart and gleamed ape-like under his scant brows. His enormous cheek bones and jaws seemed to protrude beyond the ears and almost hide them."[52]

In addition to systematically dehumanizing African Americans, Dixon insisted in several of his novels that African Americans could not be improved or developed because of their inherent racial limitations. For Dixon's protagonist in *The Sins of the Father* (1912), African Americans were "the lowest of all human forms, four thousand years below the standard of the pioneer white Aryan who discovered this continent and peopled it with a race of empire builders."[53] In *The Leopard's Spots,* Dixon's protagonist told his interlocutor to "ask history" whether African Americans could contribute anything to American progress: "The African has held one-fourth of this globe for 3,000 years. He has never taken one step in progress . . . except as the slave of a superior race. . . . He has had one hundred years of trial in the northern states of this Union with every facility of culture and progress, and he has not produced one man who has added a feather's weight to the progress of humanity."[54] Given this assessment of African-American inferiority, clothing African Americans with "the full powers of citizenship under the flag of Democracy" was a "great crime" that had to be undone.[55]

For Dixon, education, even industrial education of the sort promoted by Booker T. Washington, was a disservice to African Americans: "Education increases the power of the human brain to think and the heart to suffer. Sooner or later these educated Negroes feel the clutch of the iron hand of the white man's unwritten laws on their throats. . . . The South is kinder to the Negro when he is kept in his place."[56] Even industrial and agricultural training will lead to an inevitable "war of races," once increasingly wealthy African Americans begin to demand rights that whites would never grant them.[57] The only careers that African Americans should be given involved "menial service," and banning education for African Americans was in the best interests of both races.[58]

Dixon argued that African Americans and Anglo-Saxons could never comfortably cohabit the same geographic space. While Dixon once had opposed the colonization (or deportation) of African Americans to Africa, he eventually became one of the last regular and enthusiastic advocates of that cause, which he mentioned in his first novel, *The Leopard's Spots,* his last novel, *The Flaming Sword* (1939), and almost every other novel dealing with race that he wrote.[59] Dixon hoped to see the "Negro problem" resolved by the removal of all African Americans from the continent, as African Americans, by dint of their racial inferiority, could never be assimilated or be anything other than second-class citizens. As Dixon once remarked, "who thinks of a Negro when he [sic] says 'American'?"[60] If African Americans were to remain in the United States, then their total subordination to white rule would be necessary. While admitting that his novels may have been "hard reading for a Negro," Dixon nevertheless insisted that his assertions of black racial inferiority were unquestionable and that African Americans, in denouncing his books, were "unwittingly denouncing one of their best friends."[61] Dixon's prescriptions for racial separation, he maintained, were in the best interests of both Anglo-Saxons and African Americans.

Two plausible interpretations for Dixon's conversion from paternalism to outright hostility toward African Americans have been offered.[62] Initially, James Kinney has argued that Dixon's attitude toward African Americans and his politics were simply inconsistent with the optimism and reform spirit of fin de siécle America. Dixon's work was "moving counter to the main current of his time," Kinney has maintained, and therefore Dixon was presumably not a genuine Progressive. In contrast, Maxwell Bloomfield has argued that Dixon was a progressive reformer in his own strange way, "a muckraker in all but name, specializing in the 'black peril' rather than 'Wall Street' or 'the demon rum.'"[63] Dixon's proposal to remove African

Americans from the country of their birth, according to Bloomfield, was perfectly consistent with his commitment to social progress for both whites and blacks.

Bloomfield, like C. Vann Woodward, also noted that the imperialism of the time reinforced the belief in Anglo-Saxon superiority among the white citizenry; this commitment led to Dixon's increasing hostility toward African Americans.[64] Dixon not only crusaded against the black beast, as Bloomfield has noted, but also advocated white unity to protect American democracy from decline. For example, in *The Clansman* white Northerners and Southerners united symbolically through marriage to confront the shared racial threat posed by African Americans. No non-white race had proven itself capable of comprehending, preserving, and making appropriate use of democratic privileges, so, in the wake of the Spanish-American War, Dixon's protagonist in *The Leopard's Spots* maintained that "God has raised up our race, as he ordained Israel of old, in this world-crisis to establish and maintain for weaker races . . . the principles of civil and religious Liberty and the forms of Constitutional Government."[65] In Dixon's view, the intractable struggle over race in the United States impeded progressive reforms by preventing white unity.

Dixon's midlife switch to a rhetoric of subjugation parallels several rhetorical and material changes in U.S. politics. First, the U.S. acquisition of the Philippines and Puerto Rico after the Spanish-American War made the United States a colonial power almost overnight. With colonial power came the problem of colonial subjects, and white intellectuals and politicians alike faced the uncomfortable question of what (if any) rights to extend to persons of color in the U.S. colonies. Given the theories of race popular at the time, many commentators worried about "the ill effects from so many inferior people under the American flag," and U.S. colonial subjects were denied many of the rights granted to U.S. citizens.[66] For example, Indiana senator Albert J. Beveridge argued that, where the Philippines were concerned, it "is barely possible that 1,000 men in all the archipelago are now capable of self-government in the Anglo-Saxon sense."[67] While Beveridge's rhetoric was more often developmental than subjugationist, the duty of the white ruling class in the United States was to administer the Philippines for the good of their inhabitants, rather than to extend political rights to Filipinos for which they were not qualified.

Defenders of racial segregation in the United States, especially those typically using the rhetoric of subjugation, quickly seized the opportunity to point out how the social practices and Jim Crow laws of the former slave states resembled the colonial policies of the U.S. government. As Woodward has observed, the race theories that "justified and rationalized American imperialism in the Philippines, Hawaii, and Cuba differed in no essentials from the race theories by which Senator Benjamin R. Tillman of South Carolina and Senator James K. Vardaman of Mississippi justified white supremacy in the South."[68] Dixon understood this tension, asking whether white folk should "reverse the order of nature, and make these black people [of the Orient] our rulers? If not, why should the African here, who is not their equal, be allowed to imperil our life?"[69]

A Republican administration and its supporters at the century's turn were thus in the awkward position of endorsing political subordination for nonwhite residents of U.S. colonies while criticizing (however halfheartedly) manifestations of that same ideology in the post-Reconstruction South. Tillman, one of the leading "fire-eaters" on issues of race, could not resist reminding Republicans that their own president was responsible for thousands of "murdered Filipinos, done to death because they were fighting for liberty" that was denied to them by the U.S. government.[70] Making the point more bluntly, Congressman Hardwick of Georgia noted that "it is the most brazen of inconsistencies for the National Government to guarantee the suffrage to black men in the South while it denies it to brown men in the Philippines and to white men in Porto Rico."[71]

In short, advocates of imperialism were hard-pressed to oppose even the most glaring examples of domestic racial disparities without appearing inconsistent. With novelists, scientists, and politicians endorsing theories of white supremacy as an inevitable fact of life, efforts to enshrine this inequality in law became increasingly difficult to resist.[72] In fin de siécle America, the "Negro problem" was limited to the former Confederate states in the white popular imagination, despite the growth of the African-American population in many Northern cities. With the popular and intellectual resurgence of white supremacy at the end of the nineteenth century, Northern and national sentiment against "Southern race policy" was difficult to sustain. After the failure in 1890 of the U.S. Senate to pass the "Force Bill," which Henry Cabot Lodge designed to ensure the voting rights of African Americans in the South, decades would pass before Congress would again seriously consider such legislation.[73]

Beyond the influence of imperialism, the unique character of nascent Southern progressivism, perversely enough, made the enactment of laws segregating the races in the former Confederate states more likely. Circumstances varied widely from state to state, and references to the South as a monolithic political and cultural entity invariably risk oversimplification. However, the repeated failure of Southern Populists such as Georgia's Tom Watson to forge alliances between working-class whites and African Americans, along with the national economic problems of the early 1890s, may have led many Populists to cooperate with the most outspoken and vicious detractors of African Americans to remove African Americans from the political scene.

Ultimately African Americans were perceived as unreliable coalition partners by both populist and conservative forces among white Southerners, and beliefs about African-American racial inferiority made disfranchisement an intuitive reform. As Georgia congressman Thomas W. Hardwick asserted, "the rule is that any negro, rich or poor, educated or uneducated, will sell his vote, his chief concern being to obtain the highest possible price for it."[74] In the same document Hardwick maintained that African Americans had no right to demand the franchise, as African Americans were members of a race "that never yet founded a government or built a state that did not soon lapse into barbarism; a race that never yet made a single step toward civilization, except under the fostering care and guidance of the white man."[75] The inherent racial inferiority of African Americans made disfranchisement a reform for the good of democracy itself, whether accomplished via the poll tax, the grandfather clause, or some other device.

After the century's turn, white politicians in the South no longer competed for the black vote. Instead, they emphasized their commitment to white supremacy and their absolute opposition to any form of equality for African Americans, including the franchise. The political equality that was implied by the ballot would come with the "natural, indeed the irresistible, tendency" to social equality and race amalgamation, which were anathema to the subjugationist position on the permanent inferiority of African Americans.[76] Subjugationist rhetoric on the dangers posed by unqualified voters and the eventual threat posed by social equality made Jim Crow laws "essential, instead of hostile, to the nation's constitution" and to the preservation of law and order.[77]

The removal of African Americans from the ranks of registered voters thus constituted a "reform" supported by Southern Progressives. As Steven J. Diner has argued, having "removed African-Americans from the polity," many Southern politicians and reformers felt they could better address "the issues of democratic governance (for whites) and corporate power that dominated the nation's politics elsewhere."[78] Even James Vardaman, the infamous white-supremacist governor of Mississippi, established a reputation as a Progressive because he improved educational and social services for whites and put new controls in place for corporations.[79]

Northern white observers showed little interest in challenging this Southern version of progressivism, as future president Woodrow Wilson observed in 1902.[80]

ROOSEVELT AND DEVELOPMENTAL RHETORIC

Assessing the role played by Roosevelt in the Progressive movement and the commitment of Roosevelt to a reform agenda has been frustrating for historians and rhetoricians alike. As Richard Hofstadter says of Roosevelt's behavior during his presidency, "it is hard to understand how Roosevelt managed to keep his reputation as a strenuous reformer."[81] After reviewing evidence that Roosevelt lacked much enthusiasm for trust-busting and other progressive passions, Hoftstadter maintains that Roosevelt was a conservative nationalist who wished to put only the most modest reforms in place. Progressives such as Robert La Follette of Wisconsin who sought more systemic social change and economic reform were perceived by many business leaders and "standpatters" as far more dangerous and radical than Roosevelt.[82] In contrast, Stephen E. Lucas argues that Roosevelt, while still opposed to radicalism or "revolutionary sentiment," grew increasingly sympathetic to sweeping progressive reform efforts from the last years of his presidency to his 1912 campaign for the presidency as a Bull Moose Progressive.[83] Lucas claims that Roosevelt's famous "Man with the Muck-Rake" speech of 1906 "reflected TR's increasing disenchantment with political and economic conservatism" and was "a milestone along his movement to the left."[84]

Whatever one's assessment of Roosevelt's enthusiasm for progressivism, Roosevelt's treatment of African Americans was not ungenerous when judged by the political climate of his time. As president, Roosevelt did continue the Republican practice of appointing some African Americans to government offices when that practice was increasingly coming under fire in the former Confederate states. Further, Roosevelt has been complimented for his "generous enthusiasms" in such matters as inviting Booker T. Washington to the White House for dinner, a meeting that infuriated advocates of racial segregation and opponents of social equality.[85] In 1900, Roosevelt maintained that the citizens of a successful democracy must have "a firm and lofty purpose to do justice to all men and guard the rights of the weak as well as the strong," and he repeatedly expressed his wish that African Americans be given equal opportunities.[86]

In other ways, however, Roosevelt's treatment of African Americans was less progressive. First, Roosevelt's dismissal of African-American soldiers on the basis of rather thin evidence after an incident in Brownsville, Texas, alienated many of his African-American supporters. Second, Roosevelt made few African-American appointments in the South, though he never retracted an appointment once it was made. Many of the African Americans he did appoint were from the North, where such appointments entailed less political risk. Third, once the political drawbacks of meeting African Americans in social settings became clear, Roosevelt no longer issued dinner invitations to African-American leaders during his presidency. In one letter written some time after his evening spent with Washington, Roosevelt expressed regret that he ever had issued that invitation.[87]

Roosevelt's concerns about the Booker T. Washington meeting appeared to be typical of his attitude toward African Americans. For Roosevelt, the race problem was a constant irritant, a distraction that drew him away from more important matters. As he wrote in one letter in 1913, "Ugh! There is not any more puzzling problem in this country than the problem of color. It is not as urgent, or as menacing, as other problems, but it seems more utterly insoluble."[88] Roosevelt's behavior in the months leading up to his 1912 presidential candidacy certainly demonstrates his willingness to engage in political compromise where African-American political involvement was concerned. In an attempt to gain white supporters in the South, Roosevelt caved in to pressure from "lily white" Southern Progressives and cooperated in the barring of African Americans from membership in the state progressive parties of the former Confederate states. (This strategy ultimately failed, since Southern whites still perceived him as too friendly to African-American interests. In the 1912 election, Roosevelt lost badly in all the Southern states.)[89]

Beyond matters of political pragmatism, Roosevelt's consistent use of a developmental rhetoric may explain his seemingly mixed record on the racial politics of his day. Roosevelt employed such a rhetoric consistently, whether in his references to Filipinos, Native Americans, or African Americans.

Concerning the Philippines, Roosevelt maintained that U.S. occupation of the islands was of great help to Filipinos. In 1901 Roosevelt declared that, following U.S. acquisition of the islands, "a greater measure of material prosperity and of governmental honesty" had been attained in the Philippines "than ever before in their history."[90] However, the development of the Filipino capacity for self-government would not be quick or easy: "It is no light task for a nation to achieve the temperamental qualities without which the institutions of free government are but an empty mockery. Our people are now successfully governing themselves, because for more than a thousand years they have been slowly fitting themselves, sometimes consciously, sometimes, unconsciously, toward this end. What has taken us thirty generations to achieve, we cannot expect to see another race accomplish out of hand, especially when large portions of that race start very far behind the point which our ancestors had reached even thirty generations ago. In dealing with the Philippine people we must show both patience and strength, forbearance and steadfast resolution."[91]

Such patience would help Filipinos "to rise higher and higher in the scale of civilization," but the Philippines were "as yet totally unfit" for independence.[92] After another generation the independence of the Philippines might be possible, but no one could "prophesy the exact date" when it would be "wise to consider independence as a fixed and definite policy."[93] In accord with the typical rhetoric of development, the inferiority of Filipinos meant that only very slow progress would be possible in the direction of complete self-government. If anything, Roosevelt worried that the United States was "proceeding too rapidly in the direction of granting a large measure of self-government" to the Philippines.[94]

Roosevelt also suggested that the development of Native Americans would be slow and deliberate: "The progress of the Indians toward civilization, though not rapid, is perhaps all that could be hoped for in view of the circumstances."[95] In attempting to "lift up the savage," the education provided to Native Americans should be "elementary and largely industrial," given the current conditions on reservations.[96] While some individual Native Americans were "absolutely indistinguishable in point of social, political, and economic ability from their white associates," Native Americans as a group were not ready for "immediate absorption into some more highly developed community."[97] Again, the long-term development of an inferior race was the goal outlined by Roosevelt.

In discussing the status of African Americans, Roosevelt was also consistent in calling for development. For example, in his most famous statement on lynching, Roosevelt blamed the alleged African-American proclivity for rape for most lynchings. While denouncing lynching as "a bestial deed," Roosevelt also described rape as "even worse than murder" and hinted that the willingness of African Americans to hide accused rapists from law enforcement officers was even worse than the crime of lynching itself.[98] Curiously, the solution to the twin crimes of lynching and rape was the industrial education associated with Booker T. Washington: "The graduates of these schools turn out well in the great majority of cases, and hardly any of them become criminals."[99] Conveniently, such industrial training also helped the African American to "do most for himself and be most helpful to his white neighbors."[100]

The development of African Americans, as with Filipinos and Native Americans, would be slow. The African-American race had "to wait and bide its time; to prove itself worthy by showing its possession of perseverance, of thrift, of self-control. The destiny of the race . . . must be worked out patiently and persistently along these lines."[101] In the meantime, white folks were obligated to "treat well the colored man who shows by his life that he deserves such treatment."[102] As with Native Americans, Roosevelt counseled respect for *individual* accomplishments while proscribing more development for the *group* that remained inferior to the dominant white race.

Whether dealing with Filipinos, Native Americans, or African Americans, Roosevelt argued for incremental development of inferior races, yet Roosevelt appreciated the accomplishments of talented individuals, whatever their race. This bifurcation of race and individual in Roosevelt's rhetoric is consistent with his dinner with Washington and his defense of African-American political appointees, while also explaining his lack of effort on behalf of an inferior race that had not yet earned equality. Kelly Miller, a leading African-American intellectual in the early twentieth century, explained Roosevelt's character: "There is little room for the weak and helpless in a strenuous philosophy which glorifies the valiant man. What hope has the feeble and the heavy laden in a dispensation whose gospel relegates the hindermost to the mercy of his satanic captor? Roosevelt has never been the champion of manhood rights. But rather, . . . he believes in manhood first and rights afterward. He has little of the humanitarian sentimentalism that would stoop to the infirmities of the weak. . . . [I]f some men allow themselves to be pushed down, the overthrowers rather than the overthrown command his higher respect because they manifest the greater degree of power."[103]

Miller, however, did not recognize the import of his own analysis. In the same essay, he complained that Roosevelt lacked "consecutiveness and persistence of policy and purpose."[104] Instead, Roosevelt's policy decisions were perfectly consistent with the rhetoric of development. The interests of the superior race trumped those of the inferior race. While individuals of ability and talent should be well and fairly treated, most African Americans were consigned to the slow development of their abilities while Roosevelt's attention was turned elsewhere.

Conventional wisdom has it that Roosevelt became more sympathetic to reform as he neared the end of his presidency and especially by the time of his Bull Moose campaign. Whether this general conclusion also applies to Roosevelt's attitude toward African Americans is not certain. Even in 1912, his discourse displayed the same penchant for African-American development that had marked his earlier rhetoric. For example, in 1912 Roosevelt, not surprisingly, advised African Americans that neither Democrats nor Republicans took them seriously or dealt with them honestly. In contrast with the two major parties, Roosevelt's most specific plan for improving race relations was to "try for the worthy colored man of the South by frankly giving the leadership of our movement to the wisest and justest white men of the South." In doing so, Roosevelt hoped to secure "the right of free political expression" for the African American "who shows that he possesses the intelligence, integrity, and self-respect which justify such right of political expression in his white neighbor."[105] Roosevelt also approvingly quoted Julian Harris, a white Georgia Progressive who claimed that the "patriotic, sensible white men of the South desire to see the negro built up in character and stimulated to a sense of personal responsibility."[106]

These passages suggest no major rhetorical shift for Roosevelt where African Americans were concerned. That only "worthy" African Americans would receive the franchise meant that no serious increase in African-American voting would result. To earn the right of political expression, African Americans would have to demonstrate that they were as politically competent as their white counterparts, which Roosevelt could not have perceived as likely in the foreseeable future. While Roosevelt demanded that individual accomplishments be respected by the limited expansion of voting rights, his promise here made no concession to African Americans as a group. Further, Roosevelt emphasized the need for white leadership in fostering African-American progress. In short, the Roosevelt of 1912 still employed the rhetoric of development.

Roosevelt's penchant for developmental rhetoric is not surprising, as developmental rhetoric has been described as marking typical progressive attitudes toward race. This conclusion is understandable, as Booker T. Washington's famous Atlanta Exposition address of 1895 employed a developmental rhetoric and is sometimes taken as indicative of progressive attitudes toward African Americans. In his address, Washington essentially conceded the inferiority of African Americans at that time, as he contended that they should start "at the bottom of life" with agricultural and industrial pursuits, rather than "at the top" with the pursuit of political influence. In a famous metaphor Washington also denied an imminent African-American interest in social equality: "In all things that are purely social we can be as separate as the fingers, yet one as the hand in all things essential to mutual progress." While concentrating at the present on economic improvement, Washington proclaimed that his goals were "the highest intelligence and development of all" and "the fullest growth of the Negro."[107]

Washington never renounced the goals of full political, economic, and social equality for African Americans in his Atlanta Exposition address. Instead, he emphasized only that political and social equality would not be a priority for the immediate future. The opportunity "to earn a dollar just now" was "worth infinitely more than the opportunity to spend a dollar at the opera-house."[108] Further, Washington prophesied that economic progress for African Americans would eventually mean full equality, as "no race that has anything to contribute to the markets of the world is long in any degree ostracized."[109] In making such claims, Washington signified faith in racial development, and his expectations for the speed with which such development would take place seemed much more optimistic than the predictions of white developmentalists on this point. Ultimately, however, the rhetoric of development when used by Washington was a tacit assent to the passage of Jim Crow laws, and white developmentalists and subjugationists could agree to support such laws, even if they disagreed on the rationales for their passage.

Thus far, I have suggested that the rhetorics of subjugation and development marked two different trajectories in progressive rhetoric on race. Inspired in part by the new U.S. experience with imperialism, the rhetorical status of African Americans during the Progressive Era moved from being a chronic regional, Southern problem to the domestic manifestation of a national and international concern. How should a nation that identified itself as white deal with the non-white other? The two answers most frequently made to this question were (1) to describe all other races as permanently inferior or (2) to conclude that such races were currently inferior but could be improved with sufficient instruction and supervision. Both rhetorics legitimized the imperialist experiment, and both supported a series of domestic reforms that rendered U.S. domestic racial policy consistent with the emerging U.S. colonial policy toward subject races. These progressive reforms and the arguments that sustained them would outlast the Progressive Era itself to become major influences on twentieth-century debates on race. One rhetorical legacy of the racial attitudes of the Progressive Era was the twentieth-century Ku Klux Klan.

Progress and the Ku Klux Klan

While the rhetorics of subjugation and development were prominently featured during the Progressive Era and were consistent with progressive reforms, those rhetorics continued to circulate long after Jim Crow laws were firmly in place and early fears about U.S. imperialism had subsided. These rhetorics of subjugation and development both were featured by those associated with the twentieth-century Ku Klux Klan. While the rhetoric of subjugation was by far the most prevalent in the Klan texts of the 1920s, both developmental and subjugationist rhetorics were the effluvia of progressivism found in the advocacy of Ku Klux Klan supporters. In the discussion that follows I describe the rebirth of the Ku Klux Klan in 1915 and show how the Klan was, in a sense, a rhetorical legacy of progressivism.

THE KU KLUX KLAN REBORN

The nineteenth-century Klan was founded in Pulaski, Tennessee, in the years immediately following the Civil War. The Klan's secrecy and strange hooded regalia provided an ideal cover for night-riding and vigilantism. Many Southern whites devoutly maintained at the time and in later decades that the original Klan was necessary to maintain order in the chaotic Reconstruction era. Eventually, tales of Klan violence and state and federal anti-Klan laws combined to reduce and, ultimately, to end Klan organizing. In 1869, ex-Confederate General Nathan Bedford Forrest, the Klan's grand wizard, announced the disbanding of the Klan and ordered Klan records destroyed. While scattered Klan activity persisted for years, the end of Reconstruction in 1876–77 gave Southern whites institutional options for reasserting their political control in the states of the former confederacy.[110] The Klan then lay dormant for several decades, remembered by some white Southerners with affection and by others with disgust and antipathy. For the next forty years the Klan lived only as a historical curiosity, a memory of bygone Southern days.

The individual responsible for recreating the Klan in 1915 was curiously non-threatening. An unsuccessful minister and circuit rider, an undistinguished veteran of the Spanish-American War, and a one-time lecturer in Southern history at a failing Atlanta University, William Joseph Simmons was notable most of all for his enthusiasm for the fraternal organizations popular in his day. While recuperating in bed from an injury, Simmons claimed to have had a vision that inspired him to form a new fraternal organization, a revived Ku Klux Klan, and the showing of *The Birth of a Nation* in Atlanta and other events in 1915 encouraged him to go through with his plans. On Thanksgiving Day, 1915, Simmons chartered a bus and took fifteen men to Stone Mountain for a Klan initiation ceremony. In all, there were thirty-five charter members of Simmon's fledgling Klan, two of whom allegedly had been involved in its Reconstruction era predecessor.

While the first five years for the new, "second" Klan were not marked by impressive membership gains (only Georgia and Alabama had significant Klan enrollment), events after World War I combined with Simmons's agreement with a public relations firm to produce rapid Klan membership gains in all parts of the United States; the two states with the largest Klan membership in the mid 1920s were Indiana and Ohio. Klan membership would expand from under one hundred thousand (mostly in the South) in 1921 to over one million Klan members in every region of the country by 1925.[111] In late 1922, a group of Klan faithful used duplicitous tactics to persuade the administratively inept Simmons to accept the impressive but powerless post of emperor and to hand over the office of imperial wizard to Hiram Wesley Evans.[112] Evans would preside over the most successful years in the history of any Klan organization, though the Klan's membership declined substantially after the mid 1920s.[113]

THE PROGRESSIVE KLAN

Most scholars mark the end of the Progressive Era between 1915 and 1920, as struggles over modernism and its consequences began to dominate the political and cultural landscape. For example, Diner concludes his study of the Progressive Era by arguing that, after World War I, "postwar politics turned decisively against progressive social engineering. . . . Strikes increased, workers lost ground, repression of radicals reached new heights, and racial violence flared in the bloody summer of 1919."[114] The aftermath of World War I did present new problems and prospects for politicians and their constituents, and the Red Scare of 1919 did much to foster nativist sentiment following the war.

However, the Progressive movement did not magically disappear. In many ways progressivism remained influential in the South throughout the 1920s. The Commission on Interracial Cooperation, for example, combated Southern lynchings and blatant forms of racial injustice during the 1920s, though it carefully avoided any appearance of challenging white supremacy. Southern Progressives, often in alliance with rural interests, also challenged trusts and campaigned against political machines. Finally, Southern Progressives crusaded against a hodgepodge of moral vices in the 1920s, including violation of prohibition laws.[115]

The connection between progressivism and the new Ku Klux Klan of the twentieth century has received relatively little attention. The traditional histories of the Klan provided by such scholars as David M. Chalmers and Wyn Craig Wade essentially ignore the Progressive movement altogether, preferring instead to explain the Klan's founding and growth as the products of nativism, religious fundamentalism, a reactionary fear of modernization, and so on. While these factors all played some role in the Klan from 1915 to 1925—reasons for the Klan's growth varied wildly from state to state[116]—I wish to develop Dewey W. Grantham's provocative statement as my thesis for the remainder of this chapter: "The Klan for all its prejudice and violence, was in part a reform movement with a heritage from prewar progressivism. Community morals were an overriding concern of the organization's members, whose activities represented, among other things, a general quest for moral and social conformity."[117] Where race was concerned, such reforms were described using the familiar progressive rhetorics of subjugation or development.

Not surprisingly, the second Klan was pledged to white supremacy from its beginning in 1915 and used many of the same arguments for white supremacy found in earlier subjugationist rhetorics. For example, as one unnamed "exalted cyclops" of the Klan explained in 1923, "The Klan is fulfilling a needed mission in urging upon Americans the duty of preserving America's precious race heritage. This country was founded by the finest elements of the white race. This Government was established by the same superior types of the white race. They passed it on to posterity to be maintained by white men as a white man's country for white men. They bequeathed to their descendants the responsibility of preserving the integrity of the race by keeping pure the blood of the white man's race."[118] While there might be different types of white racial stocks, the preservation of white supremacy by maintaining white racial purity was a multigenerational obligation. The Klan had "no fight to make upon the Negro," but African Americans were "recognized as an inferior race." The Klan also was sworn, conveniently enough, to help African Americans preserve the "purity" of their race. While the "moral and spiritual being" of African Americans might be elevated by the Klan's efforts, the inferior race was to be kept separate from other, superior genetic stocks.[119]

For the Klan, white supremacy was required for democracy to work, as the racial characteristics of whiteness had led to the development of democratic institutions and were uniquely compatible with democracy. The permanent subjugation of nonwhites to white political influence and the separation of the superior race from the corrupting influence of inferior races was the logical consequence of this position. As an unidentified "grand titan" from Georgia insisted, "the hope and destiny of the nation rests in white supremacy. It will preserve the doctrines of popular liberty which lie at the foundation of our government, these ideals which are enshrined in the constitution of the republic and our free institutions." The white and, more specifically, the Anglo-Saxon racial identity of Washington, Jefferson, Hamilton, and Madison was held up as evidence of white supremacy where democratic institutions were concerned.[120] The exalted cyclops quoted above also explicitly linked white racial purity to the preservation of democracy, as "by amalgamation of bloods the people of America will be mongrelized; and . . . by political amalgamation the Government of the United States will be mongrelized."[121]

The permanent inferiority of nonwhite peoples made their political subjugation essential to the preservation of robust democratic institutions; without their subjugation democracy could not work. That democratic decision-making authority was not extended to nonwhite folk was not terribly problematic, as nonwhites were incapable of democratic government in any event. There were "nations and races" that could never be "Americanized" in their commitment to democratic institutions, because there was "no way of changing a snake into a man, or a sheep into a bull-dog."[122]

Complicating the white supremacy of the Klan was the presence of nominally white U.S. citizens who were Roman Catholics and, consequently, whose allegiance to the pope allegedly compromised their loyalties as citizens. After all, the dangers posed to America by Catholicism were discussed more often by national Klan leaders than was any other issue. How could whites adhere to a religion that had "always opposed the fundamental principle of liberty for which America stands," according to Evans?[123] The solution to the problem of white ideological and religious divisions was to parse distinctions between different kinds of whiteness, as did race theorists of the period such as Lothrop Stoddard.[124] In contrast with Anglo-Saxons, who were descended from the Protestant peoples of northern Europe, Evans identified "Celts" and "Mediterraneans" as "unstable" groups whose first loyalties were to the "Roman church." While Evans conceded that "a slight mixture of Celtic blood" was "valuable to the Anglo-Saxon race," he dismissed Mediterraneans as people "of mixed blood" who came "from lands where incompetence and laziness can survive." In addition, "Alpines" were the peasants of eastern Europe who contributed "nothing to leadership, initiative and independence." Alpines also were "controlled and dominated by the Roman Church."[125]

The racialized identity of the Roman Catholic, whose Catholicism was rhetorically linked to her or his subaltern racial standing, explained why these white Catholics were "so steeped in allegiance different from that of the American group" that they could not "become loyal members of our national body."[126] Joining the ranks of those nonwhite races who could not and would not ever be American were the inferior branches of the white race that were infected by Roman Catholicism. When Evans maintained that it was "the klan's object to create and sustain a civilian authority incomparably equipped by heredity, by experience, by the sum of its qualities" to lead America effectively, he was arguing for the political supremacy of a certain kind of white folk who were both Protestant and Anglo-Saxon.[127] The political marginalization of those possessing the wrong kind of whiteness was the logical extension of the earlier rhetoric of subjugation aimed at African Americans and other nonwhite peoples.

Restriction of immigration, disfranchisement of African Americans, mandatory attendance at public schools, and Protestant Christian religious instruction in the public schools were perceived by the Klan as *reforms* aimed at reducing or eliminating influences incommensurable with American democracy. For example, Evans maintained that saving "true democracy" in the United States required that the Roman Catholic effort to "de-Americanize our schools" be thwarted. The remedy proposed by Evans was quite clear: "As a matter of fact, if our schools are to teach Americanism, there should not be in them a single teacher whose first allegiance is to a foreign temporal sovereign."[128]

Evans's solution to the problems posed by inferior races or groups, whether white or not, included the goal of drastically restricting immigration to the United States for those belonging to races that could not be assimilated, and he expressed approval for the extant ban on Chinese and Japanese immigration to the United States. In dealing with non-Anglos already living in the United States, the exclusion of such peoples from social or political equality was required because they were not suited to or qualified for equality. For example, where African Americans were concerned, the African American "cannot be assimilated. Intermarriage with him on a wholesale scale is unthinkable. . . . He cannot attain the Anglo-Saxon level. . . . It is not in his best interests any more than in the interests of our white population that he should seek to assume the burdens of modern government."[129] Again, subjugation was the goal announced and pursued by Evans. Evans's position on African Americans was supported in part by his reading of Booker T. Washington's Atlanta Exposition address as consistent with subjugation: "Booker T. Washington, the greatest of Negro leaders, exhorted his brethren to cast aside their political and social ambitions. The Klan stands where he stood upon this phase of the question."[130] Washington's insistence that African Americans would eventually be treated as equals was ignored by Evans.

In summary, advocacy of nativist policies was meant to do nothing other than guarantee good government by ensuring the production of citizens committed to the inseparable principles of American democracy and Protestant Christianity. Oddly enough, given the beliefs of Klan adherents, the Klan's policy proposals are not hard to understand as reform measures consistent with the preservation of political power for those favoring the related causes of white supremacy and Protestant political domination. As Georgia governor Clifford Walker explained when addressing a Klan convention in 1924, he would "build a wall of steel . . . against the admission of those Southern Europeans who never thought the thoughts or spoke the language of a democracy." Governor Walker would admit only a "reasonable number of Swedes, of Norwegians or of any other type of those Northern and Western States of Europe" as immigrants, and even they would have to learn English quickly and attend an "academy of democracy" to stay in the U.S.[131] Such immigration restrictions, when combined with the social and political marginalization of lesser racial groups, would preserve American democracy.

While the rhetoric of subjugation was more prevalent in Klan discourse than the rhetoric of development, developmental arguments also can be found in Klan artifacts from the 1920s. For example, Klan member Blaine Mast, a district attorney from Pennsylvania, noted in 1924 that the Klan had been "originally organized to combat unscrupulous and criminal negroes," but the Klan was "in nowise opposed to the black man" and wished "to help the colored race."[132] Indeed, the Klan gave "great credit to the colored people for the rapid strides" of the previous half-century. According to Mast, "How . . . can the K.K.K. be opposed to the negro? The Klan is looking hopefully forward to the day when all prejudices shall disappear, when mob-law and lynchings shall become things of the past, and when all the disagreeable things, the crimes of which we read and we deplore and execrate, shall

RHETORIC AND RACE IN
THE PROGRESSIVE ERA

329

be regarded by future generations, much as we regard the ghost and witch stories of past ages!"[133]

How was this future to be reached? For Mast, a future without prejudice would come to pass once "the leaders of the black in America" had "train[ed] and educate[d] their less fortunate brothers to become law-abiding citizens, honoring and fearing God, respecting their white neighbors, . . . and working with others of paler hue for the up-building of all that is best and noblest in our New World civilization."[134] While the responsibility for African-American development belonged primarily to African Americans and no timetable for this optimal future was suggested, Mast embraced the possibility of a world in which African Americans participated more fully in public life. In contrast, such a possibility was incommensurable with the rhetoric of subjugation more commonly found in Klan discourse.

Whether using the rhetoric of subjugation or development in their talk of race, race was often featured in Klan texts that called for various reforms. While the issues of interest to Klan members varied widely from one state "realm" or local "klavern" to another, Klan members and sympathizers frequently saw themselves as enforcing "moral standards" in an increasingly lax and tolerant society.[135] For example, where African Americans were concerned, Mast maintained that the Klan was "not hostile to the colored race" but was "opposed to 'bad niggers'" and would "do all in its power to deter such from the commission of unnamable [sic] crimes, which, too often are perpetrated in our communities, both north and south. . . . Colored men who are guilty of such deeds will bring down condign punishment on their heads, especially if the proper authorities do not act promptly."[136] While Mast defended the rule of law, he also insisted that outrages committed by African Americans would risk white "mob-rule" in any part of the United States.[137] Mast hoped that the moral authority of the Klan could force lawful authorities to do their duty and "curb the law-violaters, whether bootleggers, brewers, distillers, saloon-keepers, or the 'higher-ups.'"[138]

Because progressivism, especially in its Southern manifestations, emphasized the cultivation of virtue, the connections between the Klan's moral reform efforts and progressivism are not difficult to see. As one Klan member optimistically remarked, when the Klan "began to function, bootleggers and joint runners, drunkards, wife-beaters, deserters, and the lawless element generally began to fade away."[139] The Klan, insisted a pro-Klan Louisiana minister, stood for the "upholding of the law" and provided the "back bone" to oppose "boot-leggers, horse thieves, black-leg gambler ano [sic] immoral profligates running rempant [sic]."[140]

The Ku Klux Klan as a progressive reform movement strains the imagination today. Like its Reconstruction predecessor, the Klan of the 1920s had an infamous record of violence and mayhem, despite the insistence of its national leaders that the second Klan was nonviolent. Yet most white citizens of the time did not perceive any inconsistency between the Klan name and its alleged moral, reform-oriented purpose. Given the received history of the Reconstruction Klan, especially in the South, the new Klan was credible as a progressive reform movement because its anti-immigrant, anti-Catholic stance and its white supremacy were entirely consistent with the defense of traditional morality and the advocacy of political reforms. Indeed, where race was concerned the Klan largely borrowed the two rhetorical vectors found in earlier progressive movements: the rhetoric of subjugation and the rhetoric of development. Only multiple national scandals eventually deprived the Klan of its moral authority as a reform movement.[141]

Conclusion: The Price of Progress

We return to the original problem described in the epigraph for this chapter: Was democracy expansive enough during the Progressive Era to include anyone other than white citizens of Anglo-Saxon descent? The answer for African Americans, at least, was no. The two white rhetorics dealing with race that were found most often during the Progressive Era denied that African Americans were suited for full U.S. citizenship. The subjugationist did not believe that African Americans could or should ever be citizens, while the developmentalist concluded that African Americans were not yet ready for full citizenship. The anastomosis of the subjugationist and developmentalist positions was the systematic exclusion of African Americans from meaningful participation in democratic institutions and, ultimately, exclusion from white society itself.

In *Crafting Equality: America's Anglo-African Word*, Celeste Michelle Condit and John Louis Lucaites note that white supremacists during the 1870s employed two different rhetorics. According to Condit and Lucaites, "fire-eaters" emphasized the permanent inferiority of African Americans, while paternalists argued for African-American disfranchisement and segregation until African Americans "could be helped to achieve an elevated position in society."[142] However, Condit and Lucaites maintained that by the 1880s "the voices of the patriarch and the fire-eater gradually merged in the national public arena," and "the tone of the fire-eater came to predominate the white supremacist voice."[143] By the end of the nineteenth century, they conclude, white supremacists, who now spoke essentially with one voice, "had achieved an entrenched, de facto control of the race issue in America, especially in the South."[144]

While the rhetoric of the fire-eaters was consistent with later subjugationist voices and the paternalistic rhetoric of the 1870s foreshadowed later developmental discourse, this chapter suggests that white supremacy split again during the Progressive Era. Perhaps in part because of the African-American challenge, white supremacists during the heyday of progressivism used both subjugationist and developmental rhetorics in their attempts to defend past and present "reforms" designed to disfranchise African Americans and exclude them from public life. Subjugationists, rather than rejecting reform measures and appealing to tradition, most often embraced the language of reform to describe their treatment of African Americans. Developmental Progressives, rather than exemplifying the "mild egalitarianism" outlined by Condit and Lucaites, described the development of African Americans in terms that suggested their development toward full citizenship would take a century or more.[145] Given this timeline, developmentalists could embrace a progressive cause while remaining loyal to the tenets of white supremacy for the foreseeable future. Developmental Progressives occupied a third, middle position between subjugation and egalitarianism that presumably made white supremacy more palatable.

This chapter also suggests that closer attention should be paid to the connections between progressivism and the Ku Klux Klan. Scholars generally have not considered the relationship between progressivism and the Klan. For example, Richard Hofstadter notes that the Klan was a defensive social movement valorizing the "older American type" and opposing "the intelligentsia who were trying to kill" that type.[146] In making these observations, however, Hofstadter does not consider the Klan's embrace of law-and-order causes such as prohibition that were not the primary concerns of an earlier age. For Hofstadter the Klan provided evidence only of the fundamentalist Christian's critique of modernism. Several histories of the Klan also have described the Klan as a last-ditch defense against the social changes of the 1920s. Both views have ignored the rhetorical similarities between the Klan and the movements or causes of previous eras, with the exception of nativist groups such as the Know-Nothings.[147]

More recently, Shawn Lay's study of the 1920s Klan in Buffalo, New York, emphasizes the Buffalo klavern's gradual "embrace [of] the cause of moral reform," with local Klan members lobbying for better enforcement of prohibition and vice laws in Buffalo.[148] Klan members launched highly public investigations of criminal activity in their city, and letters to Buffalo city officials bearing the Klan seal even reported on "illegal Sunday theatrical performances."[149] Lay describes the Buffalo Klan as nonviolent and committed generally to social reform. Ultimately, though, Lay concludes that the Klan's embrace of reform issues in Buffalo was a pragmatic effort to avoid "total political impotence" by forcing "officials to modify their policies."[150] Again, the potential comparison of the Klan to earlier reform or protest movements is not made, despite the common causes shared by many Progressives with Klan members two decades later.

Rather than explaining the Klan's influence during the 1920s as a product of antimodernist sentiment or the pragmatic search for political influence, this chapter has suggested the third possibility that progressive rhetorics had a significant influence on Klan discourse. At least where race is concerned, the Klan owed much of its rhetoric to the developmental and, more centrally, the subjugationist rhetoric of the Progressive Era. While we might date the end of progressivism to the time of World War I, the rhetoric of the Progressive Era lingered long after the conclusion of that war, circulating once again in response to racial tension and religious antipathy. While developmentalists played a part in the Klan, the rhetoric of the subjugationist Progressives played the dominant role in defining the relationship of whiteness to the nonwhite other, all in the name of moral and political reform. Klan members frequently cast themselves as reformers with an appreciation for racial differences, much as had their subjugationist and developmental predecessors two decades earlier.

The rhetoric of subjugation and the rhetoric of development shared core commitments to white supremacy, and the course of action endorsed by these rhetorics did not differ in any meaningful way. Nevertheless, informed in part by the U.S. experience with imperialism, these two voices during the Progressive Era figured in the emergence of a rhetorical climate in which African Americans made nothing that we would recognize today as progress. The legacy of these two progressive rhetorics should not be ignored.

Notes

1. The terms "racist" and "racism" would not come into common use until the late 1930s. Like Thomas G. Dyer, I use the terms "racist" and "racism" in this chapter as synonymous "with one who practices race prejudice and race discrimination," phrases that were in use during the Progressive Era. Thomas G. Dyer, *Theodore Roosevelt and the Idea of Race* (Baton Rouge: Louisiana State University Press, 1980), xii n. 1.
2. Robert H. Wiebe, *The Search for Order, 1877–1920* (New York: Hill and Wang, 1967), 165. Throughout this chapter, I use the label "white" to refer to those who described themselves as "white," independent of whether this label makes anthropological or historical sense. David R. Roediger and other scholars have described the ways in which the rhetorical construction of whiteness has evolved over time. See James Barrett and David R. Roediger, "Inbetween Peoples: Race, Nationality, and the 'New Immigrant' Working Class," *Journal of American Ethnic History* 16 (1997): 3–44; Matthew Frye Jacobson, *Whiteness of a Different Color: European Immigrants and the Alchemy of Race* (Cambridge: Harvard University Press, 1998); Mae M. Ngai, "The Architecture of Race in American Immigration Law: A Reexamination of the Immigration Act of

1924," *Journal of American History* 86 (1999): 67–92; David R. Roediger, *The Wages of Whiteness: Race and the Making of the American Working Class* (London: Verso, 1991); and David R. Roediger, *Towards the Abolition of Whiteness* (London: Verso, 1994).

3. C. Vann Woodward, *The Strange Career of Jim Crow*, 3d ed. (New York: Oxford University Press, 1974), 74. For Woodward's responses to some criticisms of the so-called Woodward thesis, see C. Vann Woodward, *American Counterpoint: Slavery and Racism in the North/South Dialogue* (Oxford: Oxford University Press, 1971), 234–60.

4. Woodward, *Strange Career*, 74.

5. Kelly Miller, *Race Adjustment: Essays on the Negro in America* (New York: Neale, 1908), 21.

6. W. E. B. Du Bois, *W. E. B. Du Bois Speaks: Speeches and Addresses, 1890–1919*, ed. Philip S. Foner (New York: Pathfinder, 1970), 170.

7. James Weldon Johnson, *The Autobiography of an Ex-coloured Man* (1912; reprint, New York: Hill and Wang, 1960), 76.

8. David H. Bennett, *The Party of Fear: From Nativist Movements to the New Right in American History* (1988; reprint, New York: Vintage-Random House, 1990), 179.

9. Samuel Eliot Morison and Henry Steele Commager, *The Growth of the American Republic* (London: Oxford University Press, 1942), 2:356.

10. Ibid., 2:378.

11. Hoke Smith, as quoted in T. Harry Williams, *Romance and Realism in Southern Politics* (Baton Rouge: Louisiana State University Press, 1966), 60–61.

12. Robert Bennett Bean, "The Negro Brain," in *The Development of Segregationist Thought*, ed. I. A. Newby (Homewood, Ill.: Dorsey, 1968), 47.

13. Ibid.

14. Ibid., 53.

15. Thomas W. Hardwick, "A Defense of Negro Disfranchisement," in *The Development of Segregationist Thought*, 103.

16. Hubert Howe Bancroft, "A Historian's View of the Negro," in *The Development of Segregationist Thought*, 83.

17. Bancroft, "A Historian's View," in *The Development of Segregationist Thought*, 80.

18. Brian R. McGee, "Thomas Dixon's *The Clansman*: Radicals, Reactionaries, and the Anticipated Utopia," *Southern Communication Journal* 65 (2000): 308.

19. Howard W. Odum, *Social and Mental Traits of the Negro: Research into the Conditions of the Negro Race in Southern Towns* (New York: Columbia University Press, 1910), 39.

20. William Benjamin Smith, *The Color Line: A Brief in Behalf of the Unborn* (New York: McClure, Phillips, 1905), 165.

21. Odum, *Social and Mental Traits*, 41.

22. Hardwick, "A Defense," in *The Development of Segregationist Thought*, 101.

23. Quoted in Quincy Ewing, "The Heart of the Race Problem," *Atlantic Monthly* 103 (1909): 392.

24. Nathaniel Southgate Shaler, "The Permanence of Racial Characteristics," in *The Development of Segregationist Thought*, 60.

25. Bean, "The Negro Brain," in *The Development of Segregationist Thought*, 48.

26. Frank Clark, "A Politician's Defense of Segregation," in *The Development of Segregationist Thought*, 95.

27. Ibid., 97.

28. Odum, *Social and Mental Traits*, 289, 290.

29. John E. White, "Prohibition: The New Task and Opportunity of the South," *South Atlantic Quarterly* 7 (1908): 136–37.

30. A. J. McKelway, "State Prohibition in Georgia and the South," *Outlook*, 31 August 1907, 948, 949.

31. A. J. McKelway, "Local Option and State Prohibition in the South," *Charities and the Commons*, 25 January 1908, 1453.

32. Frank Foxcroft, "Prohibition in the South," *Atlantic Monthly* 101 (1908): 632.

33. A. J. McKelway, "The Atlanta Riots 1: A Southern White Point of View," *Outlook*, 3 November 1906, 562.

34. John Carlisle Kilgo, "Our Duty to the Negro," *South Atlantic Quarterly* 2 (1903): 372.

35. Ibid., 373.

36. Ibid., 374–75.

37. Ibid., 375.

38. Ibid., 379.

39. Ibid., 379, 380, 384.

40. Ibid., 379.

41. Ibid., 375–76.

42. Ibid., 374.

43. Edgar Gardner Murphy, "Backward or Forward," *South Atlantic Quarterly* 8 (1909): 35–36.

44. "Stirring Up the Fires of Race Antipathy," *South Atlantic Quarterly* 2 (1903): 304.

45. Jack Temple Kirby, *Darkness at the Dawning: Race and Reform in the Progressive South* (Philadelphia: Lippincott, 1972), 155.

46. On Dixon's career, see Raymond Allen Cook, *Fire from the Flint: The Amazing Careers of Thomas Dixon* (Winston-Salem, N.C.: Blair, 1968); Raymond Allen Cook, *Thomas Dixon* (New York: Twayne, 1974).

47. Joel Williamson, *The Crucible of Race: Black-White Relations in the American South since Emancipation* (New York: Oxford University Press, 1984).

48. Martha Groves Perry, "Reinventing the Nation: Anglo-Saxon Romantic Racial Nationalism from Dixon to James" (Ph.D. diss., University of California, Santa Cruz, 1994), 53, 54.

49. Thomas Dixon Jr., "When Will the Negro Be Free?" *Christian Union* 41, no. 21 (1887): 730.

50. Thomas Dixon Jr., as quoted in Samuel K. Roberts, "Kelly Miller and Thomas Dixon, Jr. on Blacks in American Civilization," *Phylon* 41 (1980): 203.

51. Thomas Dixon Jr., *The Leopard's Spots: A Romance of the White Man's Burden, 1865–1900* (New York: Grosset and Dunlap, 1902), 5. The only African Americans described sympathetically by Dixon are those who cheerfully and faithfully obeyed the orders of their white superiors. For example, Nelse, an African-American servant portrayed in *The Leopard's Spots,* was allowed to manifest the desirable characteristics of devotion, good humor, and empathy.

52. Thomas Dixon Jr., *The Clansman: An Historical Romance of the Ku Klux Klan* (New York: Grosset and Dunlap, 1905), 216.

53. Thomas Dixon Jr., *The Sins of the Father* (New York: D. Appleton-Century Co., 1912), 201.

54. Dixon, *The Leopard's Spots,* 441.

55. Dixon, *The Sins of the Father,* 203.

56. Dixon, *The Leopard's Spots,* 265.

57. Ibid., 338.

58. Ibid., 265.

59. Thomas Dixon Jr., *The Flaming Sword* (Atlanta: Monarch, 1939).

60. Thomas Dixon Jr., "Booker T. Washington and the Negro," *Saturday Evening Post,* 19 August 1905, 2.

61. Ibid., 1.

62. I have omitted here as unconvincing two other explanations for Dixon's adoption of the rhetoric of subjugation. Joel Williamson argues that Dixon's books were "a sort of attenuated ink blot test" in which Dixon worked through his otherwise-unexpressed anger with his father for marrying his mother when she was only thirteen. While Williamson offers some evidence for this explanation, his theory fails to account for the younger Dixon's more generous paternalistic attitude toward African Americans. Williamson, *Crucible of Race,* 165.

    A different theory is attributed to African-American journalist Edward Bruce, who discovered that Thomas Dixon may have had a black half-brother produced by the union of his father and the family's African-American cook. However, the evidence does not seem sufficient to support Luker's claim that Dixon's novels "undoubtedly grew out of an intimate knowledge of interracial sexual exploitation" (Ralph E. Luker, *The Social Gospel in Black and White: American Racial Reform, 1885–1912* [Chapel Hill: University of North Carolina Press, 1991], 299-300).

63. James Kinney, "The Rhetoric of Racism: Thomas Dixon and the 'Damned Black Beast,'" *American Literary Realism, 1870–1910* 15 (1982): 145; Maxwell Bloomfield, "Dixon's *The Leopard's Spots:* A Study in Popular Racism," *American Quarterly* 16 (1964): 400.

64. Samuel K. Roberts's assessment is similar to that of Bloomfield. If nonwhite subjects in the newly acquired colonies were unsuited to democracy, then the same conclusion also would hold for African Americans. Dixon, therefore, "reversed his earlier sympathetic views toward Negroes and launched a vitriolic crusade against those who appeared to him to be distinctly inferior" (Roberts, "Kelly Miller and Thomas Dixon," 203).

65. Dixon, *The Leopard's Spots*, 439.

66. Wiebe, *Search for Order*, 242.

67. Albert J. Beveridge, *The Meaning of the Time and Other Speeches* (Indianapolis: Bobbs-Merrill, 1905), 65.

68. Woodward, *Strange Career*, 73. This was the same Vardaman who, when campaigning for governor of Mississippi in 1900, declared that an African American was a "lazy, lying, lustful animal which no conceivable amount of training can transform into a tolerable citizen" (quoted in Thomas F. Gossett, *Race: The History of an Idea in America* [Dallas: Southern Methodist University Press, 1963], 271). After Vardaman was elected governor, he drastically reduced state funding for African-American public schools and closed all state universities for African Americans. According to Vardaman, "education is ruining our Negroes. They're demanding equality" (quoted in Gossett, *Race*, 277).

69. Dixon, *The Leopard's Spots*, 439.

70. Woodward, *Strange Career,* 73.

71. Hardwick, "A Defense," in *The Development of Segregationist Thought*, 105.

72. For a summary of the contributions of science and social science to racist thought in the early twentieth century, see I. A. Newby, *Jim Crow's Defense: Anti-Negro Thought in America, 1900–1930* (Baton Rouge: Louisiana State University Press, 1965), 19-51.

73. Gossett, *Race*, 267–68.

74. Hardwick, "A Defense," in *The Development of Segregationist Thought*, 102.

75. Ibid., 104.

76. Ibid., 103.

77. Perry, "Reinventing the Nation," 31.

78. Steven J. Diner, *A Very Different Age: Americans of the Progressive Era* (New York: Hill and Wang, 1998), 212.

79. Ibid.

80. Woodrow Wilson, *Reunion and Nationalization*, vol. 5 of *A History of the American People* (New York: Harper and Brothers, 1902), 300.

81. Richard Hofstadter, *The American Political Tradition* (New York: Vintage-Random House, 1948), 225.

82. Ibid., 233–34.

83. Stephen E. Lucas, "Theodore Roosevelt's 'The Man with the Muck-Rake': A Reinterpretation," *Quarterly Journal of Speech* 59 (1973): 460.

84. Ibid., 458–59.

85. Hofstadter, *American Political Tradition*, 228.

86. Theodore Roosevelt, as quoted in David H. Burton, *Theodore Roosevelt, American Politician: An Assessment* (London: Associated Universities Presses, 1997), 25.

87. Concerning the Brownsville incident, see Dyer, *Theodore Roosevelt*, 114–16. On the dinner with Booker T. Washington, see Gossett, *Race*, 269.

88. Quoted in John A. Gable, *The Bull Moose Years: Theodore Roosevelt and the Progressive Party* (Port Washington, N.Y.: Kennikat Press, 1978), 66.

89. Ibid., 60–74.

90. Theodore Roosevelt, *American Problems*, vol. 17 of *The Works of Theodore Roosevelt*, National ed. (New York: Charles Scribner's Sons, 1926), 128.

91. Ibid.

92. Ibid., 307.

93. Ibid., 633.

94. Ibid., 447.

95. Ibid., 279.

96. Ibid., 281, 151.

97. Ibid., 190, 191.

98. Ibid., 412.

99. Ibid., 416.

100. Theodore Roosevelt, *American Problems*, vol. 17 of *Works*, 472.

101. Ibid., 475.

102. Roosevelt, *State Papers*, 413.

103. Miller, *Race Adjustment*, 278.

104. Ibid., 288.

105. Theodore Roosevelt, *Social Justice and Popular Rule*, vol. 19 of *Works*, 416.

106. Ibid., 418.

107. Booker T. Washington, *Up from Slavery* (1901; reprint, New York: Penguin, 1986), 218, 220–22.

108. Ibid., 224.

109. Ibid., 223.

110. The only Reconstruction Klan history written by a self-confessed Klansman (and a knowledgeable co-author) is J[ohn] C. Lester and D[aniel] L. Wilson, *Ku Klux Klan: Its Origin, Growth, and Disbandment* (1905; reprint, New York: Da Capo Press, 1973). Several sources provide discussions of the first Klan, including David Chalmers, *Hooded Americanism: The History of the Ku Klux Klan* (New York: New Viewpoints, 1976), 8–21; Eric Foner, *Reconstruction: America's Unfinished Revolution, 1863-1877* (New York: Harper and Row, 1988), 425–44; Gregory Robert Miller, "America Run Amok: The Rhetoric of the Ku Klux Klan" (Ph.D. diss., University of Southern California, 1991); and Wyn Craig Wade, *The Fiery Cross: The Ku Klux Klan in America* (New York: Touchstone-Simon and Schuster, 1987), 31–111.

    The books by Chalmers and Wade also address the twentieth-century Klan. On the twentieth-century Klan, see also Kathleen M. Blee, *Women of the Klan: Racism and Gender in the 1920s* (Berkeley and Los Angeles: University of California Press, 1991); Kenneth Earl Harrell, "The Ku Klux Klan in Louisiana, 1920–1930" (Ph.D. diss., Louisiana State University, 1966); Shawn Lay, *War, Revolution and the Ku Klux Klan: A Study of Intolerance in a Border City* (El Paso, Tx.: Texas Western Press, 1985); Nancy MacLean, *Behind the Mask of Chivalry: The Making of the Second Ku Klux Klan* (New York: Oxford University Press, 1994); my "Klannishness and the Ku Klux Klan: The Rhetoric and Ethics of Genre Theory" (Ph.D. diss., Ohio State University, 1996); Leonard J. Moore, "Historical Interpretations of the 1920's Klan: The Traditional View and the Populist Revision," *Journal of Social History* 24 (1990): 341–57; and Norman Frederic Weaver, "The Knights of the Ku Klux Klan in Wisconsin, Indiana, Ohio and Michigan" (Ph.D. diss., University of Wisconsin, 1954), 299–301.

    The rebirth of the Klan in the twentieth century encouraged some 1920s Klan investigators to reexamine Reconstruction Era Klan violence. In a short 1923 monograph, J. A. Rogers concluded his review of Klan history by observing that the "klan of today is running true to form" where violence was concerned. J. A. Rogers, *The Ku Klux Spirit* (1923; reprint, Baltimore: Black Classic Press, 1980), 35.

111. Estimates of Klan membership in the 1920s vary considerably. The problems inherent in determining Klan membership include the secrecy surrounding Klan records, the sloppy record keeping for which the Atlanta Klan headquarters was known, and the frequency with which disillusioned Klan members would become inactive or renounce their membership, even while new Klan members were initiated in record numbers. Kenneth T. Jackson argued that the "commonly accepted figure of about four million" Klan members was far too high. Jackson's best guess at the number of men and women initiated into the Klan or Klan auxiliaries between 1915 and 1944 barely exceeds two million. Kenneth T. Jackson, *The Ku Klux Klan in the City, 1915–1930* (New York: Oxford University Press, 1967), 235.

112. For Simmons's version of his betrayal by Evans, see William Joseph Simmons, *America's Menace, or The Enemy Within* (Atlanta: Bureau of Patriotic Books, 1926).

113. On the rhetoric of Hiram Wesley Evans, see my "Klannishness"; my "Speaking about the Other: W. E. B. Du Bois Responds to the Klan," *Southern Communication Journal* 63

(1998): 208–19; and my "Rehabilitating Emotion: The Troublesome Case of the Ku Klux Klan," *Argumentation and Advocacy* 34 (1998): 173–88.

114. Diner, *A Very Different Time*, 263.

115. Dewey W. Grantham, *Southern Progressivism: The Reconciliation of Progress and Tradition* (Knoxville: University of Tennessee Press, 1983), 413–14.

116. As Robert Alan Goldberg explains in his study of the Colorado Klan, local Klan "leaders and needs shaped [an] already pliable [recruiting] program to fit a particular time and place. Each klavern program distinctively fused issue and non-issue appeals, drawing a heterogeneous membership" (*Hooded Empire: The Ku Klux Klan in Colorado* [Urbana: University of Illinois Press, 1981], 163).

117. Grantham, *Southern Progressivism*, 415. Admittedly Grantham's statement here is essentially an aside, found in the conclusion of his monograph on progressivism and depending on the most superficial of footnotes. The argument needs further development, which I hope to supply.

118. *Papers Read at the Meeting of Grand Dragons, Knights of the Ku Klux Klan* (1923; reprint, New York: Arno, 1977), 132.

119. Ibid., 125.

120. Ibid., 16–17. Lothrop Stoddard, the famous apologist for white supremacy who was sometimes quoted or paraphrased by Klan leaders, argued in 1927 that American politics and culture were inherently the products of the nation's whiteness: "'America' . . . was founded by White men, who evolved institutions, ideals, and cultural manifestations which were spontaneous expressions of their racial temperament and tendencies. . . . [O]nly so long as the American people remains White will its institutions, ideals, and culture . . . continue to endure" ("The Impasse at the Color-Line," *The Forum* 78 [1927]: 513).

121. *Papers Read*, 132.

122. *Proceedings of the Second Imperial Klonvokation* (n.p.: Knights of the Ku Klux Klan, 1924), 67.

123. Hiram Wesley Evans, "The Klan: Defender of Americanism," *The Forum* 74 (1925): 810. Evans devoted an enormous amount of attention to Catholicism. For example, see Hiram Wesley Evans, "For New Marriage Laws," *The Forum* 77 (1927): 730–39; and H[iram] W[esley] Evans, *The Rising Storm: An Analysis of the Growing Conflict over the Political Dilemma of Roman Catholics in America* (Atlanta: Buckhead, 1930).

124. Lothrop Stoddard, *The Rising Tide of Color against White World Supremacy* (New York: Charles Scribner's Sons, 1920). For a perceptive analysis of Stoddard's monograph, see Ronald Walter Greene, *Malthusian Worlds: U.S. Leadership and the Governing of the Population Crisis* (Boulder, Colo.: Westview, 1999), 39–43.

125. *Proceedings*, 145–46.

126. Ibid., 146.

127. *Is the Ku Klux Klan Constructive or Destructive?: A Debate between Imperial Wizard Evans, Israel Zangwill and Others* (Girard, Kans.: Haldeman-Julius, 1924).

128. *Proceedings*, 152.

129. *Is the Ku Klux Klan*, 15–16.

130. *Proceedings*, 151.

131. Ibid., 26–27.

132. Blaine Mast, *K. K. K. Friend or Foe: Which?* (n.p., 1924), 72.

133. Ibid., 81.

134. Ibid.

135. Alma White, *Heroes of the Fiery Cross* (Zarephath, N.J.: Good Citizen, 1928), 13.

136. Mast, *K. K. K.*, 73–74.

137. Ibid., 78.

138. Ibid., 79.

139. *Proceedings*, 138. MacLean indicates, however, that more than "a few Klan members . . . harassed their own estranged wives," and there was ample evidence that many 1920s Klan members violated prohibition laws (*Behind the Mask*, 123).

140. "Endorses Ku Klux Klan," *Morehouse Enterprise* (Bastrop, La.), 23 June 1922, 1.

141. The most famous Klan scandal of the 1920s was the highly publicized conviction on rape and murder charges of Indiana's D. C. Stephenson, for a time the most successful

grand dragon in the nation (Wade, *Fiery Cross*, 238–45). In a less shocking but equally telling example, Frank Beall, the grand dragon of Maryland, resigned in 1926 because of the "shamefully crooked" and "shockingly immoral" conduct of many Klan recruiters, who would recruit anyone, no matter how questionable their background, who could pay the required initiation fee or "klectoken" (Chalmers, *Hooded Americanism*, 160–61).

142. Celeste Michelle Condit and John Louis Lucaites, *Crafting Equality: America's Anglo-African Word* (Chicago: University of Chicago Press, 1993), 117.

143. Ibid., 129–30.

144. Ibid., 155.

145. Ibid., 161.

146. Richard Hofstadter, *Anti-intellectualism in American Life* (New York: Knopf, 1962), 123–24.

147. On nativism, see Bennett, *Party of Fear*.

148. Shawn Lay, *Hooded Knights on the Niagara: The Ku Klux Klan in Buffalo, New York* (New York: New York University Press, 1995), 67.

149. Ibid., 73.

150. Ibid., 67.

Woman Suffrage in the Progressive Era: A Coming of Age

Jennifer L. Borda

10

In her pathbreaking study of the woman suffrage movement, *A Century of Struggle*, Eleanor Flexner characterized the years from 1896 to 1910 as "a period of unrelieved 'doldrums' as far as woman suffrage was concerned," while the years from 1910 to 1915 were "a contradictory mixture of awakening, confusion, and continued paralysis."[1] Because suffragists made little progress in state referenda, won the vote in no new states, and made negligible advances in efforts to win a federal amendment, Flexner and other historians of the movement have devoted little sustained attention to these foundational years in the suffrage struggle. In recent years, however, a few historians have disputed the idea that the suffrage movement achieved little during the Progressive Era. As Anne Firor Scott and Andrew Mackay Scott have written, "Close examination of what was going on both within NAWSA [National American Woman Suffrage Association] and in many local communities shows that beneath the quiet surface the currents were running strongly, and activity which would become increasingly visible by 1910 was already building up."[2] Recognizing this period as one of intense growth and renewal, Sara Hunter Graham has suggested a label very different from the "doldrums": "the suffrage renaissance."[3]

It would indeed be surprising if, as Flexner and others have suggested, the women's movement stood still as "convulsive reform movements swept across the American landscape from the 1890s to 1917."[4] And, in fact, the historical evidence suggests that this period in the woman suffrage movement was marked by a number of important developments, including the emergence of new leadership, the recruitment of a wider diversity of supporters, and the modernization of campaign techniques. According to historian Michael McGerr, "The early twentieth century was a distinctive era in the political history of women, rich in possibilities, when the suffrage movement developed a variety of alternatives"—alternatives that ultimately would carry the campaign to its successful culmination.[5] The years between 1896 and 1915 were, in short, critical to the woman suffrage movement. During this period, the movement intersected with the reform impulse of progressivism and cultivated the "progressive ethos"—a revivalistic vision of democracy and an idealism tempered by political pragmatism.[6] The inspired campaign of the suffrage activists also contributed significantly to the reform legacy of the Progressive Era.

A number of studies of the Progressive Era acknowledge the special impact of the many transformations then occurring in society—the rise of industrialism, increased immigration, and the deterioration of urban life–on the lives of women.[7] During this time, greater numbers of women began to move outside the home and into the workplace or into society as volunteers or social reformers. Historians have emphasized the important role played by women in many Progressive Era reform movements, including the temperance and social settlement movements. According to George E. Mowry, women became involved in moral and social crusades during the Progressive Era in numbers not seen since abolition and the Civil War.[8] Women's social welfare work, including the contributions of suffragists, has been given credit for many changes in public policy at both the state and local levels. According to Nell Irvin Painter, "Women had begun to leave the private sphere to obtain prohibition or the vote, but by the 1910s they were pursuing a wide range of issues. . . . To a very great degree, women's institutions laid down the agenda for public health and social welfare reforms that in the twentieth century softened the impact of industrialization on working people."[9]

Historical scholarship also highlights political reform as a definitive achievement of the Progressive Era. According to most historians, the Progressive Era marks a watershed in American politics, as electoral reform and changes in party structures opened up the system. The woman suffrage movement played an important role in this democratization of American politics, as the movement made the case for expanding the electorate and incorporating women's views in political decision making. In the process, the suffrage campaign developed and refined many of the modern campaign techniques now associated with the Progressive Era: increased attention to organization, voter education, lobbying, and "pressure politics," and the use of marketing and public relations techniques in politics.[10] Ellen Carol DuBois notes that because woman suffrage was a mass political movement—perhaps the first mass movement of the modern era—historical investigation of the suffrage movement illuminates our understanding of all Progressive Era politics.[11]

In this essay, I discuss the evolution of the woman suffrage movement between the last decade of the nineteenth century and the passage of the Nineteenth Amendment in 1920. I situate my examination of this phase of the movement within the social, political, and intellectual context of the Progressive Era in order to examine how this "very different age" impacted the leadership, organizational strategies, and rhetorical tactics of the suffrage cause.[12] I demonstrate how the imprint of progressivism may be seen in the work of three prominent suffrage leaders: Carrie Chapman Catt, Alice Paul, and Harriot Stanton Blatch. I argue that the progressive influence is evident in these three leaders' strict commitment to pragmatic politics, efficiency, and organization; in their attempts to bring order to the movement and to society; in their optimistic faith in the inevitability of progress; and in their efforts to insure that the promise of democracy would include all people, men *and* women. In the end, I argue that the suffrage movement's embrace of these progressive ideals helped propel the energetic final push for the federal amendment in 1920. I also argue that the activities and tactics of the suffrage movement, in turn, shaped the progressive agenda in ways that contributed to the distinctive political character of the Progressive Era in America.

Carrie Chapman Catt, NAWSA president during the final years of the movement, has long been recognized for leading the suffrage cause to victory through her exceptional educational and organizational skills. Alice Paul, founder of the Congressional Union (and later the National Woman's Party), often shares credit with Catt for orchestrating the campaign efforts necessary for the eventual passage of the Nineteenth Amendment. Paul also is noted for the introduction of radical reform strategies designed to gain recognition for federal woman suffrage in congressional politics. Harriot Stanton Blatch, the daughter of Elizabeth Cady Stanton, remains an often overlooked and underappreciated figure in the history of the suffrage movement.[13] Blatch's suffrage career, however, epitomized the new leadership of the movement's second generation through the successful fusion of the woman suffrage tradition and progressive politics. Although all three women have been the focus of historical scholarship, little has been written about the rhetoric of these three women and how each represented a different strategic approach to advancing women's rights in the twentieth century.[14]

I begin my discussion of these activists' innovative efforts to create a progressive identity for the woman suffrage movement with a brief review of the origins of the suffrage movement, its early leadership, and its established rhetorical traditions. I then discuss the emergence of the second generation of suffragists and how their efforts intersected with those of other progressive reformers during this most interesting historical moment. In exploring how progressivism shaped the careers of these three suffrage leaders—Catt, Paul, and Blatch—I show how different elements of progressive ideology influenced the development of three distinct strains of suffrage leadership. As the suffrage movement made its crucial transition into the new century, it became a distinctively progressive movement, yet like progressivism itself, it remained a diverse and ever-changing movement throughout the period.

The Woman Suffrage Tradition: A Brief History

The origins of the woman's rights movement traditionally have been traced to "the first public protest against women's political, economic, and social inferiority" held in Seneca Falls, New York, in 1848.[15] Prior to the public meeting, Elizabeth Cady Stanton and fellow abolitionist Lucretia Mott decided to create a declaration for the new cause, a tactic they were familiar with from their experiences in antislavery gatherings. The resulting "Declaration of Sentiments," penned by Stanton, announced, "because women do feel themselves aggrieved, oppressed, and fraudulently deprived of their most sacred rights, we insist that they have immediate admission to all the rights and privileges which belong to them as citizens of the United States."[16] This statement announced the genesis of the woman's rights movement, as well as its prescribed course of action—equal rights for women, most notably the vote. This goal would remain a constant motivator throughout a turbulent movement that would encounter numerous setbacks, ongoing ideological tensions, frequent organizational splintering, and, at times, a tumultuous leadership in the seven decades to come.

The "Declaration of Sentiments" mobilized the movement through a specific call to action by proclaiming, "we shall use every instrumentality in our power to effect our object. We shall employ agents, circulate tracts, petition the State and National legislatures, and endeavor to enlist the pulpit and the press in our behalf."[17] Over the next decade national woman's rights conventions were held every year, except in 1857. These meetings allowed attendees to state their dissatisfaction with woman's status, work toward agreed upon movement objectives, and develop an ideology that would refute critics and win new adherents. From these annual conventions "emerged a body of thought, new and dedicated leadership, wide publicity, and new recruits."[18] The campaign principles conceived at these conventions would allow the suffrage movement to endure through organizational tensions and changing leadership.

The movement was largely eclipsed during the Civil War but emerged again in full force during the winter of 1865 with Stanton and Susan B. Anthony's petition to Congress for the inclusion of women in the Fourteenth Amendment. When the amendment was ratified in 1868—and the word "male" introduced into the Constitution as a criterion for representation—the beginning of years of discord surfaced among woman's rights pioneers. Conservative veterans of the abolition movement, such as Lucy Stone and her husband Harry Blackwell, believed that efforts toward emancipation and Negro suffrage should not be compromised by a push to add women to the amendment. Stanton and Anthony, however, held their ground and continued their fight to have citizenship on the basis of "sex" written into the Fifteenth Amendment, which read: "The right of citizens of the United States to vote shall not be denied or abridged by the United States or any State, on account of race, color, or previous condition of servitude."[19]

May 1869 marked the first actual split in the woman's movement when Stanton and Anthony organized the National Woman Suffrage Association (NWSA), for women only. In November of that year a second organization founded by Stone and Blackwell—the American Woman Suffrage Association (AWSA)—came into being. For the next twenty years the two organizations operated separately on the basis of opposing viewpoints on *how* the goal of woman suffrage could be won. The more conservative American association worked for the franchise through state campaigns and viewed woman suffrage as a means to change the laws denying women civil status. The NWSA was considered more radical in its belief that these laws did not constitute the totality of women's oppression, which they believed also was the result of social institutions such as marriage and religion.[20] For the women of the NWSA, woman's right to vote was just one means of reform for the broader cause of woman's rights.

The now-divided woman's movement made considerable progress on the suffrage issue in the 1870s and 1880s through demonstrative, legal, and political activity. Campaign techniques such as organizing state suffrage associations, educating public opinion, conducting several state campaigns for suffrage referenda, and maintaining pressure for a federal amendment fueled the suffrage cause. As a result, these two decades saw a profound change in public attitude. As Chafe writes, the woman's movement "had moved from being an isolated radical group into being a moderate reform coalition."[21] The principles of the AWSA and the NWSA began to overlap as the movement became more mainstream. A formal merger of the two groups took place in February 1890, resulting in the National American Woman Suffrage Association (NAWSA) and the beginning of a new era in woman suffrage history.

Stanton became the first president of the NAWSA at the age of seventy-five. Regarded as the intellectual philosopher of the movement, Stanton's leadership was one of ideas, particularly thoughts about how the vote would help fulfill the development of women's potential. Stanton's vision of woman's rights consisted of the attainment of lofty ideals such as liberty, freedom, and sovereignty. With Stanton's resignation in 1892, Anthony took the helm as the prodigious organizer who, although lacking Stanton's humor and eloquence, worked daily to sustain the movement's force and direction. Anthony, believing that the vote was the key to women's emancipation, traveled the country, speaking, pleading, and building the cause from 1892 to 1900. Carrie Chapman Catt succeeded Anthony and served as NAWSA president until 1904, when she had to withdraw due to her husband's ill health. Catt's successor, Anna Howard Shaw, was the movement's most brilliant orator. Shaw, however, lacked the organizational abilities to maintain the political energy of the movement and is often blamed for the alleged stagnation of the movement during the first decade of the twentieth century. In 1915, Catt resumed the presidency and "transformed the huge, disorganized, and aimless group of women into a purposeful organization, each part of which carried out its assigned task in its leader's grand strategy for victory."[22]

Through efforts to attract female recruits and a public base of support, the NAWSA became a truly national movement in the last decade of the nineteenth century. Nancy Woloch notes that as "the suffrage movement gained cohesion and clout, it functioned mainly as an educational crusade, a propaganda machine. Its arguments, presented in resolutions, testimony at hearings, convention speeches, and suffrage publications, took on a new tone."[23] For many years, the staple of suffrage argument was woman's inalienable right to political liberty. The suffrage pioneers had based their ideology on the romantic idealism of a "Christian Republic," which had been passed down from their Revolutionary forefathers, who had battled to establish representative government and natural freedoms in opposition to British aristocracy. Stanton, in particular, used her suffrage discourse to revise the "shining city on a hill" into an ideal inclusive of women as well.[24] Suffragists supported the view that all men *and* women were created equal, and thus deserving of the same inalienable rights; suffrage arguments were made on the basis of woman's human character—that is, her likeness to man.

Perhaps the most famous expression of this sentiment was Stanton's 1892 address "The Solitude of Self," in which she emphasized "the individuality of each human soul; our Protestant idea, the right of individual conscience and judgment; our republican idea, individual citizenship." In the speech, Stanton argued that women are members of the same great nation and share duties and responsibilities to civilization equal to men. In an early recognition of culturally created sex subordination, Stanton explained that "it is only the incidental relations of life, such as mother, wife, sister, and daughter, that may involve some special duties and training." Stanton's overarching argument, however, was the crux of natural rights philosophy—that woman's birthright to self-sovereignty and the responsibility of her individual life requires that she be granted a voice in the government under which she lives.[25]

Suffrage arguments began to change at the turn of the century, however, in response to new social realities. The entrance of large numbers of women into the social reform movement provided an opportunity for suffragists to shift their arguments from claims to natural rights to a focus on expediency. As Margaret Finnegan notes, "expediency arguments worked in two ways: they offered quick excuses for why men should grant women the franchise, and they presented woman suffrage as a simple solution to social problems."[26] The shift in suffrage ideology reflected the changing exigencies to which the movement was forced to respond, especially the changing American culture at the time. This was just one of the many ways that the women political activists adapted to contemporary culture in the Progressive Era.

By 1900, the movement's old guard was beginning to fade as Stanton stopped attending conventions and Anthony stepped down as NAWSA president. A new generation of suffragists entered the crusade over the following years, and soon there was a resurgence of youthful energy into the campaign. Although the progressive spirit was already evident in the larger society—with masses of people becoming involved in social and political action—it was several years before this impulse was reflected in the NAWSA. The women who would become the movement's most prominent leaders in the coming decade, however, were a part of this reform generation. Between 1900 and 1910, Catt, Paul, and Blatch were each beginning to develop allegiances to the cause. A combination of contemporary progressive ideals and nostalgia for the early activism of the suffrage pioneers would shape the three women's individual perspectives on how to most effectively wage the battle for women's rights.

The Age of Progressive Reform

It is important to understand how the Progressive Era and progressivism as a movement have been conceptualized through historical scholarship before an account can be made as to the influence of this movement on woman suffrage. For generations, historians have struggled to understand and characterize the Progressive Era. So many different conclusions emerged from these studies that, by the 1970s, historians no longer could agree about whether it made sense to talk of a "Progressive movement" at all. According to Peter G. Filene, most historians agree in their assessment of progressivism's goals, namely those stated by Benjamin Park De Witt in his 1915 treatise *The Progressive Movement:* the exclusion of privileged interests from political and economic control, the expansion of democracy, and the use of government to benefit the weak and oppressed members of American society. Practically all scholars of this era concede that this period, as contrasted with the years preceding and following, was characterized by an amazing amount of political change. Disagreements over the interpretation of the progressive period, however, revolve around several major issues. Substantial differences exist regarding the origin of the movement, the nature of its leadership, its general social objectives, the social value it contributed to American society, as well as its degree of success.[27] Still, progressivism may be defined and used meaningfully in the broadest sense, which, according to Arthur S. Link and Richard L. McCormick, is "the way in which a whole generation of Americans defined themselves politically and responded to the nation's problems at the turn of the century."[28]

The Progressive movement emerged during the rapid and, at times, uneasy transition from a largely agrarian society to the burgeoning conditions of modern urban life. Between the last decade of the nineteenth century and the end of the First World War, America saw profound social and economic changes, which inspired reform movements designed to deal with the pressing problems that emerged. For many, societal transformations such as the rise of gigantic corporations, the growth of industrialization, and mass immigration represented forces out of control. Progressivism became defined by vast numbers of educated, urban, middle-class individuals or small groups seeking to intervene into these uncontrolled forces of rapid modernization. According to Robert Wiebe, an "organizational revolution" occurred during this period in which Progressives applied their social knowledge and skills to impose order upon what they saw as a chaotic society.[29] Relying on organization, social-scientific expertise, and the values of efficiency and rationality to achieve their goals, Progressives sought to improve the conditions of life and labor through largely bureaucratic means.

Progressivism also embodied a moralistic spirit that aimed directly at the reform of individuals and behavioral habits in an effort to create social stability. Richard Hofstadter has described progressivism as "a rather widespread and remarkably good-natured effort of the greater part of society to achieve some not very clearly specified self-reformation. Its general theme was the effort to restore a type of economic individualism and political democracy that was widely believed to have existed earlier in America . . . and with that restoration to bring back a kind of morality and civic purity that was also believed to have been lost." The Progressive Era was characterized by impulses toward both criticism of American society and ameliorative reform to solve the nation's problems. The faith in progress that guided these impulses also was characterized by a belief in human ability, through purposeful action and some help from government, to improve the environment and conditions of life.[30]

In spite of their pointed critique of American society and politics, most Progressives were optimists because they were fundamentally environmental determinists. These men and women believed in inevitable progress because they were confident that the changes they would bring through social reform would transform American society for the better. For this ambitious group, the wise and public-spirited "will of the people" was enough to insure an optimistic and sanguine future. As a result, progressive reform was marked by both enthusiasm and frantic activity.[31] This energetic activism began to transform the larger culture at the turn of the century and, consequently, became a defining characteristic of the second wave of the woman suffrage movement.

Woman Suffrage in the Era of Progressive Reform

As largely middle-class, white reformers, the majority of the new generation working for the suffrage cause were easily caught up in the progressive wave sweeping the nation. The progressive attitude soon began to color the behavior, thought, and especially the discourse of the woman suffrage movement. Leaders began to identify the suffrage cause with the larger progressive coalition and its efforts to extend democracy and work for social justice. As a result, the votes-for-women campaign broadened its appeal as "both the rhetoric and substance of the suffrage movement meshed with the ethos of reform."[32]

Stephen J. Diner argues that most discourse in the Progressive Era was funded by three assumptions: humans are basically rational, so the American citizenry, if properly informed and empowered, would ensure that the government works for the common good; since the environment is shaped by people, most social ills could be cured by altering social conditions; and that a faith in inherent human goodness would allow reformers to demand justice and do what was morally right.[33] Discourse about woman suffrage, and by suffragists themselves, reflected these assumptions, revising them when necessary to fit the movement's needs. Prominent themes in the rhetoric of the suffrage movement were built on the notions of "the will of the people," "justice," and "democracy." As such, popular arguments for the cause included allusions to the inevitable onward progress of democracy, which would extend the rights of citizenship to women; the necessity of strategic planning and organization for educating the public about votes for women; women's contributions to the uplift of society; and, most important, the changing condition of women brought on by their social and political evolution.

In the 9 October 1915 issue of the *New Republic*, a special supplement was dedicated to votes for women. The magazine had a distinguished editorial staff made up of well-known and respected American intellectuals who were committed to progressive ideals and the liberal education of American opinion. Herbert Croly, author of the widely read 1909 book, *The Promise of American Life*, was the editor-in-chief. Croly selected a notable staff, including journalist Walter Lippmann and liberal economist Walter Weyl.[34] All three contributed editorials regarding the woman suffrage debate, as did historian and educator Charles A. Beard, whose wife, Mary Ritter Beard, was a prominent suffragist. An analysis of the writings included in this supplement clearly illustrates the way progressive themes influenced the thought and discourse of pro-suffrage rhetoric.

Charles Beard's essay, excerpted from an address he gave in New York titled "Historical Woman Suffrage," was influenced by the assumption that the march of progress would demand justice for women. Beard explained that, by taking the long view of woman suffrage, it would become evident that the movement was not "a battle of wits" or "a temporary episode of current politics," but "an age-long battle of the common mass of people upward from serfdom to freedom, a battle which began in a dim and dateless past and will continue as long as new hopes and new visions arise in the human mind." Given this view of the suffrage battle as part of a larger history of democratic progress, Beard argued that votes for women was the inevitable next step. Consideration of woman suffrage as part of a universal battle, Beard argued, would prove that "women in the long run are destined to win."[35] Similarly, in "Working for the Inevitable," Walter Weyl wrote, "if society continues to develop as it has developed during the last century, it will be inconceivable that women will not wish to take their place beside men in the great affairs of life, and inconceivable that men will not wish it so." Both Beard and Weyl based their appeals on the progress of history toward greater democracy, including the revolt against aristocracy, the rise of male suffrage, and the abolishment of slavery. The rational conclusion of their arguments was that women's emancipation deserved support as an inevitable next step in the nation's democratic development, because, as Weyl noted, "woman suffrage [is] a link in a chain already forged. In that sense it is 'inevitable.'"[36]

Both Croly and Lippmann spoke to the expedience of woman suffrage in terms of women's moral uplift of society and women's advancements in the areas of education and politics, which the authors believed led to their equality with men. In "The Vote as Symbol," Lippmann argued that the vote is "a symbol of a new outlook upon life and a new position in the world" that women had already achieved. Lippman also stated that women "have only to point out the enormous changes which machinery and education have brought to them" to prove to "conventional males and sheltered anti[suffragist]s" that they live in a different world than the one dangled before them. Because women had already evolved into equal citizens, according to Lippman, giving them the vote would merely affirm, not require, their political evolution.[37] Croly extended this argument by noting that, since women had already proven themselves, granting them suffrage would allow them to improve their work in society. In Croly's view, the advent of woman suffrage would strengthen relations between men and women and the betterment of society by adding "to the bonds of passion and affection, the bond of [men and women's] joint responsibility for the political welfare of society and a joint effort to redeem it." As far as Croly was concerned, the "obligation of the vote" would be a benefit to all.[38] These same kinds of arguments also would appear in the speeches and writings of Catt, Paul, and Blatch.

Last, the discourse of the woman suffrage movement was impacted by the most promising development in woman's situation in the Progressive Era: the opening up of the boundaries between the public and the private. As Dye writes, "When we view reform through women's eyes, redefining the relationship between home and the community—the private sphere and the public—emerges as central to progressivism." Women Progressives, as well as woman suffragists, viewed gender difference and changing conceptions of the relationship between the home and the polity as crucial to social and political reform.[39] Carol Pateman also comments on the significance of changing views of the private and public spheres when she writes, "The dichotomy between the private and the public is central to almost two centuries of feminist writing and political struggle; it is, ultimately, what the feminist movement is about."[40] For the suffrage movement, the shifting definitions of the public and the private at the turn of the century provided women with the opportunity to form an early analysis of gender relations through their discourse and tactics. Suffragists, in order to be recognized as individuals qualified to participate in social life, worked to challenge and overturn cultural constructions of femininity and female sexuality. The discourse of woman suffrage in the Progressive Era identified these cultural constructions as at the heart of women's exclusion from the political order. Based on arguments for more than political equality, this struggle over sexual power came to define the latter part of the movement.[41] Ultimately, the emergence of a feminist challenge to the social order in the campaign's rhetoric and tactics was instrumental in empowering the suffrage cause with new energy and persuasive arguments for women's rights.

Carrie Chapman Catt and the Organization of NAWSA's Suffrage Strategy

From the beginning of Carrie Chapman Catt's involvement in the national movement for woman suffrage her distinctive style of leadership, organizational strategy, and political tactics infiltrated the campaign at every level. Catt emerged into a recognized leadership position in 1892 when Susan B. Anthony, the current president, abolished NAWSA's old executive committee and transferred its duties to the business committee—later to be chaired by Catt. As Jacqueline Van Voris writes, "The 1892 convention was the real beginning of a transition in which the new members with fresh ideas began to replace the old guard."[42] Catt quickly took advantage of her new role and created an extended network of suffrage clubs, local organizers, and lecturers for the promotion of suffrage education and recruitment across the continent. Within a decade she would expand her organizational strategy beyond the United States to the rest of the world with the establishment of the International Woman Suffrage Alliance. Catt promised that she would "organize the women of the world for woman suffrage" and proudly boasted in 1911 that "the sun *now* never sets upon Woman Suffrage activities."[43] In nearly three decades of work for women's right to vote, Catt brought order and vision to the national campaign for women's rights and drew worldwide attention to the issue of woman's dignity and rightful place in democratic government.

Catt was born in 1859, the same eventful year that witnessed John Brown's raid on Harper's Ferry and the publication of Karl Marx's *Treatise on Political Economy* and Charles Darwin's *The Origin of Species*. Catt's lifetime of eighty-eight years encompassed an exciting era in world history marked by the great expansion of human thought and rapidly changing social customs—of which Catt's own contributions to the cause of woman suffrage were a part.[44] Born to Lucius and Maria Clinton Lane, Catt spent an ordinary childhood with her two brothers on the family farm in Ripon, Wisconsin, and then on another farm outside of Charles City, Iowa. Catt entered Iowa State Agricultural College in March 1877 and received her B.S. in the General Science Course for Women four years later. While at school, Catt's interests in feminism and organization were already developing. Within two years she established the first women's military drill, the Ladies Military Company, to encourage women's exercise and comradeship. She also won the right for women to speak in the Crescent Literary Society, which allowed them the same opportunities for training in public speaking and debate as their male counterparts.[45]

After college, Catt began to prepare for a career in law before discovering her talents for teaching and administration—skills she would later apply to her work for women's enfranchisement. For several years she served as a teacher and principal at a high school in Mason City, Iowa. In February of 1885 she married Leo Chapman and joined him as co-editor of a Mason City newspaper, the *Republican*.

Her writings at this time reflected her interest in women's rights, and she consistently reminded readers that their support for woman suffrage was useless without organization. Catt also attended a variety of women's rights conventions in Iowa and initiated the Mason City suffrage organization. In May 1886 a newspaper scandal erupted over accusations of criminal libel based on an editorial Leo wrote about an elected county official. To escape a trial before the county grand jury, Leo fled to California, where he died of typhoid fever shortly before Catt's arrival. Catt remained in San Francisco for several years and began writing and lecturing professionally for women's rights until her return to Charles City in 1890. In that year she attended the NAWSA convention in Washington, D.C., as an Iowa delegate and gave her first speech for the association, "The Symbol of Liberty." In June she quietly married George Catt in Seattle and with his full support continued her dedicated work for suffrage in the Midwestern states. After several campaign tours as Anthony's apprentice, Catt was asked to join the NAWSA in an administrative capacity.[46]

ORGANIZATION, MOTIVATION, AND PRACTICAL POLITICS

It was Catt's discipline and dedication to organization that won her Anthony's respect—and which remains the most significant aspect of Catt's legacy. According to Van Voris, "Catt was a compelling speaker, she knew how to inspire workers, and she understood the importance of education and agitation. Above all, she believed that 'organization is the only assurance of final triumph of any cause.'"[47] Robert Booth Fowler attributes this aspect of Catt's leadership to her progressivism. He writes, "That Carrie Catt was a supreme organizer of the suffrage crusade was acknowledged in her time—and has been since. She was a paradigm for Progressivism's cult of organized reform—'reform' as an act of modernization to be accomplished by organization, bureaucracy, and efficient leadership."[48]

The summer of 1892 presented Catt with the first opportunity to apply her organizational and managerial skills to the woman suffrage movement through her orchestration of the Mississippi Valley Conference at Des Moines. Because of her inexperience, Catt neglected to notify the NAWSA of her plans, but still invited Anthony, the Blackwells, and numerous members of the official board to attend. Impressed, Anthony immediately asked Catt to take the position of NAWSA finance chairman and three years later invited her to head the newly established organizational committee. Catt drew up an ambitious plan of work for the committee, which she announced at the 1895 NAWSA convention. The proposal included correlating the national, state, and local branches, proposing courses in politics and government for local suffrage clubs, investigating laws and legislation affecting women and children, and creating a program of concrete aims for each region, as well as a finance committee to fund them. Recognizing in Catt the energy and confidence needed to move the campaign forward, after listening to Catt's proposal, Anthony remarked, "There never yet was a young woman who did not feel that if she had had the management of the work from the beginning, the cause would have carried long ago. I felt just that way when I was young."[49] In just a few years, Catt already had begun to prove herself as a competent leader capable of advancing the cause.

For Catt, organization was the support structure of the suffrage campaign, and this became a prominent and consistent theme in her speeches. Fowler remarks, "Without doubt Catt personified what Wiebe argues was the spirit of the age: faith in organization. She believed completely that organization was the pathway to victory for women's enfranchisement. And she had the remarkable practical talent to translate her faith into reality."[50] At the close of her report at the 1898 national convention, Catt bluntly assessed the NAWSA's desperate need for structure and

collective effort, stating: "If I were asked to name the chief cause obstructing organization, I should not hesitate to reply. It is not to be found in the antisuffragists nor
in ignorance nor in conservatism. . . . It is to be found in the hopeless, lifeless,
faithless members of our own organization." She concluded her criticism of the association's practices with a call to action, suggesting, "Let us encourage any criticism offered with the intention of replacing present methods with better ones, but
let us frown upon . . . aimless fault-finding, and let us banish from our vocabulary
the word 'can't.' Let our watchword be 'Organization and Union.'"[51] Always one to
speak her mind, Catt felt compelled to use her administrative talents to restructure
the NAWSA into a purposeful association with the ultimate goal of a suffrage victory within a generation.

Catt believed that only reform movements consisting of the rare combination
of organization, concentration, systematic method, and education would find success—and these progressive values formed the basis of her NAWSA presidency and
leadership strategy between 1900 and 1904.[52] The nineteenth century ended with
Anthony's retirement as NAWSA president and the election of a leader from the
next generation. To the surprise of many members, Anthony chose Catt over her
good friend Anna Howard Shaw. Throughout her first tenure as president, however,
Catt made only modest progress toward her organizational goals for the national
movement. Still, this period allowed Catt to test some of her ideas and to lay the
groundwork for future plans. As Fowler notes, as the result of Catt's efforts "a major
start towards a serious national organization was in place and, above all, 'suffragists [were] beginning to see the truth . . . that organization [was] the watchword of
the hour.'"[53]

The first term of Catt's presidency demonstrates clearly her modernist leanings
toward education, bureaucracy, and social-scientific management—especially the
efficient management of people, policies, and politics. As evidenced through her
tongue-lashing of the delegates to the 1898 convention, Catt believed one of the
greatest obstacles to the movement was not external opposition, but the indifference of American women—including ambivalent NAWSA members and the legions of women who remained uneducated about woman suffrage. In 1902, Catt
declared, "We must educate and agitate, agitate and educate until a full understanding . . . shall have reached the remotest man and woman."[54] Soon after her
election to the presidency in 1900, Catt introduced plans to recruit greater numbers of women into the national organization. According to Graham, "Catt asked
Business Committee members to compile lists of influential clubwomen, ministers, and politicians from which to solicit new members, and included well-heeled
men as well as society women in her recruitment scheme."[55] By 1904 the association acknowledged the "Society Plan" at the annual convention and made recommendations for greater suffragist activity in civic, charitable, and educational
groups within their communities.

The women of the club movement were a crucial audience for the NAWSA's
recruitment efforts. In 1902 membership in the clubs under the umbrella of the
General Federation of Women's Clubs had reached two hundred thousand. The
middle-class women of these clubs were a significant part of the reform impulse
that characterized the Progressive Era and were largely responsible for many of the
social reforms of the period. Catt recognized the power of this influential mass of
middle-class women and singled them out as the focus of the NAWSA's recruitment efforts. NAWSA members began attending the "parlor meetings" of women's
clubs across the nation to provide short talks and updates on the national and
local campaigns. During the General Federation's biannual convention in 1904, it
appeared Catt had accomplished her goal when newly elected president Sarah
Platt Decker of Colorado stated: "Ladies, you have chosen me your leader. Well, I
have an important piece of news to give you. Dante is dead. He has been dead for

several centuries, and I think it is time that we dropped the study of his *Inferno* and turned our attention to our own."[56] Catt's society plan was not without its critics. Some suffragists thought it smacked of impropriety and elitism; others, such as Harriot Stanton Blatch, complained about the association's gradualism. Yet the NAWSA's entrance into the club movement established woman suffrage as an imperative progressive reform measure.[57]

At the same time Catt was introducing woman suffrage as a national issue of social reform within the American political consciousness, she also was making great strides to promote women's rights as a political issue internationally. The International Woman Suffrage Alliance (IWSA) was founded in Washington, D.C., on 12 February 1902 during the NAWSA's thirty-fourth annual convention. Representatives from seven countries attended, including Germany, Great Britain, Turkey, Sweden, and Russia, among others. Catt viewed the woman suffrage fight as a universal reform movement and believed that organization and unification on a world scale would strengthen arguments for women's enfranchisement in every country. At the June 1908 IWSA conference in Amsterdam, Catt commented: "In this common cause, women have clasped hands over the mountains and over the seas, and have become in truth a world army. . . . As they march on to self-respect, liberty and opportunity, along the self-same road, they will encounter there the same obstacles, the same experiences. . . . We represent the solidarity of a sex. We oppose a common enemy, whose name is not man, but conservatism. Its weapons are the same in all lands—tradition, prejudice and selfishness. We too have a common weapon—an appeal to justice and fair play."[58] Catt devoted much of her time to her work abroad with the IWSA. Her international efforts allowed for the expansion of her progressive principles to societies throughout the world as she worked to advance women's equality on a global scale. Between the years 1904 and 1915 she was the alliance's primary leader, and her work for the women of the world remained consistent even through her own personal crises. In 1904, Catt stepped down as president of the NAWSA, citing her concern for her husband's health as the cause. When he passed away shortly after, Catt often depended on her world travel as a means of dealing with her depression.

After four years in which she had remained largely distant from the U.S. movement, Catt returned in 1908 to devote herself to suffrage work in New York. Her strategy became more focused toward practical political impact, and she began to organize New York women along precinct lines—work that the following year would result in the formation of the Woman Suffrage Party. Van Voris writes, "The Woman Suffrage Party was an attempt by Catt to draw into a compact, active organization the various clubs that had discussed suffrage academically for years. Her strategy was to organize on the lines of the political machine." Catt's primary objective for the next several years was to direct and finance an army of volunteers skillful and aggressive enough to achieve the passage of a New York suffrage amendment. She believed that if New York state were won, there would be enough strength in Washington to force debate on the national amendment.[59] It took many years of publicity, campaign and election district lobbying, public speaking, and two full-fledged Empire State amendment campaigns before New York was won in 1917. By that time Catt had been reelected as president of the NAWSA and was applying her political strategy to work for the national amendment as well.

THE "WINNING PLAN"

Anna Howard Shaw had taken up the NAWSA presidency in 1904 after Catt's departure, and she remained at the helm through 1915. Although Shaw had presided over the growth of the organization from seventeen thousand to two hundred thousand members, the later years of her presidency were characterized by poor administration, relational turmoil between the national and state associations, and the exceedingly slow pace of the campaign for state-by-state enfranchisement.[60] To her dismay, Catt was reelected to the presidency at the 1915 convention (she believed the post should have gone to someone younger). Catt spent the next six months reacquainting herself with the organization, including visits to state conventions, conferences, and meetings of all kinds in twenty-three states. The outcome of this tour was that "everything she saw and heard reinforced her conviction that the final push must be made strong and immediate."[61]

In September 1916, Catt issued a call for an emergency NAWSA meeting to be held in Atlantic City, New Jersey. A crucial turning point was upon the movement, as was announced in the convention call: "Our cause has been endorsed in the platforms of every political party. In order to determine how most expeditiously to press these newly won advantages to final victory this convention is called."[62] Catt planned to take advantage of this opportunity—which she defined as "The Crisis"—by urging members to shift their focus and resources to a new strategy. According to Karlyn Kohrs Campbell, the "Winning Plan" that Catt announced during the convention was "an administrative and tactical masterpiece designed to put maximum political pressure on Congress to pass a suffrage amendment, based on a hard-nosed analysis of what realistically could be achieved."[63]

Catt began her address to the convention stating, "a crisis has come in our movement which, if recognized and the opportunity seized with vigor, enthusiasm and will, means the final victory of our great cause in the very near future." This is one of Catt's most famous speeches, often credited with setting in motion the final push necessary for passage of the federal amendment. The long speech was highly systematic, as Catt's addresses usually were, but it was also energetic and motivational. The purpose of the speech was to set a new pace for the movement in the final effort necessary for "turning the crisis into victory." Catt used the speech to remind her audience of the movement's long and honored history, and to let them know that faith in eventual victory was no longer enough. At the close of the speech, Catt explained, "The slogan of a movement sets its pace. The old one counseled patience; it said, there is plenty of time; it pardoned sloth and half-hearted effort. It set the pace of an educational campaign. The 'Woman's Hour has struck' sets the pace of a crusade which will have its way."[64]

After her address to the convention, Catt spoke to the NAWSA's executive committee to rally the members into action by demanding that they embrace all of the values she had always applied to the suffrage campaign throughout her leadership. Pragmatic, logical, and systematic, Catt's proposal urged the delegates to engage in a vigilant practical politics; she instructed their aggressive organization in every precinct nationwide for the crucial education and agitation of state legislatures and assemblies. For the first time, Catt also recommended suffrage activity directed toward Congress and lobbying for the federal amendment. The Susan B. Anthony amendment, as it was later named, had frequently been brought before Congress by the NWSA.[65] After 1872, however, the increasingly conservative movement focused on state work, and eventually the federal amendment had become a dormant issue for the NAWSA. Urging the association to recommit to the federal campaign, Catt concluded with a clear and rational plan that would shift emphasis to the federal level while maintaining pressure at the state level, especially in states that already had strong pro-suffrage forces.

Catt's strategy called for equal suffrage states to pass resolutions requesting Congress to submit the federal amendment; for several states, including New York, to campaign for state constitutional amendments to enfranchise women; and for the remaining states to try for the right to vote for presidential electors or, at the least, to make an attempt to get suffrage in the primaries. She concluded with a detailed procedure for how to put the plan into practice and argued that an immediate start was imperative. Catt believed this was the necessary course of action to put the association back on track toward a political victory. Catt's speech was a way of persuading members to overcome the lack of "cohesion, organization, unity and consequent momentum" that had plagued the movement for so long. Catt gave her address in Atlantic City "determined to sound a call for action so loud and compelling that it would send the suffragists straight to enfranchisement. She wanted them to see victory as a possibility instead of a dream."[66]

Many members initially resisted this new tactic, as Maud Wood Park recalled in her autobiographical account of the last years of the suffrage fight. Park, who later effectively led the NAWSA's congressional lobbying, wrote, "To [Catt's] preamble, which was a brief restatement of reasons for undertaking a more energetic drive for the amendment, I listened with a good deal of inner protest." Park was only convinced once she realized that Catt "had no intention of letting her federal program lessen efforts to secure state action." In later years, however, speaking the sentiments of many suffragists who had served under Catt, Park concluded, "That women all over the United States were able to vote in 1920 is due, I believe, to the carrying out of the plan prepared and presented by an incomparable leader."[67]

"FAILURE IS IMPOSSIBLE"

Because she is best remembered for her organizational expertise, Catt's rhetorical accomplishments are often overlooked or viewed as incomparable to the virtuoso style of Shaw or Stanton. Having felt that the suffrage crusade had been based too long on words rather than practical political action, Catt was "more than a little ambivalent" about speeches. Yet in her many years as a leader of both the NAWSA and the IWSA, Catt emerged as a prolific speaker who toured the United States and the world as a distinguished orator for woman suffrage. She also published numerous articles and pamphlets for women's rights and used her suffrage addresses and writings to educate the public and organize the movement's proponents into active political involvement for the cause.[68] Catt's discourse characterized the woman suffrage movement along four lines: as a necessary part of a true democracy, as essential for the dignity of women, as a means of social uplift, and as an inevitable consequence of natural evolution.

At a meeting of the World Movement for Woman Suffrage, Catt announced: "It is because they know the unanswerable logic behind our demands and the irresistible force of our growing army that Suffragists throughout the world repeat in unison those thrilling words of the American leader, Susan B. Anthony, 'Failure is impossible.'"[69] Catt frequently quoted Anthony's famous phrase as a slogan to motivate her suffrage workers. This catchphrase also symbolized her philosophy about the inevitable success of the movement under her own leadership and functioned as the overarching logic of her arguments. As a dedicated Progressive, Catt remained inherently optimistic throughout the long suffrage battle. She believed that progress would bring social change—and with it a change in woman's place in the social order. This faith in progress and loyalty to the ultimate goal of a true democracy colored Catt's broad vision for equal rights.

In her attempt to reach a mass audience with her appeals for women's enfranchisement, Catt often linked her arguments to the widely accepted, mainstream appeals that had supported male suffrage during the Revolutionary era. A great number of Catt's addresses were directed at her opposition, and she would systematically recite such emotive phrases as "Taxation without representation is tyranny," "Governments derive their just powers from the consent of the governed," and "The will of the people." In a 1910 article written for *The Forum*, Catt asserted, "The [woman suffrage] movement is a part of the world's evolution of democracy. Its reason for existence, is the same as that of each preceding struggle for man suffrage. Its appeal presents no new arguments; it merely repeats the old. Women are people; and as such consideration is invited to the same claims which have won the vote for other classes of people."[70] As far as Catt was concerned, it was time the U.S. government put the abstract language of rights into practice by applying the wisdom of democracy to all citizens. Catt was aware that these tenets of Western liberalism with revolutionary resonance were "so pervasive in the American experience and culture that her appeal could not be ignored."[71] In 1917 she asked, "Our country professes to mean 'the people.' But does it? Is it sincere? Is our own nation governed by consent of the people? *No.*"[72] For the better part of her life, Catt would use a number of rhetorical strategies to try to change the answer to that question to one that American women deserved.

One of Catt's strategies was to point out the inconsistencies of America's democratic promise. Catt often incorporated the words of respected philosophers, such as John Stuart Mill, and American political leaders, such as Daniel Webster, into her speeches to emphasize America's long devotion to representative government and democracy. One quote she used repeatedly was from David Starr Jordan, president of Stanford University, who wrote: "It is not the mission of democracy to make governments good, but to make men strong. . . . The purpose of self-government is to intensify individual responsibility, to promote attempts at wisdom through which true wisdom may come at last."[73] Catt used this quote to point out what she believed was faulty logic: If governments exist for men and democracy is a means of making them strong, what is the rationale for keeping women weak? Catt knew the answer to this question: sex prejudice. Arguments designed to educate and agitate men and women regarding this issue became yet another prominent theme in Catt's discourse.

Catt recognized that sex prejudice was the key issue undermining women's inclusion in the republic, and her analysis of women's subordination was one of the earliest attempts to understand the roots and consequences of sexism.[74] In a 1902 speech, Catt stated, "sex-prejudice is a pre-judgment against the rights, liberties and opportunities of women. A belief, without proof, in the incapacity of women to do that which they have never done. Sex-prejudice has been the chief hindrance in the rapid advance of the women's rights movement to its present status, and it is still a stupendous obstacle to be overcome." According to Catt, argument based in the realm of sex prejudice "flies entirely outside the domain of reason . . . where neither logic or common sense can dislodge it." In her analysis of sexual oppression, Catt concluded that the subjection of women stems from four causes: obedience, ignorance, the denial of personal liberty, and the denial of rights to property wages. She attributed the blame for this condition "not in [women's] natural endowment, but in the environment which warped her growth."[75] A strong desire to right these wrongs would become the core of Catt's feminism, which she described as "a world-wide revolt against all artificial barriers which laws and customs interpose between women and human freedom." This desire, which echoed Stanton's humanistic individualism of the nineteenth century, would drive Catt's mission to secure women's equal rights.[76]

According to Fowler, the heart of Catt's case for woman's right to vote "remained her belief in the ideal of women's self-mastery, that suffrage would be a step toward their self-realization as dignified, free beings in command (as much as possible) of their own lives."[77] Based on this belief, Catt generally tried to walk the line between arguments based on justice and those based on expedience in her discourse for woman suffrage. She often stated that she did not know whether suffrage was a right, a duty, or a privilege, but that "whatever it is women want it."[78] Many of Catt's appeals, however, used the old argument for woman's natural rights to emphasize the need to promote and protect woman's dignity. The abolishment of women's humiliation and the advocation of their uplift to equal men's status were significant aspects of Catt's personal crusade for women's rights the world over, as she expressed in 1902: "The whole aim of the woman movement has been to destroy the idea that obedience is necessary to women; to train women to such self-respect that they would not grant obedience and to train men to such comprehension of equity they would not exact it."[79]

Yet the progressive belief that the law of "natural" evolution was often aided through human intervention also was pervasive in Catt's discourse. Through such arguments, woman suffrage became "linked in the public mind with the Progressive movement for political and economic reform."[80] Catt invoked the ideals of social uplift and expediency into her arguments because appealing to these values seemed to be a profitable way of securing support for her principal goal: votes for women. In 1911, Catt reminded her audience of the movement's mission, stating: "This modern movement demands political rights for women. It demands a direct influence for women upon the legislation which concerns the common welfare of all the people. It recognises the vote as the only dignified and honorable means of securing recognition of their needs and aspirations." She also informed her audiences of the social benefits that would be sure to follow women's enfranchisement, indicating that the promise of social uplift should also provide suffragists stamina for the battle ahead: "the belief that we are defending the highest good of the mothers of our race and the ultimate welfare of society makes every sacrifice seem trivial, every duty a pleasure. The pressing need spurs us on, the certainty of victory gives us daily inspiration." And in a 1914 pamphlet published by the NAWSA, "Do You Know?" Catt asked, "Do you know that extending the suffrage to women increases the moral vote . . . that in all the factors that tend to handicap the progress of society, women form a minority, whereas in churches, schools and all organizations working for the uplift of humanity women are a majority?" In these speeches, Catt effectively appealed to popular beliefs in woman's moral supremacy to advance the claim that women were needed in government to clean out political corruption.[81]

All of these strategies were supplemented by Catt's progressive emphasis on natural evolution, which threaded its way through most of her discourse. Catt frequently argued that the progress of democracy, as well as women's demonstrated political and moral evolution, made passage of woman suffrage inevitable. This theme echoed throughout almost every speech Catt gave over her thirty-year struggle for women's right to vote.

At times, Catt spoke poetically about the inevitability of women's enfranchisement, declaring that "woman suffrage is as sure to follow [man suffrage] as are the stars to move on their appointed course," or "The handwriting on the wall of human destiny announces the inevitable coming of woman suffrage. All the signs point in that direction and none points the other way." In a 1917 speech at the NAWSA national convention, Catt warned, "'There is one thing mightier than kings and armies'—aye, than Congresses and political parties—'the power of an idea when its time has come to move.'"[82]

At other times, Catt spoke in the language of nature and the physical sciences. Many of her speeches expounded the linear argument that "hard upon the track of the man-suffrage movement presses the movement for woman suffrage, a logical step onward" because the "law of evolution is guiding the world ever onward and upward." On another occasion, she declared that, "justice, like the physical forces of nature, always moves on by the 'paths of least resistance.'" In a speech before the IWSA in 1911 she similarly proclaimed, "Two things are certain: first, Woman suffrage is not a receding wave—it is a mighty incoming tide which is sweeping all before it, second, no *human* power, no university professor, no Parliament, no

Government, can stay its coming. It is a step in the evolution of society, and the eternal verities are behind it."[83] These arguments, which emphasized the movement's natural and evolutionary character, served to both persuade reluctant male agents of change and to raise the morale of the movement's followers.[84]

When Catt stood before worldwide audiences in the first two decades of the twentieth century, she was the face of woman suffrage. During the Progressive Era, the women's rights crusade was voiced largely through Catt's rhetoric. In writings and speeches that were "a triumph of strategy, logic, and realistic assessment," Catt brought international attention to the important issue of women's rights.[85] By infusing her discourse with progressive idealism, revolutionary fervor, and an intellectual critique of prejudice against women, Catt was able to motivate her adherents and at least win a hearing, if not conversion, from her political opponents. As the woman suffrage movement entered its final years, Catt continued to organize the NAWSA's efforts and became confident that she would witness the results of her long sacrifice during her presidency.

A PERSISTENT FAITH AND THE TRIUMPH OF VICTORY

"We have come upon a new time, which has brought new and strange problems. Old problems have assumed new significance. In the adjustment of the new order of things we women demand an equal voice; we shall accept nothing less."[86] These words, spoken by Catt in 1911, show her recognition of the tumultuous context for the last stages of the struggle for women's right to vote. She saw this period of change as a challenge—but also as an opportunity to reorder social customs in a way that would allow women to reemerge with greater dignity and individual freedom. During her second presidency, Catt was confident that she would see this goal to its fruition. In fact, on the day the woman suffrage amendment passed the House in January 1918, Catt ran right out and commissioned a new dress to wear when she stumped the states for ratification. It would be more than eighteen months before the amendment passed through the Senate, and Catt's ratification dress had to be remodeled before she had a chance to wear it. She donned the famous dress as she continued to lead the NAWSA's suffrage battle through the ratification debate in Tennessee, the final state required for passage of the amendment. On 26 August 1920, Catt arrived in New York City to participate in a procession in her honor outside of Pennsylvania Station. Marching to the sounds of "Hail the Conquering Hero Comes," Catt proudly accepted her place in history as the distinguished leader who led the suffrage movement to victory.[87]

Catt's triumph for woman suffrage represented the culmination of years of directing the NAWSA to a high degree of organizational coherence, practical politicking, and educational programs moderate enough to sustain the campaign for as long as necessary. In 1920, she was still organizing women through her plans for the League of Women Voters, announcing at the New York parade in her honor, "Now that we have the vote let us remember we are no longer petitioners. We are not wards of the nation but free and equal citizens. Let us do our part to keep it a true and triumphant democracy."[88] The values that had sustained Catt throughout the long fight—a commitment to order, education, and social reform—were principles that allowed her to address the world as she knew it and to forge a new world in which men and women shared equal status. As Fowler notes, "Carrie Catt was a prophet of the new organizational era of the turn of the last century. She reflected and expressed the Progressive Era's drive towards modernization—organization, bureaucracy, control, discipline, and the rest."[89] Catt would strive to attain those ideals throughout the rest of her life.

In the final years of the suffrage crusade—the years for which Catt is best remembered—she was not alone at the front lines of the fight. A younger and more radical presence had made itself felt in the campaign's last decade and would continue to work independently of the NAWSA through 1920. In the last years of Catt's presidency she was acutely aware of the woman with whom she would ultimately share the credit for suffrage victory: Alice Paul, the *other* leader of the woman suffrage movement.

Disrupting the Order: Alice Paul and the Militant Suffrage Campaign

When Jane Addams petitioned the NAWSA executive board in 1912, asking that a young suffragist named Alice Paul be sent to organize a committee in Washington, D.C., for work on the constitutional amendment, no one could have foreseen the impact that the twenty-seven-year-old activist would have on the woman suffrage movement. The cause had been grinding on for more than sixty years, and Paul brought a fresh outlook to the national campaign. In Paul's view, the NAWSA's strategy was far too moderate to accomplish any real change within a reasonable time. She believed the suffrage fight must be made dramatic and immediate, and that suffrage would be won only through direct political action on the congressional level rather than through the slow process of education and state-by-state amendments. Paul would soon "institute a suffrage campaign so swift, so intensive, so compelling—and at the same time so varied, interesting, and picturesque"—that by 1916 suffrage news was common in the daily press, often garnering front-page coverage.[90]

Paul, like Catt, was influenced by progressivism and shared Catt's commitment to a new democratic order.[91] In their leadership and strategy, however, Paul and Catt could not have been more different. While Catt's progressivism was expressed through a devotion to efficiency, bureaucratic management, and organization, Paul's progressive ideals inspired her confrontational tactics. Whereas Catt argued that, if the suffragists persisted, the evolution of democracy would bring women the vote eventually, Paul argued that the disfranchised could not wait.

Paul pushed the suffrage movement's progressive principles of democracy and orderly reform to their limits, and through her unique political tactics she challenged the promises of progressivism outright. Although Paul, like other Progressives, was still searching for balance and equality in a disorderly society, for a time her confidence in America's "inevitable" progress was shaken. She became uncertain about whether a well-ordered society and a true democracy could ever really be achieved. Her progressive search for order led her to seek a political solution for improving women's position in society. Unlike most other progressive reformers, however, she brought to the movement "an impatient, militant spirit."[92] During the years 1913 to 1920, Alice Paul changed the image of both Progressive Era reform and the woman suffrage campaign in an ambitious effort to gain for women "the right without which all others are insecure, the right of a full and equal voice in the government under which they live."[93]

A NEW KIND OF SUFFRAGE LEADER

Vivian Gornick writes of Alice Paul, "What she has been . . . and what she is at this moment, is the embodiment of the revolutionary's narrow intensity and burning energy for 'the cause.' Her life has been a vessel into which the necessity of women's rights has been poured. She *is* the cause itself." Paul was a proponent of "the cause" from childhood, even though she did not know of its existence at the time. She once told an interviewer that her interest in women's rights "wasn't something I had to think about. When the Quakers were founded in England in the 1600s, one of their principles was and is equality of the sexes. So I never really had any other idea." What she failed to realize, however, was that the rest of the world did not feel the same. According to Gornick, when Paul discovered that most people did not honor women as men's equals, "the discovery came as a visceral shock, the kind of shock that gives sudden form to that which has been inchoate. She realized that she was political to the bone, that her deepest being was aroused by the political. She saw the disfranchised condition of women in the light of political struggle, and she would never again see it otherwise."[94]

Paul was born into a Quaker reformist family in Moorestown, New Jersey, in 1885. The eldest of four children, Paul learned the Hicksite Quaker values of "a nonviolent life guided by an inward light, and the strong tradition of gender equality."[95] Before Paul entered the movement for women's rights, she was a diligent intellectual and reformer who earned a number of college degrees and devoted much of her time to social service. In 1905, Paul received a B.A. from Swarthmore College, founded by her Quaker grandfather, and from the University of Pennsylvania she received an M.A. in 1907 and a Ph.D. in 1912. In the years between her academic work in the United States, Paul graduated from the New York School of Philanthropy in 1906, studied in England at the Woodbrooke Settlement for Social Work and the University of Birmingham between 1907 and 1908, and was enrolled in graduate courses in sociology and economics at the University of London between 1908 and 1909. It was during her years in England that she first entered the movement for women's rights as a protégée of the British suffragettes, Emmeline and Christabel Pankhurst.[96]

The tactics Paul learned from the Pankhursts' Women's Social and Political Union (WSPU) would inspire her political activism throughout her life. When Paul returned to the United States in 1910, she gave a speech at the NAWSA convention defending the actions of the British militants. Paul explained to the U.S. suffrage constituency: "the magnificently defiant deeds of the last four years have at last wakened Great Britain out of her lethargy. They have played the part of the town crier's bell calling the people to attend this great question. It has become impossible to forget 'votes for women.'" Paul urged the American women to see the positive results that militancy brought to the British movement. She tried to sell the conservative audience on the "new spirit" of defiant protest. The members of the mainstream movement were not ready to embrace the rebellious attitudes of their British sisters, however, nor would many of them ever be converted to militancy as a means of protest. As a result, Paul took it upon herself to infuse the American movement with the energy she believed was crucial to make "votes for women" a national reform measure in the United States.[97]

After spending the summer of 1911 organizing open-air meetings for the Pennsylvania Suffrage Association in Philadelphia, Paul and Lucy Burns, whom she had met working with the WSPU in England, devised a way to begin working for the Susan B. Anthony amendment in Washington. Prior to the NAWSA's Philadelphia Convention in 1912, the women approached Harriot Stanton Blatch, who then convinced Jane Addams to urge the NAWSA executive board to give the women a chance. The board approved and appointed a congressional committee consisting of Paul as chairman, Burns as vice chairman, and Crystal Eastman, who would later become a notable socialist-feminist radical. The committee would be allowed to use the NAWSA's reputable name but would have to provide its own funding. Paul arrived in Washington in December to find that the NAWSA's D.C. headquarters was nonexistent, and the list of names she was given of people who could help proved outdated and useless. Most of the women had either relocated or were deceased. Paul also spoke with the woman who formerly had been in charge of the NAWSA's congressional committee activities. As further evidence of the NAWSA's stalled federal campaign, the woman told Paul that she had been given ten dollars to fund her efforts, and at the end of the year she had returned change.[98]

Intent on quickly lifting the congressional campaign out of its rut, Paul began plans for a massive suffrage procession to be held on 3 March 1913, the day before Woodrow Wilson's first inauguration. The parade would be remembered as much for its pageantry as for the scandalous mob riot it incited. The procession turned out to be a notable political spectacle, which effectively directed the attention of both Congress and the nation to the issue of woman suffrage. An elaborate march of more than eight thousand women, complete with floats, artistic tableaux, stirring music, and colorful banners and sashes, could not be ignored. Several women were dressed in flowing white robes and sat atop white horses to signify the purity of the women and the movement. Women from coast to coast mobilized to support the cause and to usher in a new era of national suffrage politics. Paul's tactical expertise transformed Washington into a stage on which suffrage women acted out their vision of the free women of the future. The parade ended abruptly, however, as heckling spectators numbering in the thousands suddenly turned into an angry mob and swarmed the marchers on Pennsylvania Avenue. Hundreds of parade participants were injured and U.S. troops from Fort Myer had to be called in to restore order.

Coming off of the publicity success of the Washington parade, Paul got down to the business of organizing the committee's efforts toward passage of the Anthony amendment. The primary goal of the congressional committee—and every organization headed by Paul thereafter—was to keep the eye of the country on the suffragists. The committee's political strategy, however, was to keep pressure on Congress and the president for passage of the federal amendment.

Before Paul entered the movement, interest in the federal woman suffrage amendment had been at an all-time low. Interest had been reawakened to an extent when Theodore Roosevelt decided to run on the progressive ticket with a woman suffrage plank in his platform. Convinced that the movement could profit from these developments, Paul and the members of her committee made remarkable progress in their federal work within the first few months. To educate President Wilson, Paul sent delegations to the White House almost every week to state the case of woman suffrage. She also arranged hearings before the Woman Suffrage Committee of the Senate and before the Rules Committee in the House. Congress also received a constant barrage of petitions, resolutions, processions, and suffrage "pilgrims" from all parts of the country. Finally, in late April, Paul founded a national political organization called the Congressional Union for Woman Suffrage (CU). Paul was appointed president, and within a short time the CU had recruited over a thousand members.[99]

The CU's sole purpose was to secure an amendment to the Constitution. Paul had realized that, in order to achieve this goal, it would take more than the five women the NAWSA had appointed to the congressional committee. The CU was initially approved by Shaw and the NAWSA as an auxiliary. Within the next year, however, difficulties arose between the two organizations, which led to Paul's secession and independence for the CU. The CU's core membership, officers, and organizers represented two types of progressive feminists: the more traditional, mature, "clubwomen" reformers, such as Alva Smith Vanderbilt Belmont, who had abundant resources and passion for the cause; and the younger, educated, liberal, "new women" reformers of the middle class who had "a strong desire for economic independence, personal freedom, and a greater, more inclusive democracy, away from patriarchal control." Paul later described the kind of women who were attracted to the CU: "Women of every experience and every walk of life you find have this same feeling for building up respect for their own sex, power for their own sex, and lifting it up out of a place where there is contempt for women in general. . . . Some people are just born feminists." CU organizers were often handpicked by Paul for their combination of independence, motivation, managerial skills, and speaking talent. They also had to prove that they were politically astute, creative, and hard as nails before Paul would send them out to work in the field.[100]

As a leader, Paul was a combination of military general and spiritual guide—forceful and demanding of her workers, but also an inspirational visionary for the movement. Co-worker Crystal Eastman wrote, "it is rare to find in one human being this passion for service and sacrifice combined first with the shrewd calculating mind of a born political leader, and second with the ruthless driving force, sure judgment and phenomenal grasp of detail that characterize a great entrepreneur." She believed these qualities were united in Alice Paul. Paul's political charisma and knack for publicity were well known, but her interpersonal skills were considerably lacking. An article written on Paul in *Everybody's Magazine* in July 1916 described her as: "very shy; she is not a really first-class platform speaker . . . she is awkward and blundering, not only in her personal estimates of people, but in her personal contacts with them." Despite these inadequacies, the author was quick to admit that, "a great multitude of women, all over the United States, give her in return unfaltering, enthusiastic loyalty; and she deserves every bit of it." Paul's success has been attributed to her method of motivating workers, which included rotating them among the different types and phases of work needed to be done, and keeping her organization in a state of "perpetual change . . . perpetual movement . . . the onward rush of an exhilarating flood." [101]

Paul's greatest accomplishments for suffrage came from her ability to draw attention to the suffrage cause through the infusion of spectacle, drama, youth, and energy—all of which translated into widespread publicity. Some of Paul's most notable early tactics included delivery to Congress of an eighteen-thousand-foot-long petition that had traveled with suffragist Sara Bard Field across the country and contained more than five hundred thousand signatures; the *Suffrage Special*, a train bedecked with purple, white, and gold banners (the CU colors) to transport members to the Chicago convention and on a tour of the western states; and on Valentine's Day, 1916, one thousand suffrage valentines dispatched to senators and representatives. In addition to these publicity events, Paul devised a number of ongoing strategies intended to raise awareness of the need for federal woman suffrage. Orchestrated to induce cooperation from politicians and the president, Paul's most notable tactics included punishing the political party in power, instituting White House pickets, and, in the very last stages of Paul's reign, outright civil disobedience.

ESTABLISHING WOMEN'S POLITICAL POWER

In December 1913 at the forty-fifth annual NAWSA convention in Washington, Lucy Burns stated the position of the CU regarding the Democratic Party: "Rarely in the history of the country has a party been more powerful than the Democratic Party is today. . . . It is in a position to give us effective and immediate help. We ask the Democrats to take action now. Those who hold power are responsible to the country to use it. . . . Inaction establishes just as clear a record as does a policy of open hostility."[102] With this pronouncement began the CU's policy of holding the party in power responsible and the beginning of concerted political action against the Democrats. The following August the Advisory Council of the CU held a meeting at Marble House, the Newport estate of Alva Belmont, during which Paul outlined the proposed election program that would put the policy into practical operation.

Once Paul had asked the press to withdraw, she asked the council, "who is our enemy and then, how shall that enemy be attacked?" Her answer was a pointed assessment of the political situation and a plan to use women's political strength in the suffrage states to put pressure on the party in power: "Now the time has come, we believe, when we can really go into national politics and use the nearly four million votes that we have to win the vote for the rest of us." She continued, "The question is whether we are good enough politicians to take four million votes and organize them and use them so as to win the vote for the women who are still disfranchised." By the end of Paul's motivational speech, she had transformed the women of the council, and soon the entire CU, from suffrage reformers to professional campaign organizers. According to Christine Lunardini, "The meeting at Marble House marked a new departure in the history of woman suffrage in the United States. For the first time, enfranchised women would be able to help their unenfranchised sisters in purely political fashion by disavowing party commitment in favor of sex solidarity."[103]

As far as Paul was concerned, suffragists would no longer politely ask for votes; the time had come when women would demand them. In March 1915, Paul declared: "We want to make Woman Suffrage the dominant political issue from the moment Congress reconvenes. We want to have Congress open in the midst of a veritable Suffrage cyclone." Paul's ambitious rhetoric attracted women to the CU who were tired of the NAWSA's traditional educational approach and were prepared to undertake more aggressively political strategies. The CU and its policies attracted many women because, as Nancy Cott notes, their approach "symbolized women exercising the power they had, forcing government to pay attention to them, fighting rather than begging for the ballot."[104]

The policy of holding the party in power responsible was highly controversial from the NAWSA's standpoint. Fearing that a policy of opposing Democrats would mean working to defeat loyal suffragists from the West, the NAWSA pleaded with the CU to stop their "partisan" campaigning. The NAWSA cited the long tradition of nonpartisanship within the movement. Paul, however, would not be persuaded; she stood behind her organization's political activism and denied accusations of partisanship. In fact, in a two-hour-long suffrage hearing before the House Judiciary Committee in 1915, Paul told the representatives: "I want to emphasize just one point, in addition, that we are absolutely non-partisan. We are made up of women who are strong Democrats, women who are strong Republicans, women who are Socialists, Progressives—every type of women. We are all united on this one thing—that we put Suffrage before everything else. In every election, if we ever go into any future elections, we simply pledge ourselves to this—that we will consider the furtherance of Suffrage and not our party affiliations in deciding what action we shall take."[105] Paul and the CU were prepared to continue to show Congress that they could deliver votes—either for them or against them—for as long as it would take. Faced with the presidential election in 1916, the Woman's Party, consisting of enfranchised women of the CU, was formed at the Congressional Union convention in Chicago. This method of pressuring Congress from below through voter strength became only one part of the CU's strategy in coming years, however. Their next task was to find another source of power that could effect a change in congressional voting practices. For this, Paul and her cohorts went straight to the person in power.

PICKETING THE PRESIDENT

Paul and the CU believed that calling upon the support of women voters in the West would have considerable influence on upcoming campaigns and suffrage support in Congress. Yet they also believed that lobbying for political reforms was futile without the support of the president. "Win the president and you win the battle" was a slogan of sorts for Paul, and this notion was the impetus for the next phase of CU activity.[106] Due to the crisis surrounding the war in Europe, Wilson had stopped receiving delegations of suffragists. The women had to find a new way to continue their agitation. The first suffrage pickets arrived outside the White House with messages for the president on 10 January 1917.

The pickets were probably the most effective rhetorical device of Alice Paul's campaign for women's enfranchisement. Known as the "Silent Sentinels," women from a variety of backgrounds, classes, and affiliations marched daily in front of the White House gates. The purple, white, and gold banners contained messages such as "MR. PRESIDENT, WHAT WILL YOU DO FOR WOMAN SUFFRAGE?" and "HOW LONG MUST WOMEN WAIT FOR LIBERTY?" The messages to the president created powerful arguments for women's votes, while at the same time maintaining women's presence in a dignified manner. The pickets drew attention to the cause more consistently than any other method applied by the woman suffrage movement up to that point. As the picketers persisted day after day, the patience of the president and the nation began to wear thin. At first the press flocked to cover the extraordinary spectacle of women marching in front of the president's gates, but before long some of the coverage had turned against the women. The *New York Times* and other reports accused the women of acting "unnatural" and called them "crazy," "hostile," and "unwomanly."[107]

By March of 1917, the CU and the Woman's Party had merged into the National Woman's Party (NWP) and continued the previous tactics of publicity, lobbying, political activism, and constant picketing. The most impressive and inspired of the NWP's actions occurred on the day of Wilson's second inauguration, 4 March 1917. Hoping to get Wilson to commit to suffrage during his second term, one thousand delegates formed a dramatic picket line ready to present various resolutions to the president. The suffragists marched through stinging sleet and howling wind. Thousands of spectators lined the street to watch the procession, and two bands played amidst the driving rain. When it came time to present the resolutions, the pickets found that all the gates had been locked and that guards had been advised to bar the women from entry. The women continued to march for more than four hours and still were denied access to the president. NWP member Doris Stevens wrote, "All the women who took part in that march will tell you of the passionate resentment that burned in their hearts that dreary day. This one single incident probably did more than any other to make women sacrifice themselves." Although this had been intended as the final picket, the indignity felt by the women that day led them to plan further protest—and to extend their activities to the gates of Congress as well.[108]

Paul frequently took time from planning to join the pickets or to offer her encouragement. She believed persistence would lead to action and explained the strategy this way: "If a creditor stands before a man's house all day demanding payment of his bill, the man must either remove the creditor or pay the bill."[109] While Wilson's war efforts took him on a European tour, the NWP began appropriating phrases from his war speeches onto their banners. A line from the president's war message of 2 April 1917 became a slogan for their banners: "WE SHALL FIGHT FOR THE THINGS WHICH WE HAVE ALWAYS HELD NEAREST OUR HEARTS— FOR DEMOCRACY, FOR THE RIGHT OF THOSE WHO SUBMIT TO AUTHORITY TO HAVE A VOICE IN THEIR OWN GOVERNMENT." The final planned assault, later known as the Russian banner incident, not only brought international attention to the NWP, but also precipitated the first outbreak of violence at the previously peaceful public demonstrations.

On 20 June 1917, members of the Russian Republic, which had just enfranchised women, were officially received by President Wilson. As they passed the gates, Lucy Burns and a fellow NWP picketer unfurled a banner reading: "PRESIDENT WILSON AND ENVOY ROOT ARE DECEIVING RUSSIA. THEY SAY, 'WE ARE A DEMOCRACY. HELP US WIN THE WAR SO THAT DEMOCRACIES MAY SURVIVE.' WE WOMEN OF AMERICA TELL YOU THAT AMERICA IS NOT A DEMOCRACY. TWENTY MILLION WOMEN ARE DENIED THE RIGHT TO VOTE. PRESIDENT WILSON IS THE CHIEF OPPONENT OF THEIR NATIONAL ENFRANCHISEMENT. HELP US MAKE THIS NATION REALLY FREE. TELL OUR GOVERNMENT THAT IT MUST LIBERATE ITS PEOPLE BEFORE IT CAN CLAIM FREE RUSSIA AS AN ALLY." After the Russian delegates passed, a spectator outside the gates leaped at the banner and destroyed it, which antagonized the crowd into rushing the women. Later a member of the Russian Republic told an American politician, "You know, it was very embarrassing for us, because we were in sympathy with those women at the gates."[110] As it became evident that the pickets were beginning to have an effect on Wilson's world leadership, the NWP strategy began to draw fire from government officials, and soon a threat of arrests was made. The first arrests were executed two days later, and Paul and the NWP entered into the most militant stage of their campaign.

CIVIL DISOBEDIENCE AND THE CRITIQUE OF AMERICAN DEMOCRACY

Of the protests and stubborn determination of the NWP, Linda Ford writes, "Here indeed were most annoying women—women who 'reversed the social order' by insisting on their legitimate say as citizens. . . . The CU stance was a 'demanding one,' informing the government: 'Here is what you are not doing for us, this is what we intend to do for ourselves.'"[111] The demands would continue in light of almost daily arrests. The NWP decided to use civil disobedience and claims that those arrested were political prisoners to gain sympathy for the cause. In a flyer titled "Why We Picket," the NWP explained: "instead of assisting women to win freedom, the Government is trying to intimidate those who ask for freedom. And the women are determined to go on asking for it, knowing well that the very effort of the Government to suppress them is carrying their message all the more clearly to the whole people."[112] Because the women felt the rights they did have as citizens were being violated, they began to operate outside the traditional social and political channels to make their voices heard. The NWP justified their transgression of the boundaries of the law by arguing that if they had no say in government, they could not be subjected to its rule.

The NWP's civil disobedience continued for months with more than ninety women, including Alice Paul, sentenced to jail and then to the Occoquan Workhouse in Virginia to serve their sentences. The workhouse was infamous for its foul air, rancid food, and enforcement of hard labor. To protest their wrongful imprisonment— they were jailed on an obscure "obstruction of traffic" law—the women went on hunger strikes and were force-fed by prison authorities. The inhumane treatment transformed the prisoners into martyrs—and gained even more sympathy for the cause. Within five weeks President Wilson stepped in and ordered the commutation of the women's sentences. Upon her release, Paul stated: "We hope that no more demonstrations will be necessary, that the amendment will move steadily on to passage and ratification without further suffering or sacrifice. But what we do depends entirely on what the Administration does."[113] It would be another two years before the administration would succumb, and Paul's NWP quickly reverted back to staging public events intended to criticize the president and his policies.

After the prison episodes, many of the NWP activists lost faith in the democratic process. These feelings only spurred more radical efforts, including more demonstrations and more arrests. In the final years of the suffrage fight, the NWP continued to invent increasingly high-profile publicity stunts. First, they sponsored *The Prison Special,* a train tour throughout the country that gave women the chance to speak about their prison experiences. Then, after the House passed the national amendment on 10 January 1918, the NWP turned its attention to the Senate. One hundred women dressed in white met at the base of Lafayette Park, across from the White House. Numerous speeches and flags demanded in the name of liberty that the Senate pass the suffrage amendment in the present session. Forty-eight women were arrested but not charged with any offense, which further inflamed the women's sense of political injustice. After the amendment was defeated in the Senate by two votes in September, the NWP's impatience mounted. President Wilson had gone to France on war business and, since they could no longer meet with him, the suffragists began igniting "watch-fires of freedom" in which they would burn Wilson's speeches hourly as a bell tolled outside the NWP headquarters. The watch-fires, arrests, convictions, hunger strikes, and even an image of the president burned in effigy were continued as symbolic demonstrations of the suffragists' contempt for the government's humiliation of women and their cause. For more than a year Paul was forced to invent strategic new ways of keeping the suffrage fight in the forefront of the national agenda until finally, on 4 June 1919, the Senate passed the measure and the Susan B. Anthony amendment was submitted to the states for ratification.

A MILITANT LEGACY

As the brainchild of Alice Paul, the CU (and later the NWP) established a brand of political activism that elevated woman suffrage to prominence among the many reform measures seeking national support in the Progressive Era. She was able to keep woman suffrage a burning issue even in the face of the nation's entrance into World War I. Paul implemented strategies and tactics that had never before been instituted by women working for suffrage reform. The tactics employed by Paul and the NWP achieved a variety of goals for the movement. The processions, pickets, and other events within the public arena demonstrated "in the most vivid fashion possible the intensity of the women's desire for the ballot and the strength of their commitment to the cause."[114] The NWP's confrontational rhetoric also challenged patriarchal oppression by the government and society and insisted on a more inclusive democracy. For seven years Paul continued the struggle without pause in order to show the president, Congress, and the world that women deserved equality and would not stop fighting until it was won.

Paul's dedication to the cause stemmed from her belief in the progressive spirit: hers was a mission to seek out injustice and to find a way to end it. Like other Progressives, Paul felt that her reform work was a way to improve society and to increase the moral uplift of the nation's people. In the summer of 1913, at the beginning of her career as a national leader in the suffrage movement, Paul wrote to Iowa socialist leader John E. Nordquist that "this Woman Suffrage question is above every question of the time, because; for one thing, it is so vitally the very next step in the process of Moral Evolution." Part of this evolution, Paul believed, would be new and wider roles for women in both society and politics. The vote for women was viewed as a desirable progressive goal and, since government was clearly the base for social change, Paul knew that her cause must be made political.[115] From the beginning, Paul's intention was to organize the movement around a single political objective. As Amelia Fry notes, "Although

Alice Paul's operation covered the continent from ocean to ocean . . . although her domain was as large as any American political figure of the day, and even though she was in sympathy with the many Progressive social reforms, she held the NWP to a one-issue goal: gender equality in the body politic."[116] With her own courage, determination, and focus, Paul created an organization that made evident to the nation that women could be powerful, political, and tenacious in achieving their goals.

On the day the secretary of state announced that the Nineteenth Amendment had become law, Alice Paul emerged onto the balcony of the NWP headquarters and hung the suffrage flag in victory. Like the NAWSA, the NWP would take credit for the ultimate success of the woman suffrage campaign. In a 1973 interview, Paul commented on the NWP's importance to the final passage of the Nineteenth Amendment. She stated that in the last seven years of the campaign, "the women in the Woman's Party succeeded in increasing the support and arousing the enthusiasm of women all over the United States to an extent that it had never been aroused before." She also credited her plan of holding the party in power responsible, and using women's political power as voters in the western states to do so, as the most important factor in passing the federal amendment.[117] History, however, would accord credit to both parties for the substantial political achievement.

CARRIE CHAPMAN CATT AND ALICE PAUL: LEADERS IN OPPOSITION

When, in 1913, the NAWSA presented Paul with an ultimatum—either step down as chair of the congressional committee or as chair of the CU—and then accused Paul of misappropriating NAWSA funds, it had become obvious that the two groups could not continue to work together amicably. Catt had been one of the first to question Paul's motives by accusing her of "a dark conspiracy to capture the entire 'National' for the militant enterprise."[118] From that moment on the relationship between the older and younger leader became one of antagonism and distrust, prompting Paul to recall Catt years later as one of the few suffragists "who seemed to have her heart very much in animosity."[119] Historians have compared the division between the NAWSA and the CU to the earlier cleavage between Stanton and Anthony's National Association and Stone's American. Back then Stone had emphasized moderation to avoid extreme reactions and the antagonism of neutrals, while Stanton and Anthony were committed to expressing their views no matter who took offense. In 1913, the NAWSA had become the relatively conservative and cautious party operating against the more radical CU, which was in favor of bolder and more unconventional strategies.[120]

Given that both Catt and Paul were brilliant tacticians and extraordinary organizers and motivators, one can only speculate what might have been accomplished if the two had joined forces. Instead, between 1913 and 1920, the two women worked at opposite ends of the movement; Catt was the moderate who believed in education and polite politicking, while Paul was the militant who embraced civil disobedience. Lunardini describes the leaders' distinctive roles in this way: "Catt belonged to the forces of order and Paul to the forces of movement."[121] The difference in ideologies between Catt and Paul also led to differences in tactics, which was the greatest source of conflict between the two.

One of Catt's main concerns was that Paul and her allies were not being politically pragmatic, but rather self-indulgent in their radical actions. According to Fowler, Catt believed "the Woman's Party was another part of America out of control in a country already blighted by too many instances of the same thing."[122] Catt and the NAWSA were convinced that the actions of the NWP would compromise the suffrage cause by losing the votes of men who resented attacks on the Democratic Party, which supported a number of other progressive issues. Further, Catt and her fellow NAWSA members believed woman suffrage "to be the inevitable byproduct of the slow evolution of democracy, of the replacement of force by reason as the basis of government." As a result, they relied on persuasion and the skillful organization of existing sentiment to achieve the "inevitable" victory. From Paul's and the NWP's perspective, Catt and the association's belief that "even a rock eventually gives way under the constant dripping of water" was a form of gradualism and inaction the cause could not afford.[123]

Another disjuncture between the two parties erupted when the NWP instituted the White House pickets. Ironically, Catt had earlier endorsed the suffrage militancy of England's WSPU, stating in an article in the 31 May 1913 issue of the *Woman's Journal*, "The suffrage campaign in the United States is a dull and commonplace affair when compared with the sizzling white heat of the British struggle." Although Catt credited the WSPU with the "arrest of public attention" and "the compulsion of public discussion in every country in the world," she herself could not embrace militant techniques. In an earlier article entitled "Suffrage Militancy," Catt stated: "I am not militant in theory or practice. . . . Reason, and not physical force, to my mind is the standard of true civilization. I believe in education, persuasion, agitation and political warfare as the means which ought to be employed to gain and establish political reforms."[124] Due to her own allegiances, Catt could not approve of militancy within the American movement and felt the NWP was a liability and an embarrassment to the cause. Believing that it was unseemly for women to resort to force, and that the women of the movement must be reasonable and respectable representations of American womanhood, Catt and the NAWSA set out to distance their campaign from Paul and the NWP. The NAWSA officers begged newspaper editors to explain in their reports the differences between radical and nonradical suffragists. Despite the NAWSA's efforts to undermine the work of her party, Paul continued to argue for women's equality—and the changing image of women that came with that struggle.[125]

By 1916, the two camps did finally agree on something; both the NWP and the NAWSA were pursuing the federal amendment. Once the forces of the two committees joined and directed their energy toward the same goal, advances came relatively quickly. After remaining dormant in Congress since 1872, the Susan B. Anthony amendment frequently was brought before sessions of the House and Senate between 1917 and 1918, and woman suffrage became a key campaign issue for both of the political parties. Common wisdom now holds that both the NAWSA and the NWP—and therefore the leadership of both the traditional Catt and the radical Paul—were necessary for this advance to take place. The steady work of Catt and the NAWSA over three long decades helped secure mainstream respectability for the movement, as well as the loyalty of many of the states necessary for ratification. Paul and the NWP reenergized the movement, and their tactics also served to challenge the NAWSA, leading to its eventual revitalization and pursuit of the amendment. In the end, it took two national organizations with divergent strategies and distinctive leaders to push the cause of suffrage through to its successful conclusion.

In most historical accounts and in subsequent public memory, Carrie Chapman Catt and Alice Paul are positioned as the dual representatives of the suffrage fight in its concluding years. As the suffrage ranks divided between "moderate" and "militant" camps on their way toward victory, however, Harriot Stanton Blatch represented a third approach to women's rights in the Progressive Era. As DuBois writes, "While Alice Paul and the militants pulled in the direction of civil disobedience, and Carrie Chapman Catt and the moderates stuck to the path of congressional lobbying, Harriot tried to combine both approaches into a militant but explicitly political challenge." Blatch's prominence in the movement reached its peak around 1910, during Catt's hiatus from the national movement and a few years before Paul's entrance. Through the practice of political protest and the assertion of women's claims to public life, Blatch reignited the woman suffrage movement by emphasizing social change and generating mass support. As the chief political strategist for the New York campaign, the largest in the Union, Blatch was a pivotal figure who brought much-needed national attention to the suffrage crusade. She also was responsible for pushing the stalled movement into new directions and linking the cause of women's rights to other progressive causes.[126] As such, an understanding of Catt and Paul's leadership tells only part of the story of suffrage in the Progressive Era. An exploration of the career of Harriot Stanton Blatch, an innovator and visionary equal to Carrie Chapman Catt and Alice Paul, helps to provide a more complete account of the intersection of the suffrage tradition and progressivism in America.

Contesting the Social and Political Order: Harriot Stanton Blatch's Suffrage Rhetoric

Harriot Stanton Blatch's leadership in the woman's rights movement seemed to be directly inherited from her famous mother. That Blatch would continue the legacy of her mother's crusade for suffrage was unquestioned by movement members. Yet what she would do with that legacy remained uncertain. Having begun her career with the women's movement in England, Blatch was quick to distinguish herself from her mother's legacy. Blatch's contributions to woman suffrage ultimately spanned more than thirty years, and throughout her career she modernized the struggling movement. Blatch was a dedicated Progressive and she infused the movement with these ideals. DuBois notes that Blatch regarded woman suffrage as "a crucial part of a larger vision of social democracy, economic equality, and political justice."[127] Based on her commitment to these ideals, Blatch's leadership epitomized the revitalization of the second generation of the movement. Blatch combined political activism and progressive-feminist rhetoric to expand the movement through the inclusion of all classes of women, including professional and working women. She also worked to revise women's role in the body politic by providing explicit examples of women's capacity for work, independence, civic participation, and, ultimately, equal citizenship.

Blatch effectively challenged gender relations, men's and women's traditional roles, and the gendered construction of the private and the public. Blatch's suffrage career unfolded in three distinct phases. In her early work for suffrage both in England and in the New York campaign, Blatch took up the cause of working and professional women to prove women's worth and their need for a political voice. By 1910, Blatch began to introduce publicity tactics into the campaign, particularly suffrage parades and outdoor demonstrations. By encouraging female activism in the public sphere, Blatch worked to subvert traditional representations of womanhood and the sexual order as a protest of women's exclusion from civic democracy. In the last years of her involvement in the suffrage crusade, and just before the amendment was passed, Blatch released a book titled *Mobilizing Woman-Power*. This work functioned as an analysis of gender oppression by contesting the social constructions of masculinity and femininity and arguing for women's rightful claims to democratic citizenship.

A NEW VISION FOR THE SUFFRAGE MOVEMENT

On the first page of her memoirs, *Challenging Years,* Blatch wrote: "I was born on January 20, 1865, to that great woman, born in the very cradle of the feminist movement, for it was in my native village of Seneca Falls, New York, that the first Woman's Rights Convention of the world met in 1848." As the daughter of suffrage pioneer Elizabeth Cady Stanton, Blatch demonstrated from an early age her own determination to challenge the limitations others had placed on her sex. One of Blatch's childhood memories recalls the early formation of this lifelong ambition: "In time I took to climbing [trees], and with my skill was connected a most emphatic feminist revolt. I was high in a heavenward journey in a big chestnut tree . . . when my father happened to see me, and called out in some agitation: 'My daughter come down, come down, you will fall.' Poised calmly on the branch, I instantly argued, 'Why don't you tell Bob to come down, he's three years younger and one branch higher?'"[128] Such incidents, Blatch claimed, helped to shape the ideas about feminism and equality that would later inspire her steadfast commitment to the woman suffrage movement.

Although Blatch's early dedication to the cause for woman's rights was no doubt inherited from her mother, she spent the better part of her life trying to differentiate herself from the venerable founder of the suffrage movement. Blatch began to find her own path during her college years at Vassar where she came to the realization that "politics were the breath of [her] nostrils." On discovering Blatch's inclination for politics, Vassar president John H. Raymond suggested a course of reading for Blatch in economics and politics. Blatch later persuaded a professor to offer a class in political economy and created the first debating club. After graduation in 1878, Blatch followed her mother's advice and enrolled in the Boston School of Oratory to continue her training in public speaking so that she could then join Stanton on the lyceum circuit.[129] After just one season, Blatch realized that she needed space to grow professionally independent of her famous mother. She left for Europe in May 1880, where she would spend the greater part of the next two decades.

Blatch traveled between Germany, France, and the United States for several years before settling in Basingstoke, England, after her marriage to Harry Blatch in November 1882. Of this time in England, Blatch recalled: "Interested as I was in politics, those twenty years were absorbing. Beginning with the great changes in educational control, there went on under my eyes the upbuilding of district councils, county councils, indeed all the machinery necessary for local self-government."[130] Blatch became involved in numerous political societies, including the Women's Local Government Society, the Women's Franchise League (WFL), the Women's Liberal Federation, and the Fabian Society of London.

In a study of both Stanton's and Blatch's transatlantic work for woman suffrage, Sandra Stanley Holton argues that in the 1890s their work for the Women's Franchise League may be viewed as the beginnings of a radical current that "left a significant legacy for the twentieth-century movement in both Britain and the United States."[131] Blatch's work with the WFL was based primarily on a demand for the vote that emphasized a broad appeal for women's citizenship, including the ending of coverture. According to Susan Kingsley Kent, under the law of coverture, married women had no rights or existence apart from their husbands; women's legal rights to her property, earnings, body, and children all resided in her husband. Deeming these rights essential for the autonomous development of the individual and a necessary component of true citizenship, radical-liberal suffragists such as Blatch believed that extending the vote to married women should be central to arguments for the franchise.[132]

As secretary of the WFL, Blatch gave an address in 1891 on a bill to allow married women the vote in municipal elections. In this speech, Blatch challenged arguments against women's voting, including those relating to child-rearing: "Another objection you may urge, is that motherhood and wifehood presuppose such absorbing duties, that a married woman has no time to form solid political opinions. Behind your contention lies the fallacy—that while maternal cares are all-absorbing, paternal cares are light as air. No, gentlemen, in this work-a-day world paternity, just as maternity, means responsibility—never light at best."[133] Here Blatch challenged the social fallacy that a woman's role in raising her children was different from that of a man's. If equality naturally existed in parental duties, she suggested, there should also naturally be equality in politics.

Throughout her days in England, Blatch continued to stay abreast of the suffrage movement in the United States and often contributed her own transatlantic perspective on woman's rights through letters to the *Woman's Journal*. Blatch first established herself as an advocate for U.S. suffrage in an open debate with her mother, which was documented through these public letters. In a December 1894 response to Stanton's plea for strict education qualifications for enfranchisement, Blatch wrote: "Because you overlook the fact that the conditions of the poor are so much harder than yours or mine, you are led to argue that 'the ignorant classes do not need the suffrage more than the enlightened, but just the reverse.' Every working man needs the suffrage more than I do, but there is another who needs it more than he does, just because conditions are more galling, and that is the working woman."[134] Blatch had recently received a master's degree from Vassar College, where her study of the rural poor in England ignited her interest in American social classes. The public debate distinguished Blatch from her mother, provided a forum for her to voice her own political ideology, and allowed her to form an independent identity as an advocate of working-class interests within the American suffrage campaign.

Blatch was soon dividing her time between England and the United States and promoting a fresh conception of women's claims to citizenship based on their labor, both paid and unpaid.[135] This idea was expressed in a 1906 magazine article Blatch wrote, entitled "Specialization of Function in Women." In the essay, Blatch argued: "The woman's 'cause' is probably a question of dollars and cents, and is not to be won solely by right to vote and hold office, or by freedom to enter every profession and trade. . . . The pivotal question for women is how to organize their work as home-builders and race-builders, how to get that work paid for, not in so-called protection, but in the currency of the state." Blatch expanded on this principle in a 1898 speech she gave to a U.S. congressional hearing on woman suffrage. In this address, titled "Progress by Proved Worth," Blatch argued that women have proven their capacity for citizenship through political clubs, through local governments, and, most important, through the economic value of their work. Blatch concluded the speech with the statement: "If we recognize the democratic side of our cause, and make an organized appeal to industrial women on the ground of their need of citizenship, and to the nation on the ground of its need that all wealth-producers should form part of its body politic, the close of the century might witness the building of a true republic in the United States." For Blatch, the cause of the working woman was the key to winning suffrage in the twentieth century; she believed it was the masses of women wage-earners who were transforming the role of woman in the modern age.[136]

With Stanton's death imminent, Blatch left England permanently in 1902. After the death of Susan B. Anthony four years later, Blatch assumed a leadership role within the U.S. movement. Beginning with her active role in the New York City suffrage campaign, Blatch began to call for a more inclusive movement, embracing both working-class and professional women. This blending of democratic ideals and pleas for social justice was typical of progressive rhetoric, but it represented a new philosophy for the suffrage movement. As a driving force during the movement's last two decades, Blatch helped recast suffrage discourse in more pragmatic terms, with an emphasis on economic effects. Blatch believed in conducting her feminist work in the trenches to ensure that woman suffrage would result in tangible benefits for working women.

Having worked with the socialist Fabians in England, Blatch was well-versed in the tenets of social progressivism. Her reform agenda led naturally to her affiliation with the Progressive Party. In her autobiography, Blatch wrote: "The Progressive Party appeared to me to be the one hope of awakening from its stupor the thought and conscience of the nation. It was bringing real issues before the people."[137] For Blatch, the "real issues" had always been the poor material conditions affecting the lower strata, especially immigrants and the working class. Inspired by the optimism of the Progressive Era, Blatch initiated a more energetic and broad-based suffrage campaign that could link up with the labor movement, particularly women of the Socialist Party and the Women's Trade Union League.

As the founder of the Equality League for Self-Supporting Women in 1907, Blatch stressed that women's productive labor, both industrial and professional, required a political voice.[138] Regarding Blatch's influence on the suffrage movement at large, DuBois writes, "Turning away from nineteenth-century definitions of the unity of women that emphasized their place in the home, their motherhood, and their exclusion from the economy, and emphasizing instead the unity that productive work provided for all women, Blatch wrote feminism in its essentially modern form, around work." Blatch saw women's unity as essential to the collective effort needed to achieve rightful citizenship for the nation's women. At the sixtieth anniversary of the Seneca Falls Woman's Rights Convention in 1908, Blatch informed the NAWSA attendees that "women are getting the sense of solidarity by being crowded together in the workshop; they are learning the lesson of fellowship. . . . They know now that they form a class." For Blatch, the notion of paid labor for all women held the promise of both resolving the differences between men and women and creating an argument for woman suffrage based on notions of equality. Along these lines, Blatch's rallying cry in numerous speeches was "The suffrage will be won by women who are economically independent . . . the woman who supports herself has a claim upon the state, which legislators are coming to realize."[139] Like Catt and Paul, Blatch's arguments contested women's exclusion from the rights of self-government and democracy.

Blatch is best remembered as the suffrage leader who lifted the movement out of its rut by focusing on the link between women's economic equality and political rights. In order to do this, however, Blatch believed the movement had to identify itself as a political movement. She articulated this in her memoirs, writing: "We all believed that suffrage propaganda must be made dramatic, that suffrage workers must be politically minded. We saw the need of drawing industrial women into the suffrage campaign and recognized that these women needed to be brought in contact, not with women of leisure, but with business and professional women who were out in the world earning a living." Blatch believed from the start that the movement's success could only be achieved if she were to "guide the suffrage ship into political channels" and put women's education and professional achievement to work for the cause.[140] By showing the rapid expansion of women's social roles through their position as workers in all professions, Blatch built a case for women's inclusion in politics. Next, she would take that argument to the streets.

PUBLIC PROTESTS AND VOTES FOR WOMEN

In a 1912 article written for the *New York Tribune,* Blatch explained why suffragists organized annual parades. "Men and women," she wrote, "are moved by seeing marching groups of people and by hearing music far more than by listening to the most careful argument."[141] Blatch understood the rhetorical force of a parade's visual imagery. Parades as celebratory performance had been a distinct feature of American civic discourse since the early days of the republic.[142] Cognizant of the procession's significance in American culture, Blatch envisioned the parade as a strategy designed to move suffrage politics from the drawing rooms into the streets.

The first annual suffrage parade, organized by Blatch's Equality League, was held on 21 May 1910. Until this time, large groups of women had never before marched in a public demonstration on such a diverse and massive scale.[143] In the many civic ceremonies of the nineteenth century, men were the social actors and women mere observers.[144] The parades Blatch orchestrated for the woman suffrage movement appropriated this public expression—previously used to celebrate republican manhood—as a conscious transgression of the rules of social order. The spectacle of the yearly suffrage parades held between 1910 and 1913 constituted both public celebration and political protest. Blatch also introduced a number of other campaign tactics into the movement during this time, including open-air meetings, street corner speeches, and trolley car campaigns. These initial demonstrations displayed women's collective mobilization and visually symbolized their challenge to prescribed societal roles. Consequently, a new set of methods of tactical resistance was established within the movement.

Suffrage tactics first moved into the public sphere with the help of the American Suffragettes, a group initiated by Bettina Borrman Wells, a visiting member of the Women's Social and Political Union of England (WSPU).[145] In the tradition of the British suffragettes, the American Suffragettes began holding open-air meetings and attempted an all-woman parade in February 1907. The parade was unsuccessful, with only twenty-three participants, who were far outnumbered by curious onlookers. Nonetheless, Blatch soon extended these new suffrage strategies into the national campaign through the activities of her larger, better-established Equality League.

Along with large, open-air meetings, the trolley campaigns and other new methods fulfilled Blatch's mission of taking suffrage out of the parlor and into the streets—and gained much-needed publicity for the woman's movement. Years before Paul began her militant protests, Blatch instructed suffrage women to spread their messages throughout American cities by wearing sandwich boards advertising the cause and giving soapbox orations on street corners. Initially characterized as "militant," particularly by more conservative members of the NAWSA, Blatch's tactics changed the personality of the American suffrage campaign to fit women's new public persona. By violating the standards of "femininity," these tactics broke through the "press boycott" that had plagued the campaign for years. Even the staid *New York Times* began reporting regularly on woman suffrage in 1908—and the more controversial the event, the more prominent the coverage.[146]

Finnegan discusses how suffragists emulated popular commercial strategies to "sell" the movement. Finnegan writes that suffragists "helped shape contemporary equations between political campaigning and political salesmanship by recognizing the importance of image management, consumption, and mass, multimedia exposure."[147] Blatch and others used these tactics to launch woman suffrage as a mainstream movement worthy of political consideration. The consequences of these strategies were clear to Blatch, who reported to the *New York Tribune:* "As this is an advertising age, leaders of any movement do well to study somewhat the methods of the press agent. The mere words 'Votes for Women,' 'Votes for Women,' repeated over and over again would at least carry the idea of the political freedom of women into many obtuse minds; brain cells would begin to be agitated; thoughts would begin to flow around the idea of suffrage for women, and we know that when one begins to think, really think, about this last step in democracy, conversion is sure to result."[148] By promoting the idea of woman suffrage to vast audiences, Blatch also was advancing the image of the "new woman," fit to enter into the body politic. Blatch's coordination of organized political reform for women pushed the movement into public spaces and thrust the concept of women's personal and political autonomy into the national consciousness.

One of the most significant reform strategies Blatch devised was the yearly suffrage procession. The women of the suffrage movement, in an effort to reconstitute their own social identity, seized the spectacle of the parade as an expression of resistance. By taking over the public space of the streets, the suffragists were able to invite spectator participation in an otherwise accepted democratic ritual. The parade also served to expand the audience for suffrage rhetoric. In Blatch's words, "a parade moves the emotions of men and brings finally conviction to our opponents, and a parade proves that an increasing number of women are urging that they be given liberty to fulfill to the uttermost their public duties in the state."[149] For the suffrage movement, the parade was a means of persuasion through visual imagery—an "agitation by symbol"—used to articulate an argument for a new pattern of social life in which women would serve a greater role.[150]

The initiation of annual parades served several functions for the woman suffrage movement. The demonstrations attracted the attention of the press, and the mobilization of women fed the enthusiasm of the suffrage army. This latter function was significant. In the act of presenting the cause to the public gaze, women experienced their own collectivity. Most important, however, the parade communicated the passion behind the cause. "Conviction is largely a matter of feeling," explained Blatch, "It is because we know this that we use the argument of the procession to convert our opponents."[151] Four major suffrage parades were held during Blatch's leadership of the movement, each further demonstrating women's capacity for organized and sustained resistance.

The most successful of these parades was held in New York on 4 May 1912 and reportedly included ten thousand men and women. Held a year before Alice Paul's D.C. procession, Blatch's parade set a precedent for massive political suffrage spectacle intended to captivate the attention of an entire city. The front page of the *New York Times* reported on the parade, "the like of which New York never knew before," and commented that the crowd was "far larger than that which greeted the homecoming of Theodore Roosevelt."[152] The parade clearly demonstrated broad support for women's votes, which Blatch felt was essential to the movement's success. The parade also convinced the marchers, who represented women of diverse economic status, that their united voice would be heard and would make a difference.

Inez Milholland, a notable suffrage leader, led the march on horseback. A lawyer and social activist, Milholland had been dedicated to the suffrage cause since her early days as a student at Vassar College. Leading roles in both this and the CU's Washington, D.C., parade fixed Milholland firmly in American suffrage imagery as the "Woman on the Horse," which conjured the militant yet godly figure of Joan of Arc, the patron saint of the British suffrage movement. With Milholland in the lead, the parade symbolized the leadership of righteous women in a patriotic "Holy War," a cause of self-sacrifice for God and country. The spectacular iconography demonstrated to the American public that, in addition to heroism and political savvy, suffragists also possessed beauty and personality.[153]

Acting out Blatch's vision of a victorious suffrage movement, the 1912 parade brought "together the extremes of wealth and poverty in a perfect representation of Progressive Era hopes for class cooperation." Women of all ages, classes, and colors banned together in communal sisterhood. Every detail of the parade was expertly planned to express the women's unity: women marched in unison, there was a uniform costume of dress, and the group exhibited impeccable discipline from start to finish. As a demonstration of women's collective power and capacity for organized resistance, the parade articulated an argument for women's right to enter the polity.[154]

For three years suffrage parades functioned as political advertising and, more important, visual argument. The parade spectacle informed spectators of the who, what, and why of the cause and laid down the grounds for women's claims to enfranchisement. Through the use of banners, diverse delegations, songs, and ceremonial speeches, the suffrage parade articulated a persuasive argument for women's right to vote and enlisted the help of supporters along the way. Various public tactics introduced into the campaign by Blatch also provided the women's movement with an innovative form of propaganda. As women's most dramatic invasion of American popular political culture, the parades opened a new space for reform and reached a broader public audience than ever before. As tactics of resistance, these public events allowed women to contest their association with the qualities and values invoked to exclude women from democratic citizenship, the public realm, politics, and the vote. The suffragists unapologetic intrusion into the public sphere, however, remained a source of controversy both inside and outside the movement.

WOMEN IN THE STREETS

For the woman suffrage movement, the appropriation of public campaign tactics represented an assertion of agency. Suffragists of the Progressive Era were the first to invade the public sphere in such a bold and dramatic fashion and to tactically manage the space of the dominant to their own ends. Blatch viewed these sites of public celebrations and political events as critical arenas for the expression of civic democracy. The suffragists readily "incorporated themselves into traditionally male-centered rituals of active citizenship, and they redefined the sexual hierarchy of streets, plazas, theaters, and convention halls."[155]

The assertion of female citizenry into the public domain was not without its price, however. Critics of the movement identified women *in* the streets with the degrading notion of women *of* the streets. Expressions of disapproval ranged from dismay to outright hostility. A group of suffragists speaking on Wall Street in 1908 were pelted with "apple cores, wet sponges, coils of ticker tape, and bags of water dropped from upper windows."[156] The general reaction to women's growing presence in the public sphere questioned the integrity of reformers. Members of the public less familiar with the suffrage cause immediately deemed street-parading suffragists as deviants. Women's appropriation of public spaces also provided anti-suffragists with increased leverage against the women's movement. The anti-suffragists characterized suffrage women as unfeminine, abrasive, and unruly. These stereotypes fueled arguments against suffrage and allowed anti-suffragists to couch their rejection of the movement in moral terms. One anti-suffragist, distressed over the New York parade, was quoted in the newspaper saying, "I never imagined that such a spectacle could be staged on the streets of New York. There were in the line women who were dressed in a manner which was so shocking that five years ago it would not have been allowed or tolerated by the police."[157] The anti-suffragists were not the only ones rejecting women's emerging publicness; the suffragists heard from dissenters within their own ranks as well.

Although parades and other street tactics were initiated by Blatch to mobilize more women to the cause, the decision to move into public spaces created friction within the movement. More conservative suffragists considered public campaign strategies—especially parade marching—unladylike and immature. Blatch was told by both the New York State Suffrage Association and the NAWSA that a parade would set suffrage back fifty years.[158] The NAWSA leaders, particularly Catt, eventually did come to realize the benefits of public demonstrations. For the first few years, however, the introduction of street tactics divided the campaign.

The suffrage parades, demonstrations, and publicity tactics introduced by Blatch into the national campaign suggested a new vision of women's emancipation. Through these public displays, women were able to appropriate the form of public demonstration into a cultural negation that allowed them to reconstitute the political and sexual hierarchy of the sexes. The women truly believed that the audience would realize the beauty of this vision and make the suffragists' cause its own. Through dramatic narratives, the women attempted to bridge the intellectual distance between their view of the struggle for voting rights and the spectators' interpretations. The public, however, was not ready for conversion. It took seven more years of parades, protests, and petitioning before the Nineteenth Amendment was finally passed. Blatch's suffrage parades alone may not have won the battle, but they contributed to the visual legacy of the suffrage fight. Soon the country would find itself immersed in another battle—World War I. And Blatch would use this event as well to ensure that women remained in the fight for democratic rights.

REVISIONING GENDER POLITICS: THE WAR AND WOMEN'S ROLE IN DEMOCRACY

In 1917 Blatch turned her attention—and energy—from woman suffrage to a larger national concern, the Great War. Blatch was a major supporter of the war; she welcomed the opportunity for the social "reconstruction" she felt the war effort would bring. In 1918, she published a book combining democratic, progressive, and feminist themes, *Mobilizing Woman-Power*.[159] In this book, Blatch called upon Americans to change the way they viewed women.

Mobilizing Woman-Power is best seen as an enlightened Progressive Era manifesto calling for men and women to do their part in conserving civilization. It gave expression to a visionary gender politics focusing on women's capacity for change in the context of wartime patriotism. Blatch reconstituted traditional gender demarcations to assert that women—by breaking through the old, customary barriers—could serve their country equally with men and should be rewarded with equal rights. In her call for the mobilization of women, Blatch brought the notion of woman power to the forefront of wartime discourse and helped make women's equality a salient proposition even in wartime America.

Mobilizing Woman-Power reenvisioned the gender divide as it demonstrated women's rightful place in the war effort and in the democratic polity. By issuing a call to action on behalf of American men and women, Blatch advocated progressive ideals while tapping into general public sentiment about the war. The rhetorical tactics Blatch employed to advance her argument highlighted faith in progress, the supremacy of democratic values, and the importance of women to the achievement of both. In the book, Blatch contended that women's combined virtues of strength and nurturance made them specially qualified for national service. She asked American women to back men in the war effort and asked the men to let them. *Mobilizing Woman-Power* also established a causal link between women's collective labor and the ability to enact great social change, which worked to emphasize the relation of women's war work and the battle for suffrage. Finally, Blatch argued that by expanding their traditional roles and fulfilling heroic duties, women would eventually be rewarded with the vote.

Blatch supported the war as an opportunity for collective effort and believed women's defense work would create a general appreciation of their value. This, she believed, would eventually bring them nearer to emancipation.[160] In a letter to fellow suffragist Anne Martin, Blatch wrote: "I am red hot for the war, I want ten million men put on the firing line as soon as they can be got there and I want women organized by women to enter on work here and free men for the army."[161] Like other pro-war Progressives, Blatch viewed the war as an opportunity for social progress. She did not worry that the glorification of war might pose a threat to the women's movement; instead she exploited the war to push the cause forward.

In short, Blatch's strategy was to incorporate war discourse—which by 1918 had infiltrated the States—into a call for women's collective action that would "point the way after the war to practical, applied feminism."[162] Convinced that WWI was a war for the future of universal democracy, Blatch wrote *Mobilizing Woman-Power* to highlight the necessary contributions of women during wartime. Blatch clearly expressed her belief that American women should not be left out of the fight or excluded from the democratic principles for which it was being waged.

THE WAR RHETORIC OF *MOBILIZING WOMAN-POWER*

Blatch organized *Mobilizing Woman-Power* to allow the reader to view the war as she saw it. Dedicated to "The Able and Devoted Women of Great Britain and France," the book celebrated the Allied women as "an unswerving second line of defense against the onslaught upon the liberty and civilization of the world."[163] Convinced that the war would serve as a turning point for women, Blatch used the book to educate the public about the war. Through her assessment of the war's effects on women both at home and abroad, Blatch argued that the war would provide the "fairer sex" a chance to demonstrate their strength and the opportunity to protect their nation in a time of crisis. With the book, Blatch made a strong case for American women's qualifications both to serve in the war effort and to exercise the vote. She did this by drawing a parallel between the international battle and women's long battle for equal rights.

The comparison of suffrage to a heroic war for democracy was a common trope in early feminist rhetoric. Michael Osborn writes, "feminist orators exploited the human fascination for wars in the symbols they created. The price they paid for these heroic, dramatic portraits of woman's struggle was to romanticize the very mentality many of them professed to despise."[164] For Blatch, however, the romanticism was intentional—she loved the idea of war and of women fighting the good fight. In a speech delivered after the 1913 New York suffrage parade, Blatch defended Emmeline Pankhurst and the militancy of the British suffragettes. In her address Blatch declared: "I have an enormous amount of Revolutionary blood in my veins. My great-grandmother loaded guns in the Revolution and she aimed to kill her country's enemy. If you had such a great-grandmother would you honor her less if she had loaded guns to fight for the freedom of women as she did to fight for the freedom of men? I am not blinded to the fact that public sentiment in the twentieth century is against our going to war for our cause."[165] Fond of celebrating the perils of war as a great character-building opportunity for both men and women, Blatch penned *Mobilizing Woman-Power* with the same "revolutionary" fervor. To further emphasize her rhetoric of war, Blatch asked Theodore Roosevelt to write the book's forward—and he readily agreed.

THEODORE ROOSEVELT AND THE MANLY VIRTUES

At the turn of the century, as Rebecca Edwards writes, "aggressive masculinity validated dramatic new forms of state activism," and Theodore Roosevelt became the most popular symbol of the "manly virtues" in politics.[166] Many people put this rhetoric to their own uses, including Blatch, who, ironically, capitalized on TR's celebration of manly virtues in *Mobilizing Woman-Power*. Blatch executed a rhetorical coup in persuading one of the most popular presidents in history to write an extended forward to the volume. TR's praise of Blatch lent intellectual credibility to the work and enhanced the political and social impact of her appeal.

Roosevelt had always shared his own values forcefully with the public. In an 1894 essay, "The Manly Virtues and Practical Politics," TR instructed voters that "we must be vigorous in mind and body . . . able to hold our own in rough conflict with our fellows, able to suffer punishment without flinching and, at need, repay it in kind with full interest." Roosevelt's explicitly masculine politics equated virility with honesty, vigor, and a willingness to sacrifice for the public good.[167] TR had deemed these qualities essential to a strong and patriotic nation in many stump speeches, including his famous April 1899 address in Chicago, "The Strenuous Life." In that speech TR proclaimed: "The man must be glad to do a man's work, to dare to endure and to labor; to keep himself, and to keep those dependent upon him. The woman must be the housewife, the helpmeet of the homemaker, the wise and fearless mother of many healthy children." Roosevelt's views were widely accepted by the general public, and feminist scholars have viewed his emphasis on the manly virtues in politics as an obstacle to public acceptance of women's political role.[168]

The emphasis on virility and martial virtue in Roosevelt's foreword to *Mobilizing Woman-Power*, however, legitimized Blatch's appeal for women's service in terms with which the public was already familiar. Extending his support within the context of women's rights discourse, Roosevelt wrote: "I join with [Blatch] in the appeal that the women shall back the men with service, and that the men in their turn shall frankly and eagerly welcome the rendering of such service *on the basis of service by equals with equals for a common end.*"[169] Roosevelt's words resonated with Blatch's arguments, particularly her emphasis on the patriotic virtues of heeding the nation's call to action. TR's words also addressed the subsequent instability of traditional gender roles, and his calm reassurance lent ethos to Blatch's feminist ideas.

Echoing his earlier promotion of virility and vigor in political service, Roosevelt concluded that "It is just as good for women as for men that they should have use of body and mind, that they should not be idlers. As [Blatch] puts it, 'Active mothers insure a virile race.'"[170] The aggressive spirit of the Progressive Era, invoked in both TR's foreword and in Blatch's prose, was further substantiated by the patriotic virtues of national force, power, and duty associated with the war. With Roosevelt's support, Blatch was able to add a new dimension to the war discourse—the integral role of the nation's women.

HEROIC WOMEN FOR A HEROIC AGE

Throughout *Mobilizing Woman-Power*, Blatch employed the concept of Roosevelt's "manly virtues" to argue that women participating in the war effort could embody those same qualities. Blatch tried to convince the American public that women would transcend traditional gender boundaries through fulfillment of their patriotic duties. Blatch divided the book into twelve short chapters, each written with a clear purpose; the entire work totals fewer than two hundred pages. Each chapter provided the reader a privileged insight into the state of the nation and contributed to Blatch's overarching ambition: to make the American public recognize the natural relationship between women, work, and war, and to stress the importance of mobilizing woman-power.

In the first three chapters, Blatch outlined the changes she believed were necessary to win the war at home using Great Britain and France as examples. The observations made by Blatch on her trip abroad were translated into a prophesy of the changes imminent for U.S. domestic policies. Blatch provided detailed evidence of European women's drastic transformation. Although Blatch had expected to find women subservient and beaten down, she found the opposite: British women were "heroically cheerful in 'doing their bit.'" By demonstrating how these women had "found themselves" through their use of brain and muscles, Blatch argued that: "Great Britain is not talking about feminism, it is living it." Blatch concluded that American women would equally benefit from the conditions of war, as long as they "answer[ed] their country's call."[171]

With the premise "War!—it does make the blood course through the veins," Blatch complimented women on their initiative and organizing abilities, which she saw evidenced through the success of the Red Cross. She confirmed that women's traditional roles had already spurred women to do their part in raising social consciousness. Blatch noted that in Britain most of the work was started in volunteer societies and had proven successful before "there was an official laying on of hands." Women's essential qualities prepared them for such duties, according to Blatch, since "a woman with sympathy sees a need, she gets an idea, and calls others about her." In these passages, Blatch appeals to the accepted beliefs that women are prepared by nature to carry out the public responsibilities of social welfare. She uses this assumption as a basis to argue that the war afforded women an opportunity to both display and expand their heroism. In addition to "binding up the wounds and conserving civilization," Blatch contended that the war would allow women to "go up the scaling ladder and out into All Man's Land."[172]

In the book, Blatch described women's new occupations as they started to "go over the top." Blatch argued that women "certainly have muscles and are tempted to use them vigorously at three dollars a day" as they worked with zest to trim the ballast and wield heavy tools. Blatch championed the working women, both in terms of their comparable ability with men and the respect they had gained through their application of skill. Peppered with catchy phrases, such as "When men go a-warring, women go to work," *Mobilizing Woman-Power* documented America's great industrial and social change and predicted important consequences for both men and women.[173]

According to Blatch, working women demonstrated "not only eagerness but fitness to substitute for man-power." She began chapter 7, "Eve's Pay Envelope," with the line: "No woman is a cross between an angel and a goose." With this opening, Blatch refuted the arguments for women's moral virtue and reproductive value, which had confined them to the domestic sphere for so long, and argued instead for woman to be viewed "as a human creature."[174] The strict gender boundaries separating men's from women's work no longer held in Blatch's view, and through this book she explored this radical departure. Blatch argued that women were being roused to exertion and were employing the "manly virtues" advocated by Roosevelt. Blatch continually made a case for the similarities between men and women. In diverse jobs, such as railroad worker, elevator operator, and train conductor, woman "gained the confidence of her public" through a demonstration of skill and strength that could challenge any man. Women only needed to be given a chance. Just like men, Blatch argued, women responded to freedom. Eve's Pay Envelope brought gratification and would improve women's ability to contribute to society.

Blatch foresaw the changes brought on by the war as a chance for women to "break down sex prejudice and overcome government opposition." By blurring the lines of gender, Blatch demonstrated how war created a context in which men and women could work side-by-side, united in pride for their nation. Blatch invited her readers to envision the long-term effects of men's and women's equality. She wrote: "Dropping their old segregation, women are going forth in fellowship with men to meet in new ways the pressing problems of the new world."[175] For Blatch, war was not only an opportunity for women, but an opportunity for broader social reform. Women worthy of fighting for men's democratic rights, she suggested throughout the book, deserved to exercise those same rights in their own country. Blatch emphasized the solidarity of both men and women as they united for democracy, as well as women's particular stake in that battle: the opportunity to earn full citizenship for themselves.

Blatch concluded the book by offering women's economic status as proof of their worth as citizens. She proposed: "for this reason, the coming of women as paid workers over the top may be regarded as epoch-making." Blatch touted the possibility that "complete service to their country in this crisis may lead women to that economic freedom which will change a political possession into a political power." In this way, Blatch hoped that women's self-discipline and service to country would have long-lasting consequences. For Blatch, the war surely would be the savior of the women's movement and most likely would complete the final push toward political freedom—as long as women were up to the challenge and willing to heed the call. Blatch's final lines advised: "Women can save civilization only by the broadest cooperative action, by daring to think, by daring to be themselves. The world is entering an heroic age calling for heroic women."[176]

Women's activities had been dramatically transformed by the cultural changes of the Progressive Era, and especially by the requirements of war; women had asserted their presence in public, in the workplace, and in politics. Blatch utilized the changing discourses about women's proper role to frame her argument that women's new status as active and virile citizens demonstrated the necessary qualifications for civic responsibility and the vote. Within this framework, Blatch was able to successfully argue that if women could serve their country equally with men through economic independence, civic participation, and war work, they deserved the same democratic equality. In her final years working for the suffrage cause, Blatch rhetorically employed the universal appeal of wartime nationalism and the changes brought about due to the war to invite her audience to view the status of women in a new light. Once this new way of thinking was accepted by the public, the movement toward women's rights would not be far behind.

Blatch's progressive ideals and her knowledge of the salient issues of the day contributed greatly to her rhetorical style. Blatch exploited the unique demands for women's active public role in industry, reform, and the war as evidence that women could work side-by-side with the nation's men and successfully fight their half of the battle. Combining contemporary progressive discourse with practical appeals for women's national service, Blatch articulated a larger argument for the passage of woman's suffrage in the new century. An integral part of this argument, however, was providing the public with an enlightened view of women and their potential contributions. Women were creating new identities for themselves through their capacity for work and their presence in the polity—and at the same time blurring the boundaries between the public and the private.

In the final chapter of *Mobilizing-Woman Power*, Blatch predicted that the disturbed balance of the sexes would right itself within one generation. This optimistic prediction may not have come true, but Blatch's belief in progress and the abilities of women expressed throughout her woman suffrage career certainly succeeded in throwing the gender imbalance into bold relief.

Conclusion

The years between 1890 and 1920 were a vital period for modern America that witnessed many changes in the nation's social, political, and intellectual landscape. These years also represented a coming of age for the woman suffrage movement, a period when "the collective power of women, which had been building throughout the nineteenth century, reached its apex in a massive push for political reform and woman suffrage."[177] Along with various other reform movements of the time, the suffrage movement aimed to rehabilitate the American promise of democracy by working for electoral reform and social justice. The suffrage campaign aimed at revising the democratic order to include those members who were still being denied power. To fulfill this goal, the movement's leaders tried to change the image and status of American women in this new era of exciting possibilities.

Woman suffrage became a mass movement in the Progressive Era by attracting large numbers of adherents through its association with various women's reform issues, including the social settlement, labor, and women's club movements. As a broad-based interest group, the suffrage movement emerged as a national platform working to secure women's rights in the twentieth century, and soon woman suffrage was recognized by many as a formidable reform coalition. In the years between 1910 and 1915, nearly two hundred articles appeared in popular magazines concerning woman suffrage; the movement had garnered the nation's attention and was quickly amassing pro-suffrage sentiment.[178] Consequently, for the first time, the opposition also organized on a national scale, and the debate over woman suffrage became a prominent issue in the public domain.[179]

Part of the reason for this build-up in prominence and momentum was the infusion of new vigor and youthful energy into the aging movement. The women of the suffrage movement's second generation were living in a different age than their pioneering foremothers, and they sought ways that would allow them to adapt to the evolving social and political culture. Carrie Chapman Catt, Alice Paul, and Harriot Stanton Blatch led the movement's second-wave revolution. Guided by the progressive values of the era, these three women reignited the stalled campaign through their efficient and innovative leadership. Through the employment of practical politics, publicity stunts, and the inspired mobilization of movement members, these three leaders resurrected the radicalism of Elizabeth Cady Stanton and Susan B. Anthony. Along the way, they also revived the woman suffrage movement's founding resolution: to *insist* on the rights and privileges belonging to women as equal citizens of the United States.

The women of the twentieth-century suffrage movement were weary of a social and political system that precluded them and were ready to force "full recognition of their individuality, equality, and right to participate fully and directly in making the laws under which they lived."[180] Catt, Paul, and Blatch were instrumental in orchestrating the movement's transition into the new century. Through their combined leadership, these three women thrust suffragists into the body politic and brought new enthusiasm and imagination to an issue that had become stale and predictable. Each woman brought her own distinctive style and ideas to the suffrage campaign, but collectively they were responsible for leading women into the public culture of electoral politics and demonstrating to the nation that women were equally qualified to participate fully in civic life.

The leaders of the woman suffrage movement forged the first paths in what later would be recognized as a great age for women in politics. Early in her career, Catt viewed politics as mainly educational, circulating literature and letters to recruit prominent politicians to the pro-suffrage ranks. In the first decade of the century, Catt raised the political issue of woman suffrage to its greatest level by organizing the International Woman Suffrage Alliance. The cause of women's rights had worldwide resonance as a result, and Catt used the gradual enfranchisement of the world's women in the coming years to put pressure on the U.S. government. Throughout her career, Catt used her speeches and writings to rally NAWSA troops into a cohesive and unified organization, to keep motivation high by faithfully advocating justice and fair play for women, and to promise inevitable victory. As NAWSA president in the campaign's final years, Catt focused more intently on congressional politicking. Her methods, however, remained grounded in educational lobbying, which she accomplished through polite meetings with legislators and, eventually, with President Wilson.

In direct contrast to Catt, Paul forced the issue of woman suffrage by confronting politicians head-on. By initially organizing western women to use their votes to put pressure on the Democrats, Paul brought the suffrage campaign directly into the realm of electoral politics. In later years, with tactics that could not be ignored, Paul and the women of the NWP engaged in direct political protests against Congress and the president. Paul's tactics persisted in the form of pickets and other public demonstrations for nearly three years in an effort to keep woman suffrage a prominent issue. When she and her fellow suffragists were jailed for their political activism, they continued to pursue the cause as political prisoners. For seven years, Paul showed the nation that women were powerful, persistent, and ready to demand equal rights as citizens of a democratic nation.

During her leadership, Blatch worked through both the NAWSA's and the NWP's political channels. Her own contribution to the movement, however, was to encourage a broad political vision that would allow the campaign to spread in new and diverse directions. Blatch successfully increased the movement's political cachet by joining the cause with the salient issues of the day, such as women's labor and the national war effort. Like Catt, Blatch worked hard to cultivate a relationship with politicians, most notably Theodore Roosevelt, which she would then use to advance the campaign. Knowing that the movement also needed public support, Blatch initiated a variety of strategies in the New York campaign to showcase women's civic participation. These strategies moved women's activism into the public sphere, gained significant publicity for the cause, and would later be adopted by Paul and the NWP in Washington, D.C. Blatch's rhetoric and tactics demonstrated the expansion of women's social and political roles and offered proof of their qualification for political participation and the vote.

The collective efforts of Catt, Paul, and Blatch provided direction for the movement over several decades and lent increased strength and substance to the suffrage fight. Their organizational talent, campaign tactics, and consciousness-raising efforts also contributed to the character of American political reform in the Progressive Era. By examining all three leaders, it becomes clear that the victory of woman suffrage was the result of an ever-changing movement made up of distinctive personalities and diverse strategies. Throughout its seventy-two years, however, the movement remained united under one goal: to secure woman's right to vote.

Catt, Paul, and Blatch may have shared similarities, particularly their progressive values, but they each brought their own vision to the movement. For this reason, the study of the three different leaders reveals the various contours and tensions of the woman suffrage movement throughout its life cycle more clearly. Viewed in this manner, the suffrage movement may be remembered as a multifaceted response to the challenges of a changing era. Within this period of progress and hope, three individual leaders entered the woman suffrage movement in the new century inspired by a faith in democracy. By 1920 they emerged victorious, and the American promise was finally extended to the nation's women.

Notes

1. Eleanor Flexner, *A Century of Struggle: The Woman's Rights Movement in the United States,* rev. ed. (1959; reprint, Cambridge: Harvard University Press, 1996), 255.

2. Anne Firor Scott and Andrew Mackay Scott, *One Half the People: The Fight For Woman Suffrage,* rev. ed. (1975; reprint, Urbana: University of Illinois Press, 1982), 24.

3. Sara Hunter Graham, "The Suffrage Renaissance: A New Image for a New Century, 1896–1910," in *One Woman, One Vote: Rediscovering the Woman Suffrage Movement,* ed. Marjorie Spruill Wheeler (Troutdale, Ore.: New Sage Press, 1995), 157–78.

4. Arthur S. Link and Richard L. McCormick, *Progressivism* (Arlington Heights, Ill.: Harlan Davidson, 1983), 1.

5. Michael McGerr, "Political Style and Women's Power, 1830–1930," *Journal of American History* 77 (1990): 864–85.

6. The term "progressive ethos" is borrowed from Clyde Griffen, "The Progressive Ethos," in *The Development of an American Culture,* ed. Stanley Coben and Lorman Ratner (Englewood Cliffs, N.J.: Prentice-Hall, 1970), 120–49.

7. Works that focus on women in the Progressive Era include Noralee Frankel and Nancy S. Dye, eds., *Gender, Class, Race, and Reform in the Progressive Era* (Lexington: University Press of Kentucky, 1991); William H. Chafe, *The Paradox of Change: American Women in the Twentieth Century* (New York: Oxford University Press, 1991); William L. O'Neill, *Everyone Was Brave: The Rise and Fall of Feminism in America* (Chicago: Quadrangle Books, 1969); Dorothy Schneider and Carl J. Schneider, *American Women in the Progressive Era, 1900–1920* (New York: Facts on File, 1993); Ellen Condliffe Lagemann, *A Generation of Women: Education in the Lives of Women Progressive Reformers* (Cambridge: Harvard University Press, 1979); Rebecca Edwards, *Angels in the Machinery: Gender in American Party Politics from the Civil War to the Progressive Era* (New York: Oxford University Press, 1997); Robyn Muncy, *Creating a Female Dominion in American Reform, 1890–1935* (New York: Oxford University Press, 1991); Ellen Fitzpatrick, *Endless Crusade: Women Social Scientists and Progressive Reform* (New York: Oxford University Press, 1990); and Margaret Finnegan, *Selling Suffrage: Consumer Culture and Votes for Women* (New York: Columbia University Press, 1999).

8. See George E. Mowry, *The Progressive Era, 1900–1920: The Reform Persuasion* (Washington, D.C.: American Historical Association, 1972), 7–9.

9. Nell Irvin Painter, *Standing at Armageddon: The United States, 1877–1919* (New York: W. W. Norton and Co., 1987), 252.

10. Lewis L. Gould, "Introduction: The Progressive Era," in *The Progressive Era,* ed. Lewis L. Gould (Syracuse, N.Y.: Syracuse University Press, 1974), 1–10. See also Link and McCormick, *Progressivism,* 52–55; and McGerr, "Political Style," 867–74.

11. Ellen Carol DuBois, "Working Women, Class Relations, and Suffrage Militance: Harriot Stanton Blatch and the New York Suffrage Movement, 1894–1909," *Journal of American History* 74 (1987): 34–58.

12. Steven J. Diner borrows the phrase "a very different age" from a 1912 address by Woodrow Wilson for the title of his book about how diverse Americans lived in the era between 1890 and World War I. Diner uses the phrase, I believe, as I have intended, to allude to the liminal moment between two eras, one reflective of a century almost past and infused with established traditions and the promise of a new one replete with exciting possibilities. See Steven J. Diner, *A Very Different Age: Americans of the Progressive Era* (New York: Hill and Wang, 1998).

13. Historian Ellen Carol DuBois has contributed the only definitive scholarship on Blatch and her woman suffrage contributions. Her works include *Harriot Stanton Blatch and the Winning of Women Suffrage* (New Haven: Yale University Press, 1997); "Harriot Stanton Blatch and the Transformation of Class Relations among Woman Suffragists," in *Gender, Class, Race, and Reform in the Progressive Era,* ed. Noralee Frankel and Nancy S. Dye (Lexington: University Press of Kentucky, 1991); and "Working Women." A discussion of Blatch's early suffrage career in England is included in Sandra Stanley Holton, "'To Educate Women into Rebellion': Elizabeth Cady Stanton and the Creation of a Transatlantic Network of Radical Suffragists," *American Historical Review* 99 (1994): 1112–36.

14. One exception is Karlyn Kohrs Campbell's chapter on Catt, Paul, and Anna Howard Shaw in *A Critical Study of Early Feminist Rhetoric*, vol. 1 of *Man Cannot Speak for Her* (Westport, Conn.: Greenwood, 1989), 157–79.

15. Aileen S. Kraditor, *The Ideas of the Woman Suffrage Movement, 1890–1920* (New York: W. W. Norton and Co., 1981), 1.

16. Flexner, *A Century of Struggle*, 69; Elizabeth Cady Stanton, Susan B. Anthony, and Mathilda Joslyn Gage, eds., *The History of Woman Suffrage* (Rochester, N.Y.: Fowler and Wells, 1881), 1:71.

17. Stanton, Anthony, and Gage, *The History of Woman Suffrage*, 71.

18. Flexner, *A Century of Struggle*, 76.

19. As quoted in ibid., 141.

20. Sherna Gluck, introduction to *From Parlor to Prison: Five American Suffragists Talk about Their Lives*, ed. Sherna Gluck (New York: Vintage Books, 1976), 6.

21. Chafe, *The Paradox of Change*, 4.

22. Kraditor, *Ideas of the Woman Suffrage Movement*, 11, 13.

23. Nancy Woloch, *Women and the American Experience* (New York: Alfred A. Knopf, 1984), 337.

24. See Blanche Glassman Hersh, *The Slavery of Sex: Feminist Abolitionists in America* (Urbana: University of Illinois Press, 1978), 121–52.

25. Elizabeth Cady Stanton, "The Solitude of Self," in *Key Texts of the Early Feminists*, vol. 2 of *Man Cannot Speak for Her*, by Karlyn Kohrs Campbell (Westport, Conn.: Praeger Publishers, 1989), 372.

26. Finnegan, *Selling Suffrage*, 26.

27. For an excellent summary of the confusion over the Progressive movement in the historical literature see Peter G. Filene, "An Obituary for 'the Progressive Movement,'" *American Quarterly* 22 (1970): 20–34. See also John D. Buenker, John C. Burnham, and Robert M. Crunden, *Progressivism* (Cambridge, Mass.: Schenkman Publishing, 1977), which uses Filene's essay as a point of departure in creating a new synthesis of progressivism; and Mowry, *The Progressive Era*, 29.

28. Link and McCormick, *Progressivism*, 3.

29. See Robert H. Wiebe, *The Search for Order, 1877–1920* (New York: Hill and Wang, 1967).

30. Richard Hofstadter, *The Age of Reform: From Bryan to F. D. R.* (New York: Vintage Books, 1955), 5–6; Link and McCormick, *Progressivism*, 21–22.

31. John C. Burnham, "Essay," in Buenker, Burnham, and Crunden, *Progressivism*, 10–18.

32. Chafe, *The Paradox of Change*, 17.

33. See chapter 8 in Diner, *A Very Different Age*.

34. For more on the *New Republic* and progressive thought, see chapters 2 and 3 of David W. Noble, *The Paradox of Progressive Thought* (Minneapolis: University of Minnesota Press, 1958).

35. Charles A. Beard, "Historical Woman Suffrage," *New Republic*, 9 October 1915, 1–3.

36. Walter E. Weyl, "Working for the Inevitable," *New Republic*, 9 October 1915, 15–16.

37. Walter Lippmann, "The Vote as Symbol," *New Republic*, 9 October 1915, 4.

38. Herbert Croly, "The Obligation of the Vote," *New Republic*, 9 October 1915, 5.

39. See Nancy S. Dye, introduction to *Gender, Class, Race, and Reform in the Progressive Era*, ed. Noralee Frankel and Nancy S. Dye (Lexington: University Press of Kentucky, 1991), 4, 8.

40. Carol Pateman, *The Disorder of Women: Democracy, Feminism, and Political Theory* (Stanford, Calif.: Stanford University Press, 1989), 118.

41. For an excellent discussion of these critiques of gender relations as taken up by the women of the British suffrage movement, and the arguments that informed my own on this issue, see Mary Maynard, "Privilege and Patriarchy: Feminist Thought in the Nineteenth Century," in *Sexuality and Subordination: Interdisciplinary Studies of Gender in the Nineteenth Century*, ed. Susan Mendus and Jane Rendall (London: Routledge, 1989), and Susan Kingsley Kent, *Sex and Suffrage in Britain, 1860–1914* (Princeton: Princeton University Press, 1987). See also Kay Sloan, "Sexual Warfare and the Silent Cinema: Comedies and Melodramas of Woman Suffragism," *American Quarterly* 33 (1981): 412–36, for a discussion of sexual politics in the American suffrage movement.

42. Jacqueline Van Voris, *Carrie Chapman Catt: A Public Life* (New York: Feminist Press at City University of New York, 1987), 30.

43. "Great Welcome to Mrs. Catt," *Woman's Journal*, 16 November 1912, 361; Carrie Chapman Catt, "Is Woman Suffrage Progressing?" in *The Presidential Address Delivered at Stockholm to the Sixth Convention of the International Woman Suffrage Alliance on Tuesday, June 13, 1911*, Cornell University Collection of Women's Rights Pamphlets, 1814–1912 (Wooster, Ohio: Bell and Howell, 1974), microfiche, 97.

44. Mary Gray Peck, *Carrie Chapman Catt: A Biography* (New York: H. W. Wilson Co., 1944), 17.

45. Van Voris, *Carrie Chapman Catt*, 8.

46. See ibid., chap. 2.

47. Ibid., vii.

48. Robert Booth Fowler, *Carrie Chapman Catt: Feminist Politician* (Boston: Northeastern University Press, 1986), xix.

49. Susan B. Anthony, as quoted in Peck, *Carrie Chapman Catt*, 84. Also see pp. 69–84.

50. Fowler, *Carrie Chapman Catt*, 105.

51. Catt as quoted in Peck, *Carrie Chapman Catt*, 96.

52. Carrie Chapman Catt, "Address at the National Suffrage Convention in Washington," *Woman's Journal*, 20 February 1904, 61.

53. Fowler, *Carrie Chapman Catt*, 108.

54. Carrie Chapman Catt, "Presidential Address, 1902," as quoted in *Man Cannot Speak for Her*, 2:479.

55. Graham, "The Suffrage Renaissance," in *One Woman, One Vote*, 163.

56. Sarah Platt Decker, as quoted in Gluck, *From Parlor to Prison*, 12–13.

57. Graham, "The Suffrage Renaissance," in *One Woman, One Vote*, 165.

58. Carrie Chapman Catt, "Mrs. Catt's International Address at the Congress in Amsterdam, June 15, 1908," in *History of Women* (New Haven: Research Publications, 1977), microfiche, 9051.

59. Van Voris, *Carrie Chapman Catt*, 79, 117.

60. Fowler, *Carrie Chapman Catt*, 25.

61. Van Voris, *Carrie Chapman Catt*, 131.

62. Harper, *History of Woman Suffrage*, 480.

63. Campbell, *Man Cannot Speak for Her*, 1:165.

64. Carrie Chapman Catt, "The Crisis," in *Man Cannot Speak for Her*, 2:483–84, 485, 501.

65. The Susan B. Anthony amendment stated: "The right of citizens of the United States to vote shall not be denied or abridged by the United States or by any State on account of sex."

66. Catt, "The Crisis," as quoted in *Man Cannot Speak for Her*, 2:499; Van Voris, *Carrie Chapman Catt*, 133.

67. Maud Wood Park, *Front Door Lobby* (Boston: Beacon Press, 1960), 16, 18.

68. Kraditor describes Catt as having "a winning manner on the platform" but notes that she "did not have Miss Shaw's oratorical brilliance." Campbell, also comparing Catt to Shaw, notes that "Catt was a competent but not a great speaker." See Kraditor, *The Ideas of the Woman Suffrage Movement*, 12–13; Campbell, *Man Cannot Speak for Her*, 1:165; and Fowler, *Carrie Chapman Catt*, 124–26.

69. Catt, "Is Woman Suffrage Progressing?" 5.

70. These arguments are the focus of numerous speeches and writings, including Carrie Chapman Catt, "Address to the United States Congress, 1917," as quoted in *Man Cannot Speak for Her*, 2:503–32; Carrie Chapman Catt, "The Will of the People," *Forum*, June 1910, p. 596; Carrie Chapman Catt, "War Aims Message to the American People," in *History of Women*, microfiche, 9155; and Catt, "The Will of the People," 596.

71. Fowler, *Carrie Chapman Catt*, 69.

72. Catt, "War Aims," in *History of Women*, 5–6.

73. Catt, "The Will of the People," 600–1.

74. Campbell, *Man Cannot Speak for Her*, 1:166.

75. Catt, "Presidential Address, 1902," in *Man Cannot Speak for Her*, 2:470, 470–71, 475.

76. Carrie Chapman Catt, "Feminism and Suffrage," in *History of Women*, microfiche, 9198.

77. Fowler, *Carrie Chapman Catt*, 76.

78. Kraditor, *The Ideas of the Woman Suffrage Movement*, 45.

79. Catt, "Presidential Address, 1902," in *Man Cannot Speak for Her*, 2:479.

80. Victoria Bissell Brown, "Jane Addams, Progressivism, and Woman Suffrage," in *One Woman, One Vote*, 187. See Link and McCormick, *Progressivism*, 21–23.

81. Catt, "Is Woman Suffrage Progressing?" 2, 13–14; Catt, "Do You Know?" in *Woman Suffrage: History, Arguments and Results*, ed. France Maule Björkman (New York: National American Woman Suffrage Association, 1913), 166.

82. Catt, "Mrs. Catt's International Address," in *History of Women*, 7; Carrie Chapman Catt, "Woman Suffrage Must Win," *Independent*, 11 October 1915, 58; Catt, "Address to the United States Congress, 1917," as quoted in *Man Cannot Speak for Her*, 2:530.

83. Catt, "Presidential Address, 1902," as quoted in *Man Cannot Speak for Her*, 2:467; Catt, "Address at the National Woman Suffrage Convention in Washington," *The Woman's Journal*, 20 February 1904, p. 64; Catt, "Is Woman Suffrage Progressing?" 7, 3.

84. Campbell, *Man Cannot Speak for Her*, 1:166.

85. Ibid., 1:171.

86. Catt, "Is Woman Suffrage Progressing?" 14.

87. Van Voris, *Carrie Chapman Catt*, 149, 161.

88. Carrie Chapman Catt, as quoted in untitled article *Woman Citizen*, 4 September 1920, 364.

89. Fowler, *Carrie Chapman Catt*, 119.

90. Inez Haynes Irwin, *The Story of Alice Paul and the National Women's Party* (Fairfax, Va.: Denlinger's Publishers, 1977), 4.

91. Nancy F. Cott, *The Grounding of Modern Feminism* (New Haven: Yale University Press, 1987), 62.

92. See Linda G. Ford, *Iron-Jawed Angels: The Suffrage Militancy of the National Woman's Party, 1912–1920* (Lanham, Md.: University Press of America, 1991), 45–46.

93. Alice Paul, editorial, *Suffragist*, January-February 1920, 1.

94. Vivian Gornick, *Essays in Feminism* (New York: Harper and Row, 1978), 178; Alice Paul, , "I was arrested, of course . . . ," interview by Robert S. Gallagher in *American Heritage*, February 1974, 17; Gornick, *Essays*, 172.

95. Ford, *Iron-Jawed Angels*, 16.

96. See Irwin, *The Story of Alice Paul*, 7–9.

97. "Miss Alice Paul's Address," *Woman's Journal*, 17 May 1910, 76.

98. Irwin, *The Story of Alice Paul*, 13, 19.

99. Flexner, *A Century of Struggle*, 255; Margaret Hope Bacon, *Mothers of Feminism: The Story of Quaker Women in America* (San Francisco: Harper and Row, 1986), 191–95; Harper, *History of Woman Suffrage*, 378–80.

100. Ford, *Iron-Jawed Angels*, 91; Alice Paul, as quoted in Christine A. Lunardini, *From Equal Suffrage to Equal Rights: Alice Paul and the National Woman's Party, 1910–1928* (New York: New York University Press, 1986), 63.

101. Crystal Eastman, "Personalities and Powers: Alice Paul," in *On Women and Revolution*, ed. Blanche Wiesen Cook (New York: Oxford University Press, 1978), 64; "A New Leader—Alice Paul—Why She Is," *Everybody's Magazine*, July 1916, 127; Irwin, *The Story of Alice Paul*, 128.

102. Lucy Burns, as quoted in Irwin, *The Story of Alice Paul*, 43.

103. Paul, as quoted in ibid., 75–77; Lunardini, *From Equal Suffrage*, 62.

104. Paul, as quoted in Irwin, *The Story of Alice Paul*, 100; Cott, *The Grounding of Modern Feminism*, 54.

105. Paul, as quoted in Irwin, *The Story of Alice Paul*, 118; see also Kraditor, *The Ideas of the Woman Suffrage Movement*, 226–37.

106. Lunardini, *From Equal Suffrage*, 25.

107. Reports were quoted in the *Suffragist*, 31 January 1917, 11, and appeared in the *New York Times*, 11 January 1917, 13. See also Lunardini, *From Equal Suffrage*, 108, and Ford, *Iron-Jawed Angels*, 128–29.

108. Doris Steven, *Jailed for Freedom: American Women Win the Vote*, rev. ed., ed. Carol O'Hare (Troutdale, Oreg.: New Sage Press, 1995), 66.

109. Paul, as quoted in Sarah Hunter Graham, *Woman Suffrage and the New Democracy* (New Haven: Yale University Press, 1996), 106.
110. Irwin, *The Story of Alice Paul*, 215.
111. Ford, *Iron-Jawed Angels*, 67–68.
112. "Why We Picket,"1917, NAWSA Papers, reel 33, Library of Congress Manuscript Division.
113. Paul, as quoted in Stevens, *Jailed for Freedom*, 130.
114. Campbell, *Man Cannot Speak for Her*, 1:172.
115. Paul, as quoted in Ford, *Iron-Jawed Angels*, 105, 46.
116. Amelia R. Fry, "Alice Paul," in *The Influence of Quaker Women on American History: Biographical Studies*, ed. Carol Stoneburner and John Stoneburner (Lewiston, N.Y.: Edwin Mellen Press, 1986), 389.
117. Alice Paul, "Conversations with Alice Paul: Woman Suffrage and the Equal Rights Amendment," interview by Amelia R. Fry, 1973, Suffragists Oral History Project, University of California at Berkeley (1976), 399.
118. Carrie Chapman Catt and Nettie Rogers Shuler, *Woman Suffrage and Politics: The Inner Story of the Suffrage Movement* (Seattle: University of Washington Press, 1969), 244.
119. Paul, *Conversations with Alice Paul*, 115.
120. Scott and Scott, *One Half the People*, 32.
121. Lunardini, *From Equal Suffrage*, 44.
122. Fowler, *Carrie Chapman Catt*, 153.
123. See Kraditor, *The Ideas of the Woman Suffrage Movement*, 245, 246.
124. "Parliament Fans Flames," *Woman's Journal*, 31 May 1913, 169; Catt, as quoted in Edith F. Hurwitz, "Carrie C. Catt's 'Suffrage Militancy,'" *Signs: Journal of Women in Culture and Society* 3 (1978): 741.
125. Ford, *Iron-Jawed Angels*, 58; Finnegan, *Selling Suffrage*, 7.
126. See DuBois, *Harriot Stanton Blatch*, 4 (also see pp. 1–6, 274–78); see also Phyllis Eckhaus, "Feminist Foremother," *Nation*, 29 December 1997, 27–28.
127. DuBois, *Harriot Stanton Blatch*, 2.
128. Harriot Stanton Blatch and Alma Lutz, *Challenging Years: The Memoirs of Harriot Stanton Blatch* (New York: G. P. Putnam's Sons, 1940), 3, 5.
129. Ibid., 36, 39; DuBois, *Harriot Stanton Blatch*, 31.
130. Blatch and Lutz, *Challenging Years*, 70.
131. Holton, "'To Educate Women into Rebellion,'" 1115.
132. Kent, *Sex and Suffrage*, 27; Holton, "'To Educate Women into Rebellion,'" 1114.
133. Harriot Stanton Blatch, "Speech on the Bill for Qualifying Women to Vote"; Women's Franchise League, *Married Women and Municipal Elections*, Cornell University Collection of Women's Rights Pamphlets, 1814–1912 (Wooster, Ohio: Bell and Howell, 1974), microfiche, 45.
134. Harriot Stanton Blatch, "Open Letter to Mrs. Stanton," *Woman's Journal*, 22 December 1894, 402–3.
135. Holton, "'To Educate Women into Rebellion,'" 1115.
136. Harriot Stanton Blatch, "Specialization of Function in Women," *Gunton's Magazine*, 10 May 1896, 350; Harriot Stanton Blatch, "Progress by Proved Worth," *Woman's Journal*, 9 April 1898, 114; DuBois, *Harriot Stanton Blatch*, 3.
137. Blatch and Lutz, *Challenging Years*, 284.
138. Cott, *The Grounding of Modern Feminism*, 24.
139. DuBois, "Working Women," 42; Blatch, as quoted in Harper, *History of Woman Suffrage*, 482; Blatch, as quoted in DuBois, "Harriot Stanton Blatch," in *Gender, Class, Race, and Reform*, 165.
140. Blatch and Lutz, *Challenging Years*, 94, 91.
141. Harriot Stanton Blatch, "Why Suffragists Will Parade on Saturday," *New York Tribune*, 3 May 1912, 1.
142. See Mary Ryan, "The American Parade: Representations of the Nineteenth-Century Social Order," in *The New Cultural History*, ed. Linda Hunt (Berkeley: University of California Press, 1989), and Simon P. Newman, *Parades and the Politics of the Street: Festive Culture in the Early American Republic* (Philadelphia: University of Pennsylvania Press, 1997).

143. Blatch herself frequently claimed to have pioneered many of the suffrage movement's publicity techniques, however, Sharon Hartman Strom makes a compelling argument that many of these tactics actually originated in the Massachusetts campaign during the spring of 1909. See Sharon Hartman Strom, "Leadership and Tactics in the American Woman Suffrage Movement: A New Perspective from Massachusetts," *Journal of American History* 62 (1975): 296–315. See also Blatch and Lutz, *Challenging Years*, 107.

144. See Ryan, *Women in Public*. Ryan notes the inclusion of a few women in the 1858 Erie Canal celebration in New York. These wives of the city elite participated in a procession of boats that sailed to Long Island Sound and, after disembarking, walked in a body from the Battery to Bowling Green in what Ryan characterizes as "a brief and rare women's parade." The women were not part of the prosaic parade that signified the actual celebration, however. See also Ryan, "The American Parade," in *The New Cultural History*.

145. DuBois, "Working Women," 53.

146. Ibid., 55–56.

147. Finnegan, *Selling Suffrage*, 12.

148. Blatch, "Why Suffragists Will Parade," 2.

149. Ibid., 1.

150. The phrase "agitation by symbol" was initially coined in a British suffrage newspaper (*Common Cause*, 15 July 1909, 173). Lisa Tickner recovers the phrase as the subject of her study of the imagery of the British suffrage campaign. See Lisa Tickner, *The Spectacle of Women: Imagery of the Suffrage Campaign, 1907–1914* (Chicago: University of Chicago Press, 1988).

151. Blatch, "Why Suffragists Will Parade," 2; Tickner, *The Spectacle of Women*, 60.

152. "Suffrage Army out on Parade," *New York Times*, 5 May 1912, 1.

153. Stevens, *Jailed for Freedom*, 26–27. In Stevens's description of Milholland's life, the Joan of Arc persona may be seen as quite prophetic. Several years after the parades, Milholland collapsed of exhaustion while delivering a suffrage address. Ten weeks later, she died as the result of her strenuous work for the cause and is honored and remembered as a suffrage martyr. Her last words, uttered during that fateful speech, were "Mr. President, how long must women wait for liberty?"

154. DuBois, *Harriot Stanton Blatch*, 140, 142.

155. Finnegan, *Selling Suffrage*, 46.

156. "Editorial Notes," *Woman's Journal*, 7 March 1908, 37.

157. "Ten Thousand Marchers in Suffrage Line," *New York Times*, 4 May 1913, 1.

158. Blatch and Lutz, *Challenging Years*, 129.

159. Harriot Stanton Blatch, *Mobilizing Woman-Power* (New York: Woman's Press, 1918).

160. O'Neill, *Everyone Was Brave*, 187–89.

161. Harriot Stanton Blatch, as quoted in DuBois, *Harriot Stanton Blatch*, 206.

162. Blatch, *Mobilizing*, 284.

163. Ibid., 1.

164. Michael Osborn, "Patterns of Metaphor among Early Feminist Orators," in *Rhetoric and Community: Studies in Unity and Fragmentation*, ed. J. Michael Hogan (Columbia, S.C.: University of South Carolina Press, 1998).

165. Blatch, as quoted in DuBois, *Harriot Stanton Blatch*, 206.

166. Edwards, *Angels in the Machinery*, 155.

167. Theodore Roosevelt, "The Manly Virtues and Practical Politics," *Forum*, July 1894, 553.

168. Theodore Roosevelt, "The Strenuous Life," in *American Voices: Significant Speeches in American History, 1640–1945*, ed. David Zarefsky and James R. Andrews (New York: Longman, 1989), 382; Edwards, *Angels in the Machinery*, 155–57.

169. Theodore Roosevelt, foreword to *Mobilizing Woman-Power*, 6. Italics in original.

170. Ibid., 9.

171. Blatch, *Mobilizing Woman-Power*, 54, 58, 34.

172. Ibid., 24, 39, 176, 86.

173. Ibid., 86, 88.

174. Ibid., 104, 106, 106.

175. Ibid., 134, 163.

176. Ibid., 104, 184.

177. Sara M. Evans, *Born for Liberty: A History of Women in America* (New York: Free Press, 1989), 145.

178. Brown, "Jane Addams," in *One Woman, One Vote*, 182.

179. The first national anti-suffrage organization, the National Association Opposed to Woman Suffrage, was formed in 1911. Due to the scope of this essay, I have only briefly addressed anti-suffrage sentiment. For the best summaries of anti-suffrage argument, see Scott and Scott, *One Half the People*, 25–27, and Kraditor, *The Ideas of the Woman Suffrage Movement*, 14–42.

180. Marjorie Spruill Wheeler, ed., *One Woman, One Vote: Rediscovering the Woman Suffrage Movement* (Troutdale, Ore.: New Sage Press, 1995), 14.

From Hull House to The Hague: Jane Addams's Rhetoric of Pacifism, 1898–1917

Carl R. Burgchardt

11

Jane Addams was one of the most significant and influential activists of the Progressive Era. Perhaps she is best known for her role as co-founder of Hull House in 1889, which placed her at the vanguard of the settlement house movement. Through Hull House, Addams strove to better understand the causes and cures for the poverty she found in the crowded tenements of Chicago. Hull House provided housing, education, and social services for destitute immigrants, but it also served as an intellectual center for labor leaders, sociologists, and political reformers. Ultimately, Hull House became a laboratory for conducting research on the social ills caused by rapid population growth, industrialization, and urbanization.

In conjunction with her activities at Hull House, Addams publicly advocated woman's suffrage, child labor laws, improved working conditions for women, compulsory school attendance, welfare reform, and worker's compensation. Moreover, Addams was politically influential. She became the first American woman to make a nominating speech at a national political convention when, in 1912, she seconded Theodore Roosevelt's presidential nomination for the Progressive Party.

Addams's fervent reform efforts on both the domestic and international levels were expressed through prolific writing and speaking. Her famous autobiography, *Twenty Years at Hull-House* (1910), was instrumental in promulgating her ideology. In all, she published eleven books during her lifetime, as well as hundreds of articles that appeared in both popular and scholarly outlets. In addition, she delivered scores of speeches and lectures before a variety of clubs, educational institutions, and legislatures.[1]

By all accounts, Addams was an effective public speaker. Primarily, she addressed middle-class, largely female audiences who were unaware of the horrifying social conditions that existed in many American cities. In Mary Lynn McCree

Bryan's analysis, Addams was particularly influential with female listeners because she drew "upon women's experiences as outsiders to create sympathy, understanding and a willingness to become involved in working for change." Because of Addams's fame and charismatic presence, she received numerous invitations to deliver speeches and lectures.[2]

Addams enjoyed widespread celebrity and approval for her work with settlement houses and domestic reform, but her outspoken pacifism was another matter. She publicly condemned American imperialism as early as 1898, but she was not vilified for her views until the outbreak of World War I in Europe. She vigorously opposed American entry into the war, and, in 1915, she helped establish the Woman's Peace Party (WPP). That same year she was named chair of the International Congress of Women, which later became the Women's International League for Peace and Freedom. Many Americans interpreted Addams's devout pacifism as disloyalty, and she was severely criticized for her views. However, she remained steadfast in her opposition to imperialism and warfare. Addams received the Nobel Peace Prize in 1931 in recognition of her lifelong efforts.[3]

The purpose of this essay is to analyze Addams's anti-war discourse from the Progressive Era. I will evaluate twenty-eight of Addams's anti-war speeches from the period of 1898 to 1917. While most commentators have treated Addams's pacifist discourse from this time as essentially unified, I contend that her anti-war rhetoric breaks neatly into two periods, 1898–1909 and 1915–1917. Although, as I will prove, there is significant continuity between the first and second periods of her rhetoric, there are also important differences.

During both periods, Addams's pacifist arguments grew directly out of her reform efforts at Hull House, which served as her primary reference point. Addams thought of Hull House as a kind of analogy for the world at large. If something worked at Hull House, she reasoned, it would probably work anywhere. This faith may account for the unwavering sense of optimism Addams expressed from 1898 to 1917. In addition, throughout both periods, Addams maintained that women and immigrants had special roles to play in bringing about peace.

Another aspect of Addams's discourse that extended through both periods was intellectual rigor. From 1898 to 1917, Addams argued logically, systematically, and powerfully. This view of Addams as a rational debater challenges the more conventional picture of her as an emotional, anecdotal speaker. For example, Christopher Lasch claimed that Addams's public discourse was largely autobiographical; that is to say, Addams spoke and wrote from the details of her daily experience. In the words of Fran Hassencahl, this resulted in discourse with a "personal touch." Moreover, Lasch thought that poignant, descriptive vignettes were the most persuasive features of her rhetoric. Delvenia Shadwell made a similar case: emotional appeals dominated Addams's speeches more than logical appeals. Daniel Levine went so far as to declare that, on international topics, Addams "was not very good at thinking analytically in larger theoretical terms." Although Addams certainly employed pathos and autobiographical narrative in her rhetoric, I will demonstrate that rational, systematic argument was much more pronounced.[4]

A final characteristic that extended through both periods of Addams's anti-war discourse was the centrality of rhetoric to her thinking. First, she spent much of her time creating persuasive messages on behalf of Hull House and pacifism; thus, Addams was a practicing rhetorician. More important, she viewed rhetoric as the key to understanding both the causes and solutions for war. She criticized pacifists of her day because they employed ineffective persuasive messages. Further, Addams argued consistently that war could be ended only by changing human perceptions, and the tool for achieving this was language.

Although Addams's anti-war discourse from 1898 to 1917 was consistent in many respects, there were crucial differences that explain why she was so well accepted by the public in the first period, but not in the second. For one thing, Addams's rhetoric from 1898 to 1909 was not even primarily about war and imperialism, as such. She employed the topic of pacifism as a means of calling attention to her domestic reform agenda. Moreover, Addams cloaked her "anti-war" arguments in the language and theoretical concerns of sociology, one of the emerging scientific disciplines of the Progressive Era. In analyzing warfare, Addams rejected philosophical and theological reasoning. Instead, she called for sociological study that was grounded in practical, objective observation.

Because Addams did not challenge specific military or foreign policy objectives of the United States in the first period, her rhetoric caused little controversy. When, in 1915, Addams departed from her familiar, saintly emphasis on helping impoverished immigrants, women, and children, the public reacted negatively. Indeed, her opposition to World War I caused many to question her loyalty. In the face of such harsh criticism, Addams, to a large extent, retreated from her sociological perspective. Her discourse became less detached and more emotional than in the first period. Ultimately, Addams was forced into a cautious, defensive rhetorical posture.

First Period, 1898–1909

Prior to the Spanish-American War, Jane Addams seemed unconcerned about pacifism. She was preoccupied with Hull House and the myriad of domestic issues associated with it. The outbreak of war with Spain, however, ended her indifference to matters of war and peace. From 1898 to 1909, Addams presented a series of well-attended lectures that criticized war and offered avenues to peace.[5]

Addams first criticized the Spanish-American War in a speech delivered to the Academy of Political and Social Sciences on 20 December 1898. She argued that "the spectacle of war has been a great setback to the development and growth of the higher impulse of civilization." War was dangerous and disturbing because "the predatory spirit is so near the surface in human nature." In condemning the human "predatory spirit," Addams echoed William James and G. Stanley Hall. Along with James, Addams would later try to develop a theory for "sublimating" destructive war impulses into constructive ventures. Like James, Addams ultimately sought a "moral equivalent for war."[6]

Although Addams was not a founding member of the Anti-imperialist League, she endorsed its principles in the summer of 1898 and became a member of the Chicago chapter. Addams agreed with George Hoar and Carl Shurz, among others, that the Philippines should not be annexed. Although she was "uplifted" by Shurz's political attacks on President McKinley's imperialistic doctrine, she avoided partisan denunciations of the president. Instead, Addams took an expansive, sociological view of warfare. In her analysis, the stimulation and gratification of military conquest needed to be turned in a peaceful direction. Addams developed this theory in a speech entitled "Democracy or Militarism," delivered to a Chicago Liberty Meeting held at the Central Music Hall on 30 April 1899. She continued this line of analysis ten months later in Saint Louis.[7]

Addams traveled to Chautauqua, New York, in July of 1902, during "Social Settlement Week," to present a series of lectures on peace. On 7 and 9 July, she delivered "The Newer Ideals of Peace," in which she urged productive alternatives to the powerful but destructive impulses of war. Said Addams, "All war . . . has been so much wasted force, and worse than wasted; it has raised anger and prejudice so that it is longer before men can use their reason." Addams insisted, "In the end men must settle questions by reason." Instead of armed conflict, she proposed that men cultivate a kind of "commercial interdependence" that would foster fair, nonviolent competition in the business arena. Moreover, she condemned the practice of child labor and pleaded with the nation to develop a new kind of patriotism, one that "holds up a standard of life for its people." On 10 and 11 July, Addams lectured on Leo Tolstoy. By all reports, her lectures were popular. According to the *Chautauqua Assembly Herald*, the "Hall was crowded" and "many were unable to get within sound of her voice."[8]

During 3–8 October 1904, Addams appeared in Boston, along with William James and others, to give a series of well-attended speeches at the thirteenth Universal Peace Conference. Her remarks at the Peace Conference banquet, which followed a speech by Booker T. Washington, were delivered to a capacity crowd of five hundred. Three years later, she presented two formal speeches to the National Arbitration and Peace Congress, held in New York City from 14 to 17 April 1907. Again, the sessions were packed with enthusiastic participants. To a large extent, all of these speeches recapitulated the major concepts of her Chautauqua lectures. Her first address to the National Arbitration and Peace Congress, entitled "New Ideals of Peace," for example, acknowledged that war represented "a series of ideas and emotions which have been very dear to men from the beginning of time." She urged conference participants to "dream that we may abolish war by supplementing these historic emotions by others . . . as heroic, as noble and as well worth while as those which have sustained this long struggle of warfare."[9]

Addams refined her ideas and published them in a 1907 book, *Newer Ideals of Peace*—a title that she had used previously for lectures. The first and last chapters of the book reiterated arguments she had made in her speeches since 1898. The middle chapters returned to Addams's familiar sphere of immigration, urbanization, child and woman labor, and city government. Thus, most of the book was not concerned with war and peace per se, but rather domestic problems in the cities. Overall, Addams attempted to shift the public's attention from military issues to domestic reform.[10]

Although William James loved the book, it did not sell well, and it received negative reviews. Some critics condemned *Newer Ideals of Peace* because it was not really about peace; others chastised the poor organization or the impression that it was an assortment of largely unrelated essays. Theodore Roosevelt ridiculed the book, calling the author "Foolish Jane Addams." Overall, however, the book generated little serious controversy. Addams enjoyed an excellent reputation because of her work with the poor, and most simply ignored her ideas on war and peace.[11]

Addams spoke before the National Peace Congress in 1909. In this address, entitled "Woman's Special Training for Peacemaking," she focused on the special role of women in bringing about peace. She claimed it would be difficult to present new ideas on peace to such a conference, "but perhaps there are some special things which might be said to an audience of women that would not be so applicable to an audience of men." Addams's address before the National Peace Congress concluded the first phase of her pacifist rhetoric, which spanned the decade after the Spanish-American War.[12]

THE PROBLEM OF WAR

In the first phase (1898–1909), Addams supported her pacifist views in a systematic, logical manner. First, she established that armed conflict should be eliminated because it damaged people and institutions. Addams presented a number of problems with war and imperialism, ranging from broad, social consequences to specific, practical harms. For example, Addams argued that war was bad because it interrupted human progress. Prior to the Spanish-American War, Addams believed that the world had changed, that war no longer drove human affairs. As she explained in the 1899 speech "Democracy or Militarism," she trusted "That we were ready to accept the peace ideal, to be proud of our title as a peace nation; to recognize that the man who cleans a city is greater than he who bombards it, and the man who irrigates a plain greater than he who lays it waste." Addams thought that the country had been evolving toward the peace ideal, but "Then came the Spanish war, with its gilt and lace and tinsel, and again the moral issues are confused with exhibitions of brutality." Thus, one of Addams's main objections to war was that it caused humanity to revert from the normal upward progress of human civilization. As Addams said at Saint Louis in 1900, adopting imperialism meant "that practically no progress has been made since the Persian Cyrus or the Roman Cesar [sic] believed that a conquering nation had every right to enslave the conquered." She compared the barbaric conquests of the Roman Empire and the imperialistic policies of the United States at the turn of the century: "At a time like this the difference between the civilizing Roman and the civilizing Anglo-Saxon seems very slight—the motives are almost identical, the methods differ but little. The results are justified by the same phrases; brutal commercialism, with a varnish of patriotism and morality"[13]

In Addams's social-scientific analysis, the regression from peace to war had other negative consequences. One major harm of war was that violence was not confined to the battlefield. Addams believed that "the fighting instinct" was very powerful. It did not "end in mere warfare," but aroused "these brutal instincts latent in every human being." Addams interpreted the particular dangers of the Spanish-American War through her experiences at Hull House: "For ten years I have lived in a neighborhood which is by no means criminal, and yet during last October and November we were startled by seven murders within a radius of ten blocks." Addams claimed that, by analyzing the causes of the killings, it was "not in the least difficult to trace the murders back to the influence of the war." War was so powerfully seductive that even hearing about it could cause unsophisticated people to behave violently: "Simple people who read of carnage and bloodshed easily receive its suggestions. Habits of self-control which have been but slowly and imperfectly acquired quickly break down under the stress." Under peaceful circumstances, flawed individuals could painstakingly exercise restraint, but the bad influence of war unhinged them.[14]

Addams cited "psychologists" who theorized that people would behave in a manner consistent with the object of their attention: "The newspapers, the theatrical posters, the street conversations for weeks had to do with war and bloodshed. The little children on the street played at war, day after day, killing Spaniards." The damage was not limited to children, however. The brutality of the war incited adults as well to behave cruelly in Chicago. Addams claimed the Spanish-American War caused the people of Chicago to tolerate "whipping for children in our city prison." Only during time of war could the Illinois legislature move to reestablish the "whipping post."[15]

In the period from 1898 to 1909, Addams rarely made pragmatic arguments addressed solely to the self-interest of her listeners. However, she did so in "Democracy or Militarism," her 1899 address to the Chicago Liberty Meeting: "There is a growing conviction among workingmen of all countries that, whatever may be accomplished by a national war, however high the supposed moral aim of such a war, there is one inevitable result—an increased standing army, the soldiers of which are non-producers and must be fed by the workers." Based on the examples of Russia and Germany, Addams claimed that ordinary citizens would be taxed to feed armies, as well as to support the social institutions such as hospitals and orphanages that were necessitated by the immoral behavior of soldiers. As she delicately stated, "The countries with the large standing armies are likewise the countries with national hospitals for the treatment of diseases which should never exist, of large asylums for the care of children which should never have been born."[16]

Addams also abhorred how the military squandered valuable resources. For one thing, armies wasted "muscular force in drilling," when it could be turned to useful occupations. Moreover, the "mental force" of soldiers was wasted on "thoughts of warfare." Finally, "The mere hours of idleness conduce mental and moral deterioration." Addams's analysis of the military reveals her criteria for judging social institutions, which were rooted in her daily experiences at Hull House. Do institutions feed or nurture people? Do they improve human relationships? By these criteria, war failed.[17]

In addition to her sociological objections to war, Addams criticized the particular circumstances of the Spanish-American War and its aftermath in the Philippines, although not as vehemently as one might expect from a celebrated pacifist. She argued that the rationale for the Spanish-American War was false, and that the rationale for keeping the Philippines was equally false: "To 'protect the weak' has always been the excuse of the ruler and tax-gatherer, the chief, the king, the baron; and now, at last of 'the white man.'" At the Universal Peace Congress in 1904, Addams maintained it was wrong for one country to invade another in order "to bring to it the blessings of civilization and self-government. . . . In the process of establishing law and order [imperialism] may crush out the very beginnings of self-government." In making this criticism, Addams's ideas seem more in tune with the values of the twenty-first century than 1904. She wanted to "nourish" other cultures, not necessarily like her own: "Perhaps we shall be able to prove that some things that are not Anglo-Saxon are of great value, of great beauty."[18]

In Addams's mind, one of the more abstract harms of imperialism was the damage it did to American principles. In brief, imperialism was essentially un-American. Holding the Philippines by force violated cherished American values. This conventional anti-imperialism argument appeared in three of her speeches from the first period. In "Democracy or Militarism" (1899), she asked the rhetorical question, "Are we going to trust our democracy, or are we going to weakly imitate the policy of other governments, which have never claimed a democratic basis?" She argued that the United States should not abandon its essential nature just because it had been thrust upon the international stage. The next year, in Saint Louis, Addams proclaimed that, in conquering Spain, the United States was merely imitating England, "because we followed her methods of the conquest and government of remote and alien peoples. We gave her the sincere admiration which imitation always implies." In 1904 she urged America to be different from Europe, which had "established forts in Africa or Asia or some other place. It seems to me that here in America is the place for experiment." In these examples Addams attempted to use a nationalistic appeal to combat the jingoism of pro-imperialism advocates. Simply put, Addams argued, in effect: We are better than Europe; let's not stoop to imitating it.[19]

BARRIERS TO PEACE

After making the case that war caused harms to individuals and society, Addams next addressed the barriers that prevented the cessation of war. In her extensive and rather scholarly analysis, the first obstacle to peace was its perceived unattractiveness as compared to war. Addams realized that warfare often called forth "strenuous endeavor," "heroic self-sacrifice," and "fine courage and readiness to meet death." Placed opposite the martial excitement of war and imperialism, peace was not likely to attract many followers. The plain fact was, Addams admitted, war excited people. Her analysis of war calls to mind Kenneth Burke's study of *Mein*

Kampf: Hitler's anti-Semitism, as Burke argued, was a *"bad* filling of a *good* need." Addams thought that human beings innately needed glory, nobility, and strenuous effort, but that war was a bad expression of these natural human tendencies.[20]

Addams lamented the popular fascination with war, which "tends to fix our minds on the picturesque." War was popular, rather than peace, because "it seems so much more magnificent to do battle for the right than patiently to correct the wrong." According to Addams, "We allure our young men not to develop but to exploit. We turn their imaginations from the courage and toil of industry to the bravery and endurance of war." She told a story to illustrate her point: "I remember once making a feeble attempt to present the prosaic thing picturesquely." A gymnastics class at Hull House wanted to perform military drills. She convinced the boys to drill with "long, narrow, sewer spades, instead of bayonets. [She] made the simple argument that it was quite as noble to maneuver as if to clean the city in order to prevent disease and save life as it was to maneuver as if to charge into an enemy and kill our fellow men." This technique worked, so long as Addams continually reinforced her concept. However, when the boys were left alone with the spades for a single evening, they soon "pretended the spades were guns and went back to military tactics. I honestly doubt if now I could even get them to touch a spade, so besotted have we all become with the notion of military glory."[21]

In addition to the inherent appeal of war, Addams claimed, peace advocates had not used effective arguments against war and imperialism. She claimed there were four main types of anti-war arguments, all of which were defective: "the appeal to pity and mercy"; the appeal to prudence, which objected to war because it was expensive, and because human life "is too precious"; "the appeal to the sense of human solidarity"; and the appeal to the "sense of righteousness." Addams concluded that all of these anti-war appeals must inherently be ineffective, or they "would not have failed so completely." As she remarked at the Chautauqua Institute, "one despairs of arousing enthusiasm for peace unless it is done more positively than any of the present peace societies are able to do it. No one listens to the people who preach or write over and over again." The problem with the typical anti-war appeals, she argued at the 1904 Universal Peace Congress, was that they were not "in accord with our present line of thinking." They failed because they were too "theoretical and sentimental."[22]

As a female, Addams wondered why other women did not speak more forcefully against war. What was the barrier that prevented them from working for peace? She found the explanation in historical gender differences. Once again employing a sociological perspective, she maintained in 1909 that "we are children of the past. The things which we are now are the results of the things which have gone before us." As Addams explained in "New Ideals of Peace" (1907), when people lived in the "tribal stage," women stayed home, and men "learned to act together, to incite themselves by war cries or by the calls of the chase, to lean upon each other for defense and achievement. . . . This broad division between the work of women and men has held throughout the centuries, women's work tending to center in the home, and man's work, even after he organized industry and commerce, still being carried on in groups."[23]

Because of historical gender differences, Addams claimed, women were not used to organizing politically and working for peace in groups. Recently, however, women's "family isolation" had been "rudely broken in upon. Her historic activities are carried on in great factories, . . . in inter-relation with hundreds of other people." Because women were learning to work together, they now had the potential to bring about peace. The problem was that women had difficulty visualizing the actual effects of war. In Addams's analysis, "there would not be another war" if women would only understand "that it was going to kill thousands of little children. . . . We fail to bring about the end of war simply because our imaginations are feeble." In Addams's mind women had the power to stop war if they became really concerned. The major challenge for Addams and other pacifists was to devise ways to stir the imaginations of women and cause them to visualize the awful effects of war.[24]

SOLUTIONS

Addams generated an impressive number of possible solutions to the problems of war and imperialism—some specific, and some more general. The overarching principle of her solutions, however, revolved around the art of persuasion. Not only did Addams use rhetoric to convince people to endorse her solutions, in a very real sense her proposals were rhetorical in nature. Her solutions involved changing public attitudes. Moreover, Addams actually argued *for* peace rather than *against* war. She wanted to shift the public's attention away from soldiers and battles to social reform. Finally, she perceived war, imperialism, and international politics through the lens of Hull House, which she used to reason about pacifism, to illustrate her points, and to test the practicality of her solutions.

As mentioned previously, Addams condemned the old, worn approaches of pacifists in the past. Appeals to pity, prudence, human solidarity, and dogma did not work. Instead, at the Universal Peace Congress of 1904, Addams suggested "something a little more active and practical, less theoretical and sentimental than some of the old preachings of peace." As she explained at the Chautauqua Institute, "active labor and service . . . does much to make war impossible." In her judgment, "What arouses attention is something that is done." Addams believed she could capture the attention of the nation, if not the world, by making a concrete difference in the lives of real people. Such an achievement would lessen the possibility of war, and that kind of accomplishment could not be ignored, unlike abstract preaching. Thus, Addams attempted to extend the lessons she learned at Hull House into the international arena of war and peace.[25]

Addams's proposed solution was intensely rhetorical. She sought to influence public perception, and her tool for accomplishing this was language. Her method was changing the subject from military topics to domestic matters. For instance, Addams attempted to shift the public's attention from pitying poor soldiers dying in the field to sympathy and common understanding for "the poor people—those who do the roughest work with their hands, wear the meanest clothes, whom we allow ourselves to feel a little differently towards." In "France, America and England," she maintained, various writers had tried to arouse pity for the poor. She cited Dickens in England, Zola in France, and "a long line of realistic novels" in the United States. According to Addams, these rhetorical efforts were gradually changing the way Americans spoke about needy people: "Certain words are almost dropping out of our vocabulary. When you know such a person in literature, he has become individualized. We are dropping such hateful words as 'slum,' 'the lower classes,' because when we use them we think of fine people we have met to whom, after we know them, we could not possibly apply such terms."[26]

Similarly, Addams argued that the anti-war appeal to prudence should be transformed into concern for ordinary people dying of starvation and disease. She claimed it was "imprudent" for nations to allow sickness and starvation. Addams attempted to adapt this appeal to the concerns of imperialists and capitalists: "There are economists who are beginning to assert very firmly that any nation that allows its people to be underfed and diseased is committing a great economic imprudence." A country with a weakened population would not compete successfully in the world arena. Also, impoverished folks had to be "cared for by the taxes of people more fortunate." In sum, Addams maintained, "in the great world-struggle that nation is going to go down which does not hold up a high standard of industrial labor." Clearly, Addams tried to draw attention to the domestic problems of the United States by framing the debate in international terms. Why should we care for the poor? To win the great world-struggle.[27]

Addams proposed the same type of rhetorical transformation for the concept of human solidarity, although this topic was not as well developed as the previous two. Instead of the solidarity that came from war, Addams wanted to glorify peaceful coexistence: "When we once surround human life with the same kind of heroism and admiration that we have surrounded war, we can say that this sense is having such an outlet that war will become impossible." In practical terms, this meant increasing the "educational efforts of government," attempting to eradicate diseases like smallpox and scarlet fever, and implementing welfare programs such as the old-age pensions in Germany.[28]

Although the heart of Addams's proposals for peace centered on correcting domestic social ills, she advocated other approaches to ending war. For instance, Addams encouraged individuals around the world to refuse to fight. This was a kind of direct action that went beyond the abstract. However, courageous pacifistic individuals, such as the Russian Doukhobors, were scattered about the globe in isolated pockets. Since they were disorganized, they were generally not heard. To remedy this problem, Addams argued that national governments should officially refuse to fight: "So one comes to believe that the only way to get at it [peace] is through the expression of national legislation, so that nations shall put themselves on record as conserving national life." If this were done, if countries stated publicly and officially their opposition to the destruction of war, "Then, perhaps, the responsibility concerning national life may extend some time beyond the boundaries of the nation." Addams believed that government action was "more active," quicker, and "more efficient" than the "slow" method of individuals "abstaining" from war. This being the case, she thought that anti-war efforts ought to be aimed at national governments.[29]

As Americans, Addams expected her fellow citizens to adopt a new morality that transcended the primitive urges of human conquest. In her mind, the debate over imperialism was a moral test. If the United States passed that test, she explained in "Democracy or Militarism" (1899), it would truly put into practice American ideals: "it is exactly in such a time as this that we discover what we really believe." Addams claimed that "new conditions are ever demanding the evolution of a new morality," one that would extend "our nationalism into internationalism" and "thrust forward our patriotism into humanitarianism." She admitted in 1904 that it was easier for a nation to behave selfishly and violently, "But if we have the spirit of moral adventure, if we believe, as we pretend to believe in America, in democracy, then we shall be ready to take another course, even if it be much more difficult." Addams urged her fellow citizens to "proceed in a different way. We must do our work on the highest plane. We have a higher ideal than the old one which has been incorporated in the rule of first gaining government control by force and making things safe."[30]

If Addams's solution to war was creating a new morality, how was this to be achieved? Her answer again involved rhetoric. She realized that national attitudes had to change for the public to cherish peace. One possible way to change these attitudes was to redefine some of the central terms in the debate over war. For example, Addams identified the dull connotations of "peace" as a barrier that needed to be overcome. Her solution for overcoming this barrier was to promote a new definition of "peace" that would be more exciting. At the Universal Peace Congress, 1904, Addams stated her goal simply: "If we could only convert our men and women, and make them see that war is destructive, that peace is creative, that if a man commits himself to warfare he is committing himself to the played-out thing, and not to the new, vigorous and fine thing along the lines of the highest human development, we should have accomplished very much." The rhetorical task was clear: to "convert," to "make them see." She portrayed war as destructive, but peace as "creative," not dull, uninteresting, or passive. Peace looked to the future; it was "vigorous" and "new," not "played-out." Peace was "fine" and devoted to the "highest" human "development."[31]

Addams gamely tried to adapt her new definition of peace to stereotypically masculine ideals of adventure. She attempted to reverse the notion that the pacifist was cowardly, while the imperialist was brave. Addams reasoned that anyone could go into a foreign country once it had been defeated in battle. It took more nerve to do business in a land that was not defeated: "The man with courage would be the man who would prefer to go without the warships, just as a brave young man walks the streets of Chicago without arms, while the coward carries brass knuckles and a revolver in his hip pocket." Addams did not want peace to be "sissified." She tried to make peace strong, active, virile, and brave. On the other hand, she portrayed warfare as cowardly and un-American.[32]

In addition to redefining peace as more muscular, Addams sought to redefine patriotism. She envisioned a kind of patriotism that involved peaceful international trade rather than military conquest. Her ideal of patriotism was "not preaching, not the saluting of the flag which we call patriotism in the public school, but in many cases, bold, self-seeking commerce." The goal of this "economic patriotism" would be fair and noble competition: "Call that national patriotism which holds up a standard of life for its people, which sees that it shall compete on the highest possible plan[e]." In Addams's analysis, the chances for warfare would be lessened by "commercial interdependence, an understanding of the interdependence of one nation with another."[33]

Another redefinition of a patriotic act would be to abolish child labor. Addams thus used the issues of war and imperialism to focus the public's attention on her domestic reform agenda. She explained that "Every civilized country in Europe, even Russia, has child-labor legislation," whereas in the U.S., only twenty-four states had legislation prohibiting child labor. The states that did not regulate child labor "form almost the only spot in the civilized world where such legislation is not found." Here Addams appealed to national pride. The United States looked bad when compared to Europe on the issue of child labor reform. Addams envisioned a kind of patriotism where the United States would compete with the rest of the world to be the most humane and enlightened nation. To bolster her humanitarian plea, Addams also proposed a scientific argument for abolishing child labor. She claimed that "By actual measurements it is found that the children in the factories weigh less than those children of the same age and family who are kept in school; that they are shorter in stature and can do various things less well." Addams's type of patriotism would rescue child laborers to achieve a "national conservation of life." In sum, stunted children did not help a country win the race with other nations.[34]

The specific proposals for changing the public's attitudes, ideas, and values reduced to one primary concept in Addams's mind: finding a "moral substitute" for war. She declared in 1904, "the thing that is incumbent on this generation is to discover a moral substitute for war, something that will appeal to the courage, the capacity of men, something which will develop their finest powers without deteriorating their moral nature, as war constantly does." This concept, which paralleled William James's thinking, had been evolving for years in Addams's mind. The problem was, what should this ideal substitute be? Although Addams recognized clearly the problems of war, the solution was less evident. She admitted in 1907 that finding a moral substitute for war would be difficult: "It is needless to say that it is hard to formulate it; that although this power of devotion to the human cause is no mean force, it is difficult to put it over against the pomp of war."[35]

In "Newer Ideals of Peace," Addams proposed a specific pursuit that could be a moral substitute for war: construction. This was a dangerous occupation, yet society did not glorify construction workers: "When structural iron workers build a bridge, almost exactly the same percentage of them are wounded and killed as of men who engage in battle, but as yet we utterly fail to regard them as an example of industrial heroism, and they fall not as heroes, but as victims." Addams's proposal was that, as a nation, we should "pour into industry something of that comradeship which has so long belonged to war, something of that glamour which Tolstoy declares adheres in the drum itself, so that when men hear a certain beat they leave everything to follow the call. Cannot we formulate a call for industrial service?"[36]

FEASIBILITY

After analyzing the harms and causes of war and proposing solutions, Addams argued that her plans would in fact help bring about peace, if only they were given a chance. Once people understood the pleasures of peace, she claimed, they would never go back to war: "these childish notions of power, these boyish ideas of adventure, these veritable rabble conceptions of what pleasure and manliness and courage consist in" would "fall away from them as the garments of a child are dropped off from his growing form." To Addams, war was immaturity; peace was maturity. War was boyish, representing misconceptions about pleasure and manliness. Although Addams did not say so directly, she assigned some stereotypically feminine traits to her proposed solution: "I do not imagine that, if the race once discovered the excitement and the pleasure and the infinite moral stimulus and the gratification of the spirit of adventure to be found in the nourishing of human life, in the bringing of all the world into some sort of general order and decent relationship with one another, they would look back with very much regret, and wish they might again go opening new lands because they found therein their only joy and their only pleasure." Clearly, she believed that men would stop soldiering if they experienced "nourishing," "bringing . . . order," and fostering "decent relationship[s]." In short, if men simply tried her alternative, they would put an end to war.[37]

From 1898 until 1906, Addams assumed that her ideas for peace would be implemented by workers. She believed that "workingmen" were at the vanguard of the peace movement. In her analysis, workers were the first to "formulate it and give it international meaning." The common laborers "in all ages have borne the heaviest burden of privation and suffering imposed on the world by the military spirit." Workers shared a "supreme interest" of common humanity and common economic plight. Seen from the perspective of workers, war was nothing more than "systematic murder." Addams claimed that "No one urges peaceful association with more fervor than the workingman." Because workers held these attitudes, Addams assumed they would embrace her proposals.[38]

In explaining why workers would lead the peace movement, Addams attributed her own womanly virtues to them. Thus, in a subtle way, Addams "feminized" workers. Who, she asked, should "protest against this destruction? Who should band together for preserving human life, for keeping the fields free from the tramping of soldiers, from the destruction of the precious bread that men love to have? I say it is the workers, who year after year nourish and bring up the bulk of the nation." Given Addams's definitions, the roles of women and workers were similar. They were both on the bottom of society; they both nourished; they both brought up the nation. In conclusion, said Addams, "The peace movement should be in the hands of those who produce, and not be allowed to fall into the hands of those who destroy."[39]

By 1907, Addams had stopped lauding workers as the hope of the peace movement. Instead, she turned to women as natural pacifist leaders. At the National Arbitration and Peace Conference, for example, Addams appealed to women as the one group that could bring about the changes she advocated. Addams believed that women, now that they were organized in an industrial society, "have the opportunity of carrying on their legitimate work in groups and definite inter-relations, not only with each other but with all society." She wanted to transform the traditional role of women by projecting it outside the home into international politics: "What might not happen if women realized that the ancient family affection, that desire to protect and rear little children which they have expressed so long in isolation, might now be socialized and be brought to bear as a moral force on the current industrial organization."[40]

Another group that Addams believed could help bring about peace was the immigrants of large cities such as Chicago. She based this opinion on her observations of immigrant behavior in the Hull House neighborhood. At the Universal Peace Congress in 1904, Addams explained how Italian immigrants demonstrated the moral equivalent of war: "almost every Sunday our Italian friends come out and beat their drums and wave their flags and wear their uniforms to celebrate the fact that they have formed a little bit of a Benefit Society. . . . All over America we have these societies; they are taking to themselves uniforms and the fife and the drum and a good deal of the paraphernalia of war." Such activities converted martial impulses into wholesome events: celebration instead of destruction. The implication was, if immigrants could find a moral equivalent for war, then this solution could work for society as a whole.[41]

Addams believed "there is arising in these cosmopolitan centers a sturdy, a virile and an unprecedented internationalism which is fast becoming too real, too profound, too widespread, ever to lend itself to warfare." The cosmopolitan attitude of immigrants promoted peace, because "if the people who have entered into this new internationalism are to be led into warfare, they must be led against their next-door neighbors." The new internationalism "is growing and developing in this America of ours as it is nowhere else, because nowhere else does it have the same opportunity." Because immigration changed attitudes about war in a positive direction, Addams thought that peace could be achieved.[42]

Clearly, Addams argued in a logical, systematic way. She claimed that warfare and imperialism caused significant harms to people, analyzed the barriers that prevented the cessation of war, proposed some plans for obtaining peace, and maintained that her proposals would work, if given a chance. Although reason and scientific detachment were the dominant features of her discourse in the first period, there were several other significant themes.

NARRATIVE

Scholars who have analyzed Addams's discourse emphasize her use of autobiographical narrative as a mode of argument. Admittedly, Addams's personal stories tend to linger in the mind. Perhaps they are the most obvious and accessible feature of her discourse. However, when one considers the volume of anti-war speeches she delivered between 1898 and 1909, the autobiographical stories are actually quite infrequent. In the first period, I discovered five clear-cut, vivid stories. Two of them involved Russia, and one was an apocryphal story about Shakespeare.[43]

Only two of the stories could be considered autobiographical. The first, which I have already discussed, was the story of the boys at Hull House who were asked to drill with sewer spades. This famous anecdote was later reprinted in *Twenty Years at Hull-House*. By far the most powerful anecdote from the first period came in support of her campaign to make domestic social work a kind of acceptable patriotism. To illustrate the horrors of child labor, Addams painted a vivid picture of a little child she personally met working in a Southern mill: "We saw at this mill a little girl of five working all night. She was very dropsical, I noticed, as she went along pushing her box. The foreman was quite proud of her. He said she worked about three nights a week. She was dipping snuff. I asked her if I might see her snuff stick, and when she opened her mouth I saw she had still her baby teeth. . . . A child of that sort will soon become utterly destroyed." This story sears itself into the memory because of the specifics. The fact that Addams witnessed this herself contributed to the poignancy of the account, as well as the fact that this story supported an argument on domestic reform, where her heart really was. However, one poignant vignette over a decade hardly constitutes a notable pattern.[44]

TOLSTOY

Count Leo Nikolayevich Tolstoy's presence in Addams's discourse from the first period is so pronounced that it deserves special consideration as a rhetorical feature. Tolstoy inspired Addams and provided authority for many of her arguments about pacifism. In addition, Tolstoy provided a general philosophy that undergirded her analysis of imperialism and warfare. Central to her understanding of Tolstoy was the concept of action. The count had acted on his convictions, giving up a life of leisure and celebrity to live among the Russian peasants. Addams quoted Tolstoy: "'If one has a glimmering of a moral principle, he should put it into action, and if one does not put it into action he does not believe it at all.'" Clearly, this idea guided much of Jane Addams's career.[45]

Addams quoted Tolstoy and related incidents from his life on a steady basis during the first period of her anti-war discourse. She actually had visited him in person on one of her earlier European tours, and she used this experience to good effect in her speeches. In one of her lectures on Tolstoy delivered in 1902, Addams explained why he was such a fascinating figure to her: "the study of human life is gradually shaping itself from the study of the individual to the contemplation of men at the base of society," the workers, farmers, and manual laborers. If one were interested in studying the masses, then Tolstoy was a pertinent source. Moreover, such a perspective squared nicely with her basic sociological approach.[46]

In retrospect, Addams's fascination with Tolstoy seems natural, considering her own decisions to abandon a life of wealth and privilege and to live among the common immigrants of Chicago in Hull House. Tolstoy inspired Addams and validated her vocational choices. He could also be brought into play as evidence to bolster an argument. Here was a male, an international celebrity, who agreed with many of her positions. For example, Tolstoy's commitment to the importance of physical labor supported Addams's practice of direct action in Chicago and helped buttress her early ideas that workingmen would lead the peace movement. According to Addams, part of Tolstoy's philosophy was to "Live in right relationships with the people about you. Insist on knowing them on the better side, and maintain a recipience involving affection." Further, Addams claimed, Tolstoy was "able to make a synthesis between such divergent classes as the peasant and the Russian noble, the type of the uneducated and the educated." These concepts describe well the philosophy that Addams lived out at Hull House. When Addams praised Tolstoy because "He stands there as an example of his own teaching," or because, in his life, "It is the sermon which the deed preaches," she might just as well have been speaking about herself.[47]

OPTIMISM

Another general characteristic of Addams's rhetoric was a strong sense of optimism. In the face of substantial evidence to the contrary, Addams believed in 1907 that conditions were gradually improving: "War, the old enemy of industry and of the home, many of us believe is passing out of society." Coupled with her sense of optimism was a wistful quality to her discourse. For example, when arguing for a new policy to bring about peace, she stated, "one longs to make this suggestion," as though she realized her proposals were not entirely realistic, that they reflected her desire for a utopian future as much as practical solutions for imperialism. She concluded her 1909 speech by declaring, "I hope that is not fantastic, and I hope we will show that it is true." Considering the functions of these peace meetings, maintaining a sense of optimism and purpose were important organizational goals.[48]

During the first period of her pacifist discourse, Addams focused on creating concern for a problem more than on providing specific solutions. Perhaps what is most striking is how she defined the causes of war, as well as the remedies for it, in rhetorical terms. Her main task was getting people to change their perceptions about warfare and imperialism, and persuasive language was the means by which this task could be accomplished. Significantly, her anti-war arguments always circled back to domestic reform issues. She believed pacifists could devise a moral equivalent for war that would be creative rather than destructive, and she saw hopeful signs of this in workers, women, and immigrants. Unquestionably, Addams's experiences at Hull House fortified her sense of optimism. Given the fact that the United States was not actively fighting a war for most of the first period, it is not surprising that her arguments were abstract, detached, scholarly—consistent with the language of the new social sciences that were emerging during the Progressive Era. After 1915, however, Addams would face a radically changed set of circumstances. In the face of adversity, she would be forced to adapt her rhetoric in unfamiliar ways, and this contributed in no small part to the largest crisis of her career.

Second Period, 1915–1917

Addams resumed her anti-war rhetoric in 1915 after a lull of about five years. Interestingly, the interim period of 1910 to 1914 coincided with the height of Addams's national popularity. According to Allen F. Davis, "In the years before World War I, she was a symbol of the best American Democracy, the best of American womanhood, and a semi-religious figure who explained all mysteries and assured everyone that despite poverty and tragedy everywhere, in the end, right would prevail." After war erupted in Europe, peace advocates looked to Addams for leadership because of her stellar reputation and national influence. She had lectured on war and peace since the turn of the century, promulgated Tolstoy's ideas, and written *Newer Ideals of Peace*. Without question, she was one of the leading women of her day.[49]

Pacifists asked Addams to preside over an organizational meeting for the Woman's Peace Party, held at the Grand Ball Room of the New Willard Hotel in Washington, D.C. She delivered the keynote address, entitled "What War Is Destroying," on 10 January 1915, to an overflow audience of three thousand. This was a women's conference, and Addams concentrated on discussing the impact of the war on women. She analyzed the destruction to principles and values in which women "have held a vested interest." Even though the husbands or sons of American women were not dying in battle, Addams attempted to motivate the audience to take action against war. During this meeting, Addams was elected chair of the Woman's Peace Party. The outcome of the conference was a resolution calling for the neutral nations of the world to continuously attempt to mediate between warring countries. Despite Addams's best organizing efforts, newspapers declined to cover the Washington meeting. As Davis notes, in 1915, "Women organizing for peace was not an especially newsworthy event."In a few months, however, pacifists would trigger intense controversy.[50]

After the Woman's Peace Party meeting, the International Congress of Women invited Addams to attend a peace conference, held at The Hague, Netherlands, from 28 April to 1 May 1915. ICW organizers asked Addams to preside over the meeting. Although she was skeptical the conference would accomplish much, she felt duty bound to do what she could for the cause of peace. By all reports, Addams did a splendid job of chairing the proceedings at The Hague. As Elizabeth Glendower Evans recalled, "Again and again, when she rose to speak and when she closed, the audience would stand and applaud—until one pitied her for this challenge to her gentle modesty."[51]

As head of The Hague meeting, Addams delivered her "Presidential Address" on 1 May 1915. She expressed special admiration for women who had come from the warring countries and characterized their actions as heroic. She also recognized the challenges to women attending the conference from neutral countries, who often had to withstand negative political pressures from home. Why were fifteen hundred women willing to come to the Congress, Addams asked? They believed that "the solidarity of women would hold fast and that through it as through a precious instrument they would be able to declare the reality of those basic human experiences ever perpetuating and cherishing the race."[52]

The women delegates to The Hague passed a resolution that conference representatives should meet with officials of neutral and warring European nations, as well as with the president of the United States. Addams was elected a representative, but she thought the entire scheme was "hopelessly melodramatic and absurd." Nonetheless, she went with the other delegates to the belligerent countries at considerable personal danger to herself, and she talked to people from both sides. On the basis of this experience, she concluded that "rational persuasion was more important than the threat of force." Instead of staying in Europe for a follow-up conference, however, Addams returned to the United States. This caused her to be criticized by some of the more radical pacifists, including Rosika Schwimmer.[53]

The American public reacted to Addams's trip in various ways. Some were proud that a United States citizen was chosen as leader of a world conference. Most newspapers doubted that the conference would accomplish much of value, but, as the *Charlotte Observer* said, "they will at least have given voice to the humane instincts of the world and they will have been true to their own conception of duty." The *New York Evening Mail* asked, "It may seem that their work has been in vain, but who shall make bold to call it a failure?" The *New York Times* opined, "Miss Addams is a citizen too highly valued for any one to see her engaged in such melancholy enterprises without a feeling of pain." In a letter to Mrs. George Rublee, Theodore Roosevelt declared the women's efforts "both silly and base" because they wanted "peace at any price." According to press accounts, Roosevelt also called Addams "one of the shrieking sisterhood" and "poor bleeding Jane." For the most part, though, The Hague conference did not damage Addams's prestige. Most disagreed with her methods, but admired her goals.[54]

Addams returned from Europe on 5 July 1915. Four days later, she delivered an address before a crowd of three thousand at Carnegie Hall, New York. The meeting was sponsored by the Woman's Peace Party, the Church Peace Union, and other groups and prominent individuals. Addams spoke extemporaneously from some brief notes but had not planned all of her remarks. The purpose of the speech was to share her experiences from the European trip. Addams observed joyously that the large audience was interested in peace: "It is very fine that peace can be rousing almost as war." She was buoyed by spirited applause and loud cheering from the balconies. Addams warned the audience how difficult it was to generalize about her trip to Europe. The situation was so confusing, she hesitated to say anything that was not absolutely factual, "And one does not come back . . . from these various warring countries with any desire . . . to let loose any more emotion upon the world."[55]

Most of the speech reported what she had discovered about the war during her travels. As a kind of gratuitous afterthought, Addams explained that "the young men in these various countries" particularly hated bayonet charges. The young soldiers exclaimed, "That is what we cannot think of." The next sentence Addams uttered almost destroyed her career: "You know of course that all of the countries make their men practically drunk before they can get them to charge, that they have a regular formula in Germany, that they give them rum in England, and absinthe in France. They all have to give them the dope before the bayonet charge is possible." Addams concluded her speech uneventfully and went home, unaware of what she had done.[56]

The reaction to Addams's Carnegie Hall speech was immediate and negative. Headlines blared, "Troops Drink-Crazed, says Miss Addams." One newspaper editorialized, "Her dabbling in politics, her suffrage activity and her ill-advised methods of working for peace have very materially lowered her in the esteem of hundreds of former admirers." The *New York Topics* concluded: "Jane Addams is a silly, vain, impertinent old maid, who may have done some good charity work at Hull House, Chicago, but is now meddling with matters far beyond her capacity." Richard Harding Davis, a noted war correspondent, refuted Addams's charges in a letter to the *New York Times:* "Miss Addams denies him [the soldier] the credit of his sacrifice. She strips him of honor and courage." Davis called Addams's remarks "untrue and ridiculous," and most of the newspaper editorials agreed with him. In addition, a score of citizens wrote angry letters directly to Addams.[57]

Addams had not intended to attack cherished public ideals at Carnegie Hall. She was simply trying to document what she hoped was rising resistance against war. At the same time, Addams tried to alter the perception that war was glamorous. Nevertheless, many people interpreted her remarks as an assault against the treasured social values of honor, duty, and country. The fact that she was discussing foreign soldiers made little difference to the public outcry. For the first time in her career, according to Davis, Addams had stepped out of the mainstream: "By challenging the part of the American dream that saw war as glorious and patriotic she had fallen from grace. The animosity of the attack can only be explained by the fact that she had been an important symbol for Americans."[58]

On 22 July Addams delivered a major speech to four thousand people at the Chicago Auditorium in which she repeated many of the themes of her Carnegie Hall address. In light of the negative reaction she had received two weeks earlier, the 22 July speech was more reserved. She cautioned her audience, "before I begin, I want to guard myself in one or two particulars." She explained that, on her tour of the European countries, she had met primarily with pacifist sympathizers. Therefore, she admitted, "I do not speak for the military in any sense, nor can we report general public opinion, altho[ugh] I am sure we report with great clearness and unmistakably the opinion of many people in every country." When Addams later generalized about the "divided mind" of soldiers in the trenches, she admonished the audience: "That sort of [doubt about war], I am sure, is in the minds of many young men—let me say a *few* young men, because I am very sure of a *few*—who are fighting upon every side of this conflict. . . . Again I wish to guard myself and say that altho[ugh] I met this type of man in these countries, I do not know how many there are."[59]

Near the end of the speech, Addams commented on her famous "bayonet charge" remarks: "I should like to make an explanation about the bayonet charge,—we heard in many countries that men who were willing to shoot, that many who with great good will fired shells and did their share in the artillery corps, found a bayonet charge very loathsome. I do not mean to say that many soldiers voice that feeling." Although Addams clearly retreated from her earlier generalization, she did not withdraw her statement or apologize for it. On the contrary, she offered more evidence: "I had a letter today from my traveling companion who reminded me exactly what was said to her by three different persons in different countries, that certain men under certain conditions—especially where they had been for a long time opposite each other—would not make a charge until stimulants had been provided." However, she quickly qualified her claim: "I can't give chapter and verse and number for these statements. I can only say these things were said to me. I did not go to the front; I did not see a bayonet charge, nor see the men before they went into action."[60]

By the end of July 1915, Addams's self-confidence had been shaken by attacks on her character and negative publicity. At first, she was uncertain how to recover. Eventually, Addams concluded that the best way to achieve peace was through a mediation process that involved neutral parties, and she looked to Woodrow Wilson for leadership. Following several delays, Addams managed to meet with Wilson, but he would not agree to her proposal. In light of German submarine attacks, the president was skeptical that mediation would work, and his advisors were clearly against it. Despite these obstacles, Addams hoped the president could be persuaded to organize a conference of neutral nations.[61]

Because Wilson was uncooperative, peace advocates sought other means to achieve their goals. In November 1915, Addams, among others, met with Henry Ford, who had recently declared his pacifism. Ford chartered an ocean liner to take a group of peace advocates to Europe for a conference of neutrals. Initially, Addams decided to go on the ship, even though the idea was ridiculed by the press. However, she became too ill to go and canceled the trip. A European peace conference was held without her in January of 1916, but it was a calamity from the start. Addams took much of the blame for the disastrous outcome of the peace ship, even though it was Henry Ford's initiative, and she did not even attend.[62]

Addams traveled to Washington, D.C., in January 1916, for the first annual meeting of the Woman's Peace Party. Despite her illness, she delivered a keynote speech on 9 January. She reminded the WPP delegates that a conference of neutral nations was part of their platform from a year earlier. However, Addams said, the Wilson administration, "doubtless with the very best of reasons, felt that the time had not yet come for action, a decision concerning which we never for a moment felt critical as the Government has much more information than we have." Because Wilson refused to organize a conference of neutrals, the Woman's Peace Party advocated "a possible conference of neutrals that should be non governmental, not to take the place of a governmental conference but to prepare the way for it."[63]

Two days later, Addams testified before the House Committee on Foreign Affairs. Her appearance coincided with the annual Woman's Peace Party conference. Addams opposed increasing "Army and naval preparations." As she told the committee, her purpose was "to present to you what seems to us the outline of the program which would forestall any necessity for such a phenomenal increase in our armament." Addams strove to appear humble before the committee: "I find myself a little embarrassed, because we seem to be instructing you. That is not what we intended to do at all."[64]

On 13 January, Addams, as president of the WPP, addressed the House Committee on Military Affairs. Once again, she cultivated an unpretentious image for the congressmen: "while I realize that it is more or less absurd for women to appear before the Committee on Military Affairs in connection with a bill concerning the Army, I also realize that the general policies of the United States are very largely determined by committees of this sort, and that women in time of war, as in peace, are very much affected by the national policies of the country." Addams opposed increased funding for the military: "we suggest that you at least postpone this plan for a large increase of the Army and Navy until the war is over." She also proposed "a commission appointed by Congress to investigate the present expenditure for the Army and Navy, to see whether the money is absolutely efficiently expended."[65]

Addams was tough and canny in responding to questions from the congressmen. She kept their attention focused on her message and refused to be diverted into criticizing Theodore Roosevelt or discussing the situation in Mexico. She declined to call for disarming the U.S. military; instead, she advocated preventing rapid increases of the army and navy. William Jennings Bryan approved of her testimony: "Your very presence was an argument. The manner in which you answered the questions put to you must have impressed the committee." The press, however, did not present a positive view. The *Minneapolis Journal* opined, "Somebody ought to lead Miss Addams back to social service. . . . She may know how long it will take Hull House to get a job for a woman out of work, but does she know how long it takes to turn raw recruits into seasoned troops?" The *Providence Journal* criticized Addams for her "unjustifiable and hysterical utterances which her pacifist ardor has led her to make." One journalist declared that Addams needed "a strong, forceful husband."[66]

Despite the harsh attacks, Addams continued to testify before congressional committees. On 12 December 1916, she addressed the Committee on Foreign Affairs concerning the relations between Asia and the United States. Addams supported a bill to investigate "relations between the United States and its vigorous neighbor on the other side of the Pacific [Japan]," in order to avert misunderstandings that might lead to war. If possible conflicts could be identified, she claimed, then the United States could avoid a future war.[67]

In January of 1917 Wilson gave his "Peace without Victory" speech in which he argued for a worldwide association dedicated to peace. Moreover, he advocated cessation of fighting before one of the belligerents won the war. Addams, naturally, approved of Wilson's ideas. However, by February of 1917, the United States had severed diplomatic ties with Germany over the issue of submarine attacks, and Wilson had concluded that America must intervene in the war in order to influence the peace settlement. Addams tried to change Wilson's mind, but he was not to be persuaded.[68]

After American entry into the war, Addams continued to testify in Congress to support her pacifist policies. On 9 April 1917, she responded to the Espionage Bill before the House Committee on the Judiciary. As usual, she represented the Woman's Peace Party of America. Addams opposed the Espionage Bill because it restricted freedom of speech. However, she framed her arguments as questions rather than bold assertions. She assumed the guise of one merely seeking clarification. For example, she asked the committee, "Are we at liberty to go out and say that? Can we say, in time of war, if such a bill as is proposed is passed—we do not wish to talk against war in time of war—we do believe, in spite of fighting, that in the end things must be settled upon some other point of view than a pure nationalistic point of view. Are we at liberty to say that or not?" Understandably,

Addams's testimony had a defensive quality: "Certainly, we are law-abiding citizens, although we are some times [sic] called hard names. I think no one could say seriously that we were not law-abiding, and we do not wish to do anything that is not according to law."[69]

Addams synthesized her ideas about government censorship in a public oration, "Patriotism and Pacifists in Wartime," delivered on 15 May 1917 to the City Club of Chicago. She gave the same address later at the University of Chicago and at the First Congregational Church of Evanston, Illinois. Addams recognized that a change in rhetorical strategy was needed: "The position of the pacifist in time of war is most difficult, and necessarily he must abandon the perfectly legitimate propaganda he maintained before war was declared. When he, with his fellow countrymen, is caught up by a wave of tremendous enthusiasm and is carried out into a high sea of patriotic feeling, he realizes that the virtues which he extols are brought into unhappy contrast to those which war, with its keen sense of a separate national existence, places in the foreground." Once war was declared, the public felt "unspeakable contempt for him who, in the hour of danger, declares that fighting is unnecessary." Because of this, Addams maintained, "we pacifists are not surprised" when "we should not only be considered incapable of facing reality, but that we should be called traitors and cowards."[70]

Addams received a "cool, but not especially hostile" response at the City Club and the University of Chicago. When she concluded her oration at the First Congregational Church in Evanston, however, "There was not even a ripple of applause," as reported by the *Chicago Examiner*. According to the *New York Times*, "Profound silence followed an address by Miss Jane Addams." Worse yet, during the question period, said the *Times*, Illinois Supreme Court Judge Orrin Carter "jumped to his feet" and disagreed with Addams's ideas. Justice Carter stated, "No pacifist measures, in my opinion, should be taken until the war is over." With that, the meeting concluded suddenly and discordantly. The press reported the incident as proof that Addams's reputation had deteriorated further. The *Survey*, her most dependable print outlet, refused to publish the speech because the editorial board feared her concepts might drive away readers.[71]

A few people commended Addams for "Patriotism and Pacifists in Wartime," but most responses were negative, even hostile. One letter writer said, "My dear Miss Addams, believe me, you are an awful ass, truly awful." In the minds of many, her speeches were now "unpatriotic and pro-German." The newspapers criticized her roundly, calling her unrealistic, foolish, and disloyal. According to Davis, "During the early months of the war she became the symbol for everything anti-American, the betrayer of her country, the antithesis of what she had stood for so many years."[72]

"Pacifism and Pacifists in War Time" was the last recorded anti-war speech Addams gave during the Progressive Era. As her former associates abandoned her, she felt isolated and worthless. Because Addams's audience had disappeared, she stopped receiving invitations to speak, and her usual publishers refused to print her work. She questioned herself and thought it was "unnatural" to hold opinions so out of line with those of the majority. For all of these reasons, Addams ceased discussing the war in public. When she discovered that she was being investigated by the Justice Department, she became even more wary.[73]

In March of 1918, Addams discovered a way to redeem herself. Herbert Hoover invited her to give a series of speeches on the topics of food production and conservation. This was a job that was perfectly suited to her interests and experience, and Addams joyfully threw herself into the work. According to Levine, "She toured thousands of miles between November of 1917 and May of 1918, making scores of speeches on food conservation." As she confided to Paul Kellogg,

"I am out here speaking for the Food Administration and thankful that there is something I can do."[74]

In "The World Food Supply and Woman's Obligation," Addams urged women to save and grow more food. This was a positive, active, life-giving activity that could not possibly be criticized as disloyal during wartime. Much to Addams's relief, she could plausibly regard her work as patriotic. The following passage reveals a great deal about Addams's motives: "From the time we were little children we have all of us, at moments at least, cherished overwhelming desires to be of use in the great world, to play a conscious part in its progress. The difficulty has always been in attaching our vague purposes to the routine of our daily living, in making a synthesis between our ambitions to cure the ills of the world on the one hand and the need to conform to household requirements on the other." The job of feeding hungry people allowed "world purpose" and "domestic routine" to coincide. What is more, this job was acceptable for women to perform in 1918, and it was perfectly consistent with Addams's lifework at Hull House and her saintly image.[75]

Addams began to repair her reputation by returning to the familiar routine of addressing meetings around the country. Unfortunately for Addams, she continued to face some criticism from the press. Ironically, she was also condemned by some of her pacifist colleagues for cooperating with the government. Although most of her listeners did not adulate her as before the war, she had an audience once again. People were willing to listen to Addams when the topic was food, not peace.[76]

In the first phase of her pacifist discourse, 1898–1909, Addams tried to create concern about imperialism and to focus the attention of the United States on pressing domestic concerns, which she defined as a "newer ideal of peace." From 1915 to 1917, however, Addams did not need to create concern for war, which was much more than a theoretical possibility. People were concerned, and they were paying attention to the European conflict. After the United States entered the fight, American audiences were even more attentive to issues of war and peace. Although Addams addressed the theoretical problems of war, her analysis was not as well developed as in the previous period. Instead, she strongly shifted the focus of her discourse to women's concerns. This was done in no small part because she headed the Woman's Peace Party and participated in conferences and meetings that were outlets for women's political activity. But, as I will demonstrate, Addams's attention to feminist themes went beyond mere audience adaptation. She was expressing bedrock convictions about the relationship between women and war.

THE PROBLEM OF WAR

In discussing the harms of the European conflict, Addams continued to advocate the more enlightened definition of patriotism that she had tried to popularize previously. Over thousands of years, Addams maintained, patriotism had evolved to mean more than blind loyalty to nationality. The newly evolved definition of patriotism contained "liberty as well as loyalty." However, with World War I, men marched off to battle under the more primitive meaning of patriotism. This degraded definition was "a tribal conception which ought to have left the world long since." The biggest problem with this regressive, tribal ideal of patriotism was that it excluded women, who had no meaningful place in a "world put back upon a basis of brute force—a world in which they can play no part." Thus, Addams deplored war because it repressed and marginalized women. Her objection to the male-centered definition of patriotism would not be out of place among recent feminist critiques of twenty-first century social institutions.[77]

Addams stated another feminist objection to the European war in 1915: "sensitiveness to human life so highly developed in women has been seriously injured by this war." Addams and her pacifist allies had persuaded themselves that war was virtually extinct: "Thousands of people in the United States and Europe had become so convinced that the sanctity of life was an accepted tenet of civilization that they deemed war had become forever impossible." Now, she had to admit, "That belief has been rudely overturned and we are now at the foot of the ladder, beginning again to establish the belief that human life is secured above all else that the planet contains."[78]

Addams did not assert that "women are better than men," but she posited that "there are things concerning which women are more sensitive than men, and that one of these is the treasuring of life." In a lengthy section, she analyzed the "five aspects concerning this sensitiveness, which war is rapidly destroying." According to Addams, the first aspect was "the protection of human life." Here she made a link to one of her cherished domestic reform efforts: reduction of infant mortality. Prior to 1914, progress was being made, but "All that effort has been scattered to the winds by the war. No one is now pretending to count the babies who are dying throughout the villages and countrysides of the warring nations." The second aspect of women's sensitiveness was the desire to "nurture . . . human life." Women cared for boys who later became soldiers, and "War overthrows not only the work of the mother, the nurse and the teacher, but at the same time ruthlessly destroys the very conception of the careful nurture of life." According to Addams, the third aspect of women's sensitiveness was "the fulfillment of human life." Mothers imagined their children growing into successful adults, "But no one in Europe in the face of war's destruction can consider any other fulfillment of life than a soldier's death." The fourth aspect of women's sensitiveness was "the conservation of human life; that which expresses itself in the state care of dependent children, in old age pensions, the sentiment which holds that every scrap of human life is so valuable that the human family cannot neglect the feeblest child without risking its own destruction." But war made it impossible to "cherish the aged and infirm. . . . Little children and aged people are dying, too; in some countries in the proportion of five to one soldier killed on the field; but the nation must remain indifferent to their suffering." The last aspect was "the ascent of human life." Addams claimed that women especially cherished "the hope that the next generation shall advance beyond the generation in which [one] lives." But, she averred, future generations in Europe faced bleak prospects.[79]

Although most of Addams's opposition to war stemmed from women's experiences, she did make a few pragmatic arguments against war that were based on expediency rather than principle. For example, at the Chicago Auditorium in 1915, she condemned war because it was wasteful and pointless. Addams cited a statistic that, on an average day, thousands of men were killed as a result of the two entrenched armies exchanging shots: "From the purely military standpoint[,] the situation [was] exactly the same as the day before, and yet two thousand young men had been killed, and had been sent out of life." Addams made another practical argument in January of 1916 when she opposed an expanded military in the United States because preparedness "increases the burdens of taxation for every country."[80]

BARRIERS TO PEACE

As she had done previously, Addams spent considerable effort in the second period analyzing the barriers that prevented peace. She continued to recognize that a major obstacle to peace was the attractiveness of war. Addams conceded the potential for glory, nobility, sacrifice, and just plain excitement caused by war. Her realism in admitting this belies the claims made by some that she was a hopeless idealist. At the Chicago Auditorium in 1915, she spoke longingly of the sense of common purpose engendered by war: "[M]en, women and children [are] united in a common cause and in a belief not only that they are defending the national ideals and those standards of life and conduct inaugurated for generations, but [they are] also brought together in that close community which self defense engenders. It is as if the consciousness of one person overflowed into the consciousness of another, so that one scarcely knew what belonged to himself and what to his fellow citizens. I think of course war is too high a price to pay for it, but I am almost ready to say that anything less is not too high a price to pay for it." Even in 1917, after the United States had entered the war, Addams continued to admit its appeal. War engendered "some of the noblest qualities of the human spirit" and "superb heroisms and sacrifices which we also greatly admire." Of course, once the United States became actively involved in the war, Addams had to avoid the impression of disloyalty. She was wise to praise the heroism and sacrifices of war, particularly in light of the controversy sparked by her remarks about bayonet charges. In sum, however, Addams recognized that a major barrier to peace was the fact that people loved war.[81]

A second barrier to peace concerned the perceptions of the warring nations. Both sides believed they were fighting to preserve cherished national values against an evil aggressor. At Carnegie Hall in 1915, Addams related her experiences meeting with government officials from nine different countries involved directly or indirectly in the war. Addams noticed that "everywhere one heard the same phrases. The identical phrases given as the causes and as the reasons for the war were heard everywhere. Each warring nation, I solemnly assure you, is fighting under the impulse of self defense." Because both sides viewed themselves as wronged victims of unwarranted aggression, it was unlikely that either side would initiate peace talks.[82]

Along the same lines, Addams claimed all of the warring parties said that "a nation at war cannot make negotiations, that a nation at war cannot even express a willingness to receive negotiations," or else "the enemy will at once construe it as a symptom of weakness." She repeated the comment nearly two weeks later in Chicago. In each nation, the government officials said the same thing: "A country at war can only go on fighting. It may not ask for negotiations." The combatants could not be the first to sue for peace because that looked like a surrender.[83]

A different kind of barrier to peace was the lack of communication between those who wanted peace within the belligerent nations. As she stated at Carnegie Hall, on both sides, "the longer the war went on, the more the military power was breaking down all of the safeguards of civil life and civil government." Foremost among these safeguards was freedom of speech. Invariably, said Addams, the warring nations instituted censorship. Groups of pacifists in Germany and England were not able to speak to each other. Thus, the pacifists "[a]t present . . . have no communication."[84]

Yet another barrier to peace was "the belief that it [militarism] can be crushed by a counter militarism." Addams called this idea "one of the greatest illusions which can possibly seize the human mind." She said it was "foolish to think that if militarism is an idea and an ideal, that it can be changed and crushed by counter militarism or by a bayonet charge." Thus, the present system of warfare to stop "militarism" was not a system that could work. Clearly, a new plan was needed.[85]

SOLUTIONS

According to Addams's analysis, warfare was inherent in the system that existed at the time, and peace would not come by itself. Therefore, something different needed to be done. Over the course of the second period, Addams proposed a number of solutions. Because circumstances changed quickly over this time, her proposals are perhaps not as consistent as in the first period. They ranged from the very abstract to the more precise, but at no time did she propose a plan with specific, legalistic language.

As was the case in the first period, Addams thought one of the keys to ending the war was changing society's conception of certain key terms. For example, she wanted to shift the public's perception of peace advocates from passive to active: "we pacifists, so far from passively wishing nothing to be done, contend on the contrary that this world crisis should be utilized for the creation of an international government able to make the necessary political and economic changes when they are due."[86]

In another attempt to alter public perception, Addams tried to redefine pacifists as brave rather than cowardly: "When as pacifists we urge a courageous venture into international ethics, which will require a fine valor as well as a high intelligence, we experience a sense of anti-climax when we are told that because we do not want war, we are so cowardly as to care for 'safety first,' that we place human life, physical life, above the great ideals of national righteousness." In Addams's estimation, being a pacifist took guts: "But surely that man is not without courage who, seeing that which is invisible to the majority of his fellow countrymen, still asserts his conviction and is ready to vindicate its spiritual value over against the world." If people would view pacifists as they really were, she maintained, they would see them as brave and admirable rather than cowardly and despicable.[87]

Addams also wanted to redefine pacifists as patriotic: "In reply to the old charge of lack of patriotism, we claim that we are patriotic from the historic viewpoint as well as by other standards." Before the war, said Addams, pacifists maintained that "the United States was especially qualified by her own particular experience to take the leadership in a peaceful organization of the world." Thus, the pacifists were American promoters and loyalists. They believed the United States was the best country to bring about peace. Moreover, they hoped that the rest of the world could be persuaded to adopt American principles of democracy and justice: "Stirred by enthusiasm over the great historical experiment of the United States, it seemed to us that American patriotism might rise to a supreme effort." Pacifists did not criticize their country. On the contrary, they held it up as a special beacon for the rest of the world. In addition, Addams pointed out, pacifists had agreed entirely with "the recognition of international obligation set forth by President Wilson as reasons for our participation in the great war." Far from being disloyal, pacifists simply concurred with the president.[88]

Overall, Addams thought that peace could come through genuine human understanding. If people could recognize each other's common humanity and learn to communicate, peace would result. Addams called for "some careful understanding, some human touch, if you please, in this over involved and over-talked-up situation." She believed that war could be ended "if the thing can be released instead of being fed and kept at the boiling pitch as it is all the time by outrages here and there and somewhere else."[89]

Addams was careful to keep her main solution for the war from becoming too specific. She advocated more of a general approach than a specific course of action. At Carnegie Hall, she recommended a panel of experts to consider the sources of conflict in Europe and to mediate solutions that would be fair to all involved. The warring nations, Addams advised, should "submit your case to a tribunal of fair minded men. If your cause is as good as you say it is, or you are sure it is, certainly those men will find the righteousness which adheres within it." This panel would make proposals to each of the governments as a starting point for negotiations.

Then, she asked rhetorically, if not naïvely, "Now that does not seem an impossible thing, does it?"[90]

Addams stated the essence of her plan quite clearly, and it had a strong rhetorical core: "We believe that reason and good will can settle any difficulty between any sets of men, whether they be groups of men or groups of nations." The key factor for Addams was to find disinterested, wise participants: "I think the best way is to have a commission appointed, composed of men of open minds, who will be able to deal with the matter in an open-minded way."[91]

As hope for a commission of impartial experts waned, Addams also advocated a conference of neutral countries that, "even if unofficial, could do two things. One was that there could be a public forum where these peace measures could be discussed—even though never carried out they could be discussed—and further it would bring the moral pressure of the neutral nations . . . and their influence might at least shorten the process of warfare." As Addams stated on 9 January 1916, a conference of neutrals might "begin to put forward measures approaching peace. No one expects them to end the war. The war must be ended by the accredited representatives of the governments, but a Conference of Neutrals may make it impossible that the war should end by the secret diplomacy with which it began."[92]

In order to end the war, Addams argued, women would need to act. This theme strongly carried over from the first period of her discourse. As she stated in "What War Is Destroying" (1915), if women were more sensitive than men in nurturing and valuing life, then "it is certainly true that this sensitiveness, developed in women, carries with it an obligation." Addams proposed to pass a resolution to "express that which is grounded in the souls of women all over the world." If the women of Europe got a strong, supportive message from their sisters in America, perhaps they would find the strength to stop the war. So, the instrument for stopping war was a "message from the women of America solemnly protesting against this sacrifice, that they may take courage to formulate their own." Addams's plan was based on rhetoric. She had faith in words to bring about change, first in the minds and hearts of other women, later in the entire world.[93]

FEASIBILITY

After showing the harms of war, identifying the obstacles to peace, and proposing some solutions, Addams then argued that her ideas would actually help end the violence. In part, she believed her proposals would work because she was fundamentally optimistic. Addams saw hopeful signs everywhere she looked during her tour of European countries. She believed peace could be achieved because both sides of the conflict had similar thoughts and attitudes; they were more alike than they realized. As Addams commented in Chicago, "my general experience in human nature is that nobody is altogether unlike anybody else." This line garnered a big ovation from the audience. The idea that people were fundamentally alike was a major premise of Addams's pacifist discourse, along with the concept that neither side was evil. This was the same perspective she had acquired through her experiences at Hull House. Addams viewed the war as tragic precisely because there was no clear-cut villain: "What is tragedy? It is not a conflict between good and evil. Tragedy from the time of Aeschylus has been the conflict between one good and another." In sum, Addams maintained, we cannot prefer one side to another on the basis of goodness. Both sides were good, and both worth saving.[94]

Addams consistently argued that the belligerents had much in common. For example, on the basis of her travels, she concluded that each country had a civilian group that feared the domination of society by the military. Because both England and Germany had pacifist groups that longed for a settlement, Addams saw this as an encouraging starting point for negotiations: "Now, that is something to work upon."[95]

Addams also held out hope for the future because of the generational differences between the young men called upon to do the fighting and the old men who made the decisions to fight. According to Addams, many (though not all) people said, "this was an old man's war; that the young men who were dying, the young men who were doing the fighting, were not the men who wanted the war, and were not the men who believed in the war." The older and middle-aged people had "established themselves and had convinced themselves that this was a righteous war," but the young people resented the fact that "young fellows have to do the fighting." Addams must have sensed this was a potentially explosive statement because she quickly added, "Now, this is a terrible indictment, and I admit that I cannot substantiate it. I can only give it to you as an impression."[96]

Addams provided examples from both sides to support her contention that many young men hated war. In one case, she described a German soldier who had been wounded and was dying of tuberculosis. The man believed he would be sent back to the trenches, where he thought he would die. He told Addams that "never during [combat] had he for once shot his gun in a way that could possibly hit another man. . . . That nothing in the world could make him kill another man. He could be ordered into the trenches; he could be ordered to go through the motions, but the last final act was in his own hands and with his own conscience." She also cited the example of "five young Germans" who "committed suicide" rather than be returned to the front, "not because they were afraid of being killed, but because they were afraid they might be put into a position where they would have to kill some one else." Addams concluded, "there are surprising numbers of young men and older men who will not do any fatal shooting."[97]

Addams claimed that young men from both sides did not believe in war as a means of settling disputes. They were living in an international world; they saw the interconnectedness of countries. They prized valuable worldwide exchanges in business, science, and literature. They shared global information from reading the newspapers. Said Addams, "That is what the younger men said—the world has become internationalized tremendously during the last twenty-five years." The older men did not share this appreciation for people being interconnected.[98]

As she had argued in the first period, Addams thought her plan would work because of the internationalism and cosmopolitanism of American immigrants living in great cities such as Chicago. Immigrants came from different nationalities and varying backgrounds, yet they opposed war as a solution for problems. This perspective, of course, came directly from her personal observations at Hull House. In Chicago, Addams observed, the immigrants "are beginning to ask, is this the way to attain the end? Is there not some other method, better fitted to the ends we seek than this method of warfare?" As she observed in testimony before the House Committee on Military Affairs, "Immigrants, simply because they represent all the nations, and simply because they are a cosmopolitan population, have already achieved an international understanding."[99]

Addams illustrated this point with a story from Hull House. In response to a question about introducing military training into the public schools, she was adamantly opposed: "I think that it is outrageous and that it is very much to be deplored. May I refer, in that connection, to an experience of ours at Hull House. We had a troop of Boy Scouts there, although instead of guns they had staves. The Russians, the Italians, and other immigrants who lived about us came to us and said, 'We did not come to America for this; this is what we came to America to get away from,' and we gave up the drilling because it gave the impression that we were standing for the sort of thing which is against American traditions." Addams suggested, ironically, that immigrants could see much clearer than native-born citizens how un-American militarism truly was. Addams explained that the foreign-born population of the United States would constitute a special advantage in negotiating peace: "our very composition would make it easier for us than for any other nation to establish an international organization." The immigrants "are a source of great strength in an international venture. . . . These ties of blood, binding us to all the nations of the earth, afford a unique equipment for a great international task if the United States could but push forward into the shifting area of internationalism."[100]

One of the main reasons Addams thought that negotiations for peace could be successful was because the belligerents expressed a willingness to work with a neutral country such as the United States. The warring parties stated they would be "glad to receive such service. Now, that came to us unequivocally." Europe trusted the United States because, "in the minds of many people," America provided "the nearest approach to a fair minded judge." In her 1916 House testimony, Addams told the congressmen that five of the neutral nations would participate in an international conference, "provided the United States came in."[101]

Finally, Addams suggested that mediation was a viable solution because logic dictated the war would inevitably end with negotiations, so why not begin them now and avoid the bloodshed and privation? She posed the question, "has not the time come for beginning some sort of negotiation? Is it not true that in the end some negotiation must take place? This war cannot go on forever—it is not conceivable that year after year it shall continue until exhaustion, financial and otherwise, shall end it. That moment will come at the end, and why cannot some sort of negotiation begin now." As she succinctly concluded, "Why not come to it early as well as late?"[102]

Addams answered a possible objection to her plan for peace. Critics scoffed that women were simply being foolish if they thought they could influence the course of the war. She maintained that her plan to have women intervene in the war was feasible, and she cited evidence to support her position. This was a steady theme through 1915 and 1916. At Carnegie Hall, she provided the example of one European official who encouraged women to become involved. When Addams remarked that it might seem "foolish" to have women making suggestions, the minister replied: "'Foolish? Not at all. These are the first sensible words that have been uttered in this room for ten months." Indeed, as she stated in Chicago, it was a woman's duty to intervene because no one could accuse her of cowardice: "This is what they [the ministers] all said: it seemed to them quite preeminently a woman's part. One said he had wondered many times why women had kept silent so long, because, as he said, women are not expected to fight and why could not they long ago have made some protest against war, which is denied to men?"[103]

OPPOSITION

One important difference between the first and second periods of Addams's pacifist discourse was that, in the latter period, she argued against war-related policies in the United States Congress. She opposed three major proposals in 1916: increased spending for military preparedness; an espionage bill that would restrict freedom of speech; and a conscription bill. The rhetorical process of opposition was different from the constructive arguments she made before, but Addams acquitted herself well. She crafted sound objections to proposed legislation and adapted her appeals to the congressmen in the audience. Addams was sensitive to the fact that she represented an unpopular view. In deference to her audience, she always expressed appreciation for being given a respectful hearing.

Addams continued to use classic argumentative approaches to oppose pro-military legislation. For instance, when she disagreed with increased military preparedness, she maintained that there was no need for elevated spending on arms because the United States was in no danger of attack from the European powers. If England and Germany engaged in a prolonged naval battle, which seemed likely, they would destroy each other. Therefore, Addams reasoned, the United States did not need more ships. In addition, England and Germany would be impoverished financially at the end of the war and would need to reduce their armaments. Thus, the United States did not need to increase its navy at the present time. Addams maintained Congress should wait for a real national threat "before we start to prepare for a hypothetical enemy who does not exist now and who may never exist."[104]

On 9 April 1917, Addams argued a proposed espionage bill would damage the United States because it violated freedom of speech and the "moral consent" of the American people. In making her case, she reasoned that the harms to cherished freedoms outweighed any supposed benefits of the bill. Addams averred, "I think to push our law ahead of the moral consent of the people, and make a law which would be against the moral impulse of a large number of people, would be a great detriment to the development of this country." Another harm of the espionage bill concerned the morale of the U.S. fighting men. She argued that soldiers would fight harder for the United States during wartime if the country preserved fundamental rights such as freedom of speech: "Of course, we are all anxious that this war, now that it has been declared, should be waged as a republic only can wage war, and that it should have in it those elements of moral sanction, the actual participation of a man's mind and spirit as well as his bodily presence in the ranks, which will cause the hastening of complete peace, and that can only come through the fullest discussion."[105]

ANALOGY

In the second period, Addams used few autobiographical anecdotes, metaphors, or other kinds of figurative language. By contrast, one of the most prominent rhetorical features from 1915 to 1917 was argument from analogy. This was consistent with her fundamentally logical approach to advocating peace. She used different types of analogies in the second period, including historical, domestic, and refutative.[106]

Addams looked to history to find a basis for arguing about the future. For example, in "What War Is Destroying" (1915), Addams asserted that, in the past, mothers were the ones who called a stop to sacrificing their children on the altar: "The women led a revolt against the hideous practice which had dogged the human race for centuries, not because they were founding a new religion, but because they were responding to their sensitiveness to life." If mothers caused human sacrifice to be halted in the past, Addams reasoned, then mothers could halt the sacrifice of their sons to the battlefields of Europe.[107]

Addams also looked to the past for proof that the peace movement would survive into the future. She noted that, for the past three hundred years, the "modern peace movement . . . has been kept alive throughout many great wars and during the present war." Pacifist groups had existed in countries around the world, even those at war. Because that was true in the past, it would likely be true in the future, particularly in America: "Surely the United States will be as tolerant to pacifists in time of war as those countries have been, some of which are fighting for their very existence."[108]

Because of her experiences in Europe with censorship, Addams predicted negative consequences in the United States if espionage legislation were to pass. For example, England had approved an espionage bill similar to the one being considered in the United States. When Addams attended "peace meetings" in England, "the men who took part in them said that technically those meetings could have been stopped. Since [then] such meetings have been stopped." Addams concluded if an espionage bill were passed in the United States, peace meetings would be prohibited, just as they had been in England.[109]

Along the same lines, Addams explained that Australia and Canada, which were similar to the United States, did not have a draft, even though they were fighting on behalf of England. The Australians rejected the draft in a referendum because "it was against the whole idea of democratic government," while the "Canadians have not even dared propose it, because they think it is so un-American." If opposing conscription was good policy in those countries, it was also good policy in the United States.[110]

On the other hand, when Addams referred to Prussia, she used it as a negative analogy. Prussia instituted the draft after the Napoleonic Wars. The Prussian army used conscription to train men for short periods of service. When the Great War did eventually come, Prussia had accumulated a large, highly trained army. Because President Wilson had declared the United States needed to combat Prussianism, the draft was an absurd way to do it: "Now, if we are going to fight Prussianism, if that is what we are fighting, . . . do not let us begin by taking the most offensive system of Prussianism and adopting it in this country." In sum, Addams argued, the Prussians had a draft; the Prussians started a war. Therefore, if we wanted to avoid acting like Prussians, we should not institute a draft.[111]

Domestic analogies were the most common type Addams used. These comparisons came from common, everyday life experiences. For Addams, many of these analogies originated from Hull House. At Carnegie Hall in 1915, for instance, she compared the international situation to squabbling children. A mother would separate two fighting children and insist they stop the cycle of hurt feelings and retaliation. If this was a good solution for a family, Addams reasoned, it would be a good solution for World War I. Similarly, if boys fought with each other in a social club at Hull House, the adult supervisor would say: "I won't go into the rights and wrongs of this; this thing must stop, because it leads nowhere and gets you nowhere." As she remarked at Chicago Auditorium, "great nations cannot conduct their operations from the standpoint of reprisals. That is not an admissible method of human life even among small groups, even among children."[112]

One analogy, which she used twice, referred to the death of a loved one. The death analogy conveyed to people untouched by the tragedy of war a small measure of the grief, helplessness, and emotional devastation caused by the European conflict. According to Addams, when Americans read about the slaughter overseas, "It is like hearing of a death by letter, which may stun you, but does not bring the same horror, the same poignancy, as though you stood by the bedside." In the same speech, she used a death analogy to explain why pacifists could not simply urge "peace" on the warring nations: "It is too much as if one went into a family in which there had been a death and reproached that family for something they had done or had not done which might have averted the calamity. It cannot be done. Your tongue cleaves to the roof of your mouth."[113]

Domestic analogy worked well for Addams because it allowed her to compare a familiar situation from the "woman's sphere" with the world outside the home. Domestic analogies were meaningful for Addams's frame of reference as well as for her predominately female audiences. The significance is deeper than this, however. Addams's entire way of thinking was one big analogy based in Hull House, which she saw as a microcosm for the larger world. If things worked a certain way at Hull House, she had faith that they could work that way on a larger scale, even an international one. She believed that people were basically good and basically the same, whatever the circumstances. This belief in consistency and similarity is why she used analogical reasoning so much in her anti-war discourse.

Addams was at her most formidable when she used analogy to refute the arguments of an opponent. In 1916, she clashed with Congressman Tilson over the validity of an analogy. Tilson attempted to argue that the United States should be prepared for war, even if there was no urgency at the present. He compared the need for an adequate national defense to the need for hospitals: "If everybody followed strictly the laws of heath and hygiene, I suppose we would not need hospitals, and yet you would not advocate that we stop building hospitals for that reason." Addams replied, "But I would not go out on an open prairie where there are no people who are ill and build a hospital. I should wait until there were sick people to move into a new hospital." This retort to Tilson explained perfectly why the United States should not spend more money on defense when there was no clear enemy and no pressing need for a larger military.[114]

In 1917, Addams tangled with Congressman Greene over a conscription analogy. During questioning, Greene claimed it would be pointless to draft an army that would always remain within the borders of the United States. To defend America, the military must be able to go outside the country and meet the enemy. Greene asked, "Then if there was a conflagration going on down the street and it was approaching your home, are you justified in going off your premises to blow up a building next to you in order that the fire may not reach you, and still call it protecting your home?" Addams replied, "I think that has nothing to do with conscription. If I was to conscript somebody to blow up the building—" At this point, Greene interrupted: "I am asking you about the term 'home defense' and not the means by which you do it." Addams retorted, "We are talking about conscription," to which Greene stated, "I understand, and it is for home defense." Addams responded: "And I quarrel with your figure. Of course I would save my home in any way I could, but your figure is that our house is going to burn if we do not blow up somebody else's house, and I do not believe that." Addams concluded, "I quarrel with your metaphor as not being analogous to the situation."[115]

EMOTIONAL APPEALS

Addams did not use emotional appeals to the extent that one would expect of an anti-war advocate. Certainly, a pacifist in 1915 might have manipulated the emotions of an audience through vivid depictions of torn bodies, ravaged cities, starvation, and disease, but Addams generally avoided this. Considering the huge controversy triggered by her off-the-cuff remarks about drunken bayonet charges, this was a wise policy. For the most part, she eschewed inflammatory materials after Carnegie Hall because she did not want another round of vilification and condemnation. However, her reticence to use emotional appeals was deeper than mere self-preservation.

Addams openly discussed her reluctance to use emotional appeals in her speeches. Simply put, she respected the awesome power of words. This was consistent with Addams's rhetorical interpretation of the nature of the war problem and how one would use language to bring about peace. Words were not something to be used lightly. As she stated at Carnegie Hall, "one is afraid to add one word that is not founded upon absolutely first-hand impressions and careful experience, because for the world one would not add a bit to this already overwhelming confusion." Ironically, she added: "And one does not come back . . . from these various warring countries with any desire . . . to let loose any more emotion upon the world." In sum, Addams feared that sensational reports or blatant emotional appeals could make it more difficult to bring about peace. In her analysis, emotion was the ally of the war mongers. Just as one could not use the force of arms to conquer militarism, one could not use heated emotions to overcome fighting.[116]

Despite her reservations about emotional appeals, she did use a few of them. The most notorious, of course, was her assertion that European soldiers needed to be drunk or drugged before they would undertake a bayonet charge. Nearly two weeks after that accusation, Addams relayed the story of a young French soldier who suggested that the army would "'squirt petroleum into the trenches on the other side so that everything will catch fire.'" When Addams expressed her horror, the man said, "'Yes, . . . but think of the [poison] gas!'" Another vivid example depicted the hardships of soldiers freezing in the Carpathian Mountains. A young woman "had given a concert to a little group of 69 men, and there were only 55 feet among those 69 men because their feet had been frozen in the long winter in the mountains."[117]

Significantly, Addams made a major exception to her reticence concerning emotional appeals. When she used pathos, it was most often directed to women. To some extent, this was a function of the fact that her audiences were predominately female. No doubt, Addams understood the types of appeals that would motivate women to work for peace. However, her selection of women as targets for emotional appeals also stemmed from her belief that they were not as excitable as men. Thus, women could be trusted with emotional appeals.

Addams conceded during her 1915 "Presidential Address," delivered at The Hague, that the peace movement may have failed because it was too rational. This was in contrast to her later statements about how dangerous emotions could be. Nonetheless, in analyzing why peace advocates had not enjoyed much success, Addams thought that too many appeals had been based on "reason and sense of justice. . . . Reason is only a part of the human endowment, emotion and deep-set radical impulses must be utilized as well, those primitive human urgings to foster life and to protect the helpless of which women were the earliest custodians."[118]

Addams tailored her emotional appeals to a mother's instinct to protect and aid her children: "They tell us that wounded lads lying in helpless pain and waiting too long for the field ambulance, call out constantly for their mothers, impotently beseeching them for help." She reminded the mothers of the world that they had raised their sons through sickness and adversity, and now their boys were being sent off to the slaughter. Such an appeal would likely motivate concerned mothers to agitate for peace.[119]

Another poignant emotional appeal concerned the conversations between wounded soldiers and their female nurses. Addams quoted a soldier who asked his nurse, "'Cannot the women do something about this war? Are you kind to us only when we are wounded?'" Men did not dare to speak to their fellows, claimed Addams, but they revealed their true feelings to the women who nursed them. When Addams constructed this particular appeal, she always gave the soldier some heartrending dialogue. The wounded man pleads with his nurse, who represents all of womankind: "'You are so good to us when we are wounded; you do everything in the world to make life possible and restore us: why do you not have a little pity for us when we are in the trenches, why do you not put forth a little of this same effort and this same tenderness to see what might be done to pull us out of these miserable places?'"[120]

Another common emotional appeal was the idea that men secretly blamed women for not stopping the war, because women could ask for an end to the fighting without being accused of cowardice. Addams read a letter from a young soldier: "'Ever since I have been in the trenches I have been wondering what is the matter with the women. . . . Why are they holding back?'" She warned her female listeners at The Hague that men would say "women refused to accept the challenge and in that moment of terror failed to assert clearly and courageously the sanctity of human life." Addams strove to make women feel guilty and to encourage them to save their men through political action.[121]

Gender differences played a role in Addams's attitude about using emotional appeals to advocate pacifism. During her 1916 House testimony, Addams stated that men were emotional: "I do not like to say that men are more emotional than women, but whenever I go to a national political convention and hear men cheering for a candidate for 1 hour and 15 minutes, it seems to me that perhaps men are somewhat emotional. I think the same thing is true in regard to this war; men feel the responsibility of defending the country and they feel that it is 'up to them' to protect the women and children, and therefore they are much more likely to catch this war spirit and respond to this panic." On the other hand, "Women are not quite so easily excited. They go on performing their daily tasks, in spite of hypothetical enemies, and they are not so easily alarmed." According to Addams, "A woman in the midst of household duties, occupied with the great affairs of birth and death, does not so quickly have her apprehensions aroused because possibly sometime, somewhere, somebody might attack the shores of the American Republic."[122]

Typically, Addams attributed the difference between the excitability between men and women to human evolution: "Perhaps our attitude indicates a survival of the old difference between the woman surrounded by a group of helpless children, who in case of supposed danger wants to move a little more slowly than the man who rushes out as soon as the bushes begin to move, quite convinced that an enemy is in ambush." Ironically, Addams characterized the (largely female) peace community as more calm and conservative, while the (male) military preparedness advocates were "quickly paralyzed with fear and rush into danger before they are quite sure that the danger is there."[123]

DEFENSIVENESS

One of the most noticeable differences between the first and second periods was the need for Addams to defend herself after 1915—an unprecedented position for her career. Redefinition, which was one of her main strategies for solving the problem of war, also functioned to defend her character against jingoistic accusers. Addams strove to define pacifism as brave, loyal, and patriotic rather than cowardly and disloyal. What her critics defined as negative, Addams defined as positive.[124]

In addition, Addams was forced to explain her connection with the Henry Ford peace ship, which proved to be a disaster. She declined to travel on the ship because of illness; nonetheless, she was criticized for associating with the enterprise. She disavowed Ford's project at the first annual Meeting of the Woman's Peace Party in 1916. The WPP was "grateful when Mr. Ford became interested in the idea of a conference of neutrals and expressed his willingness to further it." The "special peace ship" was his idea alone, however: "The Woman's Peace Party, as such, . . . had nothing whatever to do with the peace ship or with the slogans which became attached to it. But we did greatly admire Mr. Ford's energy and devotion and several of us regretted very much our inability to take part in the effort." Addams all but admitted Ford's effort was doomed from the start, but she rationalized it: "Personally, I am not afraid of failure in anything of this sort, because if you simply blaze the way and you lie down your bones are there and will tell other men which way you went. Then, perhaps you will be of some use."[125]

After her negative experiences with the bayonet charge remarks, Addams was quick to qualify her comments, especially during congressional testimony. She did not want to be misquoted or misconstrued. When she related something the pope had said to her, she swiftly added, "I do not mean that is the Pope's exact language; he does not use such informal language, but that is practically what he said, and that is what was said in substance everywhere we went." After commenting that men were quite emotional, she hastened to add that her comments were about "men in general," not, of course, about "the gentlemen of this committee whom, I am sure, are exceptions to any such unbalanced tendency."[126]

OPTIMISM

Throughout the second period, Addams still maintained a strong sense of optimism, a trait she also displayed in the first period. For example, at The Hague she predicted success for the resolutions passed by the conference participants: "We have formulated our message and given it to the world to heed when it will, confident that at last the great Court of International Opinion will pass righteous judgment upon all human affairs." At the Woman's Peace Party meeting in 1916 she stated, "Some of us believe that this informal conference . . . may perform the valuable social function of bringing open democratic discussion into international affairs." She was similarly optimistic during her 13 January 1916 congressional testimony concerning the war panic that was drawing the United States closer to entering the European conflict: "Indeed, it seems to be subsiding, even now. The papers are a little less vociferous about the necessity for the increase in the Army and Navy than they were six weeks ago."[127]

As was the case in the first period, Addams's discourse had a wistful quality. Her heartfelt longing for peace was reflected in her language. Regarding her hope that the American public would reject military conscription, she said: "Now I know that is exactly the kind of reaction we are going to get in America; at least, I should be awfully disappointed if men and women do not feel that way. I know thousands of them that will feel that way." But thousands hardly constituted a majority in the United States in 1917. She was thinking of thousands of pacifists, the people with whom she associated and spoke, but the world was larger than Hull House or the collections of pacifist organizations in which she dwelt.[128]

Conclusion

I have demonstrated that Addams's pacifist discourse falls into two distinguishable periods. Although these two periods differ in significant regards, there are also important continuities between them. For one thing, in both periods, Addams devoted a great deal of attention to analyzing the causes of war. This was an expression of her logical, systematic nature, but it was also the most salient issue. Why, indeed, was the present system incapable of delivering peace? If she could solve that puzzle, Addams believed that she could profoundly change the world.

In both periods, she admitted the powerful attraction of war, and in both periods, Addams thought that public perception was the main cause of conflict. As a consequence, she strove to redefine central terms such as "peace," "patriotism," and "pacifism." Addams believed that lack of communication, including the problem of censorship, was a major barrier to peace. Thus, she had faith in resolutions, in the power of words, to bring about change. Communication, Addams preached, was the key to genuine human understanding.

In both periods, Addams believed that immigrants and women would lead the world toward peace. Her work at Hull House, which revolved around women and immigrants, strongly influenced these perceptions. Indeed, almost every aspect of her discourse in both periods is grounded in the Chicago settlement house. Addams sought to expand the scope of Hull House from the home, to larger society, to the international domain. Hull House was the lens through which she viewed every problem, including war itself. If a solution worked there, Addams saw no reason why it would not work on a global level.

Clearly, gender played a central role in her rhetoric. Addams's discourse reflected women's concerns, and it was largely directed toward women. War was bad because of the special impact it had on women. Because of their gender, Addams argued, women had a special duty to oppose war. Moreover, she believed that men and women behaved in certain ways because of historical gender differences. When Addams employed emotional appeals, they were aimed at women's roles as caregivers, mothers, and nurturers. Interestingly, Addams openly analyzed how to break through women's reticence and apathy. When she argued that women had a special role to play in securing peace, at least part of her motivation may have been to establish a vocation for herself. Just as Ralph Waldo Emerson struggled to define his role as an American scholar, Addams worked ceaselessly to create and nurture a public arena where she could do her work.

Finally, optimism extended through both periods. No doubt, this personality trait enabled Addams to persevere in her pacifist efforts from 1898 to the end of her life. On a pragmatic level, though, optimism was an important leadership trait for her to possess. A strong sense of optimism helped Addams motivate her antiwar colleagues to continue in the face of overwhelming opposition. The converse of this rhetorical trait is a lack of negativism. Throughout both periods, there are only a few instances of Addams making negative predications about the future. Addams sought to inspire rather than discourage.

The first period (1898–1909) did have some distinctive characteristics. Primarily, Addams was actually *pro*-peace rather than *anti*-war. She framed her domestic reform efforts in terms of pacifism; however, the topic of war was almost a ruse to shift the public's attention to child labor or public sanitation. Addams knew the seductiveness of war, and she cast about for a means of tapping its appeal. Her real love (and competence, I might add) was still Hull House and its constituents. The reason Addams's "anti-war" discourse did not cause controversy prior to 1915 was because, to a large extent, it was not about overcoming war but rather about fostering peace through social justice. Moreover, her discourse had a pronounced sociological or "scientific" character; she was detached and scholarly in her approach. After 1915, however, she became tangled in a hot controversy and enraged the public by challenging conventional beliefs about duty, loyalty, patriotism, and proper behavior for a woman.

Several important themes from the first period do not extend into the second. First, references to Tolstoy almost disappear. Addams probably found his courtly, idiosyncratic, nineteenth-century philosophy increasingly less relevant to the nature of warfare and international politics in the twentieth century. Second, after numerous disappointments, Addams virtually stopped praising workers as the vanguard of the peace movement. She noticeably shifted her hopes from workingmen to women after 1915. Finally, she abandoned the concept of finding a moral substitute for war in the second period, probably because war was already raging in Europe. Finding a means of stopping a real war became more important than theorizing about a substitute for armed conflict.

In the period from 1915 to 1917, Addams began to see the limits of using rational discourse to solve problems. The circumstances of the second period were much more emotional for her. Thus, it was natural for Addams to use emotional appeals in her discourse, even though she mistrusted them and was reluctant to use them. In addition, in the second period, Addams was forced to adapt her discourse to changing events more so than before. In the first period, Addams almost exclusively proposed constructive measures for solving war and imperialism. Her ideas and activities were widely admired. After 1915, however, she argued against pro-war congressional legislation. The rhetorical posture of attack was unfamiliar, uncomfortable, and dangerous territory. Moreover, Addams was compelled to defend herself against attacks on her character. She had to answer charges that pacifists were cowardly and disloyal. Addams even had to apologize for Henry Ford's peace ship. As a result of these pressures, she ultimately became much more cautious in the second period. Addams carefully qualified all generalizations because she did not want to repeat another "bayonet charge" controversy.

Previous critics have concluded that Addams's discourse was fundamentally autobiographical and emotional. As I have demonstrated, these generalizations do not hold true for Addams's anti-war rhetoric from 1898 to 1917. She used autobiographical narrative in a limited way. Moreover, she used a surprisingly small number of emotional appeals, considering the subject matter. Without question, Addams employed examples from her experiences at Hull House, but most of them are not the poignant vignettes that Lasch described. I contend that Addams's analytical abilities deserve to be appreciated more they have been in the past. When Addams's discourse is studied as a whole, its strong logical character emerges. In both periods, Addams addressed issues of war and peace as a skilled debater. She showed that a problem existed, identified barriers that prevented the present system from solving the problem, proposed solutions, and argued that her solutions would work.

Finally, most commentators have undervalued the importance of rhetoric to Addams's pacifist efforts. Her life's work was, essentially, rhetorical. Not only did she convey her ideas through persuasive discourse, but she viewed the causes and solutions for war as rhetorical in nature. Addams did not believe that war sprang from material conditions, as a Marxist would. On the contrary, from 1898 to 1917 Addams argued that war was caused by bad thoughts and inappropriate words. Her method for ending war involved shifting focus, redefining terms, and trying to change perceptions. Beyond that, Addams excelled as a critic of the peace movement's own rhetoric. Much of her discourse analyzed why pacifist arguments had not worked in the past or why women were not motivated to speak out against war. Ironically, her rhetoric included a perceptive explanation for its own ineffectiveness with the general public. She criticized pacifist appeals of the past for being too "theoretical." Unfortunately for Addams, her own discourse fell prey to the same weakness.

Notes

1. Mary Lynn McCree Bryan, ed., *The Jane Addams Papers: A Comprehensive Guide* (Bloomington, Ind.: Indiana University Press, 1996), 95.
2. Ibid., 95–96; Fran Hassencahl, "Jane Addams," in *Women Public Speakers in the United States, 1800–1925*, ed. Karlyn Kohrs Campbell (Westport, Conn.: Greenwood Press, 1993), 7.
3. Allen F. Davis, *American Heroine: The Life and Legend of Jane Addams* (New York: Oxford University Press, 1973), 212–50.
4. Christopher Lasch, ed., *The Social Thought of Jane Addams* (Indianapolis: Bobbs-Merrill, 1965), xxvi, 22–23; Hassencahl, "Jane Addams," in *Women Public Speakers*, 7, 9; Delvenia Gail Shadwell, "A Rhetorical Analysis of Selected Speeches by Jane Addams" (Ph.D. diss., University of Illinois, 1967), 69–70, 128–30; Daniel Levine, *Jane Addams and the Liberal Tradition* (Madison, Wis.: State Historical Society of Wisconsin, 1971), 211. Also see Bryan, *Jane Addams Papers*, 95; Davis, *American Heroine*, 152.
5. Davis, *American Heroine*, 139–40.
6. Ibid.; speech of 20 December 1898, quoted in ibid.,140.
7. Davis, *American Heroine*, 141–43.

8. Shadwell, "Rhetorical Analysis," 77; Davis, *American Heroine*, 143; Jane Addams, "The Newer Ideals of Peace," *Chautauqua Assembly Herald*, 8 July 1902, Jane Addams Memorial Collection, the University of Illinois at Chicago (hereafter JAMC), 5; Addams, "The Newer Ideals of Peace," *Chautauqua Assembly*, 10 July 1902, JAMC, 6–7; Jane Addams, "Count Tolstoy," *Chautauqua Assembly Herald*, 11 July 1902, in Jane Addams, *Jane Addams on Peace, War, and International Understanding, 1899–1932*, ed. Allen F. Davis (New York: Garland, 1976), 26.

9. Shadwell, "Rhetorical Analysis," 37, 81, 83–84; Davis, *American Heroine*, 143; *Official Report of the Thirteenth Universal Peace Congress*, Boston, 3–8 October 1904, in *Jane Addams on Peace*, 44–50; Jane Addams, "New Ideals of Peace," *National Arbitration and Peace Congress Proceedings 1*, in *Jane Addams on Peace*, 51; Jane Addams, "The New Internationalism," *National Arbitration and Peace Congress Proceedings 1*, in *Jane Addams on Peace*, 56–59.

10. Jane Addams, *Newer Ideals of Peace* (New York: Macmillan, 1915).

11. Davis, American Heroine, 148–49; Theodore Roosevelt, as quoted in Davis, *American Heroine*, 148, 149; James Weber Linn, *Jane Addams: A Biography* (New York: D. Appleton-Century Co., 1935), 293–95.

12. Jane Addams, "Women's Special Training for Peacemaking," in *National Peace Congress, Proceedings* (1909), JAMC, 252–54.

13. Jane Addams, "Democracy or Militarism," in *The Chicago Liberty Meeting, Liberty Tracts, no. 1* (Chicago: Central Anti-imperialist League, 1899), JAMC, 39; Jane Addams, "Commercialism Disguised as Patriotism and Duty," *Saint Louis Post-Dispatch*, 18 February 1900, in *Jane Addams on Peace*, 16, 17. Also see Addams, "The Newer Ideals of Peace," 8 July 1902, JAMC, 5, for a similar argument.

    Addams's case for peace conformed to what is known in argumentation theory as the "stock issues model." For a discussion of this model, see David L. Vancil, *Rhetoric and Argumentation* (Boston: Allyn and Bacon, 1993), 62–73; George W. Ziegelmueller, Jack Kay, and Charles A. Dause, *Argumentation: Inquiry and Advocacy*, 2d ed. (Englewood Cliffs, N.J.: Prentice-Hall, 1990), 38–46.

14. Addams, "Democracy or Militarism," JAMC, 37, 39; also see Addams, "Commercialism," in *Jane Addams on Peace*, 15–16. Lasch commented perceptively on Addams's social-scientific approach: "Like other progressives, she wanted to substitute explanation and analysis for moral exhortation" (*Social Thought*, 124). For a discussion of Addams's central role in the development of sociology as a discipline, see Mary Jo Deegan, *Jane Addams and the Men of the Chicago School* (New Brunswick, N.J.: Transaction Books, 1988), 1–24.

15. Addams, "Democracy or Militarism," JAMC, 39.

16. Ibid., 37–38.

17. Ibid., 37.

18. Addams, "Democracy or Militarism," JAMC, 38; Jane Addams, "The Responsibilities and Duties of Women toward the Peace Movement," Universal Peace Congress, *Official Report* (1904), JAMC, 121–22.

19. Addams, "Democracy or Militarism," JAMC, 36, 38; Addams, "Commercialism," in *Jane Addams on Peace*, 16; Addams, "Responsibilities," JAMC, 121.

20. Addams, "Democracy or Militarism," JAMC, 38; Kenneth Burke, "The Rhetoric of Hitler's Battle," in *Readings in Rhetorical Criticism*, ed. Carl R. Burgchardt (State College, Penn.: Strata Publishing, 1994), 218.

21. Addams, "Commercialism," in *Jane Addams on Peace*, 17–18. Also see Addams, "Democracy or Militarism," JAMC, 38; Addams, "New Internationalism," in *Jane Addams on Peace*, 58.

22. Addams, "The Newer Ideals of Peace," 8 July 1902, JAMC, 5; Addams, "The Newer Ideals of Peace," 10 July 1902, JAMC, 6–7; Addams, "Responsibilities," JAMC, 120.

23. Addams, "Woman's Special Training for Peacemaking," JAMC, 253; Addams, "New Ideals of Peace," 51–52.

24. Addams, "New Ideals of Peace," 52, 53. Also see Addams, "Woman's Special Training for Peacemaking," JAMC, 252.

25. Addams, "Responsibilities," JAMC, 120; Addams, "Newer Ideals of Peace," 8 July 1902, JAMC, 5; Addams, "The Newer Ideals of Peace," 10 July 1902, JAMC, 6.

26. Addams, "The Newer Ideals of Peace," 8 July 1902, JAMC, 5.

27. Ibid.

28. Ibid.

29. "The Newer Ideals of Peace," 10 July 1902, JAMC, 6.

30. Addams, "Democracy or Militarism," JAMC, 36; Addams, "Responsibilities," JAMC, 121–22.

31. Addams, "Responsibilities," JAMC, 121. Also see Addams, "Democracy or Militarism," JAMC, 36.

32. Addams, "Responsibilities," JAMC, 122.

33. Addams, "The Newer Ideals of Peace," 10 July 1902, JAMC, 6–7. Also see Addams, "Responsibilities," JAMC, 122.

34. Addams, "The Newer Ideals of Peace," 10 July 1902, JAMC, 6–7.

35. Jane Addams, "Address of Miss Jane Addams [second speech]," *Official Report of the Thirteenth Universal Peace Congress,* Boston, 3–8 October 1904, in *Jane Addams on Peace,* 47; Addams, "New Internationalism," in *Jane Addams on Peace,* 58. Also see Addams, "New Ideals of Peace," 51.

36. Addams, "New Ideals of Peace," 54, 55.

37. Jane Addams, "Address of Miss Jane Addams [third speech]," *Official Report of the Thirteenth Universal Peace Congress,* Boston, 3–8 October 1904, in *Jane Addams on Peace,* 49.

38. Addams, "Democracy or Militarism," JAMC, 36–37, 38. Also see Addams, "Address of Miss Jane Addams [second speech]," in *Jane Addams on Peace,* 47.

39. Addams, "Address of Miss Jane Addams [second speech]," in *Jane Addams on Peace,* 47, 48.

40. Addams, "New Ideals of Peace," 53; Also see Addams, "Woman's Special Training for Peacemaking," JAMC, 253–54.

41. Addams, "Address of Miss Jane Addams [third speech]," in *Jane Addams on Peace,* 50. Also see Addams, "New Internationalism," in *Jane Addams on Peace,* 57.

42. Addams, "New Internationalism," in *Jane Addams on Peace,* 57, 58.

43. The first story, which was not autobiographical, involved an aristocratic Russian who had been imprisoned with a common criminal. The educated Russian was contemptuous toward his fellow convict until the man proved his extraordinary intellect by devising an escape. Then the lowly convict demonstrated his superior courage by helping a woman whose house was on fire, even though it resulted in his own recapture. The Russian aristocrat admitted that he would not have had the courage or generosity of spirit to help a fellow person in distress during an escape attempt. Addams spelled out the moral of the story. Said the Russian aristocrat, "I have a better trained mind, but that has nothing to do with human equality." According to Addams, false feelings of superiority came from misunderstanding and hatred (Addams, "The Newer Ideals of Peace," 8 July 1902, JAMC, 5).

    Another story that she repeated at least three times was also based in Russia. Addams related the plight of the Doukhobors, a religious sect that refused to fight. A young conscientious objector was brought before a sympathetic Russian judge, who asked the youth why he would not join the army. The young man answered that he was only following the teachings of Jesus. The judge agreed with him, in principle, but argued that, because of pragmatic difficulties, the time had not yet come to put the teachings of Jesus into practice. "The young man replied, 'The time may not have come for you, your honor, but the time has come for us.'" Addams used the tag line as a call to action for her audiences. In at least one of these speeches, the anecdote garnered an appreciative chuckle from the crowd (Addams, "Address of Miss Jane Addams [third speech]," in *Jane Addams on Peace,* 50. Also see Addams, "Newer Ideals of Peace," 10 July 1902, JAMC, 6–7; Jane Addams, "Chicago Auditorium Speech," 22 July 1915, stenographic transcription, 20, JAMC).

    Significantly, the Russian Doukhobor anecdote was one of the only times Addams referred to Jesus or Christianity in her anti-war discourse from the first period. Another Christian reference occurred in 1902 when she characterized Russia as "the land of the New Testament." She claimed that "many Russian peasants are doing the things they believe the New Testament bids them to do" (Addams, "Count Tolstoy," in *Jane Addams on Peace,* 26). Also see Jane Addams, "Count Tolstoy's Theory of Life," *Chautauqua Assembly Herald,* 14 July 1902, in *Jane Addams on Peace,* 34.

Addams also told an apocryphal story about a "London showman" who displayed two skulls that were reputed to be from the same man—Shakespeare. One of "Shakespeare's" skulls came from when he was a young, lawless poacher, and the other from when he was a successful playwright. The showman thought it more likely that Shakespeare was created twice (and thus had two separate heads) than that the same man could be so disparate in the same life. Again, this story probably evoked smiles and laughter from Addams's appreciative audience. The point of the anecdote was to demonstrate that societies, as well as people, could mature and evolve into a higher state (Addams, "Address of Miss Jane Addams [third speech]," in *Jane Addams on Peace,* 49).

A few other examples, such as Addams's description of Italian immigrant celebrations, could be construed as narrative (Addams, "Address of Miss Jane Addams [third speech]," in *Jane Addams on Peace,* 49–50). I excluded them because they were not vivid, well-developed stories.

44. The sewer-spade anecdote can be found in Addams, "Commercialism," in *Jane Addams on Peace,* 17–18. The little-girl story appears in Addams, "The Newer Ideals of Peace," 10 July 1902, JAMC, 7.

45. John C. Farrell, *Beloved Lady: A History of Jane Addams' Ideas on Reform and Peace* (Baltimore: Johns Hopkins University Press, 1967), 141–43; Linn, *Jane Addams,* 282–92; Addams, "Count Tolstoy," in *Jane Addams on Peace,* 31.

46. Addams, "Count Tolstoy," in *Jane Addams on Peace,* 26.

47. Ibid., 30; Addams, "Count Tolstoy's Theory of Life," in *Jane Addams on Peace,* 34, 41, 37.

48. Addams, "New Ideals of Peace," 55; Addams, "Woman's Special Training for Peacemaking," JAMC, 254.

49. Davis, *American Heroine,* 198, 211, 212–13.

50. Jane Addams, *Peace and Bread in Time of War* (1922; reprint, Silver Springs, Md.: NASW Classics Series, 1983), 7–10; Farrell, *Beloved Lady,* 151–52; Shadwell, "Rhetorical Analysis," 89–91; Jane Addams, "What War Is Destroying," in *Addresses Given at the Organization Conference of the Woman's Peace Party, Washington, D.C., January 10, 1915* (Chicago: Woman's Peace Party, [1915]), JAMC, 10; Levine, *Liberal Tradition,* 203; Davis, *American Heroine,* 217.

51. Levine, *Liberal Tradition,* 204, 206; Farrell, *Beloved Lady,* 153–54; Shadwell, "Rhetorical Analysis," 47; Davis, *American Heroine,* 217–19; Linn, *Jane Addams,* 303–5; Elizabeth Glendower Evans, as quoted in Davis, *American Heroine,* 220.

52. Jane Addams, "Presidential Address [at the International Congress of Women, The Hague, 1915]," in [Congress] *Report* (1915), JAMC, 19.

53. Farrell, *Beloved Lady,* 156–58; Levine, *Liberal Tradition,* 206–10; Shadwell, "Rhetorical Analysis," 48; Linn, *Jane Addams,* 305–7; Addams, as quoted in Davis, *American Heroine,* 220, 222.

54. Quoted in Davis, *American Heroine,* 222–24; *New York Times,* 6 July 1915, 8.

55. *New York Times,* 10 July 1915, 3; Farrell, *Beloved Lady,* 158–59; Davis, *American Heroine,* 224; Levine, *Liberal Tradition,* 212; Shadwell, "Rhetorical Analysis," 48–49, 93; Jane Addams, "Address of Miss Jane Addams Delivered at Carnegie Hall, Friday, July 9, 1915," stenographic transcription carbon, JAMC, 1.

56. Addams, "Carnegie Hall," JAMC, 28.

57. Addams, *Peace and Bread,* 135–37; quoted in Davis, *American Heroine,* 226, 229; *New York Times,* 13 July 1915, 10; Levine, *Liberal Tradition,* 212–213; Shadwell, "Rhetorical Analysis," 94; Davis, *American Heroine,* 226–28; Linn, *Jane Addams,* 313–15.

58. Addams, *Peace and Bread,* 137; Davis, *American Heroine,* 226, 241, 229.

59. Jane Addams, "Address by Jane Addams, Chicago Auditorium, July [22], 1915," stenographic transcription, JAMC, 2–3, 4, 9–10; Levine, *Liberal Tradition,* 213.

60. Addams, "Chicago Auditorium," JAMC, 18, 19.

61. Farrell, *Beloved Lady,* 163–65; Levine, *Liberal Tradition,* 213; Davis, *American Heroine,* 233–35.

62. Davis, *American Heroine*, 237–40; Shadwell, "Rhetorical Analysis," 51; Levine, *Liberal Tradition*, 214; Linn, *Jane Addams*, 316–17; Farrell, *Beloved Lady*, 165–67.

63. Jane Addams, "Address to the First Annual Meeting of the Woman's Peace Party," 9 January 1916, MSS., JAMC, 1–2.

64. Levine, *Liberal Tradition*, 216; Jane Addams, "Statement [on mediation] of Miss Jane Addams and Others," House Committee on Foreign Affairs, Commission for Enduring Peace. Hearings before the Committee on Foreign Affairs on H.R. 6921 and H.J. Res. 32, 11 January 1916, 64th Cong., 1st sess., 1916, JAMC. 3, 11, 14.

65. Shadwell, "Rhetorical Analysis," 96; *New York Times*, 14 January 1916, 5; Levine, *Liberal Tradition*, 216; Jane Addams, "Statement [on preparedness] of Miss Jane Addams, of Chicago, Ill., Representing the Woman's Peace Party," House Committee on Military Affairs, to Increase the Efficiency of the Military Establishment of the United States. Hearing before the Committee on Military Affairs, 13 January 1916, 64th Cong., 1st sess., 1916, JAMC, 3, 4, 6.

66. Levine, *Liberal Tradition*, 217; Addams, "Statement [on preparedness]," 7–15; quoted in Davis, *American Heroine*, 240.

67. Jane Addams, "Statement [on a Commission on Relations between the U.S. and the Orient] of Miss Jane Addams, of Chicago, Ill.," House Committee on Foreign Affairs, United States and the Orient. Hearings before the Committee on Foreign Affairs on H.R. 16661, 12 December 1916, 64th Cong., 2d sess., 1916, JAMC, 10–11.

68. Levine, *Liberal Tradition*, 218–19; Farrell, *Beloved Lady*, 168–69; Davis, *American Heroine*, 242–43; Shadwell, "Rhetorical Analysis," 53; Linn, *Jane Addams*, 325–26.

69. Levine, *Liberal Tradition*, 220; Jane Addams, "Statement [on the Espionage Bill] of Miss Jane Addams, of Chicago, Ill.," House Committee on the Judiciary, Espionage and Interference with Neutrality. Hearings before the Committee on the Judiciary on H.R. 291, April 9 and 12 1917, 65th Cong., 1st sess., 1917, JAMC, 51.

70. Addams, *Peace and Bread*, 109–11; Davis, *American Heroine*, 244–45; Levine, *Liberal Tradition*, 221; Jane Addams, "Patriotism and Pacifists in War Time," in *City Club [of Chicago] Bulletin*, 16 June 1917, JAMC, 184. 71. Davis, *American Heroine*, 245; Chicago Examiner, quoted in Davis, *American Heroine*, 245; *New York Times*, 11 June 1917, 2; Shadwell, "Rhetorical Analysis," 102; Levine, *Liberal Tradition*, 221; Farrell, *Beloved Lady*, 17–19.

72. Levine, *Liberal Tradition*, 221; Davis, *American Heroine*, 245–46; Farrell, *Beloved Lady*, 19, 172–73.

73. Davis, *American Heroine*, 247; Linn, *Jane Addams*, 332–34; Levine, *Liberal Tradition*, 222–23; Addams, *Bread and Peace*, 139–44.

74. Linn, *Jane Addams*, 335–37; Levine, *Liberal Tradition*, 224–25; Addams, as quoted in Davis, *American Heroine*, 247; Farrell, *Beloved Lady*, 177–81.

75. Jane Addams, "The World's Food Supply and Woman's Obligation," *General Federation of Women's Clubs, Biennial Convention Official Report* (1918), JAMC, 256, 258. Also see Jane Addams, "The World's Food and World Politics," *National Conference of Social Work, Proceedings* (1918), JAMC, 650–56; Jane Addams, "The Corn Mother," *World Tomorrow*, November 1918, in *Jane Addams on Peace*, 155–64.

76. Davis, *American Heroine*, 249–50.

77. Addams, "What War Is Destroying," JAMC, 10.

78. Ibid.

79. Ibid., 10, 11.

80. Addams, "Chicago Auditorium," JAMC, 15; Addams, "Statement [on preparedness]," JAMC, 4.

81. Addams, "Chicago Auditorium," JAMC, 4; Addams, "Patriotism and Pacifists in War Time," JAMC, 184. Also see Addams, "Statement [on preparedness]," JAMC, 13.

82. Addams, "Carnegie Hall," JAMC, 5. Also see Addams, "Chicago Auditorium," JAMC, 5; Addams, "Statement [on preparedness]," JAMC, 5–6; and Jane Addams, "Statement [on conscription] of Miss Jane Addams, Hull House, Chicago, Ill.," House Committee on Military Affairs, Volunteer and Conscription System. Hearings before the Committee on Military Affairs, 14 April 1917, 65th Cong., 1st sess., 1917, JAMC, 22.

83. Addams, "Carnegie Hall," JAMC, 6-7; Addams, "Chicago Auditorium," in JAMC, 12. Also see Addams, "Statement [on mediation]," JAMC, 16.

84. Addams, "Carnegie Hall," JAMC, 9, 12. See also Addams, "Chicago Auditorium," JAMC, 5–6.
85. Addams, "Carnegie Hall," JAMC, 27, 28. See also Addams, "Chicago Auditorium," JAMC, 14.
86. Addams, "Patriotism and Pacifists in War Time," JAMC, 185.
87. Ibid., 190.
88. Ibid., 185, 186, 188.
89. Addams, "Carnegie Hall," JAMC, 1, 25.
90. Ibid., 21, 30, 24. See also Addams, "Chicago Auditorium," JAMC, 22; Addams, "Statement [on the U.S. and the Orient]," JAMC, 10.
91. Addams, "Statement [on the U.S. and the Orient]," JAMC, 10, 12.
92. Addams, "Statement [on mediation]," JAMC, 14; Addams, "First Annual Meeting," JAMC, 4.
93. Addams, "What War Is Destroying," JAMC, 11, 12.
94. Addams, "Chicago Auditorium," JAMC, 13, 9.
95. Addams, "Carnegie Hall," JAMC, 13.
96. Ibid., 13, 14.
97. Ibid., 15–16.
98. Addams, "Chicago Auditorium," JAMC, 7, 8.
99. Ibid., 16; Addams, "Statement [on preparedness]," JAMC, 4.
100. Addams, "Statement [on preparedness]," JAMC, 12; Addams, "Patriotism and Pacifists in War Time," JAMC, 187.
101. Addams, "Carnegie Hall," JAMC, 7; Addams, "Chicago Auditorium," JAMC, 17; Addams, "Statement [on mediation]," JAMC, 15; Addams, "First Annual Meeting," JAMC, 1.
102. Addams, "Chicago Auditorium," JAMC, 11, 15.
103. Addams, "Carnegie Hall," JAMC, 27; Addams, "Chicago Auditorium," JAMC, 13. Also see Addams, "Statement [on mediation]," JAMC, 17–18; Addams, "First Annual Meeting," JAMC, 1.
104. Addams, "Statement [on preparedness]," JAMC, 4–5.
105. Addams, "Statement [on the Espionage Bill]," JAMC, 52. On another occasion, Addams objected to a conscription bill because of dire, unintended consequences. In her estimation, the draft would result in civil disorder: "you are going to have draft riots and all sorts of things like that" (Addams, "Statement [on conscription]," JAMC, 21).
106. According to Vancil, "we argue in an analogy that if two cases resemble each other in essential points, whatever is true of case one will be true of case two" (*Rhetoric and Argumentation*, 138).

In the first period, Addams used relatively little autobiographical narrative. In the second period, she employed vivid, well-developed stories even less: a total of three anecdotes, and only two were autobiographical. She had used one before: the story of the Doukhobors and the young man who faced the Russian judge (Addams, "Chicago Auditorium," JAMC, 20). The second story, already discussed, was about the Boy Scout troop at Hull House that imitated soldiers by training with staves instead of guns (Addams, "Statement [on preparedness]," JAMC, 12). The final anecdote, which was also covered previously, told the story of the German solider with tuberculosis who refused to shoot enemy soldiers (Addams, "Carnegie Hall," JAMC, 14–15). Each one of these narratives had a moral that supported her case for pacifism. One could make an argument that other examples constitute "narrative." However, considering the total amount of discourse for this three-year period, autobiographical narrative was clearly not a driving force in her anti-war rhetoric from this era.

Similarly, Addams used relatively few metaphors, although she employed more than in the first period. Interestingly, her metaphors fell into three categories: water, disease, and insanity. She used water metaphors in several speeches. At Chicago, Addams declared, "It seems impossible that the wave of patriotism has held high so long" (Addams, "Chicago Auditorium," JAMC, 16). In "Patriotism and Pacifists in Wartime," Addams alluded to a "wave of tremendous enthusiasm" and a "high sea of patriotic feeling" (Addams, "Patriotism and Pacifists in War Time," JAMC, 184). At Carnegie Hall, Addams said, "This fanatic feeling which is so high in every country, and which is so fine in every country cannot last. The wave will come down of course. The crest cannot be held indefinitely" (Addams, "Carnegie Hall," JAMC, 26). In these cases, water represented a colossal disaster. The tidal wave was a kind of unthinking, powerful impulse that swept all before it. She viewed the hysterical patriotism of the United States prior to World War I in precisely this way. It was an irresistible, violent force that swept away reason.

The most prominent negative metaphor Addams used was to characterize war as a disease, a "war contagion," that spread rapidly like an epidemic. Addams feared America would "become infected with the militaristic spirit" (Addams, "Statement [on preparedness]," JAMC, 10). In her statement opposing conscription, she combined a disease metaphor with an attack on imitation. She condemned "this curious war contagion which is going on all over the country and this queer imitation we are making of being like Europe and doing everything they do" (Addams, "Statement [on conscription]," JAMC, 21). She viewed imitation as a malicious spirit that had the unhealthy propensity to spread (Addams, "Statement [on the Espionage Bill]," JAMC, 51).

Addams also characterized war as a kind of insanity or panic. As she stated in January of 1916, the country was experiencing a "war contagion and panic," but, Addams felt "your constituencies will thank you later if you withstand such a panic." To underscore this notion of panic, she told the story of a man in Kansas who was so frightened by burglaries in New York City that he "armed himself against the advent of burglars, although there were none in Kansas. . . . His panic would be purely subjective and the result of what he read was happening elsewhere" (Addams, "Statement [on preparedness]," JAMC, 14, 3,).

107. Addams, "What War Is Destroying," JAMC, 11–12.
108. Addams, "Patriotism and Pacifists in War Time," JAMC, 184.
109. Addams, "Statement [on the Espionage Bill]," JAMC, 52.
110. Addams, "Statement [on conscription]," JAMC, 20.
111. Ibid., 21.
112. Addams, "Carnegie Hall," JAMC, 24–25; Addams, "Chicago Auditorium," JAMC, 21.
113. Addams, "Chicago Auditorium," JAMC, 18, 1.
114. Addams, "Statement [on preparedness]," JAMC, 14.
115. Addams, "Statement [on conscription]," JAMC, 22.
116. Addams, "Carnegie Hall," JAMC, 1. Also see Addams, "Chicago Auditorium," JAMC, 1.
117. Addams, "Chicago Auditorium," JAMC, 20–21, 10. Also see references to dead babies in Addams, "What War Is Destroying," JAMC, 11.
118. Addams, "Presidential Address," JAMC, 21.
119. Ibid.; Addams, "Carnegie Hall," JAMC, 20. Also see Addams, "Chicago Auditorium," JAMC, 16.
120. Addams, "Presidential Address," JAMC, 21; Addams, "Carnegie Hall," JAMC, 20.
121. Addams, "Chicago Auditorium," JAMC, 9; Addams, "Presidential Address," JAMC, 22.
122. Addams, "Statement [on preparedness]," JAMC, 5.
123. Ibid., 6-7.
124. In the classical stasis system, this is the issue of "definition." See Vancil, *Rhetoric and Argumentation*, 55–59.
125. Addams, "First Annual Meeting," JAMC, 2; Addams, "Statement [on mediation]," in JAMC, 17.
126. Addams, "Statement [on mediation]," JAMC, 18; Addams, "Statement [on preparedness]," JAMC, 7.
127. Addams, "Presidential Address," JAMC, 22; Addams, "First Annual Meeting," JAMC, 5; Addams, "Statement [on preparedness]," JAMC, 6. See also Addams, "Carnegie Hall," JAMC, 26, where she predicted that fanatic feelings could not stay high forever.
128. Addams, "Statement [on conscription]," JAMC, 20.

Charlotte Perkins Gilman, Progressivism, and Feminism, 1890–1935

Judith A. Allen

> *It is hard to be progressive, but glorious.*
>
> CHARLOTTE PERKINS GILMAN, "The Women Who Won't Move Forward," 1914

> *She never says a dull thing, but her satire is so keen it spares no one and the play of it is like the needle spray of ice water. She is slender, dark, alert. Her eyes are full of humor, her mouth indicative of sympathy. Her hair is jet black and is worn coiled neatly on her neck, letting the splendid curves of her head reveal themselves . . . her great grandfather was Lyman Beecher, her kinspeople Henry Ward Beecher and Harriet Beecher Stowe. On the other hand, the New England Perkins were splendid stock, fighters and orators from protectorate days in old England.*
>
> "WOMEN," *Chicago Journal*, 29 December 1898

12

The American public first encountered Charlotte Perkins Gilman (1860–1935) as a serious lecturer on "the great issues of the day." Reports on her lectures appeared regularly in major and minor newspapers, especially from the turn of the twentieth century until the mid-1920s.[1] Her Yankee abolitionist pedigree figured in many commentaries on her qualifications to adopt the unusual profession of *woman* preacher and podium speaker.[2] Reviewing her early career, a journalist recalled the incident propelling her to national attention. In San Francisco in 1890, she spoke about dress reform and women's health. Dramatizing the horrors of tight-lacing corsets—prescribed fashion for white women of her class—on a stage decorated with a statue of Venus de Milo and a tailor's dummy, she produced an illustration of a racehorse with a corset around its middle: "The whole bulk of the animal's middle body was squeezed into a narrow space within which no breath could possibly penetrate, while the outraged flesh bulged out at both the forequarters and hind quarters in a manner ludicrous beyond description. The audience recognized instantly the telling satire and roared its applause and Charlotte Perkins, then Mrs. Stetson, was a made woman. Newspapers east, west, north and south copied the picture and those who saw it never forgot it or Mrs. Stetson. How we did laugh at that horse laced up in a corset!"[3]

Gilman's prolific body of speeches and publications founded her reputation as the most important feminist theorist of the Progressive Era, "the Veblen of the women's movement."[4] Her biographer, Mary Armfield Hill, describes her as a "brilliant theorist for the women's movement, a charismatic 'new woman' lecturer and writer," while Alice Rossi identified her as "the leading intellectual of the women's movement during the first two decades of the twentieth century."[5] Widely praised as the movement's greatest mind, feminist contemporaries such as Alice Stone

Blackwell wrote her: "You have more gray matter inside your head than all these critics put together."[6]

Contemporary scholars also acclaim Gilman as the most important feminist theorist in turn-of-the-century America, noting her international recognition in her own lifetime. Her published works won critical acclaim throughout Europe and the British Empire, while translations reached Asia, Africa, and the Middle East. Between 1883 and 1935 she wrote verse, short stories, novels, and plays amounting to some 683 fiction items, as well as 1,580 extant nonfiction books, articles, and lectures.[7] Her autobiography was published posthumously in 1935.[8] Moreover, her estate included scores of unpublished lectures, sermons, and informal talks through which she supported herself.

Gilman's motivation in social reform was to prove "that a woman can love and work too," touching feminists of her own generation and after.[9] Criticizing women's economic dependence on men (at least in her own race and class), she concentrated on issues related to marriage, prostitution, and reproduction. Her concerns included the poor and inefficient state of household work, motherhood and childbearing, and unsafe, unhygienically designed homes, towns, and cities.

Appalled at the hyper-femininity of women raised to secure their living from men through sexual relations, Gilman presented prostitutes as the most extreme case, highlighting the venereal diseases, birth defects, and marital unhappiness attending men's nonmonogamy. Appropriating the word "androcentrism" for feminist analysis, she proposed a theory of women's subordination by men at once consistent with evolutionary theory yet justifying change. Increasingly, she addressed global population characteristics, intervening into debates over immigration restrictions (which she favored), eugenics, and the place of overpopulation in the genesis of war. She located birth control as more a pacifist than a feminist imperative. Her significant contribution to rhetorical history resides in her embrace of Progressive Era imperialism and reform through the lens of fin de siècle feminism.

Studying Gilman's spoken and written feminist discourse permits an evaluation of the relationship between the terms "progressivism" and "feminism" at this historiographically revisionist moment. A survey of prevailing commentary on her extensive oeuvre is in order. The existing scholarly focus on only a small sampling of her fiction writing—itself only a third of her published legacy—to the relative neglect of her nonfiction invites explanation. A turn to this so-far understudied Gilman work is overdue.[10]

The material conditions for her performance as a Progressive Era public intellectual repay examination. Lecturing subsidized her extensive publishing career, and she left rich logistical and financial records. Through her 1897–1900 letters to her cousin, George Houghton Gilman (1867–1932), soon to be her fiancé, then husband, a candid and often painful picture emerges of the challenges facing a woman having the temerity to take to podium and lectern throughout America. She experienced both elation and vulnerability in establishing herself as a public figure, especially through proposals she advanced for reforming prevailing relations of the sexes.

Analysis of her lectures identifies Gilman's abiding preoccupations and rhetorical strategies. Speech bore a direct relationship to her publications, especially those concerned with sexuality and its hypothesized links with species decay, racial theoretics, and eugenics. Her anxieties about these matters recurred in her discussion of birth control, woman suffrage, home, work, fashion, childbearing, immigration policy, and city planning. Her rhetorical rereading of social Darwinism strategically articulated her concerns. Integrating feminism and reform Darwinism resulted in distinctly "Gilmanesque" animal analogies. The category of "race" was important too in her analyses. Finally, her interventions on prostitution, birth control, and immigration—three quintessentially Progressive Era preoccupations—illuminate rhetorical links between feminism and progressivism.

Writing about Progressivism, Feminism, and Gilman

Revisionist scholarship in American studies and history has profound implications for evaluating Gilman's public rhetoric between 1883 and 1935. With critical interrogation of such Progressives as Theodore Roosevelt and Frederick Jackson Turner, the racism and imperialism of key Progressives has eroded faith in the term "Progressive" itself.[11] Some argue that because of its imprecision and "tangle of factors involved with the term, it has become meaningless and clear definition impossible."[12] Yet even before the loss of faith in the term "Progressive," few insights emerged about women Progressives such as Jane Addams (1860–1935), Gilman's exact contemporary.[13] Feminism received scant mention in the classic texts of progressive history.[14] Even in newer texts, feminism receives only passing mention, forbidding any conclusion that feminism was central to progressive political philosophy. Today's social and cultural historians have continued their predecessors' marginalization of Progressive Era feminism.[15] Most mentions of Gilman concentrate on her classic treatise *Women and Economics* (1898), which at the time Jane Addams described as "simply brilliant."[16]

Was American feminism between 1890 and 1920 "progressive"? Is writing feminism into histories of progressivism important, when it is absent due to sexism, misogyny, and gender blindness—intellectual and methodological flaws that together imperil the accuracy and comprehensiveness of all historical accounts? Alternatively, if feminism is marginal within existing histories, does this indict the category "progressivism"? Put differently, if the inattention to Progressive Era feminism passes unlamented, without delegitimizing this whole subfield of American historiography, is this the more significant problem to address? Should scholars again "add women and stir," embracing the remedialism that has been a hallmark of a quarter of a century of feminist disciplinary scholarship?[17] Such work, too, often, has added substantial new knowledge without necessarily interrogating the causes of the need for this new addition in the first place.[18] Speaking of women's history, as Kay Daniels wrote in 1977, it is not as if women somehow, accidentally, slipped out between the grids of historical intelligibility.[19] Rather, the methods, procedures, privileged evidence, and criteria of historical significance adopted by the discipline eliminated a focus on half of humanity, whatever their race, ethnicity, or class.

Historiographical revisionism has posed penetrating new questions related to Progressive Era race relations, ethnicity, aboriginality, class, region, population patterns, urbanization, religion, nativism, American exceptionalism, sexuality, and cultural imperialism.[20] Still, the question remains: what is the significance of feminism for defining progressivism itself? "Progressive" involves both periodization and characterization, but is its characterization premised upon the exclusion of the gendered analysis impelled by feminism?[21] Would integration of feminism alter the meaning of "progressive"?

If analysis of Gilman's rhetorical relation to progressivism poses these questions for "mainstream" accounts, it raises different questions for the history of American feminism. Can historians of feminism benefit from designating figures such as Gilman as "feminist Progressives" or "progressive feminists"? Was there a variety of feminism belonging to the Progressive Era, distinct from Gilded Age feminism on the one hand, and that between the two world wars on the other? While there is no lack of studies of women's campaigns, feminism, and feminists set within these periods, usually their authors do not anchor or interpellate feminism within these conventional eras of American history.[22] Yet neither have prevailing histories of feminism in the period 1875–1939 proposed new feminism-specific periodizations, unbound by such historicist cages as "the Gilded Age" and "the Progressive Era." Existing work suggests that, for prominent historians of American feminism, conventional periodizations have offered little analytic purchase, while alternative chronologies have been of less pressing priority than other projects.

Gilman's contemporary fame did not last. By 1956, Carl Degler described her as forgotten, thereby diminishing our understanding of historical developments in her era.[23] Although Degler focused principally on her two most important nonfiction texts, *Women and Economics* (1898) and *The Man-Made World, or Our Androcentric Culture* (1911), subsequent scrutiny has not followed this focus. There have been three strands in Gilman scholarship.

The first is the biographical strand. Its exponents concern themselves principally with the facts of her life, either in relation to her fiction writing or to illustrate the conflicts, constraints, and pressures facing American women in the Gilded Age. A striking feature of the biographical focus is the disinterest of most of its scholars in Gilman's later life. Gilman in her twenties, subjected to Dr. Silas Weir Mitchell's "rest cure" and author of its chilling fictionalization, "The Yellow Wallpaper," mesmerizes scholars of Gilman as (white) American woman.[24] Two historians have contributed biographies—Ann J. Lane and Mary Armfield Hill—among biographical essayists mainly literary in orientation. The result is a relative neglect of Gilman's rhetorical context. Several kinds of context are relevant. Comparison of Gilman's feminism with other United States feminists of her period is one critical framework, while another is her location within international feminism, 1870–1930. The absence of this latter frame has limited the effectiveness of existing work, needlessly producing parochial analysis.[25]

Reducing Gilman's feminism to biographical factors is problematic. While many women faced comparable situations, upbringing, and resource constraints, few became feminists. The diversity of feminist backgrounds resists simple biographical causality.[26] Few scholars have resisted the somewhat heroic retelling of Gilman's own account of her life as the genealogy of her feminism: the deserting New England father; the repressed and controlling mother; the loss of homosocial love, Martha Luther, to marriage; the disastrous marriage to romantic young artist Charles Walter Stetson; childbirth, mental breakdown, separation, divorce, and personal experiments in between; her later, happy remarriage to her thirty-three-year-old cousin when she was forty, permitting pursuit of both work and love and, according to some scholars, "healing."[27] In this retelling, the "rest cure" unleashes the victim/heroine's path to independence and feminism.

The second strand of Gilman scholarship is grounded in feminist literary criticism, most addressing "The Yellow Wallpaper," written in 1890 and published in the *New England Magazine* in 1892.[28] The extraordinary significance accorded to this thirteen-page story itself invites analysis.[29] Recently, more feminist literary criticism addresses her utopian novel, *Herland* (1915), first serialized in her monthly journal, *The Forerunner*, across 1915.[30] Moreover, her 1890s short stories and novellas are receiving increasing attention, particularly her "Gothic," critique-of-marriage stories and other utopian/futuristic novels foreshadowing *Herland*.[31] Literary scholarship has been selective, even though literary critics dominate among authors of work on Gilman. Other Gilman fiction attracting critical attention spans either end of her writing career: her poetry anthology of 1893, *In This Our World*, and one of her final previously unpublished novels, a murder mystery entitled *Unpunished*, completed in 1929.[32] Occasionally, literary critics have delved intertextually into her nonfiction, to illuminate concerns of the literary Gilman. Even those literary scholars seeking greater context than textual analysis alone can yield, however, often situate her in relation to other literary figures.[33]

Despite the focus on the literary Gilman, Gilman herself contended that she had neither literary skill nor any passion for "art for art's sake." Always, her fictional purpose was didactic: the message was the point.[34] Professional literary critics have ignored this self-assessment, concentrating upon her genres, rhetoric, language, composition, and creative characteristics as a writer. Her fiction receives diverse interpretation in the hands of critics with allegiances ranging from Lacanian psychoanalysis through postmodernism, antiracism, and queer theory.

The third, and much less developed, trajectory in Gilman scholarship involves close analysis of her nonfiction theoretical and political writing. Such analysis has been offered by anthologizers of Gilman's writings, and to some degree by her three principal biographers.[35] Analysis of her feminist theory appears in journal articles or anthology chapters on particular themes—race, class, social Darwinism, eugenics, social science, ethics, history of philosophy, utopian and dystopian thought, theology, religion, architecture, and town planning.[36] Philosophers, sociologists, theologians, historians, economists, and urban studies and American studies scholars inhabit the sparser field of Gilman *nonfiction* analysis. Discussions turn upon the way a selected Gilman text (or group of texts) relevant to their scholars' disciplines illuminates a particular issue, in relation to other thinkers on the same topic.[37] For the figure dubbed America's most significant "first wave" feminist theorist, there is surprisingly little commentary and analysis of her theoretical and other nonfiction writing.

Most Gilman scholars have also been feminist scholars. Arguably, Gilman's nonfiction often expounded themes at least problematic, if not wholly anathema, to modern feminist ethics. While these themes, concerning race, ethnicity, religion, social Darwinism, eugenics, sexuality, contraception, abortion, "Americanism," immigration, class, policing, and urban life, are present in her fiction, their purchase may seem muted relative to her strident nonfiction formulations. The historical preeminence of literary critics among the founders of women's studies and feminist scholarship in the United States—indeed the "foundational" role of "The Yellow Wallpaper" in launching 1970s (white) feminist literary criticism in the United States—preordained the focus on the literary Gilman, even her canonization.[38] Meanwhile, the more that emerged about her nonfiction, the less congenial to late-twentieth-century concerns did the hitherto admirable and prescient Gilman seem. If she was a feminist, then the overlay of Progressive Era concerns alienated later feminist scholars. Gilman's nonfiction anchors the analysis of the progressivism-feminism connection.

What were the key strands of Gilman's nonfiction? Theoretical works on what she called the sociological, scientific, economic, and ethical issues of the day numbered six separately published and several more serialized books, a formidable output by any reckoning. Additionally, she wrote hundreds of articles, not only published within the journals she edited—*The Impress* (1894–95) and *The Forerunner* (1909–16)—but also within popular, political, scholarly, professional, and other special-interest journals, magazines, newspapers, and newsletters. She published the first of these in 1883, when she was twenty-three, on the topic of women and physical fitness; and the last, on the right to suicide of the terminally ill, in 1935, the year she died at the age of seventy five.[39] Most of her nonfiction publications began as lectures. An important corollary of their spoken origins was this: for the era's most profound critic of women's enforced economic dependency, these lectures were her livelihood.

On the Lecture Circuit

Mrs. Stetson is a most brilliant and effective platform speaker. She speaks as she thinks, clearly, concisely, and in a perfectly straightforward and simple manner, but her utterances are always striking and she never fails to rivet the attention of her hearers. Last season she made a tour of the south and aroused more interest than any lecturer upon similar subjects has created in that section for years and her addresses in England last summer before the International Congress of Women and elsewhere attracted favorable notice from the best public in London . . . her gift of ready and eloquent speech seems inborn . . . developed by incessant labor.

—*Oakland Enquirer*, 1900

For Gilman, the personal crisis of "getting her living" through the marriage contract emerged soon after her 1884 wedding to the Rhode Island artist Charles Walter Stetson (1858–1911). That crisis was aggravated by the pregnancy and then the birth of Katharine in 1885, Gilman's only child. Only a week after their wedding, the bride's diary recorded the couple's first fight on 9 May: "Get a nice little dinner. I suggest that he pay me for my services and he much dislikes the idea. I am grieved at offending him, mutual misery. Bed and cry."[40] With ensuing depression, her prenatal diaries resentfully recount the mindless drudgery of dishwashing, cleaning, tidying, sewing, cooking, and marketing, which were supposed to fill her hours and justify her financial support as "wife." The diaries hinted, too, at the problematic dimensions of the sexual side of the bargain.[41]

During temporary separations from Stetson from 1888 prior to divorce, Gilman repaired to California and tried to fully support herself as a journalist and editor. Taking on the care of her dying mother and a live-in relationship with a journalist colleague, who shared the work of also running their home as a boarding house, made Gilman ill and exhausted. With her mother's death she cut her other personal ties in the Bay Area. Proud of her Yankee, abolitionist, Beecher family heritage and blessed from all accounts with considerable public speaking talent, she took to the road, spreading the gospel of social reform in the family tradition. Her divorce became final in 1894. Stetson promptly married Gilman's best friend, Grace Ellery Channing (1862–1937) of Pasadena, and the newlyweds accepted custody of Katharine. Thereafter, Gilman gradually moved back from the West to the East Coast, via paid speaking opportunities and a stay with Jane Addams at Hull House in 1894–95.

Her romance with Manhattan attorney George Houghton Gilman, her first cousin, finally drew her back to New York by the end of the 1890s. Nonetheless, she resisted the gender convention that she favor love over professional life. She left Houghton in no doubt of her priorities: "I wish you could have heard me last Sunday night. I never spoke better in my life. A full church. A big platform all to myself. And it came. It just poured in a great swelling river and all these people sat and took it in . . . I forget everyone in the audience when I speak."[42] She finally agreed to marry Houghton, but so important was her professional identity that their wedding in 1900 was "on the road"—he joined her in Detroit because she had speaking engagements there.[43] She married him only after elaborate negotiations on the wifely duties she would, and would not, fulfill. Of her preference for itinerant lecturing over "housekeeping" she wrote: "Cheerfully I will run around the rest of my life—a tentless Arab—living in a pair of handbags and a sleeping car—cheerfully will I forgo the comforts of home . . . than to suffer again as I have suffered for years and years."[44]

Throughout the three decades of her second marriage, until her husband's death in 1934, Gilman insisted on trying to support herself. These lectures formed a crucial part of her renegotiation of the marriage contract prior to the wedding ceremony: "You need not worry about my lecturing. I shan't lecture any more than I can help, and shall call it half a years work and rest two or three months after it—rest and play with you. Guess I'll do it, hereafter, in the late winter and spring, so as to rest in summer. Then I'll write in the autumn. A book in the fall, a trip in the spring, a long vacation in the winter and summer."[45] Her lecturing success led her to reassure Houghton. His reported annual income as an unassuming, conservative Wall Street lawyer was only six hundred dollars, his life's great passion being New York's Seventh Regiment.[46] At the height of her popularity as a speaker, in the wake of *Women and Economics* 1898, the bride-to-be crowed about her estimated income of four thousand dollars.[47] Her earning power declined significantly in her later years, to her profound disappointment. Still, speech was her living, literally, for portions of her adult life, with implications for her published work.

Her nonfiction articles, chapters, and books began as speeches. She kept meticulous records of her speaking engagements—places, dates, topics, fees paid, and correspondence related to logistics and organization. In the years 1896–1900, she presented an average of fifty lectures a year. Her range was nationwide, and her venues included universities, women' clubs, municipal leagues, religious bodies, and all manner of civic and community groups.

Presenting fewer lectures when book writing, she also reduced them during the years in which she edited *The Forerunner* (1909–16). Once she finished production of a monthly issue, however, she would undertake lecture tours before returning to produce the next month's issue, her fees helping defray costs.[48] Ceasing publication of *The Forerunner* after 1916, the Gilmans subsequently moved to Norwich Town, Connecticut. In the 1920s and 1930s, her advertising circulars described her as principally devoting her time to the lecture circuit, under the management of a Boston agency.[49]

Her papers display the mechanics of freelance lecturing in rich detail, including precise economic details. Writing in 1915 to a lecture agent, she answered questions about a Los Angeles tour:

> 1st. Yes, I could make a special trip, any time after Jan.1st, but it would cost ten days travel and all of three hundred dollars. I should want to see at least a thousand dollars engaged to do it.

> 2nd. Yes I will take single engagements as well as "weeks," and rather think those are all I shall get this December. Terms are $100 for one lecture. For Socialists, or Suffragists . . . I will cut as far back as $50.00, and in some *especial* cases . . . for as little as $75.00, but *never state that* . . . Other lecturers of my standing get $200.00 and $300.00. My present price is a fair one, and should be insisted on.[50]

At this point, Gilman was paying her agents 25 percent of the total takings. The agent paid the publicity, advertising, and venue rental in advance, to be reimbursed by the profits. Often she negotiated travel and accommodation expenses; otherwise all expenses reduced the total audience takings. A parlor for receiving visitors formed a critical function in setting up further venues and lecture tours. Gilman advertised single lecture fees of $100 (approximately $1,600 today), with lower rates per lecture when she offered a subscription series, and her interactions with lecture agents in each city or region toured reveal her professionalism. She calculated the assorted costs involved and the necessary profit levels for tours to be viable.

In the 1910s, Gilman calculated her minimum expenses for lecture courses in towns and smaller cities: printing circulars, window cards, subscription cards and coupon tickets, local notices and postage, $30; speaker's local traveling expenses, including a private parlor and entertainment, $15, for a total of $45. Her minimum "returns" included $300 for a class of one hundred subscribers at $3 each for multiple lectures, with a further sixty single-lecture admissions at 75¢ each, totaling $45, and one further outside lecture during the trip for $100. From total returns of $445 ($6,000 today), expenses of $45 plus the $100 agent's commission ($1,600 today) were deducted, leaving $345 (about $4,750 today).

Alternatively, large cities involved higher costs for travel, accommodations (including a parlor), a paid assistant, and local travel expenses. These costs accrued over days, even weeks, since Gilman would not lecture more than once a day. While these expenses, including the advance publicity and printing costs, might amount to as much as $300 ($4,500 today), returns in large urban areas "should be more than commensurate." For here she claimed that she might realistically anticipate classes of two hundred subscribers for six lectures at $5 each, and at least one-hundred single admissions at $1 (about $16 today) each, in addition to $400 from the four outside lectures. This meant that with the deduction of the $300.00 in expenses, the profits anticipated from large city lecture tours was $1200, split as $300 for the agent and $900 for Gilman ($4,500 and $13,500 today).

Many of the audiences most enthusiastic about Gilman as a speaker could not pay the advertised fee. As noted above, socialists, suffragists, and some religious groups were exceptions she made to her fee schedule. Constantly, she lectured for $10 or $15 (about $125 to $175 today).[51] She confessed to Houghton while they were courting that, despite the best intentions, "in the money making line, I can't seem to keep to it," in reference to yet another occasion on which she agreed to travel and lecture—in this case in Chicago—for nothing more than her costs.[52] Generally, she offered a series of six closely spaced lectures as a subscriber series, presented across one or two weeks. That so many women signed on for whole series, despite the greater cost than for single lectures, attests to the popularity of her mission to educate and improve women. The commitment of her audience members might resemble a modern subscriber to a film festival over consecutive days. Probably, these were mainly white, Protestant women with domestic help, moderate to small families, and enough disposable time and income to attend consecutively. One of the most critical parts of Gilman's lecture enterprises, then, was the advance identification and solicitation of subscription audiences.

The subjects of Gilman's lectures varied across her paid speaking career. At first, the auspices for her lectures related to her editing work, employment, and political commitments. Nationalism, socialism, dress reform, women's health, the labor movement, and literary topics framed her talks. Economic themes across the 1890s, culminating in *Women and Economics* (1898), followed her own situation and impelled a focus on both prostitution and marriage. By 1900, she offered three categories of paid speeches: general lectures, lectures for clubs and parlor meetings, and sermons. Most addressed issues related to marriage, motherhood, children, and the home.[53] Her focus sharpened by World War I, concentrating on woman suffrage and citizenship, masculinity, feminism, war and peace, and international issues. In 1915, she offered "A Gilman Week"—a series of hourly lectures followed by a one-hour discussion, daily. Four courses, each with six lecturers, enticed possible sponsors: "I. The Larger Feminism . . . II. Studies in Masculism . . . III. Brain Training . . . IV. War and the World Hope."[54] The context of world war inspired a further series of lectures that Gilman classified as "General Topics."[55] She also advertised a new public lecture, "War and Hope." In 1916, as the war progressed and deepened in its implications for Americans, Gilman offered six lectures in a new series, "The World War and Its Effects on Women." The cost was $3.00 for the course or 75¢ for each lecture.[56]

Gilman was received favorably by audiences nationwide. Women dominated Gilman's paying public as her natural constituency. She wrote to Houghton in 1898 that she expected female audiences to like her, whereas men's approval surprised her: "I don't know why you should be so surprised about the women. Women are human and so am I, I know women best and care more for them. I have an intense and endless love for women—partly reverence for their high estate, partly in pity for their feebleness, their long ages of suffering."[57] In North Carolina, she reported that "My welcome is among the women here. They like me much better than I expected."[58]

Yet if women were the audience for her hallmark critique of women's economic dependency and its disastrous ramifications, ironically, it was largely *men's* money that supported Gilman. Often her engagements were during men's working hours, at women's clubs and other cultural or civic bodies. Audience members usually were wives with the funds needed to subscribe. This implied breadwinner support. Meanwhile, for evening lectures, when men might accompany their wives, Gilman had to appeal to at least some men. She was preoccupied with male audience members' attitudes toward her. When she impressed men, she bragged unapologetically, as on the occasion when she won over a curmudgeon in Saint Louis: "The Beecher reputation weighs heavily in my favor so far—which I had not expected. A big old man got up last night and declared that he felt himself 'in the grip of the master mind of Henry Ward Beecher' and that now he was in favor of women on the rostrum—though he never had been before."[59] Similarly, her stay with a wealthy Southern family, the Bordens, was crowned with the success of converting a rich old banker patriarch. His wife confided that "he was reluctant to go— had never heard a woman speak—but thought he ought to go once. He sat through the whole thing with unswerving interest and has since been telling everyone to go and hear me with many praises. She said that another man, a lawyer, also reluctant to go said it was the best address he had ever heard anywhere."[60]

Later she reported proudly that "the South loves oratory and dislikes 'progressive women' and I feel much gratified as a woman speaker." Experiences like these left her exhilarated and wildly optimistic about prospects for change, and she presented them as further grounds for Houghton to accept an unconventional marriage. She would not do housekeeping. Housekeeping would not be appropriate, for if ever "there was a sense of a call, I think I've got it."[61] She accelerated this message once she agreed to marry him, in case consent threatened her lecturing. In accepting her greatness, he should diminish conventional manly demands of her: "I have been given unusual powers of expression and I truly hope that my life will count for much good to the world—as Darwin's did and Galileo and many other blessed souls who have given high place to serve the world . . . But when it comes to the woman of me, my fitness and desirability for marriage, all this counts against me. By virtue of what I have of greatness I am the less desirable wife."[62]

All these hopes for her great impact could be dashed by men's disapproval, which made her unsettled and morose. For instance, on a lecture in a Southern town she noted: "I have met almost no men here and those I have, married and staid show no signs of more than polite tolerance to an eccentric stranger."[63] Another occasion was worse, "Last night was the women one. I had a good house and well, expected much, but I did not please the men of the place—for which I am truly sorry. . . . The women liked it however. . . . But I wanted the men to get a better feeling toward the women's movement—and I feel as if I had not succeeded at all—rather the other way."[64]

Her comments on her audiences reveal emotional vulnerability, challenging her confidence in gendered ways. Reporting on a lecture that did not go well, she observed that "Some people like me, others don't. Your father don't, your aunts don't," a reference to his family's recent dismay upon learning that the thirty-three-year-old Houghton proposed to marry his divorced, nearly forty-year-old first cousin: "Some people in our audience come up and shake hands and say nice things. Many more go out silent. How do I know what they think? . . . When I meet disapproval I feel that I am indeed a naughty girl and deserve all I get."[65]

Gilman's rattled responses to audience disapproval highlighted the gender transgression involved in constructing herself as a female public intellectual. Asserting herself as an advanced thinker, she presumed to educate her fellow women. Since only a small minority of white women between the ages of twenty and seventy received higher education at the time, and while only a tiny handful had academic careers, Gilman's lecture series readily resembled adult education for women.[66] The bonds of white womanhood united Gilman with her Progressive Era audiences. Unlike her brother Thomas, educated at the Massachusetts Institute of Technology, Gilman was denied university education on the grounds of sex. The genteel poverty of her mother, deserted by her librarian and writer husband, only accentuated the cultural pattern of privileging sons' educations and not daughters.' In Gilman's only alternative—to educate *herself*—the booklist forwarded by her father, Frederick Beecher Perkins, when she was seventeen was critical. Its strongly Darwinian, scientific, historical, and anthropological bias inflected her entire subsequent development.[67] Mastering difficult texts outside the experience of most women of her race and class, Gilman constructed the lecturing persona of "advanced thinker" and "forward-looking woman." This gave her enough of an expertise or edge over her audiences to be preacher and teacher, but was not too far beyond their experience to prevent them from identifying with her.

What did their subscription fees buy Gilman's audience members? Arguably, Gilman founded extramural women's studies in the Progressive Era. Audiences heard a challenging rewriting of history and alternative readings of the development of human societies. Once upon a time there was gynaecocracy: cultures centered on motherhood and the nurture of children. Somehow in ancient history, men became dominant and enslaved women, though Gilman admitted she and other theorists remained mystified on the means and periodization involved. The successor culture was "androcentric," man-centered, and lopsided, deploying only half of the available human talents in politics, industry, religion, art, and education.

War, competition, death-worship, prostitution, and women's dependent weakness and vanity were lamentable consequences of androcentrism. Home was women's unhygienic, poorly designed, tastelessly decorated prison, established for the private cooking of the male breadwinner's meals by his dependent, untrained helpmate. It was inimical to the needs of children placed in care there.

Excluded from the affairs of the world, ignorant women stagnated at a primitive earlier stage of evolution, causing a serious evolutionary gap between the sexes. Unable to fend for themselves, dependent wives held a poor marital bargaining position. Despite the naturalness of sexual periodicity attached to reproduction, androcentric man captured woman and forced her to submit to constant sexual relations on demand. Too many births resulted, providing incentives for unpalatable birth control choices such as abortion. Moreover, dependent wives endured infidelity, with prostitutes or others, and suffered venereal diseases and birth defects.

The solution was a "human" world, one in which both sexes shared work, politics, child rearing, and all cultural activities, cured of all androcentric bias. Women needed access to paid work, suffrage, higher education, and other outlets for their energy and talents. They needed good nutrition, exercise, physical fitness, and dress reform, and to discard corsets, high heels, and long, elaborate hair styles, as well as wasteful fashion fripperies, like feather-plumed hats, frills, and jewelry. Household work and child rearing needed to be disaggregated, with its parts collectivized and professionalized, especially cooking and cleaning. Sexuality and reproduction should again match women's needs and desires, both limited to manageable levels. Prostitution had to be ended.

Rhetorically, Gilman took women to task for their poor performance as household managers and mothers as part of her case that her sex was retarded. However, her message could seem unthreatening to breadwinners, husbands and fathers, especially those of the business and professional classes, the core of Gilman's target female and mixed sex audiences. This was because, initially, many of Gilman's talks appeared framed by what Susan Gubar has called "feminist misogyny," or what Nancy F. Cott identifies as the paradox of the Janus face of recognizable feminism—a tension between dislike of present forms of patriarchally constructed femininity—women as they are—and support for, even celebration of, present forms of the feminine, in an attempt to counter misogyny and degradation of women as they are.[68] With titles and content appearing to criticize women, men of even the most misogynist views might find themselves in unexpected agreement.

Preparing her own publicity materials, Gilman lavished praise upon her own published works. She also used written testimonials, accounts of her successful European tours, and comparisons of her own philosophy to that of other leading women thinkers of the day, such as Olive Schreiner (1855–1920) and Ellen Key (1849–1926).[69] Noting that her name headed a New York newspaper's list of the twelve greatest living American women, her publicity circular reported her designation as one of only four leading women "meriting the title 'great.'" Gilman's promotional self-description claimed, first, that she "has had an enormous influence upon American life," and second, that her *Women and Economics* "utterly revolutionized" attitudes toward "woman's place," not only nationally, but thanks to European and Asian language translations, internationally as well.[70] By 1925, her circular named Gilman's eight most significant published works, two fiction ("The Yellow Wallpaper" and *In This Our World*) and six nonfiction books. Even when handled by an agent, she controlled promotion, despite her disclaimers. For instance, when arranging a trip to upstate New York in 1920, she wrote her agent:

> You asked for some publicity material, and with great distaste I have endeavored to manufacture some. These press notices I think you had before, but am not sure. It occurs to me that something might be done by asking a number of Syracuse women "What Mrs. Gilman Means to You?" That would make good newspaper stuff, and if you only asked friendly ones it ought to help the lectures. Then someone might make little funny or sharp extracts from my books or the Forerunner, call 'em "Gilmanisms," perhaps some paper would run a few. I'm not good at this publicity stunt, if I were I should be richer. . . . You see I am particularly anxious for you people to make a real success of this, so that I can convince other clubs that I am not an Expense Account only. . . . How about a sermon on the 3rd to get more folks roused up? I love to preach better than anything, have done it often.[71]

Gilman's Progressive Era handbills evinced ambivalence about "feminism," a term that entered the American political lexicon in the 1910s.[72] Noting her nomination as the most significant feminist of the era, she disdained this term in preference for the term "humanist." She claimed to focus on women simply because their social, economic, and cultural retardation obstructed human progress.[73] While Gilman's unease about "feminism" needs further analysis, her reservations may also reveal a management of image necessary to keep her living viable. She could not afford to represent herself as too far from "main street" if she hoped to maximize her fee-paying audiences in cities and towns all across America. This pertains to her occasional downplaying of the importance of woman suffrage, despite her deep commitment to it. She actually received agent feedback that an uncompromising pro-suffrage advocacy would lose her audiences in some locales. Men might not permit their wives to attend.

Gilman's anxieties about her self-representation had a material basis. In 1914, a lecture scheduled at an Ohio school, partly sponsored by the Joseph Fels Fund of America, was canceled due to parent protests against Gilman's advocacy of woman suffrage. As the fund committee chair explained to Gilman's New York lecture manager and agent, William B. Feakin: "Mrs. Gilman's lecture was canceled simply because many of the mothers of the pupils . . . warned the head of the school that if Mrs. Gilman was allowed to speak there, they would take their daughters away from the school . . . this feeling . . . wholly because of Mrs. Gilman's attitude on the suffrage. Very few people among our comfortable and well to do people are favorable to suffrage."[74]

In her lectures, Gilman's mainly women subscribers heard early prototypes of her subsequent publications. The germs of most of her articles and books could be seen months, years, and sometimes decades before in unpublished lectures. Through lectures, she brainstormed new ideas or novel formulations of existing ones, reported on her reading, commented on current issues, or debated prevalent views. Resumed later, these speeches found new life on the printed page, often little changed.

Thus, much of Gilman's published writing has a spoken, conversational character. Like any effective speech, its passage through main points was lively, colored with graphic examples, amusing anecdotes, and other devices designed to maintain a listener's attention. Determined to be self-supporting, she had no one paying her a salary, affording her time and space to carefully reconsider, rephrase, and further research the more contentious of her lectures. Many of her re-presentations and repetitions of previously spoken or published work were not verbatim, but close to the original in substance and spirit. Her dogmatism and certainty enabled her to write speeches and articles very rapidly—at least by academic standards.

Financially, she had to seek and accept paid speaking and publishing opportunities. With her genius for reconfiguring well-worked texts into new contexts, each piece seemed distinct and self-contained, a material aspect of her legacy as a public intellectual pertinent to her nonfiction. Insofar as each publication usually drew upon lectures, forging an unusually close relationship between her spoken and published words, her living though her pen was paid by spoken piece—she was a pieceworker—unlike salaried academics or journalists.

Gilman's Rhetorics: Animals, Races, and the Rise of Androcentrism

Overturning commonsense assumptions, scolding audiences, and seeking to instruct them via a higher authority (such as science), Gilman's lectures pitted reason against passion or prejudice. She set developmental tasks for her audiences. Rather than simply conveying information to passive listeners, each talk established an audience goal, a revised interpretation for them to comprehend, a new or renewed commitment to a reform campaign. Moreover, her arguments allowed no conclusion but her own, though she permitted caveats on minor points. She began her lectures conversationally, captivating audiences with anecdotes and examples. Once listeners were engaged, she would reconfigure the advertised topic in startling ways. Her lectures' trademarks were challenge, confrontation, even repudiation of her audience's conventional stance on the matter at issue.

Beginning her 1891 lecture, "Our Maternal Duties," she informed her audience that as mothers, in our present culture, "we" were pathetically unfit, inadequate, ignorant, and untrained. She lambasted the fabled "maternal instinct" as fine for rearing the "thick-skulled baby" of the cave era, but completely insufficient for infant inheritors of twentieth-century human progress.[75] Appeals to instinct only excused women's smugness, laziness, or ignorance and served well opponents of women's higher education. Far from instinctual, Gilman contended that motherhood was a skilled business, appropriately accorded training, remuneration, and respect. For children equipped to contribute human progress, mothers had to fully develop their own humanity. To correctly rear children, mothers needed to understand history, sociology, biology, zoology, ethics, and other salient branches of knowledge.[76] Countering naturalizing and essentialist rhetoric about motherhood, she insisted that something so vital to the future of human race required a cultural investment in mothers as professionals.

Gilman's lectures featured animal analogies and comparisons. The corseted horse exemplified human folly. Typically, the animal emerged from the comparisons more favorably than human, a strategy to shame audiences into recognition. "Noble" animals—leopards, lions, horses, and gazelles—showed the human idiocy of "excessive sex distinction," by which men dominated industry, public life, and all other advanced human "race" activities to the exclusion of women. Lacking common attributes, with only the bonds of sex and "whatever mutual delight" they might entail, immense evolutionary gaps separated the sexes. By contrast with the nimble leopard, where the distinctions of sex were "in their place" rather than artificially heightened as they were among humans, no obstacle prevented males and females of the species from working together, defending each other and their young, hunting and killing food, climbing trees, and the full range of great-cat activity. Comparing female animals with women, she stressed the strength, skill, and prowess of female animals. She exhorted women to cultivate these qualities and resources, so far virtually monopolized by men. The rationale here was equalitarian. If female cheetahs and leopards could participate equally in species development, why not female humans?

So distinct had human cultures made the sexes, that it was as if each sex was a distinct species, a "race" of its own, inhabiting different planets. Unless altered, marriage could not be a shared life. Instead, mating men and women together made little "race" development sense. It was like mating a lion and a sheep, an eagle and a hen, a clam and a salmon. Just as two hens have more in common than a hen and an eagle, two women had more in common than a man and a woman. While opposites might well "attract," retorted Gilman to the old adage, "like" was more likely to keep, bond, and endure in attachment.[77]

Gilman offset her positive animal analogies with other negative references to animals and to animality generally. Disputing women's submission to coitus on demand, Gilman characterized this as the "lowest" of animal instincts, contrasted with the higher state of "humanness." Other cultural discourses portrayed women as closer to nature through reproduction, with men the custodians of mind, culture, and civilization. The feminist impulse behind Gilman's response here is significant. She portrayed men as behaving like animals, closer to nature than women. Women had to elevate men into civilized culture. In lectures addressing sexuality, "animal" was synonymous with rapacious masculinity.

Meanwhile, "humanness" implied a sexual order attuned to women's reproductive periodicity and voluntary motherhood. She advanced this feminist notion of human civilization, in which husband and wife equally were breadwinners and parents, notwithstanding the prevailing discourse of masculinity, animality, and nature. The Progressive Era had Theodore Roosevelt's "Rough Riders" and obsessive writings upon manhood and "race suicide," as well as fiction such as

Burroughs's *Tarzan, Lord of the Apes*. Civilization was being recast through the very male line that Gilman sought to represent as animalistic and uncivilized. The "brute" in man became the dynamic of "racial" advance and higher civilization, in rhetorical moves inimical to Gilman's. At the very moment that her discourse demanded women's entry into the human world of race improvement and species work, the domain of animal instincts received recharacterization as both inherently manly and civilized.[78] Once again, to her chagrin, women were shut out.

The theme of excessive sex distinction depriving humanity of evolutionary advancement recurred throughout Gilman's lectures. The words "race" and "racial" saturated her publications and lectures. In many contexts, she used "race" to mean the human race—Homo sapiens—as distinct from anthropoid species and other mammals. She also used "race" synonymously with "species," referring for instance to "insect races." Alternatively, "race" also signified country or nation, in principle without any connotations beyond factual description. Yet often enough she in fact used "race" in this sense when discussing national and ethnic groups from what today are called "developing" countries, whose sexual customs she criticized. Turks, Chinese, Indians, and "Abyssinians" were some of the "races" she referred to in this way. Finally, Gilman unquestionably used "race" to designate the alleged superiority of white Euro-Americans and northern Europeans—Aryan or Nordic peoples. Only these groups, she claimed, could hear her Progressive Era message and implement reform. She provided racialized explanations of the emergence of androcentric culture at one evolutionary point, now to be superseded by a *human* culture of intersex partnership and equality. "Primitive" women, as inventors of industry as part of their nurture and care of the young, were rich in secure sources of food and domestic needs. Their lives compared favorably with the uncertain and uncomfortable existence of male hunters. At some point, via unclear means, primitive men enslaved women, usurping their industries, goods, and skills, forcing women into dependency relationships. This historic period of androcentrism permitted men to catch up to women, increasing their civilization quotient.[79]

An unresolved problem in Gilman's overall Progressive Era theory, which sought a biological basis for feminism in social Darwinist terms, was how to explain women's enslavement. This was important for her claim that androcentrism permitted men to demand frequent coitus as the human norm, overturning millennia of female-initiated and reproduction-related sexual periodicity among Homo sapiens. Feminist scholars have scrutinized Gilman's racial, ethnic, and class biases, but her use of Darwinian zoology and theories of sex selection to mandate women's renegotiation of conjugal sexuality, to reduce sexual demands, and to institute voluntary motherhood bear upon those racial and ethnic biases.[80]

Gilman, like many, many women of her generation, recoiled from prevailing forms of heterosexuality. After initially positive responses to conjugality, she withdrew from the controlling and demanding aspects of Walter Stetson's "love," which had resulted in rapid pregnancy, postnatal depression, and an acute fear of successive pregnancies.[81] As well as temporary separations and living in separate apartments within the marital home, she also undertook the highly significant sexualized insubordination of abandoning her corsets and high-heeled shoes. She began strenuous exercise at the local gymnasium.[82] In the context of late-nineteenth-century gender, class, and race norms, her insistence on professional and financial independence was sexual insubordination.[83]

If our libertarian era cannot comprehend an intelligent woman voluntarily choosing celibacy or intercourse only for reproduction, understanding Gilman's sexual world is the challenge.[84] For her, women's dependent and parasitic relations to men underpinned androcentric sexuality. "The sex relation *itself*" was the rationale for this near-universal parasitism, though effective strategies for altering existing patterns proved difficult. Rejecting Progressive Era "masculism," Gilman believed that male sexual expectations were neither necessary nor immutable. Gilman claimed that humans, the only species capable of altering its evolutionary fate culturally, had taken a mistaken path in establishing women's economic dependence on men via sexual relationships, and thereby their sex subjection.[85] From this flowed all evils retarding the species.[86]

Her claim depended upon an account of the history, origins, and progress of human sexuality. If she could not persuade her readers and audiences that at some earlier time, women had enjoyed freedom from sexual subjection, how could the feminist case for women's humanity, emancipation from sex slavery, and economic independence, plus a full platform of related reforms, be secured? She needed evidence, present traces of the past. Admitting this problem, she wrote in 1925: "It is no light matter to seek to change a relation which is almost as old as the human race, but neither was it a light matter to change one a million times older. . . . In any case, it is of visible importance to understand how it happened, to see what forces operated upon us that we should thus overturn the order of nature, as it were, and succeed in our audacious revolution. It is needless to explain that such a discovery depends on deduction purely. There were no records at that time, and the change was not one to alter the bones we unearth. Yet with some knowledge . . . it is not difficult to reconstruct the . . . easy, gradual, perfectly natural and unconscious steps by which this radical alteration was made."[87]

Gilman hypothesized the emergence of sex itself and sex differentiation as historical developments. Prior species reproduced without either or both. She sought both a positive account of the emergence of sex differentiation and yet a rationale for controlling the evolutionary damage of androcentrism. Sex originated, she claimed, as a means of species strengthening and diversification: "Sex was a later development, with a further purpose. There was something to be done by the real Life Force besides live and multiply. The big business . . . was growth, development, evolution . . . sex was an indispensable element of race progress, and has not ceased to operate in human variation and civilization. Its introduction through the segregation of the male element, and its gradual attainment of race equality allowed variation and selection previously impossible. . . . The other line of change, through natural selection, was still wider, but whatever the source of a modification, it was transmitted through the functions of sex."[88]

What went wrong? Gilman's answer was that the more highly evolved form of motherhood accompanying the extended pregnancy, lactation, and rearing of Homo sapiens infants led to women's development of industries—work of economic value. Beyond the "natural" and periodic phase during which women permitted men carnal indulgence for reproduction, cohabitation with mothers began to have added attractions for primitive men—economic attractions.[89] For the care mothers dispensed to children might be claimed by men as well:

> The male savage found in his female an attraction no other male had known, economic value. She was useful to him aside from the gratification of desire. His own father-service of hunting and fighting was strengthened and augmented by her labors. It is obvious that a savage who had a woman to take care of him could hunt and fight to better advantage than one who had to take care of himself. In this new relationship, with motherhood extended to benefit the father as well as the child, begins the swiftest stage of human advance. . . . Mother-care, given to the adult-male, seemed as nutritive as mother's milk given to the child. But the new attraction of service, added to the old attraction of sex, made the woman so desirable that they became necessary possessions, and as possessions they were unable to avoid the quite natural abuse of their original function. From this point follows a divided influence of sex upon our progress; the wholly beneficial original effect, and later ones widely varying.[90]

She lacked explanation for mothers becoming "possessions." Sometime "between those dim beginnings and the time when history is possible, something happened to reverse the hitherto unbroken leadership of the mother sex."[91] Men's enslavement and subordination of women was an event in ancient history. Hitherto, women controlled industry, produced wealth, and were fully independent. In the sequel to *Herland* (1915), a novel entitled *With Her in Ourland*, a conversation between the hero and heroine, Van and Ellador, expressed Gilman's own inability to explain the origins of women's oppression:

> "Of course, there is no getting around Lester Ward," I began slowly. "No one can study biology and sociology much and not see that on the first physiological lines the female is the whole show, so to speak, or at least most of it. All the way up she holds her own, even into early savagery, till Mr. Man gets into the saddle. How he came to do it is a mystery that I don't believe even you can explain."
>
> "No," she agreed, "I can't. I call it 'The Great Divergence.' There is no other such catastrophic change in all nature—as far as I've been able to gather . . ."
>
> "Well, he did take the reins somehow," I resumed, "and we began our historic period. . . . But in all this time, as far as I can make it out, he has never even been fair to women, and has for the most part treated her with such an assortment of cruelty and injustice as makes me blush for my sex."[92]

Ultimately, Gilman's explanation rested upon sexual economics: men, hunting erratic prey, naturally lazy and parasitic, faced an economically uncertain world. Realizing that nonhunting woman—the gatherer, agriculturalist, artisan, trader, and manufacturer—enjoyed prosperity and predictable sustenance, men jealously participated, then took over women's industries, advancing them into their modern forms over thousands of years.[93]

Force was the key element in Ward's account of the emergence of androcentrism. He held that sexualized violence secured all "primitive" men intercourse on demand against the inclinations of "primitive" women. While Gilman was more sceptical about the role of violence, she held that the abuse of sex differentiation retarded the "race." Arguably, this association between male "primitivism" and sexual subjugation fueled her hostility to non-Aryan influences upon American culture. The association between "primitivism" and rape facilitated the racialization of elements of her Progressive Era feminist discourses.[94]

Androcentrism, with its culture of primitive violence, was no longer appropriate for white Americans, whose evolutionary superiority impelled an egalitarian "human world" with women contributing to "race progress," no longer still specialized by sex, like lesser races. For Europeans and Euro-Americans, androcentrism involved women's stagnation. Now women needed to catch up with men. For other groups, such as African Americans, the salutary and civilizing potential of the androcentric era of male dominance and female dependency had yet to work its magic. Minority men remained less evolved than white men.[95] She suggested that black men learning to support their women still served a useful evolutionary purpose. For whites, this stage now was past.[96]

Gilman portrayed African Americans either negatively or humorously, despite admissions of American injustice towards them.[97] Diathna Bell's expression of humorous amazement at the multiple marriages, man trouble, and fertility of her African-American cook, Julianna, in *What Diathna Did* deployed prevailing stereotypes.[98] Ignoring the complicity of white Americans in the consequences of slavery and failures of Reconstruction, her 1908 essay "A Suggestion on the Negro Problem" proposed work camps for most black adult males.[99] Lest we suppose that discussion in such terms is only and would always be judged racist, offensive, unscholarly, and extremist, we must note that the *American Journal of Sociology* saw fit to publish this and another article by Gilman on social Darwinism.[100] *Women and Economics* (1898) had established her as a serious critic of national and international note. Her interventions were received as interesting and appropriate, horrifying as they may be to the late-twentieth-century reader.

Gilman's racialized positions partly developed through her feminist analysis of prostitution, sexuality, birth control, and eugenics. A key challenge is to reach an understanding of her uses of these discourses, their relationship with her central ideas and claims, and her use of them to make her feminism more intelligible to her Progressive Era peers. Some critics have approached Gilman's racialized discourses by placing her views in their historical context, noting these same prejudices among most serious intellectuals of her era while denouncing them as reprehensible and unforgivable.[101] In contrast with this contextual approach, other recent critics urge that since late-twentieth-century feminism draws significantly from her theoretical legacy, it cannot escape contamination from her racialized cosmology. Failing to repudiate her racism renders feminist successors complicit.[102]

Gilman made creative use of contemporary racial theoretics and prejudices to buttress her critique of androcentrism, male sexuality, birth control, and psychoanalysis. Racism sharpened her analysis. She assumed intelligibility when, in differentiating between the forms and types of women's subordination, she wrote, "As helplessly sold, given, or seized by force, they lost their power of selection; the male alone did the selecting, and his choice did not depend on her strength or intelligence—quite the contrary . . . our use of sex has contributed to race progress a deteriorating influence. It can be roughly indicated that those peoples whose women are most completely denied freedom and growth remain the least progressive."[103] Who were these "least progressive" peoples? In her view, any culture with a history of polygamy or harems, or in which women were secluded radically, utterly dependent, and without nondomestic community, education, or industrial function. Africa provided "proof enough of the hopelessly low status of a people whose men only hunt and fight and live on the work of women."[104] Knowing scandalously little of the facts or context of women and girls' lives in cultures beyond the United States and parts of Europe, she characterized (and often homogenized) the situation of women as worst in Asia (which she usually called "the Orient"), the Middle East, Africa, and the Pacific Rim, as well as in any indigenous or aboriginal situation whatsoever.

Ann J. Lane astutely observes that the social scientists whom Gilman admired, such as Lester Ward and Thorstein Veblen, postulated common human evolutionary origins that coexisted with developmental differences which were, in effect, permanent.[105] This seems to have been exactly her position. Highlighting the alleged barbarism toward women of cultural "others," she advanced nativist, American exceptionalist arguments that the best hope for women' status and all progressive change for humanity was the United States. Subliminally, derogatory cross-cultural examples pressured the resisting reader or listener into disassociation with such backward peoples.

Beyond passively reproducing prevailing racial, ethnic, and evolutionary discourses, Gilman juxtaposed arguments in novel ways. Thereby, she exceeded mere use of discourses established by others, transforming them by sexualizing them in previously unthought ways. She made original contributions. Hers was a political unconscious, "in which questions of race permeate questions of sex."[106] Acknowledging this is not praise or endorsement. Her racializing of "sex slavery" was fully intelligible to her contemporaries. Indeed, it is likely that so embedding the analysis enhanced the overall effectiveness of her arguments to her readers and audiences. By simultaneously sexualizing the implications of race differences and attributes, she enlarged her reception as a serious contributor to Progressive Era social-policy debate.

Through her preoccupations with economic dependency, with the quality and conditions of motherhood, and with animal and human comparisons in her analysis of sex distinctions, race, and the pace of evolution, Gilman rhetorically advanced particular concerns. One was the elimination of prostitution, a Progressive Era obsession, taken as a metaphor for the malfunctions of modern, industrial, urban society. Her concerns went deeper and further than those of many of her contemporaries. Prostitution was a cardinal feature of androcentrism, its elimination a prerequisite for a more "human" world.

Reforming Prostitution

[M]an . . . has insisted on maintaining another class of women . . . subservient to his desires; a barren, mischievous unnatural relation, wholly aside from parental purposes, and absolutely injurious to society. This whole field of morbid action will be eliminated from human life by the normal development of women. . . . Many, under the old mistaken notion of what used to be called "the social necessity" of prostitution, will protest the idea of its extinction. . . . An intelligent and powerful womanhood will put an end to this indulgence of one sex at the expense of the other and to the injury of both. In this inevitable change will lie what some men will consider a loss. But only those of the present generation. For, the sons of the women now entering upon this new era of world life, will be differently reared. With all women full human beings, trained and useful in some form of work, the class of . . . idlers . . . will disappear as utterly as will the prostitute . . . No woman with real work to do, work she loved and was well fitted for, work honored and well-paid, would take up the Unnatural Trade. . . . One major cause of the decay of nations is "the social evil"—a thing wholly due to androcentric culture.

CHARLOTTE PERKINS GILMAN, *The Man-Made World or, Our Androcentric Culture*

Gilman, like other Progressive Era feminists, critically analyzed the interface between the two key sexual contracts: marriage and prostitution.[107] Arguably, the depth and intensity of her concern about prostitution remain "under-read" in existing commentaries.[108] Prostitution epitomized the evils of women's situation.[109] Identifying it among "the three great evils most strictly due to our androcentric culture—war, intemperance, and prostitution," she noted that prostitution, because it is accompanied by "its train of diseases," had won for itself the distinct and grave title of the "the Social Evil."[110] References to it haunted her lectures, as well as both *Women and Economics* (1898) and *The Man-Made World* (1911), her two most significant Progressive Era texts. Prostitution was the centerpiece of one of her last nonfiction publications, "Parasitism and Civilized Vice" (1931).[111] In *Women and Economics*, references to prostitution anchored key parts of the argument: "[T]he personal profit of women bears but too close a relation to their power to win and hold the other sex. . . . When we confront this fact boldly and plainly in the open market of vice, we are sick with horror. When we see the same economic relation made permanent, established by law, sanctified by religion, covered with flowers and incense . . . we think it innocent, lovely and right. The transient trade we think evil. The bargain for life we think good. But the biological effect is the same. In both cases the female gets her food from the male by virtue of her sex relationship to him."[112]

Her longstanding concern about the evolutionary impact of prostitution was evident from some of her first paid public lectures. For instance, in her 1890 Pasadena lecture on prostitution and venereal diseases, "Causes and Cures," she argued that everyone—men, women, and children—were endangered by women kept in ignorance about prostitution by lies, subterfuge, and "delicacy" in public discourses. Meanwhile, the selective prosecution of prostitutes, but not their clients, was useless. The view that prostitution was inevitable, warranting official fatalism and resignation, was for Gilman "simply wrong" and "utterly mistaken."[113] Prostitution could be ended, but only with a conscious plan to change approaches to sexuality in human life. Conditions for ending prostitution had to be created, a project justified by the great collective cost of this androcentric institution. She vehemently used repetition for emphasis, indicting the passivity of key authorities: "There is no physician who can deny the immeasurable extent of disease and death which have been brought upon us from this evil alone. There is no lawyer who can deny the immeasurable extent of crime and death which have been brought upon us from this evil alone. There is no minister who can deny the immeasurable extent of pain and death which have been brought upon us by this evil alone. . . . The evil exists—the evil is great. In one way or another we all suffer from it."[114]

Women's economic independence formed the cornerstone of Gilman's vision for raising new generations of men no longer believing that every woman had her price. Since many of her suggestions challenged the inevitability of men's demand for prostitution—a provocatively counterintuitive position—she gave a certain ground to the sexual double standard by holding women's participation more heinous and unnatural than men's. Criticizing the criminalization of women but not men, she granted that the offense was not equally grave for both sexes. Thus, police hounded prostitutes but not their clients. Gilman in part condoned this. While clients indulged, albeit to excess, natural urges, the prostitute "is . . . in most cases showing the falseness of the deed by doing it for hire—physical falsehood—a sin against nature."[115] At this early point in her career she abhorred the ascetic and celibate strands of Christian culture, sympathetic instead to the natural needs of animals to mate. She shared the pervasive cultural notion that "womanless" men met their erotic desires, one way or another. It was a man's world. Condemnation of prostitutes was proof that humanity regarded it as unnatural. Yet tolerance of the institution was ensured because it served men's interests.[116]

Much was at stake in interpreting prostitution. Gilman wished to apply evolutionary theory to justify enhanced options for women. For social Darwinism to emancipate rather than enslave women, odious features of their situation needed designation as perversions of "nature," impeding human progress.[117] Rather than "natural," prostitution specifically, and women's economic dependence generally, should appear as a monstrous distortion of evolution threatening human survival: "Some hidden cause has operated continuously against the true course of natural evolution, to pervert the natural trend toward a higher and more advantageous sex-relation; and to maintain lower forms, and erratic phases, of a most disadvantageous character. . . . That peculiar sub-relations which has dragged along with us all the time that monogamous marriage has been growing to be the accepted form of sex union—prostitution—we have accepted, and called a 'social necessity.' We also call it 'the social evil.' We have tacitly admitted that this relation in the human race must be more or less uncomfortable and wrong, that it is part of our nature to have it so."[118]

How did Gilman account for the prevalence of prostitution? Women, unlike the females of any other animal species, depended on men for food. Resistance to economic dependence was checked by their lack of other means to independent survival. This fostered feminine attributes, securing men's economic support. Heightening sex distinctions between men and women, minimizing androgyny, flowed from this culturally made female dependence, unauthorized by nature. Men called women "the sex," a chilling designation of female humanity's prescriptive raison d'etre.[119]

Thereby men reduced economic competition for resources. Depending on their area of economic specialization, men could bargain for decent livelihoods across a wide range of trades, crafts, professions, businesses, and skills. By contrast, the other half of humanity, with marriage its only means of livelihood, created an oversupply and increased competition. Oversupplied trades provided their workers with poor conditions and remuneration, and little protection from occupational hazards. Moreover, these oversupplied conditions meant that currently unmarried women readily became judged "ineligible" or "undesirable" candidates for the smallest mistakes.[120]

Under these evolutionary circumstances, women who failed to please men did not reproduce themselves. Those with secure biological inheritances were the hyper-feminine or "overfeminized." In nature, Gilman observed, "the male carries ornament and the female is dark and plain." Males compete to be most appealing to the females, who select the best, most fit mates. By contrast, among humans, "the females compete in ornament, and the males select."[121] This bizarre reversal was culturally generated, with direct eugenic consequences, and increased the demand for prostitution. Consequently, the least vigorous women became overrepresented in "the stock."[122] Idealized, their characteristics passed on to their sons, the fathers of the next generation, resulting in a general weakening of the species. "Breeding out" vigorous female strains contracted genetic diversity and weakened men, creating a gloomy prognosis for the survival of the species.[123]

Overfeminization artificially inflated demands for carnal relations. Observing the animal kingdom, she insisted that natural sexual desire was periodic, linked to reproduction. Increased human erotic desire, a product of excessive sex distinction, arose from women's forced economic dependence. Nor did men confine unchecked sexual indulgence to their wives, though its effects were injurious enough upon married women and the next generation.[124] Late-nineteenth-century feminists criticized women and girls' vulnerability to sexual assault, seduction, pregnancy out of wedlock, and recruitment to prostitution. Gilman argued that androcentric culture enjoined single women to cooperate in excessive sex distinction in order to secure their own living, making these hazards inevitable. The double standard of sexual morality supplied women for prostitution, providing men the option of the purchase of sexual mastery without requiring reciprocal desire: "[W]here . . . man inherits the excess in sex-energy and is never blamed for exercising it, and where he develops also the age-old habit of taking what he wants from women . . . what should naturally follow? . . . We have produced a certain percentage of females with inordinate sex-tendencies and inordinate greed for material gain. We have produced a certain percentage of males with inordinate sex-tendencies and a cheerful willingness to pay for their gratification. And as the percentage of such men is greater than the percentage of such women, we have worked out the most evil methods of supplying the demand."[125]

Many contemporary feminists argue that prostitution is women's work, comparable with other jobs assigned to women via the sex division of paid labor.[126] Why did Gilman, with her distinctive focus on work and economics, decline this view? This could have left her critique of the economic dependence of wives on marriage intact. Was there not a fundamental difference between the prostitute and the wife, in that during her "currency," the prostitute earned the highest wages available to women? Gilman's feminist version of social Darwinism obstructed her from embracing prostitutes as workers like any other and so precluded solidarity with them. Since living through the artificial enhancement of sex division, sex attraction, and sex indulgence had exiled women from "race development," prostitution was the most extreme example of androcentric femininity.

Though men were far worse than women in their demand for excessive sex indulgence, such indulgence did not retard them, because it was not, simultaneously, their occupation.[127] Men developed, worked, invented, produced, mastered problems, and generally partook in diverse activities that developed them into higher forms of humanity—which Gilman called "race development." Exiled from race development by economic dependence, women had only the option of putting their intelligence and creativity into "sex development."[128] The results were catastrophic.

Gilman showed a clear and realistic understanding of the systemic factors that led to women's recruitment into the trade. Nonetheless, she saw prostitutes as a group—as an entity in sexual politics—as the enemies of women's advancement. They weakened the bargaining position of all women. They helped sex-indulgent men deteriorate "the race."[129] War was evil because sex-segregated men used prostitutes, and upon returning home, infected their sweethearts and wives, damaging generations to come.[130] Prostitutes were the agents of all that was worst in men. They offered the most extreme example of the reversal of nature by which women exhibited sex-attraction plumage. In the frequent and needless changes called "fashion," prostitutes led the way, so as to please men's sex-indulgent demand for variety.[131]

The urban framework of Progressive Era America facilitated these dynamics. In rural and agricultural contexts, a wife was a productive partner. Men and women married young, and their sex attraction was "natural" and "normal."[132] In the industrialized Northeast and Mid-Atlantic cities, by contrast, wives only consumed, supported by husbands. Men delayed marriage until they could provide fully for their own consumer. For the unfortunate fatherless adult son with a mother and sisters to support, marriage might be delayed indefinitely, until husbands prepared to support his sisters appeared.[133] Delaying marriage to an "unnatural" age artificially heightened the demand for prostitution. Sex ratios and marriage markets skewed, their "balance thrown out," as Gilman put it.[134] Some desire for sex was "natural" in mature animals, making prostitution appear inevitable.

Gilman's definition of feminism placed a central focus on responsible motherhood of "the race" (Homo sapiens). Feminism postulated "a womanhood free, strong, clean and conscious of its power and duty. This means selective motherhood, the careful choosing of fit men for husbands. . . . This means a higher standard of chastity, both in marriage and out, for men as well as women. It means a recognition of the responsibility of socially organized mothers for the welfare of children."[135] This intensified her concern about the ubiquity of prostitution. This evil institution potentially (if not actually) affected all women, but also children, born and unborn, through inherited syphilis and gonorrhea.[136] Gilman proposed the elimination of prostitution as a key institution of "Our" Androcentric Culture." In the development of a human world, superseding androcentrism, women and men would be partners in productive labor. Both the demand and the supply for prostitution would cease, she projected, within one generation.

Gilman's position on prostitutes as *women* (as distinct from prostitution the institution[137]) can disturb or offend current feminist sensibilities.[138] She proposed a reconfiguration of "vice," placing the focus on the male demand for prostitution. It was a trade, a living for women, albeit an injurious and obnoxious one. For men, however, it was an indulgence, a recreation, a pleasure, a form of sexuality, with dangerous consequences for women, children, and "the race." Prostitution must be swept away as a precondition for progressive change for women. She urged legal reform. Practices presently legal or considered only trivial offenses needed serious punishment. Seducing girls into prostitution, living off the earnings and related extortion from prostitutes, knowingly infecting a wife, and "poisoning" an unborn child—all these practices had to end.[139] Gilman's concerns about prostitution should be analyzed in the framework of her feminist evolutionary arguments.[140] The consequences of prostitution, then, had to be faced by "clean" women, to right eugenic wrongs and to put the prostitute out of business.

Arguably, prostitution's analytic significance accelerated within Gilman's lectures and writing, heightening in the 1910–16 period of wider international and wartime concern about "the red menace" of venereal diseases.[141] Her prostitution-disease focus drew upon wartime xenophobia and anti-Semitism, as eastern European Jewish immigration to Manhattan suddenly soared to two million. Women and girls formed 43 percent of the Jewish Poles, Lithuanians, Russians, and Hungarians immigrating to America, many arriving without families or friends.[142] Moreover, her interest in population issues, eugenics, sex ratios, marriage markets, and "race progress" propelled her concern with the allegedly deteriorating American "stock," including birth defects and venereal disease-related hereditary disabilities.[143] These concerns widened her focus from prostitution to all women's increased "sex indulgence," their "aping" of the sexual mores of men, and the resulting "race" consequences. Ironically, this enlarged concern diluted the earlier specificity of her views on the prostitution problem, lending to a more general critique of what she called the "sexolatry" of the modern age, including sex relations involving no direct monetary exchange: "Another obstacle is that resurgence of phallic worship set before us in the solemn phraseology of psychoanalyses. This pitifully narrow and morbid philosophy presumes to discuss sex from observation of humanity only. It is confronted with our excessive development and assumes it to be normal. It ignores the evidence of the entire living world below us, basing its conclusions on the behavior and desires of an animal which stands alone in nature for misery and disease in sex relation."[144]

Prostitution began its place in Gilman's analysis as an issue of sexual economics and masculine distortion of nature in libidinous excess. She had not anticipated masculine sexual "excess" becoming normative, nor that women's equality could extend to erotic equality, with male sexuality recast as paradigmatic for both sexes. This sidelined her earlier feminist analysis of prostitution. If it remained significant for feminist analysis, changed understandings of sexuality eclipsed prostitution's emblematic status, even in the era of the Great Depression, when other issues were foregrounded.

Declining focus on prostitution coincided with Gilman's concerns about "sex and race progress," as an increased rather than reduced indulgence of sex on demand represented a distortion of nature. Now all women—not just those set apart—experienced pressure to meet men's sexual demands. In the solemn dictates of popularized Freudianism, women received the brainwashing message that constant sexual indulgence was natural, no longer to be unhealthily repressed. These developments threatened her long-predicted political unification of women as a sex against the common menace of prostitution and forced sexual service to men.[145]

Gilman had sought to end prostitution as a prerequisite for changing men's sexual behavior to more resemble women's. As author of *Women and Economics*, she did not anticipate in 1898 that ending women's dependence on prostitution might coincide with women's sexual behavior increasingly resembling men's.[146] If she began her theoretical career by analyzing the prostitution-economics-disease connection, spotlighting men, she ended it by confronting the prostitution-sexuality continuum—for *women*.

If Gilman imagined a "human world" resting upon white, racially progressive men (perhaps like her husband Houghton) accepting conjugal periodicity, partial celibacy, and no prostitution, her optimism was difficult to sustain. Her impassioned diatribes against psychoanalysis, sexology, sexual promiscuity, and virtually birth control for women confronted her 1920s contemporaries' proclivities.[147] Prostitution, as a target for eradication, was one dimension of her wider critique of androcentric sexuality. Analysis of this sexual critique helps to explain her ambivalent and changing approach to birth control.

Race Degeneration, "Sexolatry," and Birth Control

Gilman represented motherhood as "natural," the desirable glory of every woman's life. On the other hand, she argued that maternity led to women's oppression, confinement to dependency, and primitive domestic seclusion in the home. Seeking to deconstruct the supposed "naturalism" of motherhood and insisting on adult women's right to paid work and economic independence, Gilman might be expected to have supported universal access to birth control. Yet she did not, opposing it until the latter 1920s, in the belief that it disempowered women.

Her earliest writings endorsed reduced childbearing, taking smaller families as a proxy for "race progress." Quoting Spencer and Galton, she declared that "Reproduction is in inverse relation to individuation."[148] The more advanced a civilization, the lower its birthrate, and the higher its quality of motherhood and child rearing. She offered two or three children as the ideal for Progressive Era America. Yet women faced difficult sexual struggles to limit reproduction to this level. Men's expectations of conjugal rights could mean constant pregnancy, while the alternative options looked problematic. Ovulation was misunderstood. An erroneous theory put the fertile period late in the menstrual cycle and during the menstrual period and declared midcycle "safe." Efforts to prevent excessive births by careful timing of intercourse were rewarded with frequent conception.[149] Perhaps this was Gilman's experience. The present theory of ovulation, twelve to sixteen days before the next period, was not published in medical journals until 1928, long after Gilman's reproductive life.[150] Some of her writings also concerned women dying in childbirth.[151] Gilman lived before penicillin dramatically had reduced puerperal risks.

These circumstances generated a huge demand for criminal abortion, resulting in sensationalized press stories of tragic fatalities and illnesses throughout the Progressive Era. Gilman was not the only feminist or reformer to oppose abortion as a solution to women's dependence, subjugation, and cruel treatment by men.[152] Wartime conditions spotlighted abortion and its grim toll on women in New York City.[153] It is no accident that the fictionalized women of *Herland* (1915) greeted their visitors' news that abortion took place in "Ourland" with quiet horror.[154] Gilman resisted the rhetoric about a population explosion in the 1920s, particularly the moral burden it placed upon women to affect "control," while men's sexual "excess" and "irresponsibility" remained unchallenged. The "menace" of women's reproduction, as articulated by the eminent population biologist Raymond Pearl, irritated her because it pathologized maternity.[155] It was a sorry day when women judged conditions so disadvantageous to motherhood that they declined this basic corporeal function.

Unquestionably Gilman supported "voluntary motherhood," as did her feminist peers in the United States and around the world.[156] She disputed the proposed means, however, dreading the sexual implications of birth control. Compulsory birth control conscripted women into male-serving sexual behavior. It further enlarged men's demand for unlimited sexual indulgence, removing one of few disincentives: unwanted offspring. Moreover, it pointed away from women's emancipation through reducing the emphasis on sex functions, permitting women to rejoin human "race" progress.[157] When fully enslaved and helplessly under dominant male tutelage, women were used for pleasure: "The real trend of the woman's movement is away from the long abuse of this relationship. It postulates freedom of the woman from that abuse, not freedom to join in it. The misused movement we call 'birth control' is intended to protect the mother from enforced childbearing, and has been most beneficial to the crowded poor. But in the present mishandling of the movement it has come to be, as it were, a free ticket for selfish and fruitless indulgence, and an aid in the lamentable misbehavior of our times, affecting both men and women."[158]

In Gilman's view, a women's version of a sexuality consistent with "race progress" needed cultural space. Sex indulgence under present conditions hindered rather than fostered "race progress." Connecting sexual excess and women's enslavement, birth control obstructed women from "naturally" limiting sexual intercourse to reproduction. The loss of women's freedom retarded "race progress" through disease and frightful outcomes, including "the wholesale weakening of old civilizations . . . allowing their easy conquest by fresher races, not yet rich enough to follow the same road." Repeating her interest in historical perspective, Gilman ventured that it would be most illuminating to have "a chart, marking in deepening color the effect of increasing misuse of sex on the progress of one people after another."[159] The problem for women, then, lay in the sex relation itself, and all its retarding ramifications.[160] Racialized discourses supplied analogies and comparisons to advance her arguments. Her claims would have been less persuasive to her readers without such well-worn, ill-informed, and familiar stereotypes: "We find social progress differing widely in degree and in rate of advancement among different races, but we do not find that they differ commensurately in sex development, or that sex is the acting cause of their progress. Is the contrasting record of Holland and Ireland traceable to any similar contrast in sex-power or habit? Is the stationary culture of Abyssinia due to lack of sex impulse? Is the sudden and amazing progress of Japan based on as sudden and amazing a development of sex activity? No, real race progress has no such relation. Whether we look at sex as a simple physical phenomenon, or as of the highest psychic development in noble emotion, it remains an individual affair; whereas civilization, in all its advance, stagnation or collapse, is a social affair."[161]

At best, birth control was the least of other evils, already signifying women's disadvantage. Birth control was damage control. The disastrous state of the human sex relation required change.[162] She believed that the promotion of birth control, coinciding with the popularization of psychoanalysis, conspired to defeat the new generation of women. Lurking behind demographic justifications for birth control, an unspoken masculinist position asserted itself: coitus was recreation, and women its more willing participants if they did not fear pregnancy. Gilman's hypothesized alliance between birth control advocacy and psychoanalysis approached a conspiracy theory. Faced with the aspirations of newly enfranchised women citizens, men counterattacked. Women had challenged hydraulic accounts of male sexuality, with their alleged need for constant indulgence: "The overdeveloped sex instinct of men, requiring more than women were willing to give, has previously backed its demands by an imposing array of civil and religious laws requiring feminine submission, has not scrupled to use force or falsehood, and held final power through the economic dependence of women. . . . But now that the woman no longer admits that 'he shall rule over her,' and is able to modify the laws; now that she has become the braver, and above all is attaining financial freedom, her previous master has no hold upon her beyond natural attraction and—persuasion."[163]

All over the feminist world, texts, tracts, speeches, and sermons had repudiated this androcentric maxim. So androcentric discourse shifted: "Whereas in the past women were taught that they had no such 'imperative instincts' as men, the wooer, even the husband, sought to preserve this impression, now it is quite otherwise. All that elaborate theory of feminine chastity, that worship of virginity, goes by the board, and women are given a reversed theory—that they are just the same as men, if not more so; our 'double standard' is undoubled and ironed flat—to the level of masculine desire. Clothed in the solemn, newly invented terms of psychoanalysis, a theory of sex [is] urged upon us which bases all our activities upon this one function. It is exalted as not only an imperative instinct, but as *the* imperative instinct, no others being recognized save the demands of the stomach. Surely never was more physical a theory disguised in the technical verbiage of 'psychology.'"[164]

Gilman deplored psychoanalysis taking the masculine to be the human, since it thereby worked against her efforts to reconfigure sexuality in what she called "human" terms. Nonetheless, she understood how feminist equality implied for younger women equal sexual indulgence: "We should not too harshly blame the ingenious mind of man for thinking up a new theory to retain what the old ones no longer assured him; nor too severely criticize the subject class, so newly freed, for committing the same excesses, the same eager imitations of the previous master, which history shows in any recently enfranchised people. Just as women have imitated the drug-habits of men, without the faintest excuse or reason, merely to show that they can, so are they imitating men's sex habits, in large measure."[165] This phase of emulation would pass, Gilman suggested, perhaps over about three generations. A central finding had emerged from a half-century of sexology: women, almost universally, desired less intercourse than was their marital experience, and men desired more.[166] This finding and its ramifications defined androcentric heterosexuality. It had to change.

Moreover, birth control had other connections. Gilman insisted that the world's future population must be determined by women, as an index of women's judgment about their conditions.[167] Her involvement in newly racialized discourses complicated her longstanding analysis of androcentric sexuality and birth control. Critics approvingly represent her change, sometime during the 1920s, from apparent condemnation of birth control to endorsement as progress toward a "woman's right to choose," a position recognizable to late-twentieth-century feminists.[168] Arguably, this is a presentist reading, distorting the racialized, eugenic basis of Gilman's argument.[169]

For Gilman, the emancipation of women should lead to a woman-regulated population without man-serving, man-controlled birth control—and the "unreconstructed" sexuality it implied. This aspiration collided, however, with the pressing reality of the majority of women's situations. Gilman faced the fact that most women lived with men who were entitled by law to conjugal rights and who allegedly "needed" frequent intercourse for health, sanity, fidelity, and the stability of their support for their families. Without birth control, women risked excessive childbearing, which was detrimental to race progress, or impairment and death from the "loathsome" practice of abortion.[170] To this extent, then, she allowed birth control as a "feminist" issue. However, she represented feminist approaches to birth control as individualistic and emotional, rather than as social or collective in import: "Perhaps since birth is woman's business it is right that she have some voice in discussing its control. . . . Mrs. Sanger's appeal for the over-burdened mother is a just one, it is enough to warrant prompt action, to justify birth control; but there is far more to be considered than any personal feeling, however strong . . . we are slow to grasp the distinct proposition that it is her place to regulate the population of the earth. . . . An active sense of social motherhood is desperately needed among the women of today, if we are to put a stop to war, to cease producing defectives, and to begin conscious improvement of our stock."[171] The question of the "stock" moved Gilman from her utopia of voluntary motherhood to active support for birth control. With no prospect of the population reducing excessive forms of sex indulgence, restrictions on birth control imperiled the human future. Contraception might be the only way to reduce the evolutionary menace of "the unfit" specifically, and the ill consequences of excessive sex indulgence more generally.[172] Thus, Gilman did not finally support birth control as a *women's* right, or as a practice for all women. Some "stocks," meaning Aryan and educated, risked extinction.[173] Gilman eventually saw birth control as a class obligation of the least fit of parents. Archaic laws suppressing contraceptive knowledge and the pernicious effects of backward religious prohibitions against birth control all had to end.[174]

An immediate context framed Gilman's shift to pro-birth control: mass immigration of European peoples with cultural attributes uncongenial to her Yankee disposition and cultural background. As Lanser has argued, America had become a culture "obsessively preoccupied with race as the foundation of character, a culture desperate to maintain Aryan superiority in the face of massive immigrations from Southern and Eastern Europe, a culture openly anti-Semitic, anti-Asian, anti-Catholic, and Jim Crow."[175] These sentiments underpinned Gilman's advocacy of birth control more than feminist arguments.[176]

The Immigrant Threat to the Feminist Polity

Gilman had been familiar with eugenic and anti-immigrant sentiments since the late nineteenth century. Yet her earlier work showed impatience and even bemusement with both of these allied positions. Reporting to her fiancé Houghton Gilman on a lecture she would give at the headquarters of progressivism, Jane Addams's Hull House in Chicago in 1898, she specified her position on immigrants: "Tonight I speak at Hull House on 'Our Social Progress.' . . . People get so blue, the best people—and don't see her move at all. America in especial I want to speak of—touching on the public phenomena we groan over, and show how healthy we are after all. Take the immigrant question—look at it from the standpoint of progress in history—show the thing to be noted is not the incidental disturbance caused by hasty assimilation of varied racial elements—but here is a land where all the nations of the earth can live together, compelled by the same free and enlightening popular spirit. Show that these 'lower classes' we so condemn as immigrants are healthier grafts upon our body politic than those highly specialized branches would be and facts prove their rapid assumption of citizenship."[177] With her support for the woman suffrage movement, her sentiments were both sincere and strategic in citing new immigrants as strengthening American democracy by adding diverse new elements, a clear argument for women's petition to become part of that same body politic. She wrote to Houghton that she found woman suffrage as an autonomous subject more difficult to advocate enthusiastically than when it connected with other issues. In this case, immigration helped her make broader points. While she remained a noncitizen on the basis of sex, she remained relatively generous on the topic of immigrants. Moreover, in her article of 1904 "Malthusianism and Race Suicide," she asserted that "elevate human life and the birthrate will take care of itself. The American fear is that some people will increase faster than others—as indeed they perceptibly do. We complain that our 'American stock' does not increase fast enough, and that the 'foreign stock' does. This is an amusing distinction—as if none were Americans save those whose foreign stock came over in a certain century, charter members as it were—all later additions inferior."[178]

Defense of immigrants within America, however, did not amount to multiculturalism. Nativism dominated her anguished letter to Houghton when in 1900 her ex-husband, Walter Stetson, and his wife, Grace, proposed to take her daughter, Katharine, to live with them in Italy: "I don't want her foreignized. . . . She need not be a 'reformer,' but she shall at least be an American if I can fix it."[179] Furthermore, she had difficulty accepting or respecting religions and ethics of non-Western cultures: "All this eastern thought gives me mental nausea—always did. It is one of the most sharply defined instincts I have. Anything occult, psychic—metaphysical quite sickens me."[180]

Twenty years later her position on immigration strongly resembled that which she had criticized in 1897 and 1904. To the defenders of unlimited immigration, she responded that, while it was true that "Americans" were a mixed race, some blends were better than others. Summarizing Gilman's view of the connection between immigration and feminism, Lanser has written that "for Gilman, an educated, Protestant, social democratic Aryan, America explicitly represented the major hope for feminist possibility. . . . The immigrant 'invasion' thus becomes a direct threat to Gilman's program for feminist reform."[181]

An unrepentant opponent of mass immigration by the 1920s, Gilman published critiques of public policy, addressed public meetings, and worked on the executive boards of eugenics and Americanization societies.[182] Now a citizen, she also was increasingly alienated from younger feminists, in the role of grand old woman commentator on "the new generation of women."[183] She could even be found on public platforms playing the female curmudgeon in panel debates with titles such as "This Freedom of Women" and "Has Woman Suffrage Failed?"[184] Feeling alienated and offended that her advice was being ignored, she gravely pronounced feminist achievements imperiled from many quarters, most notably by ignorant, undemocratic immigrants from backward patriarchal cultures. Importantly, she now lived in Houghton's childhood home in Norwich, Connecticut, claiming that they were driven out of New York City—displaced—by obnoxious immigrants.

One part of the context for the anti-immigrant tilt to her rhetoric in the 1910s and 1920s was the largest influx ever of Jewish immigrants to the eastern United States. Whereas the only previous period of Jewish immigration (principally from Germany) brought about 50,000 Jews to the United States between 1840 and 1870, the second wave came principally from eastern Europe, with 2 million Jews immigrating between 1870 and 1924. This Jewish immigration formed a large portion of a more general acceleration in immigration to the United States. The highest rates either before or since came in the years 1905–14, with over a million immigrants annually in almost all of these peak years. The highest point of the tide was 1,285,349 in 1907. The total number of immigrants entering the United Stated between 1890 and 1917 was 17,991,486.[185] Moreover, while the 1910 census showed the foreign born as only 14.5 percent of the total population, as it had in 1860, the distribution had become quite different. Almost 80 percent of the immigrants in the Gilded Age and Progressive Era were concentrated in urban industrial areas of the Northeast, the Mid-Atlantic, and the eastern third of the United States.[186]

Confronted with this massive population change, Gilman asserted her distinguished Yankee roots. She shared the anxiety of Progressive Era intellectuals such as Frederick Jackson Turner that these aliens were replacing "the old American stock in the labor market," lowering the standard of living and increasing "the pressure of population upon the land."[187] Gilman approved of President Theodore Roosevelt's creation of a commission to analyze the immigrants arriving after 1883 in sociological, psychological, and eugenic terms and supported annual quotas.[188] The 1921 law, upheld by the courts in 1924, restricted the percentage of any given immigrant group to their percentage of the population in the 1890 census. Since the largest influx of eastern European Jews came after 1890, the measure most especially targeted Jewish immigration.[189] Gilman supported this reduction of

Jewish immigration, as well as the administration of literacy tests to immigrants, always aimed at "ignorant" eastern European Jews, southern European Catholics, and the equally Catholic Irish.[190]

Gilman's ethnocentric nativism was not an incidental or unfortunate aberration that, once rebuked or contextualized, can be shunned in favor of analysis of interesting other works of the Progressive Era, such as her *His Religion and Hers* (1923). For that text shared the year of 1923, creatively speaking, with Gilman's fiercest condemnation of immigration, "Is America Too Hospitable?" This article and others like it earned her a place not only in women's magazines and newspapers, but also in major mainstream journals such as *The Century, North American Review, Forum,* and *Nation.*[191] She was treated as an intelligent contributor to mainstream public debate.

Her use of nativist discourses was too active and inventive to represent a mere passive reflection of her era's beliefs, with which she was quietly brainwashed against her will. Rather, she took a principled and strategic stand against immigration, integrated with her concern to define a distinct American "race":

> It is quite true that we ourselves are a mixed race—as are all races today—and that we were once immigrants. All Americans have come from somewhere else. But all persons who come from somewhere else are not therefore Americans. The American blend is from a few closely connected races. . . . With glowing enthusiasm we have seized upon one misplaced metaphor, and call our country now a "melting pot" instead of an asylum. Our country is our home. Any man who wants to turn his home into an asylum of a melting pot is—well, he is a person of peculiar tastes. Why did we ever so stupidly accept that metaphor? . . . The American people, as a racial stock, are mainly of English descent, mingled with the closely allied Teutonic and Scandinavian strains, of which indeed the English are compounded, together with some admixture of the Celt and Gael. . . . The American people, as representing a group culture, brought with them from England and Holland and Scandinavia the demand for freedom and the capacity to get it . . . they made rapid growth and were able to add to their inherited tendencies a flexible progressiveness, and inventive ingenuity, a patience and broad kindliness of disposition which form a distinct national character.[192]

"Is America Too Hospitable?" (1923) was a spirited attack upon the "melting pot" representation of America. Equally a polemic against the exploitation of America by immigrants practicing cultural separatism, she criticized immigrants for speaking only their native languages, producing their own newspapers, opening their own universities, seeking to infiltrate "ours," and ungratefully criticizing American culture and society. Wartime revealed how few foreigners would fight for America: "Even so long established residents as the Irish remain Irish,—they are not Americans. They would willingly sacrifice the interests of this country, or of the world as a whole for the sake of Ireland."[193]

Most offensive to modern eyes are the sections of the article concerned with the ill effects of the intermingling of incompatible races, replete with analogies from cookery, dog breeding, agriculture, horticulture, and botany.[194] As if to foreshadow the welfare debates of the later twentieth century, Gilman offered reasons immigrants should not be permitted to continue exploiting the kindly American national character. Earners were taxed to support those unable to earn. Prisoners provided a particularly sore example of this. She urged that able-bodied prisoners pay entirely for their own upkeep through supervised, waged work, and she objected to the unnatural situation in which the "best is handicapped by the worst, and this increasingly so as we learn new ways of keeping incompetents alive." Those who objected to sterilization of the "patently unfit" she described contemptuously as "tender hearts."[195] As for the well-known attraction of America as a rich country, she responded: "But Africa is a great rich country too; why not go there? They do not wish to go there; the country is 'undeveloped;' there are savages in it. True, but this country was undeveloped, when we came here, and there were savages in it. Our swarming immigrants do not wish for a wilderness, nor for enemies. They like an established nation, with free education, free hospitals, free nursing, and more remunerative employment than they can find at home."[196]

Passing glibly over the colonization of Native American lands and the attempted genocide of the so-called savages, Gilman symbolically turned the Yankee Americans, and perhaps those assimilated by the 1890 census, into the true "native" Americans. Meanwhile, the insectile connotations of "swarming" analogized immigrants with so-called savages, rendering them at best subhuman, and implicitly nonhuman. Portraying immigrants as rapacious, grasping, and greedy, she claimed that they were not entitled to the services and opportunities they sought. They exploited "real" Americans.

Gilman believed that the most vigorous and able of the immigrant nations stayed at home. America thus received the least robust of the world. How long could a nation so substantially infused with the human refuse remain preeminent in the world? She offered a scathing reply to the defense that such immigration fostered democracy around the world and contributed special gifts to American life. Any country that wanted a democracy could have one. No one could stop them. But immigrants from nondemocratic nations dragged down and retarded the development of the precious American democracy, just as it was finally admitting its women to citizenship. They "mix our physical stock and clog the half-grown 'body politic' with all manner of undemocratic peoples."[197]

Moreover, the special cultural gifts of each nation and ethnic group were gifts to the world only when offered from their home context. They were not gifts within America. Instead, these transplanted "gifts" became liabilities and sources of friction. She warned her countrypeople to resist and fear the "mongrelization" of America, the looming threat of the era: "It is also a mistake to suppose that social evolution requires the even march of all races to the same goal. . . . The sea-weeds and mosses have not all become oaks and roses. . . . Evolution selects, and social evolution follows the same law. If you are trying to improve corn, you do not wait to bring all the weeds in the garden to the corn level before going on."[198]

Confronted with difference, then, Gilman asserted the importance of race purity, noting that the wise of both the white and black races in America concurred on the undesirable outcomes of "interbreeding." She considered the Eurasian combination the "most unfortunate."[199] Fear of "yellow" was especially pervasive in her writing, and as Lanser explains, "yellow" was the ascribed color for a diverse range of peoples who were neither dark-skinned nor Nordic.[200] For Gilman, certain groups—some "yellow," some not—especially posed a threat: the eastern Europeans, the Jews of all kinds, the Chinese, the Irish, and the southern Europeans. Though earlier in the Progressive Era, Gilman dismissed as ludicrous the notion that superior peoples risked domination by inferior ones, war taught that "a conquering people is not necessarily superior to the conquered, and that social progress has been most seriously retarded by the destruction of more advanced societies by the less so."[201]

This made the social Darwinist article of faith that the stronger and more civilized naturally and therefore justly prevailed over the weaker and inferior "most unsatisfactory."[202] Gilman's eugenically inspired conversion to birth control advocate responded to the horrors of war and the hopes for peace. By 1927, she contended that nations with unchecked birthrates pursued imperialist expansion. Russia, China, and Africa loomed as threats to world peace, as Germany had just done, "so, we are faced with a choice of three courses: shall we allow the unchecked increase of population, till all . . . peoples either mixed, or stratified in castes? Shall we allow that unchecked increase and fight continually for our places in the sun? Or shall we keep population within rationally chosen limits?"[203] By the end of her life, Gilman had forged new connections between feminist reform and a cluster of stances related to the regulation of population characteristics, including eugenics, birth control, and restrictions on immigration.

Conclusion: Feminist Progressivism or Progressive Feminism?

How might Gilman's rhetoric in her lectures and nonfiction publications, especially in relation to the themes of sexuality, population, race, and gender, illuminate the meaning of "feminist progressivism" or "progressive feminism"? Do her preoccupations with these topics sketch a distinctly *feminist* take on progressive theory and reform—notwithstanding her ambivalent public utterances on the term "feminist" itself?[204]

Gilman's feminism appeared nowhere more progressivist than in her articulations about prostitution. Reformers depicted the increased visibility of prostitution as an evil side effect of urban, industrial capitalism, deploring the conspiracy of silence that accepted it as ineradicable. If she accepted parts of this Progressive Era reform analysis, she regarded it as fundamentally lopsided. Her distinct focus was on demand, refusing its view as "natural," sharing a minority Progressive Era contention that epidemics of incurable venereal diseases impelled aggressive strategies to end demand, permitted by men's desires, fostered widespread infection. Prostitution should be eliminated, not just purged of its diseased workers. This meant ending the demand for prostitution through education and campaigns to stigmatize its clients.[205]

Gilman's concern with prostitution then was representatively "progressive." Yet she took analysis of it as an androcentric institution and sexual practice considerably further than most of her Progressive Era contemporaries. Her analysis centered on her reworked, neo-Darwinian, eventually eugenic accounts both of women's degradation within androcentric culture and on her "race" regenerating solutions. The "human" rather than the androcentric world would be without either demand for prostitution or humans motivated to supply it under any circumstances.

Her more general discourse upon sexuality embraced stances uncongenial and even ludicrous to late-twentieth-century readers. These included her virulent attack on libertarian sexual mores, Freudian psychoanalysis, and artificial birth control; her insistence that the project of feminism must be the restoration of sexual periodicity and female-initiated sex selection; her advocacy of a feminist-inflected version of eugenics, immigration quotas, and aggressive campaigns of Americanization of all immigrants; and her belated advancing of birth control as a check on the proliferation of "the unfit." All of these ideas related to her increasing anti-Semitism, racism, ethnocentrism, and nativism. Arguably, Gilman could not have reached her particular feminist insights without adherence to these sentiments. She both racialized the pivotal claims about sex and human progress and sexualized Progressive Era racial tropes and theoretics. Beyond merely *using* prevailing discourses, she deepened their ramifications by grafting onto them analysis of sex and gender.

If feminists today find this too drastic, revealed thereby may be an investment in feminist innocence, assuming feminist marginality to mainstream discourses to reside elsewhere, undefiled. At most, for adherents of this stance, past feminists may suffer influence from powerful others. As a path-breaker in these problematic Progressive Era discourses, Gilman challenges present critics to take her words seriously, understanding (as distinct from endorsing) her contribution, reconnecting the various dimensions of her thought, and grasping her racialized feminism and feminist racism in their mutual implications. Her concerns with sexuality, reproduction, and population attributes, arguably, were quintessentially progressive. Yet she exceeded conventional Progressive Era discourses, contributing original and critical dimensions and destabilizing existing verities.

Her interventions here were integral to her developing feminism. Over a century of challenging women's abject subordination in Nordic cultures (now crowned with symbolic Progressive Era victories, such as the vote) might be stalled by the immigrant "swarm," the threat of war, and "melting pot" cultural philosophies. Confronting such dire postwar threats, she reversed her previous opposition to birth control, tolerance for immigrants, and skepticism about eugenics.

Most fundamentally, Gilman resisted the twentieth-century shift separating reproduction and sexuality and valorizing the latter as only further degrading women. She was not alone in this conviction, and dubbing it "conservative" or "puritanical" sheds little light on her interventions into debates on sexuality, gender, and reproduction. If a "human world" was the desirable successor to the androcentric era, contemporary trends—especially developments in psychoanalysis, sexual libertarianism, and birth control movements—left little hope of its advent. Meanwhile, the "infestation" of America with "less-developed" peoples posed an immediate threat.[206]

Gilman's progressive feminism was caught between two discursive moments, formed after the vogue of reform Darwinism but before the full impact of psychoanalysis and scientific sexology within Anglophone cultures. In her shrill charges of "sexolatry," "phallic worship," and "sex obsession," she registered the magnitude of these developments. Had she lived longer, she may have seen them in different terms, standing as she did on the brink of a reanalysis of sexuality that extolled sexual expression and experimentation and lifted taboos. Claiming to free women erotically, libertarianism threatened her theoretical legacy, which blended sexual economics and modified social Darwinism.[207] Insisting on the desirability of human return to the "natural" order of periodic sex relations for reproduction, she ended her life rejecting that increasingly orthodox new view of sexuality.

Gilman demonstrated the integration of feminist theory within Progressive Era discourses, its intelligibility within public debates, and the limited utility of certain progressivist tenets. Despite her criticisms of economic dependency and its sexual implications, Gilman saw marriage as inevitable for women's "race-function" as mothers.[208] Feminism's task was to guide women toward renegotiating the labor description of "wife" and "mother," combining them with paid work.

Some of the most historically significant feminist analysts, by definition, have not worn well. The more integrated and effective these analyses were within discourses of their own period, the less likely that they will withstand the application of presentist criteria often used by historians of feminism. Gilman's feminist preoccupations, so absolutely of the Progressive Era, may be an important caution against the search for worthy foremothers of whom today's feminists can approve. Not only was Gilman a significant exemplar of progressivism, notwithstanding its present historiographical instabilities, her record and currency for at least twenty years of the period placed feminism firmly within the progressivist agenda. Her preoccupations and rhetorical strategies can contribute to a recasting of tangled debates presently generating nihilism around "progressivism" itself. Gilman was what progressivism was, what feminism was, warts and all. Her feminist discourses on prostitution, sexuality, birth control, and eugenics racialized these domains, obtaining impetus from Progressive Era racism, ethnocentrism, anti-Semitism, and nativism. She sexualized unfolding interwar discourses on race, immigration, and American national identity, to the detriment of those non-Americans and non-Aryans whom she identified as threat to women's claims to "race progress." As America's most significant first-wave feminist theorist, the "Veblen" of the women's movement, her integration into vexed Progressive Era discourses impels serious reevaluations of the history of feminist thought and American rhetoric.

Notes

1. See for instance "The Mother's World," *Geneva Evening World*, 20 December 1902, "Woman Created First," *New York Tribune*, 17 October 1903, p. 7; "Adam the Real Rib Mrs. Gilman Insists," *New York Times*, 19 February 1914, p. 9; "A Feminist Revision of History," *New York Times*, 3 April 1914, p. 10; "Great Duty of Women after War," *Boston Post*, 26 February 1918, p. 2; "Fiction of America Being a Melting Pot Unmasked by Charlotte Perkins Gilman," *Dallas Morning News*, 15 February 1926, p. 9 and 11, Charlotte Perkins Gilman Papers (CPGP) 177/266 and 287.

2. For an account of the newness and controversial status of women speakers in the early and mid-nineteenth century, see Davis Yoakim, "Pioneer Women Orators of America," *Quarterly Journal of Speech* 23 (1937): 251–59.

3. "Charlotte Perkins Gilman: The Apostle for Women," unidentified journal offprint, pencil-dated "1905" in Gilman's handwriting, CPGP, Arthur and Elizabeth Schlesinger Library on the History of Women in America, 177/266/1.

4. Carl N. Degler, "Charlotte Perkins Gilman and the Theory and Practice of Feminism," *American Quarterly* 8 (spring 1956): 21.

5. Mary Armfield Hill, ed., *A Journey From Within: The Love Letters of Charlotte Perkins Gilman, 1897–1900* (Lewisburg, Pa.: Bucknell University Press, 1995), 17; Alice Rossi, *The Feminist Papers* (New York: Bantam, 1973), 568.

6. Alice Stone Blackwell to Charlotte Perkins Gilman (hereafter CPG), 4 April 1912, CPGP, 141/1.

7. For a full and complete numbered listing of most surviving items, see Gary Scharn-horst, *Charlotte Perkins Gilman: A Bibliography* (Metuchen, N.J.: Scarecrow Press, 1985).

8. Gail Bederman, *Manliness & Civilization: A Cultural History of Race & Gender in the United States, 1880–1930* (Chicago: University of Chicago Press, 1995),132. The most significant CPG works were "The Yellow Wallpaper," *The New England Magazine* 5 (January 1892): 647–55; *In This Our World* (Oakland, Calif.: McCombs and Vaughan, 1893); *Women and Economics* (1898; reprint, Berkeley and Los Angeles: University of California Press, 1998); *Concerning Children* (Boston: Small, Maynard, and Co., 1900); *The Home: Its Work and Influence* (New York: McClure, 1903); *Human Work* (New York: McClure, Phillips and Co., 1904); *What Diathna Did* (New York: Charlton Co., 1910); *The Crux* (New York: Charlton Co., 1911); *Moving the Mountain* (New York: Charlton Co., 1911); *The Man-Made World, or Our Androcentric Culture* (New York: Charlton Co., 1911); *Herland* (1915; reprint, New York: Pantheon, 1979); *His Religion and Hers: A Study of the Faith of Our Fathers and the Work of Our Mothers* (New York: Century Co., 1923); and *The Living of Charlotte Perkins Gilman: An Autobiography* (New York: D. Appleton-Century Co., 1935).

9. Hill, *A Journey From Within*, 17; and Gary Scharnhorst, *Charlotte Perkins Gilman* (Boston: Twayne Publishers, 1985), 5.

10. Bernice Hausman, "Sex Before Gender: Charlotte Perkins Gilman and the Evolutionary Paradigm of Utopia," *Feminist Studies* 24 (fall 1998): 489–510.

11. See for instance Bederman, *Manliness & Civilization*, 121–69.

12. Robert M. Crunden, "Progressivism," in *The Reader's Companion to American History*, ed. Eric Foner and John A. Garraty (Boston: Houghton Mifflin, 1995), 869.

13. The contrast between CPG and Jane Addams (1860–1935) is that the former is usually called the most famous feminist of the era, and Addams, the most famous *woman*. While some of Addams's prolific writings directly concerned women, the framework

of her preoccupations are cited as quintessentially progressivist, including *Democracy and Social Ethics* (New York: Macmillan, 1902); *Newer Ideals of Peace* (New York: Macmillan, 1907); *The Spirit of Youth and the City Streets* (New York: Macmillan, 1909); *Women and Public Housekeeping* (New York: National Women's Suffrage Publishing Co., 1910); *A New Conscience and an Ancient Evil* (New York: Macmillan, 1912); *Women at The Hague* (New York: Macmillan, 1915); *The Long Road of Women's Memory* (New York: Macmillan, 1916); *The Child, the Clinic, and the Court* (New York: Macmillan, 1927); and *Forty Years at Hull House* (New York: Macmillan, 1935). Most Addams scholarship was published before 1990, most notably James Weber Linn, *Jane Addams: A Biography* (New York: D. Appleton-Century Co., 1935); Winifred Esther Wise, *Jane Addams of Hull House* (New York: Harcourt Brace and Co., 1935); Margaret Tims, *Jane Addams of Hull House, 1860–1935: A Centenary Study* (New York: Macmillan, 1961); Christopher Lasch, ed., *The Social Thought of Jane Addams* (New York: Irvington, 1965); Cornelia Meigs, *Jane Addams, Pioneer for Social Justice: A Biography* (Boston: Little Brown, and Co., 1970); Daniel Levine, *Jane Addams and the Liberal Tradition* (Madison: Historical Society of Wisconsin, 1970); Allen Freeman Davis, *American Heroine: The Life and Legend of Jane Addams* (New York: Oxford University Press, 1973); John C. Farrell, *Beloved Lady: A History of Jane Addams' Ideas on Reform and Peace* (Baltimore: Johns Hopkins University Press, 1967); and Mary Jo Deegan, *Jane Addams and the Men of the Chicago School, 1892–1918* (New Brunswick, N.J.: Transaction Books, 1988). More recent work on Addams, mainly shorter articles, comes from fields such as urban history, philosophy, social work, and medicine, as well as women's studies. See also Stanley Lemmons, *The Woman Citizen: Social Feminism in the 1920s* (Charlottesville: University Press of Virginia, 1973); and "What's in a Name? The Limits of 'Social Feminism,' or Expanding the Vocabulary of Women's Political History," *Journal of American History* 76 (December 1989): 809–30.

14. See for instance Richard Hofstadter, *The Age of Reform: From Bryant to F. D. R.* (New York: Vintage, 1955), and *The Progressive Historians: Turner, Beard, and Parrington* (New York: Alfred Knopf, 1968).

15. In the following critical works, for instance, both published since 1980, Gilman's work receives token mention: Sean Dennis Cashman, *America in the Age of Titans: The Progressive Era and World War I* (New York: New York University Press, 1988), 248–49; David B. Danbom, *"The World of Hope": Progressives and the Struggle for an Ethical Public Life* (Philadelphia: Temple University Press, 1987), 186. In most of the "classic" and debated "revisionist" studies of the Progressive Era, however, Gilman receives no systematic analysis. See for instance Andrew Feffer, *The Chicago Pragmatists and American Progressivism* (Ithaca, N.Y.: Cornell University Press, 1993); Kenneth Finegold, *Experts and Politicians: Reform Challenges to Machine Politics in New York, Cleveland, and Chicago* (Princeton: Princeton University Press, 1995); Eldon J. Eisenach, *The Lost Promise of Progressivism* (Lawrence: University Press of Kansas, 1994); David W. Southern, *The Malignant Heritage: Yankee Progressives and the Negro Question, 1901–1914* (Chicago: Loyola University Press, 1968); William A. Link, *The Paradox of Southern Progressivism, 1880–1930* (Chapel Hill: University of North Carolina Press, 1992); Edward F. Haas, *Political Leadership in a Southern City: New Orleans in the Progressive Era, 1896–1902* (Ruston, La.: McGinty Publications, 1988); John Lugton Safford, *Pragmatism and the Progressive Movement in the United States: The Origin of the New Social Sciences* (Lanham, Md.: University Press of America, 1987); Lewis L. Gould, *Reform and Regulation: American Politics from Roosevelt to Wilson* (New York: Knopf, 1986); Paul D. Casdorph, *Republicans, Negroes, and Progressives in the South, 1912–1916* (University: University of Alabama Press, 1981); Morton Keller, *Regulating a New Society: Public Policy and Social Change in America, 1900–1933* (Cambridge: Harvard University Press, 1994); Martin Paulsson, *The Social Anxieties of Progressive Reform: Atlantic City, 1854–1920* (New York: New York University Press, 1994); Ronald L. Feinman, *Twilight of Progressivism: The Western Republican Senators and the New Deal* (Baltimore: Johns Hopkins University Press, 1981); John Whiteclay Chambers, *The Tyranny of Change: America in the Progressive Era, 1890–1920* (New York: St. Martin's Press, 1992); Noralee Frankel and Nancy S. Dye, eds., *Gender, Class, Race, and Reform in the Progressive Era* (Lexington, Ky.: University

Press of Kentucky, 1991); and Thomas G. Dyer, *Theodore Roosevelt and the Idea of Race* (Baton Rouge, La.: Louisiana State University Press, 1980).

16. Robert M. Crunden, "Progressivism," in *Reader's Companion,* 870; and Jane Addams to CPG, 19 July 1898, and Florence Kelley to CPG, 26 July 1898, CPGP, 177/137.

17. See for instance Judith Stacey and Barrie Thorne, "The Missing Feminist Revolution in Sociology," *Social Problems* 32 (1985): 301–16; and see also my "Evidence and Silence: Feminism and the Limits of History," in *Feminist Challenges: Social and Political Theory* ed. Carole Pateman and Elizabeth Grosz (Boston: Northeastern University Press, 1986), 173–89.

18. Elizabeth A. Grosz, "Feminist Theory and the Challenge to Disciplines," *Women's Studies International Forum* 10 (1987): 475–80.

19. Kay Daniels, introduction to *Women in Australia: A Guide to Records,* ed. Kay Daniels, Mary Murnane, and Anne Picot (Canberra: Australian Government Printing Office, 1976), xiii.

20. See for instance Carl N. Degler, *In Search of Human Nature: The Decline and Revival of Darwinism in American Social Thought* (New York: Oxford University Press, 1991); Donald K. Pickens, *Eugenics and the Progressives* (Nashville, Tenn.: Vanderbilt University Press, 1968); Nicole Hahn Rafter, *Creating Born Criminals* (Urbana, Ill.: University of Illinois Press, 1997); and Marouf A. Hasian, *The Rhetoric of Eugenics in Anglo-American Thought* (Athens: University of Georgia Press, 1996).

21. Political theorists and philosophers have demonstrated how the core paradigm could not simply include women because its tenets were predicated upon or defined by their exclusion. See Genevieve Lloyd, *The Man of Reason: "Male" and "Female" in Philosophy* (London: Jonathan Cape, 1984); and Sandra Harding, *Whose Science? Whose Reality? Thinking from Women's Lives* (Ithaca, N.Y.: Cornell University Press, 1991).

22. See for instance Nancy F. Cott, *The Grounding of Modern Feminism* (New Haven: Yale University Press, 1987); Rosalind Rosenberg, *Beyond Separate Spheres: Intellectual Roots of Modern Feminism* (New Haven: Yale University Press, 1982); Sarah Slavin Schram, *Plow Women Rather Than Reapers: An Intellectual History of Feminism in the United States* (Metuchen, N.J.: Scarecrow Press, 1978), esp. 37–39, 97–98, 267–69, and 387–89; Barbara Ryan, *Feminism and the Women's Movement: Dynamics of Change in Social Movement, Ideology, and Activism* (New York: Routledge, 1992); Linda K. Kerber, *Toward an Intellectual History of Women: Essays* (Chapel Hill: University of North Carolina Press, 1997); Suzanne M. Marilly, *Woman Suffrage and the Origins of Liberal Feminism in the United States, 1820–1920* (Cambridge: Harvard University Press, 1996); William L. O'Neill, *Feminism in America: A History* (New Brunswick, N.J.: Transaction Books, 1989); and Christine Bolt, *Feminist Ferment: "The Woman Question" in the USA and England, 1870–1940* (London: UCL, 1995).

23. Degler, "Charlotte Perkins Gilman," 21–39.

24. See for instance Mary Armfield Hill, *Charlotte Perkins Gilman: The Making of a Radical Feminist, 1860–1896* (Philadelphia: Temple University Press, 1980), and "Charlotte Perkins Gilman: A Feminist's Struggle with Womanhood," *Massachusetts Review* 21 (fall 1980): 503–26; Carol Ruth Berkin, "Private Woman, Public Woman," 150–73; Carol Farley Kessler, "Charlotte Perkins Gilman, 1860–1935," in *Modern American Women Writers,* ed. Elaine Showalter (New York: Charles Scribner's and Sons, 1991); Ann J. Lane, *To Herland and Beyond: The Life and Work of Charlotte Perkins Gilman* (New York: Pantheon, 1990); Sheryl L. Meyerling, introduction to *Charlotte Perkins Gilman: The Woman and Her Work,* ed. Sheryl L. Meyerling (Ann Arbor, Mich.: UMI Research Press, 1989), 1–11; and Elaine Hedges, afterword to *The Yellow Wallpaper* by Charlotte Perkins Gilman (Old Westbury, N.Y.: Feminist Press, 1973), 37–63.

25. For a critique of the effects of such parochialism on histories of feminism, see my "Contextualizing Late Nineteenth Century Feminism: Problems and Comparisons," *Journal of the Canadian Historical Association* 1 (1990): 17.

26. Judith A. Allen, *Rose Scott: Vision and Revision in Feminism, 1880–1925* (Melbourne: Oxford University Press, 1994), 33–34.

27. See for instance Lane, *To Herland and Beyond,* 225–56.

28. See for instance Eugenia C. DeLamotte, "Male and Female Mysteries in 'The Yellow Wallpaper,'" *Legacy* 5, no. 1 (1988): 3–14; Karen Ford, "'The Yellow Wallpaper' and

Women's Discourse," *Tulsa Studies in Women's Literature* 4, no. 2 (1985): 309–14; Lo-ralee MacPike, "Environment as Psychopathological Symbolism in 'The Yellow Wall-paper,'" *American Literary Realism, 1870–1910* 8 (summer 1975): 286–88; Jean Kennard, "Convention Coverage, or How to Read Your Own Life," *New Literary History* 13 (autumn 1981): 69–88; Beate Schopp-Schilling, "'The Yellow Wallpaper': A Redis-covered 'Realistic' Story," *American Literary Realism* 8 (summer 1975): 284–86; Carol Thomas Neely, "Alternative Women's Discourse," *Tulsa Studies in Women's Literature* 4, no. 1 (1985): 315–22; Paula A. Treichler, "The Wall behind 'The Yellow Wallpaper': A Response to Carol Neely and Karen Ford," *Tulsa Studies in Women's Literature* 4, no. 2 (1985): 323–30; Mary Beth Pringle, "La poetique de l'espace in Charlotte Perkins Gilman's 'The Yellow Wallpaper,'" *The French-American Review* 3 (winter-spring 1978): 15–22; Jeannette King and Pam Morris, "On Not Reading between the Lines: Models of Reading in 'The Yellow Wallpaper,'" *Studies in Short Fiction* 26 (fall 1989): 23–32; Diane Herndl, "The Writing Cure: Charlotte Perkins Gilman, Anna O., and 'Hysterical Writing,'" *NWSA Journal* 1, no. 1 (1988): 52–74; William Veeder, "Who Is Jane? The Intricate Feminism of Charlotte Perkins Gilman," *Arizona Quarterly* 44 (autumn 1988): 40–79; Georgia Johnston, "Exploring Lack and Absence in the Body/Text: Charlotte Perkins Gilman Prewriting Irigaray," *Women's Studies* 21 (1992): 75–86; Greg Johnson, "Gilman's Gothic Allegory: Rage and Redemption in 'The Yellow Wallpaper,'" *Studies in Short Fiction* 26 (fall 1989): 521–30; and Lisa Kasmer, "Charlotte Perkins Gilman's 'The Yellow Wallpaper': A Symptomatic Reading," *Literature and Psychology* 36 (fall 1990): 1–15.

29. Susan S. Lanser, "Feminist Criticism, 'The Yellow Wallpaper,' and the Politics of Color in America," *Feminist Studies* 15 (fall 1989): 416–23.

30. See for instance K. Graehme Hall, "Mothers and Children: 'Rising with the Resistless Tide' in *Herland*," in *Charlotte Perkins Gilman*, 161–72; Christopher P. Wilson, "Char-lotte Perkins Gilman's Steady Burghers: The Terrain of *Herland*," in *Charlotte Perkins Gilman*, 173–90; and Susan Gubar, "*She* in *Herland*: Feminism as Fantasy," in *Charlotte Perkins Gilman*, 191–202; Kathleen M. Lant, "The Rape of the Text: Charlotte Perkins Gilman's Violation of *Herland*," *Tulsa Studies in Women's Literature* 9 (fall 1990): 291–308; Laura Donaldson, "The Eve of Destruction: Charlotte Perkins Gilman and the Feminist Recreation of Paradise," *Women's Studies* 16 (1989): 373–87; and Thomas Galt Peyser, "Reproducing Utopia: Charlotte Perkins Gilman and *Herland*," *Studies in American Fiction* 20 (spring 1992): 1–16; CPG, *Herland*, ed. Ann J. Lane (New York: Women's Press, 1979).

31. Denise Knight, "The Reincarnation of Jane: Gilman's Companion to 'The Yellow Wall-paper,'" *Women's Studies,* 20 (1991): 87–102; Juliann E. Fleenor, "The Gothic Prism: Charlotte Perkins Gilman's Gothic Stories and Her Autobiography," in *The Female Gothic*, ed. Juliann E. Fleenor (Montreal: Eden, 1983), 227–41; and Michelle A. Masse, "Gothic Repetition: Husbands, Horrors, and Things That Go Bump in the Night," *Signs* 15 (1990): 679–709.

32. See for instance CPG, "The Giant Wisteria," *The New England Magazine* 4 (June 1891): 480–85, and CPG, *Unpunished*, ed. Catherine J. Golden and Denise K. Knight (1931; reprint, New York: Feminist Press, 1997); and on this novel see Lillian S. Robinson, "Killing Patriarchy: Charlotte Perkins Gilman, the Murder Mystery, and Post-feminist Propaganda," *Tulsa Studies in Women's Literature* 10 (fall 1991): 273–76.

33. See for instance Jane Atteridge Rose, "Image of the Self: The Example of Rebecca Hard-ing Davis and Charlotte Perkins Gilman," *English Language Notes* 29 (June 1992): 70; Charlotte Goodman, "Bitter Harvest: Charlotte Perkins Gilman and the Writing of Edith Summers Kelly's *Weeds*" (paper presented at the Second International Confer-ence on Charlotte Perkins Gilman, Skidmore College, 26–29 June 1997).

34. CPG to Caroline Hill, 4 December 1921, CPGP, 177/143.

35. Scharnhorst, *Charlotte Perkins Gilman*, 57–113; Lane, *To Herland and Beyond*, 229–306; and Larry Ceplair, *Charlotte Perkins Gilman: A Nonfiction Reader* (New York: Columbia University Press, 1992), 84–93.

36. Lanser, "Feminist Criticism," 415–41; Elizabeth Ammons, "Writing Silence: 'The Yel-low Wallpaper,'" in *The Yellow Wallpaper*, ed. Thomas L. Erskine and Connie L. Richards (New Brunswick, N.J.: Rutgers University Press, 1993), 257–76; Polly Wynn Allen,

Building Domestic Liberty: Charlotte Perkins Gilman's Architectural Feminism (Amherst: University of Massachusetts Press, 1988); Carol Farley Kessler, *Charlotte Perkins Gilman: Her Progress toward Utopia with Selected Writings* (Syracuse, N.Y.: Syracuse University Press, 1995); Lois N. Magner, "Darwinism and the Woman Question: The Evolving Views of Charlotte Perkins Gilman," in *Critical Essays on Charlotte Perkins Gilman*, ed. Joanne B. Karpinski (New York: G. K. Hall and Co., 1992), 115–28; Jane S. Upin, "Charlotte Perkins Gilman: Instrumentalism beyond Dewey," *Hypatia* 8, no. 2 (1993): 38–63; Maureen Egan, "Evolutionary Theory in the Social Philosophy of Charlotte Perkins Gilman," *Hypatia* 4, no. 1 (1989): 102–19; Ann Palmeri, "Charlotte Perkins Gilman: A Forerunner of a Feminist Social Science," in *Discovering Reality: Feminist Perspectives on Epistemology, Metaphysics, Methodology, and Philosophy of Science*, ed. Sandra Harding and Merrill B. Hintikka (Dordrecht: Reidel, 1983), 97–120; and Hausman, "Sex before Gender," 497–500.

37. Hayden for instance examines Gilman's "kitchenless houses" and feminist urban design plans in the context of other utopian architecture visions, rather than in relation to the rest of Gilman's philosophy and reform proposals. Similarly, Palmeri examines Gilman's *Women and Economics* (1898), *The Home: Its Work and Influence* (1901), *Concerning Children* (1903), and *Human Work* (1904) in relation to the broader development of feminist social science. Ethicists and political theorists compare her work to that of John Dewey, Lester Ward, and Thorstein Veblen. This work has a tendency to be ahistorical, interested in Gilman's contribution and usefulness for ongoing issues of concern to contemporary feminist commentators. Consequently, its scholars often apply anachronistic criteria of value to Gilman's beliefs without apologies. Gilman's context is not their particular concern. For all the diversity of subjects upon which some of her prolific publications prove pertinent then, it remains true that nonfiction Gilman commentary is minor, uneven, and often out of context.

38. Lanser, "Feminist Criticism," 415.

39. CPG, "The Providence Ladies Gymnasium," *Providence Journal* (23 May 1883): 8, and CPG, "The Right to Die" *Forum* 94 (November 1935): 297–300.

40. CPG, *1879–87*, vol. 1 of *The Diaries of Charlotte Perkins Gilman*, ed. Denise D. Knight, (Charlottesville, Va.: University Press of Virginia, 1991), 280.

41. CPG, diary, 7, 15, and 16 August 1884, CPGP, 177/27/19.

42. CPG to George Houghton Gilman [hereafter GHG], 5 June 1897, CPGP, in Hill, *A Journey from within*, 64.

43. Hill, *A Journey from within*, 380.

44. CPG to GHG, 7 June 1897, CPGP, in *A Journey from within*, 65.

45. GHG to CPG, 26 January 1900, CPGP, in *A Journey from within*, 343.

46. CPG to GHG, 19 December 1898, CPGP, in *A Journey from within*, 218.

47. CPG to GHG, 10 November 1899, CPGP, in *A Journey from within*, 310.

48. CPG to Mrs. Williams, 17 June 1915, CPGP, 177/153.

49. [Unpublished circular], "Charlotte Perkins Gilman, Author and Lecturer," February 1925, CPGP, 177/10.

50. CPG to Mrs. Williams, 20 June 1915, CPGP, 177/153.

51. Ibid.

52. CPG to GHG, 9 January 1899, CPGP, in *A Journey from within*, 224.

53. The general lectures included the titles "The Social Organism," "Our Brains and What Ails Them," "The Servant Question Answered," "The Power behind the Throne," "The New Motherhood," "Home: Past, Present, and Future," "Our Unknown Children," "Why We Work," "Modern Myths," and "America's Place Today." Meanwhile, her 1900 club and parlor meeting titles were "The Club Conscience," "Social Science," "The Responsibility of the Purchaser," "What We Need to Know," "The Sense of Beauty in Women," "Duties, Domestic and Other," "To Improve Our Minds," "Child Labor," "Domestic Service," and "The Body, the Dress, and the Health." Her sermons, imbued with a thoroughly secular and nontheological temper, described by her as "ethical" in character, had titles such as "Right and Wrong," "Collective Ethics," "The Joy of Life," "Moral Gymnastics," "Relative Virtues," "The Heroes We Need Now," "Truth," "Body and Soul," and "Heaven."

54. The 1915 four discussion lecture courses were entitled as follows: series 1, "The Biological Base," "The Economic Relation," "'Love': Love and Marriage," "The Home: Past, Present, and Future," "Motherhood: Personal, and Social," and "The Normal Woman and the Coming World"; series 2, "Our Male Civilization," "Its Influence on Women," "On the Family, the Child, and the Home," "On Business, Government, Warfare," "On Education, Art, Literature," and "On Ethics, Religion, Progress"; series 3, "Our Brains and What Ails Them," "The Years That Cripple Us," "What Schools Should Be," "Specialization: Its Use and Danger," "Feeling, Thinking and Doing," "and "Social Parentage"; and series 4, "What Humanity Is for," "War, Waste, and Social Economy," "The Life We Have a Right to," "Where Women Come in," "How to Make World Citizens," "Old Religions and New Hopes."

55. This collection included "The Wicked Waste of Housework," "War and Women," "The Meaning of Feminism," "The Dress of Women," "A Place for Babies," "A Reasonable Socialism," "Common Sense and Equal Suffrage," "America's Place Today," "Men, Women, and People," "Social Ethics," and "World Federation." This advertising flyer lists "The Charlton Co.," 67 Wall Street, Houghton Gilman's business address, as the contact point for "Terms and Dates" for Gilman lectures, CPGP, 177/10.

56. The individual lecture titles in this 1916 series were "Mother Service," "Industry and Women," "Food Service," "Citizenship," "World Service, " and "Our Losses and Our Gains."

57. CPG to GHG, 22 May 1898, CPGP, in *A Journey from within*, 144.

58. CPG to GHG, 25 May 1898, CPGP, in *A Journey from within*, 147.

59. CPG to GHG, 18 January 1899, CPGP, in *A Journey from within*, 228–29.

60. CPG to GHG, 18 May 1898, CPGP, in *A Journey from within*, 141.

61. CPG to GHG, 9, 31 January 1899, CPGP, in *A Journey from within*, 224.

62. CPG to GHG, 22 May 1898, CPGP, in *A Journey from within*, 145.

63. CPG to GHG, 25 May 1898, CPGP, in *A Journey from within*, 147.

64. CPG to GHG, 20 May 1898, CPGP, in *A Journey from within*, 142.

65. CPG to GHG, 22 May 1898, CPGP, in *A Journey from within*, 144.

66. According to the U.S. Department of Education, in 1889–90, when CPG began her lecturing career, a total of 2,682 women and 12,837 men received bachelor's, 194 women and 821 men received master's, and 2 women and 147 men received doctoral degrees. See National Center for Education Statistics, *Digest of Education Statistics* (Washington, D.C.: Department of Education, Office of Education Research and Improvement, 1995), NCES 95–0291.

67. Key texts he suggested included Edward B. Tylor, *Researches into the Early History of Mankind and the Development of Civilization* (1865) and *Primitive Culture* (1871); John Lubbock, *Prehistoric Times, as Illustrated by Ancient Remains and the Manners and Customs of Modern Savages* (1869) and *The Origin of Civilization and the Primitive Condition of Man* (1870). For discussion, see Bederman, *Manliness and Civilization*, 126.

68. Susan Gubar, "Feminist Misogyny: Mary Wollstonecraft and the Paradox of 'It Takes One to Know One,'" in *Feminism beside Itself*, ed. Diane Elam and Robyn Wiegman (New York: Routledge, 1995), 133–54; and Cott, *The Grounding of Modern Feminism*, 6–8.

69. Despite her ambivalence about the term feminism as applied to herself, she was reluctant to cede the domain of feminist commentary to these two peers. She criticized Key in review articles, including "Comment and Review," *The Forerunner* 2 (October 1911): 280–82, and "On Ellen Key and the Woman Movement," *The Forerunner* 4 (February 1913): 35–38. Alternatively, her comments on Schreiner, though admiring, insisted on her own share of the glory, as shown in a letter to Houghton: "Do read in Nov. Cos. Olive Schreiner."

70. 1915 lecture circular, CPGP, 177/10.

71. CPG to Mrs. Roantree, 15 September 1920, CPGP, 177/153.

72. Cott, *The Grounding of Modern Feminism*, 3–10.

73. [Circular], "Charlotte Perkins Gilman: Author and Lecturer," February 1925.

74. Daniel Kiefer to William B. Feakin, 8 June 1914, CPGP, 177/139/2.

75. CPG, "Our Maternal Duties" unpublished lecture, Oakland, Calif., 17 November 1891, CPCP, 177/166, 13.

76. Ibid., 10.

77. CPG, "She Who Is to Come," unpublished lecture, 10 March 1891, CPGP, 177/165, 5–6.

78. Bederman, *Manliness and Civilization*, 156–61.

79. Gilman addressed this origins story in many sources during her rhetorical career. See for instance "Wash Tubs and Women's Duty: Is a Mother's Business Child Culture or Housework?" *The Century Magazine* 110 (June 1925): 152–59.

80. Unfortunately, presentist assumptions about sexuality, framed in a contemporary context that is post-Kinsey, post-Masters and Johnson, and post-contraceptive pill, and near-universal marital recourse to birth control in Western countries, powerfully inflect most historians' contributions to the history of both sexuality and feminism in the United States. Historians tend to characterize nineteenth-century feminist sexual thought as conservative, puritanical, and erotophobic. Although these judgments are understandable, when commentators confront alien and uncongenial sexual philosophies, they have a tendency to seriously decontextualize the history of feminism. See for instance Ellen Carol DuBois and Linda Gordon, "'Seeking Ecstasy on the Battlefield': Danger and Pleasure in Nineteenth Century Sexual Thought," *Feminist Studies* 9 (1983): 17.

81. CPG to GHG, 11 September 1897, CPGP, in *A Journey from within*, 99.

82. Jane Lancaster, "'I could easily have been an acrobat': Charlotte Perkins Gilman and the Providence Ladies' Gymnasium, 1881–1884," *The American Transcendental Quarterly* 8 (March 1994): 33–52.

83. CPG, *Herland* (New York: Pantheon, 1915), 44.

84. For instance, CPG, "A Garden of Babies," *Success* (June 1909): 370–71; *What Diathna Did*, 53; and *The Crux*, 141–43.; see also William Veeder, "Who Is Jane?: The Intricate Feminism of Charlotte Perkins Gilman," *Arizona Quarterly* 44 (1988): 59–60.

85. CPG, "With Her in Ourland," *The Forerunner* 7 (November 1916): 296–97; and "Wash Tubs and Women's Duty," 154–55.

86. Among these evils, she included war, disease, birth defects, prostitution, women's bodily weakness and cultural backwardness, waste, extravagance, fashion, infant mortality, and children's accidents. See CPG, *The Home*, 96–97, and *His Religion and Hers*, 218–30.

87. CPG, "Wash Tubs and Women's Duty," 153.

88. CPG, "Sex and Race Progress," in *Sex in Civilization*, ed. Samuel D. Schmalhausen and V. F. Calverton (New York: MacCaulay, 1929), 109.

89. Ibid., 109 and 112.

90. CPG, "Wash Tubs and Women's Duty," 153.

91. Ibid., 153–54.

92. CPG, *With Her in Ourland*, excerpted in Carol Farley Kessler, *Charlotte Perkins Gilman: Her Progress toward Utopia with Selected Writings* (Syracuse, N.Y.: Syracuse University Press, 1995), 243–44.

93. CPG, *Women and Economics*, 102–17.

94. For fuller explication of this argument, see Gail Bederman, "Naked, Unfettered, and Unashamed: Charlotte Perkins Gilman, Anti-feminism, and the Figure of the Savage Rapist" (paper presented at the Second International Charlotte Perkins Gilman Conference, Skidmore College, Saratoga Springs, N.Y., 26–29 June 1997).

95. *New Orleans Daily Picayune*, 1904, CPGP, 177/266.

96. Bederman, *Manliness and Civilization*, 131–32 and 128–34.

97. CPG, "Race Pride," *The Forerunner* 4 (April 1913): 90.

98. CPG, *What Diathna Did*, 160–61.

99. CPG, "A Suggestion on the Negro Problem," *American Journal of Sociology* 14 (July 1908): 78–85.

100. CPG, "Social Darwinism," *American Journal of Sociology* 12 (March 1907): 713–14.

101. See for instance Ceplair, *Charlotte Perkins Gilman*, 272.

102. Lanser, "Feminist Criticism," 435.

103. CPG, "Sex and Race Progress" in *Sex in Civilization*, ed. V. F. Calverton and Samuel D. Schmalhausen (New York: Macaulay, 1929), 112.

104. Ibid., 112.

105. Lane, *To Herland and Beyond*, 18.

106. This is not the same as saying, as contemporary critics continually do, that we must see "gender," "race," and "class" as continually "intersecting." The latter verb is not equal to the task of characterizing the place of race in Gilman's feminism. Rather, for her "patriarchy is a racial phenomenon": it is primarily non-Aryan "yellow" peoples whom Gilman holds responsible for originating and perpetuating patriarchal practices, and it is primarily Nordic Protestants whom she considers capable of change. See Lanser, "Feminist Criticism," 435.

107. CPG, *Women and Economics*, 63. For full discussion of the category "sexual contract" and of marriage and prostitution as specific and central sexual contracts in modern, "fraternal" democracies, see Carole Pateman, *The Sexual Contract* (Cambridge, Eng.: Polity Press, 1988).

108. The analytical centrality of prostitution in Gilman's key texts receives little or no discussion in major biographical studies to date nor in more minor essays and commentaries published during her lifetime and since her death.

109. Susan Kingsley Kent, *Sex and Suffrage in Britain, 1860–1914* (Princeton: Princeton University Press, 1987), 33.

110. CPG, "The Oldest Profession in the World," *The Forerunner* 4 (March 1913): 63.

111. Gilman used prostitution-related analogies and direct examples drawn from prostitution in many texts. See for instance CPG, *The Home*, 97; *Human Work*, 253; *His Religion and Hers*, 41; "The Oldest Profession in the World," 63-64; and "Parasitism and Civilized Vice," in *Woman's Coming of Age: A Symposium*, ed. Samuel D. Schmalhausen and V. F. Calverton (New York: Horace Liveright, 1931), 110–26.

112. CPG, *Women and Economics*, 63.

113. CPG, "Causes and Cures," unpublished lecture, Pasadena, Calif., 26 June 1890, CPGP, 177/163, 2–3.

114. Ibid., 2.

115. CPG, *Women and Economics*, 95.

116. Ibid., 94–95.

117. Ibid., 33.

118. Ibid., 28–29.

119. Ibid., 49.

120. Her arguments here make interesting comparison with those of acclaimed actress and expatriate suffragette Cicely Hamilton, author of *Marriage as a Trade* (1909; reprint, London: Women's Press, 1981).

121. CPG, *Women and Economics*, 53.

122. Ibid., 45.

123. Ibid., 72.

124. Ibid., 42.

125. Ibid., 96.

126. See for instance Kate Millett, *The Prostitution Papers* (New York: Ballantine, 1976); Lori Rottenberg, "The Wayward Worker: Toronto's Prostitute at the Turn of the Century," in *Women at Work: Ontario, 1850–1930*, ed. Janice Acton, Penny Goldsmith, and Bonnie Shepard (Toronto: Canadian Women's Educational Press, 1974); and Mariana Valverde, *The Age of Light and Soap and Water: Moral Reform in English Canada, 1880–1925* (Toronto: McClelland Stewart, 1991).

127. CPG, *Women and Economics*, 44.

128. Ibid., 45–46.

129. CPG, *Man-Made World*, 63–64.

130. Ibid., 169.

131. Ibid., 175.

132. CPG, *Women and Economics*, 93.

133. This was the desperate plight of Ross, the fiancé of Diathna, in Gilman's novel *What Diathna Did* (1910). See also CPG, *Women and Economics*, 93–94.

134. CPG, *Women and Economics*, 94.

135. CPG, "Feminism" in Ceplair, *Charlotte Perkins Gilman*, 184–86.

136. CPG's short story "The Vintage" (1916) explores the horrifying consequences of a man, Rodger Moore, marrying his beloved Leslie. His doctors warned that he

remained syphilitic from a past infection, contracted in a "brief black incident in his past . . . long since buried." One frail withered son, followed by stillborns and miscarriages, was the outcome of their union. See "The Vintage," *The Forerunner* 7 (October 1916): 253–57.

137. Pateman argues that modern feminists carefully distinguish between condemnation of prostitution as an institution oppressive to women as a sexed group and condemnation of prostitutes as women, just as the Marxist opposes capitalism, not the worker. See *The Sexual Contract,* 209, and her "Defending Prostitution: Charges against Ericsson," *Ethics* 93 (April 1982): 557–62.

138. See CPG, "Is America Too Hospitable?" *Forum* 70 (October 1923): 1983–89, and "A Suggestion on the Negro Problem," 78–85. These latter positions and prejudices are pervasive throughout Gilman's journals, in correspondence, and in anecdotal examples in her major texts. The so-called Orientals of China receive most hostile representation in her work, fond as she was of claiming women were most oppressed and degraded in Asian societies. Middle Eastern cultures were another frequent target or illustration of the worst case of female dependence. As she aged, ever-more shrill condemnation of Jewish cultural separatism and distinctiveness appeared in her personal and some published writings. Meanwhile, aboriginal populations of the world appear uniformly as barbaric peoples, doomed by evolution to extinction, including the savage Bushmen of Australia or the squaw laborer of the ancient Americas.

139. CPG, *Man-Made World,* 205.

140. CPG, "Feminism or Polygamy?" *Forerunner* 5 (October 1914): 260–61.

141. See for instance Allan Brandt, *No Magic Bullet: A History of Venereal Disease in the United States since 1880* (New York: Oxford University Press, 1985).

142. Leonard Dinnerstein, *Uneasy at Home* (New York: Columbia University Press, 1987), 15–18.

143. See for instance CPG, "Prisons, Convicts, and Women Voters," *The Forerunner* 4 (April 1913): 92; "Humanness," *The Forerunner* 4 (February 1913): 52–53; "Sex and Race Progress," in *Sex in Civilization,* 109–26; "Is America Too Hospitable?" 1983–89; "Progress through Birth Control," *North American Review* 224 (December 1927): 622–29; "Divorce and Birth Control," *Outlook* 125 (25 January 1928): 130–51; "Birth Control, Religion, and the Unfit," *Nation* 134 (January 1932): 108–9; and "What May We Expect of Eugenics?" *Physical Culture* 31 (March 1914): 219–22.

144. CPG, "The New Generation of Women," *Current History* 18 (August 1923): 731–37; "Progress through Birth Control," 628; "Toward Monogamy," in *Our Changing Morality,* ed. Freda Kirchwey (New York: Albert and Charles Boni, 1924), 65, and "Parasitism and Civilized Vice," in *Woman's Coming of Age,* 124–26 and 123.

145. CPG, "The Oldest Profession in the World," 63.

146. CPG, "Toward Monogamy," in *Our Changing Morality,* 59.

147. Ibid., 63.

148. CPG, "Birth Control," *The Forerunner* 6 (July 1915): 180.

149. Janet Brodie Farrell, *Contraception and Abortion in Nineteenth Century America* (New York: Macmillan, 1994), 32.

150. Jeffrey Weeks, *Sex, Politics and Society: The Regulation of Sexuality since 1800* (London: Longman, 1981), 48.

151. CPG, "The Giant Wisteria" *New England Magazine* 4 (June 1891):480–85; and "My Poor Aunt," *Kate Field's Washington* (7 January 1891): 9–11.

152. Allen, *Rose Scott,* 182.

153. Marvin Olansky, "Abortion News in the Late 1920s: A New York City Case Study," *Journalism Quarterly* 66, no. 3 (1990): 724–26.

154. CPG, *Herland,* 73.

155. See for instance Raymond Pearl, *The Biology of Population Growth* (New York: Alfred A. Knopf, 1925).

156. CPG, "Malthusianism and Race Suicide," *The Woman's Journal,* 3 September 1904, 282.

157. CPG, "Back of Birth Control," *Birth Control Review* 6 (March 1922): 32–33.

158. CPG, "The New Generation of Women," *Current History* 18 (April 1923): 736.

159. CPG, "Sex and Race Progress," in *Sex in Civilization,* 114.

160. CPG, *The Home,* 176–83 and 294–99.

161. CPG, "Sex and Race Progress," in *Sex in Civilization*, 116.

162. CPG, "Back of Birth Control," 180.

163. CPG, "Feminism or Polygamy," *The Forerunner* 5 (October 1914): 261.

164. CPG, "Toward Monogamy," in *Our Changing Morality*, 57.

165. Ibid., 58.

166. See for instance Robert Latou Dickinson and Laura Ella Beam, *A Thousand Marriages* (Baltimore: Williams and Wilkins, 1931).

167. CPG, "Masculinism at Its Worst," *The Forerunner* 5 (October 1914): 259.

168. See for instance Ceplair, *Charlotte Perkins Gilman*, 274.

169. CPG, "Progress through Birth Control," 623, 627.

170. CPG, *Herland*, 73.

171. CPG, "Progress through Birth Control," 627–28.

172. CPG, "Birth Control, Religion, and the Unfit," 108–9.

173. CPG, "Progress through Birth Control," 629.

174. CPG, "Birth Control, Religion, and the Unfit," 108.

175. Lanser, "Feminist Criticism," 236.

176. For examples of feminist birth control arguments from the period, see Mary Ware Dennett, *Birth Control Laws: Shall We Keep Them, Change Them, or Abolish Them?* (New York: DaCapo Press, 1926); *The Sex Side of Life: An Explanation for Young People* (New York: Astoria, 1928). And also see Constance Marian Chen, *"The Sex Side of Life": Mary Ware Dennett's Pioneering Battle for Birth Control and Sex Education* (New York: New Press, 1996); and John M. Craig, *"The Sex Side of Life:* The Obscenity Case of Mary Ware Dennett," *Frontiers* 15 (spring 1995): 145–67. Margaret Sanger's important writings include *Biological and Medical Aspects of Contraception* (Washington, D.C.: National Committee on Federal Legislation for Birth Control, 1934); *The Case for Birth Control* (New York: Modern Art Printing Co, 1917); *Debate on Birth Control: Margaret Sanger and Winter Russell and Shaw vs Roosevelt on Birth Control* (Giraud, Kans.: Haldeman-Julius, 1921). On Sanger's work, see David M. Kennedy, *Birth Control in America: The Career of Margaret Sanger* (New Haven: Yale University Press, 1970); Madeline Gray, *Margaret Sanger: Biography of the Champion of Birth Control* (New York: Marek, 1979); Virginia Coigray, *Margaret Sanger: A Rebel with a Cause* (Garden City, N.Y.: Doubleday, 1955); and Ellen Chesler, *Woman of Valor: Margaret Sanger and the Birth Control Movement in America* (New York: Simon and Schuster, 1992).

177. CPG to GHG, 4 December 1898, CPGP, in *A Journey from within*, 214.

178. CPG, "Malthusianism and Race Suicide," 282.

179. CPG to GHG, 6 January 1900, CPGP, in *A Journey from within*, 307.

180. CPG to GHG, 24 August 1897, CPGP, in *A Journey from within*, 81.

181. Lanser, "Feminist Criticism," 430–33.

182. For example, her involvement in anti-immigrant, Americanization, and eugenics movements can disquiet commentators. Once she and her husband George Houghton Gilman left New York City in 1922, partly in distaste for its ethnic diversity, and moved into Houghton's inherited family home in Norwich Town, Connecticut, they were in the new "heartland" of immigration restriction movements. They became members of the Norwich Americanization Institute, described as "An Institution Training the Foreign Born for Intelligent and Useful Citizenship," and for "Keeping Up the Fight for Americanism." Meanwhile, the American Eugenics Society headquartered itself in New Haven throughout the 1920s. CPG's annotated copies of such organizations' printed materials are located in CPG 177/143 and 145. For analysis of these movements, see Barbara Miller Solomon, *Ancestors and Immigrants: A Changing New England Tradition* (Chicago: University of Chicago Press, 1989).

183. CPG, "The New Generation of Women," *Current History* 8 (August 1928): 731–37.

184. Society of Arts and Sciences, "This Freedom of Women," 26 December 1922, and Women's Committee for Political Action, "Has Woman Suffrage Failed?" 8–11 May 1924, CPGP, 177/143/2 and 144/1.

185. Of these, eastern, southern, and central Europeans, the cause of Gilman's consternation, formed over 70 percent of the influx, while the migrants of whom she could more easily approve, those from northwestern Europe, were only 20 percent. Even then, a considerable portion of the latter were Irish Catholics, against whom she

directed the sectarian prejudice common amongst American Protestants. See Cashman, *Age of Titans*, 146–47.

186. This meant that almost half of that foreign-born population was concentrated into just four states: Massachusetts, New York, place of Gilman's home and work from 1900 until 1922, Illinois, and Pennsylvania. New England received the bulk of the Irish and Italians. By 1910, three-quarters of the population of the cities of Boston, New York, Detroit, Chicago, and Cleveland were first- or second-generation immigrants; Providence, city of Gilman's childhood and first marriage in the 1880s, and Philadelphia, where she went for the "rest cure," were only somewhat less in the rate of new immigrant population. Meanwhile, the comparable immigrant proportion in the population of San Francisco area, where Gilman lived and worked for part of the 1890s, was 72 percent. See Cashman, *Age of Titans*, 169.

187. Frederick Jackson Turner, "Pioneer Ideals and the State University," *Indiana University Bulletin* 8 (June 1910), reprinted in John Mack Faragher, *Rereading Frederick Jackson Turner* (New York: Henry Holt and Co., 1994), 109.

188. Bernard A. Weisenberg, "Genes, Brains, and Bunk," *American Heritage* 46 (April 1995): 28–29.

189. The comparison of later rates of Jewish immigration, two million, and over eighteen million immigrants overall during the Gilded Age and Progressive Era, is dramatic. From the implementation of the 1924 restrictions onward, through the interwar decades of European crisis, including the rise of Third Reich and Hitler's Europe-wide anti-Semitic offensive, until the postwar refugee aftermath, by 1953, only three hundred sixty-five thousand Jewish immigrants came to the United States. See Leonard Dinnerstein, *Uneasy at Home* (New York: Columbia University Press, 1987), 36.

190. Hans Voight, "Division and Reunion: Woodrow Wilson, Immigration, and the Myth of Unity," *Journal of American Ethnic History* 13 (spring 1994): 24–51; and Thomas J. Curran, *Xenophobia and Immigration, 1820–1930* (Boston: Twayne Publishers, 1975).

191. See for instance CPG, "Vanguard, Rearguard, and Mudguard," *The Century Magazine* 104 (July 1922): 348–53; "The New Generation of Women, 731–37; "Is America Too Hospitable?" 1983–89; "Women's Achievements since the Franchise," *Current History* 27 (October 1927): 7–14; "Progress through Birth Control," 622–29; "Divorce and Birth Control," 130–31; "Birth Control, Religion, and the Unfit," 108–9; and "The Right to Die," 297–30.

192. CPG, "Is America Too Hospitable?" 1984–86.

193. Ibid., 1989.

194. Ibid., 1984–86, 1989, and 1986.

195. CPG, "Prisoners, Prisons, and Women Voters," *Forerunner* 4 (April 1913): 91–92, and "Progress through Birth Control," 627.

196. CPG, "Is America Too Hospitable?" 1983.

197. Ibid., 1986

198. Ibid.

199. Ibid., 1985, 1986.

200. Lanser, "Feminist Criticism," 430.

201. CPG, "Progress through Birth Control," 626.

202. Ibid.

203. Ibid.

204. CPG, "Is Feminism Really So Dreadful?" *The Delineator* 85 (August 1914): 6; "As to 'Feminism,'" *The Forerunner* 5 (February 1914): 45; and "The Biological Anti-Feminist," *The Forerunner* 5 (March 1914): 64–67; and "What Feminism Is and Isn't," *Ford Hall Folks* 2 (April 1916): 1–2, 4; "What Is Feminism?" *Boston Sunday Herald*, 3 September 1916.

205. Jeffrey Moran demonstrates how thoroughly this message inflected Progressive Era sex education programs in cities such as Chicago. Counsel against sex outside marriage in the 1910s was practically indistinguishable from counsel against resort to prostitutes for sexual gratification. See Jeffrey P. Moran. "Modernism Gone Mad: Sex Education Comes to Chicago, 1913," *Journal of American History* 83 (September 1996): 481–513.

206. CPG, "Birth Control, Religion, and the Unfit," 109.

207. See for instance Samuel D. Schmalhausen, "The Sexual Revolution," in *Sex in Civilization*, 349–436, and Smith Ely Jelliffe, "The Theory of the Libido," in *Sex in Civilization*, 456–71; G. V. Hamilton, "The Emotional Life of Modern Woman," in *Woman's Coming of Age*, 207–29, and V. F. Calverton, "Are Women Monogamous?" in *Woman's Coming of Age*, 475–88; Floyd Dell, "Can Men and Women Be Friends?" and Beatrice M. Hinkle, "Women and the New Morality," in *Our Changing Morality*, 183–96, 235–49.

208. See for instance CPG, "Feminism or Polygamy," 260–61; and "The New Generation of Women," 734.

CONCLUSION
Memories and Legacies
of the Progressive Era

J. Michael Hogan

For "generations of historians," as Nancy S. Dye has observed, "progressivism has exuded powerful fascination." And for Dye, the reasons are clear: "the Progressive Era marks the beginning of contemporary America, and within it we can trace the roots of institutions, policies, and values that still define the United States as a nation nearly a century later."[1] Historians may disagree whether historical progressivism was radical or conservative, "a democratic movement of popular political protest or a movement dominated by a few large businessmen and industrialists bent upon creating a centralized liberal state."[2] But nobody disputes that the "progressive tradition . . . has had an enduring influence on politics and government in the United States."[3] From the income tax to the direct election of senators, from a host of federal regulatory agencies to the beginnings of the welfare state itself, the legacy of the Progressive Era remains deeply ingrained in our political culture.

Still, we continue to struggle with many of the same political and social problems that first gave rise to historical progressivism. As Robert Putnam has observed, Americans in the Progressive Era confronted challenges that were "strikingly similar to those that we must now address": technological change, economic inequality, environmental degradation, racial tensions, loss of community, and political disaffection. Then, as now, Putnam writes, "optimism nurtured by recent economic advances battled pessimism grounded in the hard realities of seemingly intractable social ills." Then, as now, "new concentrations of wealth and corporate power raised questions about the real meaning of democracy." Then, as now, "massive urban concentrations of impoverished ethnic minorities posed basic questions of social justice and social stability." Then, as now, "older strands of social connection were being abraded—even destroyed—by technological and economic and social

471

change."[4] With so many parallels, it comes as little surprise that there has been a revival of historical interest in the Progressive Era. Indeed, preaching the "lessons" of the Progressive Era has become something of a cottage industry.

The progressive voices heard throughout this volume resist such sermonizing. The lessons they teach are diverse and sometimes idiosyncratic, and they are rooted in a particular historical context—a context that was, in many ways, unique. What are the common political lessons to be learned from Theodore Roosevelt and Woodrow Wilson? What can the iconoclastic William Jennings Bryan teach us about the progressive response to social change? What are we to make of W. E. B. Du Bois, who often seemed to speak not to his contemporaries but to generations as yet unborn? And what can the illiberal and ethnocentric teachings of a Charlotte Perkins Gilman contribute to contemporary thought about sexuality or immigration?

Questions such as these complicate the whole business of drawing lessons from the Progressive Era. They also should make us skeptical of all who claim to represent *the* progressive legacy. They remind us that the turn of the last century was a very different age, and that our memories of the Progressive Era are themselves, in some measure, historical fictions. Recalling lessons from the Progressive Era inevitably risks historical oversimplification, for the Progressives left a complex and often contradictory legacy.

Still, the *rhetorical* legacy of the Progressive Era remains instructive. As we confront the democratic dilemmas of the twenty-first century, it offers hope that we might find ways to reinvigorate public discussion and combat civic decay. Confronted with challenges similar to those we face today, the Progressives reinvented America's democratic institutions and encouraged public deliberation. They rewrote the rules of democratic debate and encouraged a broader range of citizens to participate. Above all, they rediscovered the art of rhetoric and found the courage to "test" their ideas in the public forum. As political leaders, as social activists, and as ordinary citizens, Americans of the Progressive Era took seriously their obligations to listen, speak, write, and debate. They considered it not only a right but a responsibility of citizenship to discuss and debate the issues of the day with their fellow citizens.

As they grappled with the challenges posed by urbanization and industrialization, Americans in the Progressive Era addressed some of the most fundamental philosophical questions of democratic life: What are the purposes and limitations of government? Who should assume the responsibilities of leadership in a democratic state? And how and when should public opinion decide important questions of public policy? As they struggled with such questions, Progressives drew upon both the Hamiltonian and Jeffersonian traditions, and they forged both a "Christian" and a "scientific" approach to progressive reform.[5] Yet whatever their philosophical or ideological differences, Progressives shared a common commitment to democratic speech and public deliberation. They left a *rhetorical* legacy of robust democratic deliberation that still might inspire us in the twenty-first century.

The New Progressivism

In a commencement address at Princeton University in 1996, President Bill Clinton proclaimed that we are "living through another time of great change, standing on the threshold of a new progressive era."[6] As Peter Levine has noted, Clinton was not alone in proclaiming this "revival" of progressivism. First Lady Hillary Clinton, Senators Bill Bradley and Ted Kennedy, Representative Dick Gephardt, and even Republican presidential candidates Patrick Buchanan and Steve Forbes all "made similar predictions."[7] In addition, a number of academics, journalists, and other social commentators have published books and articles announcing a New Progressive movement. These New Progressives argue that, like the original Progressives, we live in revolutionary times and face a crisis of democratic governance. Like the original Progressives, all propose far-reaching reforms but differ significantly over specific policies and programs.

For some, Bill Clinton himself has represented the leading edge of this New Progressive movement. According to E. J. Dionne Jr., for example, the Clinton administration's efforts to "reinvent government" reflected the reform spirit of the original Progressives, and Clinton won reelection with a rhetoric that "harkened back directly to the original Progressive project." Not only did Theodore Roosevelt emerge as the president's role model in 1996, but the "Progressive idea"—the idea that "government could help ease the country through a promising but difficult economic transition"—became "the focal point of his campaign." Clinton's "Bridge to the 21st century" was "built with materials provided by our Progressive forebears," according to Dionne, and it reflected much the same view of government as Roosevelt's Square Deal or Wilson's New Freedom. Like the original Progressives, Clinton understood that "while governments in authoritarian societies oppress, governments in democratic societies have the capacity to liberate." And according to Dionne, that assumption is the foundation of a new progressivism—a progressivism that, like the original, is "resolutely experimental rather than reflexively ideological, in constant search of new methods, insistent on continuous reform but always committed to a more equitable distribution of opportunity and power."[8]

Other New Progressives have distanced their cause from Clinton and the so-called New Democrats. Joel Rogers, for example, has complained that "the leadership of the Democratic Party has moved steadily to the right" over the past twenty years, and that the Clinton administration was "hopelessly compromised" if not "proudly ensconced on the wrong side" of every major issue of concern to Progressives. According to Rogers, the liberalism of the Democratic Party is "not just corrupt, but dying," while an "insurgent corporate Right aims squarely at democracy's destruction." Rogers thus advocates a new progressivism, not within the Democratic Party, but built around specific grassroots initiatives and a new third party.[9] Writing in 1995, Rogers probably never imagined that a progressive third-party challenge would come so soon. But when Ralph Nadar challenged Al Gore in the 2000 election, New Progressives confronted an old dilemma: whether to "waste" their vote on a genuinely progressive candidate or to vote for the candidate with a chance to win.

The same tension between progressive ideals and political pragmatism has been evident in the intellectual manifestoes of the new progressivism, such as Jacob Weisberg's *In Defense of Government*. At first glance, Weisberg's book delivers just what the title promises: a spirited defense of governmental activism. Beginning with the story of Pam Jackson, a black single mother who escaped the drug- and rat-infested public housing projects on Chicago's South Side with help from "an unfashionable entity called big government,"[10] Weisberg makes the case for a new progressivism that remains committed to the original Progressives' "broad aspirations for a more humane and equitable society."[11] "Government is *us*, collectively," Weisberg reminds us, and an activist government—"one with courage, confidence, and the nation's support"—*can* do good, as evidenced by "Pam Jackson's apartment, the preservation of the American wilderness, the rise of labor standards, the WPA, the Social Security system, the defeat of Hitler, integration, the landing on the moon, and the victory over communism."[12] As "the first modern liberals," Weisberg writes, the original Progressives had a "disposition toward activism," and like all liberals they believed that government not only had "the potential to better society" but a "moral obligation to do so."[13] And that, according to Weisberg, is precisely the sort of government we need today: "We need an activist government more than ever to heal the injuries of race and to reverse our growing stratification based on class."[14]

At the same time, however, Weisberg concedes that modern liberals—the "legatees of the Progressive tradition"—have "fallen out of favor" because they allowed government to become too large and intrusive.[15] Like most New Progressives, Weisberg invokes Herbert Croly's *The Promise of American Life*—"the greatest single work to come out of the Progressive movement"—as the "foundation stone of modern liberalism." Yet Weisberg denies that Croly advocated unbounded governmental activism, and he advocates a government that heeds Alexander Hamilton's call for "an energetic and intelligent assertion of the national good" without becoming overbearing or paternalistic.[16] According to Weisberg, liberals "lost the support of the nation" not because the public rejected their "ideals," but "as a result of the flawed way they put them into practice." Weisberg concludes that a "liberalism that wants to be popular again must free itself from sentimentality and adopt a stance of hard-headed pragmatism."[17]

Weisberg's vision of a pragmatic new progressivism embraces such traditionally liberal causes as safeguarding the environment, combating poverty and discrimination, and funding intellectual and artistic endeavors. Yet he ranks none of these causes among his top priorities, and he chastises his fellow liberals for assuming that governmental action can mitigate all risk in society, for clinging stubbornly to outmoded governmental programs, and for accepting only "grudgingly" that "the armed forces and police are important."[18] Weisberg also urges liberals to reject the "multicultural view that sorts the country into racial and ethnic compartments" and to embrace instead a new "nationalism." "*Nationalism* is not a word that comes easily to liberal lips," he concedes, as liberals "instinctively shrink from its small-minded and superpatriotic connotations." But the term need not "imply bigotry," he insists; "it can mean the simple assertion of a common American identity, a sense that for all our diversity we are part of a unified culture with certain shared values, interests, and aspirations."[19]

Weisberg thus calls not so much for a new progressivism as for a *return* of the old progressivism–a progressivism that, by his account, was activist and pro-government, yet also pragmatic and nationalistic. According to Weisberg, this is the true legacy of Alexander Hamilton, and it is the tradition later upheld by Lincoln, both Roosevelts, Wilson, and Kennedy. Only in recent years has that tradition been abandoned, as government has become "overdrawn and overextended," its purposes "muddied."[20] Weisberg thus urges his fellow Progressives to revive not only the ideals of the original Progressives but also their pragmatic reform spirit—something that he considers sorely lacking in the politics of contemporary liberalism: "Looking back to the old Progressives we find a liberalism without a century's accretion of bad habits, without mawkishness or excess. We find a practical, democratic approach to bettering the country. By reviving progressive ideas, liberals can fit themselves for governing again. By resurrecting the term, we can indicate a break with our recent past and our link to an older tradition."[21]

Not all New Progressives would agree with Weisberg's assessment of the failings of modern liberalism. Yet by definition, all agree that we have much to learn from the Progressive Era, and most identify three characteristics of the original Progressives worth emulating: (1) their nationalistic spirit, (2) their emphasis on morality in public life, and (3) their faith in ordinary citizens. Each of these characteristics presumably distinguished the original Progressives, not just from their political opponents, but also from liberals who later *claimed* their legacy. According to the New Progressives, liberalism went astray precisely because it lost touch with these *genuinely* progressive ideals.

The first of those ideals is, of course, the most controversial: New Progressives advocate not just an activist national government, but also a spiritual and cultural nationalism. Rejecting multiculturalism, they emphasize the need for a strong national identity, a renewed sense of community, and a common sense of purpose. One the most prominent New Progressives, Michael Lind, has advocated a new "liberal nationalism," combining a "color-blind, gender-neutral regime of individual rights" with "governmental activism promoting a high degree of substantive social and economic equality."[22] More than a program of political reform, however, Lind's vision ultimately rests upon a "national awakening" in which Americans become a "self-conscious community" united by language, culture, and custom.[23] Similarly, Michael Sandel's influential neoprogressive manifesto, *Democracy's Discontent*, emphasizes how "the nationalizing project that unfolded from the Progressive era to the New Deal to the Great Society succeeded only in part," because it created "a strong national government," but "failed to cultivate a shared national identity."[24] Like most New Progressives, Sandel invokes Herbert Croly in support of his view that "the success of democracy" requires "more than the centralization of government"; it also requires "the nationalization of politics." Croly understood that the "nationalizing" of American life meant not just "Federal centralization," but also "inspiring in citizens a new sense of national identity." In Croly's words, the people had to be fashioned "into more of a nation"; there needed to be a "nationalization of the American people in ideas, in institutions, and in spirit."[25]

Second, the New Progressives call for moral renewal. Again, Michael Sandel emphasizes this theme, as he laments how American politics and culture have lost their moral grounding. "With a few notable exceptions," he writes, "our political discourse in recent decades has come to reflect the liberal resolve that government be neutral on moral and religious questions, that matters of policy and law be debated and decided without reference to any particular conception of the good life." That is the hallmark of what Sandel calls a "procedural" conception of republican governance, and in his view, such a conception "cannot contain the moral energies of a vital democratic life": "It creates a moral void that opens the way for narrow, intolerant moralisms. And it fails to cultivate the qualities of character that equip citizens to share in self-rule. . . . The procedural republic cannot secure the liberty it promises, because it cannot sustain the kind of political community and civic engagement that liberty requires."[26]

Sandel acknowledges that the original Progressives "tried to render government less dependent on virtue among the people by shifting decision-making to professional managers, administrators, and experts." In this sense, they "gestured toward the version of liberalism" that would later "inform the procedural republic." Ultimately, however, they emphasized "the formative ambition" of an older tradition, "the republican tradition," and "sought new ways to elevate the moral and civic character of citizens."[27] This was especially true of Theodore Roosevelt, for whom "Progressive politics was emphatically an enterprise of moral uplift." And even Herbert Croly, while embracing Hamilton's vision of an "energetic" national government, still "shared Jefferson's conviction that economic and political arrangements should be judged by the qualities of character they promote." For Croly, as for Jefferson and later Roosevelt, "democracy had as its highest purpose the moral and civic improvement of the people."[28]

Finally, the New Progressives distinguish themselves by professing faith in the American people. According to Joel Rogers, this is the key difference between Progressives and liberals; Progressives "actually believe in democracy," insisting that "people of ordinary means and intelligence, if properly organized and equipped, can govern themselves," while liberals "lack such confidence in ordinary people." Indeed, according to Rogers, liberals are convinced of "the essential stupidity of man."[29] Of course, Rogers's own attitude toward the American people—"if properly organized and equipped," he suggests, they are "no more stupid or corrupt than any other"—stops well short of the rallying cry of the democratic purist: *Vox*

Populi, Vox Dei. But as Sidney Milkis has argued, the original Progressives' "faith in public opinion" was also "far from complete." Although they tried "to close the space between the cup of power and the lips of the people, championing government *of* the People directly *by* the People," their reforms also empowered experts and "insulated government decisions from the vagaries of public opinion and elections."[30]

However qualified their democratic faith, New Progressives remain optimistic that the American people would "support a new progressive program"—if only "currently divided progressives" could unite "to offer them one."[31] This, of course, is the central theme of E. J. Dionne Jr's best-selling political manifesto, *They Only Look Dead: Why Progressives Will Dominate the Next Political Era.* We are "on the verge of a second Progressive Era," Dionne argues, an era in which the aspirations of Theodore and Franklin Roosevelt, Woodrow Wilson and Harry Truman will dominate over the "ideas of William McKinley and Calvin Coolidge."[32] According to Dionne, the Republican electoral sweep of 1994 was not, in fact, a "decisive ideological verdict," but merely an expression of anger at "government that has proven ineffectual in grappling with the political, economic and moral crises that have shaken the country."[33] Dionne argues that the electorate is "skeptical" of Newt Gingrich's "particular brand of radicalism,"[34] and he envisions the very same voters who swept Republicans into office in 1994—that great mass of worried yet nonideological voters that he dubs the "Anxious Middle"—forming the "core constituency" of the new progressivism.[35] Progressives need only create a "vision" that captures both the spirit of the progressive project and the yearnings of the "Anxious Middle." Well aware of past liberal failures, however, Dionne concludes on a cautionary note: "But Progressives will not create an effective competing vision unless they learn from past liberal mistakes, speak with genuine conviction about government's purposes and reexamine the tradition from which they sprung."[36]

Not surprisingly, the new progressivism has its critics. Some on the Left not only resist the assault on multiculturalism, but also worry that an emphasis on moral character and the responsibilities of citizenship might be exclusionary, even coercive.[37] More fundamentally, critics on the Left are skeptical of the New Progressives' vision of a rational, enlightened, and politically engaged citizenry. Jeffrey C. Isaac, for example, has criticized the assumption that the "active promotion of the 'truth' about the causes of our problems" could, "in time, lead to 'progressive,' forward-looking remedial change." This vastly overestimates the possibilities for an enlightened public opinion, according to Isaac; it assumes victory in "a steeply uphill battle against the indifference, cynicism, and attention deficit disorder of American mass culture."[38] The New Progressives overlook the fact that the "kind of rational discourse that the left requires is anathema to the mass media and has been marginalized in our society"—a point made by Baudrillard, Habermas, and "many other social theorists as well." This is not to say that ordinary Americans are "morons," according to Isaac; it simply acknowledges a "sociological reality": that the "the mass-mediated form of our culture at large" has rendered "large-scale agendas of mass mobilization and coherent social reform . . . deeply problematic."[39]

Political conservatives, of course, are also suspicious of the new progressivism. In 1994, a group of conservatives led by Lamar Alexander and Chester E. Finn Jr. gathered at the Hudson Institute specifically to reflect upon the legacy of Croly's *The Promise of American Life.* Not surprisingly, the Hudson group not only rejected Croly's "cult of governmentalism,"[40] but also the assumption of progressive elites in general that public affairs has been so "complicated by modernity" that "the average citizen" can "no longer hope to understand or manage them."[41] It is precisely Croly's "prescription" for centralized government, they concluded, that is now "making us sicker."[42] At the same time, however, the Hudson group insisted that

Croly, were he still alive, would be puzzled by today's "contentious arguments about multiculturalism and diversity." In his era, "the question of national identity" was simply "not at issue."[43] In addition, Croly "possessed a keen sense of the virtues," according to Charles E. Finn Jr., and he "urgently wanted these to dominate both private lives and public policies." In this respect, Croly resembled "today's social conservatives" more than modern liberals. According to Finn, liberalism failed not because Croly was wrong, but because political "pragmatism" won out over Croly's "moralism." As a result, we ended up with "the worst of both worlds: the all-encompassing governmentalism of the 'New Nationalism' *without* the moral foundation that Croly would have placed under it."[44]

Conservatives thus agree with New Progressives that multiculturalism and a morally neutral government betray the progressive legacy. Conservatives object to the "governmentalism" of the progressive tradition, but New Progressives such as Wiesberg deny that the Progressives ever envisioned the intrusive, paternalistic governmentalism of the liberal welfare state. Nor are New Progressives guilty of the attitude that Lamar Alexander attributes to today's "liberal establishment" in Washington: that "the rest of America is too stupid to get up in the morning and make good decisions about what to do the rest of the day."[45] New Progressives, like conservatives, profess faith in the ability of ordinary people to govern themselves.

New Progressives, of course, qualify their faith in popular sovereignty. Like many of the original Progressives, they worry that the American people lack the skills and forums to deliberate productively. Yet finding inspiration in the ways that early-twentieth-century reformers "rethought, repaired, and revived their democratic institutions,"[46] New Progressives aspire, as Jefferson did, to create the spaces where citizens might "educate themselves and participate in their own self-government." They hope to rebuild democratic institutions that will, "within the confines of the modern world, sustain a democratic public and public-minded values, not just private, commercial motivations."[47] Proposing a variety of reforms in America's civic and cultural institutions, New Progressives envision another "civic renaissance like the one that took place between 1900 and the First World War."[48]

Yet the original Progressives did more to revive deliberative democracy than simply reform America's political and social institutions. They also presided over a remarkable rebirth of interest in the theory and practice of public speaking and persuasion. Progressive reformers took seriously their obligations as public advocates. They studied the great speakers and writers of the past, and they prided themselves on their own rhetorical achievements. In short, they rediscovered the art of rhetoric—an art lost for a time in the crass and corrupt political climate of the Gilded Age. This *rhetorical renaissance,* in the final analysis, may be the most significant and instructive legacy of the Progressive Era.

The Rhetorical Legacy of the Progressive Era

As an era "uncannily like our own," as Robert Putnam has argued, the Progressive Era offers "many instructive parallels" for revitalizing America's civic life. In this "most fecund period of civic innovation in American history," Putnam writes, Americans invented or refurbished most of the "major community institutions in American life today,"[49] and in the process they regenerated the nation's stores of "social capital"—that productive human energy that arises out of "social networks and the norms of reciprocity and trustworthiness that arise from them."[50] For Putnam, the lesson is clear. We "desperately need" a similar burst of "civic inventiveness," he argues, to "create a renewed set of institutions and channels for a reinvigorated civic life that will fit the way we have come to live." We need to "reinvent the twenty-first century equivalent of the Boy Scouts or the settlement house or the playground or Hadassah or the United Mine Workers or the NAACP."[51]

Yet civic decay is more than institutional problem; it also poses ideological and rhetorical challenges. As Michael Sandel argues, a vibrant civic life *does* require the "public spaces that gather citizens together, enable them to interpret their condition, and cultivate solidarity and civic engagement."[52] But it also requires a public philosophy and a public discourse that cultivate civic virtue, a shared identity, and a common sense of purpose. Today's public philosophy—the philosophy of a "procedural republic"—makes for an "impoverished civic life" because it "banishes moral and religious argument from political discourse" and forces citizens to negotiate the "sometimes overlapping, sometimes conflicting obligations" of multiple political identities.[53] In the end, it encourages a "drift toward storylessness," or a condition that leaves citizens "unable to weave the various strands of their identity into a coherent whole": "Political community depends on the narratives by which people make sense of their condition and interpret the common life they share; at its best, political deliberation is not only about competing policies but also about competing interpretations of the character of a community, of its purposes and ends. A politics that proliferates the sources and sites of citizenship complicates the interpretive project. At a time when the narrative resources of civic life are already strained—as the soundbites, factoids, and disconnected images of our media-saturated culture attest—it becomes increasingly difficult to tell the tales that order our lives. There is a growing danger that, individually and collectively, we will find ourselves slipping into a fragmented, storyless condition."[54]

In offering the republican tradition as a "corrective to our impoverished civic life,"[55] Sandel thus fashions a moral and even spiritual solution to civic decay. Republican theory, he notes, dictates that "citizens possess, or come to acquire, certain qualities of character, or civic virtues."[56] As such, it "regards moral character as a public, not merely private concern," and in this sense "it attends to the identity, not just the interests, of its citizens."[57] But because republican theory envisions citizens "deliberating with fellow citizens about the common good,"[58] it also implies certain rhetorical competencies: knowledge of public affairs, some level of historical and cultural literacy, the ability to speak and write persuasively, and an understanding of the processes and "rules" of public deliberation. It is not enough that citizens have the institutional "spaces" to deliberate, as Sandel suggests. They also must have some knowledge of public affairs and know *how* to deliberate.

Clearly, there has been an erosion of these deliberative competencies in American politics and culture. As Mattson has argued, America has not "paid enough attention to nurturing democratic practices among regular citizens." Not only do many citizens lack an understanding of the role of a citizen in a democracy, but they also lack "the skills necessary for the health of a democratic public: listening, persuading, arguing, compromising, and seeking common ground."[59] In some measure, this is indeed an institutional problem: the schools no longer teach rhetoric or debate as training for democratic citizenship, and America is "bereft" of other sorts of "civic institutions" that might "teach citizens the skills of self-government and dialogue."[60] Yet the decline of deliberative competencies is also a larger, *cultural* problem. It reflects—and is exacerbated by—the rhetoric of images and "sound bites" on television news, the substitution of "synecdochic phrases" and "visual dramatization" for well-reasoned political speech,[61] and the strident, uncompromising "grammar of hostility" in today's mass-mediated "culture wars."[62] Given the character of the contemporary public dialogue, it should come as little surprise that citizens confuse images and anecdotes with substantive arguments, name-calling and emotions with information and ideas.

A healthy democracy requires more than institutional spaces for public deliberation. It also requires a common store of historical and political knowledge and familiarity with the American rhetorical tradition. It requires appreciation for the well-crafted argument and the eloquent speech, as well as the ability to recognize and resist the diversions and deceptions of the demagogue. For self-government to succeed, there must not only be some common understanding of the methods and conventions of public discussion, but also a shared rhetorical ethic and a commitment to "serious speech": speech "in search of truth"; speech designed not just to defeat political adversaries, but to aid citizens in their "common search for understanding"; speech that *engages* citizens in "a continuous and ongoing effort to balance worthy but competing values, to mediate conflicts, to resolve disputes, to solve problems."[63] "Serious speech" may be rare in today's acrimonious political environment, but for the original Progressives it was the foundation of social reform.

The progressive concern with "serious speech" was most obviously reflected in the educational reforms of the day. In the Progressives' "vision of progress," as Katherine Adams has written, "new leaders would work with a well-educated populace, giving them the right information to choose the right nominees, laws, and national reforms." This, in turn, dictated "a more active and complete form of education for citizenship," with an emphasis on speaking, persuasion, and civic engagement.[64] In elementary schools, the reformers gave students "more experience with active language use, with the oral communication skills citizens would need to work together and to effect change," while at the university level they trained a new generation of "communication experts to further educate citizens and persuade them to accept new political principles that could improve their lives."[65] Ironically, as Adams concludes, many of these new, university-trained experts in persuasion eventually went to work for big business and other interests opposed to progressive reform. Nevertheless, the emphasis on education for citizenship helped revitalize the public sphere in the Progressive Era and gave rise to a "new view of the populace—as a powerful body to be persuaded and organized but never ignored."[66]

The new legitimacy and authority ascribed to public opinion made almost inevitable the emergence of the so-called rhetorical presidency—the modern style of presidential leadership emphasizing direct appeals to "the people."[67] It also was reflected in the professionalization of journalism and the emergence of the muckraking press, as reporters took it upon themselves to initiate and mediate the great public debates over the trusts, political corruption, race relations, and other issues. Above all, the new authority of public opinion was evident in the day-to-day talk of politics and reform in the Progressive Era. As politicians, intellectuals, civic and labor leaders, and social activists pled their causes before the "jury" of public opinion, they forged a paradigm of "serious speech" that continuously reaffirmed the sovereignty of "the people." For some historians, the Progressive Era may be the age of the bureaucrat or the expert. But far more significant—both in their own day and in our public memories of the Progressive Era—were the great public advocates who led the rhetorical renaissance in the Age of Reform.

Scholars have long recognized the contributions of the two great progressive presidents to this rhetorical renaissance. Despite their political differences and personal rivalry, Theodore Roosevelt and Woodrow Wilson contributed to the same legacy of presidential speech: a legacy of intelligent, bold, and visionary speech, grounded firmly in moral principle and in a considered philosophy of rhetorical leadership. Neither Roosevelt nor Wilson is remembered for pandering to popular sentiment. Both took unpopular positions, and both refused to compromise their core principles and values. Historians may continue to debate where the two progressive presidents rank among the great presidents in history, but in an age of presidential rhetoric fashioned by focus groups and polling, their legacy of "serious speech" remains an inspiration for genuine leadership from the "bully pulpit."

Looking beyond the great progressive presidents highlights still more lessons to be learned from the rhetorical renaissance of the Progressive Era. Today's environmentalists might take inspiration from the first conservationists, who successfully forged a public mandate for protecting the wilderness and other natural resources. Modern journalists, faced with their own "crisis of confidence,"[68] might follow the lead of their progressive predecessors and rethink their professional canons and their democratic mission. Inspired by Justice Holmes, jurists might benefit from more serious reflection on the role of the law in American public life, while politicians of all stripes might take inspiration from William Jennings Bryan's celebration of Jeffersonian ideals. In some ways, the voices of progressivism are deeply rooted in a unique historical context. Yet the rhetorical lessons they teach are universal: great political and social challenges demand "serious speech," and the best hope for democracy in the modern world remains robust public deliberation.

While sometimes defiant of traditional rhetorical conventions, the voices of dissent in the Progressive Era are no less instructive. With the union movement moribund, Eugene Debs represents at least one alternative for returning working-class issues to the "main stage" of American politics, as James Darsey put it: a genuinely radical, "working class eloquence." In a similar vein, Du Bois and Garvey articulated alternative visions of the black experience that still speak to the dilemmas faced by African Americans, while the larger progressive debate over race—however offensive in retrospect—grappled with the persistent challenges of a multicultural America. In the diversity of women's voices from the Progressive Era, we might discern lessons of interest not just to feminists but to all social movements. Carrie Chapman Catt, Alice Paul, and Harriot Stanton Blatch chose very different strategies and styles of leadership, but each contributed in her own way to the victory of the suffrage crusade, while Jane Addams taught an important lesson the hard way: humiliated by the failure of her anti-war speech, she retreated to protect the legacy of Hull House. Even Charlotte Perkins Gilman, while perhaps "uncongenial," even "ludicrous" to modern ears, also teaches an important lesson: that democratic deliberation is served, not just by the compromisers and consensus-builders, but also by those who challenge conventional wisdom.

Whether highlighting presidents or protestors, the rhetorical history of the Progressive Era tells a remarkable story of public advocacy and democratic deliberation in America. It tells the story of new modes of presidential leadership, new ways of thinking and talking about American institutions and social problems, and new strategies for engaging "the people" in democratic self-governance. It tells the story of a diverse array of talented public advocates who embraced the responsibility of putting the great questions of the day before the "jury" of public opinion. It is the story of a revival of "serious speech" and public deliberation in America—a revival that not only changed the course of history but also pointed the way toward a rhetorical renaissance in our own day.

In our age of televised images, sound bites, and poll-driven leadership, it may be hard to imagine such a rhetorical renaissance. Perhaps, as Jeffrey Isaac suggests, rational discourse itself is "anathema" to the modern mass media and is simply no longer possible in our postmodern age.[69] Yet as legal scholar Cass Sunstein has suggested, what people prefer and believe at this particular moment in history may not be the inevitable result of our mass mediated culture, but merely the product of "insufficient information, limited opportunities, legal constraints, or unjust background conditions." People may think and act as they do, not because of irremediable defects in our democratic institutions or culture, but simply because they have not been "provided with sufficient information and opportunities." In

Sunstein's view, democratic deliberation is not precluded by this state of affairs; it is, instead, the corrective. "It is not paternalistic, or an illegitimate interference with competing conceptions of the good for a democracy to promote scrutiny and testing of preferences and beliefs through deliberative processes," Sunstein concludes.[70] And that, in the final analysis, may be the most important lesson to be learned from the rhetorical history of the Progressive Era.

Notes

1. Nancy S. Dye, introduction to *Gender, Class, Race, and Reform in the Progressive Era*, ed. Noralee Frankel and Nancy S. Dye (Lexington: University Press of Kentucky, 1991), 9.

2. Ibid.

3. Sidney M. Milkis, "Introduction: Progressivism, Then and Now," in *Progressivism and the New Democracy*, ed. Sidney M. Milkis and Jerome M. Mileur (Amherst: University of Massachusetts Press, 1999), 1.

4. Robert D. Putnam, *Bowling Alone: The Collapse and Revival of American Community* (New York: Simon and Schuster, 2000), 28, 381–82.

5. See David B. Danbom, *"The World of Hope": Progressives and the Struggle for an Ethical Public Life* (Philadelphia: Temple University Press, 1987), 80–149.

6. Bill Clinton, remarks at the Princeton University commencement, 4 June 1996, quoted in Peter Levine, *The New Progressive Era: Toward a Fair and Deliberative Democracy* (Lanham, Md.: Rowman and Littlefield Publishers, 2000), x.

7. Levine, *The New Progressive Era*, x.

8. E. J. Dionne Jr., *They Only Look Dead: Why Progressives Will Dominate the Next Political Era* (New York: Touchstone Books, 1997), 10–11, 15.

9. Joel Rogers, "How Divided Progressives Might Unite," *New Left Review*, no. 210 (March-April 1995): 3–32.

10. Jacob Weisberg, *In Defense of Government: The Fall and Rise of Public Trust* (New York: Scribner, 1996), 14.

11. Ibid., 157.

12. Ibid., 29.

13. Ibid., 157.

14. Ibid., 28.

15. Ibid., 157.

16. Ibid., 189–91.

17. Ibid., 157–58.

18. Ibid., 164–75.

19. Ibid., 188–89.

20. Ibid., 28.

21. Ibid., 158.

22. Michael Lind, *The Next American Nation: The New Nationalism and the Fourth American Revolution* (New York: Free Press, 1995), 15.

23. Ibid., 300.

24. Michael J. Sandel, *Democracy's Discontent: America in Search of a Public Philosophy* (Cambridge: Harvard University Press, 1996), 346.

25. Ibid., 219–20.

26. Ibid., 24.

27. Ibid., 208–9.

28. Ibid., 218–20.

29. Rogers, "How Divided Progressives Might Unite," 3–4.

30. Milkis, "Introduction," 7–8.

31. Joel Rogers, "Response to 'The Poverty of Progressivism,'" *Dissent* 43 (fall 1996): 56.

32. Dionne, *They Only Look Dead*, 9.

33. Ibid., 10, 12.

34. Ibid., 9.

35. Ibid., 277.

36. Ibid., 277–78.

37. As Michael Sandel has noted, the republican tradition does require that citizens "possess certain excellences," and this in turn implies that "citizenship cannot be indiscriminately bestowed." Yet while early republican theorists, such as Aristotle, assumed "that the capacity for civic virtue corresponds to fixed categories of birth or condition," that assumption "is not intrinsic to republican political theory, and not all republicans have embraced it." Good citizens are "made, not found," Sandel argues. There is some danger that cultivating virtue and "forging a common citizenship among a vast and disparate people" will produce coercive forms of "soulcraft," or efforts to force citizens to embrace a "unitary" and "uncontestable" conception of the "common good." Again, however, Sandel insists that civic education is not necessarily coercive. Embracing a republican politics that is "more clamorous than consensual," the "agencies of civic education" might "inculcate the habit of attending to public things" without dictating how political disagreements are resolved. See Sandel, *Democracy's Discontent*, 317–21.

38. Jeffrey C. Isaac, "The Poverty of Progressivism: Thoughts on American Democracy," *Dissent* 43 (fall 1996): 43–44.

39. Jeffrey C. Isaac, "The Poverty of Progressivism: A Response to My Critics," *Dissent* 44 (winter 1977): 113–14.

40. Chester E. Finn Jr., "Herbert Croly and the Cult of Governmentalism," in *The New Promise of American Life*, ed. Lamar Alexander and Chester E. Finn Jr. (Indianapolis: Hudson Institute, 1995), 27–46.

41. Michael S. Joyce and William A Schambra, "A New Citizenship, A New Civic Life," in *The New Promise of American Life*, 143.

42. Lamar Alexander and Chester E. Finn Jr., introduction to *The New Promise of American Life*, 2.

43. Diane Ravitch, "The Future of American Pluralism," in *The New Promise of American Life*, 74.

44. Finn, "Herbert Croly and the Cult of Governmentalism," in *The New Promise of American Life*, 40–41.

45. Lamar Alexander, "The New Promise of American Life," in *The New Promise of American Life*, 15.

46. Levine, *The New Progressive Era*, 10.

47. Kevin Mattson, *Creating a Democratic Public: The Struggle for Urban Participatory Democracy during the Progressive Era* (University Park, Pa.: Pennsylvania State University Press, 1998), 4, 8.

48. Levine, *The New Progressive Era*, xiii.

49. Putnam, *Bowling Alone*, 367–68.

50. Ibid., 19.

51. Ibid., 401.

52. Sandel, *Democracy's Discontent*, 349.

53. Ibid., 349–50.

54. Ibid., 350–51.

55. Ibid., 6.

56. Ibid., 5–6.

57. Ibid., 25.

58. Ibid., 5.

59. Mattson, *Creating a Democratic Public*, 3–4.

60. Ibid., 3.

61. Kathleen Hall Jamieson, *Eloquence in an Electronic Age: The Transformation of Political Speechmaking* (New York: Oxford University Press, 1988), 90–117.

62. James Davison Hunter, *Culture Wars: The Struggle to Define America* (New York: Basic Books, 1991), 143–58.

63. Dionne, *They Only Look Dead*, 261.

64. Katherine H. Adams, *Progressive Politics and the Training of America's Persuaders* (Mahwah, N.J.: Lawrance Erlbaum Associates, 1999), xvi–xvii.

65. Ibid., 21.

66. Ibid., 109.

67. See Jeffrey K. Tulis, *The Rhetorical Presidency* (Princeton: Princeton University Press, 1987).

68. The scholarship criticizing the news media and documenting declining public confidence in media institutions is abundant, of course, but the "crisis of confidence" in journalism is perhaps best described and accounted for by those who have experienced it first-hand: the journalists themselves. Two such accounts are James Fallows, *Breaking the News: How the Media Undermine American Democracy* (New York: Pantheon Books, 1996), and Howard Kurtz, *Media Circus: The Trouble with America's Newspapers* (New York: Times Books, 1994).

69. Isaac, "The Poverty of Progressivism: A Response to My Critics," 113.

70. Cass R. Sunstein, *Democracy and the Problem of Free Speech* (New York: Free Press, 1993), 19–20.

BIBLIOGRAPHY

Adams, Katherine H. *Progressive Politics and the Training of America's Persuaders.* Mahwah, N.J.: Lawrence Erlbaum Associates, 1999.

Addams, Jane. *The Child, the Clinic, and the Court.* New York: Macmillan, 1927.

———. *Democracy and Social Ethics.* New York: Macmillan, 1902.

———. *Forty Years at Hull House.* New York: Macmillan, 1935.

———. *Jane Addams on Peace, War, and International Understanding, 1899–1932.* Edited by Allen Freeman Davis. New York: Garland, 1976.

———. *The Long Road of Women's Memory.* New York: Macmillan, 1916.

———. *A New Conscience and an Ancient Evil.* New York: Macmillan, 1912.

———. *Newer Ideals of Peace.* New York: Macmillan, 1907.

———. *Peace and Bread in Time of War.* 1922. Reprint, Silver Springs, Md.: NASW Classics Series, 1983.

———. *The Social Thought of Jane Addams.* Edited by Christopher Lasch. 1965. Reprint, New York: Irvington, 1982.

———. *The Spirit of Youth and the City Streets.* New York: Macmillan, 1909.

———. *Women and Public Housekeeping.* New York: National Women's Suffrage Publishing Co., 1910.

———. *Women at The Hague.* New York: Macmillan, 1915.

Alexander, Lamar, and Chester E. Finn Jr., eds. *The New Promise of American Life.* Indianapolis: Hudson Institute, 1995.

Allen, Judith A. *Rose Scott: Vision and Revision in Feminism, 1880–1920.* Melbourne: Oxford University Press, 1994.

Andrews, William L., ed. *Critical Essays on W. E. B. Du Bois.* Boston: G. K. Hall and Co, 1985.

Axson, Stockton. *"Brother Woodrow": A Memoir of Woodrow Wilson.* Edited by Arthur S. Link. Princeton: Princeton University Press, 1993.

Baker, Liva. *Justice from Beacon Hill: The Life of Oliver Wendell Holmes, Jr.* New York: Harper Collins, 1991.

Baker, Ray Stannard. *Following the Color Line: American Negro Citizenship in the Progressive Era.* 1908. Reprint, New York: Harper and Row, 1964.

Baskerville, Barnet. *The People's Voice: The Orator in American Society.* Lexington, Ky.: University Press of Kentucky, 1979.

Bederman, Gail. *Manliness and Civilization: A Cultural History of Race and Gender in the United States, 1880–1930.* Chicago: University of Chicago Press, 1995.

Beveridge, Albert J. *The Meaning of the Time and Other Speeches.* Indianapolis: Bobbs-Merrill, 1905.

Blatch, Harriot Stanton, and Alma Lutz. *Challenging Years: The Memoirs of Harriot Stanton Blatch.* New York: G. P. Putnam's Sons, 1940.

Blum, John Morton. *The Republican Roosevelt.* 2d ed. Cambridge: Harvard University Press, 1977.

Boorstin, Daniel J. *The Americans: The Democratic Experience.* New York: Random House, 1973.

———. *The Americans: The National Experience.* 1965. Reprint, London: Sphere Books, Cardinal, 1988.

Brands, H. W. *T. R.: The Last Romantic.* New York: Basic Books, 1997.

Brigance, William Norwood, ed. *A History and Criticism of American Public Address.* 2 vols. New York: McGraw-Hill, 1943.

Broderick, Francis L. *Progressivism at Risk: Electing a President in 1912.* New York: Greenwood, 1989.

Brommel, Bernard J. *Eugene V. Debs: Spokesman for Labor and Socialism.* Chicago: Charles H. Kerr, 1978.

Bryan, Mary Lynn McCree, ed. *The Jane Addams Papers: A Comprehensive Guide.* Bloomington, Ind.: Indiana University Press, 1996.

Bryan, William Jennings, and Mary Baird Bryan. *Memoirs of William Jennings Bryan.* Chicago: John C. Winston Co., 1925.

Buenker, John D. *Urban Liberalism and Progressive Reform.* New York: Scribner, 1973.

Buenker, John D., and Nicholas C. Burckel. *Progressive Reform: A Guide to Information Sources.* Detroit: Gale Research Co., 1980.

Buenker, John D., John C. Burnham, and Robert M. Crunden. *Progressivism.* Cambridge, Mass.: Schenkman Publishing, 1977.

Burgchardt, Carl R. *Robert M. La Follette, Sr.: The Voice of Conscience.* New York: Greenwood, 1992.

Burton, David H. *Theodore Roosevelt, American Politician: An Assessment.* London: Associated Universities Presses, 1997.

Byerman, Keith E. *Seizing the Word: History, Art, and Self in the Work of W. E. B. Du Bois.* Athens: University of Georgia Press, 1994.

Campbell, Karlyn Kohrs. *Man Cannot Speak for Her.* 2 vols. Westport, Conn.: Greenwood, 1989.

Casdorph, Paul D. *Republicans, Negroes, and Progressives in the South, 1912–1916.* University: University of Alabama Press, 1981.

Cashman, Sean Dennis. *America in the Age of Titans: The Progressive Era and World War I.* New York: New York University Press, 1988.

Catt, Carrie Chapman, and Nettie Rogers Shuler. *Woman Suffrage and Politics: The Inner Story of the Suffrage Movement.* 1926. Reprint, Seattle: University of Washington Press, 1969.

Chalmers, David Mark. *The Muckrake Years.* Huntington, N.Y.: Robert E. Krieger Publishing Co., 1980.

Chambers, John Whiteclay. *The Tyranny of Change: America in the Progressive Era, 1890–1920.* New York: St. Martin's Press, 1992.

Cherny, Robert W. *Populism, Progressivism, and the Transformation of Nebraska Politics, 1885–1915.* Lincoln: University of Nebraska Press, 1981.

———. *Righteous Cause: The Life of William Jennings Bryan.* Boston: Little, Brown, and Co., 1985.

Chrislock, Carl H. *The Progressive Era in Minnesota, 1899–1918.* St. Paul: Minnesota Historical Society Press, 1971.

Cmiel, Kenneth. *Democratic Eloquence: The Fight over Popular Speech in Nineteenth-Century America.* New York: Morrow and Co., 1990.

Coletta, Paolo E. *William Jennings Bryan.* 3 vols. Lincoln: University of Nebraska Press, 1964–69.

Collin, Richard H. *Theodore Roosevelt and Reform Politics.* Lexington, Mass.: D. C. Heath and Co., 1972.

Commager, Henry Steele. *The American Mind: An Interpretation of American Thought and Character since the 1880s.* New Haven: Yale University Press, 1950.

Connolly, James J. *The Triumph of Ethnic Progressivism: Urban Political Culture in Boston, 1900–1925.* Cambridge: Harvard University Press, 1998.

Cooper, John Milton Jr. *Breaking the Heart of the World: Woodrow Wilson and the Fight for the League of Nations.* Cambridge: Cambridge University Press, 2001.

———. *Pivotal Decades: The United States, 1900–1920.* New York: W. W. Norton and Co., 1990.

———. *The Warrior and the Priest: Theodore Roosevelt and Woodrow Wilson.* Cambridge: Harvard University Press, 1983.

Cott, Nancy F. *The Grounding of Modern Feminism.* New Haven: Yale University Press, 1987.

Croly, Herbert. *The Promise of American Life.* 1909. Reprint, Boston: Northeastern University Press, 1989.

Cronon, E. David. *Black Moses: The Story of Marcus Garvey and the Universal Negro Improvement Association.* Madison: University of Wisconsin Press, 1955.

Crunden, Robert M. *Ministers of Reform: The Progressives' Achievement in American Civilization.* 1982. Reprint, Urbana: University of Illinois Press, 1984.

———. "Progressivism." In *The Reader's Companion to American History,* edited by Eric Foner and John A. Garraty, 868–71. Boston: Houghton Mifflin, 1995.

Cutright, Russell. *Theodore Roosevelt: The Making of a Conservationist.* Urbana: University of Illinois Press, 1985.

Danbom, David B. *"The World of Hope": Progressives and the Struggle for an Ethical Public Life.* Philadelphia: Temple University Press, 1987.

Darsey, James F. *The Prophetic Tradition and Radical Rhetoric in America.* New York: New York University Press, 1997.

Davis, Allen Freeman. *American Heroine: The Life and Legend of Jane Addams.* New York: Oxford University Press, 1973.

———. *Spearheads for Reform: The Social Settlements and the Progressive Movement, 1890–1914.* New York: Oxford University Press, 1967.

Debs, Eugene V. *Debs: His Life, Writings and Speeches.* Chicago: Charles H. Kerr and Co., 1908.

———. *Eugene V. Debs Speaks.* Edited by Jean Tussey. New York: Pathfinder, 1972.

———. *Gentle Rebel: Letters of Eugene V. Debs.* Edited by J. Robert Constantine. Urbana: University of Illinois Press, 1995.

———. *Walls and Bars.* 1927. Reprint, Chicago: Charles H. Kerr and Co., 1973.

———. *Writings and Speeches of Eugene V. Debs.* Edited by Arthur Schlesinger Jr. New York: Heritage Press, 1948.

Deegan, Mary Jo. *Jane Addams and the Men of the Chicago School, 1892–1918.* New Brunswick, N.J.: Transaction Books, 1988.

Degler, Carl N. *In Search of Human Nature: The Decline and Revival of Darwinism in American Social Thought.* New York: Oxford University Press, 1991.

Deverell, William Francis, and Tom Sitton, eds. *California Progressivism Revisited.* Berkeley and Los Angeles: University of California Press, 1994.

Diner, Steven J. *A Very Different Age: Americans of the Progressive Era.* New York: Hill and Wang, 1998.

Dionne, E. J., Jr. *They Only Look Dead: Why Progressives Will Dominate the Next Political Era.* New York: Touchstone Books, 1997.

Dixon, Thomas, Jr. *The Clansman: An Historical Romance of the Ku Klux Klan.* New York: Grosset and Dunlap, 1905.

———. *The Leopard's Spots: A Romance of the White Man's Burden: 1865–1900.* New York: Grosset and Dunlap, 1902.

———. *The Sins of the Father.* New York: D. Appleton and Co., 1912.

DuBois, Ellen Carol. *Harriot Stanton Blatch and the Winning of Women Suffrage.* New Haven: Yale University Press, 1997.

Du Bois, W. E. B. *The Autobiography of W. E. B. Du Bois: A Soliloquy on Viewing My Life from the Last Decade of Its First Century.* New York: International Publishers, 1968.

———. *Darkwater: Voices from within the Veil.* New York: Kraus-Thomson, 1921.

———. *Dusk of Dawn: An Essay toward an Autobiography of a Race Concept.* New York: Harcourt, Brace and Co., 1940.

———. *The Souls of Black Folk.* New York: Penguin Books, 1989.

———. *W. E. B. Du Bois Speaks: Speeches and Addresses, 1890–1919.* Edited by Philip S. Foner. New York: Pathfinder, 1970.

Dyer, Thomas G. *Theodore Roosevelt and the Idea of Race.* Baton Rouge: Louisiana State University Press, 1980.

Ebner, Michael H., and Eugene M. Tobin, eds. *New Perspectives on the Progressive Era.* Port Washington, N.Y.: Kennikat Press, 1977.

Eisenach, Eldon J. *The Lost Promise of Progressivism.* Lawrence: University of Kansas Press, 1994.

Ekirch, Arthur A., Jr. *Progressivism in America: A Study of the Era from Theodore Roosevelt to Woodrow Wilson.* New York: New Viewpoints, 1974.

Farrell, John C. *Beloved Lady: A History of Jane Addams' Ideas on Reform and Peace.* Baltimore: Johns Hopkins University Press, 1967.

Feffer, Andrew. *The Chicago Pragmatists and American Progressivism.* Ithaca, N.Y.: Cornell University Press, 1993.

Feinman, Ronald L. *Twilight of Progressivism: The Western Republican Senators and the New Deal.* Baltimore: Johns Hopkins University Press, 1981.

Ferrell, Robert H. *Woodrow Wilson and World War I.* New York: Harper and Row, 1985.

Filene, Peter G. "An Obituary for 'The Progressive Movement,'" *American Quarterly* 22 (1970): 20–34.

Filler, Louis. *Appointment at Armageddon: Muckraking and Progressivism in the American Tradition.* Westport, Conn.: Greenwood, 1976.

Finegold, Kenneth. *Experts and Politicians: Reform Challenges to Machine Politics in New York, Cleveland, and Chicago.* Princeton: Princeton University Press, 1995.

Fink, Leon. *In Search of the Working Class: Essays in American Labor History and Political Culture.* Urbana: University of Illinois Press, 1994.

———. *Progressive Intellectuals and the Dilemmas of Democratic Commitment.* Cambridge: Harvard University Press, 1997.

———, ed. *Major Problems in the Gilded Age and the Progressive Era.* Lexington, Mass.: D. C. Heath and Co., 1993.

Finnegan, Margaret. *Selling Suffrage: Consumer Culture and Votes for Women.* New York: Columbia University Press, 1999.

Fitzpatrick, Ellen. *Endless Crusade: Women Social Scientists and Progressive Reform.* New York: Oxford University Press, 1990.

Flexner, Eleanor. *Century of Struggle: The Woman's Rights Movement in the United States.* Rev. ed. 1959. Reprint, Cambridge: Harvard University Press, 1996.

Flint, Winston A. *The Progressive Movement in Vermont.* Washington, D.C.: American Council on Public Affairs, 1941.

Folsom, Burton W. *No More Free Markets or Free Beer: The Progressive Era in Nebraska, 1900–1924.* Lanham, Md.: Lexington Books, 1999.

Forcey, Charles. *The Crossroads of Liberalism: Croly, Weyl, Lippmann, and the Progressive Era, 1900–1925.* New York: Oxford University Press, 1961.

Ford, Linda G. *Iron-Jawed Angels: The Suffrage Militancy of the National Woman's Party, 1912–1920.* Lanham, Md.: University Press of America, 1991.

Fowler, Robert Booth. *Carrie Chapman Catt: Feminist Politician.* Boston: Northeastern University Press, 1986.

Frankel, Noralee, and Nancy S. Dye, eds. *Gender, Class, Race, and Reform in the Progressive Era.* Lexington: University Press of Kentucky, 1991.

Gable, John A. *The Bull Moose Years: Theodore Roosevelt and the Progressive Party.* Port Washington, N.Y.: Kennikat Press, 1978.

Garvey, Marcus M. *More Philosophy and Opinions of Marcus Garvey.* London: Cass, 1997.

———. *Philosophy and Opinions of Marcus Garvey.* 2 vols. New York: Atheneum, 1967.

Geiger, Louis G. "Muckrakers: Then and Now." *Journalism Quarterly* 62 (autumn 1966): 469–76.

Gilman, Charlotte Perkins. *Charlotte Perkins Gilman: A Nonfiction Reader.* Edited by Larry Ceplair. New York: Columbia University Press, 1992.

———. *Concerning Children.* Boston: Small, Maynard, and Co., 1900.

———. *The Crux.* New York: Charlton Co., 1911.

———. *The Diaries of Charlotte Perkins Gilman.* 2 vols. Edited by Denise D. Knight. Charlottesville: University Press of Virginia, 1991.

———. *Herland.* 1915. Reprint, New York: Pantheon, 1979.

———. *His Religion and Hers: A Study of the Faith of Our Fathers and the Work of Our Mothers.* New York: Century Co., 1923.

———. *The Home: Its Work and Influence.* New York: McClure, 1903.

———. *Human Work.* New York: McClure, Phillips and Co., 1904.

———. *A Journey from within: The Love Letters of Charlotte Perkins Gilman, 1897–1900.* Edited by Mary Armfield Hill. Lewisburg, Pa.: Bucknell University Press, 1995.

———. *In This Our World.* Oakland, Calif.: McCombs and Vaughan, 1893.

———. *The Living of Charlotte Perkins Gilman: An Autobiography.* New York: D. Appleton-Century Co., 1935.

———. *The Man-Made World, or Our Androcentric Culture.* New York: Charlton Co., 1911.

———. *Moving the Mountain.* New York: Charlton Co., 1911.

———. *What Diathna Did.* New York: Charlton Co., 1910.

———. *Women and Economics.* 1898. Reprint, Berkeley and Los Angeles: University of California Press, 1998.

———. *The Yellow Wallpaper.* Edited by Thomas L. Erskine and Connie L. Richards. New Brunswick, N.J.: Rutgers University Press, 1993.

Gilmore, Grant. *The Ages of American Law.* New Haven: Yale University Press, 1977.

Goble, Danney. *Progressive Oklahoma: The Making of a New Kind of State.* Norman: University of Oklahoma Press, 1980.

Gordon, Robert W., ed. *The Legacy of Oliver Wendell Holmes, Jr.* Stanford, Calif.: Stanford University Press, 1992.

Gould, Lewis. *The Presidency of Theodore Roosevelt.* Lawrence: University Press of Kansas, 1991.

———. *Reform and Regulation: American Politics from Roosevelt to Wilson.* New York: Knopf, 1986.

———, ed. *The Progressive Era.* Syracuse, N.Y.: Syracuse University Press, 1974.

Graham, Otis L. *The Great Campaigns: Reform and War in America, 1900–1928.* 1971. Reprint, Huntington, N.Y.: R. E. Krieger, 1980.

Graham, Sarah Hunter. *Woman Suffrage and the New Democracy.* New Haven: Yale University Press, 1996.

Grantham, Dewey W. *Southern Progressivism: The Reconciliation of Progress and Tradition.* Knoxville: University of Tennessee Press, 1983.

Haas, Edward F. *Political Leadership in a Southern City: New Orleans in the Progressive Era, 1896–1902.* Ruston, La.: McGinty Publications, 1988.

Harlan, Louis. *Booker T. Washington in Perspective.* Jackson: University Press of Mississippi, 1988.

———. *Booker T. Washington: The Making of a Black Leader, 1856–1901.* New York: Oxford University Press, 1972.

Harrison, John M., and Harry H. Stein. *Muckraking: Past, Present and Future.* University Park: Pennsylvania State University Press, 1973.

Hasian, Marouf A. *The Rhetoric of Eugenics in Anglo-American Thought.* Athens: University of Georgia Press, 1996.

Haynes, Irwin Inez. *The Story of Alice Paul and the National Women's Party.* Fairfax, Va.: Denlinger's Publishers, 1977.

Hays, Samuel P. *The Response to Industrialism, 1885–1914.* Chicago: University of Chicago Press, 1957.

Hibben, Paxton. *The Peerless Leader: William Jennings Bryan.* New York: Farrar and Reinhart, 1929.

Hill, Mary Armfield. *Charlotte Perkins Gilman: The Making of a Radical Feminist, 1860–1896*. Philadelphia: Temple University Press, 1980.

Hofstadter, Richard. *The Age of Reform: From Bryan to F. D. R.* 1955. Reprint, New York: Alfred A. Knopf, 1959.

———. *The American Political Tradition and the Men Who Made It.* 1948. Reprint, New York: Vintage Books, 1954.

———. *The Progressive Historians: Turner, Beard, and Parrington.* New York: Alfred Knopf, 1968.

———, ed. *The Progressive Movement.* Englewood Cliffs, N.J.: Prentice-Hall, 1963.

Hogan, J. Michael. *The Panama Canal in American Politics.* Carbondale: Southern Illinois University Press, 1986.

———. ed. *Rhetoric and Community: Studies in Unity and Fragmentation.* Columbia: University of South Carolina Press, 1998.

Holmes, Oliver Wendell, Jr. *The Essential Holmes: Selections from the Letters, Speeches, Judicial Opinions, and Other Writings of Oliver Wendell Holmes, Jr.* Edited by Richard Posner. Chicago: University of Chicago Press, 1992.

Howe, Mark DeWolfe. *Justice Oliver Wendell Holmes.* 2 vols. Cambridge: Harvard University Press, 1957–63.

Janick, Herbert F. *Government for the People: The Leadership of the Progressive Party in Connecticut.* New York: Garland, 1993.

Johnson, Robert D. *The Peace Progressives and American Foreign Relations.* Cambridge: Harvard University Press, 1995.

Johnson, Roger T. *Robert M. La Follette, Jr. and the Decline of the Progressive Party in Wisconsin.* Madison: State Historical Society of Wisconsin, 1964.

Jones, Howard Mumford. *The Age of Energy.* New York: Viking Press, 1970.

Juergens, George. *News from the White House: The Presidential-Press Relationship in the Progressive Era.* Chicago: University of Chicago Press, 1981.

Karpinski, Joanne B., ed. *Critical Essays on Charlotte Perkins Gilman.* New York: G. K. Hall and Co., 1992.

Karsner, David. *Debs: His Authorized Life and Letters.* New York: Boni and Liveright, 1919.

Keller, Morton. *Regulating a New Society: Public Policy and Social Change in America, 1900–1933.* Cambridge: Harvard University Press, 1994.

Kessler, Carol Farley. *Charlotte Perkins Gilman: Her Progress toward Utopia with Selected Writings.* Syracuse, N.Y.: Syracuse University Press, 1995.

Kirby, Jack Temple. *Darkness at the Dawning: Race and Reform in the Progressive South.* Philadelphia: Lippincott, 1972.

Kloppenberg, James T. *Uncertain Victory: Social Democracy and Progressivism in European and American Thought, 1870–1920.* New York: Oxford University Press, 1986.

Koenig, Louise W. *Bryan: A Political Biography of William Jennings Bryan.* New York: G. P. Putnam's Sons, 1971.

Kolko, Gabriel. *The Triumph of Conservatism: A Reinterpretation of American History, 1900–1916.* 1963. Reprint, New York: Free Press, 1977.

Kraditor, Aileen S. *The Ideas of the Woman Suffrage Movement, 1890–1920.* New York: W. W. Norton and Co., 1981.

———. *The Radical Persuasion, 1890–1917: Aspects of the Intellectual History and Historiography of Three American Radical Organizations.* Baton Rouge: Louisiana State University Press, 1981.

Kraig, Robert Alexander. "The 1912 Election and the Rhetorical Foundations of the Liberal State." *Rhetoric and Public Affairs* 3 (2000): 363–95.

Kuhlman, Erika A. *Petticoats and White Feathers: Gender Conformity, Race, the Progressive Peace Movement, and the Debate over War, 1895–1919.* Westport, Conn.: Greenwood, 1997.

La Follette, Robert M. *La Follette's Autobiography: A Personal Narrative of Political Experiences.* 1913. Reprint, Madison: University of Wisconsin Press, 1960.

Lagemann, Ellen Condliffe. *A Generation of Women: Education in the Lives of Women Progressive Reformers.* Cambridge: Harvard University Press, 1979.

Lawson, Linda. *Truth in Publishing: Federal Regulation of the Press's Business Practices, 1880–1920.* Carbondale: Southern Illinois University Press, 1993.

Lemmons, Stanley. *The Woman Citizen: Social Feminism in the 1920s.* Charlottesville: University Press of Virginia, 1973.

Levine, Daniel. *Jane Addams and the Liberal Tradition*. Madison: Historical Society of Wisconsin, 1970.

Levine, Lawrence W. *Defender of the Faith, William Jennings Bryan: The Last Decade, 1915–1925*. New York: Oxford University Press, 1965.

Levine, Peter. *The New Progressive Era: Toward a Fair and Deliberative Democracy*. Lanham, Md.: Rowman and Littlefield Publishers, 2000.

Lewis, David L. *W. E. B. Du Bois: Biography of a Race, 1868–1919*. New York: Henry Holt and Co., 1993.

Link, Arthur S., and Richard L. McCormick. *Progressivism*. Arlington Heights, Ill.: Harlan Davidson, 1983.

Link, William A. *The Paradox of Southern Progressivism, 1880–1930*. Chapel Hill: University of North Carolina Press, 1992.

Linn, James Weber. *Jane Addams: A Biography*. New York: D. Appleton-Century Co., 1935.

Lippmann, Walter. *Drift and Mastery*. 1914. Reprint, Englewood Cliffs, N.J.: Prentice-Hall, 1961.

———. *The Essential Lippmann*. Edited by Clinton Rossiter and James Lare. Cambridge: Harvard University Press, 1982.

———. *Public Opinion*. 1922. Reprint, New York: Free Press, 1997.

Lucas, Stephen E. "Theodore Roosevelt's 'The Man with the Muck-Rake': A Reinterpretation." *Quarterly Journal of Speech* 59 (1973): 452–62.

Luker, Ralph E. *The Social Gospel in Black and White: American Racial Reform, 1885–1912*. Chapel Hill: University of North Carolina Press, 1991.

Lunardini, Christine A. *From Equal Suffrage to Equal Rights: Alice Paul and the National Woman's Party, 1910–1928*. New York: New York University Press, 1986.

Mann, Arthur, ed. *The Progressive Era: Major Issues of Interpretation*. Hindsdale, Ill.: Dryden Press, 1975.

Marable, Manning. *W. E. B. Du Bois: Black Radical Democrat*. Boston: Twayne, 1986.

Margulies, Herbert F. *The Decline of the Progressive Movement in Wisconsin, 1890–1920*. Madison: State Historical Society of Wisconsin, 1968.

Marilly, Suzanne M. *Woman Suffrage and the Origins of Liberal Feminism in the United States, 1820–1920*. Cambridge: Harvard University Press, 1996.

Mattson, Kevin. *Creating a Democratic Public: The Struggle for Urban Participatory Democracy during the Progressive Era*. University Park: Pennsylvania State University Press, 1998.

Maxwell, Robert S. *La Follette and the Rise of the Progressives in Wisconsin*. 1956. Reprint, New York: Russell and Russell, 1973.

May, Henry F. *The End of American Innocence: A Study of the First Years of Our Own Time, 1912–1917*. New York: Knopf, 1969.

McFarland, Gerald W. *Mugwumps, Morals, and Politics, 1884–1920*. Amherst: University of Massachusetts Press, 1975.

McGeary, M. Nelson. *Gifford Pinchot: Forester-Politician*. Princeton: Princeton University Press, 1960.

McGee, Brian R. "Thomas Dixon's *The Clansman*: Radicals, Reactionaries, and the Anticipated Utopia." *Southern Communication Journal* 65 (2000): 300–17.

Meigs, Cornelia. *Jane Addams, Pioneer for Social Justice: A Biography*. Boston: Little, Brown, and Co., 1970.

Meyerling, Sheryl L., ed. *Charlotte Perkins Gilman: The Woman and Her Work*. Ann Arbor, Mich.: UMI Research Press, 1989.

Milkis, Sidney M., and Jerome M. Mileur, eds. *Progressivism and the New Democracy*. Amherst: University of Massachusetts Press, 1999.

Miller, Nathan. *Theodore Roosevelt: A Life*. New York: William Morrow and Co., 1992.

Mowry, George E. *The California Progressives*. Chicago: Quadrangle Books, 1963.

———. *The Era of Theodore Roosevelt and the Birth of Modern America, 1900–1912*. New York: Harper and Row, 1958.

———. *The Progressive Era, 1900–1920: The Reform Persuasion*. Washington, D.C.: American Historical Association, 1972.

———. *Theodore Roosevelt and the Progressive Movement*. New York: Hill and Wang, 1946.

Noble, David W. *The Paradox of Progressive Thought*. Minneapolis: University of Minnesota Press, 1958.

————. *The Progressive Mind, 1890–1917.* Chicago: Rand McNally and Co., 1970.

Novick, Sheldon. *Honorable Justice: The Life of Oliver Wendell Holmes.* Boston: Little, Brown, and Co., 1989.

Nye, Russel B. *Midwestern Progressive Politics: A Historical Study of Its Origins and Development, 1870–1958.* East Lansing: Michigan State University Press, 1959.

Olin, Spencer C., Jr. *California's Prodigal Sons: Hiram Johnson and the Progressives, 1911–1917.* Berkeley and Los Angeles: University of California Press, 1968.

Oliver, Robert T. *A History of Public Speaking in America.* Boston: Allyn and Bacon, 1965.

Painter, Nell Irvin. *Standing at Armageddon: The United States, 1877–1919.* New York: W. W. Norton and Co., 1987.

Papachristou, Judith. *Bibliography in the History of Women in the Progressive Era.* Bronxville, N.Y.: Sarah Lawrence College, 1985.

Paulsson, Martin. *The Social Anxieties of Progressive Reform: Atlantic City, 1854–1920.* New York: New York University Press, 1994.

Pease, Otis A., ed. *The Progressive Years: The Spirit and Achievement of American Reform.* New York: G. Braziller, 1962.

Peck, Mary Gray. *Carrie Chapman Catt: A Biography.* New York: H. W. Wilson Co., 1944.

Pegram, Thomas R. *Partisans and Progressives: Private Interest and Public Policy in Illinois, 1870–1922.* Urbana: University of Illinois Press, 1992.

Phillips, David Graham. *The Reign of Gilt.* New York: James Pott and Co., 1905.

Pickens, Donald K. *Eugenics and the Progressives.* Nashville, Tenn.: Vanderbilt University Press, 1968.

Pinchot, Gifford. *The Fight for Conservation.* New York: Doubleday, Page, 1910.

Pinkett, Harold R. *Gifford Pinchot: Private and Public Forester.* Urbana: University of Illinois Press, 1970.

Pittenger, Mark. *American Socialists and Evolutionary Thought, 1870–1920.* Madison: University of Wisconsin Press, 1993.

Pringle, Henry F. *Theodore Roosevelt: A Biography.* New York: Harcourt, Brace and Co., 1931.

Putnam, Robert D. *Bowling Alone: The Collapse and Revival of American Community.* New York: Simon and Schuster, 2000.

Rampersad, Arnold. *The Art and Imagination of W. E. B. Du Bois.* Cambridge: Harvard University Press, 1976.

Reed, Adolph. *W. E. B. Du Bois and American Political Thought: Fabianism and the Color Line.* New York: Oxford University Press, 1997.

Resek, Carl, ed. *The Progressives.* Indianapolis: Bobbs-Merrill, 1967.

Richardson, Elmo R. *The Politics of Conservation: Crusades and Controversies, 1897–1913.* University of California Publications in History. Vol. 70. Berkeley and Los Angeles: University of California Press, 1962.

Roosevelt, Theodore. *Theodore Roosevelt: An Autobiography.* New York: Charles Scribner's Sons, 1929.

————. *The Works of Theodore Roosevelt.* 20 vols. National ed. New York: Charles Scribner's Sons, 1926.

Rosenberg, Rosalind. *Beyond Separate Spheres: Intellectual Roots of Modern Feminism.* New Haven: Yale University Press, 1982.

Rossi, Alice. *The Feminist Papers.* New York: Bantam, 1973.

Rozwenc, Edwin Charles, and A. Wesley Roehm, eds. *The Status Revolution and the Progressive Movement.* Boston: Heath, 1963.

Safford, John Lugton. *Pragmatism and the Progressive Movement in the United States: The Origin of the New Social Sciences.* Lanham, Md.: University Press of America, 1987.

Salvatore, Nick. *Eugene V. Debs: Citizen and Socialist.* Urbana: University of Illinois Press, 1982.

Sanders, Elizabeth. *Roots of Reform: Farmers, Workers, and the American State, 1877–1917.* Chicago: University of Chicago Press, 1999.

Scharnhorst, Gary. *Charlotte Perkins Gilman.* Boston: Twayne Publishers, 1985.

Schneider, Dorothy, and Carl J. Schneider. *American Women in the Progressive Era, 1900–1920.* New York: Facts on File, 1993.

Schudson, Michael. *Discovering the News: A Social History of American Newspapers.* New York: Basic Books, 1978.

Scott, Anne Firor, and Andrew Mackay Scott. *One Half the People: The Fight for Woman Suffrage.* Rev. ed. 1975. Reprint, Urbana: University of Illinois Press, 1982.

Shannon, David A., ed. *Progressivism and Postwar Disillusionment, 1898–1928.* New York: McGraw-Hill, 1966.

Sinclair, Upton. *The Industrial Republic.* New York: Doubleday, Page and Co., 1907.

Sklar, Martin J. *The Corporate Reconstruction of American Capitalism, 1890–1916.* New York: Cambridge University Press, 1988.

Smith, Page. *America Enters the World: A People's History of the Progressive Era and World War I.* New York: McGraw-Hill, 1985.

Smith, Willard H. *The Social and Religious Thought of William Jennings Bryan.* Lawrence, Kans.: Coronado, 1975.

Southern, David W. *The Malignant Heritage: Yankee Progressives and the Negro Question, 1901–1914.* Chicago: Loyola University Press, 1968.

Stanton, Elizabeth Cady, Susan B. Anthony, and Mathilda Joslyn Gage, eds. *The History of Woman Suffrage.* 6 vols. Rochester, N.Y.: Fowler and Wells, 1881–1922.

Stettner, Edward A. *Shaping Modern Liberalism: Herbert Croly and Progressive Thought.* Lawrence: University Press of Kansas, 1993.

Stid, Daniel D. *The President as Statesman: Woodrow Wilson and the Constitution.* Lawrence: University Press of Kansas, 1998.

Sullivan, Mark. *Our Times, 1900–1925.* New York: Charles Scribner's Sons, 1936.

Swanberg, W. A. *Pulitzer.* New York: Charles Scribner's Sons, 1967.

Tapia, John E. *Circuit Chautauqua: From Rural Education to Popular Entertainment in Early Twentieth Century America.* Jefferson, N.C.: McFarland and Co., 1997.

Thelen, David P. *The New Citizenship: Origins of Progressivism in Wisconsin, 1885–1900.* Columbia: University of Missouri Press, 1972.

———. *Robert M. La Follette and the Insurgent Spirit.* Madison: University of Wisconsin Press, 1985.

Tickner, Lisa. *The Spectacle of Women: Imagery of the Suffrage Campaign, 1907–1914.* Chicago: University of Chicago Press, 1988.

Timberlake, James H. *Prohibition and the Progressive Movement, 1900–1920.* New York: Atheneum, 1970.

Tims, Margaret. *Jane Addams of Hull House, 1860–1935: A Centenary Study.* New York: Macmillan, 1961.

Tulis, Jeffrey K. *The Rhetorical Presidency.* Princeton: Princeton University Press, 1987.

Van Voris, Jacqueline. *Carrie Chapman Catt: A Public Life.* New York: Feminist Press at the City University of New York, 1987.

Walker, Robert H., ed. *The Reform Spirit in America.* New York: G. P. Putnam's Sons, 1976.

Warner, Hoyt L. *Progressivism in Ohio, 1897–1917.* Columbus: Ohio State University Press, 1964.

Watson, Richard L., Jr. *The Development of National Power: The United States, 1900–1919.* Boston: Houghton Mifflin, 1976.

Weaver, Richard. *The Ethics of Rhetoric.* 1953. Reprint, Davis, Calif.: Hermagoras Press, 1985.

Weinstein, James. *The Corporate Ideal in the Liberal State, 1900–1918.* Boston: Beacon Press, 1968.

Wesser, Robert F. *A Response to Progressivism: The Democratic Party and New York Politics, 1902–1918.* New York: New York University Press, 1986.

Wheeler, Marjorie Spruill, ed. *One Woman, One Vote: Rediscovering the Woman Suffrage Movement.* Troutdale, Ore.: New Sage Press, 1995.

White, G. Edward. *Justice Oliver Wendell Holmes: Law and the Inner Self.* New York: Oxford University Press, 1993.

Wiebe, Robert H. *Businessmen and Reform: A Study of the Progressive Movement.* 1962. Reprint, Chicago: Ivan R. Dee, 1989.

———. *The Search for Order, 1877–1920.* New York: Hill and Wang, 1967.

Wilson, R. Jackson. *In Quest of Community: Social Philosophy in the United States, 1860–1920.* London: Oxford University Press, 1970.

Wilson, Woodrow. *Constitutional Government in the United States.* 1908. Reprint, New York: Columbia University Press, 1961.

————. *Papers of Woodrow Wilson.* 69 vols. Edited by Arthur S. Link. Princeton: Princeton University Press, 1966–94.

Wise, Winifred Esther. *Jane Addams of Hull House.* New York: Harcourt Brace and Co., 1935.

Woodward, C. Vann. *The Strange Career of Jim Crow.* 3d ed. New York: Oxford University Press, 1974.

Zamir, Shamoon. *Dark Voices: W. E. B. Du Bois and American Thought, 1888–1903.* Chicago: University of Chicago Press, 1995.

ABOUT THE AUTHORS

JUDITH A. ALLEN is Professor of History and Chair of Gender Studies at Indiana University, Bloomington. She is the author of *Sex and Secrets: Crimes Involving Australian Women Since 1880* (1990) and *Rose Scott: Vision and Revision in Feminism* (1994).

JAMES ARNT AUNE is Associate Professor of Speech Communication at Texas A &M University. He is the author of *Rhetoric and Marxism* (1994) and *Selling the Free Market: The Rhetoric of Economic Correctness* (2001).

DOUGLAS BIRKHEAD was Associate Professor in the Department of Communication at the University of Utah. He was a former newspaper reporter and editor. He wished to thank Christine Oravec and Malcolm Sillars for many thoughtful discussions on the phenomenon of rhetoric. Douglas Birkhead died 29 July 2002.

JENNIFER L. BORDA is Assistant Professor in the Department of Communication at the University of New Hampshire. Her work on the rhetoric of the woman suffrage movement has appeared in the *Western Journal of Communication*. She wishes to thank J. Michael Hogan for help in the development of this essay.

CARL R. BURGCHARDT is Professor in the Department of Speech Communication at Colorado State University. He is author of *Robert M. La Follette, Sr. The Voice of Conscience* (1992) and editor of *Readings in Rhetorical Criticism* (1995, 2000).

JAMES DARSEY is Associate Professor of Communication at Georgia State University. He is the author of *The Prophetic Tradition and Radical Rhetoric in America* (1997). He wishes to thank Rich Rados, whose research assistance on this project was indispensable, and Jim Millhorn of Founders Library, Northern Illinois University.

LEROY G. DORSEY is an Associate Professor of Speech Communication at Texas A&M University. His work has been published in the *Quarterly Journal of Speech, Rhetoric and Public Affairs,* and *Presidential Studies Quarterly.* He is editor of *The Presidency and Rhetorical Leadership*

(2002). For research assistance with this essay, he wishes to thank Wallace Dailey, Curator of the Theodore Roosevelt Collection in the Houghton Library, Harvard University.

J. MICHAEL HOGAN is Professor and Graduate Officer in the Department of Communication Arts and Sciences at the Pennsylvania State University. He is the author of *The Panama Canal in American Politics* (1986) and *The Nuclear Freeze Campaign* (1994), and the editor of *Rhetoric and Community* (1998). For research assistance with this volume, he would like to thank Jennifer Young and Steve Martin.

ROBERT ALEXANDER KRAIG is the Wisconsin State Political Director for the Service Employees International Union (SEIU). He has published in *Rhetoric and Public Affairs* and *Communication Studies,* and he is the author of the forthcoming book, *Woodrow Wilson and the Lost World of the Oratorical Statesman* (2003).

BRIAN R. MCGEE is associate professor and chair of the Department of Communication Studies at Spalding University. His research has been published in *Argumentation and Advocacy, Southern Communication Journal,* and *Western Journal of Communication.*

CHRISTINE L. ORAVEC is Professor Emerita of Communication at the University of Utah. Her publications include several arcticles on the origins of the conservation movement and a book co-edited with James G. Cantrill, *The Symbolic Earth: Discourse and Our Creation of the Environment* (1996). The foundations of this chapter rest upon Professor Michael Calvin McGee's outstanding contributions to rhetorical studies. Nickieann Fleener and Douglas Birkhead, Associate Professors at the University of Utah, supplied useful references.

MALCOLM O. SILLARS is Professor Emeritus of Communication at the University of Utah. He is coauthor of *Argumentation and Critical Decision-Making* and *Communication Criticism: Rhetoric, Social Codes, Critical Studies.* He is the author of numerous articles on argumentation and American public address. For research assistance in preparing his article he wishes to thank David Werling.

ROBERT E. TERRILL is Assistant Professor in the Department of Communication and Culture at Indiana University. His has published essays in the *Quarterly Journal of Speech, Critical Studies in Media Communication, Rhetoric & Public Affairs,* and *Rhetoric Review.* He thanks the editor of this volume, J. Michael Hogan, for helpful comments on earlier drafts of this essay.

ERIC KING WATTS is an Associate Professor in the Department of Communication at Wake Forest University. Watts received his Ph.D. from Northwestern University and is the author of several essays on African American culture, the Harlem Renaissance, and W.E.B. DuBois in journals including *Quarterly Journal of Speech, Rhetoric and Public Affairs,* and *Critical Studies in Media Communication.*

INDEX

INDEX

166–67; romantic realism of, xviii, 147, 163; and Santayana, 147, 152, 180n. 53; as scientist, 175–76; as a social Darwinist, 173, 174; as a speaker, 146; sublime, 159, 163; themes of, 149, 153, 155–57; on truth, 149. **Opinions**: *Abrams v. United States*, 167, 170–74, 184n. 139; *Buck v. Bell*, 147, 151, 174–75; *Frank v. Magnum*, 151; *Lochner v. New York*, 146, 147, 151, 164–67, 168, 170, 175; *Masses Publishing Company v. Patten*, 168; *Moore v. Dempsey*, 151; *Schenk v. United States*, 168–70. **Speeches**: "Law," 163; "Memorial Day Address," 146, 147, 154–57; "Path of the Law," 146, 147, 148, 151, 154–57, 158–64, 175; "Soldier's Faith," 146, 147, 157–58. **Works**: *Collected Legal Papers*, 158; *Common Law*, 151, 158, 175; *Occasional Speeches*, 158. *See also* Constitution; jingoism
"Holmes and the Judicial Figure" (Ferguson), 148, 152
Holt, Hamilton, 134
Holt, Thomas C., 270, 279
Holton, Sandra Stanley, 367
Homestead, Pennsylvania, 230, 232, 236
Hoover, Herbert, 405
Hope, John, 300, 309n. 169
Hopkinson, Chris, 152
Horizon, 290, 291, 292, 304n. 48
Howard, W. G., 13
Howe, Mark, 176
Hudson, Frederic, 124
Hudson Institute, 476–77
Hugo, Victor, 242–45, 248, 249
Hull House: cofounder Addams, 387, 480; work of, xx, 388–89, 391, 393–94, 411, 414, 419–20. *See also* Addams
Hurwitz, Howard, 53
Hyde, William, 129, 142n. 103

Illinois, 185, 186; progressivism, xii
Illinois College, 185
imagery, of Holmes, 164
immigration, 187; and feminism, 452–56; Gilman on, xxi, 448, 468n. 185, 469n. 186, 189; and peace, 398, 411, 418
imperialism, xviii; Addams as foe of, 388, 389, 392, 393, 394, 396; British, 316; and Bryan, 198, 200–5, 217, 218; Debs on, 249–50; and Gilman, 428; harms of, 392; opposition, 389; Philippine, 320, 323; and progressivism, 200; and racism, 320; and Roosevelt, xx
Impress, The, 431
In Defense of Government (Weisberg), 473
Independent, 134, 231

Indianapolis, Indiana, 201
industrialization, 131–35, 187–88. *See also* journalism
Ingersoll, Robert, 17
Inland Waterways Commission (IWC), 94, 97, 98
Inner Civil War, The (Frederickson), 154
International Congress of Women (ICW, The Hague), 388, 401, 416, 418
International Socialist Review, 233
International Woman Suffrage Alliance (IWSA), 347, 350, 352, 354
International Workers of the World (IWW), 231, 234, 238
Interstate Commerce Commission (ICC), 61
Iowa, 22, 159, 347
Iowa State Agricultural College, 347
irony, 154; Holmes', 155, 157, 159–161, 172
Irwin, Will, 117, 118, 123, 128, 130; on industrialization and power, 132, 134–35; and professionalism, 136
Isaac, Jeffrey C., 476

Jackson, Andrew, 10, 11, 189
James, William, 150, 273, 276, 281, 304n. 37; influenced Addams, 389, 390
Jamieson, Kathleen, 58
Jefferson, Thomas, xviii, 20, 189; 1st Inaugural Address of, 187
Jeffersonian liberal: Bryan as a, 187, 189–91, 194, 201, 202, 205, 215
Jennison, James, 150
Jim Crow: in America, 452; and Du Bois, 280; laws, xii, 86, 197, 199, 285, 311, 317, 320–21, 325–26
jingoism, 146, 157, 158, 181n. 82, 392
Johnson, Andrew, 11
Johnson, Hiram, 19, 21, 199
Johnson, James Weldon, 300, 312
Johnson, Robert, 66, 73
Jones, Howard Mumford, 132
Jordan, David Starr, 353
journalism, xviii, 8; antebellum, 114, 118, 121–22, 125; as a business, 116, 118–22, 129, 133–35, 137–38; decline of, 124–28; the editor-publisher in, 125, 126, 128, 129, 133, 134; as "fourth estate," 124, 126, 129; function of, 125, 128, 141n. 62; mass appeal of, 113–14; New York City, 119–20; Penny Press, 124, 125; power of, 123, 128, 132, 134–35; professional development of, 114, 115–18, 124, 129–31, 136–38, 188; progressive voice of, 113, 114–16; and public opinion, 115–16; reporter's role in, 117; schools, 137–38; technology of,

118–20, 123, 131–32; "yellow," 113, 135. *See also* muckraker
"judicial activism," 164
Judson, Clara Ingram, 153

Kansas City Star, 73, 74
Key, Ellen, 437
Keene, New Hampshire, 154
Kellogg, Paul, 405–6
Kelly, Howard A., 213
Kennedy, Anthony, 163
Kent, Susan Kingsley, 367
Kidd, Benjamin, 211
Kilgo, John Carlisle, 316–17
Kimball, Arthur Reed, 133–34
Kinney, James, 319
Kirby, Jack Templeton, 318
Knapp, George L., 100
Knapp, Samuel, 8
Know-Nothing Party, 332
Kolko, Gabriel, xi
Kraig, Robert Alexander, xvii, xxi
Ku Klux Klan: and Bryan, 200; Colorado, 337nn. 116, 120, 139, 141; in film, 318, 326; Garvey on the, 299; grand dragons, 338n. 141; grand titan, 328; grand wizards, 326; history, 326, 327, 329, 336n. 110; imperial wizards, 326; membership, 326, 336n. 111; New York, 332; and progressivism, 327–30; rhetoric of the, 312, 326–32; resurgence of the, xx, 293, 326–27, 330, 336n. 110. *See also* Dixon

labor movement. *See* class; Debs; Pullman strike; unions
Labor Party, 301
La Follette, Robert, 15; *Autobiography*, xvii; as a Chautauquan, 27; criticized, 24; dismissed Roosevelt, xvii; on oratory, 18; as a progressive, 188, 198; and public discourse, xiii; reputation of, 21, 22, 24, 322; as Wisconsin governor, 26
Lahav, Pnina, 173
Lamarck (Lamark), Jean Baptiste, 93. *See also* conservation
Lane, Ann J., 430, 443
Lanser, Susan, 452, 453, 455
Lasch, Christopher, 388, 420
Laski, Harold, 162; and Holmes, 150, 152, 170, 171, 174
Laughlin, Harry, 174
law(s): "bad man" theory of, 151, 159, 160, 162; conservation, 87, 89; Jim Crow, xii, 86, 197, 199, 285, 311, 317, 320–21, 325–26; "limits of the," 160; and "narrative theory," 148; and religion,

151; Sherman Antitrust Act, 121; and tort, 151
"Law, The" (Holmes)
Law and Letters in American Culture (Ferguson), 152
Law and Literature (Posner), 148, 165
Lawson, Thomas, 114
Lay, Shawn, 332
League of Nations, 26, 28, 32, 203, 205
League of Women Voters, 355
Lectures on American Literature (Knapp), 8
Leopard's Spots, The (Dixon), 318, 319, 320
Lerner, Max, 169
Lester, John C., 336n. 110
Leuba, James H., 209
Leupp, Francis, 127, 128
Levine, Lawrence W., 216
Levine, Peter, ix, x, xxv, xvi; on democracy, xv; on LaFollette, xi; on progressivism revival, 472; on Wilson, xvi
Lewis, David Levering, 273, 279, 284
Lewis, William, 147, 163
Liberal Club of New York, 54
liberalism: Bryan's "modern," xix
Licht, Walter, 232, 239
Lichtenstein, Alex, 284
Life of Reason (Santayana), 152
Lincoln, Abraham, 154
Lind, Michael, 475
Link, Arthur S., 3, 51, 53, 59, 73, 344
Lippmann, Walter, 162, 345; *Drift and Mastery* by, xv, 231–32; *Public Opinion* by, xv; on suffrage, 346
Llewellyn, Karl, 176
Lloyd, Henry Demarest, 218
Lochner v. New York, 146, 147, 151, 164–67, 168, 170, 175
Locke, John, 4, 34n. 5
Lodge, Henry Cabot, 10, 20, 27, 321
Log Cabin Campaign, 12, 13
logos, 149, 153
London, England, 203
London Times, 137
Louisville Courier-Journal, 125
Lowell, James Russell, 11
Lowell Institute lectures, 146
Luban, David, 159, 162
Lucaites, John Louis, 331
Lucas, Stephen E., 322
Lull, Richard S., 212
Lunardini, Christine, 364
Luther, Martha, 430
lyceum, 14, 21, 367
Lyman, Stanford, 54

Madison, James, 4, 5, 11
"Mammonism in America," 278, 286, 304n. 54

Pulitzer, Joseph, 114, 116, 119, 122, 126, 133; and business school, 137–38
Pullman strike, 222n. 29, 230, 23; and Debs, 230, 231, 241
Purcell, Edward A., 145, 147
Puritanism, 188; and class, 233; Holmes,' 146, 150, 156, 176
Putnam, Carleton, 53
Putnam, Robert, 471, 477

Quaker, 357
Quintilian, xvii, 3, 10, 15, 24

Rabban, David, 168, 170, 183n. 132
race: Bryan on, 197–200, 201; and class, 299; Du Bois on, 282–83, 295, 311–12; and Gilman, 442–43, 449, 452–56, 466n. 138; and KKK rhetoric, 312, 326–32; and progressivism, xii, 199, 284–86
"race progress," 449, 450
racism: Debs on, 245–46, 320; defined, 332n. 1; Dixon's, 334nn. 52, 62; in the progressive era, xiii, xix–xx, 311–12; and religion, 328–29; and rhetoric, xix–xx, 313, 317; and segregation, 86. See also Dixon; Jim Crow; Ku Klux Klan
railroads, 133; and Roosevelt, 57, 58, 61; and the *Suffrage Special*, 359; unions, 230
Rampersad, Arnold, 274, 277–78, 280, 286, 294
Randolph, A. Philip, 294
rape, 442
Raymond, H. J., 122, 133
Raymond, John H., 367
reasonable man premise, 165
Reckner, James, 72
Redkey, Edwin S., 308n. 159
Reed, Adolph, 271, 274, 276, 277, 278, 281, 284
Reed, Thomas B., 20, 23, 24, 25
reform, x. See also Imperialism; Ku Klux Klan; pacifism; progressivism; racism; suffrage; Wilson, Woodrow
Reid, Whitelaw, 133, 134
rights. See law; suffrage; women
religion: and Debs, 240–41, 249, 254. See also evangelical Protestantism; Puritanism; Quaker; Roman Catholicism; Social Gospel
Republican, 347
Republican Convention of 1912, 64
Republican Party, 191, 195, 197, 476, 482n. 37; Bryan on the, 201
reversal, 154
Review of Reviews, 54

rhetoric: and alliteration, 165; and anaphora, 158, 165; and aphorisms, 175; and apodeictic, 240; and class consciousness, 230; and conservation, 92–93, 97, 99; of development, xix, xx, 312, 313–14, 315–17, 331–32; in education, 4, 6, 8, 14–15, 148; eloquent, 148; epideictic, 153–63, 252; historically, 3–4, 174; and imagery, 164; Jacksonian, 10–11; legal, xviii, 148; and logos, 153; and metaphor, 148, 150, 165; and metonymy, 154, 166, 229–30; movements, 154,159, 165; and "narrative theory," 148; and opposition, 412–13; and parallelism, 165; presidential, 472, 479; progressive, x, xxi; power of, xvii; presidential, 28–33; and propaganda, xvi; of race, xix, xx, 313; republican, 6, 26; repetitive structure of, 165; and reversal, 154; Scottish, 6; of subjugation, xix, xx, 312, 313–15, 317–21, 331–32, 334n. 62; sublime, 159, 163; theorists, 177; in visual imagery, 370; war, 374; whiteness, 332n. 2. See also Addams; analogy; alliteration; Blatch; Bryan; Catt; Debs; Dixon; Du Bois; ethos; Garvey; Gilman; Holmes; irony; Ku Klux Klan; metaphor; metonymy; muckraker; oratory; pacifism; pathos; Paul; Stanton
"rhetorical presidency," 30
"rhetorical progressivism," 51, 60, 62, 63, 67, 68, 73, 76–77
Rhode Island, 58
Richardson, Elmo, 103
Ridge, Martin, x, xii
Rieke, Richard, 295
Roberts, Samuel K., 335n. 64
Rockefeller, John D., 57, 135, 233
Rogat, Yosal, 176, 181n. 79
Rogers, James Edward, 133
Rogers, Joel, 473, 475
Roman Catholicism and racism, 328
Romanes, George, 209, 212, 225n. 130
romantic realism, xviii, 147, 163
Roosevelt, Theodore, xiii–xiv; attacked, Addams, 390, 401; attacked Wilson's policies, 73; and Blatch, 374–75; and the Bull Moose party, xvii, 64; "bully pulpit" of, xvi, 21, 28, 51, 76; campaign oratory by, 17, 19, 20, 64–65; career of, 52–56, 64, 66, 68; and class, 230–31; as a conservationist, 87, 90, 100; conservative policies of, xvii–xviii, 50, 51–52, 59; contradictory, 76; Croly on, 61, 63, 204; death of, 73; Debs on, 230–31; developmental rhetoric of, 317, 322–25; education of, 52, 66; enigmatic,

xvii; expeditions of, 73; family of, 52, 53, 66; final years of, 62–65, 73–75; foreign policy of, 51, 52, 66–68, 69, 70; in *Forum*, 54; and free speech, xiv; ghostwriter for, 94; as governor, 53, 54, 55–56; and the Great White Fleet, 66, 72; influenced by Holmes, 146, 157; and imperialism, xx; Link on, 51, 53, 59; masculine politics of, 375–76; and military strength, 65, 66, 67–69, 71, 72–74; and moral responsibility, 53–56, 58–60, 61, 63, 65, 67–69, 76; and muckrakers, 58–59; "New Nationalism" of, 52, 62–63, 64; on Native Americans, 323; and patriotism, 375; on "the People," 98; and the Philippines, 67, 68, 69; as president, 57–65, 68–73; as a progressive, 188, 204, 357; and the Progressive Party, 20, 50, 64–65, 387; and progressivism, 50, 51–77; and racism, 56, 198–99, 291, 322–23; and railroads, 57, 58, 61; as a reactionary, 50; as a reformer, xxivn. 73, 50, 51, 53–54, 55–77; reputation of, xvii, 20, 216; rhetoric of, xvii, 323–25; and his "rhetorical progressivism," 51, 60, 62, 63, 67, 68, 73, 76–77; on rights, 234; as a role model, 473; sermonic rhetoric of, 74, 75; speaking tours of, 28–29, 54, 62–63, 67–72, 98, 100; as a spellbinder, 27, 28–29; and statesmanship, 10; style of, xxi, 29; and suffrage, 358; and trusts, 57–59, 60, 61, 65; and Washington, 198, 199, 322; in WWI, 73–75. **Speeches**: "Confession of Faith," 52, 64–65; "Fourth Annual Message," 69; "Man with the Muck-Rake," xiii–xiv, 59, 322; "Manly Virtues and Practical Politics," 56; "New Nationalism," 52, 62–63, 64, 164; "Second Annual Message," 69; "Special Message to Congress," 70; "Square deal," 61; "Strenuous Life," 68, 375; "Third Annual Message," 70; "War Message," 74; "Washington's Forgotten Maxim," 68. **Works**: *Autobiography*, 52, 57; "Fear God and Take Your Own Part," 75; "German Hatred of America," 74; *Naval War of 1812*, 66, 67; "Pillar-of-Salt Citizenship," 74; *Rough Riders*, 66; " . . . Shadow Huns," 74; "Summing Up," 75; *Winner of the West*, 66, 67

Roosevelt Club, 102

Roosevelt Corollary to the Monroe Doctrine, 69–70

Rosenberg, Neil, 176

Ross, Edward Alsworth, 188, 199, 212

Ross, Herold Truslow, 25

Rossi, Alice, 427

Rountree, Mrs., 437

rural progressivism, xi

Rush, Richard, 7, 9

Saint Louis, Missouri, 192, 389, 391

Saint Louis Dispatch, 122

Salem, Illinois, 185, 186

San Antonio, Texas, 59

Sandel, Michael, 475, 478, 482n. 37

San Francisco, California, 427

Santayana, George, 26, 151–52, 180n. 56, 273; and Holmes, 147, 152, 180n. 53

Sarbah, John Mansah, 291

Scallon, Eileen, 165

Schenk v. United States, 168–70

Schlesinger, Arthur M., Jr., 51

Schmoller, Gustav von, 273

Schreiner, Olive, 437

Schwarz, Joan, 148, 162

Science: and Holmes, 175–76; and social issues, 238–39, 241

Science, 110n. 64

Science of Power (Kidd), 211

scientific progressivism, xv–xvi, 101, 104–6; literature of, 131; and technology, 131–34. *See also* journalism

Scopes, John, 219

Scopes Trial, 185, 186; Bryan at the, 205, 206–7, 208–10, 214, 219, 225n. 133; Darrow at the, 206–7, 209–11, 225n. 133

Scott, Andrew Mackay, 339

Scott, Anne Firor, 339

Scott, William Berryman, 213

Scribner's Magazine, 123

Sedition Act (1798), 171, 172

segregation, 317, 318, 319–20; NAACP on, 300

Seneca Falls, New York, 341, 367, 369

"separate as the fingers . . . hand" (Washington), 285–86, 325, 329

Separatism, and Garvey, 295–97, 299, 308n. 148

sexism, 353; Gilman on, 443–52. *See also* gender issues

Shadwell, Delvenia, 388

Shaw, Anna Howard, 343, 349, 350, 358

Sherman Antitrust Act, 121

Shurz, Carl, 389

Sierra Club, 87

Sillars, Malcom O., xviii–xix

"Silent Sentinels," 361

Simmons, A. M., 233

Simmons, William Joseph, 326

Sinclair, Upton, 132

Skinner, Elliot P., 289, 294

slaves, 8, 296; suffrage for, 318

Turner, George K., 132
Tuskegee Institute, 285, 316, 304n. 61
Twenty Years at Hull House (Addams), 387, 399

Union League Club, 60, 69
unions: AFL, 230; American Railroad Union, 230; CU, 341, 358–64; and Debs, 237–38; IWW, 231, 234, 238; WSPU, 357, 365, 370; Women's Trade Union League, 369. *See also* railroads
Universal Negro Improvement and Conservation Association (UNIA), 293, 294, 295, 296, 298–99
Universal Peace Conference (1904), 390
Universal Peace Congress (1904), 392, 393–94, 395, 398
University of Iowa, 159
University of Pennsylvania, 72, 273
University of Wisconsin, xiv
Untermeyer, Samuel, 215
Up From Slavery (Washington), 286
urban progressivism, xi, 187
U.S. Forest Service, 100–1, 102–4, 105
U.S. Geological Survey, 87

Van Hise, Charles R., 91
Van Voris, Jacqueline, 347, 350
Vardaman, James K., 314, 320, 321, 335n. 64
Vassar, 367, 368, 371
Vaughan, Stephen, xxivn. 67
Veblen, Thorstein, 427, 443
Vermont progressivism, xii
Villard, Oswald Garrison, 25
Virginia, 174
"Vote as Symbol, The" (Lippmann), 346

Wade, Wyn Craig, 327
Wagner, Adolf, 273
Walker, Clifford, 329
Walker, S. Jay, 284
Wander, Philip, 163
Ward, Lester, 443
Warner, Charles Dudley, 18, 129
Washington, Booker T.: Atlanta Exposition address, 285–86, 325, 329; death of, 289, 293; and feud with Du Bois, xix, 269, 279, 283, 285–90; influenced Garvey, 293, 297; metaphors of, 325; pacifist, 390; and progressivism, 284–86; visited Roosevelt, 198, 199. **Speeches**: "separate as the fingers . . . hand," 285–86, 325, 329. **Works**: *Up From Slavery*, 286
Watson, Richard, Jr., 49, 57, 66
Watson, Thomas W., 321
Watterson, Henry, 125

Watts, Eric King, xix
Webster, Daniel, 3, 8, 13, 353; campaign speeches by, 12, 33; and Hayne debate, 32, 33; on Jackson, 11; reputation of, 18, 23; style of, 12. **Speeches**: "Whig Principles and Purposes," 13
Weisberg, Joel, 473–74
Wells, Bettina Borman, 370
Wells, Ida B., 292
Weyl, Walter, 345, 346
Whig Party: ideal orator, 31; orators, 2, 7, 11–14, 16, 18
White, G. Edward, 151, 156, 157, 158, 173–74; on Holmes' brevity, 164; on Holmes' image, 175–76
White, John, 284
White, John E., 315
White, Walter, 300–1
White, William Allen, 21
Whitehead, A. E., 15
Whitman, Walt, 153
"Why We Picket" (NWP), 362
Wiebe, Robert, xii, xx, 124, 231, 233, 344, 348
Wilberforce, U. of Pennsylvania, 273
Williamson, Joel, 318, 334n. 62
Willis, George, 150
Wilson, Daniel L., 336n. 110
Wilson, Edmund, 153, 163
Wilson, Joseph Ruggles, 15
Wilson, Woodrow: and Addams, 403, 404; and Bryan, 185, 194, 199, 202, 223n. 91; campaigns of, 185; on capitalism, 121; Columbia University lectures by, 29; conservative appeal of, 24; health of, 32; and the League of Nations, 26, 28, 32, 203, 205; and muckrakers, xi; as New Jersey governor, 21, 24; 1912 contest oratory by, 20; 1919 speaking tour of, 28–29, 32–33; oratory tradition and, 15, 16, 27, 33; as president, 25, 26, 28–29, 32–33, 65; as a Princeton orator, 14, 15–16, 24; as a progressive, 188; as a reformer, 21; reputation of, 27, 28, 29–30, 31; on rhetoric, 1, 14–15, 16; rhetorical presidency of, 30, 32; and Russia, 171; and scientific progressivism, xvi; as a statesman, 24; and suffrage, 197, 358, 361–65; as a traditionalist, 31; Whiggish, 16. **Speeches**: "An Address on Robert E. Lee," 1; "Peace Without Victory," 404; "swing around the circle," 18–19. **Works**: *Constitutional Government*, 28, 30, 31, 32
Winchester, Tennessee, 185, 208, 211
Wingate, Charles, 125
"Winning Plan" (Catt), 350–52